THE RORSCHACH: A COMPREHENSIVE SYSTEM

Volume
1

Third Edition

THE RORSCHACH

A COMPREHENSIVE SYSTEM

VOLUME 1: BASIC FOUNDATIONS

THIRD EDITION

JOHN E. EXNER, JR.

John Wiley & Sons, Inc.

New York • Chichester • Brisbane • Toronto • Singapore

To My Sons and Daughter

John, Michael, Christopher, James, and Andrea

In recognition of the importance of preserving what has been written, it is a policy of John Wiley & Sons, Inc., to have books of enduring value published in the United States printed on acid-free paper, and we exert our best efforts to that end.

This publication is designed to provide accurate and
authoritative information in regard to the subject
matter covered. It is sold with the understanding that
the publisher is not engaged in rendering legal, accounting,
or other professional services. If legal advice or other
expert assistance is required, the services of a competent
professional person should be sought. *From a Declaration
of Principles jointly adopted by a Committee of the
American Bar Association and a Committee of Publishers.*

Library of Congress Cataloging-in-Publication Data

Exner, John E.
    The Rorschach : a comprehensive system / John E. Exner, Jr. — 3rd
  ed.
      p.   cm. — (Wiley series on personality processes)
     Includes bibliographical references and indexes.
     Contents: v. 1. Basic foundations.
     ISBN 0-471-55902-4 (v. 1 : alk. paper)
     1. Rorschach Test. I. Title. II. Series.
  BF698.8.R5E87   1993
  155.2'842—dc20   93-9878

Printed in the United States of America

10 9

Series Preface

This series of books is addressed to behavioral scientists interested in the nature of human personality. Its scope should prove pertinent to personality theorists and researchers as well as to clinicians concerned with applying an understanding of personality processes to the amelioration of emotional difficulties in living. To this end, the series provides a scholarly integration of theoretical formulations, empirical data, and practical recommendations.

Six major aspects of studying and learning about human personality can be designated: personality theory, personality structure and dynamics, personality development, personality assessment, personality change, and personality adjustment. In exploring these aspects of personality, the books in the series discuss a number of distinct but related subject areas: the nature and implications of various theories of personality; personality characteristics that account for consistencies and variations in human behavior; the emergence of personality processes in children in adolescents; the use of interviewing and testing procedures to evaluate individual differences in personality; efforts to modify personality styles through psychotherapy, counseling, behavior therapy, and other methods of influence; and patterns of abnormal personality functioning that impair individual competence.

IRVING B. WEINER

University of Denver
Denver, Colorado

Preface

If anyone present in 1970, during the assemblage of the first pieces of the Comprehensive System, which, in retrospect, involved simplistic decisions concerning seating, instructions, and the basics of scoring, had predicted that the project would continue into the 1990s, they would not have been taken seriously. The task seemed, at that time, relatively straightforward, namely, to merge into a single format all of the empirically defensible features of other approaches. It was naively assumed that almost all of the elements necessary for the use and understanding of the test already existed. Thus, no one could have foreseen the extended research odyssey that has evolved. In fact, by the end of 1973, when the manuscript for the first edition of this work was completed, naivete continued to exist. It was obvious that the issue of Special Scores was still to be resolved and that larger standardization samples of data would be necessary. Projects designed to accomplish these tasks were already underway. But, in reality, most of us believed that we had completed most of the work to achieve the goal of presenting the "best" of the Rorschach. But, as it turned out, the "best" was yet to come.

As new projects were completed, the data often raised more questions than were answered, thereby necessitating the design of many more studies than were originally anticipated. The breadth of data that had accumulated by 1976 was much more extensive than could easily be scattered through a series of articles and a decision to create *Volume 2* was made. Although *Volume 2* did provide an avenue through which to expand and clarify the basic work, focus on younger clients remained pitifully inadequate, and *Volume 3* was a natural consequence. Additions and changes to the Comprehensive System were so numerous between 1978 and 1985 that the original edition of *Volume 1* had little utility. The second edition was published in 1986, but research and additional data analyses have provoked more changes and additions and the second edition has also become woefully outdated.

Hopefully, this third edition of *Volume 1,* plus the second edition of *Volume 2,* released in 1991, represent some sort of culmination in the development of the Comprehensive System. This does not mean that the work is finished, for the Rorschach continues to pose many unanswered questions. Nonetheless, the basic system seems in place and does appear to meet the primary objective for the project from which it developed—namely, to provide a standardized method of using the test which is easily taught, manifests a high interscorer reliability, and for which the interpretive premises will withstand validation demands.

The term *Comprehensive* remains appropriate. The system does reflect the hard-won wisdoms of those who researched and developed the test long before this project was initiated, plus the new information that has unfolded through the work of many practitioners and researchers during the past 25 years. The early success of the project was due in no small part to the encouragement of four of the five Rorschach systematizers, Samuel Beck, Marguerite Hertz, Bruno Klopfer, and Zygmunt Piotrowski. In some ways, the original idea for the project may have been stimulated by David Rapaport who, in 1954, cautioned me to know *all* of the Rorschach, but its actual inception was provoked by Bruno Klopfer and Samuel Beck, who viewed each other with very low regard. In 1967, they both endorsed a project to research the empirical sturdiness of their respective approaches to the test and, in 1968, the first of a series of investigations to address that issue began. By 1970, when the results clearly indicated that each of the approaches, including those of Hertz, Piotrowski, and Rapaport had considerable merit, but that all were also seriously flawed in one way or another, I proposed to Beck and Klopfer that some integration of approaches seemed to be the logical extension of the work. Neither was very pleased with the findings nor the proposal, but they also were able to rise above their personal animosities and offer a cautious endorsement to the idea, as did Hertz and Piotrowski shortly thereafter. In retrospect, I doubt that any of the four believed in the project, but I do think that all four were intrigued with it.

As the project progressed, each showered me with suggestions, comments, and criticism, but beyond that, they all offered support and inspiration. The support came through their suggestions and comments. The inspiration was fomented by their kind and generous encouragement, and most of all by their warm friendship. It served as a powerful motivation to persist at the task. In effect, they are the Godfathers and Godmother of the Comprehensive System. They have all passed on, but their legacy remains. Much of their work and many of their ideas are firmly embedded in the Comprehensive System.

Much of the later development of the Comprehensive System has been derived from the suggestions of practitioners and the efforts of a small army of researchers. Among the latter is a group who deserve special recognition. They have served on the staff of the Rorschach Research Foundation *(Rorschach Workshops)* for varying intervals as project directors and assistants with a seemingly tireless enthusiasm. Their efforts often went well beyond what might have been expected and their contributions have insured the continuing accumulation of new data that added enormously to the bank of information concerning the nature of the test and its interpretation. They have trained and/or supervised more than 800 examiners who have participated in more than 550 investigations. They include:

Gerald Albrecht	Terry Cross
Doris Alinski	Robert Cummins
Michael Allen	Mark Edwards
Franscesca Antogninni	Frederick Ehrlich
William Baker	Gail Famino
Miriam Ben Haim	John Farber
Jeffrey Berman	Ronda Fein
Carol Bluth	Gary Fireman
Peter Brent	Roy Fishman
Evelyn Brister	Jane Foreman
Richard Bruckman	Benjamin Franklin
Edward Caraway	Dorothy Frankmann
Eileen Carter	Christy George
Andrew Chu	Katherine Gibbons
Michael Coleman	Nancy Goodman
Susan Colligan	Laura Gordon
William Cooper	Carolyn Hafez

Nancy Haller
Doris Havermann
Dorothy Helinski
Lisa Hillman
Sarah Hillman
Milton Hussman
Geraldine Ingalls
Susan James
Marianne Johnston
Lester Jones
Katsushige Kazaoka
Mary Lou King
Richard Kloster
Beth Kuhn-Clark
Nancy Latimore
Carol (TC) Levantrosser
Arnold Lightner
Richard McCoy
Denise McDonnahue
Marianne McMannus
Louis Markowitz
Andrew Miller
Beatrise Mittman
Lynn Monahan
Ralph Nicholson
Michael O'Reilly
Carmen Penzulotta
George Pickering
Doris Price

Beth Raines
Virginia Reynolds
Felix Salomon
Joseph Schumacher
Whitford Schuyler
Barbara Seruya
Jane Sherman
Sherill Sigalow
Kenneth Sloane
Frederick Stanley
Louise Stanton
Eva Stern
Sarah Sternklar
Robert Theall
Vicki Thompson
Peter Vagg
Alice Vieira
Donald Viglione
Edward Walker
Jane Wasley
Richard Weigel
Donna Wiener-Levy
Robert Wilke
Elizabeth Winter
Leslie Winter
Helen Yaul
Tracy Zalis
Nancy Zapolski
Mark Zimmerman

Our examiners have included many professional psychologists and psychology graduate students, but nearly half come from more varied backgrounds, ranging from a professional musician and a retired tailor to an extremely talented high school senior. Other examiners have included physicians, dentists, nurses, social workers, homemakers, and a few very adept secretaries who learned that administering the Rorschach is almost as boring as typing a letter. The ability of these laypeople to learn to administer and score the test in a standardized format has been among the very reassuring aspects of the system.

The project has also included some very special people who deserve mention. They have served as core staff or in senior advisory roles. Joyce Wylie served as our project coordinator from 1969 to 1978, and without her persistence and organizing talents we might have faltered along the way. During the same period, Elaine Bryant was our overseer for laboratory experiments. She devised some remarkable innovations to improve on our designs. Antonnia Victoria Leura was our recruiter for nearly 10 years and during that time obtained more than 8000 subjects for our various studies. I will never cease to be amazed at her ingenuity. Barbara Mason was also with us for more than a decade, serving as trainer, teacher, researcher, and clinician. Her versatility was continuously impressive.

George Armbruster and Eugene Thomas each served more than a decade as our research "purists." Both contributed much more than can be described in a few words and both epitomize the very best of psychology. John Roger Kline was our first computer consultant and despite knowing little about the Rorschach, he devised programs for storage and analysis that enabled us, for the first time, to addressed large chunks of data with an amazing ease. Joel Cohen replaced John, and has been mainly responsible a variety of sophisticated programs that broadened our capacity to store and analyze data. He and Howard McGuire are also responsible for our computer interpretation assistance programs.

Ten people deserve particular recognition. They were involved in the terrible task of rescoring thousands of records each time some new change in the format occurred: Doris Alinski, Earl Bakeman, Eileen Carter, Ruth Cosgrove, Lisa Hillman, Nancy Latimore, Theresa Sabo, John Talkey, Eugene Thomas, and Edward Walker. I appreciate their diligence and admire their frustration tolerance.

There are also many in the international community who have been extremely helpful in testing out the system, teaching it to their colleagues, and contributing significantly to our data base. They include Anne Andronikof-Sanglade (France), Bruno Zanchi (Italy), Anne Helene Skinstad (Norway), Leo Cohen (Netherlands), Noriko Nakamura and Toshiki Ogawa (Japan), and Vera Campo, Monserrat Ros Plana, and Conception Sendin (Spain). Their contributions reaffirm the fact that the test is universal and that people are people, no matter where they live.

Luis Murillo has been an exceptional friend to Rorschach Workshops. He generously opened Stony Lodge Hospital to our efforts in 1970, and supported our research there for nearly 15 years. He has been a superb colleague and a true model for psychiatry. Irving Weiner has also been a faithful friend, advisor, and critic since the inception of the project. He is directly responsible for many features of the system and has shared a host of workshops with me, thereby lightening the burden and increasing the enjoyment.

I must also acknowledge an unpayable debt to my wife, Doris, who probably often felt that she married an inkblot. She has been involved in most every aspect of the work at Rorschach Workshops and has been a continuing source of support and encouragement to all of us.

Finally, a word for the prospective Rorschach researcher. There is no apparent end in sight to the continuing research questions posed by this awesome test. Although many of its mysteries have been solved, many remain. We are still unsure about many of the stimulus properties of the blots and some conceptual links between data clusters and personality or behavioral correlates require more study. The issue of personality styles has received far too little attention, not only with regard to the Rorschach but to assessment instruments in general. These are challenges that must be addressed if the Rorschach, and assessment in general, is to reach the level of contribution for which we have strived, that is, understanding people and aiding in their times of quandary. The quest for knowledge about people is always difficult, but the rewards can endure for a lifetime.

J.E.E.

Asheville, North Carolina
February 1993

Contents

18.   CLUSTER INTERPRETATION I—THE COGNITIVE TRIAD,   449

19.   CLUSTER INTERPRETATION II—AFFECT, SELF-PERCEPTION, INTERPERSONAL PERCEPTION,   489

PART V   APPLICATIONS

Tables

Figures

PART I

The History and Nature
of the Rorschach

CHAPTER 1

Introduction

The 10 inkblots that constitute the stimuli of the Rorschach test were first unveiled to the professional public in September 1921, with the release of Hermann Rorschach's famed monograph, *Psychodiagnostik*. Since that time the test has generated much interest, extensive use, and considerable research. For at least two decades, the 1940s and 1950s, its name was almost synonymous with clinical psychology. During those years the primary role of the clinician focused on assessment or psychodiagnosis. But even as the role of the clinician broadened and diversified during the 1960s and 1970s, the Rorschach remained among the most commonly used tests in the clinical setting, and that status continues today. It is a test from which considerable information can be derived if *properly* administered, scored, and interpreted. Some of this information is relevant to diagnostic decisions, the formulation of intervention plans, or making predictions. But most of the test data provide descriptive information about the psychological characteristics of the subject.

Although the test has become an important clinical tool, its history has been marked by much controversy. It has often proved baffling to researchers and very irritating to those advocating the stringent application of psychometric principles to any psychological test. Criticism of the test, some real and some unreal, became especially widespread during the 1950s and 1960s. During that period many openly judged its worth with contempt and advocated its abandonment as a test for clinical work (Jensen, 1958; Zubin, Eron, & Schumer, 1965). There is no question that many Rorschach advocates had overestimated its potential usefulness and often made unrealistic claims about its efficacy. Some even likened it to an X-ray of the mind in spite of a growing number of publications that appeared during the 1950s and 1960s, which reported negative findings for issues such as diagnostic accuracy, reliability, and validity. On the other hand, many of the criticisms were naive and unjust, often fomented from bias, ignorance, or simply a misunderstanding of the method and the principles that led to its exploration by Rorschach.

EARLY HISTORY

Rorschach did not conceive of his work as having yielded a test per se. Instead, he regarded his monograph as a report of findings from an investigation in perception that he believed might ultimately lend itself to a sophisticated diagnostic approach for the differentiation of schizophrenia. Obviously, he used inkblots as stimulus figures, but this was not an original Rorschach idea. Quite the contrary, there had been several attempts to use inkblots as some form of test well before Rorschach began his investigation. Binet and Henri (1895, 1896) had tried to incorporate them into their early efforts to devise an intelligence test. They were like many of their day, believing that the inkblot stimulus might be useful to the study of visual imagination. They abandoned the use of inkblot stimuli in their effort because of group administration problems. Several other investigators in the United States and Europe published articles about the use of inkblot stimuli to study imagination and creativeness (Dearborn, 1897, 1898; Kirkpatrick, 1900; Rybakov, 1911; Pyle, 1913, 1915; Whipple, 1914; Parsons, 1917). It is doubtful that any of this work stimulated Rorschach's original study, but it is quite likely that he became familiar with much of it before he wrote his monograph.

The reasons for Rorschach's decision to study the use of inkblots are not fully clear. There is little doubt that, like most children of his time, he often played the popular *Klecksographie* (Blotto) game as a youth. In fact, he even had the nickname "Klex" during his last two years in the Kantonsschule, which might have reflected his enthusiasm for the game or may simply have evolved from the fact that his father was an artist (Ellenberger, 1954). It is also clear that his continued close friendship with a classmate from the Kantonsschule, Konrad Gehring, played a role in stimulating his exploration of the use of inkblots with patients. The Blotto game had flourished in Europe for nearly 100 years by the time Rorschach began his psychiatric residency in 1909. It was a favorite of adults and children and had several variations. Inkblots (*Klecksen*) could be purchased easily in many stores or, as was more commonplace, players of the game could create their own. Sometimes the "game" was played by creating poem-like associations to the blots (Kerner, 1857). In another variation the blot would be the centerpiece for charades. When children played the game, they usually created their own blots and then competed in developing elaborate descriptions.

Konrad Gehring became a teacher at an intermediate school close to the Munsterlingen hospital where Rorschach did his residency, and he and his pupils often visited the hospital to sing for patients. Gehring had also discovered that if he contracted with his students to work diligently for a period of time and then permitted them to play the Blotto game, his classroom management problems were reduced considerably. Rorschach became intrigued with the management potential that the game seemed to offer, but was also interested in making comparisons between the Blotto responses of Gehring's male adolescent students and his own patients. Thus in a very casual and unsystematic manner, they worked together for a brief period, making and "testing out" different inkblots during 1911.

Probably little would have come from the Rorschach-Gehring "experiment" had not another event occurred during the same year. This was the publication of Eugen Bleuler's famed work on Dementia Praecox in which the term *schizophrenia* was coined. Bleuler was one of Rorschach's professors and supervisors. In fact, he directed Rorschach's Doctor's Thesis, which concerned hallucinations. The Bleuler concepts intrigued the psychiatric community, but they also posed the very important issue of how to differentiate the schizophrenic from those forms of psychosis reflected in organically induced dementia. As almost a passing matter, Rorschach noted that patients who had been identified as schizophrenic seemed to respond quite differently to the Blotto game than did others. He made a brief report of this to a local psychiatric society, but little interest was expressed in his apparent finding. Thus Rorschach did not pursue the matter with any thoroughness for several years.

In 1910 he had married a Russian, Olga Stempelin, with plans to ultimately practice in Russia. He completed his residency in 1913 and moved on to Moscow, but for reasons unknown remained in Russia for only about seven months before returning to accept a position at Waldau; then, in 1915, he moved on to a position as Associate Director of the Krombach hospital in Herisau. It was at Herisau in late 1917 or early 1918 that Rorschach decided to investigate the Blotto game more systematically.

It is likely that the stimulus to that decision was the publication of the "Doctor's Thesis" of Syzmond Hens, a Polish medical student who studied under Bleuler at the Medical Policlinic in Zurich. Hens developed his own series of eight inkblots which he administered to 1000 children, 100 nonpatient adults, and 100 psychotic patients. His thesis focused on how the contents of responses were both similar and different across these three groups, and he suggested that a classification system for the contents of responses might be diagnostically useful. This approach to classification was quite different than the one Rorschach and Gehring had conceived of in their casual 1911 exploration. Whereas the Hens approach emphasized classifying content, Rorschach was more interested in classifying the more salient characteristics of the response. It seems clear that he was quite familiar with much of the literature on perception and apparently was especially intrigued with, and influenced by the concepts of Ach, Mach, Loetze, and Helmholtz, and particularly with the notion of an *apperceptive mass*. That concept is pervasive in much of his writing concerning his findings.

Rorschach used about 40 inkblots in his investigation, administering 15 of them much more frequently than the others. Ultimately, he collected data from 405 subjects of which 117 were nonpatients that he subdivided into "educated" and "noneducated." The sample also included 188 schizophrenics which were his basic target population. True to his casual 1911 observations, the schizophrenic group did respond to the inkblots quite differently than did the other groups. His major thrust avoided and/or minimized content, but instead focused on the development of a format for classifying responses by different characteristics. Thus he developed a set of codes, following largely from the work of the Gestaltists (mainly Wertheimer), that would permit the differentiation of response features. One set of codes, or scores as they have come to be called, was used to represent the area of the blot to which the response was given, such as W for the whole blot, D for large detail areas, and so on. A second set of codes concerned the features of the blot that were mainly responsible for the image perceived by the subject, such as F for form or shape, C for chromatic color, M for the impression of human movement, and so on. A third set of codes was used to classify contents, such as H for human, A for animal, An for anatomy, and so on.

By early 1920, the sample sizes of Rorschach's groups were sufficient for him to demonstrate that the inkblot method he had devised offered considerable diagnostic usefulness, especially in identifying the schizophrenic. But in the course of the investigation he had also discovered that clusterings of high frequencies of certain kinds of responses—mainly movement or color responses—appeared to relate to distinctive kinds of psychological and/or behavioral characteristics. Thus the method seemed to have both a diagnostic potential and the possibility of detecting some qualities of the person which, in the terminology of contemporary psychology, would probably be called personality traits, habits, or styles.

Several of Rorschach's colleagues were impressed with his findings, and Bleuler was particularly enthusiastic about its diagnostic potential. Collectively they encouraged him to publish his findings in a form from which others could learn to use the method. His first manuscript, based on the 15 blots that he used most frequently, was rejected by several publishers. One did accept it but with the proviso that the number of blots be reduced to six because of printing costs. Rorschach rejected this offer but continued with his investigation, adding more and more subjects to his sample. In 1920 he rewrote the manuscript to include his new data and again submitted it to several publishers. The work might not have been published if it were not for the efforts of Walter Morgenthaler, a colleague of Rorschach's who became an informal solicitor on Rorschach's behalf. In 1920 Morgenthaler obtained a contract for Rorschach from a small publisher in Bern, The House of Bircher. But a compromise was necessary. Like other publishers, Bircher objected to the reproduction of 15 or more inkblots because of printing costs. Thus Rorschach agreed to rewrite the manuscript to include only 10 blots that he used most often. The manuscript was finally published in late June 1921, but with it came a new problem to be addressed. When the inkblots were reproduced, Bircher made them smaller and altered some of the colors slightly.

But another change was much more important. The blots that Rorschach used in his research contained no shading; they were all solid colors. When Bircher reproduced them, very marked differences in the saturation levels occurred. Shading differences appeared in almost every area of every blot, resulting in very different stimulus figures than Rorschach had used. But Rorschach is reported to have been more excited than dismayed with this printing error. According to Ellenberger (1954), "he was seized with a new enthusiasm, and understood at once the new possibilities that the prints offered." Thus he decided to continue his research using the new multishaded blots.

When he wrote the monograph, Rorschach chose to call his method a *Form Interpretation Test,* and cautioned that his findings were preliminary and stressed the importance of much more experimentation. It is apparent that he looked forward to much more research with the "method" and invested himself vigorously in it during the next several months. But then tragedy struck. On April 1, 1922 he was admitted to the emergency room at the hospital at Herisau after having suffered abdominal pains for nearly a week. He died the next morning! He was only 37 years old and had devoted less than four years to his investigation of the "Blotto Game." Had he lived to extend his work, the nature of the test and the direction of its development might have been much different than proved to be the case.

There is little doubt that Rorschach was disappointed about the indifference to his work that was apparent after the publication of *Psychodiagnostik.* The only Swiss psychiatric journal gave no review to it, and other European psychiatric journals did little more than publish brief summaries of the work. The monograph was a financial disaster for the publisher. Only a few copies were sold before Rorschach died and before the House of Bircher was to enter bankruptcy. Fortunately the subsequent auction of Bircher goods left the monograph and the 10 plates in the hands of a larger and highly respected publishing house in Bern, Verlag Hans Huber. Huber's reputation for quality publications plus a few favorable reviews of the monograph stimulated interest and the use of the method persisted. However, Rorschach's absence and the fact that a new set of blots had been created posed a significant problem for those who would try to continue his work. But that was only the beginning of the problem for those who became interested in developing and using Rorschach's method.

THE RORSCHACH SYSTEMS

Although several of Rorschach's colleagues continued to use his method after his death, none followed a systematic empirical approach to data collection as he had done. Instead, they attempted to focus on clinical and/or vocational applications of the method. Rorschach had deliberately avoided theorizing about the nature of his method and, as noted earlier, cautioned repeatedly in the monograph about the limitations of his data and the need for more research. He also tended to discount the importance of content per se, postulating that content analysis would yield little about the person. But this did not detract many users of the test from trying to apply it more directly to the increasingly popular Freudian theory.

Three of Rorschach's colleagues became the strongest advocates of the *Form Interpretation Test*. They were Walter Morgenthaler, Emil Oberholzer, and Georgi Roemer. At the beginning they based their advocacy on the premise that the method was well suited for the differentiation of schizophrenia, but like many others in the psychiatric community, felt that Rorschach's work was incomplete *mainly* because of the lack of content interpretation. Roemer tried to extend Rorschach's work by using a new set of blots and ultimately formulated several interesting but not well-received positions concerning the "test." Morgenthaler and Oberholzer remained quite faithful to Rorschach's blots and to his method for scoring answers, but each sought to extend his work by giving considerably greater emphasis to the use of the content. Oberholzer in particular was to play an important role in the ultimate expansion of the use and understanding of the test.

Actually, none of the early European users of the method exploited the use of content interpretation inordinately, but at the same time none seemed equipped, by reason of understanding or motive, to extend Rorschach's postulates concerning the perceptual properties of the method. No new scores were added to the format until 1932, when Hans Binder published an elaborate scheme for scoring achromatic and shading responses. But unlike Rorschach, Binder's scoring format was logically intuitive rather than empirically developed.

Many people and events were to become influential in determining the expansion and growth of Rorschach's method. Emil Oberholzer was among the first catalysts to that growth. By the mid-1920s he had become a widely respected psychoanalyst who included a specialty in children among his varied talents. Because of that reputation, an American psychiatrist, David Levy, petitioned for and received a grant to study with Oberholzer in Switzerland for one year. During his year with Oberholzer, Levy learned about Rorschach's work and on his return to the United States brought along several copies of the blot photos (they were not yet routinely mounted on cardboard), with the intent of exploring their use with children. Other interests deterred Levy from his intent to use and study the test but he did publish a translation of one of Oberholzer's papers about it in 1926. At that time Levy was a staff psychiatrist at the Institute of Guidance in New York City. The Institute was interdisciplinary and was a resource for the New York City schools to serve the needs of children, mainly those whose academic performances were substandard, but also to provide psychiatric consultation and service to disturbed children from the greater New York area. Thus it was a natural training facility for students in psychiatry and psychology.

In 1927, Samuel J. Beck, who was a graduate student at Columbia University, was awarded a student fellowship at the Institute. Typically, he worked a few hours each week, learning to administer and interpret various tests of intelligence, aptitude, and achievement. By 1929 Beck was actively searching for a research topic that might be acceptable for a dissertation. In a casual conversation one afternoon, Levy mentioned to Beck that he had brought copies of the Rorschach blots with him on his return from Switzerland; he showed them to Beck and loaned him a copy of Rorschach's monograph. Beck became intrigued with the method, as a test, and practiced with it under Levy's supervision at the Institute. Subsequently, with Levy's encouragement, Beck broached the idea of a standardization study to his dissertation advisor, the famous experimental psychologist Robert S. Woodworth. Woodworth was not specifically aware of Rorschach's work but was familiar with some of the experiments of the Gestaltists in which inkblots were used as a part of the stimulus field. After reviewing the test with Beck, Woodworth agreed that a standardization study using children as the subjects might contribute to the literature on individual differences. Thus nearly seven years after Rorschach's death, the first systematic investigation concerning his test was initiated, one which would launch Beck into a career that was to make him one of the truly great figures of the test.

Beck took nearly three years to collect and analyze the data for his study. It involved the testing of almost 150 children. During that period he maintained contact with two close friends who he had first met some 10 years earlier while working as a newspaper reporter in Cleveland; they were Ralph and Marguerite Hertz. It was shortly after Beck began his dissertation study that the Hertzes visited New York. At that time Marguerite Hertz was also a psychology graduate student, studying at Western Reserve University in Cleveland. During the visit Beck shared some of his notions about Rorschach's work with her and she was quick to recognize the vast potential of the method. As a result she also petitioned to do her dissertation about the test and devised a study similar to Beck's, but with several variations in sampling. Thus the second systematic investigation of the test began. Both dissertations were completed in 1932. After graduating, Hertz accepted a position involving a very elaborate multidisciplinary study of children at the Brush Foundation in Cleveland, whereas Beck took a joint position at the Boston Psychopathic Hospital and Harvard Medical School.

Neither Beck nor Hertz added any new components to Rorschach's format for coding or scoring answers in their dissertation works. Their findings did add important data concerning how children responded, but probably more important than the data as such was the breadth of experience each gained that led to a better comprehension of the conceptual framework used by Rorschach. Both completed their work with a marked awareness of how much more research was needed. If one were to have predicted the developmental future of the Rorschach Test at that time, it is doubtful that any anticipation of future controversy would have been mentioned. Both Beck and Hertz were trained in psychology programs with stringent empirical orientations. Many of their findings were similar as were most of the conclusions that they developed. But events of the world would ultimately alter this seemingly harmonious beginning very significantly.

Probably the most important of those events was the rise to power of Adolph Hitler in Germany. The ultimate chaos that was created affected the lives of three other psychologists markedly and, as a result, each became extensively involved with Rorschach's test. The first to experience the grave impact of the power of the Nazis in Germany was Bruno Klopfer. Klopfer had completed his Ph.D. in 1922 at the University of Munich. He became a specialist in children and focused much of his work on emotional problems as related to academic progress or lack thereof. Ultimately, he became a senior staff member at the Berlin Information Center for Child Guidance. It was an institute similar in design and scope to the Institute for Child Guidance in New York where Beck did his early research. But unlike Beck who by 1932 had become deeply interested in the test and its use, Klopfer had no interest in the Rorschach. Both his training and subsequent orientation were strongly phenomenological, and his abiding interest was in the Freudian and Jungian psychoanalytic theories. He had begun personal analysis in 1927 and training analysis in 1931, with the ultimate objective of becoming a practicing analyst. By 1933 the many directives from the government to the Berlin Information Center for

Children concerning studies on, and services for Aryan and non-Aryan children, as well as the increasing pressure on Jews, led Klopfer to decide to flee the country. Klopfer's training analyst, Werner Heilbrun,[1] aided him in contacting many professionals outside of Germany, seeking assistance for him. One who responded positively was Carl Jung, who promised a position for Klopfer if he could reach Zurich, which he did during 1933.

The position that Jung found for Klopfer was that of a technician at the Zurich Psychotechnic Institute. The Institute served many functions, among which was psychological testing of candidates for various types of employment. The Rorschach test was among the techniques used routinely, and thus Klopfer was required to learn how to administer and score it. His instructor was another technician, Alice Garbasky. During the nearly nine months that he held this post, Klopfer became intrigued with some of the postulates offered by Rorschach in the monograph, *Psychodiagnostik,* but he did not become strongly interested in teaching or using the test. Instead, his first love remained psychoanalysis and his stay in Zurich provided the opportunity for considerable personal experience with Jung. His role of a technician was far less satisfying to him than had been his much more prestigious position as a senior staff member in Berlin. Consequently he persisted in soliciting other employment, both in Switzerland and other countries. Ultimately he was offered, and accepted a position as a research associate in the Department of Anthropology at Columbia University and immigrated to the United States in 1934. Interestingly, this was about the same time that Beck went to Switzerland, under a Rockefeller Fellowship, to study with Emil Oberholzer for a year. Beck anticipated that his study in Switzerland would lead him to a better understanding of Rorschach's concepts, and particularly of his notions concerning the use of the multishaded blots that had been created with the publication of the monograph.

By 1934 Beck had already published nine articles describing the potential merits of the Rorschach for the study of personality organization and individual differences. The first three of these appeared before Beck completed his dissertation, so that by 1934 considerable interest had began to develop about the test in the United States.[2] This interest was evident in both psychiatry and psychology and was similar to the interest that had developed in Europe during the first decade after Rorschach's death. But unlike the situation on most of the European continent, where the test had gradually gained widespread use, the American student of the test was faced with two problems. First Rorschach's monograph was not readily available, but even if a copy were located, the reader had to be quite skilled in reading German, because it was not translated into English until 1942. Second, and much more important at that time, was the fact that it had not gained the widespread use as was the case in Europe. Consequently, there were relatively few opportunities to learn the techniques of administration and scoring, or the principles of interpreting the results.

Beck had taught the method at Harvard Medical School and the Boston Psychopathic Hospital for about two years, and Hertz was teaching the method to technicians at the Brush Foundation and to students at Western Reserve University. David Levy left New York in 1933 to head a new children's unit at Michael Reese Hospital in Chicago, and he

[1]About four years after aiding Klopfer's flight from Germany, Heilbrun left his own practice to join the International Brigade in the Spanish Civil War. He was to become immortalized in some of Ernest Hemingway's writing as he was the model for "the physician" about who Hemingway wrote.

[2]Woodworth was very enthusiastic about Beck's project and pressed him to publish early and frequently about it. Beck admitted (Personal Communication, June 1963) that Woodworth's status as an editor for the *American Journal of Psychology* made this easy to do.

trained a few technicians there how to administer the test. But other than those three locations, no formal instruction in the test existed. Thus it was not uncommon for the interested student to experience some frustration, because formal training about the test was not readily available. It was this situation that would have a major impact on the career of Bruno Klopfer and ultimately lead him into a role as one of the most significant figures in the Rorschach community.

In late 1934 some of the graduate students at Columbia learned that Klopfer had gained considerable experience with the test in Zurich and petitioned their department chairman, Woodworth, for a seminar about the test to be conducted by the Research Associate from Anthropology. Woodworth was very reluctant to arrange a joint appointment for a relative unknown to his department, and instead suggested that he would try to arrange for some formal training in the test by Beck after Beck's return from Switzerland. The students were not to be deterred from their interest however, and enticed Klopfer to conduct an informal seminar in his apartment two evenings a week. Klopfer agreed to do so with the proviso that at least seven students would participate, each paying a small stipend for the 6-week seminar.

It had been Klopfer's intention to teach the fundamentals of administration and scoring during that first private seminar, but that format was subverted by the incompleteness of Rorschach's work. At almost every meeting, when participants would discuss responses that they had collected in their practice with the test, the lack of precise designations for the variety of blot areas—that is, whether an area being used was *common* or *unusual*—created much disagreement. More important, the lack of codes or scores to differentiate the variety of responses that emphasized the shading of the blots led to debates that would often continue well into the night. Klopfer readily perceived that the future of the test could easily hinge on the resolution of these problems. Klopfer was a masterful teacher and an excellent organizer, and as he found his own intrigue with the test rekindled by the enthusiasm of the students, he became excited about the challenge posed by the incompleteness of the test.

By the end of the six weeks the students had already decided to continue for a second six-week seminar, and other students from Columbia and New York University asked Klopfer to form a second group. The second led to a third and so on. In each of these seminars possible new scores for location designations, and to encompass those responses that included reference to the shading features were discussed, and decisions were made to add them to the existing scoring format. By late 1935 several new scores had been added, and more were being considered. The Klopfer groups approached the problem of the shading answers by drawing extensively from Binder's (1932) suggestions, but then redefining some, and creating others.

By 1936 Klopfer was devoting most of his time to the test. It is quite important to note that during the time when Klopfer and his pupils were seeking to develop the test, the atmosphere was not readily conducive to new innovations. American psychology looked askance on phenomonology during that period, having established itself as closely aligned with the traditions of "pure science." Behaviorism was a byword, and anyone willing to depart from the rigors of empiricism or unwilling to accept its tenets would often be regarded with a somewhat jaundiced eye. This was to create a significant problem for Klopfer and even more so for the development of the test.

Klopfer was quick to recognize the need to disseminate information about the Rorschach, especially because in each of his seminars new scores were being adopted or new formulations about the test evolved. In 1936 he began to publish a mimeographed newsletter that he called *The Rorschach Research Exchange,* which was later to become the *Journal of Projective Techniques,* and ultimately the *Journal of Personality Assessment.* Its basic purpose was to provide updates concerning the developments of the test, as they had evolved in the many seminars that Klopfer conducted privately and in the supervisory seminars he had begun teaching at Columbia. But there was another purpose. He perceived the *Exchange* as having the potential to serve as a vehicle to share data, ideas, and experiences with the test. In that context, he invited Beck, Levy, Hertz, and Oberholzer to contribute and anticipated that a dialogue among those experienced with the test would stimulate more rapid development. But this was not to be the case.

Shortly before the first issue of the *Exchange* appeared, an article was published by Beck (1936) in another journal that was extremely critical of some of the Swiss psychiatrists, especially Bleuler and his son Manfred, who were applying the test in ways Beck felt were far too subjective, especially in the way that the responses were being scored. The title of the article, "Autism in Rorschach Scoring," provides some indication of the vigor with which Beck attacked deviations from the coding or scoring format that Rorschach had developed. As he had done in previous articles, Beck pointed to the need for careful, systematic research that would lead to fixed standards for administration, scoring, and interpretation. It is not surprising then, in light of that firm position, to find that Beck reacted to Klopfer's movement to expand the scoring format for the test with very marked coolness. There is no question that the scoring format the Klopfer group developed, which was presented in the first issue of the *Exchange,* (Klopfer & Sender, 1936) was well organized and carefully thought through. But the absence of any data base plus the fact that the format diversified the scoring well beyond any points that Rorschach had conceptualized or defined, or that either Beck or Hertz had explored in their work, made it, at best, difficult and probably impossible for anyone committed to an empirical framework for the test to accept.

Things went from bad to potentially disastrous in early 1937. After Beck received an invitation to write for the *Exchange* in 1936, he sent a copy of a manuscript that he had been preparing for nearly two years. It was his first book, *Introduction to the Rorschach Method,* published as the first monograph of the American Orthopsychiatric Association in 1937, which later became known as "Beck's Manual." Klopfer decided to devote a major portion of a 1937 issue of the *Exchange* to a review of Beck's Manual (Klopfer, 1937). As might be expected, the review was more negative than positive, discussing Beck's reluctance to add scores and his criteria for the definition of good versus poor form quality responses. Naturally it provoked a reply from Beck, which Klopfer published in the second volume of the *Exchange* (Beck, 1937b). That article, "Some Rorschach Problems," was very critical of the Klopfer approach and clearly documents the fact that a very important schism existed between the two orientations. In the next issue of the *Exchange* a series of comments on the Beck article was published, most of which were written by followers of Klopfer or by those who tended to favor his orientation. Obviously many were very critical of Beck and some were openly hostile. Collectively they only served to strengthen Beck's resolve.

Marguerite Hertz, much to her disappointment, also became caught up in the controversy between Beck and Klopfer. Like Beck, she was among the earliest to identify the need for further development of the test and her commitment to that need never waned after her first contact with it. Her relation with Klopfer, first through correspondence and then personal contact, led her to take a positive stance toward his efforts for a consolidated approach to studying the test. But like Beck, she was committed to careful investigation. When the Beck-Klopfer schism became so apparent in the *Exchange,* she attempted to assume the role of a mediator. Her first effort was put forth in a 1937 article that appeared in the *Exchange,* in which she noted the relatively limited data base from which Beck had drawn many of his conclusions, and at the same time criticized the Klopfer group for, "refining scoring to the extent of becoming involved in a maze of symbols. . . ." Although the article did little to reconcile Beck and Klopfer, it did point to the potential flaws of each approach. Nonetheless she remained hopeful for some more unified approach to the test and periodically would issue a new plea for reconciliation and compromise (Hertz, 1939, 1941, 1952).

In spite of the efforts of Hertz and others to strike some form of compromise between Beck and Klopfer, the schism continued to grow and by 1939 reached a point where reconciliation was no longer considered possible by either. After that time no further communication, verbal or written, was to occur between them. After his return from Switzerland, Beck was enticed by his old mentor, David Levy, to accept a joint appointment at the Michael Reese Hospital and the University of Chicago. During the period from 1944 to 1952 he published a three-volume series concerning the Rorschach, representing his approach to its use (Beck, 1944, 1945, 1952). Klopfer remained in New York, holding appointments at Columbia University and the City University of New York until the end of World War II. Then he accepted a professorship at the University of California at Los Angeles. His first book about the test appeared in 1942, coauthored by Douglas Kelley. Between 1954 and 1970 he and his colleagues also published a three-volume series which generally reflects the system he organized for using the test (Klopfer, Ainsworth, Klopfer, & Holt, 1954; Klopfer et al., 1956; Klopfer, Meyer, Brawer, & Klopfer, 1970).

Marguerite Hertz remained in Cleveland as a professor at Western University. She published more than 60 articles concerning the test plus a very elaborate set of frequency tables, which were revised several times, for use in scoring form quality (Hertz, 1936, 1942, 1951, 1961, 1970).[3] In effect, each went their own way, developing the Rorschach in the context of their own theoretical and/or empirical bias. As such the Rorschach became fragmented into three separate systems that were quite different from each other. But further diversification of the test was also to occur.

Among the participants in Klopfer's first seminar was Zygmunt Piotrowski, a postdoctoral fellow at the Neuropsychiatric Institute in New York. Piotrowski had been trained as an experimental psychologist, obtaining his Ph.D. in 1927 from the University of Poznan in Poland. He wanted to broaden his education by studying at a variety of universities, and after obtaining his degree spent two years at the Sorbonne in Paris; he then accepted a position as an instructor and postdoctoral fellow at the Columbia University College of Physicians and Surgeons. His primary objective in accepting that appointment was to learn more about neurology because, at that time he was very interested in the development of symbolic logic. He knew little about the Rorschach test, although

---

[3]Hertz began a manuscript describing her own approach to the test during the mid-1930s. It included large quantities of data collected at the Brush Foundation. When the Foundation closed, it was inadvertently destroyed, a tragedy that she described in personal correspondence (1968):

> One day it was decided to dispose of the material that was no longer in use and which the authorities felt was worthless. I was called and told that I may have my material. I went over at once with graduate students and a truck, but to my dismay I learned that my material had already been burned by mistake. All the Rorschach records, all the psychological data, all the worksheets, plus my manuscript went up in smoke. Of course the loss was irreparable.

he had been a subject, while a graduate student, for someone learning to use the test. From that experience, he had a vague notion about the nature of the test, but had little interest in it. As a postdoctoral fellow at Columbia he came into contact with many of the graduate students from psychology, and on the encouragement of one of them he decided to attend Klopfer's first seminar. The result of that somewhat casual decision was the onset of considerable intrigue with the test, not so much concerning its development as Klopfer encouraged, but more with the potential of the test to differentiate creativeness. He was especially interested in how those with neurologically related problems might function in the relatively ambiguous test situation. Piotrowski continued in a close relationship with Klopfer during the period of the first few Klopfer seminars, contributing ideas for some new scores that would become permanent fixtures in the Klopfer System. But as the Beck criticisms of the Klopfer approach became more intense, he backed away from the Klopfer group and devoted more time to studies of the neurologically impaired under the tutelage of Kurt Goldstein, and with the intent of returning to his homeland in 1939.

The German invasion of Poland, which began September 1, 1939, caused Piotrowski to alter his course and he accepted a position at the Jefferson Medical School in Philadelphia where he was able to continue his studies of the neurologically impaired and at the same time, test out some of his own ideas about the Rorschach method. Ten years later (1950) he published a monograph that contained the nucleus for his own unique approach to the test. Later he published an elaborate text about the use of the test, *Perceptanalysis* (1957), in which he integrated his own wisdoms about perceptual interpretation into a system for using the test. Thus a fourth approach to the Rorschach, different than Beck, Klopfer, or Hertz, came into being.

But even before Piotrowski completed his work with the test, another figure was to have a significant impact on the development and use of the Rorschach test in the United States. This was David Rapaport. Like so many others of his time Rapaport fled Europe in 1938, shortly after completing his Ph.D. at the Royal Hungarian Petrus at Pazmany. His orientation was strongly psychoanalytic and during his training he had become intrigued with the process of thinking, especially pathological thinking. He had some limited experience with the Rorschach, but no strong commitment to it or any other psychological test. His forte was theory, and primary among his professional dreams was to augment contemporary concepts about the functions of the ego in the classic analytic model. After coming to the United States he worked briefly at the Mount Sinai Hospital in New York and then took a position at a state hospital in Oswatomie, Kansas. His decision to accept the Kansas position came partly from financial need, but mainly because it brought him closer to the mecca of psychoanalytic thinking and practice, The Menninger Foundation. His position at Oswatomie afforded him frequent contact with Menninger's, and when a staff position opened there in 1940, he was appointed to it and became head of the psychology department two years later. His work with the Rorschach and other tests convinced him that they could be used to study ideational activity. He was also strongly influenced by the writing of Henry Murray (1938), concerning the process of projection and its relation to the study of personality.

Following a directive of Karl Menninger, he organized an elaborate project to study the efficacy of several psychological tests for the purpose of deriving a broad picture of the psychological functioning of the person. He was aware that his own training did not equip him well for psychometric research, but was able to surround himself with a brilliant research team, drawn both from the staff of the Foundation and from the graduate study body at the University of Kansas. This team included Merton Gill, who was a staff psychiatrist at the Foundation, and Roy Schafer who was an intern there and a graduate student at the University of Kansas. That project culminated in a masterfully written two-volume series, *Psychological Diagnostic Testing* (1946) which focused on the clinical applications of eight psychological tests, including the Rorschach. That work has been largely responsible for the notion that a battery or group of tests will provide the sorts of data from which an integrated and rich understanding of the person can evolve.

Rapaport was very aware of the dispute between Beck and Klopfer and took pains to avoid taking sides. The approach to the Rorschach that he ultimately selected is similar to Klopfer in some ways, yet also quite different from Klopfer and much more influenced by his allegiance to psychoanalytic propositions. The two volumes were frequented with charts and graphs that highlighted data, but the conclusions often ignored or went well beyond the data, reflecting much of Rapaport's logic about the psychology of the person. Had the Rapaport and Klopfer groups merged in their respective efforts to develop the test, the result might have been much more striking and ultimately influential concerning the use of the Rorschach; and some of Rapaport's tendencies to deviate markedly away from Rorschach's basic methodology might have been thwarted. But this was not to be, and by 1946 the seeds of a fifth approach to the test were firmly sown in ways that were incompatible with each of the other four approaches. Following the publication of the two volumes Rapaport was to drift away from psychological testing and back to his first love, developing a more detailed model about ego functioning. Nonetheless the system he had developed was to influence many users of the Rorschach and was to be marked once more by a classic work by Roy Schafer, published in 1954. That book, *Psychoanalytic Interpretation in Rorschach Testing,* not only added considerably to the basic Rorschach model that Rapaport had created, but also represents a milestone in the use of content analysis to derive a broad review of the dynamics of personality. In effect, what Rapaport began, Schafer extended enormously.

And thus during a period of slightly more than 20 years (1936–1957), five American Rorschach Systems developed. They were not completely different from one another, but most of the similarities among them consisted of the elements that each had incorporated from Rorschach's original work. Beyond those features the five systems were incredibly different, so much so in some respects that they defied comparison for many issues of scoring and the approach to interpretation (Exner, 1969). In spite of this the Rorschach *method* flourished as one of the mainstays in psychodiagnosis. Practitioners and researchers alike often tended to ignore the presence of five markedly different approaches to the method. Either they were not fully cognizant of the breadth of the differences that existed across the five separate systems, or they minimized those differences unrealistically. Most preferred to believe that a single test—*the* Rorschach—existed which could be described in laudatory or critical terms depending on one's perspective about it. That notion probably persisted because of another common thread that was to link the systems together by altering the way in which the method was characterized.

THE CONCEPT OF PROJECTION AND PROJECTIVE TECHNIQUES

During the first three decades of the twentieth century, applied psychology was mainly involved with the use of tests to study intelligence, and operations related to intelligence, such as aptitudes, achievement levels, motor skills, and the like. There were methods devised to study some features of personality, but typically they were designed to measure single traits, such as introversion, dominance, flexibility, and so on. In those instances when a personality description or diagnosis was called for, a thorough interview and social history provided the bulk of data (Louttit, 1936). Tests that were used were constructed on traditional psychometric principles whereby specific scores could be judged against group means, with little or no regard for the contents of a subject's response.

Most of the early Rorschach research, such as that of Beck and Hertz, followed that same format. The concept of projection as applicable in psychological testing, had not really been formulated beyond the implications offered in Jung's Word Association Test (1910, 1918), which focused more on the issue of emotional arousal than projection as such. In Rorschach's experiment he concentrated on score frequencies to develop a psychogram. He noted that "occasionally" the content of responses might offer some information about the characteristics of the subject but expressed skepticism that this would be of major value in the method, stressing the fact that the task required adaptation rather than being one to evoke a stream of associations (pp. 122–123). It would be nearly *two decades* later before the notion of projection would be applied to Rorschach's method.

At about the same time that Klopfer began his first seminar, Morgan and Murray (1935) introduced the Thematic Apperception Test, which was based in part on the premise that people reveal something of their own personality when confronted with an ambiguous social situation. Three years later, Murray (1938) offered an elegant description of how the process of projection operates in an ambiguous stimulus situation. Murray's concept was, in part, derived from Freud's postulate about projection as a form of ego defense (i.e., the translation of internally experienced dangers into external dangers), thereby making them easier to deal with (Freud, 1894, 1896, 1911), and later as a natural human process (Freud, 1913). Murray drew largely from Freud's 1913 concept of projection, describing it as a more natural process in which defense, as such, may or may not be relevant. Thus Murray's concept of projection was formulated simply as the tendency of people to be influenced by their needs, interests, and overall psychological organization in the cognitive translation or interpretation of perceptual inputs whenever the stimulus field included some ambiguity. This concept was neatly crystallized by Frank (1939) in a paper in which the term *projective hypothesis* was coined. Frank suggested the label "projective methods" for a variety of techniques useful to the clinician in evoking this kind of action. Obviously the Rorschach was cited as one technique with this potential.

The *Zeitgeist* of psychology and psychiatry was ripe for this movement, and very quickly the availability of methods such as the Rorschach and the TAT began to change the orientation of clinicians away from one based largely on nomothetic comparisons toward a more intense effort to study the idiography of the person. Psychodynamic theory was gaining in popularity and this change in direction, which emphasized the unique needs, interests, conflicts, and styles of the individual, afforded the clinician a new status among professionals. By the early 1940s case studies, research papers, opinions, and arguments concerning projective methods were appearing in the professional literature in a virtual torrent. During that decade and the next, many new projective techniques were developed. Louttit and Browne (1947) found that a 60% turnover occurred among the 20 tests used most frequently in clinical settings between 1935 and 1946. Sundberg (1961) repeated the Louttit and Browne survey using data through 1959, and found that the turnover rate between 1936 and 1959 had reached 76% for the 20 most frequently used tests. In the Louttit and Browne survey the Rorschach and TAT ranked fourth and fifth among the most frequently used instruments. In the Sundberg survey they ranked first and fourth, respectively. It seems clear that the emphasis on projective methodology became broadly pervasive in clinical testing during the 1940s and 1950s, and that emphasis has continued. Lubin, Wallis, and Paine (1971) collected data about test use through 1969 and found that the Rorschach ranked third and the TAT seventh. In a 1982 replication of that survey, Lubin, Larsen, and Matarazzo (1984) found the Rorschach to rank fourth and the TAT fifth among the 30 most frequently used tests.

Although these surveys indicate the popularity of the Rorschach and of projective methods in general, they fail to illustrate the extensive controversy that has swirled around projective techniques. The controversy has been lengthy and often bitter, and unfortunately created a schism among many psychologists interested in measurement, individual differences, and personality assessment. One of the most unfortunate by-products of this controversy has been the tendency to categorize psychological tests into either of two classifications: (1) *objective* or (2) *projective.* The implication of this scheme is that objective tests have been developed in accord with fundamental measurement principles. In other words, they are scoreable, have been standardized, and have been demonstrated to have credible reliability and validity. Conversely, the implication regarding projective tests is that they lack some or all of the measurement features, and that data derived from them are interpreted more subjectively. Although there is some evidence for those implications, the dichotomy itself is grossly oversimplified.

Theoretically, any stimulus situation that evokes or facilitates the process of projection, as defined by Murray and Frank, can be considered a projective method. This is quite independent of whether or not the basic rules of measurement have been used in developing the test. Put more simply, any stimulus situation *that is not structured to elicit a specific class of response,* as are arithmetic tests, true-false inventories, and the like, *may evoke* the projective process. Intelligence tests are typically regarded as being objective tests because they are structured and developed in the basic psychometric framework. However, some intelligence tests include items, or whole sections, that permit a relatively open-ended form of response. For instance, several of the subtests in the Wechsler Scales are designed to permit open-ended responses. In the Comprehension subtest, the best answer to the question, "Why does the state require people to get a license before they get married?" is that it is for purposes of record keeping. If the response given is, "To prevent unsuspecting women from getting Herpes," the answer is not only less than satisfactory but also conveys some peculiarities about the respondent. A special interest or preoccupation has been projected into the response.

Many psychological tests have been designed to permit a broad range of responses, and the TAT is obviously one of them. The original Morgan and Murray format for its use included a technique of scoring for needs and presses in each story, using a scale from 1 to 5. But during the more than 50 years since its publication, approaches to its use and interpretation have proliferated extensively. By the late 1940s at least 20 different approaches had been published, ranging from the strictly qualitative, emphasizing content analysis, to those that are more score oriented. Unfortunately, none of the latter have been pursued to the point of establishing a sturdy empirical basis for their use. Thus it is appropriate to identify the TAT as a projective test, and that is essentially what it was designed to be. But other tests, also designed to evoke the process of projection, such as some sentence-completion tests, also meet the standards for an objective test. For instance, the sentence completion developed by Rotter and Rafferty (1950) has included an elaborate format for scoring, and has been sufficiently researched to establish extensive normative data and address the issues of reliability and validity quite successfully. It is a projective technique, yet is it also an objective test, and to force classification into one or the other of the two categories is very misleading.

As noted earlier, the Rorschach was *not* designed as a projective method nor developed as such during the first two decades of use. But the nature of the test procedure and the ambiguity of its stimuli do permit a broad range of responses. And often the elaborations about responses can be very revealing about the subject. Consequently, it is not surprising that it became hailed as an important test in the projective movement of the early 1940s. As such, it was also to become conspicuously listed among the projective tests in the objective-projective dichotomy. This does not mean that efforts to establish psychometric credibility for the test were abandoned. Beck and Hertz remained in the forefront among many researchers working toward that goal by studying the wide array of test variables. Their efforts were joined by many others who sought to demonstrate its efficacy as an objective method.

By the early 1950s, some of that research had a positive yield. Both Beck and Hertz had published useful normative data, and each had also published actuarially based tables for the discrimination of adequate form fit of responses. Several hundred very sound research articles had also appeared in the literature, offering data related to the validity of many of the scoring variables. But they constituted a very modest segment of Rorschach literature which, by that time, had burgeoned to more than 3000 books and articles. Many were clinical studies and many were research works containing negative or contradictory findings. Critics of projective methods often cited the latter as evidence for the conclusion that *the* Rorschach was of little use if gauged against psychometric or scientific standards.

Unfortunately, the rush into the projective movement had more or less overlooked the fact that there were five markedly different approaches to the test, or technique as some now preferred to call it. Both advocates and critics of the method ignored or downplayed those differences as being irrelevant to the larger issue of whether the method had merit. Many of the critics of the Rorschach, and of projective methods in general, were also critics of psychoanalytic theory and often naively linked the two. The erroneous assumption was that the process of projection, as formulated by Murray, was directly related to unconscious operations as defined in the Freudian concept (Lindzey, 1961; Sargent, 1945; Symonds, 1946; Wiggins, Renner, Clore, & Rose, 1971). Actually, very few projective methods are strictly theory based, least of all the Rorschach. But many clinicians trained during the 1940s and 1950s were strongly imbued with psychodynamic concepts and that model was commonly used as the framework for interpreting any test data.

Paul Meehl (1954) published an important work, *Clinical Versus Statistical Prediction,* that served to define and perhaps broaden the schism that was developing between those favoring a stringent psychometric approach and those aligned with a more global approach to assessment. He reviewed 20 studies, all but one of which showed that the actuarial method was equal to or better than the "clinical" technique, which customarily included the use of projective methods. He argued for an abandonment of the clinical approach to assessment, favoring less time-consuming techniques that are actuarially based, such as the MMPI, to allow clinicians more time for other important work, especially psychotherapy. Later, Gough (1963) and Sawyer (1966) published surveys of predictive studies that appear to provide support for Meehl's argument, although Gough did observe that no adequate test of the clinician's forecasting skills had yet been carried out.

Holt (1958, 1970), in two excellent rejoinders to the Meehl argument, has pointed out that many of the studies cited by Meehl used extremely inadequate or even contaminated criteria. In his 1970 paper Holt called attention to the fact that another survey of predictive studies (Korman, 1968) reported positive findings for the clinical method. Holt noted, with a sense of dismay, that the Sawyer and Korman studies were published within two years of each other, but their respective bibliographies showed absolutely no overlap. That finding illustrates very well how a selective use of literature could be used to support almost any bias, and especially those concerning the objective-projective, or actuarial-clinical issues. Both Holt (1970) and Weiner (1972) have noted the focus of the Meehl position is prediction, whereas the major focus of the diagnostician is description and understanding.

In spite of the controversy, the use of the Rorschach continued to be widespread during the 1960s, a decade during which the very character of clinical psychology changed extensively. Through the 1950s the major role of the clinician was psychodiagnosis but with the early 1960s the profession began to broaden its scope and role. New models of behavior and intervention became popular, and most clinicians found themselves much more involved in planning and conducting intervention. Some universities had reduced or even discontinued training for assessment using tests by the end of the decade. But in the clinical settings *assessment* (a term that had come to replace psychodiagnosis) continued as a way of life for the professional, and the Rorschach remained one of the standard methods used. But to some extent it remained in a developmental state of limbo. In part this was because of the gradual deemphasis on psychological testing and the corresponding reductions in the number of broad-based studies that had marked the 1940s and 1950s. But the older *Rorschach problem* was probably much more responsible in fomenting this developmental lag.

INTERSYSTEM DIFFERENCES

All of the Rorschach Systems were firmly in place by 1957 and none of the systematizers were oriented toward integration or compromise. Some of the research published between 1950 and 1970 was system specific, but much was not. It was common for authors, readers, and practitioners to interpret almost any report in the literature, whether positive or negative, as applicable to *the* Rorschach. In effect, a substantial disregard for the differences among the systems existed.

A comparative analysis of the five approaches was ultimately published in *The Rorschach Systems* (Exner, 1969). That comparison was provoked by both Beck and Klopfer. Earlier, they had been encouraged to participate in a face-to-face discussion of their respective positions, but both declined. In doing so, however, each recommended that their differences be carefully reviewed in a journal article (Beck, 1961; Klopfer, 1961). That project seemed simple at the onset, yet the significant following of those trained in, or aligned with the Hertz, Piotrowski, or Rapaport-Schafer approaches to the use of the test argued for a broader comparison that would include the five approaches. Thus what was to be an article became a book and required nearly seven years to complete, because the literature concerning each of the systems was extensive, scattered, and sometimes very distorted.

The final yield of the comparison illustrated the enormous magnitude of the differences across the five Systems. For instance, only two of the five used the same seating arrangements and none of the five used the same instructions to the subject. In fact, none of the instructions to the subject, as given in one system, were even remotely similar to those used in any of the other systems. Obviously, each system collected the data of the test differently, making any comparison of the respective yields questionable. If the differences between the Systems had involved only seating and instructions, some resolution could have occurred easily through a systematic study of the effects of those differences on test performance. But the differences went far beyond these two easily studied variables.

Each systematizer had developed his or her own format for coding or scoring responses, and they were markedly different. All had included most of Rorschach's original scoring symbols, but most altered some or all of the criteria for their application. Ultimately, 15 different codes or scores were formulated among the five Systems to identify the *location* or area of the blot used in a response. *Not one* of those 15 codes was defined in the same way across all of the Systems. All five included Rorschach's scoring symbol *F* to denote that the form features or contours of the blot were important to the response, but each of the five used a different criterion to determine whether the form had been used accurately. *None* of the five scored the perception of movement the same as any of the other four, and each even defined the presence of a movement percept differently than the other four. Sixteen symbols existed among the Systems to code the presence of chromatic color in a response, but even when the same symbol appeared in more than one System, the criterion for its application was likely to be different than in the other Systems. The greatest disagreement for scoring among the Systems concerned the use of shading or achromatic color in a response. Each System had a relatively unique set of symbols and criteria for their application. This is not surprising because Rorschach's original work did not include this feature as his blots did not become shaded until the monograph was published.[4]

Obviously, the differences in scoring led to many differences concerning interpretation. They differed significantly about which scores should be calculated in a quantitative summary of the record and what relationships between scores would be important to interpretation. They differed concerning the meaningfulness of many variables and which configurations of variables might be interpretively important. In spite of their substantial differences, several interpretive postulates appeared in each of the Systems that were the same or similar. For the most part these were drawn from Rorschach's original work, but to the casual observer that common thread could easily convey the impression that the Systems were much more similar than was actually the case. Major differences existed across the Systems for issues about which Rorschach was not definitive or had offered no procedures or postulates.

The major conclusion drawn from the comparative analysis presented in *The Rorschach Systems* was that the breadth of differences among the Systems was so great that the notion of *the* Rorschach was more myth than reality. In effect, *five uniquely different Rorschach tests had been created.* They were similar only in that each used the same Swiss stimulus figures, and that each had included most of Rorschach's original scores and basic interpretive postulates, but even some of those had been uniquely embellished by some of the systematizers.

---

[4]Rorschach did become concerned with the need to score responses based on the shading features that appeared in the new blots which had been created by the publisher, Bircher. He began to use the score *(C)*, describing this in an unfinished paper that was published posthumously in 1923 on his behalf by Emil Oberholzer, and which has been included as a part of the monograph, *Psychodiagnostik* since 1942.

THE COMPREHENSIVE SYSTEM

Two questions were implicit in the yield of the comparative analysis of the five approaches to the Rorschach method: "Which of the five demonstrated the greatest empirical sturdiness?" and "Which of the five had the greatest clinical utility?" In 1968 the *Rorschach Research Foundation* was established to address those issues.[5] Among the first projects completed at the Foundation were three surveys, conducted to determine how clinicians were using the Rorschach method, and what problems in design and analysis were being encountered by those doing research with the method.

The first of the three surveys (Exner & Exner, 1972) involved the use of a relatively brief questionnaire, which was sent to 750 clinicians whose names were drawn randomly from the membership listings of the Division of Clinical Psychology of the American Psychological Association and the Society for Personality Assessment. The 30 items asked in which of the five Systems the respondent had received formal training, which of the five did he or she use in everyday practice, and a number of items pertaining to seating, instructions, scoring, and interpretation. A total of 395 (53%) usable questionnaires were returned and the results were very striking. Nearly three of every five responding had received some formal training in the Klopfer method and about one in every two in the Beck approach. Only about one in every five had received some formal training in the Piotrowski System, and about 10% had received training in either the Hertz or Rapaport methods. Although that distribution was not necessarily unexpected, two other findings were very much so.

First, nearly 22% of the respondents had abandoned scoring altogether. They used the method exclusively for the subjective analysis of contents. Second, 232 of the 308 respondents who did score the test admitted to *personalizing* the scoring, by integrating scores from one system to another system, and/or adding unique scores developed from personal experience with the test. An overwhelming majority also admitted that they did not necessarily follow the prescribed tactics for administration specified in the system from which they derived most of their scoring, and the same was true for interpretive postulates. In other words, one might administer the Rorschach using the Rapaport face-to-face seating (which was disavowed in all other systems), score responses using criteria drawn from Klopfer, Beck, and Piotrowski, and draw from at least as many sources to develop interpretive postulates concerning the resulting data.

Thus it was common to find that clinicians using the Rorschach method tended to piece together an assortment of features from the several Systems, and from their own experience with the test, to generate a final product that they identified as *the* Rorschach. The five major approaches to the method had become astronomically proliferated into almost as many different tests as there were test users.

In retrospect, the findings, although striking, should not have been surprising. Jackson and Wohl (1966) had conducted a survey of university Rorschach instructors. They found that 12% did not teach scoring, and that the variability of methods for administration, scoring, and interpretation was remarkable. They also found that approximately 60% of those teaching Rorschach in the university setting had little or no postdoctoral training with the test, and that 46% would have preferred to be teaching something else. The Jackson and Wohl data highlighted the failure to standardize the teaching of the

---

[5]Although the legal title, Rorschach Research Foundation, continues to exist, the Foundation has actually become more widely known by its nickname, *Rorschach Workshops.*

test, emphasized that those teaching it at that time were often less well qualified to do so than might be desired, and indicated that the generation of clinicians produced during the 1960s might be led to use the test in ways that could be substantially deviant from those for which the test was intended.

The second survey conducted by the Foundation involved the use of a more elaborate 90-item questionnaire, which was mailed to 200 Diplomates of the American Board of Professional Psychology. The return yielded 131 completed questionnaires, but 20 were discarded because the respondents indicated that they used the Rorschach fewer than 20 times per year. The remaining 111 questionnaires provided information about the practices and opinions of clinicians who used the test at least 20 times per year and who averaged 12 years of postdoctoral experience. Eighty-three of the respondents (75% had received formal training in at least two of the systems, usually either Beck or Klopfer plus one or two of the others, and 95 (85%) considered themselves knowledgeable in at least three of the systems. Only seven had discontinued scoring, but 62 (56%) admitted that they intermixed the procedures of administration and scoring from more than one system, and almost all used interpretive postulates drawn from more than one of the systems. In effect, the same broad proliferation of approaches indicated in the results of the first survey also existed among this group of highly qualified practitioners who were using the method with a substantial frequency. In fact, when the data from the two surveys were combined, it was revealed that only 103 of the 506 respondents (20%) faithfully followed any single system. Obviously, the divergence of Rorschach methodology into five major approaches, and the subsequent proliferation of those approaches, did little to promote a more thorough understanding of the method, as a test, or to enhance its development.

The third survey consisted of a 55-item questionnaire concerning issues of design and analysis in Rorschach research. It was mailed to 100 authors who had published research-based articles concerning the method between 1961 and 1969. The return yielded 71 usable replies. Nearly half of those responding, 34, had abandoned Rorschach research in favor of a different topic. Those persisting were typically focusing their efforts on the study of single scores or the development of new scores to address specific issues such as anxiety, body boundary, cognitive development, ego defense, and the like. The majority had received training in more than one system, but almost all were following research plans specific to a system. The results highlighted three broad areas of concern to most investigators.

The first concerned difficulties in recruiting subjects and/or the problem of requiring multiple examiners to avoid an experimenter bias effect. The second involved the complexities of data analysis, especially the applicability of parametric statistics to some data and/or the problem of controlling for the number of responses. The third represented the most common complaint, that of adequacy of control groups and/or the lack of extensive normative data to use for general comparisons. The respondents uniformly agreed that the complexities of the Rorschach often generated more discouragement than reinforcement to the researcher. Most identified important research objectives concerning the method, but many also elaborated on the difficulties that made the achievement of those goals seemingly impossible.

Concurrent with the three surveys, another project was completed at the Foundation in 1970 which involved a systematic review of all published Rorschach research. The purpose of the project was to categorize, cross-reference, and evaluate studies as they related to the variables of administration, scoring, and the interpretive postulates that had evolved in each of the five Systems. By 1970 the Rorschach literature consisted of more than 4000 articles and 29 books, plus Rorschach's monograph. In spite of that voluminous literature, a surprisingly large number of issues had not been researched systematically. For example, seating arrangements had never been subject to experimental manipulation and only one study compared different instructions, and for only two systems. No research had been published for 16 scoring variables and only a handful of studies had appeared concerning six other scores. Similarly, many interpretive postulates had not been addressed through research, and for many others, the data were equivocal because of problems in research design and/or data analysis. In fact, problems in design and/or analysis marked a very large number of the published research studies concerning the Rorschach.

About 2100 of the more than 4000 articles that had appeared concerning the Rorschach were purportedly research works. When scrutinized against *contemporary* standards for adequacy of design and/or data analysis however, more than 600 were judged to be seriously flawed to the extent that the conclusions probably were not valid. Another group of nearly 800 also contained flaws that rendered them of questionable value. It is important to emphasize that those findings should not be interpreted to mean that most Rorschach research was shoddy, incompetent, or illogical. The majority of studies reviewed in this project were published between 1938 and 1958, an era in which the tactics of design and data analysis for *all* of psychology were continually being improved so that works deemed adequate by the standards of one period might be considerably less sophisticated when compared with the methodology of another. This was especially the case for much clinical research. For instance, by 1970, 24 studies had been published addressing the issue of "blind analysis" in Rorschach interpretation. Although all were well intended, no more than nine of the 24 would meet contemporary standards for adequacy of design to test the issue. Similarly, 26 studies were published prior to 1970 focusing on the stimulus characteristics of the blots. Less than half would be considered to be free of flaws by contemporary standards.

It is also important to note that the project to evaluate the Rorschach literature yielded more than 700 research works which were clearly methodologically appropriate, and the data from those studies had been carefully and appropriately analyzed. Collectively, those works provided a data bank from which many elements of the various systems could be evaluated. The majority of these reported positive findings, but many also reported negative or equivocal results. In some instances, two or more adequately designed and analyzed studies reported contradictory findings. Many of these were works involving small samples, a finding that argued for replication using a larger number of subjects.

The most important project undertaken at the Foundation during the first two years was the creation of a data pool to permit direct comparison of the five Systems. By early 1970, that pool consisted of 835 Rorschach records. These protocols were submitted by 153 psychologists in response to a mailing request for 600 members of the Division of Clinical Psychology of the American Psychological Association and instructors of Rorschach courses at eight universities. The 835 were selected from more than 1300 that were submitted.[6] Each was accompanied by a data questionnaire concerning the

---

[6]Those selected to receive the mailing were professionals whose place of work was shown in the *Directory* of the American Psychological Association to be a hospital or clinic. A total of 1342 protocols was submitted but 507 were discarded because of illegibility, no completed data sheet, no inquiry, or because the procedures used in taking the record were grossly different from those recommended in any of the five systems.

demographic features of the subject, purpose of the examination, and information concerning the training and test procedures of the examiner. The protocols included 204 from nonpatient subjects and 631 from a variety of inpatient and outpatient psychiatric groups. When subdivided for the procedures of administration by system, the breakdown was: Klopfer, 329; Beck, 310; Rapaport, 78; Piotrowski, 66; and Hertz, 52. Numerous comparisons of the records of each system with the others were completed and most of the results confirmed the main operational hypothesis, namely, that protocols of one system would be substantially different from those of the other systems in several ways. For instance, they differed significantly for the average number of responses, ranging from 23.9 answers if the Klopfer (original Rorschach) instructions were employed to 31.2 responses using the Beck instructions, 33.8 using the Piotrowski method, and 36.4 responses if the Rapaport instructions were used. This finding was not surprising because each system included instructions and procedures for administering the test that were very different than each of the other systems.

By early 1971 the data accumulated at the Foundation tended to support three broad conclusions. First, that the intersystem differences in procedures did produce five relatively different kinds of records. Second, that each system included some scores, scoring criteria, and interpretive postulates for which no empirical support existed or for which negative findings had been discovered. Third, that each of the systems did include many empirically sturdy elements. In fact, if any system were applied faithfully for administration, scoring, and interpretation, a considerable positive yield would result. On the other hand, some of that positive yield might be offset by the flaws of the system, either in scoring or interpretation.

Those findings, plus the fact that the surveys concerning the use of the test indicated that fewer than 20% faithfully followed any single system, led to a decision to alter the main objective of the Foundation. The thrust was changed from one designed to study each system for its merits and liabilities to one designed to integrate the features of all systems for which empirically defensible data existed or could be established. During the next three years, the pool of protocols was increased to nearly 1200, and more than 150 investigations were completed concerning the array of elements involved in the use of the Rorschach.

In the early phases of the project, focus was on fundamental issues such as seating, instructions, recording and inquirying responses, and the selection of the codes or scores to be used. The issue of interscorer reliability was broached so that no scoring category was included in the "new" system unless a minimum .85 level could be achieved easily for groups of 10 to 15 scorers across at least 10 to 20 protocols in which the target score occurred frequently. Interestingly, this caused the initial rejection of many seemingly useful scores that have subsequently been added to the system by using a revision of the criteria for their application. Each of dozens of interpretive postulates was explored and no procedure or score was included in the new system unless it met fundamental requirements for validation. In the course of this research several new approaches to coding or scoring answers evolved, and several derivations of scores for interpretive purposes were discovered. Computer technology aided enormously to the search for *the* Rorschach. It permitted easy data storage and very complex analyses to be performed quickly, which only a decade earlier could have required inordinate periods.

The beginning of the final product was published in 1974 under the appropriate rubric, *Comprehensive System,* for indeed it reflected an integration of the hard won, empirically demonstrable wisdoms that marked the growth of the test from the time of Rorschach's monograph in 1921 to the most current thinking and research of the early 1970s. It represents the works of all of the systematizers, plus the findings of many dedicated researchers who contributed to the study of a complex tactic used to generate information about personality structure and functioning.

As more information about the Rorschach method has evolved, a fundamental reality pervades. The method has not changed very much, if at all. The same 10 inkblots constitute the primary stimulus elements that were noted more than 70 years ago when Rorschach pursued his experiment. What has changed is that his experimental method has developed into a test. Its psychometric properties have been established and most of the other basic requirements for a psychological test have been met. Much of the research that has been conducted on and about it, especially during the past 20 years, indicates that it is *not* a magical X-ray of the mind, as some have purported it to be. Rather, it is a procedure that provokes many of the psychological operations of the subject. There is no question that the process of projection often occurs during the test, but it is misleading to label it simplistically as a projective technique. It is much more than that, and as the data concerning it have evolved through research, it has become clearer how the test stimuli provoke a complex set of psychological features into action. Some understanding of that process is necessary for the user of the test, because it helps to clarify why certain procedures are important, why scoring is crucial, and how interpretive postulates are generated.

REFERENCES

Beck, S. J. (1936) Autism in Rorschach scoring: a feeling comment. *Character & Personality,* **5,** 83–85.

Beck, S. J. (1937a) *Introduction to the Rorschach method: A manual of personality study.* American Orthopsychiatric Association Monograph, **1.**

Beck, S. J. (1937b) Some recent research problems. *Rorschach Research Exchange,* **2,** 15–22.

Beck, S. J. (1944) *Rorschach's Test I: Basic Processes.* New York: Grune & Stratton.

Beck, S. J. (1945) *Rorshach's Test II: A variety of personality pictures.* New York: Grune & Stratton.

Beck, S. J. (1952) *Rorschach's Test III: Advances in interpretation.* New York: Grune & Stratton.

Beck, S. J. (1961) Personal communication.

Binder, H. (1932) Die helldunkeldeutungen in psychodiagnostischen experiment von Rorschach. *Schweiz Archives Neurologie und Psychiatrie,* **30,** 1–67.

Binet, A., and Henri, V. (1895–1896) La psychologie individuelle. *Annee Psychologique,* **2,** 411–465.

Dearborn, G. (1897) Blots of ink in experimental psychology. *Psychological Review,* **4,** 390–391.

Dearborn, G. (1898) A study of imaginations. *American Journal of Psychology,* **9,** 183–190.

Ellenberger, H. (1954) Hermann Rorschach, M.D. 1884–1922. *Bulletin of the Menninger Clinic,* **18,** 171–222.

Exner, J. E. (1969) *The Rorschach Systems.* New York: Grune & Stratton.

Exner, J. E. (1974) *The Rorschach: A Comprehensive system. Volume 1.* New York: Wiley.

Exner, J. E., and Exner, D. E. (1972) How clinicians use the Rorschach. *Journal of Personality Assessment,* **36,** 403–408

Frank, L. K. (1939) Projective methods for the study of personality. *Journal of Psychology,* **8,** 389–413.

Freud, S. (1894) The anxiety neurosis. *Collected papers.* Volume 1. London: Hogarth Press, 1953,

76–106.

Freud, S. (1896) Further remarks on the defense of neuropsychoses. *Collected papers.* Volume 1. London: Hogarth Press, 1953, 155–182.

Freud, S. (1911) Psychoanalytic notes on an autobiographical account of a case of paranoia. *Collected papers.* Volume 3. London: Hogarth Press, 1953, 387–396.

Freud, S. (1913) Totem and taboo. *Collected papers.* Volume 3. London: Hogarth Press, 1955.

Gough, H. G. (1963) Clinical versus statistical prediction in psychology. In L. Postman (Ed.) *Psychology in the making.* New York: Knopf.

Hertz, M. R. (1936) *Frequency tables to be used in scoring the Rorschach ink-blot test.* Brush Foundation, Western Reserve University.

Hertz, M. R. (1937) Discussion on "Some recent Rorschach problems." *Rorschach Research Exchange, 2,* 53–65.

Hertz, M. R. (1939) On the standardization of the Rorschach method. *Rorschach Research Exchange, 3,* 120–133.

Hertz, M. R. (1941) Rorschach: Twenty years after. *Rorschach Research Exchange, 5,* 90–129.

Hertz, M. R. (1942) *Frequency Tables for Scoring Rorschach Responses.* Cleveland: Western Reserve University Press.

Hertz, M. R. (1952) *Frequency Tables for Scoring Rorschach Responses.* Cleveland: Western Reserve University Press.

Hertz, M. R. (1952) The Rorschach: Thirty years after. In D. Brower, and L. E. Abt (Eds.) *Progress in Clinical Psychology.* New York: Grune & Stratton.

Hertz, M. R. (1961) *Frequency Tables for Scoring Rorschach Responses.* Cleveland: Western Reserve University Press.

Hertz, M. R. (1970) *Frequency Tables for Scoring Rorschach Responses.* Cleveland: Case Western Reserve University Press.

Holt, R. R. (1958) Clinical and statistical prediction: A reformulation and some new data. *Journal of Abnormal and Social Psychology, 56,* 1–12.

Holt, R. R. (1970) Yet another look at clinical and statistical prediction: Or, is clinical psychology worthwhile? *American Psychologist, 25,* 337–349.

Jackson, C. W., and Wohl, J. (1966) A survey of Rorschach teaching in the university. *Journal of Projective Techniques and Personality Assessment, 30,* 115–134.

Jensen, A. R. (1958) Personality. *Annual Review of Psychology, 9,* 395–422.

Jung, C. G. (1910) The association method. *American Journal of Psychology, 21,* 219–269.

Jung, C. G. (1918) *Studies in Word Association.* London: Heineman.

Kerner, J. (1857) *Klexographien:* Part VI. In R. Pissen (Ed.) *Kerners Werke.* Berlin: Boag & Co.

Kirkpatrick, E. A. (1900) Individual tests of school children *Psychological Review, 7,* 274–280.

Klopfer, B. (1937) The present status of the theoretical development of the Rorschach method. *Rorschach Research Exchange, 1,* 142–147.

Klopfer, B. (1961) Personal communication.

Klopfer, B., Ainsworth, M. D., Klopfer, W. G., and Holt, R. R. (1954) *Developments in the Rorschach Technique. I. Technique and Theory.* Yonkers-on-Hudson, N.Y.: World Book.

Klopfer, B. et al. (1956) *Developments in the Rorschach Technique. II. Fields of Application.* Yonkers-on-Hudson, N.Y.: World Book.

Klopfer, B., and Kelley, D. (1942) *The Rorschach Technique.* Yonkers-on-Hudson, N.Y.: World Book.

Klopfer, B., Meyer, M. M., Brawer, F. B., and Klopfer, W. G. (1970) *Developments in the Rorschach Technique. III. Aspects of Personality Structure.* New York: Harcourt Brace Jovanovich.

Klopfer, B., and Sender, S. (1936) A system of refined scoring symbols. *Rorschach Research*

Exchange, **1,** 19–22.

Korman, A. K. (1968) The prediction of managerial performance. *Personnel Psychology,* **21,** 295–322.

Lindzey, G. (1961) *Projective Techniques and Cross Cultural Research.* New York: Appleton-Century-Crofts.

Louttit, C. M. (1936) *Clinical Psychology.* New York: Harper & Row.

Louttit, C. M., and Browne, C. G. (1947) Psychometric instruments in psychological clinics. *Journal of Consulting Psychology,* **11,** 49–54.

Lubin, B., Wallis, R. R., and Paine, C. (1971) Patterns of psychological test usage in the United States: 1935–1969. *Professional Psychology,* **2,** 70–74.

Lubin, B., Larsen, R. M., and Matarazzo, J. D. (1984) Patterns of psychological test usage in the United States: 1935–1982. *American Psychologist,* **39,** 451–454.

Meehl, P. E. (1954) *Clinical Versus Statistical Prediction.* Minneapolis: University of Minnesota Press.

Morgan, C., and Murray, H. A. (1935) A method for investigating fantasies: The Thematic Apperception Test. *Archives of Neurology and Psychiatry,* **34,** 289–306.

Murray, H. A. (1938) *Explorations in Personality.* New York: Oxford University Press.

Parsons, C. J. (1917) Children's interpretation of inkblots (A study on some characteristics of children's imagination). *British Journal of Psychology,* **9,** 74–92.

Piotrowski, Z. (1950) A Rorschach compendium: Revised and enlarged. In J. A. Brussel et al. *A Rorschach Training Manual.* Utica, N.Y.: State Hospitals Press.

Piotrowski, Z. (1957) *Perceptanalysis.* New York: Macmillan.

Pyle, W. H. (1913) *Examination of School Children.* New York: Macmillan.

Pyle, W. H. (1915) A psychological study of bright and dull children. *Journal of Educational Psychology,* **17,** 151–156.

Rapaport, D., Gill, M., and Schafer, R. (1946) *Diagnostic Psychological Testing. Volumes 1 & 2.* Chicago: Yearbook Publishers.

Rorschach, H. (1921) *Psychodiagnostik.* Bern: Bircher (Transl. Hans Huber Verlag, 1942).

Rotter, J. B., and Rafferty, J. E. (1950) *Manual: The Rotter Incomplete Sentences Blank.* New York: Psychological Corporation.

Rybakov, T. (1911) *Atlas for Experimental Research on Personality.* Moscow: University of Moscow.

Sargent, H. (1945) Projective methods: Their origins, theory, and application in personality research. *Psychological Bulletin,* **42,** 257–293.

Sawyer, J. (1966) Measurement and prediction, clinical and statistical. *Psychological Bulletin,* **66,** 178–200.

Schafer, R. (1954) *Psychoanalytic Interpretation in Rorschach Testing.* New York: Grune & Stratton.

Sundberg, N. D. (1961) The practice of psychological testing in clinical services in the United States. *American Psychologist,* **16,** 79–83.

Symonds, P. M. (1946) *The Dynamics of Human Adjustment.* New York: Appleton-Century-Crofts.

Weiner, I. B. (1972) Does psychodiagnosis have a future? *Journal of Personality Assessment,* **36,** 534–546.

Whipple, G. M. (1914) *Manual of Mental and Physical Tests.* Two volumes. Baltimore: Warwick & York.

Wiggins, J. S., Renner, K. E., Clore, J. L., and Rose, R. J. (1971) *The Psychology of Personality.* Reading, Mass.: Addison-Wesley.

Zubin, J., Eron, L. D., and Schumer, F. (1965) *An Experimental Approach to Projective Techniques.* New York: Wiley.

CHAPTER 2

The Nature
of the Rorschach

It is very important for anyone using the Roschach test to understand how it works. How can the responses to 10 inkblots provide much information about an individual? This is an intriguing issue that has often baffled advocates of the test and has sometimes provided grist for the mill of the skeptic. At first glance it does seem incredulous. Such skepticism was probably increased as the projective movement reached its zenith. During that time major emphasis was on content analysis, and thus the test was usually conceptualized in terms of the projective process. Some attempted a direct symbolic interpretation of specific kinds of contents (Phillips & Smith, 1953). Others sought to equate the blot stimuli with universal symbolic meanings, generating faulty notions about a father card, mother card, sex card, interpersonal card, and so on (Halpern, 1953; Meer & Singer, 1950; Pascal, Ruesch, Devine, & Suttell, 1950). Although emphasis on projected material in interpretation served to enhance the usefulness of the test, it also detracted from a broader understanding of the true nature of the test, and detracted from the research on Rorschach's original thinking about the method.

RORSCHACH'S CONCEPT OF THE METHOD

The process of the test obviously intrigued Rorschach and he did formulate some hypotheses related to the response operation. He postulated that responses are formed through an integration of memory traces with the sensations created by the stimulus figure. He argued that this integration, or effort to match the sensations of the stimulus with existing engrams, is a *consciously realized* operation. In other words, the subject is aware that the blot is not identical to objects stored in memory. Consequently, the method requires a willingness by the subject to identify the blot, or blot area, as being something that it is not, but to which it has some similarity. He described this as an associational process. He postulated that differences in "thresholds" exist among people for the ability to assimilate or integrate the stimulus sensation with the existing engrams. He believed that the differences in threshold were the main cause for the broad array of responses that occurs. It was on this premise that he rejected the notion that unconscious elements might be influential in forming a response. He viewed the response process as one of perception and/or apperception.

He also argued, quite persuasively, that imagination had little or nothing to do with the *basic* process of the test, but that it could manifest in embellishments to responses. He felt that these reflected the creative quality of imagination. It seems likely that if Rorschach had lived long enough to consider Murray's concept of projection (1938), or Frank's formulation of the *Projective Hypothesis,* he would have been intrigued with them as relevant to the response process. But it is equally likely that he would have disavowed the concept of projection as representing a major component in the response process. Whatever might have been had Rorschach lived longer, there is no question that the nature of the test, and of the response process, were sorely neglected areas of research for several decades following his death. This neglect probably contributed substantially to the broad divergence that occurred among those attempting to develop the test. Interestingly, as that much-needed research has accumulated, considerable support for most of Rorschach's postulates has been generated. It would seem that he was correct in his basic hypotheses about the response process, but he probably oversimplified the cause for the great diversity that occurs for responses. The method, or test, is considerably more complex than he conceived of it. Numerous operations occur before a response is actually delivered, and they occur within a time frame that few recognized during the early days of the development of the test.

THE RORSCHACH AS A PROBLEM-SOLVING TASK

Rorschach was apparently correct in his assumption that the response is formulated after some awareness that the blot is not identical to existing memory traces. But the subject has some awareness of this well before the first blot is exposed. Cattell (1951) probably best described the task of the subject who is taking the Rorschach for the first time, in his effort to describe the projective situation. He noted that in this situation the subject is required to provide something that is not actually there. Essentially, the task requires the subject to "misperceive" the stimulus, according to Cattell, and through that misperception is encouraged to project something of himself or herself into the response.

Although Cattell may be correct in describing the projective situation, that description can be quite misleading when applied to the circumstances of the Rorschach, depending on whether the term *misperceive* is translated to mean how the stimulus is *translated* or how the stimulus is *identified*. This is a very important distinction, because the first implies that the subject neglects the fact that the stimulus is an inkblot, whereas the second does not carry that implication. Rorschach, of course, believed that identification is one of the essential operations in the response, but he also encountered subjects in his experiment who would concretely and redundantly name the blots. He concluded that they were so seriously debilitated by reason of intellectual limitations, neurological impairment, or active psychosis that the associational or integrative operations failed or decayed.

Most professionals who have used the Rorschach extensively will have encountered the kinds of subjects who are so impaired that they simply cannot respond to the task, or who are so detached from reality that they offer only hallucinatory type of responses when confronted with a blot (e.g., "My God, that sounds terrible, take it away."). But these are very rare subjects. The overwhelming majority of those who take the test are fully aware that they are responding to an inkblot. As noted earlier, that awareness is reinforced when the test is introduced.

Most examiners will usually alert the adult subject by saying something such as, "Now we are going to do the inkblot test." But even if the introduction to the test does not include the use of the word *inkblot,* as is commonly the case when testing younger clients, one would be hard-pressed to argue that the subject is not aware of the fact. For instance, when the records of 500 patient and nonpatient 5- and 6-year-olds were reviewed, it was found that 207 gave comments or responses at the onset implying an awareness of the nature of the stimulus (Exner, 1980). These varied from responses such as, "It's an inkblot" or "It's a bunch of ink," to comments such as, "I know how to make these" or "We make prettier ones than this." In reality, those children gave the only truly correct answer. The stimulus is only an inkblot! But if that correct answer is delivered as the *first* response, it is *not* accepted. Instead, the examiner encourages some other identification, usually by saying, "Yes, I know. This is the inkblot test, but what might it be?"

In effect, the nature of the test situation forces the subject to convert the blot into something that it is not. A *problem-solving* situation is created which requires some violation of reality. At the same time the subject remains concerned with his or her own personal integrity. Thus the requirement to *misidentify* the stimulus provokes a complex of psychological operations into activity that ultimately culminates in decision making and the delivery of answers.

DECISION CHOICES

The problem posed by the need to misidentify the stimulus would be quite simple for most subjects if only one alternative to the answer "inkblot" occurred, but that is not the case. Many misidentifications, or potential answers, are formed very quickly after the blot is presented. Thus one component of the problem situation that the subject must address in taking the test is which of the potential answers to verbalize and which to discard.

Interestingly, for several decades after the test was published, most who used and researched it were unaware of the substantial frequency of potential answers that are available to most subjects. There are probably several reasons for this, beginning with Rorschach's report of his experiment. He noted that most subjects gave between 15 and 30 responses, with depressed, "sullen or unobliging" subjects tending to give the fewest. He noted that most subjects delay before giving answers and suggested that those who gave several responses very quickly were probably "scattered" in their perception or ideation. Rorschach did not record reaction times for first responses, or total times per blot, but his notion of "scattered," plus another hypothesis concerning "shock," caused those who followed him to stress the faithful recording of those times. As a result, many interpretive hypotheses were formulated about short and long records, and about reaction time data. The latter became particularly widespread across the several systems.

Rorschach used the term *color shock* to describe those instances in which a subject appeared to have considerable difficulty in forming a response to Card VIII, the first of the totally chromatic blots, although responding to the prior blots at a seemingly natural rate. He speculated that this apparent helplessness indicated some form of emotional repression. All of the systematizers, and many other researchers of the test were quick to incorporate and expand this concept to other chromatically colored blots, and also to formulate the notion of "gray-black shock" with regard to the achromatic blots. The latter was postulated to equate with forms of anxiety, whereas both were thought to represent neurotic characteristics (Beck, 1945; Klopfer & Kelley, 1942; Miale & Harrower-Erikson, 1940; Piotrowski, 1957). A variety of lists was developed that hypothetically identified those test characteristics related to color or gray-black shock. Although the lists differed, each included as the first or main feature a long reaction time for the first response to a blot. The implication, in both concepts, was that the subject was somehow traumatized by the blot features and therefore struggled to form a response.

A second factor that tended to mislead most Rorschachers about the availability of potential answers has been the variety of published norms. Although they have varied depending on the system employed, the mean number of responses for adults has generally ranged from about 22 to 32 responses, with standard deviations ranging from five to eight (Beck, Beck, Levitt, & Molish, 1961; Exner, 1974, 1978). The data concerning children yielded even lower means for R (Ames, Learned, Metraux, & Walker, 1952; Ames, Metraux, & Walker, 1971; Beck, 1961; Exner, 1978; Exner & Weiner, 1982). These data appeared to indicate that the average subject might be expected to find, or misidentify, two or three objects per blot, and few would have argued with the position that some subjects have difficulty formulating more than one answer to some of the blots. That conclusion was afforded further support by hundreds of research studies in which the average number of responses given by the subjects studied would generally fall within the "normal" range.

Another element contributing to the false notion that subjects of the test would formulate only a small number of answers per blot was the infrequent (but not uncommon) occurrence of card rejections—that is, instances in which subjects would report that they could not find or see anything other than the blot itself. Rorschach noted that some of his subjects did give "refusals" and suggested that this might be the result of an insurmountable blocking process. Klopfer and Kelley (1942) tended to agree with that postulate, but Beck (1945) argued that the rejection, or tendency to reject, might also be generated by problems in the perceptual organizing process, especially for the more "difficult" blots. This issue stimulated several interesting studies on card difficulty in which *reaction time* was used as an index of the difficulty or complexity of the stimuli (Dubrovner, VonLackum, & Jost, 1950; Matarazzo & Mensh, 1952; Meer, 1955; Rabin & Sanderson, 1947). Meer's findings were based on a transformation of reaction times and form accuracy data from 12 studies to formulate decisions about blot difficulty levels. Frequency data collected at the Rorschach Research Foundation suggest that most of his conclusions were correct concerning blot difficulty and/or complexity levels (Exner, Martin, & Cohen, 1983). However, findings such as those reported by Meer only served to reinforce the faulty notion that subjects often had to struggle to find or "misidentify" more than one object in each blot. Few practitioners or researchers entertained the notion that most subjects form potential answers quickly and with relative ease, yet this fact appears to be supported by a series of studies regarding the input-output process. Possibly the most important of these studies was not published until 57 years after Rorschach's monograph had been published.

The Range of Potential Responses   An issue of concern during the development of the Comprehensive System was the impact of the examiner on the subject. A considerable literature had evolved, suggesting that some features of Rorschach responses can be altered under conditions that vary from the standard procedures. For example, different instructional sets, such as asking the subject to find more things, find things moving, find more small objects, and so on, will usually produce more of the kinds of responses for which the set is established (Coffin, 1941; Hutt, Gibby, Milton, & Pottharst, 1950; Abramson, 1951; Gibby, 1951). Similarly, it has been demonstrated that differences among the basic instructions used by the various Rorschach Systematizers will produce significant differences in the average length of a record.

Goetcheus (1967) used 16 examiners in a crossover design to test for differences between the Beck and Klopfer instructions. Each examiner administered eight tests using the Beck instructions and eight using the Klopfer instructions. She found that the Beck instructions, which included, "Tell me everything you see," produced records that, on the average were six responses longer than those administered by the Klopfer format. One of the early studies at the Rorschach Research Foundation involved the comparison of 346 protocols representing the procedures used in the five different systems. The pool consisted of 75, each collected using the Beck and Klopfer procedures, 78 collected by the Rapaport method, 66 using the Piotrowski system, and 52 using the Hertz method. The Klopfer instructions, which are essentially the same as those used by Rorschach in his experiment, and also adopted for use in the Comprehensive System, produced the lowest average number of answers, 23.9. The other instructional formats, all of which encourage subjects to give more answers, turn cards, practice before beginning, or supplement information after each card, produced significantly more answers (Beck = 31.2, Hertz = 32.9, Piotrowski = 33.8, Rapaport = 36.4).

Several studies have also demonstrated that reinforcement, both verbal and nonverbal, can alter the frequencies of some kinds of responses (Wickes, 1956; Gross, 1959; Dinoff, 1960; Magnussen, 1960; Hersen & Greaves, 1971). As it turns out, all, or most all of these designs were tapping into the fact that most subjects generate many misidentifications, or potential responses when confronted with the blot. Although some hints of this fact can be culled from some of the early research on the response process, no one did so. It was not until the late 1970s that this fact became apparent, causing a much more careful review of the operations involved in the response process. This occurred somewhat serendipitously.

In a pilot investigation concerning the effects of reinforcement, two groups of 10 subjects each were instructed to give as many responses as they could, with a time limit of 60 seconds per blot (Exner & Armbruster, 1974). The subjects were reinforced with a payment of 10 cents per response, which was paid immediately as each response was delivered. The first group consisted of 10 nonpatients, and they averaged 104 answers to the 10 blots, with a range of 68 to 147 responses. The second group consisted of 10 nonschizophrenic outpatients. They averaged 113 responses, with a range of 71 to 164 answers. These strikingly large numbers of answers raised several questions. First, to what extent did the reinforcement of the dimes alter the Rorschach response process? Second, to what extent did the exposure time of 60 seconds force subjects to rescan the stimulus field, thereby forming responses that might not have been formulated under the standard administration conditions. Third, did the reinforcement condition cause subjects to violate the use of accurate form more frequently than might be typical? Finally, because only one examiner was used in the pilot, would subjects give unusually large numbers of responses if several examiners were used? These questions led to the design of a more sophisticated study.

Exner, Armbruster, and Mittman (1978) used 12 experienced examiners to administer the test to five groups of 20 subjects each: (1&2) 40 adult nonpatients, ranging in age from 20 to 41 years, subdivided into two groups of 20 each by a median split of their distribution of scores on the K Scale of the MMPI; (3) 20 nonpatient children, ranging in age from 11 to 13 years; (4) 20 inpatient depressives, aged 29 to 51 years; and (5) 20 inpatient schizophrenics, ranging in age from 24 to 42 years. None had been administered the Rorschach previously. The examiners were randomly assigned to subjects so that none tested more than four subjects from a single group or more than 10 subjects in all. All of the subjects had volunteered to participate in a *standardization* study concerning the inkblot test. The procedure followed the standardized method, except that prior to the onset of the association period each subject was told that he or she would have the blot for a 60-second interval, which would be terminated by a beep from a timer, and that during that time the subject should report as many things as he or she could find in the blot.

The responses were audio recorded, and a silent signal was entered on the tape at 15-second intervals. The examiners would rewind the tape after the responses to all 10 cards had been given, and play them back, one at a time, to inquire for the location of the responses. This permitted a review of the answers for the accurate use of form. The average number of responses given by each group, to all 10 blots, is shown in Table 1, which also shows the average number given during the first 15-second interval, the second 15-second interval, and the last 30 seconds of exposure.

The average number of responses given under *standard* procedures is about 22. The data in Table 1 indicate that all five groups gave more than two to four times that number under this experimental condition. The lowest average number was given by the depressed group, which under standard conditions would be expected to give fewer than 23 answers. The data are even more revealing when the average number of responses given during the first 15 seconds of blot exposure are examined. The three nonpatient groups all gave at least one-third more answers during that interval than is usually the case under the standard conditions of administration, in which most subjects retain the cards for between 40 and 55 seconds. Both psychiatric groups gave at least as many answers during the first 15 seconds of exposure to the blots as they would be expected to give when the test is administered under standardized conditions.

In addition to the striking finding that subjects can give many answers when instructed to do so, the data regarding the appropriate use of form are quite important. Table 2 shows the mean X+%'s for each of the groups for the total exposure period, plus those for the first and second 15 seconds, and last 30 seconds of exposure. Table 2 also includes the average number of Popular responses given by the groups during each of those intervals.

Table 1.   Average Number of Responses Given by Each of Five Groups during Four Intervals of Blot Exposure

	First 15 Seconds		Second 15 Seconds		Second 30 Seconds		Total 60 Seconds	
	M	SD	M	SD	M	SD	M	SD
Nonpatients, upper half, MMPI K scale $N = 20$	30.4	4.1	31.2	5.8	21.7	4.1	83.3[a]	9.2
Nonpatients, lower half MMPI K scale $N = 20$	38.1	6.8	32.2	6.1	30.4	7.8	100.6	10.4
Nonpatient children $N = 20$	38.9	7.1	30.7	4.3	24.5	8.3	94.1	9.8
Inpatient schizophrenics $N = 20$	22.7[b]	6.2	18.1[b]	5.1	22.4	6.7	63.2[b]	9.4
Inpatient depressives $N = 20$	14.8[b]	4.4	17.1[b]	5.7	19.3	7.8	51.2[b]	7.8

[a] Statistically fewer than nonpatient adult group scoring in the lower half of the MMPI K Scale distribution, $p < .05$

[b] Statistically significant difference from nonpatient groups, $p < .05$

Table 2.   Means for X + % and Popular Responses for Each of Five Groups during Four Intervals of Blot Exposure

	First 15 Seconds		Second 15 Seconds		Second 30 Seconds		Total 60 Seconds	
	M	SD	M	SD	M	SD	M	SD
Nonpatients, upper half, MMPI *K* scale *N* = 20								
X + %	88.9	11.1	81.4	9.9	89.3	9.6	85.1	10.2
P	5.2	2.1	3.5	1.3	3.2	1.1	10.8	2.8
Nonpatients, lower half MMPI *K* scale *N* = 20								
X + %	83.2	9.7	79.6	7.6	78.1	8.7	79.9	9.8
P	5.0	1.9	2.4	1.1	1.9	0.9	9.3	3.1
Nonpatient children *N* = 20								
X + %	84.6	7.8	80.1	8.5	84.1	7.8	83.3	8.1
P	5.3	1.8	2.4	1.1	2.0	1.1	9.7	2.2
Inpatient schizophrenics *N* = 20								
X + %	63.2[a]	10.8	54.6[a]	11.7	49.3[a]	11.4	53.6	12.7
P	2.4[a]	1.6	1.7	1.0	4.3[a]	1.7	8.4	3.8
Inpatient Depressives *N* = 20								
X + %	77.1	6.8	72.3	7.1	68.7	8.3	71.9	8.9
P	6.2	3.1	3.1	1.4	0.9	0.7	10.2	4.3

[a] Statistically significant difference from all other groups, *p* < .05.

As revealed in Table 2, none of the four nonschizophrenic groups violated form accuracy markedly during any of the intervals of exposure to the blots. The X+% does decline slightly for the Low K nonpatient group, but not significantly so. The High K nonpatient group and the nonpatient children actually show a higher mean X+% during the last 30 seconds of blot exposure than during the second 15-second interval. The depressives also declined slightly from the first 15 seconds to the last 30 seconds, as did the schizophrenics, but these reductions are not statistically or interpretively significant. In effect, each group gave about as many responses with well-defined and appropriate use of form during the first quarter minute as during the entire time of exposure, or stated differently, the significant majority of responses given by all but the schizophrenic group approximated the contours of the blot area used in the response.

The data concerning the Popular answers are also important in this context. Popular answers are the ones given most frequently. The criterion for a response to be defined as Popular is that it occurs at least once in every three records. At the time of this study 17 Popular responses were listed.[1] All of the nonschizophrenic groups averaged about eight Popular

[1] Current norms show only 13 responses meeting the criterion for popularity. The number of Popular responses can be expected to differ slightly across cultures, and within a culture over extended time intervals.

answers during the first 30 seconds of exposure, with about two-thirds of those occurring during the first 15 seconds with the blots. Thus with a relatively brief exposure period, the nonschizophrenic subjects gave as many or more answers than is customary when the test is given under standard conditions, and they also gave the types of answers that are commonly given under the standard conditions.

To say that these findings were surprising is an understatement! The average time for the first response to most blots for most of the groups was less than 2 seconds, a phenomenon Rorschach thought represented scattered perception or ideation; and none of the 100 subjects attempted to reject a blot! There is a considerable variance for the average number of answers per card, but even that performance is relatively consistent across groups when the ratio of responses to each card is considered in light of the total number of responses given. The most solid blots—IV, V, VI, and IX—generally yielded the lowest average number of answers for each group, whereas the most broken blots—III, VIII, and X—yielded the highest average number of answers.

The results of this study indicate that subjects, including those with severe pathology, can form multiple potential responses that are generally congruent with the blot stimuli, in a relatively brief interval after the blot is exposed. The shortest nonpatient record contained 56 answers, and the shortest patient record (from one of the depressed subjects) contained 34 answers. When the yield of responses to the 10 blots during the first 30 seconds of exposure is considered, the lowest number of answers from the nonpatient groups is 23, the highest being 89. One depressed patient gave only 10 responses during the first 30-second interval, but 32 of the 40 psychiatric subjects averaged 16 or more responses to the 10 blots in those intervals, the largest number being 51 given by a schizophrenic subject.

These findings are in sharp contrast with normative data which reveal that most adult groups average between 20 and 23 answers, and that most groups of adolescents and children average between 17 and 22 responses. This narrow range of means appears to be universal. For instance, in the United States, nonpatient adults average about 22 responses. Sendin (1981) has reported that the mean R for a large group of Spanish subjects is about 23. Nonpatient samples ranging in size from 40 to 150, collected in various countries by the Rorschach Research Foundation yield similar results (Canada = 21.6; Japan = 23.2; Malaysia = 22.4; Mexico = 21.2; Micronesia = 20.4; Phillippines = 21.3).

THE RESPONSE PROCESS

If subjects generate many potential answers to each blot, why is it they deliver far fewer than are available when the test is administered in the standardized manner? Extrapolating from the Exner, Armbruster, and Mittman study, it seems reasonable to suggest that many subjects will deliver fewer than 25% of the potential answers that they have available. Any attempt to understand why this occurs, and its importance to the interpretation of the test data, must include consideration of several elements involved in the response process. These include: (1) the input or encoding of the stimulus field, (2) the classification of the field and/or its parts, (3) discarding some potential answers by reason of economy and rank ordering, (4) discarding some potential answers through censorship, (5) selection from the remaining potential responses because of styles and/or traits, and (6) also selection of answers because of psychological states that are activated by the task demand.

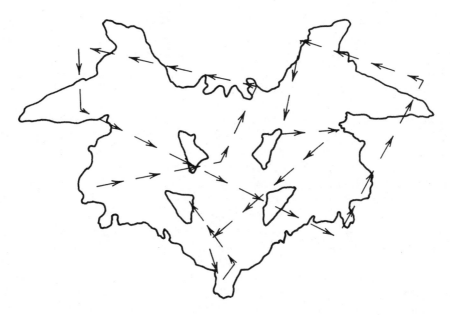

Figure 1.   Visual Scanning by a 19-Year-Old Female during the First 500 ms of Blot Exposure.

1. *The Input Process.* Sometimes it is difficult to appreciate the capacities of the human being to process information. The Rorschach blots are, of course, a form of visual stimulation and the processing of visual information occurs quite rapidly. Although theories of visual processing remain open to discussion (Hochberg, 1981; Neisser, 1976; Pomerantz & Kubovy, 1981), an extremely large number of studies have demonstrated that pattern and/or picture recognition can occur very quickly (Fisher, Monty, & Senders, 1981). Although the number of studies concerning visual processing has increased dramatically during the last two decades (probably as a result of increasingly sophisticated technology), the methodology was not applied to Rorschach research until recently. Exner (1980, 1983) has studied the visual scanning activity of nonpatient adults to some of the blots. Figure 1 is a crude facsimilie of the eye-scanning activity of a 19-year-old female viewing Card I for approximately 500 ms.[2]

The arrows each represent the focal point of the visual field of the subject. It is not certain how far the peripheral visual field extends, but if a 1-inch area on either side of the centerpoint is used as a conservative estimate, it would appear that this subject has clearly viewed all of the blot, and some parts more than once. The importance of this finding is that the average reaction time for the first answer to Card I is 5.79 seconds ($SD = 2.38$) for 125 nonpatient adults, using a voice-accuated timer to insure precision. If this subject, or most like her, were allowed as much as twice the scanning time shown here (1000 ms) for the visual input and encoding of the stimulus field, slightly less than

[2]A Gulf & Western Model 200 Eye Movement Monitor was used to record the scanning activity. The subject's head was held in a retainer to minimize random head movement. The blots were presented tachistoscopically on a small screen in the center of the subject's visual field. The eye movements were recorded through infrared sensors attached to spectacle frames worn by the subject and transmitted in an analog model to a computer and a digital model to a converter, which reproduced the activity on a video display.

5 seconds would remain before she might be expected to offer her first answer. Figure 2 is a crude facsimilie of the scanning action of a 23-year-old nonpatient male presented with Card III. It reflects his eye activity during the interval of 1100 ms after the blot was shown.

This subject scanned Card III at about the same pace as other subjects in the study. A review of his eye activity indicates that he has viewed all of the features of this broken blot at least once, and some segments more than once during this interval. The average reaction time for the first response to this card is 7.74 seconds ($SD = 3.1$), indicating that the majority of subjects offer their first answer to the blot in a period of about 4.5 to nearly 11 seconds. In other words, an interval of between 5 and 9 seconds elapses *after* the input occurs until the first answer is given.

The importance of these findings is not so much that the subject is able to input the stimulus quickly; that information should have been obvious from the many studies on eye activity. The importance rests in confirmation of the *delay period* that exists between the input and the output. It is that critical interval of a few seconds, in which the many substantive operations take place, that lead to the decisions of how the subject will use the potential answers that he or she classified after being exposed to the stimulus.

2. *Classification of the Stimulus and/or Its Parts.* It seems quite probable, drawing from information concerning perception, that once the input is made it is encoded and held in a form of short-term storage, and the process of classification begins. Data from long-term storage are used as the basis for comparison to classify, or misidentify, the stimulus field and/or its parts. In some instances, the field as a whole, or some of its

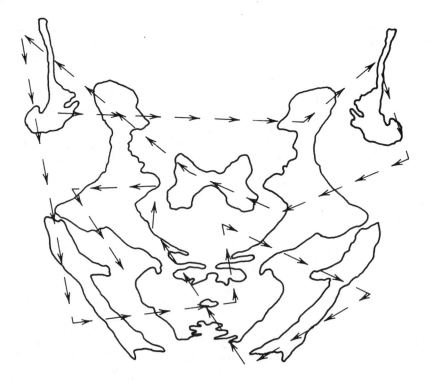

Figure 2.   Visual Scanning by a 23-Year-Old Male during the First 1100 ms after Blot exposure.

parts, may not be classified because of their apparent ambiguity to the subject. But almost all subjects, with the probable exception of those with severe intellectual or neurologically related deficits, will classify some elements in the field as being sufficiently approximate to a known or imagined object to create potential answers.

It seems clear that some parts of the stimulus field have much more similarity to real or imagined objects than others. Thus they are easier to classify or misidentify. As a consequence, some whole blots or blots areas have a greater likelihood of being included among the responses that are actually delivered when the rank ordering and discarding procedures are completed. In some cases it seems likely that a greater effort will be made to classify some blot areas simply because the other areas are much more ambiguous. For example, the contours of the $D1$ area on Card VIII probably have a greater similarity to a known object, an animal, than any whole blot or any other areas of the blots. It has components that are very similar to the legs, body, and head of a four-legged animal. In addition, its location is somewhat discrete in relation to the remainder of the blot. Thus even though the coloring of this area (pink) is incongruous to a four-legged animal, the preciseness of the contours and its discrete location, plus the fact that other areas of the blot are less easily identified, a response to Card VIII that includes the use of this area as an animal is highly predictable. More than 90% of all nonpatient adults and children and more than 80% of all nonschizophrenic psychiatric subjects include the use of this area, as an animal, among their responses. Almost 65% of schizophrenics also give this type of response even though, as a group, they tend to give significantly fewer of the common or Popular answers on other blots.

There are also some characteristics of the blots that are critical to the formation of a potential answer—that is, bits or parts of the blots which have a high valence for belonging to a particular class of objects. The coloring of Card I and the contours of a relatively small area of the blot are a good illustration of this. The most frequently given answer to Card I is a bat, using the whole blot. Nearly 60% of all subjects, psychiatric and nonpsychiatric, identify Card I as a bat. Exner (1959) demonstrated that if the achromatic coloring of the blot is changed to chromatic, holding all other features constant (size, shading, etc.), the frequency of the bat response is sharply reduced. In fact, some chromatic colors such as yellow and blue eliminate the bat response completely. Thus it can be surmised that the achromatic coloring of the blot is a stimulus bit that is quite important to the classification or misidentification of the stimulus field as a bat. But two other elements in the stimulus field are at least as important as the coloring, if not more so, to the formation of the bat response. These are the $Dd34$ projections that extend outward from either side of the top of the blot. Exner and Martin (1981) used a photographic technique to eliminate these areas and administered the entire test with the modified Card I to 30 adult nonpatient volunteer subjects. Not one bat response was given by the group and, in fact, the frequency of butterfly, moth, and bird responses all fell to nearly zero. Obviously, those projections play an important role in classifying the blot as a winged object.

Sometimes critical stimulus elements that contribute significantly to the classification process are not readily apparent. For instance, the most common answer given to the blue-colored $D1$ area in Card X (which is a multichromatic and broken stimulus field) is a spider. The response "crab" to this same area is the second most frequently given answer to this blot. For unknown reasons, schizophrenics do not give either of these responses very often. Exner and Wylie (1976), pursuing the hypothesis that the blue creates a dissonant effect, used a dye-coupling technique to alter the color of that blot area, making it a reddish-brown. The entire test was administered to two groups of 50 subjects each, one of nonpatients and one of schizophrenics. A random half of the subjects in each group were administered the standard Card X and the other half the altered version. The groups administered the altered version of Card X gave significantly fewer spider and crab responses than did the controls. This finding seemed puzzling until it was noted that the subjects in the experimental groups gave significantly more responses to another area of the blot, $D6$, which is colored blue. A 30-item questionnaire was hastily contrived and administered to the 50 nonpatient subjects who had participated in the experiment. It contained one critical item, "What is your favorite color?" Of the 50 subjects, 41 responded with the answer, "blue."

Thus it was hypothesized that although the contours of $D1$ can be judged as similar to those of a crab or spider, the blue coloring of the area increases the stimulus valence of the area, causing subjects to attend more to it during the classification process. Exner and Wylie (1977) created a completely achromatic version of Card X to test this hypothesis. They administered the entire test to 30 nonpatient volunteers, half of whom were administered the standard version of Card X and half the achromatic version. Only three subjects in the experimental group gave spider or crab responses to the $D1$ area, whereas 12 subjects in the control group did so.

There is still much to be learned about the cognitive activity involved in the classification procedure and, in turn, how that procedure relates to the total response process. It does seem clear that classification can occur very quickly after the blot is entered into the visual field of the subject. The first clue to this, generally disregarded by the Rorschach community, was evidenced in a study published in 1949 by Morris Stein. He presented the blots tachistoscopically to two groups of subjects, each of which was administered the test four times. The first, named the "ascending group," was shown the blots for intervals of 0.01 seconds in the first administration, 0.10 seconds in the second administration, 3.0 seconds in the third, and given an unlimited time exposure in the fourth. The control group, "descending," also received four administrations of the test, but with the exposure times reversed as compared with the ascending group (i.e., starting with the unlimited time exposure). Unfortunately the time intervals between testings were very brief and this rapid retest procedure probably confounded some of the results.

But some clues about the rapidity of the response formulation may be gleaned from the results for the ascending group. In their first trial, with the blots exposed for only 10 milliseconds, the subjects averaged nearly 10 answers, with a range of five to 14 responses. When the blots were exposed for a full 3.0 seconds, two trials later, the average number of answers had increased only slightly, to about 12, with a range of eight to 17. Stein noted that as the exposure times increased, so too did the frequencies of answers based exclusively or primarily on the contours of the blots. At the third trial, using the 3.0-second exposure, a significantly greater number of Popular responses were given than had been the case when the blots were exposed for the much briefer intervals. In other words, once the blots were exposed long enough to permit a full scan of the stimulus, considerable homogeneity occurred among the responses given.

In a related study, Horiuchi (1961) presented Cards III and VI tachistoscopically to groups of 80 nonpatients, 80 neurotics, and 80 schizophrenics for intervals of .10 seconds, .30 seconds, 1.0 second, and unlimited time. She found that 60 of the 80 nonpatients and nearly half of the neurotics and schizophrenics gave at least one response per blot with the exposure time of 100 ms. When the exposure time was increased to 300 ms, all of the nonpatients gave at least one response per blot, but the frequency of answers for the neurotic and schizophrenic groups did not increase. She also found that some subjects from the neurotic and schizophrenic groups continued to have difficulty forming a differentiated response when the blots were exposed for a full second. She concluded that some of the mediational activity necessary to form an answer is inhibited in conditions of psychopathology.

Colligan and Exner (1985) tested three groups of 36 subjects each—schizophreniform inpatients, orthopedic inpatients, and nonpatients—using a tachistoscopic presentation of the blots. They randomized each group into three subgroups of 12 subjects each and exposed the blots to one for 200 ms, the second for 400 ms, and the third for 600 ms. Subjects were instructed to give their responses after a tone sounded. The tone occurred 900 ms after the exposure to allow sufficient time for the decay of the icon. They found that 62 of the 72 nonpsychiatric subjects were able to give at least one response to each blot, and 9 of the 10 who gave refusals were in the subgroups with time exposures of 200 ms or 400 ms. Several of the nonpsychiatric subjects in each of the subgroups gave between 12 and 15 answers. There were many more refusals among the schizophrenic subjects at each of the exposure levels. In all, 17 of the 36 schizophrenics gave fewer than 10 answers. Eight of those 17 were in the 600 ms subgroup. These findings may support Horiuchi's postulate that mediational activity is impaired by psychopathology; however, it might be more accurate to suggest that the schizophrenics were much more defensive in the test situation. Six of the 19 schizophrenics who did not give refusals gave between 12 and 15 responses.

Another important finding from the Colligan and Exner study concerns the appropriate use of the blot contours. Nearly 70% of all responses given by the nonpsychiatric subgroups included an appropriate use of contours. An examination of those answers in which the contours of the blot were violated reveals that many occurred to the more broken blots—II, III, VIII, and X. Many of the answers given to those blots seem to reflect the principle of closure; that is, the subjects created an imaginary line to encompass the parts of the blots. For example, seven of the 72 nonpsychiatric subjects reported that Card III was a "face." Classification of this very broken blot in that way requires some closure operation. If such an answer occurs under the standardized procedures of administration, it is considered a serious violation of reality. The fact that it occurs with a considerable frequency among nonpsychiatric subjects faced with the task of classifying a field very quickly may provide a clue about why the female subject whose eye scan of Card I (Figure 1) was able to encompass almost all of the blot in about a half second, whereas the male subject scanning Card III (Figure 2) took approximately 1.1 seconds to complete a full scan of the blot. The more broken the stimulus field, the more time will be necessary for the procedure of encoding and classifying. This seems to confirm the notion that some blots or blot areas are classified very quickly and easily, whereas other blots or blot areas may require more scanning time.

Assuming that this is true, the differences in required scanning and classification time are not so substantial to account for the relatively lengthy delay that occurs between the presentation of the blot and the delivery of the first answer. Extrapolating conservatively from the eye-tracking data and the Stein, Horiuchi, and Colligan and Exner studies, it seems reasonable to assume that a period of 2 to 3 seconds after exposure is more than sufficient for encoding the stimulus and classifying at least three, if not more, potential answers. Why then, do most subjects take at least twice that time, and often much longer, before delivering their first answer? It seems probable that the procedures of ranking and discarding are mainly responsible for the delay.

3. *Discarding Potential Answers by Ranking.* The instructions to the subject are deliberately brief. No requirements or limits are implied concerning the number of responses that should be delivered. Subjects who give only one answer to Card I are encouraged to "Take your time and look a bit more and you'll probably find something else." The implication for that group is that only one response may not be sufficient. Subjects who give more than one response to Card I receive no confirmation that the yield is sufficient, except by the passive acceptance of the examiner. Some subjects seek direction by asking, "Is that enough?" "Do you want more?" or "How many should I give?" If only one answer has been given to Card I, the prompt is used, but if the subject has given more than one answer to Card I, the response to such queries remains open-ended: "It's up to you." This requires the subject to decide how many of the potential answers that have been formulated to deliver.

The majority of subjects appear to be influenced by an economy principle in their decisions about how many responses to give. There are occasional compulsive-like subjects who seem prepared to give an infinite number of answers to each blot, but they are deterred from this by withdrawing the card after the fifth response, if this occurs early in the test. But most subjects are much more conservative with their yield of answers, and this probably accounts for the fact that most groups average about 22 responses. Whether the orientation to economize is a simple matter of efficiency, or whether it is more a matter of defensive concealment is not certain, but probably both of these issues are involved. Practically all subjects, even children, have some conception of psychological testing, and often will have some vague awareness of the "inkblot test." Unfortunately, many of these concepts are based on faulty assumptions. People tend to think of testing in terms of educational models, which include right and wrong answers, high versus low scores, and passing or failing. Even when the competent examiner properly devotes time to an explanation of procedures and arranging for feedback with the subject, most will still approach the testing continuing to be influenced by prior sets and/or experiences of apprehension. The desire to complete the test quickly and effectively is natural in such a situation and probably contributes to some of the economy orientation.

A second factor contributing to the economy orientation is the rank ordering process. As noted earlier, some blots or blot areas are easier to classify than others. Quite often a single blot or blot area will be classified or misidentified more than once. For example, the whole Card I might be classified as a bat, a bird, and a butterfly. Some subjects elect to give two of those three potential answers, and occasionally a subject may give all three, or even more from the same general classification of winged objects. But most subjects will give only one of those responses. In doing so they withhold or discard the others. The selection of which of the three to deliver is based, at least in part, on some form of ranking, such as it looks more like a bat than either a bird or a butterfly. This same process occurs whether the multiple potential answers are generated from the same blot area or from a variety of areas. For instance, a subject might classify the whole Card I as a bat and a butterfly, the $D4$ area as a woman, the $D2$ area as an animal, the $D7$ area as a bird, and the $DdS29$ areas as triangles, but deliver only two or three of those six possibilities. This form of paired comparison rank ordering appears to contribute significantly to the process of selection and discarding. In a pilot study, Martin and Thomas (1982) presented the blots twice, using a slide projector, to a class of 28 high school students. In the first presentation each blot was exposed for 1 minute. The students were instructed to *write* three responses per blot on a form provided. After all 10 blots had been presented, they were shown again in the same order with exposure times of 15 seconds. Prior to the second exposure the students were instructed to look at the blots again and select one of the three answers they had written to be "scored," and also to write, in a space provided, a brief statement about why they selected that answer. Of the 280 statements, 159 could easily be catagorized under the heading, "It looks most like that."[3]

Although it seems clear that some form of paired comparison ranking, based on a similarity to known objects, does occur, it would be erroneous to assume that this procedure is *mainly* responsible for the selection of those answers to be delivered. There are at least three other elements that play a significant role in determining which of the potential answers will be delivered and which will be discarded.

4. *Discarding through Censorship.* As noted earlier, most subjects will approach psychological testing with some preconceptions or sets. Some of these may be specific to psychological testing or even to the Rorschach in particular. Generally they result from bits and pieces of information concerning testing that the subject has accumulated. However, many of the sets with which a subject approaches the test are derived from the more broadly based values that the subject has developed. Whatever the origins, this composite of attitudes will often be very influential on the procedures of discarding and selecting. For example, the MMPI K Scale has been demonstrated to have some relation to the orientation to make socially acceptable responses (Dahlstrom, Welsh, & Dalhstrom, 1972). In the Exner, Armbruster, and Mittman (1978) study, the 40 nonpatient adults were also administered the MMPI and subdivided into two groups based on a median split of the distribution of their scores on the K Scale. The results show that the 20 subjects scoring in the upper half of that distribution averaged 17 fewer responses than did those scoring in the lower half. In other words, those subjects more oriented toward making acceptable responses tended to withhold or discard more responses than did the subjects not so oriented. These findings have provoked several other studies regarding the circumstances in which subjects may be more or less prone to withhold or discard responses.

In a second study reported by Exner, Armbruster, and Mittman (1978), 10 therapists were asked to recruit two each of their own patients who had never taken the Rorschach. Those patients were randomized so that each therapist tested one of his or her patients and the patient of another therapist with whom the examining therapist had no prior contact. The results show that those patients tested by their own therapist averaged 10 more responses to the test than did the controls, including significantly more sex responses (4.3 versus 0.8). Leura and Exner (1978) trained 10 junior high school teachers to administer the test and then used them in the same design. Each teacher was asked to recruit two volunteers from his or her classes, the criterion for selection being that the students were progressing quite well in that class. All of the recruited students were from seventh-grade classes. As with the patients in the Exner, Armbruster, and Mittman study, they were randomized so that each teacher tested one of his or her own pupils and a student from another school with whom the examining teacher had no prior contact. Subjects tested by their own teacher averaged nearly 16 more responses than did the controls.

---

[3]The comments for the total group varied considerably from "I don't know" to "I like those," but all categorized under the rubric of "It Looks Most Like That" ranged from form specified responses such as, "It has the wings and body like they are," to "It looks more like that than anything else there."

The results of these studies seem to indicate that subjects who feel emotionally and/or intellectually close to their examiner will deliver more and conceal less. This should not be translated to suggest that the well-trained examiner can or will have a significantly influential effect on how many responses are delivered. If the test is administered in the standardized manner, examiners can expect to obtain a normal distribution of responses from their subjects, unless they do a high frequency of testing with unusual populations such as the neurologically impaired, newly admitted criminals, and so on. Exner (1974) has demonstrated that some novice examiners may, because of their own difficulties and discomfort about learning the procedures of the test administration, cause fewer responses to be delivered than might ordinarily be the case. Apparently the discomfort of the examiner increases the apprehensiveness of the subject and leads to more withholding. But this is easily corrected with supervised experience in administration.

Goodman (1979) studied the effect of sex differences among examiners, using a design in which 10 male and 10 female examiners each tested two male and two female subjects. She also rated the examiners on an interpersonal "warmth" scale, using videotapes of them administering the TAT to a collaborator subject. Her results indicate no significant effects for the same-sex versus cross-sex pairings. She did find that the more experienced examiners, who also tended to be rated as "warmer" in their interactions with subjects, elicited a greater number of human responses than did the less experienced examiners. She also found that the experienced examiners obtained more records of average length (17 to 27 responses) than did the examiners who were still in graduate school training.

Although the element of rapport between the examiner and subject will contribute to censorship based discarding of potential answers, it seems likely that much censoring occurs because of sets about the test and value judgments concerning the acceptability of answers. Exner and Leura (1976) used 60 nonpatient adults, 30 males and 30 females, in a pilot study concerning the ease with which objects can be perceived in the blots. None had prior exposure to the test. They were randomized into two groups of 30 each and seated at opposite ends of a hotel ballroom, each at their own small table. The groups were separated by a thick sliding wall. Each subject was provided with a list of five answers per blot plus a location sheet on which all 50 answers were outlined. Each group of five answers was randomized for the ordering sequence so that no answer appeared at the same point in the list for more than six subjects in each group. Each group of five answers included a Popular response to the blot, two commonly given responses, and two others that are not given frequently. One of the five answers, the *target* response, had a content implying sexuality, injury, or violence.

For example, the five answers listed for Card I were, a bat, a mask, an animal, a bell, and the target answer, a naked woman. Subjects were instructed to look carefully at each blot as it was projected on a screen for an interval of 165 seconds, review the areas outlined on the location sheet, and decide the ease with which each could be recognized as compared with the remaining four answers, and assigning the rank of 1 for the easiest to see, 2 for the next easiest to see, and 5 for the one most difficult to see. The only difference between the two groups was that one was told that the responses they would be ranking were among those given *most frequently by normal subjects,* whereas the second group was told that the responses represented those given *most often by severely disturbed psychiatric patients.*

When the groups were compared for their rankings, a significant difference at .05 or less occurred for 22 of the 50 answers, including eight of the 10 target responses. For example, only four of the 30 subjects who thought the responses came from psychiatric subjects ranked the target response (naked woman) 1 or 2. In fact, 17 of the 30 ranked the target response 4 or 5, and 15 of those 17 assigned the rank of 5. Conversely, 19 of the 30 subjects told that the answers were given frequently by normal subjects ranked the target answer 1 or 2, and 14 of those 19 assigned the rank of 1. The responses listed for Card VI included an animal skin, a totem pole, a human profile, a dog, and the target response, a penis. One of the subjects set to believe that the answers came from psychiatric patients ranked the target answer 2, a second ranked the target answer 3, and the remaining 28 ranked the target answer 4 or 5, including 23 who assigned the rank of 5. In the group set to believe that the responses came from normal subjects, 19 ranked the target answer 1, and 4 others assigned the rank of 2. Only three subjects ranked the target answer 4 or 5.

Thomas, Exner, and Leura (1977) used another group of 60 nonpatients, naive to the test, in a modification of this same design. Again, the group was randomized into two groups of 30 each and seated at opposite ends of a ballroom separated by a sliding wall. They were provided with the same lists of five responses per blot used in the previous study, but with location sheets on which there were *no* outlines of the answers. These groups were given similar, but more distinctive sets concerning the origins of the responses. One group was told that the answers were given most commonly by *very successful businessmen,* whereas the second group was told that the responses were those given most often by *inpatient schizophrenics.* Instead of projecting the blots on a screen, each subject was provided with a set of the Rorschach cards. The subjects were instructed to study each blot carefully, using as much time as might be necessary, and *find* each of the objects listed and, using a black marking pen, to outline each on the location sheet. After locating and outlining all five, they were to decide which was the easiest to see, the next easiest, and so on, using the same rankings of 1 to 5 that had been used in the pilot investigation.

The results of this study are similar to those of the pilot study. The groups differed significantly for their rankings of 21 of the 50 responses, including nine of the 10 target responses. The 10 target responses and the frequencies for rankings are shown in Table 3. The ranks of 1 and 2, and 4 and 5 have been collapsed to represent the "easier" versus "more difficult" to see.

In both of these studies *all* of the subjects could see the responses listed, whether outlined on the location sheet as in the pilot study, or not. The difference between the groups in each study lies in the rankings or weights assigned with regard to how *easily* each could be seen. It is important to note that all of the target responses involve larger and/or more discrete areas of the blots than others in the five response groupings and two of them *occur with a relatively high frequency when the test is administered under standard conditions.* These are the figure of the woman on Card I, and the anatomy response on Card VIII. The "blood" areas on Cards II, III, and X, and the penis area on Card VI are all very discrete blot areas. Because sets were employed concerning the origins of the responses, it seems logical to postulate that the negative set (i.e., the responses were given by psychiatric subjects) caused many to rank some responses as being more difficult to perceive, whereas those with the positive set felt less need to do so.

Although studies of this kind are inconclusive about the censoring operations that occur, they do appear to provide some clues about how the process may work. Thus even though the ranking operations might cause a potential answer to be ranked highly in terms

Table 3.   Frequencies of Rankings for 10 Target Responses Given by Two Groups, with Ranks 1 and 2, and 4 and 5 Collapsed

Card	Area	Responses	Group 1 Schizophrenia Set 1–2	3	4–5	Group 2 Businessmen Set 1–2	3	4–5
I	D4	Naked woman	5	4	16[a]	18[a]	9	3
II	D2	Blood smears	1	10	19	14[a]	5	11
III	D2	Blood running down	5	11	14	16[a]	6	8
IV	W	Monster looming	21	6	3	20	9	1
V	W	Rams fighting	7	15	8	18[a]	10	2
VI	D2	Penis	3	9	18[a]	21[a]	5	4
VII	D6	Vagina	0	7	23[a]	13[a]	9	9
VIII	W	Open chest cavity	4	7	19	14[a]	5	11
IX	D6	Buttocks	0	12	18[a]	11[a]	11	8
X	D9	Blood stains	5	13	11	15[a]	7	8

The "Rankings" label spans above the 3 column between the two groups.

[a]Statistically significant larger number of this rank, $p < .05$.

of object similarity, the censoring operation might cause the response to be discarded because the subject places a negative value judgment on it in light of the test situation. But there are still two remaining elements that may override the ranking and censoring operations in the discarding and selection decisions.

5. *Styles and Traits and the Selecting Process.* It seems obvious that the basic psychological characteristics of the individual play a dominant role in determining which of the potential answers will be delivered. These are the features of people that cause them to be relatively consistent in many of their psychological operations and manifest behaviors. Historically, they have been identified as psychological habits, traits, styles, or dispositions. Whatever nomenclature is used, it represents the composite of the more dominant elements of the personality structure that breed behavioral preferences and create a tendency to redundancy in the selection of many coping responses.

These features are often reflected in the descriptions of a person rendered by those who know him or her well. For example, some people may be described as being quiet and reserved, whereas others may be described as more spontaneous and emotional. Some may be described as forceful or assertive, whereas others may be described as more passive. Some may be considered as strong in the face of stress and others as easily disorganized, and so on. If the person offering the description has frequent and close contact with the person being described, it is very likely that the description will be reasonably accurate.

These characteristics are especially influential to many of a person's decision operations that relate to coping and/or problem solving. In that the task of the Rorschach creates a form of problem-solving demand, it is only natural that the subject will be influenced by these characteristics in the final decisions concerning which responses to deliver. In effect, the tendency toward behavioral redundancy becomes manifest in Rorschach-related operations by creating a greater probability that certain classes of responses will be selected for delivery than other classes of responses that are also available. This creates one of the strengths of the Rorschach, as a test—its reliability over time.

During the often stormy history of the Rorschach, those who disavowed its usefulness as a test frequently pointed to problems of establishing satisfactory evidence of reliability. Unfortunately, most of the efforts to do so approached the issue by attempting to demonstrate that the test is internally consistent, using a split-half technique (Vernon, 1933; Hertz, 1934; Ford, 1946; Orange, 1953). Although most of the results were statistically significant, very few of the correlation coefficients fall into the .80 or higher range that would be required if a test is to be judged as truly internally consistent. The problem with this approach to reliability is the required assumption that the stimuli are equivalent, and will be equally likely to promote any class of response. The Rorschach blots are not equivalent stimuli. They differ for levels of complexity and are clearly different for the kinds of responses they are likely to generate. It was because of this problem that much of the work at the Rorschach Research Foundation has focused on the issue of reliability by studying the temporal consistency of classes of response. The operational hypothesis posed is that people do have preferred response styles that manifest in the majority of their responses, and evidence for those styles should be consistently evident in repeated testings.

Earlier, Holzberg (1960) had questioned the usefulness of the test-retest model as applied to the Rorschach, arguing that personality variables might not be consistent over time, and that a different set might occur during the second testing because of the memory input created by the earlier testing. Neither of these objections is very convincing. A host of data exist indicating that many so-called personality traits do remain consistent over time (London & Exner, 1978), and the findings of the Exner, Armbruster, and Mittman (1978) study suggest that if memory is an important variable, it is *less contingent on recalling what was seen, and more on recalling what was reported.*

By late 1983 more than 30 temporal consistency studies had been completed at the Rorschach Research Foundation, using many different groups of adults and children, patients and nonpatients. The intervals between first and second tests have varied from a few days to many months. When viewed in relation to the consistency of response styles or dispositions, the more important of these involve retesting after reasonably lengthy intervals. Data from two such studies are available and appear to support the consistency hypothesis. In the first, 100 nonpatient adults, 50 male and 50 female, were retested after 36 to 39 months (Exner, Armbruster, & Viglione, 1978). In the second, completed for this volume, 50 nonpatient adults, 25 male and 25 female, were retested after 12 to 14 months (Exner, Thomas, & Cohen, 1983). The retest correlations from each of these studies, for 25 variables, are show in Table 4.

An examination of the data for the 50 subjects retested after approximately 1 year reveals that two of the correlations exceed .90, and 13 others fall between .81 and .89. Only five of the correlations fall below .72, a finding that is not surprising, because all five relate to *state* rather than *trait* features. The data for the retests taken at approximately three years are quite similar. One of the correlations falls at .90, and 12 others are between .80 and .87. Again, only five, all related to state conditions, fall below .70.

The psychometric purist might argue, with some merit, that correlations falling below .80, or even below .85, are not sufficient to support a claim of stability or consistency for a variable. This argument is most relevant to those variables having retest correlations between .70 and .79. Five of these appear in the data for the 1-year retest, and seven in the data for the 3-year retest. Obviously the features and/or operations related to these variables are not as consistent as the features and operations related to the variables with higher retest correlations, yet each accounts for more than one-half of the variance. Thus it seems reasonable to postulate that these variables relate to

Table 4.   Correlation Coefficients for Nonpatient Groups of 50 Adults Retested after 12 to 14 Months and 100 Adults Retested after 36 to 39 Months

Variable	Description	1-Year Retest	3-Year Retest
		r	r
R	No. of Responses	.86	.79
P	Popular responses	.83	.73
Zf	Z Frequency	.85	.83
F	Pure Form	.74	.70
M	Human Movement	.84	.87
FM	Animal Movement	.77	.72
m	Inanimate Movement	.26	.39
a	Active Movement	.83	.86
p	Passive Movement	.72	.75
FC	Form Color Responses	.86	.86
CF	Color Form Responses	.58	.66
C	Pure Color	.56	.51
CF + C	Color Dominant Responses	.81	.79
Sum C	Sum Weighted Color	.82	.86
T	Texture Responses	.91	.87
C'	Achromatic Color Responses	.73	.67
Y	Diffuse Shading Responses	.31	.23
V	Vista Responses	.87	.81
Ratios & Percentages			
L	Lambda	.78	.82
X + %	Extended Good Form	.86	.80
Afr	Affective Ratio	.82	.90
3r + (2)/R	Egocentricity Index	.89	.87
EA	Experience Actual	.83	.85
es	Experienced Stimulation	.64	.72
D	Stress Tolerance Index	.91	.83

characteristics having some considerable stability, but which are also more subject to influence by other conditions, including lengthy time intervals.

It is also important to note that none of the 18 single variables listed in Table 4, *taken alone,* have a critical impact on the interpretation of the test. The seven ratios and percentages shown in Table 4 have a much more important role in interpretation, and most of those do have retest correlations of .80 or greater. Those having correlations of less than .80 are much more related to state influences.

Whereas the data in Table 4 indicate that most of the characteristics represented by Rorschach scores are very stable among nonpatient adults over long periods, the same is not true for children. Exner and Weiner (1982) have reported relatively low retest correlations for 6-year-olds who were retested at age 8, and for 9-year-olds retested when they were 12. The results of an 8-year longitudinal study of 57 nonpatient youngsters, tested first at age 8 and retested at each 2-year interval through the age of 16, show that retest correlations for most variables tend to remain low until the interval between 14 and 16 years of age (Exner, Thomas, & Mason, 1985). However, this should not be interpreted to mean that the traits or styles of the child are not stable over briefer intervals, or that those features will have little influence on the selection of responses. Retest correlations for most variables are quite high, for both children and adults, when the second test is taken in less than 1 month. Table 5 includes the results of three such studies. One concerns 25 nonpatient 8-year-olds retested after 7 days (Exner & Weiner, 1982). In the other two, involving 35 nonpatient 9-year-olds and 35 nonpatient adults, the retest was administered after approximately 3 weeks (Thomas, Alinsky, & Exner, 1982).

The correlations for the 8-year-olds retested after 7 days include eight which are at .90 or greater and seven others between .81 and .89. Those for the 9-year-olds include eight at .90 or greater, and 11 others falling between .80 and .89. The correlations for the adults include three at .90 or greater and 14 between .81 and .89.

The large number of high correlations developed from these brief interval retest studies tends to favor the postulate that these styles and characteristics do play an important role in the selection of answers to be delivered. It could be argued, following from Holzberg (1960), that the memory factor may play a more important role when brief interval retesting is done, thereby causing some correlations to be spuriously elevated. But there is evidence to indicate that this is not the case.

Table 5. Correlation Coefficients for 25 Nonpatient 8-Year-Olds Retested after 7 Days, 35 Nonpatient 9-Year-Olds, and 35 Nonpatient Adults Retested after Approximately 3 Weeks

Variable	Description	8-Year-Olds Seven-Day Retest	9-Year-Olds Three-Week Retest	Adults Three-Week Retest
		r	r	r
R	No. of Responses	.88	.87	.84
P	Popular responses	.86	.89	.81
Zf	Z Frequency	.91	.92	.89
F	Pure Form	.79	.80	.76
M	Human Movement	.90	.87	.83
FM	Animal Movement	.75	.78	.72
m	Inanimate Movement	.49	.20	.34
a	Active Movement	.91	.91	.87
p	Passive Movement	.86	.88	.85
FC	Form Color Responses	.90	.84	.92
CF	Color Form Responses	.76	.74	.68
C	Pure Color	.72	.64	.59
CF+C	Color Dominant Responses	.89	.92	.83
Sum C	Sum Weighted Color	.88	.87	.83
T	Texture Responses	.86	.92	.96
C'	Achromatic Color Responses	.77	.74	.67
Y	Diffuse Shading Responses	.42	.17	.41
V	Vista Responses	.96	.93	.89
Ratios & Percentages				
L	Lambda	.82	.84	.76
X+%	Extended Good Form	.95	.92	.87
Afr	Affective Ratio	.91	.91	.85
$3r+(2)/R$	Egocentricity Index	.94	.86	.90
EA	Experience Actual	.85	.87	.84
es	Experienced Stimulation	.74	.70	.59
D	Stress Tolerance Index	.93	.91	.88

Exner (1980) recruited 60 nonpatient 8-year-olds from four elementary schools under the guise of needing *practice* subjects for examiners in training. Thus each child volunteered for the study by his or her parents anticipated being tested at least twice, during regular school hours, in a five- to seven-day interval. Ten highly experienced examiners were used. None had any awareness of the nature of the study, assuming that they were collecting data in a routine reliability investigation. When the first test was administered, the project director accompanied the child from the classroom to the testing room provided by the school and introduced the examiner. The second test was administered three or four days later. The 60 subjects had been randomized previously into two groups of 30 each, and the procedure for the Control subjects was the same for the second test as the first; that is, the project director accompanied the youngster from he classroom to the test location and introduced the new examiner. This procedure was altered for the subjects in the Experimental group. While accompanying them to the testing room, the project director would pause and ask the child to assist in the solution of an important problem concerning the training of the examiners. The "problem," as outlined quickly by the project director, was that the "trainees" were hearing the same answers repeatedly, and that the training would be enhanced considerably if the child would "try hard" to remember the answers that he or she gave in the first test and promise not to repeat any of those in the test to be taken. In return, the project director offered a reward of 50 cents. All of the children in the Experimental group promised to change their answers.

The retest correlations of the two groups are almost identical, with two exceptions. In the retest, the subjects in the Experimental group gave significantly fewer Pure Form responses than they had in the first test and significantly more responses that included the achromatic or shading features of the blots. Otherwise, the correlations are essentially no different for the two groups, and very similar to those shown in Table 5 for the eight-year-olds retested after only seven days. Five of the correlations for the Experimental group are at .90 or greater and eight others fall between .81 and .89. A critical issue for this study is whether or not the youngsters in the Experimental group actually gave different answers. This issue was addressed by randomizing the 60 pairs of records into three groups of 20 pairs each and assigning each group to one of three judges who were told that the records were from a reliability study. The judges were instructed to read each pair of records and check all responses in the second test that were the same (or nearly the same) as those in the first test. The comparisons revealed that 481 of the 546 responses (86%) given in the second test by the Control subjects were replications or near replications of answers that they had given in the first test. On the other hand, only 77 of the 551 answers (14%) given by Experimental subjects in the second test were the same or similar to the answers they had given in the first test. Thus even though the youngsters in the Experimental group generally did honor the promise to give different responses in the second test, the answers that they tended to select show a distribution of scores, subject by subject, similar to those of the first test.

There are other structural data, not shown in Tables 4 or 5, which are also important to the study of the consistency hypothesis as related to the selection of answers. These include three relationships, or ratio directions, that exist between data sets. Each is important to the interpretation of the test, either because of the directionality shown in the relationship (i.e., which of the data sets are greater) and/or the magnitude of the difference. The first, the *Erlebnistypus* (*EB*) was conceptualized by Rorschach and relates to the coping style of the subject. It involves the relationship of *M* (human movement) to the weighted sum of chromatic color responses (*Sum C*). Both direction and magnitude are important to the interpretation of this relationship. A minimum two-point difference is considered necessary before the data would be interpreted as indicating a preference in coping habits. In the one-year retest study of 50 adult nonpatients cited earlier, the first tests of 41 subjects showed an *EB* in which one side of the ratio was two or more points greater than the other side. In the second test, 38 of those 41 subjects continued to show at least a two-point difference in the *EB,* and *none* had changed for the direction of the difference. In the study involving the retest of 100 nonpatient adults after 3 years, 83 of the first test records showed at least a two-point difference in the *EB*. In the retest, 77 of those 83 continued to have the difference of two points or more and only two had changed directionality.

A second important ratio concerns the relationship between *FC* (Form Color Responses) and *CF + C* (Color Dominant Responses). It relates to the modulation or control of discharged emotion. Again, both direction and magnitude are important. In the one-year retest study, 36 of the 50 first records showed one side of that ratio to be two points or greater than the other side. The retests showed that 32 of those 36 subjects continued to have at least a two-point difference between these variables, and *none* had changed for directionality. In the 3-year retest study, 57 of the 100 first records had a difference of two points or more for this ratio. In he retest, 50 of the 57 continued to have the two or more point difference and none had changed directionality.

The third is the ratio of active (*a*) to passive (*p*) movement. In this relationship, more active movement is always expected but the magnitude of the difference is also important. It provides some information about the flexibility of thinking and/or values. In the 1-year retest study, 39 of the records from the first test showed a two or more point difference in this ratio, with 31 of the 39 being higher for active movement. The retest protocols showed that 30 of the 31 "high active" records remained two or more points greater on the active side, and all eight of those higher on the passive side in the first test also remained so. In the three-year retest, a two-point or more difference was noted in 76 of the first records, with 60 being higher for active movement. In the retest, 57 of those 60 were still two or more points higher on the active side, and 11 of the original 16 "high passive" records remained at least two points higher in that direction.

The composite of data regarding the consistency of Rorschach scores and ratios, during both lengthy and brief intervals, and even under conditions where different responses are generated, affords substantial support for the proposition that the traits or styles of the subject will be quite influential in the selection of which potential answers to deliver. Yet, there is still one more element that will often play a crucial role in the final decisions about which responses to deliver.

6. *Psychological States and the Selection Process.* The relative consistency of many personality characteristics and their consequent behaviors is contingent upon some relative consistency in the stimulus conditions that evoke them. In other words, the habits, traits, or response styles of a person are probabilistic. Certain classes of behaviors are likely to occur under certain classes of stimulus conditions. The stimulus conditions include *both internal and external elements.* The person who is an athletic-outdoor enthusiast may be far less likely to engage in such activities if the outside temperatures fall well below zero or above 115°. Sedentary activity may replace some of the common activities. That same person may also be less likely to engage in the athletic activities if his or her own temperature exceeds 101° or if an irritating stomach upset occurs. The

person has not changed, but external or internal conditions have changed in a way to cause other behaviors to be evoked.

These changes, or alterations in behavior, may also result from changes in the psychological state of the individual. Increases or decreases in needs and/or emotions, or the unexpected experience of stress or the onset of various psychopathologial states can have the effect of evoking new behaviors that add to, or replace, preexisting orientations. In most instances, the basics of the person do not change, but some unexpected behaviors occur. In some cases, the behaviors of the person may shift slightly as in the instance of the normally sedate person who becomes flustered under recognition. In other instances, the deviations from expected behaviors may be much more marked as in the case of the individual who becomes panic-stricken and disorganized under moderate stress. These are *state* phenomenon, which tend to supersede the routine psychological functioning of the person, or at least will stimulate the addition of behaviors that are not ordinarily part of the psychological routine.

Rorschach responses can be viewed as a sampling of problem-solving behavior. Thus if a psychological state exists that will alter, or add to the routine functioning of the person, that state can also influence the selection of responses to be delivered during the test. For example, two of the scoring variables listed in Tables 4 and 5 show very low retest reliabilities, over both lengthy and brief retest intervals. These are m, scored for inanimate movement, and Y, scored for the articulation of diffuse shading. The means for both, from nonpatient samples, are quite low as are the standard deviations. Thus although either might occur once in a record, they are not expected to appear more frequently. Research has shown that both relate to situational stress (Shalit, 1965; Armbruster, Miller, & Exner, 1974; Exner, Armbruster, Walker, & Cooper, 1975; Exner, 1978; Exner & Weiner, 1982). Thus if the frequencies for either or both are elevated in a protocol, it signals that the presence of some situationally related phenomenon that is stimulating the mental and/or emotional experiences which occur when concerns about loss of control and feelings of helplessness or paralysis exist.

Another illustration of how the selection of Rorschach answers may be influenced by a state condition is exemplified in the texture (T) responses. The average number of texture responses, for various age groups of nonpatients, is about 1.0, with a standard deviation of less than 1.0. This variable tends to distribute on a J-Curve. Approximately 80% of all nonpatient adults give one texture answer. For this reason, the retest reliabilities for texture responses usually range from the middle .80's to the low .90's in both short- and long-term retest studies. Less than 10% of nonpatient adults give more than one texture answer; however, if the subject has recently experienced a significant emotional loss, the average number of texture responses will usually increase significantly.

Exner and Bryant (1974) found an average of nearly *four* texture responses in the records of 30 nonpatient adults who had recently separated from close emotional relationships. The subjects were retested approximately 10 months later. Twenty-one of the 30 reported that they had established new relationships or reconstructed the one that had been fractured earlier. They gave substantially fewer texture responses in the second test than in the first. Conversely, the nine subjects who reported a continuing sense of loss all gave three or more texture responses in the second test.

Although many psychological states are transient, others can form a more enduring overlay to the primary personality structure. Many psychopathological states have this characteristic, and just as they influence a broad spectrum of behaviors, they are also quite influential in the selection of Rorschach answers. Severe and/or enduring depression is an example of this. Depressed patients tend to give much higher frequencies of vista (*V*) and achromatic color (*C*'s) responses than do other groups. They also have more answers that are marked by a clear morbidity (*MOR*), and are usually low on a index of self-esteem. Haller and Exner (1985) used a retest design similar to that employed by Exner (1980) with nonpatient children. Fifty first-admission patients, presenting symptoms of depression and/or helplessness, were retested three or four days after the first test had been administered. A randomly selected half of the subjects were asked to give different answers in the second test than in the first. That group repeated about one-third of their answers from the first test in the second, whereas the control subjects repeated nearly 70% of their first test responses in the second test. In spite of the fact that the experimental group gave more than 68% new answers in the second test, the retest reliabilities for both groups were quite high, very similar to those reported by Exner for nonpatient children used in essentially the same design. Moreover, the group did not differ significantly for any of the variables related to depression.

As the state endures, so does its influence, and the more severe the state may be, its impact on decision making will be greater. Exner, Thomas, and Mason (1985) found that the retest reliabilities for the major indices of depression remained very high among inpatient adolescents diagnosed as major depressive disturbance even after having been in treatment for nearly one year. On the other hand, as the state dissipates, so too does its influence on the selection of Rorschach answers. In a study completed for this work, Exner, Cohen, and Hillman (1984) retested 46 subjects, diagnosed initially using DSM-III criteria as major depressive disorder, at the termination of their treatment. All had begun treatment as inpatients and continued treatment as outpatients for a period averaging almost 2 years. The retest correlations for each of the variables related to depression were very low, ranging from .19 for the vista variable, to .33 for the presence of Morbid Content responses.

In effect, the psychological state of the person taking the Rorschach will contribute in the final selection of the answers that are delivered. The influence of the state in the selection process will probably be proportionate to its impact on the individual, and its continuing influence will be proportionate to its durability. It will not always supersede other influencing traits, styles, or habits, *but it may.*

A SUMMARY OF THE OPERATIONS IN THE RESPONSE PROCESS

It is in the very few seconds before a response is delivered that all of these operations occur. The bulk of data concerning information processing and cognitive activity support the notion that some overlap occurs between these six operations during the total process. Quite possibly, there is some merit in considering the six operations as they occur in three phases of the response process, because they probably occur before the delivery of the first answer.

Phase I: 1. Visual input and encoding of the stimulus and its parts.
           2. Classification of the stimulus and/or its parts and a rank ordering of the many potential responses that are created.

Phase II: 3. Discarding potential answers that have low rankings.
           4. Discarding other potential answers through censorship.

Phase III: 5. Selection of some of the remaining responses by reason of traits or styles.

6. Selection of some of the remaining responses because of the state influences.

After these phases or operations have occurred, the delivery of the first answer to a blot is given.

THE ROLE OF PROJECTION IN THE RESPONSE

Does projection occur in the selection and/or discarding of all responses? That position could be argued *only* if the definition of projection is extended to include all decision operations, but this seems a simplistic and overinclusive position. If the selection of a response is based exclusively on the classification and rank ordering operations, it seems highly unlikely that projection is involved. The more common, somewhat simplistic responses that are formulated mainly by using the contours of the blots, such as a bat, two dogs, a butterfly, a tree, and so on, are the best examples of answers for which there is no evidence of projection. Similarly, much or all of the discarding that ensues, during and after classification, probably does not include much, if any, of the influences of the projective process. Most of this is directed more by attitudes and values of the subject, and his or her perception of the test situation.

In a similar context, it is difficult to reason that the traits or styles of the subject are significantly impacted by projection as such. To the contrary, these are enduring characteristics that will be influential in directing the projective process when it does occur. The same relationship exists between state influences and projection; that is, the presence of the state may give direction to the projective process *if* it occurs. In fact, when a state is intense and broadly encompassing, it can easily give rise to much rich projective material.

Obviously, projections can and do occur in the Rorschach and their presence often adds considerably to the interpretive yield of the test, but it is very important to discriminate projected material from that which is not. Exner (1989) has presented data suggesting that there are probably two types of projected responses: One is formed during the Phase I operations and the second is formed during the Phase II or Phase III operations.

Projection and Phase I   The first type of projection that may occur in Rorschach answers apparently provokes some sort of distortion and/or misperception during the input-classification process. For instance, most people who are shown a ball and asked what it is will usually respond that it is a ball. The distinct stimulus features of the object (ball) reduce the parameters of its definition rather sharply. It can be identified functionally (e.g., "Something you throw") or even synchretistically (e.g., "It's a thing that is made by humans"), but the range of adequate responses is quite limited. If a subject who is not perceptually impaired misidentifies the ball by calling it an airplane, or a devil, or a kidney, and so on, it is not unreasonable to assume that some element of projection has occurred because the stimulus field has been markedly distorted and/or ignored. In other words, although the potent stimulus elements within each blot tend to facilitate the formation of certain responses or classes of response, the demands or restrictions created by their characteristics also tend to reduce the likelihood that projection will be involved in most Phase I operations. Nonetheless, classifications of blots or blot areas in ways that violate or ignore these prevalent features do occur. Technically, they are minus answers, and if they are not the product of some neurophysiologically related dysfunction in perceptual operations, it seems logical to postulate that they are the result of some form of cognitive mediation in which internal psychological sets or operations have superseded a reality-oriented translation of the field. Thus, some form of projection may be involved.

Projection and Phases II and III   Although it is possible that projection may play a role during the Phase I classifications of the blot, it seems much more likely that the impact of the process, if it occurs, will be greater during the Phase II and III operations. During these operations, a type of imaginative projection may become involved if the subject overelaborates on, or departs from, the stimulus field. For instance, as noted earlier, most people who are shown a ball and asked what it is will answer that it is a ball. But even within the parameters of that narrow stimulus field, a subject might projectively embellish the answer such as, "It is a ball that was made by a very conscientious person." Likewise, most people who are asked, "How much are two times two?" will answer "four," but again, the answer could be embellished in a projected manner such as, "The answer is four, which is my favorite number because it represents the four seasons of the year that are so important to the cycle of life." Such an elaboration clearly seems to reflect something about the person who gave it because there is nothing in the stimulus field or in the question posed that provokes it. In each of these examples, the nature of the tasks, that is, multiplying numbers or identifying an object reduces the probability that projection will occur. It can occur but usually will not because the parameters of the task and the field are so narrow. But in the Rorschach, the parameters of both the task and the field are broader. While the limited ambiguity of the stimulus field plus the nature of the task do not encourage projection, they do not prohibit or discourage the unique translations or embellishments that almost certainly have some projected properties. As a result, projected characteristics do occur in the formation of some answers, and they continue to be weighed positively during the Phase III operations and ultimately appear in the protocol.

The majority of answers that include this kind of projection do not require much interpretive translation because the embellishment is usually obvious by its departure from, or overelaboration of the stimulus field such as occurs in many movement responses or answers in which an object is described with excessive specificity. Many such projections occur in movement answers, but many others occur in responses in which there is no movement but in which the subject embellishes his or her description of the object considerably. When they occur with a higher than average frequency, these types of answers are probably very direct reflections concerning the feelings and/or behaviors of people.

It is important to recognize that not all of the responses, or all of the verbiage represent projected material. In fact, the majority of nonpatient records have more responses that contain no projections than those that do have that feature. It is less common, but not infrequent, to find records in which no projected material appears to exist. Usually these are closely guarded, relatively short protocols in which each response is limited to a few words. Those records are no less valid than the more elaborated protocols, but they do lack the rich, idiosyncratic features of the subject that tend to appear in projections and which, at times, contribute much in fleshing out a description of the subject.

SUMMARY

Although the process of the Rorschach is very complex, provoking an abundance of perceptual and cognitive operations, and laying open the psychological door for projection to occur, it is not a complicated assessment tool for the adept user. The procedures by which the data of the test are obtained are simplistic, but also delicate. If they are violated by intent or naiveté of the user, the method becomes reduced from a test to a composite of verbiage, the efficacy of which will depend largely on the clinical skills of the user plus a great deal of good fortune. Conversely, when the standard procedures for collecting the data are employed faithfully, the yield is very substantial. It provides information about habits, traits, and styles, and about the presence of states, and about many other variables that can be listed under the broad rubric encompassed by the term *personality.*

As noted earlier, the test is not an x-ray of the mind or soul, but it does afford, in a brief glimpse, a picture of the psychology of the person, as it is, and to some extent as it has been, and to some extent as it will be. It is not difficult to interpret the basics of the test, but the more sophisticated interpreter will always be able to glean more information from the data of the test because of his or her understanding of how the test works.

REFERENCES

Abramson, L. S. (1951) The influence of set for area on the Rorschach Test results. *Journal of Consulting Psychology,* **15,** 337–342.

Ames, L. B., Learned, J., Metraux, R. W., and Walker, R. N. (1952) *Child Rorschach Responses.* New York: Hoeber-Harper.

Ames, L. B., Metraux, R. W., and Walker, R. N. (1971) *Adolescent Rorschach Responses.* New York: Brunner/Mazel.

Armbruster, G. L., Miller, A. S., and Exner, J. E. (1974) Rorschach responses of parachute trainees at the beginning of training and prior to the first jump. Workshops Study No. 201 (unpublished), Rorschach Workshops.

Beck, S. J. (1945) *Rorschach's Test II: A Variety of Personality Pictures.* New York: Grune & Stratton.

Beck, S. J., Beck, A. G., Levitt, E. E., and Molish, H. B. (1961) *Rorschach's Test I: Basic Processes* (3rd Ed.) New York: Grune & Stratton.

Cattell, R. B. (1951) Principles of design in "projective" or misperceptive tests of personality. In H. Anderson and G. Anderson (Eds.) *Projective Techniques.* Englewood Cliffs, N.J.: Prentice-Hall.

Coffin, T. E. (1941) Some conditions of suggestion and suggestibility: A study of certain attitudinal and situational factors in the process of suggestion. *Psychological Monographs,* **53,** Whole No. 241.

Colligan, S. C., and Exner, J. E. (1985) Responses of schizophrenics and nonpatients to a tachistoscopic presentation of the Rorschach. *Journal of Personality Assessment,* **49,** 129-136.

Dalhstrom, W. G., Welsh, G. S., and Dahlstrom, L. E. (1972) *An MMPI Handbook. Volume 1* (rev.) Minneapolis: University of Minnesota Press.

Dinoff, M. (1960) Subject awareness of examiner influence in a testing situation. *Journal of Consulting Psychology,* **24,** 465.

Dubrovner, R. J., VonLackum, W. J., and Jost, H. (1950) A study of the effect of color on productivity and reaction time in the Rorschach Test. *Journal of Clinical Psychology,* **6,** 331–336.

Exner, J. E. (1959) The influence of chromatic and achromatic color in the Rorschach. *Journal of Projective Techniques,* **23,** 418–425.

Exner, J. E. (1974) *The Rorschach: A Comprehensive System. Volume 1.* New York: Wiley.

Exner, J. E. (1978) *The Rorschach: A Comprehensive System. Volume 2. Recent Research and Advanced Interpretation.* New York: Wiley.

Exner, J. E. (1980) But it's only an inkblot. *Journal of Personality Assessment, 44,* 562–577.

Exner, J. E. (1983) Rorschach Assessment. In I. B. Weiner (Ed.) *Clinical Methods in Psychology.* New York: Wiley.

Exner, J. E. (1989) Searching for projection in the Rorschach. *Journal of Personality Assessment, 53,* 520–536.

Exner, J. E., and Armbruster, G. L. (1974) Increasing R by altering instructions and creating a time set. Workshops Study No. 209 (unpublished) Rorschach Workshops.

Exner, J. E., Armbruster, G. L., and Mittman, B. (1978) The Rorschach response process. *Journal of Personality Assessment, 42,* 27–38.

Exner, J. E., Armbruster, G. L., and Viglione, D. (1978) The temporal stability of some Rorschach features. *Journal of Personality Assessment, 42,* 474–482.

Exner, J. E., Armbruster, G. L., Walker, E. J., and Cooper, W. H. (1975) Anticipation of elective surgery as manifest in Rorschach records. Workshops Study No. 213 (unpublished) Rorschach Workshops.

Exner, J. E., and Bryant, E. L. (1974) Rorschach responses of subjects recently divorced or separated. Workshops Study No. 206 (unpublished) Rorschach Workshops.

Exner, J. E., Cohen, J. B., and Hillman, L. B. (1984) A retest of 46 major depressive disorder patients at the termination of treatment. Workshops Study No. 275 (unpublished) Rorschach Workshops.

Exner, J. E., and Leura, A. V. (1976) Variations in the ranking Rorschach responses as a function of situational set. Workshops Study No. 221 (unpublished) Rorschach Workshops.

Exner, J. E., and Martin, L. S. (1981) Responses to Card I when shown with Dd34 eliminated. Workshops Study No. 279 (unpublished) Rorschach Workshops.

Exner, J. E., Martin, L. S., and Cohen, J. B. (1983) Card by card response frequencies for patient and nonpatient populations. Workshops Study No. 276 (unpublished) Rorschach Workshops.

Exner, J. E., Thomas, E. E., and Cohen, J. B. (1983) The temporal consistency of test variables for 50 nonpatient adults after 12 to 14 months. Workshops Study No. 281 (unpublished) Rorschach Workshops.

Exner, J. E., Thomas, E. E., and Mason, B. (1985) Children's Rorschachs: Description and prediction. *Journal of Personality Assessment, 49,* 13–20.

Exner, J. E., and Weiner, I. B. (1982) *The Rorschach: A Comprehensive System. Volume 3: Assessment of Children and Adolescents.* New York: Wiley.

Exner, J. E., and Wylie, J. R. (1976) Alterations in frequency of response and color articulation as related to alterations in the coloring of specific blot areas. Workshops Study No. 219, (unpublished) Rorschach workshops.

Exner, J. E., and Wylie, J. R. (1977) Differences in the frequency of responses to the D1 area of Card X using an achromatic version. Workshops Study No. 237 (unpublished) Rorschach Workshops.

Fisher, D. F., Monty, R. A., and Senders, J. W. (Eds.) (1981) *Eye Movements: Cognition & Visual Perception.* Hillsdale, NJ: Erlbaum Associates.

Ford, M. (1946) *The Application of the Rorschach Test to Young Children.* University of Minnesota, Institute of Child Welfare.

Frank, L. K. (1939) Projective methods for the study of personality. *Journal of Psychology, 8,* 389–413.

Gibby, R. G. (1951) The stability of certain Rorschach variables under conditions of experimentally induced sets: I. The intellectual variables. *Journal of Projective Techniques, 15,* 3–26.

Goetcheus, G. (1967) The effects of instructions and examiners on the Rorschach. Unpublished M.A. Thesis, Bowling Green State University.

Goodman, N. L. (1979) Examiner influence on the Rorschach: The effect of sex, sex-pairing and warmth on the testing atmosphere. Doctoral Dissertation, Long Island University.

Gross, L. (1959) Effects of verbal and nonverbal reinforcement on the Rorschach. *Journal of Consulting Psychology,* **23,** 66–68.

Haller, N., and Exner, J. E. (1985) The reliability of Rorschach variables for inpatients presenting symptoms of depression and/or helplessness. *Journal of Personality Assessment,* **49,** 516–521.

Halpern, F. (1953) *A Clinical Approach to Children's Rorschachs.* New York: Grune & Stratton.

Hersen, M., and Greaves, S. T. (1971) Rorschach productivity as related to verbal reinforcement. *Journal of Personality Assessment,* **35,** 436–441.

Hertz, M. R. (1934) The reliability of the Rorschach ink-blot test. *Journal of Applied Psychology,* **18,** 461–477.

Hochberg, J. (1981) Levels of Perceptual Organization. In M. Kubovy and J. R. Pomerantz (Eds.) *Perceptual Organization.* Hillsdale, NJ: Erlbaum Associates.

Holzberg, J. D. (1960) Reliability Re-examined. In M. Rickers-Ovsiankina (Ed.) *Rorschach Psychology,* New York: Wiley.

Horiuchi, H. (1961) A study of perceptual process of Rorschach cards by tachistoscopic method on movement and shading responses. *Journal of Projective Techniques,* **25,** 44–53.

Hutt, M., Gibby, R. G., Milton, E. O., and Pottharst, K. (1950) he effect of varied experimental "sets" upon Rorschach test performance. *Journal of Projective Techniques,* **14,** 181–187.

Klopfer, B., and Kelley, D. M. (1942) *The Rorschach Technique.* Yonkers-on-Hudson, NY: World Book.

Leura, A. V., and Exner, J. E. (1978) Structural differences in the records of adolescents as a function of being tested by one's own teacher. Workshops Study No. 265 (unpublished) Rorschach Workshops.

London, H., and Exner, J. E. (1978) *Dimensions of Personality.* New York: Wiley.

Magnussen, M. G. (1960) Verbal and nonverbal reinforcers in the Rorschach situation. *Journal of Clinical Psychology,* **16,** 167–169.

Martin, L. S., and Thomas, E. E. (1982) Selection of preferred responses by high school students. Workshops Study No. 278 (unpublished) Rorschach Workshops.

Matarazzo, J. D., and Mensh, I. N. (1952) Reaction time characteristics of the Rorschach Test. *Journal of Consulting Psychology,* **16,** 132–139.

Meer, B. (1955) The relative difficulty of the Rorschach cards. *Journal of Projective Techniques,* **19,** 43–53.

Meer, B., and Singer, J. L. (1950) A note on the "father" and "mother" cards in the Rorschach inkblots. *Journal of Consulting Psychology,* **14,** 482–484.

Miale, F. R., and Harrower-Erikson, M. R. (1940) Personality structure in the psychoneuroses. *Rorschach Research Exchange,* **4,** 71–74.

Murray, H. A. (1938) *Explorations in Personality.* New York: Oxford University Press.

Neisser, U. (1976) *Cognition and Reality.* New York: Appleton-Century-Crofts.

Orange, A. (1953) Perceptual consistency as measured by the Rorschach. *Journal of Projective Techniques,* **17,** 224–228.

Pascal, G., Ruesch, H., Devine, D., and Suttell, B. (1950) A study of genital symbols on the Rorschach Test: Presentation of method and results. *Journal of Abnormal and Social Psychology,* **45,** 285–289.

Phillips, L., and Smith, J. G. (1953) *Rorschach Interpretation: Advanced Technique.* New York: Grune & Stratton.

Piotrowski, Z. (1957) *Perceptanalysis.* New York: Macmillan.

Pomerantz, J. R., and Kubovy, M. (1981) Perceptual Organization: An Overview. In M. Kubovy and J. R. Pomerantz (Eds.) *Perceptual Organization.* Hillsdale, NJ: Erlbaum Associates.

Rabin, A. I., and Sanderson, M. H. (1947) An experimental inquiry into some Rorschach procedures. *Journal of Clinical Psychology,* **3,** 216–225.

Sendin, C. (1981) *Respuestas Populares al test de Rorschach in sujetos Espanoles.* Proceedings of the 10th International Rorschach Congress, Washington, D.C.

Shalit, B. (1965) Effects of environmental stimulation on the *M, FM,* and *m* responses in the Rorschach. *Journal of Projective Techniques and Personality Assessment,* **29,** 228–231.

Stein, M. I. (1949) Personality factors involved in the temporal development of Rorschach responses. *Rorschach Research Exchange,* **13,** 355–414.

Thomas, E. E., Alinsky, D., and Exner, J. E. (1982) The stability of some Rorschach variables in 9-year-olds as compared with nonpatient adults. Workshop Study No. 441 (unpublished) Rorschach Workshops.

Thomas, E. E., Exner, J. E., and Leura, A. V. (1977) Differences in ranking responses by two groups of nonpatient adults as a function of set concerning the origins of the responses Workshop Study No. 251 (unpublished) Rorschach Workshops.

Vernon, P. E. (1933) The Rorschach inkblot test. II. *British Journal of Medical Psychology,* **13,** 179–205.

Wickes, T. A. (1956) Examiner influence in a testing situation. *Journal of Consulting Psychology,* **20,** 23–26.

PART II

Administration
and Scoring

CHAPTER 3

Decisions and Procedures

Before laying hand to the Rorschach cards, the person responsible for the assessment must make some important decisions. One of the most important of these concerns the appropriateness of the Rorschach for the task at hand. The Rorschach *does not* provide data from which answers to all questions can be derived. The data that unfold from the test are essentially descriptive in substance. The data represent a report from the subject of what he or she has seen or imagined when confronted with the 10 inkblots. That report is a complex specimen of behavior which, when scored and compared with norms and studied for its apparent idiosyncrasies, can be translated into a series of descriptive statements concerning the subject. This description can be quite lengthy, converging on such features as response styles, affectivity, cognitive operations, motivations, preoccupations, and interpersonal-interenvironmental perceptions and response tendencies. Ordinarily, the description will include reference both to overt and covert behaviors, the characterization of either being determined mainly by the richness of the protocol. Many statements may be made with considerable sureness, whereas others may be more speculative; but most will represent the subject as he or she is, rather than how the subject may have been, or will be. It is common for the description to include some information concerning etiological factors, and possibly to offer predictions, but generally these kinds of statements are derived less directly from the data of the protocol. More likely they are the product of using inductive and deductive logic to integrate the data from the record with other available information concerning the subject. As such, they are more speculative and rely heavily on the accumulated knowledge of the interpreter regarding personality, response styles, psychopathology, and behavior. Rorschach data can be used legitimately for some speculations about the past or the future. For instance, piecing together data concerning the variety of assets and liabilities of the subject, *as manifest* in Rorschach data, can lead to logical recommendations about intervention objectives and alternatives. Similarly, an evaluation of the apparent strengths and/or relationships of certain responses tendencies can generate logical speculation about the chronicity, or even the origins of such tendencies.

But speculation can be carried on *ad absurdum.* It would seem that, too frequently, clinicians have been enticed by the intrigue of questions (or by their own grandiosity) into issuing verdicts about people and their behaviors, after reviewing a Rorschach, which have little relevance to the data found in the record. In good assessment practice, it follows that the assessor will use procedures appropriate to the questions for which answers are being sought. For instance, questions concerning parent interaction, religious preference, hobbies, supervisor or teacher ratings, sibling relationships, sexual preference, or the frequency of intercourse can be relevant in some cases. Any or all may be important questions but at best, most Rorschach data will be only indirectly related to any of them. There are much better methods than the Rorschach to gain these kinds of information. A good interview or a thorough social history should provide most of it. Just as questions of this sort are inappropriate to the Rorschach, so too are certain classes of prediction, such as success or attrition in some types of training, marital success, ultimate family size, length of hospitalization, or the probability of parole violation. Most of these are intelligent questions and the well-equipped psychologist, given appropriate information and adequate criterion measures, might attack them with considerable success, *but not from the Rorschach alone, and possibly not using the Rorschach at all.*

There are other questions often asked of the clinician that may seem more compatible with the Rorschach method but are not necessarily so. These are questions concerning intellectual functioning and problems of neurological involvement. Both have been considered in research with the Rorschach and some positive relationships have been found. Some elements in the Rorschach do correlate positively with indices of intelligence, but not to the extent that the Rorschach can be used in a reliable and valid manner to substitute for an intelligence test. Similarly, there are some elements in the Rorschach that have a reasonably high probability of occurrence in some conditions of neurologically related dysfunctioning, but *none* have proven to be diagnostically differentiating except in those cases where the dysfunction is so severe that it can easily be detected by visually observing the subject. Thus if the primary purpose of the assessment relates to questions of intelligence or cognitive functioning, the Rorschach is not the test of choice. It may be useful in the overall assessment of the subject, but only as an adjunct to provide some information concerning the personality of the subject if that seems relevant.

THE RORSCHACH AND THE TEST BATTERY

The strength of the Rorschach rests with its yield concerning some of the psychological functioning of the subject. In many cases it is important to integrate this yield with data and information from other sources. In some instances, the yield may be sufficient to address the assessment issues that have been raised.

In the historical framework of psychodiagnostics or assessment, the clinician usually is inclined to use multiple procedures. The mainstay of this approach has been the interview and the "test battery." The latter sometimes may include as few as two or three tests, but not uncommonly it has been comprised of more than three, and often more than five. The rationale for the use of the test battery has been expounded considerably (Rapaport, Gill, & Schafer, 1946; Piotrowski, 1958; Harrower, 1965). The premises underlying the test battery approach are essentially twofold. The first is that no test is so broad in its scope to test everything. Different tests focus on different dimensions or functions of the subject, and thus the test battery provides a broader data base from which to evaluate the *total* person. Second, various tests do overlap to some extent, thereby affording the possibilities of cross-validating information derived from any single test. The test battery procedure is argued to minimize error and maximize accuracy. Proponents of the test battery approach have suggested that it can be viewed as multiple samples of behavior, noting that data from a single instrument will generate greater speculation, whereas the composite of data from several instruments provides for greater certainty in conclusions.

The positions supporting the test battery approach have been challenged in several studies (Sarbin, 1943; Kelly & Fiske, 1950; Gage, 1953; Kostlan, 1954; Giedt, 1955). Data from each point to the fact that clinicians often do not use all of the data available to them, or if they do, they are prone to weigh some segments inordinately. These critics also argue that a ceiling of predictive accuracy is usually reached quickly and adding more data provides only slight, if any, increase in the predictive correlation. Several studies appear to refute these criticisms about the test battery approach, demonstrating that it does work well in the clinical situation (Vernon, 1950; MacKinnon, 1951; Stern, Stein, & Bloom, 1956; Luborsky & Holt, 1957). In each, validity is increased as the data are increased. Holt (1958, 1970) has probably offered the most cogent arguments about the additive process and how it can be essential for some kinds of descriptive or predictive conclusions.

Support for the test battery approach does not mean that it should be used always; nor does it mean that the same composite of tests should be used when a battery is required. One of the most important decisions in the assessment process concerns which procedures to use. This decision usually will evolve from consideration of the questions to be addressed, but the decision does not always end there. In some situations a subject may react to a procedure in a very unpredicted manner, providing new questions and forcing the assessor to alter the planned procedures. For example, a subject whose WAIS performance is extremely bizarre and psychotic-like probably need not be administered the Rorschach if the prime question to be answered concerns the presence of a psychotic state. Similarly, the subject rendering 25 rich Rorschach responses might not be administered the TAT unless important unanswered questions remain after the Rorschach has been examined, and which the TAT might best address. Many clinicians are prone to administer both the MMPI and the Rorschach to their clients on the premise that they are complimentary, but offer data derived from different task sources (i.e., self-report and cognitive-perceptual activity). Although it is true that they compliment each other, there may be many instances when the MMPI alone may suffice, or other instances where the Rorschach might be the preferred instrument because of the nature of the questions posed.

Unfortunately, there remain far too many instances where a clinician perseverates in the use of a "standard" test battery no matter what the appointed task, and no matter what data become available during the testing process. This tactic of assessment harks back to the 1940s and 1950s when the primary role of the clinician was diagnostics and much less was known about tests, procedures, personality, and psychopathology. It may have been important then, to provide a sort of security blanket for those confronted with the task, but that is no longer true. Great chunks of data are not necessarily required for most assessment goals. It is also clear that the amount of time consumed in administering test after test is often disproportionate to the objectives of the process, a situation that is made even worse when the clinician does not use all of the data obtained from the lengthy procedure. Unfortunately, hospital and clinic files have become filled with psychological test reports of varying lengths, many of which replay information given in the interview and provide little description from the test data even though 5 to 10 hours of testing occurred. No clinician should insult the dignity of the subject with such a piece of work. If a test battery is used, then all of the data obtained should be interpreted.

Another important decision that must be made by the assessor is the placement of each procedure in the process. For instance, Van de Castle (1964) found that test order could alter the incidence of human content responses in the Rorschach. Grisso and Meadow (1967) reported differences in WAIS performances depending on whether the WAIS was administered prior to or after the Rorschach. Exner and Hark (1979) studied 200 WAIS records, 100 of which were administered prior to the Rorschach and 100 administered after the Rorschach. No significant differences were found for any of the WAIS subtest scores *or* for the distributions of Rorschach scores. Nonetheless, good judgment should be exercised in the placement of any test in an assessment process. For example, Exner and Hark (1980) found that Rorschachs administered after three hours of prior testing do have a significantly lower average number of responses than those administered after only 90 minutes of prior testing. It is also probable, although not proven, that Rorschach productivity will be affected by almost any procedures in the assessment process that are stressful to the subject.

For example, subjects with some cognitive dysfunctioning will often have difficulties on the Categories Test, or the Tactual Performance Test of the Halstead-Reitan Battery. Thus it is probably not wise to administer the Rorschach *immediately* after either of these procedures unless the subject has performed quite well on them. Similarly, it is probably best not to administer the Rorschach *immediately* after the MMPI. Although the MMPI can yield very important information concerning a subject, it can also produce a fatigue effect that could impact Rorschach performance.

Whenever a test battery approach is selected, the time factor can be critical. Usually, when neuropsychological issues are not involved, the total assessment process can be completed within a three-hour time frame. Weiner (1966) presented an exceptionally fine summary of those indicators relevant to the diagnosis of schizophrenia using a test battery that should take less than three hours. In contemporary assessment that would be targeted toward a reasonably full picture of the person, three tests might best be considered as forming the nucleus of the assessment procedure: (1) one of the Wechsler Intelligence Scales, (2) the Rorschach, and (3) the MMPI. Each is empirically sturdy and each provides a wealth of information from which the sophisticated clinician can generate many important and meaningful hypotheses concerning the subject.

None of the foregoing should be interpreted to mean that the Rorschach should always be used as a part of a test battery. It can stand alone quite well and provide much data concerning a subject, descriptive data which ordinarily will go well beyond that extracted from other tests. One need only to review the extensive literature concerning the yield of the test to gauge the wealth of information that it can provide, either from the quantitative analysis or from the qualitative analysis of the projected material (Beck, 1937, 1945, 1952, 1960; Exner, 1969, 1978, 1991; Klopfer & Kelly, 1942; Klopfer et al., 1954; Hertz, 1969; Piotrowski, 1958, 1969; Schafer, 1954). In this context, the assessor should not be adverse to using the Rorschach alone if the assessment questions are specific to the yield of the test.

It is also important to reaffirm that some questions are unanswerable from any assessment procedure, whether Rorschach, interview, observation, or other tests. Other questions can only be addressed in a speculative manner. If, however, the prime question concerns a description of the psychological operations, needs, styles, habits, and so on of the subject, the Rorschach is probably the best instrument to accomplish that task, of those procedures currently available. It is a worthy but sometimes delicate method that will generate great amounts of information about its subject if used wisely. The interpretation of the test requires much training. It is not a simplistic, "this equals that" technique, but with appropriate training the clinician should be able to provide a broad spectrum of information about the subject of the test.

PROCEDURES OF ADMINISTRATION

Once the decision to use the Rorschach in the assessment process has been made, it is vitally important that the test be used appropriately. Factors such as seating, instructions, recording responses, and Inquiry all become critical to generating the data bank from which many conclusions will be reached. Sometimes these items seem incidental to the task at hand, but they are not. The procedures employed with the inkblots can often dictate whether a protocol is truly valid or whether it should be reduced to the level of a free-wheeling interview. Alterations in procedure can influence such elements as the number of answers and the characteristics of the response as reported. These serve only to minimize the ultimate data available to the interpreter and, in the instance of the more naive user, can create some alterations in the final description rendered.

Seating   The preferred seating for Rorschach administration is where the subject and examiner *sit side-by-side*. This can be done at a table, or using two comfortable chairs with a small table between them, or any of several variations of this. There are two reasons for the side-by-side seating. The first, and most important, is to reduce the effects of inadvertent and unwanted cues from the examiner that may influence the subject. Second, the side-by-side position affords the examiner a much better view from which to see the features of the blot as they are referred to by the subject.

Rorschach apparently had some awareness of the potential for examiner influence and used side-by-side seating in his experiment. However, the systematizers who extended his work varied the seating arrangement in accord with their own positions concerning the test. Klopfer and Hertz continued to use the side-by-side seating; Piotrowski also recommended the side-by-side position, but stressed that it should not be used if it necessitated a change in the regimen used in interviewing or prior testing; Beck preferred to sit behind the subject; and Rapaport recommended a face-to-face seating on the assumption that it is the most natural for interviewing and testing. Actually, there is no psychological test that requires the face-to-face arrangement. Even when materials must be laid before the subject, as in some intelligence testing, the examiner can sit next to the subject.

The impact of the examiner, or cues given by the examiner, should not be regarded lightly in any testing situation, and especially one in which the Rorschach is involved. Coffin (1941) demonstrated that when factors intended to provoke projection exist (such as the ambiguity and novelty of the Rorschach situation), an increase in the subject's susceptibility to influence or suggestions is likely to occur. Schachtel (1945) was among the first to offer a major conceptual position concerning this element. He stressed the subject's problem in reacting to the total test situation, which includes apparent freedom yet simultaneous control, compounded by the relationship between the examiner and subject. He argued that the subject tends to create a "subjective definition" of the situation. Schafer (1954) extended this idea considerably, emphasizing the interaction between the subject and the dynamics of the situation. He suggested that factors such as required levels of communication, violation of privacy, the lack of situational control, and the danger of premature self-awareness arouse anxiety and defensiveness from which specific reactions to the examiner evolve. Neither Schachtel nor Schafer posited that the Rorschach performance can be altered completely by the examiner-subject relationships, but both warned that many of the test variables can be affected.

Research on the subject of examiner influence has revealed some important findings. Lord (1950) used three female examiners in a counterbalanced design to test 36 male subjects. Each subject was tested three times, once by each of the examiners who varied their examiner roles across three models. One was designed to make the subject feel accepted and successful, a second to make the subject feel rejected and a failure, and the third a more standard procedure of affective neutrality. Her results were clouded by the complexity of the retest design, but many significant differences did occur across the different rapport models; however, the largest and most frequent differences occurred across examiners, regardless of the rapport model that they employed.

Baughman (1951) studied the protocols obtained from 633 subjects by 15 examiners. He found that the records obtained by most of the examiners were highly comparable, but that records obtained by some examiners continually deviated quite markedly. He attributed those deviations to variations in procedure *or* to the examiner-subject relationship. Gibby, Miller, and Walker (1953) also found substantial differences among examiners for length of protocol and certain classes of scores, especially pure form, color, and shading.

Masling (1965) hypothesized that unintentional reinforcement by examiners could be a major factor underlying the observation that subjects produce different responses for different subjects. He created an especially clever design to test this proposition, using 14 graduate students, naive to the Rorschach, who volunteered for special training in the test which would be quick and efficient. Randomized into two groups, all received identical instruction except that one group was given the set that experienced examiners always elicit more human than animal responses. The second group of trainees were given the opposite set. After the training sessions were completed, each student tested two subjects. The sessions were audio recorded with the expectancy of finding evidence for verbal conditioning by the student examiners. The two groups did differ in the predicted direction for the ratio of human to animal responses, *but no evidence* was found for verbal conditioning. Masling logically concluded that the examiners influenced subjects with postural, gestural, and facial cues.

Exner, Leura, and George (1976) used a modification of the Masling design to test the impact of seating on the outcome. They trained 24 student volunteers, randomized into four groups of six each, to administer the test. Two of the groups used a face-to-face seating, whereas the second two groups were trained to sit side-by-side. One face-to-face group and one side-by-side group were given the set that competent examiners obtain more human responses and the other two groups were set to believe the opposite. After the training was complete, each student examiner tested three subjects and the sessions were videotaped. The two groups using the face-to-face seating did differ from each other in the predicted direction for the ratio of human to animal responses, and behavioral ratings of the videotapes confirmed Masling's hypothesis that more postural, gestural, and facial cues would occur when the subject gave a response related to the set. Similar differences in the behavioral ratings for postural, gestural, and facial activity were found for the two groups giving the test using the side-by-side seating, *but they did not differ for the ratio of human to animal response.*

The foregoing should not be interpreted to suggest that all, or most all Rorschach variables can easily be altered through some subtle set given either to the examiner or the subject. As noted earlier in the Exner (1980) and Haller and Exner (1985) studies, the distributions of most scores do not differ even though subjects, by instruction, give different responses in a retest than they did in the first test. In the same context, Fosberg (1938) found no major differences in a retest design in which subjects were asked to give their best and worst impressions. Carp and Shavzin (1950) used the same technique and obtained similar results. Similarly, the basic features of the protocol do not change as a product of ego-altering sets (Cox & Sarason, 1954); by requests to respond as quickly as possible (Williams, 1954); when the test is introduced as one of imagination (Peterson, 1957), or when the subject is led to believe that there are right and wrong answers (Phares, Stewart, & Foster, 1960). Even when the face-to-face position is used, some variables are not affected although sets are given to the examiner concerning desirable responses. In two studies (Strauss, 1968; Strauss & Marwit, 1970) examiners were "set" to expect records in which a higher number of human movement (M) or a higher number of chromatic color responses (FC, CF, C) would occur, and also created an expectancy for long or short records. The results indicate no significant differences for any of the sets. On the other hand, the results of the Goodman (1979) study, described in the preceding chapter, indicate that more experienced examiners will generally be rated as warmer in their interactions with a subject, and will also be more likely to obtain records in which an average number of answers occur.

It would be folly to assume that the side-by-side seating eliminates all examiner influence, but it does reduce the prospect of the subject being influenced inordinately by the nonverbal behaviors of the examiner, and this is probably true of any test. Unfortunately, the accumulated information concerning behavior modifying techniques has made considerably less impact on assessment procedures than should logically have been the case. The examiner who fails to weigh the potential impact of those behaviors in the assessment situation only makes his or her task more difficult and may even provide a disservice to the subject.

Introducing the Test   Ordinarily, no special elaboration concerning the nature of the Rorschach should be required *if the subject has been prepared properly for the overall assessment process*. In most cases this will be done after a relatively brief interview, during which the examiner seeks to insure that the subject has a reasonable awareness of the purpose of the assessment. Most subjects are aware of the general purpose of assessment, but unfortunately much of that awareness includes some negative or erroneous assumptions. In instances when a subject is self-referred the responsibility for clarifying the purpose will rest with the examiner. In cases where the subject is referred for assessment by someone else, it is the responsibility of that person to explain why the referral has been made. Similarly, it is the responsibility of the examiner to provide the subject with an overview of the procedures in the assessment process.

An important purpose in providing the introductory overview concerning procedures is to ease any mistrust or anxiety that the subject may have about the situation. But beyond that, the subject is entitled to know what will be happening and what will be done with the results—when they will be available and who will receive them. The routine should be honest, but the description of the procedures need not be overly elaborate. The purpose is to describe the procedures, not how they are interpreted. For example, if a Bender Gestalt and a WAIS are planned as a part of the routine, the examiner might say, "I am going to have you copy some designs and then we will do a test that has several different parts. In one I'll ask you to remember some numbers, in another I'll ask you create some designs using some blocks, in another I'll ask you to tell me what different words mean, and so on."

In the course of the overview a statement such as, "And we will be doing the inkblot test, maybe you've heard of it" can be included. The brevity of the statement is not meant to circumvent a longer explanation about the test and sometimes more information may be required. But most subjects are "test-wise," because testing has become an integral part of the culture, and most will have taken tests for different reasons, such as job placement and academic achievement. Similarly, most subjects will have some familiarity with the inkblot method, whether it is the child who has made inkblots in the first grade or the adult who has formulated some ideas about the test through the media, educational experience, games, or relationships with others who have been administered the Rorschach.

If the subject expresses naiveté about inkblots, and wants to pursue the issue of why the test is to be used, the response should be honest (e.g., "It is just some inkblots that I'll show you and ask you what they might be.") Depending on the circumstances, a statement can be added to the effect that it is a test that provides some information about some of the characteristics of a person or, it helps us to understand something about the personality of an individual. Occasionally a subject may want to discuss some of the procedures in greater detail, including the Rorschach and especially how it works. It is probably best to avoid more detailed explanations of any of the procedures prior to testing, and instead offer the subject an opportunity to raise more questions after all of the data have been collected.

Assuming that the seating is appropriate, and that the subject has been prepared for testing, the procedure of administering the Rorschach becomes relatively simple. Some sort of alert to the subject is in order (e.g., "Now we are going to do the inkblot test."). The specific content of the alert will depend largely on what dialogue ensued when the examiner did the overview of all procedures. Thus there are some instances when the test might be identified as the Rorschach, but the term *inkblot* will probably be preferable in most cases, and can be used freely. In a few instances some explanation about how inkblots are made is appropriate, especially if the subject is a young child. In other instances the particularly anxious subject may ask something about correct answers, and the standard response should be to the effect that people see all sorts of things in the blots. But this kind of commentary should be avoided whenever possible and, most specifically, *it should not* include any reference to card turning, right or wrong answers, or any statement that might create a set about the quantity of answers to be given. The ultimate nature of the pretest phase of Rorschach administration must be left to the judgment of the examiner. No two subjects or testing situations will be completely identical; however, it is important that the examiner accomplish the pretest procedures as smoothly as possible within the realities of the test situation.

Usually, the blots will be visible to the subject, stacked *face down,* and in the appropriate order, with Card I on top. They should be within easy reach of the examiner *but not* of the subject. The Location Sheet that will be used during the Inquiry phase of the test should not be visible at this time. Because all responses will be recorded verbatim, the examiner should be well prepared with plenty of paper, and an extra pen or pencil can sometimes prove very important.

Instructions   The test begins by handing the subject the first blot and asking, *"What might this be?"* That is the basic instruction to the subject and nothing need be added.

If, in spite of the pretest preparation, the subject comments, "It's an inkblot," the examiner should counter with an acknowledgment plus a restatement of the basic instruction, such as, "That's right. This is the inkblot test, and I want you to tell me what it might be."

The Response (Association) Phase   The period during which the subject is giving responses to the blots has often been called the Free Association (Exner, 1974, 1978; Exner & Weiner, 1982), but that label can be misleading because the subject is not really associating to the blot. Instead, he or she is defining it and selecting responses for delivery from those definitions. Whatever the nomenclature, it is a time when the examiner's responsibilities become somewhat more complex than during the pretest preparation.

The examiner must record all verbal material *verbatim,* quickly and efficiently, field questions on occasion, and in some instances provide a nondirective form of encouragement. The examiner must avoid injecting any set, bias, or direction into the situation except in those few instances when encouragement is required. Silence by the examiner is the rule, interrupted only during the exchange of cards or when a comment is necessary, but even then the verbalizations from the examiner should be formulated with care. As noted earlier, it is the perfunctory utterance that has the potential to impinge on the ambiguity of the situation. Even the most simple response, such as "mmm-hmm," can operate as a significant influence without any awareness by the subject.

The subject should *hold the card.* If some reluctance to do so is manifest, the examiner should say, "Here, take it." If the subject opts to place the card on the table, the examiner should not interfere, but initially it should be placed in the subject's hand.

Questions and Encouragement   It is not uncommon for subjects to ask a variety of questions, especially early into the test. The response from the examiner should be nondirective, conveying the general notion that people respond to the blots in different ways. The following are examples of questions commonly asked, and responses that would ordinarily be appropriate.

S: Can I turn it?

E: It's up to you.

S: Should I try to use all of it?

E: Whatever you like. Different people see different things.

S: Do you want me to show you where I see it?

E: If you like. (It is probably best at this point to avoid any mention of the Inquiry.)

S: Should I just use my imagination?

E: Yes, just tell me what you see. (It is more appropriate to use the word *see* rather than *reminds you of* to questions of this sort, stressing perception rather than association.)

S: (After giving a response) Is that the kind of thing you want?

E: Yes, just whatever it looks like to you.

S: Is that the right answer?

E: There are all sorts of answers.

S: Does it look like that to you?

E: Oh, I can see a lot of things.

S: How can you make anything out of what I see?

E: Why not wait until we are done and I'll try to explain it a bit more.

S: Do you buy these or just make them?

E: We buy them.

S: Do you always show people the same ones?

E: Yes.

S: How many of these are there?

E: Just 10.

S: How long will this take?

E: Not very long.

There is another class of question, the response to which will depend on the point at which it occurs in the Response Phase. These are questions concerning how many responses should be given. Often, before giving any answers or after giving only *one* response to Card I, a subject will ask, "How many things should I find?" The standard response by the examiner should be, *"If you take your time I am sure that you will find more than one."* If the subject gives only *one* response to Card I and then attempts to return the card to the examiner, a similar prompt is employed, *"If you take your time and look some more I think that you will find something else, too."*

The objective of the prompt is to "set" the subject to give a record of sufficient length to permit a valid interpretation. If, however, the subject fails to give a second answer to Card I, the examiner should *accept* that decision. If the subject does give *more than one* response to the first card and then asks, "How many should I see?," the standard response is, *"It's up to you."* This same response should be used if the subject raises a question about the quantity of answers while viewing cards *after* Card I.

THE PROBLEM OF BRIEF PROTOCOLS

Most brief records, that is, those containing less than 14 answers probably are not valid. Research findings make it clear that the overwhelming majority of brief records will not have the level of reliability prerequisite to the assumption of interpretive validity (Exner, 1988). Brief records are often given by highly resistive subjects who are simply attempting to avoid the many demands of the test situation. In effect, these performances depict subtle refusals to take the test. There is no easy way to distinguish the low R record that is valid from one that is not.

Thus, as a rule, protocols in which the number of responses is less than 14 should probably be discarded on the premise that they are unreliable and as such are not interpretively valid. There will be some obvious exceptions, but these will be the protocols of severely disturbed patients in which the $X+\%$ is extremely low, the $X-\%$ is quite high, and two or three bizarre responses occur, and for which other data exist confirming the magnitude of the disability.

Unfortunately, brief records occur much more often than might be expected. Many reflect a form of subtle resistance to the test, but in other instances the brief record simply may be the result of a subject following instructions very concretely and failing to generalize from encouragement given during Card I. Some subjects, especially young children, want to go through the test as quickly as possible and their haste produces a short record. Whatever the cause, a record of less than 14 answers should not be accepted. In fact, it should not even be inquired.

When a brief record is taken, the examiner/interpreter should consider either of two options. The first is simply to discard the test and rely on other assessment data that are available to formulate an evaluation of the subject. On the other hand, a second option exists if Rorschach data seem to be of importance to the assessment issue(s) that have been posed. It involves an immediate retest following the Response Phase of the test. To do so, the examiner should interrupt the standard procedure, which ordinarily means proceeding to describe the purpose of the Inquiry, and explain to the subject:

Now you know how it's done. But there's a problem. You didn't give enough answers for us to get anything out of the test. So we will go through them again and this time I want you to make sure to give me more answers. You can include the same ones you've already given if you like but make sure to give me more answers this time.

Some subjects seek direction under this new circumstance and ask, "How many should I really give?" The response should depend mainly on whether the examiner feels that the subject had tried to be cooperative. For example, if the subject seemed cooperative, it is appropriate to say, "Well, it's really up to you, but you only gave _____ answers and I really need more than that to get anything out of the test." If a subject obviously has been more resistive or guarded, the examiner should be more directive if a question is asked about how many answers are required, such as, "Well, it's up to you but I really need several more answers than you gave."

Potential Rejections   In a few cases, especially with very resistant subjects, an attempt is made to reject the card. Usually the subject will say, "It doesn't look like anything to me" or, "I just don't see anything there" or, "All I can see is an inkblot, nothing else." If this occurs in responding to Card I, or to Card II after the subject has given only one answer to Card I, it may be an indication that the examiner has not created sufficient rapport with the subject during the overview of purposes and procedures. If this is true, it will be necessary to stop the administration and review the purpose of the assessment with the subject once again. Conversely, some subjects simply do not want to be tested and, unfortunately, there is no magic formula that will insure their cooperation. If this proves to be the case, efforts to administer the Rorschach should be abandoned. The latter is usually a very unusual instance that occurs with the extremely guarded and hostile subject, or occasionally with some who are extremely disorganized because of the psychological chaos created by an active psychotic state. The subject who is chaotically psychotic should not have been referred. As for the angry and guarded subject, the judgment and skills of the examiner must dictate the matter of disposition.

The most common attempts to reject cards do not occur with Cards I or II. Instead, they tend to occur later in the test, and quite often with Card IX, which seems to have the highest level of difficulty. If a subject has been giving responses to the preceding cards, the attempted rejection can be taken as an indicator of the discomfort that the subject is experiencing as the task proceeds. But it *does not mean that the subject cannot respond.* To the contrary, it suggests that he or she is having difficulty in the discarding and selection operations. Some reassurance can be helpful such as, *"Take your time, we are in no hurry."* If the subject persists in the rejection attempt, the examiner should be more firm, responding with, *"Look, take your time, everyone can find something. We've got all day if we need it."* This sort of pressure should be applied only in the exceptional circumstance where no other tactic can be used to avoid the rejection. It is likely that the remainder of the record will be brief and possibly more guarded than might otherwise be the case, but unfortunately, the alternative is to have a record that is missing responses to one or more cards, and it will probably not be valid.

THE PROBLEM OF LENGTHY RECORDS

Whereas the most common problem in Rorschach administration involves the excessively short record, some subjects become overly involved in the task, and because of their obsessive style, will give endless numbers of answers if permitted to do so. In the early days of the Rorschach, and extending through the 1960s, examiners had no guidelines to use to halt a subject if he or she seemed determined to provide very large numbers of answers to each blot. Exner (1974) found that the Beck tactic of encouraging for more than one response on each of the first five blots yielded an increase in the average R of nearly 10 responses; however, the majority of the increase consists of answers in which a common detail area (D) is used, that are based on pure form (F), and involve animal (A) content. In effect, the increased number of responses does not contribute significantly to the interpretive yield.

In a study completed for this work, protocols from various patient and nonpatient groups, ranging in length from 45 to 85 answers, were drawn from the data pool for study. Each of these 135 records were retyped, but including no more than the first five responses per blot. Both sets of records, the original full-length one and the reduced one, were interpreted by at least two of a group of six judges, working independently of each other, and they were also processed through a computer interpretation program. When the interpretive descriptions and conclusions were examined in pairs (i.e., one derived from the original and one derived from the reduced version for each subject), the interpretations were strikingly similar. In some instances, the longer record produced a more firm conclusion that the subject was obsessive or pedantic, but few other differences evolved, and they were not consistent. These findings suggest that it is reasonable to limit the number of answers that a subject is permitted to deliver, *under some circumstances.*

If a subject delivers *six* responses *to the first blot,* the examiner should intervene and take the blot from the subject. Subsequently, *if the same subject* delivers *five* answers to Card II, the same procedure should be employed, and so on. However, *anytime the subject delivers fewer than five answers to a blot, no further intervention should occur.*

This tactic has some hazards, and should be employed cautiously. For instance, the calculations for both the Affective Ratio and the Egocentricity Index may be affected as R is being controlled. Several other ratios and percentages might also be affected, and the application of normative data, even though done proportionally, may be of questionable use for some variables. This procedure is a trade-off to replace the inordinately long record, which may be extremely time-consuming to administer and score, and equally problematic to interpret. It is important to note that if the subject gives fewer than *six* answers on Card I, *no intervention* will occur, *regardless of the number of answers on any subsequent blot.*

RECORDING THE RESPONSES

All responses must be recorded verbatim. This may seem like a difficult feat, especially for the Rorschach novice, but it is not as arduous as it might appear. Most Rorschachers use a relatively common scheme of abbreviations in recording answers. These combine the use of phonetics, the coding abbreviations for response content, and some logically derived abbreviations not unlike those found in speed writing. Some of the more common abbreviations are shown in Table 6.

There are two reasons that responses must be recorded verbatim. First, the examiner must be able to read them later to decide on the coding (scoring) for the response. The codes or scores are based on the presence of specific words or phrases. Responses that are not recorded verbatim cannot be coded accurately, and the record will not be valid. Second, the verbatim recording creates a permanent record of the test so that others can

Table 6. Abbreviations Commonly Used for Recording Rorschach Responses

Phonetically Derived		Logically Derived		Derived from Scores	
Abbreviation	Meaning	Abbreviation	Meaning	Abbreviation	Meaning
b	be	abt	about	h	human
c	see	a.t.	anything	a	animal
g	gee	bc	because	bl	blood
o	oh	bf	butterfly	cg	clothing
r	are	cb	could be	cl	cloud
u	you	dk	don't know	ex	explosion
y	why	e.t.	everything	fd	food
		frt	front	fi	fire
		j	just	ge	geography
		ll	looks like	hh	household
		mayb	may be	ls	landscape
		ss	some sort	na	nature
		st	something	sc	science
		wm	woman	sx	sex
		-g	ing	xy	x-ray

also read the record and know *exactly* what the subject said. This is important for purposes of consultation, be even more so if the subject is retested at another time to cross-validate the findings, or to review changes that may have occurred as the result of treatment. The latter cannot be overestimated in importance. If the responses in the first administration are illegible, or not recorded verbatim, the comparison of the two records becomes difficult or impossible.

It is also important for the examiner to record the position of the blot when the response is given. The use of carat marks for this purpose were suggested by Loosli-Usteri (1929), using the peak of each angle to represent the direction of the top of the card, <, V, >, with no mark entered when the card is upright. A circle (0) may also be useful in noting instances when the subject has rotated the card completely *without stopping,* but this should not be confused with those instances when a subject deliberately turns the card to each side and examines each view before giving a response, <, V, >.

The format for recording responses should not vary from examiner to examiner. It is best to use 8½ by 11-inch paper, which is easiest to file, and to record the responses on the sheet *horizontally* rather than vertically, that is, with the 11-inch margin at the top. This provides ample room to record the Response Phase and the Inquiry Phase and still have room for recording the card number and a column for entering the scores. This format is illustrated in Figure 3.

INQUIRY PHASE

The procedure for administering the Rorschach becomes more complex for the examiner during the Inquiry. It is conducted *after* all responses are given to all 10 cards. The purpose of the Inquiry is to gain whatever additional information is necessary in order to score the response accurately, *as it occurred.* In other words, the Inquiry is *not* used to

Card	Response	Inquiry	Scoring
I	1. Ths ll a bat 2 me	E: U said ths ll a bat to me S: Yeah, it has the wgs & som feelrs E: I'm not sur where u r seeing it S: Oh, all of it	
	(S wants to return card) E: I thk if u tak ur time u'll c sthg else too < V >		
	2. I supp ths cb a wm in the cntr	E: And then u said I supp this cb a wm in the cntr S: Yeah, c here (outlines), her shape, & she's got her hands up. lik she's waving or sthg E: I'm not sur wht maks it ll tht S: Just the way it is, curvy, lik a wm, c her legs r here & the hands up here	
II	v3. Ths way it ll an ex	E: Here u said it ll an ex S: Yeah, c ths part here (points) E: I'm not sur I'm see-g it the way u r S: C the way the lines go out, kinda up, lik an ex, lik a blast E: A blast? S: Its all red lik a blast is, lik fire	
	That's all I c		

Figure 3. Format for Recording Rorschach Responses.

generate new information from the subject, but simply to clarify what was perceived during the Response Phase. But this is easier said than done, and the procedure requires the examiner to work within some very narrow parameters to avoid injecting new sets into the situation.

First, it is *critically important* that the subject be prepared for the Inquiry. This is best accomplished if the examiner explains the procedure and its purpose clearly. The preface to the Inquiry will vary slightly, depending on the characteristics of the subject, but it should generally follow this format:

> O.k., we've done them all. Now we are going to go back through them. It won't take long. I want you to help me see what you saw. I'm going to read what you said, and then I want you to show me where on the blot you saw it and what there is there that makes it look like that, so that I can see it too. I'd like to see it just like you did, so help me now. Do you understand?

The crux of these instructions is that the examiner wants to see the object, *as the subject sees it.* If that happens, the response is scored easily.

Once the subject implies an understanding of the Inquiry procedure, it can begin. Card I is handed to the subject and the examiner says, "All right, here you said. . . ," and finishing the statement with a *verbatim* reading of what was given in the first answer. If the subject has understood the nature of the task, he or she will proceed to point out the main features of the object reported. Conversely, if the subject simply replies with, "Yes that's right," the examiner should reaffirm the Inquiry purpose by saying something such as, *"Wait now, remember why we are doing this. I want to see it like you do. So help me. Show me where it is and what there is that makes it look like that."*

Each response should be inquired by first rereading, verbatim, the subject's answer. The reasonably cooperative subject will comprehend the task quickly and will usually provide the examiner with enough information to score the response accurately. Under these optimal conditions, very few questions or comments from the examiner will be required, and in some circumstances the need for questions is eliminated. In fact, there are occasions when the ideally cooperative subject is sufficiently articulate during the Response Phase that an answer need not be inquired, but before making this decision the examiner should review the response carefully to insure that information about the location and determinant(s) has been given.

Obviously, the examiner must know how to code a response to conduct the Inquiry properly. As the subject elaborates on the answer the examiner must review the information given in light of all scoring possibilities. Nothing should be assumed, and codes are assigned *only* when warranted by the articulations of the subject. Unfortunately, the Inquiry sometimes has been the most misunderstood and abused features of the test. When done correctly, it enhances the richness of the data. When it is done in a negligent or distorted manner however, it can muddle the record terribly. It must not be done hastily, and the decision to inject a comment or question should be weighed intelligently.

Appropriate Questions   In considering whether to inject a question during the Inquiry, the examiner focuses on the three major components of coding: (1) Location (Where is it?), (2) Determinants (What makes it look like that?), and (3) Content (What is it?). Most problems for the novice examiner occur arise from the second of the three, determinants, because the subject will usually say where it is and the response itself indicates what it is. But why it looks like that can be another matter. Objects may be perceived in the blots because of the shape of the contours, color, shading, apparent movement, or any combination of these. The report of the subject should reveal which of these elements has been important to the formulation of the answer. It would simplify the process if the subject could be asked directly about each of the elements, but several studies indicate that the number of answers based exclusively on the form features will decrease, and the number of answers that include the use of color, movement, or shading will increase if this direct method is employed (Gibby & Stotsky, 1953; Klingensmith, 1956; Baughman, 1958, 1959; Zax & Stricker, 1960). Only one study suggests that this will not be the case (Reisman, 1970). The Rapaport et al. (1946) approach to the test included the Inquiry after each card. When records taken using that method were compared with those employing the Inquiry after all 10 cards, a significant increase was found in the frequencies of movement, color, and shading answers (Exner, 1974). Thus the traditional method of using subtle, nondirective questions, free of any cues, should always be followed.

In most instances, routine kinds of questions can be used. *"I'm not sure that I'm seeing it as you are,"* is a standard form of prompting to remind the subject of the task at hand. It should not, however, be repeated endlessly and thus other nondirective questions should also be employed. *"I'm not sure I know where you are seeing it,"* is a standard prompter when the location is in doubt. *"I'm not sure what there is there that makes it look like that,"* focuses on the determinant issue by asking the subject for clarification.

Occasionally, a very resistive subject will be extremely vague during the Inquiry, by saying, "It just looks like that." Here, the examiner must also be resistive and not permit the subject to be evasive. Again, it may be necessary to restate the purpose of the procedure, but sometimes a comment such as, *"I know it looks like that to you, but help me see it too,"* may suffice. If a subject is vague about location, there can be some value in directing, *"Run your finger around it and show me some of the parts."* As a last resort some examiners may feel that it is appropriate to ask the subject to trace the object on the Location Sheet with a pen or pencil, but this is not an ideal tactic, and if it is used, the examiner should make sure that the subject does not draw on the blot itself.

There is another category of questions that is sometimes required in instances when a subject has used a *key word* in the response, or spontaneously at the onset of the Inquiry. Most key words are adjectives, but not always, and the examiner must be alert to any word that implies the presence of a determinant. For instance:

RESPONSE	INQUIRY
It cb a very pretty flower	*E:* (Repeats S's response verbatim)
	S: Yes, ths cb the stem & here r the petals

At this point the subject has provided the basic location and has implied the use of contours in forming the answer, but a key word has occurred in the Response that must be pursued. The word is *pretty,* implying the possible use of color in the response.

E: U mentioned that it is pretty

If the subject had not used the word *pretty* in the response, the examiner would not have posed any question in the Inquiry, *even if the response were given to a chromatically colored area of the blot.* Inquiry questions are posed only when there is a substantial implication that an unarticulated determinant exists. Consider another example:

RESPONSE	INQUIRY
It 11 2 peopl doing sthg at nite	*E:* (Repeats *S*'s response) *S:* Yes, c here thy r, their heads and legs & thes r the arms

Again, the location and form features have been delineated, and movement has also been given. But even though the response already includes the movement determinant, two issues remain in doubt. There is no indication about whether the movement is active or passive, and the subject has used the word *night,* implying the possible use of the achromatic features of the blot. It is usually best to avoid addressing both of these issues in a single question such as, "You said doing something at night?" Instead, it would be more appropriate to separate the issues into two questions, "You said they are doing something?" and, if no clarification about the word night is generated, to ask a second question, "You also said it was at night?"

In some cases the key word does not occur in the response, but does occur, *spontaneously,* in the Inquiry. The decision to pursue it must be conservative. If the word occurs at the onset of the Inquiry, the issue is not in doubt and the word should be pursued. But if the word occurs in response to a question, the examiner must proceed very cautiously in asking another question. For example:

RESPONSE	INQUIRY
That 11 2 bears to me	*E:* (Rpts *S*'s response) *S:* Yeah, c 1 here & 1 here, like they r fighting

The word *fighting* signals active movement and the score should be assigned to the response, but the word *fighting* also raises the issue about whether color might be involved. Because the word is offered spontaneously, it should be questioned, "You said like they are fighting?" And if the subject replies, "Yes, that red looks like blood, like they are hurt," the score for color would be assigned. However, presume that the answer is given in the following manner:

RESPONSE	INQUIRY
That 11 2 bears to me	*E:* (Rpts *S*'s resp) *S:* Yeah, c 1 here & 1 here, like thyr do-g sthg *E:* Doing sthg? *S:* Yeah, maybe thyr fit-g or sthg

In this instance, the score for the active animal movement would be assigned, but the indecisiveness of the subject suggests that the issue should not be pursued further. Conversely, had the subject said, "Well it looks like they are hurt so they've probably been fighting," a question concerning the word *hurt* would clearly be in order.

The rule about whether or not to pose a question when a key word appears in the Inquiry is more ambiguous than might be desired. If the key word relates to something said in the original response, it should be questioned. If there is reason to believe that the subject is simply reporting something that he or she saw during the Response Phase, it should be questioned. On the other hand, if the examiner has been asking many questions as the Inquiry proceeds, the issue of whether those questions may have provoked *new* information, not present in the original response, must be weighed by the examiner. It is clear that if the subject is simply reexamining the response in an effort to assist the examiner in seeing the object reported, no further questioning should ensue. These decisions are never made easily, but conservatism should always be the guideline.

Inappropriate Questions   There are some classes of question that should never be posed during the Inquiry. These are the direct or leading questions, or questions that are oriented to elicit material that is not related directly to the coding issue. Direct questions such as, "Did the color help?" or "Are they doing anything?" can only serve to cloud the scoring issue and create unwanted sets about the procedure. The same is true of leading questions such as, "Which side of the skin is up?" or "Can you tell me anything else about it?" which create the same sort of unwanted sets. It is sometimes very tempting to ask a subject to elaborate on a response such as, "Are they males or females?" or "Why do you think he feels sad?" These are questions that are completely foreign to the coding issue, and although the answers might appear to be clinically useful, the questions only serve to contaminate the test.

The Inquiry should be viewed as a delicate procedure. It is the "soft underbelly of the test," and it is a procedure in which the examiner has several tasks. The verbiage must be recorded *verbatim,* the Location Sheet must be completed, and the material must be carefully reviewed with an eye to whether questioning is necessary. It is a crucial segment of the test that can be likened to an Achilles' heel and botched badly when done by the unskilled or casual examiner. There is no absolute cookbook listing of questions to be asked. The examiner should not feel compelled to ask about the possible presence of every determinant. Brevity should be the rule, and the questions must be nondirective. And finally, the examiner must be aware that the subject is now operating under a new set of guidelines which Levin (1953) has likened to a second test. In some instances it can promote a sense of relief for the subject as the task is now more well defined. If this occurs it is not uncommon for subjects, especially children, to offer new responses during the Inquiry. Those *additional* answers should be faithfully recorded, because they may have some qualitative usefulness, but they are not coded or used directly in the basic interpretation of the test. Conversely, the new guidelines of the Inquiry can provoke a sense of threat in other subjects because of the perceived need to justify the responses that were reported earlier. In some such cases the subject may accuse the examiner of a recording error such as, "I didn't say that. You must have wrote it wrong." In other instances a subject may attempt to avoid a response by saying either, "That's not what I really saw," or "It doesn't look like that now," or "I can't find it now."

The examiner who encounters this form of resistance in the Inquiry should proceed tactfully but firmly. In the case where the subject denies the response, the examiner should counter with something such as, "No, I'm sure I wrote every word, here look at what I wrote. Now let's find it so you can show it to me." If the subject states that it does not look like that now, or worse, reports that it cannot be found, the examiner should be firmly reassuring, saying something such as, "Sometimes things look different when you look again, but let's try to see it like you did before. Take your time, and let me tell you again what you said."

The following are some illustrations of how resistance during the Inquiry might be handled:

RESPONSE PHASE	INQUIRY
Maybe sk of animal	*E:* (Rpts *S*'s resp)
	S: I dk, mayb here (vaguely outlines)
	E: I'm not sur I c it
	S: Just there
	E: Wait now, I kno u c it but help me c it
	S: Ok, the head & legs here

(This is sufficient and no further questions are required.)

A face	*E:* (Rpts *S*'s resp)
	S: I don't c it now
	E: Take ur time, u saw it once I'm sur u can find it again
	S: Nope, its not there
	E: Keep trying, don't hurry
	S: It's not there
	E: Do u remember what kind of face?
	S: I dk, an A I guess
	E: Try a little longer

(If *S* continues to deny the response, the Inquiry effort concerning the response should be abandoned and a minus form quality score assigned such as, *Ddo* F-Ad.)

Maybe an airplane	*S:* (Rpts *S*'s resp)
	S: Yeah it could b
	E: Show me where u c it
	S: All of it
	E: I'm not sur what makes it ll an airplane
	S: It just does
	E: I kno it does to u but help me c it too
	S: I dk it just does
	E: Show me some parts of it
	S: C the wgs lik a plane

(This is sufficient and no further questions are required.)

A parachute	*E:* (Rpts *S*'s resp)
	S: It doesn't ll tht now, it ll a tree
	E: Ok, we'll talk about the tree in a minute, but first let's try & c it as a parachute

> *S:* But its not lik that now
>
> *E:* I kno, but it did before, let's try to c it tht way 1st
>
> *S:* Well I thot of ths big top here
>
> *E:* Run ur finger around it 4 me
>
> *S:* (Outlines)

(This should be sufficient to score, and at this point the examiner should record and inquire about the additional tree response.)

Although redundant, it seems important to reaffirm the importance of preparing the subject for the Inquiry. If this is accomplished skillfully, the examiner will be free to use a greater latitude in questioning the subject that otherwise might provoke extreme resistance to the process by the subject.

THE LOCATION SHEET

Another important task of the examiner during the Inquiry is recording the locations used for the responses. This is done on the Location Sheet that has been developed for use with the test. It is a single page on which the blots are reproduced in miniature. The recording is done by outlining the area designated by the subject on the miniature, using an ink or a felt-tip pen, and recording the number of the response close to the outline. If the whole blot has been used, the scoring symbol *W* is recorded on the Location Sheet together with the number of the response.

The importance of completing the Location Sheet carefully cannot be overstated. It provides a permanent record that will be used when the test is scored, and is available later for others to review the test with an awareness of which blot areas have been used. The competent examiner will also take the time to identify some of the features of the object reported *if* they are not obvious to the casual observer. The less common the response, the greater the likelihood that these added notations will be important during the scoring or in a later review of the protocol.

If the response involves a human or animal, some notation concerning the areas in which the nose, legs, or arms have been identified can be helpful. Similarly, some responses include several separate objects such as, "a man riding a bicycle with a child running in front of him as they are passing a pond." Here, each of the four features (man, bicycle, child, and pond) should be noted on the Location Sheet.

DIRECT INQUIRY AND TESTING OF LIMITS

There are instances when information developed during the Inquiry may seem insufficient even though several questions have been posed to the subject. Thus the examiner is faced with the dilemma of asking too many questions or abandoning an issue prematurely. Usually these are instances when a subject has been overly vague about a response in spite of one, two, or even three questions. It will also often occur when the form quality of the response is minus. The decision about whether to pursue the matter further should be made conservatively. In a few cases, added questions may seem critical, but when this is not the case, the examiner should proceed to the next response. *After* the Inquiry has been completed, an examiner still troubled by this quandary can opt to return to the issue, using either a direct questioning method (Zax & Stricker, 1960), or a more subtle paired-comparison form of question (Baughman, 1958) to attempt to resolve the issue. Although the new information may be clinically useful, however, it *should not be used in coding the response.* The reason this added information should not be used in the coding decision is that it is collected under questioning which is much too directive to insure that the new material is truly reflective of the cognitive operations that occurred originally, as the response was formulated and delivered.

A second form of post-Inquiry questioning may be much more important. This is the Testing-of-Limits procedure, recommended originally by Klopfer and Kelley (1942). It was designed to test out hypotheses that responses (objects) may have been classified but later rejected in the response process. The procedure can be taken to extremes and, as such, has no useful purpose to the interpretation of the record. Nonetheless, there are instances, especially with schizophrenic subjects, when a very low number of Popular responses have been delivered in the record and the question arises about whether the subject did not classify, *or* simply failed to report the commonly reported object. This is especially important to differentiate the subject whose perceptual processes are so impaired to cause a marked perceptual distortion versus those who discard the obvious in favor of more idiosyncratic answers.

Testing-of-Limits proceeds with the examiner selecting blots to which the most common Popular response ordinarily occur, but have not in a particular protocol, and simply asking the subject if he or she might see that object there. The directions are simplistic—*"Sometimes people see . . . here. Do you see anything that looks like that?"* Often this procedure will provide valuable information, useful in discriminating perceptually impaired persons from those who are less prone to offer the conventional responses. These findings can be especially important for the treatment planning for schizophrenics.

COMMENT OR RESPONSE?

Occasionally a subject will say something when viewing a blot that may be a response, but might simply be a comment. For instance, if a blot has chromatic coloring, a subject might say, "Oh, blue and pink," which, if a response, would be coded as color naming (*Cn*) but if a comment about the blot, would not be pursued in the Inquiry. Or a subject might say, "That's an ugly-looking thing," raising the issue of whether this is comment concerning the blot or the identification of an ugly-looking object. In instances such as this the examiner should, at the appropriate point in the Inquiry, read what the subject said verbatim and ask, "Did you mean that as an answer?" Most subjects will offer clarification quickly and the examiner should proceed accordingly.

SUMMARY

The task of administering the Rorschach is not simple, but it is not difficult to learn. The key to the procedure is proficiency in coding. As noted earlier, no one can be competent in the tactics of administering the Rorschach unless they can code responses easily and accurately. Once the decision is made that the data of the Rorschach will be relevant to the assessment issues, the examiner becomes committed to a complex procedure that relies heavily on coding expertise. But competent administration of the Rorschach is not contingent *only* on that skill. Good examiners also exercise good judgment in the process of administering the test, and deal with their subjects in a tactful, sensitive, and very human manner.

REFERENCES

Baughman, E. E. (1951) Rorschach scores as a function of examiner differences. *Journal of Projective Techniques,* **15,** 243–249.

Baughman, E. E. (1958) A new method of Rorschach Inquiry. *Journal of Projective Techniques,* **22,** 381–389.

Baughman, E. E. (1959) An experimental analysis of the relationship between stimulus structure and behavior on the Rorschach. *Journal of Projective Techniques,* **23,** 134–183.

Beck, S. J. (1937) *Introduction to the Rorschach Method: A manual of personality study.* American Orthopsychiatric Association Monographs, No. 1.

Beck, S. J. (1945) *Rorschach's Test. II: A variety of personality pictures.* New York: Grune & Stratton.

Beck, S. J. (1952) *Rorschach's Test. III: Advances in interpretation.* New York: Grune & Stratton.

Beck, S. J. (1960) *The Rorschach Experiment: Ventures in blind analysis.* New York: Grune & Stratton.

Carp, A. L., and Shavzin, A. R. (1950) The susceptibility to falsification of the Rorschach diagnostic technique. *Journal of Consulting Psychology,* **3,** 230–233.

Coffin, T. E. (1941) Some conditions of suggestion and suggestibility: A study of certain attitudinal and situational factors influencing the process of suggestion. *Psychological Monographs,* **53,** Whole No. 241.

Cox, F. N., and Sarason, S. B. (1954) Test anxiety and Rorschach performance. *Journal of Abnormal and Social Psychology,* **49,** 371–377.

Exner, J. E. (1969) *The Rorschach Systems.* New York: Grune & Stratton.

Exner, J. E. (1974) *The Rorschach: A Comprehensive System. Volume 1.* New York: Wiley.

Exner, J. E. (1978) *The Rorschach: A Comprehensive System. Volume 2. Current research and advanced interpretation.* New York: Wiley.

Exner, J. E. (1980) But it's only an inkblot. *Journal of Personality Assessment,* **44,** 562–577.

Exner, J. E. (1988) Problems with brief Rorschach protocols. *Journal of Personality Assessment,* **52,** 640–647.

Exner, J. E. (1991) *The Rorschach: A Comprehensive System. Volume 2: Interpretation.* New York: Wiley.

Exner, J. E., and Hark, L. J. (1979) Order effects for WAIS and Rorschach scores. Workshops study No. 262 (unpublished) Rorschach Workshops.

Exner, J. E., and Hark, L. J. (1980) Frequency of Rorschach responses after prolonged cognitive testing. Workshops study No. 271 (unpublished) Rorschach Workshops.

Exner, J. E., Leura, A. V., and George, L. M. (1976) A replication of the Masling study using four groups of new examiners with two seating arrangements and video evaluation. Workshops study No. 256 (unpublished) Rorschach Workshops.

Exner, J. E., and Weiner, I. B. (1982) *The Rorschach: A Comprehensive System. Volume 3: Assessment of children and adolescents.* New York: Wiley.

Fosberg, I. A. (1938) Rorschach reactions under varied instructions. *Rorschach Research Exchange,* **3,** 12–30.

Gage, N. L. (1953) Explorations in the understanding of others. *Educational and Psychological Measurement,* **13,** 14–26.

Gibby, R. G., Miller, D. R., and Walker, E. L. (1953) The examiner's influence on the Rorschach protocol. *Journal of Consulting Psychology,* **17,** 425–428.

Gibby, R. G., and Stotsky, B. A. (1953) The relation of Rorschach free association to inquiry. *Journal of Consulting Psychology,* **17,** 359–363.

Giedt, F. H. (1955) Comparison of visual, content, and auditory cues in interviewing. *Journal of Consulting Psychology,* **18,** 407–416.

Goodman, N. L. (1979) Examiner influence on the Rorschach: The effect of sex, sex pairing and warmth on the testing atmosphere. Doctoral Dissertation, Long Island University.

Grisso, J. T., and Meadow, A. (1967) Test interference in a Rorschach-WAIS administration sequence. *Journal of Consulting Psychology,* **31,** 382–386.

Haller, N., and Exner, J. E. (1985) The reliability of Rorschach variables for inpatients presenting symptoms of depression and/or helplessness. *Journal of Personality Assessment,* **49,** 516–521.

Harrower, M. (1965) Differential diagnosis. In B. Wolman (ed.) *Handbook of Clinical Psychology.* New York: McGraw-Hill.

Hertz, M. R. (1969) A Hertz interpretation. In J. E. Exner *The Rorschach Systems.* New York: Grune & Stratton.

Holt, R. R. (1958) Clinical and statistical prediction: A reformulation and some new data. *Journal of Abnormal and Social Psychology,* **56,** 1–12.

Holt, R. R. (1970) Yet another look at clinical and statistical prediction. *American Psychologist,* **25,** 337–349.

Kelly, E. L., and Fiske, D. W. (1950) The prediction of success in the V.A. training program in clinical psychology. *American Psychologist,* **4,** 395–406.

Klingensmith, S. W. (1956) A study of the effects of different methods of structuring the Rorschach inquiry on determinant scores. Doctoral Dissertation, University of Pittsburgh.

Klopfer, B., and Kelley D. M. (1942) *The Rorschach Technique.* Yonkers-on-Hudson, N.Y.: World Book.

Klopfer, B., Ainsworth, M. D., Klopfer, W. G., and Holt, R. R. (1954) *Developments in the Rorschach Technique. I: Technique and theory.* Yonkers-on-Hudson, N.Y.: World Book.

Kostlan, A. A. (1954) A method for the empirical study of psychodiagnosis. *Journal of Consulting Psychology,* **18,** 83–88.

Levin, M. M. (1953) The two tests in the Rorschach. *Journal of Projective Techniques,* **17,** 471–473.

Loosli-Usteri, M. (1929) Le test de Rorschach applique a differents groupes d'enfants de 10-13 ans. *Archives de Psychologie,* **21,** 51-106.

Lord, E. (1950) Experimentally induced variations in Rorschach performance. *Psychological Monographs,* **60,** Whole No. 316.

Luborsky, L., and Holt, R. R. (1957) The selection of candidates for psychoanalytic training. *Journal of Clinical and Experimental Psychopathology,* **18,** 166–176.

MacKinnon, D. W. (1951) The effects of increased observation upon the accuracy of prediction. *American Psychologist,* **6,** 311 (abstract).

Masling, J. (1965) Differential indoctrination of examiners and Rorschach responses. *Journal of Consulting Psychology,* **29,** 198–201.

Peterson, L. C. (1957) The effects of instruction variation on Rorschach responses. Unpublished M.A. Thesis, Ohio State University.

Phares, E. J., Stewart, L. M., and Foster, J. M. (1960) Instruction variation and Rorschach performance. *Journal of Projective Techniques,* **21,** 28–31.

Piotrowski, Z. A. (1958) The psychodiagnostic test battery: Clinical application. In D. Brower, and L. E. Abt (Eds.) *Progress in Clinical Psychology.* Vol. 3. New York: Grune & Stratton.

Piotrowski, Z. A. (1969) A Piotrowski interpretation. In J. E. Exner *The Rorschach Systems.* New York: Grune & Stratton.

Rapaport, D., Gill, M., and Schafer, R. (1946) *Diagnostic Psychological Testing.* Vol 1. Chicago: Yearbook.

Reisman, J. M. (1970) The effect of a direct inquiry on Rorschach scores. *Journal of Projective Techniques and Personality Assessment,* **34,** 388–390.

Sarbin, T. R. (1943) A contribution to the study of actuarial and individual methods of prediction. *American Journal of Sociology,* **48,** 593–602.

Schachtel, E. G. (1945) Subjective definitions of the Rorschach test situation and their effect on test performance. *Psychiatry,* **8,** 419–448.

Schafer, R. (1954) *Psychoanalytic Interpretation in Rorschach Testing.* New York: Grune & Stratton.

Stern, G. G., Stein, M. I., and Bloom, B. S. (1956) *Methods in Personality Assessment.* Glencoe, Ill.: Free Press.

Strauss, M. E. (1968) Examiner expectancy: Effects on Rorschach Experience Balance. *Journal of Consulting Psychology,* **32,** 125–129.

Strauss, M. E., and Marwit, S. J. (1970) Expectancy effects in Rorschach testing. *Journal of Consulting and Clinical Psychology,* **34,** 448.

Van de Castle, R. L. (1964) Effect of test order on Rorschach human content. *Journal of Consulting Psychology,* **28,** 286–288.

Vernon, P. E. (1950) The validation of civil service selection board procedures. *Occupational Psychology,* **24,** 75–95.

Weiner, I. B. (1966) *Psychodiagnosis in Schizophrenia.* New York: Wiley.

Williams, M. H. (1954) The influence of variations in instructions on Rorschach reaction time. *Dissertation Abstracts,* **14,** 2131.

Zax, M., and Stricker, G. (1960) The effect of a structured inquiry on Rorschach scores. *Journal of Consulting Psychology,* **24,** 328–332.

CHAPTER 4

Scoring:
The Rorschach Language

The full value of the Rorschach is realized only from the complete sum of its parts. A neglect of any available Rorschach data, whether quantitative or qualitative, is an abuse of the test and a disservice to the subject. This principle has been emphasized by all of the Rorschach Systematizers. Beck (1945, 1967), Klopfer (1942, 1954) and Rapaport-Schafer (1946, 1954) have each stressed the importance of using the total *configuration* of the record. Hertz (1952, 1963) has accented the same principle in her "interactionist approach" and Piotrowski (1957) has elaborated on this in his "principle of interdependent components." In essence, the concept of *total* Rorschach acknowledges that few if any single test variables will have a consistently high correlation with any internal or external behavior. Instead, this concept is predicated on the notion that an understanding of any feature of an individual can be useful only when it is judged in the context of other features. It is the knowledge of how the characteristics of a person merge together in a series of complex interrelationships that breeds a reasonable understanding of that person.

Much rich information concerning the characteristics of a person, and the interrelationship of those characteristics, is derived from the scoring summary of the Rorschach. These are the data that provide the nucleus of interpretation. The issue of scoring and the symbols to be used have been topics of much discussion in the literature. In fact, it was the scoring issue that formed the original seeds of divergence among the various systematizers and ultimately led them in different directions in extending Rorschach's work (Exner, 1969). It was also on this issue that the major criticisms of the Rorschach unfolded during the 1950s and 1960s. Much of the research published during that period focused on single variables rather than constellations or configurations of variables. The result was a sizable body of literature concerning the test which reported negative or equivocal findings, provoking some, such as Zubin et al. (1965), to argue that the test should not be considered in the "measurement" framework at all.

To some extent, critics such as Zubin have been correct in the assumption that all Rorschach "scores" do not meet some of the psychometric characteristics that are common in most psychological tests. For instance, many scores are not normally distributed, making the application of parametric statistics at best, difficult. Others are valid but not temporally consistent, and some have levels of temporal consistency or reliability that account for less than one-half of the variance. Moreover, the test is open-ended; that is, all protocols are not of the same length. Even when the total number of responses is the same for two records, it is highly unlikely that the distribution of codes or scores to each of the 10 cards will be the same. This is both an asset and a liability for the test. It is a liability because it restricts the full usefulness of normative comparisons and thus makes for greater difficulty in establishing useful normative data (Cronbach, 1949). Holtzman et al. (1961) pointed out, "Providing a subject with only ten inkblots and permitting him to give as many or as few responses as he wishes characteristically results in a set of unreliable scores with sharply skewed distributions."[1] The Cronbach-Holtzman criticism concerning the variability of the number of responses cannot be denied, but they erred in suggesting that this makes the test psychometrically unapproachable. It is quite true that this composite of *measurement* problems constitutes a difficult problem for the statistician, and a virtual nightmare for the psychometric purist, but none have been unresolvable in the context of contemporary statistical methods plus the use of reasonably large samples of data.

As noted in Chapter 2, much of the criticism of the test was fomented by a lack of understanding about the nature of the test. But some of the misunderstanding was also generated by a misuse or overgeneralization of the term *score*. The procedure of translating Rorschach responses into Rorschach symbols traditionally has been called scoring. Unfortunately, the use of the word *score* carries with it, in the realm of psychology, some concepts of measurement that are not always useful or appropriate to Rorschach scoring. Once a protocol has been collected from a subject, each response is *coded*. The coding is called scoring, but most of the code assigned does not involve numbers. They are not ordinal scores as used in an intelligence or achievement test. In effect, the coding procedure reduces the response into a logical and systematic format, a special Rorschach language. It is like a system of shorthand used to record various components that exist in a response. It is only in very rare instances that the score or code for any single response becomes interpretively important. For instance, a response scored *Do Fo A* simply indicates that the subject responded to a common detail area of the blot, and gave a frequently reported animal response using the contours of the blot to delineate the animal.

The Rorschach scores that are crucial to interpretation are the frequency scores for each of the codes and the numerous percentages, ratios, and other metrically useful derivations that are calculated from them. Collectively, they represent the *Structural Summary* of the record. Thus although some substance of the response is lost in the coding or scoring translation from words to symbols, the data derived from those codes allow an evaluation of response styles and other psychological features of the subject that otherwise would not be possible. Obviously, the procedure of scoring or coding each response is critically important, because each contributes to the Structural Summary of the protocol.

The codes that have been selected for use in the Comprehensive System represent a combination of those derived from other systems for which empirical support has been established, plus some new codings that have evolved as the System has matured. Most of Rorschach's original symbols are included. He recognized the importance of coding responses and devised a simplistic format for doing so that consisted of five categories: (1) Location (to which feature(s) of the blot did the subject respond?), (2) Determinant (What features of the blot contribute to the formulation of the answer?), (3) Form Quality (Is the object described appropriate for the blot contours used?), (4) Content (What is the class of content to which the response belongs?), and (5) Popular (Does

---

[1] In fact, Holtzman devised an inkblot test consisting of 45 blots in which subjects are permitted to give only one response per blot. By controlling for the number of responses, statistical manipulations are accomplished more easily and the use of a psychogram is appropriate. Although considerable normative and reliability data have been reported for the Holtzman Inkblot Method, data concerning validity are somewhat more limited.

the response occur with a high frequency in the general population?). Each of the systematizers retained this basic format in their own systems and it has proved useful.

Beck (1937) and Hertz (1940) added a sixth category for Organizational Activity, to account for responses involving the meaningful integration of blot features. Rapaport et al. (1946) also added a category of Special Scores designed to note strange verbiage and pathognomic features in responses. The work of Friedman (1952) has led to the development of an eighth category related to the location selection, which concerns the Developmental Quality of that selection. Although the number of specific codes or scores within each category has increased or decreased as the result of research findings, each of these eight categories remains useful to the ultimate richness of interpretation that is derived from the structural data. Some responses are scored or coded for as few as five of these categories, whereas others will be marked by coding from six, seven, or all eight.

There is only one symbol (*P*) if the response is Popular, used for each of 13 very high frequency answers. Each of the remaining seven categories has multiple symbols. There are three symbols for the Location, *W* (whole blot), *D* (common detail area), and *Dd* (unusual detail area), and the symbol *S* is added to any of the three if white space is also involved. One of four Developmental Quality symbols is added to the Location coding. Many more options exist when coding the Determinants. Symbols are used to denote the use of form, chromatic color, achromatic color, each of three kinds of shading, and each of three kinds of movement. One of four symbols is used to signify the appropriateness of the form use. The symbols for coding the content of the responses are logical abbreviations, such as *H* for human, *A* for animal, *Bt* for botany, and so on. When responses involve integrating or organizing the blot or blot areas in a complex manner, a score for Organizational Activity, a numerical value, is also assigned to that answer. Two kinds of Special Scores are used. They are also abbreviations. One kind notes the presence of cognitive slippage in the response, such as *DV,* which is the abbreviation for deviant verbalization. The second set of Special Scores is used to note unique characteristics of the response, such as *AG,* which is employed for movement answers in which the action is aggressive.

The constancy of the Rorschach language permits interpreters to recognize the same characteristics in a single record, and across records. The composite frequencies for each code yield a base of data, and when those frequencies are numerically translated into ratios and percentages, the breadth of information concerning personality features and/or psychopathology becomes very substantial.

The *cardinal rule* of coding (or scoring) Rorschach responses is that the code (or score) should represent the cognitive operation that occurred at the time the subject gave the answer. Obviously this is a very difficult objective to achieve, and this is the main reason that the Inquiry creates some hazards to the overall process. Nonetheless, the objective of coding *only* the process reflected in the original response cannot be emphasized enough, particularly to the Rorschach novice. The coder-interpreter must resist the temptation to consider the original response and the information developed in the Inquiry as being continuous, for this is an illogical assumption. Many events transpire between the original response and the Inquiry and, as noted earlier, the latter occurs under a much different structure than the former.

Although the *cardinal rule* in coding is easy to understand (although not always easy to apply), the second most important rule in coding is that *all of the components that appear in the response should be included in the coding.* Rorschach endorsed this principle, although his scheme for coding was much less elaborate than developed by those following in his footsteps.[2] Each of the Rorschach Systems developed after his death made some provision for this, although Klopfer later deviated from this principle.[3]

Some illustrations of the coding process may be useful before addressing the complexities of each of the eight coding categories. Each of these illustrations involves a relatively common or Popular response to Card III.

RESPONSE	INQUIRY
III Ths 11 a person, mayb a man *I guess*	E: (Rpts S's response) S: Yes, right here (points to D9) E: I'm not sure I'm seeing it lik u r, help me. S: Here is his head & body & legs

This is a very simplistic response. The subject has reported only one figure, whereas most people report two in this blot. Nonetheless, it is still a very common answer. The coding for this answer is:

Location Developmental Quality	Determinant Form Quality	Content	Popular
Do	*Fo*	*H*	*P*

The coding of *Do Fo H* indicates that the subject used a common detail area of the blot (*D*) and identified it as a single or unitary object (*o*). The Determinant of *F* indicates that only the form or contours of the blot area were identified to justify the object. The Form Quality code (*o*) indicates that the use of the form was conventional, and the Content of the response (*H*) signifies that it is fictional or mythological human. The code *P* indicates that it is a frequently given response.

A second response to Card III shows how the coding will become more complex as the response increases in complexity.

RESPONSE	INQUIRY

III Ths 11 2 wm stirring sthg in
  a pot
	E: (Rpts S's response)
	S: That's right, thy r here (points to D1) &
	  ths 11 a pot tht thy r stirring sthg in it

---

[2]Rorschach's format for coding is considerably briefer than developed by other systematizers for two reasons. First, his premature death left much of his work incomplete, but possibly even more important is the fact that the blots used in his investigation contained no shading. The shading components that exist in the blots now used were apparently created through a printing error at the time his monograph was published. In the subsequent development of the test several newer codes have been required in consideration of responses that include the use of the shading.

[3]In the early 1940s Klopfer, out of concern that determinants were being scored too liberally, decided to adopt the position that only one determinant should be given full weight in the interpretation. Thus instead of using the principle of blended determinants that had been suggested by Rorschach, he moved to a tactic of scoring only one determinant as the "main" determinant, and all others in a response were called "additional" and quantitatively assigned half weight. In a private interview in 1965 at Asilomar, California, Klopfer expressed some regret about that decision. He did maintain, however, that the Main-Additional dichotomy he created did, in fact, preclude the interpreter from overemphasizing determinants that may not have existed in the response proper but which might have been provoked by questioning in the Inquiry.

In this example, the subject provides most of the information necessary for coding the response when giving the response. He or she reports the commonly identified human figures in the blot and includes the frequently reported human movement associated with them. The Inquiry to the response correctly begins with the repeating of the subject's response and, in this instance, is designed to confirm the location of the objects reported, but with the awareness that the subject may *spontaneously* add other features not previously reported. If this occurred, they would be pursued in the Inquiry. This subject did not add any features to the original response that would be related to the coding, thus the code will be:

Location Developmental Quality	Determinant Form Quality	Pair	Contents	Popular	Organization Activtiy
D +	$M^a o$	(2)	H, Hh	P	3.0

This code (or score) also shows that the subject used a common detail area of the blot (*D*), and that in doing so, some form of synthesizing activity occurred (+); that is, the subject mentally broke up the area into separate objects and then organized them in a meaningful way. The Determinant of *Ma* indicates that the response was form based and involved active human movement. The notation of a pair (2) indicates that the subject reported two similar objects, using the symmetrical features of the blot as the basis for this impression. The Contents of the response are human (*H*) and household (*Hh*). It is a Popular response, and because it is complex, it is assigned an Organizational Activity score of 3.0, which is the value used when the objects organized are in adjacent detail areas on this blot. Some responses will have multiple determinants, and can have more than one Special Score as in the following example.

RESPONSE	INQUIRY
III It's a cpl of skeletons in a battle, really vicious	*E:* (Rpts S's response) *S:* Yeah wow, c here thy r (points to *D*1) c the heads & legs *E:* U said in a battle, really vicious *S:* Yeah, its lik thy r fighting w eo & thy got bld all over ths wall in the back, c the red splotches r lik bld on the wall

This response is a good illustration of how, at times, information developed spontaneously in the Inquiry will contribute to the coding of the response. It is not until after the examiner has asked for clarification (U said in a battle, really vicious), that the subject reveals the presence of two determinants that were not obvious in the basic response. Because they have been given without provocation, they will be included in the Determinant coding of the response. When multiple determinants occur in a response, each is separated from the next by a dot (.) which notes a determinant *Blend*. The complete coding or scoring for this response is:

Location Developmental Quality	Determinants Form Quality	Pair	Contents	Organizational Activity	Special Scores
WS +	$M^a.C.F Do$	(2)	(H), Bl	5.5	FABCOM, AG

In the response the subject used the entire blot (W), plus white space (S). Thus the Location scoring is *WS*. There is synthesis of the reported objects and so a Developmental Quality code of + is added to the location scoring, *WS* + . There are three determinants in the response, active human-like movement (M^a), the use of chromatic color without including any form features in its use (C), and dimensionality, the blood is on a wall in the background (FD). Thus the blend of $M^a.C.FD$. Although the response is strange, the use of the form features is appropriate, and the Form Quality code of *o* (ordinary) has been added to the Determinant code, $M^a.C.FDo$. There are two similar objects reported (skeletons), using the symmetry of blot as the basis, and so a 2 is included to note the pair. The Content codes are (H), used to denote human-like figures, and *Bl* for blood. There is organizing activity involved and a score for that, 5.5, has also been entered. Finally, there are two Special Scores assigned. The first identifies the highly implausible relationship of the skeletons that has been reported. Skeletons do not fight, except in cartoons and there is no implication that this is a cartoon. Also skeletons do not bleed. When these sorts of highly implausible relationships are reported, they are called Fabulized Combinations, and scored as *FABCOM*. The second Special Score is used to note the characteristic of the movement. It is clearly aggressive, and the score *AG* is included in the coding.

In most instances the coding for a single response will have little or no interpretive significance, regardless of whether it is simple and uncomplicated as in the first illustration, or quite complex as in the last example. As noted earlier, these codes are converted into frequency data, and from those frequencies a variety of ratios and percentages is derived. The frequencies are derived by first listing each of the codes or scores separately in consecutive sequence. This is called the Sequence of Scores. A computer printout of a scoring sequence for a protocol is shown in Figure 4. The numbers that have been entered after the Location codes identify which area of the blot has been used for the response.

The Sequence of Scores makes it easy to tally the frequency for each of the variables, and they are entered in the upper section of the Structural Summary. The ratios and percentages that form the basis of the interpretive process are then calculated and entered in the lower section of the Structural Summary. A printout of the Structural Summary, derived from the Sequence of Scores shown in Figure 4, is presented in Figure 5.

SEQUENCE OF SCORES

CARD	NO	LOC	#	DETERMINANT(S)	(2)	CONTENT(S)	POP Z	SPECIAL SCORES
I	1	WSo	1	FC'o		A	P 3.5	DV
	2	Wv	1	C'Fu		Cl		PER
	3	W+	1	Fo	2	Art,A,Bt	4.0	ALOG
II	4	Dv	2	C		Bl		
	5	DS+	5	ma.CFo		Sc,Fi	4.5	
III	6	Do	2	FDu		Sc		
	7	Do	9	Fo	2	H	P	
	8	Do	3	Fo		A		
IV	9	Wo	1	FDo		(H)	P 2.0	
	10	Wo	1	F-		Sc	2.0	PER
V	11	Wo	1	Fo		A	P 1.0	INC
	12	Wo	1	Fu		A	1.0	INC
	13	W+	1	FVu	2	Ls,Id	2.5	PER
VI	14	Wo	1	Fu		Ay	2.5	DV
	15	W+	1	FMa.mp.C'Fu		A,Fi	2.5	FAB,PER
VII	16	W+	1	Fo	2	(H),Art	P 2.5	DV
VIII	17	W+	1	FMao	2	A,Ls	P 4.5	
IX	18	W+	1	Ma.CFu	2	(H),Fi	P 5.5	PER
X	19	Dv	1	C	2	Na		
	20	Wv	1	C		Art,Ay		

Copyright (c) 1976, 1985, 1990 by John E. Exner, Jr.

Figure 4.   Illustration of a Sequence of Scores.

STRUCTURAL SUMMARY
===

LOCATION	DETERMINANTS		CONTENTS	S-CONSTELLATION
FEATURES	BLENDS	SINGLE		YES..FV+VF+V+FD>2
			H = 1, 0	NO..Col-Shd Bl>0
Zf = 13	m.CF	M = 0	(H) = 3, 0	NO..Ego<.31,>.44
ZSum = 38.0	FM.m.C'F	FM = 1	Hd = 0, 0	NO..MOR > 3
ZEst = 41.5	M.CF	m = 0	(Hd)= 0, 0	NO..Zd > +- 3.5
		FC = 0	Hx = 0, 0	YES..es > EA
W = 14		CF = 0	A = 6, 1	YES..CF+C > FC
(Wv = 2)		C = 3	(A) = 0, 0	YES..X+% < .70
D = 6		Cn = 0	Ad = 0, 0	NO..S > 3
Dd = 0		FC'= 1	(Ad)= 0, 0	NO..P < 3 or > 8
S = 2		C'F= 1	An = 0, 0	YES..Pure H < 2
		C' = 0	Art = 2, 1	NO..R < 17
DQ		FT = 0	Ay = 1, 1	5.....TOTAL
........(FQ-)		TF = 0	Bl = 1, 0	
+ = 7 (0)		T = 0	Bt = 0, 1	SPECIAL SCORINGS
o = 9 (1)		FV = 1	Cg = 0, 0	Lv1 Lv2
v/+ = 0 (0)		VF = 0	Cl = 1, 0	DV = 3x1 0x2
v = 4 (0)		V = 0	Ex = 0, 0	INC = 2x2 0x4
		FY = 0	Fd = 0, 0	DR = 0x3 0x6
		YF = 0	Fi = 0, 3	FAB = 1x4 0x7
		Y = 0	Ge = 0, 0	ALOG = 1x5
FORM QUALITY		Fr = 0	Hh = 0, 0	CON = 0x7
		rF = 0	Ls = 1, 1	SUM6 = 7
FQx FQf MQual SQx		FD = 2	Na = 1, 0	WSUM6 = 16
+ = 0 0 0 0		F = 8	Sc = 3, 0	
o = 9 5 0 2			Sx = 0, 0	AB = 0 CP = 0
u = 7 2 1 0			Xy = 0, 0	AG = 0 MOR = 0
- = 1 1 0 0			Id = 0, 1	CFB = 0 PER = 5
none= 3 -- 0 0		(2) = 7		COP = 0 PSV = 0

===
RATIOS, PERCENTAGES, AND DERIVATIONS

R = 20	L = 0.67		FC:CF+C = 0: 5	COP = 0	AG = 0
			Pure C = 3	Food = 0	
EB = 1: 6.5	EA = 7.5	EBPer= 6.5	Afr =0.25	Isolate/R =0.35	
eb = 4: 4	es = 8	D = 0	S = 2	H:(H)Hd(Hd)= 1: 3	
	Adj es = 7	Adj D = 0	Blends:R= 3:20	(HHd):(AAd)= 3: 0	
			CP = 0	H+A:Hd+Ad =11: 0	
FM = 2 : C'= 3	T = 0				
m = 2 : V = 1	Y = 0		Zf =13	3r+(2)/R=0.35	
a:p = 4: 1	Sum6 = 7	P = 7	Zd = -3.5	Fr+rF = 0	
Ma:Mp = 1: 0	Lv2 = 0	X+% =0.45	W:D:Dd =14: 6: 0	FD = 2	
2AB+Art+Ay= 5	WSum6 = 16	F+% =0.63	W:M =14: 1	An+Xy = 0	
M- = 0	Mnone = 0	X-% =0.05	DQ+ = 7	MOR = 0	
		S-% =0.00	DQv = 4		
		Xu% =0.35			

SCZI = 2	DEPI = 5*	CDI = 4*	S-CON = 5	HVI = No	OBS = No

===

Figure 5. Illustration of a Structural Summary.

When completed, the Structural Summary provides a wealth of information concerning some of the psychological characteristics of the subject. Obviously, it is vital that each of the codes be applied accurately. They have been selected and defined to minimize ambiguity and to maximize the research yield concerning each variable. Numerous studies have been conducted at the Rorschach Research Foundation to insure adequate interscorer reliability for each variable, using a *minimum* standard of 90% agreement among coders or a .85 intercorrelation. Two such studies have been completed for the revision of this work, one involving 20 "scorers" and 25 nonpatient records and the second involving 15 scorers and 20 psychiatric records. The results of these studies are included in the various sections of the next several chapters, in which the codes (or scores) that constitute this special Rorschach language are described in detail for each of the eight basic categories.

REFERENCES

Beck, S. J. (1937) *Introduction to the Rorschach Method.* American Orthopsychiatric Association Monograph No. 1.

Beck, S. J. (1945) *Rorschach's Test. II: A variety of personality pictures.* New York: Grune & Stratton.

Beck, S. J., and Molish, H. B. (1967) *Rorschach's Test. II: A variety of personality pictures.* (2nd Ed.) New York: Grune & Stratton.

Cronbach, L. J. (1949) Statistical methods applied to Rorschach scores: A review. *Psychological Bulletin,* **46,** 393–429.

Exner, J. E. (1969) *The Rorschach Systems.* New York: Grune & Stratton.

Friedman, H. (1952) Perceptual regression in schizophrenia: An hypothesis suggested by the use of the Rorschach test. *Journal of Genetic Psychology,* **81,** 63–98.

Hertz, M. R. (1940) *Percentage Charts for use in computing Rorschach scores.* Cleveland: Brush Foundation and the Department of Psychology, Western Reserve University.

Hertz, M. R. (1952) The Rorschach: Thirty years after. In D. Brower and L. E. Abt (Eds.) *Progress in Clinical Psychology.* New York: Grune & Stratton.

Hertz, M. R. (1963) Objectifying the subjective. *Rorschachiana,* **8,** 25–54.

Holtzman, W. H., Thorpe, J. S., Swarz, J. D., and Herron, E. W. (1961) *Inkblot Perception and Personality.* Austin: University of Texas Press.

Klopfer, B., and Kelley, D. M. (1942) *The Rorschach Technique.* Yonkers-on-Hudson, N.Y.: World Book.

Klopfer, B., Ainsworth, M. D., Klopfer, W. G., and Holt, R. R. (1954) *Developments in the Rorschach Technique. I: Technique and Theory.* Yonkers-on-Hudson, N.Y.: World Book.

Piotrowski, Z. (1957) *Perceptanalysis.* New York: Macmillan.

Rapaport, D., Gill, M., and Schafer, R. (1946) *Diagnostic Psychological Testing: The theory, statistical evaluation, and diagnostic application of a battery of tests. Volume II.* Chicago: Yearbook Publishers.

Schafer, R. (1954) *Psychoanalytic Interpretation in Rorschach Testing.* New York: Grune & Stratton.

Zubin, J., Eron, L. D., and Schumer, R. (1965) *An Experimental Approach to Projective Techniques.* New York: Wiley.

CHAPTER 5

Location and Developmental Quality: Symbols and Criteria

The first, and probably easiest, of the coding decisions concerns the location of the response; that is, to which part of the blot did the response occur? The open-endedness of the test permits either of two approaches in formulating answers. The subject may decide to use the entire blot or may select only a portion of it. When the former occurs, it is a *whole* response and the coding is simple and straightforward, using the symbol *W*. In the latter case it is a *detail* response, and the symbol used in coding the location will depend on whether the area selected is one that is commonly used. If so, the symbol *D* will be employed to note this. Conversely, if the area selected is not among those used frequently by subjects, the symbol *Dd* is employed. As noted in the preceding chapter, whenever the subject includes use of the white space (ground), the symbol *S* is added to the location code.

The symbols and criteria used in the Comprehensive System for coding location are essentially those described in the Beck methodology, which follows from Rorschach's suggestion. The discrimination between *D* and *Dd* has been based on empirical findings, thus avoiding some of the arbitrary or overinclusive features that exist in some of the other approaches to coding location.

In some instances the information necessary for deciding on the location code will be given in the response, such as, "Well the whole thing looks like . . . ," or "If I use only this upper part it could be . . ." When this occurs, only a brief verification concerning location area is required in the Inquiry. In many responses, however, the subject does not specify the area of the blot being used during the response, and this matter becomes an important target during the Inquiry. Ordinarily, it is easily derived, especially when the subject has been prepared properly for the Inquiry, which will include mention of this objective. Nonetheless, some subjects remain vague about location and when that occurs, the examiner must persist by using instructions such as, "Run your finger around it carefully," or "Point to some of the features so that I can see it, too."

The four symbols used in coding location and the criterion for each are shown in Table 7.

THE *W* RESPONSE (WHOLES)

The criterion for coding or scoring *W* constitutes an either-or issue. Either the subject uses the entire blot, or less than the entire blot. Only the former is coded *W*. It is quite important that the examiner verify that the entire blot has been used in a response. Occasionally, a subject will report a response that is like those commonly given to the whole, but in fact, the subject has not used the entire blot in forming the answer. For example, the response,

Table 7.   Symbols Used for Coding the Location of Rorschach Responses

Symbol	Definition	Criterion
W	Whole response	Where the entire blot is used in the response. All portions must be used.
D	Common detail response	A frequently identified area of the blot
Dd	Unusual detail response	An infrequently identified area of the blot
S	Space response	A white space area is used in the response (scored only with another location symbol, as in *WS*, *DS*, or *DdS*)

"bat," is the most frequently given answer to both Cards I and V. About 97% of subjects who give either of those responses use the entire blot, but a small minority exclude some portions of the blot in order to be more precise about the answer. Those kinds of responses are *not* coded as *W* even though only a few small segments are omitted.[1]

Under the routine conditions of administration there should be no reason for misidentification of whole answers. In two interscorer reliability studies, one involving 20 scorers and 25 records and the second involving 15 scorers across 20 records, the percentage of agreement for coding *W* is 99% in both, with the disagreements resulting from scorer error.

THE *D* RESPONSE (COMMON DETAILS)

The criterion for coding *D* follows the suggestion of Rorschach. He referred to these as "Normal" details of the plates. He suggested that the differentiation of these areas from other areas of the blots should be based on the frequency with which subjects respond to them. During the early development of the Rorschach, several efforts were made to codify the obvious detail areas with numerical designations to provide easy identification of the areas. These efforts were not always based on the same format for decision making, nor did those involved always agree on Rorschach's intent. The result was several schemes for identifying the different blot areas. When the nucleus of the Comprehensive System was formulated in 1972, it was decided to use the Beck method of coding detail areas. That decision was based on three considerations. First, Hertz (1970) had compared her format for designating details with that used by Beck, Piotrowski, and Klopfer. She noted that she and Beck agreed on 90 of 97 areas, which she had designated as being appropriate for scoring *D*. Second, the Beck scheme includes the designation of 25 other areas that Hertz does not consider. Third, in two surveys of Rorschach practitioners (Exner, 1974; Exner & Exner, 1972) it was noted that considerably more were already familiar with the Beck format.

[1]Two of the systematizers, Klopfer and Hertz, added a second type of *W* response, that of the cut-off whole, using the symbol *W* for coding. The rationale was that Rorschach sometimes coded a *W* for Card III even though the outside red areas were omitted in the response. Klopfer later defined the cutoff whole as any response using at least two-thirds of the blot. Investigation of this code revealed low interscorer reliability, and no empirical basis for interpreting it differently than *Dd* responses. Thus it was excluded from those variables integrated into the Comprehensive System.

In preparation for the 2nd edition of this volume, two random samples, each consisting of 1500 records drawn from a much larger protocol pool, were used to review the frequency of responses by subjects to each of the 103 blot areas designated as *D* by the Beck format. One sample included 750 nonpatient adults and children and 750 nonschizophrenic adult and children outpatients. The second sample consisted of 750 psychiatric inpatients, including 150 schizophrenics, and 750 nonpatient adults and children. The distribution of the responses by the various groups, including schizophrenics, is not significantly different from those given by any of the other groups. Because the purpose of the review was to provide some cross-validation for the Beck format of distinguishing common (*D*) from uncommon (*Dd*) detail areas, a cutoff criterion of 5% was established. Therefore an area would continue to be designated as *D* if at least 5% of the *subjects* gave at least one response to the area. The results of this review indicate that 29 of the 103 areas designated by Beck as *D* fall short of the 5% criterion. This is not too surprising, because Beck apparently tended to number *D* areas in terms of the frequencies that he observed in his relatively small samples. In other words, he assigned the designation *D*1 to the area most frequently used, *D*2 to the next most frequently used, and so on. Most of the *D* areas specified by Beck that do not meet criterion involve higher numbers, such as *D*7, *D*8, and so on.

In addition to the discovery that 29 areas previously specified as *D* should be reclassified as *Dd,* it was also found that there are five areas, one each on Cards IV, VI, VII, VIII, and IX, that had not been numbered by Beck to which more than 5% of subjects respond. These have been added to the listing of *D* areas. Thus the current format for the Comprehensive System includes 79 blot areas that are designated as *D* areas. Obviously, some are used much more frequently than others; that is, they have a higher valence as discrete or semidiscrete stimuli in the field, or they may be areas that are more easily misidentified as possible responses because of their similarity to known or imagined objects. For instance, about 95% of all subjects taking the test include the selection of the card VIII, *D*1 area as a separate object, usually an animal. It is both discrete and has contours that are very similar to an animal. The *D*1 and *D*2 areas on Card VII, and the *D*1 areas on Cards II and III are also used in forming answers by a very high percentage of subjects taking the test.

Many *D* areas encompass large segments of the blot, but this is not always the case. Several involve only small portions of the total blot. The numbering of the *D* areas is shown for each of the 10 cards in figures included in Table A in Chapter 11 of this work.

THE *Dd* RESPONSE (UNUSUAL DETAILS)

The *Dd* coding is afforded responses that are given to areas of the blots which are used infrequently. A criterion of less than 5% of use by *subjects* has been established to define *Dd* areas. It could be argued that a cutoff of 5% is too low. Although that is possible, it is important to note that most *D* areas are selected by 20% or less of the subjects taking the test. It is true there is a rather sharp demarcation differentiating a few *D* locations that are selected by a high percentage of subjects (40% or more), from a second grouping that are selected for use by between 15% and 20% of the subjects. In fact, this second grouping is also significantly different for selection frequency from a third grouping of *D* areas that is selected by between 5% and 10% of the subjects. This finding could be used as a basis to favor a differentiation of two or three types of common details. But there is no empirical support for such a differentiation. Klopfer attempted this, but research conducted in relation to the formation of the Comprehensive System indicates that such a differentiation has no empirically based interpretive usefulness. It is conceivable that, at some future time, a subclassification of the *D* areas might be found to relate to different forms of information processing, but that is very speculative at this time.

None of the areas identified as *Dd* approach the 5% selection frequency criterion. A few are selected by as many as 3% of subjects, but most have selection frequencies of 1 or 2%, and many are selected by less than 1% of the subjects taking the test. These are areas that attract little attention for the overwhelming majority of subjects taking the test, or if they do attract attention, the potential responses generated from them are apparently discarded with a very high frequency. Beck (1937, 1944) found it useful to provide numerical designations for some *Dd* areas. His listing has been expanded in the Comprehensive System by adding to it those areas that he had specified as *D*, but which do not meet the 5% criterion, plus some other areas that have been studied in the research at the Rorschach Research Foundation.

The majority of *Dd* areas involve small segments of the blots, but size is not necessarily a determining factor. In many instances, a subject may deliberately eliminate some small areas of the whole blot, or of a common detail area in an effort to be more precise. This creates a *Dd* area. The majority of *Dd* selections used by subjects are *not* included among those afforded numerical designations in Table A. Indeed, they are so rare that they have not been recorded systematically. Obviously, any response that is not a *W* or a *D* is coded as *Dd*.

THE *S* RESPONSE (WHITE SPACE DETAILS)

The symbol *S* is included in the Location coding whenever a white space area of the card is included in the response. The use of white space can occur in either of two ways. The subject may integrate the white space with other blot areas, or may elect to deliver a response that involves only a white space area. Regardless of which form of space use occurs, the *S* is never scored alone as a location code. Instead it is always used in conjunction with one of the three primary location codes, as in *WS, DS,* or *DdS.* The rationale for using *S* only with another location code is to maintain consistency in evaluating the three primary types of location selections. Some space answers, particularly on Cards I, II, and VII occur with a much greater frequency than space answers on other cards. If the *D* versus *Dd* criteria are applied, it is clear that some *S* responses are clearly *DS,* whereas most will be *DdS.*

LOCATION CODING FOR MULTIPLE *D* AREAS

Some responses will involve the use of two or more *D* areas. In some of these responses, the appropriate coding will be *D,* whereas in other instances the coding of *Dd* is correct. Some *D* areas are, in fact, a combination of other *D* areas. For example, the *D*1 area on Card III is actually the composite of the two *D*9 areas plus *D*7. Similarly, the composite of *D*1 and *D*3 on Card IX equals the *D*12 area. Naturally, a response to any area listed as *D* will be coded as *D*. However, there are instances when subjects will combine *D* areas to form a new area that is not commonplace. *If* that combination involves only one object, the answer will be coded *Dd*. Conversely, if the subject is using each of the combined *D* areas to identify a separate object, the appropriate location code will still be *D* even though more than one common detail area is involved. These are synthesized responses and will be noted as such by the coding for Developmental Quality.

For example, on Card III a subject might report a person (*D*9) working on some pottery (*D*7). In this answer the integrity of each *D* area is maintained by reporting separate objects, one being used for the person and one for the pottery. On the other hand, the same two areas might be integrated more uniquely if the response were a person (*D*9) with a grotesque hand (*D*7). Here, the subject is reporting the composite of the two areas as a single area, a very uncommon event, and requiring the coding of *Dd*.

Once a coder has become familiar with the *D* areas, as identified in Table A, misidentifications of *D*, *Dd*, and *S* should not occur unless the coder is negligent. In the two interscorer reliability studies mentioned previously, the percent agreement for *D* is 99%, for *Dd* is 99%, and for *S* is 98%. When disagreement occurred, it was the result of coder neglect.

CODING FOR THE DEVELOPMENTAL QUALITY OF THE RESPONSE

The full interpretive value of the data concerning location selection is increased substantially by the addition of a second code to differentiate the *quality* of the area specification. All whole responses are not selected or organized in the same manner. Neither are the specifications involved in the selection of common or unusual details, or the use of space in forming a response. Rorschach recognized these differences and discussed them as "Apperceptive" approaches (*Erfassungstypen*), suggesting that some subjects manifest a "keen imagination" in forming responses, whereas others approach the blot in a more simplistic or even concrete manner. All of those involved in the development of the test after Rorschach's death have described these differences in cognitive processing, using such words as unorganized, simple, organized, combinatory, and superior.

For example, the unorganized response is one in which the subject uses the blot in a manner that does not require specifications of features. Responses such as clouds, blood, paint, dirt, an island, and so on are examples of this concrete and somewhat nonchalant use of the stimulus field. It has been identified in a manner that circumvents the necessity to organize specific stimulus features in meaningful relationships. A cloud, an island, a skin, and so on can take any of a broad variety of external shapes and, similarly, there are no specific form demands concerning the internal characteristics of the object.

At a higher, but still somewhat simplistic and economical level, the blot is defined as a single object that requires greater specificity, such as, a bat, a person, a maple tree, the skin of a leopard, the island of Barbados, and so on. In these types of answers the cognitive activity includes the necessity of organizing some of the stimulus features in a meaningful way. Combinatory or superior responses require a much higher level of cognitive action, such as "two people picking up a large boulder," or "a woman running after a child up a small hill," or "a submarine gliding through the water with its shadow being cast in the moonlight." The location codes do not provide information concerning the quality of the specification involved in the response. Consequently, a second code is necessary to identify this characteristic.

Meili-Dworetzki (1939, 1956) was among the first to recognize the potential in the Rorschach for differentiating levels of mental complexity and flexibility. She studied levels of location selection in children of various ages, designing her investigations based on the assumptions of Rorschach (1921), Piaget (1924), and Beck (1933). She found a general "enrichment" in location selection and integration with increasing age levels, and suggested the possibility of studying cognitive development through a differentiation of various types of location responses. Rapaport et al. (1946) obviously perceived the same potential and suggested an experimental approach to differentiate types of *W* responses. Friedman (1952, 1953) developed the most elaborate method for differentiating location specification. His work is based on Werner's (1948, 1957) theory of cognitive development. It is similar to, but much more inclusive than the Rapaport approach, being applicable to both whole and detail responses. The Friedman approach employs six categories for evaluating location specification, three of which are considered "developmentally high" codes or scores, and three reflecting "developmentally low" scores. The research on the Friedman method has been considerable and appears to establish that the technique can be useful for the study of developmental levels of cognitive functioning.[2]

Early attempts to integrate the Friedman approach for coding developmental quality into the Comprehensive System encountered three problems. First, two of the categories tend to overlap for criteria, creating considerable difficulty in establishing adequate levels of interscorer reliability. Second, two other categories are based on a questionable assumption that five of the blots are markedly different than the remaining five in terms of stimulus unity. Third, and possibly most important, one of the developmentally low categories is directly correlated with the inaccurate use of the blot contours—that is, the form quality of the response. The developmental quality codes relate the levels of cognitive functioning, whereas the coding for form quality relates to perceptual accuracy or conventionality. Although there is probably some relationship between the two, it is far less than is implied by the direct correlation used in the Friedman method.

When the Comprehensive System was first published (Exner, 1974), no solution to the overlap problem between developmental quality and form quality was readily apparent; however, the other two issues were resolved by reducing the number of categories from six to four. The four categories were represented by the symbols + (synthesis), *o* (ordinary), *v* (vague), and − (arbitrary). The arbitrary code (−) is the one that correlated directly with form quality, and considerable research ensued during the next several years to resolve the interpretive problem created by that spurious relationship. The issue was ultimately resolved by reviewing findings concerning levels of cognitive activity that had been differentiated in a series of problem-solving studies, plus data that had been collected using the Halstead-Reitan neuropsychological test battery. Each data set was divided into quartiles and the first and fourth quartiles compared with special attention to responses that had been coded either *v* or − for developmental quality, but which also included some synthesis activity. Those types of answers were assigned either of two experimental developmental quality scores, *v*/+ or −/+ (Exner, 1983). As hypothesized, subjects with a higher frequency of synthesized responses (+, *v*/+, and −/+) fall significantly more often in the upper quartile; that is, they demonstrate higher levels of performance in analysis-synthesis operations in problem solving, concept formation, and have better performances on the conceptual tests in the Halstead-Reitan battery. Conversely, subjects with few synthesis responses and a higher than average frequency

---

[2]Although the Friedman method does distinguish differences in children, as identified by chronological and mental age, it probably deals more specifically with general cognitive operations. Thus the concept of development, as used traditionally in psychology in the study of children, is not directly applicable.

of − and v responses in their Rorschachs, fall in the lowest quartile of the distribution based on these kinds of performance.

The second step in this analysis was to determine if the presence of the arbitrary code, −, contributed significantly to the differentiation of subjects in the first and fourth quartiles of the distribution. The results are essentially negative; that is, the arbitrary DQ codings do occur only slightly, but not significantly more often among subjects in the lowest quartile.

These data led to the elimination of the arbitrary code for developmental quality, and the addition of another code to signify synthesis activity occurring in responses that previously would have been coded as v (vague). The new code is v/+. It is designed to identify answers in which some synthesizing activity has occurred, but the objects reported have no form demand. Thus four developmental quality codes remain in the Comprehensive System. The criterion for each is presented in Table 8. In the two previously cited studies concerning interscorer reliability, the percent agreement for the + code is 95%, for the v/+ is 94%, for the o is 96%, and for the v is 95%. As with the coding for location selection, interscorer disagreements occurring in the two studies cited resulted from scorer neglect.

Some elaboration concerning the criteria for the DQ coding is in order, because there are some key words in each. For each of the two types of synthesis (+ and v/+) responses the criterion statement includes, ". . . separate but related." More than one object must be involved *and* it must be reported in a meaningful relationship to the other objects in the response. For example, "two birds sitting on a fence" would be coded + because there are three objects in the response and all are interrelated. The two birds are sitting on the fence. If the response had been, "two birds," alluding to the symmetry of the blot, the DQ code would be o (ordinary) because there is no meaningful relationship between them. No integration has occurred. If the separate objects involve clothing on a figure, the clothing *must* be identified in a way that alters the natural contour of the figure, or be a discrete blot area itself.

Table 8. Symbols and Criteria Used for Coding Developmental Quality

Symbol	Definition	Criterion
+	Synthesized response	Unitary or discrete portions of the blot are articulated and combined into a single answer. Two or more objects are described as separate but related. At least *one* of the objects involved must have a specific form demand, or be described in a manner that creates a specific form demand.
v/+	Synthesized response	Unitary or discrete portions of the blot are articulated and combined into a single answer. Two or more objects are described as separate but related. None of the objects involved have a specific form demand, or are articulated in a way to create a specific form demand.
o	Ordinary response	A discrete area of the blot is selected and articulated so as to emphasize the outline and structural features of the object. The object reported has a natural form demand or the description of the object is such to create a specific form demand.
v	Vague response	A diffuse or general impression is offered to the blot or blot area in a manner that avoids the necessity of articulating specific outlines or structural features. The object reported has no specific form demand, and the articulation does not introduce a specific form demand for the object reported.

For example, subjects often report one or two human figures on Card III. Occasionally the figure is described as wearing a tuxedo, which is defined because the figure is dark in coloring. This is *not* coded + because the same blot area is being used for both the figure and the clothing. Conversely, if the figure (D9) were described as wearing big mittens (Dd16), a + would be appropriate because discrete blot areas have been used.

Some other very important key words in the criteria are, "specific form demand." This means that the object being reported generally has a consistent form; that is, when the noun identifying the object is used, some specific shapes are implied. For example, the words *man, bird, butterfly, spider, lion, ship, house,* and so on each identify a class of objects that has some specific form characteristics even though some variations may exist within each class. Men may be short or tall, thin or fat, and so on, but men cannot take an infinite number of shapes. On the other hand, words such as *cloud, lake, island, foliage, blood, paint, desert,* and so on represent classes of objects that can take any of a wide variety of shapes. There is no specific form demand. Thus if the object reported

Table 9.   Examples of Coding the Location Component

Card	Response	Location Coding
I	Two witches dancing around a woman (W)	W+
	A piece of coral (D1)	Dv
	Two ghosts (DdS30) climbing up a hill (Dd24)	DdS+
II	Two dogs rubbing noses (D6)	D+
	Some sort of colorful map (W)	Wv
	Icicles (Dd25)	Ddo
III	Some pieces of a puzzle (W)	Wv
	A person seeing his reflection in a mirror (D1)	D+
	A catfish (D2)	Do
IV	A man sitting on a tree stump (W)	W+
	Some storm clouds coming together (W)	Wv/+
	A couple of boots, one on each side (D6)	Do
V	A bat (W)	Wo
	An x-ray of some insides (W)	Wv
	A map of the United States (W)	Wo
VI	A piece of torn fur (D1)	Dv
	A bearskin rug (D1)	Do
	Some shrubs or something on a hill (D3)	Dv/+
VII	A necklace (W)	Wo
	An island in the ocean (WS)	WSv/+
	A bird (Dd25) gliding toward his nest (D6)	Dd+
VIII	A brightly lit chandelier (W)	Wo
	Some insides of a dissected animal (W)	Wv
	Some torn cloth hanging on a stick (D5)	Dv/+
IX	A big explosion (W)	Wv
	An atomic explosion with the mushroom cloud (W)	Wo
	A dried-up bloodstain (Dd28)	Ddv
X	A lot of underwater creatures swimming around these rocks, like fish and eels (W)	W+
	A whole lot of things like you see in the water, like fishes (D2) and crabs (D1) and other things (W)	Wo
	A Buddha (DdS29) with a jewel for a navel (D3)	DdS+

does have a form demand, the *DQ* coding must be *o* (ordinary) or + (synthesis) if it is meaningfully combined in relation to another object, *regardless of whether the other object has form demand.* If the object reported has no specific form demand, the *DQ* coding will be *v* (vague), or *v/+* (synthesis) if it is meaningfully combined with another object *that also has no form demand.*

It is important to note that, at times, a subject will report an object that has no specific form demand, but in elaborating on the object may inject a form demand. For example, the response, "cloud" will usually be coded *v*; however, a subject might elaborate, "like the kind that build up in a funnel shape, like those dangerous storm clouds." This elaboration has injected a form demand, requiring the coding of *o* rather than *v*. Similarly, the response, "a lake" that is not elaborated for specification will be coded *v,* but Lake Michigan, which does have a specific shape, would be coded *o.*

Examples The location component of each response will always include two symbols—one for the area used and the second for the developmental quality. Some examples of the various types of codings are shown in Table 9.

Accuracy in coding location is essential. Although the criteria are reasonably straightforward, the process may seem to be more simplistic than is actually the case, and caution is always in order. The overall impact of the location coding to the interpretation of the protocol can be considerable. Several interpretive hypotheses concerning cognitive functioning, perceptual scanning, needs for achievement, awareness of convention, and proneness to economize are often based on the composite of these data. If they are accurate, so too will be the interpretive postulates, but if they are inaccurate, the interpretive yield can suffer significantly.

REFERENCES

Beck, S. J. (1933) Configurational tendencies in Rorschach responses. *American Journal of Psychology,* **45,** 432–443.

Beck, S. J. (1937) *Introduction to the Rorschach Method: A Manual of Personality Study.* American Orthopsychiatric Association, Monograph No. 1.

Beck, S. J. (1944) *Rorschach's Test. I: Basic Processes.* New York: Grune & Stratton.

Exner, J. E. (1974) *The Rorschach: A Comprehensive System. Volume 1.* New York: Wiley.

Exner, J. E. (1983) *1983 Alumni Newsletter.* Bayville, N.Y: Rorschach Workshops.

Exner, J. E., and Exner, D. E. (1972) How clinicians use the Rorschach. *Journal of Personality Assessment,* **36,** 403–408.

Friedman, H. (1952) Perceptual regression in schizophrenia: A hypothesis suggested by the use of the Rorschach test. *Journal of Genetic Psychology,* **81,** 63–98.

Friedman, H. (1953) Perceptual regression in schizophrenia: An hypothesis suggested by the use of the Rorschach test. *Journal of Projective Techniques,* **17,** 171–185.

Hertz, M. R. (1970) *Frequency Tables for Scoring Rorschach Responses.* (5th Ed.) Cleveland: Case Western Reserve Press.

Meili-Dworetzki, G. (1939) Le test Rorschach et l'evolution de la perception. *Archives de Psychologie,* **27,** 111–127.

Meili-Dworetzki, G. (1956) The development of perception in the Rorschach. In B. Klopfer et al. *Developments in the Rorschach Technique. II: Fields of Application.* Yonkers-on-Hudson, N.Y: World Book.

Piaget, J. (1924) *Le Judgement et le Raisonnement chez l'Enfant.* Neuchatel: Delachaux & Niestle.

Rapaport, D., Gill, M., and Schafer, R. (1946) *Diagnostic Psychological Testing. Volume 2.* Chicago: Yearbook Publishers.

Rorschach, H. (1921) *Psychodiagnostik.* Bern: Bircher.

Werner, H. (1948) *Comparative Psychology of Mental Development.* (Rev. Ed.) Chicago: Follett.

Werner, H. (1957) The concept of development from a comparative and organismic point of view. In D. B. Harris (Ed.) *The Concept of Development.* Minneapolis: University of Minnesota Press.

CHAPTER 6

Determinants:
Symbols and Criteria

The most important, and possibly the most complex, of the coding decisions concerns the response determinant(s), that is, the blot features that have contributed to the formation of the percept. The object of determinant coding is to provide information concerning the complex perceptual-cognitive process that has produced the response. There are many stimulus characteristics in the blots, each of which generally falls into one of three descriptive classifications: (1) those involving form, (2) those involving color, and (3) those involving the grey-black or shading features. Determinant coding would be a relatively easy task if all responses could be discretely identified as falling into one of these three categories, but that is not ordinarily the case. In many instances, more than one of the three categories is involved as in, "a yellow rose with a long stem," or "a man in the dark shadows." The first involves both form and color, whereas the second involves both form and shading. In other instances, a single coding classification of stimulus characteristics fails to differentiate the ways in which the stimulus is used. For example, form features can be used to create the impression of movement as in "a person bowing," or "a bat flying." Sometimes the symmetry of the blot is used as a reflection as in, "a woman seeing herself in a mirror." In still other instances, the form may be used simply for purposes of identification as in, "It looks like a bat because of the shape of the wings and the body."

The numerous ways in which the stimulus characteristics of the blots can be used to create responses have continually posed a challenge to those seeking to offer a systematic coding for the test. Recommendations for determinant codes have varied considerably from system to system and have often been focal points of Rorschach controversy. Rorschach had originally suggested five symbols for the scoring of determinants, one for form (*F*), one for human movement (*M*), and three for color (*FC, CF,* and *C*), two of which were selected to indicate the relative importance of form in the color answer (1921). It was a relatively simple system that discounted the importance of separate codings for responses marked by animal or inanimate movement, perceived dimensionality, reflections, or the use of the achromatic coloring as color. It obviously contained no codes for shading type responses because the blots with which Rorschach did most of his work *did not* contain shading. He did begin working with shaded blots shortly before his death, and introduced a sixth scoring symbol (*C*) in his last, posthumously published, paper (1923), to be used for "chiaroscuro" responses. The six symbols provided the base from which others continued to study and refine the test. Unfortunately, each Rorschach systematizer preferred to use symbols and criteria that, more often than not, are different than those selected by another systematizer, and in some instances even different than those that Rorschach had suggested. The end product was an astonishing lack of agreement. Even where the same symbol appears in two or more systems, the criterion for the use of that symbol probably differs. In fact, there is no single symbol the criterion for which was agreed upon by all five American Rorschach systems, and there are only a few determinant symbols the criteria for which were agreed upon even by two of the systems (Exner, 1969). For example, 16 different symbols representing 12 different types of color response were suggested. An even greater number of symbols had been recommended for the shading responses.

The selection of the symbols and criteria for determinants in the Comprehensive System would be relatively uncomplicated if any one system could be demonstrated as clearly superior to the others, but that is not the case. Some are overly elaborate, including components without the logic of a sound empiric base or providing "subscorings" that tend to misrepresent summary data. Others have omitted important components, or have altered component criteria in such a way as to be inconsistent with symbol definitions. Consequently, the symbols and criteria selected for the Comprehensive System constitute a composite of several systems plus those developed from research findings that have evolved since 1970. Each of the possibilities from each system has been considered and evaluated against research findings. This process has yielded 24 symbols, representing nine determinant categories. These nine categories are: (1) Form, (2) Movement, (3) Color (chromatic), (4) Color (achromatic), (5) Texture (shading), (6) Dimensionality (shading), (7) General Shading, (8) Dimensionality (form), and (9) Pairs and Reflections. The symbols used in each of these categories, plus the criterion for the symbol, are presented in Table 10.

Table 10.   Symbols and Criteria for Determinant Coding

Category	Symbol	Criteria
Form	F	*Form answers.* To be used separately for responses based exclusively on form features of the blot, or in combination with other determinant symbols (*except M & m*) when the form features have contributed to the formulation of the answer.
Movement	M	*Human movement response.* To be used for responses involving the kinesthetic activity of a human, or of an animal or fictional character in human-like activity.
	FM	*Animal movement response.* To be used for responses involving a kinesthetic activity of an animal. The movement perceived must be congruent to the species identified in the content. Animals reported in movement *not* common to their species should be coded as *M*.
	m	*Inanimate movement response.* To be used for responses involving the movement of inanimate, inorganic, or insensate objects.
Chromatic Color	C	*Pure color response.* To be used for answers based exclusively on the chromatic color features of the blot. *No* form is involved.
	CF	*Color-form response.* To be used for answers that are formulated *primarily* because of the chromatic color features of the blot. Form features *are* used, but are of secondary importance.
	FC	*Form-color response.* To be used for answers that are created mainly because of form features. Chromatic color is also used, but is of secondary importance.
	Cn	*Color naming response.* To be used when the colors of the blot or blot areas are identified *by name,* and with the intention of giving a response.
Achromatic Color	C'	*Pure achromatic color response.* To be used when the response is based exclusively on the gray, black, or white features of the blot, when they are clearly used as color. *No* form is involved.

Table 10 (Continued)

Category	Symbol	Criteria
	$C'F$	*Achromatic color-form response.* To be used for responses that are formulated *mainly* because of the black, white, or gray features, clearly used as color. Form features *are* used, but are of secondary importance.
	FC'	*Form-achromatic color response.* To be used for answers that are based *mainly* on the form features. The achromatic features, clearly used as color, are also included, but are of secondary importance.
Shading-Texture	T	*Pure texture response.* To be used for answers in which the shading components of the blot are translated to represent a tactual phenomenon, with no consideration to the form features.
	TF	*Texture-form response.* To be used for responses in which the shading features of the blot are interpreted as tactual, and form is used secondarily, for purposes of elaboration and/or clarification.
	FT	*Form-texture response.* To be used for responses that are based *mainly* on the form features. Shading features of the blot are translated as tactual, but are of secondary importance.
Shading-Dimension	V	*Pure vista response.* To be used for answers in which the shading features are interpreted as depth or dimensionality. *No* form is involved.
	VF	*Vista-form response.* To be used for responses in which the shading features are interpreted as depth or dimensionality. Form features are included, but are of secondary importance.
	FV	*Form-vista response.* To be used for answers that are based *mainly* on the form features of the blot. Shading features are also interpreted to note depth and/or dimensionality, but are of secondary importance to the formulation of the answer.
Shading-Diffuse	Y	*Pure shading response.* To be used for responses that are based exclusively on the light-dark features of the blot that are completely formless and do not involve reference to either texture or dimension.
	YF	*Shading-form response.* To be used for responses based primarily on the light-dark features of the blot. Form features are included, but are of secondary importance.
	FY	*Form-shading response.* To be used for responses that are based *mainly* on the form features of the blot. The light-dark features of the blot are included as elaboration and/or clarification and are secondary to the use of form.
Form Dimension	FD	*Form based dimensional response.* To be used for answers in which the impression of depth, distance, or dimensionality is created by using the elements of size and/or shape of contours. *No* use of shading is involved in creating this impression.
Pairs & Reflections	(2)	*The pair response.* To be used for answers in which two identical objects are reported, based on the symmetry of the blot. The objects must be equivalent in all respects, but must *not* be identified as being reflected or as mirror images.
	rF	*Reflection-form response.* To be used for answers in which the blot or blot area is reported as a reflection or mirror image, because of the symmetry of the blot. The object or content reported has no specific form requirement, as in clouds, landscape, shadows, etc.
	Fr	*Form-reflection response.* To be used for answers in which the blot or blot area is identified as reflected or a mirror image, based on the symmetry of the blot. The substance of the response is based on form features, and the object reported has a specific form demand.

It will be obvious to the experienced Rorschacher that, in addition to including the five original Rorschach symbols (*F, M, FC, CF, C*) and his criteria for them, many of the symbols are drawn from the Beck and Klopfer systems. The familiarity of the symbol, however, does not necessarily mean that the criterion is identical. This is not the case in some instances, particularly where a symbol has been used in two or more systems with different criteria. This matter is clarified as each of the symbols, its criterion, and reason for selection is discussed more extensively.

THE FORM DETERMINANT (*F*)

The selection of the symbol *F* for the Form answers should require little explanation. It was used by Rorschach to denote answers based on form and has been incorporated into all subsequent systems, using essentially the same criterion. The Form answer has been the focus of some intersystematizer disagreements, but the issues have not concerned the basic criterion. Rather, these disagreements have centered on methods of evaluating form quality (which are discussed in the next chapter), or have related to other determinant criteria, the inclusion or exclusion of which determines what is a "Pure" Form answer. *F* is coded for any response that includes Form as one of the determinant features, and is coded separately when no other determinant is involved.

Generally, the inclusion of Form as a response determinant is easily identified. Subjects frequently use the words *form* or *shaped*, or, in most cases, describe the details of the object perceived so as to emphasize the form features. For instance, in elaborating on the response of "a bat" to Card I, the subject may add, "These outer parts look like wings and the center looks like the body part." Even without further elaboration it seems clear that the Form features of the blot have been used. Responses based exclusively on the Form features usually comprise the largest single determinant category in a record, and ordinarily Form features will be included in more than 95% of all responses given.

THE MOVEMENT DETERMINANTS

Three kinds of movement responses may occur in the Rorschach: (1) those involving humans or human-like behaviors, (2) those involving animals, and (3) those involving inanimate or inorganic objects or forces. Rorschach scored for only one type of movement, that involving humans or human behaviors. He specifically discounted animal movement as having the same meaning as human movement and thus provided no scoring for it. Beck (1937, 1944, 1961) vigorously defended Rorschach's position and also excluded any formal scoring for animal or inanimate movement in his method. Klopfer (1936, 1942, 1954), Hertz (1942, 1951, 1970), and Piotrowski (1937, 1947, 1957) have each taken the opposite position and include scorings for animal and inanimate movement, using the same scoring symbols but with differing criteria for the scoring of inanimate movement.

An examination of each of these positions seems to indicate that both are at least partially correct. There is very little empirical evidence to suggest that the three types of movement all represent different levels of the same psychological process as has been implied by Klopfer and Piotrowski. Quite the contrary, work that has been reported encourages the notion that the three types of responses represent relatively different psychological operations. In that context, Rorschach and Beck have been correct in discouraging separate scorings for animal and inanimate movement so as not to confuse the interpretation of human movement responses. On the other hand, animal and inanimate responses do occur, the former with considerable frequency. Research findings indicate that, just as they are different from human movement responses, they are different from answers based only on form.

Human Movement (*M*)   The symbol *M*, and its criterion, is derived from Rorschach's original work. Each of the systems developed after Rorschach includes this symbol for human movement answers and three of those (Beck, Klopfer, & Hertz) use Rorschach's criterion. The Piotrowski (1947, 1957) and Rapaport-Schafer (1946) systems both include modifications of Rorschach's criterion. Piotrowski restricts the scoring of *M* to responses occurring to an area sufficiently ambiguous as to make any type of movement or posture equally plausible. It is a caution designed to avoid scoring *M* falsely, as in responses where movement is injected to explain form features. Rapaport restricts the scoring of *M* to responses that include complete, or nearly complete, human figures. Neither of the arguments for these criterion restrictions follows from an empirical base, nor is the logic strongly persuasive. The Piotrowski position appears to depend excessively on subjective judgments concerning the intent of the subject in his or her use of movement. The Rapaport restriction appears to eliminate the scoring of *M* in some instances where *M* does occur. It is quite true that movement perceived in whole human figures is interpreted differently from movement perceived in partial human figures, but in each, the movement has been perceived and should be scored.

The *M* is scored for human activity. The movement may be active such as in running, jumping, fighting, and arguing, or it may be passive, such as in sleeping, thinking, smiling, and looking. In either instance *M* is scored.

The symbol *F* is *not used* when *M* is scored. Ordinarily, the *M* assumes form, although there are rare instances in which no form exists in an *M* response, such as when the only content is a human experience such as "Depression," or "Happiness." The existence of *M* should not be assumed simply because human figures are perceived. The movement itself must be articulated for a response to be scored *M*. In *most cases*, the movement is reported when the response is delivered. In *fewer instances*, the movement is not reported in the response phase, but instead is reported *spontaneously* at the onset of the Inquiry to the response. For example, a subject might respond to Card III, "It looks like two people here." This response appears to be based on form only and would not be scored *M*. If, however, after the examiner begins the Inquiry to the response by simply restating *S*'s response and *S* offers, "Yes, they are right here, it looks like two people doing something," it seems logical to assume that movement had been perceived during the response phase but had not been articulated. Spontaneity must be the guideline and *M should never be scored* if there is reason to believe that the movement was provoked by the Inquiry questioning of the examiner. This rule holds true for all determinants.

Although most *M* responses involve human figures, *M* may also occur where the content is animal, but only when the movement described involves a human activity that is not common to the animal species. For example, "two beetles arguing" would be coded *M*, as would "two bears playing gin rummy." Conversely, "two beetles fighting over something," or "two bears playing together," *would not* be scored *M*, but instead would be coded using the symbol for animal movement, *FM*.

Animal Movement (*FM*)   This coding was originally suggested by Klopfer and Sender (1936). His justification for the use of *FM* was based primarily on Rorschach's 1923 article, in which Rorschach referred to a special consideration for responses that are essentially form based but which also tend toward the use of movement or color. Because some of Rorschach's examples included animals in movement, it was natural for Klopfer to include designation of animal movement in this category. By 1942, Klopfer had decided to use a different symbol to represent "tendencies toward" (→), and selected *FM* for use exclusively in animal movement responses. The criterion selected for use in the Comprehensive system is that of Klopfer. It is to be scored for any response involving animals in activity that is common to the species, such as "a dog barking," "a bat flying," and "a leopard stalking its prey." In extremely rare instances, an animal will be perceived in an animal activity that is not common to its species, such as "a snake flying along in the air." In these cases, *M* is entered as the determinant to reflect the human fantasy that has been involved in forming the answers.

Although most *FM* answers include a whole animal, some will involve only a partial animal figure such as "two animals scampering behind a bush, you can only see their legs," on Card V. Occasionally, the content of the animal movement response will be a mythological animal such as a dragon or a unicorn. The scoring in these unusual types of responses continues to be *FM*, and the uniqueness of the animal is accounted for in the Content scoring. The scoring of *FM*, like that of *M*, is contingent on the spontaneous reporting of movement by the subject.

Inanimate Movement (*m*)   The third type of movement response that may occur in the Rorschach involves inanimate, inorganic, or insensate objects. The symbol *m*, which has been selected to denote such responses, was first suggested by Piotrowski (1937) during a time when he was closely identified with Klopfer's efforts to develop the Rorschach. Klopfer and Hertz continued to use the symbol in their systems of the test, but with a substantially broader criterion than is used by Piotrowski, including in it phallic forces, facial expressions, and human abstracts.

It is essentially the Piotrowski criterion and method that have been selected for the coding of inanimate movement in the Comprehensive System. The criterion is reasonably precise and does not overlap with either the *M* or *FM* categories, as does the broader criterion of Klopfer and Hertz. Thus *m* is scored for any movement perceived that involves nonhuman and nonanimal objects. The most common types of inanimate movement responses include fireworks, explosions, blood dripping, water falling, and trees bending. Some other types of inanimate movement that occur with considerably less frequency include skins stretched tightly, a leaf floating, seaweed drifting, a bullet smashing, and such. The *m* is scored for any of these or similar responses. In very rare cases, inanimate objects are perceived in humanlike activity, such as "trees dancing a waltz." In this kind of response, the scoring should be *M*, rather than *m*.

In the studies concerning interscorer agreement, the 20 coders working with 25 protocols have a 96% agreement for *M*, 97% for *FM*, and 93% for *m*. In the group of 15 coders and 20 records, the percent agreement for *M* is 96%, for *FM* is 98%, and for *m* is 95%. Most of the disagreements concerning *M* and *FM* were caused by coder error; however, some legitimate disagreements occurred about coding *M* or *FM* for science fiction creatures in human-like behavior. Most of the disagreements concerning *m* involved answers in which an object was reported in a form of passive or static movement, such as a coat hanging on a post, which should be coded *m* because of the unnatural tension state, or a rug lying on the floor, which should not be coded as *m* because no unnatural tension state exists.

ACTIVE-PASSIVE SUPERSCRIPTS

A second important coding that must be added to *all* movement answers is a superscript that notes whether the movement is active or passive ([a] for active, [p] for passive). Rorschach suggested the importance of evaluating movement answers in terms of "Flexion" (moving toward the center of the blot) or "Extension" (moving away from the center of the blot). Beck et al. (1961) called attention to a third movement stance, *static.* Piotrowski (1957, 1960) has studied various kinds of movement answers extensively and suggested differentiations such as active-passive, cooperative-noncooperative, and aggressive-friendly. Research findings generated from several studies designed to test some of Piotrowski's hypotheses indicate that the active-passive dimension provides the most consistently valid interpretive yield.

One of the more frustrating issues associated with the development of the Comprehensive System has involved attempts to establish precise criteria for the application of the [a] and [p] superscripts. That objective has not been achieved. Nevertheless, most people do seem able to agree on the meaning of the terms *active* and *passive* when applied to movement answers. Reliability studies, in which trained coders are instructed to differentiate large numbers of movement answers as either active or passive, have a surprisingly positive yield. For example, 10 postdoctoral fellows show a 93% agreement for 150 movement answers, whereas 10 briefly trained high school students show a 94% agreement for the same 150 answers (Exner, 1978). In another study, 20 nonpatient adults (none trained in psychology) and 20 second-year psychology graduate students, completing a course in assessment that included training in Rorschach, were asked to code 300 words, most of them verbs, as either active or passive. The lay group was provided with a few examples to create a conceptual framework, such as "leaping," "brawling," and "zooming" to illustrate active movement and "gliding," "thinking," and "languishing" to illustrate passive movement. The students were asked to code in the context of their Rorschach training. The majority of subjects from both groups agreed on the coding for 275 of the 300 words. The students agreed unanimously on 213 of the 300 words, whereas the lay group agreed unanimously on only 112. More important, the overall percentage of agreement among the student group was 95%, and for the lay group it was 86%. In other words, even when coding occurs *without the context of the full response,* there is very high agreement among those with formal training, and very substantial agreement among those who have no training.

Table 11 shows the 300 words used in this study, and includes the coding for each agreed to by the majority of subjects, plus the actual number of subjects in each group that constitute that majority. It has been included here as a *general reference* for those learning to make the active-passive differentiation; *however, it should not be considered as a definitive guide for scoring decisions.* The final decision to code active or passive must be made in the context of the complete response. Empirical findings, derived from research concerning the interpretation of the relationship between active and passive movement suggest that "talking" should always be coded *passive.* Thus, "talking" serves as a benchmark against which questionable issues are judged. In that context, "whispering," "standing," "looking," and the like are easily defined as passive, whereas "yelling" and "arguing" are

Table 11.　Results of an Active-Passive Word Study for Two Groups for 300 Items, Showing the Majority Score for Each Item for Each Group Plus the Number of Subjects Represented by That Majority, with * Indicating Group Disagreements

Item	Lay Group N = 20 Score	N	Students N = 20 Score	N	Item	Lay Group N = 20 Score	N	Students N = 20 Score	N
Abandoned	p	19	p	18	Challenging	a	18	a	20
Accelerating	a	20	a	20	Charging	a	20	a	20
Accusing	a	20	a	19	Chasing	a	20	a	20
Acting	a	17	a	18	Chewing	a	18	a	20
Admonishing	a	19	a	20	Clapping	a	19	a	20
Aggravated (looks)	a	18	a	16	Climbing	a	20	a	20
Aggressive	a	20	a	20	Clinging (helplessly)	p	20	p	20
Agitated	a	18	a	19	Clutching	a	18	a	20
Ailing	p	16	p	19	Composed (looks)	p	16	p	18
Aimless (feeling)	p	20	p	20	Confused (looks)	p	17	p	20
Alarmed	a	18	a	20	Creeping (animal)	a	18	a	20
Amazed (looks)	p	14	p	15	Crouched (animal)	p	16	p	20
Amused (looks)	p	15	p	18	Crying	p	17	p	20
Anchored	p	20	p	20	Cuddled	p	18	p	20
Angry (looks)	a	20	a	20	Dancing	a	20	a	20
Anguished (looks)	p	16	p	14	Dealing (cards)	a	18	a	20
Animated	a	15	a	18	Deciding	a	14	a	17
Annoyed (looks)	p	14	p	16	Defensive (looks)	p	15	p	19
Anxious	a	17	a	15	Defeated (looks)	p	19	p	20
Apologizing	p	16	p	14	Demanding	a	20	a	20
Arguing	a	20	a	20	Demoralized	p	18	p	20
Ascending (smoke)	p	19	p	20	Depressed	p	20	p	20
Aware (looks)	p	14	p	13	Deprived (looks)	p	17	p	20
Bad (looks)	a	11 *	p	12	Deteriorating	p	20	p	20
Baffled	p	16	p	17	Determined (looks)	a	17	a	19
Baking	p	18	p	16	Determined (feels)	a	19	a	20
Balancing (a top)	a	17	a	20	Disappointed (feels)	p	18	p	20
Basking (in the sun)	p	19	p	20	Discussing	a	17	a	20
Bathing	a	14	a	16	Disturbed (upset)	a	14 *	p	13
Battering	a	20	a	20	Dreaming	p	16	p	20
Battling	a	20	a	20	Dripping (water)	p	20	p	20
Beaming (the sun)	p	16	p	20	Drowning	a	13 *	p	18
Bending (in wind)	p	19	p	20	Dropping (leaf)	p	20	p	20
Bewildered (looks)	p	18	p	20	Dying	p	20	p	20
Bleeding	p	20	p	20	Ejecting	a	16	a	18
Blissful (looks)	p	17	p	20	Embarrassed	p	13	p	17
Blowing (hair)	p	18	p	20	Erect (penis)	a	19	a	20
Boasting	a	20	a	20	Euphoric (looks)	a	14	a	15
Bouncing (ball)	a	20	a	17	Excited	a	20	a	20
Breaking	a	18	a	16	Exhausted	p	20	p	20
Bumping (balls)	p	14	p	15	Exploding	a	20	a	20
Burning (fire)	p	13	p	17	Facing	p	14	p	20
Calmly	p	19	p	20	Falling	p	20	p	20
Calling	a	20	a	20	Feeling (physical)	a	16	a	14
Carrying	a	20	a	20	Feeling (mental)	p	18	p	16
Carving	a	18	a	20	Ferocious	a	20	a	20
Casual (looks)	p	17	p	20	Fighting	a	20	a	20
Catching	a	20	a	20	Filling (a pool)	p	14	p	19
Celebrating	a	20	a	20	Firm (muscle)	a	15	a	18

Table 11 (Continued)

Item	Lay Group N = 20 Score	N	Students N = 20 Score	N	Item	Lay Group N = 20 Score	N	Students N = 20 Score	N
Fixing	a	20	a	20	Leading	a	17	a	20
Flapping (in wind)	p	20	p	20	Leering (a wolf)	a	15	a	20
Flapping (bird)	a	18	a	20	Leaning (against)	p	17	p	20
Fleeing	a	20	a	20	Lifting	a	20	a	20
Floating	p	20	p	20	Limping	a	14	a	13
Flowing (river)	p	19	p	20	Loading (cargo)	a	20	a	20
Flying	a	20	a	20	Longing (looks)	p	14	p	18
Frightened (looks)	p	18	p	20	Loosely (held)	p	11	p	16
Gambling	a	16	a	20	Loving (2 people)	a	18	a	20
Gasping (for breath)	a	17	a	12	Lustful (looks)	a	15	a	20
Gazing	p	18	p	20	Lying (down)	p	20	p	20
Glaring (at someone)	a	17	a	20	Mad (looks)	a	17	a	20
Graciously (standing)	a	14 *	p	16	Magical	a	14 *	p	13
					Making (a cake)	a	20	a	20
Grinding	a	17	a	19	Mashing	a	20	a	20
Growing (plant)	a	15 *	p	14	Mean (looks)	a	16 *	p	15
Hallucinating	a	13 *	p	17	Meditating	p	14	p	20
Hammering	a	20	a	20	Menstruating	p	16	p	20
Hanging (man)	p	18	p	20	Miserable (looks)	p	20	p	20
Happy (looks)	a	17	a	19	Mixing	a	20	a	20
Harassed (looks)	p	14	p	17	Modeling (standing)	p	14	p	20
Helping	a	20	a	20	Modeling (clay)	a	11	a	18
Hesitant	p	15	p	19	Mounting	a	20	a	20
Holding	a	17	a	20	Moving	a	20	a	20
Hostile (looks)	a	20	a	17	Mugging	a	20	a	20
Hunting	a	20	a	20	Murdering	a	20	a	20
Hurting	a	20	a	20	Musing (alone)	p	15	p	20
Idle	p	19	p	20	Nervous (feels)	a	13 *	p	18
Imagining	a	13 *	p	18	Nervous (looks)	p	12	p	20
Impatient (looks)	a	14 *	p	14	Nodding (to sleep)	p	20	p	20
Impulsive	a	18	a	20	Noticing (someone)	a	17 *	p	20
Inclining	p	13	p	20	Numb (feels)	p	18	p	20
Inert	p	20	p	20	Objecting	a	20	a	20
Injured	p	20	p	20	Oblivious	p	20	p	20
Inspecting	a	16 *	p	14	Observing	p	16	p	20
Intercourse	a	20	a	20	Offensive (looks)	a	13 *	p	14
Interested	a	13	a	17	Oozing	p	20	p	20
Isolated (feels)	p	18	p	20	Opening (a door)	a	16	a	20
Jeering	a	20	a	20	Opposing	a	18	a	20
Jerking	a	19	a	20	Outraged	a	20	a	20
Jogging	a	20	a	20	Pacing	a	20	a	20
Joining (2 people)	a	18	a	20	Painful (feels)	p	14	p	20
Jovial (looks)	a	17	a	18	Panting (a dog)	p	13 *	a	16
Jumping	a	20	a	20	Passing	a	20	a	20
Kidding (2 people)	a	20	a	19	Peaceful (looks)	p	20	p	20
Killing	a	20	a	20	Perplexed (looks)	p	15	p	20
Knowingly (looks at)	p	14 *	a	17	Picking up	a	20	a	20
Laboring	a	20	a	20	Playing	a	20	a	20
Landing (plane)	a	18	a	16	Pleased (feels)	p	13	p	17
Laughing	a	15	a	13	Pleased (looks)	p	15	p	20
Laying	p	20	p	20	Pondering	p	12	p	20

Table 11 (Continued)

Item	Lay Group N = 20		Students N = 20		Item	Lay Group N = 20		Students N = 20	
	Score	N	Score	N		Score	N	Score	N
Preaching	a	20	a	20	Smoking (fire)	p	17	p	20
Pretending (sleep)	p	11	p	16	Smoking (person)	a	18	a	20
Prowling	a	20	a	20	Sniffing	a	11 *	p	19
Puffed (balloon)	p	14	p	20	Speaking	a	16	a	14
Pulling	a	20	a	20	Spilling (water)	p	14	p	20
Pushing	a	20	a	20	Springing	a	16	a	20
Putting (golf)	a	20	a	20	Squall (rain)	a	14	a	18
Queer (looks)	p	16	p	20	Stabbing	a	20	a	20
Querulous (looks)	p	15	p	20	Standing	p	13	p	20
Quiet	p	20	p	20	Steaming water	p	18	p	20
Quivering	a	13 *	p	14	Stormy	a	13	a	20
Racing	a	20	a	20	Stroking	a	11	a	16
Raging (river)	a	20	a	20	Struggling	a	20	a	20
Raising (a log)	a	20	a	20	Stuck (in mud)	p	20	p	20
Ramming (2 cars)	a	20	a	20	Subdued (looks)	p	16	p	20
Rapturous	a	16 *	p	18	Suffering	a	13 *	p	17
Reaching	a	20	a	20	Suspicious (looks)	p	12	p	20
Ready (to run)	a	20	a	20	Swimming	a	20	a	20
Reckless (looks)	a	12 *	p	20	Taking	a	18	a	20
Refreshed	p	13	p	11	Talking	a	13 *	p	18
Remorseful	p	15	p	17	Tapping	a	20	a	20
Reposing	p	20	p	20	Tearful	p	17	p	20
Resigned	p	16	p	20	Telling	a	14 *	p	18
Resolute (looks)	a	13	a	15	Terrorized (feels)	p	16	p	20
Reticent (looks)	p	11	p	17	Thrilled	a	14	a	13
Revolving	a	17	a	20	Throwing	a	20	a	20
Riding (a horse)	a	20	a	20	Thumping	a	20	a	20
Ringing (bell)	a	14	a	18	Tilted	p	14	p	20
Ripping fabric	a	20	a	20	Toasting (people)	a	17	a	20
Roaring (lion)	a	20	a	20	Tormented (feels)	p	15	p	20
Roaring (water)	a	13 *	p	18	Touching (2 people)	a	14	a	17
Rolling (ball)	p	17	p	20	Tranquil (looks)	p	20	p	20
Rowing	a	20	a	20	Troubled (looks)	p	13	p	20
Running	a	20	a	20	Turning (around)	a	20	a	16
Sad (looks)	p	18	p	20	Unconscious	p	20	p	20
Sad (feels)	p	20	p	20	Unsteady	p	14	p	20
Sagging	p	16	p	20	Upset (feels)	p	13	p	20
Sailing (boat)	p	14	p	20	Vaulting (animal)	a	18	a	20
Satisfied (feel)	p	13	p	19	Vibrating	a	20	a	20
Screaming	a	20	a	20	Vigorous	a	20	a	20
Seated	p	17	p	20	Violent	a	20	a	20
Seeing	p	15	p	20	Waiting	p	16	p	20
Seething	a	16	a	20	Walking	a	20	a	20
Shaking	a	16	a	18	Wanting	p	11	p	16
Shocked	p	13	p	20	Watching	a	13 *	p	20
Singing	a	20	a	20	Weary (feels)	p	15	p	20
Sinister (look)	a	13	a	16	Whirling	a	20	a	20
Skimming	a	17	a	14	Wounded	p	17	p	20
Sleeping	p	20	p	20	Writing	a	20	a	20
Slipping	p	15	p	20	Yielding	p	18	p	20
Smelling	a	12 *	p	17					

easily defined as active. It is important to note that the decision to use "talking" as the upper parameter for the passive category was not derived casually, even though the logic of doing so may not be readily apparent, especially to the Rorschach novice.

Some movement responses are always coded as *passive*. They are the answers in which the movement reported is *static*. The static feature of the response is usually created by qualifying the answer to make it an abstract, a caricature, or a picture. These are all coded p regardless of the description of the movement reported. Many static responses involve inanimate movement such as, "an abstract of fireworks exploding on the Fourth of July." The described movement, "exploding," is clearly active but it is qualified by the word *abstract* and thus would be scored m^p. Similarly, "a painting of two people struggling to lift something," or "a drawing of two lions climbing a mountain" both involve active movement that has become static because of the qualifications of "a painting . . ." and "a drawing . . ." These responses would be coded M^p and FM^p, respectively. It is important to make sure that the subject has qualified the response rather than simply used a qualifying word as a manner of articulation. Children often use the words *picture* or *painting* in their responses. Differentiation between the static response and the articulation style is sometimes difficult, but in most cases involving articulating style, the subject will use the same qualifying word in other responses that do not include movement.

Some examples of the three types of movement answers and the active-passive coding are shown in Table 12. Most include only the original response, although critical parts of the Inquiry are included in parentheses when essential to the coding decision.

THE COLOR DETERMINANTS (CHROMATIC)

The symbols used for coding chromatic color responses are the same as used by Rorschach, and the criteria for them are very similar to those that he prescribed. He observed that subjects frequently are impressed with the chromatic colors and use them as factors in forming their responses to the five blots that contain chromatic features. He differentiated these responses into three basic categories: (1) those based exclusively on the color features (*C*), (2) those based primarily on the color features but also involving form (*CF*), and (3) those based primarily on form but also involving color (*FC*). He also used a special scoring (*CC*) in one of his example protocols to note an instance of color naming. Each of the Rorschach systematizers incorporated Rorschach's three basic scoring categories for chromatic color responses into their respective systems, but some have altered the criteria for their application. Beck remained most faithful to the Rorschach criteria, and Klopfer and Rapaport have deviated most from them.

Each of the systematizers, except Beck, also proliferated the chromatic color scoring categories somewhat extensively. Special scorings for "color projections," "color denial," "crude color," "color description," "color symbolism," "arbitrary color," and "forced color" are found in the various systems. All of the systems except Beck's also include color naming, although the criterion varies from system to system. There are no empirical findings to support the usefulness of the variety of proliferated categories for coding chromatic color answers, with the possible exceptions of color naming and color projection. The data concerning color projection suggest that it should be coded separately rather than as a determinant. Thus the Comprehensive Systems include four symbols for coding responses that include the use of chromatic color, *C* (Pure Color), *CF* (Color-Form), *FC* (Form Color), and *Cn* (Color Naming).

Table 12.   Examples of the Three Types of Movement Responses

Card	Location	Response	Coding
I	$D4$	A wm stndg w her arms raised	M^p
I	W	Two witches dancing arnd some symbol	M^a
I	W	A bf glidding along	FM^p
I	W	A bat zoomg in to strike	FM^a
I	$Dd24$	A church bell ringing (Dd 31 is clapper)	m^a
I	W	A fallen leaf disintegrating (S: Ths little pieces out to the sides r prts fallg off)	m^p
II	W	Two clowns dancing in a circus	M^a
II	$D3$	Menstruation	M^p
II	$D6$	Two dogs fighting	FM^a
II	$D4$	An erect penis	M^a
II	$DS5$	A top spinning	m^a
III	$D1$	Two people leaning over something	M^p
III	$D1$	Two people picking something up	M^a
III	$D3$	A bf flyg between two cliffs	FM^a
III	$D2$	A bat hanging upside down, asleep	FM^p
III	$D2$	Blood running down a wall	m^p
IV	W	A man sitting on a stump	M^p
IV	W	A giant looming over you	M^a
IV	$D1$	A caterpillar crawling along	FM^a
V	W	A bf floating along	FM^p
V	W	Someone dressed up like a bunny doing a ballet dance	M^a
V	W	Two people resting against each other	M^p
VI	$D3$	An erect penis	M^a
VI	$<D4$	A ship passing silently in the night	m^p
VI	$Dd19$	A speedboat racing up a river	m^a
VII	$D2$	A little boy looking in the mirror	M^p
VII	$\vee W$	Two wm dancing	M^a
VIII	Dd	(Half of blot including $D1$) An animal climbing up something	FM^a
VIII	$D4$	A frog leaping over something	FM^a
VIII	$D5$	Two flags waving in the breeze	m^p
IX	W	Intercourse ($D9$ male, remainder of blot female)	M^a
IX	$>D1$	A wm running after a child	M^a
IX	$\vee W$	An atomic explosion	m^a
IX	$DS8$	A waterfall	m^p
X	$D1$	A crab grabbing something ($D12$)	FM^a
X	$D2$	A collie dog sitting down	FM^p
X	Dd	(Upper $D9$ each side) Two boys talking to each other	M^p
X	$\vee D10$	Someone swinging in a swing ($D5$ is the person, $D4$ is the swing)	M^a
X	$\vee D6$	Two people reaching out to each other	M^a
X	W	Fireworks	m^a
X	$D7$	A deer jumping	FM^a
X	$D3$	A seed dropping to earth	m^p
X	W	A lot of seaweed floating along	m^p
X	Dd	(Center parts including $D9$, $D3$, $D6$, and $D10$) A flower that is opening up to the sun	m^p
X	$D11$	Two animals trying to climb a pole	FM^a

The Pure Color Response (C)   The C response is based exclusively on the chromatic features of the blot. It occurs with least frequency of any of the three basic types of color answers and is identified by the complete lack of form. The decision to code pure C is usually based on the fact that color alone has been specified or implied in the response with no attempt to articulate form features. Among the more common examples of the pure C response are blood, paint, water, and ice cream. Any of these might be articulated in such a manner as to include form, such as "blood running down" (Card III), and when such an articulation occurs the coding is CF rather than C. In that the clarification of the use of color is not commonly offered during the response, it is especially important that the Inquiry be cautious but specific to this point such as, "I'm not sure why it looks like that." The examiner must rely on the "spontaneity" of the Inquiry material and, for responses such as "this red is blood" given in the response phase, the C should be coded unless a form clarification is spontaneously offered *at the onset of the Inquiry.* Ordinarily, when a pure color response has been given in the response, the subject simply verifies the location of his answer at the onset of the Inquiry. Conversely, where form has also been involved, the subject usually concentrates on the form features at the onset of the Inquiry. Two similar responses, extracted from the protocol pool, serve as good examples. Both are whole responses to Card X.

RESPONSE	INQUIRY
X Gee, a lot of paint	E: (Rpts S's response)
	S: Yeah, all over like somebody threw a lot of paint there
	E: I'm not sure why it looks like paint.
	S: All those colors, that's like paint

In this response, the absence of form is implied in the response and confirmed immediately in the Inquiry, and a score of C is appropriate. The second example is somewhat different even though the response is extremely similar.

RESPONSE	INQUIRY
X Oh, a lot of paint	E: (Rpts S's response)
	S: Yes, all of it ll an abstract of somesort
	E: An abstract?
	S: Yes, it's the same on both sides as if to give each of the colors a double meaning, as if the painter was trying to convey s.t. by the design that he selected which is very pretty by the way

In this response, the subject spontaneously injects the form features of the blot at the onset of the Inquiry. In most instances, the form quality of the blot would have been implied in the response, such as "oh, an abstract painting," but this particular subject did not do so. Assuming that there has been no set offered by the examiner during the Inquiry that would produce a form orientation, this response would be coded CF rather than C. It has been suggested previously that questionable M responses might best be decided in light of the overall record. This principle also holds for the questionable *C* responses; namely, if other pure *C* responses have occurred, the questionable response should probably be coded as *C,* and vice versa. Again, caution should be exercised in the use of this guideline. It is not a hard-and-fast rule, but simply one tactic that may assist the examiner who is confronted with a coding dilemma.

Quite often, the Rorschach novice finds it difficult to discriminate the pure *C* response, being overly influenced by the fact that everything has some form. Although that fact is unrefutable, it is not an issue here. The issue is whether the subject *processes and articulates the use of the form features in creating and selecting the response.* The failure to articulate those features of the stimulus field signals some disregard and/or dysfunction in processing, mediating, or integrating the stimulus characteristics that are present. For instance, a drop of blood has a contour, but that contour can take an infinite number of shapes. If a subject identifies a drop of blood, and adds no more, the cognitive operations have, in effect, discarded or disregarded the possible use of contours. Conversely, a subject might identify "an almost perfectly round drop of blood," or "a drop of blood that looks like it has splattered outward." In each of these responses, the subject has included some meaningful, albeit not necessarily definitive, use of contour in the response and the appropriate coding is *CF.*

The Color-Form Response (*CF*)   The *CF* response is one based primarily on the color features of the blot and which also includes reference to form. These are very often answers the content of which does not require a specific form. In many instances, the presence of form articulation differentiates them from pure *C* responses as in "two scoops of ice cream sherbet" (Card VIII), or "orange flames from a forest fire" (Card IX). In other responses, the vagueness of form articulation differentiates them from the *FC* type answer as in "a lot of flowers" (Card X). Most flower responses are *FC* because the form characteristics such as petals, leaves, and stems are mentioned. In the example above, however, the subject offers no further form differentiation in the Inquiry ("Yeah, just a lot of different colored flowers"). The distinction of *CF* from *FC* is often difficult because of the vagueness or inarticulation of subjects. A seemingly large number of *CF* responses involve objects that have ambiguous form requirements such as lakes, maps, meat, foliage, minerals, or underwater scenes. Any of these contents can be *FC* if the subject provides sufficient justification by his or her emphasis on form. Conversely, many responses, such as the example to Card X, which carry specific form requirements, and which usually will be *FC* when color is used, might be *CF* if form is deemphasized by the subject.

Some Rorschach authorities, such as Klopfer and Hertz, have suggested a more definitive criterion for differentiating *FC* from *CF* by using the form requirements of the content as a guide. Thus all flowers, which have a relatively common form, are *FC,* whereas all lakes, which have only ambiguous form requirements, are *CF.* Although the intent of these differentiations is clearly worthwhile, the logic is not altogether sound, for it assumes that all subjects interpret color equally if they use the same content. This is probably no more the case for differentiating *CF* from *FC* than it would be for differentiating *C* from *CF.* Consequently, the articulation of the subject must be weighed carefully and a cautious but nondirective Inquiry is always in order. Where doubt remains, the examiner may use the remainder of the protocol as a basis for decision making.

The Form-Color Response (*FC*)   The *FC* response represents the most controlled use of color. It involves an answer where the form features of the blot are primary in forming the percept and color is also used for purposes of elaboration or clarification. The overwhelming majority of *FC* responses have specific form such as in "a red butterfly" (Card III), "an anatomy chart with the lungs (*D*1), the rib cage and the lower organs" (Card VIII), or "daffodils" (Card X). These form features are also given considerable elaboration, either in the Response or in the Inquiry. Some inarticulate subjects do not offer much elaboration regarding form features but do mention color. Here, as with decisions about other determinants, the total protocol proves a useful guide and the limited articulation will be noted in noncolor responses. If the issue remains in doubt, a conservative approach to coding *CF* versus *FC* is in order, because one is generally interpreted to mean a more limited modulation of affective displays than the other. In either instance, it is quite important that the *FC not be rejected* simply because the content reported does not have a specific form requirement. Numerous contents of ambiguous form requirement, such as anatomy, foliage, sea animals, and even blood cells, can be offered in a manner that emphasizes the form features while also including reference to color. In such cases, the code is *FC*.

Some Guidelines　Quite often, objects that have no specific form demand will be *CF*, but that *is not* a hard-and-fast rule. For example, a subject might say, *"This green is colored like leaves, like a leaf from a bush."* If no further form elaboration occurs, the answer should be coded *CF*. However, the same response could be elaborated, as in *"This green, it is colored like a leaf, a leaf from a bush, like a berry bush, see the way that it comes to a point like, what are they, raspberries I think, they're shaped like that."* The precise form elaboration would require a coding of *FC*. A more important guideline is the Step-Down Principle. The distinction between *C* and *CF* is usually less of a dilemma. The *C* answers are often blatant, *"This red, it's like blood, all red like that,"* or *"It's blue so it could be water,"* or *"Just a lot of different colored paint, that's all,"* or *"It's blue, like ice gets blue sometimes."* These illustrations are the obvious *C* responses, but sometimes an object that ordinarily would be scored as *C* must be coded as *CF* because it is *touching* a formed object.

For instance, "The red must be blood, it's *on* these bears that are probably fighting with each other." Whereas red blood would typically be coded *C*, the coding is stepped down one interval to *CF* because of the direct proximity to a form-dominated object. If the response had been, "Two bears that are fighting, maybe they are hurt because this red back here in the background is like blood," the coding would remain *C* because the blood is not on the bears, even though it is associated with them.

Confirming Color Use　Sometimes a quandary will arise about the coding of color because a subject has reported an object in a colored area of the blot, and it seems "almost certain" that color has influenced the formation of the answer. But the subject *has not reported* the color, either directly or through implication. For example, "This looks like a very beautiful flower." In the Inquiry, the examiner strikes at the key word, "You mentioned it is beautiful?" to which the subject responds, "Yes, it looks very thin and very delicate." Color is not coded for this response, even though the entire area used might be colored. The coding *must* reflect the verbalization of the subject. There are responses in which the way that a subject articulates a color makes it clear that the color is being used as a determinant. These are instances in which the color and content converge. For instance, "That red sure looks like blood to me," "That orange looks like a forest fire," "The blue is the water." In these responses, the use of color seems unequivocal and should be scored. However, most color use is not so obvious, even in responses in which the color and content appear to converge. For example: "That red could be blood," "The orange might be a fire or something," "This blue part might be water."

In these answers, the subject has not been definite. Instead, there is equivocation (could be, might be). Thus, the examiner should inquire further to test the color use by asking, "I'm not sure what makes it look like _____?" or "What is there about it that makes it look like _____?"

The Color Naming Response (Cn)   Rorschach gave little attention to color naming other than to score it *CC* and to note that he observed it in the records of deteriorated epileptics. Piotrowski (1936) introduced the use of the symbol *Cn* for color naming in his studies of the protocols of organics. He does not consider it to be a genuine color response but rather an acknowledgment of the presence of color. The research that has been reported on color naming suggests that it can be an important diagnostic clue and that it does occur with sufficient frequency among the more severely disturbed to warrant special scoring. The criterion adopted for *Cn* in the comprehensive system follows Klopfer and Rapaport; that is, that it is intended as a response. Naturally, it is important that *Cn*, as is the case with any other unique or dramatic response, be interpreted in the context of the total configuration of the protocol. Thus a *Cn* response followed by a *CF* response, using the same or nearly the same blot areas, will be interpreted differently than will be a *Cn*, which is the only response given to a card. In either instance, the *Cn* should be scored, provided that the subject actually identifies one or more chromatic areas by name (red, green, blue, etc.) and intends that identification as a response. The examiner should not confuse occasional spontaneous comments, which some subjects give when presented with chromatically colored cards, with color naming. Comments such as "Oh, how pretty," or "My, look at all the colors," *are not* color naming. They are interpretively important comments but should not be considered as the same as, or even similar to, the *Cn* answer. Most *Cn* responses are given with an almost mechanical or detached flavoring, manifesting the difficulties that the subject has in cognitively integrating the complex stimulus material.

Some examples of the four types of chromatic color responses are provided in Table 13. The Inquiry material included consists *only* of that which is relevant to the coding decision, so that in some instances, the Inquiry is omitted and in other instances only a portion of the Inquiry is shown.

The decision to code color is sometimes complicated by the approach of the subject to the test. Under ideal conditions, subjects will identify color responses by a statement,

Table 13.   Examples of the Four Types of Chromatic Color Responses

Card	Location	Response		Inquiry	Coding
II	D3	This red ll blood	S:	Its all reddish	C
II	D3	A red bf			FC
II	D2	A fire, like a bonfire	S:	Well its all red like a bonfire sort of blazing upward	CF.m[a]
II	W	Two clowns, in a circus	S:	I thought of a circus because of the red hats	FC
III	D2	Bad meat	S:	The color makes it look spoiled to me	C

Table 13 (Continued)

Card	Location	Response		Inquiry	Coding
III	VD2	Blood running down a wall or s.t.	S:	Its red & u can c it like its running down	$CF.m^p$
III	D3	A hair ribbon	S:	Its a pretty red one	FC
VIII	W	A dead animal	S:	It looks like the insides, all decayed	CF
			E:	Decayed?	
			S:	Yes all the different colors ll decay & u can c some bones	
VIII	D5	Two blue flags			FC
VIII	W	Pink and orange & blue			Cn
VIII	D4	A frog	S:	Well the legs r out & it has a froggy like body & it has a froggy like color to it	FC
VIII	D2	An ice cream sundae	S:	It ll orange & raspberry ice cream, like two scoops	CF
IX	W	A forest fire	S:	Well the fire here (D3) is coming up over ths trees & stuff	$m^a.CF$
			E:	Trees & stuff?	
			S:	C, the green here cld b trees & ths other cld b bushes	
IX	D9	Pink here	S:	Right down here	Cn
IX	D4	A newborn baby	S:	U can c the head, that's all, it must b newborn because its pinkish	FC
IX	VW	An atomic explosion	S:	The top prt is the mushroom cld & dwn here the orange is the fire blast & the green area cld b smoke	$m^a.CF$
X	VD4	A seahorse	S:	It has that shape & its green	FC
X	D9	Coral	S:	Its colored like coral	C
X	W	Some sort of really neat abstract	S:	Well the artist has taken pains to make it the same on both sides the shapes are identical on each side & he's represented his different thoughts with different colors, really neat	FC
X	W	An abstract painting of some kind	S:	abstract thought I guess, its pretty good	CF
X	D13	A potato chip	S:	Well it's kind of shaped like a potato chip & it has the same color as one	FC
X	D15	A flower	S:	I don't kno what kind, it is a pretty yellow, there isn't much of a stem tho u can only c the flower part itself, like the petals and that	FC
X	D12	A leaf	S:	Its green like a leaf	CF

such as "It looks like that because of the color." Unfortunately, many subjects are not that cooperative or articulate. For example, a subject may give a response such as "blood" to the *D*3 area of Card III. When the response is inquired, the subject may state, "Yes, here in this red part." The question is legitimately raised concerning the necessity to inquire further to verify the actual use of color. It is indeed a rare subject who would give a blood response to a red area and then deny that color was influential; however, it does happen occasionally. These rare instances do necessitate some inquiry approach by the examiner to establish the fact that color is used. It is *not,* however, necessary for the examiner to repeat the same Inquiry routine to evoke the word *color* to every response that apparently involves color. The skilled examiner will detect the pattern of articulation early in the Inquiry, and it is appropriate for him or her to use that information wisely in forming subsequent Inquiry questions. The use of good judgment by the examiner will both save time and probably avoid some irritation to the subject. Thus, if a subject gives several color responses in a protocol but does not articulate the word *color* easily in the Inquiry, the examiner should rely on the consistency of articulation as a guide once the color element has been established as being important. This is not to imply that color should be automatically assumed in one response because it has been used in another response, for that should never be the case. It is, however, necessary for the examiner to manifest some flexibility in his or her communications with the subject. The inflexible examiner takes the risk of creating a "color set" for the subject so that, as the questioning is repeated and prolonged, the tendency to articulate color to the last three cards is exaggerated, and color may be offered as an elaboration when, in fact, color was not used in the response.

The examiner must also be careful not to assume the use of color simply because the subject identifies a location area by its color, as in "This red part looks like a butterfly," or "This blue reminds me of a crab." These *are not* color responses as they stand. Naturally, if there is reason to believe that color might be used, it should be inquired; however, the use of color to specify location should not be confused with the use of color as a response determinant.

THE COLOR DETERMINANTS (ACHROMATIC)

Rorschach did not suggest a special scoring for responses that include the use of achromatic color as color in determining a response. The first formal scoring for these kinds of responses was devised by Klopfer and Miale (1938), using the symbol *C'*. Klopfer's decision to create a separate scoring for the achromatic color response was, at least in part, based on Rorschach's apparent disregard of the determinant, plus the subsequent writing of Binder (1932), who proposed an elaborate system for evaluating "chiaroscuro" responses. Binder, like Rorschach, did not suggest a separate scoring for the achromatic color responses, but did imply that they are interpretively different than responses using the light-dark features as "shading." Klopfer defined the *C'* response as one in which the black, gray, or white areas of the blot are used as color. This symbol and criterion were adopted by Rapaport and variations of it are in the Piotrowski and Hertz methods.

Campo and de de Santos (1971) reviewed the literature regarding approaches to coding responses based on the light-dark features of the blots and concluded that the *C'* type of answer is discrete from other categories. Similarly, the accumulation of research findings indicate that *C'* responses represent different operations than do the shading responses, and as such, the coding provides useful interpretive information. In that context, the symbols and criteria employed by Klopfer to identify these responses have been incorporated into the Comprehensive System, and follow a form-related continuum similar to that used for the coding of the chromatic color answers.

The Pure Achromatic Color Response (C')   The C' response is one based exclusively on the achromatic features of the blot. It is very uncommon and is identified by the complete absence of form. In some cases, the achromatic color will be used directly in the response, as in "white snow" (DS5 area of Card II). In most cases, a formless content is offered in the response and elaborated as having been perceived by the achromatic color in the Inquiry. Two responses, both to Card V, serve as good examples.

	RESPONSE	INQUIRY
V	It ll mud to me	E: (Rpts S's response)
		S: Yeah, it's black
		E: I'm not sure I c it as u do
		S: All of it here, it's black just like mud
V	Some coal	E: (Rpts S's response)
		S: It's dark
		E: I'm not sure I c it as u do
		S: It must b coal, it's dark like coal

In each of these responses the subject has made no effort to develop the form characteristics and, in each case, has offered achromatic color spontaneously. If the second response had been "a piece of coal," *accompanied* by some attempt at form differentiation, such as jagged, the coding would not be C' but rather C'F.

The Achromatic Color-Form Response (C'F)   The C'F response is one based primarily on the achromatic color features, and form is used secondarily for purposes of elaboration or clarification. In almost all of these responses, it is clear that the answer would not have been formulated without the achromatic features of the blot being involved, and the form features are vague and often undifferentiated.

	RESPONSE	INQUIRY
I	A black sky with white clouds	E: (Rpts S's response)
		S: It's all black & ths thgs r like white clouds (DdS26)
VII	Pieces of black coral	E: (Rpts S's response)
		S: There r 4 of them, thyr black like pieces of coral, black coral, they mak jewlry out of it

In the first example, the differentiation, by content, of the blackness of the whole blot from the white spaces is a vague form use, sufficient to warrant scoring C'F rather than

C'. In the second example, the differentiation of blot into "pieces" also justified the inclusion of *F* into the scoring. Occasionally, subjects will perceive "smoke" because of the achromatic color and, depending on the extent of form use, the scoring will be *C'* or *C'F*. Most "smoke" responses, however, are perceived because of the shading features rather than the achromatic color and the scoring decision must be formulated carefully, with regard to the report of the subject. It is not uncommon for subjects to use the word *color* to articulate shading features, and in even more frustrating circumstances, subjects may include the specific achromatic element, such as "the blackness of it." This is not necessarily an achromatic color answer, and the examiner needs to ensure that it is not simply a way of describing the shading features.

The Form-Achromatic Color Response (*FC'*) The *FC'* response is one in which form is the primary determinant and achromatic color is used secondarily, for elaboration or clarification. It is the most frequent of the achromatic color responses and is usually easy to identify because of the emphasis on specific form features offered by the subject. Among the more common *FC'* responses are "a black bat" (Cards I and V); "Halloween figures in ghost costumes" (*DdS*26 area of Card I), clarified as ghost costumes because they are white; "African figures" (Card III), elaborated as being African because they are black or dark; a silhouette of a tree (Card IV), elaborated as being a silhouette because it is black or dark; and ants or insects (*D*8, Card X), elaborated as being gray or dark.

The *key* words on which any of the achromatic color codings are based are black, white, gray, dark, and light. Unfortunately, these same words are sometimes used to specify the location of an object, as in, "This black part looks like . . ." Obviously, it is important to ensure that the word is being used to denote the use of the achromatic feature as color before applying the *C'* coding. It is also unfortunate but true that some of these words are also used to note the use of shading rather than achromatic color, as in ". . . it is blacker here, like it would be deeper" (vista), or ". . . it is lighter up here like the top of a cloud" (diffuse shading). The examiner's decision to use one of the *C'* symbols is usually not difficult, for the majority of these responses will include the words *black, white,* or *gray* in a manner conveying the use of the achromatic color, *as color,* quite clearly. Greater difficulty in the decision is encountered when the words *dark* or *light* are employed. The decision to use one of the *C'* symbols versus one of the symbols for diffuse shading should be made cautiously, and following the rule that *the intent of the subject is clear and unequivocal.* If the intent of the subject to use the grey, black, or white as color is not obvious, the code for diffuse shading should be used.

THE SHADING DETERMINANTS

The coding of responses in which the light-dark features of the blot are used as a determinant has been one of the most controversial aspects of the Rorschach. Although discussed extensively, it has been the least researched of the major determinant categories. It has been previously noted that Rorschach made no mention of shading or "chiaroscuro" features in his original monograph because the cards on which his basic experiment was based contained no variations in hue. These characteristics of the blots were created through a printing error, and according to Ellenberger (1954), Rorschach immediately perceived the possibilities created by the new dimension. Rorschach, during the brief period in which he worked with shaded cards, scored all references to shading as (*C*) to denote the *Hell-Dunkel* interpretations. Binder (1932) was the first to systematically develop a more extensive scoring for the shading features, following from some of the inferences that had been offered by Rorschach. The Binder approach differentiates four basic types of shading responses but suggests scorings for only two of these. The two that Binder codes are Helldunkel (scored using the symbol *Hd*), which includes answers based on "the diffuse total impression of the light and dark values of the whole card," and *F(Fb)* responses in which shading is differentiated within the blot area used. Binder also noted that subjects sometimes use the shading contour as form-like, or use the light-dark features as achromatic color. Because neither meet his criteria for *Hd* or *F(Fb)*, he offers no special codings for them.

Binder's work has been quite influential to the decisions of the systematizers in their respective approaches to shading answers. Piotrowski, in addition to coding for achromatic color, used two categories for shading responses. One, *c* or *Fc*, is for shading and/or texture responses prompted by the light shades of gray. The second, *c'* or *Fc'*, is used where the dark nuances of the blot are involved, or when a dysphoric mood is expressed. Rapaport also included two categories for shading. The first, *Ch, ChF,* or *FCh*, represents all shading responses except those falling into the second category. The second, scored *(C)F* or *F(C)*, is for the chiaroscuro answer in which the shading components specify important inner details, or for Color-Form responses that include reference to texture.

Hertz includes three categories of shading response, in addition to achromatic color. The first, *c, cF,* or *Fc*, is for responses in which the shading features produce a textural, surface, or reflective quality. The second, employing the symbols *(C), (C)F,* and *F(C)*, is for answers where shading precipitates the interpretation of a three-dimensional effect. The third, *Ch, ChF,* or *FCh*, is used for all other shading responses. Beck also used three categories for shading responses. One, *T, TF,* or *FT*, denotes answers in which the shading features create the impression of texture. The second, *V, VF,* or *FV*, is for responses in which shading contributes to the interpretation of depth or distance, and the third, *Y, YF,* or *FY*, is used for all other types of shading responses and is also used when achromatic color is involved.

The Klopfer approach to shading is the most complex. Klopfer was actually the first, after Binder, to formulate multiple categories for the coding and interpretation of shading responses. In addition to *C'* for achromatic color, Klopfer formulated four categories of shading. The first, *c, cF,* or *Fc*, is used for responses in which shading is interpreted to represent textural, surface, or reflective qualities. It is the same coding and criterion incorporated by Hertz and the criterion is nearly the same as used by Beck in his coding of *T*. The second utilizes the symbols *K* and *KF* to note responses in which the shading is perceived as diffuse. It is very similar to Binder's *Hd*, the Rapaport and Hertz *Ch*, and the Beck *Y*. The third, *FK*, represents instances where shading is used for vista, linear perspective, reflections, and landscapes. Some components of this criterion are similar to the Hertz use of *(C)* and the Beck *V*. These three shading categories appeared in Klopfer's original 1936 work. In 1937, Klopfer added a fourth category, *k, kF,* or *Fk*, defined as a three-dimensional expanse projected on a two-dimensional plane. The *k* category, as used in the Klopfer system, applies to X-ray or topographical map responses. The Klopfer approach to the shading responses is made considerably more complex by a number of idiomatic rules for specific types of responses. The product of these rules is that some responses are provided a shading code, even though the response determinant does not meet the criterion for the category. The majority of these idiomatic rules require the use of the *Fc*, although some call for the use of *FK*. For example, "transparencies" are *Fc,* as are answers in which achromatic color is interpreted as "bright" color. Similarly, most responses that emphasize "roundness" are *Fc* rather than *FK,* and *Fc* is also used when the "fine differentiations" in shading are designated to specify parts of objects. The *FK* idioms include both vista and reflection responses *even though* shading is not mentioned.

The selection of symbols and criteria for the coding of shading responses in the Comprehensive System is based on several considerations. The first concerned the possible use of the Klopfer method because it is the most comprehensive. Campo and de de Santos, in their evaluation of the various approaches to the scoring of shading, make a strong logical argument favoring the Klopfer method, but they neglect the complications created by the variety of idiomatic scorings. These scoring idioms not only tend to violate the scoring criteria but also imply the feasibility of interpreting relatively different types of responses as the same. The empirical data available concerning shading responses are somewhat complex, because it is difficult to translate findings derived by one method of coding to another coding approach. It is clear, however, that reflection answers are interpretively different from vista responses, and that percepts that include an emphasis on roundness are different from transparencies. A notable lack of empirical support for the separate *k* category also argues against the Klopfer approach. Data which have been reported suggest that the kind of shading perceived in X-ray responses is different than that used in topographical maps, the former being either achromatic color or diffuse shading, the latter involving the use of shading as vista.[1]

The factors that argue against the Klopfer system also argue in favor of an approach in which the criteria are distinct, which avoids idiomatic scorings, and which neatly differentiates the various types of shading responses. None of the systems accomplish these tasks completely. The three-category approach appears clearly preferable to the two-category method of Binder, Piotrowski, and Rapaport. The symbols selected for the Comprehensive System are those of Beck (*T, V,* and *Y*), but the criteria for two of these three are *more restricted* than that suggested by Beck. The *V* category includes *only* responses in which shading is present, and the *Y* category *excludes* achromatic color responses.

THE TEXTURE DETERMINANT

The shading features of the blots are often interpreted to represent "tactual" stimuli. In these types of answers, the subject elaborates on the composition or texture of the object. The elaboration carries with it, explicitly or implicitly, the conceptualization that the object is differentiated by its tactual features such as soft, hard, smooth, rough, silky, grainy, furry, cold, hot, sticky, and greasy. Texture is coded when the shading components of the blot area are used to justify or clarify these kinds of responses. Texture *should not* be assumed simply because words such as those listed above are used. They are legitimate clues to the probability that shading is involved but this is not always the case; thus Inquiry skill of the examiner is often extremely important. It is not uncommon, for example, to obtain responses in which words such as *rough, shaggy,* or *furry* are

---

[1]Klopfer remarked during a 1964 interview with me that he had been continuously dissatisfied with the various criteria for the scoring of shading responses in his system, especially the *k* category. He quickly added, however, that he felt his own approach was superior to others developed, and expressed the belief that it would be unrealistic to attempt to change his own system in that it had been in use for 30 years by that time.

used as form elaborations, with no concern for shading features. Similarly, objects may be perceived as "hot" or "cold" because of color. In the optimal situation the subject will indicate the use of shading when giving the response, but this is the exception rather than the rule. In most cases, the response will contain some clue that texture may be included, such as using words like *shaggy, furry, hot,* and so on; or the nature of the object itself may raise the possibility as in a rug, a coat, some ice, and such. These clues form the basis of Inquiry questions if they are required. Some subjects, especially children, will actually *rub* the blot but not necessarily articulate the shading. *This is sufficient evidence of the tactile impression to code texture.* The texture determinant is coded in one of three ways, depending on the extent of form involvement.

The Pure Texture Response (*T*) The *T* response is the least common of the three kinds of texture. It is used for answers in which the shading components of the blot are represented as "textural," with no form involvement. The criterion for differentiating a *T* from a *TF* answer is essentially the same as for differentiating *C* from *CF*. In other words, no effort is made by the subject to use the form features of the blot, even in a secondary manner. Responses such as "wood, flesh, ice, fleecy wool, grease, hair, and silk" all represent examples that *might* be scored *T* provided shading is involved and has been perceived as texture, *and* no form is used. Where the form configuration of the blot area is included, even though it is relatively ambiguous or formless, the coding should be *TF* rather than *T.*

The Texture-Form Response (*TF*) The *TF* response is one in which the shading features are interpreted as texture and form is used secondarily for purposes of elaboration and/or clarification. In most instances, the object specified will have an ambiguous form such as "a chunk of ice," "an oily rag," "a piece of fur," or "some very hard metal." Less commonly, a specific form is used but it is clear, from the response or information offered spontaneously in the Inquiry, that the shading features precipitated the response; for example, "Something breaded, like a,—well like shrimp, yeah, that's it, fried shrimp" (Card VII). Usually this response will be scored *FT,* because most subjects giving it emphasize the form features and mention the texture as a clarification. In this example, however, the subject, responds first to the texture and then integrates the form in a meaningful way. The scoring of *TF* for objects of specific form must meet the criterion requirement that the interpretation of shading as texture is primary in the response, and that the form features have been used secondarily in the percept. In most cases, the issue is clarified by the response itself, and that must be considered before information given in the Inquiry is weighed. In some situations, the first information given in the Inquiry elaborates shading. This should not automatically be interpreted by the examiner to mean that shading was perceived as the primary feature in forming the response, particularly if the response itself suggests that the object reported might have been form determined. Three very similar responses to Card VI provide examples of how form and texture may vary in importance.

RESPONSE	INQUIRY
VI Gee, ths is a funny one, I guess it could b a skin, like an A skin.	*E:* (Rpts *S*'s response) *S:* Well, yeah its all kinda fuzzy and spotted, ths here cld b legs

In this example, there is no indication in the response that form has been primary. Quite the contrary, the subject is somewhat vague in the response formulation and uses the word *skin* first, and then clarifies it as an animal skin. In addition, the first material offered in the Inquiry concerns shading ("kinda fuzzy"), and only after that is some reference to form injected. This response is *TF*. In a second example, the response is similar but the coding is different.

RESPONSE	INQUIRY
VI It ll an A skin to me	*E:* (Repeats *S*'s response)
	S: Well, the shading gives it a very furry appearance and the edging is very rough like an A skin wld b & there is the distinct impression of legs and & the haunch part too

The appropriate code for this response is *FT*, even though the shading features are mentioned first in the Inquiry. The decision to code *FT* rather than *TF* is based on the fact that the response is reasonably definitive and *could be* form dominated, and the bulk of the *spontaneously given* Inquiry material is form oriented. The necessity of weighing the possibility of form domination in the response is demonstrated by a third example.

RESPONSE	INQUIRY
VI Well, it cld b an A skin	*E:* (Rpts *S*'s response)
	S: Yes, its not very well done either, it ll the skinner didn't get as much of the front prt as he could have
	E: I'm not sure what u see that ll an A skin
	S: Well all of it except ths top part looks that way, here r the rear legs & I suppose ths r the ft legs

This response involves no shading, or at least the subject has not articulated shading. The total emphasis of the subject is on the form features and the coding must be *F*. The Rorschach skeptic may argue that, because most animal skin responses to Card VI do involve the use of shading as texture, the coder would be justified in scoring *FT*, even though it is not articulated. Empirical findings argue against such a procedure. Baughman (1959) obtained animal skin responses to cards presented in silhouette form and to those in which shading features had been eliminated. It has also been demonstrated (Exner, 1961) that the frequency of "skin" responses to Card IV and VI is not altered if the gray-black features of the cards are made chromatic.

The Form-Texture Response (*FT*)   *FT* is used for responses in which form is the primary determinant and the shading features, articulated as texture, are used secondarily for purposes of elaboration and/or clarification. Most responses coded as *FT* will involve objects that have specific form requirements. For example, the commonly perceived animals on Cards II and VIII are sometimes elaborated as "furry" because of the light-dark features. Similarly, the human figure often reported to Card IV is frequently perceived as wearing a "fur coat." There is, however, a glaring exception to the guideline that *FT* will ordinarily involve objects of specific form requirement. This is the animal skin response to Card VI, which is the most frequently given of all texture responses. A random selection from the protocol pool at the Rorschach Research Foundation of 250 adult nonpatient records and 850 records of adult nonschizophrenic patients yielded 22,311 responses, of which 851 have a texture coding. The 851 include 364 responses (43%) to Card VI, of which 337 are the common animal skin responses and 318 of those are coded *FT.* The distribution of texture responses to Card IV is the second largest for this group, constituting 202 (24%) of the answers, of which 161 are *FT,* about equally divided between animal skin responses and human or human-like figures with fur or fur coats. Only 112 of the texture responses (13%) occurred to Cards I, II, III, and V, whereas 173 of these answers (20%) occurred to Cards VII, VIII, IX, and X. A total of 727 of the 851 texture responses (85%) are coded as *FT,* 107 (13%) are *TF,* and only 15 (2%) are pure *T.*

THE SHADING-DIMENSIONALITY DETERMINANT (VISTA)

The least common use of the light-dark features of the blot involves the interpretation of depth or dimensionality. These responses are marked by the use of the shading characteristics to alter the flat perspective offered by the blot stimulus. The most frequent type of vista response is one in which the contours created by the shading are used to convey the general impression of depth. Three codings are used for the vista responses.

The Pure Vista Response (*V*)   The pure *V* answer is extremely rare. The coding of *V* requires that the subject report depth or dimensionality based exclusively on the shading characteristics of the blot, with no form involvement. These responses, when they occur, are somewhat dramatic because they ignore the form qualities of the stimulus. Some examples are "depth," "perspective," "deepness," and "It's sticking out at me." Any of these similar responses might have some elaboration which involves the form features of the blot. When this occurs, the coding is *VF* rather than *V.*

The Vista-Form Response (*VF*)   The *VF* responses include primary emphasis on the shading features to represent depth or dimensionality and incorporate the form features of the blot for clarification and/or elaboration. Most *VF* responses have contents of nonspecific form requirement, such as "one of those maps like you use in a geography class with the mountains and plateaus shown," "rain clouds, one behind the other," or "a deep canyon with a river running in there." If the topographical map were to be more specifically defined, such as "a topographical map of the western part of the United States," or the canyon and river were more specifically defined, as in "an aerial view of the Colorado River," wherein the form features are given greater emphasis, the coding would be *FV* rather than *VF.* The *VF,* like *TF,* is contingent on the primary emphasis being given to the shading features.

The Form-Vista Response (*FV*)   The *FV* response is one in which form is the primary feature and the shading component is used to represent depth or dimensionality for purposes of clarification and/or elaboration. Most *FV* responses will have contents with a relatively specific form requirement but that is not necessarily an adequate guideline for differentiating the *FV* and *VF* answers. For example, "a well" has a reasonably specific form requirement, yet most "well" responses are *VF* rather than *FV,* the differentiation being based on whether primary emphasis is given to the form characteristics or the shading. The response that is *FV* will generally include considerable emphasis or elaboration on form. Almost any content, ranging from frequently perceived human or animal figures to very unusual answers, may involve vista. Bridges, dams, and waterways are among the more frequently given *FV* responses; however, the vista component may be reported in almost any form-dominated response. For example, the human figure often reported to the center *D* of Card I is sometimes perceived as "behind a curtain" because of the shading difference, or the lower center *D* area of Card IV is often perceived as a worm or caterpillar "coming out from in under a leaf." Both are scored *FV, provided* shading contributes to the percept. The *FV* answer is the most common of the three types of vista.

Some examples of the different types of texture and vista responses are provided in Table 14. The Inquiry material included consists *only* of that which is directly relevant to the scoring decision; therefore, in some instances the Inquiry is omitted, and in other instances, a portion of the Inquiry is presented.

The differentiation between texture and vista answers is not always precise and can make for difficult decisions. For example, a response such as "the convolutions of the brain" to the center area of Card VI will ordinarily be scored *VF* because of the emphasis on dimensionality. The same response, however, might be elaborated as "It looks bumpy, like if you touched it you could feel the bumps." This elaboration, which emphasizes the tactual interpretation, meets the criterion for the scoring of *TF.* The guideline that should be used for the scoring decision requires consideration of the "interpretive emphasis" offered by the subject. If, in the example cited, the elaboration on "bumpy" features appears to have been injected for purposes of clarification, the scoring remains *VF.* Conversely, if the tactual emphasis is injected in the basic response, or is offered spontaneously *at the onset* of the Inquiry, the scoring should be *TF.* Fortunately, in most cases, the subject provides material from which the "interpretive emphasis" can be identified easily. For example, "rough mountain peaks" (vista) is easy to differentiate from "a rough piece of sandpaper" (texture). The word *rough* occurs in each, but mountain peaks are not associated tactually, and sandpaper is not perceived dimensionally. In those few responses where doubt may remain after the Inquiry has been completed, the examiner should review the remainder of the record with concern for the occurrence of other texture or vista answers. If the record contains no other vista responses but does have texture answers, the texture code should be used, and vice versa. Accurate coding of vista and texture is quite important, because each carries significantly different interpretive assumptions.

THE DIFFUSE SHADING DETERMINANT

A frequent use of the shading features of the blots is in a nonspecific, more general manner than is the case in either vista or texture answers. It is this type of shading response with which Rorschach concerned himself in developing the scoring of (*C*). The shading features may be used in this way as primary to the formation of a percept, or secondary to provide greater specification to a form answer. The coding for diffuse shading incorporates all shading answers which are neither vista nor texture.

Table 14. Examples of the Different Types of Texture and Vista Responses

Card	Location	Association	Inquiry	Coding
I	W	A dried up leaf	S: Pts r missing & fallg off & its crinkly E: Crinkly? S: It looks rough, the way the colors are there	FT
I	D4	A wm behind a curtain	S: U can't c all of her, just the lowr prt of her body (D3) & ths is like a curtain u can c thru	FV
I	W	An old torn rag w oil spots on it	S: Its all black and oily looking to me	TF
II	D4	A circumcised penis	S: U can c the folds left thr in the cntr	FV
II	D1	A teddy bear	S: It has that shape & it has all that fur there (rubs)	FT
II	DS5	Somethg deep, lik a hole mayb	S: U can c the round edges there, like a bottomless pit, it gets drkr as it goes dwn & I don't c any bottom	VF
III	D1	Two gentlemen in velvet suits	E: U mentioned velvet suits S: Yes, it looks velvet to me, dark shiny velvet	FT
III	D3	A bow tie	S: It has a big bulging knot there in the middl of it, the drk lines r lik bulges	FV
IV	W	Hunters boots prop'd up against a post	S: The post is behind them u can tell bec it looks further away E: Further away? S: Well u c where they come together the color is different like the post was further back	FV
IV	W	An old bearskin	S: It looks like the fur is pretty well worn, smooth (rubs)	FT
IV	Dd30	A red hot spike	S: Its a lot lighter on the outside like very hot metal	FT
V	W	A person in a fur cape	S: U c mostly the cape, it looks like fur to me (rubs fingers on card)	FT
V	W	It looks sticky if u touched it	S: Ugh, it just ll a sticky mess	T
V	W	The rite half is lower than the left	S: Thers a deep crack rite dwn the cntr, c the drkr prt, & it ll the rite side is lower	V
V	W	A rabbits head behnd a big rock	S: Its here (D6), u can't c much of it, just the outline, the drkr prt is the rock in frt	FV
VI	D1	An irrigation ditch	S: Its dwn in the cntr there, the shades help u to c how the diffrnt amounts of waterg have effected the land @ it	FV

Table 14 (Continued)

Card	Location	Association	Inquiry		Coding
VI	D4	A chunk of ice	S:	Its cold lookg like ice wld b, all diff colors of grey	TF
				Most of it ll the furry skin c the diff lines, & u can still c the head prt here (points)	
VI	∨Center Dd	A deep gorge	S:	Ths prt (D12) is the bttm & u can c the sides comg up to the top	VF
VII	>D2	A scotty dog	S:	He has more fur on his chin & ft legs, where its drkr	FT
VII	W	Rocks	S:	It just ll 4 rocks next to e.o., u can c that they r round, especially the bottom 2, thyr drkr at the bottom	VF
VII	Dd25	It ll a dam back in there	S:	Well the dam is here, ths liter prt (Dd25 ceter) & the frt prt is like the waterfall part, or mayb a river comg ths way	FV
VII	∨W	Hair, a lot of hair	S:	It all looks hairy to me (rubs)	T
VIII	D5	An aerial view of a forest	S:	Yeah, thes drkr prts wld be the bigger trees stckg up	VF
VIII	D2	Ice cream sherbet	S:	It looks grainy like sherbet is grainy	TF
IX	D6	Cotton candy, its al fluffy	S:	It has like rolls, like it was fluffy like cotton candy is fluffy	VF
IX	DS8	There's a plant inside a glass	S:	U can just c the stem (D5) & it looks hazy like u were seeg it inside the glass or bowl	FV
IX	DS8	Like u were lookg into a cave or s.t.	S·	It ll an opening & u can c back into it, its drkr there, like the cave mouth	VF
X	D9	Ths pink part ll a map of a chain of mts	S:	Its like a map that is used in schls or s.t. to show the way mts r formed, some r higher than others, the drkr areas	VF
X	D13	A piece of leather	S:	Its rough, like it hasn't been tanned	TF
			E:	Rough?	
			S:	U c the different colors there, they make it ll that	
X	D3	A maple seed	S:	The pods r a drkr color, like they r thicker, round like	FV

The Pure Shading Response (Y) The scoring of Y is used for percepts based exclusively on the light-dark features of the blot. No form is involved, and the content used typically has no form feature as in mist, fog, darkness, and smoke. A response in which pure Y is the only determinant is quite rare.

The Shading-Form Response (YF) The YF response is one in which the light-dark features of the blot are primary to the formation of the response and form is used secondarily for purposes of elaboration and/or clarification. The content of the YF answer ordinarily has an ambiguous or nonspecific form requirement as in clouds, shadows, nonspecific types of X-rays, and smoke associated with a specific form object such as "smoke coming out of this fire." The main factor that differentiates YF from pure Y is the intent of the subject to delineate form features, even though vague, in the response. Similarly, the YF response is usually differentiated from the FY answer by the lack of specificity or emphasis on form. Contents having a specific form requirement are rarely coded $YF,$ occurring only in those cases where the shading features are clearly of primary importance to the formation of the percept.

The Form-Shading Response (FY) The FY code is used for responses in which form characteristics are primary to the formation of the percept, and shading is used for purposes of specification and/or elaboration. Shadows associated with specific content, X-rays, and elaborations concerning characteristics of form specific objects, such as dirty face, are among the more commonly reported FY responses. Ordinarily, the FY response can be identified by the fact that the content could be given as a pure form response, whereas this is not usually the case in the YF or pure Y answer. A notable exception to this rule is the "cloud" response *which can be* based purely on form. When the shading features are associated with the cloud answer, the code is usually $YF,$ but in some instances, such as "cloudiness," may be pure $Y,$ and in other cases, where form is strongly emphasized, may be $FY.$

Some examples of the various types of diffuse shading responses are provided in Table 15. The Inquiry material included consists only of that related to the scoring decision. It is important to emphasize that, at times, the shading features of the blots are used as form contour. For example, the $D3$ area of Card I is sometimes perceived as the lower part of a person and delineated by "these dark lines." Similarly, a dark spot may be sometimes identified as an eye. These *are not* shading responses per se and should be scored as form answers. They do have interpretive importance because the subject has chosen to respond to the "internal" form features of the blot, but they should not be confused with the shading answer.

The Form-Dimension Response (FD) This is a new category, developed out of the research related to the formation of the Comprehensive System. There is no coding comparable to it in the other Rorschach systems, although both Beck and Klopfer have noted the existence of such answers. Klopfer had idiomatically included such responses in the FK category, even though no shading is involved. Beck has been prone to score these answers $FV,$ but only in instances where the unarticulated use of shading seems very probable. Beck specifically avoided the scoring of FV for perspective or dimensionality based on size discrimination.

The potential usefulness of a separate scoring for dimensional responses based exclusively on form was first noted during some System related research concerning the

Table 15. Examples of Diffuse Shading Responses

Card	Location	Association		Inquiry	Coding
I	W	An x-ray of a pelvis	S:	It's drk lik an xy & ll a pelvis	FY
I	<D8	A Xmas tree at night	S:	Its dark like it wld b at night	FY
I	W	Ink	S:	It's just all dark like ink is dark[a]	Y
II	D3	A very delicate bf	E:	U mentioned that it is delicate	FY
			S:	You can c the differnt colors, their shades I guess, in the wgs	
II	D4	A church steeple	S:	It looks like light is in the top, it's lighter there as if the sun was shining on it	FY
III	D7	Some sort of x-ray	S:	It is different colors like an an x-ray	YF
IV	W	Darkness	S:	It just ll darkness to me, I can't tell u why	Y
IV	D3	A multi-colored flower	S:	It has different colors in it, like the petals r a different color fr the middle part	FY
V	W	A piece of rotten meat	S:	Some of it is more rot'd than the rest	YF
			E:	More rotted?	
			S:	The colors r different	
VI	D2	A highly polished bedpost	S:	Its very shiny lookg	FY
VI	D4	It ll a sailing ship cruising in the nite	S:	Its all darkish so it must be in the nite	m[a].FY
VII	W	It could be clouds I guess	S:	Its pretty irregular like clouds would be & it has dark and lite color to it like clouds, mayb like cumulus clouds	FY
VII	W	Storm clouds	S:	They'r dark like a storm cloud formation is dark	YF
VII	D2	A granite statue	S:	Its dark like granite	FY
VIII	D1	An animal with dirt all over its face	S:	This drkr part is the circle around the eye like dirt, ther's more there too, more dirt	FY
IX	∨W	A lot of smoke and fire	S:	The orange part is the fire & the rest is the smoke, u can see how the colors go together	CF.YF
X	D11	Some bones that r drying out	S:	It ll bones drying up, ths prt is lighter so it must be drier	YF

[a] Had the subject indicated that it is *black* like ink the scoring would be *C'*.

meaningfulness of vista answers. This research, which is presented in detail in chapters on interpretation, included examination of 60 protocols obtained from subjects prior to suicide or a suicidal gesture. It was noted that a significant number of form determined dimensional-perspective responses occur in this group when compared with a nonpsychiatric group. A closer inspection of an additional 150 protocols revealed that the *FD* type of answer occurs with considerable frequency in the records of a variety of subjects, both psychiatric and nonpsychiatric. The number of *FD* answers is greater than the number of vista answers for most groups. When it is interpreted in the context of other information in the protocol, it appears related to factors such as introspectiveness and self-awareness.

The *FD* is for responses which include perspective or dimensionality based *exclusively* on form, interpreted by size or in relation to other blot areas. The most common *FD* is the Card IV human figure, seen as "leaning backward," or "lying down." The elaboration to this response usually includes mention that the "feet" portion is much larger; thus the head must be further away. Although the *FD* response occurs most frequently to Card IV, it has been noted in every card. In some answers, such as "leaning backward" on Card IV, another determinant is involved, but in most instances only the form features are used. Some examples of *FD* responses are provided in Table 16.

Many of the examples offered in Table 16 are of responses in which the dimensionality or perspective is based on the size of the blot area used. In other instances, the relationship between two blot areas creates the effect, wherein the "absence" of features is interpreted to support a percept of dimensionality or perspective. For example, the response to Card V, shown in Table 16, notes the leg of an animal is showing, whereas the larger portion of the blot is interpreted as a bush. The interpretation is of an animal jumping behind a bush because only the leg is obvious. Whether or not this is the same type of percept as "a person lying down" to Card IV is still open to investigation. At this time, it seems appropriate to code both responses as *FD* because both imply perspective.

PAIR AND REFLECTION RESPONSES

Another category incorporated in the Comprehensive System, which is not found in any of the other Rorschach systems, is related to the reflection response. This category, like the *FD* scoring, was discovered somewhat accidentally during an investigation regarding "acting out," which was conducted during 1966 and 1967. In that investigation, which included the collection of a large number of protocols from patients in an installation for the "criminally insane," it was noted that overt homosexuals and "psychopaths" tend to offer a significantly greater number of reflection responses than do other psychiatric subjects or nonpsychiatric subjects. Originally, these data were interpreted as an index of "narcissism" (Exner, 1969, 1970); however, because of the complexity of the concept narcissism, it seems more appropriate to use the concept of *egocentricity*. A sentence completion test, patterned after one developed by Watson (1965), was developed to study the characteristic of egocentricity in greater detail, and to relate those findings to the occurrence of reflection answers in the Rorschach. This work has confirmed a high correlation between a high "self-centeredness" score on the sentence completion blank and the reflection answer in the Rorschach. A variety of independent measures of egocentricity (or self-centeredness) has been used, and the results seem clearly to indicate that subjects who are highly egocentric or self-focusing tend to give significantly more

Table 16. Examples of Form-Dimensional Responses

Card	Location	Association		Inquiry	Coding
I	< D2	A tree off on a hill	S:	Its a lot smaller so it must be far off	FD
II	D4 + DS5	Some sort of temple at the end of a lake	S:	This (DS5) is the lake & here (D4) is the temple, u have to thk of it in perspective	FD
III	V Dd20	Two trees off on a hill with a path leading up to them	S:	These (D4) r the trees & this (D11) is the path	FD
			E:	U said off on a hill	
			S:	It doesn't hav to b a hill, its just that they'r small & the path is pretty wide so they r off a ways	
IV	W	A person laying down	S:	His feet r out in front, like toward me & his head is way bk there, like he was flat on his back	Mᵖ.FD
V	D4	An animal jumping behnd a bush, u only c his leg	S:	Well here is where the bush ends & ths is the leg so it has to be behind	FMᵃ.FD
VI	W	A religious statue on a hill-top	S:	Well its a lot smler so it wld b off in the distance like ths cld b a hill here if u stretch u'r immagin	FD
VII	Dd19	A city off in the distance	S:	U can c the bldgs there	FD
			E:	U said off in the distn.	
			S:	Its so small, it must b a long ways off	
VIII	D4	Two people stndg off on a hill	S:	U can c the people here (Dd24) & this wld b the hill	Mᵖ.FD
IX	< Dd26	A person stndg out on a ledge	S:	Yeah, here's a ledge (most of D3) & there's this person way out there, leaning up against a tree or s.t., its quite far out there	Mᵖ.FD
			E:	Quite far?	
			S:	He's so small, it's fairly hard to even see him	
X	V D6	Two men pushing s.t. out in front of them	S:	Their bodies r shaped like they were bending forward & their arms r extended outward like they were pushing this thing in front of them	Mᵃ.FD

reflection responses than do subjects who are not highly egocentric. These types of reflection answers are based *on the symmetry of the blot,* and are different from the extremely rare reflection answer that does not use symmetry. The nonsymmetrical reflection ordinarily involves shading, and thus is usually scored either *V* or *Y.*

Numerous studies have been completed to validate the usefulness of the sentence completion blank as an index of egocentricity (Exner, 1973) and to investigate the reflection answer in more detail. During the course of these investigations, which are described in detail in the chapters on interpretation, a second Rorschach phenomenon was discovered that appears to be related to the reflection answer. This is the *pair* response, in which the perceived object is reported as two identical objects because of the card symmetry. The pair type of response occurs with considerable frequency in most records, usually including about one-third of the responses. The pair frequency increases significantly in the more egocentric subjects and is almost nonexistent in the protocols of subjects who have little regard for themselves.

The selection of appropriate symbols to record the reflection and pair answers created some problem because, like the *FD* answer, they are based on the form of the blot, and yet the form is used somewhat differently than in selection of content. The symbol *r* seems a logical choice. The symbol selected for the pair response is the Arabic numeral 2. Because the pair answer occurs with considerable frequency, it was decided that the coding should be entered apart from the regular determinant scoring and in parentheses, so as to avoid "cluttering" the determinant code and also to make the number of pair answers easy to tabulate for the Structural Summary. There is only one coding for the pair answer (2), whereas two are used for different types of reflection answers.

The Reflection-Form Response (*rF*)   The *rF* is used for responses in which the symmetry features of the blot are primary in determining the answer, and form is used nonspecifically, or ambiguously, as an object being reflected. The *rF* type of reflection is very uncommon, and always involves content with nonspecific form requirements such as clouds, rocks, shadows, and rain. In some instances, the subject may select a content that is nonspecific in form requirements but provides sufficient articulation of the perceived object to warrant the scoring of *Fr* rather than *rF.* The most common example of this is when landscape is perceived as being reflected in a lake or pond. In almost all of these cases, the appropriate code is *Fr.*

The Form-Reflection Response (*Fr*)   *Fr* is for responses in which the form of the blot is used to identify specific content, which, in turn, is interpreted as reflected because of the symmetry of the blot. In many cases, movement is also associated with the reflection as in "a girl seeing herself in the mirror." The critical issue in coding either *rF* or *Fr* is that the subject *uses* the concept of reflection. This may be manifested directly through the use of the word *reflection* or it may be implied by other wording such as *mirror image,* and "seeing himself in the lake." The identification of "one on each side" or "there is two of them" is *not a reflection* answer and is coded simply as a pair response.

The Pair Response (2)   The symbol (2) is used whenever the symmetry features of the blot precipitate the report that "two" of the perceived object are present. The pair is independent of form specificity or the form quality used in the answer. The pair coding (2) *is not* used when the object is interpreted as being reflected, because the reflection code already denotes that two of the objects are being seen. The articulation of pairs

Table 17. Examples of Reflection and Pair Responses

Card	Location	Association		Inquiry	Coding
I	< D2	A couple of donkeys, there's one on each side			$F(2)$
I	D1	Two little birds who r peeking their heads out of a nest			$FM^p(2)$
II	< D6	A rabbit sliding on an ice pond, he's being reflected in the ice	S:	Ths white is the ice & u can c his reflection in it	$FM^a.Fr$
II	W	Two bears doing a circus act	S:	They have red hats on like a circus act & they have their paws touchg	$FM^a.FC(2)$
III	D1	Two people picking s.t. up			$M^a(2)$
III	D1	A person inspecting himself in the mirror	S:	He's bending forward like he's looking at himself	$M^p.Fr$
IV	< W	If u turn it ths way it ll a reflection of s.t., mayb a cloud	S:	Well all of ths on one side is being reflected here, its like a cloud I guess	$YF.rF$
			E:	I'm not sure how u c it as a cloud	
			S:	Well its all dark like a cld at nite. There's not much shape to it	
IV	D6	A pair of boots			$F(2)$
V	W	Two people laying back to back			$M^p(2)$
VI	> W	All of ths is the same down here	S:	I don't kno what it is, mayb rocks of s.t., it's the same on both sides like a reflection	rF
VI	< D1	It ll a submarine in the nite being reflected in the water	S:	Its all black like nitetime, u can c the conning tower & the hull & here its all reflected	$FC'.Fr$
VII	D2	Ths ll a little girl, there's one on each side			$F(2)$
VII	D2	A little girl looking in the mirror			$M^p.Fr$
VIII	D5	A pair of flags			$F(2)$
VIII	< W	An A crossing over some rocks or s.t. like in a creek, u can c his reflection there, he's looking down at it			$FM^a.Fr$
IX	< D5	Its like u r out in the water & u can c ths coastline off in the distance	S:	Well, its being reflected in the water, c here is the waterline (points to midline), its all so small it must b way off in the dist. U really can't make much out, mayb some trees or s.t. like that	$FD.rF$
IX	D3	Two halloween witches	S:	They r colored like for halloween, all orangish & they'r leaning back like they r laughing	$M^a.FC(2)$

Table 17 (Continued)

Card	Location	Association		Inquiry	Coding
X	D1	A couple of crabs	S:	There's one on each side, they'r the same on both sides	F (2)
X	D7	Deer, like they'r jumping	S:	One here & one here, they'r the same, w. their legs out-stretched like they were jumpg	FM^a (2)

varies considerably among subjects. Some will actually use the word *pair,* but more commonly the word *two* is used, and in many responses, the subject comments, "There is one here and one here." The pair code is used *only* when the symmetry is involved; thus clarification of the location areas used is important. It is not uncommon, for example, for a subject, looking at Card X, to report, "A couple of bugs." The response appears to be a pair, but the Inquiry reveals that the subject is using the upper D1 area as one bug, and the side D7 area as a second bug.

Some examples of pair and reflection responses are provided in Table 17. It will be noted that either the reflection or pair answers can occur in responses that have other determinants as well.

INTERSCORER AGREEMENT

The percentage of agreement among coders in the two reliability studies completed for this work, for each of the Determinant codes, and by category, is shown in Table 18.

As will be noted from examination of Table 18, the agreement levels in both studies are quite respectable for all variables. As might be expected, the greatest percentage of disagreement occurs in coding the *active-passive* dimension of movement. Most important, however, is the fact that when a total category is reviewed—that is, was texture coded, regardless of whether it was coded *FT, TF,* or *T,* or was chromatic color coded, regardless of whether the coding was *FC, CF,* or *C*—the agreements are very high. These data indicate that trained examiners, as were used in these studies, will generally apply the same coding to the same responses. Some will err, and some will disagree from time to time, but overall the levels of agreement fall well within acceptable limits for a task as complex as coding Rorschach determinants.

SUMMARY

The 26 symbols that are used for coding the nine determinant categories contribute much to the nucleus of the structural data of the Rorschach. None have exacting correlations with behavior or with personality characteristics, but collectively they are used to form a caricature of response styles and personality characteristics. There are still other features of the response that, when coded or scored accurately, add considerably to the structural data. Three of these are described in the next chapter.

Table 18.   Percentage of Coder Agreement for Two Reliability Studies

Variable	20 Coders 25 Records	15 Coders 20 Records
	% Agreement	% Agreement
M	96%	96%
FM	96%	98%
m	93%	95%
Movement coded	97%	98%
a	90%	91%
p	88%	89%
C or Cn	89%	91%
CF	90%	92%
C or CF	95%	96%
FC	97%	96%
Chromatic Color Coded	98%	99%
C'	98%	97%
C'F	91%	90%
FC'	94%	96%
Achromatic Color Coded	96%	95%
T	99%	99%
TF	96%	94%
FT	94%	91%
Texture Coded	97%	97%
V	—	99%
VF	98%	96%
FV	97%	95%
Vista Coded	99%	98%
Y	89%	90%
YF	87%	89%
FY	94%	92%
Diffuse Shading Coded	95%	97%
FD	97%	95%
rF	92%	94%
Fr	93%	93%
(2)	98%	99%
F	90%	91%

REFERENCES

Baughman, E. E. (1959) An experimental analysis of the relationship between stimulus structure and behavior on the Rorschach. *Journal of Projective Techniques, 23,* 134–183.

Beck, S. J. (1937) *Introduction to the Rorschach Method: A Manual of Personality Study.* American Orthopsychiatric Association Monograph, No. 1.

Beck, S. J. (1944) *Rorschach's Test: Basic Processes.* New York: Grune & Stratton.

Beck, S. J., Beck, A. G., Levitt, E. E., and Molish, H. B. (1961) *Rorschach's Test. I: Basic Processes.* (3rd Ed.) New York: Grune & Stratton.

Binder, H. (1932) Die Helldunkeldeutungen im psychodiagnostischen experiment von Rorschach. *Schweizer Archiv fur Neurologie und Psychiatrie.* **30,** 1–67, 232–286.

Campo, V., and de de Santos, D. R. (1971) A critical review of the shading responses in the Rorschach I: Scoring problems. *Journal of Personality Assessment,* **35,** 3–21.

Ellenberger, H. (1954) The life and work of Hermann Rorschach. *Bulletin of the Menninger Clinic,* **18,** 173–219.

Exner, J. E. (1961) Achromatic color in Cards IV and VI of the Rorschach. *Journal of Projective Techniques,* **25,** 38–40.

Exner, J. E. (1969) *The Rorschach Systems.* New York: Grune & Stratton.

Exner, J. E. (1969) Rorschach responses as an index of narcissism. *Journal of Projective Techniques and Personality Assessment,* **33,** 324–330.

Exner, J. E. (1970) Rorschach manifestations of narcissism. *Rorschachiana,* **IX,** 449–456.

Exner, J. E. (1973) The self focus sentence completion: A study of egocentricity. *Journal of Personality Assessment,* **37,** 437–455.

Exner, J. E. (1978) *The Rorschach: A Comprehensive System. Volume 2: Current research and advanced interpretation.* New York: Wiley.

Hertz, M. R. (1942) *Frequency Tables for Scoring Rorschach Responses.* Cleveland, Ohio: The Press of Western Reserve University.

Hertz, M. R. (1951) *Frequency Tables for Scoring Rorschach Responses.* (3rd Ed.) Cleveland, Ohio: The Press of Western Reserve University.

Hertz, M. R. (1970) *Frequency Tables for Scoring Rorschach Responses.* (5th Ed.) Cleveland, Ohio: The Press of Case Western Reserve University.

Klopfer, B., and Sender, S. (1936) A system of refined scoring symbols. *Rorschach Research Exchange,* **1,** 19–22.

Klopfer, B. (1937) The shading responses. *Rorschach Research Exchange,* **2,** 76–79.

Klopfer, B., and Miale, F. (1938) An illustration of the technique of the Rorschach: The case of Anne T. *Rorschach Research Exchange,* **2,** 126–152.

Klopfer, B., and Kelley, D. (1942) *The Rorschach Technique.* Yonkers-on-Hudson, N.Y.: World Book.

Klopfer, B., Ainsworth, M., Klopfer, W., and Holt, R. (1954) *Developments in the Rorschach Technique. I: Theory and Technique.* Yonkers-on-Hudson, N.Y.: World Book.

Piotrowski, Z. (1936) On the Rorschach method and its application in organic disturbances of the central nervous system. *Rorschach Research Exchange,* **1,** 148–157.

Piotrowski, Z. (1947) A Rorschach compendium. *Psychiatric Quarterly,* **21,** 79–101.

Piotrowski, Z. (1957) *Perceptanalysis.* New York: Macmillan.

Piotrowski, Z. (1960) The movement score. In M. Rickers-Ovsiankina (ed.) *Rorschach Psychology.* New York: Wiley.

Rapaport, D., Gill, M., and Schafer, R. (1946) *Diagnostic Psychological Testing.* Vol. 2. Chicago: Yearbook Publishers.

Rorschach, H. (1921) *Psychodiagnostik.* Bern: Bircher.

Rorschach, H., and Oberholzer, E. (1923) The application of the form interpretation test. *Zeitschrift fur die Gesamte Neurologie und Psychiatrie,* **82.**

Watson, A. (1965) Objects and objectivity: A study in the relationship between narcissism and intellectual subjectivity. Unpublished Ph.D. Dissertation, University of Chicago.

CHAPTER 7

Blends, Organizational Activity, and Form Quality

Three very important elements, for which all Rorschach responses must be evaluated, are (1) the blend, wherein two or more determinants have been used in an answer; (2) the organizational activity, which represents those responses in which some synthesis of the blot stimuli has occurred; and (3) the form quality, which is an evaluation of the "fitness" of the blot features to the object described. Each of these response characteristics carries considerable interpretive significance, especially because they are *not common* to all responses. A modest proportion of the answers in most records have multiple determinants. Similarly, it is unusual to find a large proportion of the responses marked by the synthesis features of organizational activity. Conversely, most responses will be evaluated for form quality. These response features yield important data concerning the idiographic dimensions of the subject; thus accurate evaluation of responses for their presence is vital.

THE BLEND RESPONSE (.)

The term *blend* signifies that more than one determinant has been used in the formulation of a response. When this occurs, each determinant should be entered, separated from each other by a dot (.), as in *M.YF,* which represents the answer containing both human movement and a shading-form component. The frequency of blend responses varies considerably from record to record. A sample of 2000 protocols, for example, shows that slightly more than 20% of the responses are blends, but the variance is considerable, with some records yielding more than 50% blends and others containing no blend answers. Any combination of determinants is theoretically possible in a response, and each should be scored. The majority of blend answers contain two determinants, but in unusual instances three, and even four, separate determinants may occur.

There has been some disagreement among Rorschach systematizers concerning the appropriate method for scoring and evaluating the blend answer. Most have followed Rorschach's lead in the scoring procedure. He simply scored multiple determinants together when they occurred, as in *MC* (1921). The protocols published by Rorschach contain relatively few blend responses, mainly because his basic work was accomplished using blots which contained no shading features. Klopfer (1942, 1954) deviated most from Rorschach's approach to the multiple determined responses. He postulated that only one determinant can be "primary" to the formation of a percept, and subdivided the "Main" or primary determinant, from other determinants, coded as "Additional." Accordingly, Klopfer weighs the interpretive importance of the Main determinants differently than Additionals. This procedure is possibly one of the major limitations to the Klopfer system, and is compounded by the fact that a somewhat arbitrary "hierarchical" scheme is used to distinguish Main from Additional determinants in answers where the relative importance is not clear; M is given preference, with chromatic color, texture, and achromatic color ranked in that order of importance. Klopfer did not begin his Rorschach system with the Main-Additional distinction. He originally followed Rorschach's technique of entering multiple scores but, as his recommended technique of Inquiry became more elaborate, and as the number of scoring categories was proliferated, he perceived the fact that large numbers of multiple determinant scores would create much difficulty in interpretation. In addition, he became convinced that determinants relevant only to a part of a concept, or those given somewhat reluctantly in the Inquiry, were not as important to the "basic" personality as the "primary" determinant. By this time (1938), he began scoring some of the "questionable" determinants as Additional, although he continued to use multiple determinant scores where the issue seemed clear. Subsequently, he decided that it was impractical to expect all scorers to be consistent in these decisions and by the time his first text on the Rorschach was published (1942), he had settled on the principle of giving only one score for the Main determinant.[1]

The other systematizers differ only slightly from each other, and from Rorschach, in scoring multiple determined answers. Beck (1937) introduced the use of the dot (.), as a convenient method of identifying and tabulating the blend response. In each of the systems except Klopfer's, all determinants are given equal weight in forming interpretive postulates.

The decision to include the Blend in the Comprehensive System is based on two elements. First, four of the five Rorschach systems endorse this approach. Second, and more important, is a series of three studies completed to gather more data concerning the multiple determinant answer. The first of the three was designed to evaluate the relationship of the multiple determinant response to intelligence. The protocols of 43 nonpsychiatric subjects, for whom Otis Intelligence Test scores were also available, were rescored using the Comprehensive System by one of three scorers. These subjects were selected because the I.Q. scores manifest a considerable range, 84 to 122, with a median of 103. The Rorschach protocols were divided on the basis of an I.Q. median split, with the midranking protocol discarded, thus creating two groups of 21 each. The mean I.Q. for the upper half is 113.4, and for the lower half 93.7. The number of blend responses was tallied for each protocol and the data subjected to chi-square analysis, which indicates that subjects in the upper half give significantly more blend answers than do subjects in the lower half. In fact, 17 of the 21 protocols of subjects in the upper half contain at least one blend, whereas only eight of the 21 protocols in the lower half contain at least one blend. The number of blends in a given protocol does not correlate highly with I.Q. ($r = .32$), but the tendency to give a blend answer apparently does require at least average intellectual ability. In view of these findings, a second study was undertaken using 28 psychiatric out-patients for whom WAIS I.Q. scores were also available. These I.Q.'s ranged from 97 to 132, with a median of 110. Using the same procedure of a median split and tallying the number of blend answers for upper and lower half, the resulting chi-square *was not* significant. Twelve of the subjects in the upper half gave blend answers,

---

[1]In a private interview in 1965 at Asilomar, California, Klopfer expressed some regret concerning that decision. He alluded to the fact that the interpreter, relying "too heavily" on the psychogram, could be misled in some instances. He maintained, however, the belief that the Main-Additional dichotomy in determinant scoring did, in fact, preclude the interpreter from "overemphasis" of determinant scores which might be developed in the inquiry.

whereas 10 of the 14 protocols in the lower group contained blends. An interesting by-product of these two investigations is the fact that the psychiatric group tended to give proportionally more blends per protocol than did the subjects in the upper half of the nonpsychiatric group (31% versus 19%). This finding generated a third study, using two protocols from each of 21 "neurotic" outpatients. The first protocol from each subject was collected at the onset of intervention, whereas the second was taken at intervention termination, which varied from 9 to 17 months later. A comparison of the pre- and post-treatment protocols for total number of blends *is not* significantly different, although there is a tendency toward decrease. Conversely, when the actual number of pre- and posttreatment records containing blend answers is compared, a significant difference is discovered. Twenty of the 21 pretreatment protocols contain blend responses as contrasted with 13 of the 21 posttreatment records. It is possibly of even greater interest to note that the kinds of determinants used in the blend answers change substantially when the pre-and posttreatment records are compared, the former containing more shading blends, and more determinants in which form is secondary such as *CF* and *TF.* The latter records yield fewer shading blends, more *FD* type determinants, and more determinants in which form is primary. These data appear to indicate that the blend, although somewhat related to intellect, is very possibly a useful index of the complexity of the subject's psychological process. This interpretation is generally consistent with Beck's hypothesis concerning the blend (1944, 1961), and argues for a method of coding multiple determinant answers which gives equal weight to each of the determinants involved. The Beck procedure has been incorporated into the Comprehensive System.

The symbols entered in the blend *are the same* as would be used if any of the determinants were scored separately. Some examples of blend responses are shown in Table 19.

The majority of blend responses involve complex answers, and typically, but not always, the whole blot or a large segment of it is used. The coding of *F* (pure Form) in a blend is *extremely rare.* A review of nearly 15,000 protocols in the pool at the Rorschach Research Foundation yields only 26 such responses. Almost all are in records collected from neurologically impaired or intellectually limited subjects. They are responses in which two or more separate contents are identified, at least one of which is based exclusively on form, *and which is not reported in relation to the other(s).* These responses occur with the greatest frequency to Card III, such as "There are two people, and a butterfly, and they are picking something up." The answer sounds like two responses, people picking something up as one, and the butterfly as the second, and if the subject does not distinguish them as separate answers in the Inquiry, or organize them meaningfully (it's flying between them), the examiner should ask, *"Did you mean that all as one answer?"* If the subject answers, "yes," and still fails to integrate the objects reported, the *F* should be included in the blend with the other determinant. In this example, the coding will be $M^a.F$. These responses indicate a significant cognitive dysfunction in either processing or mediating the stimulus field. Any examiner deciding to code an *F* in a blend should review the responses very carefully, because they are extremely unusual and interpretively quite significant.

Most blends containing multiple objects will include a proximate and/or meaningful relation between the objects as in, "a woman standing with smoke all around her" to Card I. In this response, both proximity and direct relationship are present. Here the coding is $M^p.YF$, and if the response had been "a woman with smoke all around her," with no inference of movement offered in the response or spontaneously in the Inquiry, the coding would be simply *YF.*

Table 19. Examples of Blend Responses

Card	Location	Response		Inquiry	Coding
I	W	A wm stndg in the cntr w her arms raised w a lot of smk around her	E:	(Rpts S's resp)	M^p.YF
			S:	Rite here, ths r her arms & ths is her body & all ths (points to each side) is all dark & hazy like smoke	
II	W	Two bears fitg, they'v got ther paws togethr & ther's bld on ther heads & feet	E:	(Rpts S's resp)	FM^a.CF
			S:	C, heads, paws, bodies, feet & the red ll bld	
III	W	Ths ll 2 butlers bowing to e.o.	E:	(Rpts S's resp)	M^a.FC.FC'
			S:	Its like at a party, thes r ss of red decorations & ths r the butlers in their formal suits sort of bending frwd like they were bowing	
			E:	Format Suits?	
			S:	Yes, they r black, like a tuxedo.	
			E:	U said red decorations?	
			S:	Yeah, just som red thgs	
IV	∨ W	Ths ll a snake or a worm crawling out from in under a leaf	E:	(Rpts S's resp)	FM^a.FY.C'F.FD
			S:	Well u can just c the head, I thk its a snake bec it has the different markgs on it	
			E:	And the leaf?	
			S:	Yeah, all the rest of it ll a leaf, its dead and dried up	
			E:	Dead & dried up?	
			S:	Yeah, its all black like dead leaves get after a while	
			E:	U said it was crawling out from in under the leaf	
			S:	Yeah, the way it is there he must be under it bec u can only c the head	
IV	W	A guy sitting on a stump in a fur coat, like an old raccoon coat	E:	(Rpts S's resp)	M^p.FT.FD
			S:	He's leaning backward, like he was laughg or s.t., c heres the feets, big feets & his head & little arms	
			E:	U mentioned a fur coat, like an old raccoon coat	
			S:	Yeah, it looks all furry to me (rubs card)	
VI	D1	Its a deep gorge with a river I guess, it must b cause it overflowd not too long ago	E:	(Rpts S's resp)	FV.YF
			S:	This cntr looks really deep, c how dark it is & yet all the land around it looks differnt colors like it was partly water	

Table 19 (Continued)

Card	Location	Response		Inquiry	Coding
VII	D2	A cpl of kids w mud or dirt on their faces like they r makg faces at e.o.	E:	(Rpts S's resp)	MP.FY
			S:	U just c the upper part of 'em, 2 little girls I guess stickg their lips out like makg a face	
			E:	U mentioned that they hav mud or dirt on their faces	
			S:	Its all dark like dried mud or dirt wld b	
VIII	D2	Down here it ll some strawberry & orange Italian ices	E:	(Rpts S's resp)	CF.TF
			S:	See here is the pink like strawberry & the orange	
			E:	U said they ll ices	
			S:	Rite, I did. They look icy to me, not like real ice cream, more like ice chips, the different colors in there make them look icy, colder	
IX	VW	Wow, an explosion w a lot of fire & smoke	E:	(Rpts S's resp)	m^a.CF.YF
			S:	Yeah, its all shootg up & u c the fire here, its orange & all ths green ll the smoke	
			E:	I'm not sure why it ll smoke	
			S:	Well u c how the diff colors come togethr, like fire & smoke all mixed together	
X	D9	Ths ll bld thats dryg	E:	(Rpts S's resp)	m^p.C.Y.
			S:	Well its red lik blood o.k., there's no question about that & u can tell that its drying because these outside parts r darker	

One further scoring caution concerning the blend answer seems important, particularly for the novice. This concerns the shading determined responses. The light-dark features of the blot, when used to delineate a feature of a percept, are usually perceived as only one of the three types of shading. Responses containing multiple shading determinants are quite unusual and, when they do occur, a vista component is frequently involved. When shading blends occur, they are identifiable by the fact that different contents, or different characteristics of a single content, are articulated, for example, "muddy fields on each side of a deep gorge" (Card VI). In this response two contents, muddy fields and deep gorge, are offered, each of which includes a shading determinant, yielding a coding of YF.FV. Obviously, the possibilities exist for any combination of shading determinants to be given in a single response so that blends such as FV.FY, V.T, FT.YF, or even YF.TF.VF are noted occasionally. It is quite important, however, that the coder not confuse the shading blend with the sometimes complex articulation of a single shading determinant; for instance: "These dark differences in the shading make it look bumpy, like velvet. Its all very soft looking like it is the soft folds in a blanket" (Card IV). Even though the articulation is complex, including words relevant to each of the three types of shading (dark differences, bumpy like velvet, soft looking), the content is essentially singular and only one use of the shading is manifest. Thus the response is scored only once, for texture. A similar response is, in fact, a shading blend: "This looks like a piece of material, something very fuzzy, that has been bunched together, like it was pleated, these lines here are the folds." The Inquiry to this answer confirms that the subject perceived both texture ("It seems fuzzy bec of the diff colors") and vista ("the dark lines ll folds") and the scoring is *TF.VF.*

ORGANIZATIONAL ACTIVITY (Z)

The scoring for organizational activity has been one of the most neglected of the Rorschach components. At least three factors appear to contribute to the general lack of interest among Rorschachers in this type of scoring. First, the systems differ considerably in approaching this feature. Beck was the first to introduce an organizational score (1933), using a scheme of weighing organized responses depending on the type of organization and the complexity of the stimuli involved (Z score). Hertz used a method in which all organized responses are weighed equally (g score, 1940), whereas Klopfer (1944) included some recognition of organizational activity in his Form Level Rating but also included other elements in this score; thus it does not represent organizational activity per se. The other systems do not include a formal scoring for organization activity, nor did Rorschach, although he appears to have offered some description of the process in his discussion of *Assoziationsbetrieb*. Second, most of the literature concerning a scoring for organizational activity focuses on the Beck Z score, the procedure for which sometimes appears to be much more complicated than is actually the case. Third, and possibly most important, is the *misconception* that the clinical utility of a scoring for organizational activity is centered mainly on estimates of I.Q. Unfortunately, Beck's own words, "These totals (ZSums) vary directly as the intelligence of *S*," (1945), plus the fact that a considerable segment of the research on organizational activity scores has concerned the relationship to intelligence test performance, seems to have encouraged this misconception.

There is no question but that organizational activity scores, whether weighed as in Beck or unweighed as in Hertz, do correlate positively with some components of intelligence testing. A variety of positive correlations have been reported for both types of scoring, some of which are statistically significant well beyond the .01 level. Wishner (1948) reports a .536 correlation between Wechsler-Bellevue I.Q. and the weighted Z score. Sisson and Taulbee (1955) obtained correlations of .43 and .52 between Wechsler I.Q. and weighted and unweighted ZSums, respectively. Blatt (1953) found correlations of .49 and .46 between weighted ZSums and the verbal and reasoning sections of the Primary Mental Abilities Test. The Wishner findings seem especially important to understanding the kind of relation that seems to exist between organizational activity and intellect. He reports correlations for each of the individual subtests in the Wechsler-Bellevue, including data both for the regular weighed Z scores and using a method that eliminates Z scores for the so-called unorganized Whole answers such as the Bat response on Cards I and V. The standard Beck ZSum correlates significantly with two verbal subtests (vocabulary .605 and information .365) and two performance subtests (picture completion .346 and digit symbol .308) with other correlations ranging as low as .102 for block design. The modified ZSum correlates quite differently with the Wechsler subtests, ranging from a high of .306 for similarities to −.059 for object assembly.

In other words, these data seem to suggest that the weighted method of assigning Z scores, as used by Beck, does correlate significantly with some types of intellectual operations but not with others. Even this issue is cast in some doubt when it is noted that Wishner's data are collected from only 42 psychiatric (neurotic) cases. Hertz (1960) has reported substantially lower correlations between the Beck ZSum and Otis I.Q. (.174) and Stanford-Binet M.A. (.113) for 12-year-olds. She also reports low positive correlations between her g score and I.Q. and M.A. (.256 and .249). At the lower end of the intellectual spectrum, Jolles (1947), using "feebleminded" subjects, found correlations of .08 between weighted ZSum and Binet I.Q. and .15 with Wechsler I.Q. Kropp (1955), in reviewing most of the studies on the Z score, concluded that it relates highly to W, and to M, but that it does not relate to intelligence as operationally defined by intelligence tests.

Obviously, intelligence appears to have some relationship to organizational activity, but this relationship apparently varies with certain response styles, a variation which is especially notable in some instances of psychopathology. Schmidt and Fonda (1953) have shown that Z scores are significantly higher in manics than in schizophrenics. Varvel (1941) and Hertz (1948) both report lower levels of organizational activity in depressed patients, whereas Beck (1952) and Molish (1955) find high organizational activity in patients prone to "project conflicts" in a systematized delusional operation. It would seem that intelligence is prerequisite to organizational activity, but other factors influence the frequency and characteristics of the organizing activity.

The variety of empirical data seems to argue in favor of including some form of organizational activity scoring in the Comprehensive System. A major question appears to be whether such a scoring should include weighing different kinds of responses as suggested by Beck, or considering all organized responses equally as purported by Hertz. An interesting work, published by Wilson and Blake (1950), appears to support the Hertz approach. They correlated Z scores, as weighed in the Beck method, using a count of one for each organized response, with the weighed ZSums for 104 subjects, and derived a .989 correlation. However, the Wilson and Blake sample included 81 "normals" and only 23 psychiatric cases of which only eight were psychotic. The sample limitations in their study appeared to suggest that a larger psychiatric group would be worthwhile to study. In this context, two groups of 60 protocols each were randomly selected from the protocol pool, one representing nonpsychiatric subjects and the second a psychiatric group comprised of 26 schizophrenics and 34 nonschizophrenics. Each of the protocols was rescored using the Beck weighted Z score method and also with the Wilson-Blake method of assigning a value of 1 to each response manifesting organizational activity. The correlation for the "normal group" was consistent with the Wilson-Blake findings, .984; however, the correlation for the psychiatric group was considerably lower, .708. A closer examination of the data from the group of psychiatric protocols revealed that in approximately 25% of the cases, the sum of Z differed from the Wilson-Blake estimated sum of Z by four or more points. In fact, using an arbitrary cutoff value for a difference score (d) of 3.0, nearly one-third (32%) of the psychiatric group is identified, whereas only two of the "normal" subjects fall in this range.

Following the discovery that the Wilson and Blake table of estimated ZSums is significantly less accurate in predicting the actual ZSum for psychiatric subjects than for nonpatients, a series of studies concerning this issue have been completed at the Rorschach Research Foundation (Exner, 1978). The findings from these studies indicate that those subjects with a ZSum greater than +3.0, or less than −3.0 from the estimated ZSum (Zest), derived from the Wilson and Blake table, do exhibit markedly different features in scanning and/or processing visual or auditory information. The former exert much more effort in processing and tend to be overly thorough and cautious, whereas the latter are often hasty and negligent in the scanning effort. In view of these findings, the Beck method of assigning weights for responses that are marked by organizational activity has been incorporated into the Comprehensive System.

A Z score is assigned to any response that *includes form and meets at least* one of the following criteria: (1) it is a W response that has a *DQ* coding of +, v/+, or o (answers that are Wv are not assigned a Z score); (2) it is a response that *meaningfully* integrates two or more adjacent detail areas; (3) it is a response that *meaningfully* integrates two or more nonadjacent detail areas; or (4) it is a response in which white space is *meaningfully* integrated with other details of the blot. Form *must always* be involved to score Z; thus pure C, T, Y, or V answers *are never scored Z.*

The specific Z score assigned to an organized response will depend on which of the scoring criteria have been met, and to which card the response has been given. The weighted Z values for each of the four types of organizational activity are shown, by card, in Table 20.

Whenever a response meets *two or more* of the criteria for scoring Z, the higher of the values is assigned. For example, a W response to Card I is ordinarily assigned a Z score of 1.0; however, if the whole blot is used in a manner so that adjacent detail areas are specifically organized as in "a woman standing in the center with two creatures dancing around her," the value of 4.0 (Adjacent Detail weighted score) would be assigned.

The issue of meaningfulness of organization in responses is critically important to the decision to score Z, in both whole and detail responses. It should be obvious that the component parts of the blot used in the response are related to each other in some meaningful way. For instance, "two figures, pointing in different directions" on Card VII is not scored Z, because the response does not manifest any *meaningful* relationship. The same two figures, ". . . arguing about which way to go," is scored Z in that a meaningful relation does obviously exist. Some examples of organizational activity scores are provided in Table 21. Inquiries are included only where they are relevant to the decision concerning the Z score.

Table 20.   Organizational (Z) Values for Each of the Ten Cards

Card	Type of Organizational Activity			
	W (*DQ*+, v/+, o)	Adjacent Detail	Distant Detail	White Space with Detail
I	1.0	4.0	6.0	3.5
II	4.5	3.0	5.5	4.5
III	5.5	3.0	4.0	4.5
IV	2.0	4.0	3.5	5.0
V	1.0	2.5	5.0	4.0
VI	2.5	2.5	6.0	6.5
VII	2.5	1.0	3.0	4.0
VIII	4.5	3.0	3.0	4.0
IX	5.5	2.5	4.5	5.0
X	5.5	4.0	4.5	6.0

Source: This table is taken from Beck, S. J., Beck, A., Levitt, E., and Molish, H. *Rorschach's Test,* Vol. 1. New York: Grune & Stratton, 1961. Those familiar with the Beck system will note that Beck's special z scoring for W with Adjacent Detail, which Beck uses for some responses to Cards III, VI, and VII, has been omitted in preference for criteria that are consistent across all cards.

Table 21. Examples of Z Score Assignment for Responses to Each of the 10 Rorschach Cards

Card	Response	Inquiry	Z Scoring
I	A bat	(Confirms W)	1.0
I	A halloween mask	S: The white parts are the eyes & mouth so the rest is a mask	3.5
I	A dead leaf lying on the snow	S: U can c the snow thru the holes in the leaf	3.5
I	Two big birds, thy'r lookg at a couple of mountains off in the distance ($D2$ = Birds; $Dd22$ = Mountains)		6.0
II	Two clowns kicking e.o.	[The lower ($D3$) area represents the kick]	4.5
II	Two dogs rubbing noses		3.0
II	A rocket ship taking off w the fire coming out	(Confirms $DS5 + D4$ is rocket, $D3$ is flame)	4.5
II	Two hens getting ready to fite, lik fiting cocks	($D2$)	5.5
III	Two witches brewing s.t. in their den w trophies hung all over	(W)	5.5
III	Two wm pickg up a basket	($D1$)	3.0
III	Two wm looking at e.o.	($D9$ only, $D7$ not includ)	4.0
IV	A big giant sitting on a stump	($D1$ is stump)	4.0
IV	A bear hide	(W)	2.0
IV	∨Two witches arguing w e.o.	($Dd26$)	3.5
IV	∨Like Hansel & Gretel taking a bite off a candy tree	($DdS24$ are Hansel & Gretel, $D1$ is the candy tree)	5.0[a]
V	A butterfly	(W)	1.0
V	An alligator's head, there's one on each side		No Z score
VI	Ths ll a totem pole sitting high up on a mountain	($D3$ is totem, the rest of the card is the mt)	2.5
VI	I c a submarine being reflectd	($D4$ is the submarine)	2.5
VI	∨There r 2 littl birds in a nest	($Dd28$)	2.5
VI	∨There r 2 birds calling to e.o.	($Dd21$)	6.0
VI	Ths whole thg cld b an island	(W)	No Z score[b]
VII	Two wm smiling at e.o.	($D1$)	3.0
VII	Two wm talkg to e.o. standg behind ths rock	(W, $D2$ are wm, $D4$ is rock)	1.0
VII	∨Two can-can dancers	S: Their heads r almost touchg here & u can only c one leg bec the other is kicked out	3.0[c]
VII	A mountain range and a lake	S: Ths white part ($DS7$) is the lake & the rest r mountains, like u were lookg thru them to see the lake down below	4.0
VIII	Two rats climbing up a garbage heap of s.s.	(W)	4.5
VIII	Two animals, one on each side		No Z score

148

Table 21 (Continued)

Card	Response	Inquiry	Z Scoring
VIII	A bear climbing a tree	(*D*1 is a bear, *D*4 is tree)	3.0
VIII	∨A milk bottle balanced on a log	(Center small white space is milk bottle, *D*5 is the log)	4.0
VIII	Somebody splattered paint here	(*W*) Names colors	No *Z* score[d]
IX	∨The whole thg ll an atomic explosion	(*W*, with *D*6 being the cloud, the green area being smoke, & the orange area being fire)	5.5
IX	A man playing a saxaphone	(*D*1, with the man being the major portion of the area used and the saxaphone the remaining part):	2.5[e]
IX	Two witches having a good joke together	(*D*3) *S*: They are leaning backward as if they are laughing about a joke	4.5
IX	Like an explosion on the sun where gas is shot off	(Top of *D*8 is sun, *Dd*25 is the gas shooting off) *S*: U can c the space in between the sun and where the gas rises (*DdS*32)	5.0
X	An artist's abstract, its symmetrical with each pair of object having a special significance	(*W*)	5.5
X	A lot of paint, like s.b. thru alot of paint on it	(*W*)	No *Z* score[f]
X	A fraternity paddle	(*D*11 is the handle, upper *DdS*30 is the paddle, *D*3 is a design on on the paddle)	6.0
X	Two dogs, they'r each sitg up	(*D*2)	No *Z* score
X	Two dogs, they'r both sitg w their heads raised as if they r howling at the moon	(*D*2)	4.5
X	Two creatures trying to climb a pole	(*D*8 are animals, *D*14 is the pole)	4.0
X	A lot of undersea things, I c 2 crabs and 2 lobsters & 2 fish:	(*D*1 are crabs, *D*7 are lobsters, *D*13 are fish)	No *Z* score[g]

[a] Hansel and Gretel alone would be assigned the value for distant detail (3.5); however, the fact that they are related meaningfully to the "candy tree" requires the value of 5.0 (space integrated with detail).

[b] The Developmental Quality coding for a nonspecific island will be *v*. *Wv* responses are not assigned a Z score.

[c] The *Z* value for distant detail is assigned here because the figures are not perceived as adjacent even though the portions of the blot used actually do touch.

[d] No *Z* score is assigned as no basic form is used.

[e] This is an example of an organizational activity which involves a break-up and synthesis of a single *D* area. In this instance the *Z* value for "adjacent detail" is assigned.

[f] In the first example to Card X the response clearly includes reference to meaningful relationships of the component detail. In the second example no such reference occurs.

[g] This response, although similar in basic content to *W* responses of "an underwater scene" which would have a *Z* score of 5.5, is essentially three separate detail responses. The whole blot is not used nor is there any indication of a meaningful synthesis of the pairs of "undersea things" identified.

An accurate scoring of organizational activity in the Rorschach protocol, both in terms of frequency of Z and the sum of Z scores, can provide very useful data from which some aspects of cognitive activity can be evaluated.

FORM QUALITY

The issue of "goodness of fit" of the response to the area of the blot used was, during the time of the Rorschach's development, a major point of contention. Each of the systematizers has agreed that form quality or "fit" is one of the most important of the "quantifiable" elements of the test. They have also generally agreed that responses can be differentiated into two basic categories—those with good form and those with poor form. This is consistent with Rorschach's recommendation. Beyond these two basic points of agreement, the systematizers differ concerning the "best" method of evaluating the appropriateness of the form used in the response. Beck et al. (1961) and Hertz (1970) followed Rorschach's suggestions most closely. They, like Rorschach, used the symbol + for good form answers, and the symbol − for poor form answers. The assignment of the plus or minus symbols is, essentially, based on the statistical frequency with which any given type of response occurs to specific location areas.

Kinder, Brubaker, Ingram, and Reading (1982) have traced the development of Beck's decisions concerning the assignment of the + and − symbols, and suggest that many of Beck's decisions were more subjectively based than may have been implied in Beck's description of his work. Both Beck and Hertz have published elaborate tables, by card and location areas, to define which responses are + and which are −. The two differ in that they do not always use the same location areas, but Hertz has reported a relatively high agreement level between her table and that of Beck.

Piotrowski (1957) and Rapaport both endorse the concept of using statistical frequencies to determine the adequacy of form fit, but neither has developed frequency distributions for use. In Klopfer's early work he also used the symbols + and −, but he was generally opposed to statistical frequency as a determining criterion. Rather, he preferred to defend the appropriateness of the subjective evaluation of the examiner in determining the goodness of form fit of the response. Ultimately, he discarded the plus-minus symbols in favor of a Form Level Rating (Klopfer & Davidson, 1944).

Early in the development of the Comprehensive System it was decided that decisions concerning form quality should be based on an empirical approach to insure intercoder reliability, and to maintain a consistency in evaluating form fit that could be subject to a variety of validation studies. A method based on statistical frequency, such as that of Beck and Hertz, has broad applicability and appears to be effective in assuring high interscorer reliability. This seems especially important in that the proportion of good and poor form answers in a protocol is often an important clue in some differential diagnoses (Weiner, 1966). Statistical frequency methods are, however, somewhat limited by the fact that all + responses are not of equal quality, nor are all − answers equally poor in form fit. Rapaport (1946) noted this in his work, and suggested that form quality might be differentiated into six categories (plus, ordinary, vague, minus, special plus, and special minus). Rapaport argued that such a differentiation of form quality would provide a clearer understanding of the "reality testing" operations of the subject.

Mayman (1966, 1970), following from Rapaport's suggestion, developed a method of evaluating form quality which has six categories ranging from exceptionally good form to exceptionally poor form. The categories and criterion for each are as follows:

$F+$ (highest level):   Representing a successful combination of imagination and reality congruence.

Fo (ordinary level):   Representing the obvious, easily noticed answers, requiring little or no creative effort. This category includes almost all responses that would be considered commonplace.

Fw (weak level):   Representing a significant shift away from the reality adherence characteristic of the $F+$ or Fo answers. Mayman suggests that some Fw answers border on the adequate (scored $Fw+$) when the general contours do not clash with the answer, whereas other Fw answers are less than adequate (scored $Fw-$) when some of the blot area used makes the form fit somewhat incongruous.

Fv (vague level):   Representing answers in which the content avoids the necessity of specific shape.

Fs (spoiled level):   Representing an essentially adequate use of form that has been spoiled by an oversight or distortion.

$F-$ (minus level):   Representing the wholly arbitrary percept where there is substantial disregard for the structural properties of the blot areas used.

Mayman has been able to demonstrate that this method of differentiation of form quality yields data of substantially greater diagnostic usefulness than does the simple plus and minus differentiation. He reports very respectable correlations with ratings of health, tolerance for anxiety, motivation, ego strength, and quality of interpersonal relations. He also reports a reasonably high level of agreement between scorers for most of the six categories.

At first glance it appeared that the Mayman method for evaluating form quality might be appropriate for the Comprehensive System, especially if it could be integrated with a format based on statistical frequency. A pilot study concerning its usefulness was conducted in which four predoctoral clinical psychology interns were given approximately 90 minutes of instruction in the Mayman method, plus preinstructional readings, and asked to code independently 20 protocols randomly selected from the protocol pool. Their codings were only for form quality, and they were also permitted to use the Beck Tables of Good and Poor Form as a guideline. The results were somewhat disappointing in that the levels of agreement among the four scorers ranged from 41 to 83%. Checking the levels of agreement among only three of the four scorers yielded only slightly higher percentages. An analysis of the discrepancies rendered some insight into the low reliability problem. First, there was considerable disagreement in the scoring of responses as $Fw+$ or $Fw-$. Second, there was substantial disagreement in the use of the Fv category, partly because some of the responses that might be scored Fv in the Mayman scheme are listed as $+$ by Beck, whereas others are listed $-$ by Beck, and partly because the levels of articulation varied considerably in these types of responses. Mayman also reported the lowest level of agreement for this category. Third, there was considerable disagreement for the scoring of Fs versus $F-$. As a consequence of these findings, it was decided to investigate a modification of the Mayman method, in which

Fv and *Fs* would be eliminated from the format, and all *Fw* answers would be considered as a single score rather than attempt to differentiate *Fw* + and *Fw* −. The same four predoctoral interns independently scored a second set of 20 randomly selected protocols, using this modified format. The results of this scoring were quite encouraging. The percentage of agreement among all four scorers ranged from 87 to 95%. It was even more encouraging to discover that almost all instances of disagreement occurred either between the scoring of *Fw* or *F* −, or between the scoring of *F* + or *Fo*. In other words, if the *F* + and *Fo* answers are all considered as representing "good" form, the scorers agreed in 99% of the responses. Similarly, if the *Fw* and *F* − answers are all considered as representing "poor" form, the scorers agreed in 98% of the responses. These high levels of agreement were generated essentially through the use of Beck's Tables of Good and Poor Form, with instances of disagreement occurring where the response in question did not appear on the Beck listing.

These findings promoted a decision to select a method of form quality evaluation for the Comprehensive System which utilizes the frequency distribution method favored by Beck and Hertz, and which *also* permits some differentiation regarding the goodness or poorness of the form used in the response. This format consists of four categories, derived from Mayman's work, two of which represent form which is used appropriately with good fit, one of which accounts for responses in which the appropriate use of form is not violated significantly, but which has a content reported by a very low frequency of subjects, and the fourth that represents those answers in which the form use has been inappropriate and/or distorted. These four categories and the criterion for each are shown in Table 22.

The appropriate symbol for form quality is entered at the end of the determinant coding. For instance, responses based exclusively on form will be coded as *F* +, *Fo, Fu,* or *F* −. Similarly, when determinants other than pure Form are present in the answer, the placement of the form quality coding remains the same, as in $M^a o$, *TFu, FC.FD* −, $FM^p.FC' +$.

The decision process concerning which symbol to employ will begin with an examination of Table A, which is one of the working tables included in Part III. Table A provides a

Table 22.   Symbols and Criteria for Coding Form Quality

Symbol	Definition	Criterion
+	Superior-overelaborated	The unusually precise articulation of the use of form in a manner that tends to enrich the quality of the response without sacrificing the appropriateness of the form use. The + answer need not be original, but rather unique by the manner in which details are defined and by which the form is used and specified.
o	Ordinary	The obvious, easily articulated use of form features to define an object reported frequently by others. The answer is commonplace and easy to see. There is no unusual enrichment of the answer by overelaboration of the form features.
u	Unusual	A low-frequency response in which the basic contours involved are not significantly violated. These are uncommon answers that are seen quickly and easily by the observer.
−	Minus	The distorted, arbitrary, unrealistic use of form in creating a response. The answer is imposed on the blot structure with total, or near total disregard for the structure of the area being used in creating the response. Often arbitrary contours will be created where none exist.

listing of responses, card by card, and by location areas. It was constructed using 7500 protocols that include 162,427 responses. These include the records of 2500 nonpatient adults (56,478 responses), 2500 nonschizophrenic outpatients (57,898 responses), and 2500 nonschizophrenic-nonpsychotic inpatients (48,051 responses). It replaces an earlier version that was published in the first edition of this work, which had been constructed using only 1200 records containing slightly more than 26,000 responses.

Each item in Table A is identified as *ordinary (o), unusual (u),* or *minus (−)*. If the item is designated as *ordinary (o),* and involves a *W* or *D* area, this signifies that the object was reported in at least 2% (150 or more) of the 7500 records, and that it involves blot contours that do exist. If the item listed as *o* involves a *Dd* location, this signifies that the *area* was used by at least 50 subjects, that the object was reported by no fewer than two-thirds of those using the area, and involves blot contours that do exist. If the response is listed as *ordinary* in Table A, the coding for form quality must always be either *o* or +. Most of these responses will be coded *o,* because the frequency of + responses is quite low in all groups. Responses that should be coded + are usually easy to distinguish, because the subject identifies many more form details than is commonplace. Nonetheless, the decision to code + versus *o* includes the subjective judgment of the coder.

If the item in Table A is designated as *unusual (u),* and involves a *W* or *D* area, this indicates that it was reported by fewer than 2% of the 7500 subjects, but in the unanimous opinion of at least three judges, working independently of each other, the object is seen quickly and easily and is appropriate to the contours that are used. If the item designated as *u* involves a *Dd* area, this signifies that it was reported by fewer than 50 subjects, but in the unanimous opinion of at least three judges, working independently of each other, it is seen quickly and easily and is appropriate to the contours that are involved. Although Table A encompasses a large number of items, it does not include all possible responses.

If an examiner-coder is confronted with a response that is not in Table A, a judgment call is required that will involve either of two steps. First, an effort should be made to extrapolate conservatively from the answers in Table A. For instance, a "gyroscope might not be listed for a specific area but a "top" might be included in the list. In that they are very similar objects, it is reasonable to assign the coding given in the list for top for the gyroscope response. If, on the other hand, the object reported only has a remote similarity to items listed in Table A, the attempt at extrapolation should be abandoned and the criteria for distinguishing *u* from − answers should be reviewed carefully and faithfully. If the response can be seen *quickly and easily,* it should be coded *u.* Otherwise it should be coded −. Some examiners are loath to code a response −, apparently influenced by a faulty impression that a minus answer will have great interpretive significance. This is not true, however. The overwhelming majority of subjects from all groups give one or more minus responses. Minus answers become interpretively important when the frequency is significantly high, or in some cases, when they all involve a single content.

Many responses will contain multiple objects that do not all have the same form quality. As a rule, the "lowest" form quality is assigned for the entire response; however, this rule is only applied to objects that are important in the overall response. For example, a response to Card II might be, "Two bears (*D*1) stepping on a heart (*D*3). The *D*1 area is listed in Table A as ordinary for bear, but the *D*3 area is listed as minus for heart. Thus, the form quality for the entire response is minus because both objects are important to the overall response. On the other hand, if one object that is not very important to the overall response has a listed lower form quality than the other objects in the answer, the higher form quality score should be assigned. For instance, another response to Card II might be, "Two bears (D1) playing together, it looks like they are stepping on something red there (D3), maybe a flower." Again, the bears are listed as ordinary, but a flower for D3 is listed as unusual. In this response, the specification of flower was casual and relatively unimportant. The important features of the answer are the two bears playing, stepping on something. Thus, the form quality scoring of ordinary seems more appropriate.

The items listed as *minus* in Table A generally are those that occur with low frequencies and are not congruent with the contours of the blots. But all are not necessarily low-frequency answers for all groups. For instance, the response of a face, using all of Card X inverted, is relatively commonplace among some groups of adolescents, both patients and nonpatients. It is a curious phenomenon that is not well understood, and which apparently occurs because those subjects tend to perceptually "close" the broken figure. Nonetheless, it is properly coded as − because the subject must create contours that do not exist in the blot. The majority of minus answers do have some contours that are congruent with the object reported, but the overall "fit" of the object(s) tends to violate the contours considerably. As a rule of thumb it is best to code questionable responses as −, following the principle that one or two minus responses will not contribute significantly to the overall interpretation of the record.

It is practical to question the cut-off of 2% in determining the *ordinary* responses in Table A for W and D location areas, and the requirement of at least 50 answers to a Dd location area, with two-thirds including the reported object to be designated ordinary or commonplace. These are somewhat arbitrary cut-off points, but they are not drawn randomly or carelessly. As noted earlier, the frequency of responses to the D areas is somewhat bimodal. Some D areas attract a great deal of attention, with response rates well into the hundreds, whereas other areas designated as D are used for considerably fewer responses. An examination of all of the responses included in Table A reveals that some occur with frequencies greater than 1000. These are typically responses defined as *Popular* in the next chapter. A second group of answers has frequencies ranging between 150 and 500. The majority of items listed in Table A as *o* have such frequencies. Interestingly, there are very few items listed in Table A that have response frequencies falling between 125 and 150. To the contrary, most with frequencies of less than 150 occur less than 100 times. Thus the mark of 150 seems to be a good breakpoint.

A second factor arguing in favor of the 150 cut-off concerns the protocols of antisocial or asocial subjects. Nearly 400 of these subjects are included among the 2500 outpatients and nearly 500 are included among the 2500 inpatients used in the construction of Table A. Antisocial and asocial people typically do not violate reality. Instead, they interpret it in a way to coincide with their own needs and orientation toward unconventionality. This is reflected in the *unusual* response. *Practically all subjects* give some unusual answers, and this represents their individuality. But if the premise is true, that antisocial and asocial people do this to an extreme, they should have a significantly higher frequency of *u* answers as contrasted with *o* or − responses. An analysis of the records of 868 subjects in the Table A construction pool, who meet the DSM-III criteria for antisocial or asocial personalities, reveals that the use of "good" form quality, (i.e., *o* or +) is significantly lower than for nonpatients, but the frequency of − answers is not significantly greater than for nonpatients. In other words, they give substantially more unusual answers.

A third factor that tends to support the construction principles used in creating Table A is derived from data concerning the protocols of schizophrenics and psychotic subjects. *None* of these were used in constructing Table A on the premise that either group—but especially the schizophrenic group—might have a high frequency for some responses that would not appear among the nonpatient, or nonschizophrenic groups. One of the characteristics of schizophrenics, and many psychotic subjects, is perceptual inaccuracy. They distort the perceptual input in translating it, or possibly their psychological disarray causes them to dysfunction during the input operation. In either event, they do not interpret reality adequately in many more instances than is true for nonpatients or nonschizophrenics. When taking the Rorschach, they tend to give significantly more minus responses than do other groups (Exner, 1978, 1981; Weiner, 1966). The protocols of 320 first admission schizophrenics, drawn randomly from the protocol pool at the Rorschach Research Foundation, were recoded for form quality, using Table A as the guideline. They were compared with equal-sized groups of nonpatients and nonschizophrenic inpatients, drawn randomly from the Table A construction pool. The results show that an average of 31% of the responses from schizophrenics are minus, as contrasted with an average of 15% minus responses among the nonschizophrenic inpatients, and only 6% of minus responses among the nonpatients.

The two studies regarding interscorer reliability indicate that considerable agreement does occur when Table A is used as a guideline for coding form quality. For the group of 20 coders and 25 records the percentages of agreement are: $+$ = 93%, o = 97%, u = 94%, and $-$ = 94%. For the group of 15 coders and 20 records, the percentages of agreement are: $+$ = 96%, o = 97%, u = 95%, and $-$ = 93%.

Mayman (1970) has offered an important caution to all Rorschachers concerning the coding of form quality. He states,

> Many clinicians seem to feel that there is little they can learn from form level scores that they do not already know from their impressionistic scanning of Rorschach protocols. Those who do score form quality often settle for a rough-and-ready classification of responses as either "acceptable" or "poor" . . . The form quality of Rorschach responses indicates in microcosm the attitude with which a person maintains his hold on is object world.

Presumably, the modification of Mayman's technique for coding form quality included in the Comprehensive System goes well beyond the "rough-and-ready" classifications to which Mayman alludes. It will afford a more sophisticated glimpse into the world of the subject and his object relations than do the more simplified methods of good form–poor form that have been used in the past.

REFERENCES

Beck, S. J. (1933) Configurational tendencies in Rorschach responses. *American Journal of Psychology,* **45,** 433–443.

Beck, S. J. (1937) *Introduction to the Rorschach Method: A Manual of Personality Study.* American Orthopsychiatric Association Monograph, No. 1.

Beck, S. J. (1944) *Rorschach's Test. I: Basic Processes.* New York: Grune & Stratton.

Beck, S. J. (1945) *Rorschach's Test. II: A Variety of Personality Pictures.* New York: Grune & Stratton.

Beck, S. J. (1952) *Rorschach's Test. III: Advances in Interpretation.* New York: Grune & Stratton.

Beck, S. J., Beck, A., Levitt, E., and Molish, H. (1961) *Rorschach's Test. I: Basic Processes.* (3rd Ed.) New York: Grune & Stratton.

Blatt, H. (1953) An investigation of the significance of the Rorschach z score. Unpublished Ph.D. dissertation, University of Nebraska.

Exner, J. E. (1978) *The Rorschach: A Comprehensive System. Volume 2. Current research and advanced interpretation.* New York: Wiley.

Exner, J. E. (1981) The response process and diagnostic efficacy. 10th International Congress of Rorschach and Projective Techniques. Washington, D.C.

Hertz, M. (1940) *Percentage Charts for Use in Computing Rorschach Scores.* Brush Foundation and Department of Psychology, Western Reserve University.

Hertz, M. (1948) Suicidal configurations in Rorschach records. *Rorschach Research Exchange,* **12,** 3–58.

Hertz, M. (1960) Organization Activity. In M. Rickers-Ovsiankina (Ed.), *Rorschach Psychology.* New York: Wiley, pp. 25–57.

Hertz, M. (1970) *Frequency Tables for Scoring Rorschach Responses.* (5th Ed.) Cleveland: Case Western Reserve University Press.

Jolles, I. (1947) The diagnostic implications of Rorschach's Test in case studies of mental defectives. *Genetic Psychology Monographs,* **36,** 89–198.

Kinder, B., Brubaker, R., Ingram, R., and Reading, E. (1982) Rorschach form quality: A comparison of the Exner and Beck systems. *Journal of Personality Assessment,* **46,** 131–138.

Klopfer, B., and Tallman, G. (1938) A further Rorschach study of Mr. A. *Rorschach Research Exchange,* **3,** 31–36.

Klopfer, B., and Kelley, D. (1942) *The Rorschach Technique.* Yonkers-on-Hudson, N.Y.: World Book.

Klopfer, B., and Davidson, H. (1944) Form level rating: A preliminary proposal for appraising mode and level of thinking as expressed in Rorschach records. *Rorschach Research Exchange,* **8,** 164–177.

Klopfer, B., Ainsworth, M., Klopfer, W., and Holt, R. (1954) *Developments in the Rorschach Technique. I: Technique and Theory.* Yonkers-on-Hudson, N.Y.: World Book.

Kropp, R. (1955) The Rorschach "Z" score. *Journal of Projective Techniques,* **19,** 443–452.

Mayman, M. (1966) Measuring reality-adherence in the Rorschach test. American Psychological Association Meetings, New York.

Mayman, M. (1970) Reality contact, defense effectiveness, and psychopathology in Rorschach form-level scores. In B. Klopfer, M. Meyer, and F. Brawer (Eds.), *Developments in the Rorschach Technique. III: Aspects of Personality Structure.* New York: Harcourt Brace Jovanovich, pp. 11–46.

Molish, H. (1955) Schizophrenic reaction types in a naval hospital population as evaluated by the Rorschach Test. Bureau of Medicine and Surgery, Navy Department, Washington, D.C.

Piotrowski, Z. (1957) *Perceptanalysis.* New York: Macmillan.

Rapaport, D., Gill, M., and Schafer, R. (1946) *Diagnostic Psychological Testing.* Vol. 2. Chicago: Yearbook Publisher.

Rorschach, H. (1921) *Psychodiagnostics.* Bern: Bircher (Transl., Hans Huber Verlag, 1942).

Schmidt, H., and Fonda, C. (1953) Rorschach scores in the manic states. *Journal of Projective Techniques,* **17,** 151–161.

Sisson, B., and Taulbee, E. (1955) Organizational activity of the Rorschach Test. *Journal of Consulting Psychology,* **19,** 29–31.

Varvel, W. (1941) The Rorschach Test in psychotic and neurotic depressions. *Bulletin of the Meninger Clinic,* **5,** 5–12.

Weiner, I. (1966) *Psychodiagnosis in Schizophrenia.* New York: Wiley.

Wilson, G., and Blake, R. (1950) A methodological problem in Beck's organizational concept. *Journal of Consulting Psychology,* **14,** 20–24.

Wishner, J. (1948) Rorschach intellectual indicators in neurotics. *American Journal of Orthopsychiatry,* **18,** 265–279.

CHAPTER 8

Content Categories
and Populars

Another task in coding the Rorschach response involves two steps. First, an appropriate symbol must be selected to represent the content of the response. Second, the response should be checked against a listing of "Popular" answers, that is, those given quite frequently in Rorschach records. Neither of these procedures is complex, but both are quite important for the interpretive process.

CONTENT

All responses are coded for content. The symbol used for the content score should be reasonably representative of the object or of the class of objects reported in the response. Rorschach (1921) used only six different symbols for content scoring. They are *H* (Human), *Hd* (Human Detail), *A* (Animal), *Ad* (Animal Detail), *Ls* (Landscape), and *Obj* (Inanimate Objects). In the early development of the test it became obvious that these six categories did not provide adequate differentiation of many frequently reported classes of objects. Therefore each of the Rorschach systematizers has expanded Rorschach's original listing considerably to provide for a greater discrimination among responses. There is considerable agreement among the systems concerning the more commonly appearing contents; however, the agreement is far from unanimous. The lists of categories vary considerably, differing notably in length. Beck used the longest (35 categories), and Klopfer and Davidson (1962) the shortest (23 content categories). Slight variations also occur across the listings regarding the actual symbol to be used. For instance, Beck used the symbol *An* to score anatomy content, whereas Klopfer used the symbol *At* for the same category.

The list of content symbols used in the Comprehensive System was developed in three phases. First, a random sample of 600 protocols was selected from the protocol pool. These records constitute 13,542 responses, each of which was coded for content using the Beck listing of symbols, because that list is the longest for any of the systems. A frequency tally was then derived for each of the 35 content scores, and any category that did not show a frequency of 20 or more was deleted form the list. This procedure reduced the length of the Beck listing from 35 to 21 content categories.[1] The rationale for this procedure is that any content occurring with very limited frequency is probably quite "idiographic" when it does occur; thus it is better represented in a summary of codes in

---

[1] The 14 Beck Content scorings eliminated by this procedure are *Aq* (Antiquity), *Ar* (Architecture), *As* (Astronomy), *Dh* (Death), *Im* (Implement), *Mn* (Mineral), *Mu* (Music), *My* (Mythology), *Pr* (Personal), *Rc* (Recreation, *Rl* (Religion), *Ru* (Rural), *Tr* (Travel), and *Vo* (Vocational).

written-out form. For example, contents such as a candle, a milk bottle, ice tongs, and flags appear in Rorschach records very infrequently. Although each could be coded in a general category, such as object (*obj*), the full uniqueness of the content would not be readily evident in a summary as it would be in written-out form.

The second phase in developing the list of content scorings was comprised of a reexamination of the 21 remaining content categories to determine if any one might be including two or more frequently occurring, but relatively different, classes of objects. Two such categories were discovered. The scoring of Anatomy (*An*) included 179 responses of anatomy and 97 X-ray responses. Although Beck had decided to score both under the single rubric of *An,* it was decided to create a separate scoring for X-ray. Similarly, the scoring of Fire (*Fi*) include two relatively separate kinds of answer. The most frequent was "explosion" ($N = 248$), approximately half of which included reference to fire. A somewhat different kind of response, also scored *Fi,* is "fire," involving no explosion ($N = 69$). These findings seem to warrant a separate content scoring for explosion answers.

In addition, many of the human and animal responses were of fictional and mythological humans or animals, such as witches, giants, monsters, unicorns, and devils. More than 20% of the human content responses and more than 10% of the animal content responses in the sample of 600 records are of this variety. Thus it seemed logical, following the approaches of Klopfer, Piotrowski, and Rapaport, to add four categories—(*H*), (*Hd*), (*A*), and (*Ad*)—to account for these types of contents. A new category, *Hx,* was also added to account for responses involving human emotions and sensory experiences.

The final listing selected for use in the Comprehensive System is comprised of 26 categories. These categories and the symbol and criterion for each are shown in Table 23.

CODING MULTIPLE CONTENTS

Many responses will contain more than one content. *All* should be included in the coding *with two exceptions* that concern the categories Nature, Botany, and Landscape.

Na always takes priority over *Bt* or *Ls.* In other words, if a response includes *Na* and *Bt* and/or *Ls,* only *Na* is scored. For example, "This is an animal stepping on some stones that

Table 23.   Symbols and Criteria Used for Coding Content

Category	Symbol	Criterion
Whole Human	*H*	Involving the percept of a whole human form. If the percept involves a *real* historical figure, such as Napoleon, Joan of Arc, etc., the content code *Ay* should be added as a secondary code.
Whole Human (fictional or mythological)	(*H*)	Involving the percept of a whole human form that is fictional or mythological, such as clowns, fairies, giants, witches, fairy tale characters, ghosts, dwarfs, devils, angels, science fiction creatures that are humanoid, human-like monsters.
Human Detail	*Hd*	Involving the percept of an incomplete human form, such as an arm, leg, fingers, feet, the lower part of a person, a person without a head.
Human Detail (fictional or mythological)	(*Hd*)	Involving the percept of an incomplete human form that is fictional or mythological such as, the head of the devil, the arm of a witch, the eyes of an angel, parts of science-fiction creatures that are humanoid, and all masks.
Human Experience	*Hx*	Involving the percept of human emotion or sensory experience such as love, hate, depression, happiness, sound, smell, fear, etc. Most answers in which *Hx* is coded will also include the use of *AB* as a special score.
Whole Animal	*A*	Involving the percept of a whole animal form.

Table 23 (Continued)

Category	Symbol	Criterion
Whole Animal (fictional or mythological)	(A)	Involving the percept of a whole animal that is fictional or mythological, such as a unicorn, dragon, magic, frog, flying horse, Black Beauty, Jonathan Livingston Seagull.
Animal Detail	Ad	Involving the percept of an incomplete animal form, such as the hoof of a horse, claw of a lobster, head of a dog, animal skin.
Animal Detail (fictional or mythological)	(Ad)	Involving the percept of an incomplete animal form that is fictional or mythological such as the wing of Pegasus, the head of Peter Rabbit, the legs of Pooh Bear.
Anatomy	An	Used for responses in which the content is skeletal, muscular, or of internal anatomy such as, bone structure, skull, rib cage, heart, lungs, stomach, liver, muscle fiber, vertebrae, brain. If the response involves a tissue slide, the code Art should be added as secondary.
Art	Art	Involving percepts of paintings, drawings, or illustrations, either abstract or definitive, art objects, such as statues, jewelry, chandelier, candelabra, crests, badges, seals, and decorations.
Anthropology	Ay	Involving percepts that have a specific cultural or historical connotation such as totem, Roman helmet, Magna Carta, Santa Maria, Napolean's hat, Cleopatra's crown, arrowhead, prehistoric axe.
Blood	Bl	Involving the percept of blood, either human or animal.
Botany	Bt	Involving the percept of any plant life such as bushes, flowers, seaweed, trees, or parts of plant life, such as leaves, petals, tree trunk, root.
Clothing	Cg	Involving the percept of any article of clothing such as, hat, boots, belt, necktie, jacket, trousers, scarf.
Clouds	Cl	Used specifically for the content cloud. Variations of this category, such as fog or mist are coded Na.
Explosion	Ex	Involving percepts of a blast or explosion, including fireworks.
Fire	Fi	Involving percepts of fire or smoke.
Food	Fd	Involving the percept of any edible, such as fried chicken, ice cream, fried shrimp, vegetables, cotton candy, chewing gum, steak, a filet of fish.
Geography	Ge	Involving the percept of a map, specified or unspecified.
Household	Hh	Involving percepts of household items, such as bed, chair, lamp, silverware, plate, cup, glass, cooking utensil, carving knife, lawn chair, garden hose, rug, (excluding animal skin rug, which is coded Ad).
Landscape	Ls	Involving percepts of landscape, such as mountain, mountain range, hill, island, cave, rocks, desert, swamp, or seascapes, such as coral reef or underwater scene.
Nature	Na	Used for a broad variety of contents from the natural environment that are not coded as Bt or Ls, such as sun, moon, planet, sky, water, ocean, river, ice, snow, rain, fog, mist, rainbow, storm, tornado, night, raindrop.
Science	Sc	Involving percepts that are associated with, or are the products of science or science fiction, such as microscope, telescope, weapons, rocket ships, motors, space ships, ray guns, airplane, ship, train, car, motorcycle, light bulb, TV aerial, radar station.
Sex	Sx	Involving percepts of sex organs or activity of a sexual nature, such as penis, vagina, buttocks, breast (except if used to delineate a female figure), testes, menstruation, abortion, intercourse. Sx is usually scored as a secondary content. Primary contents are typically H, Hd, or An.
X-ray	Xy	Used specifically for the content of x-ray and may include either skeletal or organs. When Xy is coded, An is not included as a secondary code.

are in the water, he's trying to get to this bush." This answer contains four contents, animal (*A*), stones (*Ls*), water (*Na*), and bush (*Bt*), but the correct content coding is *A, Na*.

If a response does not include *Na* but contains both *Bt* and *Ls,* only one of the two is scored. Thus, if the response were, "An animal stepping over some stones next to this bush," the correct content coding would be *A, Bt* or *A, Ls*.

The reason for the rule concerning Nature, Botany, and Landscape is that all are included in the calculation of the *Isolation Index,* and the rule is designed to ensure that no single answer will contribute excessively to that calculation.

When multiple contents are entered, they are separated by a comma, with the first representing the content that is *most* central to the response. Usually, but not always, the main content will be the first item mentioned in the response. For instance, the response, "A painting of a person with a large hat on, standing next to a tree," would be *Art, H, Cg, Bt*. Here, the painting is the main content, and the substance of the painting forms the secondary contents.

In a response such as, "Let's see, this could be a tree I suppose, and there is a person standing there, next to the tree, she's got a big hat on," the central feature is the person even though the tree was mentioned first. Thus, the coding would be *H, Bt, Cg*.

It is quite important to include all of the contents in an answer in the coding. Some of the interpretive ratios are based on the total number of contents, and omissions in content coding can create misleading data.

Unusual Contents   Some responses will include contents that do not fit easily into one of the standard content categories. When that occurs, the unique content should be written out and entered under idiographic contents (*Id*) on the Structural Summary Blank. It is important however, to make sure that the item does not fit into one of the standard content categories before deciding to enter it idiographically. For example, a "test tube" is a very unusual response, and at first glance, it may seem appropriate to list it idiographically because of its rarity. Nonetheless, it does fit neatly into the *Sc* category, and should be coded as such. Similarly, a carousel is also a fairly unusual content. Technically, it could be scored as *Sc*, using the premise that it can be considered as a product of science, but it might be more appropriate to score it as *Art*.

POPULAR RESPONSES

Rorschach made no mention of the commonly given, or Popular, answers in his original work (1921). He did, however, call attention to these types of responses in his posthumously published 1923 paper, referring to them as "Vulgar" answers. Rorschach defined the Vulgar or Popular responses as those occurring at least once in every three protocols, suggesting that they represent the capability for conventional perception. Each of the Rorschach systematizers has included the Popular, or *P,* scoring as an important feature of the test; however, there exists considerable variation across the systems concerning the listings of responses to be scored *P*. These intersystem differences have generally been created by disagreements concerning the criterion of *P,* although in some instances sampling differences have contributed to the variations. Most of the systematizers broadened Rorschach's criterion of limiting the *P* scoring to answers occurring at least once in three records. Rapaport et al. (1946) recommended the scoring of *P* for responses occurring once in every four or five records. Beck et al. (1961) list as Popular, responses occurring at least three times as frequently as the next most commonly occurring answer to a blot, provided that it is given not less than once by at least 14% of his adult sample. Piotrowski (1957) included responses given at least once in every four records. Hertz (1970) used the broadest criterion, defining as Popular any answer which occurs at least once in six protocols, and presents the longest listing of Populars, although not substantially longer than that developed by Beck. The Klopfer et al. (1962) listing of Populars has considerably fewer answers, having been developed from "clinical experience," using Rorschach's guideline of responses occurring once in three protocols.

The absence or deficiency of Popular answers has been noted in several empirical works (Rickers-Ovsiankina, 1938; Rapaport et al., 1946; Beck, 1954; Bloom, 1962), and is a consistent finding across systems. Unfortunately, the interpretive conclusions concerning the incidence of high or low numbers of Popular answers is often system-specific and not easily generalized.

Because the concept of *Popular* reflects the *very* conventional answers, it was decided to use Rorschach's suggestion to define them as any response occurring at least once in every three records. The 7500 protocols used in the construction of Table A (2500 nonpatient adults, 2500 nonschizophrenic outpatients, and 2500 inpatient nonschizophrenic and nonpsychotic patients) were computer tallied for response frequencies. Any specific response that occurred at least 2500 times in this sample is designated as *Popular* in the Comprehensive System. The analysis yielded 13 Popular responses, which are shown in Table 24 with the percentage of nonpatient and nonschizophrenic groups that gave each response also included.

The listing in Table 24 replaces the 13 *classes* of Popular responses that were published in the first edition of this work. The 1974 list combined the bat and butterfly responses to Cards I and V and the spider and crab responses to Card X. The current list eliminates five responses that were found to be Popular a decade ago, and includes two answers that meet the Popular criterion now. Interestingly, the current listing, with the exception of the Card IX Popular, is essentially the same as reported by Sendin (1981), using a sample of 294 Spanish adult patients and nonpatients.

The one-in-three criterion may seem somewhat stringent to some. It is true that there is great variation in the frequencies by which each of the 13 answers are reported. The least frequent of the 13, however, the Popular for Card IX, occurs significantly more than the next most frequent response in the sample, which is the female figure reported in the center $D4$ area to Card I. In that context, the selection of the one-in-three criterion can be justified on a statistical basis. The female figure to $D4$ in Card I occurred in 25% of the total sample and, as such, does meet a one-in-four criterion, but it does not occur significantly more often than five other answers that have response frequencies between 18 and 24%. They are an animal face or mask to WS on Card I (24%), a rocket ship to $DS5$ on Card II (19%), a butterfly to $D3$ on Card III (21%), an animal skin to the whole of Card IV (22%), and a totem pole to $D3$ on Card VI (18%). In addition, there are more than 50 other responses that have frequencies of between 13 and 17%.

Piotrowski (1957) has suggested that the listing of Populars may vary across cultures. Some support for this hypothesis is noted by the failure of the Card IX Popular to reach the criterion frequency in Sendin's sample of Spanish adults, and by the findings of Fried (1977) who found that subjects in Finland deliver the response "Christmas elves" to Card II with a Popular frequency. These differences are more likely to exist among the Popular answers that barely meet criterion in one culture, but it is unlikely that the higher frequency answers will differ cross-culturally. Some support for this postulate is derived

Table 24.   Popular Responses Selected for the Comprehensive System Based on the Frequency of Occurrence of at Least Once in Every Three Protocols Given by Nonpatient Adult Subjects and Nonschizophrenic Adult Patients

Card	Location	Criterion	% Nonpatient Reporting	% Nonschizophrenic Reporting
I	*W*	Bat. The response always involves the whole blot	48	38
I	*W*	Butterfly. The response always involves the whole blot.	40	36
II	*D*1	Animal forms, usually the heads of dogs, bears, elephants, or lambs; however, the frequency of the whole animal to this area is sufficient to warrant the scoring of *P*.	34	35
III	*D*1 or *D*9	Two human figures, or representations thereof, such as dolls and caricatures. The scoring of *P* is also applicable to the percept of a single human figure to area *D*9.	89	70
IV	*W* or *D*7	A human or human-like figure such as giant, monster, science fiction creature, etc.	53	41
V	*W*	Butterfly, the apex of the card upright or inverted. The whole blot *must* be used.	46	43
V	*W*	Bat, the apex of the card upright or inverted, and involving the whole blot.	36	38
VI	*W* or *D*1	Animal skin, hide, rug, or pelt. The *P* is also scored when a whole animal is given, provided reference is made to the back, skin, or hide.	87	35
VII	*D*1 or *D*9	Human head or face, specifically identified as female, child, indian, or with gender not identified. If *D*1 is used, the upper segment (*D*5) is usually identified as hair, feather, etc. If the response includes the entire *D*2 area, *P* is coded if the head or face are restricted to the *D*9 area. If *Dd*23 is included as part of the human form, the response is *not* coded as *P*.	59	47
VIII	*D*1	Whole animal figure. This is the most frequently perceived common answer, the content varying considerably, such as bear, dog, rodent, fox, wolf, and coyote. All are *P*. The *P* is also coded when the animal figure is reported as part of the *W* percept as in a family crest, seal, and emblem.	94	91
IX	*D*3	Human or human-like figures such as witches, giants, science fiction creatures, monsters, etc.	54	24
X	*D*1	Spider with all appendages restricted to the *D*1 area.	42	34
X	*D*1	Crab with all appendages restricted to the *D*1 area. Other variations of multilegged animals are not *P*.	37	38

from the examination of a group of 293 protocols that were collected in 12 countries for the Rorschach Research Foundation (Argentina = 15, Australia = 25, France = 37, India = 9, Italy = 16, Japan = 14, Malaysia = 22, Mexico = 60, Micronesia = 33, Philippines = 40, Switzerland = 8, and New Zealand = 14). None of these samples is large enough to test for Populars, but when combined, 11 of the 13 Populars listed in Table 24 occur in at least 40% of the records. The two that fall below the one-third criterion are the Populars on Cards II and IX, with percentages of 31 and 26%, respectively.

The high frequencies with which the Popular responses occur suggest that they represent the most distinctive contours or other stimulus features of the blots, and thus are most easily misidentified. Nonetheless, there are some marked differences in response rates among patients and nonpatients for the Populars on Card VI and Card IX, which merit further study. Similarly, there are also some subtle sex differences for some of the Populars that do reach levels of statistical significance. They warrant further study. Females report the Popular butterfly responses on both Cards I and V more frequently than males, whereas males report the bat responses on Cards I and V more frequently than females. Similarly, males report the Card X crab with a higher frequency than females, whereas the reverse is true for the Card X spider response. On Card VII, females identify the Popular human figures as women much more often than they report children or Indians. The reverse is true for male subjects. The same pattern of difference occurs for the Card VIII Popular. Males report larger and nondomestic animals most often, whereas females report smaller and domestic animals more frequently.

The two interscorer reliability studies show percentages of agreement for both groups for coding P to be 99%. There is no room for error in coding P. Similarly, high percentages of agreement occurred for both groups in coding *primary* content, that is, the basic content of the response. The 20 coders and 25 records yielded a 95% agreement for primary content, whereas the 15 coders and 20 records had a 96% agreement. However, the percentage of agreement for both groups was considerably lower for the coding of *secondary* contents. In the past, and in the first edition of this work, little emphasis has been afforded the importance of coding secondary contents. Research during the past decade indicates that they are much more important than implied heretofore. In the reliability study involving 20 coders and 25 records, a very modest 78% agreement occurred for secondary content, and only slightly better, 82%, for the 15 coders and 20 records. The disparity for each group was created much more by omissions rather than actual disagreements. Several contents such as Art, Botany (*Bt*), Clothing (*Cg*), Fire (*Fi*), Nature (*Na*), Landscape (*Ls*), and Science (*Sc*) occur far more frequently as secondary contents than as primary contents. The conscientious examiner will scan each answer carefully and code for each additional content that may exist. In many cases the presence of secondary contents will add very little to the interpretive yield, but in some instances the accumulated frequencies for one or two, or for some combinations of contents, will contribute significantly to the overall interpretation.

REFERENCES

Beck, S. J. (1954) *The six schizophrenias.* American Orthopsychiatric Association. Research Monograph No. 6.

Beck, S. J., Beck, A., Levitt, E., and Molish, H. B. (1961) *Rorschach's Test. I: Basic Processes.* (3rd ed.) New York: Grune & Stratton.

Bloom, B. L. (1962) The Rorschach Popular response among Hawaiian schizophrenics. *Journal of Projective Techniques,* **26,** 173–181.

Fried, R. (1977) Christmas elves on the Rorschach: A Popular Finnish response and its cultural significance. 9th International Congress of Rorschach and Projective Techniques. Fribourg, Switzerland.

Goldfried, M. R., Stricker, G., and Weiner, I. B. (1971) *Rorschach Handbook of Clinical and Research Applications.* Englewood Cliffs, N.J.: Prentice-Hall.

Hertz, M. R. (1970) *Frequency Tables for Scoring Rorschach Responses.* (5th ed.) Cleveland: The Press of Case Western Reserve University.

Klopfer, B., and Kelley, D. (1942) *The Rorschach Technique.* Yonkers-on-Hudson. N.Y.: World Book.

Klopfer, B., and Davidson, H. (1962) *The Rorschach Technique. An Introductory Manual.* New York: Harcourt Brace Jovanovich.

Piotrowski, Z. (1957). *Perceptanalysis.* New York: Macmillan.

Rapaport, D., Gill, M., and Schafer, R. (1946) *Diagnostic Psychological Testing.* Vol. 2. Chicago: Yearbook Publishers.

Rickers-Ovsiankina, M. (1938) The Rorschach Test as applied to normal and schizophrenic subjects. *British Journal of Medical Psychology,* **17,** 227–257.

Rorschach, H. (1921) *Psychodiagnostics.* Bern: Bircher, (Transl. Hans Huber Verlag, 1942).

Rorschach, H., and Oberholzer, E. (1923) The application of the interpretation of form to Psychoanalysis. *Zeitschrift fur gesamte Neurologie und Psychiatrie,* **82,** 240–274.

Schafer, R. (1954) *Psychoanalytic Interpretation in Rorschach Testing.* New York: Grune & Stratton.

Sendin, C. (1981) Identification of Popular responses among Spanish adults. 10th International Congress of Rorschach and Projective Techniques. Washington, D.C.

Weiner, I. B. (1966) *Psychodiagnosis in Schizophrenia.* New York: Wiley.

CHAPTER 9

Special Scores

The final task in coding the Rorschach response is to determine whether the answer has any of the features that require the addition of a *Special Score*. Like most other components in the Rorschach language, Special Scores are actually codes, rather than numerical scores, which signal the presence of an unusual characteristic in the response. The use of Special Scores permits quantification of many features of responses that have been interpreted more qualitatively in the past.

Rapaport et al. (1946) were the first to recognize the importance of systematically identifying unusual features of answers, and they devised 25 special categories for this purpose. Unfortunately, as Rapaport cautioned, many had overlapping criteria and, as a consequence, the interscorer reliability for most has been modest at best. As a result, the issues of validation have been quite difficult to approach. Currently, there are 14 basic Special Scores in the Comprehensive System, which, including subdivisions, comprise 18 categories. Ten of these categories are derivations from one or more of Rapaport's categories. Six of the basic 14 concern unusual verbalizations, and 4 of the 6 are subdivided into Levels, which create 10 categories. Two more are used for perseverations and integration failure, 4 involve special characteristics of content, 1 is used when the answer is personalized, and 1 is used for a special color phenomenon. None of the 14 was included when the Comprehensive System was first published (Exner, 1974) because of problems with criteria, interscorer reliability, or a lack of convincing validation data. The first 5, all dealing with unusual verbalizations, were published approximately two years later (Exner, Weiner, & Schuyler, 1976), developed from research based on the works of Rapaport, Schafer (1954) and Weiner (1966). Two each were added with the publications of Volumes 2 (Exner, 1978) and 3 (Exner & Weiner, 1982). The remaining 7 have been developed since that time through research at the Rorschach Research Foundation (Exner, 1990, 1991).

UNUSUAL VERBALIZATIONS

Unusual verbalizations are an important element in the study of cognitive activity, and more particularly, cognitive slippage. When some form of cognitive disarray occurs, whether momentary or for a longer interval, it will often manifest verbally. It is evidenced in Rorschach responses in any of three ways: (1) Deviant Verbalizations, (2) Inappropriate Combinations, or (3) Inappropriate Logic. Six Special Scores are used to note the presence of these sorts of disarray in Rorschach answers, two for the Deviant Verbalizations, three for the Inappropriate Combinations, and one for Inappropriate Logic.

LEVEL 1—LEVEL 2 DIFFERENTIATIONS

The two scores used for Deviant Verbalizations (*DV* and *DR*) and two of the three scores used to identify Inappropriate Combinations (*INCOM* and *FABCOM*) are also differentiated for degrees of bizarreness and designated as either *Level* 1 or *Level* 2. This is necessary because a considerable range of cognitive dysfunction exists within each category. Therefore, it is important to attempt to discriminate between those responses that represent mild to modest forms of slippage and those that reflect more serious forms of disarray.

Level 1 Responses   A value of 1 is assigned to those answers in which a mild or modest instance of illogical, fluid, peculiar, or circumstantial thinking is present.

Although the Level 1 responses meet the criterion for the assigned special score, usually they are not markedly different from the cognitive slips that often occur when people do not pay close attention to how they are expressing themselves or to the judgments that they are making. Level 1 special scores often sound as if they are the product of immaturity, limited education, or judgments that are not well thought through.

Level 2 Responses   A value of 2 is assigned to those answers in which a moderate or severe instance of dissociated, illogical, fluid, or circumstantial thinking is present. They deviate markedly in the flawed judgment that is conveyed and/or in the very unusual mode of expression that is used. Level 2 responses stand out because of their bizarreness and seldom leave doubt concerning their scoring.

In those instances in which a scorer has legitimate doubts about whether a response meets the Level 2 criterion, a conservative stance should be taken and the Level 1 score assigned. Extraneous elements such as age, educational level, or cultural background *should not be considered* in making the differentiation between Level 1 and Level 2.

DEVIANT VERBALIZATIONS (*DV* AND *DR*)

There are two Special Scores for Deviant Verbalizations, one of which is restricted to the brief form of slippage and the second which concerns a larger segment of the response. Both are characterized by idiosyncratic modes of expression that impede the subject's ability to communicate clearly.

    1. Deviant Verbalization (*DV*)   *DV* is assigned to those answers that have either of two characteristics, both of which create the impression of oddity in the answer.

    a. *Neologism.* Involving the use of an incorrect word, or neologism, in place of a correct word that falls well within the subject's verbal capacity. Examples are: "A woman with a *disretheal* air about her" (*DV*2), "Some bacteria you might see under a *telescope*" (*DV*1), "A cat sticking her *purr* up" (*DV*2), "The *pubic* arch of somebody" (*DV*1). "Some *sexsnot* like you dig out of your ear" (*DV*2).

    b. *Redundancy.* Involving the odd use of language that cannot be justified in terms of subcultural idioms or limited vocabulary skills, in which the subject identifies *twice* the nature of the object(s) reported. Examples are: "The two *twin* lips of a vagina" (*DV*2), "A pair of *two* birds" (*DV*1)," "The backward *reversed* propeller of an airplane" (*DV*2), "A *trio* of three people" (*DV*2), or "A tiny little dog" (*DV*1). *DV* responses are usually easy to detect because the inappropriate word stands out quite markedly.

2. Deviant Response (*DR*). *DR* is assigned to answers that have a strange or peculiar quality. This may be manifested in either of two ways.

a. *Inappropriate Phrases*. Involving the inclusion of phrases that are inappropriate or completely irrelevant to the response. For example: "A bird, *but I was hoping to see a butterfly*" (*DR*2),"Some kind of bug but I've never seen one like it, *neither has anyone else for that matter*" (*DR*2), "It's a cat, *my father always hated cats*" (*DR*1), "It's a womb, *it's not nice this way cause the baby is gone*" (*DR*2), "A dancer with a pink robe, a blue bra, and a green G-string, *she's perfectly anonymous cause you can't see her body*" (*DR*2), "An abstract of President Carter *if you look at it from a Democratic perspective*" (*DR*2).

b. *Circumstantial Responses*. Involving answers that are fluid or rambling in which the subject becomes inappropriately elaborative or has marked difficulty in achieving a definition of the object. Examples are: "I'm not sure what this could be, something like an animal nose, maybe equine or bovine, *like in that play that was so filled with passions and psychological drama and thrills and so many tensions. I had to see it twice*. Yes, the nose of a horse" (*DR*2). "It looks like a map of two continents, *I can tell because I've traveled a lot and that middle line is something like the Arabs would do, dividing it all up like a map that represents darkness and light*. It's probably a map of Africa and Eastern Asia" (*DR*2). "*I'm a scientist*. I can see legs, a head, and a tail like an insect *but I'm having trouble seeing it. I see unilateral and bilateral symmetry and it's very interesting in the phylogenetic scheme of things, but I don't see what I know*. I'll just say an insect." (*DR*2) "It could be part of a crab, *I'm just trying to think of the angle we're looking at it from, maybe it's a stone crab, I really like those. If you are ever in Maine try them, the only thing you ever get is the leg cause they're only allowed to harvest the legs*" (*DR*2).

Caution should be exercised to avoid confusing the circumstantial *DR* response with the elaborate but appropriate answer. In the latter, the subject remains *on target* and simply verbalizes the organization of the answer. For example: "These might be some flowers and a walkway, like it is in a garden or a park, and you know this part in the top could be like a tower or a fountain if you look at it in perspective. In fact you could even think of it as the Eiffel Tower as you might see it across a park with many pretty flowers lining the walkway."

In the *DR* response the subject tends to wander *off target*, sometimes aimlessly, and may never actually return to the response object. For example: "Oh dear, I know I've seen something like that in a magazine, like a person from Samoa or someplace like that, *I'm always doing a lot of reading because it sharpens your mind and you can learn a lot of things about people and the world if you devote yourself to self-improvement by making sure to read something new every day without fail*." The circumstantial verbiage in the *DR* answer is not necessarily bizarre. In the preceding example the commentary about reading and self-improvement might be quite appropriate in a different situation, but is inappropriate for the task at hand. Rapaport suggested that responses such as these indicate a loss of distance from the task.

Most examiners find the circumstantial *DR* easy to identify because so much of the verbiage has little if any relevance to the actual response. Some *DR* answers will also contain a *DV.* When this occurs, *only* the *DR* is coded.

INAPPROPRIATE COMBINATIONS (*INCOM, FABCOM, CONTAM*)

These combinative responses involve the inappropriate condensation of impressions and/or ideas into responses that violate realistic considerations. They are answers in which unreal relationships are inferred between images, objects, or activities attributed to objects. There are three types of inappropriate combinations, each of which has a separate code.

1. Incongruous Combination (*INCOM*). Involving the condensation of blot details or images that are inappropriate merged into a single object. For example: "A *four-* legged chicken" (*INCOM*2), "A butterfly with his *hands* out" (*INCOM*1), "A frog with a *mustache*" (*INCOM*2), or "A woman with the *head of a chicken*" (*INCOM*2). Sometimes the incongruity will be manifested by the inappropriate combination of color and form as in "*Red* bears" (*INCOM*1), "*Black* snow" (*INCOM*1), or "An *orange* man" (*INCOM*1). The *INCOM* is coded *only* when the combination involves a single object.

2. Fabulized Combination (*FABCOM*). Involves an implausible relationship that is posited between two or more objects identified in the blot. These answers *always* include two or more discrete details of the blot. Examples are: "Two chickens holding *basketballs*" (*FABCOM*1), "A woman attacking a *submarine*" (*FABCOM*2), "Mice biting the *fingers of a martian*" (*FABCOM*2), or "Two ants fighting over a *baseball bat*" (*FABCOM*1). *FABCOM* is also coded for implausible transparencies, most of which will be coded as Level 2, such as "There is a big man sitting there and you can see his *heart pumping*" (*FABCOM*2), or "This is a vagina and here are her *fallopian tubes*" (*FABCOM*2).

3. Contamination (*CONTAM*). This is the most bizarre of the inappropriate combinations. The *CONTAM* represents two or more impressions that have been fused into a single response in a manner that clearly violates reality. The process of fusion causes impairment to the adequacy of either impression in contrast to the situation where they might be reported separately. Whereas the *INCOM* answers fused impressions from discrete blot areas into a single implausible object, the *CONTAM* response involves the use of a single discrete area. One response has been psychologically overlaid above another as in a photographic double exposure. Contaminations often (but not always) include the use of a neologism or other peculiar verbalizations to describe the object. A classic illustration of the neologistic *CONTAM* is the condensation of the front view of a bug and the front view of an ox into *"The face of a bug ox."* Another involves carefully viewing Card III upright, and then inverted, and then concluding that the *D*3 area is *"No doubt, a butterflower,"* apparently fusing the impressions of a flower and a butterfly. In other instances, the strained logic that apparently characterizes the *CONTAM* is more directly manifest as in *"It looks like blood here, and an island, it must be a bloody island,"* or *"It must be a bird dog cause it's got the body like a dog and the nose of a bird."*

In the past it has been suggested that all *CONTAM* responses be assigned a form quality coding of −, but this is a faulty rule. Form quality concerns perceptual accuracy, whereas the *CONTAM* signals cognitive or ideational impairment that may or may not involve perceptual distortion. If the object reported is nonexistent, as a bug-ox or a butterflower, it will obviously be coded as − for form quality. If the form is appropriate to the blot area used, however, the form quality may be *u,* or in some cases may be *o.*

INAPPROPRIATE LOGIC (*ALOG*)

The *ALOG* is used whenever the subject, *without prompting,* uses strained reasoning to justify his or her answer. The logic involved is clearly not conventional. Instead it represents a form of loose thinking. Sometimes the *ALOG* response is easily identified because the subject calls attention to size features or spatial elements of the blot. For example, "This is a very small lion *because it is only a part of the picture,*" or "This green must be lettuce *because it's next to the rabbit,*" or "It must be a man and a woman *because they're together,*" or "It's the North Pole *because it's at the top.*" In each of these statements, the reasoning becomes attached to, and dependent upon, the size, positioning, or number of objects included in the response. In other *ALOG* responses, other stimulus features become the focal point from which the strained reasoning evolves. For instance, "It's black so it must be evil," or "They are laying down so they must be dead."

It is important to reemphasize that *ALOG* is coded *only* when the impaired logic is offered *spontaneously.* There are instances when a subject may offer a complex answer, and in the attempt to use the entire card, or as much as possible, includes features in a more "qualified" way, as in the statement ". . . and I suppose this could be a . . . if you stretch your imagination." These kinds of qualifications are *not* scored *ALOG.* Similarly, it is not uncommon for some "strained" logic to be manifest in the inquiry *after* the examiner has asked for clarification of a percept. *ALOG* would not be scored in these instances, inasmuch as the element of spontaneity has been removed by the examiner's questioning.

PERSEVERATION AND INTEGRATION FAILURE

In some records two or more almost identical responses will be given to the same blot. In other cases, a response given previously will be alluded to again to a different blot. In some records, the same answer will be offered redundantly across several blots, and in still other instances an answer will be overgeneralized to the whole blot by using only an area of the blot. These sorts of answers represent a form of cognitive dysfunction or a marked psychological preoccupation. Two Special Scores are included in the System to indicate the presence of these answers.

PERSEVERATION (*PSV*)

There are at least three types of perseveration that may occur. Although they are different, all are assigned the same Special Score (*PSV*).

Within Card Perseveration   The within card *PSV* responses are those that use *exactly* the *same* location, the *same* determinant(s), the *same* content, the *same DQ* and *FQ,* and the *same Z* scoring if it has been involved, *as the preceding response.* The content may change slightly, but it will remain in the same general content category. Special Scores need not be the same in both answers. The most common examples of this form of *PSV* response occur in Cards I and V, when the subject gives two Popular answers in *consecutive* order. For instance:

1. "This could be a bat." (described by form and to the *W* and coded *Wo Fo A P* 1.0) followed by,
2. "Or, it could be a butterfly, too." (described by the form to the *W* and coded *Wo Fo A P* 1.0 *PSV*)

It is quite important to establish the fact that the subject *does* mean to give two responses and not simply an alternative, as is often the case. Usually, when the alternative type of answer is intended, it will be revealed by the selection of one of the two answers as being most appropriate, as in "Well the more I look at it it seems like a butterfly rather than a bat." In other instances, a subject may give an alternative type response, "Well it might be a bat, or it could be a butterfly too," but then will clearly differentiate the two in the inquiry. For example, "Well it really could be a bat because it's all black too," *Wo FC'o A P* 1.0; and "Of course it would be a good butterfly if you ignore the coloring," scored *Wo Fo A P* 1.0.

The real issue in a within card form of *PSV* is that the subject does deliver essentially the same answer *in the context* of the coding, with *no intervening answers*.

Content Perseveration   Whereas within card *PSV* is only for consecutive answers within a card, Content Perseveration characterizes responses that are not necessarily within the same card or to consecutive cards; but the content is *identified as the same seen earlier*. The coding of the new response may be quite different than for the answer in which the object was initially perceived, but the subject makes it quite clear that it is the same object(s). For instance, a subject may identify "Two people in a fight" on Card II, and to Card III report, "Oh, there are those *same* two people but the fight is over now and they're bowing to each other." It is not uncommon for some subjects, especially children, to see a bat on one card, usually Card I or V, and then report, "Oh, there's *that bat again*" to a subsequent card.

Mechanical Perseveration   A third type of perseverative response is seen more frequently among subjects who are intellectually handicapped and/or neurologically impaired. For the most part, this kind of perseveration is noted in very brief records, and it is easily identified because the subject gives essentially the same answer over and over, in an almost mechanical way. For example, a subject with severe organic impairment gave the answer "A bat" to each of the first seven cards, with no other responses intervening. When Card VIII was presented, he said, "Oh, this bat is colored," and finally on Card IX said, "Where did it go; it's not there anymore." These subjects will often inadvertently emphasize their perceptual rigidity by saying, "Oh, another . . . ," or "This one looks like a . . . too," or "My, they all look like . . . to me." Typically, subjects who manifest this form of perseveration are not good candidates for the Rorschach, and because they are so mechanistic, they are usually distinguished easily from the very resistive subject who is more clearly uncooperative and attempting to conceal through comments such as, "Man, they just don't look like nothing. They all look the same, all bats or something."

CONFABULATION (*CONFAB*)

In rare instances, a subject attends only to a detail area of the blot, but generalizes a response from that detail to a larger area, or to the entire blot. In most of these responses the contours of the detail selected will be used and/or described appropriately, but the overall response will be inappropriate for the total area involved. For instance, a subject might focus on the $D1$ area of the Card I and respond, "It's a claw, it's a lobster." In the Inquiry the subject establishes that the entire blot is included for the response, but when the examiner pursues the features of the response, the subject persists in justifying the answer because of the presence of the claw. There is no meaningful integration of the remainder of the blot even though the subject insists that the entire blot is included in the answer. The coding for this response would be *Wo F* − A *CONFAB*. A *Z* score is *not* assigned to the Confabulated answer.

It is important that the examiner insure that integration failure has truly occurred. Some very resistive subjects, especially adolescents, become irritated and/or threatened by the requirements of the Inquiry. If asked, "What is there that makes it look like . . . ?" they often respond, "I don't know, it just does," and are quite vague about any details of the object or the location used. Occasionally these subjects will point out one feature such as, "There's a foot there," for a response involving a whole human or whole animal. These are *not* typically *Confabulated* responses, but rather instances of lazy or resistive articulation. Usually, a caution to the subject by the examiner will clarify the issue as in, "Look, I know it looks like that to you, but you have to help me see it, too. Take your time. We are in no hurry. Now show me . . . ."

The true *CONFAB* is more mechanistic, and often the subject will seem mystified by the fact that the examiner does not appear to understand. A hint to the possible presence of a *CONFAB* sometimes will occur in the original association such as, "A claw, a lobster." The response has a stilted quality that strikes the ear of the listener. Unfortunately, some *CONFAB* answers are not identified as such until the Inquiry, because the subject gives only a single-word response in the original association. For example, a subject might give the response, "A lobster," and in the Inquiry report, "Sure, see the claw?" It is only when the examiner pursues the matter further that the *CONFAB* becomes apparent, because the subject will persist in focusing the single detail such as, "Look, see the claw, it's a lobster." Sometimes the subject will even manifest the very strained *ALOG*-like reasoning in attempting to defend the answer: "It's got a claw, it must be a lobster cause they have claws." Even if the *ALOG* is manifest it is *not* coded, because the *CONFAB* coding reflects the serious pathognomic quality of the answer and the perceptual-cognitive impairment that it includes.

SPECIAL CONTENT CHARACTERISTICS

Some of the studies completed at the Rorschach Research Foundation have focused on the special issues of content, and especially those features of responses that can be argued to reflect the characteristics of *projection*. In other words, those features of an answer that go beyond the level of classification. Although criteria to define various codes for this purpose are relatively easy to establish, the matter of validating their interpretive usefulness is more difficult to achieve. Sufficient work has been completed to warrant the incorporation of three of these codes into the Comprehensive System. They are important to the overall study of self-image, interpersonal perception, and behavior, and sometimes contribute information about the characteristics of thinking.

AGGRESSIVE MOVEMENT (*AG*)

The *Ag* coding is used for any movement response (*M, FM,* or *m*) in which the action is clearly aggressive, such as fighting, breaking, tearing, stalking, exploding, arguing, looking angry, and so on. The aggressive action must be occurring. Caution should be exercised to avoid coding *Ag* for responses in which the object *has been* subjected to aggression, such as a bear that has been shot, or a ship that has been bombed. These are *not Ag* responses. Similarly, an explosion per se is not *Ag*, but something being destroyed by an explosion *is Ag*.

COOPERATIVE MOVEMENT (*COP*)

The *COP* coding is assigned to any movement response (*M, FM,* or *m*) involving two or more objects in which the interaction is *clearly* positive or cooperative. The positive or cooperative characteristic of the interaction must be unequivocal. Thus, looking or talking are not scored *COP*. Some examples are: "Two men lifting something up," "Two insects trying to knock down this post," "Two people leaning toward each other, sharing a secret," "Three people doing a dance together," "A bird feeding her young," "Two children playing on a seesaw," "Two wolves attacking some other animal."

MORBID CONTENT (*MOR*)

The *MOR* coding is used for any response in which an object is identified by either of two classes of characteristics:

1. Identification of the object as dead, destroyed, ruined, spoiled, damaged, injured, or broken (e.g., a broken mirror, a dead dog, a worn out pair of boots, a bear that is hurt, a ripped piece of cloth, a wound, a torn coat, a decaying leaf, and so on).
2. Attribution to an object of a clearly dysphoric feeling or characteristic (e.g., a gloomy house, a sad tree, an unhappy person, a person crying, depression, and so on).

OTHER SPECIAL FEATURES OF RESPONSES

There are three other special responses charactistics which, when they occur, should be coded. Each reflects a type of defensive psychological activity that can be quite important to the development of any understanding of the subject.

ABSTRACTIONS (*AB*)

The *AB* coding is used for two classes of answers. The first are those for which the content code Human Experience (*Hx*) has been used to note human emotion or sensory experience. The second are responses in which the subject articulates a clear and specific symbolic representation. Abstract paintings are not scored *AB* unless a specific representation is included. Some examples of *AB* answers are: "A statue representing communist tyranny," "It just reminds me of depression," "A modern dance representing the beauty of women," "It's just a horrible smell, please take it back," "A mask that represents evil," "A poster of two dancers from the musical *Chorus Line*, "A Blake painting of man's struggle for purity."

PERSONALIZED ANSWERS (*PER*)

Many responses contain personal pronouns such as *I, me, my,* or *we*. Most are used naturally in the course of articulating a response such as, "It looks like a bat to me," or "I think that it looks like two people." There are, however, instances in which these forms of self-reference are used somewhat differently, and when that occurs, a Special Score is required because it signals a form of defensiveness.

Personal (*PER*)   The *PER* code is assigned to any response in which the subject refers to personal knowledge or experience as part of the basis for justifying and/or clarifying a response. Examples are: "We had one like that once," "I see them all the time in the yard," "I used to make them like this," "My father showed me some once," "I remember seeing one in a magazine," and so on.

Ordinarily the *PER* response will include the use of a personal pronoun—I, me, my, or we—but in some instances the personal knowledge or experience may be conveyed without a personal pronoun being employed. For instance, "It's an amoeba, if you ever took a biology course you've seen them," or "They make you wear ones like this in the Army." In either case the examiner should be convinced that the subject is injecting personal knowledge or experience rather than commentary. Comments such as "They used them a long time ago, I think," or "I've never seen one but I think they are like that," or "I think they are popular among children" are *not PER*.

COLOR PROJECTION (*CP*)

In most instances, subjects identifying chromatic colors will do so correctly—that is, red as red, green as green, and so on. In rare instances, some subjects misidentify chromatic colors. If this occurs, the examiner should pursue the issue cautiously in the Inquiry to determine whether a verbal lapse may have occurred. If the subject makes an appropriate correction, the response should be coded *DV* to indicate the verbal slip. Conversely, if no correction is made, an appropriate examination for color vision should be conducted. If color vision is intact, the response is a *DV;* however, there is another special phenomenon involving color for which a Special Score (*CP*) exists.

The *CP* coding is assigned to any response in which a subject identifies an achromatic blot or blot area as being chromatically colored. These are rare responses, occurring most frequently to Cards IV or V. In most, the chromatic coloring is hinted at but not specified in the original response, such as "Oh, what a beautiful butterfly." Obviously, the key word *beautiful* should be pursued in the Inquiry, and some subjects do report that the blot has "a pleasant purple coloring," or "different yellows and blues" and the like. There are no data to suggest that responses such as these are related to deficiencies in color vision, and research suggested by Piotrowski (1957) indicates that they do have a special interpretive significance.

Table 25.   Percentage of Coder Agreement for 12 Special Scores in Two Reliability Studies

Special Score	Symbol	20 Coders 25 Records % Agreement	15 Coders 20 Records % Agreement
Deviant Verbalization	*DV*	96%	97%
Deviant Response	*DR*	94%	95%
Incongruous Combination	*INCOM*	97%	97%
Fabulized Combination	*FABCOM*	98%	97%
Inappropriate Logic	*ALOG*	93%	95%
Contamination	*CONTAM*	99%	99%
Perservation	*PSV*	None present	99%
Confabulation	*CONFAB*	None present	None present
Aggressive Movement	*AG*	97%	96%
Cooperative Movement	*COP*	98%	99%
Morbid Content	*MOR*	98%	99%
Abstract Content	*AB*	96%	95%
Personal	*PER*	96%	97%
Color Projection	*CP*	99%	None present

CP is coded only when the subject specifically identifies the presence of chromatic coloring in the achromatic blot area. Most subjects who give *CP* answers tend to delineate the chromatic colors by using the shading features of the blot, thus requiring a determinant coding for diffuse shading (*FY, YF,* or *Y*).

The percentages of agreement in the two interscorer reliability studies, for each of the 12 Special Scores, are shown in Table 25.

REFERENCES

Exner, J. E. (1974) *The Rorschach: A Comprehensive System. Volume 1.* New York: Wiley.

Exner, J. E. (1978) *The Rorschach: A Comprehensive System. Volume 2. Current Research and Advanced Interpretation.* New York: Wiley.

Exner, J. E. (1990) *A Rorschach Workbook for the Comprehensive System* (3rd Ed.). Ashville, N.C.: Rorschach Workshops.

Exner, J. E. (1991) *The Rorschach: A Comprehensive System. Volume 2: Interpretation.* New York: Wiley.

Exner, J. E., and Weiner, I. B. (1982) *The Rorschach: A Comprehensive System. Volume 3. Assessment of Children and Adolescents.* New York: Wiley.

Exner, J. E., Weiner, I. B. and Schuyler, W. (1976) *A Rorschach Workbook for the Comprehensive System.* Bayville, N.Y.: Rorschach Workshops.

Piotrowski, Z. (1957) *Perceptanalysis.* New York: Macmillan.

Rapaport, D., Gill, M. M., and Schafer, R. (1946) *Diagnostic Psychological Testing. Volume II.* Chicago: Yearbook Publishers.

Schafer, R. (1954) *Psychoanalytic Interpretation in Rorschach Testing.* New York: Grune and Stratton.

Weiner, I. B. (1966) *Psychodiagnosis in Schizophrenia.* New York: Wiley.

CHAPTER 10

The Structural Summary

The objective of coding each response accurately is to be able to complete the *Structural Summary*. The Summary represents the composite of code frequencies plus many ratios, percentages, and numerical derivations. They are the data base from which Rorschach interpretation begins, and from which many important postulates concerning psychological functioning are generated. There are three simple procedures involved in creating the Structural Summary: (1) listing the Sequence of Scores, (2) recording frequencies for each variable, and (3) performing various calculations required to obtain the ratios, percentages, and derived scores. The protocol of a 26-year-old male has been included here to illustrate each of these steps.

SEQUENCE OF SCORES

The first step is the listing of the codes for each response in the order of occurrence, that is, Card by Card and with the responses numbered consecutively. This consolidation of the coding makes it easier to do the frequency tallies that are required, and the Sequence itself is often an additional source of important interpretive data. The Sequence of Scores page of the *Structural Summary Blank* includes columns for Card number, response number, and each of the major categories of coding used. It *also* has a column after the *Location* section headed *No.* that can be used to record the Location number involved in the response, such as *D*3, *DdS*26, and so on. If an area used is not numbered in Table A, the number 99 is used. The listing of location numbers in the Sequence of Scores will, occasionally, contribute to the interpretation of individual records, but generally they are much more useful for research purposes, and essential if a computer interpretation of the Structural Summary is to be generated. The Sequence of Scores for the protocol of L.S. is shown in Table 26.

FREQUENCY TALLIES

The second step in preparing the Structural Summary is the entry of frequency tallies for each of the codes on the *Structural Summary Blank*.

1. Location Features. Each of the three basic location codes is tallied separately. Spaces are also included to enter the frequencies of *Wv* and *S* responses, although *neither* of these frequencies is subtracted from the tallies for the three basic location codes of *W, D,* or *Dd.* Frequencies are also entered for each of the developmental quality codes, disregarding the type of location used.

2. Determinants. Each of the determinants is tallied separately, *except* when occurring in a blend. Each blend is entered in its entirety in the separate section under *Blends,*

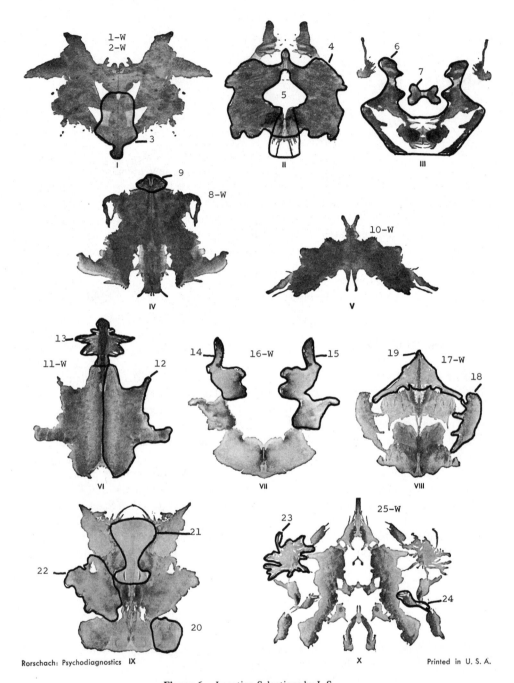

Figure 6. Location Selections by L.S.

The L.S. Protocol

Card	Response	Inquiry	Scoring
I	1. ll a bat gliding along	E: (Rpts S's resp) S: It has the outstrchd wgs & the small ft feet & ths cntr part wld b the body	Wo FMp_o A P 1.0
	2. It cld also b a modrn dance of s.s. w a wm in the cntr w her hands in the air & 2 creatures dancg around her	E: (Rpts S's resp) S: Yes, it ll her hands r raised in sort of supplication & ths creatures on the side reprsnt s.t. symbolic of whatever she's doing E: Symbolic S: They rem me of those wgd A's in Greek mythology, I can't rem the name.	$W+$ Mp^{-o}_o (2) $H, (A), 4.0 AB, COP$
	3. Say, ths lowr prt c.b. a bell	E: (Rpts S's resp) S: It has a pretty good shape of one w the clapper here	Ddo Fo Sc Bell
II	4. It cld b a cpl of dogs touchg noses	E: (Rpts S's resp) S: Its ths drkr areas (points), it ll the upper prts of dogs, thr noses r touchg, ths wld b the ear E: Upper parts? S: Its just the neck & head, u can't c the rest of the body	$D+$ FMp_o (2) Ad P 3.0
	5. The cntr cld b a rocket ship taking off & ths red cld b the exhaust fire	E: (Rpts S's resp) S: It has a delta shape & the way the color is there u get the impression of firey exhaust & upward motion	$DS+$ $m^a.CFo$ Sc, Fi 4.5
III	6. A cpl of men bendg ovr to lift s.t. up	E: (Rpts S's resp) S: U can c the gen outlins of thm, the forehead & a long nose, the neck & body, the arm reaching down, thyr bending forward, the hips r tilted backwrds, the legs, it ll thyr about to lift s.t. up but I can't tell what it is, prob som big rocks	$D+$ $M^a + (2) H, Ls P$ 3.0 COP

177

The L.S. Protocol (Continued)

Card	Response	Inquiry	Scoring					
	7. The cntr red area c.b. a bowtie	E: (Rpts S's resp) S: Well, the red attracted my attention to it, made me thk of those big red bowties that clowns wear sometimes	Do	FCo		Cg		
IV	8. It cld b a gorilla sittg on a stump	E: (Rpts S's resp) S: Yeah, it looks all furry lik a big A, lik a gorilla w the feet here (points), sorta lik he's leaning bkward bec the ft r so much bigger E: U said it looks furry S: Yes, all of the color variation makes it ll that	W+	$FM^pFD.FTo$	A, Bt	P	4.0	
	9. A delicate flower	E: (Rpts S's resp) S: I don't kno the name, my wife grows them, they almost ll velvet w ths contour & coloring effect E: Coloring effect? S: Yes, all the different shades in there	Do	FYo	Bt		PER	
V	10. It cld b a bat or a bf, I thk more a bf now that I look at it bec I said bat before.	E: (Rpts S's resp) S: Well it has the wgs & antennae & the split tail lik som bf's hve E: I'm not sure where u see it S: All of it I suppose, the W thg	Wo	Fo	A	P	1.0	DR
VI	11. Wld u believe an A skin?	E: (Rpts S's resp) S: I don't kno what kind of A, prob from the cat family bec of the stuff around the head E: The stuff around the head? S: Well actually, the W thg looks furry & spotted, the diff spots give a furry impress, lik from a tiger or s.t. & ths r whiskers	Wo	FTo	Ad	P	2.5	
	<12. Ths c.b. a submarine crusg along in the drkness	E: (Rpts S's resp) S: It has a pretty good shape of a sub, & the fact its all blk makes me thk	Do	$m^a.FYo$	Sc			

of darknss, like at night, the blacknss is like a shadowy effect, lik a nite, u get a good effect of the superstructure, the conning tower part here (points) & the long bow (points)

E: (Rpts S's resp)
S: The gen form of it rem me of kind of carving u mite c on a totem, usually a wgs effect like ths has to it

13. U kno, tht c.b. a totem too

Do Fo Ay

VII
14. A cpl of kids

E: (Rpts S's resp)
S: Just the heads, lik they hav feathers in their hair
E: I'm not sure why they ll tht
S: U can c the gen features, chins, noses, foreheads, that sort of thg

$D+$ Fo (2) Hd,ld P 1.0

<15. Ths way the side ll a scotty dog

E: (Rpts S's resp)
S: It has the blunt nose, thes r the short legs, & here's the tail

Do Fo A

V16. Ths way it ll a cpl of wm doing the can-can

E: (Rpts S's resp)
S: Thy hav big hairdos, sort of flat headed, c the neck is here (points) & their upper body & the skirt or dress ends here & thyr dancg on one leg, sort of throwg backward

$W+$ M^{a+} (2) H,Cg 3.0 COP

17. The W thg cld b an emblem, very colorful

E: (Rpts S's resp)
S: Yes, its like a family crest of s.s., being symmetrical & quite colorful

Wo CFo H,Sc 4.5

18. Ths thg on the side c.b. A's of s.s.

E: (Rpts S's resp)
S: There's 2 of 'em, one on each side
E: Can u tell me how u c them
S: Well thy c.b. mice or s.t. of the rodent family, c (points) here r the legs & head & tail

Do Fo (2) A P

19. U kno, ths top prt c.b. a sand crab, lik it was leapg forward, going away from u

E: (Rpts S's resp)
S: The pincers r here (points) & the area where the eyes r & it has the legs ex-

Do $FM^a.FDu$ A

The L.S. Protocol (Continued)

Card	Response	Inquiry	Scoring			
		tended lik it was leaping out, prob going away fr u the proportions give that effect				
IX	20. Ths ll T. Roosevelt's head	E: (Rpts S's resp) S: Rite here in the pink, its got the mustache & the flat forehead, its just the head, it really ll tht	Do	Fo		Hd
	21. Tht cntr prt c.b. a vase	E: (Rpts S's resp) S: Its just shaped lik a vase to me	Do	Fo		Hh
	<22. U kno, ths way it ll a person on a motorcycle or bike	E: (Rpts S's resp) S: Ths W green prt, most of it ll the person, I guess a heavy set man, & he's holdg the handlebars. The bike isn't too clear but the way his head is formed there u can get the impression of his hair flying bk in the breeze	D+	$M^a.mp$+		H, bike 2.5
X	23. Ths blue thg ll crabs	E: (Rpts S's resp) S: Thy just giv tht impress w all the legs	Do	Fo	(2)	A P
	24. Ths brwn c.b. a deer jumpg	E: (Rpts S's resp) S: The legs r outstrtchd & u can c the antlers here (points)	Do	FM^ao		A
	V25. Ths way it ll a floral scene, w a huge flower in the cntr & smaller flwrs around it	E: (Rpts S's resp) S: Well, the cntr flwr made me thk of it & I stretched it abit about the other thgs E: I'm not sure what u were seeing S: Its very colorful, the pink c.b. a daffodil & the blue pom poms but I can't really identify the rest. Its very pretty tho like a floral display	W +	CFo	(2)	Bt 5.5

180

Table 26.   Scoring Sequence for Protocol L.S.

CARD	NO	LOC	#	DETERMINANT(S)	(2)	CONTENT(S)	POP	Z	SPECIAL SCORES
I	1	Wo	1	FMpo		A	P	1.0	
	2	W+	1	Ma-po	2	H,(A)		4.0	AB,COP
	3	Ddo	24	Fo		Sc			
II	4	D+	6	FMpo	2	Ad	P	3.0	
	5	DS+	5	ma.CFo		Sc,Fi		4.5	
III	6	D+	1	Ma+	2	H,Ls	P	3.0	COP
	7	Do	3	FCo		Cg			
IV	8	W+	1	FMp.FD.FTo		A,Bt		4.0	
	9	Do	3	FYo		Bt			PER
V	10	Wo	1	Fo		A	P	1.0	DR
VI	11	Wo	1	FTo		Ad	P	2.5	
	12	Do	4	ma.FYo		Sc			
	13	Do	3	Fo		Ay			
VII	14	D+	1	Fo	2	Hd,Id	P	1.0	
	15	Do	2	Fo		A			
	16	W+	1	Ma+	2	H		3.0	COP
VIII	17	Wo	1	CFo		Art		4.5	
	18	Do	1	Fo	2	A	P		
	19	Do	4	FMa.FDu		A			
IX	20	Do	4	Fo		Hd			
	21	Do	8	Fo		Hh			
	22	D+	1	Ma.mpo		H,Sc		2.5	
X	23	Do	1	Fo	2	A	P		
	24	Do	7	FMao		A			
	25	W+	1	CFo	2	Bt		5.5	

and the determinants are not counted again as each of the frequencies for single determinants are entered.

3. Form Quality. There are four distributions to be entered concerning form quality. The first, shown by the heading on the Structural Summary Blank as *FQx* (Form Quality Extended), includes *all* of the responses in the record. It includes spaces to enter the tallies for each of the four types of form quality, plus one for the frequency of responses in which no form quality has been coded. The second is headed as *FQf* (Form Quality-Form) on the Summary. It is for the *FQ* frequencies of those responses in which pure *F* is the only determinant. The third is headed *M* Quality, and is for the distribution of *FQ* for all of the Human Movement responses. The last is headed *SQx,* and is for the distribution of FQ for all of the Space responses.

4. Contents. The column headed Contents includes each of the 27 categories. In some instances, *two* entries are required for a single category, one indicating the frequency of responses in which the category represents *the primary content* and the second, separated from the first by a comma, representing the frequency of responses in which the category has been used as *an additional or secondary content.* For example, two responses may have Botany (*Bt*) as the primary content, such as "A tree," and "Some flowers," but a third response may have *Bt* as an additional content, such as, "A man sitting on a tree stump." Thus the entry for the *Bt* category will be *Bt* = 2,1. A second column of blank lines is included on the Summary to enter the idiographic contents.

5. Organizational Activity. Three entries are required at the top of the Summary for organizational activity. The first, *Zf (Z Frequency),* is the number of times a Z response has occurred in the record. The second, *ZSum,* is for the summation of the weighted Z scores that have been assigned. The third, *Zest,* is a prediction of what the *ZSum* should be, based on *Zf.* It is derived from Table 27, a copy of which is reproduced in the Structural Summary Blank. L.S. gave 13 answers that were scored for Z; thus the *Zest* is 41.5.

6. Populars, Pairs, and Reflections. There are three other entries at the top of the Summary. One represents the number of Popular answers, the second (2) is for the total number of pair responses, and the third, *Fr + rF,* is for the number of reflection responses in the protocol.

7. Special Scores. The last set of frequencies to be entered includes those for each of the 12 Special Scores, and a calculation is required to enter a *Weighted Sum* for the first six (*WSUM6*). The values assigned are: Each *DV* = 1, each *DR* = 3, each *INCOM* = 2, each *FABCOM* = 4, each *ALOG* = 5, and each *CONTAM* = 7.

The Structural Summary for the protocol of L.S. is shown as Table 28, illustrating how each of the frequencies has been entered in the upper portion, and how various ratios, percentages, and derivations are entered in the lower section.

Table 27. Best Weighted ZSum Prediction When *Zf* Is Known[a]

Zf	Zest	Zf	Zest
1	*	26	88.0
2	2.5	27	91.5
3	6.0	28	95.0
4	10.0	29	98.5
5	13.5	30	102.5
6	17.0	31	105.5
7	20.5	32	109.0
8	24.0	33	112.5
9	27.5	34	116.5
10	31.0	35	120.0
11	34.5	36	123.5
12	38.0	37	127.0
13	41.5	38	130.5
14	45.5	39	134.0
15	49.0	40	137.5
16	52.5	41	141.0
17	56.0	42	144.5
18	56.0	42	144.5
18	59.5	43	148.0
19	63.0	44	152.0
20	66.5	45	155.5
21	70.0	46	159.0
22	73.5	47	162.5
23	77.0	48	166.0
24	81.0	49	169.5
25	84.5	50	173.0

[a]Taken from Beck, S. J., Beck, A., Levitt, E., and Molish, H. *Rorschach's Test I: Basic Processes* (3rd ed.) New York: Grune & Stratton, 1961.

Table 28.   Structural Summary for Protocol L.S.

```
===============================================================================
LOCATION            DETERMINANTS              CONTENTS       S-CONSTELLATION
FEATURES              BLENDS         SINGLE                  NO..FV+VF+V+FD>2
                                              H   = 4, 0     NO..Col-Shd Bl>0
Zf   = 13        m.CF            M   = 3      (H) = 0, 0     NO..Ego<.31,>.44
ZSum = 39.5      FM.FD.FT        FM  = 3      Hd  = 2, 0     NO..MOR > 3
ZEst = 41.5      m.FY            m   = 0      (Hd)= 0, 0     NO..Zd > +- 3.5
                 FM.FD           FC  = 1      Hx  = 0, 0     YES..es > EA
W   =  8         M.m            CF  = 2      A   = 8, 0     YES..CF+C > FC
 (Wv = 0)                        C   = 0      (A) = 0, 1     NO..X+% < .70
D   = 16                         Cn  = 0      Ad  = 2, 0     NO..S > 3
Dd  =  1                         FC'= 0      (Ad)= 0, 0     NO..P < 3 or > 8
S   =  1                         C'F= 0      An  = 0, 0     NO..Pure H < 2
                                 C' = 0      Art = 1, 0     NO..R < 17
     DQ                          FT  = 1      Ay  = 1, 0     2....TOTAL
.........(FQ-)                   TF  = 0      Bl  = 0, 0
  +  =  9  ( 0)                  T   = 0      Bt  = 2, 1     SPECIAL SCORINGS
  o  = 16  ( 0)                  FV  = 0      Cg  = 1, 0         Lv1    Lv2
 v/+ =  0  ( 0)                  VF  = 0      Cl  = 0, 0     DV  =  0x1    0x2
  v  =  0  ( 0)                  V   = 0      Ex  = 0, 0     INC =  0x2    0x4
                                 FY  = 1      Fd  = 0, 0     DR  =  1x3    0x6
                                 YF  = 0      Fi  = 0, 1     FAB =  0x4    0x7
                                 Y   = 0      Ge  = 0, 0     ALOG =  0x5
  FORM QUALITY                   Fr  = 0      Hh  = 1, 0     CON  =  0x7
                                 rF  = 0      Ls  = 0, 1       SUM6  = 1
      FQx  FQf  MQual  SQx        FD  = 0      Na  = 0, 0       WSUM6 = 3
  +  =  2   0    2     0          F   = 9      Sc  = 3, 1
  o  = 22   9    2     1                       Sx  = 0, 0     AB  = 1    CP  = 0
  u  =  1   0    0     0                       Xy  = 0, 0     AG  = 0    MOR = 0
  -  =  0   0    0     0                       Id  = 0, 1     CFB = 0    PER = 1
none=  0   --    0     0          (2) =  8                    COP = 3    PSV = 0
===============================================================================
             RATIOS, PERCENTAGES, AND DERIVATIONS
```

```
Core                                   Affect              Interpersonal
R = 25          L =  0.56              FC:CF+C = 1: 3      COP = 3     AG = 0
-----------------------------------    Pure C  =  0        Food   = 0
EB = 4: 3.5  EA =  7.5   EBPer= N/A    Afr    =0.56        Isolate/R =0.16
eb = 8: 4    es = 12        D  = -1    S      = 1          H:(H)Hd(Hd)= 4: 2
         Adj es =  9   Adj D =  0      Blends:R= 5:25      (HHd):(AAd)= 0: 1
-----------------------------------    CP     = 0          H+A:Hd+Ad  =13: 4
FM = 5  :  C'= 0   T = 2
m  = 3  :  V = 0   Y = 2
                         Mediation          Processing         Self Perception
Ideation                 P   = 8             Zf  =13            3r+(2)/R=0.32
a:p   =  8: 5   Sum6  = 1  X+% =0.96          Zd  = -2.0         Fr+rF  = 0
Ma:Mp =  4: 1   Lv2   = 0  F+% =1.00          W:D:Dd = 8:16: 1   FD     = 2

2AB+Art+Ay= 4   WSum6 = 3  X-% =0.00          W:M = 8: 4         An+Xy  = 0
M-   = 0       Mnone = 0  S-% =0.00          DQ+ = 9            MOR    = 0
                           Xu% =0.04          DQv = 0
-------------------------------------------------------------------------------
SCZI = 0    DEPI = 2    CDI = 1    S-CON = 2    HVI = No    OBS =YES
===============================================================================
```

RATIOS, PERCENTAGES, AND DERIVATIONS

Once the data have been organized into frequencies, the Structural Summary can be completed by doing the various calculations required for the entries in the lower portion of the Summary which is divided into seven data blocks. At the very bottom of the lower section there are six special indices, the *SCZI, DEPI, CDI, S-CON, HVI,* and *OBS,* that are completed last using the *Constellations Worksheet,* which is shown for the L.S. protocol at the end of this chapter.

THE CORE SECTION

The Core Section is at the upper left of the lower section of the *Structural Summary*. It contains 16 entries. Seven entries are frequency data. They include *R* (total number of responses), and the total number for each of the determinants *FM, m, C', T, V,* and *Y.* (The latter four include all variations so that *C'* includes *FC', C'F,* and *C';* *T* includes *FT, TF,* and *T;* etc.)

The other nine entries are ratios and derivations. They are:

1. *Lambda (L).* The second entry is for *Lambda (L).* This is a ratio that compares the frequency of pure *F* responses with all other answers in the record. It relates to issues of economizing the use of resources. It is calculated as:

$$L = \frac{F \text{ (Number of Responses having only Pure } F \text{ determinants)}}{R - F \text{ (Total } R \text{ minus Pure Form answers)}}$$

In the L.S. record, out of 25 responses, there are 9 pure *F* responses and 16 answers with other determinants, which yields $L = (9/16) = 0.56$.

2. Erlebnistypus *(EB).* This is a relationship between two major variables, human movement *(M)*, and the weighted sum of the chromatic color responses. It is entered as *Sum M:Weighted Sum Color.* The *Weighted Sum Color (WSumC)* is obtained by multiplying each type of chromatic color responses by a weight. Color naming responses, *Cn,* are *not* included in the *WSumC*.

$$WSumC = (0.5) \times FC + (1.0) \times CF + (1.5) \times C.$$

The L.S. protocol contains 4 *M* responses, 1 *FC* response, 3 *CF* answers, and 0 *C* responses. Thus, $WSumC = (0.5) \times (1) + (1.0) \times (3) + (0) \times (1) = 3.5$, yielding an *EB* of 4:3.5.

3. Experience Actual *(EA).* This is a derivation that relates to available resources. It is obtained by adding the two sides of the *EB* together, that is, *Sum M + WSumC.* In the L.S. protocol, it is $4 + 3.5 = 7.5$.

4. EB Pervasive *(EBPer).* This is a ratio concerning the dominance of an *EB* style in decision-making activity. It is calculated by dividing the larger number in the *EB* by the smaller number. In the L.S. protocol, no calculation for *EBPer* is required because *EBPer* is calculated *only* when a marked style is indicated in the *EB*. In other words, if the value of *EA* is 10.0 or less, one side of the *EB* must be *at least two points* greater than the other side, or if the value of *EA* is more than 10.0, one side of the *EB* must be *at least* 2.5 points greater than the other.

5. Experience Base *(eb).* This is a relationship comparing all nonhuman movement determinants *(FM* and *m)* with the shading and achromatic color determinants. It provides information concerning stimulus demands experienced by the subject. It is entered as *Sum FM + m:Sum all C' + all T + all Y + all V.*

The data in the right side of the ratio include *all* determinants in which any of the four components exist. For example, "all *T*" includes *FT, TF,* and *T*. In the L.S. protocol, as indicated by the entries made just below the boxed area, there are 5 *FM* and 3 *m* determinants, plus 2 *Achromatic color* answers *(C')*, and 2 *Texture answers (T)*. Thus the *eb* is 8:4.

6. Experienced Stimulation *(es).* This is a derivation obtained from the data in the *eb.* It relates to current stimulus demands. It is obtained by adding the two sides of the *eb* together, that is, *Sum FM+m+all C'+all T+all Y+all V.* In the L.S. record it is $8 + 4 = 12$.

Table 29.   *EA − es D* **Score Conversion Table**

EA − es Raw Score	*D* Score
+13.0 to +15.0	+5
+10.5 to +12.5	+4
+8.0 to +10.0	+3
+5.5 to +7.5	+2
+3.0 to +5.0	+1
−2.5 to +2.5	0
−3.0 to −5.0	−1
−5.5 to −7.5	−2
−8.0 to −10.0	−3
−10.5 to −12.5	−4
−13.0 to −15.0	−5

7. The *D* Score *(D)*. The *D* Score provides important information concerning the relationship between *EA* and *es*. This concerns stress tolerance and elements of control. It is obtained by first calculating the raw score difference between the two variables, that is, *EA − es,* and including the appropriate sign. The raw difference score is then converted into a scaled difference score, based on standard deviations, in which each *SD* has been rounded to equal 2.5.

Thus, if the raw score difference of *EA − es* falls between +2.5 and −2.5, there is no significant difference between the two values and the *D* Score is 0. If the raw score of *EA − es* is greater than +2.5, the *D* Score will increase by units of +1 for each 2.5 raw score points. If the raw score of *EA − es* yields a value of less than −2.5, the *D* Score will decrease by units of −1 for each 2.5 points. Table 29 is the Conversion Table for obtaining the *D* Score.

In the L.S. protocol, the difference *EA − es* is 7.5 −12 = −4.5, yielding a *D* Score of −1.

8. Adjusted *es (Adj es)*. Whereas the *D* Score provides information concerning stress tolerance and available resources, it is important to determine if the score has been influenced by situational elements. The first step in doing this is to subtract from the *es* most of the elements that are related to situational phenomena. The tactic is simple. All but 1 *m* and 1 *Y* (including *FY* and *YF*) are subtracted from the *es* to create the *Adj es*. In the L.S. record, there are 3 *m* determinants and 2 *Y* determinants. Thus, a value of 3 (2 *m* + 1 *Y*) is subtracted from *es* and the *Adj es* has a value of 9.

9. Adjusted *D* Score *(Adj D)*. The *Adj D* is obtained by using the formula *EA − Adj es*. The result is applied against the *D Score Conversion Table*. In the L.S. record, the result is 7.5 − 9 = −1.5, which yields an *Adj D* of 0.

THE IDEATION SECTION

This section contains eight entries. Four of the eight are frequency data (*M −* and *M* with no *FQ*, *Raw Sum*6, number of Level 2 responses), and a fifth (*WSum*6) has already been calculated. The remaining three consist of two ratios and one index. They are:

1. Active:Passive Ratio *(a:p)*. This relationship concerns flexibility in ideation and attitudes. It is entered as the total number of *Active* movement answers ($M^a + FM^a + m^a$)

on the left and the total number of *Passive* movement responses ($M^p + FM^p + m^p$) on the right. Movement determinants with $^a - ^p$ superscripts are added to both sides. The L.S. record shows an $a:p$ of 8:5.

2. *M* Active:Passive Ratio ($M^a:M^p$). This variable concerns some characteristics of thinking. It includes *only* human movement responses with total Active entered on the left and total Passive entered on the right. $M^a - ^p$ answers are added to both sides. The L.S. record has an $M^a:M^p$ of 4:1.

3. The Intellectualization Index—$2AB + (Art + Ay)$. This index includes the special score *AB* (Abstract) and the contents Art and Anthropology. It is calculated as two times the number of *AB* answers plus the number of *Art* and *Ay* contents. Both primary and secondary contents are included. In the sample record, there is 1 *AB* response plus 1 *Art* content and 1 *Ay* response, yielding and Index value of 4.

THE AFFECT SECTION

This section includes six entries. Three are frequency data (*Pure C, S,* and *CP*), and the remaining three are the following ratios:

1. Form-Color Ratio ($FC:CF + C$). This ratio relates to the modulation of affect. It is entered as shown, with the total number of *FC* determinants on the left and the sum of the $CF + C$ determinants on the right. The chromatic color determinants are each weighed equally in this ratio as contrasted with the *WSumC* used in the *EB* and *EA*. The L.S. protocol has 1 *FC* response, 3 *CF* responses. Thus, the ratio is 1:3.

2. Affective Ratio (*Afr*). This is a ratio that compares the number of answers to the last three cards with those given to the first seven cards. It relates to interest in emotional stimulation. It is calculated as:

$$Afr = \frac{\text{Number Responses to Cards VIII} + \text{IX} + \text{X}}{\text{Number Responses to Cards I} + \text{II} + \text{III} + \text{IV} + \text{V} + \text{VI} + \text{VII}}$$

In the sample record, the subject gave 9 responses to the last three cards and 16 responses to the first seven cards, yielding an $Afr = (9/16) = 0.56$.

3. Complexity Index (Blends:R). This relationship is usually *not* reduced to a ratio, but instead entered as indicated with the total number of blends on the left and the number of responses on the right. In the sample record, there are five blends yielding a ratio of 5:25.

THE MEDIATION SECTION

This section contains six entries, one for the frequency of Popular (P) responses and five percentages:

1. Conventional Form ($X + \%$). This variable concerns the extent to which form use is conventional. It is calculated as:

$$X + \% = \frac{\text{Sum } FQx + \text{ and } o}{R}$$

In the L.S. record, there are 2 + answers and 22 *ordinary* responses, yielding an $X + \%$ of 0.96.

2. Conventional Pure Form ($F+\%$). This variable concerns the conventional use of contour in the pure F responses. It is calculated as:

$$F+\% = \frac{\text{Sum } F+ \text{ and } Fo}{\text{Sum } F}$$

The L.S. record contains 9 Pure F responses, all of which are *ordinary*. This calculates for an $F + \%$ of 1.00.

3. Distorted Form ($X-\%$). This variable concerns the proportion of perceptual distortion that has occurred in the record. It is calculated as:

$$X-\% = \frac{\text{Sum } FQx-}{R}$$

The L.S. record contains no minus answers, leading to an $X - \%$ of 0.00.

4. White Space Distortion ($S-\%$). This variable concerns the proportion of distorted form answers that include the use of white space. It is calculated as:

$$S-\% = \frac{\text{Sum } SQ-}{\text{Sum } FQx-}$$

The L.S. record contains 1 S response but no minus answers. Thus the $S - \%$ equals 0.00.

5. Unusual Form ($Xu\%$). This variable concerns the proportion of answers in which contours have been used appropriately but unconventionally. It is calculated as:

$$Xu\% = \frac{\text{Sum } FQxu}{R}$$

In the L.S. record, there is only 1 *unusual* response, yielding an $Xu\%$ of 0.04.

THE PROCESSING SECTION

This section contains six entries, three of which are frequency data (Zf, $DQ+$, and DQv). Two of the remaining three are ratios and the third is a difference score:

1. Economy Index ($W:D:Dd$). This relationship is entered as shown with the total number of W responses on the left, the total number of D responses in the center, and the total number of Dd answers at the right.

2. Aspirational Ratio ($W:M$). This relationship usually is not reduced to a ratio, but instead entered as indicated with the total number of W responses on the left and the total number of M answers at the right.

3. Processing Efficiency (Zd). The Zd is a difference score obtained by the formula $ZSum - Zest$, with the appropriate sign recorded. In the L.S. protocol, the $ZSum = 39.5$ and the $Zest = 41.5$, yielding a Zd score of -2.0.

THE INTERPERSONAL SECTION

This section contains seven entries, three of which are frequency data (the number of COP responses, the number of AG responses, and the number of primary and secondary $Food$ contents). The remaining four are ratios, the first of which requires some calculation:

1. Isolation Index (*Isolate/R*). This variable is related to social isolation. It involves the primary *and* secondary contents in five categories (Botany, Clouds, Geography, Landscape, and Nature), with the raw sum for two categories being doubled. It is calculated as:

$$Isolate/R = \frac{Bt + 2Cl + Ge + Ls + 2Na}{R}$$

The L.S. record contains 3 *Bt,* and 1 *Ls* for a weighted sum of 4, which yields an Index value of 0.16.

2. Interpersonal Interest—(*HH*) + *Hd* + (*Hd*). This entry provides information about interest in people. The entry includes both primary and secondary contents. The sum of *Pure H* responses is entered on the left and the sum of the other human contents entered on the right.

3. (*H*) + (*Hd*):(*A*) + (*Ad*). This summary entry provides some information about the extent to which conceptions of others may be based more on imagination than real experience. The entry includes both primary and secondary contents.

4. *H* + *A* : *Hd* + *Ad*. This summary entry provides information about the frequencies of whole human and animal contents as contrasted with human and animal detail answers. Both primary and secondary contents are included and entered as shown.

THE SELF-PERCEPTION SECTION

This section contains five entries, four of which are frequency tallies. They include the sum *Fr* + *rF,* the number of Form Dimension (*FD*) responses, the number of answers that have morbid content (*MOR*), and the sum of responses that contain Anatomy (*An*) or X-ray (*Xy*) contents, either primary or secondary. The sixth entry is a ratio.

1. Egocentricity Index (3*r* + (2)/*R*). This index relates to self-esteem. It represents the proportion of reflection and pair responses in the total record, with each reflection determinant weighed as being equal to three pair responses. It is calculated as:

$$3r + (2)/R = \frac{3 \times (Fr + rF) + Sum\ (2)}{R}$$

The L.S. record contains no reflection answers and 8 pair responses leading to an Egocentricity Index = [(3) × 0 + 8]/(25) = 0.32.

SPECIAL INDICES

At the bottom of the *Structural Summary* there are six special indices, the Schizophrenia Index (*SCZI*), the Depression Index (*DEPI*), the Coping Deficit Index (*CDI*), the Suicide Constellation (*S-CON*), the Hypervigilance Index (*HVI*), and the Obsessive Style Index (*OBS*).

The variables included for each are shown on the *Constellations Worksheet,* shown as Table 30 for the L.S. protocol, with boxes provided to check those that are positive. The total number of positive variables should be entered at the bottom of the *Structual Summary* for the *SCZI, DEPI, CDI,* and *S-CON.* Notations of *Yes* or *No* should be entered for the *HVI* and the *OBS*.

Table 30. Constellations Worksheet for the L.S. Protocol

```
=====================================================================
  SCZI (SCHIZOPHRENIA INDEX):
    Positive if 4 or more conditions are true:

    No...EITHER: (X+% < .61) AND (S-% < .41)
        OR...: (X+% < .50)
    No...(X-% > .29)
    No...EITHER: (FQ- >= FQu)
        OR...: (FQ- > FQo + FQ+)
    No...(Sum Level 2 Sp. Sc. > 1) AND (FAB2 > 0)
    No...EITHER: (Raw Sum of 6 Spec. Scores > 6)
        OR...: (Weighted Sum of 6 Sp. Sc. > 17)
    No...EITHER: (M- > 1)
        OR...: (X-% > .40)


  DEPI (DEPRESSION INDEX):          CDI (COPING DEFICIT INDEX):
    Positive if 5 or more             Positive if 4 or 5
    conditions are true:              conditions are true:

    No...(FV+VF+V > 0)  OR  (FD > 2)  No...(EA < 6)  OR  (AdjD < 0)
    No...(Col-Shd Blends > 0)  OR     No...(COP < 2)  AND  (AG < 2)
        (S > 2)                       No...(Weighted Sum C < 2.5)
    YES...(3r+(2)/R > .44  and  Fr+rF=0)  OR  (Afr < .46)
        OR  (3r+(2)/R < .33)          No...(Passive > Active+1)  OR
    No...(Afr < .46)  OR  (Blends < 4)    (Pure H < 2)
    No...(SumShading > FM+m)  OR      YES...(Sum T > 1)  OR
        (SumC' > 2)                       (Isolate/R > .24)  OR
    YES...(MOR > 2)  OR                   (Food > 0)
        (2AB+(Art+Ay)  > 3)
    No...(COP < 2)  OR
        ( Isolate/R  > .24)


  HV (HYPERVIGILANCE INDEX):        OBS (OBSESSIVE STYLE INDEX):
    Positive if Condition 1 is
    true and at least 4 of the        No...(1) Dd > 3
    others are true.                  YES...(2) Zf > 12
                                      No...(3) Zd > +3.0
    No...(1) FT+TF+T = 0              YES...(4) Populars > 7
- - - - - - - - - - - - - -          YES...(5) FQ+ > 1
    YES...(2) Zf > 12                - - - - - - - - - - - - - -
    No...(3) Zd > +3.5               Positive if one or more is true:
    No...(4) S > 3                     No...Conditions 1 to 5
    No...(5) H+(H)+Hd+(Hd) > 6               Are All True
    No...(6) (H)+(A)+(Hd)+(Ad) > 3   No...2 or more of 1 to 4
    YES...(7) H+A:Hd+Ad < 4:1              are true AND FQ+ > 3
    No...(8) Cg > 3                  YES...3 or more of 1 to 5
                                          are true AND X+% > .89
                                      No...FQ+ > 3  AND  X+% > .89
=====================================================================
```

SUMMARY

Once the Structural Summary has been completed, the interpretation can proceed. It is not a lengthy process, but the interpretive yield is directly dependent on the element of accuracy—accuracy in coding each response, accuracy in entering each of the frequencies, and accuracy in completing the variety of calculations necessary to generate the ratios, percentages, and derivations. *If* the total data base is accurate, the resulting interpretation of the record is far less likely to be blemished by inappropriate or inaccurate conclusions.

The novice Rorschacher may find the procedures required to collect, collate, and complete the calculations cumbersome and time-consuming, but the time requirements are reduced quickly as experience builds. The experienced Rorschacher will ordinarily devote little more than 30 minutes to code the responses in an average length record, even though some of the responses are quite complex. Completing the Structural Summary should take little more than 10 to 15 minutes for those who are comfortable with the procedures, and the interpretation, although involving many principles and rules, can usually be completed in considerably less than 1 hour.

PART III

Working Tables
and Descriptive Statistics

CHAPTER 11

Working Tables

This chapter contains five tables, each of which is used frequently in coding decisions concerning responses. The first, Table A, includes figures of each of the 10 blots showing the revised location numbering system for the common and unusual detail areas. Approximately 70% of those location numbers are extracted directly from Beck's work, with the remaining 30% generated by the procedures described in Chapter 5. The bulk of Table A is comprised of listings of responses, by card and location area. Each is designated as *o* (ordinary), *u* (unusual), or − (minus), depending on whether it meets the frequency or judgment criteria described in Chapter 7.

Table A could be expanded considerably with the addition of a large number of minus answers, selected either from the more than 162,000 responses against which the frequency criteria were applied, or from psychotic or schizophrenic records not included in that data base. The overwhelming majority of those answers occur with an extremely low frequency, however, typically less than once per 1000 records. Their inclusion would probably detract (more than assist) from the usefulness of the table by making it much longer. Thus a frequency criterion of 10 or more has been used in selecting the minus responses that are included for the W and D areas, and three or more for inclusion in the listings for Dd areas.

As noted in Chapter 7, decisions to code a response as *FQ*+ involves some subjective judgment. They reflect an unusual detailing of form features that may be very creative, or may simply represent a tendency toward greater preciseness. Table B provides a few illustrations of responses in which the form features have been articulated extensively, thus warranting the *FQ* coding of +. All could be delivered with less emphasis on the specific form elements and, if so, would be coded as *o*. In each of these examples the subject has gone well beyond the necessities of form elaboration to enrich the answer. It is important to restrict the coding of + to answers that, with less elaborate form articulation, would be coded *o*. The vast majority of responses in the *FQ* data base that include an unusual elaboration of form elements also meet the criterion to be coded *o*. It is true that unusual answers, especially those that are very creative, may include a precise and/or elaborate articulation of the form features. Even so, the *FQ* coding of *u* is required. Some examiners may wish to note the unusual form elaboration by using the experimental coding of *u*/+ to denote the superior use of the form. If the *u*/+ code is assigned, however, the response should continue to be treated as *u* in all of the Structural calculations.

The Z values by card have also been entered in Table A. Table C has been included here to provide the entire array of those values. Table D provides the estimated weighted ZSum (*Zest*) from which the *Zd* score is derived.

The criterion for Popular responses is also included, by card, in Table A. Table E provides the entire listing of Populars.

USING TABLE A

It has been noted in Chapter 7 that the listing of responses in Table A should be fairly inclusive because of the size of the sample involved in its construction. Nonetheless, some objects may not appear in the table with the same specificity that occurs in a response. Obviously, it is appropriate to attempt *conservative* extrapolation from the Table A data when that occurs. For example, some specific animals may appear in a listing for a given location area, but "cougar" may not be in the list. If this is the case, it should not be difficult to extrapolate from the available items to the appropriate coding decision for "cougar." If the scanning of the list reveals an animal similar to a cougar, such as a tiger or cat, it is appropriate to assign the code listed for them for the cougar response. In other cases extrapolation can occur by using the rule of similarly shaped objects, such as extrapolating from a worm to a snake, a branch to a stick, a stick to a cane, a human-like figure to an angel, and so on. Unfortunately, some coding decisions will remain more subjective. Generally, the following principles, derived from the *FQ* criteria, should be observed: (1) If a specific item is not listed and extrapolation does not occur easily, it should be coded either as *u* or − by applying principles 2 or 3; (2) if a specific item does not appear in the list, but can be perceived *quickly and easily,* and involves no substantial contour distortions, it should be coded *u;* (3) if a specific item does not appear in the list, and can be perceived only with difficulty, or not at all, it should be coded as −.

Sometimes it may be necessary to review the listings for more than one location area before making a decision concerning extrapolation. For instance, a response might involve two or three different anatomy items. The list for the total area used might indicate a *FQ* code for anatomy "(Unspecified)." In this case, the listings for the areas used for each of the specific anatomy components should be reviewed to determine if codes are available for any of those items.

Some responses will contain multiple objects that do not all have the same form quality. As a rule, the "lowest" form quality is assigned for the entire response; however, this rule is applied only to objects that are important to the overall response. For example, on Card III a subject reports, "Two people (*D*9) bending over looking at some lungs (*D*7) down here." *D*9 as a human figure is listed as *o* in Table A and, in fact, is also a Popular response. However, *D*7, as lungs, is listed in Table A as *minus.* Thus, the form quality for the response is *minus.* On the other hand, if one object that is not very important to the overall response has a listed form quality that is lower than the other objects in the answer, the higher form quality is assigned. For instance, another response to Card III might be "Two people (*D*9) dancing around this thing in the center (*D*7), maybe a drum." Again, the people are listed as *o* in Table A but *D*7, as a drum, is listed as *unusual.* In this response, the important objects are the two people and the drum is added somewhat casually, "maybe a drum." Thus, the form quality scoring of ordinary seems to be the more appropriate. This issue occurs most frequently on Card X when a subject, describing several insects or underwater creatures, most of which are listed as *ordinary,* includes one that may be listed as *unusual* or even *minus.* Assuming the the one listed as *unusual* or *minus* is not critical to the overall answer, the correct coding should be *ordinary.*

Caret marks (<v>) have been included for some responses to indicate the direction for the apex of the blot. If no caret mark appears next to an item, it signifies that the *FQ* coding listed is appropriate only when the apex of the card is in the upright position.

Table A.   Figures Showing Common (*D*) and Unusual (*Dd*) Location Areas by Card, Listings of Ordinary (*o*), Unusual (*u*) and Minus (−) Responses and Response Classes by Location Areas, Plus Populars and Z Values for Each Card

CARD I

P Is to *W*:   Bat or Butterfly

Z Values:	*W* = 1.0	Adjacent = 4.0	Distant = 6.0	Space = 3.5

Location	FQ	Category	Location	FQ	Category
W	−	Abalone	o		Bug (Winged)
	−	Abacus	−		Bullet
	−	Abdomen	o		Butterfly
	u	Abstract drawing	u	v	Cabin
	u	Airplane (Top view)	u		Cocoon
	−	Airplane (Front view)	−		Cactus
	−	Albacore	−		Cage
	u	Amoeba	−		Cake
	−	Anchor	u	v	Cap (Snow)
	o	Angel	u		Cape
	−	Animal (Not winged)	−		Car
		(*Note:* This class of response includes a	−		Cart
		large group of animals that do not have	u	v	Castle
		wings or flappers such as bear, cat,	−		Cat
		dog, lion, etc.)	u	v	Catamaran (Front view)
	u	Animal (Winged but unspecified)	−		Cattle (Herd)
	−	Ant	u		Cave
	−	Anteater	o	v	Chandelier
	u	v Astrodome	−		Chest
	−	Australia	−		Chevron
	−	Baboon	−		Chinese Art
	o	Badge	u		Cinder
	o	Bat	u	v	Circus Tent
	−	Battleship	−		Cistern
	−	Bear	−		Citrus Tree
	−	Beard	−		Clamp
	u	Bee	−		Clitoris
	u	Beetle	u		Cloak
	−	Bell	−		Clock
	u	v Bellows	u		Cloud(s)
	−	Bib	−		Clove
	o	Bird	u		Coal (Piece)
	−	Blanket	−		Coat
	−	Boat	u		Coat of Arms
	−	Body	−		Codfish
	−	Body (Split)	u		Coral
	−	Book	−		Cow
	−	Bookmark	o		Crab
	u	Bone (Skeletal)	−		Crate
	u	Bowl (With handles)	−		Crater
	−	Brain	u		Crawfish
	u	Brain (Cross section)	u		Crow
	−	Breast	o	v	Crown
	−	Bridge (Man-made)	o		Dancer (In costume or cape)
	u	Bridge (Natural)	−		Dandelion
	−	Buckle	u		Demon (Caped)
	−	Bug (Unspecified, not winged)	u		Design

Table A (Continued)

Location	FQ	Category	Location	FQ	Category
	—	Dirigible		u	Fog
	u	Dirt		—	Foliage
	o	Disc (Anatomy)		—	Food
	u	v Dome		—	Forest
	—	Door		u	Fossil
	u	Dracula		o	v Fountain
	—	Dragonfly		—	Frog
	—	Dream		u	Fur (Piece)
	—	Dress		u	Fuzz (Piece)
	—	Drill		u	Gnat
	—	Drillpress		—	Garden
	u	Duck		u	v Gazebo
	u	Dust (Speck)		o	Girls (Dancing or standing in a
	o	Eagle			circle)
	—	Egg		u	v Hair (Styled)
	—	Elves (Group)		o	v Hat (Woman's)
	o	Emblem			Head (See face)
	—	Explosion		o	v Headdress
		Face		—	Helicopter

(*Note:* Most faces are *o* or *u*, provided *Dd*34 is used as ears, and *DDS*29 and 30 are used for eyes & mouth and the content is *(Hd), Ad,* or *(Ad);* however, some faces are inappropriate for the contours. A partial list is given below.)

Location	FQ	Category	Location	FQ	Category
	u	Abstract		o	v Helmet
	o	Animal (Unspecified)		u	v Hill
	—	Ant		—	Hive (Insect)
	u	Bear		u	v House
	—	Bird		—	Human
	o	Cat		o	Human (Winged or caped)
	u	Cow		u	Humans (2 facing midline)
	u	Dog		—	Humans (2 turned away)
	—	Fish		o	Humans (3)
	o	Fox		—	Ice
	—	Goat		u	Inkblot
	—	Horse		—	Insect (Not winged)
	—	Human		o	Insect (Winged)
	u	Monster		u	Island
	u	Mouse		—	Jellyfish
	—	Racoon		—	Keel (Boat)
	u	Robot		—	Kidney(s)
	—	Seal		—	Lamp
	o	Tiger		u	Landscape
	—	Turtle			
	o	Wolf			

(*Note:* This category includes rocks, rocky terrain, and broad landscape expanse such as a mountainside.)

Location	FQ	Category	Location	FQ	Category
	—	Fan		o	Leaf
	—	Fern		—	Lungs
	—	Fiddle		—	Map (Specific)
	—	Fire		u	Map (Unspecified)
	—	Flag		o	Mask

(*Note:* This category includes a wide variety of animal, Halloween, monster, party, voodoo, etc., masks.)

Location	FQ	Category	Location	FQ	Category
	u	Flea		—	Mat (Door)
				—	Meat
	u	Fly		u	Medusa
				—	Melon
				u	Monster

Table A (Continued)

Location	FQ	Category	Location	FQ	Category
	u	v Mountain		u	v Train (As D4 crossing a trestle)
	u	Mosquito		—	Tree
	o	Moth		—	Tuning Fork
	u	Mud		—	Turtle
	—	Neck		u	Urn
	—	Neckbone		—	Valve
	—	Nest		u	Vase
	—	Net		—	Washing Machine
	—	Nose		u	Wasp
	—	Note (Musical)		—	Wave
	o	Opera Singers (2 or 3)		—	Weathervane
	o	Ornament		—	Weed
	—	Owl		o	Witches (2 or 3)
	—	Pau (Cooking)		o	Woman (Winged or caped)
	—	Parking Meter		—	Wood
	o	Pelvis		o	X-ray (Chest)
	—	Pick (Guitar)		—	X-ray (Heart)
	—	Plant		—	X-ray (Lungs)
	—	Plymouth Emblem		o	X-ray (Pelvis)
	—	Pot		—	X-ray (Stomach)
	—	Printing Press		o	X-ray (Unspecified)
	—	Rib(s)		—	Yacht
	—	Roadmap			
	u	Robot	D1	—	Angels
	u	v Rock		—	Ants
	u	v Rocketship		o	Antennae
	u	Rower (In boat)		u	Antlers
	—	Rudder		—	Apes
	—	Rug		—	Birds
	—	Sailboat		o	Bird Heads
	—	Sawhorse		—	Bones
	o	Sea Animal (With D2 or Dd34 as flappers)		—	Bugs
	—	Seed		u	Butterflies
	—	Ship		o	Claws
	—	Shrimp		—	Clip
	—	Skeleton (Unspecified)		—	Crabs
	o	Skull (Human or animal)		—	Dancers
	—	Smile		u	Duck Heads
	—	Snowflake		u	Eagle Heads
	u	Spaceship		—	Elves
	—	Sperm		o	Feelers
	—	Spider		o	Fingers
	—	Sponge		—	Flags
	—	Spring (Metal)		—	Fork
	o	Statues (2 or 3)		u	Ghosts
	—	Steeple		—	Gun
	u	Stone (Carved)		o	Hands
	—	Stove		—	Heads (Animal)
	—	Sundial		o	Heads (Birds)
	—	Tank (Army)		u	Heads (Monster)
	u	v Tent		u	Heads (Reptile)
	o	Totem (Winged)		o	Horns
	—	Tornado		o	Humans
				—	Insect

Table A (Continued)

Location	FQ	Category	Location	FQ	Category
	o	Mittens		–	Pig
	u	Monsters		–	Rodent
	–	Penis		–	Sky
	o	Pincers		–	Tree
	u	Puppets		u	< Tree(s) & Foliage
	u	Rock		o	Wing(s)
	–	Rocket		–	Wolf
	–	Roots		u	Woodpecker (Profile)
	u	Sculpture (Abstract)		–	X-ray (Specified or unspecified)
	–	Shrimp			
	–	Tooth	D3	u	Alligator
	u	Thumb		u	Alligator (Reflected)
	–	Tree		o	v Bowling Pin
	–	Waves		–	Brain Stem
				–	Candle
D2	o	Acrobat		–	Candle Holder
	–	Airplane		–	Face
	–	Anatomy		–	Gun
	o	Angel		o	Human (Lower half)
	o	Animal (Specified as long-eared, such as donkey, elephant, some varieties of dogs.)		–	Insect
				o	Legs
				o	Mummy Case
	–	Animal (Specified as short-eared, such as cat, cow, and some varieties of dogs.)		–	Nose
				–	Ornament
				–	Penis
	o	Animal (Cartoon)		u	Robot
	u	Animal (Unspecified)		–	Snake
	–	Bat		u	Spaceship
	–	Beetle		u	Spinal Cord
	o	Bird (With Dd34 as wings)		o	Statue
	u	Bug (With Dd34 as wings)		o	Totem Pole
	–	Bug (Not winged)		–	Tree
	–	Cat		–	Vagina
	–	Chicken		o	Vase
	–	Cow		u	Violin
	u	Cloud			
	o	Dancer	D4	–	Alligator
	o	Demon		–	Anatomy
		Dog (See Animal)		–	Animal (Unspecified)
	–	Dragon		–	Ant
	o	Face (Animal, Bird Cartoon, or Monster with Dd34 as nose)		u	Baboon
				o	Beetle
	–	Face (Animal, Bird, Cartoon or Monster with Dd34 as ear)		–	Bird
				–	Bone Structure
	–	Face, Human		o	Bug (With D1 as antennae or feelers)
	–	Fish			
	o	Head, Bird		–	Bullet
	o	Human		–	Cat
	o	Human-like Figure		o	Cello
	o	Landscape		–	Centipede
	u	Map (Unspecified)		–	Clitoris
	–	Map (Specified)		–	Crab
	o	Pegasus		u	Crown (Ceremonial)

Table A (Continued)

Location	FQ	Category	Location	FQ	Category
	−	Door		u	Pot (Dd34 as handle)
	−	Face		u	Rock
	−	Fish		−	Skull
	−	Frog		o	Sphinx
	o	Gorilla		o	Statue (Bird)
	o	Human (Whole)		u	Weathervane
	o	Human (Headless)		o	Wings
	o	Humans (2)			
	o	Insect (Unspecified with D1 as antennae or feelers)	Dd21	−	Anatomy
				o	Bug (D1 as feelers)
	−	Island		u	Crab
	u	Jack-in-the-Box		−	Foliage
	−	Lamp		−	Heart
	−	Lobster		−	Jellyfish
	o	Monster		u	Landscape
	u	Monument		o	Nest
	−	Nose		−	Sea Animal
	−	Plant		u	Shield
	−	Reptile		−	Statue
	u	v Rocket			
	u	v Rocketship	Dd22	−	Balls
	−	Spider		u	Breasts
	o	Statue		u	Boulders
	−	Turtle		−	Buttocks
	u	v Tree		−	Heads (Animal)
	−	Wasp		u	Heads (Human)
	o	Woman		o	Hills
	u	Vase		u	Labia
	u	Viola		o	Mountains
				−	Trees
D7	−	Animal (Not winged)			
	o	Animal (Winged)	Dd23	−	Airplanes
	u	Arrowhead		u	Birds
	o	Bird		−	Dots
	−	Bone		−	Flies
	u	Cliff		u	Insects
	u	Cloud		o	Islands
	o	Crow		−	Notes (Musical)
	u	Duck		−	Symbols
	o	Eagle			
	u	Face, Animal (With Dd34 as nose)	Dd24	o	Bell
				−	Bug
	u	Face, Cartoon (With Dd34 as nose)		o	Cello
				u	Emblem
	−	Face, Human		−	Head
	−	Hat		u	Helmet
	−	Insect (Not winged)		−	Human (Whole)
	u	Insect (Winged)		u	Human figure (Lower half)
	o	Landscape		u	Lamp
	−	Map (Specific)		u	Lantern
	u	Map (Unspecified)		u	Monster
	u	Nest		−	Plant
	−	Plant			

Table A (Continued)

Location	FQ	Category	Location	FQ	Category
	u	Skirt		−	Lungs
	−	X-ray		u	Snow
				−	Trees
Dd25	−	Animal			
	−	Animal Rump	Dd31	u	Feet
	o	Face, Human-Abstract		−	Hammer
	u	Face, Human		u	v Head (Rabbit)
	−	Trees		−	Head (Unspecified)
				−	Nose
DdS26	o	Clouds		−	Root
	o	Eyes		−	Skull
	o	Ghosts		u	Tooth
	o	Mask Details			
	u	Snow	DdS32	u	Bay
	−	Trees		−	Bird
				u	Canyon
Dd27	u	Boat (With midline)		−	Mask
	o	Buckle		−	Vase
	u	Elevator (With midline)			
	−	Face	Dd33	−	Ball
	−	Head		−	Bell
	−	Heart		−	Bone
	u	Shield		−	Head (Animal)
	u	Spaceship		u	v Head (Human)
	−	Top		−	Lamp
	−	Ulcer		u	v Mushroom
				u	Tail
Dd28	u	'Arrowhead		o	v Tree
	−	Bird (Whole)			
	u	Hat	Dd34	u	Arrowhead
	−	Head (Animal)		u	Blade (Knife)
	o	Head (Bird)		o	Cliff
	−	Head (Human)		−	Face
	−	Pole		o	Fin
	−	Shoe		u	< Ghost
	u	Tree		−	Head
				−	Insect
DdS29	o	Eyes (Abstract)		o	< Mountain
	−	Eyes (Human)		u	Nose (Cartoon)
	u	Flying Saucers		u	Rock
	o	Ghosts		u	Saw
	o	Holes		u	< Seal
	u	Mountains		u	< Shrub
	u	Pyramids		u	< Tower
	u	Snow		o	< Tree (Fir)
	u	Spaceships		u	< Tree (Unspecified)
	u	Triangles		u	< Umbrella (Closed)
	u	Tents			
	u	Wings	Dd35	u	< Dog
				−	Face (Animal)
DdS30	o	Eyes		−	Face (Bird)
	o	Ghosts		u	v Face (Human)
	u	Human (In costume)			

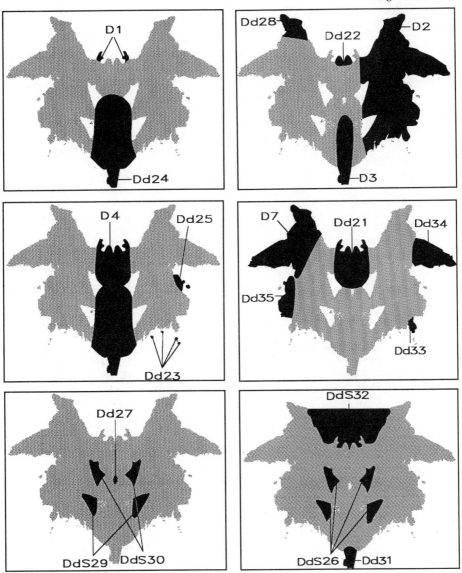

Figure 7.   *D* and *Dd* Areas for Card I.

Table A (Continued)

CARD II

P Is to D1: Bear, Dog, Elephant or Lamb, Head or Whole Animal

Z Values: W = 4.5 Adjacent = 3.0 Distant = 5.5 Space = 4.5

Location	FQ	Category	Location	FQ	Category
W	–	Anatomy (Specific)	D1	–	Amoeba
	u	Anatomy (Unspecified)		u	Animal (Unspecified)
	u	Art (Abstract)		o	Bear
	–	Badge		–	Bird
	–	Bat		u	< Buffalo
	o	Bears		o	< Cat
	–	Bird		u	Cloud
	–	Body		–	Clown
	u	Bookends		u	v Coat
	–	Bug		o	Cow
	u	v Bug (Winged)		u	v Demon
	o	v Butterfly		o	Dog
	u	Cave		o	Elephant
	o	Dancers		–	Fish
	u	Design (Abstract)		u	v Gorilla
	o	Devils		–	Hat
	–	Disc (Anatomy)		–	Heart
	u	Emblem		–	Human
	o	v Explosion		o	v Human
	–	Face		o	Lamb
	o	Fire & Smoke		u	Landscape
	–	Fly		–	Map
	u	Gorillas		–	Machine
	–	Heart		o	v Mountain(s)
	o	Humans or Human-like figures		–	Monument
	–	Insect		o	v Monster
	u	Insect (Winged)		o	< Rabbit
	–	Intestines		u	Rock
	–	Kidneys		–	Sponge
	–	Lungs		–	Tree
	–	Map		–	Turtle
	u	Mask		–	Wing
	(Note: This category includes a variety of animal, cartoon, Halloween, party, etc., masks)		D2	u	Angel
				o	Bird
	–	Meat		o	Blood
	–	Mouth		–	Boot
	o	Ornament		–	Bug (Not winged)
	u	v Pelvis		u	Bug (Winged)
	–	Plant		o	Butterfly (Side view)
	–	Rectum		o	Cap
	–	Spaceship		–	Candle
	o	Statues		–	Cell (Blood)
	–	Stomach		u	Chicken
	–	Throat		o	Creature (Cartoon)
	u	v Torches (With smoke)		u	Devil
	–	Vagina		u	Finger Painting
	u	Volcano		–	Finger Print
	–	X-ray		u	Footprint

Table A (Continued)

Location	FQ	Category	Location	FQ	Category
	–	Hand		–	Head (Bird)
	o	Hat		–	Head (Human)
	–	Head (Animal)		u	v Headset (Radio)
	u	Head (Bird)		–	Heart
	–	Head (Human)		u	Insect
	u	Head (Human-like)		u	Jellyfish
	u	v Holster		–	Kidney
	u	v Italy (Map)		–	Lobster
	–	Kidney		–	Lung
	–	Lantern		u	Manta Ray
	u	Lava		–	Mask
	–	Leg		u	Monster
	o	Mask (Animal, bird, cartoon, human-like)		u	Meat
				u	Menstruation
	–	Mitten		u	Moth
	–	Penis		–	Octopus
	o	Puppet (Hand)		o	Paint
	u	Rabbit		u	Plant
	–	Rat		u	Snail
	o	Seal		u	Spaceship
	–	Shoe		o	v Sun
	u	Snail		o	v Torch
	u	v Sock		o	Vagina
	u	v South America (Map)		–	Uterus
	–	Tongue			
	–	Tooth	D4	o	Arrow
	o	Torch		o	Arrowhead
	–	Vase		–	Bat (Baseball)
	–	Worm		–	Bell
				–	Bottle
D3	u	Anemone (Sea)		o	Bullet
	–	Ant		u	Candle
	–	Anus		o	Capsule (Space)
	–	Beetle		u	Castle
	o	Blood		–	Crucifix
	–	Bug (Not winged)		–	Crucifixion
	o	Bug (Winged)		u	Dome
	o	Butterfly		u	v Drill
	–	Clamp		–	Face
	u	Coral		u	Hands (Praying)
	o	Crab		u	Hat
	–	Crawfish		–	Head
	u	Embryo		u	Helmet
	o	v Explosion		–	Knife
	–	Face (Animal)		o	Missile
	u	Face (Devil or monster)		u	Monument
	–	Face (Human)		–	Mountain
	u	Fan		–	Nose
	o	Fire		u	Penpoint
	–	Fish		u	Penis
	u	Flower		u	Pliers
	–	Fly		u	Pyramid
	–	Head (Animal)		o	Rocket

Table A (Continued)

Location	FQ	Category	Location	FQ	Category
	–	Snake		–	Animal
	o	Spaceship		u	Animals (2 unspecified)
	u	Spear (Tip)		o	Animals (2, each meeting
	o	Steeple			criterion for o as D1)
	–	Tail		–	Bat
	o	Temple		–	Bird
	o	Tower		u	Butterfly
	u	Tree (Fir)		u	Cloud(s)
	–	Tree (Unspecified)		–	Insect (Not winged)
	–	Vase		u	Insect (Winged)
				u	Island
DS5	o	Airplane		–	Lungs
	u	Archway		–	Map (Specific)
	u	Basket		u	Map (Unspecified)
	–	Bat		u	Moth
	u	Bell		o	v Pelvis
	–	Bird		–	Rug
	–	Boat		u	Spinal cord (Slice, may include
	u	Bowl			DS5)
	–	Butterfly		o	v X-ray (Pelvic)
	o	Castle (May include D4)		–	X-ray (Specific other than pelvic)
	o	Cave		u	X-ray (Nonspecific)
	o	Chandelier			
	o	Church	Dd21	–	Beak
	u	Crown		–	Bird
	u	Dome		–	Ear
	–	Dress		–	Frog
	u	Fountain		o	Head (Animal)
	u	Goblet		–	Head (Bird)
	u	Hat (Woman's)		–	Head (Fish)
	–	Heart		–	Head (Human)
	u	Helmet		o	Mountain
	o	Hole		--	Nest
	u	Island		–	Seal
	u	Kite		–	Shrub
	o	Lake		–	X-ray
	o	Lamp			
	o	Light	Dd22	o	v Bush
	–	Mask		–	Chicken
	o	Missile		–	Head (Animal)
	–	Mouth		u	v Head (Human)
	o	Ornament		u	v Rabbit
	u	Pendant		u	v Rock
	o	Rocket		–	Tree
	o	Spaceship			
	u	Steeple	Dd23	u	Bush
	u	Sting Ray		–	Frog
	–	Stomach		–	Head
	o	Top		u	v Mountain
	o	Tunnel		u	v Rock
	u	Vagina		–	Tree
	o	Vase			
			Dd24	u	Anus
D6	–	Anatomy		u	Bowling Pin

Table A (Continued)

Location	FQ		Category	Location	FQ		Category
	u		Bullet		*u*		Claw
	u		Candle		−		Nail
	−		Doorway		−		Tail
	−		Face		−		Wall
	u		Ghost				
	−		Human	*Dd*28	*u*		Bloodstain
	u		Human-like Figure		−		Head
	u		Penis		−		Turtle
	u		Rocket		*u*		Varnish
	−		Tooth		*u*		Wood (Stained)
	u		Totem		−		X-ray
	o		Vagina				
	u	v	Waterfall	*DdS*29	*u*		Cave
					u		Cup
*Dd*25	*o*		Antennae		*u*		Dome
	o		Antlers		*u*	v	Goblet
	u		Feelers		*u*		Pottery
	o		Horns		*u*		Tunnel
	u		Icicles				
	u		Needle	*DdS*30	−		Clam
	u		Spike		−		Eyes
	u		Spear		−		Head
	u		Spike		*u*		Inlet
	u		Stick		−		Oyster
	−		Tail				
	−		Tusk	*Dd*31	*u*		Beak
					−		Claw
*Dd*26	*o*		Blood		*u*	v	Ears (Animal)
	u		Caterpillar		−		Head (Animal)
	o		Fire		*u*		Head (Human)
	u		Sunset		*u*		Head (Human-like)
	−		Walrus		*u*	<	Mountains
	u		Worm		*u*		Stone Sculpture
					−		Trees
*Dd*27	*u*		Bridge (Draw)				

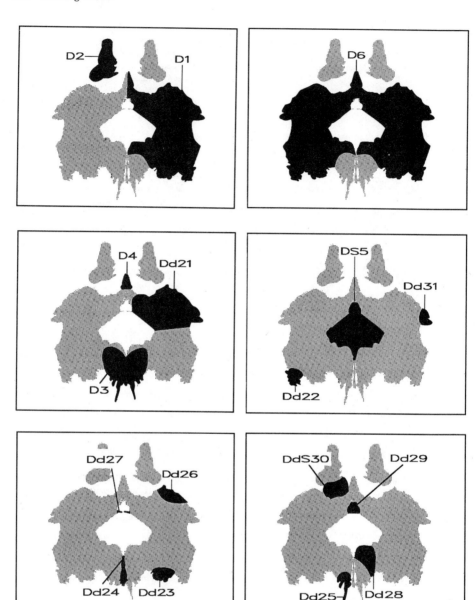

Figure 8.   *D* and *Dd* Areas for Card II.

Table A (Continued)

CARD III

P Is to D1 or D9: Human Figure or Representation Thereof

Z Values:	W = 5.5	Adjacent = 3.0	Distant = 4.0	Space = 4.5

Location	FQ	Category	Location	FQ	Category
W		(*Note:* Most W responses that involve a single object will be coded – as the blot is broken. In a few instances, response frequencies argue in favor of a *u* coding for answers that conform to the contours and are not largely dependent on arbitrarily created contours. W responses coded *o* will usually involve multiple objects.)		*u*	v Monster
				–	Noose
				–	Rib Cage
				–	Skeleton
				–	Spider
				u	v Vase (With handles and design)
				–	X-ray
	–	Anatomy	D1	–	Animal
	–	Animal		*u*	Animals (2 Unspecified)
	o	Animals (As D1 in a scene with other objects, such as in a circus. All other objects included must be codable as *o* if reported separately.)		–	Ant
				u	v Arch
				–	Bird
				o	Birds (2)
				o	Bone Structure
	–	Ant		–	Bug
	u	Art (Abstract)		*u*	v Cave Entrance
	u	Badge		–	Dog
	o	Birds (As D1 in a scene with other objects such as in a cage. All other objects included must be codable as *o* if reported separately.)		*o*	Dogs (2 with D7 as separate object)
				o	Dolls (2)
				–	Human
				o	Humans (2 with D7 as separate object)
	u	Bowl (With handles and design)		*u*	v Humans (With D5 as arms)
	–	Bug		–	Insect
	–	Butterfly		*u*	Keel (Boat with D5 as supports)
	–	Cat		*o*	v Landscape
	u	Chandelier		–	Lobster
	–	Crab		–	Map (Specific)
	u	Emblem		–	Map (Unspecified)
	–	Face		*u*	Map (Unspecified)
	–	Flower		*o*	Monkeys (With D7 as separate object)
	–	Fly			
	–	Gorilla		*u*	Monster
	–	Human		*o*	Ostrich (2)
	o	Humans or Human-like Figures (As D1 in a scene with other objects each of which would be coded as *o* if reported separately, such as in ceremonies, parties, playgrounds, etc.)		*o*	Pelvic Structure
				o	Sheep (2, or Lambs)
				–	Skeleton
				–	Skull
				–	Spider
				–	Trees
				u	Vase
	–	Insect		*o*	X-ray (Pelvis)
	u	v Islands		*u*	X-ray (Unspecified)
	–	Jack-O-Lantern			
	–	Jellyfish	D2	–	Anchor
	u	v Landscape		*u*	Amoeba
	–	Map (Specific)		*o*	Animal (Long-Tailed)
	u	Map (Unspecified)		–	Animal (Not long-tailed)

Table A (Continued)

Location	FQ	Category	Location	FQ	Category
	−	Artery		o	Pot (Hanging)
	o	Bird		o	v Puppet
	o	Blood		−	Rabbit
	−	Bone		u	Robot
	−	Brain		u	Sea Horse
	−	Bug		−	Snail
	−	Cocoon		−	Snake
	u	Chandelier		u	Statue (Abstract)
	o	Chicken (Hanging)		u	Statue (Animal)
	u	Coral		o	Statue (Human)
	−	Club		−	Stick
	o	Decoration (Unspecified)		u	Stomach
	o	Devil		o	Symbol (Abstract)
	−	Dog		u	v Tree
	−	Dragon		o	Umbilical cord (With placenta)
	−	Duck		−	Vase
	o	Embryo			
	u	Esophagus	D3	−	Antennae
	o	Fire		−	Antlers
	−	Fish		u	Bellows
	−	Flesh		−	Bat
	u	v Flower		−	Bird
	−	Fly		−	Brain
	u	Germ		o	Blood
	u	Guitar		u	Bone
	o	Hat (Clown or costume)		o	Bow
	−	Head (Animal)		o	Bowtie
	−	Head (Bird)		u	Brassiere
	−	Head (Human)		−	Breasts
	u	Head (Human-like)		−	Breastbone
	−	Heart		o	Butterfly
	u	Hook		−	Crab
	o	Human (This class of response includes many variations of the human figure such as acrobat, child, gymnast, etc.)		u	Dam (Between hills)
				o	Decoration (Unspecified)
				−	Dragonfly
				u	Dumbbell
	o	Human-like Figure (This class of response includes many variations of cartoon, mythological, or science fiction figures such as devil, dwarf, elf, imp, etc.)		u	Emblem (Abstract)
				u	Eye Shades
				−	Eye Glasses
				u	Exercise Apparatus
				o	Fire
	−	Insect		−	Fly
	−	Intestine		u	Fossil
	u	Island		−	Girdle
	u	Kidney		u	Hang Glider
	−	Lung		−	Heart
	o	Meat (Hung)		−	Helmet
	o	Monkey		−	Human(s)
	o	Neuron		−	Insect (Not winged)
	u	Note (Musical)		u	Insect (Winged)
	o	v Parrot		u	Island
	u	v Pipe		−	Intestine
	u	v Plant		u	Kidney
				−	Lips

Table A (Continued)

Location	FQ	Category	Location	FQ	Category
	o	Lungs		—	Buckle
	—	Mask		—	Butterfly
	u	Mosquito		—	Cactus
	o	Moth		o	Cauldron
	—	Mouth		u	Coal (Piece)
	—	Nose		o	Crab
	—	Oranges		u	Drum
	o	Pelvic Structure		—	Eye Glasses
	o	Ribbon		—	Face
	—	Seed		o	Fireplace
	—	Skeleton		u	Gate
	u	Spinal Cord (Cross section)		—	Head
	u	Sun Glasses		—	Heart
	—	Testicles		u	Island
	u	Wasp		—	Kidney
	u	Wing		—	Lungs
	—	Wishbone		u	v Mushrooms
				o	Nest
D5	u	Arm		o	Pelvis
	u	Arrow		o	Rock(s)
	—	Bird		u	Shadows
	u	Bomb		u	Smoke
	—	Bone		—	Stomach
	—	Bug		o	v Trees
	u	*Bullet*		—	Vagina
	u	Claw		u	Vertebrae
	u	Club		o	X-ray (Pelvis)
	o	Fish		—	X-ray (Specific other than pelvis)
	—	Gun		u	X-ray (Unspecified)
	—	Hand			
	u	Island	D8	o	Bones
	o	Leg (Animal)		—	Brain Stem
	o	Leg (Bird)		—	Chest
	o	Leg (Human)		u	Crab
	u	Limb (Tree)		—	Dragon
	u	Log		u	Hour Glass
	—	Map		u	Lamp
	u	Missile		u	Lake (In mountains)
	u	Peninsula		u	Monster
	u	Rocket		—	Pumpkin
	o	Shark		o	Ribs
	—	Snake		u	Skeletal (Specific other than ribs)
	u	Spaceship		o	Skeletal (Unspecified)
	u	Spear		u	Stone
	u	Stick		u	v Torch
	u	Torpedo		—	Vagina
	—	Tree		u	v Vase
	—	Vine		u	v Wine Glass
				—	X-ray
D7	—	Anatomy			
	—	Animal	D9	—	Anatomy
	o	Basket		u	Animal (Unspecified)
	—	Beetle		—	Ant
	o	Bones		o	Bird

Table A (Continued)

Location	FQ		Category	Location	FQ		Category
	–		Bug		*u*		Cloud
	o		Cartoon Figure		*u*		Ghost
	u		Chicken		–		Head
	u		Cloud		*u*		Water
	u		Demon				
	o		Dog	*DdS*24	*u*		Bowl
	o		Doll		–		Face
	u		Duck		–		Head
	–		Foliage		*u*		Lake
	u		Ghost		*u*	v	Lamp
	o		Human		*u*	v	Mushroom
	–		Insect		*u*		Snow
	u		Jack-In-The-Box		*u*	v	Statue
	–		King Kong		*u*		Vase
	o		Lamb				
	u	v	Landscape	*Dd*25	*u*		Esophagus
	o		Monkey		–		Face
	u		Monster		–		Head
	u	v	Mountain		*u*		Root
	u		Parrot		–		Spear
	o		Puppet		*u*		Stick
	–		Rabbit		*u*		String
	–		Root		*u*		Tail
	o		Sheep		–		Tool
	u		Skeleton		*u*		Tube
	–		Spider		*u*		Umbilical cord
	u		Statue		*u*		Worm
	–		Tree				
	o		Witch	*Dd*26	*u*		Fin
	–		X-ray		–		Head
					–		Leg
*Dd*21	*u*		Bird		*o*		Penis
	–		Bomb		*u*		Stump
	u		Cliff				
	–		Dog	*Dd*27	*o*		Breast
	–		Head (Animal)		–		Building
	o		Head (Bird)		*o*		Head (Animal)
	o		Head (Fish)		*o*		Head (Bird)
	–		Head (Human)		*u*		Head (Fish)
	u		Landscape		–		Head (Human)
	o	v	Mountain		*u*	<	Mountain
	u		Pensula		*u*		Nose
	u	v	Tree		–		Skull
*Dd*22	–		Animal	*Dd*28	*u*		Corset
	o		Bird		*u*		Dam
	–		Bone		*u*		Doors (Swinging)
	u		Cloud		–		Face
	u		Human (Upper half)		–		Head
	u	v	Landscape		*u*		Net
	–		Rodent		–		Tooth
	u		Statue				
				*Dd*29	–		Airplane
*DdS*23	*u*		Bird		–		Arrow

Table A (Continued)

Location	FQ	Category	Location	FQ	Category
	u	Arrowhead		–	Ball
	u	Bird		u	Clam
	u	Breast		u	Coconut
	u	Butterfly		–	Egg
	u	Cartoon Character		–	Eye
	–	Fetus		–	Fish
	–	Head		–	Head (Animal)
	–	Heart		o	Head (Bird)
	–	Human		o	Head (Human)
	–	Insect		u	Mask
	–	Tent		u	Oyster
	u	< Valentine		u	Rock
				u	Statue
Dd30	u	Arm			
	–	Club	Dd33	u	Claw
	–	Foot		u	Finger
	–	Hand		u	Foot
	–	Head		–	Fork
	u	Icicle		u	Hand
	–	Missile		–	Head (Animal)
	u	Log		u	Head (Bird)
				–	Head (Human)
Dd31	–	Anatomy		o	Hoof
	u	Animal		–	Penpoint
	o	Ball		o	Shoe
	u	Balloon		–	Spear
	o	Basket			
	u	Bones	Dd34	–	Animal
	u	Cloud		o	Bird
	–	Earmuffs		–	Fish
	–	Embryo		o	Human (Upper part)
	–	Eyes		–	Insect
	–	Face		o	v Landscape
	u	Gourd		o	v Mountains
	–	Hat		–	Skeletal
	–	Head (Animal)		–	X-ray
	o	v Head (Human)			
	o	v Head (Skeletal)	Dd35	u	Arch
	u	Kettledrums		o	Birds (2)
	–	Lamp		u	Bones
	–	Lungs		u	Bowl
	u	Mittens		–	Crab
	–	Mountains		–	Frog
	o	Pot		u	Islands
	o	Skeletal		o	v Landscape
	o	v Skull		u	Mountains (Aerial view)
	o	Stones		o	Pelvis
	o	v Trees		–	Trees
	–	Turtle		o	X-ray (Pelvis)
	–	Womb		–	X-ray (Specific other than pelvis)
Dd32	–	Animal		u	X-ray (Unspecified)

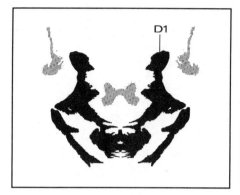
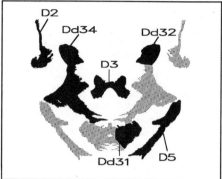
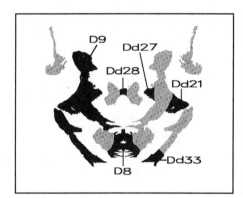
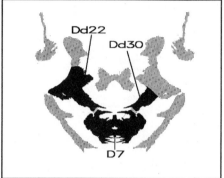
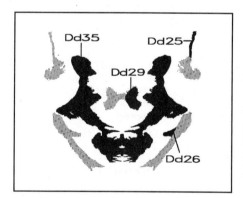
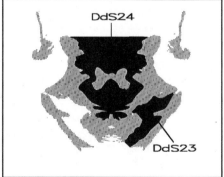

Figure 9.   *D* and *Dd* Areas for Card III.

Table A (Continued)

CARD IV

P Is to *W* or *D*7: Human or Human-Like Figure

Z Values:		*W* = 2.0	Adjacent = 4.0	Distant = 3.5	Space = 5.0

Location	FQ		Category	Location	FQ		Category
	−		Amoeba		*u*		Kite
	o	v	Anchor		*o*	<	Landscape (Reflected)
	o		Animal		*o*		Leaf
	o	v	Badge		−		Lettuce
	o	v	Bat		−		Lobster
	u		Bell		−		Lung(s)
	u	v	Bird		−		Map (Specific)
	o		Boots (On pole)		*o*		Map (Topographic, nonspecific)
	−		Brain		*u*		Map (Unspecified)
	−		Bug		*u*		Mask
	−		Bull		*o*		Monster
	o		Bush(es)		*u*	v	Moth
	o		Butterfly		*u*		Mountain
	−		Candle		−		Mud
	u		Carcass (Animal)		*o*		Pelt
	u	v	Chandelier		*o*	v	Pelvis
	u		Cloud(s)		*o*		Plant
	o		Coat (On pole)		*u*		Robe
	−		Coral		*u*		Rock
	−		Crab		−		Root
	o	v	Crest		*o*		Rug
	u		Design (Abstract)		*o*		Sea Animal
	u	v	Eagle		*u*		Sea Weed
	o	v	Emblem		*o*		Skin (Animal)
	−		Embryo		*u*		Smoke
	−		Face		−		Snail
	u		Flower		−		Snowflake
	u		Fountain		*u*		Sponge
	u		Fossil		*u*		Squid
	u		Frog		*u*		Squirrel (Flying)
	o		Giant		*u*		Statue
	o		Gorilla		*o*	v	Sting Ray
	u		Head (Animal)		*u*		Temple
	−		Head (Bird)		*o*		Tree
	−		Head (Human)		*u*	v	Urn
	−		Helmet		*o*		X-ray (Pelvis)
	o		Hide (Animal)		−		X-ray (Specific other than pelvis)
	o		Hunchback		*u*		X-ray (Unspecified)
	o		Human				
	(*Note:* This class of response may			D1	−		Alligator
	involve *W* as the human figure or *D*7 as				−		Animal
	the human figure with *D*1 as a second				*u*		Bug
	object, such as bike, seat, stump, etc.				*o*		Bush(es)
	The card *must* be upright.)				*o*	v	Cactus
	u		Ice Cream Cone		*u*	v	Candle
	−		Insect		*u*	v	Castle
	u		Island (Unspecified)		*u*		Caterpillar
	−		Jello		−		Crab
	−		Jellyfish		−		Crawfish

Table A (Continued)

Location	FQ	Category	Location	FQ	Category
	u	v Crown		−	Map (Specific other than Africa
	−	Fish			or South America)
	o	v Head (Animal, horned or horse)		*u*	Map (Unspecified)
	−	v Head (Animal, specific not		*u*	Peninsula
		horned or horse)		*o*	< Pig
	u	v Head (Animal, not specific)		*u*	Rock
	u	v Head (Bird)		*o*	< Seal
	−	v Head (Human)		*o*	Shoe
	o	v Head (Insect)		*u*	Sphinx
	u	v Head (Monster)		*u*	Statue
	−	v Head (Reptile other than turtle)		*u*	< Totem
	u	v Head (Turtle)		*u*	Wing
	−	Human		−	X-ray
	u	Hydrant			
	o	Insect	D3	−	Anus
	−	Intestines		*u*	Brain
	−	Lamp		*o*	Bud (Flower)
	u	v Lighthouse		*u*	Bush
	u	Medulla		*u*	Butterfly
	−	Penis		*u*	Cabbage
	−	Shell		*u*	Clam
	o	Shrub		*u*	Crown
	u	Skull		−	Face
	u	Snail		*u*	Fan
	−	Snake		*o*	Flower
	o	Spinal Cord		*o*	Head (Animal, flat-faced such as
	o	Stool			cat, monkey, owl, etc.)
	o	Stump		−	Head (Animal, specific but not
	u	Tail			flat-faced)
	o	Tree Trunk		*u*	Head (Animal, unspecified)
	o	Vertebrae		*u*	Head (Bird)
	−	X-ray		−	Head (Human)
				u	Head (Monster or science fiction)
D2	*o*	< Bear		−	Insect (Not winged)
	−	Boat		*u*	Insect (Winged)
	−	Bone		*u*	Mushroom
	u	Cliff		*u*	Leaf
	u	Cloud		*o*	Sea Shell
	−	Cow		*u*	Shrub
	o	v Dog		*u*	Tam o' Shanter
	−	Emblem		*u*	Vagina
	o	Foot			
	o	< Head (Animal, flat or stubby	D4	−	Animal
		nose such as bear, dog, pig, seal,		*u*	Arm
		etc.)		−	Arrow
	u	< Head (Animal, not specific)		*o*	Bird (Long-necked)
	−	Head (Bird)		*o*	Branch (Tree)
	u	v Head (Camel)		*u*	Cap (Stocking)
	o	< Head (Human)		*o*	Claw
	−	Head (Insect)		*o*	Diver (Back flip)
	−	Head (Reptile)		−	Ear
	u	Landscape		*u*	Eel
	u	Map (Africa or South America)		−	Fish

Table A (Continued)

Location	FQ	Category	Location	FQ	Category
	o	Handle		—	Sea Animal
	—	Head (Animal)		u	Shoe
	o	Head (Bird)		u	Smoke
	u	Horn (Animal)		u	Wing
	o	Human (Bending or diving)			
	o	Icicle	D7	u v	Anchor
	—	Leg		o	Animal
	o	Lizard		u v	Badge
	u	Nail (Bent)		o v	Bat
	u	Peninsula		u	Bird
	—	Penis		—	Bug
	u	Root		—	Crab
	o	Snake		—	Face
	u	Tail		u	Fossil
	u	Trunk (Elephant)		o	Giant
	o	Vine (Hanging)		o	Gorilla
				—	Head
D5	o	Bone (Skeletal)		u	Helmet
	o	Canyon		o	Hide (Animal)
	o	Column		o	Hunchback
	—	Crayfish		o	Human
	u	Drill		u	Island
	—	Fish		o	Mask
	u v	Fountain		o	Monster
	o	Gorge		u	Mountain
	—	Insect		o v	Pelvis
	o	Pole		u	Statue
	o	River			
	u	Rocket	Dd21	—	Apple
	o	Spinal cord		u	Crown
	—	Statue		o	Face (Human, profile)
	u	Totem		—	Head (Animal)
	—	Tree		o	Head (Human)
	o	Vertebrae		u	Hut
	o	Waterway		u	Landscape
	u	X-ray (Specific other than spine)		u	Temple
	o	X-ray (Spine)		u	Tent
	u	X-ray (Unspecified)		—	Wart
D6	o	Animal (As D2 on hill or rock)	Dd22	—	Eye
	o	Boot		—	Face
	—	Face		—	Head
	o	Foot		—	Moon
	u v	Head (Camel)		—	Shrub
	u v	Head (Cartoon animal)			
	o <	Human (As D2 sitting in chair or on a hill)	Dd23	u	Beak
				—	Head (Animal)
	u	Italy		o	Head (Bird)
	o	Leg		—	Head (Human)
	o	Map (Italy)		u	Head (Reptile)
	—	Map (Specific other than Italy)			
	u	Map (Unspecified)	DdS24	u	Clouds
	u	Rudder		u	Ghosts

Table A (Continued)

Location	FQ	Category	Location	FQ	Category
	−	Head(s)		u	Flower
	u	Snow		−	Heart
				−	Human
Dd25	−	Face		u	Nail
	−	Human(s)		o	v Rocket
	−	Human-like Figure(s)		u	Tack
	u	Landscape (Aerial view)		u	Tee (Golf)
				−	Tongue
Dd26	−	Clitoris		u	Tooth
	u	Feet		u	Waterfall
	u	Fingers			
	u	v Ghosts	Dd31	−	Animal
	−	Heads (Animal)		−	Bird
	u	Heads (Bird)		u	Ghost
	−	Heads (Human)		−	Head (Animal)
	−	Human		−	Head (Bird)
	u	v Human-like Figures		−	Head (Human)
	u	Legs		u	v Head (Human-like)
	u	Snakes		−	Human
	−	Teeth		−	Rock
	−	Trees		−	Root
	u	Worms		u	v Seal
				u	v Statue
Dd27	u	Bridge		−	Tree
	u	Cliff		u	v Witch
	−	Foot			
	−	Tail	Dd32	−	Fist
				u	v Head (Animal with flat or stubby nose)
Dd28	o	Antennae			
	−	Claws		u	v Head (Human)
	−	Feet		u	Rock
	u	Horns		u	Toe
	−	Legs			
	−	Roots	Dd33	o	Bone (Skeletal)
				o	Canyon
DdS29	u	Clouds		u	Drill
	u	Ghosts		o	Gorge
	u	Lakes		u	Pole
	u	Monsters		o	River
				o	Spine
Dd30	u	Beak		o	Waterway
	−	Face			

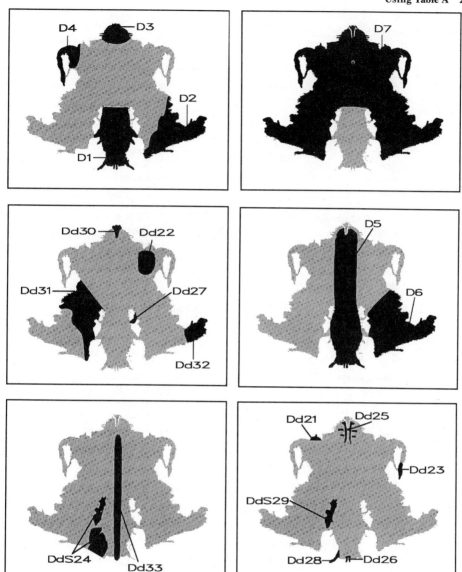

Figure 10. *D* and *Dd* Areas for Card IV.

Table A (Continued)

CARD V

P Is to *W*: Bat or Butterfly

| Z Values: | | *W* = 1.0 | Adjacent = 2.5 | | Distant = 5.0 | Space = 4.0 |

Location	FQ	Category	Location	FQ	Category
	u	v Acrobat (Doing handstand)		*o*	Insect (Winged)
	u	Airplane		—	Kangaroo
	—.	Anatomy		*u*	Kite
	—	Anchor		—	Kidney
	u	Angel		*o*	Landscape
	—	Animal		*u*	Leaf
	o	Animals (2 butting heads)		—	Lung(s)
	—	Badge		—	Machine
	o	Bat		—	Map
	u	Bee		—	Microorganism
	—	Beetle		*u*	Monster
	o	Bird		*u*	Mosquito
	u	Bookends		*o*	Moth
	—	Bug (Not winged)		*u*	Mustache
	u	Bug (Winged)		—	Neckbone
	o	Butterfly		*u*	Ornament
	u	Cape		*u*	Ostrich
	—	Cat		*u*	Pelvis
	u	Cloth (piece)		*o*	v Pelvis
	u	Cloud(s)		—	Propeller
	—	Clove		—	Pump
	u	Coal (Piece)		—	Ribs
	—	Coat		*u*	Rower (In boat)
	—	Coral		—	Sailboat
	u	Crow		—	Skeleton
	o	Dancer (In costume)		*u*	v Smoke
	u	Demon		*u*	Spaceship
	o	Dracula		—	Spider
	u	Duck		*u*	Stole (Fur)
	u	Eagle		*u*	Stone
	—	Elves		—	Tent
	—	Explosion		*u*	< Tornado (Reflected)
	—	Fern		—	Umbrella
	—	Flag		*o*	Vampire
	u	Fly		*o*	Vulture
	u	Flea		*u*	Wings
	u	Flower		*u*	v Wok (Cooking)
	u	Foliage		*o*	X-ray (Pelvis)
	—	Gnat		—	X-ray (Specific other than pelvis)
	—	Grasshopper		*u*	X-ray (Unspecified)
	—	Hairpiece			
	—	Head		*u*	Arm
	u	Hill (With trees)		—	Arrow
	—	Human		*o*	Bone
	o	Human (In costume)		—	Cylinder
	o	Humans (Back to back)		—	Eel
	u	Human-like Figure (Specified		—	Fish
		with giant arms or wings)		*u*	Foot (Animal)
	—	Ice		—	Foot (Human)
	—	Insect (Not winged)		—	Head (Animal)

Table A (Continued)

Location	FQ	Category	Location	FQ	Category
	u	Head (Cartoon animal)		o	Head (Animal, with horns or
	—	Head (Human)			long ears)
	o	Head (Reptile)		u	Head (Animal)
	o	Leg (Animal)		o	Head (Insect)
	o	Leg (Human)		—	Head (Human)
	u	Limb (Tree)		o	Head (Human, in costume or
	u	Log			with mask)
	u	Muscle		u	< Head (Reptile)
	—	Nose		u	Insect (With antennae)
	u	Root		u	Pliers
	u	Skull (Animal)		u	v Robot
	—	Spear		u	v Sawhorse
	u	Stick		u	Scissors
	—	Wrench		u	Slingshot
				u	Statue
D4	o	Animal (With head at D7)		—	Tuning Fork
	—	Anteater		—	Vase
	u	Blanket		u	Wishbone
	o	Bush(es)			
	u	Cloud	D7	o	Animal (Horned or long-eared)
	—	Crab		—	Animal (Not horned or long-
	—	Driftwood			eared)
	u	Fan		—	Beetle
	—	Head (Animal)		—	Bone
	—	Head (Bird)		u	Bug (With antennae)
	o	Head (Human, profile)		o	Demon
	o	Human (Reclining)		o	Devil
	—	Insect		—	Fish
	—	Jellyfish		—	Human
	—	Kangaroo		o	Human (In costume)
	u	Landscape		u	Humans (2, with arms raised)
	—	Leaf		u	Insect (With antennae)
	—	Leg		u	Monster
	u	Leg (Chicken or turkey cooked)		o	Rabbit
	—	Mud		—	Skeleton
	u	Plant		—	Tree
	o	Rock			
	u	Shoulder Pad (Football)	D9	u	Beak
	—	Skin		u	v Bells
	u	Sleeping Bag		u	v Brooms
	o	v Smoke		v	v Birds (2, long-necked)
	—	Tree		u	Chopsticks
	u	Weed		u	Clamp
	u	Wing		u	Cleaners (Vacuum)
				—	Feet (Animal)
D6	u	Antennae		o	Feet (Bird)
	u	Badge		—	Feet (Human)
	—	Bird		o	v Flamingos
	u	Clippers		o	v Geese
	u	v Elves		—	Head
	o	Face (Animal, long-eared)		u	Heads (2, Birds)
	—	Face (Human)		—	Insect(s)
	o	Face (Human with mask)		u	Legs (Animal)
	u	Hat (Mickey Mouse)		o	Legs (Bird)

Table A (Continued)

Location	FQ	Category	Location	FQ	Category
	−	Legs (Human)	Dd25	u	Cannon
	o	Swans		−	Hat
	u	Tail(s)		−	Penis
	o	Tweezers		u	Rock
	−	Vagina		−	Thumb
	o	Wishbone		−	Tree
D10	u	Bones	Dd26	u	v Bird (In flight)
	−	Coral		u	Branch (Tree)
	−	Head (Animal)		−	Head
	u	Head (Bird)		−	Reptile
	u	Head (Cartoon)		−	Tree
	o	Head (Reptile)			
	−	Insect	DdS27	u	Cone
	u	Legs (Animal)		u	Ghost
	−	Legs (Bird)		u	Inlet
	u	Legs (Human)		u	Tower
	−	Nose		u	Spike
	u	Peninsula		u	v Vase
	u	Pipewrench			
	o	Roots	DdS28	u	Cup
	u	Wood (Driftwood, logs, or sticks)		−	Helmet
				u	v Hill
				u	Inlet
Dd22	o	Arrow		u	v Mountain
	u	Bayonet		u	Vase
	u	Crutch			
	−	Finger	DdS29	u	Inlet
	−	Head (Animal)		u	River
	u	Head (Bird)		−	Snake
	−	Head (Human)			
	−	Insect	Dd30	−	Ball
	o	Limb (Tree)		−	Face (Animal except cat or rabbit)
	−	Leg (Animal)			
	u	Leg (Bird)		u	Face (Bird)
	−	Leg (Human)		u	Face (Cat)
	o	Reptile		−	Face (Human)
	o	Spear		u	Face (Rabbit)
	o	Sword		u	Head (Animal)
	o	Tail		u	Head (Bird)
				−	Head (Human)
Dd23	u	Coastline		o	Mask
	−	Head (Animal)		−	Skull
	−	Head (Human)			
	u	Landscape	Dd31	o	Bone
				o	Ear (Animal)
Dd24	u	Bird		u	Elf
	−	Breast		u	Finger
	u	Ghost		−	Foot
	−	Human		−	Head
	u	Monster		−	Human
	u	Nipple		u	Leg
	u	Tent		u	Penis
	u	Tree		u	Stick

Table A (Continued)

Location	FQ	Category	Location	FQ	Category
	−	Tree		u	Clippers
	u	Worm		u	Elves
				−	Heads (Animal)
Dd32	u	Antenna		−	Heads (Birds)
	o	Beak		−	Heads (Human)
	o	v Bird (Long-necked)		u	Heads (Insect)
	u	Bone		u	Heads (Reptile)
	u	Club		o	Horns
	−	Finger		−	Humans
	o	Head (Bird)		u	Human-like Figures
	−	Match		u	Legs
	−	Root		u	< Mouth (Animal or bird)
	−	Snake		u	Pliers
	o	v Swan		u	Scissors
	−	Tree		u	v Stool
				−	Trees
Dd33	−	Breast			
	−	Head (Animal)	Dd35	−	Breast
	−	Head (Human)		−	Head (Animal)
	u	Head (Human-like)		−	Head (Bird)
	o	Hill		o	Head (Human, profile)
	o	Mountain		u	Human (Sitting or lying)
	o	Shrub(s)		o	Landscape
				u	Mask (Profile)
Dd34	o	Antennae		o	Mountains
	u	Bones		−	Nose
				u	Rocks

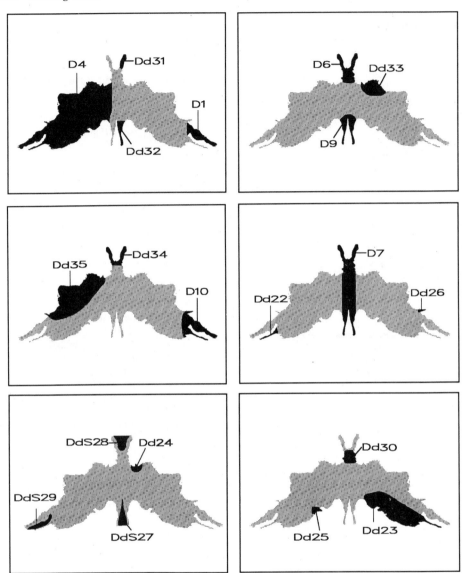

Figure 11.   *D* and *Dd* Areas for Card V.

Table A (Continued)

CARD VI

P Is to W or D1: Animal Skin, Hide, Pelt, or Rug

Z Values:		W = 2.5		Adjacent = 2.5		Distant = 6.0		Space = 6.5

Location	FQ		Category	Location	FQ		Category
W	u		Abstract Drawing		−		Frog
	u		Airplane		o		Fur Pelt
	−		Amoeba		−		Genitals (Male)
	−		Anchor		−		Gnat
	u		Animal (In natural form, canine		u		Guitar
			or feline, such as cat, dog, lynx,		−		Hair
			tiger, wolf, etc.)		o	<	Iceberg (Reflected)
	−		Animal (In natural form, *not*		−		Insect (Not winged)
			canine or feline, such as anteater,		u		Insect (Winged)
			elephant, giraffe, etc.)		u		Island
	o		Animal (In unnatural form such		−		Lamp
			as flattened, skinned, etc.)		o	<	Landscape (Reflected)
	o		Animal Pelt or Skin		u		Leaf
	−		Artichoke		u		Leather (Piece)
	−		Badge		−		Lungs
	−		Bat		−		Map (Specific)
	−		Bear		u		Map (Unspecified)
	o		Bearskin		u		Mask (Science fiction)
	−		Bee		u	v	Mirror (Hand)
	−		Beetle		o		Missile Launch (With missile at
	u		Bird				D6 and pad or smoke at D1)
	−		Body		u		Monster (Animal)
	−		Brain		u		Monster (Sea)
	−		Brainstem		−		Mosquito
	−		Bug (Not winged)		−		Moth ·
	u		Bug (Winged)		−		Mud
	−		Butterfly		−		Note (Musical)
	o		Candle (With D1 as base)		−		Pan
	−		Chest		o		Pelt
	o	v	Coat (Hanging on post)		u	v	Plant
	−		Club		−		Pot
	−		Crab		o		Rocket Launch (With rocket at
	−		Crow				D3 and pad or smoke at D1)
	−		Doll		u		Rudder
	−		Dragonfly		o		Rug
	u	v	Drill		u	v	Scarecrow
	−		Duck		u	v	Shield
	u	v	Duster (With handle)		o	<	Ship (Reflected with D3 as
	−		Emblem				second object(s))
	u		Explosion		−		Shrimp
	−		Face		o		Skin (Animal)
	o	v	Fan		−		Snail
	−		Fish		−		Spider
	u	v	Flag		u	v	Sponge
	−		Flea		u	v	Statue
	u	v	Flower		u	v	Sting Ray
	−		Fly		o		Totem (As D3 with D1 as hill or
	u		Forest (Aerial view)				expanse)
	u		Fountain (Abstract)		o	v	Tree

Table A (Continued)

Location	FQ	Category	Location	FQ	Category
	o	Waterway (As D5 with other areas landscape)		u	Map (Topographic)
				u	Map (Unspecified)
	–	X-ray (Specific)		u	v Monkeys (Back to back)
	u	X-ray (Unspecified)		u	v Monsters
				o	< Mountain Range (Reflected)
D1	u	Amoeba		u	Mud
	–	Anatomy		u	Ornament
	–	Animal		o	Pot (With handles)
	u	v Animals (Back to back)		u	Rock
	–	Artichoke		o	Rug
	u	Badge		–	Shell
	u	Bib		u	Shield
	o	Blanket		o	Ship (Reflected)
	–	Body		o	Skin (Animal)
	u	Bookends		–	Skull
	u	Bowl (With handles)		u	Smoke
	–	Brain		u	Sponge
	–	Bug		–	Star
	–	Butterfly		–	Starfish
	u	v Cape		o	Statues
	–	Chest		–	Turtle Shell
	u	Cloak		u	Urn
	u	Cloud(s)		o	Waterway (As D5 with other areas as landscape)
	u	Coal (Piece)		–	X-ray (Specific)
	o	Coat		u	X-ray (Unspecified)
	u	v Crown			
	–	Disc (Anatomy)	D2	o	Alligator
	u	Doors (Swinging)		–	Animal
	u	Emblem		o	Banister Spindle
	–	Face		o	Bedpost
	u	Face (Monster)		u	Bone
	u	Filet (Fish or meat)		–	Bug
	–	Flesh		o	Candle
	–	Flower		o	Candlestick
	u	Foliage (Aerial view)		–	Caterpillar
	u	Forest (Aerial view)		u	Club
	u	Gate		u	Crocodile
	–	Head		u	Drill Bit
	–	Heads (Animal)		u	Eel
	u	Heads (Human, profile, back to back)		–	Fish
				o	Giant
	u	v Hive (Bee)		o	Human
	–	Human		o	Human-like Figure
	u	Humans (Back to back)		–	Insect
	u	Ice		u	Knife
	o	v Iceberg (Reflected)		o	Lamp (Ornamental)
	u	Island		o	Lamp Post
	u	v Jacket		o	Lamp (Street)
	o	Landscape		o	Missile
	o	Leaf		u	Nail
	–	Liver (Anatomy)		–	Needle
	–	Lung(s)		–	Penis
	–	Map (Specific)			

Table A (Continued)

Location	FQ	Category	Location	FQ	Category
	u	Piston		*o*	Totem Pole
	u	Reptile		*u*	Tree
	o	Rocket		−	Valve
	o	Statue (Human-like)		*u*	Wasp
	u	Sword	D4	*o*	< Aircraft Carrier
	u	Thermometer		*u*	v Animal
	o	Totem Pole		*o*	< Animal (As *Dd*24 and remainder
	u	Train (Aerial view)			as another object)
	−	Vertebrae		*o*	< Bathtub (With *Dd*24 as another
	−	X-ray (Specific)			object)
	u	X-ray (Unspecified)		*o*	< Battleship
D3	*u*	Airplane		*o*	< Boat (In some instances *Dd* 24
	−	Anatomy			may be reported as a separate
	−	Animal (Not winged)			object)
	u	Animal (Winged)		−	Building
	o	Bird		−	Cocoon
	u	Bug (Not winged)		*u*	Cloud
	o	Bug (Winged)		*o*	< Cloud
	u	Butterfly		*u*	Coral
	o	Cross (Abstract or modern)		*u*	< Explosion
	o	Crucifix (Abstract)		*u*	< Gun (Science fiction)
	u	Crucifixion		−	Head (Animal)
	o	Duck (Flying)		−	Head (Bird)
	o	Emblem		*o*	Head (Human, profile)
	−	Face		*u*	v Human
	u	Flower		*u*	v Human-like Figure
	u	Fly		*o*	Iceberg
	u	Flying Fish		−	Insect
	o	Goose (Flying)		*o*	Landscape
	u	Head (Animal, with whiskers)		−	Map (Specific)
	−	Head (Bird)		*u*	Map (Unspecified)
	−	Head (Human)		*o*	Mask
	−	Head (Insect)		*o*	< Mountain(s)
	−	Head (Reptile)		*o*	Rock
	−	Human		*o*	< Rower (In boat)
	o	Human (Abstract)		*o*	< Sailboat
	o	Human (In costume)		*o*	< Ship
	o	Human-like Figure		*o*	Statue
	u	Insect (Not winged)		*o*	< Submarine
	o	Insect (Winged)		*u*	< Tank (Army)
	o	Lamp			
	o	Match (With fire)	D5	−	Animal
	o	Ornament		*o*	Backbone
	−	Owl		*o*	Bone
	−	Penis		*o*	Canal
	u	Pole (Electric or telephone)		*o*	Canyon
	u	Rocket		−	Caterpillar
	o	Rocket (With fire or smoke)		−	Eel
	o	Scarecrow		−	Fern
	u	Shrub(s) (Reflected)		*u*	Foliage (Aerial view)
	−	Skull		*o*	Gorge
	o	Statue		−	Human

Table A (Continued)

Location	FQ	Category	Location	FQ	Category
	–	Insect		o	Cross (On hill)
	–	Knife		o	Crucifix (Abstract)
	o	Missile Launch (With missile as		o	Crucifixion (On hill)
		D2 or D6 and remainder as		o	Flower (In pot)
		smoke and/or fire)		o	Fountain
	u	Pole		u	Head (Animal, whiskered)
	u	Reptile		–	Head (Bird)
	o	River		–	Head (Human)
	o	Road		–	Head (Reptile)
	o	Shaft		o	Lighthouse
	u	Spear		–	Map
	o	Spinal cord		o	Plant
	u	Thermometer		o	Scarecrow
	–	Tree		–	Spinal cord
	u	Tube		o	Statue (Human-like)
	o	Waterway		o	Totem Pole
	u	Worm		u	Tree
	–	X-ray (Specific other than spine)		–	Turtle
	o	X-ray (Spine)		–	X-ray
	u	X-ray (Unspecified)	D12	–	Arrow
D6	–	Animal		u	Burner (Bunsen)
	u	Arm (With fist at Dd23)		o	Canal
	o	Bullet		o	Candle
	u	Carving		o	Canyon
	u	Club		o	Gorge
	u	Cylinder		–	Human
	u	Eel		u	Missile
	–	Fish		–	Needle
	–	Head		u	Pencil
	–	Human		–	Penis
	u	Insect		–	Rectum
	u	Log		u	Road
	o	Missile		o	River
	u	Mummy Case		u	Rocket
	–	Neck		o	Shaft (Mine)
	u	Parking Meter		u	Spear
	o	Penis		u	Spinal cord
	o	Pole		u	Vagina
	o	Reptile		o	Waterway
	u	Road			
	o	Rocket	Dd21	o	v Claw
	–	Skull		–	Hand
	u	Statue		–	Head (Animal)
	–	Valve		o	v Head (Bird)
	u	Weapon (Unspecified)		–	Head (Human)
D8	–	Animal		o	v Head (Reptile)
	u	Airplane		u	v Horn
	u	Bird (Statue)		o	v Pincer
	–	Bug		o	v Tongs
	u	Bug (Winged, crawling from	Dd22	–	Arms
		object)		u	Birds (2, Profile)
	–	Butterfly		u	Branch(es)

Table A (Continued)

Location	FQ	Category	Location	FQ	Category
	u	< Cactus		—	Reptiles
	o	Feathers		u	Sticks
	u	Flames		u	Whiskers
	—	Flowers			
	u	Geese (Flock)	Dd27	—	Anatomy
	—	Ice		—	Buttocks
	u	Light Rays		u	v Eggs
	—	Pelt		—	Eyes
	u	v Shrub(s)		—	Heads
	—	Tree(s)		—	Humans
	o	Water (Splashing)		—	Testicles
	o	Whiskers		—	Vagina
				u	v Waterfall
Dd23	—	Bug			
	—	Eyes	Dd28	u	v Claws
	u	Fist		—	Heads
	u	Hands (Clasped)		u	v Reptiles
	—	Head (Animal)		—	Trees
	u	Head (Bird)			
	—	Head (Human)	Dd29	u	Coastline
	u	Head (Monster)		—	Head
	u	Head (Reptile)		—	Human Profile
	—	Heads (2)			
	u	Nob (Door)	DdS30	—	Cup
	—	Nose		u	Inlet
				—	Vase
Dd24	u	v Animal (Sitting)			
	—	Boot	Dd31	u	Bird
	u	v Castle		—	Head
	o	Cliff		—	Human
	u	v Head (Animal, with upper body)		u	Iceberg
	—	Head (Bird)		—	Nose
	—	Head (Human)		u	Shaker (Salt or pepper)
	—	Leg			
	—	Paw	Dd32	u	Boat
	o	Peninsula		—	Brain
	o	Rock		u	Butterfly
	o	< Seal		—	Egg
	o	< Smokestack		—	Eyes
	u	< Statue		u	Flames
	u	< Walrus		—	Kidney(s)
				—	Lung(s)
Dd25	u	Carving		u	Shell (Opened)
	u	Doll		—	Tonsils
	u	Foot (Human)		u	Waterwings
	—	Head			
	u	Human	Dd33	u	v Canyon (May include waterfall)
	—	Mountain		u	Inlet
	u	Paw		u	Landscape
	—	Penis		o	v Nest
	u	Shoe		u	Tongs
	u	Statue		u	Tweezer
				u	Vagina
Dd26	u	Antennae			

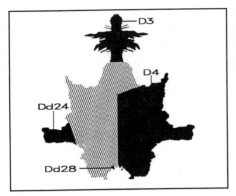

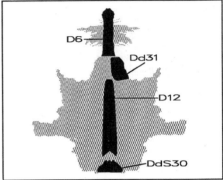

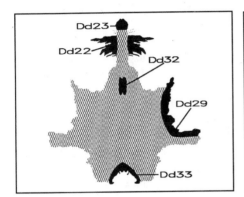

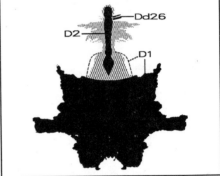

NOTE: The D1 location may also include the dashed area.

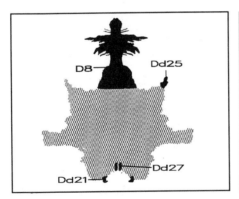

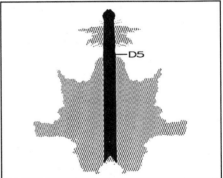

Figure 12. *D* and *Dd* Areas for Card VI.

Table A (Continued)

CARD VII

P Is to *D*1 or *D*9: Human Heads or Faces

Z Values:		*W* = 2.5	Adjacent = 1.0	Distant = 3.0	Space = 4.0

Location	FQ	Category	Location	FQ	Category
W	*u*	Abstract Drawing	*o*		Food (Breaded or fried)
	−	Amoeba	−		Frog
	−	Anchor	*u*		Froglegs (Food)
	−	Anatomy	−		Giant
	−	Animal	*o*	v	Girls
	u	Animals (2, cartoon with each as one-half of the blot)	*o*		Harbor (Includes *DS*7)
	−	Animals (2, real, with each as one-half of the blot)	*u*		Horseshoe
	o	Animals (2, as *D*2 and identified as cat, cartoon monkey, or rabbit, with *D*4 as a separate object)	−		Human
			u		Humans (2)
			o		Humans (As *D*2 with *D*4 as separate object)
		(*Note:* If the animals reported as *D*2 are not cat, cartoon, monkey, or rabbit, they should be coded as *u* if the contours are used in an appropriate way, or − in other cases. Examples of *u* include flat-faced animals such as some dogs. Examples of − include fox, elephant, horse, lion, etc.)	*o*	v	Humans (2)
			−		Insect
			o		Island(s)
			−		Keel (Boat)
			u	v	Lamp (Ornamental)
			−		Leaf
	u	v Arch	*u*		Leaf (Torn)
	−	Beard	−		Legs
	−	Bird	−		Map (Specific)
	−	Body (Lower half)	*u*		Map (Unspecified)
	−	Body (Split)	*u*		Monument
	u	Bones (Unspecified)	−		Moth
	−	Bug	−		Mouth
	−	Butterfly	−		Neck
	o	Canyon	−		Neckbone
	u	v Cap (With ear flaps)	*u*		Necklace
	u	Carving	−		Plant
	u	v Cave	*u*		Puzzle
	o	v Chair (Includes use of *DS*10)	*u*		Reef
	o	Cloud(s)	*u*		Rocks
	−	Coat	*u*		Rocking Horse
	−	Cookie (Includes broken)	−		Sea Animal
	−	Conch Shell	*u*		Sculpture
	−	Cracker (Includes broken)	−		Shrimp
	u	Crown	*u*		Shrimps (4)
	o	v Dancers (2)	−		Shrub(s)
	−	Dogs	−		Skull
	u	Dolls	*u*		Smoke
	o	Dolls (As *D*2 with *D*4 as separate object)	*u*		Spaceship
			o		Statues (As *D*2 with *D*4 as base)
	u	v Doorframe	*u*		Stool
	o	Elves (As *D*2 with *D*4 as separate object)	*u*		Swing
			−		Table
	−	Face	−		Vagina
	u	v Face (Photo negative and includes use of *DS*7 or *DS*10)	*u*		Vase
			u	v	Wig
			−		Womb
			−		X-ray (Specific)
			u		X-ray (Unspecified)

Table A (Continued)

Location	FQ		Category	Location	FQ		Category
D1	–		Anatomy		–		Animal (Large)
	–		Animal		–	v	Animal
	u	v	Animal (Small, long-tailed with nose at Dd24)		u	v	Animal (Cartoon)
					–		Bird
	u	<	Animal (Cartoon with D5 as long nose or beak)		u		Bush
					o		Cherub
	u		Art (Abstract)		–		Chicken
	–		Bird		u		Chicken Wings (Breaded or fried)
	u		Cactus				
	u	v	Cap (Coonskin)		o		Cloud(s)
	–		Cat		–		Cow
	u		Chair		o	<	Dog
	–		Chicken		–		Dragon
	o		Cliff		–		Donkey
	o		Cloud(s)		o		Dwarf
	u		Commode		o	v	Elephant (Cartoon or toy)
	–		Eagle		–		Fish
	–		Fish		u		Food (Breaded or fried)
	u		Fist (With finger pointing upward)		–		Fox
					–		Frog
	u		Foliage		–		Head
	o		Head (Animal, as cat, cartoon, monkey, or rabbit)		u		Hill
					–		Horse
			(Note: If animal head reported is not cat, cartoon, monkey, or rabbit, it should be coded as u if the contours are used appropriately, as for some dog heads, or – if that is not the case.)		o		Human (Child, Indian, female, or unspecified, may be whole human or head and upper body)
					u		Human (Adult male)
					o		Human-like Figure
	u	v	Head (Animal, with D5 as trunk)		o		Island(s)
	o		Head (Human, as child, Indian, female, or unspecified)		u		Lamb
					u		Landscape
	u		Head (Human, adult male)		–		Meat (Raw)
	o		Head (Human-like)		u		Mountains
	–		Horse		o		Rabbit
	–		Insect		u		Shrimp (2, breaded or fried)
	u		Ladle		o		Snowman
	u		Landscape		o		Statue
	–		Map (Specific)		–		Tiger
	u		Map (Unspecified)		o		Toy (Human or animal)
	u		Mask		–		Tree(s)
	–		Mountain		–		X-ray
	o		Rabbit (With nose as D8)				
	u	v	Rudder	D3	–		Animal
	–		Sea Animal		–		Beard
	o		Shrimp (Breaded or fried)		u		Candy (Cotton)
	o		Statue		–		Cap
	–		Tree		u		Cleaver
	–		X-ray		u		Cliff
					u		Cloud
D2	o		Angel		–		Cup
	o		Animal (Small, with D5 as ear and Dd 21 as tail, such as cat, dog, monkey, rabbit)		–		Dog
					u		Fish (Tail as Dd21)
					u		Fist (Thumb as Dd21)
	o		Animal (Cartoon)		–		Hairpiece

Table A (Continued)

Location	FQ	Category	Location	FQ	Category
	—	Ham		u	Kite
	—	Hand		u	Landscape
	o	Head (Animal, with Dd21 as ear or horn)		—	Lung(s)
				—	Map (Specific)
	u	v Head (Animal, with Dd21 as nose or trunk)		u	Map (Unspecified)
				—	Mountain(s)
	o	Head (Animal, cartoon or toy)		u	Paper (Torn)
	u	v Head (Bird, with Dd21 as beak)		o	Pelvis
	—	Head (Human)		u	Plateau (Aerial view)
	u	Head (Human-like)		—	Rib Cage
	—	Head (Reptile)		o	Rock(s)
	—	Insect		—	Sea Animal
	u	Island		—	Shell
	u	Kite (With Dd21 as tail)		—	Shoes
	u	Landscape		—	Shrub(s)
	—	Map		—	Skull
	o	Mask		—	Tent
	—	Nest		—	Vagina
	u	Peninsula		u	Wings
	u	Rock		o	X-ray (Pelvis)
	—	Sack		—	X-ray (Specific other than pelvis)
	u	Shrimp (Breaded or fried)		u	X-ray (Unspecified)
	—	Shrub			
	u	Statue	D5	—	Animal
	—	Tree		—	Arrow
	—	X-ray		u	Arrowhead
				—	Bird
D4	—	Anatomy		o	Blade (Knife)
	—	Animal(s)		u	< Boat
	o	v Bat		u	Bone
	o	Bird		u	< Canoe
	u	Bookends		u	Caterpillar
	—	Boots		u	Claw
	o	Bow		u	Comb (Decorative)
	u	Bowtie		—	Drill
	—	Bowl		—	Eel
	—	Bridge (Man-made)		o	Feather
	u	Bridge (Natural)		u	Finger
	—	Bug (Not winged)		—	Gun
	u	Bug (Winged)		u	Hair (Groomed or styled as in hairpiece or pony tail)
	o	Butterfly			
	—	Buttocks		—	Head
	—	Chest		u	Headdress
	o	Cloud(s)		u	Horn
	u	Cushion(s)		—	Human
	u	Doors (Swinging)		u	v Icicle
	—	Emblem		—	Insect
	—	Fly		u	Leg
	u	Hang Glider (May include D6 as person)		—	Log
				—	Penis
	—	Head		u	Pick (Guitar)
	—	Human		u	Plant
	—	Insect (Not winged)		—	Rifle
	u	Insect (Winged)		u	Sabre

Table A (Continued)

Location	FQ	Category	Location	FQ	Category
	–	Sausage		u	v Helmet
	u	Saw		u	Lake
	–	Smoke		o	v Lamp
	u	Stalamite		o	v Mushroom
	u	Sword		u	v Pagoda
	u	Tail		u	Pot
	u	Totem		o	v Sphinx
	–	Tree		o	v Statue
	u	Wing		–	Tree
	–	Worm		u	Vase
D6	–	Animal	D8	u	City (In distance)
	u	Anus		u	Cliff(s)
	–	Bone		–	Dragon
	–	Bug		o	Forest
	o	Canal		–	Head
	o	Canyon		u	Humans (Several on cliff or hill)
	–	Caterpillar		u	v Icicles
	u	Clitoris		o	Landscape
	u	Crack		u	Nest
	u	Dam		u	Sea Animal
	u	Doll		u	Snail
	–	Drill		u	Stalagmites
	–	Fish		u	Towers (Electric)
	o	Gorge		u	Trees
	–	Head		o	Village
	o	Hinge (Door)		u	Whale
	o	Human			
	o	Human-like Figure	D9	u	Cliff
	–	Insect		u	Cloud
	u	Missile (Often with Dd28 as pad		o	Head (Animal, small such as cat,
		or smoke)			dog, monkey, etc.)
	u	Monster (Animal)		–	Head (Animal, large)
	–	Penis		u	v Head (Animal)
	o	River		–	Head (Bird)
	u	Rocket (Often with Dd28 as pad		o	Head (Human)
		or smoke)		o	Head (Human-like)
	–	Spine		–	Insect
	–	Tower		u	Landscape
	–	Tree		–	Sea Animal
	o	Vagina		o	Statue (Bust)
	o	Waterway			
			DS10	o	Bowl
DS7	–	Anatomy		u	Entrance
	u	Arrowhead		–	Face
	–	Bell		o	Harbor
	o	Bowl		o	v Hat (Historical)
	–	Cloud		–	Head
	u	Entrance		o	Helmet
	–	Face		u	Lake
	o	Harbor		o	Lampshade
	u	v Hat (Historical)		u	Mushroom (Cap)
	–	Head		u	Tent

Table A (Continued)

Location	FQ	Category	Location	FQ	Category
Dd21	–	Ant		–	Cloud
	u	Arm		u	Dirt
	–	Bird		–	Head
	u	Caterpillar			
	–	Face	Dd25	u	Bird
	o	Finger		u	Landscape
	–	Head		u	Seagull
	u	Horn		–	Vagina
	u	Paw		u	Waterfall
	u	Peninsula			
	–	Penis	Dd26	o	Canyon
	–	Rifle		o	Gorge
	u	Tail		u	Human
	u	Thumb		u	Human-like Figure
	u	Trunk (Elephant)		o	River
				o	Statue
Dd22	–	Animal		o	Vagina
	u	Animal (Cartoon or toy)			
	–	Bones	Dd27	–	Animal
	u	v Doll		u	Anus
	u	Human		–	Human
	o	Human-like Figure		–	Teeth
	u	v Human		–	Vagina
	u	Puppet		–	Window
	u	Statue			
			Dd28	–	Animal
Dd23	–	Animal		–	Bird
	u	Brick		–	Buttocks
	u	Cloud		u	Face (Animal)
	u	Hat (Fur)		–	Face (Human)
	–	Head (Animal except bear or dog)		u	Face (Monster)
				u	Humans (2)
	o	Head (Animal, bear or dog)		u	v Parachute (With D6 or Dd26 as person)
	–	Head (Human)		–	Plant
	u	Pillow		u	Statue(s)
	u	Rock		u	Water
	–	Shoe		o	v Waterfall
				u	v Waves
Dd24	u	Cave			

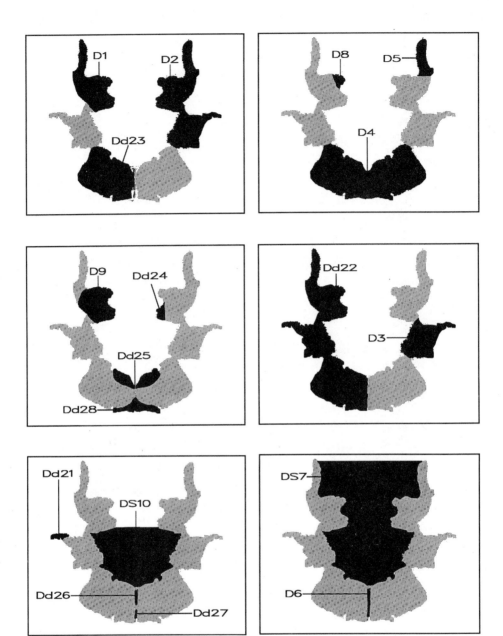

Figure 13. *D* and *Dd* Areas for Card VII.

Table A (Continued)

CARD VIII

P Is to *D*1: Whole Animal Figure

Z Values:		$W = 4.5$	Adjacent = 3.0		Distant = 3.0	Space = 4.0

Location	FQ	Category	Location	FQ	Category
W	—	Airplane		u	Island(s)
	—	Anatomy (Specific)		—	Jacket
	o	Anatomy (Unspecified)		—	Jellyfish
	—	Animal		—	Kidney(s)
	o	Animals (As *D*1 with other areas identified as object(s) that are consistent with contours)		u	Kite
				u	Lamp (Decorative)
				o	Landscape (Often as aerial view)
	o	Art (Abstract)		u	Lantern (Oriental)
	u	Badge		u	Leaf
	—	Bat		u	Lights (Colored as created by strobes)
	—	Bird			
	—	Bones (Skeletal)		—	Lobster
	o	Bowl (Ornamental)		—	Lung(s)
	—	Brain		—	Machine
	—	Butterfly		—	Map (Specific)
	u	Cage (Bird)		u	Map (Unspecified)
	o	Carousel		u	Mask
	—	Cake		—	Meat
	o	Chandelier		o	Medical Illustration (Parts are representative rather than real)
	u	Christmas Tree			
	u	Circus Tent		u	Monument
	—	Cloud(s)		—	Moth
	o	Coat-of-Arms		u	Mountain
	u	Coral		o	Ornament
	—	Crab		u	Pagoda
	u	Crown		—	Pelvis
	o	Design (Abstract)		o	Plant (Often in pot)
	o	Emblem		o	Poster (Abstract)
	—	Explosion		o	Poster (Nature)
	—	Face		—	Pyramid
	—	Fish		u	Robot
	u	Flag		u	Rocket
	o	Floral Design		u	Rubbish
	o	Flower		—	Sea Animal
	u	Foliage		u	Sea Shell
	o	Fountain		o	Ship (With sails, view from end)
	—	Frog		—	Skeleton
	u	Garden		—	Skull
	u	Gazebo		—	Snowflake
	—	Head (Animal)		—	Spider
	—	Head (Bird)		u	Statue
	—	Head (Human)		—	Stomach
	—	Head (Insect)		u v	Torch
	u	Head (Monster)		u	Totem Pole
	u	Headdress (Ornamental)		—	Tree
	u	Helmet (Science fiction)		u	Tree (Abstract or cartoon)
	—	Human		u	Vegetation (Tropical)
	—	Insect		u	Vegetation (Underwater)
	—	Intestines		u	Vase

Table A (Continued)

Location	FQ	Category	Location	FQ	Category
	u	Volcano (Erupting)		–	Crown
	–	X-ray		–	Disc (Spinal)
				–	Dog
$D1$	–	Anatomy		–	Emblem
	o	Animal (Four-legged, and		u	Fire
		appropriate to contours. This		–	Flesh
		class of response includes a wide		o	Flower
		variety of animals, including		–	Frog
		some considered to be		–	Hat
		prehistoric. The most commonly		u	v Head (Animal, short-eared or
		reported include badger, bear,			horned)
		cat, dog, gopher, lion, mouse,		–	Head (Animal, not short-eared or
		possum, rat, and wolf. Four-			horned)
		legged animals that are not		–	Head (Bird)
		appropriate for the contours		–	Head (Human)
		should be coded as –, such as		–	Head (Insect)
		elephant, giraffe, horse,		u	Head (Monster)
		kangaroo, etc.)		o	Ice Cream
	–	Bird		–	Insect
	u	Blood		u	v Jacket
	–	Camel		u	Jell-O
	–	Dolphin		u	Landscape
	–	Fish		o	Lava
	–	Flower		u	Leaf
	–	Frog		–	Meat
	u	Iguana		u	Mountain(s)
	–	Insect		u	Painted Desert
	u	Lizard		–	Pelvis
	–	Lung		u	Pot
	u	Petal (Flower)		u	Rock(s)
	–	Porpoise		u	Rug
	–	Reptile (Other than iguana or		u	Scab
		lizard)		u	Slide (Biological)
	–	Seal		–	Stomach
	–	Shrimp		–	Vagina
	–	Tree		–	Vertebrae (Cross section)
	–	Turtle	$D3/DS3$	u	< Animal (Reflected)
	–	X-ray		–	Badge
$D2$	–	Anatomy		o	Bone Structure
	–	Animal		–	Cave
	–	Bat		u	Corset
	u	Bowl (Decorative)		–	Door
	–	Brain		–	Face
	u	Bug		–	Head
	o	Butterfly		u	Ice
	–	Buttocks		o	Mask
	u	Cake		–	Net
	u	Canyon		o	Rib Cage
	u	v Cape		u	Skeleton
	–	Chest		o	Skull (Animal)
	u	v Coat		–	Skull (Human)
	u	Coral		u	Snow
	–	Crab		u	v Spaceship

Table A (Continued)

Location	FQ	Category	Location	FQ	Category
	u	v Tepee	D5		(*Note: D4 + D5 = D8*)
	u	v Tent		−	Animal
	u	v Tree (Fir)		u	Bat
	o	Vertebrae		u	Bird
	−	Web		o	Bird (Prehistoric or science fiction)
D4		(*Note: D4 + D5 = D8*)		−	Bone
	u	Airplane		o	Butterfly
	−	Animal		u	Cliff(s)
	u	v Antlers		o	Cloth
	−	Bat		u	Cloud(s)
	−	Bridge (Man-made)		−	Face
	−	v Bridge (Natural)		o	Flags
	u	Boomerang		−	Flower
	−	Butterfly		−	Head(s)
	u	Castle (On mountain)		o	Ice
	u	Cliff(s)		−	Kidney(s)
	−	Cloud		o	Landscape (Often as aerial view)
	u	Crab		−	Leaves
	−	Crawfish		−	Lung(s)
	−	Crown		−	Pelvis
	−	Face		u	Pillow(s)
	u	Face (Science fiction)		−	Rib Cage
	−	Fish		u	Sails
	o	Frog		−	Skull(s)
	−	Head		−	Sky
	u	Head (Science fiction)		o	Water
	−	House		−	X-ray
	−	Human(s)			
	u	Ice	D6	−	Anatomy (Specific)
	u	Iceberg		o	Anatomy (Unspecified)
	u	Insect		u	Art (Abstract)
	−	Jellyfish		−	Bird
	−	Lobster		−	Bones
	u	Mask (Science fiction)		−	Brain
	o	Monster		u	Chandelier
	o	Mountain		u	Christmas Tree
	−	Octopus		−	Crab
	u	v Pelvis		−	Face
	u	Robot		o	Flower
	u	Rocket		u	Glacier
	o	Roots		−	Head
	u	Sea Animal		u	Helmet (Science fiction)
	−	Scorpion		−	Human
	u	Shrub(s)		u	Island(s)
	−	Skull		o	Landscape (Often aerial view)
	o	Spaceship		u	Mask
	u	Spider		o	Mountain
	u	Stump (Tree)		u	Ornament
	u	Temple		u	Pagoda
	u	Tent		o	Plant
	u	Tree		u	Ship (With sails, view from end)
	u	Vine		u	Statue
	u	Waterfall		u	Vegetation

Table A (Continued)

Location	FQ	Category	Location	FQ	Category
D7	–	Animal		u	Feet (Animal)
	–	Bird		u	Glove
	o	Blood (Usually dried)		u	Hand
	–	Buttocks		u	Horn (Animal)
	u	Canyon		u	Root
	–	Chest			
	–	Face	Dd23	u	Anus
	–	Head		u	Canyon
	o	Ice Cream		–	Face
	u v	Jacket		u	Flask
	u	Jello		–	Head
	u	Landscape		–	Human(s)
	u	Leaf (Autumn)		u	Vagina
	–	Mountain		u	Waterfall
	u	Painted Desert			
	o	Rocks	Dd24	u	Antennae
	u v	Vest		–	Birds
				u	Feelers
D8		(Note: D4 + D5 = D8)		u	Fingers
	–	Anatomy		u	Horns
	u	Bird		–	Human(s)
	–	Butterfly		u v	Legs (Human)
	u v	Chandelier		u	Pincers
	–	Crab		u	Roots
	–	Face		–	Teeth
	u	Floral Display		o	Trees
	–	Flower			
	u	Glacier	Dd25	u	Alligator
	–	Head		–	Animal
	u	Helmet (Science fiction)		–	Bird
	u	Landscape		–	Fish
	u	Pagoda		–	Human
	o	Plant		u	Island
	–	Shell		–	Penis
	o	Spaceship		u	Spaceship
	u	Tent		u	Statue
Dd21	–	Animal	Dd26	u v	Cliff
	o	Bone (Skeletal)		u <	Dog
	–	Esophagus		u <	Head (Animal)
	–	Human		–	Head (Bird)
	u	Knife (And case)		–	Head (Human)
	u v	Missile Launch		u	Rock
	o	River		u <	Statue
	u	Rockets (Separating stages)			
	–	Spear	Dd27	u	Alligator
	o	Spinal cord		u	Bone
	u	Stick(s)		u	Drill Bit
	u	Waterfall		u	Hypodermic
	o	Waterway		u	Knife
				u	Missile
Dd22	–	Animal		–	Needle
	o	Arm (Human)		u	Pen
	u	Branch		u	Rocket

Table A (Continued)

Location	FQ	Category	Location	FQ	Category
	u	Spear		–	Crab
	–	Worm		–	Insect
				u	Monster (Animal-like)
DdS28	u	Cloud(s)		–	Reptile
	u	Snow		u	Root(s)
	u	Water		–	Wing
DdS29	u	v Bottle (Milk)	Dd32	u	Albatross
	u	v Bowling Pin		o	Bird
	–	Ghost		u	Butterfly
	u	v Salt Shaker		o	Gull
	–	Statue		o	Snow
	–	Tooth		u	Water
	u	v Triangle (Music)			
	u	< Whale			
			Dd33	–	Anatomy
Dd30	u	v Cane		u	Butterfly
	u	Gorge		–	Face
	u	River		u	Flower(s)
	o	Spinal Cord		u	Head (Animal)
	o	Stick		–	Head (Bird)
	–	Sword		–	Head (Human)
	u	Waterfall		u	Ice Cream
				–	Lung(s)
Dd31	–	Animal		u	Rock(s)

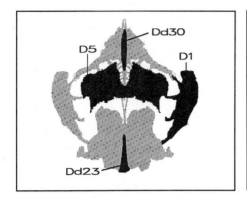

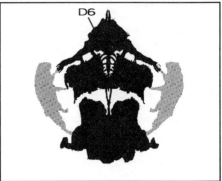

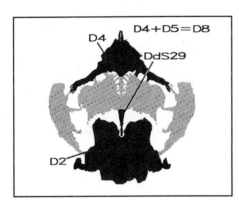

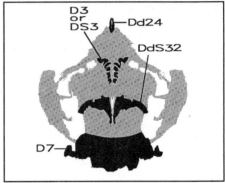

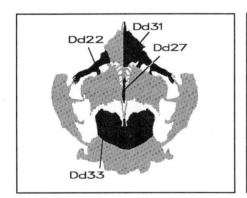

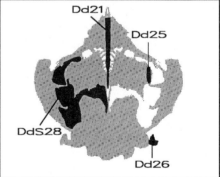

Figure 14.   *D* and *Dd* Areas for Card VIII.

Table A (Continued)

CARD IX

P Is to *D3*: Human or Human-like Figures

Z Values:		*W* = 5.5	Adjacent = 2.5			Distant = 4.5	Space = 5.0

Location	*FQ*	Category	Location	*FQ*	Category
W	–	Anatomy		*o*	Illustration (Medical)
	u	Anchor		–	Insect
	–	Ant		*u*	Island
	o	Art (Abstract)		*u*	v Jellyfish
	u	Badge		*u*	v Lamp (Ornamental)
	–	Bird		*o*	Landscape
	o	v Birds (As *D3* under tree)		–	Leaf
	o	Bowl (Ornamental)		–	Lung(s)
	–	Bug		–	Machine
	–	Butterfly		–	Map (Specific)
	u	Cactus		*u*	Map (Unspecified)
	u	Cake (With candles as *D3*)		*o*	Mask
	u	Candle (With *D6* as base)		*u*	Monster
	o	Canyon (As *D8* with other areas as foliage and/or landscape)		*u*	Ornament
				o	Paint
	u	v Cape (Theatrical)		*o*	Pallet (Artist's)
	u	Chair (Winged with *D6* as base or swivel)		*o*	Plant (Sometimes with *D6* as pot)
	u	v Clothing (Woman's)		*u*	v Robot
	–	Cloud(s)		–	Sea Animal
	–	Cocoon		*u*	Seaweed
	o	Coral		–	Seed
	–	Crab		–	Skull
	u	Crater (As *D8* with other areas as foliage and/or landscape)		*u*	Spaceship
				–	Throat
	u	Decoration		*u*	v Tree
	u	v Dummy (Dressmaker's)		–	Vagina
	u	Emblem		*o*	Vase
	o	Explosion		*o*	Waterfall (As *D5* with other areas as foliage and/or landscape)
	–	Face			
	u	Face (Clown)			
	u	Face (Monster)		–	X-ray
	o	Fire (Usually with smoke as *D1*)			
	o	Floral Arrangement	*D1*		(*Note:* *D1* + *D1* = *D11*)
	o	Flower (Often with *D6* as pot)		–	Anatomy
	–	Fly		–	Animal
	o	Foliage		*u*	< Animal (Unspecified)
	o	Fountain		*o*	< Ape
	o	Garden		*o*	< Bear
	u	Hat		–	Bird
	–	Head (Animal)		–	Bone
	–	Head (Human)		–	Bug
	–	Head (Insect)		–	Butterfly
	u	Head (Monster)		–	Cat
	o	Headdress (Ceremonial)		*u*	Cloud
	u	Helmet (Science fiction)		*u*	Coral
	–	Human		*u*	< Dog
	u	v Human (In costume)		–	Elephant
	u	v Human-like Figure		*u*	Fern

Table A (Continued)

Location	FQ	Category	Location	FQ	Category
	−	Fish		−	Cloud(s)
	o	Foliage		u	Coral
	u	Forest (Usually aerial view)		−	Crab
	−	Frog		o	Crater (As D8 with other areas as
	o	< Giant			foliage and/or landscape)
	o	Grass		u	Emblem
	−	Hat		u	Explosion
	u	Head (Animal, with snout at the		−	Face
		D5 centerline)		o	Face (Clown)
	o	Head (Animal, with snout at		u	Face (Monster)
		Dd24, often with DdS29 as eye)		o	Fire (As D3 with other areas as
	o	v Head (Animal, with snout at D5			smoke)
		centerline or at Dd24)		o	Flower
	−	Head (Bird)		−	Fly
	u	< Head (Human or human-like		o	Foliage
		with chin at Dd24)		u	Fountain
	−	Head (Insect)		u	Garden
	−	Heart		−	Head (Animal)
	−	Human		−	Head (Human)
	o	< Human (With Dd24 as head)		u	Head (Human-like)
	−	Insect		−	Head (Insect)
	o	Landscape		o	Headdress (Ceremonial)
	u	Leaf		u	Helmet
	−	Lion		−	Human
	−	Lung		u	Illustration (Medical)
	−	Map		−	Insect
	u	< Monkey		u	v Jellyfish
	u	< Monster		o	Landscape
	−	Mushroom		u	Leaf (Autumn)
	u	v Pig		−	Map
	u	Plant		o	Mask
	u	< Rabbit		u	Ornament
	−	Sea Animal		o	Plant
	o	Shrub		−	Sea Animal
	u	Smoke		−	Skull
	u	Sponge		o	v Tree
	u	< Statue		u	Vagina
	−	Tree		o	Vase
	−	Wing		u	v Waterfall (As D5 with other
	−	X-ray			areas as foliage and/or
					landscape)
D2	−	Anatomy			
	o	Anchor	D3	−	Anatomy
	u	Art (Abstract)		o	Animal (Antlered or horned)
	u	Badge		−	Animal (Not antlered or horned)
	−	Bird		u	Bird
	o	v Birds (As D3 under bush)		o	v Bird
	o	Bowl		u	Blood
	−	Bug		−	Bone
	−	Butterfly		−	Bug
	o	Canyon (As D8 with other areas		u	Carrot
		as foliage and/or landscape)		o	Cliff
	u	Chair (Wing)		u	Cloud
	−	Clothing		o	Clown

Table A (Continued)

Location	FQ	Category	Location	FQ	Category
	−	Club		−	Eye
	u	Crab		−	Fish
	o	Dancer (In costume)		u	Flower
	o	< Deer		u	Head (Animal)
	o	Demon		o	Head (Human)
	−	Dog		u	Mask
	u	Dragon		−	Meat
	−	Face		−	Pot
	o	Fire		o	Raspberry
	−	Fish		u	Rock
	o	Flower		−	Sperm
	o	Ghost		u	Sponge
	o	v Gnome		u	Strawberry
	o	Head (Animal, antlered or horned)		−	Turtle
	−	Head (Animal, not antlered or horned)	D5	−	Anatomy
				−	Animal
	o	Head (Human)		u	Arrow
	o	Head (Human-like)		o	Bone
	−	Head (Insect)		o	Candle
	o	Hill		u	Cane
	u	Human		u	Drill Bit
	o	Human-like Figure		−	Esophagus
	−	Insect		u	Flame
	o	Landscape		u	Geyser
	o	Lava		u	Gorge
	−	Leg		−	Head
	u	Lobster		−	Human
	−	Lung		−	Insect
	u	Map (Unspecified)		o	Landscape
	−	Meat		o	Match
	u	v Owl		−	Peninsula
	o	v Parrot		−	Penis
	u	Plant		u	Reptile
	−	Rodent		u	River
	o	Sand		u	Road
	−	Sea Animal		u	Sand Bar
	−	Shrimp		o	< Shoreline
	−	Skull		o	Skewer
	u	Statue		o	Spinal Cord
	u	Sun Spot		u	Stalagtite
	u	Torch		u	Stem
	o	Toy (For punching)		u	Sword
	−	Tree		−	Tree
	u	Wing		o	Waterfall (With D8 as background)
	o	Witch			
				u	Waterway
D4	−	Anatomy			
	o	Apple	D6	−	Anatomy
	o	Ball		−	Animal(s)
	u	Blood		o	Apples (4)
	−	Bug		o	Babies (2)
	o	Candy (Cotton)		o	Balloons
	−	Cocoon		−	Bird

Table A (Continued)

Location	FQ	Category	Location	FQ	Category
	o	Blood		u	v Human-like Figure
	u	v Butterfly		u	Keyhole
	−	Buttocks		u	v Lamp
	o	Candy (Cotton)		o	Light Bulb
	o	Cloud (Including mushroom cloud)		u	v Mask
				u	v Monster
	o	Embryos (2)		u	Nose (Cow or horse)
	−	Face		u	Parking Meter
	u	v Face (Insect)		u	v Robot
	u	v Face (Science fiction)		o	v Salt Shaker
	u	Fire		−	Skull
	u	Flower(s)		u	Sky
	−	Head (Animal)		−	Tree
	u	v Head (Elephant or rodent)		u	Tornado
	o	< Head (Human, reflected)		−	Vagina
	−	Human		o	Vase
	o	< Human (Sitting, reflected)		u	Violin
	−	Insect		o	Water
	−	Island		o	Waterfall
	u	Marshmallows		−	Womb
	−	Meat			
	u	v Mushroom	D9	−	Animal
	−	Pot(s)		u	Chandelier
	u	Powder Puff		u	v Corkscrew
	u	Raspberries		−	Drill
	o	Sherbet		−	Head (Animal other than elephant)
	u	v Shoulders (Human)			
	−	Skin		u	Head (Elephant)
	u	Smoke		−	Head (Human)
	u	Strawberries		−	Head (Insect)
	−	Vagina		u	v Heron (On one leg)
	−	Wing		−	Human
				o	v Flower
D8/DS8	−	Anatomy		o	Fountain
	−	Animal		u	v Lamp
	u	Blender		o	Spindle (Office)
	o	Bottle		u	v Tree
	o	Canyon		o	v Umbrella
	o	Cave		u	v Valve
	u	Chandelier			
	−	Chest	D11	−	Anatomy
	u	v Dress		u	Bat
	u	v Dummy (Dressmaker's)		u	Bird
	−	Face (Animal)		u	Bookends
	−	Face (Human)		o	Butterfly
	u	v Face (Monster)		−	Ear Muffs
	u	v Flask		−	Earphones
	o	v Ghost		o	Foliage
	−	Head (Animal)		−	Head
	−	Head (Human)		−	Human
	u	v Head (Monster)		−	Insect
	o	Hourglass		u	Insect (Winged)
	−	Human		−	Lungs

Table A (Continued)

Location	FQ	Category	Location	FQ	Category
	o	Pelvis	Dd24	u	Cliff
	u	Plant		u	Head (Animal)
	u	Shrubs		u	< Head (Human)
D12	–	Animal	Dd25	u	Claws
	u	< Dragon		u	Feelers
	o	Fire (Forest)		–	Fingers
	o	< Human (As D1 with D3 as other		u	Roots
		object such as hill, sand, etc.)		u	Tentacles
	o	< Landscape		–	Trees
	u	Leaves		u	Weeds
	–	Monster			
	–	Tree	Dd26	–	Animal
				u	Claw
Dd21	o	Claws		o	Finger
	o	Finger		–	Foot
	u	v Fins		u	Gun (Often science fiction)
	u	v Horns		u	Hose (Nozzle)
	–	Humans		–	Human
	u	Icicles		u	Key
	–	Rake		–	Nose
	u	v Rockets (Group)		u	< Scarecrow
	–	Spears		u	< Statue
	u	Stalagtites		u	Trumpet
	–	Trees			
			Dd27	–	Animal
Dd22/	u	Bowl		–	Face
DdS22	–	Candles		–	Head
	u	Cavern		–	Human
	–	Cup		u	< Tent
	–	Door(s)		u	< Top
	–	Eyes			
	–	Face (Animal)	Dd28	–	Blood
	–	Face (Human)		u	Breast
	–	Face (Insect)		u	Egg
	o	Face (Monster)		–	Head
	–	Head		u	Insect (Hard-shelled)
	–	Jar		–	Scab
	–	Jellyfish		u	Shell
	u	Lake(s)		–	Stomach
	o	Mask			
	u	Nose (Animal)	DdS29	o	Bell
	o	Pumpkin (Halloween)		–	Bug
	–	Skull		u	Eye
				–	Face
DdS23	u	Caves		o	Ghost
	u	Eyes		–	Human
	o	Holes		u	Human-like Figure
	u	Islands		u	Lake
	u	Lakes			
	u	Nostrils (Animal)	Dd30	u	Candlewax
	–	Pillows		u	Caterpillar
	–	Shells		–	Intestine

Table A (Continued)

Location	FQ	Category	Location	FQ	Category
	−	Penis	Dd34	−	Animal
	−	Reptile		u	Antlers
				u	Branches
Dd31	u	Breast		u	Bridge (Natural)
	u	v Cover (Pot)		u	Cannon (Usually science fiction)
	u	< Face (Animal)		u	Claw(s)
	u	< Face (Human)		o	Drawbridge (Often opening)
	u	Foliage		u	Horns
	−	Tree(s)		u	Hose
				−	Human(s)
DdS32	u	v Bowl		u	Lightning Flash
	u	Dome		u	Roots
	−	Helmet		−	Skeletal
	u	Moon (Upper half)		−	Trees
	u	Shell			
	u	Sun (Upper half)	Dd35	−	Animal
	u	Sunspot		u	Bathysphere
	u	Tent		−	Bird
				u	Buttocks
Dd33	o	< Alligator		u	Furnace
	o	< Crocodile		−	Head
	u	Foliage		−	Lung(s)
	u	< Head (Animal)		−	Mask
	−	Head (Human)		u	Pot
	u	< Head (Reptile)		u	Rock(s)
	u	Log		u	Stove (Iron)
	−	Mountain(s)			
	−	Tree			

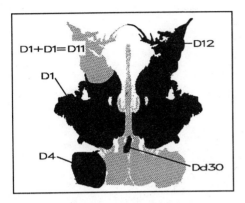
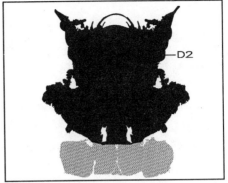
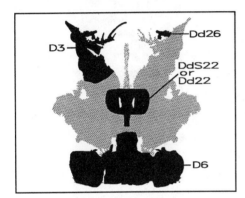
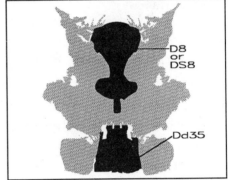
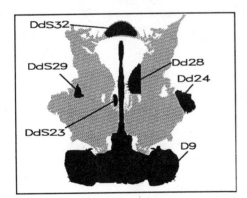
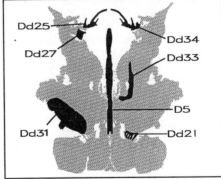

Figure 15. *D* and *Dd* Areas for Card IX.

Table A (Continued)

CARD X

P Is to D1: Spider or Crab

Z Values:	W = 5.5	Adjacent = 4.0	Distant = 4.5	Space = 6.0

Location	FQ	Category		FQ	Category
W	–	Anatomy		–	Sea Animal
	o	Animals (Marine, unspecified, or if specified, meeting appropriate contour requirements)		o	Underwater Scene
				o	Walkway (As center space and other areas as flowers and/or shrubbery)
	u	Animals (Not marine but meeting contour requirements)			
	o	Art (Abstract)	D1	o	Amoeba
	o	Aquarium		–	Animal
	u	v Aviary		u	Bug
	u	Bacteria		u	Cell (Biological)
	–	Birds		–	Cockroach
	–	Bones		u	Coral
	u	Chandelier		o	Crab
	u	Children's Play Park (With all areas included as play equipment)		u	Dragon
				u	Earring
				–	Face
	–	Christmas Tree		u	Fern
	–	Clouds		–	Fish
	u	Costume (Theatrical, hanging on wall)		u	Flower
				–	Hat
	u	Design (Abstract)		–	Head
	u	v Explosion		u	Insect
	–	Face		u	Island
	u	Fireworks Display		–	Jellyfish
	o	Floral Design		u	Landscape
	o	Flower Garden		–	Leaf
	o	v Flowers (Bouquet)		u	Lobster
	o	Garden Scene (With some areas as flowers or shrubbery and areas such as D11 and/or D6 as sculpture or architecture)		–	Map
				–	Mask
				u	Monster
				o	Octopus
	–	Headdress		u	Pom Pom
	–	Human		–	Reindeer
	o	Insects (Unspecified, or if specified, meeting appropriate contour requirements)		u	Roots
				o	Scorpion
				–	Sea Shell
	u	Islands		u	Snowflake
	u	Kaleidoscope		o	Spider
	u	Lights (Created by strobe)		o	Water (Drop)
	–	Map (Specific)		–	Web
	u	Map (Unspecified)		u	Weed
	–	Mask			
	u	Mobile (Abstract)	D2	u	Amoeba
	–	Pagoda		u	Animal (Unspecified)
	o	Painting (Modern)		–	Bee
	u	Painting (Finger)		u	v Bird
	u	Pallet (Artist's)		u	Bug
	u	Plants		u	Cat
	o	Poster (Abstract)		o	Cell (Biological)
	u	Puzzle (Pieces)		–	Chicken

Table A (Continued)

Location	FQ	Category	Location	FQ	Category
	o	Dog		o	Wishbone
	o	Egg (Broken or fried)		u	v "V"
	–	Eye			
	–	Face	D4	–	Anatomy
	u	v Fish		–	Animal
	o	Flower		u	v Animal (Prehistoric)
	u	Frog		–	Arm
	–	Head		u	Boot (Jester)
	u	Insect		–	Bug
	u	Island		o	Caterpillar
	u	Leaf		–	Cucumber
	o	Lion		o	Eel
	–	Monkey		–	Fish
	–	Monster		–	Head (Animal)
	u	Plant		u	v Head (Animal, prehistoric)
	–	Sea Animal		–	Head (Bird, except peacock or
	u	Seal			swan)
	–	Sperm		–	Head (Human)
				u	v Head (Peacock)
D3	–	Airplane		u	v Head (Swan)
	o	v Antennae (Radar or TV)		u	Horn
	u	Antennae (Insect)		–	Insect
	o	v Balloons (Weather)		u	Plant
	–	Bird		u	v Saxophone
	u	Buds		o	v Sea Horse
	–	Bug		u	Smoke
	o	Cherry Pits		u	Snail
	–	Crab		o	Snake
	u	Ear Muffs		u	Tail (Bird)
	u	Earphones		–	Tree
	–	Eyes		–	Wing
	–	Flower(s)			
	o	Governor (On motor)	D5	o	v Angel
	–	Head		–	Bug
	–	Human		u	Clothespin
	o	Instrument (Weather for wind		u	v Crucifix
		velocity)		u	v Devil
	u	Instrument (Medical)		–	Face
	u	Knocker (Door)		o	Head (Animal, long-eared)
	u	Lights (Electric)		–	Head (Animal, not long-eared)
	–	Lungs		–	Head (Human)
	u	v Necklace		u	Head (Insect, with antennae)
	–	Notes (Musical)		o	v Human
	–	Ovaries		u	v Human-like Figure
	–	Parachutist		–	Insect
	o	Pawnbroker Symbol		o	Mask
	–	Rower (In boat)		u	v Tack
	–	Scissors		u	v Tooth
	o	Seed Pod (Maple)		u	Tweezers
	u	Spaceship			
	–	Stethoscope	D6	–	Anatomy
	–	Testicles		–	Animal
	u	Tongs (Ice)		o	v Anthropoids
	u	Twig		u	Bagpipes

Table A (Continued)

Location	FQ	Category	Location	FQ	Category
	–	Bat(s)		–	Sea Animal
	u	Birds		u	Seed Pod
	u	Brassiere		u	Spider
	–	Breasts		–	Turtle
	o	Bridge (Natural)		u	Weed
	–	Cloud(s)			
	u	Coral	D8	–	Animal
	u	v Dolls		u	Animal (Cartoon or prehistoric)
	u	Ducks		o	Ant
	–	Eyeglasses		u	Bee
	–	Face(s)		o	Beetle
	u	v Flowers		o	Bug
	o	v Ghosts		–	Cat
	o	v Gorillas		–	Chicken
	–	Hands		u	Chipmunk
	u	v Heads (Animal)		u	Crab
	u	Heads (Bird)		o	Dragon
	–	Heads (Human)		u	Dwarf
	u	v Humans		u	Elf
	o	v Human-like Figures		u	Emblem
	–	Insect(s)		–	Face
	–	Jaw		–	Fish
	–	Kidneys		u	Frog
	–	Lungs		u	Gnome
	o	v Monsters		–	Goat
	u	Nest		–	Head (Animal)
	–	Nose		o	Head (Animal-like creature)
	–	Ovaries		–	Head (Human)
	u	Pipes (Smoker's)		u	Head (Human-like creature)
	u	Skeletal		o	Head (Insect)
	u	Water		–	Human
				o	Insect
D7	o	Animal (Leaping)		–	Lizard
	o	Ant		u	Mask
	–	Bird		–	Monkey
	–	Clam		o	Monster (Animal)
	u	Claw		o	Monster (Human-like)
	o	Cockroach		u	Parrot
	u	Cocoon		u	Rodent
	o	Crab		u	Roots
	o	Crayfish		–	Sea Animal
	o	Deer		–	Shrimp
	–	Dog		–	Skeletal
	–	Face		–	Spider
	–	Fish		u	Unicorn
	–	Frog		–	Witch
	o	Grasshopper			
	–	Human	D9	–	Anatomy (Except intestine)
	–	Kidney		–	Animal
	u	Lobster		u	Animal-like Creature
	o	Nest		u	Bacon
	u	Preying Mantis		o	Blood
	u	Rodent (With head toward D9)		u	Bone
	o	Roots		–	Bug

Table A (Continued)

Location	FQ	Category	Location	FQ	Category
	o	Caterpillar		—	Centipede
	u	Cloud		o	Eiffel Tower
	o	Coral		—	Face
	—	Dolphin		u	Face (Monster)
	u	Eel		u	v Flower
	o	Elf		u	v Funnel
	o	Fire		o	Helmet (Science fiction)
	—	Hair		—	Human
	—	Head		o	Insects (As D8 and D14 as
	u	Human			another object)
	o	Human-like Figure		—	Intestines
	u	Insect		—	Lungs
	u	Island		u	Mask
	—	Map		o	Missile (With smoke or on pad)
	u	Map (Topographic)		u	Mistletoe
	o	Mermaid		—	Nervous System
	o	Microorganism		u	Plant
	u	Mountain Range (Often as aerial		o	Rocket (With smoke or on pad)
		view)		o	Roots
	o	Mummy		u	Skeletal
	—	Porpoise		—	Skull
	u	Sea Horse		o	Spaceship
	o	Worm		u	Statue
				o	v Torch
D10	o	Arbor		u	v Tree
	o	Arch		—	X-ray (Specific)
	—	Anatomy		u	X-ray (Unspecified)
	u	Angel			
	—	Animal	D12	u	Bean
	u	v Bird		—	Bird
	u	v Comb (Ornamental)		o	Buffalo
	o	v Door Knocker		o	Bull
	—	Flower		o	Bug
	u	Fountain		u	Claw
	—	Funnel		o	Cow
	u	v Head (Animal, horned)		u	Dog
	—	Head		—	Fish
	o	v Horns		u	Goat
	o	v Human (As D5 with other area as		u	Grasshopper
		flags, smoke, streamers, swing,		o	Insect
		etc.)		u	Lamb
	—	Insect		o	Leaf
	u	Lyre		—	Plant
	o	v Parachutist		o	Ram
	u	v Pelvis		—	Rodent
	o	Shrub(s)		u	Seed Pod
	u	v "U"		o	Unicorn
	o	Wishbone		u	Whale
D11	u	Airplane	D13	o	< Animal (Usually lying or
	—	Animal			jumping and includes a wide
	—	Broom			variety, such as bear, buffalo,
	o	Candle (With holder)			cat, dog, lion, etc.)
	u	Castle		—	Ant

Table A (Continued)

Location	FQ	Category	Location	FQ	Category
	–	Bird		–	Jellyfish
	u	Bug		o	Rose
	u	Cloud		–	Seal
	–	Face		–	Smoke
	u	Fish		–	Walrus
	–	Flower		u	Wing
	–	Head			
	–	Human	Dd21	–	Animal(s)
	u	Insect		u	v Antennae
	u	Leaf		u	Arch
	u	Mat		u	v Bird (Flying)
	o	Potato Chip		–	Boomerang
	u	Rock		o	v Butterfly (Front view)
	–	Sea Shell		u	Canyon
	u	Sponge		u	v Chevron
	–	Tree		o	v Flower (Sometimes including D6)
D14	–	Animal		–	Human(s)
	u	Artery		–	Insect
	u	Baton		u	v Keel (Boat)
	o	Bone		u	Landscape
	o	Candle		u	v Ornament
	o	Chimney		u	Reef
	u	Crowbar		–	Tuning Fork
	–	Face		u	v Wishbone
	–	Finger			
	u	Handle	DdS22	–	Anatomy
	–	Head		u	Design (Abstract)
	–	Human		–	Face
	–	Knife		–	Head
	u	Log		u	Islands
	o	Missile		–	Map (Specific)
	u	Pencil		u	Map (Unspecified)
	u	Penis		u	Underwater Scene
	o	Post			
	o	Rocket	Dd25	u	Coastline
	u	Root		–	Head (Animal)
	u	Ruler		o	Head (Human)
	u	Shotgun		o	Head (Human-like)
	o	Spinal Cord			
	u	Statue	Dd26	–	Breast
	o	Stove Pipe		–	Face (Animal)
	u	Sword		u	Face (Human, profile)
	u	Test Tube		u	Face (Human-like, profile)
	u	Vase			
			Dd27	–	Face
D15	–	Animal		u	Insect
	o	Bird		–	Seaweed
	o	Bud (Flower)		–	Trees
	u	Butterfly			
	–	Cloud	Dd28	–	Clown
	o	Flower		u	Insect
	–	Head		u	Puppet
	–	Insect		u	Roots

Table A (Continued)

Location	*FQ*	Category	Location	*FQ*	Category
*DdS*29	*o*	Buddha	*Dd*33	*o*	Acorn
	–	Face		*u*	Ball
	o	Fan (With *D*11 as handle)		–	Eye
	u	Lantern (Sometimes with *D*11 as handle)		–	Head
				u	Orange
	u	Paddle (With *D*11 as handle)		*u*	Sun
				o	Walnut
*DdS*30	–	Skeleton			
	u	Water	*Dd*34	*u*	Basket
				–	Bullet
*Dd*31	*u*	v Head (Animal)		–	Head
	u	v Head (Caterpillar)		–	Skull
	–	Head (Human)		*u*	Tooth
	u	v Head (Human-like)			
			*Dd*35	–	Animal
*Dd*32	–	Animal		*u*	People (On a cliff)
	u	Head (Animal)		–	Reptile
	–	Head (Human)		*u*	Trees (On a cliff)

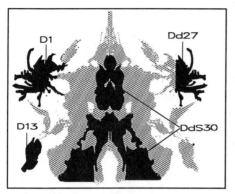
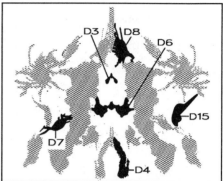
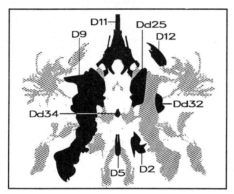
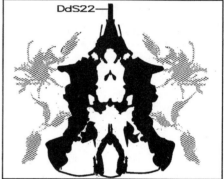
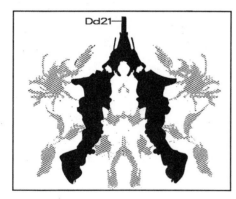
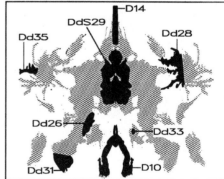

Figure 16.   *D* and *Dd* Areas for Card X.

Table B.   Illustrations of Responses That Should Be Coded *FQ* +

Card	Response		Inquiry
I	Ths ll one of those exotic bf's, it has the irregular edges & the markings & the little antennae	E: S:	(Rpts S's resp) Yes, well most bf's have wings that r straighter, but some of the one's that r rare have a more irregular structure like this. And there r the triangular white markings & here r the very small antennae & the little round nobs at the head & the tail is here
I	There is s.o. standg in the cntr & people dancing arnd her with large flowg capes on, thy have little caps on too	E: S:	(Rpts S's resp) Ths is the person, the legs, the waist & up here r her hands, her head is not apparent, mayb she's dancing too & her head is back & on each side there r other dancers, thy hav thes long flowing capes out here & their heads r here & it almost looks lik thy all have their feet down here, together, mayb its a balancing act or dance, thy seem to hav little caps on too, c up here
IV	Ths ll a fellow like sorta hunched over riding a bike or a motorcycle, he has a little helmet on & he's stickg his feet out forward	E: S:	(Rpts S's resp) Here r his big legs, comg out this way & the cntr is the tire of the motorcycle & thes r the handlebars, c how thy come to points as thy r bent downward & ths is his body & up here is lik his head only u can only c the helmet, here
V	Ths ll 2 people, sittg on the ground resting back to back, lik mayb thy hav ski caps on & thy r covered with blankets	E: S:	(Rpts S's resp) Thy r back to back, here is their heads & thes ll tassled caps lik skiers wear sometimes & their legs r out here, c the outline of them but the bodies look too full, lik they r covered lik w a blanket, u can c the bulges lik where their arms and knees might be
VI	< Ths ll a submarine in a battle, u can c the conning tower & the bomb blasts out in front of it	E: S:	(Rpts S's resp) Here is the conning tower & the bow & ths is the waterline & the hull & out here is a blast like effect, lik it was being shelled, c the splash effect here
VII	Ths is lik 2 littl childrn on a see-saw, little girls w their pony tails bouncg up in the air	E: S:	(Rpts S's resp) Yes, one here & here, c the head, the little nose & mouth & ths is the pony tail & ths is like a bar tht thy lean against & thy r lik squatting & down here is the base of the thg sorta curved upward lik the see-saw
VIII	Ths is a carousel, mayb a painting of one, lik an elaborate painting with each part detailed by a a diff color	E: S:	(Rpts S's resp) Well it has the two animals on the sides, lik standg on their hind legs & this blue square part would b the machinery & the top the tent lik effect & the round base dwn here
VIII	< Ths ll an animal that is walking over some rocks & thgs stickg up from the water to get from ths rock to ths stump here & its all reflected down here	E: S:	(Rpts S's resp) Here, the pink, c the head & the legs and the tail, c the pointed nose & ths orange is lik a big boulder & he's stepping on these smaller rocks & his front paw is on ths stump that is stickg up here & the blue is the water and all of the details r reflected dwn here
IX	< Ths ll a heavy set person chasing a littl kid up ths hill here	E: S:	(Rpts S's resp) Well here is the person, it ll a woman, sorta bulky, c the head & the body & ths is her arm & out in front of her is the kid, c the head & her body, her hair is lik flyg in the breeze & this is lik a hill, going up, mayb a sand dune caus its got the orange color, lik mayb thy r running in the sand

Table B (Continued)

Card	Response	Inquiry
X	It ll the inside of an aquarium	*E:* (Rpts *S*'s resp) *S:* There r alot of undersea creatures. The blue & this brown both ll crabs, thy hav a lot of legs sticking out, & the green ll vegetation & the pink is lik logs or coral & ths green dwn here is lik two seahorses, c the curved heads & the yellow r lik amoeba sort of thgs, not amoeba but bigger with the rounded cntr & ths brown cb sk of shell

Table C.   Organizational (Z) Values for Each of the Ten Cards

Card	W	Type of Organizational Activity		
		Adjacent Detail	Distant Detail	White Space With Detail
I	1.0	4.0	6.0	3.5
II	4.5	3.0	5.5	4.5
III	5.5	3.0	4.0	4.5
IV	2.0	4.0	3.5	5.0
V	1.0	2.5	5.0	4.0
VI	2.5	2.5	6.0	6.5
VII	2.5	1.0	3.0	4.0
VIII	4.5	3.0	3.0	4.0
IX	5.5	2.5	4.5	5.0
X	5.5	4.0	4.5	6.0

Table D.   Best Weighted Z Sum Prediction When Zf Is Known

Zf	Zest	Zf	Zest
1	*	26	88.0
2	2.5	27	91.5
3	6.0	28	95.0
4	10.0	29	98.5
5	13.5	30	102.5
6	17.0	31	105.5
7	20.5	32	109.0
8	24.0	33	112.5
9	27.5	34	116.5
10	31.0	35	120.0
11	34.5	36	123.5
12	38.0	37	127.0
13	41.5	38	130.5
14	45.5	39	134.0
15	49.0	40	137.5
16	52.5	41	141.0

Table D (Continued)

Zf	Zest	Zf	Zest
17	56.0	42	144.5
18	59.5	43	148.0
19	63.0	44	152.0
20	66.5	45	155.5
21	70.0	46	159.0
22	73.5	47	162.5
23	77.0	48	166.0
24	81.0	49	169.5
25	84.5	50	173.0

Table E. Popular Responses Used in the Comprehensive System

Card	Location	Criterion
I	W	Bat, the response *always* involving the whole blot.
I	W	Butterfly, the response *always* involving the whole blot.
II	D1	Animal, specifically identified as bear, dog, elephant, or lamb. The response is usually the head or upper body; however, responses involving the whole animal are also coded *P*.
III	D9	Human figure or representations thereof such as dolls, caricatures, etc. If D1 is used as two human figures, D7 should not be reported as part of the human figure if the coding *P* is to be applied.
IV	W or D7	Human or human-like figure such as giant, monster, science fiction creature, etc.
V	W	Bat, the apex of the blot upright or inverted and *always* involving the whole blot.
V	W	Butterfly, the apex of the blot upright or inverted and always involving the whole blot.
VI	W or D1	Animal skin, hide, rug, or pelt (the skin or hide may be reported as part of a whole animal, either in natural or unnatural state).
VII	D1 or D9	Human head or face, specifically identified as female, child, or Indian, or with gender not identified. If D1 is used, the upper segment (D5) is usually identified as hair, feather, etc. If the response includes the entire D2 area, *P* is coded if the head or face is restricted to the D9 area. If Dd23 is included as a part of the human form, the reponse is not coded as *P*.
VIII	D1	Whole animal figure, usually of the canine, feline, or rodent varieties.
IX	D3	Human or human-like figure such as witch, giant, monster, science fiction creature, etc.
X	D1	Crab, with all appendages restricted to the D1 area.
X	D1	Spider, with all appendages restricted to the D1 area.

CHAPTER 12

Normative Data
and Reference Samples

This chapter contains several tables of normative and comparative data. They are important to the understanding and utilization of the test data. If used wisely, they aid considerably in interpretation; but if applied in a more naive or casual manner, they can lead to interpretive postulates that hold the potential for disaster. Almost any normative sample will have limitations, and those presented here are no exception. The nonpatient data for adults and younger subjects have been collected as faithfully as possible by competent examiners working within the constraints of problems created by subject recruitment and sample sizes. Thus, it seems reasonable to argue that the data do reflect coding and scoring distributions that would be very similar to those obtained from different groups of nonpatients, provided those groups have geographic and socioeconomic distributions that are similar to those here.

All of the nonpatient subjects are, in one sense or another, volunteers. None had special reasons to be examined and none have any admitted psychiatric history. Among the provisions of agreement before the testing occurred was one discounting any possibility of feedback concerning results. All were informed that the project concerned standardization of the test. Of the 700 adult subjects, 486 volunteered through their places of work, usually under conditions of encouragement by supervisors or union leaders, and typically were provided with time away from work for the testing. An additional 172 adult subjects volunteered through social or interest organizations to which they belonged, such as the PTA, local Audubon groups, bowling leagues, and so on, and the remaining 42 were recruited through the assistance of social service agencies. None were financially reimbursed for their participation, although all received greeting cards of appreciation.

The 1390 nonpatient children were recruited through schools and social organizations such as Cub Scouts, Little Leagues, 4H Clubs, and such. They were "volunteered" by their parents and about 75% were tested in schools during school hours. Ideally, all of the sample sizes for each of the age groups should be larger. The original goal was to obtain a minimum of 150 subjects at each of the 12 age levels, but that objective was never achieved.

THE ADULT SAMPLE

The adult nonpatient sample consists of data generated from the protocols of 700 nonpatient adults, stratified for geographic distribution, and partially stratified for socioeconomic level. These data have accumulated over a period of more than 20 years and as a result the tables have been revised several times (Exner, 1978, 1986, 1990, 1991; Exner, Weiner, & Schuyler, 1976). The most recent revision occurred because of findings indicating that brief records, that is, those containing less than 14 answers, are likely to be invalid (Exner, 1988). These findings made it necessary to discard all records with less than 14 answers from previously developed samples. The current data have been randomly selected from a group of 1332 adult nonpatient records that were available. The final selection was stratified to include 350 males and 350 females and to reflect 140 subjects from each of five geographic areas, Northeast, South, Midwest, Southwest, and West. Attempts were made to equalize the number of males and females from each region but that was not always possible because the samples for some regions are markedly uneven for sex. Thus, the number of males and females are nearly equal for four regions but the southwest group includes 83 females and 57 males while the midwest group contains 81 males and 59 females.

The mean age for the group is 32.36 (SD = 11.93; Median = 30; Mode = 22) with a range of 19 to 70 years. The subjects average 13.25 years of education with a range of 8 to 18 years. A breakdown for demographic variables is shown in Table 31.

The data for socioeconomic level have been collapsed in Table 31. The coding for SES was done using a 9-point variation of the Hollingshead and Redlich Scale. It includes three subgroups for each of the categories, upper, middle, and lower. Thus, SES 2 equals middle-upper class, SES 5 equals middle-middle class, and so on, with SES 9 being restricted to subjects exclusively on public assistance. The sample contains no subjects from SES 1 (upper-upper) and the group shown in Table 31 as "Lower" includes 52 subjects from SES 9.

A multivariate model was used to search out significant differences among the three broad categories and among the subgroups. The only significant findings occur between the SES 9 subgroup and other subgroups. The SES 9 group does have a significantly higher average *Lambda* and significantly lower mean values for *EA* and *es*. Consequently, they have lower mean values for most of the determinants that contribute to *EA* and *es*. The data for all 700 subjects were compared with a modified sample of 648 subjects that excluded all of the SES 9 subjects. In general, it was found that the inclusion of that group in the sample does not alter means or standard deviations significantly. Apparently this is because the *N* for the group is modest, representing only 7% of the total sample.

Several descriptive statistics for 111 Rorschach variables for the adult nonpatient sample are shown in Table 32. Standard deviations are shown in brackets for many of

Table 31. Demography Variables for 700 Nonpatient Adults

Variable	N	$%$	Variable	N	$%$	Variable	N	$%$
Marital Status			*Age*			*Race*		
Single	193	28	18–25	236	34	White	567	81
Lives w/S.O.	57	8	26–35	267	38	Black	81	12
Married	332	47	36–45	100	14	Hispanic	43	6
Separated	28	4	46–55	44	6	Asian	9	1
Divorced	71	10	56–65	34	5			
Widowed	19	3	Over 65	19	3			
Education			*Residence*			*Socioeconomic Level*		
Under 12 Yrs	53	8	Urban	259	37	Upper	65	9
12 Yrs	214	31	Suburban	280	40	Middle	411	59
13–15 Yrs	346	49	Rural	162	23	Lower	224	32
16+ Yrs	87	12						

Table 32.   Descriptive Statistics for 700 Adult Nonpatients

Variable	Mean	SD	Min	Max	Freq	Median	Mode	SK	KU
R	22.67	4.23	14.00	38.00	700	23.00	23.00	0.54	1.37
W	8.55	1.94	3.00	20.00	700	9.00	9.00	1.28	8.87
D	12.89	3.54	0.00	22.00	698	13.00	14.00	−0.38	1.02
Dd	1.23	[1.70]	0.00	15.00	452	1.00	0.00	3.89	22.18
S	1.47	[1.21]	0.00	10.00	600	1.00	1.00	2.44	11.43
DQ+	7.31	2.16	2.00	13.00	700	7.00	6.00	0.27	−0.39
DQo	13.64	3.46	5.00	34.00	700	14.00	15.00	0.95	4.67
DQv	1.30	[1.26]	0.00	6.00	477	1.00	0.00	0.93	0.38
DQv/+	0.41	[0.66]	0.00	2.00	219	0.00	0.00	1.35	0.53
FQx+	0.90	0.92	0.00	5.00	427	1.00	0.00	1.21	2.26
FQxo	16.99	3.34	7.00	29.00	700	17.00	17.00	0.04	0.52
FQxu	3.25	1.77	0.00	13.00	667	3.00	3.00	0.94	3.37
FQx−	1.44	1.04	0.00	6.00	605	1.00	1.00	0.95	0.93
FQxNone	0.09	[0.33]	0.00	3.00	58	0.00	0.00	4.00	18.52
MQ+	0.55	0.73	0.00	3.00	297	0.00	0.00	1.23	1.02
MQo	3.52	1.89	0.00	8.00	693	3.00	3.00	0.46	−0.60
MQu	0.20	0.45	0.00	2.00	123	0.00	0.00	2.23	4.31
MQ−	0.03	[0.19]	0.00	2.00	22	0.00	0.00	5.90	36.99
MQNone	0.01	[0.11]	0.00	1.00	8	0.00	0.00	9.21	83.11
SQual−	0.18	[0.49]	0.00	3.00	102	0.00	0.00	3.16	11.29
M	4.31	1.92	1.00	9.00	700	4.00	3.00	0.51	−0.74
FM	3.70	1.19	1.00	9.00	700	4.00	4.00	−0.05	0.46
m	1.12	0.85	0.00	4.00	530	1.00	1.00	0.51	0.32
FC	4.09	1.88	0.00	9.00	690	4.00	5.00	0.31	−0.13
CF	2.36	1.27	0.00	6.00	670	2.00	3.00	0.40	−0.12
C	0.08	[0.28]	0.00	2.00	51	0.00	0.00	3.73	14.14
Cn	0.01	[0.08]	0.00	1.00	5	0.00	0.00	11.73	135.98
Sum Color	6.54	2.52	1.00	12.00	700	7.00	5.00	−0.04	−0.79
WSumC	4.52	1.79	0.50	9.00	700	4.50	3.50	0.02	−0.69
Sum C'	1.53	[1.25]	0.00	10.00	551	1.00	1.00	1.32	5.24
Sum T	1.03	[0.58]	0.00	4.00	620	1.00	1.00	1.35	5.39
Sum V	0.26	[0.58]	0.00	3.00	137	0.00	0.00	2.39	5.54
Sum Y	0.57	[1.00]	0.00	10.00	274	0.00	0.00	4.08	28.70
Sum Shading	3.39	2.15	0.00	23.00	689	3.00	3.00	3.03	20.65
Fr+rF	0.08	[0.35]	0.00	4.00	47	0.00	0.00	6.06	49.54
FD	1.16	[0.87]	0.00	5.00	553	1.00	1.00	1.00	2.57
F	7.99	2.67	2.00	19.00	700	8.00	8.00	0.65	1.21
(2)	8.68	2.15	1.00	14.00	700	8.00	8.00	0.06	0.63
3r+(2)/R	0.40	0.09	0.03	0.79	700	0.38	0.33	0.42	2.59
Lambda	0.58	0.26	0.14	2.25	700	0.56	0.50	2.23	9.91
FM+m	4.82	1.51	1.00	10.00	700	5.00	5.00	0.27	0.30
EA	8.83	2.18	2.00 ·	14.50	700	9.00	9.50	−0.30	0.15
es	8.20	2.98	3.00	31.00	700	8.00	7.00	1.90	10.18
D Score	0.04	1.08	−10.00	2.00	244	0.00	0.00	−3.29	24.95
AdjD	0.20	0.87	−5.00	2.00	272	0.00	0.00	−1.11	6.04
a (active)	6.48	2.14	2.00	13.00	700	6.00	6.00	0.57	−0.09
p (passive)	2.69	1.52	0.00	9.00	659	2.00	2.00	0.54	0.26
M^a	3.04	1.59	0.00	7.00	679	3.00	2.00	0.45	−0.38
M^p	1.31	0.94	0.00	5.00	568	1.00	1.00	0.59	0.34
Intellect	1.56	1.29	0.00	6.00	546	1.00	1.00	0.78	0.25
Zf	11.81	2.59	5.00	23.00	700	12.00	12.00	0.27	1.47
Zd	0.72	3.06	−6.50	9.50	644	0.50	−1.00	0.48	0.09
Blends	5.16	1.93	1.00	12.00	700	5.00	5.00	0.04	−0.37

Table 32.   (Continued)

Variable	Mean	SD	Min	Max	Freq	Median	Mode	SK	KU
Blends/*R*	0.23	0.09	0.04	0.67	700	0.23	0.26	0.76	1.55
Col-Shd *Bld*	0.46	[0.69]	0.00	3.00	252	0.00	0.00	1.45	1.66
Afr	0.69	0.16	0.27	1.29	700	0.67	0.91	0.40	0.30
Populars	6.89	1.39	3.00	10.00	700	7.00	8.00	−0.47	−0.13
X+%	0.79	0.08	0.50	1.00	700	0.80	0.80	−0.23	1.17
F+%	0.71	0.17	0.25	1.00	700	0.71	1.00	−0.24	−0.24
X−%	0.07	0.05	0.00	0.43	605	0.05	0.04	1.86	8.97
Xu%	0.14	0.07	0.00	0.37	667	0.14	0.15	0.17	0.41
S−%	0.08	[0.23]	0.00	1.00	102	0.00	0.00	2.93	7.99
Isolate/R	0.20	0.09	0.00	0.47	689	0.19	0.16	0.39	−0.23
H	3.40	1.80	0.00	9.00	694	3.00	3.00	0.90	0.30
(*H*)	1.20	0.98	0.00	4.00	499	1.00	1.00	0.41	−0.35
HD	0.69	0.89	0.00	7.00	348	0.00	0.00	2.06	8.03
(*Hd*)	0.14	0.35	0.00	2.00	99	0.00	0.00	2.14	2.95
Hx	0.01	[0.11]	0.00	1.00	8	0.00	0.00	9.21	83.11
All *H* Cont	5.42	1.63	1.00	11.00	700	5.00	6.00	0.23	−0.10
A	8.18	2.04	3.00	15.00	700	8.00	7.00	0.43	0.17
(*A*)	0.17	[0.47]	0.00	3.00	95	0.00	0.00	3.27	12.22
Ad	2.21	[1.18]	0.00	9.00	665	2.00	2.00	1.14	4.65
(*Ad*)	0.05	[0.26]	0.00	2.00	33	0.00	0.00	5.14	28.41
An	0.42	[0.65]	0.00	4.00	244	0.00	0.00	1.54	2.46
Art	0.91	0.83	0.00	4.00	448	1.00	1.00	0.50	−0.41
Ay	0.34	[0.48]	0.00	2.00	236	0.00	0.00	0.78	−1.09
Bl	0.15	[0.40]	0.00	2.00	96	0.00	0.00	2.64	6.55
Bt	2.48	1.29	0.00	6.00	652	3.00	3.00	−0.02	−0.47
Cg	1.29	0.93	0.00	4.00	572	1.00	1.00	0.62	0.12
Cl	0.15	[0.38]	0.00	2.00	102	0.00	0.00	2.32	4.54
Ex	0.13	[0.34]	0.00	1.00	93	0.00	0.00	2.17	2.71
Fi	0.42	[0.67]	0.00	2.00	221	0.00	0.00	1.33	0.44
Food	0.23	[0.50]	0.00	2.00	136	0.00	0.00	2.11	3.65
Ge	0.04	[0.21]	0.00	2.00	25	0.00	0.00	5.74	35.68
Hh	0.93	0.85	0.00	4.00	458	1.00	1.00	0.76	0.32
Ls	0.89	0.78	0.00	3.00	460	1.00	1.00	0.45	−0.50
Na	0.38	[0.60]	0.00	2.00	222	0.00	0.00	1.34	0.72
Sc	0.91	[0.97]	0.00	6.00	411	1.00	0.00	1.25	2.99
Sx	0.07	[0.39]	0.00	5.00	30	0.00	0.00	8.41	85.78
Xy	0.03	[0.18]	0.00	2.00	17	0.00	0.00	7.25	57.98
Idio	1.85	1.29	0.00	7.00	599	2.00	2.00	0.75	1.08
DV	0.70	[0.79]	0.00	4.00	373	1.00	0.00	1.12	1.20
INCOM	0.52	[0.65]	0.00	4.00	323	0.00	0.00	1.39	3.56
DR	0.15	[0.38]	0.00	2.00	103	0.00	0.00	2.30	4.44
FABCOM	0.17	[0.41]	0.00	2.00	111	0.00	0.00	2.27	4.43
DV2	0.01	[0.10]	0.00	1.00	7	0.00	0.00	9.87	95.70
INC2	0.00	[0.07]	0.00	1.00	3	0.00	0.00	15.21	229.99
DR2	0.00	[0.04]	0.00	1.00	1	0.00	0.00	26.46	700.00
FAB2	0.02	[0.13]	0.00	1.00	12	0.00	0.00	7.46	53.74
ALOG	0.04	[0.22]	0.00	2.00	29	0.00	0.00	5.23	29.28
CONTAM	0.00	0.00	0.00	0.00	0	0.00	0.00	—	—
*Sum*6 *Sp Sc*	1.62	1.26	0.00	7.00	564	1.00	1.00	0.73	0.35
*Sum*6 *Sp Sc*2	0.03	[0.18]	0.00	1.00	23	0.00	0.00	5.25	25.66
*WSum*6	3.28	2.89	0.00	15.00	564	3.00	0.00	1.07	1.15
AB	0.15	[0.40]	0.00	2.00	98	0.00	0.00	2.57	6.17
AG	1.18	1.18	0.00	5.00	466	1.00	1.00	1.04	0.62

Table 32.   (Continued)

Variable	Mean	SD	Min	Max	Freq	Median	Mode	SK	KU
CFB	0.00	0.00	0.00	0.00	0	0.00	0.00	—	—
COP	2.07	1.52	0.00	6.00	555	2.00	2.00	0.25	−0.84
CP	0.02	[0.14]	0.00	1.00	13	0.00	0.00	7.15	49.23
MOR	0.70	[0.82]	0.00	4.00	356	1.00	0.00	1.03	0.60
PER	1.05	1.00	0.00	5.00	478	1.00	1.00	1.38	3.27
PSV	0.05	[0.22]	0.00	1.00	34	0.00	0.00	4.21	15.76

Note: Standard deviations shown in brackets indicate that the value is probably unreliable and/or misleading because the variable is nonparametric.

the variables. This signifies that the variable *is not* parametric, that is, the distribution of scores for the variable deviates significantly from a normal distribution. Thus, in most instances, the standard deviation should not be used to estimate the expected or average range for the variable. Obviously, variables that have standard deviations in brackets should not be included in most types of parametric analyses.

RORSCHACH DATA AND DESCRIPTIVE STATISTICS

Several issues confront those who use normative data in professional practice. Among those problems are the integrity of the normative sample and issues of cross-validation. However, a much more important issue concerns application, that is, how best to use the data. Normative data can be abused much more easily than is readily apparent, and this is especially true for Rorschach data. Norms are meant to provide descriptive information about groups. They offer reference points against which individual subjects can be compared. Unfortunately, in many cases, some reference points do not provide adequate information from which meaningful judgments concerning conformity or deviation can be derived. Most norms are presented in terms of arithmetic means and standard deviations. In theory, these measures of central tendency provide useful reference points that are easily interpreted. But means and standard deviations are also easily misinterpreted. While providing some information about scores, they can be misleading with regard to the nature of the distribution of scores. Thus issues concerning deviation can become clouded quite easily.

Means and standard deviations are probably most revealing when the distribution of scores approaches the Gaussian or normal-shaped curve. As distributions deviate from normality, the possibilities increase that the mean and standard deviations will not provide a good representation of the true distribution. This is especially the case when scores fall on a *J*-curve, that is, one in which most of the values fall on one, two, or three data points of the curve and very few deviate from those points. The distributions for many Rorschach variables fall on *J*-curves, and this reduces the usefulness of mean and standard deviation data markedly when considering those variables.

In fact, the frequencies for some Rorschach variables have such a restricted range that efforts at scaling or smoothing the distribution are futile. This is not to suggest that means and standard deviations are useless when working with Rorschach data. To the contrary, they provide a very accurate picture for many variables, but their usefulness can be enhanced considerably if other methods are also used to describe frequency and score distributions.

Among the variety of descriptive statistics available, which can be useful in approaching the issue of variables that are not normally distributed, are the frequency, range, median, mode, skewness, and kurtosis. The frequency provides information concerning the number of subjects who have given a particular kind of response. The range describes the spread of the values for a variable, the median provides information concerning the center of the spread, and the mode indicates which value appears most frequently in the distribution.

The values for skewness and kurtosis concern the actual shape of the curve. The perfectly bell-shaped normal distribution will have a skewness value of .00. If the curve is positively skewed, that is, with the greater proportion of the scores being low or to the left of center, the skewness value will be positive. If the curve is negatively skewed, the value will be shown as a minus. The kurtosis value indicates something about the height of the curve. In the perfect bell-shaped distribution the kurtosis is .00. If the curve is *leptokurtic,* that is, with a piling up of scores in one region, the kurtosis will be positive, whereas if the curve is *platykurtic,* with the scores being more or less evenly distributed over a broad range, the kurtosis value will be minus.

The composite of these eight measures—mean, standard deviation, median, mode, range, frequency, skewness, and kurtosis—should provide a much better picture of Rorschach frequencies and scores than any one used alone, or even a composite of two or three. For example, the data in Table 32 show that the texture variable ($FT + TF + T$) has a mean of 1.03 and a standard deviation of .58. Technically, this suggests that two-thirds of the 700 subjects gave between .45 and 1.61 texture responses. Because it is impossible to give a fractional texture response, it is reasonable to postulate that those subjects all have values of 1 for texture. That postulate appears supported by the fact that the mode and median are 1, even though the range is 0 to 4. The frequency data show that 620, or about 89% of the 700 subjects gave at least one texture response. The composite of these data suggests the probability of a J-curve distribution. That notion is supported by the data concerning skewness and kurtosis. The skewness is +1.35, indicating a sharp positive distribution, whereas the kurtosis is +5.39, indicating that a marked clustering of scores exists. They confirm the presence of a J-curve. In reality, 555 of the subjects gave one texture response (about 79%), 5% gave two, 6% gave more than two, and 11% had no T answers.

In the example concerning the texture variable, the possibility of a J-curve distribution was evident early on. The Table 32 data for the C' variable illustrate circumstances in which such a finding is not nearly as obvious. Table 32 shows a mean for the C' variable as 1.53 and a standard deviation of 1.25. This suggests that two-thirds of the 700 subjects gave between .28 and 2.78 C' responses. In other words, one or two C' responses would be considered as average. But that is not consistent with other data. The mode and median are both 1, but the range is extensive, from 0 to 10, and the frequency is 551, indicating that 21% of the sample gave *no C'*. The skewness is +1.32, indicating a large number of low scores, and the kurtosis is +5.24, revealing a large cluster of scores at one or two data points. The skewness is very marked and the kurtosis quite extreme. The fact that 21% of the sample gave no C' responses, and the mode is 1, indicates that more than half of the total sample have C' values of either 0 or 1. Adding those findings to the indications provided by the skewness and kurtosis values leaves little doubt that a J-curve exists.

Table 33. Frequencies and Percentages for 33 Structural Variables for 700 Adult Nonpatients

EB Style				Form Quality Deviations		
Introversive	251	36%		$X + \% > .89$	49	7%
Pervasive	68	10%		$X + \% < .70$	71	10%
Ambitent	143	20%		$X + \% < .61$	12	2%
Extratensive	306	44%		$X + \% < .50$	0	0%
Pervasive	86	12%		$F + \% < .70$	313	45%
				$Xu\% > .20$	109	16%
D Score				$X - \% > .15$	24	3%
D Score > 0	156	22%		$X - \% > .20$	9	1%
D Score = 0	455	65%		$X - \% > .30$	2	0%
D Score < 0	89	13%				
D Score < −1	30	4%				
Adjusted D Score				*FC:CF+C Ratio*		
Adj D Score > 0	206	29%		$FC > (CF + C) + 2$	220	31%
Adj D Score = 0	428	61%		$FC > (CF + C) + 1$	345	49%
Adj D Score < 0	66	9%		$(CF + C) > FC + 1$	30	4%
Adj D Score < −1	30	4%		$(CF + C) > FC + 2$	9	1%
Zd > +3.0 (Overincorp)	127	18%		S-Con Positive	0	0%
Zd < −3.0 (Underincorp)	37	5%		HVI Positive	13	2%
				OBS Positive	14	2%

$SCZI = 6$	0	0%	$DEPI = 7$	1	0%	$CDI = 5$	3	0%
$SCZI = 5$	0	0%	$DEPI = 6$	3	0%	$CDI = 4$	18	3%
$SCZI = 4$	2	0%	$DEPI = 5$	21	3%			

Miscellaneous Variables

Lambda > .99	38	5%	$(2AB + Art + Ay) > 5$	52	7%
Dd > 3	33	5%	Populars < 4	9	1%
$DQv + DQv/ + > 2$	200	29%	Populars > 7	293	42%
S > 2	72	10%	COP = 0	145	21%
Sum T = 0	80	11%	COP > 2	271	39%
Sum T > 1	75	11%	AG = 0	234	33%
$3r + (2)/R < .33$	112	16%	AG > 2	95	14%
$3r + (2)/R > .44$	169	24%	MOR > 2	22	3%
$Fr + rF > 0$	47	7%	Lvl 2 Sp.Sc. > 0	23	3%
PureC > 0	51	7%	Sum 6 Sp.Sc. > 6	1	0%
PureC > 1	3	0%	Pure H < 2	69	10%
Afr < .40	11	2%	Pure H = 0	6	1%
Afr < .50	50	7%	$p > a + 1$	6	1%
$(FM + m) <$ Sum Shad	106	15%	$M^p > M^a$	72	10%

The issue that remains unanswered is whether a C' value of 2 should be regarded as "average" or "deviant." Although an exact answer is not easily derived, the magnitude of the standard deviation, plus the values of the range, suggest an answer. The broad range tends to magnify the standard deviation, and the curve is markedly lopsided. Because more than half of the subjects have C' values of 0 or 1, the most conservative conclusion is that a value of 2 should be considered as "unusual."

There are other, even less noticeable hazards that challenge those using Rorschach normative data. Although the sorts of descriptive statistics provided in Table 32 often are of some value in understanding the test and test results, some can be quite misleading unless clarified by other information concerning the distributions of scores. The distribution for the *Erlebnistypus* probably offers the best illustration of this. As it involves the relation between *M* and *Sum C*, those naive to the Rorschach might be prone to estimate the "average" *EB* by reviewing the normative data for those variables. The data in Table 32 indicate that the mean for *M* is 4.31 (*SD* = 1.92; Median = 4; Mode = 3) and the mean for *Sum C* is 6.54 (*SD* = 2.52; Median 7.0; Mode = 5.0).

Either of two erroneous conclusions could be drawn from those data. One is that the majority of subjects in the sample are extratensive because the mean for *Sum C* exceeds the mean for *M* by more than two points. The second is that most subjects in the sample are ambitents because there is considerable overlap among the variances for the two variables. Unfortunately, neither conclusion is correct. Table 33 includes some important information concerning the distribution of scores, with a particular focus on cutoff scores that are often critical in evaluating ratios and percentages, or defining the existence of response styles.

The Table 33 data reveal that about 36% of the sample consists of introversives, about 44% are extratensives, and only 20% are ambitents. In other words, the means and standard deviations in Table 33 are misleading because the distribution of the data is bimodal, that is, introversives tend to give more *M*'s than represented by the mean, while extratensives tend to have more *Sum C* than indicated by the mean.

ADULT NORMATIVE DATA BY STYLE

The data in Tables 32 and 33 provide an overall picture of the frequencies and scores that are generated from a reasonably large, heterogeneous sample of nonpatient subjects. They offer descriptive statistics for many variables that may serve well as guidelines from which to judge the presence of deviation. However, as noted earlier, they can be misleading in some instances because of the mixture of introversive, extratensive, and ambitent subjects. This problem is possibly best illustrated by the data in Tables 34 and 35.

Table 34 provides a comparison of the introversive, extratensive, and ambitent subjects for 22 variables drawn from the data for nonpatient adult subjects in Table 32. Subjects with *Lambda* values greater than 0.99 have been excluded even though they represent very small segments of each group. This is because they represent another very important response style that tends to be a dominating factor in processing and translating information and forming behaviors.

The Table 34 data indicate that very significant differences exist among the three groups for all but one (*CP*) of the 22 variables. Some of the differences are very dramatic. For instance, introversive subjects give an average *Pure H* that is more than twice the average for either of the other groups. Similarly, extratensive subjects average 20 times more *Blood* responses than introversives, and four times more *Blood* responses than ambitents. Conversely, only about 2% of extratensives give explosion responses while about 27% of introversives do give those answers. The data in Table 35 add to the intrigue.

Table 35 contains frequency data regarding 9 structural variables for the nonpatient introversive, extratensive and ambitent subjects who have *Lambda* values less than 1.0. It will be noted from examination of Table 35 that the three groups differ quite significantly for five of the 9 variables.

Almost all of the differences in Tables 34 and 35 appear to be important, especially when issues of deviation are studied. All 27 variables can be quite important in the interpretive routine, and these findings raise an interesting question concerning the use of

Table 34. Statistical Comparisons for 22 Variables between 295 Extratensive, 240 Introversive, and 127 Ambitent Nonpatient Adults with Protocols in Which *Lambda* < 1.0

Variable	Extratensives				Introversives				Ambitents			
	Mean	SD	Freq	Mode	Mean	SD	Freq	Mode	Mean	SD	Freq	Mode
M	2.92	0.77	295	3.00	6.47*	1.21	240	7.00	3.84^a	1.22	127	3.00
FC	5.29*	1.60	295	5.00	3.25	1.39	235	3.00	3.59	1.77	123	5.00
CF	3.35*	1.03	295	3.00	1.57	0.70	227	2.00	1.66	1.02	113	1.00
C	0.10	[0.29]	28^x	0.00	0.01	[0.11]	3	0.00	0.17	[0.43]	18	0.00
WSumC	6.13*	1.04	295	6.00	3.21	1.02	240	3.50	3.71^b	1.41	127	3.50
FM + m	4.65	1.29	295	5.00	5.04	1.40	240	5.00	5.25^a	1.69	127	6.00
EA	9.05	1.60	295	8.50	9.69^a	2.07	240	9.50	7.55*	2.37	127	7.50
es	8.12	2.31	295	7.00	7.87	2.51	240	7.00	9.66*	4.25	127	9.00
Sum Y	0.65	[0.72]	153^x	0.00	0.32	[0.79]	51	0.00	0.87	[1.63]	57	0.00
Sum Shad	3.46	1.49	295	3.00	2.83	1.75	233	2.00	4.41*	3.41	127	3.00
Blends	5.77	1.59	295	6.00	4.47*	1.89	240	3.00	5.61	2.00	127	5.00
Col-Shd Bl	0.70	[0.81]	151#	0.00	0.26	[0.49]	56	0.00	0.35	[0.60]	37	0.00
Afr	0.73*	0.16	295	0.91	0.67	0.14	240	0.67	0.64	0.15	127	0.63
H	2.44	0.81	295	3.00	5.17*	1.68	240	5.00	2.50	1.23	123	3.00
All H Cont	4.72	1.32	295	4.00	6.59*	1.35	240	7.00	5.06	1.72	127	5.00
Bl	0.25	[0.47]	70^x	0.00	0.01	[0.11]	3	0.00	0.21	[0.51]	21	0.00
Ex	0.02	[0.14]	6	0.00	0.27	[0.45]	65#	0.00	0.14	[0.35]	18	0.00
Fi	0.63	[0.78]	131#	0.00	0.26	[0.49]	56	0.00	0.30	[0.58]	30	0.00
Food	0.36	[0.59]	88#	0.00	0.12	[0.33]	29	0.00	0.18	[0.50]	17	0.00
AB	0.23	[0.46]	63^x	0.00	0.07	[0.33]	12	0.00	0.17	[0.37]	21	0.00
COP	1.88	1.32	237	2.00	2.68*	1.71	201	3.00	1.65	1.28	93	2.00
CP	0.04	[0.21]	13	0.00	0.00	[0.00]	0	0.00	0.00	[0.00]	0	0.00

* = *F* ratio indicates a value significantly different than both other groups (*p* < .001).
^{a} = Scheffe procedure indicates significant difference from extratensive group (*p* < .001).
^{b} = Scheffe procedure indicates significant difference from introversive group (*p* < .001).
= Chi-square indicates a proportional frequency different from both groups (*p* < .001).
^{x} = Chi-square indicates a proportional frequency different from introversive group (*p* < .001).

Table 35. Frequency Comparisons for 9 Structural Variables between 295 Extratensive, 240 Introversive, and 127 Ambitent Nonpatient Adults with Protocols in Which *Lambda* < 1.0

Variable	Extratensive		Introversive		Ambitent	
	N	%	N	%	N	%
EBPER > 2.4	84	28	61	25	NA	—
Adj D Score > 0	70	24	110	46*	15	12
Adj D Score = 0	205	69	124	52	79	62
Adj D Score < 0	21	7	6	3	33	26*
COP > 2	98	33	131	55*	36	28
Pure H < 2	33	11	2	1*	25	20
(FM + m) < Sum Shad	46	16	15	6*	30	24
$M^p > M^a$	53	18*	9	4	8	6
p > a + 1	2	1	2	1	2	2

* = Chi-square shows proportional frequency different from both groups (*p* < .001).

normative data. Should the data from a single record be compared with the more heterogeneous sample of all nonpatient adults, or should comparisons be made in contrast to the more homogeneous samples that represent nonpatient adults divided by basic response styles?

Unfortunately, the answer is not simple because Rorschach data will often detect the presence of any of several seemingly basic personality or response styles, and in many instances the presence of a style becomes critically important to interpretation. Some styles, such as the extratensive-introversive differentiation are the most straightforward. Unlike other styles, they pose no direct relationships to pathology or predisposition to maladjustment. They are commonplace among all subjects, both patients and nonpatients. In that context, descriptive statistics for nonpatients, subdivided by the categories of introversive, extratensive, and ambient are included in Tables 36 through 41, using the same format as for the entire nonpatient sample. The appropriate use of these data is described in the section on interpretation.

Table 36. Descriptive Statistics for 251 Adult Nonpatient Introversives

Variable	Mean	SD	Min	Max	Freq	Median	Mode	SK	KU
R	23.50	4.76	14.00	38.00	251	24.00	20.00	0.50	0.46
W	8.71	2.26	3.00	20.00	251	9.00	8.00	1.53	8.71
D	13.25	3.63	2.00	22.00	251	14.00	14.00	0.20	0.81
Dd	1.54	[1.62]	0.00	10.00	191	1.00	1.00	2.48	9.39
S	1.43	[1.39]	0.00	10.00	204	1.00	1.00	2.61	11.21
DQ+	8.48	2.29	4.00	13.00	251	9.00	8.00	−0.22	−0.72
DQo	13.15	3.88	5.00	26.00	251	12.00	12.00	0.75	0.65
DQv	1.53	[1.36]	0.00	5.00	187	1.00	1.00	0.67	−0.64
DQv/+	0.34	[0.61]	0.00	2.00	68	0.00	0.00	1.59	1.38
FQx+	0.99	1.02	0.00	5.00	161	1.00	1.00	1.39	2.78
FQxo	17.46	3.42	9.00	27.00	251	18.00	18.00	0.32	0.29
FQxu	3.63	1.73	0.00	12.00	246	4.00	4.00	0.79	3.26
FQx−	1.39	0.99	0.00	4.00	217	1.00	1.00	0.87	0.33
FQxNone	0.02	[0.15]	0.00	1.00	6	0.00	0.00	6.27	37.63
MQ+	0.59	0.81	0.00	3.00	107	0.00	0.00	1.34	1.22
MQo	5.38	1.42	1.00	8.00	251	5.00	5.00	−0.27	0.08
MQu	0.38	0.59	0.00	2.00	82	0.00	0.00	1.29	0.64
MQ−	0.04	[0.21]	0.00	2.00	8	0.00	0.00	6.32	43.98
MQNone	0.01	[0.11]	0.00	1.00	3	0.00	0.00	9.04	80.29
SQual−	0.17	[0.40]	0.00	2.00	40	0.00	0.00	2.18	3.88
M	6.40	1.23	4.00	9.00	251	7.00	7.00	−0.13	−0.48
FM	3.65	1.26	1.00	7.00	251	4.00	4.00	0.07	−0.13
m	1.38	0.84	0.00	3.00	211	1.00	2.00	−0.05	−0.65
FC	3.20	1.39	0.00	7.00	246	3.00	3.00	0.28	0.27
CF	1.54	0.71	0.00	3.00	235	2.00	2.00	−0.15	−0.20
C	0.01	[0.11]	0.00	1.00	3	0.00	0.00	9.04	80.29
Cn	0.00	[0.00]	0.00	0.00	0	0.00	0.00	—	—
Sum Color	4.75	1.62	1.00	9.00	251	5.00	5.00	0.07	0.27
WSumC	3.16	1.04	0.50	5.50	251	3.50	3.50	−0.19	0.28
Sum C'	1.21	[1.08]	0.00	4.00	168	1.00	0.00	0.49	−0.59
Sum T	0.99	[0.47]	0.00	3.00	226	1.00	1.00	0.90	5.78
Sum V	0.29	[0.56]	0.00	2.00	59	0.00	0.00	1.82	2.32
Sum Y	0.33	[0.81]	0.00	6.00	53	0.00	0.00	3.81	19.45
Sum Shading	2.82	1.75	0.00	9.00	244	3.00	2.00	1.05	1.47

Table 36. (Continued)

Variable	Mean	SD	Min	Max	Freq	Median	Mode	SK	KU
Fr + rF	0.08	[0.42]	0.00	4.00	12	0.00	0.00	7.48	63.71
FD	1.17	[0.87]	0.00	4.00	194	1.00	1.00	0.48	0.20
F	8.04	2.91	2.00	19.00	251	7.00	6.00	0.65	0.16
(2)	9.11	2.01	3.00	14.00	251	9.00	8.00	0.45	0.71
3r + (2)/R	0.40	0.08	0.25	0.79	251	0.38	0.38	1.56	4.96
Lambda	0.54	0.21	0.17	1.12	251	0.50	0.50	0.60	−0.23
FM + m	5.02	1.47	1.00	9.00	251	5.00	5.00	0.38	−0.12
EA	9.56	2.11	4.50	14.50	251	9.50	9.50	−0.16	−0.22
es	7.84	2.61	3.00	16.00	251	7.00	7.00	0.52	0.21
D Score	0.24	0.80	−3.00	2.00	90	0.00	0.00	−0.46	3.29
AdjD	0.48	0.74	−2.00	2.00	122	0.00	0.00	−0.06	0.97
a (active)	7.90	2.12	4.00	13.00	251	8.00	6.00	0.27	−0.78
p (passive)	3.55	1.60	0.00	9.00	241	3.00	3.00	−0.02	0.14
M^a	4.62	1.20	1.00	7.00	251	5.00	4.00	−0.16	0.06
M^p	1.80	1.06	0.00	5.00	224	2.00	1.00	0.18	−0.20
Intellect	1.27	1.20	0.00	5.00	176	1.00	1.00	0.90	0.26
Zf	12.65	2.92	6.00	23.00	251	13.00	12.00	0.25	1.81
Zd	−0.43	3.04	−6.50	8.50	235	−1.00	−3.00	0.53	−0.15
Blends	4.39	1.90	1.00	10.00	251	4.00	3.00	0.29	−0.80
Blends/R	0.19	0.09	0.07	0.57	251	0.17	0.12	1.18	1.70
Col-Shd Bld	0.25	[0.48]	0.00	2.00	56	0.00	0.00	1.80	2.43
Afr	0.67	0.14	0.30	1.14	251	0.67	0.67	0.58	1.54
Populars	6.78	1.28	3.00	10.00	251	6.00	6.00	−0.00	−0.16
X + %	0.79	0.07	0.56	1.00	251	0.80	0.80	−0.32	1.50
F + %	0.71	0.17	0.29	1.00	251	0.71	0.80	−0.57	−0.04
X − %	0.06	0.04	0.00	0.13	217	0.05	0.04	0.22	−0.48
Xu%	0.15	0.06	0.00	0.37	246	0.15	0.15	0.30	1.26
S − %	0.09	[0.22]	0.00	1.00	40	0.00	0.00	2.83	7.74
Isolate/R	0.19	0.10	0.00	0.47	243	0.17	0.12	0.48	−0.19
H	5.09	1.70	1.00	9.00	251	5.00	5.00	0.05	−0.47
(H)	1.04	1.06	0.00	4.00	155	1.00	0.00	0.89	0.21
HD	0.34	0.66	0.00	4.00	68	0.00	0.00	2.54	8.51
(Hd)	0.08	0.28	0.00	2.00	18	0.00	0.00	3.77	14.45
Hx	0.01	[0.11]	0.00	1.00	3	0.00	0.00	9.04	80.29
All H Cont	6.55	1.34	2.00	11.00	251	7.00	7.00	0.02	0.43
A	8.10	1.94	3.00	15.00	251	8.00	8.00	0.32	1.10
(A)	0.29	[0.58]	0.00	3.00	58	0.00	0.00	2.14	4.62
Ad	2.39	[1.12]	0.00	7.00	235	3.00	3.00	0.06	1.54
(Ad)	0.04	[0.22]	0.00	2.00	10	0.00	0.00	5.52	33.19
An	0.47	[0.70]	0.00	2.00	89	0.00	0.00	1.15	−0.05
Art	0.73	0.76	0.00	3.00	137	1.00	0.00	0.55	−0.90
Ay	0.40	[0.50]	0.00	2.00	100	0.00	0.00	0.50	−1.51
Bl	0.01	[0.11]	0.00	1.00	3	0.00	0.00	9.04	80.29
Bt	2.00	1.20	0.00	5.00	225	2.00	3.00	0.01	−0.98
Cg	1.54	1.13	0.00	4.00	206	1.00	1.00	0.36	−0.88
Cl	0.16	[0.40]	0.00	2.00	37	0.00	0.00	2.43	5.37
Ex	0.26	[0.44]	0.00	1.00	65	0.00	0.00	1.11	−0.78
Fi	0.26	[0.49]	0.00	2.00	58	0.00	0.00	1.74	2.17
Food	0.12	[0.32]	0.00	1.00	29	0.00	0.00	2.42	3.89
Ge	0.01	[0.09]	0.00	1.00	2	0.00	0.00	11.14	122.97
Hh	1.16	0.92	0.00	4.00	184	1.00	1.00	0.45	−0.01
Ls	1.22	0.82	0.00	3.00	197	1.00	1.00	−0.06	−0.87
Na	0.39	[0.65]	0.00	2.00	75	0.00	0.00	1.42	0.76

Table 36.   (Continued)

Variable	Mean	SD	Min	Max	Freq	Median	Mode	SK	KU
Sc	1.02	[1.09]	0.00	6.00	158	1.00	0.00	1.68	4.98
Sx	0.08	[0.50]	0.00	5.00	11	0.00	0.00	8.14	73.81
Xy	0.02	[0.14]	0.00	1.00	5	0.00	0.00	6.91	46.16
Idio	1.92	1.25	0.00	7.00	219	2.00	2.00	0.70	1.61
DV	0.79	[0.90]	0.00	4.00	136	1.00	0.00	1.02	0.45
INCOM	0.50	[0.71]	0.00	4.00	102	0.00	0.00	1.82	4.76
DR	0.10	[0.35]	0.00	2.00	22	0.00	0.00	3.64	13.52
FABCOM	0.19	[0.42]	0.00	2.00	45	0.00	0.00	2.05	3.38
DV2	0.01	[0.09]	0.00	1.00	2	0.00	0.00	11.14	122.97
INC2	0.01	[0.11]	0.00	1.00	3	0.00	0.00	9.04	80.29
DR2	0.00	[0.00]	0.00	0.00	0	0.00	0.00	—	—
FAB2	0.03	[0.18]	0.00	1.00	8	0.00	0.00	5.36	26.97
ALOG	0.04	[0.23]	0.00	2.00	8	0.00	0.00	6.47	44.89
CONTAM	0.00	0.00	0.00	0.00	0	0.00	0.00	—	—
Sum 6 *Sp Sc*	1.68	1.42	0.00	7.00	190	1.00	1.00	0.66	−0.11
Lvl 2 *Sp Sc*	0.05	[0.22]	0.00	1.00	13	0.00	0.00	4.07	14.68
WSum6	3.35	3.17	0.00	15.00	190	3.00	0.00	1.08	1.18
AB	0.07	[0.32]	0.00	2.00	12	0.00	0.00	5.05	25.71
AG	1.16	1.11	0.00	5.00	175	1.00	1.00	1.10	1.06
CFB	0.00	0.00	0.00	0.00	0	0.00	0.00	—	—
COP	2.63	1.70	0.00	6.00	210	3.00	3.00	−0.07	−1.05
CP	0.00	[0.00]	0.00	0.00	0	0.00	0.00	—	—
MOR	0.81	[0.90]	0.00	4.00	138	1.00	0.00	0.98	0.50
PER	1.02	0.90	0.00	5.00	170	1.00	1.00	0.82	1.76
PSV	0.03	[0.17]	0.00	1.00	7	0.00	0.00	5.77	31.53

Note: Standard Deviations shown in brackets indicate that the value is probably unreliable and/or misleading because the variable is nonparametric.

Table 37. Frequencies and Percentages for 33 Structural Variables for 251 Adult Nonpatient Introversives

EB Style			Form Quality Deviations		
Introversive	251	100%	$X + \% > .89$	12	5%
Pervasive	68	27%	$X + \% < .70$	23	9%
Ambitent	0	0%	$X + \% < .61$	4	2%
Extratensive	0	0%	$X + \% < .50$	0	0%
Pervasive	0	0%	$F + \% < .70$	106	42%
			$Xu\% > .20$	40	16%
D Score			$X - \% > .15$	0	0%
D Score > 0	72	29%	$X - \% > .20$	0	0%
D Score = 0	161	64%	$X - \% > .30$	0	0%
D Score < 0	18	7%			
D Score < −1	7	3%			
Adjusted D Score			FC:CF + C Ratio		
Adj D Score > 0	113	45%	$FC > (CF + C) + 2$	68	27%
Adj D Score = 0	129	51%	$FC > (CF + C) + 1$	115	46%
Adj D Score < 0	9	4%	$(CF + C) > FC + 1$	6	2%
Adj D Score < −1	4	2%	$(CF + C) > FC + 2$	4	2%
Zd > +3.0 (overincorp)	34	14%	S-Con Positive	0	0%
Zd < −3.0 (Underincorp)	26	10%	HVI Positive	2	1%
			OBS Positive	6	2%

SCZI = 6	0	0%	DEPI = 7	0	0%	CDI = 5	0	0%
SCZI = 5	0	0%	DEPI = 6	1	0%	CDI = 4	0	0%
SCZI = 4	0	0%	DEPI = 5	9	4%			

Miscellaneous Variables

Lambda > .99	11	4%	$(2AB + Art + Ay) > 5$	7	3%
Dd > 3	16	6%	Populars < 4	2	1%
$DQv + DQv/+ > 2$	78	31%	Populars > 7	95	38%
S > 2	27	11%	COP = 0	41	16%
Sum T = 0	25	10%	COP > 2	135	54%
Sum T > 1	18	7%	AG = 0	76	30%
$3r + (2)/R < .33$	36	14%	AG > 2	27	11%
$3r + (2)/R > .44$	61	24%	MOR > 2	12	5%
$Fr + rF > 0$	12	5%	Lvl 2 Sp.Sc. > 0	13	5%
PureC > 0	3	1%	Sum 6 Sp.Sc. > 6	1	0%
PureC > 1	0	0%	Pure H < 2	2	1%
Afr < .40	7	3%	Pure H = 0	0	0%
Afr < .50	14	6%	$p > a + 1$	2	1%
$(FM + m) < $ Sum Shad	15	6%	$M^p > M^a$	9	4%

Table 38. Descriptive Statistics for 306 Nonpatient Adult Extratensives

Variable	Mean	SD	Min	Max	Freq	Median	Mode	SK	KU
R	22.76	2.93	15.00	36.00	306	23.00	23.00	0.44	2.61
W	8.73	1.63	4.00	19.00	306	9.00	9.00	1.76	11.70
D	13.21	3.00	1.00	21.00	306	13.00	13.00	−0.75	1.69
Dd	0.83	[1.17]	0.00	11.00	163	1.00	0.00	4.48	35.43
S	1.35	[0.82]	0.00	5.00	275	1.00	1.00	0.93	2.26
DQ+	6.88	1.70	3.00	11.00	306	6.00	6.00	0.63	−0.03
DQo	14.32	2.09	8.00	23.00	306	15.00	15.00	−0.30	2.22
DQv	1.13	[1.14]	0.00	6.00	197	1.00	0.00	1.18	1.92
DQv/+	0.44	[0.64]	0.00	2.00	111	0.00	0.00	1.15	0.19
FQx+	0.93	0.86	0.00	4.00	199	1.00	1.00	0.86	1.05
FQxo	17.32	2.66	11.00	24.00	306	17.00	17.00	−0.06	0.11
FQxu	3.04	1.65	0.00	9.00	286	3.00	3.00	0.42	0.22
FQx−	1.37	1.02	0.00	4.00	258	1.00	1.00	0.89	0.40
FQxNone	0.11	[0.33]	0.00	2.00	30	0.00	0.00	3.15	9.76
MQ+	0.62	0.68	0.00	3.00	156	1.00	0.00	0.71	−0.34
MQo	2.23	0.96	0.00	4.00	303	2.00	2.00	0.07	−0.86
MQu	0.04	0.20	0.00	1.00	13	0.00	0.00	4.56	18.91
MQ−	0.00	[0.00]	0.00	0.00	0	0.00	0.00	—	—
MQNone	0.00	[0.00]	0.00	0.00	0	0.00	0.00	—	—
SQual−	0.12	[0.35]	0.00	2.00	36	0.00	0.00	2.74	7.00
M	2.89	0.78	1.00	5.00	306	3.00	3.00	−0.22	0.61
FM	3.78	0.99	1.00	6.00	306	4.00	4.00	−0.29	0.02
m	0.81	0.66	0.00	4.00	212	1.00	1.00	0.78	2.55
FC	5.16	1.70	1.00	9.00	306	5.00	5.00	0.21	−0.08
CF	3.34	1.02	1.00	6.00	306	3.00	3.00	0.29	0.65
C	0.10	[0.30]	0.00	1.00	30	0.00	0.00	2.72	5.42
Cn	0.01	[0.08]	0.00	1.00	2	0.00	0.00	12.31	150.47
Sum Color	8.61	1.59	5.00	12.00	306	8.00	8.00	−0.21	−0.38
WSumC	6.07	1.07	4.00	9.00	306	6.00	6.00	0.20	−0.25
Sum C'	1.58	[1.11]	0.00	5.00	258	1.00	1.00	0.58	0.03
Sum T	1.09	[0.58]	0.00	4.00	284	1.00	1.00	1.77	5.58
Sum V	0.19	[0.47]	0.00	2.00	47	0.00	0.00	2.53	5.78
Sum Y	0.66	[0.73]	0.00	3.00	161	1.00	0.00	0.88	0.33
Sum Shading	3.52	1.53	1.00	9.00	306	3.00	3.00	0.88	0.58
Fr + rF	0.07	[0.30]	0.00	2.00	17	0.00	0.00	4.77	23.78
FD	1.06	[0.70]	0.00	5.00	254	1.00	1.00	1.18	5.58
F	8.12	2.30	4.00	19.00	306	8.00	8.00	0.73	2.66
(2)	8.54	1.76	5.00	12.00	306	8.00	8.00	0.32	−0.82
3r + (2)/R	0.38	0.08	0.26	0.61	306	0.36	0.36	0.95	0.42
Lambda	0.58	0.23	0.24	1.88	306	0.56	0.56	1.99	9.41
FM + m	4.58	1.34	1.00	9.00	306	5.00	5.00	0.13	0.41
EA	8.96	1.65	5.50	13.00	306	9.00	8.50	0.03	−0.21
es	8.11	2.34	4.00	18.00	306	8.00	7.00	0.70	1.14
D Score	0.16	0.74	−3.00	2.00	95	0.00	0.00	−0.21	3.67
AdjD	0.20	0.70	−2.00	2.00	96	0.00	0.00	0.28	2.04
a (active)	5.44	1.57	3.00	10.00	306	5.00	5.00	0.38	−0.41
p (passive)	2.08	1.05	0.00	7.00	293	2.00	2.00	0.84	2.50
M^a	1.95	0.91	0.00	4.00	285	2.00	2.00	−0.28	−0.19
M^p	0.98	0.69	0.00	3.00	236	1.00	1.00	0.33	0.07
Intellect	1.94	1.24	0.00	6.00	282	2.00	1.00	0.84	0.67
Zf	11.59	2.02	7.00	19.00	306	11.00	11.00	0.23	0.08
Zd	1.75	2.81	−3.00	9.50	276	1.00	2.00	0.76	0.21
Blends	5.72	1.59	2.00	12.00	306	6.00	6.00	0.29	0.46
Blends/R	0.25	0.07	0.08	0.57	306	0.26	0.26	0.46	1.59
Col-Shd Bld	0.69	[0.80]	0.00	3.00	155	1.00	0.00	1.01	0.42
Afr	0.73	0.16	0.44	1.09	306	0.74	0.91	0.22	−0.47
Populars	7.07	1.31	4.00	9.00	306	7.00	8.00	−0.70	−0.12

Table 38. (Continued)

Variable	Mean	SD	Min	Max	Freq	Median	Mode	SK	KU
X + %	0.80	0.08	0.60	1.00	306	0.81	0.86	0.09	0.38
F + %	0.74	0.16	0.29	1.00	306	0.75	1.00	−0.16	−0.24
X − %	0.06	0.04	0.00	0.19	258	0.05	0.04	0.76	0.08
Xu%	0.13	0.06	0.00	0.28	286	0.13	0.14	−0.03	−0.24
S − %	0.07	[0.21]	0.00	1.00	36	0.00	0.00	3.56	12.12
Isolate/R	0.22	0.09	0.05	0.45	306	0.21	0.29	0.43	−0.64
H	2.43	0.82	0.00	5.00	304	2.00	3.00	0.14	0.73
(H)	1.19	0.86	0.00	3.00	229	1.00	2.00	0.02	−0.98
HD	0.88	0.85	0.00	4.00	197	1.00	1.00	0.97	0.93
(Hd)	0.21	0.41	0.00	1.00	65	0.00	0.00	1.41	−0.00
Hx	0.00	[0.00]	0.00	0.00	0	0.00	0.00	—	—
All H Cont	4.71	1.30	2.00	9.00	306	4.00	4.00	0.33	−0.24
A	8.27	2.03	4.00	14.00	306	8.00	7.00	0.71	−0.20
(A)	0.10	[0.37]	0.00	3.00	25	0.00	0.00	4.79	28.25
Ad	2.13	[0.91]	0.00	5.00	299	2.00	2.00	0.29	0.21
(Ad)	0.07	[0.31]	0.00	2.00	18	0.00	0.00	4.61	22.27
An	0.37	[0.55]	0.00	4.00	108	0.00	0.00	1.72	6.17
Art	1.19	0.74	0.00	4.00	258	1.00	1.00	0.40	0.60
Ay	0.30	[0.48]	0.00	2.00	91	0.00	0.00	1.04	−0.44
Bl	0.25	[0.47]	0.00	2.00	72	0.00	0.00	1.61	1.64
Bt	3.16	1.12	0.00	6.00	301	3.00	3.00	−0.02	−0.04
Cg	1.13	0.72	0.00	4.00	254	1.00	1.00	0.43	0.84
Cl	0.10	[0.30]	0.00	1.00	30	0.00	0.00	2.72	5.42
Ex	0.02	[0.14]	0.00	1.00	6	0.00	0.00	6.96	46.80
Fi	0.61	[0.77]	0.00	2.00	131	0.00	0.00	0.81	−0.87
Food	0.36	[0.60]	0.00	2.00	90	0.00	0.00	1.46	1.07
Ge	0.07	[0.28]	0.00	2.00	19	0.00	0.00	4.31	19.74
Hh	0.86	0.73	0.00	3.00	211	1.00	1.00	0.77	0.82
Ls	0.73	0.67	0.00	3.00	188	1.00	1.00	0.50	−0.17
Na	0.40	[0.56]	0.00	2.00	112	0.00	0.00	1.01	0.03
Sc	0.91	[0.92]	0.00	3.00	184	1.00	0.00	0.72	−0.39
Sx	0.03	[0.16]	0.00	1.00	8	0.00	0.00	5.97	33.85
Xy	0.00	[0.00]	0.00	0.00	0	0.00	0.00	—	—
Idio	1.99	1.32	0.00	7.00	274	2.00	1.00	0.71	0.61
DV	0.59	[0.63]	0.00	3.00	158	1.00	0.00	0.66	−0.12
INCOM	0.54	[0.56]	0.00	2.00	156	1.00	0.00	0.39	−0.85
DR	0.17	[0.39]	0.00	2.00	52	0.00	0.00	1.90	2.19
FABCOM	0.10	[0.30]	0.00	2.00	28	0.00	0.00	3.13	9.18
DV2	0.01	[0.10]	0.00	1.00	3	0.00	0.00	10.00	98.63
INC2	0.00	[0.00]	0.00	0.00	0	0.00	0.00	—	—
DR2	0.00	[0.06]	0.00	1.00	1	0.00	0.00	17.49	306.00
FAB2	0.00	[0.00]	0.00	0.00	0	0.00	0.00	—	—
ALOG	0.05	[0.22]	0.00	1.00	15	0.00	0.00	4.20	15.73
CONTAM	0.00	0.00	0.00	0.00	0	0.00	0.00	—	—
Sum 6 Sp Sc	1.46	1.05	0.00	5.00	254	1.00	1.00	0.58	−0.03
Lvl 2 Sp Sc	0.01	[0.11]	0.00	1.00	4	0.00	0.00	8.62	72.72
WSum6	2.86	2.46	0.00	13.00	254	2.00	2.00	1.19	1.65
AB	0.22	[0.45]	0.00	2.00	63	0.00	0.00	1.86	2.61
AG	1.14	1.26	0.00	5.00	186	1.00	0.00	1.11	0.57
CFB	0.00	0.00	0.00	0.00	0	0.00	0.00	—	—
COP	1.83	1.33	0.00	4.00	241	2.00	2.00	0.14	−1.10
CP	0.04	[0.20]	0.00	1.00	13	0.00	0.00	4.56	18.91
MOR	0.62	[0.72]	0.00	3.00	152	0.00	0.00	0.98	0.54
PER	1.13	1.13	0.00	5.00	217	1.00	1.00	1.61	3.27
PSV	0.05	[0.22]	0.00	1.00	16	0.00	0.00	4.04	14.43

Note: Standard deviations shown in brackets indicate that the value is probably unreliable and/or misleading because the variable is nonparametric.

Table 39. Frequencies and Percentages for 33 Structural Variables for 306 Adult Nonpatient Extratensives

EB Style			Form Quality Deviations		
Introversive	0	0%	$X + \% > .89$	28	9%
Pervasive	0	0%	$X + \% < .70$	24	8%
Ambitent	0	0%	$X + \% < .61$	2	1%
Extratensive	306	100%	$X + \% < .50$	0	0%
Pervasive	86	28%	$F + \% < .70$	115	38%
			$Xu\% > .20$	49	16%
D Score			$X - \% > .15$	13	4%
D Score > 0	68	22%	$X - \% > .20$	0	0%
D Score $= 0$	211	69%	$X - \% > .30$	0	0%
D Score < 0	27	9%			
D Score < -1	6	2%			
Adjusted D Score			*FC:CF + C Ratio*		
$Adj\ D$ Score > 0	73	24%	$FC > (CF + C) + 2$	113	37%
$Adj\ D$ Score $= 0$	210	69%	$FC > (CF + C) + 1$	166	54%
$Adj\ D$ Score < 0	23	8%	$(CF + C) > FC + 1$	19	6%
$Adj\ D$ Score < -1	6	2%	$(CF + C) > FC + 2$	3	1%
$Zd > +3.0$ (overincorp)	68	22%	*S-Con* Positive	0	0%
$Zd < -3.0$ (Underincorp)	0	0%	*HVI* Positive	1	0%
			OBS Positive	5	2%

$SCZI = 6$	0	0%	$DEPI = 7$	0	0%	$CDI = 5$	0	0%
$SCZI = 5$	0	0%	$DEPI = 6$	0	0%	$CDI = 4$	8	3%
$SCZI = 4$	0	0%	$DEPI = 5$	4	1%			

Miscellaneous Variables

Lambda $> .99$	11	4%	$(2AB + Art + Ay) > 5$	33	11%
$Dd > 3$	2	1%	Populars < 4	0	0%
$DQv + DQv/+ > 2$	81	26%	Populars > 7	139	45%
$S > 2$	22	7%	$COP = 0$	65	21%
Sum $T = 0$	22	7%	$COP > 2$	98	32%
Sum $T > 1$	35	11%	$AG = 0$	120	39%
$3r + (2)/R < .33$	58	19%	$AG > 2$	50	16%
$3r + (2)/R > .44$	52	17%	$MOR > 2$	5	2%
$Fr + rF > 0$	17	6%	$Lvl\ 2\ Sp.Sc. > 0$	4	1%
$PureC > 0$	30	10%	Sum 6 $Sp.Sc. > 6$	0	0%
$PureC > 1$	0	0%	Pure $H < 2$	35	11%
$Afr < .40$	0	0%	Pure $H = 0$	2	1%
$Afr < .50$	15	5%	$p > a + 1$	2	1%
$(FM + m) <$ Sum Shad	57	19%	$M^p > M^a$	55	18%

Table 40. Descriptive Statistics for 143 Adult Nonpatient Ambitents

Variable	Mean	SD	Min	Max	Freq	Median	Mode	SK	KU
R	21.00	5.06	14.00	38.00	143	21.00	23.00	0.87	1.21
W	7.89	1.84	3.00	13.00	143	8.00	8.00	−0.20	0.49
D	11.57	4.12	0.00	20.00	141	12.00	14.00	−0.43	−0.14
Dd	1.54	[2.46]	0.00	15.00	98	1.00	1.00	3.66	15.59
S	1.80	[1.50]	0.00	9.00	121	2.00	2.00	2.00	6.79
DQ+	6.20	1.87	2.00	9.00	143	7.00	5.00	−0.36	−0.78
DQo	13.07	4.61	5.00	34.00	143	13.00	14.00	1.86	6.62
DQv	1.28	[1.26]	0.00	5.00	93	1.00	0.00	0.90	0.40
DQv/+	0.46	[0.78]	0.00	2.00	40	0.00	0.00	1.30	−0.06
FQx+	0.66	0.84	0.00	4.00	67	0.00	0.00	1.28	1.88
FQxo	15.43	4.02	7.00	29.00	143	15.00	19.00	0.35	0.38
FQxu	3.01	1.97	0.00	13.00	135	3.00	4.00	1.94	7.78
FQx−	1.70	1.14	0.00	6.00	130	1.00	1.00	1.08	1.89
FQxNone	0.20	[0.51]	0.00	3.00	22	0.00	0.00	2.93	9.32
MQ+	0.32	0.63	0.00	3.00	34	0.00	0.00	2.17	4.59
MQo	3.02	1.42	0.00	7.00	139	3.00	3.00	0.17	−0.15
MQu	0.21	0.44	0.00	2.00	28	0.00	0.00	1.93	2.90
MQ−	0.10	[0.30]	0.00	1.00	14	0.00	0.00	2.74	5.56
MQNone	0.04	[0.18]	0.00	1.00	5	0.00	0.00	5.12	24.53
SQual−	0.33	[0.78]	0.00	3.00	26	0.00	0.00	2.38	4.61
M	3.68	1.29	1.00	7.00	143	4.00	3.00	0.26	0.11
FM	3.63	1.42	1.00	9.00	143	4.00	4.00	0.11	0.80
m	1.32	1.00	0.00	4.00	107	1.00	2.00	0.42	0.17
FC	3.37	1.81	0.00	8.00	138	3.00	5.00	0.30	−0.41
CF	1.68	1.04	0.00	4.00	129	2.00	1.00	0.40	−0.50
C	0.15	[0.41]	0.00	2.00	18	0.00	0.00	2.89	8.17
Cn	0.02	[0.14]	0.00	1.00	3	0.00	0.00	6.76	44.26
Sum Color	5.22	2.13	1.00	9.00	143	5.00	5.00	0.01	−0.80
WSumC	3.59	1.45	0.50	6.50	143	3.50	3.50	−0.06	−0.81
Sum C'	1.97	[1.61]	0.00	10.00	125	2.00	1.00	1.92	7.01
Sum T	0.95	[0.71]	0.00	4.00	110	1.00	1.00	1.05	3.58
Sum V	0.36	[0.78]	0.00	3.00	31	0.00	0.00	2.20	3.95
Sum Y	0.81	[1.56]	0.00	10.00	60	0.00	0.00	3.86	18.60
Sum Shading	4.10	3.36	0.00	23.00	139	3.00	3.00	3.07	13.36
Fr + rF	0.13	[0.33]	0.00	1.00	18	0.00	0.00	2.28	3.24
FD	1.34	[1.14]	0.00	5.00	105	1.00	2.00	0.94	1.31
F	7.65	2.97	2.00	18.00	143	7.00	7.00	0.68	1.36
(2)	8.22	2.89	1.00	13.00	143	8.00	8.00	−0.09	−0.13
3r + (2)/R	0.41	0.11	0.03	0.63	143	0.40	0.50	−0.92	2.28
Lambda	0.63	0.38	0.14	2.25	143	0.56	0.44	2.20	6.23
FM + m	4.95	1.84	1.00	10.00	143	5.00	6.00	0.12	0.01
EA	7.27	2.48	2.00	12.00	143	7.50	7.50	−0.01	−0.58
es	9.05	4.37	3.00	31.00	143	9.00	9.00	2.18	8.07
D Score	−0.54	1.72	−10.00	2.00	59	0.00	0.00	−3.04	12.73
AdjD	−0.27	1.16	−5.00	2.00	54	0.00	0.00	−1.67	4.77
a (active)	6.20	1.87	2.00	11.00	143	6.00	6.00	0.42	0.26
p (passive)	2.47	1.53	0.00	6.00	125	2.00	2.00	0.25	−0.36
M^a	2.58	0.99	1.00	6.00	143	2.00	2.00	0.75	1.11
M^p	1.13	0.82	0.00	3.00	108	1.00	1.00	0.13	−0.78
Intellect	1.27	1.35	0.00	5.00	88	1.00	0.00	0.90	−0.04
Zf	10.78	2.61	5.00	17.00	143	11.00	14.00	−0.20	−0.58
Zd	0.55	2.84	−6.50	8.00	133	0.00	−1.00	0.59	0.25
Blends	5.29	2.18	1.00	10.00	143	5.00	5.00	−0.07	−0.66
Blends/R	0.26	0.11	0.04	0.67	143	0.25	0.26	0.88	1.55
Col-Shd Bld	0.34	[0.58]	0.00	2.00	41	0.00	0.00	1.50	1.26
Afr	0.65	0.16	0.27	1.29	143	0.63	0.63	0.62	1.13
Populars	6.69	1.67	3.00	10.00	143	7.00	8.00	−0.49	−0.39

Table 40. (Continued)

Variable	Mean	SD	Min	Max	Freq	Median	Mode	SK	KU
$X + \%$	0.77	0.09	0.50	1.00	143	0.78	0.81	−0.43	1.09
$F + \%$	0.64	0.18	0.25	1.00	143	0.63	0.50	0.35	−0.02
$X - \%$	0.09	0.07	0.00	0.43	130	0.07	0.04	2.11	7.43
$Xu\%$	0.14	0.07	0.00	0.34	135	0.13	0.13	0.43	0.30
$S - \%$	0.11	[0.25]	0.00	1.00	26	0.00	0.00	2.21	3.77
Isolate/R	0.18	0.09	0.00	0.47	140	0.17	0.21	0.57	0.64
H	2.50	1.20	0.00	7.00	139	3.00	3.00	0.73	2.16
(H)	1.48	0.98	0.00	4.00	115	2.00	2.00	0.12	−0.25
HD	0.87	1.11	0.00	7.00	83	1.00	0.00	2.78	12.16
(Hd)	0.11	0.32	0.00	1.00	16	0.00	0.00	2.49	4.25
Hx	0.04	[0.18]	0.00	1.00	5	0.00	0.00	5.12	24.53
All H Cont	4.96	1.67	1.00	10.00	143	5.00	5.00	0.54	1.18
A	8.13	2.25	4.00	14.00	143	9.00	9.00	0.12	−0.40
(A)	0.11	[0.39]	0.00	3.00	12	0.00	0.00	4.64	25.84
Ad	2.05	[1.68]	0.00	9.00	131	2.00	2.00	1.97	4.99
(Ad)	0.04	[0.18]	0.00	1.00	5	0.00	0.00	5.12	24.53
An	0.45	[0.74]	0.00	3.00	47	0.00	0.00	1.73	2.61
Art	0.64	0.92	0.00	3.00	53	0.00	0.00	1.11	−0.11
Ay	0.32	[0.47]	0.00	1.00	45	0.00	0.00	0.81	−1.37
Bl	0.19	[0.49]	0.00	2.00	21	0.00	0.00	2.62	6.11
Bt	1.87	1.11	0.00	4.00	126	2.00	2.00	−0.02	−0.84
Cg	1.21	0.88	0.00	4.00	112	1.00	1.00	0.46	0.21
Cl	0.26	[0.47]	0.00	2.00	35	0.00	0.00	1.52	1.26
Ex	0.15	[0.36]	0.00	1.00	22	0.00	0.00	1.94	1.78
Fi	0.29	[0.59]	0.00	2.00	32	0.00	0.00	1.89	2.41
Food	0.16	[0.47]	0.00	2.00	17	0.00	0.00	2.99	8.15
Ge	0.03	[0.17]	0.00	1.00	4	0.00	0.00	5.79	31.93
Hh	0.64	0.88	0.00	3.00	63	0.00	0.00	1.34	1.05
Ls	0.65	0.73	0.00	3.00	75	1.00	0.00	1.09	1.19
Na	0.32	[0.61]	0.00	2.00	35	0.00	0.00	1.74	1.83
Sc	0.71	[0.82]	0.00	2.00	69	0.00	0.00	0.58	−1.27
Sx	0.13	[0.50]	0.00	3.00	11	0.00	0.00	4.65	22.59
Xy	0.10	[0.34]	0.00	2.00	12	0.00	0.00	3.74	14.51
Idio	1.43	1.24	0.00	7.00	106	1.00	1.00	1.05	2.23
DV	0.76	[0.86]	0.00	4.00	79	1.00	0.00	1.21	1.40
INCOM	0.53	[0.69]	0.00	4.00	65	0.00	0.00	1.71	4.93
DR	0.20	[0.40]	0.00	1.00	29	0.00	0.00	1.49	0.24
FABCOM	0.29	[0.52]	0.00	2.00	38	0.00	0.00	1.53	1.44
DV2	0.01	[0.12]	0.00	1.00	2	0.00	0.00	8.37	68.94
INC2	0.00	[0.00]	0.00	0.00	0	0.00	0.00	—	—
DR2	0.00	[0.00]	0.00	0.00	0	0.00	0.00	—	—
FAB2	0.03	[0.17]	0.00	1.00	4	0.00	0.00	5.79	31.93
ALOG	0.04	[0.20]	0.00	1.00	6	0.00	0.00	4.62	19.60
CONTAM	0.00	0.00	0.00	0.00	0	0.00	0.00	—	—
Sum 6 Sp Sc	1.87	1.34	0.00	6.00	120	2.00	2.00	0.68	0.47
Lvl 2 Sp Sc	0.04	[0.20]	0.00	1.00	6	0.00	0.00	4.62	19.60
WSum6	4.04	3.07	0.00	13.00	120	3.00	3.00	0.67	0.01
AB	0.16	[0.37]	0.00	1.00	23	0.00	0.00	1.87	1.50
AG	1.29	1.12	0.00	4.00	105	1.00	1.00	0.78	0.10
CFB	0.00	0.00	0.00	0.00	0	0.00	0.00	—	—
COP	1.58	1.26	0.00	4.00	104	2.00	0.00	0.19	−1.09
CP	0.00	[0.00]	0.00	0.00	0	0.00	0.00	—	—
MOR	0.69	[0.86]	0.00	3.00	66	0.00	0.00	1.00	−0.01
PER	0.93	0.87	0.00	5.00	91	1.00	1.00	0.85	1.81
PSV	0.08	[0.27]	0.00	1.00	11	0.00	0.00	3.21	8.42

Note: Standard deviations shown in brackets indicate that the value is probably unreliable and/or misleading because the variable is nonparametric.

Table 41. Frequencies and Percentages for 33 Structural Variables for 143 Adult Nonpatient Ambitents

EB Style			Form Quality Deviations		
Introversive	0	0%	$X + \% > .89$	9	6%
Pervasive	0	0%	$X + \% < .70$	24	17%
Ambitent	143	100%	$X + \% < .61$	6	4%
Extratensive	0	0%	$X + \% < .50$	0	0%
Pervasive	0	0%	$F + \% < .70$	92	64%
			$Xu\% > .20$	20	14%
D Score			$X - \% > .15$	11	8%
D Score > 0	16	11%	$X - \% > .20$	9	6%
D Score = 0	84	59%	$X - \% > .30$	2	1%
D Score < 0	43	30%			
D Score < −1	17	12%			

Adjusted D Score			FC:CF + C Ratio		
Adj D Score > 0	20	14%	$FC > (CF + C) + 2$	39	27%
Adj D Score = 0	89	62%	$FC > (CF + C) + 1$	64	45%
Adj D Score < 0	34	24%	$(CF + C) > FC + 1$	5	3%
Adj D Score < −1	15	10%	$(CF + C) > FC + 2$	2	1%
Zd > +3.0 (Overincorp)	25	17%	S-Con Positive	0	0%
Zd < −3.0 (Underincorp)	11	8%	HVI Positive	6	4%
			OBS Positive	2	1%

$SCZI = 6$	0	0%	$DEPI = 7$	1	1%	$CDI = 5$	3	2%
$SCZI = 5$	0	0%	$DEPI = 6$	2	1%	$CDI = 4$	9	6%
$SCZI = 4$	2	1%	$DEPI = 5$	8	6%			

Miscellaneous Variables

Lambda > .99	16	11%	$(2AB + Art + Ay) > 5$	12	8%
Dd > 3	15	10%	Populars < 4	7	5%
$DQv + DQv/+ > 2$	41	29%	Populars > 7	59	41%
S > 2	23	16%	COP = 0	39	27%
Sum T = 0	33	23%	COP > 2	38	27%
Sum T > 1	22	15%	AG = 0	38	27%
$3r + (2)/R < .33$	18	13%	AG > 2	18	13%
$3r + (2)/R > .44$	56	39%	MOR > 2	5	3%
Fr + rF > 0	18	13%	Lvl 2 Sp.Sc. > 0	6	4%
PureC > 0	18	13%	Sum 6 Sp.Sc. > 6	0	0%
PureC > 1	3	2%	Pure H < 2	29	20%
Afr < .40	4	3%	Pure H = 0	4	3%
Afr < .50	21	15%	p > a + 1	2	1%
(FM + m) < Sum Shad	34	24%	$M^p > M^a$	8	6%

THE NORMATIVE SAMPLES FOR CHILDREN AND ADOLESCENTS

The normative samples for younger subjects changed much more than the adult sample as a result of eliminating records of less than 14 responses. The Exner and Weiner (1982) normative samples for ages 5 to 16 included 1580 protocols, with the number for each year ranging between 105 (age 6) to 150 (ages 9, 11, and 16). A total of 239 of the 1580 protocols (15%) were discarded from the sample because of a low R.

Nearly half of the discarded records were from ages 5 through 8 thus, the data for those ages are likely to have changed most, but every age group has been affected. Some records of nonpatient children that had not been selected for use in the 1982 norms have been added to replace about 20% of those that had been discarded, but samples for all years remain smaller than the originals, and the discarding and replacement procedure has altered the stratification pattern, based on geographic distribution and socioeconomic level, that was applied in the original sample. The total sample now consists of 1390 protocols.

The 1390 records were collected by 87 examiners, for an average of 16 protocols each. Actually, 12 examiners collected between 21 and 26 protocols, but no examiner collected fewer than 7 records. Eighty-four school districts, from 33 states plus the District of Columbia, are represented. There are no more than 36 subjects from any single school district, and none contributed more than 10 records for any age group. Most minority subjects were recruited from the northeastern, southwestern, and western United States.

Table 42 provides some demographic data concerning sex, race, socioeconomic level, and residential geography in each age group.

The descriptive statistics for younger clients are shown, by age group, in Tables 43 and 44.

Table 42.   Distribution of Demographic Variables, by Age, for 1390 Nonpatient Children and Adolescents

| | Age Groups | | | | | | | | | | | |
	5	6	7	8	9	10	11	12	13	14	15	16
Total	90	80	120	120	140	120	135	120	110	105	110	140
Male	50	46	68	54	72	64	70	63	45	43	53	68
Female	40	34	52	66	68	56	65	57	65	62	57	72
Race												
White	71	60	106	88	106	97	110	87	80	76	81	107
Black	11	15	9	16	14	11	13	19	20	18	16	21
Hispanic	8	5	5	14	13	12	9	10	8	9	8	11
Asian	0	0	0	2	7	0	3	4	2	3	5	1
SES and Geographic Distribution												
Upper	22	17	21	15	21	25	27	19	14	15	20	17
Middle	47	38	63	64	80	63	77	67	68	61	57	84
Lower	21	25	36	41	39	32	31	34	28	29	33	39
Urban	31	21	34	34	45	27	41	34	37	24	43	46
Suburban	26	27	39	42	51	41	51	43	39	44	35	49
Rural	33	32	46	44	44	52	43	43	34	37	32	44

Table 43. Descriptive Statistics for 1390 Nonpatient Children and Adolescents by Age

				5-Year-Olds ($N = 90$)					
Variable	Mean	SD	Min	Max	Freq	Median	Mode	SK	KU
R	17.64	1.44	14.00	20.00	90	18.00	18.00	−0.83	−0.25
W	9.97	1.65	7.00	12.00	90	9.00	11.00	0.24	−1.35
D	7.10	2.61	3.00	12.00	90	8.00	6.00	−0.83	−0.24
Dd	0.58	[0.65]	0.00	2.00	44	0.00	0.00	0.70	−0.53
S	1.40	[1.14]	0.00	3.00	64	1.00	0.00	0.14	−1.39
DQ+	5.47	1.43	2.00	8.00	90	5.50	4.00	0.35	−1.29
DQo	10.72	2.07	7.00	13.00	90	12.00	13.00	−1.25	0.05
DQv	1.37	[0.62]	0.00	4.00	83	1.00	1.00	0.36	−0.63
DQv/+	0.09	[0.29]	0.00	1.00	8	0.00	0.00	2.94	6.78
FQX+	0.00	0.00	0.00	0.00	0	0.00	0.00	—	—
FQXo	11.54	2.50	6.00	15.00	90	13.00	13.00	−0.70	−0.52
FQXu	3.59	1.96	1.00	7.00	90	4.00	1.00	0.13	−1.19
FQX−	1.46	0.64	0.00	3.00	86	1.00	1.00	0.04	−0.19
FQXNone	0.87	[0.62]	0.00	2.00	63	1.00	1.00	0.36	−0.63
MQ+	0.00	0.00	0.00	0.00	0	0.00	0.00	—	—
MQo	1.13	0.34	1.00	2.00	90	1.00	1.00	2.19	2.88
MQu	0.38	0.66	0.00	2.00	25	0.00	0.00	1.53	1.00
MQ−	0.19	[0.39]	0.00	1.00	17	0.00	0.00	1.62	0.63
MQNone	0.00	[0.00]	0.00	0.00	0	0.00	0.00	—	—
S−	0.91	[0.69]	0.00	3.00	62	1.00	1.00	0.45	−0.83
M	1.70	1.00	1.00	4.00	90	1.00	1.00	1.26	0.36
FM	5.00	0.95	4.00	7.00	90	5.00	4.00	0.32	−1.20
m	0.78	0.80	0.00	3.00	49	1.00	0.00	0.43	−1.32
FM + m	5.78	1.19	4.00	9.00	90	6.00	5.00	0.65	0.50
FC	0.71	0.46	0.00	1.00	64	1.00	1.00	−0.95	−1.13
CF	3.02	1.41	1.00	6.00	90	3.00	3.00	0.53	−0.20
C	0.67	[0.62]	0.00	2.00	63	1.00	1.00	0.36	−0.63
Cn	0.00	[0.00]	0.00	0.00	0	0.00	0.00	—	—
Sum Color	4.40	1.10	2.00	6.00	90	4.00	4.00	−0.39	−0.11
WGSum C	4.38	1.09	2.50	6.50	90	4.00	4.00	0.27	−0.73
Sum C'	0.63	[0.48]	0.00	1.00	57	1.00	1.00	−0.56	−1.72
Sum T	0.83	[0.48]	0.00	2.00	57	1.00	1.00	0.42	2.42
Sum V	0.00	[0.00]	0.00	0.00	0	0.00	0.00	—	—
Sum Y	0.36	[0.33]	0.00	2.00	20	0.00	0.00	−0.65	2.71
Sum Shading	1.77	0.97	0.00	2.00	57	2.00	2.00	−0.56	−1.72
Fr + rF	0.38	[0.45]	0.00	2.00	29	0.00	0.00	1.01	−1.00
FD	0.28	[0.63]	0.00	1.00	16	0.00	0.00	1.77	0.58
F	6.98	1.26	4.00	9.00	90	6.00	6.00	0.19	−0.35
PAIR	9.08	1.96	5.00	11.00	90	9.00	11.00	−0.91	−0.29
3r(2)/R	0.69	0.14	0.33	1.00	90	0.60	0.64	0.28	0.57
Lambda	0.86	0.15	0.36	1.25	90	0.75	0.60	0.76	−0.52
EA	5.08	1.34	2.50	8.50	90	5.50	5.00	−0.24	−0.75
es	7.04	1.14	5.00	9.00	90	7.00	7.00	0.10	−0.60
D	−0.24	0.43	−1.00	0.00	90	0.00	0.00	−1.21	−0.55
AdjD	−0.20	0.40	−1.00	0.00	90	0.00	0.00	−1.53	0.33
a (active)	6.28	0.95	5.00	8.00	90	6.00	6.00	0.38	−0.70
p (passive)	1.20	1.37	0.00	4.00	49	1.00	0.00	0.82	−0.60
M^a	1.42	0.67	1.00	3.00	90	1.00	1.00	1.32	0.47
M^p	0.28	0.45	0.00	1.00	25	0.00	0.00	1.01	−1.00
Intellect	0.17	0.38	0.00	1.00	90	0.00	0.00	1.82	1.34
Zf	10.08	2.18	8.00	14.00	90	10.00	14.00	0.15	−1.52
Zd	−1.13	2.60	−5.00	4.50	90	−1.75	−2.50	0.70	0.09
Blends	2.86	1.92	0.00	5.00	77	3.00	5.00	−0.21	−1.56
Col Shd Bl	0.18	[0.56]	0.00	1.00	5	0.00	0.00	1.81	−2.37

Note: Standard deviations shown in brackets indicate that the value is probably unreliable and/or misleading and should not be used to estimate expected ranges. Ordinarily, these variables should not be included in most parametric analyses.

Table 43. (Continued)

Variable	Mean	SD	Min	Max	Freq	Median	Mode	SK	KU
				5-Year-Olds ($N = 90$)					
Afr	0.88	0.13	0.50	1.00	90	0.90	0.80	−0.65	−0.08
Populars	4.66	1.69	3.00	10.00	90	4.00	4.00	0.55	−0.94
X + %	0.67	0.10	0.47	0.83	90	0.68	0.72	−0.27	−0.68
F + %	0.84	0.13	0.50	1.00	90	0.83	0.83	−0.62	0.28
X − %	0.09	0.04	0.00	0.21	86	0.07	0.11	−0.03	−0.18
Xu%	0.23	0.10	0.06	0.40	90	0.22	0.06	0.08	−1.42
S−%	0.49	[0.46]	0.00	1.00	52	0.50	0.00	0.02	−1.83
Isolate/R	0.17	0.06	0.11	0.27	90	0.17	0.11	0.58	−0.88
H	2.19	0.50	1.00	3.00	90	2.00	2.00	0.38	0.34
(H)	1.46	0.50	1.00	2.00	90	1.00	1.00	0.18	−2.01
Hd	0.36	0.48	0.00	1.00	32	0.00	0.00	0.61	−1.66
(Hd)	0.46	0.57	0.00	2.00	13	0.00	0.00	1.42	1.54
Hx	0.00	[0.00]	0.00	0.00	0	0.00	0.00	—	—
All H Cont	4.00	1.15	2.00	6.00	90	4.00	3.00	0.41	−0.90
A	10.69	2.32	6.00	14.00	90	11.00	12.00	−0.88	−0.28
(A)	0.37	[0.48]	0.00	1.00	33	0.00	0.00	0.56	−1.72
Ad	0.71	[0.60]	0.00	2.00	57	1.00	1.00	0.23	−0.57
(Ad)	0.00	[0.00]	0.00	0.00	0	0.00	0.00	—	—
An	0.37	[0.49]	0.00	3.00	18	0.00	0.00	0.46	2.01
Art	0.17	0.38	0.00	1.00	15	0.00	0.00	1.82	1.34
Ay	0.00	[0.00]	0.00	0.00	0	0.00	0.00	—	—
Bl	1.13	[0.46]	0.00	2.00	86	1.00	1.00	0.54	1.30
Bt	0.28	0.45	0.00	1.00	25	0.00	0.00	1.01	−1.00
Cg	3.73	1.35	2.00	6.00	90	3.00	3.00	0.62	−0.92
Cl	0.58	[0.74]	0.00	2.00	42	0.00	0.00	1.21	0.83
Ex	0.22	[0.51]	0.00	2.00	16	0.00	0.00	2.31	4.54
Fi	0.22	[0.51]	0.00	2.00	16	0.00	0.00	2.31	4.54
Fd	0.41	[0.53]	0.00	2.00	21	0.00	0.00	2.16	2.38
Ge	0.00	[0.00]	0.00	0.00	0	0.00	0.00	—	—
Hh	0.71	0.65	0.00	3.00	61	1.00	1.00	−0.48	1.96
Ls	2.68	0.63	2.00	4.00	90	3.00	3.00	0.38	−0.65
Na	0.36	[0.51]	0.00	2.00	19	0.00	0.00	1.42	−0.39
Sc	0.52	[0.43]	0.00	2.00	37	0.00	0.00	1.35	3.58
Sx	0.00	[0.00]	0.00	0.00	0	0.00	0.00	—	—
Xy	0.00	[0.00]	0.00	0.00	0	0.00	0.00	—	—
Idio	0.14	0.35	0.00	1.00	13	0.00	0.00	2.06	2.28
DV	1.16	[1.05]	0.00	4.00	83	1.00	1.00	1.00	0.57
INCOM	1.96	[0.70]	0.00	4.00	76	1.00	1.00	0.06	−0.93
DR	0.11	[0.21]	0.00	1.00	9	0.00	0.00	4.50	18.63
FABCOM	0.89	[0.57]	0.00	3.00	72	1.00	1.00	−0.02	0.06
DV2	0.00	[0.00]	0.00	0.00	0	0.00	0.00	—	—
INC2	0.09	[0.29]	0.00	1.00	8	0.00	0.00	2.94	6.78
DR2	0.09	[0.29]	0.00	1.00	8	0.00	0.00	2.94	6.78
FAB2	0.22	[0.42]	0.00	1.00	20	0.00	0.00	1.36	−0.16
ALOG	0.61	[0.50]	0.00	1.00	57	1.00	1.00	0.37	−1.91
CONTAM	0.00	0.00	0.00	0.00	0	0.00	0.00	—	—
Sum6 Sp Sc	6.88	2.01	3.00	9.00	90	6.00	5.00	0.45	−0.65
Sum6 Sp Sc2	0.40	[0.58]	0.00	2.00	32	0.00	0.00	1.12	0.30
WSum6	14.88	4.68	4.00	22.00	90	14.00	7.00	−0.10	−1.05
AB	0.00	[0.00]	0.00	0.00	0	0.00	0.00	—	—
AG	1.23	0.67	0.00	3.00	82	1.00	1.00	0.60	0.74
CFB	0.00	0.00	0.00	0.00	0	0.00	0.00	—	—
COP	1.08	0.52	0.00	3.00	81	1.00	1.00	0.10	0.67
CP	0.23	[0.81]	0.00	1.00	2	0.00	0.00	3.38	11.55
MOR	0.78	[0.75]	0.00	2.00	53	1.00	1.00	0.39	−1.10
PER	0.18	0.41	0.00	2.00	21	0.00	0.00	0.69	4.73
PSV	0.63	[0.48]	0.00	1.00	57	1.00	1.00	−0.56	−1.72

Table 43. (Continued)

<table>
<tr><td colspan="10" align="center">6-Year-Olds ($N = 80$)</td></tr>
<tr><th>Variable</th><th>Mean</th><th>SD</th><th>Min</th><th>Max</th><th>Freq</th><th>Median</th><th>Mode</th><th>SK</th><th>KU</th></tr>
<tr><td>R</td><td>18.91</td><td>0.98</td><td>14.00</td><td>20.00</td><td>80</td><td>19.00</td><td>20.00</td><td>−0.23</td><td>−1.25</td></tr>
<tr><td>W</td><td>10.79</td><td>1.17</td><td>7.00</td><td>10.00</td><td>80</td><td>11.00</td><td>9.00</td><td>−0.56</td><td>−1.16</td></tr>
<tr><td>D</td><td>7.94</td><td>1.01</td><td>7.00</td><td>11.00</td><td>80</td><td>7.00</td><td>8.00</td><td>−1.38</td><td>2.27</td></tr>
<tr><td>Dd</td><td>0.30</td><td>[0.46]</td><td>0.00</td><td>1.00</td><td>24</td><td>0.00</td><td>0.00</td><td>0.89</td><td>−1.24</td></tr>
<tr><td>S</td><td>0.79</td><td>[0.76]</td><td>0.00</td><td>3.00</td><td>51</td><td>1.00</td><td>1.00</td><td>1.09</td><td>1.67</td></tr>
<tr><td>DQ+</td><td>4.42</td><td>0.59</td><td>3.00</td><td>5.00</td><td>80</td><td>4.00</td><td>4.00</td><td>−0.46</td><td>−0.66</td></tr>
<tr><td>DQo</td><td>11.31</td><td>1.35</td><td>9.00</td><td>13.00</td><td>80</td><td>11.00</td><td>13.00</td><td>0.11</td><td>−1.45</td></tr>
<tr><td>DQv</td><td>2.54</td><td>[1.19]</td><td>1.00</td><td>5.00</td><td>80</td><td>3.00</td><td>3.00</td><td>0.14</td><td>−0.89</td></tr>
<tr><td>DQv/+</td><td>0.45</td><td>[0.64]</td><td>0.00</td><td>1.00</td><td>38</td><td>1.00</td><td>1.00</td><td>−1.18</td><td>−0.63</td></tr>
<tr><td>FQX+</td><td>0.00</td><td>0.00</td><td>0.00</td><td>0.00</td><td>0</td><td>0.00</td><td>0.00</td><td>—</td><td>—</td></tr>
<tr><td>FQXo</td><td>13.39</td><td>1.22</td><td>12.00</td><td>16.00</td><td>80</td><td>14.00</td><td>14.00</td><td>0.25</td><td>−0.92</td></tr>
<tr><td>FQXu</td><td>4.01</td><td>1.29</td><td>3.00</td><td>7.00</td><td>80</td><td>4.00</td><td>4.00</td><td>0.75</td><td>−0.32</td></tr>
<tr><td>FQX−</td><td>0.94</td><td>0.50</td><td>0.00</td><td>6.00</td><td>66</td><td>0.00</td><td>0.00</td><td>0.21</td><td>−2.01</td></tr>
<tr><td>FQXNone</td><td>0.74</td><td>[0.48]</td><td>0.00</td><td>2.00</td><td>68</td><td>1.00</td><td>1.00</td><td>−0.58</td><td>−1.70</td></tr>
<tr><td>MQ+</td><td>0.00</td><td>0.00</td><td>0.00</td><td>0.00</td><td>0</td><td>0.00</td><td>0.00</td><td>—</td><td>—</td></tr>
<tr><td>MQo</td><td>1.96</td><td>0.75</td><td>1.00</td><td>3.00</td><td>80</td><td>2.00</td><td>2.00</td><td>0.06</td><td>−1.22</td></tr>
<tr><td>MQu</td><td>0.00</td><td>0.00</td><td>0.00</td><td>0.00</td><td>0</td><td>0.00</td><td>0.00</td><td>—</td><td>—</td></tr>
<tr><td>MQ−</td><td>0.23</td><td>[0.67]</td><td>0.00</td><td>1.00</td><td>6</td><td>0.00</td><td>0.00</td><td>1.24</td><td>4.12</td></tr>
<tr><td>MQNone</td><td>0.00</td><td>[0.00]</td><td>0.00</td><td>0.00</td><td>0</td><td>0.00</td><td>0.00</td><td>—</td><td>—</td></tr>
<tr><td>S−</td><td>0.42</td><td>[0.78]</td><td>0.00</td><td>0.50</td><td>11</td><td>0.00</td><td>0.00</td><td>0.98</td><td>3.15</td></tr>
<tr><td>M</td><td>1.96</td><td>0.75</td><td>1.00</td><td>3.00</td><td>80</td><td>2.00</td><td>2.00</td><td>0.06</td><td>−1.22</td></tr>
<tr><td>FM</td><td>4.52</td><td>0.81</td><td>4.00</td><td>8.00</td><td>80</td><td>5.00</td><td>4.00</td><td>−1.25</td><td>2.76</td></tr>
<tr><td>m</td><td>1.40</td><td>1.48</td><td>0.00</td><td>4.00</td><td>51</td><td>1.00</td><td>0.00</td><td>0.81</td><td>−0.72</td></tr>
<tr><td>FM + m</td><td>5.92</td><td>0.99</td><td>7.00</td><td>10.00</td><td>80</td><td>8.00</td><td>8.00</td><td>1.11</td><td>0.35</td></tr>
<tr><td>FC</td><td>1.11</td><td>1.09</td><td>0.00</td><td>3.00</td><td>42</td><td>2.00</td><td>0.00</td><td>0.07</td><td>−1.72</td></tr>
<tr><td>CF</td><td>3.51</td><td>0.94</td><td>1.00</td><td>5.00</td><td>80</td><td>3.00</td><td>3.00</td><td>−0.36</td><td>0.83</td></tr>
<tr><td>C</td><td>0.94</td><td>[0.48]</td><td>0.00</td><td>2.00</td><td>68</td><td>1.00</td><td>1.00</td><td>−0.58</td><td>−1.70</td></tr>
<tr><td>Cn</td><td>0.06</td><td>[0.09]</td><td>0.00</td><td>1.00</td><td>1</td><td>0.00</td><td>0.00</td><td>4.15</td><td>35.81</td></tr>
<tr><td>Sum Color</td><td>5.56</td><td>1.63</td><td>1.00</td><td>7.00</td><td>80</td><td>6.00</td><td>6.00</td><td>−0.94</td><td>0.29</td></tr>
<tr><td>WGSum C</td><td>5.02</td><td>1.42</td><td>1.00</td><td>6.50</td><td>80</td><td>5.50</td><td>5.50</td><td>−1.23</td><td>1.26</td></tr>
<tr><td>Sum C'</td><td>0.58</td><td>[0.50]</td><td>0.00</td><td>1.00</td><td>46</td><td>1.00</td><td>1.00</td><td>−0.31</td><td>−1.95</td></tr>
<tr><td>Sum T</td><td>0.83</td><td>[0.22]</td><td>0.00</td><td>1.00</td><td>69</td><td>1.00</td><td>1.00</td><td>−1.21</td><td>6.12</td></tr>
<tr><td>Sum V</td><td>0.00</td><td>[0.00]</td><td>0.00</td><td>0.00</td><td>0</td><td>0.00</td><td>0.00</td><td>—</td><td>—</td></tr>
<tr><td>Sum Y</td><td>0.54</td><td>[0.48]</td><td>0.00</td><td>1.00</td><td>37</td><td>0.00</td><td>0.00</td><td>0.70</td><td>−1.55</td></tr>
<tr><td>Sum Shading</td><td>1.95</td><td>0.88</td><td>0.00</td><td>3.00</td><td>76</td><td>2.00</td><td>2.00</td><td>−0.18</td><td>−0.89</td></tr>
<tr><td>Fr + rF</td><td>0.28</td><td>[0.40]</td><td>0.00</td><td>2.00</td><td>17</td><td>0.00</td><td>0.00</td><td>1.83</td><td>0.35</td></tr>
<tr><td>FD</td><td>0.48</td><td>[0.68]</td><td>0.00</td><td>1.00</td><td>29</td><td>0.00</td><td>0.00</td><td>1.49</td><td>2.34</td></tr>
<tr><td>F</td><td>5.77</td><td>1.47</td><td>3.00</td><td>10.00</td><td>80</td><td>4.00</td><td>4.00</td><td>3.10</td><td>10.34</td></tr>
<tr><td>PAIR</td><td>9.61</td><td>1.79</td><td>5.00</td><td>12.00</td><td>80</td><td>10.00</td><td>11.00</td><td>−0.88</td><td>0.30</td></tr>
<tr><td>3r(2)/R</td><td>0.67</td><td>0.15</td><td>0.25</td><td>0.90</td><td>80</td><td>0.66</td><td>0.60</td><td>0.38</td><td>0.61</td></tr>
<tr><td>Lambda</td><td>0.79</td><td>0.17</td><td>0.18</td><td>1.50</td><td>80</td><td>0.78</td><td>0.65</td><td>−1.56</td><td>0.64</td></tr>
<tr><td>EA</td><td>6.98</td><td>1.42</td><td>2.00</td><td>8.50</td><td>80</td><td>6.00</td><td>5.00</td><td>0.85</td><td>1.77</td></tr>
<tr><td>es</td><td>7.87</td><td>1.00</td><td>8.00</td><td>11.00</td><td>80</td><td>7.00</td><td>6.00</td><td>0.13</td><td>−1.52</td></tr>
<tr><td>D</td><td>−0.41</td><td>0.59</td><td>−2.00</td><td>0.00</td><td>80</td><td>0.00</td><td>0.00</td><td>−1.11</td><td>0.28</td></tr>
<tr><td>AdjD</td><td>−0.21</td><td>0.41</td><td>−2.00</td><td>0.00</td><td>80</td><td>0.00</td><td>0.00</td><td>−1.43</td><td>0.05</td></tr>
<tr><td>a (active)</td><td>6.03</td><td>1.27</td><td>5.00</td><td>9.00</td><td>80</td><td>6.00</td><td>5.00</td><td>0.43</td><td>−1.17</td></tr>
<tr><td>p (passive)</td><td>1.85</td><td>1.90</td><td>1.00</td><td>6.00</td><td>80</td><td>2.00</td><td>1.00</td><td>0.51</td><td>−1.49</td></tr>
<tr><td>M^a</td><td>0.98</td><td>0.84</td><td>0.00</td><td>2.00</td><td>51</td><td>1.00</td><td>0.00</td><td>0.05</td><td>−1.59</td></tr>
<tr><td>M^p</td><td>0.99</td><td>1.35</td><td>0.00</td><td>3.00</td><td>29</td><td>0.00</td><td>0.00</td><td>0.70</td><td>−1.44</td></tr>
<tr><td>Intellect</td><td>0.96</td><td>0.51</td><td>0.00</td><td>2.00</td><td>80</td><td>1.00</td><td>1.00</td><td>−0.06</td><td>0.93</td></tr>
<tr><td>Zf</td><td>10.15</td><td>1.44</td><td>6.00</td><td>12.00</td><td>80</td><td>11.00</td><td>9.00</td><td>−0.45</td><td>−1.21</td></tr>
<tr><td>Zd</td><td>−1.38</td><td>2.20</td><td>−5.00</td><td>1.00</td><td>80</td><td>0.00</td><td>0.00</td><td>−0.91</td><td>−0.93</td></tr>
<tr><td>Blends</td><td>2.16</td><td>0.49</td><td>1.00</td><td>3.00</td><td>80</td><td>2.00</td><td>2.00</td><td>0.38</td><td>0.64</td></tr>
<tr><td>Col Shd Bl</td><td>0.44</td><td>[0.64]</td><td>0.00</td><td>1.00</td><td>18</td><td>0.00</td><td>0.00</td><td>2.13</td><td>4.67</td></tr>
</table>

Note: Standard deviations shown in brackets indicate that the value is probably unreliable and/or misleading and should not be used to estimate expected ranges. Ordinarily, these variables should not be included in most parametric analyses.

Table 43. (Continued)

Variable	Mean	SD	Min	Max	Freq	Median	Mode	SK	KU
				6-Year-Olds ($N = 90$)					
Afr	0.87	0.26	0.25	1.11	80	0.82	0.78	−0.76	−0.36
Populars	5.02	1.43	4.00	9.00	80	5.00	5.00	0.14	−0.70
X + %	0.71	0.07	0.45	0.84	80	0.70	0.60	−0.30	−0.89
F + %	0.74	0.25	0.50	1.00	80	0.75	0.75	0.63	1.02
X − %	0.11	0.07	0.00	0.25	80	0.06	0.08	0.21	−1.78
Xu%	0.18	0.09	0.16	0.35	80	0.18	0.15	0.49	−0.48
S − %	0.25	[0.67]	0.00	0.00	28	0.33	0.20	0.88	2.13
Isolate	0.24	0.08	0.12	0.39	80	0.22	0.15	0.31	−1.21
H	2.63	1.14	1.00	4.00	80	3.00	3.00	−0.47	−1.24
(H)	0.78	0.50	0.00	1.00	66	1.00	1.00	−0.31	−1.95
Hd	0.64	0.62	0.00	2.00	45	1.00	1.00	0.43	−0.63
(Hd)	0.23	0.63	0.00	1.00	16	0.00	0.00	1.28	3.16
Hx	0.00	[0.00]	0.00	0.00	0	0.00	0.00	—	—
All H Cont	4.28	0.68	2.00	6.00	80	4.00	4.00	0.22	−0.83
A	8.24	0.96	6.00	10.00	80	8.00	8.00	−0.06	0.32
(A)	0.30	[0.46]	0.00	1.00	24	0.00	0.00	0.89	−1.24
Ad	0.95	[0.22]	0.00	1.00	76	1.00	1.00	−4.21	16.12
(Ad)	0.00	[0.00]	0.00	0.00	0	0.00	0.00	—	—
An	0.33	[0.50]	0.00	1.00	11	0.00	0.00	0.99	2.02
Art	0.96	0.51	0.00	2.00	68	1.00	1.00	−0.06	0.93
Ay	0.00	[0.00]	0.00	0.00	0	0.00	0.00	—	—
Bl	0.25	[0.44]	0.00	1.00	20	0.00	0.00	1.18	−0.63
Bt	1.52	0.60	0.00	2.00	76	2.00	2.00	−0.84	−0.25
Cg	1.02	0.70	0.00	3.00	49	1.00	1.00	0.47	−0.68
Cl	0.11	[0.32]	0.00	1.00	9	0.00	0.00	2.50	4.36
Ex	0.20	[0.40]	0.00	1.00	16	0.00	0.00	1.53	0.35
Fi	0.64	[0.48]	0.00	1.00	51	1.00	1.00	−0.58	−1.70
Fd	0.58	[0.50]	0.00	1.00	46	1.00	1.00	−0.31	−1.95
Ge	0.05	[0.22]	0.00	1.00	4	0.00	0.00	4.21	16.12
Hh	1.26	0.55	1.00	3.00	80	1.00	1.00	2.01	3.16
Ls	1.27	0.78	0.00	3.00	80	1.00	1.00	2.21	3.84
Na	0.81	[0.75]	0.00	2.00	49	1.00	1.00	0.32	−1.14
Sc	0.69	[0.57]	0.00	2.00	51	1.00	1.00	0.08	−0.59
Sx	0.00	[0.00]	0.00	0.00	0	0.00	0.00	—	—
Xy	0.00	[0.00]	0.00	0.00	0	0.00	0.00	—	—
Idio	0.15	0.36	0.00	1.00	12	0.00	0.00	2.00	2.04
DV	0.26	[0.24]	0.00	2.00	35	0.00	0.00	0.68	1.87
INCOM	2.35	[0.48]	2.00	3.00	80	2.00	2.00	0.64	−1.63
DR	0.78	[0.56]	0.00	2.00	36	0.00	0.00	0.57	2.76
FABCOM	0.58	[0.50]	0.00	1.00	46	1.00	1.00	−0.31	−1.95
DV2	0.00	[0.00]	0.00	0.00	0	0.00	0.00	—	—
INC2	0.15	[0.36]	0.00	2.00	13	0.00	0.00	1.94	2.56
DR2	0.00	[0.00]	0.00	0.00	0	0.00	0.00	—	—
FAB2	0.20	[0.45]	0.00	1.00	10	0.00	0.00	1.74	0.96
ALOG	0.64	[0.48]	0.00	1.00	51	1.00	1.00	−0.58	−1.70
CONTAM	0.00	0.00	0.00	0.00	0	0.00	0.00	—	—
Sum6 Sp Sc	6.63	1.38	2.00	8.00	80	6.00	5.00	−0.03	−1.54
Sum6 Sp Sc2	0.72	[0.98]	0.00	2.00	20	0.00	0.00	1.94	2.05
WSum6	13.30	5.03	4.00	20.00	80	13.00	10.00	−0.33	−1.71
AB	0.00	[0.00]	0.00	0.00	0	0.00	0.00	—	—
AG	0.30	0.56	0.00	3.00	20	0.00	0.00	1.74	2.11
CFB	0.00	0.00	0.00	0.00	0	0.00	0.00	—	—
COP	2.40	0.54	0.00	3.00	76	2.00	2.00	−4.21	16.12
CP	0.18	[0.30]	0.00	1.00	2	0.00	0.00	2.73	11.95
MOR	0.60	[0.57]	0.00	3.00	37	0.00	0.00	0.55	2.15
PER	0.23	1.06	0.00	3.00	14	0.00	0.00	0.78	3.24
PSV	0.64	[0.77]	0.00	2.00	28	0.00	0.00	1.21	3.85

Table 43. **(Continued)**

					7-Year-Olds ($N = 120$)				
Variable	Mean	SD	Min	Max	Freq	Median	Mode	SK	KU
R	19.93	1.25	14.00	24.00	120	19.00	19.00	−0.10	−0.50
W	10.33	2.01	5.00	12.00	120	9.00	9.00	0.02	−1.34
D	9.09	2.86	7.00	15.00	120	9.00	7.00	0.07	−1.77
Dd	0.82	[0.32]	0.00	3.00	74	0.00	0.00	0.42	2.91
S	1.44	[1.06]	0.00	4.00	102	2.00	2.00	−0.49	−0.38
DQ+	6.48	0.80	6.00	9.00	120	6.00	6.00	0.11	−0.41
DQo	11.15	0.98	10.00	13.00	120	11.00	11.00	0.36	−0.92
DQv	1.63	[0.58]	0.00	3.00	89	2.00	1.00	0.28	−0.71
DQv/+	0.28	[0.45]	0.00	1.00	33	0.00	0.00	1.02	−0.98
FQX+	0.00	0.00	0.00	0.00	0	0.00	0.00	—	—
FQXo	14.37	1.46	12.00	18.00	120	15.00	14.00	0.24	−1.28
FQXu	2.08	0.69	1.00	3.00	120	2.00	2.00	−0.10	−0.86
FQX−	1.99	1.27	0.00	4.00	117	2.00	1.00	0.36	−1.18
FQXNone	1.10	[0.30]	0.00	3.00	72	1.00	1.00	2.70	5.38
MQ+	0.00	0.00	0.00	0.00	0	0.00	0.00	—	—
MQo	2.51	1.16	2.00	6.00	120	3.00	2.00	1.25	0.67
MQu	0.56	0.34	0.00	1.00	13	0.00	0.00	2.20	4.96
MQ−	0.45	[0.22]	0.00	2.00	28	0.00	0.00	2.18	11.75
MQNone	0.00	[0.00]	0.00	0.00	0	0.00	0.00	—	—
S−	0.12	[0.32]	0.00	1.00	14	0.00	0.00	2.42	3.91
M	3.02	1.22	2.00	6.00	120	3.00	2.00	1.15	0.12
FM	5.92	1.20	3.00	7.00	120	6.00	6.00	−1.11	0.14
m	1.06	0.40	0.00	2.00	114	1.00	1.00	0.52	3.35
FM + m	6.08	1.14	5.00	8.00	120	7.00	8.00	−0.80	−0.79
FC	2.17	0.93	1.00	4.00	120	2.00	2.00	0.27	−1.82
CF	3.19	0.98	1.00	6.00	120	3.00	3.00	−0.71	0.47
C	0.99	[0.30]	0.00	3.00	72	0.00	0.00	2.70	5.38
Cn	0.00	[0.00]	0.00	0.00	0	0.00	0.00	—	—
Sum Color	6.15	1.39	4.00	10.00	120	5.00	5.00	0.70	−1.11
WGSum C	4.97	1.14	3.00	7.00	120	4.00	4.00	0.16	−1.17
Sum C'	1.25	[0.86]	0.00	2.00	87	2.00	2.00	−0.51	−1.47
Sum T	0.93	[0.78]	0.00	2.00	110	1.00	1.00	0.42	4.14
Sum V	0.00	[0.00]	0.00	0.00	0	0.00	0.00	—	—
Sum Y	0.23	[0.42]	0.00	1.00	37	0.00	0.00	1.33	−0.23
Sum Shading	2.48	1.12	1.00	4.00	120	3.00	3.00	−0.05	−1.37
Fr + rF	0.30	[0.39]	0.00	2.00	22	0.00	0.00	2.70	5.38
FD	0.13	[0.70]	0.00	1.00	14	0.00	0.00	1.31	−2.94
F	7.62	1.60	3.00	10.00	120	7.00	8.00	−0.68	−0.31
PAIR	9.73	1.94	7.00	12.00	120	9.00	8.00	0.03	−1.75
3r(2)/R	0.65	0.12	0.33	0.90	120	0.62	0.60	0.14	0.28
Lambda	0.79	0.16	0.20	1.25	120	0.70	0.62	−0.17	−0.32
EA	7.48	1.04	4.00	9.00	120	8.00	7.00	−0.41	−1.07
es	8.56	1.67	4.00	12.00	120	8.00	7.00	0.01	−0.98
D	−0.53	0.67	−2.00	0.00	120	0.00	0.00	−0.92	−0.32
AdjD	−0.47	0.58	−2.00	0.00	120	0.00	0.00	−0.79	−0.35
a (active)	6.97	1.24	4.00	8.00	120	7.00	8.00	−1.00	−0.19
p (passive)	3.03	1.28	2.00	6.00	120	2.00	2.00	0.91	−0.50
M^a	2.82	0.87	2.00	5.00	120	3.00	2.00	0.84	−0.07
M^p	0.20	0.40	0.00	1.00	24	0.00	0.00	1.52	0.31
Intellect	0.27	0.44	0.00	1.00	120	0.00	0.00	1.07	−0.87
Zf	11.51	1.46	10.00	15.00	120	11.00	14.00	−0.08	−1.14
Zd	−1.04	2.41	−3.50	3.00	120	−1.00	−3.50	0.39	−1.46
Blends	5.11	0.65	3.00	7.00	120	4.00	5.00	−0.72	0.74
Col Shd Bl	0.36	[0.64]	0.00	1.00	20	0.00	0.00	2.12	8.35

Note: Standard deviations shown in brackets indicate that the value is probably unreliable and/or misleading and should not be used to estimate expected ranges. Ordinarily, these variables should not be included in most parametric analyses.

Table 43. (Continued)

	7-Year-Olds (N = 90)								
Variable	Mean	SD	Min	Max	Freq	Median	Mode	SK	KU
Afr	0.79	0.09	0.45	0.83	120	0.67	0.75	0.02	−1.21
Populars	4.75	0.79	2.00	8.00	120	6.00	4.00	−0.35	−0.16
X + %	0.74	0.09	0.45	0.89	120	0.71	0.72	−0.62	−0.39
F + %	0.66	0.17	0.33	0.88	120	0.63	0.88	−0.08	−0.98
X − %	0.12	0.07	0.05	0.30	107	0.09	0.12	0.33	−1.09
Xu%	0.14	0.08	0.05	0.28	120	0.11	0.11	−0.68	−0.56
S − %	0.15	[0.14]	0.00	0.50	24	0.00	0.00	2.60	5.18
Isolate	0.25	0.05	0.17	0.35	120	0.25	0.25	0.41	−1.08
H	1.87	0.79	1.00	3.00	120	1.00	1.00	0.65	−1.10
(H)	1.64	0.88	0.00	3.00	93	2.00	2.00	−0.29	−1.00
Hd	0.38	0.49	0.00	1.00	45	0.00	0.00	0.52	−1.76
(Hd)	0.74	0.87	0.00	3.00	63	1.00	0.00	1.15	0.71
Hx	0.00	[0.00]	0.00	0.00	0	0.00	0.00	—	—
All H Cont	4.63	0.89	2.00	7.00	120	5.00	4.00	0.17	−0.94
A	9.26	0.77	8.00	10.00	120	9.00	10.00	−0.48	−1.16
(A)	1.18	[0.81]	0.00	2.00	90	1.00	2.00	−0.35	−1.39
Ad	0.68	[0.79]	0.00	2.00	57	0.00	0.00	0.65	−1.10
(Ad)	0.05	[0.22]	0.00	1.00	6	0.00	0.00	4.18	15.75
An	0.37	[0.48]	0.00	1.00	44	0.00	0.00	0.56	−1.72
Art	0.10	0.30	0.00	1.00	12	0.00	0.00	2.70	5.38
Ay	0.17	[0.37]	0.00	1.00	20	0.00	0.00	1.81	1.30
Bl	0.48	[0.45]	0.00	2.00	43	0.00	0.00	1.02	−0.98
Bt	2.11	0.56	1.00	3.00	120	2.00	2.00	0.03	0.12
Cg	1.15	0.36	1.00	2.00	120	1.00	1.00	1.98	1.97
Cl	0.38	[0.57]	0.00	1.00	21	0.00	0.00	2.78	6.10
Ex	0.41	[0.64]	0.00	2.00	19	0.00	0.00	2.46	4.84
Fi	0.48	[0.50]	0.00	1.00	57	0.00	0.00	0.10	−2.02
Fd	0.20	[0.40]	0.00	1.00	24	0.00	0.00	1.52	0.31
Ge	0.00	[0.00]	0.00	0.00	0	0.00	0.00	—	—
Hh	1.45	0.88	0.00	3.00	58	1.00	1.00	0.73	1.40
Ls	1.21	0.93	0.00	3.00	92	1.00	1.00	0.93	1.59
Na	0.96	[0.77]	0.00	2.00	82	1.00	1.00	0.07	−1.31
Sc	1.54	[1.14]	0.00	4.00	96	1.00	1.00	0.39	−0.62
Sx	0.00	[0.00]	0.00	0.00	0	0.00	0.00	—	—
Xy	0.00	[0.00]	0.00	0.00	0	0.00	0.00	—	—
Idio	0.53	0.59	0.00	2.00	57	0.00	0.00	0.64	−0.53
DV	1.39	[0.49]	1.00	2.00	120	1.00	1.00	0.45	−1.83
INCOM	1.39	[0.58]	0.00	2.00	114	1.00	1.00	−0.34	−0.71
DR	0.46	[0.63]	0.00	2.00	56	0.00	0.00	1.06	0.06
FABCOM	0.49	[0.46]	0.00	3.00	55	0.00	0.00	0.93	−1.16
DV2	0.00	[0.00]	0.00	0.00	0	0.00	0.00	—	—
INC2	0.29	[0.57]	0.00	1.00	13	0.00	0.00	2.58	5.05
DR2	0.10	[0.34]	0.00	1.00	7	0.00	0.00	2.98	7.45
FAB2	0.08	[0.26]	0.00	1.00	9	0.00	0.00	3.27	8.83
ALOG	0.48	[0.49]	0.00	2.00	55	0.00	0.00	0.52	−1.76
CONTAM	0.01	0.09	0.00	1.00	1	0.00	0.00	10.95	120.00
Sum6 Sp Sc	5.92	1.25	1.00	7.00	120	5.00	5.00	−0.31	−0.12
Sum6 Sp Sc2	0.18	[0.26]	0.00	1.00	19	0.00	0.00	3.27	8.83
WSum6	12.18	4.66	1.00	29.00	120	10.00	4.00	0.86	0.69
AB	0.00	[0.00]	0.00	0.00	0	0.00	0.00	—	—
AG	1.20	0.40	1.00	2.00	120	1.00	1.00	1.52	0.31
CFB	0.00	0.00	0.00	0.00	0	0.00	0.00	—	—
COP	1.57	0.59	0.00	4.00	108	2.00	2.00	−0.06	−0.28
CP	0.00	[0.00]	0.00	0.00	0	0.00	0.00	—	—
MOR	1.64	[0.58]	1.00	3.00	120	2.00	2.00	0.23	−0.70
PER	2.22	0.57	1.00	4.00	120	1.00	2.00	2.51	4.94
PSV	0.54	[0.50]	0.00	1.00	65	1.00	1.00	−0.17	−2.01

Table 43. (Continued)

Variable	Mean	SD	Min	Max	Freq	Median	Mode	SK	KU
R	18.73	2.46	14.00	23.00	120	18.00	16.00	0.21	−1.57
W	10.03	1.01	6.00	11.00	120	11.00	8.00	0.55	−1.05
D	7.00	1.28	7.00	11.00	120	7.00	7.00	0.41	−1.12
Dd	1.70	[0.84]	0.00	3.00	104	1.00	0.00	0.40	−1.47
S	1.73	[0.58]	1.00	3.00	119	2.00	2.00	0.08	−0.43
DQ+	6.80	1.74	4.00	10.00	120	6.00	6.00	0.64	−0.57
DQo	11.27	1.40	9.00	14.00	120	12.00	12.00	−0.04	−0.68
DQv	0.90	[0.62]	0.00	3.00	99	1.00	1.00	0.50	−0.59
DQv/+	0.17	[0.25]	0.00	1.00	19	0.00	0.00	3.56	11.07
FQX+	0.00	0.00	0.00	0.00	0	0.00	0.00	—	—
FQXo	13.22	1.83	10.00	17.00	120	13.00	12.00	0.44	−0.37
FQXu	3.47	1.37	2.00	6.00	120	4.00	2.00	0.24	−1.34
FQX−	1.72	0.76	1.00	4.00	120	2.00	1.00	0.53	−1.07
FQXNone	0.43	[0.48]	0.00	1.00	43	0.00	0.00	0.73	−1.53
MQ+	0.00	0.00	0.00	0.00	0	0.00	0.00	—	—
MQo	3.12	1.62	1.00	6.00	120	2.00	2.00	0.68	−0.97
MQu	0.20	0.40	0.00	1.00	24	0.00	0.00	1.54	0.38
MQ−	0.07	[0.25]	0.00	1.00	10	0.00	0.00	3.56	11.07
MQNone	0.00	[0.00]	0.00	0.00	0	0.00	0.00	—	—
S−	0.13	[0.34]	0.00	1.00	29	0.00	0.00	2.21	3.00
M	3.38	1.85	1.00	7.00	120	3.00	2.00	0.79	−0.49
FM	4.72	1.37	3.00	8.00	120	4.00	4.00	0.71	−0.30
m	0.57	0.50	0.00	3.00	57	0.00	0.00	0.14	−2.05
FM + m	5.28	1.56	3.00	8.00	120	5.00	4.00	0.20	−1.29
FC	1.80	0.84	1.00	3.00	120	2.00	1.00	0.40	−1.47
CF	2.73	0.78	1.00	4.00	120	3.00	3.00	−0.38	−0.01
C	0.43	[0.48]	0.00	1.00	43	0.00	0.00	0.73	−1.53
Cn	0.00	[0.00]	0.00	0.00	0	0.00	0.00	—	—
Sum Color	4.87	0.72	3.00	6.00	120	5.00	5.00	−0.90	1.37
WGSum C	4.13	0.77	3.00	6.00	120	4.00	3.50	0.80	0.22
Sum C'	1.30	[0.89]	0.00	3.00	102	1.00	1.00	0.92	−0.26
Sum T	1.08	[0.60]	0.00	2.00	107	1.00	1.00	0.76	2.58
Sum V	0.00	[0.00]	0.00	0.00	0	0.00	0.00	—	—
Sum Y	0.92	[0.85]	0.00	2.00	68	1.00	0.00	0.37	−1.54
Sum Shading	2.90	1.47	1.00	5.00	120	2.00	2.00	0.18	−1.46
Fr + rF	0.33	[0.48]	0.00	1.00	33	0.00	0.00	0.73	−1.53
FD	0.53	[0.34]	0.00	2.00	39	0.00	0.00	2.21	3.00
F	6.98	1.64	5.00	10.00	120	7.00	7.00	0.67	−0.58
PAIR	7.97	1.19	6.00	10.00	120	8.00	8.00	0.07	−0.60
3r(2)/R	0.62	0.12	0.30	0.90	120	0.67	0.60	0.28	0.39
Lambda	0.77	0.27	0.29	1.35	120	0.65	0.70	0.91	−0.21
EA	7.51	1.45	4.00	11.50	120	7.00	6.50	0.48	−0.31
es	8.18	2.51	4.00	12.00	120	7.00	6.00	0.07	−1.31
D	−0.22	0.64	−2.00	1.00	120	0.00	0.00	−1.38	2.44
AdjD	−0.15	0.61	−2.00	1.00	120	0.00	0.00	−1.82	4.40
a (active)	6.73	1.63	4.00	10.00	120	6.00	6.00	0.15	−0.34
p (passive)	1.93	1.30	0.00	5.00	112	2.00	1.00	0.89	0.20
M^a	3.12	1.66	1.00	6.00	120	3.00	2.00	0.52	−1.01
M^p	0.37	0.45	0.00	2.00	46	0.00	0.00	1.08	−0.86
Intellect	0.46	0.98	0.00	1.50	120	0.00	0.00	2.46	3.15
Zf	11.27	1.49	10.00	15.00	120	12.00	11.00	0.28	−1.27
Zd	−0.70	1.93	−4.50	5.00	120	−1.00	0.00	1.23	3.73
Blends	4.88	1.03	3.00	6.00	120	5.00	5.00	−0.54	−0.82
Col Shd Bl	0.30	[0.40]	0.00	1.00	34	0.00	0.00	1.54	0.38

Note: Standard deviations shown in brackets indicate that the value is probably unreliable and/or misleading and should not be used to estimate expected ranges. Ordinarily, these variables should not be included in most parametric analyses.

Table 43. **(Continued)**

Variable	Mean	SD	Min	Max	Freq	Median	Mode	SK	KU
				8-Year-Olds ($N = 90$)					
Afr	0.69	0.09	0.36	0.90	120	0.68	0.63	0.64	0.00
Populars	5.68	0.80	3.00	7.00	120	6.00	6.00	−0.57	−1.22
X + %	0.69	0.07	0.45	0.82	120	0.67	0.63	0.44	−0.76
F + %	0.59	0.07	0.43	0.71	120	0.60	0.60	−0.47	0.10
X − %	0.10	0.04	0.05	0.25	120	0.09	0.06	0.82	−0.25
Xu%	0.20	0.06	0.13	0.32	120	0.18	0.13	0.86	−0.07
S − %	0.06	[0.15]	0.00	0.50	24	0.00	0.00	2.38	4.02
Isolate	0.23	0.04	0.14	0.27	120	0.24	0.19	−0.66	−0.44
H	1.87	1.03	1.00	4.00	120	1.00	1.00	0.66	−1.06
(H)	1.47	0.62	1.00	3.00	120	1.00	1.00	1.00	0.00
Hd	0.27	0.45	0.00	1.00	32	0.00	0.00	1.08	−0.86
(Hd)	1.20	0.55	1.00	3.00	120	1.00	1.00	2.69	6.06
Hx	0.00	[0.00]	0.00	0.00	0	0.00	0.00	—	—
All *H* Cont	4.80	1.92	3.00	9.00	120	4.00	3.00	0.89	−0.41
A	9.27	1.45	7.00	12.00	120	9.00	8.00	0.35	−1.06
(A)	1.73	[0.58]	1.00	3.00	120	2.00	2.00	0.08	−0.43
Ad	0.33	[0.48]	0.00	1.00	40	0.00	0.00	0.73	−1.53
(Ad)	0.13	[0.34]	0.00	1.00	16	0.00	0.00	2.21	3.00
An	0.20	[0.40]	0.00	1.00	24	0.00	0.00	1.54	0.38
Art	0.59	0.64	0.00	1.00	13	0.00	0.00	2.41	4.58
Ay	0.10	[0.35]	0.00	1.00	4	0.00	0.00	4.87	11.65
Bl	0.33	[0.48]	0.00	1.00	40	0.00	0.00	0.73	−1.53
Bt	1.45	0.65	0.00	3.00	118	1.00	1.00	0.77	0.10
Cg	1.80	1.18	1.00	4.00	120	1.00	1.00	0.92	−0.92
Cl	0.13	[0.34]	0.00	1.00	16	0.00	0.00	2.21	3.00
Ex	0.43	[0.34]	0.00	2.00	35	0.00	0.00	2.20	3.13
Fi	0.33	[0.48]	0.00	1.00	40	0.00	0.00	0.73	−1.53
Fd	0.20	[0.40]	0.00	1.00	41	0.00	0.00	1.54	0.38
Ge	0.00	[0.00]	0.00	0.00	0	0.00	0.00	—	—
Hh	0.45	0.36	0.00	3.00	48	0.00	0.00	1.01	2.11
Ls	0.93	0.25	0.00	1.00	112	1.00	1.00	−3.56	11.07
Na	0.80	[0.40]	0.00	1.00	96	1.00	1.00	−1.54	0.38
Sc	2.45	[0.62]	1.00	3.00	120	3.00	3.00	−0.68	−0.46
Sx	0.00	[0.00]	0.00	0.00	0	0.00	0.00	—	—
Xy	0.00	[0.00]	0.00	0.00	0	0.00	0.00	—	—
Idio	0.53	0.62	0.00	2.00	56	0.00	0.00	0.74	−0.40
DV	1.33	[0.71]	0.00	2.00	104	1.00	2.00	−0.58	−0.80
INCOM	2.07	[0.45]	1.00	3.00	120	2.00	2.00	0.32	2.18
DR	0.47	[0.62]	0.00	2.00	48	0.00	0.00	1.00	0.00
FABCOM	0.55	[0.89]	0.00	3.00	84	1.00	1.00	1.63	1.78
DV2	0.07	[0.25]	0.00	1.00	7	0.00	0.00	3.56	11.07
INC2	0.13	[0.34]	0.00	1.00	15	0.00	0.00	2.21	3.00
DR2	0.00	[0.00]	0.00	0.00	0	0.00	0.00	—	—
FAB2	0.13	[0.34]	0.00	1.00	16	0.00	0.00	2.21	3.00
ALOG	0.73	0.45	0.00	1.00	88	1.00	1.00	−1.08	−0.86
CONTAM	0.00	0.00	0.00	0.00	0	0.00	0.00	—	—
Sum6 Sp Sc	6.15	1.96	2.00	10.00	120	6.00	5.00	0.74	0.52
Sum6 Sp Sc2	0.33	[0.48]	0.00	1.00	27	0.00	0.00	0.73	−1.53
WSum6	14.33	5.12	5.00	28.00	120	14.00	13.00	0.72	1.86
AB	0.00	[0.00]	0.00	0.00	0	0.00	0.00	—	—
AG	0.93	0.58	0.00	4.00	96	1.00	1.00	−0.00	0.11
CFB	0.00	0.00	0.00	0.00	0	0.00	0.00	—	—
COP	1.93	1.01	1.00	4.00	120	2.00	1.00	0.55	−1.05
CP	0.08	[0.40]	0.00	1.00	2	0.00	0.00	3.17	16.45
MOR	1.13	[0.34]	1.00	3.00	120	1.00	1.00	2.21	3.00
PER	0.33	0.48	0.00	2.00	40	0.00	0.00	0.73	−1.53
PSV	0.46	[0.78]	0.00	2.00	18	0.00	0.00	2.74	9.86

Table 43. (Continued)

Variable	Mean	SD	Min	Max	Freq	Median	Mode	SK	KU
				9-Year-Olds ($N = 140$)					
R	20.53	2.46	14.00	26.00	140	21.00	19.00	0.41	0.57
W	10.33	1.57	6.00	12.00	140	11.00	9.00	0.55	0.05
D	9.00	1.28	7.00	13.00	140	9.00	8.00	0.41	0.84
Dd	1.20	[0.84]	0.00	4.00	102	1.00	0.00	0.40	3.47
S	1.73	[0.58]	0.00	4.00	108	2.00	1.00	1.78	3.43
$DQ+$	6.40	1.94	3.00	12.00	138	7.00	6.00	0.64	2.57
DQo	11.67	1.80	7.00	14.00	140	11.00	10.00	−0.04	−0.68
DQv	1.61	[0.65]	0.00	4.00	72	1.00	0.00	0.50	−0.59
$DQv/+$	0.45	[0.65]	0.00	1.00	23	0.00	0.00	3.56	11.07
$FQX+$	0.26	0.31	0.00	1.00	5	0.00	0.00	4.18	13.67
$FQXo$	14.22	1.83	10.00	18.00	140	14.00	12.00	0.44	−0.37
$FQXu$	3.49	1.37	2.00	6.00	140	4.00	2.00	0.24	−1.34
$FQX-$	2.04	0.76	1.00	3.00	140	2.00	1.00	0.53	−1.07
$FQXNone$	0.38	[0.48]	0.00	2.00	31	0.00	0.00	0.73	−1.53
$MQ+$	0.00	0.00	0.00	0.00	0	0.00	0.00	—	—
MQo	3.12	1.62	1.00	6.00	140	2.00	2.00	0.68	−0.97
MQu	0.20	0.40	0.00	1.00	22	0.00	0.00	1.54	0.38
$MQ-$	0.37	[0.25]	0.00	2.00	7	0.00	0.00	3.27	10.61
$MQNone$	0.00	[0.00]	0.00	0.00	0	0.00	0.00	—	—
$S-$	0.13	[0.34]	0.00	1.00	29	0.00	0.00	2.21	3.00
M	3.12	1.85	1.00	7.00	140	3.00	2.00	0.79	−0.49
FM	4.22	1.47	3.00	9.00	140	4.00	4.00	0.71	0.64
m	0.67	0.58	0.00	3.00	66	0.00	0.00	0.14	3.65
$FM+m$	5.64	1.86	2.00	9.00	140	6.00	4.00	0.20	0.59
FC	1.89	0.86	0.00	3.00	131	2.00	1.00	0.40	2.47
CF	2.79	0.78	1.00	4.00	140	3.00	2.00	−0.38	2.01
C	0.43	[0.48]	0.00	2.00	22	0.00	0.00	0.73	2.53
Cn	0.00	[0.00]	0.00	0.00	0	0.00	0.00	—	—
Sum Color	4.15	0.72	3.00	9.00	140	6.00	5.00	−0.90	1.37
$WGSum\ C$	5.13	1.07	2.50	7.50	140	4.00	3.50	0.80	0.22
Sum C'	1.16	[0.79]	0.00	4.00	104	1.00	1.00	0.92	1.66
Sum T	0.97	[0.63]	0.00	2.00	123	1.00	1.00	0.24	3.58
Sum V	0.00	[0.00]	0.00	0.00	0	0.00	0.00	—	—
Sum Y	0.83	[0.85]	0.00	3.00	102	1.00	1.00	0.37	−1.76
Sum Shading	2.96	1.27	1.00	6.00	140	2.00	2.00	0.18	−1.46
$Fr+rF$	0.42	[0.43]	0.00	1.00	26	0.00	0.00	0.73	2.53
FD	0.63	[0.34]	0.00	1.00	64	0.00	0.00	2.45	3.13
F	9.14	1.84	5.00	11.00	140	8.00	8.00	0.67	−0.58
$PAIR$	8.97	1.69	5.00	12.00	140	9.00	8.00	0.07	−0.60
$3r(2)/R$	0.57	0.12	0.30	0.88	140	0.60	0.55	0.18	0.54
$Lambda$	0.81	0.37	0.29	1.45	140	0.85	0.70	0.91	0.21
EA	8.25	1.95	4.00	11.50	140	8.00	6.50	0.38	0.56
es	8.60	2.59	4.00	13.00	140	7.00	6.00	0.07	1.31
D	−0.18	0.54	−3.00	1.00	140	0.00	0.00	1.18	1.44
$AdjD$	−0.10	0.41	−2.00	1.00	140	0.00	0.00	−1.32	3.44
a (active)	6.26	1.23	3.00	11.00	140	7.00	6.00	0.12	0.30
p (passive)	2.51	1.40	0.00	5.00	76	2.00	1.00	0.89	0.70
M^a	2.72	1.36	1.00	6.00	134	3.00	2.00	0.52	−1.01
M^p	0.27	0.45	0.00	1.00	61	0.00	0.00	1.28	1.86
Intellect	1.03	0.98	0.00	1.00	140	0.00	0.00	2.68	10.89
Zf	11.16	1.54	7.00	15.00	140	11.00	11.00	0.28	0.47
Zd	0.40	2.03	−4.50	6.00	140	0.00	0.00	0.23	0.73
Blends	4.38	1.23	2.00	7.00	140	5.00	5.00	−0.44	−0.92
Col Shd Bl	0.90	[0.56]	0.00	3.00	59	0.00	0.00	1.04	0.34

Note: Standard deviations shown in brackets indicate that the value is probably unreliable and/or misleading and should not be used to estimate expected ranges. Ordinarily, these variables should not be included in most parametric analyses.

Table 43. (Continued)

	9-Year-Olds ($N = 90$)								
Variable	Mean	SD	Min	Max	Freq	Median	Mode	SK	KU
Afr	0.79	0.13	0.38	1.05	140	0.76	0.68	−0.44	0.03
Populars	5.78	0.63	4.00	7.00	140	6.00	5.00	−0.52	−1.02
X + %	0.74	0.09	0.53	0.90	140	0.76	0.71	−0.02	0.64
F + %	0.70	0.08	0.43	1.00	140	0.75	0.67	−0.37	0.15
X − %	0.09	0.06	0.05	0.25	140	0.07	0.09	−0.32	0.25
Xu%	0.17	0.07	0.10	0.33	140	0.18	0.15	0.81	−0.15
S − %	0.06	[0.15]	0.00	1.00	29	0.00	0.00	1.34	4.22
Isolate	0.16	0.05	0.06	0.32	140	0.14	0.17	−0.67	−0.34
H	2.87	1.03	0.00	6.00	138	2.00	2.00	0.66	−1.06
(H)	1.32	0.61	1.00	3.00	140	1.00	1.00	0.84	1.25
Hd	0.57	0.40	0.00	2.00	46	0.00	0.00	1.58	0.36
(Hd)	0.74	0.58	0.00	2.00	62	0.00	0.00	1.60	4.06
Hx	0.00	[0.00]	0.00	0.00	0	0.00	0.00	—	—
All *H* Cont	5.50	1.62	2.00	8.00	140	5.00	4.00	0.59	−0.41
A	8.28	1.59	5.00	13.00	140	9.00	8.00	0.35	0.06
(A)	0.73	[0.68]	0.00	3.00	101	1.00	1.00	0.28	1.63
Ad	0.53	[0.98]	0.00	2.00	80	1.00	1.00	−0.63	2.73
(Ad)	0.23	[0.39]	0.00	1.00	13	0.00	0.00	3.27	4.00
An	0.36	[0.60]	0.00	3.00	34	0.00	0.00	2.54	2.38
Art	0.32	0.71	0.00	2.00	31	0.00	0.00	1.38	3.09
Ay	0.13	[0.28]	0.00	1.00	11	0.00	0.00	3.94	8.28
Bl	0.33	[0.48]	0.00	1.00	28	0.00	0.00	1.03	1.33
Bt	1.45	0.65	0.00	3.00	129	1.00	1.00	0.97	1.10
Cg	1.84	1.08	1.00	4.00	133	1.00	1.00	0.92	1.92
Cl	0.16	[0.39]	0.00	1.00	40	0.00	0.00	2.01	3.34
Ex	0.26	[0.54]	0.00	1.00	21	0.00	0.00	1.93	4.06
Fi	0.69	[0.68]	0.00	1.00	68	0.00	0.00	0.33	2.73
Fd	0.18	[0.46]	0.00	1.00	15	0.00	0.00	2.54	4.38
Ge	0.00	[0.00]	0.00	0.00	0	0.00	0.00	—	—
Hh	0.59	0.36	0.00	1.00	49	0.00	0.00	2.11	2.07
Ls	0.93	0.59	0.00	3.00	107	1.00	1.00	−0.28	0.83
Na	0.70	[0.48]	0.00	2.00	96	1.00	1.00	−0.54	1.38
Sc	1.55	[0.72]	0.00	3.00	102	2.00	1.00	0.68	2.46
Sx	0.00	[0.00]	0.00	0.00	0	0.00	0.00	—	—
Xy	0.00	[0.00]	0.00	0.00	0	0.00	0.00	—	—
Idio	0.63	0.42	0.00	1.00	48	0.00	0.00	0.84	1.40
DV	1.01	[0.61]	0.00	2.00	97	1.00	1.00	−0.08	2.80
INCOM	1.37	[0.75]	0.00	3.00	81	1.00	1.00	0.32	2.18
DR	0.67	[0.72]	0.00	2.00	91	1.00	1.00	−0.73	2.00
FABCOM	1.05	[0.89]	0.00	3.00	102	1.00	1.00	0.63	1.68
DV2	0.07	[0.21]	0.00	1.00	6	0.00	0.00	1.56	12.07
INC2	0.11	[0.59]	0.00	1.00	7	0.00	0.00	1.27	11.40
DR2	0.00	[0.00]	0.00	0.00	0	0.00	0.00	—	—
FAB2	0.05	[0.39]	0.00	1.00	3	0.00	0.00	0.68	13.00
ALOG	0.61	[0.49]	0.00	1.00	56	0.00	0.00	1.08	3.86
CONTAM	0.00	0.00	0.00	0.00	0	0.00	0.00	—	—
Sum6 Sp Sc	5.95	2.16	1.00	9.00	140	6.00	6.00	0.74	0.52
Sum6 Sp Sc2	0.27	[0.51]	0.00	2.00	14	0.00	0.00	0.63	6.53
WSum6	13.06	4.72	3.00	26.00	140	12.00	11.00	0.92	0.86
AB	0.00	[0.00]	0.00	0.00	0	0.00	0.00	—	—
AG	1.37	0.78	0.00	4.00	128	2.00	1.00	0.67	1.11
CFB	0.00	0.00	0.00	0.00	0	0.00	0.00	—	—
COP	2.03	1.14	0.00	5.00	136	2.00	2.00	0.18	1.05
CP	0.00	[0.00]	0.00	0.00	0	0.00	0.00	—	—
MOR	0.87	[0.64]	0.00	4.00	116	1.00	1.00	−0.41	1.87
PER	1.16	0.78	0.00	6.00	99	1.00	1.00	0.73	−1.53
PSV	0.26	[0.61]	0.00	2.00	29	0.00	0.00	1.04	4.14

Table 43.   (Continued)

					10-Year-Olds ($N = 120$)				
Variable	Mean	S	Min	Max	Freq	Median	Mode	SK	KU
R	20.97	1.92	18.00	25.00	120	19.00	19.00	0.85	−0.39
W	9.52	0.87	9.00	12.00	120	9.00	9.00	1.59	1.46
D	10.10	1.48	8.00	13.00	120	10.00	9.00	0.31	−1.32
Dd	1.35	[0.44]	0.00	3.00	119	0.00	0.00	1.17	−0.64
S	1.48	[0.70]	1.00	3.00	107	1.00	1.00	1.12	−0.08
DQ+	7.68	0.96	3.00	9.00	120	8.00	7.00	−0.48	−0.18
DQo	12.07	1.78	9.00	17.00	120	12.00	11.00	0.08	0.01
DQv	0.53	[0.50]	0.00	2.00	64	1.00	1.00	−0.14	−2.02
DQv/+	0.38	[0.28]	0.00	1.00	36	0.00	0.00	3.05	7.45
FQX+	0.30	0.50	0.00	1.00	11	0.00	0.00	4.04	9.15
FQXo	15.80	1.98	13.00	21.00	120	15.00	15.00	0.81	0.33
FQXu	2.95	0.79	1.00	4.00	120	3.00	3.00	−0.54	0.12
FQX−	1.58	1.03	0.00	6.00	104	2.00	2.00	1.74	6.56
FQXNone	0.13	[0.34]	0.00	1.00	29	0.00	0.00	2.19	2.82
MQ+	0.08	0.21	0.00	1.00	2	0.00	0.00	4.80	13.25
MQo	3.23	1.48	1.00	6.00	120	3.00	3.00	0.22	−0.78
MQu	0.25	0.44	0.00	1.00	30	0.00	0.00	1.17	−0.64
MQ−	0.17	[0.37]	0.00	2.00	21	0.00	0.00	1.81	1.30
MQNone	0.00	[0.00]	0.00	0.00	0	0.00	0.00	—	—
S−	0.12	[0.32]	0.00	1.00	14	0.00	0.00	2.42	3.91
M	3.65	1.63	1.00	7.00	120	4.00	3.00	−0.04	−0.69
FM	5.53	1.46	3.00	7.00	120	6.00	7.00	−0.43	−1.38
m	1.08	0.28	1.00	2.00	120	1.00	1.00	3.05	7.45
FM + m	6.62	1.40	4.00	8.00	120	7.00	8.00	−0.56	−1.06
FC	2.55	0.96	1.00	4.00	120	2.00	2.00	0.44	−1.03
CF	3.68	1.29	2.00	6.00	120	3.50	5.00	0.14	−1.27
C	0.13	[0.34]	0.00	2.00	29	0.00	0.00	2.19	2.82
Cn	0.00	[0.00]	0.00	0.00	0	0.00	0.00	—	—
Sum Color	6.37	1.50	4.00	8.00	120	7.00	8.00	−0.41	−1.30
WGSum C	5.16	1.25	3.00	7.00	120	5.00	4.00	−0.23	−1.26
Sum C'	0.79	[0.85]	0.00	4.00	73	1.00	1.00	0.41	0.44
Sum T	0.98	[0.39]	0.00	2.00	106	1.00	1.00	−0.16	3.86
Sum V	0.02	[0.13]	0.00	1.00	2	0.00	0.00	7.65	57.43
Sum Y	0.43	[0.65]	0.00	2.00	34	0.00	0.00	0.82	−0.37
Sum Shading	1.83	1.32	1.00	6.00	120	3.00	4.00	0.06	−1.16
Fr + rF	0.35	[0.36]	0.00	1.00	36	0.00	0.00	1.98	1.97
FD	0.67	[0.58]	0.00	2.00	78	1.00	1.00	1.33	0.81
F	6.38	2.04	3.00	12.00	120	5.50	5.00	0.57	−0.73
PAIR	9.62	1.36	6.00	12.00	120	9.00	9.00	−0.29	0.09
3r(2)/R	0.54	0.07	0.29	0.68	120	0.52	0.47	−0.71	6.30
Lambda	0.49	0.23	0.19	1.11	120	0.36	0.36	0.90	−0.23
EA	8.81	1.36	4.00	11.00	120	9.00	7.00	−0.37	1.09
es	8.45	1.90	5.00	12.00	120	8.00	7.00	−0.33	−0.89
D	−0.15	0.44	−2.00	1.00	120	0.00	0.00	−1.89	5.07
AdjD	−0.12	0.49	−2.00	1.00	120	0.00	0.00	−1.17	3.81
a (active)	7.15	1.37	6.00	11.00	120	8.00	7.00	0.32	−0.74
p (passive)	3.27	0.66	1.00	4.00	120	2.00	2.00	1.46	1.91
M^a	2.82	1.09	1.00	5.00	120	3.00	3.00	−0.10	−0.63
M^p	0.98	0.83	0.00	3.00	88	1.00	1.00	0.93	0.76
Intellect	0.53	0.56	0.00	2.00	120	0.50	0.00	0.44	−0.81
Zf	13.52	1.19	11.00	16.00	120	13.50	13.00	−0.19	−0.27
Zd	−0.13	2.32	−5.00	5.00	120	0.00	−3.00	0.22	−0.35
Blends	5.80	1.05	3.00	7.00	120	6.00	7.00	−0.39	−0.70
Col Shd Bl	0.42	[0.13]	0.00	1.00	22	0.00	0.00	7.65	57.43

Note: Standard deviations shown in brackets indicate that the value is probably unreliable and/or misleading and should not be used to estimate expected ranges. Ordinarily, these variables should not be included in most parametric analyses.

Table 43. (Continued)

Variable	Mean	SD	Min	Max	Freq	Median	Mode	SK	KU
Afr	0.63	0.09	0.50	0.85	120	0.58	0.58	0.94	−0.05
Populars	6.O7	0.84	3.00	7.00	120	6.00	6.00	−1.01	1.55s
X + %	0.76	0.08	0.45	0.88	120	0.79	0.75	−0.86	1.39
F + %	0.55	0.14	0.33	0.82	120	0.50	0.50	0.39	−1.03
X − %	0.08	0.06	0.00	0.25	104	0.07	0.05	1.46	5.42
Xu%	0.15	0.05	0.05	0.21	120	0.16	0.16	−0.44	−0.53
S − %	0.12	[0.14]	0.00	1.00	34	0.00	0.00	2.82	6.34
Isolate	0.19	0.03	0.14	0.26	120	0.19	0.16	0.67	−0.53
H	2.47	1.12	1.00	5.00	120	3.00	3.00	0.01	−0.83
(H)	1.48	0.74	0.00	2.00	102	2.00	2.00	−1.06	−0.37
Hd	0.25	0.47	0.00	2.00	28	0.00	0.00	1.65	1.80
(Hd)	0.85	0.36	0.00	1.00	102	1.00	1.00	−1.98	1.97
Hx	0.00	[0.00]	0.00	0.00	0	0.00	0.00	—	—
All *H* Cont	5.05	1.64	2.00	8.00	120	6.00	6.00	−0.59	−0.59
A	8.92	1.18	7.00	11.00	120	9.00	9.00	0.54	−0.43
(A)	1.20	[0.77]	0.00	3.00	96	1.00	1.00	−0.14	−0.88
Ad	1.35	[1.08]	0.00	3.00	76	2.00	2.00	−0.25	−1.49
(Ad)	0.07	[0.25]	0.00	1.00	8	0.00	0.00	3.52	10.56
An	0.67	[0.57]	0.00	2.00	74	1.00	1.00	0.14	−0.66
Art	0.53	0.56	0.00	2.00	60	0.50	0.00	0.44	−0.81
Ay	0.23	[0.41]	0.00	1.00	12	0.00	0.00	2.95	11.25
Bl	0.60	[0.59]	0.00	2.00	66	1.00	1.00	0.37	−0.70
Bt	2.17	0.74	1.00	4.00	120	2.00	2.00	0.49	0.33
Cg	1.48	1.03	0.00	3.00	102	1.00	1.00	0.33	−1.10
Cl	0.08	[0.28]	0.00	1.00	10	0.00	0.00	3.05	7.45
Ex	0.08	[0.28]	0.00	1.00	10	0.00	0.00	3.05	7.45
Fi	0.75	[0.44]	0.00	1.00	90	1.00	1.00	−1.17	−0.64
Fd	0.53	[0.50]	0.00	1.00	64	1.00	1.00	−0.14	−2.02
Ge	0.00	[0.00]	0.00	0.00	0	0.00	0.00	—	—
Hh	0.60	0.49	0.00	1.00	72	1.00	1.00	−0.41	−1.86
Ls	1.00	0.45	0.00	2.00	108	1.00	1.00	0.00	2.14
Na	0.30	[0.46]	0.00	1.00	36	0.00	0.00	0.88	−1.24
Sc	2.85	[0.40]	2.00	4.00	120	3.00	3.00	−1.17	1.62
Sx	0.00	[0.00]	0.00	0.00	0	0.00	0.00	—	—
Xy	0.00	[0.00]	0.00	0.00	0	0.00	0.00	—	—
Idio	0.08	0.28	0.00	1.00	10	0.00	0.00	3.05	7.45
DV	1.03	[0.61]	1.00	3.00	112	1.00	1.00	1.72	4.91
INCOM	1.35	[0.51]	1.00	3.00	103	1.00	1.00	1.01	−0.16
DR	0.18	[0.28]	0.00	1.00	30	0.00	0.00	3.05	7.45
FABCOM	0.65	[0.48]	0.00	1.00	82	0.00	0.00	0.64	−1.62
DV2	0.00	[0.00]	0.00	0.00	0	0.00	0.00	—	—
INC2	0.23	[0.43]	0.00	1.00	5	0.00	0.00	1.28	−0.38
DR2	0.02	[0.13]	0.00	1.00	2	0.00	0.00	7.65	57.43
FAB2	0.02	[0.09]	0.00	1.00	1	0.00	0.00	8.31	69.82
ALOG	0.47	[0.48]	0.00	1.00	49	0.00	0.00	0.56	−1.72
CONTAM	0.00	0.00	0.00	0.00	0	0.00	0.00	—	—
*Sum*6 *Sp Sc*	5.15	1.20	2.00	8.00	120	4.00	4.00	1.37	0.95
*Sum*6 *Sp Sc*2	0.09	[0.44]	0.00	1.00	10	0.00	0.00	1.17	−0.64
*WSum*6	10.22	3.79	3.00	17.00	120	7.00	7.00	1.08	0.65
AB	0.08	[0.28]	0.00	1.00	2	0.00	0.00	4.15	10.34
AG	1.57	0.62	1.00	3.00	120	1.50	1.00	0.61	−0.55
CFB	0.00	0.00	0.00	0.00	0	0.00	0.00	—	—
COP	1.73	0.84	1.00	4.00	120	2.00	2.00	1.41	1.94
CP	0.00	[0.00]	0.00	0.00	0	0.00	0.00	—	—
MOR	0.75	[0.62]	0.00	3.00	78	1.00	1.00	0.67	−0.50
PER	0.75	0.44	0.00	1.00	90	1.00	1.00	−1.17	−0.64
PSV	0.05	[0.22]	0.00	1.00	6	0.00	0.00	4.18	15.75

Table 43. (Continued)

	11-Year-Olds ($N = 135$)								
Variable	Mean	SD	Min	Max	Freq	Median	Mode	SK	KU
R	21.29	2.43	15.00	27.00	135	22.00	19.00	0.93	0.29
W	9.61	0.95	9.00	12.00	135	9.00	9.00	1.49	1.06
D	10.01	1.31	9.00	13.00	135	11.00	11.00	0.05	−1.09
Dd	1.67	[1.13]	0.00	4.00	128	0.00	0.00	2.12	3.75
S	1.75	[0.68]	1.00	3.00	135	2.00	2.00	0.36	−0.81
DQ+	8.07	1.22	6.00	10.00	135	8.00	7.00	0.10	−1.08
DQo	12.08	2.14	9.00	17.00	135	12.00	11.00	0.73	0.25
DQv	0.64	[0.88]	0.00	3.00	63	0.00	0.00	1.57	1.99
DQv/+	0.50	[0.69]	0.00	2.00	41	0.00	0.00	1.98	2.39
FQX+	0.21	0.38	0.00	1.00	9	0.00	0.00	3.08	11.42
FQXo	15.83	1.40	13.00	18.00	135	16.00	17.00	−0.29	−1.09
FQXu	3.18	1.26	1.00	6.00	135	3.00	3.00	0.52	0.49
FQX−	2.20	1.87	0.00	7.00	125	2.00	2.00	1.73	2.02
FQXNone	0.18	[0.27]	0.00	1.00	18	0.00	0.00	3.09	7.69
MQ+	0.11	0.45	0.00	1.00	3	0.00	0.00	4.24	13.85
MQo	3.59	1.38	1.00	6.00	135	4.00	3.00	−0.15	−0.69
MQu	0.33	0.47	0.00	1.00	44	0.00	0.00	0.75	−1.46
MQ−	0.20	[0.40]	0.00	1.00	27	0.00	0.00	1.52	0.30
MQNone	0.00	[0.00]	0.00	0.00	0	0.00	0.00	—	—
S−	0.31	[0.46]	0.00	1.00	52	0.00	0.00	0.82	−1.34
M	4.12	1.67	1.00	7.00	135	4.00	3.00	0.08	−0.56
FM	4.48	1.21	2.00	7.00	135	6.00	4.00	−0.51	−0.65
m	1.00	0.89	0.00	2.00	122	1.00	1.00	0.84	1.69
FM + m	5.48	1.21	4.00	8.00	135	7.00	7.00	−0.51	−0.65
FC	2.93	0.95	1.00	4.00	135	3.00	4.00	−0.19	−1.29
CF	3.43	1.13	2.00	6.00	135	4.00	4.00	0.10	−1.14
C	0.28	[0.27]	0.00	1.00	17	0.00	0.00	3.09	7.69
Cn	0.00	[0.00]	0.00	0.00	0	0.00	0.00	—	—
Sum Color	6.44	1.39	4.00	8.00	135	7.00	7.00	−0.57	−0.93
WGSum C	4.02	1.15	2.50	8.00	135	5.00	4.00	−0.36	−1.06
Sum C'	1.06	[0.71]	0.00	2.00	105	1.00	1.00	−0.09	−0.99
Sum T	0.94	[0.47]	0.00	2.00	116	1.00	1.00	−0.20	1.55
Sum V	0.00	[0.00]	0.00	0.00	0	0.00	0.00	—	—
Sum Y	0.85	[0.70]	0.00	2.00	91	1.00	1.00	0.21	−0.92
Sum Shading	2.85	1.10	1.00	4.00	135	3.00	4.00	−0.32	−1.31
Fr + rF	0.21	[0.41]	0.00	1.00	29	0.00	0.00	1.40	−0.03
FD	0.91	[0.84]	0.00	2.00	92	0.00	0.00	0.59	−1.34
F	6.70	2.37	4.00	12.00	135	6.00	5.00	1.12	0.09
PAIR	9.90	1.08	7.00	12.00	135	10.00	10.00	−0.31	0.86
3r(2)/R	0.53	0.04	0.35	0.75	135	0.58	0.50	0.44	0.38
Lambda	0.68	0.22	0.27	1.50	135	0.69	0.60	0.89	−0.62
EA	8.14	1.37	7.00	12.00	135	8.00	7.00	0.57	−0.53
es	8.33	1.72	4.00	12.00	135	9.00	7.00	−0.22	−1.08
D	−0.09	0.29	−1.00	0.00	135	0.00	0.00	−2.92	6.63
AdjD	−0.06	0.34	−1.00	1.00	135	0.00	0.00	−1.00	5.32
a (active)	7.89	1.42	6.00	11.00	135	8.00	7.00	0.67	−0.27
p (passive)	2.79	1.60	2.00	8.00	135	2.00	2.00	2.08	3.12
M^a	2.81	1.01	1.00	5.00	135	3.00	3.00	0.29	−0.01
M^p	1.38	1.33	0.00	5.00	104	1.00	1.00	1.26	0.76
Intellect	0.77	0.65	0.00	2.00	135	1.00	1.00	0.26	−0.67
Zf	13.70	1.22	11.00	16.00	135	14.00	15.00	−0.30	−0.72
Zd	0.60	2.74	−4.50	4.50	135	1.00	4.50	−0.07	−1.15
Blends	6.04	1.41	3.00	8.00	135	6.00	7.00	−0.28	−1.05
Col Shd Bl	0.00	[0.00]	0.00	0.00	0	0.00	0.00	—	—

Note: Standard deviations shown in brackets indicate that the value is probably unreliable and/or misleading and should not be used to estimate expected ranges. Ordinarily, these variables should not be included in most parametric analyses.

Table 43. (Continued)

| | 11-Year-Olds (N = 90) | | | | | | | | |
Variable	Mean	SD	Min	Max	Freq	Median	Mode	SK	KU
Afr	0.62	0.09	0.47	0.80	135	0.58	0.58	0.33	−0.90
Populars	6.06	0.86	4.00	9.00	135	7.00	5.00	−0.76	−0.78
X + %	0.75	0.08	0.52	0.90	135	0.77	0.79	−1.65	2.46
F + %	0.54	0.16	0.27	1.00	135	0.50	0.60	0.75	0.92
X − %	0.10	0.07	0.00	0.26	125	0.09	0.09	1.42	1.41
Xu%	0.15	0.05	0.05	0.24	135	0.16	0.14	−0.35	−0.35
S − %	0.11	[0.19]	0.00	0.50	42	0.00	0.00	1.47	0.42
Isolate	0.20	0.05	0.14	0.37	135	0.18	0.17	2.07	4.31
H	2.80	1.27	1.00	5.00	131	3.00	3.00	0.23	−0.71
(H)	1.51	0.66	0.00	2.00	123	2.00	2.00	−1.01	−0.12
Hd	0.52	0.66	0.00	2.00	58	0.00	0.00	0.90	−0.30
(Hd)	0.87	0.33	0.00	1.00	118	1.00	1.00	−2.28	3.25
Hx	0.00	[0.00]	0.00	0.00	0	0.00	0.00	—	—
All *H* Cont	5.70	1.80	2.00	9.00	135	6.00	6.00	−0.22	0.04
A	8.58	1.25	7.00	11.00	135	8.00	8.00	0.83	−0.19
(A)	1.00	[0.83]	0.00	2.00	89	1.00	0.00	0.00	−1.54
Ad	1.54	[0.95]	0.00	3.00	101	2.00	2.00	−0.75	−0.78
(Ad)	0.16	[0.36]	0.00	1.00	21	0.00	0.00	1.92	1.72
An	0.73	[0.64]	0.00	2.00	85	1.00	1.00	0.30	−0.66
Art	0.56	0.50	0.00	1.00	76	1.00	1.00	−0.26	−1.96
Ay	0.21	[0.59]	0.00	2.00	17	0.00	0.00	2.62	5.19
Bl	0.44	[0.57]	0.00	2.00	54	0.00	0.00	0.87	−0.24
Bt	2.10	0.67	1.00	4.00	135	2.00	2.00	0.65	1.16
Cg	1.60	0.99	0.00	3.00	122	1.00	1.00	0.26	−1.15
Cl	0.16	[0.24]	0.00	1.00	18	0.00	0.00	3.77	12.44
Ex	0.23	[0.17]	0.00	2.00	14	0.00	0.00	3.61	9.92
Fi	0.85	[0.36]	0.00	1.00	72	1.00	1.00	−2.00	2.04
Fd	0.64	[0.48]	0.00	1.00	67	1.00	1.00	−0.61	−1.65
Ge	0.10	[0.27]	0.00	1.00	6	0.00	0.00	3.97	13.57
Hh	0.81	0.46	0.00	2.00	106	1.00	1.00	−0.65	0.55
Ls	1.28	0.61	0.00	2.00	124	1.00	1.00	−0.23	−0.58
Na	0.35	[0.48]	0.00	1.00	47	0.00	0.00	0.64	−1.61
Sc	2.96	[0.36]	2.00	4.00	135	3.00	3.00	−0.57	4.57
Sx	0.00	[0.00]	0.00	0.00	0	0.00	0.00	—	—
Xy	0.09	[0.29]	0.00	1.00	9	0.00	0.00	2.92	6.63
Idio	0.06	0.34	0.00	2.00	4	0.00	0.00	5.61	29.92
DV	1.21	[0.41]	1.00	2.00	135	1.00	1.00	1.46	0.13
INCOM	1.44	[0.63]	0.00	3.00	131	1.00	1.00	0.42	−0.06
DR	0.22	[0.32]	0.00	1.00	26	0.00	0.00	2.39	3.75
FABCOM	0.46	[0.48]	0.00	2.00	48	0.00	0.00	0.61	−1.65
DV2	0.00	[0.00]	0.00	0.00	0	0.00	0.00	—	—
INC2	0.12	[0.32]	0.00	1.00	16	0.00	0.00	2.39	3.75
DR2	0.03	[0.17]	0.00	1.00	4	0.00	0.00	5.61	29.92
FAB2	0.00	[0.00]	0.00	0.00	0	0.00	0.00	—	—
ALOG	0.28	[0.43]	0.00	1.00	39	0.00	0.00	1.20	−0.56
CONTAM	0.00	0.00	0.00	0.00	0	0.00	0.00	—	—
Sum6 Sp Sc	4.36	1.16	2.00	6.00	135	3.00	3.00	0.69	−0.54
Sum6 Sp Sc2	0.15	[0.36]	0.00	1.00	20	0.00	0.00	2.00	2.04
WSum6	8.93	3.04	3.00	16.00	135	8.00	7.00	0.78	1.10
AB	0.21	[0.39]	0.00	1.00	8	0.00	0.00	3.38	11.45
AG	1.42	0.57	1.00	4.00	135	1.00	1.00	0.94	−0.11
CFB	0.00	0.00	0.00	0.00	0	0.00	0.00	—	—
COP	1.56	0.50	1.00	4.00	135	2.00	2.00	−0.23	−1.98
CP	0.00	[0.00]	0.00	0.00	0	0.00	0.00	—	—
MOR	0.72	[0.57]	0.00	3.00	82	0.00	0.00	0.94	−0.11
PER	0.88	0.53	0.00	2.00	107	1.00	1.00	−0.11	0.38
PSV	0.09	[0.25]	0.00	1.00	8	0.00	0.00	4.47	18.26

Table 43. (Continued)

Variable	Mean	SD	Min	Max	Freq	Median	Mode	SK	KU
			12-Year-Olds ($N = 120$)						
R	21.40	2.05	14.00	23.00	120	20.00	22.00	-1.03	0.96
W	8.79	1.85	1.00	14.00	120	9.00	9.00	-1.94	7.05
D	10.85	1.96	1.00	13.00	120	11.00	12.00	-3.26	12.20
Dd	1.76	[1.11]	0.00	5.00	117	1.00	1.00	3.51	16.47
S	1.92	[0.76]	0.00	5.00	118	2.00	2.00	1.30	4.92
$DQ+$	8.16	1.90	2.00	10.00	120	8.00	10.00	-1.42	2.39
DQo	12.12	1.07	9.00	15.00	120	12.00	12.00	-0.13	1.90
DQv	1.03	[0.26]	0.00	2.00	72	1.00	1.00	0.65	2.43
$DQv/+$	0.38	[0.38]	0.00	2.00	16	0.00	0.00	3.62	13.45
$FQX+$	0.30	0.54	0.00	2.00	10	0.00	0.00	4.16	16.95
$FQXo$	15.34	2.32	5.00	17.00	120	16.00	17.00	-2.40	6.80
$FQXu$	3.77	0.89	1.00	5.00	120	4.00	3.00	-0.95	1.08
$FQX-$	1.95	1.04	1.00	7.00	120	2.00	2.00	3.71	16.47
$FQXNone$	0.43	[0.26]	0.00	2.00	42	0.00	0.00	2.65	7.43
$MQ+$	0.10	0.30	0.00	1.00	5	0.00	0.00	7.45	45.23
MQo	3.21	1.52	1.00	5.00	120	3.00	5.00	-0.33	-1.26
MQu	0.67	0.51	0.00	2.00	78	1.00	1.00	-0.32	-1.01
$MQ-$	0.22	[0.41]	0.00	1.00	26	0.00	0.00	1.39	-0.06
$MQNone$	0.02	[0.13]	0.00	1.00	2	0.00	0.00	7.65	57.43
$S-$	0.57	[0.62]	0.00	3.00	63	1.00	1.00	1.02	2.14
M	4.21	2.06	1.00	7.00	120	4.00	4.00	-0.22	-1.07
FM	5.02	1.66	0.00	9.00	118	6.00	4.00	-1.34	1.64
m	1.00	0.45	0.00	3.00	112	1.00	1.00	2.26	12.57
$FM+m$	6.02	1.70	1.00	9.00	120	7.00	7.00	-1.44	1.83
FC	2.87	1.17	0.00	4.00	106	3.00	3.00	-1.61	1.77
CF	3.14	1.40	0.00	5.00	112	3.00	3.00	-0.55	-0.30
C	0.39	[0.13]	0.00	1.00	38	0.00	0.00	1.65	7.43
Cn	0.00	[0.00]	0.00	0.00	0	0.00	0.00	—	—
Sum Color	6.03	2.29	0.00	8.00	119	7.00	7.00	-1.49	1.26
$WGSum C$	4.05	1.78	0.00	6.50	120	5.00	6.50	-1.17	0.69
Sum C'	1.08	[0.88]	0.00	3.00	99	1.00	1.00	0.38	-0.47
Sum T	0.88	[0.32]	0.00	1.00	106	1.00	1.00	-2.42	3.91
Sum V	0.07	[0.36]	0.00	2.00	4	0.00	0.00	5.27	26.16
Sum Y	1.01	[0.67]	0.00	2.00	108	2.00	2.00	-1.04	-0.13
Sum Shading	3.74	1.37	0.00	6.00	114	4.00	4.00	-0.98	1.25
$Fr+rF$	0.20	[0.13]	0.00	1.00	15	0.00	0.00	3.65	17.43
FD	1.48	[0.83]	0.00	2.00	94	2.00	2.00	-1.11	-0.61
F	5.84	1.65	5.00	13.00	120	5.00	5.00	2.75	7.47
$PAIR$	9.09	1.89	1.00	10.00	120	10.00	10.00	-2.89	9.00
$3r(2)/R$	0.54	0.08	0.10	0.50	120	0.55	0.50	-3.53	16.28
Lambda	0.66	0.58	0.29	4.25	120	0.70	0.50	5.18	30.28
EA	8.26	2.38	1.00	12.00	120	8.50	7.00	-1.38	1.99
es	8.97	2.59	1.00	13.00	120	8.00	6.00	-2.08	3.95
D	-0.21	0.53	-2.00	1.00	120	0.00	0.00	-1.17	2.25
$AdjD$	-0.11	0.67	-2.00	2.00	120	0.00	0.00	-0.04	1.74
a (active)	6.53	1.45	2.00	8.00	120	7.00	6.00	-1.34	2.04
p (passive)	4.00	2.01	0.00	8.00	118	3.00	2.00	0.50	-0.57
M^a	2.47	0.80	0.00	4.00	118	2.00	2.00	0.32	0.24
M^p	1.73	1.60	0.00	5.00	92	2.00	2.00	-0.06	-1.04
Intellect	1.05	0.59	0.00	4.00	120	1.00	1.00	2.96	12.69
Zf	13.14	1.96	5.00	16.00	120	14.00	14.00	-2.25	6.48
Zd	1.67	2.11	-4.50	5.00	120	1.50	1.50	-0.24	-0.26
Blends	6.67	2.29	0.00	9.00	118	7.00	8.00	-1.79	2.12
Col Shd Bl	0.05	[0.22]	0.00	1.00	6	0.00	0.00	4.18	15.75

Note: Standard deviations shown in brackets indicate that the value is probably unreliable and/or misleading and should not be used to estimate expected ranges. Ordinarily, these variables should not be included in most parametric analyses.

Table 43. (Continued)

Variable	Mean	SD	Min	Max	Freq	Median	Mode	SK	KU
				12-Year-Olds ($N = 90$)					
Afr	0.65	0.11	0.21	0.67	120	0.69	0.67	−0.80	0.75
Populars	6.22	1.10	2.00	7.00	120	7.00	6.00	−1.53	2.56
X + %	0.75	0.09	0.29	0.88	120	0.77	0.77	−3.33	14.09
F + %	0.54	0.11	0.18	0.88	120	0.60	0.60	−0.10	1.95
X − %	0.10	0.05	0.05	0.41	120	0.09	0.09	4.05	19.33
Xu%	0.15	0.04	0.05	0.29	120	0.15	0.14	−0.27	2.29
S − %	0.27	[0.28]	0.00	1.00	63	0.33	0.00	0.42	−0.71
Isolate	0.15	0.04	0.00	0.33	120	0.16	0.18	0.19	5.42
H	3.38	1.64	1.00	5.00	120	3.00	5.00	−0.37	−1.42
(*H*)	1.24	0.84	0.00	4.00	97	1.00	1.00	0.38	0.53
Hd	0.59	0.69	0.00	3.00	61	1.00	0.00	1.37	2.75
(*Hd*)	0.78	0.41	0.00	1.00	94	1.00	1.00	−1.39	−0.06
Hx	0.13	[0.34]	0.00	1.00	2	0.00	0.00	7.57	46.38
All *H* Cont	6.00	2.56	2.00	11.00	120	5.00	5.00	−0.24	−1.18
A	7.70	1.29	4.00	13.00	120	8.00	7.00	0.65	4.48
(*A*)	0.47	[0.50]	0.00	1.00	57	0.00	0.00	0.10	−2.02
Ad	1.97	[0.45]	0.00	3.00	116	2.00	2.00	−2.44	11.96
(*Ad*)	0.36	[0.54]	0.00	2.00	20	0.00	0.00	3.10	5.86
An	1.14	[0.60]	0.00	2.00	106	1.00	1.00	−0.06	−0.27
Art	0.92	0.28	0.00	1.00	110	1.00	1.00	−3.05	7.45
Ay	0.03	[0.18]	0.00	1.00	4	0.00	0.00	5.27	26.16
Bl	0.26	[0.44]	0.00	1.00	31	0.00	0.00	1.12	−0.76
Bt	1.52	0.65	0.00	2.00	110	2.00	2.00	−1.04	−0.03
Cg	1.90	1.06	0.00	4.00	116	1.00	1.00	0.12	−1.63
Cl	0.22	[0.13]	0.00	1.00	12	0.00	0.00	7.65	57.43
Ex	0.47	[0.38]	0.00	2.00	40	0.00	0.00	3.16	4.84
Fi	0.57	[0.26]	0.00	2.00	81	1.00	1.00	−1.61	12.13
Fd	0.37	[0.34]	0.00	1.00	29	0.00	0.00	2.19	4.82
Ge	0.02	[0.13]	0.00	1.00	2	0.00	0.00	7.65	57.43
Hh	0.88	0.32	0.00	1.00	106	1.00	1.00	−2.42	3.91
Ls	1.36	0.60	0.00	2.00	112	1.00	1.00	−0.36	−0.65
Na	0.10	[0.35]	0.00	2.00	10	0.00	0.00	3.79	14.82
Sc	2.47	[0.87]	0.00	3.00	112	3.00	3.00	−1.72	2.12
Sx	0.02	[0.13]	0.00	1.00	2	0.00	0.00	7.65	57.43
Xy	0.06	[0.12]	0.00	1.00	7	0.00	0.00	4.95	21.11
Idio	0.15	0.51	0.00	3.00	12	0.00	0.00	4.02	17.31
DV	1.21	[0.55]	0.00	2.00	112	1.00	1.00	0.08	−0.13
INCOM	1.35	[0.57]	0.00	3.00	116	1.00	1.00	0.34	−0.10
DR	0.44	[0.43]	0.00	1.00	39	0.00	0.00	1.22	−0.51
FABCOM	0.46	[0.53]	0.00	2.00	36	0.00	0.00	1.95	2.99
DV2	0.02	[0.16]	0.00	1.00	3	0.00	0.00	6.16	36.58
INC2	0.17	[0.56]	0.00	3.00	13	0.00	0.00	3.54	12.65
DR2	0.02	[0.16]	0.00	1.00	3	0.00	0.00	6.16	36.58
FAB2	0.04	[0.20]	0.00	1.00	5	0.00	0.00	4.65	19.91
ALOG	0.41	[0.68]	0.00	2.00	27	0.00	0.00	1.94	3.61
CONTAM	0.00	0.00	0.00	0.00	0	0.00	0.00	—	—
*Sum*6 *Sp Sc*	4.06	0.95	1.00	6.00	120	3.00	4.00	−0.47	−1.06
*Sum*6 *Sp Sc*2	0.27	[0.68]	0.00	4.00	22	0.00	0.00	3.47	14.40
*WSum*6	8.86	3.85	2.00	19.00	120	8.00	4.00	2.33	9.04
AB	0.05	[0.22]	0.00	1.00	6	0.00	0.00	4.18	15.75
AG	1.08	0.66	0.00	2.00	99	1.00	1.00	−0.09	−0.65
CFB	0.00	0.00	0.00	0.00	0	0.00	0.00	—	—
COP	1.93	0.53	0.00	4.00	114	3.00	2.00	0.18	−0.19
CP	0.00	[0.00]	0.00	0.00	0	0.00	0.00	—	—
MOR	0.67	[0.37]	0.00	3.00	58	0.00	0.00	1.81	1.30
PER	0.93	0.36	0.00	2.00	108	1.00	1.00	−0.89	4.40
PSV	0.03	[0.18]	0.00	1.00	4	0.00	0.00	5.27	26.16

Table 43. **(Continued)**

				13-Year-Olds ($N = 110$)					
Variable	Mean	SD	Min	Max	Freq	Median	Mode	SK	KU
R	21.20	3.30	14.00	33.00	110	20.00	20.00	1.07	3.51
W	8.57	2.15	1.00	14.00	110	9.00	9.00	−1.07	3.04
D	11.15	3.09	1.00	21.00	110	11.00	12.00	−0.25	3.08
Dd	1.46	[1.66]	0.00	6.00	93	1.00	1.00	2.74	7.81
S	1.33	[1.16]	0.00	7.00	106	2.00	1.00	1.93	5.93
DQ+	7.70	2.54	2.00	15.00	110	8.00	8.00	0.24	1.27
DQo	12.40	2.02	8.00	20.00	110	12.00	12.00	0.73	2.74
DQv	0.45	[0.99]	0.00	4.00	24	0.00	0.00	2.31	4.70
DQv/+	0.24	[0.57]	0.00	2.00	18	0.00	0.00	2.33	4.18
FQX+	0.20	0.59	0.00	3.00	14	0.00	0.00	3.25	10.63
FQXo	15.24	3.04	5.00	23.00	110	15.00	17.00	−0.70	2.09
FQXu	3.27	1.53	0.00	8.00	106	3.00	3.00	0.42	1.24
FQX−	2.00	1.42	0.00	7.00	108	2.00	2.00	2.15	4.81
FQXNone	0.07	[0.32]	0.00	2.00	6	0.00	0.00	4.81	23.90
MQ+	0.13	0.43	0.00	2.00	10	0.00	0.00	3.52	11.76
MQo	3.23	1.66	1.00	8.00	110	3.00	5.00	0.34	−0.38
MQu	0.54	0.66	0.00	3.00	51	0.00	0.00	1.23	2.00
MQ−	0.14	[0.51]	0.00	2.00	12	0.00	0.00	2.08	3.61
MQNone	0.02	[0.13]	0.00	1.00	2	0.00	0.00	7.31	52.42
S−	0.52	[0.81]	0.00	4.00	43	0.00	0.00	2.16	5.84
M	4.14	2.24	1.00	11.00	110	4.00	4.00	0.50	−0.01
FM	4.42	1.94	0.00	8.00	108	4.00	6.00	−0.25	−0.89
m	1.25	0.94	0.00	5.00	98	1.00	1.00	1.88	4.46
FM + m	5.67	2.10	1.00	11.00	110	6.00	7.00	−0.28	−0.34
FC	2.95	1.72	0.00	9.00	96	3.00	3.00	0.42	1.72
CF	2.70	1.50	0.00	5.00	102	3.00	3.00	−0.07	−0.98
C	0.07	[0.26]	0.00	1.00	8	0.00	0.00	3.34	9.30
Cn	0.00	[0.00]	0.00	0.00	0	0.00	0.00	—	—
Sum Color	5.73	2.61	0.00	10.00	110	6.50	8.00	−0.71	−0.33
WGSum C	4.29	1.94	0.00	7.50	110	4.75	6.50	−0.61	−0.49
Sum C'	1.20	[0.89]	0.00	3.00	87	1.00	1.00	0.48	−0.37
Sum T	0.97	[0.51]	0.00	3.00	90	1.00	1.00	0.64	4.99
Sum V	0.14	[0.48]	0.00	2.00	10	0.00	0.00	3.31	9.70
Sum Y	1.02	[0.81]	0.00	2.00	80	1.00	2.00	−0.22	−1.44
Sum Shading	3.34	1.44	0.00	6.00	104	4.00	4.00	−0.55	−0.07
Fr + rF	0.45	[0.23]	0.00	1.00	32	0.00	0.00	2.98	4.08
FD	1.27	[0.87]	0.00	3.00	82	2.00	2.00	−0.39	−1.25
F	6.90	2.52	3.00	13.00	110	6.00	5.00	0.93	−0.20
PAIR	8.64	2.30	1.00	14.00	110	9.50	10.00	−1.18	2.59
3r(2)/R	0.49	0.10	0.20	0.66	110	0.48	0.50	−1.84	4.97
Lambda	0.67	0.61	0.20	4.33	110	0.38	0.33	4.44	24.00
EA	8.43	2.69	1.00	15.00	110	9.00	7.50	−0.60	0.64
es	9.01	3.01	1.00	14.00	110	10.00	8.00	−0.83	−0.02
D	−0.09	0.82	−2.00	3.00	110	0.00	0.00	0.78	3.45
AdjD	0.10	0.84	−2.00	3.00	110	0.00	0.00	0.74	2.06
a (active)	6.23	1.89	2.00	11.00	110	6.00	6.00	−0.34	0.13
p (passive)	3.61	2.11	0.00	8.00	104	3.00	3.00	0.45	−0.49
M^a	2.49	1.30	0.00	8.00	106	2.00	2.00	1.80	6.06
M^p	1.67	1.44	0.00	5.00	84	2.00	2.00	0.12	−0.80
Intellect	1.22	0.95	0.00	4.00	110	1.00	1.00	1.24	1.45
Zf	12.64	3.02	5.00	23.00	110	13.00	11.00	0.05	2.17
Zd	1.37	2.27	−4.50	5.00	110	1.50	−0.50	−0.35	−0.40
Blends	5.81	2.43	0.00	9.00	108	7.00	7.00	−0.90	−0.34
Col Shd Bl	0.16	[0.37]	0.00	1.00	18	0.00	0.00	1.84	1.42s

Note: Standard deviations shown in brackets indicate that the value is probably unreliable and/or misleading and should not be used to estimate expected ranges. Ordinarily, these variables should not be included in most parametric analyses.

Table 43. (Continued)

Variable	Mean	SD	Min	Max	Freq	Median	Mode	SK	KU
				13-Year-Olds ($N = 90$)					
Afr	0.69	0.15	0.28	1.00	110	0.58	0.67	0.10	0.52
Populars	6.19	1.34	2.00	9.00	110	7.00	6.00	−0.59	0.79
X + %	0.76	0.11	0.30	1.00	110	0.77	0.77	−1.86	5.39
F + %	0.61	0.18	0.18	1.00	110	0.60	0.60	0.39	0.14
X − %	0.10	0.07	0.00	0.38	108	0.09	0.09	2.67	8.99
Xu%	0.16	0.07	0.00	0.33	106	0.15	0.14	−0.03	0.76
S − %	0.20	[0.28]	0.00	1.00	43	0.00	0.00	1.11	0.35
Isolate	0.16	0.06	0.00	0.33	110	0.16	0.18	0.59	1.30
H	3.09	1.72	1.00	8.00	110	3.00	5.00	0.42	−0.57
(H)	1.25	1.02	0.00	5.00	84	1.00	1.00	1.06	2.35
Hd	0.68	0.83	0.00	3.00	55	0.50	0.00	1.24	1.11
(Hd)	0.56	0.53	0.00	2.00	60	1.00	1.00	0.11	−1.21
Hx	0.00	[0.00]	0.00	0.00	0	0.00	0.00	—	—
All H Cont	5.59	2.46	2.00	11.00	110	5.00	5.00	0.13	−1.03
A	7.96	1.81	4.00	13.00	110	8.00	7.00	0.63	0.65
(A)	0.37	[0.49]	0.00	1.00	41	0.00	0.00	0.53	−1.75
Ad	2.00	[0.81]	0.00	4.00	106	2.00	2.00	0.42	1.71
(Ad)	0.00	[0.00]	0.00	0.00	0	0.00	0.00	—	—
An	0.84	[0.69]	0.00	2.00	74	1.00	1.00	0.22	−0.89
Art	0.85	0.48	0.00	2.00	88	1.00	1.00	−0.36	0.78
Ay	0.11	[0.31]	0.00	1.00	12	0.00	0.00	2.54	4.55
Bl	0.19	[0.39]	0.00	1.00	21	0.00	0.00	1.59	0.55
Bt	1.74	0.98	0.00	5.00	98	2.00	2.00	0.44	1.35
Cg	1.62	1.10	0.00	4.00	98	1.00	1.00	0.47	−0.93
Cl	0.05	[0.23]	0.00	1.00	6	0.00	0.00	3.98	14.08
Ex	0.09	[0.29]	0.00	1.00	10	0.00	0.00	2.89	6.44
Fi	0.76	[0.54]	0.00	2.00	78	1.00	1.00	−0.12	−0.23
Fd	0.42	[0.52]	0.00	2.00	46	1.00	0.00	−0.10	−1.15
Ge	0.04	[0.19]	0.00	1.00	4	0.00	0.00	5.02	23.65
Hh	1.07	0.81	0.00	4.00	90	1.00	1.00	1.35	2.87
Ls	1.10	0.97	0.00	6.00	84	1.00	1.00	2.28	10.32
Na	0.22	[0.50]	0.00	2.00	20	0.00	0.00	2.25	4.39
Sc	1.97	[1.14]	0.00	5.00	96	2.00	3.00	−0.18	−0.48
Sx	0.07	[0.42]	0.00	3.00	4	0.00	0.00	6.43	42.22
Xy	0.00	[0.00]	0.00	0.00	0	0.00	0.00	—	—
Idio	0.78	1.14	0.00	4.00	44	0.00	0.00	1.26	0.28
DV	1.01	[0.70]	0.00	3.00	86	1.00	1.00	0.32	0.05
INCOM	1.07	[0.79]	0.00	3.00	84	1.00	1.00	0.33	−0.33
DR	0.30	[0.66]	0.00	4.00	27	0.00	0.00	3.54	16.72
FABCOM	0.42	[0.71]	0.00	3.00	34	0.00	0.00	1.71	2.45
DV2	0.02	[0.13]	0.00	1.00	2	0.00	0.00	7.31	52.42
INC2	0.22	[0.60]	0.00	3.00	16	0.00	0.00	3.06	9.49
DR2	0.04	[0.19]	0.00	1.00	4	0.00	0.00	5.02	23.65
FAB2	0.07	[0.32]	0.00	2.00	3	0.00	0.00	4.81	23.90
ALOG	0.34	[0.19]	0.00	1.00	18	0.00	0.00	5.02	23.65
CONTAM	0.00	0.00	0.00	0.00	0	0.00	0.00	—	—
Sum6 Sp Sc	2.94	1.46	0.00	9.00	110	3.00	2.00	1.55	5.03
Sum6 Sp Sc2	0.34	[0.77]	0.00	4.00	24	0.00	0.00	2.73	8.42
WSum6	7.54	6.99	0.00	40.00	108	6.00	3.00	2.89	9.56
AB	0.13	[0.33]	0.00	1.00	14	0.00	0.00	2.27	3.20
AG	1.18	0.91	0.00	4.00	85	1.00	1.00	0.67	0.48
CFB	0.00	0.00	0.00	0.00	0	0.00	0.00	—	—
COP	1.84	1.22	0.00	6.00	101	2.00	1.00	1.59	3.11
CP	0.02	[0.13]	0.00	1.00	1	0.00	0.00	7.31	52.42
MOR	0.49	[0.74]	0.00	3.00	40	0.00	0.00	1.42	1.38
PER	1.05	0.89	0.00	5.00	90	1.00	1.00	2.31	7.82
PSV	0.04	[0.21]	0.00	1.00	5	0.00	0.00	3.68	14.48

Table 43. (Continued)

<table>
<thead>
<tr><th colspan="10" style="text-align:center">14-Year-Olds (N = 105)</th></tr>
<tr><th>Variable</th><th>Mean</th><th>SD</th><th>Min</th><th>Max</th><th>Freq</th><th>Median</th><th>Mode</th><th>SK</th><th>KU</th></tr>
</thead>
<tbody>
<tr><td>R</td><td>21.72</td><td>3.36</td><td>14.00</td><td>33.00</td><td>105</td><td>20.00</td><td>20.00</td><td>1.11</td><td>3.43</td></tr>
<tr><td>W</td><td>8.92</td><td>2.19</td><td>4.00</td><td>14.00</td><td>105</td><td>9.00</td><td>9.00</td><td>−1.01</td><td>2.83</td></tr>
<tr><td>D</td><td>11.13</td><td>3.16</td><td>1.00</td><td>21.00</td><td>105</td><td>11.00</td><td>10.00</td><td>−0.23</td><td>2.82</td></tr>
<tr><td>Dd</td><td>1.67</td><td>[1.70]</td><td>0.00</td><td>6.00</td><td>98</td><td>2.00</td><td>1.00</td><td>2.67</td><td>7.31</td></tr>
<tr><td>S</td><td>1.32</td><td>[1.09]</td><td>0.00</td><td>7.00</td><td>101</td><td>2.00</td><td>2.00</td><td>1.89</td><td>5.56</td></tr>
<tr><td>DQ+</td><td>7.81</td><td>2.55</td><td>2.00</td><td>15.00</td><td>105</td><td>8.00</td><td>8.00</td><td>0.33</td><td>1.36</td></tr>
<tr><td>DQo</td><td>12.69</td><td>2.06</td><td>8.00</td><td>20.00</td><td>105</td><td>12.00</td><td>12.00</td><td>0.73</td><td>2.58</td></tr>
<tr><td>DQv</td><td>0.58</td><td>[1.01]</td><td>0.00</td><td>4.00</td><td>27</td><td>0.00</td><td>0.00</td><td>2.23</td><td>4.30</td></tr>
<tr><td>DQv/+</td><td>0.65</td><td>[0.58]</td><td>0.00</td><td>2.00</td><td>48</td><td>0.00</td><td>0.00</td><td>2.25</td><td>3.79</td></tr>
<tr><td>FQX +</td><td>0.14</td><td>0.50</td><td>0.00</td><td>2.00</td><td>11</td><td>0.00</td><td>0.00</td><td>3.16</td><td>9.97</td></tr>
<tr><td>FQXo</td><td>15.17</td><td>3.09</td><td>5.00</td><td>23.00</td><td>105</td><td>15.00</td><td>15.00</td><td>−0.64</td><td>1.93</td></tr>
<tr><td>FQXu</td><td>3.27</td><td>1.56</td><td>0.00</td><td>8.00</td><td>101</td><td>3.00</td><td>3.00</td><td>0.42</td><td>1.10</td></tr>
<tr><td>FQX −</td><td>1.84</td><td>1.25</td><td>0.00</td><td>5.00</td><td>103</td><td>2.00</td><td>2.00</td><td>2.10</td><td>4.46</td></tr>
<tr><td>FQXNone</td><td>0.02</td><td>[0.53]</td><td>0.00</td><td>1.00</td><td>4</td><td>0.00</td><td>0.00</td><td>4.69</td><td>22.65</td></tr>
<tr><td>MQ +</td><td>0.11</td><td>0.44</td><td>0.00</td><td>2.00</td><td>6</td><td>0.00</td><td>0.00</td><td>3.42</td><td>11.04</td></tr>
<tr><td>MQo</td><td>3.21</td><td>1.66</td><td>1.00</td><td>8.00</td><td>105</td><td>3.00</td><td>1.00</td><td>0.43</td><td>−0.26</td></tr>
<tr><td>MQu</td><td>0.51</td><td>0.67</td><td>0.00</td><td>3.00</td><td>46</td><td>0.00</td><td>0.00</td><td>1.34</td><td>2.18</td></tr>
<tr><td>MQ −</td><td>0.13</td><td>[0.50]</td><td>0.00</td><td>2.00</td><td>11</td><td>0.00</td><td>0.00</td><td>2.18</td><td>4.01</td></tr>
<tr><td>MQNone</td><td>0.00</td><td>[0.00]</td><td>0.00</td><td>0.00</td><td>0</td><td>0.00</td><td>0.00</td><td>—</td><td>—</td></tr>
<tr><td>S −</td><td>0.39</td><td>[0.82]</td><td>0.00</td><td>3.00</td><td>31</td><td>0.00</td><td>0.00</td><td>2.24</td><td>6.00</td></tr>
<tr><td>M</td><td>4.06</td><td>2.24</td><td>1.00</td><td>11.00</td><td>105</td><td>4.00</td><td>4.00</td><td>0.59</td><td>0.16</td></tr>
<tr><td>FM</td><td>4.35</td><td>1.96</td><td>0.00</td><td>8.00</td><td>103</td><td>4.00</td><td>6.00</td><td>−0.17</td><td>−0.92</td></tr>
<tr><td>m</td><td>1.27</td><td>0.96</td><td>0.00</td><td>5.00</td><td>93</td><td>1.00</td><td>1.00</td><td>1.81</td><td>4.08</td></tr>
<tr><td>FM + m</td><td>5.62</td><td>2.14</td><td>1.00</td><td>11.00</td><td>105</td><td>6.00</td><td>7.00</td><td>−0.21</td><td>−0.42</td></tr>
<tr><td>FC</td><td>2.93</td><td>1.76</td><td>0.00</td><td>9.00</td><td>91</td><td>3.00</td><td>3.00</td><td>0.45</td><td>1.59</td></tr>
<tr><td>CF</td><td>2.70</td><td>1.53</td><td>0.00</td><td>5.00</td><td>97</td><td>3.00</td><td>3.00</td><td>−0.08</td><td>−1.05</td></tr>
<tr><td>C</td><td>0.10</td><td>[0.27]</td><td>0.00</td><td>1.00</td><td>9</td><td>0.00</td><td>0.00</td><td>3.14</td><td>7.67</td></tr>
<tr><td>Cn</td><td>0.00</td><td>[0.00]</td><td>0.00</td><td>0.00</td><td>0</td><td>0.00</td><td>0.00</td><td>—</td><td>—</td></tr>
<tr><td>Sum Color</td><td>5.71</td><td>2.67</td><td>1.00</td><td>10.00</td><td>105</td><td>7.00</td><td>8.00</td><td>−0.69</td><td>−0.44</td></tr>
<tr><td>WGSum C</td><td>4.29</td><td>1.98</td><td>0.50</td><td>7.50</td><td>105</td><td>5.00</td><td>6.50</td><td>−0.60</td><td>−0.58</td></tr>
<tr><td>Sum C'</td><td>1.11</td><td>[0.91]</td><td>0.00</td><td>3.00</td><td>82</td><td>1.00</td><td>1.00</td><td>0.44</td><td>−0.50</td></tr>
<tr><td>Sum T</td><td>0.99</td><td>[0.52]</td><td>0.00</td><td>3.00</td><td>85</td><td>1.00</td><td>1.00</td><td>0.66</td><td>4.71</td></tr>
<tr><td>Sum V</td><td>0.13</td><td>[0.50]</td><td>0.00</td><td>2.00</td><td>8</td><td>0.00</td><td>0.00</td><td>3.21</td><td>9.06</td></tr>
<tr><td>Sum Y</td><td>0.88</td><td>[0.84]</td><td>0.00</td><td>2.00</td><td>75</td><td>1.00</td><td>2.00</td><td>−0.14</td><td>−1.44</td></tr>
<tr><td>Sum Shading</td><td>3.10</td><td>1.47</td><td>0.00</td><td>6.00</td><td>99</td><td>4.00</td><td>4.00</td><td>−0.49</td><td>−0.19</td></tr>
<tr><td>Fr + rF</td><td>0.38</td><td>[0.43]</td><td>0.00</td><td>1.00</td><td>15</td><td>0.00</td><td>0.00</td><td>3.97</td><td>10.25</td></tr>
<tr><td>FD</td><td>1.24</td><td>[0.87]</td><td>0.00</td><td>3.00</td><td>71</td><td>1.00</td><td>2.00</td><td>−0.31</td><td>−1.30</td></tr>
<tr><td>F</td><td>6.96</td><td>2.56</td><td>3.00</td><td>13.00</td><td>105</td><td>6.00</td><td>5.00</td><td>0.87</td><td>−0.35</td></tr>
<tr><td>PAIR</td><td>8.59</td><td>2.34</td><td>1.00</td><td>14.00</td><td>105</td><td>9.00</td><td>10.00</td><td>−1.12</td><td>2.38</td></tr>
<tr><td>3r(2)/R</td><td>0.47</td><td>0.10</td><td>0.05</td><td>0.56</td><td>105</td><td>0.45</td><td>0.50</td><td>−1.79</td><td>4.60</td></tr>
<tr><td>Lambda</td><td>0.67</td><td>0.62</td><td>0.20</td><td>4.33</td><td>105</td><td>0.38</td><td>0.33</td><td>4.34</td><td>22.96</td></tr>
<tr><td>EA</td><td>8.34</td><td>2.70</td><td>1.00</td><td>15.00</td><td>105</td><td>9.00</td><td>7.50</td><td>−0.55</td><td>0.60</td></tr>
<tr><td>es</td><td>8.92</td><td>3.06</td><td>1.00</td><td>13.00</td><td>105</td><td>9.00</td><td>9.00</td><td>−0.76</td><td>−0.15</td></tr>
<tr><td>D</td><td>−0.09</td><td>0.84</td><td>−2.00</td><td>3.00</td><td>105</td><td>0.00</td><td>0.00</td><td>0.78</td><td>3.19</td></tr>
<tr><td>AdjD</td><td>0.09</td><td>0.86</td><td>−2.00</td><td>3.00</td><td>105</td><td>0.00</td><td>0.00</td><td>0.74</td><td>1.95</td></tr>
<tr><td>a (active)</td><td>6.20</td><td>1.92</td><td>2.00</td><td>11.00</td><td>105</td><td>6.00</td><td>7.00</td><td>−0.32</td><td>0.06</td></tr>
<tr><td>p (passive)</td><td>3.49</td><td>2.07</td><td>0.00</td><td>8.00</td><td>99</td><td>3.00</td><td>3.00</td><td>0.52</td><td>−0.35</td></tr>
<tr><td>M^a</td><td>2.59</td><td>1.32</td><td>0.00</td><td>8.00</td><td>101</td><td>2.00</td><td>2.00</td><td>1.81</td><td>5.93</td></tr>
<tr><td>M^p</td><td>1.49</td><td>1.36</td><td>0.00</td><td>5.00</td><td>89</td><td>2.00</td><td>2.00</td><td>0.17</td><td>−0.74</td></tr>
<tr><td>Intellect</td><td>1.23</td><td>0.97</td><td>0.00</td><td>4.00</td><td>105</td><td>1.00</td><td>1.00</td><td>1.18</td><td>1.22</td></tr>
<tr><td>Zf</td><td>12.56</td><td>3.06</td><td>5.00</td><td>23.00</td><td>105</td><td>13.00</td><td>14.00</td><td>0.12</td><td>2.11</td></tr>
<tr><td>Zd</td><td>1.27</td><td>2.26</td><td>−4.50</td><td>5.00</td><td>105</td><td>1.50</td><td>−0.50</td><td>−0.30</td><td>−0.38</td></tr>
<tr><td>Blends</td><td>5.74</td><td>2.46</td><td>0.00</td><td>9.00</td><td>103</td><td>7.00</td><td>7.00</td><td>−0.84</td><td>−0.47</td></tr>
</tbody>
</table>

Note: Standard deviations shown in brackets indicate that the value is probably unreliable and/or misleading and should not be used to estimate expected ranges. Ordinarily, these variables should not be included in most parametric analyses.

Table 43. **(Continued)**

			14-Year-Olds ($N = 90$)						
Variable	Mean	SD	Min	Max	Freq	Median	Mode	SK	KU
Col Shd *Bl*	0.17	[0.38]	0.00	1.00	18	0.00	0.00	1.77	1.15
Afr	0.69	0.16	0.31	0.89	105	0.68	0.67	0.03	0.47
Populars	6.02	1.17	3.00	9.00	105	7.00	6.00	−0.53	0.67
X + %	0.76	0.12	0.49	0.95	105	0.79	0.75	−1.81	5.01
F + %	0.69	0.18	0.38	1.00	105	0.60	0.60	0.34	0.03
X − %	0.09	0.07	0.00	0.27	105	0.09	0.05	2.60	8.43
Xu%	0.16	0.07	0.00	0.33	105	0.15	0.14	−0.03	0.61
S − %	0.19	[0.28]	0.00	1.00	38	0.00	0.00	1.27	0.76
Isolate	0.16	0.06	0.00	0.33	105	0.16	0.16	0.60	1.15
H	3.00	1.71	1.00	8.00	105	3.00	1.00	0.54	−0.35
(*H*)	1.23	1.03	0.00	5.00	79	1.00	1.00	1.14	2.44
Hd	0.67	0.85	0.00	3.00	52	0.00	0.00	1.28	1.07
(*Hd*)	0.56	0.54	0.00	2.00	57	1.00	1.00	0.13	−1.19
Hx	0.00	[0.00]	0.00	0.00	0	0.00	0.00	—	—
All *H* Cont	5.46	2.44	2.00	11.00	105	5.00	5.00	0.22	−0.91
A	7.97	1.85	4.00	13.00	105	8.00	7.00	0.60	0.49
(*A*)	0.39	[0.49]	0.00	1.00	41	0.00	0.00	0.46	−1.83
Ad	2.00	[0.83]	0.00	4.00	101	2.00	2.00	0.41	1.50
(*Ad*)	0.23	[0.41]	0.00	1.00	13	0.00	0.00	4.16	29.15
An	0.84	[0.71]	0.00	2.00	49	1.00	0.00	0.24	−0.97
Art	0.85	0.50	0.00	2.00	83	1.00	1.00	−0.32	0.62
Ay	0.15	[0.32]	0.00	1.00	14	0.00	0.00	2.46	4.13
Bl	0.20	[0.40]	0.00	1.00	20	0.00	0.00	1.52	0.32
Bt	1.73	1.00	0.00	5.00	91	2.00	2.00	0.44	1.22
Cg	1.55	1.08	0.00	4.00	94	1.00	1.00	0.60	−0.69
Cl	0.06	[0.23]	0.00	1.00	8	0.00	0.00	3.87	13.24
Ex	0.09	[0.29]	0.00	1.00	19	0.00	0.00	2.80	5.94
Fi	0.75	[0.55]	0.00	2.00	63	1.00	1.00	−0.06	−0.32
Fd	0.30	[0.53]	0.00	2.00	31	1.00	1.00	−0.02	−1.16
Ge	0.04	[0.19]	0.00	1.00	3	0.00	0.00	4.90	22.40
Hh	1.08	0.83	0.00	4.00	82	1.00	1.00	1.30	2.58
Ls	1.06	0.97	0.00	6.00	79	1.00	1.00	2.47	11.28
Na	0.23	[0.50]	0.00	2.00	24	0.00	0.00	2.18	4.01
Sc	1.93	[1.15]	0.00	5.00	96	2.00	3.00	−0.10	−0.48
Sx	0.08	[0.43]	0.00	1.00	3	0.00	0.00	6.27	40.17
Xy	0.04	[0.20]	0.00	1.00	5	0.00	0.00	5.18	31.60
Idio	0.82	1.16	0.00	4.00	44	0.00	0.00	1.19	0.10
DV	0.98	[0.69]	0.00	3.00	81	1.00	1.00	0.38	0.22
INCOM	1.05	[0.79]	0.00	3.00	79	1.00	1.00	0.39	−0.24
DR	0.29	[0.66]	0.00	4.00	25	0.00	0.00	3.61	16.99
FABCOM	0.44	[0.72]	0.00	3.00	34	0.00	0.00	1.64	2.18
DV2	0.02	[0.14]	0.00	1.00	2	0.00	0.00	7.14	49.92
INC2	0.12	[0.60]	0.00	3.00	6	0.00	0.00	3.06	9.40
DR2	0.03	[0.17]	0.00	1.00	2	0.00	0.00	5.74	31.57
FAB2	0.08	[0.33]	0.00	1.00	3	0.00	0.00	4.69	22.65
ALOG	0.11	[0.19]	0.00	1.00	10	0.00	0.00	4.90	22.40
CONTAM	0.00	0.00	0.00	0.00	0	0.00	0.00	—	—
*Sum*6 *Sp Sc*	2.89	1.38	0.00	8.00	103	3.00	2.00	1.61	5.11
*Sum*6 *Sp Sc*2	0.14	[0.38]	0.00	1.00	9	0.00	0.00	2.75	8.37
*WSum*6	7.42	7.14	0.00	20.00	105	6.00	3.00	2.85	9.12
AB	0.13	[0.34]	0.00	1.00	12	0.00	0.00	2.19	2.84
AG	1.30	0.92	0.00	4.00	89	1.00	1.00	0.63	0.36
CFB	0.00	0.00	0.00	0.00	0	0.00	0.00	—	—
COP	1.75	1.14	0.00	5.00	95	1.00	1.00	1.57	2.91
CP	0.00	[0.00]	0.00	0.00	0	0.00	0.00	—	—
MOR	0.61	[0.75]	0.00	3.00	48	0.00	0.00	1.35	1.17
PER	1.01	0.81	0.00	4.00	80	1.00	1.00	2.25	7.32
PSV	0.03	[0.12]	0.00	1.00	3	0.00	0.00	5.87	23.24

Table 43. (Continued)

				15-Year-Olds ($N = 110$)					
Variable	Mean	SD	Min	Max	Freq	Median	Mode	SK	KU
R	21.94	4.21	14.00	32.00	110	21.00	20.00	0.94	1.14
W	8.87	2.20	3.00	20.00	110	9.00	9.00	1.57	9.58
D	11.42	3.66	0.00	20.00	109	12.00	12.00	−0.31	1.91
Dd	1.65	[1.31]	0.00	7.00	91	1.00	1.00	1.31	3.76
S	1.44	[1.31]	0.00	5.00	104	2.00	1.00	2.66	12.86
DQ+	7.88	2.02	2.00	13.00	110	8.00	8.00	−0.33	0.15
DQo	12.67	3.62	5.00	29.00	110	12.00	12.00	1.49	5.43
DQv	0.75	[1.29]	0.00	4.00	40	0.00	0.00	1.84	2.46
DQv/+	0.14	[0.42]	0.00	2.00	12	0.00	0.00	3.22	10.13
FQX+	0.36	0.70	0.00	3.00	27	0.00	0.00	1.81	2.20
FQXo	16.35	3.34	7.00	29.00	110	16.00	15.00	0.60	2.79
FQXu	3.08	1.57	0.00	11.00	108	3.00	3.00	1.37	5.75
FQX−	1.60	0.91	0.00	6.00	99	2.00	2.00	0.81	3.89
FQXNone	0.04	[0.25]	0.00	2.00	4	0.00	0.00	6.07	39.81
MQ+	0.25	0.57	0.00	3.00	22	0.00	0.00	2.46	6.34
MQo	3.54	2.01	0.00	8.00	108	3.00	1.00	0.20	−0.91
MQu	0.44	0.52	0.00	2.00	48	0.00	0.00	0.43	−1.36
MQ−	0.12	[0.32]	0.00	1.00	13	0.00	0.00	2.40	3.82
MQNone	0.00	[0.00]	0.00	0.00	0	0.00	0.00	—	—
S−	0.38	[0.57]	0.00	2.00	37	0.00	0.00	1.22	0.52
M	4.35	2.17	1.00	9.00	110	4.00	4.00	0.06	−0.97
FM	4.82	1.73	1.00	9.00	110	5.00	6.00	−0.20	−0.80
m	1.17	0.78	0.00	4.00	97	1.00	1.00	1.49	3.79
FM + m	5.99	1.78	2.00	10.00	110	6.00	7.00	−0.14	−0.67
FC	3.14	1.14	0.00	6.00	107	3.00	3.00	−0.56	0.76
CF	2.85	1.53	0.00	6.00	101	3.00	2.00	−0.11	−0.73
C	0.03	[0.16]	0.00	1.00	3	0.00	0.00	5.88	33.24
Cn	0.02	[0.13]	0.00	1.00	2	0.00	0.00	7.31	52.42
Sum Color	6.04	2.01	1.00	10.00	110	7.00	8.00	−0.62	−0.37
WGSum C	4.47	1.68	0.50	8.00	110	4.50	3.50	−0.33	−0.64
Sum C'	1.63	[1.35]	0.00	10.00	94	1.00	1.00	2.49	12.61
Sum T	1.06	[0.51]	0.00	3.00	101	1.00	1.00	2.62	13.12
Sum V	0.18	[0.49]	0.00	2.00	12	0.00	0.00	2.75	6.73
Sum Y	1.30	[1.27]	0.00	10.00	83	1.00	2.00	3.35	20.69
Sum Shading	4.17	2.55	0.00	23.00	109	4.00	4.00	4.04	27.31
Fr + rF	0.50	[0.45]	0.00	2.00	26	0.00	0.00	6.67	53.57
FD	1.33	[0.97]	0.00	5.00	83	1.50	2.00	0.35	0.78
F	6.48	2.71	2.00	17.00	110	5.00	5.00	1.31	2.02
PAIR	9.10	2.00	1.00	14.00	110	10.00	10.00	−1.37	4.47
3r(2)/R	0.44	0.10	0.05	0.79	110	0.45	0.50	−0.58	4.63
Lambda	0.65	0.22	0.14	1.71	110	0.36	0.33	2.27	8.94
EA	8.82	2.34	2.00	13.50	110	9.50	9.50	−0.69	0.39
es	9.16	3.40	4.00	17.00	110	10.00	9.00	2.13	12.31
D	−0.45	1.39	−10.00	2.00	39	0.00	0.00	−3.73	20.85
AdjD	−0.25	1.07	−5.00	2.00	43	0.00	0.00	−1.71	5.14
a (active)	6.99	1.73	3.00	12.00	110	7.00	8.00	0.18	0.32
p (passive)	3.36	1.93	0.00	9.00	106	3.00	3.00	0.75	0.31
M^a	2.58	1.44	1.00	7.00	110	2.00	2.00	0.96	0.38
M^p	1.77	1.46	0.00	5.00	81	2.00	2.00	0.48	−0.51
Intellect	1.04	0.83	0.00	4.00	110	1.00	1.00	1.59	3.76
Zf	12.68	2.59	5.00	23.00	110	13.00	13.00	0.01	2.61
Zd	1.03	2.96	−6.50	9.00	110	0.50	−0.50	0.17	0.11
Blends	6.34	2.16	1.00	12.00	110	7.00	7.00	−0.63	0.03

Note: Standard deviations shown in brackets indicate that the value is probably unreliable and/or misleading and should not be used to estimate expected ranges. Ordinarily, these variables should not be included in most parametric analyses.

Table 43. (Continued)

Variable	Mean	SD	Min	Max	Freq	Median	Mode	SK	KU
				15-Year-Olds ($N = 90$)					
Col Shd *Bl*	0.22	[0.51]	0.00	2.00	19	0.00	0.00	2.35	4.69
Afr	0.65	0.18	0.27	1.29	110	0.67	0.67	0.97	1.69
Populars	6.33	1.23	3.00	9.00	110	7.00	7.00	−0.59	0.22
X + %	0.78	0.07	0.50	0.90	110	0.77	0.75	−0.46	2.72
F + %	0.62	0.18	0.29	1.00	110	0.60	0.60	0.54	−0.44
X − %	0.07	0.05	0.00	0.43	99	0.09	0.05	3.29	23.26
Xu%	0.14	0.06	0.00	0.37	108	0.15	0.14	0.45	1.97
S − %	0.18	[0.27]	0.00	1.00	37	0.00	0.00	1.28	0.76
Isolate	0.15	0.07	0.00	0.47	110	0.15	0.16	1.76	8.18
H	3.42	1.96	0.00	8.00	109	3.00	5.00	0.49	−0.51
(*H*)	1.04	0.90	0.00	4.00	75	1.00	1.00	0.52	−0.15
Hd	0.57	0.82	0.00	4.00	48	0.00	0.00	1.97	5.02
(*Hd*)	0.54	0.50	0.00	1.00	59	1.00	1.00	−0.15	−2.01
Hx	0.00	[0.00]	0.00	0.00	0	0.00	0.00	—	—
All *H* Cont	5.57	2.28	1.00	9.00	110	5.00	5.00	−0.15	−0.95
A	7.98	1.96	3.00	15.00	110	8.00	7.00	0.55	1.91
(*A*)	0.36	[0.55]	0.00	3.00	37	0.00	0.00	1.55	3.35
Ad	2.08	[1.20]	0.00	9.00	102	2.00	2.00	2.26	11.70
(*Ad*)	0.05	[0.30]	0.00	2.00	4	0.00	0.00	5.80	34.15
An	0.43	[0.79]	0.00	3.00	43	1.00	0.00	0.24	−1.02
Art	0.85	0.63	0.00	4.00	82	1.00	1.00	1.01	4.67
Ay	0.14	[0.34]	0.00	1.00	15	0.00	0.00	2.15	2.66
Bl	0.22	[0.41]	0.00	1.00	24	0.00	0.00	1.38	−0.09
Bt	1.68	0.82	0.00	4.00	102	2.00	2.00	−0.05	−0.06
Cg	1.47	1.11	0.00	4.00	93	1.00	1.00	0.59	−0.80
Cl	0.09	[0.35]	0.00	2.00	8	0.00	0.00	4.12	17.53
Ex	0.12	[0.32]	0.00	1.00	13	0.00	0.00	2.40	3.82
Fi	0.69	[0.52]	0.00	2.00	73	1.00	1.00	−0.23	−0.72
Fd	0.30	[0.51]	0.00	2.00	25	1.00	1.00	−0.20	−1.47
Ge	0.01	[0.09]	0.00	1.00	1	0.00	0.00	10.49	110.00
Hh	0.89	0.60	0.00	4.00	88	1.00	1.00	1.36	7.28
Ls	1.12	0.71	0.00	2.00	88	1.00	1.00	−0.18	−1.00
Na	0.12	[0.35]	0.00	2.00	12	0.00	0.00	3.02	9.12
Sc	1.70	[1.34]	0.00	6.00	77	2.00	3.00	0.03	−0.83
Sx	0.11	[0.44]	0.00	3.00	8	0.00	0.00	4.64	23.43
Xy	0.04	[0.19]	0.00	1.00	4	0.00	0.00	5.02	23.65
Idio	1.09	1.47	0.00	7.00	52	0.00	0.00	1.49	2.28
DV	0.98	[0.70]	0.00	3.00	84	1.00	1.00	0.35	0.03
INCOM	0.88	[0.74]	0.00	4.00	76	1.00	1.00	0.75	1.58
DR	0.13	[0.33]	0.00	1.00	14	0.00	0.00	2.27	3.20
FABCOM	0.23	[0.46]	0.00	2.00	23	0.00	0.00	1.87	2.73
DV2	0.03	[0.16]	0.00	1.00	3	0.00	0.00	5.89	33.24
INC2	0.01	[0.09]	0.00	1.00	1	0.00	0.00	10.49	110.00
DR2	0.01	[0.09]	0.00	1.00	1	0.00	0.00	10.49	110.00
FAB2	0.04	[0.19]	0.00	1.00	4	0.00	0.00	5.02	23.65
ALOG	0.05	[0.26]	0.00	2.00	5	0.00	0.00	5.37	31.19
CONTAM	0.00	0.00	0.00	0.00	0	0.00	0.00	—	—
*Sum*6 *Sp Sc*	2.27	1.36	0.00	5.00	110	2.00	2.00	−0.11	−0.96
*Sum*6 *Sp Sc*2	0.08	[0.27]	0.00	1.00	9	0.00	0.00	3.09	7.71
*WSum*6	4.71	3.33	0.00	15.00	110	4.00	3.00	0.60	0.27
AB	0.03	[0.16]	0.00	1.00	3	0.00	0.00	5.89	33.24
AG	1.14	0.91	0.00	4.00	82	1.00	1.00	0.53	−0.05
CFB	0.00	0.00	0.00	0.00	0	0.00	0.00	—	—
COP	1.54	0.97	0.00	5.00	98	1.00	1.00	0.75	0.98
CP	0.00	[0.00]	0.00	0.00	0	0.00	0.00	—	—
MOR	0.54	[0.83]	0.00	4.00	41	0.00	0.00	1.74	3.06
PER	0.92	0.65	0.00	5.00	89	1.00	1.00	2.31	14.11
PSV	0.04	[0.19]	0.00	1.00	4	0.00	0.00	5.02	23.65

Table 43. (Continued)

				16-Year-Olds ($N = 140$)					
Variable	Mean	SD	Min	Max	Freq	Median	Mode	SK	KU
R	22.89	5.16	14.00	31.00	140	21.00	20.00	0.94	1.70
W	8.96	2.37	3.00	20.00	140	9.00	9.00	1.70	8.32
D	11.91	3.74	0.00	21.00	139	12.00	12.00	−0.23	1.41
Dd	2.02	[1.82]	0.00	7.00	121	2.00	1.00	3.49	15.11
S	1.24	[1.23]	0.00	5.00	132	2.00	2.00	2.70	14.04
DQ+	7.94	2.04	2.00	13.00	140	8.00	8.00	−0.28	−0.13
DQo	13.12	3.47	5.00	27.00	140	12.00	12.00	1.23	4.58
DQv	0.89	[1.35]	0.00	5.00	59	0.00	0.00	1.59	1.62
DQv/+	0.84	[0.53]	0.00	2.00	46	0.00	0.00	2.21	3.98
FQX+	0.54	0.83	0.00	3.00	48	0.00	0.00	1.26	0.31
FQXo	16.43	3.36	7.00	29.00	140	16.00	15.00	0.59	2.16
FQXu	3.19	1.56	0.00	11.00	138	3.00	3.00	1.18	4.32
FQX−	1.58	0.91	0.00	5.00	126	2.00	2.00	0.70	2.97
FQXNone	0.06	[0.26]	0.00	2.00	7	0.00	0.00	5.01	27.20
MQ+	0.35	0.64	0.00	3.00	38	0.00	0.00	1.96	3.75
MQo	3.50	2.01	0.00	8.00	138	3.00	1.00	0.29	−0.86
MQu	0.37	0.50	0.00	2.00	51	0.00	0.00	0.71	−1.07
MQ−	0.09	[0.29]	0.00	1.00	13	0.00	0.00	2.84	6.13
MQNone	0.00	[0.00]	0.00	0.00	0	0.00	0.00	—	—
S−	0.34	[0.55]	0.00	2.00	43	0.00	0.00	1.32	0.81
M	4.31	2.13	1.00	9.00	140	4.00	4.00	0.20	−0.88
FM	4.58	1.66	1.00	9.00	140	4.00	4.00	0.04	−0.73
m	1.14	0.80	0.00	4.00	117	1.00	1.00	1.10	2.43
FM + m	5.72	1.78	2.00	10.00	140	6.00	7.00	0.03	−0.73
FC	3.43	1.34	0.00	8.00	137	3.00	3.00	0.14	1.16
CF	2.78	1.45	0.00	6.00	130	3.00	3.00	−0.05	−0.59
C	0.04	[0.20]	0.00	1.00	6	0.00	0.00	4.56	19.10
Cn	0.01	[0.12]	0.00	1.00	2	0.00	0.00	8.27	67.44
Sum Color	6.26	2.08	1.00	11.00	140	7.00	8.00	−0.56	−0.16
WGSum C	4.56	1.66	0.50	8.00	140	5.00	3.50	−0.42	−0.49
Sum C'	1.15	[1.27]	0.00	6.00	118	1.00	1.00	2.48	13.59
Sum T	1.02	[0.48]	0.00	3.00	128	1.00	1.00	2.44	13.39
Sum V	0.19	[0.51]	0.00	2.00	20	0.00	0.00	2.64	6.03
Sum Y	1.04	[1.21]	0.00	5.00	95	2.00	1.00	3.25	20.79
Sum Shading	3.44	2.35	0.00	23.00	139	4.00	4.00	4.25	31.18
Fr + rF	0.48	[0.41]	0.00	3.00	32	0.00	0.00	6.27	48.14
FD	1.31	[0.93]	0.00	5.00	108	1.00	2.00	0.33	0.77
F	6.85	2.69	2.00	17.00	140	6.00	5.00	0.96	0.93
PAIR	9.04	2.00	1.00	14.00	140	9.00	10.00	−0.90	3.36
3r(2)/R	0.43	0.09	0.05	0.79	140	0.45	0.50	−0.32	3.89
Lambda	0.65	0.21	0.24	1.71	140	0.68	0.63	1.85	7.03
EA	8.87	2.23	2.00	13.50	140	9.00	8.50	−0.59	0.63
es	9.21	3.29	4.00	17.00	140	10.00	8.00	2.09	12.09
D	−0.31	1.31	−10.00	2.00	140	0.00	0.00	−3.70	22.64
AdjD	−0.11	1.04	−5.00	2.00	140	0.00	0.00	−1.56	5.47
a (active)	6.82	1.71	3.00	12.00	140	7.00	6.00	0.25	0.13
p (passive)	3.22	1.89	0.00	9.00	133	3.00	2.00	0.70	0.33
M^a	2.62	1.42	1.00	7.00	140	2.00	2.00	0.88	0.20
M^p	1.69	1.38	0.00	5.00	106	2.00	2.00	0.55	−0.32
Intellect	1.14	0.93	0.00	5.00	140	1.00	1.00	1.38	2.72
Zf	12.61	2.64	5.00	23.00	140	13.00	13.00	0.37	3.18
Zd	1.12	2.96	−6.50	9.00	140	0.75	−0.50	0.09	0.15
Blends	6.11	2.13	1.00	12.00	140	7.00	7.00	−0.44	−0.26

Note: Standard deviations shown in brackets indicate that the value is probably unreliable and/or misleading and should not be used to estimate expected ranges. Ordinarily, these variables should not be included in most parametric analyses.

Table 43. (Continued)

Variable	Mean	SD	Min	Max	Freq	Median	Mode	SK	KU
				16-Year-Olds ($N = 90$)					
Col Shd *Bl*	0.24	[0.50]	0.00	2.00	28	0.00	0.00	2.08	3.56
Afr	0.65	0.17	0.27	1.29	140	0.67	0.67	0.80	1.61
Populars	6.46	1.27	3.00	10.00	140	7.00	7.00	−0.35	0.39
X + %	0.78	0.07	0.50	0.90	140	0.79	0.75	−0.42	2.27
F + %	0.74	0.18	0.29	1.00	140	0.70	0.67	0.36	−0.58
X − %	0.07	0.05	0.00	0.25	126	0.07	0.05	3.08	22.84
Xu%	0.14	0.06	0.00	0.37	138	0.15	0.15	0.45	1.42
S − %	0.16	[0.27]	0.00	1.00	43	0.00	0.00	1.48	1.38
Isolate	0.16	0.07	0.00	0.47	140	0.16	0.16	1.31	4.09
H	3.39	1.94	0.00	8.00	139	3.00	3.00	0.62	−0.28
(*H*)	1.07	0.89	0.00	4.00	97	1.00	1.00	0.36	−0.43
Hd	0.59	0.81	0.00	4.00	62	0.00	0.00	1.79	4.08
(*Hd*)	0.46	0.50	0.00	1.00	64	0.00	0.00	0.17	−2.00
Hx	0.00	[0.00]	0.00	0.00	0	0.00	0.00	—	—
A!l *H* Cont	5.51	2.12	1.00	9.00	140	5.00	5.00	−0.06	−0.76
A	8.04	1.97	3.00	15.00	140	8.00	7.00	0.46	1.18
(*A*)	0.32	[0.54]	0.00	3.00	41	0.00	0.00	1.73	3.69
Ad	2.11	[1.15]	0.00	9.00	131	2.00	2.00	1.98	10.34
(*Ad*)	0.07	[0.33]	0.00	2.00	7	0.00	0.00	4.94	24.56
An	0.41	[0.79]	0.00	4.00	32	1.00	0.00	0.45	−0.96
Art	0.83	0.68	0.00	4.00	97	1.00	1.00	0.79	2.33
Ay	0.19	[0.41]	0.00	2.00	25	0.00	0.00	1.95	2.75
Bl	0.21	[0.43]	0.00	2.00	29	0.00	0.00	1.68	1.61
Bt	1.87	1.03	0.00	6.00	130	2.00	2.00	0.62	1.27
Cg	1.39	1.06	0.00	4.00	116	1.00	1.00	0.65	−0.57
Cl	0.11	[0.36]	0.00	2.00	14	0.00	0.00	3.33	11.30
Ex	0.31	[0.32]	0.00	1.00	26	0.00	0.00	2.45	4.06
Fi	0.39	[0.57]	0.00	2.00	42	1.00	0.00	0.20	−0.76
Fd	0.31	[0.52]	0.00	2.00	31	0.50	0.00	0.13	−1.62
Ge	0.01	[0.12]	0.00	1.00	2	0.00	0.00	8.28	67.44
Hh	0.91	0.67	0.00	4.00	108	1.00	1.00	1.14	3.97
Ls	1.07	0.74	0.00	3.00	108	1.00	1.00	−0.00	−0.87
Na	0.17	[0.41]	0.00	2.00	22	0.00	0.00	2.36	5.05
Sc	1.51	[1.31]	0.00	6.00	93	2.00	0.00	0.23	−0.82
Sx	0.11	[0.41]	0.00	3.00	11	0.00	0.00	4.58	23.67
Xy	0.04	[0.19]	0.00	1.00	5	0.00	0.00	5.06	23.93
Idio	1.31	1.45	0.00	7.00	81	1.00	0.00	1.07	1.04
DV	0.99	[0.71]	0.00	3.00	107	1.00	1.00	0.39	0.11
INCOM	0.83	[0.75]	0.00	4.00	91	1.00	1.00	0.81	1.34
DR	0.14	[0.37]	0.00	2.00	19	0.00	0.00	2.48	5.51
FABCOM	0.21	[0.44]	0.00	2.00	28	0.00	0.00	1.89	2.75
*DV*2	0.02	[0.14]	0.00	1.00	3	0.00	0.00	6.68	43.26
*INC*2	0.01	[0.12]	0.00	1.00	2	0.00	0.00	8.28	67.44
*DR*2	0.01	[0.08]	0.00	1.00	1	0.00	0.00	11.83	140.00
*FAB*2	0.04	[0.19]	0.00	1.00	5	0.00	0.00	5.06	23.93
ALOG	0.05	[0.25]	0.00	2.00	6	0.00	0.00	5.49	32.88
CONTAM	0.00	0.00	0.00	0.00	0	0.00	0.00	—	—
*Sum*6 *Sp Sc*	2.22	1.34	0.00	8.00	124	3.00	2.00	0.03	−0.90
*Sum*6 *Sp Sc*2	0.08	[0.27]	0.00	1.00	11	0.00	0.00	3.17	8.14
*WSum*6	4.57	3.23	0.00	15.00	140	4.00	3.00	0.67	0.32
AB	0.06	[0.25]	0.00	1.00	9	0.00	0.00	3.59	11.06
AG	1.20	0.99	0.00	5.00	106	1.00	1.00	1.03	1.98
CFB	0.00	0.00	0.00	0.00	0	0.00	0.00	—	—
COP	1.60	1.10	0.00	5.00	120	1.00	1.00	0.69	0.45
CP	0.00	[0.00]	0.00	0.00	0	0.00	0.00	—	—
MOR	0.58	[0.81]	0.00	4.00	59	0.00	0.00	1.57	2.57
PER	0.96	0.72	0.00	5.00	110	1.00	1.00	1.60	7.12
PSV	0.04	[0.20]	0.00	1.00	4	0.00	0.00	4.56	29.10

Table 44. Frequencies for 33 Variables for 1390 Nonpatient Children and Adolescents by Age

	Age 5 (N = 90) Freq %		Age 6 (N = 80) Freq %		Age 7 (N = 120) Freq %		Age 8 (N = 120) Freq %		Age 9 (N = 140) Freq %		Age 10 (N = 120) Freq %	
EB Style												
Introversive	2	2	1	1	9	8	16	13	33	24	26	22
Pervasive	0	0	0	0	0	0	0	0	3	2	0	0
Ambitent	24	27	20	25	44	37	48	40	51	36	38	32
Extratensive	64	71	59	74	67	56	56	47	56	40	56	47
Pervasive	62	69	46	58	40	33	32	27	15	11	26	22
D Score & Adjusted D Score												
D Score > 0	0	0	0	0	0	0	6	5	7	5	2	2
D Score = 0	68	76	51	64	69	58	90	75	117	84	100	83
D Score < 0	22	24	29	36	51	43	24	20	16	11	18	15
D Score < -1	4	4	4	5	12	10	8	7	9	6	2	2
Adj D Score > 0	0	0	0	0	0	0	6	5	9	6	6	5
Adj D Score = 0	72	80	63	79	69	58	98	82	121	86	96	80
Adj D Score < 0	18	20	17	21	51	43	16	13	10	7	18	15
Adj D Score < -1	3	3	4	5	5	4	8	7	7	5	2	2
Zd > +3.0 (Overincorp)	3	3	0	0	0	0	8	7	28	20	30	25
Zd < -3.0 (Underincorp)	23	26	27	34	32	27	19	16	22	16	19	16
Form Quality Deviations												
X + % > .89	0	0	0	0	0	0	0	0	1	1	0	0
X + % < .70	51	57	28	35	22	18	56	47	48	34	12	10
X + % < .61	25	28	13	16	12	10	16	13	11	8	13	11
X + % < .50	4	4	0	0	0	0	3	3	3	2	3	3
F + % < .70	15	17	27	34	81	68	68	57	67	48	92	77
Xu% > .20	49	54	59	74	0	0	32	27	36	26	22	18
X $-$ % > .15	9	10	12	15	12	10	14	12	21	15	17	14
X $-$ % > .20	1	1	1	1	6	5	2	2	2	1	8	7
X $-$ % > .30	0	0	0	0	0	0	0	0	0	0	0	0
FC:CF + C Ratio												
FC > (CF + C) + 2	0	0	0	0	9	8	1	1	0	0	1	1
FC > (CF + C) + 1	0	0	0	0	12	10	9	8	10	7	14	12
(CF + C) > FC + 1	87	97	71	89	17	14	48	40	30	21	60	50
(CF + C) > FC + 2	43	48	49	61	11	9	32	27	19	14	21	18
Constellations & Indices												
HVI Positive	0	0	0	0	0	0	0	0	0	0	0	0
OBS Positive	0	0	0	0	0	0	0	0	0	0	0	0
SCZI = 6	0	0	0	0	0	0	0	0	0	0	0	0
SCZI = 5	0	0	0	0	0	0	0	0	0	0	0	0
SCZI = 4	0	0	0	0	0	0	0	0	0	0	0	0
DEPI = 7	0	0	0	0	0	0	0	0	0	0	0	0
DEPI = 6	0	0	0	0	0	0	0	0	0	0	0	0
DEPI = 5	0	0	0	0	0	0	0	0	0	0	0	0
CDI = 5	1	1	2	2	3	3	3	3	0	0	0	0
CDI = 4	11	12	10	13	13	11	8	7	9	6	18	15
Miscellaneous Variables												
Lambda > .99	12	12	9	11	14	12	20	17	20	14	13	11
S > 2	21	23	4	5	37	31	9	8	12	9	14	12
Sum T = 0	33	37	11	14	10	8	8	7	17	12	14	12
Sum T > 1	0	0	0	0	2	2	8	7	6	4	8	7

Table 44. (Continued)

	Age 5 (N = 90) Freq	%	Age 6 (N = 80) Freq	%	Age 7 (N = 120) Freq	%	Age 8 (N = 120) Freq	%	Age 9 (N = 140) Freq	%	Age 10 (N = 120) Freq	%
$3r + (2)/R < .33$	0	0	4	5	0	0	1	1	7	5	4	3
$3r + (2)/R > .44$	86	96	68	85	86	72	82	68	56	40	110	92
$PureC > 1$	14	16	31	39	9	8	3	3	9	6	2	2
$Afr < .40$	0	0	12	15	0	0	1	1	8	6	2	2
$Afr < .50$	13	14	19	24	9	8	12	10	16	11	16	13
$(FM + m) <$ Sum Shading	0	0	0	0	2	2	10	8	14	10	8	7
Populars < 4	6	7	8	10	3	3	4	3	0	0	4	3
$COP = 0$	13	14	13	16	12	10	6	5	4	3	6	5
$COP > 2$	6	6	5	6	16	13	30	25	37	26	21	18
$AG = 0$	8	9	40	50	0	0	24	20	12	9	3	3
$AG > 2$	4	4	4	5	3	3	13	11	19	14	18	15
$MOR > 2$	3	3	5	6	6	5	3	3	11	8	13	11
Level 2 $SpSc > 0$	32	36	16	20	19	16	13	11	14	10	10	8
Sum 6 $SpSc > 6$	19	21	22	27	22	18	32	27	23	16	21	18
Pure $H < 2$	4	4	24	30	63	52	32	27	31	22	36	30
Pure $H = 0$	1	1	8	10	2	2	4	3	2	1	4	3
$p > a + 1$	7	8	5	6	16	13	10	8	19	14	12	10
$M^p > M^a$	9	10	9	11	11	9	14	12	17	12	14	12

	Age 11 (N = 135) Freq	%	Age 12 (N = 120) Freq	%	Age 13 (N = 110) Freq	%	Age 14 (N = 105) Freq	%	Age 15 (N = 110) Freq	%	Age 16 (N = 140) Freq	%
EB Style												
Introversive	41	30	38	32	34	31	36	34	41	37	52	37
Super-Introversive	0	0	8	7	10	9	10	10	8	7	12	9
Ambitent	34	25	39	33	39	35	26	25	23	21	27	19
Extratensive	60	44	43	36	37	34	43	41	46	42	61	44
Super-Extratensive	14	10	22	18	18	16	18	17	18	16	23	16
EA − es Differences: D-Scores												
D Score > 0	0	0	4	3	14	13	10	10	9	8	14	10
D Score = 0	123	91	90	75	70	64	69	66	71	65	110	79
D Score < 0	12	9	26	22	26	24	26	25	30	27	16	11
D Score < −1	5	4	3	3	4	4	3	3	10	9	9	6
Adj D Score > 0	4	3	14	12	25	23	21	20	16	15	17	12
Adj D Score = 0	119	88	80	67	65	59	70	67	67	61	86	61
Adj D Score < 0	11	8	26	22	20	18	14	13	27	25	12	9
Adj D Score < −1	4	3	2	2	2	2	2	2	6	5	7	5
Zd > +3.0 (Overincorp)	36	27	34	28	30	27	21	20	25	23	30	21
Zd < −3.0 (Underincorp)	14	10	20	17	15	14	16	15	16	15	14	10
Form Quality Deviations												
$X + \% > .89$	2	1	0	0	2	2	1	1	7	6	8	6
$X + \% < .70$	21	16	18	15	16	15	16	15	7	6	12	9
$X + \% < .61$	14	10	6	5	8	7	8	8	3	3	3	2
$X + \% < .50$	0	0	4	3	6	5	4	4	0	0	0	0
$F + \% < .70$	117	87	91	76	82	75	57	54	77	70	72	51
$Xu\% > .20$	26	19	16	13	16	15	14	13	9	8	16	11
$X - \% > .15$	20	15	6	5	12	11	10	10	2	2	2	1
$X - \% > .20$	18	13	4	3	6	5	4	4	2	2	2	1
$X - \% > .30$	0	0	2	2	2	2	0	0	1	1	0	0

Table 44. (Continued)

	Age 11 (N = 135) Freq %		Age 12 (N = 120) Freq %		Age 13 (N = 110) Freq %		Age 14 (N = 105) Freq %		Age 15 (N = 110) Freq %		Age 16 (N = 140) Freq %	
FC:CF + C Ratio												
$FC > (CF + C) + 2$	3	2	8	7	6	5	4	4	10	9	18	13
$FC > (CF + C) + 1$	17	13	12	10	12	11	8	8	20	18	38	27
$(CF + C) > FC + 1$	45	33	24	20	19	17	16	15	23	21	23	16
$(CF + C) > FC + 2$	14	10	0	0	3	3	3	3	2	2	2	1
Constellations & Indices												
HVI Positive	3	2	4	3	3	3	1	1	0	0	1	1
OBS Positive	0	0	0	0	0	0	0	0	1	1	1	1
$SCZI = 6$	0	0	0	0	0	0	0	0	0	0	0	0
$SCZI = 5$	0	0	0	0	0	0	0	0	0	0	0	0
$SCZI = 4$	0	0	0	0	0	0	0	0	0	0	0	0
$DEPI = 7$	0	0	0	0	0	0	0	0	0	0	0	0
$DEPI = 6$	0	0	0	0	0	0	0	0	0	0	0	0
$DEPI = 5$	0	0	1	1	1	1	0	0	0	0	0	0
$CDI = 5$	0	0	0	0	0	0	0	0	1	1	1	1
$CDI = 4$	12	9	29	24	14	13	13	12	11	10	12	9
Miscellaneous Variables												
$Lambda > .99$	16	12	10	8	10	9	7	7	8	7	9	6
$S > 2$	18	13	10	8	16	15	13	12	17	15	18	13
Sum $T = 0$	19	14	14	12	20	18	17	16	6	5	12	9
Sum $T > 1$	11	8	0	0	4	4	2	2	9	8	11	8
$3r + (2)/R < .33$	0	0	6	5	18	16	18	17	7	6	10	7
$3r + (2)/R > .44$	123	91	85	71	62	56	59	56	49	45	74	53
Pure$C > 1$	0	0	0	0	0	0	0	0	0	0	0	0
$Afr < .40$	0	0	6	5	8	7	6	6	5	5	6	4
$Afr < .50$	13	10	45	38	33	30	24	23	19	17	21	15
$(FM + m) <$ Sum Shading	10	7	12	10	11	10	9	9	17	15	20	14
Populars < 4	0	0	4	3	4	4	1	1	3	3	4	3
$COP = 0$	6	4	6	5	10	9	13	12	12	11	20	14
$COP > 2$	13	10	19	16	16	15	18	17	15	14	24	17
$AG = 0$	5	4	21	18	25	23	19	18	28	25	34	24
$AG > 2$	10	7	15	13	8	7	10	10	8	7	11	8
$MOR > 2$	6	4	6	5	2	2	5	5	4	4	5	4
Level 2 $SpSc > 0$	20	15	22	18	13	12	9	9	9	8	7	5
Sum 6 $SpSc > 6$	22	16	17	14	16	15	12	11	9	8	9	6
Pure $H < 2$	27	20	30	25	28	25	18	17	23	21	14	10
Pure $H = 0$	4	3	0	0	0	0	0	0	1	1	1	1
$p > a + 1$	12	9	10	8	7	6	13	12	13	12	15	11
$M^p > M^a$	20	15	18	15	9	8	8	8	16	15	17	12

THE PSYCHIATRIC REFERENCE GROUPS

Tables 45 through 52 include data for the same variables listed in the normative tables for four groups of adult psychiatric subjects. These tables differ considerably from those published earlier as none contain records of less than 14 answers. Each group represents a random selection of between 25% and 50% of the records available for each group.

Although the records for the groups have been randomly selected from larger samples, no effort has been made at stratification, except to choose relatively equal samples of public and private hospital subjects for the two inpatient groups. Therefore, the data for these four groups *should not be considered normative* in any sense. They do provide a source of comparison with findings for adult nonpatients, and this can be useful in establishing a conceptual framework. On the other hand, there is far too much heterogenity in each group to make the data diagnostically practical.

Tables 45 and 46 present data for 320 schizophrenics, 147 from private hospitals and 173 from public hospitals, that were randomly selected from approximately 1100 available records. Tables 47 and 48 include data for 315 inpatient depressives, 184 from private hospitals and 131 from public hospitals, that were randomly selected from approximately 1300 available records. Tables 49 and 50 show data for a group of 440 outpatients beginning treatment for the first time. They reflect a considerable variety of diagnoses, although more than half presented features or complaints of depression during their initial screening. They were randomly selected from a group of nearly 900 available protocols. Tables 51 and 52 contain data for 180 outpatient character problems. Although some have forensic-related problems, none have been adjudicated. They were selected from approximately 370 available records.

Demographic data for each group concerning sex, age, race, marital status, and completed education are included for each group in the tables of frequency data.

REFERENCES

Exner, J. E. (1978) *The Rorschach: A Comprehensive System. Volume 2: Recent research and advanced interpretation.* New York: Wiley.

Exner, J. E. (1991) *The Rorschach: A Comprehensive System. Volume 2: Interpretation,* (2nd Ed.). New York: Wiley.

Exner, J. E. (1985) *A Rorschach Workbook for the Comprehensive System,* (2nd Ed.). Bayville, N.Y.: Rorschach Workshops.

Exner, J. E. (1986) *The Rorschach: A Comprehensive System. Volume 1: Basic Foundations,* (2nd Ed.). New York: Wiley.

Exner, J. E. (1988) Problems with brief Rorschach protocols. *Journal of Personality Assessment,* **4,** 640–647.

Exner, J. E. (1990) *A Rorschach Workbook for the Comprehensive System,* (3rd Ed.). Asheville, N.C.: Rorschach Workshops.

Exner, J. E., and Weiner, I. B. (1982) *The Rorschach: A Comprehensive System. Volume 3: Assessment of children and adolescents.* New York: Wiley.

Exner, J. E., Weiner, I. B., and Schuyler, W. (1976) *A Rorschach Workbook for the Comprehensive System.* Bayville, N.Y.: Rorschach Workshops.

Table 45. Descriptive Statistics for 320 Inpatient Schizophrenics

Variable	Mean	SD	Min	Max	Freq	Median	Mode	SK	KU
R	23.44	8.66	14.00	45.00	320	21.00	19.00	1.21	0.88
W	8.79	5.11	0.00	22.00	317	9.00	10.00	0.68	0.11
D	9.79	6.47	0.00	32.00	313	10.00	10.00	0.82	0.47
Dd	4.86	[5.04]	0.00	21.00	300	3.00	2.00	1.98	3.47
S	2.77	[2.49]	0.00	10.00	257	2.00	2.00	0.96	0.33
DQ+	6.93	4.32	0.00	20.00	288	7.00	6.00	0.23	−0.56
DQo	14.87	7.80	3.00	42.00	320	12.00	9.00	1.46	1.45
DQv	1.43	[1.74]	0.00	8.00	216	1.00	1.00	2.20	5.55
DQv/+	0.21	[0.45]	0.00	2.00	63	0.00	0.00	1.93	2.92
FQX+	0.07	0.31	0.00	2.00	15	0.00	0.00	5.12	26.51
FQXo	8.92	3.39	2.00	18.00	320	9.00	8.00	0.39	0.01
FQXu	4.89	3.17	0.00	14.00	316	4.00	3.00	0.83	−0.12
FQX−	8.95	5.32	0.00	27.00	317	7.00	7.00	1.24	1.30
FQXNone	0.61	[0.95]	0.00	4.00	129	0.00	0.00	1.95	3.85
MQ+	0.05	0.29	0.00	2.00	10	0.00	0.00	6.07	36.52
MQo	2.40	1.96	0.00	7.00	263	2.00	1.00	0.62	−0.63
MQu	1.06	1.17	0.00	5.00	195	1.00	0.00	1.37	2.02
MQ−	2.42	[2.46]	0.00	10.00	256	2.00	1.00	1.32	0.81
MQNone	0.07	[0.25]	0.00	1.00	21	0.00	0.00	3.53	10.49
S−	1.61	[1.77]	0.00	6.00	191	1.00	0.00	0.91	−0.21
M	6.00	4.33	0.00	16.00	289	6.00	6.00	0.57	−0.42
FM	2.41	2.43	0.00	13.00	246	2.00	1.00	1.23	1.24
m	1.18	1.17	0.00	5.00	207	1.00	0.00	1.00	0.87
FM + m	3.59	2.92	0.00	15.00	277	3.00	3.00	0.89	0.35
FC	1.54	1.60	0.00	7.00	227	1.00	1.00	1.12	0.44
CF	1.24	1.38	0.00	5.00	198	1.00	0.00	1.15	0.55
C	0.42	[0.72]	0.00	3.00	101	0.00	0.00	1.97	3.88
Cn	0.06	[0.29]	0.00	2.00	13	0.00	0.00	5.56	31.66
Sum Color	3.25	2.61	0.00	11.00	320	3.00	1.00	1.02	0.82
WGSum C	2.63	2.23	0.00	10.50	320	2.00	1.50	1.13	1.21
Sum C'	1.50	[1.57]	0.00	6.00	224	1.00	1.00	1.27	1.04
Sum T	0.46	[0.99]	0.00	7.00	97	0.00	0.00	3.88	19.29
Sum V	0.60	[1.20]	0.00	7.00	112	0.00	0.00	3.46	14.31
Sum Y	2.12	[2.62]	0.00	9.00	189	1.00	0.00	1.11	−0.07
Sum Shading	4.68	4.51	0.00	23.00	268	3.50	0.00	1.51	2.90
Fr + rF	0.17	[0.48]	0.00	2.00	41	0.00	0.00	2.83	7.15
FD	0.60	[1.08]	0.00	6.00	108	0.00	0.00	2.56	8.29
F	10.46	6.42	1.00	32.00	320	9.00	6.00	1.15	1.01
PAIR	8.53	4.90	0.00	29.00	320	8.00	7.00	0.53	0.33
3r(2)/R	0.38	0.18	0.10	0.75	320	0.37	0.33	−0.08	−0.49
Lambda	1.57	3.47	0.05	29.00	320	0.85	0.33	6.08	41.06
EA	8.63	5.39	2.00	24.00	320	8.00	8.00	0.77	0.43
es	8.27	5.99	3.00	28.00	320	6.50	2.00	0.83	0.07
D	0.14	1.58	−7.00	4.00	320	0.00	0.00	−1.10	5.39
AdjD	0.69	1.45	−4.00	4.00	320	0.00	0.00	0.37	0.74
a (active)	5.51	3.94	0.00	16.00	290	5.00	4.00	0.76	0.19
p (passive)	4.25	3.28	0.00	14.00	291	4.00	2.00	0.81	−0.17
M^a	3.38	2.76	0.00	10.00	267	3.00	2.00	0.68	−0.44
M^p	2.75	2.54	0.00	9.00	260	2.00	1.00	0.89	−0.22
Intellect	1.32	1.88	0.00	8.00	320	1.00	0.00	1.84	3.08
Zf	12.67	5.21	2.00	26.00	320	12.00	11.00	0.66	0.44
Zd	1.33	4.93	−11.50	13.50	320	1.50	−5.00	0.08	−0.21
Blends	4.28	3.97	0.00	19.00	273	3.00	0.00	1.43	2.27
Col Shd Bl	0.67	[1.26]	0.00	7.00	109	0.00	0.00	2.73	8.99

Note: Standard deviations shown in brackets indicate that the value is probably unreliable and/or misleading and should not be used to estimate expected ranges. Ordinarily, these variables should not be included in most parametric analyses.

Table 45. (Continued)

Variable	Mean	SD	Min	Max	Freq	Median	Mode	SK	KU
Afr	0.52	0.20	0.18	1.25	320	0.50	0.33	0.77	0.95
Populars	4.67	2.08	1.00	10.00	320	5.00	4.00	0.29	−0.30
X + %	0.40	0.14	0.13	0.77	320	0.40	0.35	0.22	−0.18
F + %	0.42	0.20	0.00	1.00	301	0.40	0.50	0.39	0.75
X − %	0.37	0.14	0.05	0.72	320	0.37	0.32	−0.11	0.14
Xu%	0.20	0.09	0.00	0.43	316	0.19	0.27	0.35	−0.29
S − %	0.20	[0.22]	0.00	0.83	191	0.14	0.00	0.92	−0.04
Isolate	0.15	0.13	0.00	0.54	320	0.13	0.00	1.15	1.17
H	3.17	2.44	0.00	9.00	273	3.00	2.00	0.62	−0.36
(H)	1.60	1.45	0.00	8.00	267	1.00	1.00	1.80	4.27
Hd	1.88	2.18	0.00	9.00	212	1.00	0.00	1.61	2.35
(Hd)	0.77	0.98	0.00	6.00	168	1.00	0.00	2.12	7.38
Hx	0.14	[0.49]	0.00	3.00	27	0.00	0.00	3.89	15.22
All *H* Cont	7.41	4.19	0.00	21.00	315	7.00	8.00	0.69	0.47
A	8.21	3.53	3.00	27.00	320	7.00	7.00	1.08	2.00
(A)	0.53	[0.85]	0.00	3.00	109	0.00	0.00	1.50	1.24
Ad	2.03	[1.88]	0.00	10.00	235	2.00	0.00	1.06	1.76
(Ad)	0.27	[0.62]	0.00	3.00	57	0.00	0.00	2.38	4.90
An	0.98	[1.49]	0.00	8.00	148	0.00	0.00	2.11	5.12
Art	0.73	1.41	0.00	7.00	102	0.00	0.00	2.67	7.84
Ay	0.21	[0.48]	0.00	5.00	62	0.00	0.00	3.96	29.41
Bl	0.32	[0.79]	0.00	5.00	73	0.00	0.00	4.09	20.40
Bt	0.82	1.04	0.00	5.00	162	1.00	0.00	1.54	2.85
Cg	1.83	1.88	0.00	9.00	232	1.00	0.00	1.38	1.93
Cl	0.26	[0.66]	0.00	4.00	60	0.00	0.00	3.55	15.34
Ex	0.11	[0.33]	0.00	2.00	33	0.00	0.00	3.02	8.82
Fi	0.38	[0.59]	0.00	2.00	103	0.00	0.00	1.31	0.69
Fd	0.32	[0.67]	0.00	4.00	74	0.00	0.00	2.61	7.45
Ge	0.18	[0.53]	0.00	2.00	39	0.00	0.00	2.79	6.43
Hh	0.38	0.93	0.00	6.00	72	0.00	0.00	3.38	12.92
Ls	0.44	0.85	0.00	4.00	88	0.00	0.00	2.20	4.59
Na	0.72	[1.00]	0.00	4.00	138	0.00	0.00	1.35	1.04
Sc	0.49	[0.69]	0.00	3.00	124	0.00	0.00	1.25	0.92
Sx	1.36	[2.16]	0.00	8.00	146	0.00	0.00	1.85	2.63
Xy	0.16	[0.45]	0.00	2.00	42	0.00	0.00	2.83	7.43
Idio	2.56	2.33	0.00	10.00	266	2.00	1.00	1.38	2.04
DV	0.78	[1.18]	0.00	7.00	141	0.00	0.00	2.11	5.25
INCOM	1.53	[1.44]	0.00	6.00	226	1.00	0.00	0.90	0.44
DR	0.97	[1.49]	0.00	7.00	148	0.00	0.00	2.31	6.04
FABCOM	0.72	[1.07]	0.00	5.00	140	0.00	0.00	1.99	4.37
DV2	0.28	[0.57]	0.00	5.00	75	0.00	0.00	2.96	15.03
INC2	1.17	[1.68]	0.00	7.00	157	0.00	0.00	1.76	2.78
DR2	1.90	[2.80]	0.00	14.00	182	1.00	0.00	1.97	4.04
FAB2	1.83	[2.04]	0.00	9.00	202	1.00	0.00	1.12	0.39
ALOG	0.93	[1.40]	0.00	6.00	141	0.00	0.00	1.83	3.32
CONTAM	0.13	0.41	0.00	2.00	35	0.00	0.00	3.18	9.84
Sum6 Sp Sc	9.07	3.23	2.00	15.00	320	5.00	4.00	1.09	1.29
Sum6 Sp Sc2	5.18	[4.92]	0.00	25.00	277	3.00	1.00	1.09	0.57
WSum6	44.69	35.40	0.00	173.00	320	32.00	32.00	1.07	0.74
AB	0.19	[0.45]	0.00	2.00	52	0.00	0.00	2.40	5.18
AG	1.26	1.85	0.00	9.00	161	1.00	0.00	2.05	4.49
CFB	0.05	0.26	0.00	2.00	8	0.00	0.00	6.12	38.81
COP	0.81	1.03	0.00	5.00	158	0.00	0.00	1.36	1.73
CP	0.04	[0.19]	0.00	1.00	12	0.00	0.00	4.89	22.07
MOR	1.47	[1.71]	0.00	7.00	192	1.00	0.00	1.31	1.31
PER	1.22	1.97	0.00	15.00	166	1.00	0.00	2.95	11.91
PSV	0.13	[0.37]	0.00	2.00	37	0.00	0.00	2.95	8.56

Table 46.   Frequency Data for 320 Inpatient Schizophrenics

Demography Variables

Marital Status			Age			Race		
Single	232	73%	18–25	154	48%	White	271	85%
Lives w/S.O.	0	0%	26–35	83	26%	Black	26	8%
Married	70	22%	36–45	45	14%	Hispanic	23	7%
Separated	8	2%	46–55	14	4%	Asian	0	0%
Divorced	10	3%						
Widowed	0	0%				Education		
						Under 12	47	15%
Sex						12 Years	133	42%
Male	153	48%				13–15 Yrs	94	29%
Female	167	52%				16+ Yrs	46	14%

Ratios, Percentages, and Special Indices

EB Style			Form Quality Deviations		
Introversive	191	60%	$X + \% > .89$	0	0%
Pervasive	128	40%	$X + \% < .70$	309	97%
Ambitent	95	30%	$X + \% < .61$	300	94%
Extratensive	34	11%	$X + \% < .50$	234	73%
Pervasive	19	6%	$F + \% < .70$	286	89%
			$Xu\% > .20$	142	44%
D Score & Adjusted D Score			$X - \% > .15$	290	91%
			$X - \% > .20$	288	90%
D Score > 0	99	31%	$X - \% > .30$	221	69%
D Score $= 0$	152	48%			
D Score < 0	69	22%			
D Score < -1	19	6%	FC:CF + C Ratio		
			$FC > (CF + C) + 2$	38	12%
$Adj\ D$ Score > 0	132	41%	$FC > (CF + C) + 1$	51	16%
$Adj\ D$ Score $= 0$	153	48%	$(CF + C) > FC + 1$	81	25%
$Adj\ D$ Score < 0	35	11%	$(CF + C) > FC + 2$	44	14%
$Adj\ D$ Score < -1	12	4%			
$Zd > +3.0$ (Overincorp)	121	38%	S-Constellation Positive	18	6%
$Zd < -3.0$ (Underincorp)	82	26%	HVI Positive	56	18%
			OBS Positive	0	0%

$SCZI = 6$	106	33%	$DEPI = 7$	3	1%	$CDI = 5$	22	7%
$SCZI = 5$	83	26%	$DEPI = 6$	15	5%	$CDI = 4$	57	18%
$SCZI = 4$	72	23%	$DEPI = 5$	42	13%			

Miscellaneous Variables

$Lambda > .99$	124	39%	$(2AB + Art + Ay) > 5$	38	12%
$Dd > 3$	151	47%	Populars < 4	101	32%
$DQv + DQv/+ > 2$	63	20%	Populars > 7	20	6%
$S > 2$	136	43%	$COP = 0$	162	51%
Sum $T = 0$	223	70%	$COP > 2$	23	7%
Sum $T > 1$	22	7%	$AG = 0$	159	50%
$3r + (2)/R < .33$	112	35%	$AG > 2$	53	17%
$3r + (2)/R > .44$	115	36%	$MOR > 2$	71	22%
$Fr + rF > 0$	41	13%	Level 2 Sp.Sc. > 0	277	87%
$PureC > 0$	101	32%	Sum 6 Sp.Sc. > 6	217	68%
$PureC > 1$	21	7%	Pure $H < 2$	92	29%
$Afr < .40$	99	31%	Pure $H = 0$	47	15%
$Afr < .50$	151	47%	$p > a + 1$	60	19%
$(FM + m) <$ Sum Shading	131	41%	$M^p > M^a$	111	35%

Table 47. Descriptive Statistics for 315 Inpatient Depressives

Variable	Mean	SD	Min	Max	Freq	Median	Mode	SK	KU
R	22.70	8.52	14.00	41.00	315	19.00	19.00	1.56	2.59
W	8.48	4.13	0.00	18.00	306	9.00	9.00	−0.07	−0.79
D	9.94	6.01	1.00	30.00	315	8.00	7.00	1.06	0.95
Dd	4.28	[5.25]	0.00	21.00	275	3.00	2.00	2.55	7.97
S	2.51	[2.30]	0.00	10.00	261	2.00	1.00	1.35	1.97
DQ+	5.96	3.33	0.00	18.00	308	5.00	4.00	0.77	0.82
DQo	13.99	7.86	4.00	46.00	315	12.00	11.00	1.73	3.57
DQv	2.46	[1.97]	0.00	8.00	262	2.00	1.00	0.72	−0.08
DQv/+	0.29	[0.63]	0.00	3.00	64	0.00	0.00	2.12	3.58
FQX+	0.04	0.24	0.00	3.00	11	0.00	0.00	7.80	76.85
FQXo	11.76	4.28	4.00	28.00	315	11.00	11.00	0.82	1.06
FQXu	5.20	3.24	1.00	14.00	315	5.00	2.00	0.79	0.10
FQX−	4.70	3.35	0.00	18.00	302	4.00	2.00	1.37	2.71
FQXNone	1.00	[1.29]	0.00	6.00	166	1.00	0.00	1.46	1.73
MQ+	0.02	0.18	0.00	2.00	7	0.00	0.00	7.71	65.72
MQo	2.25	1.46	0.00	6.00	288	2.00	2.00	0.69	0.12
MQu	0.64	0.95	0.00	5.00	127	0.00	0.00	1.93	5.19
MQ−	0.58	[0.81]	0.00	4.00	127	0.00	0.00	1.33	1.57
MQNone	0.08	[0.27]	0.00	1.00	25	0.00	0.00	3.13	7.83
S−	1.04	[1.21]	0.00	5.00	179	1.00	0.00	1.27	1.16
M	3.57	2.17	0.00	9.00	300	3.00	4.00	0.50	−0.31
FM	3.12	2.76	0.00	14.00	278	3.00	2.00	1.86	4.81
m	1.69	1.89	0.00	11.00	217	1.00	0.00	2.15	7.45
FM + m	4.81	3.62	0.00	15.00	294	4.00	3.00	1.06	0.89
FC	1.58	1.95	0.00	11.00	194	1.00	0.00	1.97	5.60
CF	1.58	1.38	0.00	8.00	236	1.00	1.00	1.09	2.16
C	0.72	[0.99]	0.00	4.00	142	0.00	0.00	1.51	2.00
Cn	0.03	[0.18]	0.00	1.00	10	0.00	0.00	5.37	26.98
Sum Color	3.91	2.52	0.00	12.00	291	4.00	2.00	0.53	0.11
WGSum C	3.45	2.15	0.00	9.00	291	3.50	4.00	0.27	−0.66
Sum C'	2.16	[1.79]	0.00	8.00	245	2.00	0.00	0.68	0.10
Sum T	0.86	[1.35]	0.00	7.00	136	0.00	0.00	2.29	6.25
Sum V	1.09	[1.23]	0.00	5.00	175	1.00	0.00	0.94	0.06
Sum Y	1.81	[1.40]	0.00	8.00	247	2.00	3.00	0.78	1.92
Sum Shading	5.92	3.72	0.00	18.00	309	5.00	4.00	0.90	0.48
Fr + rF	0.12	[0.36]	0.00	2.00	33	0.00	0.00	3.18	10.12
FD	0.82	[1.03]	0.00	4.00	159	1.00	0.00	1.26	1.00
F	9.20	5.68	1.00	33.00	315	8.00	9.00	1.62	3.76
PAIR	7.01	3.94	1.00	21.00	315	6.00	5.00	1.18	1.51
3r(2)/R	0.33	0.15	0.06	0.67	315	0.31	0.33	0.48	−0.47
Lambda	0.94	1.68	0.08	15.00	315	0.67	0.36	7.50	60.29
EA	7.03	3.56	2.00	18.00	315	6.00	5.00	0.81	0.60
es	10.73	5.48	1.00	27.00	315	11.00	13.00	0.34	−0.06
D	−1.22	1.72	−6.00	3.00	315	−1.00	0.00	−0.67	0.27
AdjD	−0.57	1.52	−6.00	3.00	315	0.00	0.00	−1.14	3.09
a (active)	4.79	3.19	0.00	14.00	292	5.00	6.00	0.56	−0.16
p (passive)	3.66	2.53	0.00	11.00	293	3.00	3.00	0.82	0.32
M^a	1.94	1.68	0.00	7.00	245	2.00	2.00	0.95	0.56
M^p	1.67	1.41	0.00	6.00	242	2.00	2.00	0.96	1.05
Intellect	2.39	2.10	0.00	10.00	315	2.00	0.00	0.86	0.66
Zf	11.38	4.31	1.00	25.00	315	12.00	13.00	0.15	0.11
Zd	−0.33	4.90	−12.50	13.00	315	0.50	4.50	−0.40	0.01
Blends	4.50	3.17	0.00	15.00	292	4.00	6.00	0.67	0.15
Col Shd Bl	0.95	[1.13]	0.00	5.00	179	1.00	0.00	1.44	2.03

Note: Standard deviations shown in brackets indicate that the value is probably unreliable and/or misleading and should not be used to estimate expected ranges. Ordinarily, these variables should not be included in most parametric analyses.

Table 47. (Continued)

Variable	Mean	SD	Min	Max	Freq	Median	Mode	SK	KU
Afr	0.47	0.16	0.16	1.00	315	0.43	0.36	0.85	0.85
Populars	5.22	1.90	2.00	10.00	315	5.00	4.00	0.19	−0.91
X + %	0.53	0.11	0.27	0.81	315	0.51	0.47	−0.05	−0.50
F + %	0.52	0.21	0.00	1.00	302	0.54	0.50	−0.55	0.34
X − %	0.20	0.10	0.00	0.44	302	0.18	0.13	0.15	−0.70
Xu%	0.22	0.10	0.04	0.47	315	0.24	0.24	0.03	−0.59
S − %	0.21	[0.25]	0.00	1.00	179	0.13	0.00	1.16	0.98
Isolate	0.17	0.12	0.00	0.53	315	0.16	0.00	0.50	−0.05
H	2.05	1.45	0.00	7.00	291	2.00	1.00	0.96	0.53
(H)	1.12	1.02	0.00	6.00	226	1.00	1.00	1.35	3.70
Hd	1.26	1.44	0.00	6.00	192	1.00	0.00	1.38	1.68
(Hd)	0.78	1.11	0.00	5.00	151	0.00	0.00	1.99	4.52
Hx	0.04	[0.19]	0.00	1.00	12	0.00	0.00	4.85	21.65
All *H* Cont	5.21	2.92	1.00	15.00	315	5.00	4.00	1.04	1.22
A	7.57	3.28	3.00	17.00	315	7.00	5.00	0.82	0.05
(A)	0.48	[0.97]	0.00	5.00	96	0.00	0.00	3.08	11.07
Ad	2.37	[2.69]	0.00	19.00	258	2.00	1.00	3.80	20.97
(Ad)	0.20	[0.43]	0.00	2.00	60	0.00	0.00	1.94	2.92
An	1.05	[1.57]	0.00	7.00	150	0.00	0.00	1.94	3.66
Art	1.62	1.67	0.00	9.00	215	1.00	0.00	1.24	2.10
Ay	0.27	[0.50]	0.00	2.00	76	0.00	0.00	1.69	2.01
Bl	0.48	[1.06]	0.00	6.00	73	0.00	0.00	2.95	10.48
Bt	0.94	1.22	0.00	5.00	158	1.00	0.00	1.35	1.19
Cg	1.80	1.47	0.00	8.00	267	1.00	1.00	1.36	2.90
Cl	0.29	[0.54]	0.00	2.00	78	0.00	0.00	1.71	2.02
Ex	0.17	[0.44]	0.00	2.00	46	0.00	0.00	2.61	6.30
Fi	0.57	[0.74]	0.00	3.00	140	0.00	0.00	1.26	1.25
Fd	0.37	[0.64]	0.00	3.00	93	0.00	0.00	1.71	2.49
Ge	0.16	[0.47]	0.00	4.00	42	0.00	0.00	4.48	28.11
Hh	0.53	0.87	0.00	4.00	115	0.00	0.00	2.11	5.08
Ls	1.04	1.18	0.00	5.00	175	1.00	0.00	0.99	0.27
Na	0.49	[0.71]	0.00	3.00	119	0.00	0.00	1.19	0.42
Sc	0.75	[1.10]	0.00	5.00	130	0.00	0.00	1.69	2.97
Sx	0.73	[1.22]	0.00	5.00	110	0.00	0.00	1.76	2.30
Xy	0.16	[0.46]	0.00	2.00	41	0.00	0.00	2.84	7.40
Idio	1.73	1.55	0.00	7.00	244	1.00	1.00	1.14	1.47
DV	0.69	[0.98]	0.00	6.00	136	0.00	0.00	1.96	6.54
INCOM	1.18	[1.20]	0.00	6.00	206	1.00	0.00	1.11	1.41
DR	0.88	[1.41]	0.00	5.00	116	0.00	0.00	1.49	0.91
FABCOM	0.52	[1.01]	0.00	5.00	100	0.00	0.00	2.85	9.31
DV2	0.22	[0.58]	0.00	4.00	54	0.00	0.00	3.59	16.67
INC2	0.64	[0.95]	0.00	5.00	134	0.00	0.00	1.92	4.12
DR2	0.55	[1.27]	0.00	6.00	95	0.00	0.00	2.77	7.31
FAB2	0.50	[0.85]	0.00	5.00	79	0.00	0.00	2.31	6.60
ALOG	0.13	[0.34]	0.00	2.00	39	0.00	0.00	2.49	5.06
CONTAM	0.00	0.00	0.00	0.00	0	0.00	0.00	—	—
Sum6 Sp Sc	3.40	2.20	1.00	9.00	315	3.00	3.00	0.78	0.31
Sum6 Sp Sc2	1.41	[2.18]	0.00	7.00	225	1.00	0.00	1.76	3.63
WSum6	18.20	13.68	2.00	55.00	315	16.00	4.00	0.91	0.41
AB	0.25	[0.61]	0.00	3.00	54	0.00	0.00	2.39	4.83
AG	0.56	0.93	0.00	4.00	109	0.00	0.00	1.77	2.63
CFB	0.00	0.00	0.00	0.00	0	0.00	0.00	—	—
COP	0.72	0.83	0.00	3.00	159	1.00	0.00	0.85	−0.22
CP	0.04	[0.20]	0.00	1.00	13	0.00	0.00	4.63	19.60
MOR	1.56	[1.87]	0.00	8.00	219	1.00	1.00	1.79	2.82
PER	1.85	2.40	0.00	9.00	180	1.00	0.00	1.38	1.05
PSV	0.33	[0.67]	0.00	2.00	69	0.00	0.00	1.76	1.53

310

Table 48   311

Table 48.   Frequency Data for 315 Inpatient Depressives

Demography Variables

Marital Status			Age			Race		
Single	110	35%	18–25	58	18%	White	254	81%
Lives w/S.O.	0	0%	26–35	56	18%	Black	36	11%
Married	161	51%	36–45	70	22%	Hispanic	25	8%
Separated	17	5%	46–55	75	24%	Asian	0	0%
Divorced	19	6%	56–65	24	8%			
Widowed	8	3%	Over 65	6	2%	Education		
						Under 12	43	14%
Sex						12 Years	104	33%
Male	129	41%				13–15 Yrs	69	22%
Female	186	59%				16+ Yrs	99	31%

Ratios, Percentages, and Special Indices

EB Style			Form Quality Deviations		
Introversive	80	25%	$X + \% > .89$	0	0%
Pervasive	39	12%	$X + \% < .70$	294	93%
Ambitent	177	56%	$X + \% < .61$	229	73%
Extratensive	58	18%	$X + \% < .50$	129	41%
Pervasive	33	10%	$F + \% < .70$	248	79%
			$Xu\% > .20$	193	61%
D Score & Adjusted D Score			$X - \% > .15$	188	60%
D Score > 0	37	12%	$X - \% > .20$	143	45%
D Score $= 0$	105	33%	$X - \% > .30$	51	16%
D Score < 0	173	55%			
D Score < -1	140	44%	FC:CF + C Ratio		
			$FC > (CF + C) + 2$	30	10%
Adj D Score > 0	56	18%	$FC > (CF + C) + 1$	53	17%
Adj D Score $= 0$	125	40%	$(CF + C) > FC + 1$	116	37%
Adj D Score < 0	134	43%	$(CF + C) > FC + 2$	60	19%
Adj D Score < -1	68	22%			
Zd $> +3.0$ (Overincorp)	81	26%	S-Constellation Positive	16	5%
Zd < -3.0 (Underincorp)	79	25%	HVI Positive	32	10%
			OBS Positive	0	0%

SCZI $= 6$	2	1%	DEPI $= 7$	28	9%	CDI $= 5$	50	16%
SCZI $= 5$	6	2%	DEPI $= 6$	95	30%	CDI $= 4$	88	28%
SCZI $= 4$	24	8%	DEPI $= 5$	114	36%			

Miscellaneous Variables

Lambda $> .99$	93	30%	$(2AB + Art + Ay) > 5$	94	30%
Dd > 3	110	35%	Populars < 4	59	19%
$DQv + DQv/+ > 2$	158	50%	Populars > 7	57	18%
S > 2	130	41%	COP $= 0$	156	50%
Sum T $= 0$	179	57%	COP > 2	9	3%
Sum T > 1	71	23%	AG $= 0$	206	65%
$3r + (2)/R < .33$	163	52%	AG > 2	19	6%
$3r + (2)/R > .44$	75	24%	MOR > 2	58	18%
Fr + rF > 0	33	10%	Level 2 Sp.Sc. > 0	225	71%
PureC > 0	142	45%	Sum 6 Sp.Sc. > 6	118	37%
PureC > 1	58	18%	Pure H < 2	142	45%
Afr $< .40$	107	34%	Pure H $= 0$	24	8%
Afr $< .50$	180	57%	$p > a + 1$	72	23%
$(FM + m) <$ Sum Shading	191	61%	$M^p > M^a$	107	34%

Table 49. Descriptive Statistics for 440 Outpatients

Variable	Mean	SD	Min	Max	Freq	Median	Mode	SK	KU
R	20.41	5.18	14.00	55.00	440	20.00	19.00	2.77	12.65
W	7.72	3.02	1.00	16.00	440	7.00	7.00	0.19	−0.74
D	9.59	4.18	0.00	26.00	424	8.00	5.00	1.02	1.04
Dd	3.09	[3.30]	0.00	26.00	378	3.00	1.00	3.42	19.81
S	1.97	[1.69]	0.00	7.00	324	2.00	1.00	0.80	0.17
DQ+	5.85	3.23	0.00	15.00	438	5.00	3.00	0.85	0.97
DQo	12.92	5.26	5.00	47.00	440	11.00	9.00	3.03	16.55
DQv	1.42	[1.63]	0.00	6.00	267	1.00	0.00	1.15	0.45
DQv/+	0.22	[0.57]	0.00	5.00	80	0.00	0.00	4.25	26.28
FQx+	0.61	1.38	0.00	5.00	101	0.00	0.00	2.29	3.87
FQxo	12.63	3.15	6.00	26.00	440	11.00	12.00	0.46	0.39
FQxu	3.41	2.69	0.00	17.00	412	3.00	3.00	1.86	5.30
FQx−	3.14	2.59	0.00	19.00	407	3.00	1.00	2.42	11.46
FQxNone	0.62	[0.99]	0.00	3.00	154	0.00	0.00	1.43	0.72
MQ+	0.48	1.10	0.00	4.00	89	0.00	0.00	2.23	3.60
MQo	2.31	1.65	0.00	8.00	403	2.00	1.00	0.92	0.60
MQu	0.51	0.77	0.00	3.00	161	0.00	0.00	1.51	1.69
MQ−	0.39	[0.71]	0.00	4.00	126	0.00	0.00	2.14	5.57
MQNone	0.03	[0.19]	0.00	2.00	9	0.00	0.00	7.37	36.22
SQual−	0.69	[0.98]	0.00	5.00	200	0.00	0.00	1.83	3.84
M	3.68	2.49	0.00	11.00	408	4.00	4.00	0.86	0.81
FM	2.30	1.70	0.00	8.00	372	2.00	2.00	0.79	0.55
m	1.19	1.24	0.00	5.00	267	1.00	0.00	0.88	0.17
FC	1.23	1.27	0.00	6.00	312	1.00	1.00	1.58	2.67
CF	1.82	1.42	0.00	6.00	281	2.00	1.00	1.20	1.27
C	0.64	[1.01]	0.00	4.00	163	0.00	0.00	1.57	1.62
Cn	0.02	[0.15]	0.00	1.00	10	0.00	0.00	6.43	39.48
Sum Color	3.72	1.95	0.00	9.00	424	4.00	3.00	1.03	1.26
WSumC	3.90	1.96	0.00	9.50	424	4.00	2.50	1.14	1.88
Sum C'	0.86	[1.12]	0.00	5.00	231	1.00	0.00	1.64	2.37
Sum T	0.46	[0.78]	0.00	3.00	140	0.00	0.00	1.87	2.97
Sum V	0.42	[0.78]	0.00	3.00	116	0.00	0.00	1.82	2.32
Sum Y	0.88	[0.93]	0.00	6.00	264	1.00	0.00	1.22	2.32
Sum Shading	2.81	2.32	0.00	11.00	391	2.00	1.00	1.27	0.97
Fr + rF	0.28	[0.63]	0.00	6.00	42	0.00	0.00	4.37	23.74
FD	0.87	[0.91]	0.00	5.00	269	1.00	1.00	1.36	2.96
F	8.93	5.11	2.00	39.00	440	8.00	7.00	2.47	10.43
(2)	7.83	3.79	2.00	24.00	440	8.00	6.00	1.77	4.46
3r + (2)/R	0.41	0.14	0.12	1.25	440	0.40	0.40	0.64	2.27
Lambda	1.16	1.26	0.11	7.67	440	0.77	1.00	3.00	9.96
FM + m	3.48	2.31	0.00	11.00	388	4.00	4.00	0.39	0.10
EA	6.78	3.42	0.00	16.50	439	6.50	6.00	1.03	1.34
es	6.09	3.78	1.00	17.00	440	6.00	5.00	0.60	−0.37
D Score	0.11	1.23	−4.00	5.00	199	0.00	0.00	−0.01	3.45
AdjD	0.38	1.12	−3.00	5.00	211	0.00	0.00	0.77	2.66
a (active)	3.92	2.44	0.00	11.00	414	3.00	3.00	0.55	−0.25
p (passive)	3.24	2.52	0.00	11.00	378	2.00	2.00	0.52	−0.61
M^a	1.90	1.65	0.00	8.00	349	2.00	2.00	1.08	1.10
M^p	1.78	1.53	0.00	8.00	320	2.00	2.00	0.84	1.19
Intellect	1.98	1.96	0.00	7.00	311	2.00	0.00	0.86	−0.36
Zf	10.62	3.55	2.00	23.00	440	10.00	10.00	0.34	1.04
Zd	0.10	4.09	−9.00	10.00	431	−0.50	5.00	0.46	−0.50
Blends	3.91	2.23	0.00	8.00	384	5.00	3.00	0.58	−0.65
Blends/R	0.22	0.12	0.00	0.50	384	0.19	0.16	0.63	−0.17
Col-Shd Bl	0.63	[0.78]	0.00	3.00	207	0.00	0.00	1.09	0.58
Afr	0.53	0.18	0.13	1.25	440	0.50	0.50	1.80	4.14

Table 49. (Continued)

Variable	Mean	SD	Min	Max	Freq	Median	Mode	SK	KU
Populars	5.56	2.22	0.00	10.00	428	5.50	5.00	−0.27	−0.35
X + %	0.64	0.14	0.27	0.89	440	0.64	0.63	−0.25	−0.50
F + %	0.66	0.19	0.13	1.00	440	0.67	0.71	−0.45	0.22
X − %	0.16	0.10	0.00	0.44	407	0.14	0.07	0.61	−0.14
Xu%	0.17	0.10	0.00	0.42	412	0.15	0.11	0.35	−0.47
S − %	0.21	[0.29]	0.00	1.00	200	0.00	0.00	1.36	1.03
Isolate/R	0.14	0.16	0.00	0.81	347	0.11	0.00	2.75	9.01
H	2.10	1.29	0.00	7.00	422	2.00	1.00	1.00	1.32
(H)	1.07	1.18	0.00	5.00	250	1.00	0.00	0.91	0.08
HD	1.45	2.19	0.00	18.00	311	1.00	1.00	4.58	28.90
(Hd)	0.54	0.82	0.00	3.00	156	0.00	0.00	1.33	0.70
Hx	0.06	[0.30]	0.00	2.00	16	0.00	0.00	5.74	32.95
All H Cont	5.16	3.24	0.00	27.00	424	5.00	4.00	2.98	17.20
A	7.50	2.65	3.00	15.00	440	7.00	5.00	0.61	−0.30
(A)	0.33	[0.67]	0.00	3.00	107	0.00	0.00	2.37	5.67
Ad	1.69	[1.70]	0.00	11.00	343	1.00	1.00	1.92	4.85
(Ad)	0.08	[0.29]	0.00	2.00	35	0.00	0.00	3.54	12.54
An	0.56	[0.86]	0.00	5.00	171	0.00	0.00	2.01	5.67
Art	1.22	1.22	0.00	5.00	273	1.00	0.00	0.68	−0.48
Ay	0.16	[0.37]	0.00	1.00	71	0.00	0.00	1.85	1.42
Bl	0.26	[0.61]	0.00	3.00	85	0.00	0.00	2.92	9.21
Bt	1.18	1.23	0.00	4.00	279	1.00	0.00	0.98	0.07
Cg	1.71	1.58	0.00	6.00	305	2.00	0.00	0.72	−0.21
Cl	0.14	[0.43]	0.00	2.00	47	0.00	0.00	3.21	9.76
Ex	0.19	[0.46]	0.00	2.00	70	0.00	0.00	2.45	5.40
Fi	0.25	[0.46]	0.00	2.00	102	0.00	0.00	1.60	1.52
Food	0.25	[0.53]	0.00	2.00	88	0.00	0.00	2.08	3.40
Ge	0.02	[0.13]	0.00	1.00	8	0.00	0.00	7.24	50.60
Hh	0.60	0.99	0.00	4.00	141	0.00	0.00	1.62	2.04
Ls	0.68	1.07	0.00	6.00	171	0.00	0.00	2.05	5.46
Na	0.23	[0.79]	0.00	4.00	49	0.00	0.00	4.13	16.56
Sc	0.51	[0.81]	0.00	5.00	157	0.00	0.00	2.15	7.06
Sx	0.51	[0.95]	0.00	5.00	131	0.00	0.00	2.27	5.49
Xy	0.11	[0.31]	0.00	1.00	48	0.00	0.00	2.52	4.35
Idio	0.92	1.16	0.00	5.00	222	1.00	0.00	1.26	0.93
DV	0.95	[1.18]	0.00	5.00	247	1.00	0.00	1.81	3.86
INCOM	1.01	[1.09]	0.00	4.00	264	1.00	0.00	1.04	0.45
DR	0.25	[0.72]	0.00	4.00	57	0.00	0.00	3.22	10.50
FABCOM	0.51	[0.80]	0.00	4.00	155	0.00	0.00	1.67	2.82
DV2	0.10	[0.30]	0.00	1.00	45	0.00	0.00	2.63	4.96
INC2	0.19	[0.58]	0.00	4.00	53	0.00	0.00	3.92	18.00
DR2	0.10	[0.71]	0.00	10.00	25	0.00	0.00	12.74	175.89
FAB2	0.21	[0.62]	0.00	3.00	58	0.00	0.00	3.40	11.46
ALOG	0.17	[0.49]	0.00	3.00	55	0.00	0.00	3.13	9.81
CONTAM	0.00	0.00	0.00	0.00	0	0.00	0.00	—	—
Sum 6 SpSc	3.48	2.99	0.00	21.00	407	3.00	1.00	1.67	4.97
Lvl 2 SpSc	0.60	[1.28]	0.00	11.00	156	0.00	0.00	4.63	28.43
WSum6	9.59	10.96	0.00	97.00	407	8.00	1.00	3.35	19.27
AB	0.30	[0.52]	0.00	3.00	120	0.00	0.00	1.72	3.18
AG	0.97	1.24	0.00	8.00	199	1.00	0.00	2.37	9.40
CFB	0.00	0.00	0.00	0.00	0	0.00	0.00	—	—
COP	1.09	1.20	0.00	6.00	267	1.00	0.00	1.35	2.31
CP	0.02	[0.13]	0.00	1.00	8	0.00	0.00	7.24	50.60
MOR	1.13	[1.21]	0.00	6.00	285	1.00	1.00	1.84	3.49
PER	1.06	1.60	0.00	10.00	201	0.00	0.00	2.23	7.45
PSV	0.15	[0.48]	0.00	3.00	49	0.00	0.00	3.98	17.92

Table 50. Frequency Data for 440 Outpatients

Demography Variables

Marital Status			Age			Race		
Single	132	30%	18–25	84	19%	White	341	78%
Lives w/S.O.	46	10%	26–35	170	39%	Black	47	11%
Married	175	40%	36–45	104	24%	Hispanic	41	9%
Separated	49	11%	46–55	18	4%	Asian	11	3%
Divorced	34	8%	56–65	34	8%			
Widowed	4	1%	Over 65	7	2%	Education		
						Under 12	58	13%
Sex						12 Yrs	96	22%
Male	186	42%				13–15 Yrs	211	48%
Female	254	58%				16+ Yrs	75	17%

Ratios, Percentages, and Special Indices

EB Style			Form Quality Deviations		
Introversive	134	31%	$X + \% > .89$	1	0%
Pervasive	118	27%	$X + \% < .70$	276	63%
Ambitent	193	44%	$X + \% < .61$	173	39%
Extratensive	113	26%	$X + \% < .50$	54	12%
Pervasive	81	18%	$F + \% < .70$	237	54%
			$Xu\% > .20$	151	34%
D Score			$X - \% > .15$	202	46%
D Score > 0	92	21%	$X - \% > .20$	138	31%
D Score $= 0$	261	59%	$X - \% > .30$	34	8%
D Score < 0	87	20%			
D Score < -1	25	6%			

Adjusted D Score			FC:CF + C Ratio		
Adj D Score > 0	113	26%	$FC > (CF + C) + 2$	26	6%
Adj D Score $= 0$	269	61%	$FC > (CF + C) + 1$	60	14%
Adj D Score < 0	58	13%	$(CF + C) > FC + 1$	153	35%
Adj D Score < -1	13	3%	$(CF + C) > FC + 2$	88	20%
Zd $> +3.0$ (Overincorp)	106	24%	S-Con Positive	35	8%
Zd < -3.0 (Underincorp)	123	28%	HVI Positive	19	4%
			OBS Positive	26	6%

$SCZI = 6$	1	0%	$DEPI = 7$	6	1%	$CDI = 5$	41	9%
$SCZI = 5$	2	0%	$DEPI = 6$	12	3%	$CDI = 4$	84	19%
$SCZI = 4$	5	1%	$DEPI = 5$	71	16%			

Miscellaneous Variables

Lambda $> .99$	167	38%	$(2AB + Art + Ay) > 5$	94	21%
$Dd > 3$	177	40%	Populars < 4	69	16%
$DQv + DQv/+ > 2$	108	25%	Populars > 7	98	22%
$S > 2$	148	34%	$COP = 0$	173	39%
Sum $T = 0$	280	64%	$COP > 2$	43	10%
Sum $T > 1$	41	9%	$AG = 0$	201	46%
$3r + (2)/R < .33$	121	28%	$AG > 2$	44	10%
$3r + (2)/R > .44$	136	31%	$MOR > 2$	62	14%
$Fr + rF > 0$	42	10%	Lvl 2 Sp.Sc. > 0	156	35%
PureC > 0	163	37%	Sum 6 Sp.Sc. > 6	51	12%
PureC > 1	76	17%	Pure H < 2	173	39%
Afr $< .40$	66	15%	Pure H $= 0$	18	4%
Afr $< .50$	209	48%	$p > a + 1$	124	28%
$(FM + m) <$ Sum Shad	159	36%	$M^p > M^a$	146	33%

Table 51. Descriptive Statistics for 180 Character Disorders

Variable	Mean	SD	Min	Max	Freq	Median	Mode	SK	KU
R	18.44	4.29	14.00	34.00	180	18.00	18.00	1.74	3.23
W	6.94	3.86	1.00	23.00	180	7.00	5.00	0.89	1.96
D	8.64	4.56	0.00	21.00	178	8.00	12.00	0.44	−0.05
Dd	2.84	[2.21]	0.00	10.00	161	2.50	1.00	1.00	0.94
S	1.92	[1.86]	0.00	7.00	123	2.00	0.00	0.87	0.22
DQ+	4.13	2.55	0.00	10.00	176	4.00	2.00	0.69	−0.29
DQo	12.74	5.09	4.00	27.00	180	12.00	9.00	0.67	0.33
DQv	1.12	[1.12]	0.00	4.00	108	1.00	0.00	0.64	−0.44
DQv/+	0.43	[0.72]	0.00	3.00	57	0.00	0.00	1.73	2.56
FQX+	0.03	0.16	0.00	1.00	5	0.00	0.00	5.79	31.94
FQXo	10.56	3.03	4.00	18.00	180	10.00	11.00	0.56	0.24
FQXu	3.71	2.13	0.00	9.00	169	3.00	3.00	0.34	−0.45
FQX−	3.72	2.01	0.00	10.00	174	4.00	4.00	0.97	1.89
FQXNone	0.41	[0.73]	0.00	3.00	51	0.00	0.00	1.81	2.63
MQ+	0.03	0.16	0.00	1.00	5	0.00	0.00	5.80	31.94
MQo	1.55	1.47	0.00	6.00	135	1.00	1.00	1.00	0.28
MQu	0.61	0.89	0.00	3.00	75	0.00	0.00	1.53	1.60
MQ−	0.47	[0.78]	0.00	3.00	57	0.00	0.00	1.52	1.34
MQNone	0.00	[0.00]	0.00	0.00	0	0.00	0.00	—	—
S−	0.97	[1.23]	0.00	4.00	89	0.00	0.00	1.12	0.09
M	2.66	2.54	0.00	10.00	149	2.00	1.00	1.34	1.48
FM	1.57	1.17	0.00	5.00	153	1.00	1.00	1.02	1.24
m	1.02	1.06	0.00	4.00	107	1.00	0.00	0.79	−0.26
FM + m	2.59	1.74	0.00	7.00	160	2.00	2.00	0.55	−0.07
FC	0.98	1.29	0.00	5.00	85	0.00	0.00	1.21	0.64
CF	0.86	1.08	0.00	5.00	89	0.00	0.00	1.28	1.29
C	0.47	[0.86]	0.00	3.00	49	0.00	0.00	1.68	1.60
Cn	0.01	[0.10]	0.00	1.00	2	0.00	0.00	9.41	87.45
Sum Color	2.32	2.00	0.00	7.00	180	2.00	0.00	0.45	−0.88
WGSum C	2.06	1.91	0.00	6.00	180	1.50	0.00	0.63	−0.76
Sum C'	0.83	[1.05]	0.00	4.00	88	0.00	0.00	1.26	1.14
Sum T	0.31	[0.52]	0.00	2.00	50	0.00	0.00	1.44	1.16
Sum V	0.24	[0.55]	0.00	2.00	32	0.00	0.00	2.25	3.95
Sum Y	0.65	[0.95]	0.00	4.00	77	0.00	0.00	1.71	2.71
Sum Shading	2.03	1.82	0.00	9.00	141	2.00	2.00	1.25	2.13
Fr + rF	0.47	[0.43]	0.00	4.00	36	0.00	0.00	2.62	6.45
FD	0.33	[0.65]	0.00	2.00	42	0.00	0.00	1.74	1.61
F	10.86	4.90	2.00	25.00	180	11.00	11.00	0.66	0.77
PAIR	6.87	3.55	0.00	20.00	180	6.00	4.00	1.30	2.70
3r(2)/R	0.46	0.17	0.20	0.93	180	0.48	0.30	0.68	0.81
Lambda	2.12	2.39	0.15	16.00	180	1.62	3.00	4.96	33.89
EA	4.72	3.40	0.50	14.00	180	4.00	2.50	1.16	1.50
es	4.62	3.03	2.00	13.00	180	6.00	4.00	0.81	0.25
D	0.03	1.06	−3.00	3.00	180	0.00	0.00	−0.21	2.18
AdjD	0.19	1.05	−3.00	3.00	180	0.00	0.00	−0.01	1.47
a (active)	2.82	2.31	0.00	10.00	150	2.00	2.00	0.91	0.50
p (passive)	2.43	1.89	0.00	10.00	157	2.00	2.00	1.63	4.30
M^a	1.39	1.67	0.00	8.00	115	1.00	1.00	1.83	3.81
M^p	1.27	1.30	0.00	6.00	125	1.00	1.00	1.39	2.28
Intellect	1.44	2.13	0.00	11.00	104	1.00	0.00	2.59	7.92
Zf	9.40	4.20	2.00	24.00	180	10.00	13.00	0.28	0.10
Zd	0.20	4.83	−18.50	9.00	180	0.50	−1.00	−1.14	2.26
Blends	2.14	1.90	0.00	7.00	133	2.00	0.00	0.62	−0.46
Col Shd Bl	0.32	[0.57]	0.00	3.00	51	0.00	0.00	1.95	4.71

Note: Standard deviations shown in brackets indicate that the value is probably unreliable and/or misleading and should not be used to estimate expected ranges. Ordinarily, these variables should not be included in most parametric analyses.

Table 51. (Continued)

Variable	Mean	SD	Min	Max	Freq	Median	Mode	SK	KU
Afr	0.49	0.19	0.20	1.08	180	0.46	0.50	0.75	0.38
Populars	4.93	1.67	1.00	8.00	180	5.00	6.00	0.03	−0.50
X + %	0.58	0.12	0.29	0.82	180	0.57	0.61	0.01	−0.25
F + %	0.59	0.16	0.25	1.00	180	0.58	0.50	−0.11	−0.31
X − %	0.20	0.10	0.00	0.43	174	0.20	0.20	0.15	−0.36
Xu%	0.20	0.10	0.00	0.50	169	0.20	0.20	0.10	0.10
S − %	0.24	[0.30]	0.00	1.00	89	0.00	0.00	1.08	0.13
Isolate	0.14	0.12	0.00	0.50	180	0.11	0.00	1.10	0.79
H	1.94	1.65	0.00	7.00	156	1.00	1.00	1.41	1.97
(H)	0.83	1.01	0.00	4.00	97	1.00	0.00	1.35	1.31
Hd	1.39	1.47	0.00	6.00	118	1.00	0.00	1.14	0.84
(Hd)	0.40	0.67	0.00	3.00	55	0.00	0.00	1.65	2.14
Hx	0.09	[0.35]	0.00	2.00	12	0.00	0.00	4.27	18.33
All H Cont	4.56	2.97	0.00	12.00	168	4.00	5.00	0.72	0.05
A	7.67	3.30	2.00	21.00	180	7.00	7.00	1.19	2.25
(A)	0.27	[0.49]	0.00	2.00	45	0.00	0.00	1.58	1.60
Ad	1.90	[1.57]	0.00	7.00	146	2.00	1.00	1.02	1.07
(Ad)	0.14	[0.41]	0.00	2.00	21	0.00	0.00	3.05	9.13
An	0.87	[1.33]	0.00	5.00	75	0.00	0.00	1.70	2.27
Art	0.80	0.96	0.00	4.00	93	1.00	0.00	1.14	0.70
Ay	0.11	[0.31]	0.00	1.00	20	0.00	0.00	2.50	4.28
Bl	0.26	[0.59]	0.00	3.00	34	0.00	0.00	2.51	6.29
Bt	0.86	1.02	0.00	5.00	101	1.00	0.00	1.73	4.28
Cg	0.99	1.11	0.00	4.00	101	1.00	0.00	1.03	0.39
Cl	0.14	[0.38]	0.00	2.00	23	0.00	0.00	2.72	7.06
Ex	0.08	[0.31]	0.00	2.00	12	0.00	0.00	4.27	19.31
Fi	0.22	[0.51]	0.00	2.00	32	0.00	0.00	2.29	4.38
Fd	0.17	[0.38]	0.00	1.00	31	0.00	0.00	1.75	1.08
Ge	0.15	[0.57]	0.00	4.00	18	0.00	0.00	5.38	32.48
Hh	0.29	0.50	0.00	2.00	48	0.00	0.00	1.47	1.20
Ls	0.58	0.92	0.00	4.00	65	0.00	0.00	1.62	2.03
Na	0.32	[0.55]	0.00	2.00	49	0.00	0.00	1.56	1.52
Sc	0.29	[0.61]	0.00	3.00	43	0.00	0.00	2.66	8.29
Sx	0.43	[0.83]	0.00	4.00	53	0.00	0.00	2.58	7.29
Xy	0.11	[0.31]	0.00	1.00	19	0.00	0.00	2.59	4.76
Idio	0.84	1.01	0.00	5.00	101	1.00	0.00	1.52	2.55
DV	0.76	[0.85]	0.00	3.00	98	1.00	0.00	1.04	0.54
INCOM	1.06	[1.36]	0.00	6.00	91	1.00	0.00	1.39	1.94
DR	0.35	[0.61]	0.00	3.00	52	0.00	0.00	1.85	3.56
FABCOM	0.63	[0.57]	0.00	2.00	70	0.00	0.00	1.54	1.42
DV2	0.14	[0.41]	0.00	2.00	21	0.00	0.00	3.05	9.13
INC2	0.36	[0.68]	0.00	2.00	30	0.00	0.00	2.27	5.48
DR2	0.20	[0.57]	0.00	3.00	23	0.00	0.00	3.04	8.86
FAB2	0.36	[0.79]	0.00	3.00	21	0.00	0.00	2.80	8.81
ALOG	0.30	[0.65]	0.00	2.00	25	0.00	0.00	3.77	14.60
CONTAM	0.00	0.00	0.00	0.00	0	0.00	0.00	—	—
Sum6 SpSc	2.62	2.10	0.00	9.00	180	2.00	2.00	0.83	0.44
Sum6 SpSc2	0.76	[1.29]	0.00	4.00	62	1.00	0.00	1.07	0.18
WSum6	11.31	10.77	0.00	48.00	180	8.00	7.00	1.42	1.62
AB	0.27	[0.89]	0.00	5.00	22	0.00	0.00	4.09	17.29
AG	0.41	0.67	0.00	2.00	56	0.00	0.00	1.36	0.54
CFB	0.00	0.00	0.00	0.00	0	0.00	0.00	—	—
COP	0.57	0.85	0.00	3.00	69	0.00	0.00	1.40	1.08
CP	0.00	[0.00]	0.00	0.00	0	0.00	0.00	—	—
MOR	1.07	[1.62]	0.00	7.00	76	0.00	0.00	1.73	2.77
PER	0.93	1.51	0.00	9.00	77	0.00	0.00	2.47	8.37
PSV	0.19	[0.63]	0.00	5.00	25	0.00	0.00	5.37	35.91

Table 52   317

Table 52. Frequency Data for 180 Character Disorders

Demography Variables

Marital Status			Age			Race		
Single	118	66%	18–25	57	32%	White	147	82%
Lives w/S.O.	7	4%	26–35	39	22%	Black	16	9%
Married	39	22%	36–45	12	7%	Hispanic	17	9%
Separated	2	1%	46–55	18	10%	Asian	0	0%
Divorced	14	8%	56–65	4	2%			
Widowed	0	0%	Over 65	0	0%	Education		
						Under 12	55	31%
Sex						12 Years	62	34%
Male	112	62%				13–15 Yrs	49	27%
Female	68	38%				16+ Yrs	14	8%

Ratios, Percentages, and Special Indices

EB Style			Form Quality Deviations		
Introversive	63	35%	$X + \% > .89$	0	0%
Super-Introversive	33	18%	$X + \% < .70$	147	82%
Ambitent	74	41%	$X + \% < .61$	113	63%
Extratensive	43	24%	$X + \% < .50$	37	21%
Super-Extratensive	34	19%	$F + \% < .70$	123	68%
			$Xu\% > .20$	83	46%
$EA - es$ Differences: D-Scores			$X - \% > .15$	121	67%
D Score > 0	38	21%	$X - \% > .20$	76	42%
D Score $= 0$	111	62%	$X - \% > .30$	26	14%
D Score < 0	31	17%			
D Score < -1	13	7%	FC:CF + C Ratio		
			$FC > (CF + C) + 2$	8	4%
$Adj\ D$ Score > 0	51	28%	$FC > (CF + C) + 1$	21	12%
$Adj\ D$ Score $= 0$	102	57%	$(CF + C) > FC + 1$	45	25%
$Adj\ D$ Score < 0	27	15%	$(CF + C) > FC + 2$	29	16%
$Adj\ D$ Score < -1	10	6%			
$Zd > +3.0$ (Overincorp)	50	28%	S-Constellation Positive	3	2%
$Zd < -3.0$ (Underincorp)	31	17%	HVI Positive	13	7%
			OBS Positive	0	0%

SCZI = 6	0	0%	DEPI = 7	0	0%	CDI = 5	18	10%
SCZI = 5	0	0%	DEPI = 6	1	0%	CDI = 4	69	38%
SCZI = 4	4	2%	DEPI = 5	23	13%			

Miscellaneous Variables

$Lambda > .99$	122	68%	$(2AB + Art + Ay) > 5$	17	9%
$Dd > 3$	55	31%	Populars < 4	40	22%
$DQv + DQv/+ > 2$	48	27%	Populars > 7	16	9%
$S > 2$	61	34%	$COP = 0$	111	62%
Sum $T = 0$	130	72%	$COP > 2$	8	4%
Sum $T > 1$	5	3%	$AG = 0$	124	69%
$3r + (2)/R < .33$	62	34%	$AG > 2$	0	0%
$3r + (2)/R > .44$	60	33%	$MOR > 2$	31	17%
$Fr + rF > 0$	36	20%	Level 2 Sp.Sc. > 0	62	34%
$PureC > 0$	49	27%	Sum 6 Sp.Sc. > 6	29	16%
$PureC > 1$	28	16%	Pure $H < 2$	91	51%
$Afr < .40$	54	30%	Pure $H = 0$	24	13%
$Afr < .50$	94	52%	$p > a + 1$	42	23%
$(FM + m) <$ Sum Shading	54	30%	$M^p > M^a$	64	36%

PART IV

Interpretation

CHAPTER 13

Some General Guidelines

The interpretation of Rorschach data is complex, but not nearly as complex as often is implied. It requires, as does the interpretation of any psychological test, training, skill, and experience. The fundamental requirements for interpretation include a reasonably good knowledge of personality and behavioral theories, an expertise in psychopathology, and a knowledge of the test itself. This composite background affords the core of information that is necessary to develop and review interpretive postulates in the context of the broad framework of human behaviors. Obviously, access to normative and reference data is also important to the formation and acceptance or rejection of interpretive hypotheses.

Magical thinking or crystal ball operations have no place in Rorschach interpretation. Quite the contrary, the process involves analysis and synthesis, drawing intelligently from the quantitative and qualitative material in the record. Many can learn to administer and code or score the Rorschach, but the training required for interpretation goes well beyond that level. A well-trained clerk can become a good examiner, but rarely, if ever, a qualified interpreter. A valid interpretation is the product of a well-administered and accurately scored test, plus the variety of skills reflected in the good clinician; that is, the knowledge, skills, and experience that are important to the translation of the myriad of Rorschach scores and words into a meaningful understanding of the person.

In other words, the response is the result of a complex set of operations that involve processing, translation, conceptualization, decision making, and sometimes projection. The idiography of the subject is often reflected at its most exquisite level in the projected material, but much of the idiography is often captured through the integration of structural data. No two subjects are alike and when the mixture of structural, sequential and projected material are sorted through diligently and intelligently, a picture of a singular person who is like others in many ways but unique in some ways should unfold. Some have attempted to address the Rorschach from an almost strictly nomothetic approach. Others tend to rely much more on the impressions that they glean from the content of the test. Both approaches are wrong and potentially very dangerous. Both may include conclusions that are correct, or potentially correct, but the accuracy of their conclusions is usually clouded over by other hypotheses, assumptions, or conclusions that are misleading and do an injustice to the subject. The competent interpreter will not fall into either of these mediocre and potentially unethical approaches to the test. Instead, wisdom will prevail, and all of the data, structural, sequential, and content will be used to flesh out a reasonably valid and realistic picture of the subject.

THE INTERPRETIVE PROCESS

Rorschach (1921) was very cautious about what kinds of conclusions might be drawn from the test data. He indicated that he did not know how to differentiate manifest from latent symptoms, and questioned the value of the test for studying "unconscious" characteristics of thinking. Although it seems plausible that Rorschach would have accepted Frank's projective hypothesis as applicable to the test, Rorschach himself gave no indication that he considered such a process in the test. He was especially forceful in emphasizing that the test does not provoke a continuing "stream" of thought, but rather is one requiring adaptation to external stimuli.

As the Rorschach has "matured," so too, has the process of Rorschach interpretation. Each of the authorities of the test has gone well beyond Rorschach's original position concerning interpretation. Almost all have used the bulk of Rorschach's interpretive postulates as the nucleus of their own interpretive frameworks. Most of those postulates have ultimately gained solid empirical support. But Rorschach was far less concerned with the validity of specific test factors as applied to interpretation, as he was with stressing the necessity of approaching the test data in its totality. He very accurately perceived that similar test signs or features, such as a given number of M responses, would, in different test configurations, be interpreted differently. For example, a preponderance of M answers in a protocol might indicate the existence of a strong tendency to use the inner life for gratification. Assuming that statement to be valid, it provides, at best, only a very limited understanding of the person. Important questions concerning the degree of adaptivity afforded by that inner life, or the extent to which the tendency to the inner life impairs interaction with the environment, cannot be answered simply by studying the number of M's in the protocol. In fact, if there is also a preponderance of color responses in the record, the statement itself *would not be valid.* Similarly, many other Rorschach features could alter, or negate, any statement taken from a single "sign."

Each of the Rorschach systematizers, although differing in their own approaches, has solidly agreed with Rorschach's recommendation that the totality of the test must be considered in interpretation. This has generally been referred to in the literature as the "global" approach and, in effect, it requires that *all* Rorschach data be considered in the interpretive process in a manner which is concerned with the configuration of data, as opposed to the interpretation of pieces of data in isolation. This process is essentially the same as occurs in any clinical interpretation, whether that interpretation be of data drawn from interviews, tests, or therapy sessions. Levy (1963) offers an excellent work on the subject of psychological interpretation that identifies the components of the process in more detail than is necessary here; however, extrapolating from Levy, Rorschach interpretation might best be described as a three-stage procedure. The first stage is a propositional one, whereas the second stage is one of integration. The third stage is one in which the integration of findings is used to develop conclusions that are relevant to the assessment issues that have been raised, such as diagnosis, personality description, recommendations concerning treatment or disposition, evaluation of treatment effects, and so on.

THE PROPOSITIONAL STAGE

The onset of Rorschach interpretation begins with a careful review of each of the test variables by clusters. In other words, the data are not reviewed as a group of singular variables. Instead, the data are addressed in groups of variables, each of which relates to specific characteristics of the components of the total personality. Ultimately, this approach accounts for all of the data from the Structural Summary, with all of its frequencies, ratios, and percentages, the specific scorings of responses and their sequence of occurrence, the verbalizations given during the response and, finally, the verbalizations given during the Inquiry.

Propositions concerning each category of personality can evolve only after a careful study of the many elements that relate to that feature. Unfortunately, some Rorschach interpreters follow the dangerous path of identifying or emphasizing some findings, especially liabilities, without providing a complete description of the psychology of the person, including assets, or at times, without considering apparent liabilities in the broader context of the subject's environment. This is a misuse of the test and a disservice to the subject. It need not occur, and will not if the data are addressed systematically.

Table 53 provides an alphabetical listing of seven clusters of variables (Exner, 1991). In each, the variables relate to each other, and all relate to specific psychological components or functions, which are shown in the column on the left. Some data should be available concerning each of these components in any valid Rorschach protocol. Table 53 also includes one array of variables that relate to situational stress. Those variables do not necessarily relate to each other, but all relate to situational stress experience.

Some variables appear in more than one cluster. For example, minus answers relate to both mediation and personal perception. Some movement contents appear in self and interpersonal perception. A high *Lambda* is included in both processing and mediation. This is because single variables often have a multiple input. For instance, *MOR* responses are relevant to both ideation and personal perception. The data regarding *MOR* indicate that significant elevations in the frequency by which this type of response is given signals the likelihood of two psychological characteristics: (1) the presence of more negative features in self-image, which relates to personal perception, and (2) a tendency for attitudes about the self and the world to be marked by pessimism, which in turn has influence on ideation. Thus, as the interpretive routine proceeds, information about

Table 53.   Variable Clusters Related to Several Psychological Features

Component or Function	Variables
Affective Features	*EB* (extratensive style), *EBPer, eb* (right side value [*C', T, V, Y*]), *FC:CF + C*, Pure *C* quality, *Afr, CP, S*, Blends, *COL-SHD* Blends, Shading Blends
Capacity for Control & Stress Tolerance	*D* Score, *AdjD* Score, *EA* (Sum *M*, Sum *C*), *es* (*FM, T, V, C'*), *CDI*
Cognitive Mediation	$L > .99$, *P, OBS, X + %, Xu%, X − %, S − %* (review minus answers by *S*, homogeneous clustering, levels of distortion), *CONFAB*
Ideation	*EB* (introversive style), *EBPer, eb* (left side value [*FM,m*], $a:p$, $M^a:M^p$, $2Ab + (Art + Ay)$, 6sSp Sc (*Lv*1 vs *Lv*2), *MQ*, Quality of *M* responses
Information Processing	$L > .99$, *OBS, HVI, Zf, W:D:Dd, (W:M), DQ, Zd, PSV*, Location Sequencing
Interpersonal Perception	$p > a + 1$, *CDI, Fd, T, HVI, PER, COP, AG, Isol:R*, Content of Movement Responses That Contain a Pair, All Human Content
Self-Perception	$3r + (2)/R$ (*Fr + rF*), *FD, V*, Pure *H*:Nonpure *H, An + Xy, MOR*, Content of Minus responses, Content of all movement responses
Situation-Related Stress	*D, Adj D, EA, EB* (zero values), *m, Y, T*, Blend Complexity, *COL-SHD* Blends (*m* & *Y*), Pure *C*, Formless *M, M −*

Note: EB is stylistic *only* if one side exceeds the other by 2 or more *if EA* is 10 or less, or more than 2 if *EA* is greater than 10.

more than one component or function will often develop even though the focus of interpretive attention is on a single feature.

As the various component parts of each of these Rorschach clusters are surveyed, propositions or hypotheses are formulated. At this point, it is important that no reasonable hypothesis be rejected simply because it does not seem compatible with other propositions generated from the review. It is also quite important that all of the components are studied, not simply those that are unusual or dramatic. It is true that the unusual or dramatic findings are intriguing as they often represent the idiography of the subject more distinctly. For instance, the presence of a reflection answer, the absence of a texture response, or the presence of a Color Projection each convey some very important information about the psychology of the subject. Similarly, a response such as, "the remnants of a decayed penis" cannot help but warrant some hypothesizing by the interpreter. Nonetheless, the full significance of such findings can only be judged in light of all other data, including the usual or commonplace, which are equally important in "getting at" the entire person.

The actual number of propositions generated from each cluster of data will vary with the richness of the data, plus the deductive skills of the interpreter. In some instances, findings from a cluster of data yield little more than some pedestrian-like statements concerning the psychological organization or functioning of a feature. But even those become important in the integration of findings and often cause hypotheses generated from more unique or dramatic data to be tempered considerably. It is not unreasonable to conceptualize the Rorschach as a *wideband procedure,* that is, one that yields information that can affect many different decisions. Cronbach and Gleser (1957), in discussing decision theory, have pointed out that wideband techniques often include data from which numerous hypotheses are formulated which, when confirmed, have great practical importance. They note that, although any single hypothesis may be questionable or undependable, the sequential accumulation of hypotheses will often draw attention to information that might otherwise be neglected.

SUMMARIZING THE PROPOSITIONS FOR EACH CLUSTER

When the data for a cluster have been exhausted, a summary should occur and a set of propositions, reflecting the findings concerning that specific feature of the psychology of the subject, should be developed. It continues to be in a propositional form because findings from other clusters may cause it to be modified or better understood. But for the moment, it constitutes a summary regarding the personality element that has been in the focus of attention. For example, consider the data from a cluster of data related to information-processing behavior derived from a 20-response protocol:

			Location Sequencing		
$L = 1.35$	OBS = Neg	HVI = Neg			
Zd $= -4.5$	$DQ+$ $= 6$	I W,D	V W,W	VIII D,D
Zf $= 10$	$DQv/+$ $= 1$	II D,D,Dd	VI D,D	IX D
$W:D:Dd = 5:14:1$	DQv $= 2$	III D,D	VII W,D	X D,D
$W:M$ $= 6:4$	PSV $= 0$	IV W,D		

When reviewing this cluster, only the structural and sequential data are relevant. The contents of specific responses are not used. Collectively, the data provide some information about processing habits. At this stage, it does not matter whether the subject is a child or adult, male or female, patient or nonpatient. The data are the data, so to speak, and the findings are descriptive of the processing behaviors of the subject. The first variable in the cluster (L) is quite important, leading to the proposition that the subject is markedly prone to simplify complex stimulus situations. The second and third variables (OBS, HVI) offer no significant findings. The fourth variable (Zd) reveals that the subject is somewhat negligent when scanning a stimulus field, although the fifth variable (Zf) suggests that the subject tends to try to organize a stimulus field as much as do most people, both children and adults. The sixth variable ($W:D:Dd$) indicates that the subject tends to be very conservative in processing new information, and the seventh variable ($W:M$) appears to confirm this very conservative approach. The eighth variable (comprising of the DQ distribution) indicates that the subject does organize at a more sophisticated level some of the time, but in many instances the processing behaviors are less sophisticated than expected, and seemingly concrete. The last variable (Location Sequencing) tends to confirm that the subject is quite conservative, but consistent in his or her approach.

A summary of these findings would include the propositions that (1) the subject prefers not to be too involved with complexity and has a basic style oriented toward simplification of stimulus situations, (2) the subject scans new stimulus fields in a somewhat haphazard manner that often neglects critically important stimulus bits, (3) the subject is very conservative in his or her scanning habits, preferring to deal with more easily managed aspects of a field than deal with it in its entirety, and (4) the tendency of the subject to be conservative causes goal-setting behaviors also to be quite conservative, that is, the subject usually does not set goals that are difficult to achieve or ones that may require extended effort.

All of these propositions are probably correct, but none contain speculation about causation or whether findings should be considered as assets or liabilities. If the subject is a young child, such findings are not unexpected; or if the subject is an adult who recently has experienced a neurological insult, they are not inconsistent. In fact, in the instance of the neurologically impaired subject, some of the findings, such as the tendency to simplify, economize, and set modest goals could be regarded as an asset. On the other hand, the description is not very positive and usually would be regarded as a liability, especially for an adult subject. However, it is foolish to try to draw conclusions about these findings until all of the other data of the test have been reviewed and fully integrated.

THE INTEGRATION STAGE

After the numerous propositions have been formulated by reviewing each of the clusters of data, the interpreter comes to the point of creating a meaningful description of the subject. This description is the product of a logical integration of the various postulates that have been formed. It is not simply a process of adding statements together, but instead involves the clinical conceptualization of the psychology of a person. Occasionally, propositions previously formulated from the data of one cluster may be rejected because of findings from another cluster, but this is very unusual. More commonly, propositions developed from one cluster serve to modify or clarify propositions derived from other clusters. It is here that clinicians go beyond specific data, using their propositional statements as a base and adding to that base their own deductive logic and knowledge of human behavior and psychopathology. This is the output of the Rorschach clinician. For instance, assume that the record of the subject for whom the data on processing has been presented above also contains the following data concerning affect:

$EB = 5:0.5$	$EBPer = 10$	$DEPI = 3$	Blends
$eb \quad\quad = 2.2$	$(C' = 1, T = 1, V = 0, Y = 0)$		$M.FC'$
$FC:CF + C = 1:0$	Pure $C = 0$		
$Afr \quad\quad = 0.33$	$CP = 0$	$S = 0$	Col-Shd B1 $= 0$

These findings would lead to several propositions. First, the EB reveals that the subject is very ideational and the $EBPer$ indicates that he or she uses a "thinking through" approach in almost all coping or problem-solving situations. In fact, the value for $EBPer$ suggests that this style is quite dominant and that, in most instances, the subject tries to keep feelings away from decision making, regardless of whether that psychological tactic will be the most effective in a given situation. This proposition is strengthened considerably by the datum for the Afr, which is very low, indicating that the subject does not like to be around emotion or influenced by it.

The data in the processing cluster revealed that the subject tries to simplify complex stimulus situations, often scans a stimulus field haphazardly, and generally tries to be very economical in goal setting. In light of these findings, it seems reasonable to assume that there is some relationship between the seemingly inept processing behavior, especially the orientation to oversimplify, and the apparent dislike or even fearfulness that the subject has concerning emotion. This is not an *absolute* conclusion, for there are many additional propositions to be considered, but it does seem to be a potentially viable hypothesis that has been developed from the findings of two clusters of data.

The overall yield of the integration stage is essentially descriptive, designed to aid in understanding the subject. It is predicated on a matrix of data that has led to propositions and conceptions. It is not necessarily *predictive* at this point, nor does it ultimately need to be predictive. Predictions and recommendations, although clearly a function for the psychodiagnostician, accumulate from the total information available to the clinician regarding the subject. Rorschach interpretation may be only one element of that information. For example, a Rorschach description may include information to the effect that a subject is "quick" to display emotion under stressful conditions. Assuming that statement to be valid, it provides only a limited understanding of the person and the manner in which he or she handles emotion. A major unanswered question is whether this proclivity is used adaptively, or whether it is a liability. Other Rorschach data may add some clarification to the issue. It may be determined that contact with reality is reasonably effective, that sufficient interest in people exists so as not to avoid them, that he or she is able to perceive things conventionally, and that the person apparently does not experience overwhelming feelings of tension or anxiety. All of these factors might lead the interpreter to "predict" that the subject probably handles emotions effectively, and that there is no need for concern that he or she will be dominated by these affective experiences. Such a recommendation or prediction, however, is not based on the Rorschach data, but on an intelligent hunch of the interpreter. If the same interpreter already knew that the subject had a history of temper outbursts plus some incidents of assaultiveness, it is highly unlikely that the same recommendations or predictions would be made. But that added information would not change the Rorschach-derived conclusions. The description that the subject is quick to show emotion under stress, that reality contact is reasonably effective, that he or she maintains a normal or average interest in people, and is able to perceive things conventionally remains true. The added behavioral information simply clarifies how the emotion is displayed.

Naturally, this added clarification is critically important to the clinician who may be asked to speculate concerning future emotional displays and exemplifies how inputs from many sources, including the Rorschach, contribute to the process of making recommendations or predictions. But that is not the focus or purpose of the integration stage. It is not oriented toward prediction, except that it includes information which may ultimately contribute to predictions and/or recommendations. Long ago, Sarbin (1941) suggested that any diagnostic statement is meaningful only when it has reference to the future; that is, when it is predictive. Unfortunately, Sarbin's position tended to neglect the importance of simply understanding a person. This position has been well defended by Holt (1970), and it is in the context of the Holt premise that the integrative stage of Rorschach interpretation renders its greatest yield.

In many ways, the integration stage approximates a form of *blind interpretation,* a procedure that, in the past, has been a controversial issue for the Rorschach, and one that has often been confusingly distorted. The issue of blind interpretation has probably been given more notoriety than may have been warranted. This was especially true for the period from 1935 to 1955 when the question of Rorschach validity was so frequently challenged and defended. Numerous studies using a blind methodology to evaluate the validity of the test were reported during this period. They generally fall into three design categories: (1) those using a blind interpretation to generate a *personality description* which was then compared for congruence with personality descriptions created by "expert" judges using methods other than the Rorschach, (2) those using blind analysis to derive a *diagnostic impression* versus diagnostic impressions rendered by "expert" judges, and (3) those using blind analysis versus some previously *established criteria.* A summary of 24 of these studies is shown in Table 54. It will be noted from examination of Table 54 that the results are generally mixed, although a substantial majority do provide support for the Rorschach.

The issue of blind interpretation, as has been recommended by several of the Rorschach systematizers, and the approach to the issue of the test validity using blind interpretation *are not the same issues.* The systematizers conceptualize blind interpretation as a clinical method designed to keep the interpreter free of any sets or biases. Beck (1960), Klopfer (1954), and Piotrowski (1957, 1964) all maintain that the best way to approach the test is free of any set. None suggests that the process of clinical interpretation or diagnosis necessarily ends with the Rorschach summary developed in the "blind," although each has demonstrated a phenomenal skill in being able to produce a thorough and highly accurate personality description from nothing other than a blind Rorschach interpretation. Even with this skill, however, all have remained clinical realists, recognizing the limitations of the Rorschach and the importance of other kinds of data. Each conceives of the Rorschach interpretation as a nuclear understanding of the subject, which is added to by inputs from other sources, thus providing a complete clinical evaluation. They differ only in terms of *how* additional data should be used, not *whether* they should be used.

The researchers have attempted to use the method of blind interpretation as a test of the test, as Rorschach himself had suggested. Although these have been generally legitimate designs, the goal of the researcher in using the method is different than that of the clinician using the method. The researcher uses the blind interpretation as an end in itself, which becomes compared with other criteria. The interpretation is not extended or clarified by other inputs, as is the case in the clinical setting. Unfortunately, critics of

Table 54.   Summary of Blind Analysis Studies Concerning the Rorschach

Author	N	Design	Conclusions
Abel (1942)	1	Blind analysis versus case study	Agreement with case study by Margaret Mead
Bailick and Hamlin (1954)	25	Blind estimate of I.Q. versus Wechsler scores	Four judges made valid estimates of I.Q. showing correlations of .61, .64, .69, and .73
Benjamin and Brosin (1938)	36	Accuracy of Blind analyses versus extensive case analyses	The blind analyses were as "accurate" as the extensive case analyses
Benjamin and Ebaugh (1938)	55	Blind analysis versus final clinical diagnosis	84.7% correct
Chambers and Hamlin (1957)		Twenty clinicians were asked to identify each of five protocols according to five diagnostic groupings	Selections were correct in 58 of 100 attempts
Clapp (1938)	1	Blind analysis versus clinical case data	"High agreement"
Cummings (1954)	10	Blind analysis versus established diagnoses of 10 patients in five diagnostic groups using a single Rorschach card	"Analysis significant"
Grant, Ives, and Razoni (1952)	146	Blind ratings on a 4 point scale of normal subjects by three Rorschach "experts" and two inexperienced judges	Rorschach judges placed from between 61 and 71% of subjects on the maladjusted end of the continuum with a high correlation between judges
Hamlin and Newton (1938)	2	Blind ratings of adjustment versus established evaluation	Ratings were "reasonably accurate"
Hertz and Rubenstein (1938)	1	Blind analysis versus data collected in 14 interviews	"High agreement"
Kluckhohn and Rosenzweig (1949)	2	Blind analysis versus anthropological data	"High agreement"
Krugman (1942)	20	Comparisons by three blind judges in matching interpretations by two experienced examiners for 20 subjects	The three judges made a "perfect" score in matching the pairs of interpretations to the subjects
Lisansky (1956)	40	Blind judges versus judges using life history data	Rorschach judges did not show significantly better agreement than did the life history judges
Little and Shneidman (1959)	12	Blind analyses compared to previously existing assessment and with each other	Diagnostic agreement better than chance although wide variations occurred in the assignment of diagnostic categories
Monroe (1945)	1	Blind analysis versus teacher observations	"Satisfactory agreement"
Newton (1954)	5	Blind analysis versus comprehensive case material and psychiatric evaluation	Rorschach judgements correlate significantl teria
Oberholzer (1944)	37	Blind analysis versus data collected by ethnologist	"Considerable" congruency
Palmer (1949)	28	Blind analyses to be selected by patient's therapist	In 39% of the cases the selection of the therapist was correct

Table 54.   (Continued)

Author	N	Design	Conclusions
Schachtel (1942)	3	Blind analysis versus anthropological findings	"Close convergence"
Siegel (1948)	26	Blind analysis versus psychiatric evaluations	88.5% agreement
Silverman (1959)	10	Blind analysis versus evaluations of psychotherapists using 30 blind judges each analyzing protocols for seven variables	Blind analysis agreed with therapists judgements greater than chance although validity coefficients ranged from low to moderate
Swift (1944)	26	Blind analysis versus psychiatrist evaluations	88% agreement
Symonds (1955)	1	Blind analysis by seven judges versus comprehensive case study	65% agreement
Vernon (1936)	45	Blind analysis versus personality sketches by two psychologists	Correlation of .83

the Rorschach have frequently cited the sometimes limited findings derived from the blind interpretation research works as both a criticism of the test and of the procedure as useful with the test. Such a position, of course, neglects the manner in which blind interpretation is commonly used, that is, as a beginning rather than an end.

It is in keeping with the recommendations of Beck, Klopfer, and Piotrowski that interpreters of the Comprehensive System are encouraged to begin their interpretation *in the blind*. This means developing hypotheses during the propositional stage only from the Rorschach data, and merging these postulates into a meaningful description of the subject during the integration stage. This is a difficult challenge for many Rorschachers, because the interpreter is often the one responsible for administering the test and will naturally be influenced to some extent by that event, and by the cursory review of the verbalizations which occurs during the process of scoring the test. The astute clinician is aware of this, and makes attempts to restrict interpretive logic only to the Rorschach data. If the interpreter has already developed subjective impressions, either positive or negative, concerning the subject, he or she should not create premature sets that could influence the interpretation or cause the neglect of any data. Sometimes, even data from a brief history can cause such sets, as has been illustrated quite well by Levy (1970) who found that simple demographic information, such as socioeconomic status, can have an impact on diagnostic conclusions.

THE FINAL REPORT STAGE

In the integration stage, the data of the test converge on internal organization and process and a description unfolds. The description provides a picture of the subject as he or she is *now*. The issue facing the interpreter in the third stage is how best to use that description in a way that combines it with other data available concerning the subject and create a final report in terms of the issues that have been presented in the assessment referral. It should be obvious to any well-trained clinician that the injection of feelings, prejudice, theoretical bias, or sets has no place in the interpretation as it proceeds through the propositional and integration stages. But in drawing conclusions, which usually have a predictive element, the process changes from science to more of an art form. It clearly challenges the expertise of the interpreter. It is in this stage that the accumulated wisdom of the clinician is sorely tested as the issues of diagnosis, disposition, treatment planning, treatment evaluation, or other recommendations become the focus.

ISSUES OF DIAGNOSIS

Assuming a lawfulness to the behaviors of humans, anyone with a thorough grasp of the test and a reasonably good understanding of people will have generated a valid and useful description of the subject from the Rorschach data. Unfortunately, in most instances, the description will not fall neatly into a configuration or profile that equates directly with diagnostic categories such as those described in the DSM-III, DSM-IIIR, or DSM-IV. This should not be surprising as people differ enormously and, as pointed out in the Introduction to the DSM, diagnostic labeling is not designed to classify individuals, but rather to classify "disorders that individuals have."

Obviously, the description generated during the integration stage can be used in several ways. Sometimes, it will be sufficient as a stand-alone report, or it can be used as a source of questions that might be answered from other information that might be available or could be collected. For example, additional history information might contribute significantly in developing a better understanding of how some of the subjects' stylistic features are manifested, such as in self-centeredness, passive dependency, and problems in modulating affective displays. Similarly, findings from cognitive testing might shed some light on how seriously the attention and concentration of the subject are being affected by a stress condition or some other circumstance.

In most cases, unless serious pathology is present, the final description will not have contained any specific diagnostic formulation although it can be used as a basis from which one can be generated. For instance, a case may include findings for evidence for narcissistic, dependency, and histrionic features. Although none are very desirable when considered in light of "optimal" precursors to adjustment, none are so obviously disruptive to the overall psychological organization to be considered pathological. If a DSM model for diagnosis is applied, any or all of these three features can serve as a basis for an *Axis II* decision. In some cases, the only findings that might contribute directly to an *Axis I* diagnostic formulation are those related to a current situational stress. The final conclusions may include specific recommendations for intervention, and in many instances, they clearly can serve as the basis for various intervention considerations such as long term versus short term, supportive versus uncovering, cognitive versus dynamic and so on.

TREATMENT PLANNING

A treatment plan is really a prediction concerning the potential effectiveness of an intervention strategy designed to accomplish specific objectives. The diagnosis can contribute information to this prediction in some cases. but for the most part, the validity of the prediction will improve considerably as information concerning the psychological organization and functioning of the subject is included in the array of material to be considered. Collectively, the findings from the test will reveal both general and specific information about some personality features. Most records will contain data related to ideation, emotion, coping preferences and response styles, capacity for control, self-perception, information processing, interpersonal perception, cognitive mediation, and routine defensive strategies. Collectively, these data provide much information concerning personality styles, traits, or habits. Nonetheless, it is erroneous to assume that the findings will fall into neat patterns that automatically dictate treatment recommendations. The unique psychological organization of each individual will inevitably be marked by features that, at times, may be assets but at other times may be liabilities.

In other words, there is no magic in the Rorschach from which intervention decisions can be made easily. In fact, taken alone, that is, without some knowledge about the presenting complaints and/or recent behavior of the subject, Rorschach data could easily become misleading in the formation of a treatment plan. This is because all humans are somewhat fragile and have liabilities. Most anyone can be psychologically dissected and, if judged against optimal standards, be made to appear much more pathological than is the case. Nonetheless, the use of the Rorschach for the selection of treatment targets and treatment modalities does begin with the so-called optimal state, that is, with the speculative question: What features of the test would be altered if a magic wand were available? Some Rorschach data provide valid indices of response styles, and if the composite of these data is reviewed carefully, those styles can be viewed in terms of their effectiveness, their interrelationships, and, possibly most important, whether they are assets or liabilities in the overall functioning of the subject.

For example, data presented earlier from the processing cluster of a 20-response record included a Zd score of -4.5. As noted, this indicates a rather haphazard scanning approach in which the subject often neglects stimuli, some of which may be critically important. Generally, this is a liability and typically would be included in any listing of potential treatment targets. Characteristics identified as liabilities become the focal points for treatment consideration, beginning with the question of how serious they seem to be in the total context of the personality, extending through speculation on how easily they can be altered, and ending in a framework of the immediate and long-range goals of the subject. Thus, an optimal intervention plan can be formulated which deals with the ideal condition, that is, a design to contend with those liabilities that *might* be viable intervention targets. But Rorschach data do not identify the *reality factors* that are involved in the situation. Not everyone needs or wants treatment and even for those who do, the most ideal treatment plan may not be realistic or appropriate. Some potential treatment targets will not necessarily be the most optimal when viewed in the context of the goals, motivation, or life circumstances of the subject, or the intervention resources that are available.

Any treatment recommendations or decisions should evolve in a framework that considers both internal and external relationships. The optimal intervention design will have three objectives. First, it should target the reduction or elimination of existing stresses and/or symptoms. Second, it should permit the subject to maintain whatever harmony he or she has created with the world. Third, it should improve the psychological sophistication of the subject in ways that will enhance the probability for effective adjustment, both internal and external, in the future.

These seem to be simple, straightforward objectives, but that is not always the case. For instance, the elimination of symptoms can, at times, be quite disruptive to pretreatment relationships with the world. Similarly, an increase in the psychological sophistication of a subject can become markedly disruptive to preexisting relations and patterns of behavior. Thus, any treatment formulation requires a *cost-benefit analysis* in which a myriad of factors must be afforded very careful consideration. Obviously, concern for the psychological organization of the subject is included among those factors and can often provide the core from which the cost-benefit evaluation evolves.

COOKBOOKS AND COMPUTERS

Ideally, the final interpretive yield from the Rorschach will represent an intermingling of empirically based findings, that is, those conservative interpretations that are based on research, with a conceptual framework in which links are drawn between the test data and aspects of personality functioning. Such an approach extends well beyond a "cookbook" effort at data translation, which sometimes can be overly simplistic or concrete, and even quite misleading. Many years ago, Meehl (1956) made an intelligent and intriguing appeal for a cookbook approach to diagnostics, which would simplify the task and provide more time for clinicians to perform other important tasks. Although Meehl's position was reasonable, particularly for the task of "hanging" diagnostic labels, it is not very applicable to Rorschach interpretation. There is no simple checklist of Rorschach signs that automatically can be translated as representative of aspects of personality or behavior. Unfortunately, the novice interpreter often believes that such simple equations do exist and searches for them quite diligently. This tendency has often been encouraged by some Rorschach authors who have conveyed the impression that simplistic translations of scores, or classes of response contents, are useful procedures in interpretation. That supposition is *pure nonsense,* and the unwitting interpreter who is bound to that procedure would do better to avoid the use of the Rorschach in assessment work. The test is far too complex for a simplistic sign approach, and the validity of the interpretation will depend largely on the extent to which the interpreter achieves the full measure of data integration in forming the description of the subject.

The cookbook approach to test interpretation is probably best illustrated by the several elaborate computer programs that have been developed to translate psychological test scores into an interpretive narrative. Many have been well received in the professional community, especially some of those written for *MMPI* interpretation, and evidence is building to support their usefulness (Moreland, 1984). Nonetheless, computers do only as they are instructed or programmed, and it is highly unlikely that any computer program has been written for a complex psychological test that will consider the multitude of possibilities regarding the relationships among test variables or between test variables and the history of the subject. In other words, the computer program scans variables and combinations of variables *as instructed,* but has no capacity for deviating from those instructions. As a consequence, the empirically based computer scan of test data may be very accurate in generating some important descriptive and/or diagnostic information; however, it does not integrate that information with other *nonprogrammed* variables, nor does it conceptualize. Thus anyone using a computer "cookbook" program properly for a complex psychological test will usually go well beyond the computer print or narrative in forming final descriptive, diagnostic, or recommendation statements.

Failure to do so creates a high risk that some important data will not be integrated in a meaningful way and/or that some data, relevant to final judgments or conclusions, may be neglected completely.

Matarazzo (1983) has summarized the potential hazards of computerized psychological testing quite well, and those same hazards apply to any interpretive procedure, whether human or mechanistic, that is based on the naive assumption that a checklist of signs can be translated directly into information regarding features of personality or behaviors. However, it is erroneous to conclude that the sophisticated cookbook approach, as represented in *some* computer interpretation programs, has little or no value in assessment. Any program that ensures a thorough scanning of a large number of variables and combinations of variables can provide a useful assist to interpretation because of speed and reliability. Some of the *MMPI* programs illustrate this, and the same principles can be applied to some, *but not all,* of the data of the Rorschach. For example, a computer-assist program has been developed at the Rorschach Research Foundation, The Rorschach Interpretation Assistance Program (RIAP). RIAP scans through 81 miniclusters of data, derived from 337 structural features of the test (Exner, 1983, 1984; Exner, McGuire, & Cohen, 1986, 1990). It is a large program that requires a great deal of storage space to permit the thousands of operations which are involved. Most, but not all of the scanning involves a search for unusual data, and each time such data are discovered a numbered statement is printed. In most cases, between 15 and 45 statements result, *none of which is based on single signs or data points.* If triggered, a statement indicates the presence of several findings, the composite of which is sufficient to warrant an interpretive postulate.

In effect, the computer search of the Rorschach structural data follows the same procedures that typically are used by the well-trained Rorschach interpreter when reviewing data cluster by cluster during the propositional stage of interpretation. Although it has the advantage of consistency and speed, it has the disadvantages previously mentioned; that is, it fails to integrate findings beyond points for which it is programmed. It does follow logical, decision-tree rules—that is, if datum *A* is positive, search datum *B,* and so on; but even though it follows this logical progression search, it still does not encompass all of the data available in the Rorschach. As such, it becomes a useful tool, in the propositional stage, but cannot possibly capture the full uniqueness of the subject as should be represented in the description developed during the integration stage.

CONCEPTUALIZATION AND INTERPRETIVE STRATEGIES

Interpretation should evolve conceptually, that is, each finding is integrated with other findings so that hypotheses and/or conclusions formulated during the propositional stage will be based on the total available information. In turn, the hypotheses and conclusions formed during the integration stage are merged logically with a careful view of the relationships between the numerous psychological features of the subject. As noted earlier, any valid record will contain data related to ideation, emotion, coping preferences and response styles, capacity for control, self-perception, information processing, interpersonal perception, and cognitive mediation, and may also afford some information about routine defensive strategies. Thus, the challenge for the interpreter is twofold: First, to search systematically through all of the data concerning each component and second, to weave together the resulting yield in a manner that reflects the total person.

All Rorschach protocols should not be addressed in the same way. First, the interpreter must feel assured that the record is interpretively valid. Once that is established, an interpretive strategy should be developed. Thus, before illustrating the tactics involved in the three stages of interpretation, it seems important to describe how the "stage is set" to address a record and subsequently summarize the data that pertain to variables in the seven clusters, and one array, of Rorschach variables by reviewing the data related to each variable, and illustrating how summaries of the data for each cluster are derived in the propositional stage.

REFERENCES

Abel, T. M. (1948) The Rorschach test in a study of culture. *Journal of Projective Techniques,* **12,** 1–15.

Bailick, I., and Hamlin, R. (1954) The clinician as judge: Details of procedure in judging projective material. *Journal of Consulting Psychology,* **18,** 239–242.

Beck, S. J. (1960) *The Rorschach Experiment: Ventures in Blind Diagnosis.* New York: Grune & Stratton.

Benjamin, J. D., and Brosin, H. W. (1938) The reliability and validity of the Rorschach Test. In J. D. Benjamin and F. G. Ebaugh, *The diagnostic validity of the Rorschach Test. American Journal of Psychiatry,* **94,** 1163–1168.

Benjamin, J. D., and Ebaugh, F. G. (1938) The diagnostic validity of the Rorschach test. *American Journal of Psychiatry,* **94,** 1163–1168.

Chambers, G. S., and Hamlin, R. (1957) The validity of judgments based on "blind" Rorschach records. *Journal of Consulting Psychology,* **21,** 105–109.

Clapp, H., Kaplan, A. H., and Miale, F. R. Clinical validation of Rorschach interpretations. *Rorschach Research Exchange,* **2,** 153–163.

Cronbach, L. J., and Gleser, G. C. (1957) *Psychological Tests and Personnel Decisions.* Urbana: University of Illinois Press.

Cummings, S. T. (1954) The clinician as judge: Judgments of adjustment from Rorschach single-card performance. *Journal of Consulting Psychology,* **18,** 243–247.

Exner, J. E. (1983) *A computer program to assist in Rorschach interpretation.* Bayville, N.Y.: Rorschach Workshops.

Exner, J. E. (1984) *A computer program to assist in Rorschach interpretation.* (Revised) Bayville, N.Y.: Rorschach Workshops.

Exner, J. E., McGuire, H., and Cohen, J. B. (1986) *The Rorschach Interpretation Assistance Program.* (Version 1.0). Bayville, N.Y.: Rorschach Workshops.

Exner, J. E., McGuire, H., and Cohen, J. B. (1990) *The Rorschach Interpretation Assistance Program.* (Version 2.0). Asheville, N.C.: Rorschach Workshops.

Frank, L. K. (1939) Projective methods for the study of personality. *Journal of Psychology,* **8,** 389–413.

Grant, M. Q., Ives, V., and Razoni, J. H. (1952) Reliability and validity of judges' ratings of adjustment on the Rorschach. *Psychological Monographs,* **66,** No. 234.

Hamlin, R., and Newton, R. (1952) Comparisons of a schizophrenic and a normal subject, both rated by clinicians as well adjusted on the basis of "blind analysis." *Eastern Psychological Association.* Atlantic City, N. J.

Hertz, M. R., and Rubenstein, B. B. (1949) A comparison of three blind Rorschach cases. *American Journal of Orthopsychiatry,* **19,** 295–313.

Holt, R. R. (1970) Yet another look at clinical and statistical prediction: Or, is clinical psychology worthwhile? *American Psychologist, 25,* 337–349.

Klopfer, B., Ainsworth, M. D., Klopfer, W., and Holt, R. (1954) *Developments in the Rorschach Technique.* Vol. 1. Yonkers-on-Hudson, N.Y.: World Book.

Kluckhohn, S., and Rosenzweig, S. (1949) Two Navajo children over a five year period. *American Journal of Orthopsychiatry, 19,* 266–278.

Krugman, J. (1942) A clinical validation of the Rorschach with problem children. *Rorschach Research Exchange, 5,* 61–70.

Levy, L. (1963) *Psychological Interpretation.* New York: Holt, Rinehart and Winston.

Levy, M. R. (1970) Issues in the personality assessment of lower class patients. *Journal of Projective Techniques, 34,* 6–9.

Lisansky, E. S. (1956) The inter-examiner reliability of the Rorschach test. *Journal of Projective Techniques, 20,* 310–317.

Little, K. B., and Shneidman, E. S. (1959) Congruencies among interpretations of psychological test and anamnestic data. *Psychological Monographs, 27,* No. 476.

Matarazzo, J. M. (1983) Computerized psychological testing. *Science, 221,* 323.

Meehl, P. E. (1956) Wanted—A good cookbook. *American Psychologist, 11,* 263–272.

Monroe, R. L. (1945) Three diagnostic methods applied to Sally. *Journal of Abnormal Psychology, 40,* 215–227.

Moreland, K. L. (1984) Some ruminations on the validation of automated psychological reports. National Computer Systems: Minneapolis.

Newton, R. (1954) The clinician as judge: Total Rorschach and clinical case material. *Journal of Consulting Psychology, 18,* 248–250.

Oberholzer, E. (1944) Blind analysis of the people of Alor. In C. DuBois, *The People of Alor.* Minneapolis: University of Minnesota Press.

Palmer, J. O. (1949) Two approaches to Rorschach validation. *American Psychologist, 4,* 270–271.

Piotrowski, Z. (1957) *Perceptanalysis.* New York: Macmillan.

Piotrowski, Z. (1964) Digital computer interpretation of ink-blot test data. *Psychiatric Quarterly, 38,* 1–26.

Rorschach, H. (1921) *Psychodiagnostics.* Bern: Bircher.

Sarbin, T. R. (1941) Clinical psychology—Art or science. *Psychometrika, 6,* 391–400.

Schachtel, A. H. (1942) Blind interpretation of six Pilaga Indian children. *American Journal of Orthopsychiatry, 12,* 679–712.

Siegel, M. (1948) The diagnostic and prognostic validity of the Rorschach test in child guidance clinics. *American Journal of Orthopsychiatry, 18,* 119–133.

Silverman, L. H. (1959) A Q-Sort study of evaluations made from projective techniques. *Psychological Monographs, 27,* No. 477.

Swift, J. W. (1944) Matchings of teacher's descriptions and Rorschach analysis of pre-school children. *Child Development, 15,* 217–244.

Symonds, P. M. (1955) A contribution to our knowledge of the validity of the Rorschach. *Journal of Projective Techniques, 19,* 152–162.

Vernon, P. H. (1936) The evaluation of the matching method. *Journal of Educational Psychology, 27,* 1–17.

CHAPTER 14

The Tactics
of Interpretation

The first issue that must be addressed is to make sure that the protocol is interpretively valid. For several decades, Rorschachers assumed that if a subject is presented with the 10 ink blots and gives some responses to them, the results will yield information that is both reliable and valid. That Rorschach mythology has been followed by many who have been extensively involved with the test and has led to a substantial abuse of the test. Obviously, any conclusions and/or recommendations about psychological organization and functioning that are derived from a protocol that is not reliable and/or valid can be dangerously misleading, and in some instances can contribute to disastrous recommendations. Similarly, data from invalid protocols that are included among research findings can generate very spurious information.

There are two classes of protocols that are of questionable reliability and/or validity. Each may have some usefulness under certain conditions in which the assessment issues to be addressed are both narrow and specific, but neither will afford the full breadth of information concerning personality organization and functioning that typically is available from the Rorschach.

One class of potentially invalid protocols includes records that are potentially misleading because they were administered during a time in which the psychological organization of the subject has been thrown into severe disarray by transient or situational elements. Those circumstances often create a picture that, although valid for the moment, fails to accurately detect the more salient features of the personality of the subject and can produce a distorted psychological portrait. The second includes those records in which the number of responses is too few to produce reliable data. If interpreted, those protocols are likely to produce a personality picture that is quite misleading.

RECORDS TAKEN UNDER UNUSUAL CIRCUMSTANCES

Unfortunately, some examiners do not, or cannot exercise good judgment about when to administer the Rorschach. When referrals are made, schedules and routines become fixed and do not allow for much flexibility in decision making concerning the assessment routine. This lack of flexibility appears to be most common among inpatient settings in which the need to formulate a diagnosis or plan intervention requires that data be collected shortly after admission. Although the goal is admirable, there are instances in which the patients who are tested are in an actively psychotic or toxic state. Either of these conditions will impact significantly on the test performance.

When the Rorschach is administered to a subject who is toxic or actively psychotic, the results will, no doubt, portray the presence of that state. Usually this will manifest by a low $X+\%$, a higher than average $X-\%$, an elevated number of critical Special Scores, and in general, the protocol will be marked by considerable evidence of bizarreness and/or disorientation. Almost any competent interpreter can review the record, knowing nothing about the subject, and conclude that a very serious disturbance exists. However, the data do not reveal the extent to which the presence of the disturbance conceals and/or distorts information regarding the basic personality of the subject. Stated differently, to what extent are the data regarding basic personality styles valid when the record has been taken during a time when the subject is psychotic or toxic?

The relevance of this issue is highlighted by the protocols of 100 involuntary first admissions that were contributed to the protocol pool of the Rorschach Research Foundations from 14 county and state facilities (Exner, 1991). All were admitted in state of considerable disarray, and admission notes include references to psychotic-like features and/or behaviors. Most were suspected of drug-induced toxicity, but about 30% were tentatively diagnosed as schizophrenic. The group included 42 females and 58 males ranging in age from 19 to 33 years. Fifty of the 100 subjects were tested on the 2nd, 3rd, or 4th day after admission, while the remaining 50 were tested 7 to 10 days after admission. Almost all had been prescribed some medication after admission, including 21 who were taking antipsychotic medication at the time of the testing (8 from Group 1 and 13 from Group 2). Table 55 contains data for each group regarding the interpretive range or directionality for eight variables that are often critical in defining the presence of personality or response styles.

Assuming that both groups are drawn from the same population, these findings issue a significant caution regarding the interpretation of records administered shortly after admission if the presenting picture includes a psychotic or toxic-like state. This seems especially true when the admission has been involuntary. The data suggest that conclusions regarding response styles, capacity for control, modulation of affective displays, and extent of mediational distortion can be quite misleading.

These findings should not be interpreted to mean that the data are not valid for the moment. In all likelihood, they do illustrate the disarray of the subjects correctly, but they tend to be misleading if taken to represent the basic personality structure of many of the subjects. In this instance, it appears as if the intensity of the disarray, which probably includes the products of the stressful experience of being admitted involuntarily, created

Table 55. Range or Directionality Data for Two Groups of Involuntary First Admissions Tested at Different Times

Variable	Group 1 $N = 50$ Tested 2–4 Days after Admission		Group 2 $N = 50$ Tested 7–10 Days after Admission	
	N	$\%$	N	$\%$
EB = Ambitent	37*	74	19	38
D Score < 0	44*	88	16	32
$Adj\ D$ Score > 0	34*	68	11	22
$X - \% > .30$	39*	78	17	34
$Lambda > 0.99$	8	6	2	4
$EA < 6.0$	14	28	5	10
$CF + C > FC + 3$	31*	62	18	36
$p > a + 1$	5	10	13	26

*Significantly different from Group 2 ($p < .01$).

a transient form of dysfunctioning for many of the subjects tested prematurely. As a result, the test results for some subjects probably offered a more dismal picture of the basic personality than may have been the case if the testing had been deferred until the subject had made some adjustments to the situation and the psychotic or toxic episode had subsided.

If the purpose for using the Rorschach for the cases who were tested within two to four days after admission had been to confirm the state of disarray, that objective appears to have been readily achieved. But if the purpose was to generate a valid description of the more enduring personality features, that objective was probably not achieved for many of the cases, and in some instances, intervention decisions could have been made on the basis of data that easily might have been misinterpreted.

Some Rorschach lore suggests that it is preferable to administer the test before medication, especially high potency antipsychotic medication, is prescribed; or that it is best to administer the Rorschach as soon as a subject is available to ensure that the test performance will not be affected by the onset of intervention. Neither of those presumptions are true. The Rorschach data will have the clearest yield when the subject is cooperative and coherent. Pharmacological intervention, especially when the subject has been stabilized reasonably well on the medication, will have relatively little impact on most Rorschach variables, and certainly no significant impact on those variables that relate to the core features of the personality structure. Thus, it behooves those using the test to make intelligent decisions about when it should be administered, or when the administration might best be delayed.

BRIEF RECORDS

Unfortunately, brief records, that is, those containing 13 answers or less, occur much more frequently than might be suspected. A review of response frequency data for several groups in the protocol pool at the Rorschach Research Foundation reveals that the proportion of records containing 13 or fewer answers ranges from 6% for nonpatient adults to 14% of inpatient depressives and 17% of children with conduct disorders. The impact of brief records on research findings has been suspect for quite some time. For instance, the original Suicide Constellation (S-Con) correctly identified nearly 80% of subjects who effected their own death within 60 days after taking the Rorschach (Exner & Wylie, 1977). The revised S-Con (Exner, Martin, & Mason, 1984; Exner, 1986) improved the accuracy to nearly 85% while continuing to misidentify very few as false positives. Inspection of the false negative cases shows that 60% are records in which fewer than 13 answers occurred.

A review of 10 studies that were completed at the Rorschach Research Foundation between 1974 and 1984 concerning validation issues of test variables (Exner, 1988) shed additional light on the problem of brief protocols. These studies were selected because each contained at least 70 records and the data had been subjected to some form of discriminant or correlation analysis. The data for each study were reanalyzed twice using the same statistical procedures employed originally. In the first reanalysis, protocols containing fewer than 13 responses were deleted from the sample. In the second reanalysis, all records containing fewer than 14 answers were deleted from the sample. The results were striking. When the studies were reanalyzed with records of 12 or fewer answers omitted, the levels of significance that had been detected for positive findings in the original analyses improved substantially. When protocols of 13 or fewer answers were omitted in the second reanalysis, the findings again improved significantly. None of the new findings changed the basic interpretation of the data, but *in each study,* conclusions drawn from the original findings were strengthened considerably.

The results of this elementary exercise in data manipulation raised a question about when a Rorschach can be considered as truly representative of the subject. If differences between the original analyses and the two reanalyses are used as guidelines, it would appear clear that the majority of brief records, 13 responses or less, are of questionable usefulness and the interpretation of them could be quite misleading. The findings raised a new issue. Should all brief records be discarded as interpretively suspect, or might there be some way to differentiate the useful from the invalid record? This question was addressed by studying records collected in a variety of temporal consistency studies.

Thirty-six target pairs of protocols were culled from 295 pairs of records from nine short-term retest studies. Four involved nonpatient children and five included nonpatient adults, all retested between four and 30 days (Exner, 1978, 1983, 1986; Exner & Weiner, 1982). In each of the 36 target pairs, one of the protocols contains 13 or fewer answers while the second record of the pair contains at least 15 responses. A control group of 36 pairs of records was drawn randomly from the remaining pool of 259 subjects who had given at least 15 answers in each of their two records.

The first step was a correlational analysis to establish the retest reliabilities for each group, which are shown in Table 56.

The correlations in Table 56 offer considerable evidence to support the postulate that the structural data derived from a brief record are likely to be quite different than the structural data for the same subject generated from a record that contains at least 15 answers. The retest correlations for only two variables, m and $X + \%$, are reasonably similar for both groups and the correlations for the group in which one record contained 13 or fewer responses shows only two variables with values above .75 ($X + \%, D$). It seems clear that the probability is considerable for a second record to have substantially different values for most structural variables. Nonetheless, most of the retest correlations for the group containing one brief record are statistically significant, raising the possibility that some of the retest records might be interpretively similar to the first protocol.

A second analysis involved frequency calculations concerning the interpretive consistency of 17 ratios, indices, and percentages in Test 1 versus Test 2. This was done to address the issue of whether the interpretive range would change even though the absolute values might differ substantially from one test to the other. An inspection of the 36 target pairs of records revealed that, for eight subjects, the values for *Lambda* were .85 or less in both records. None of the values for L in the brief records of the remaining 28 target pairs fell lower than 1.0, and many were greater than 1.5 (Mean = 1.48, SD = .46). However, a *Lambda* value of less than .90 occurred in 22 of the 28 longer protocols for those pairs. Thus, the group was subdivided based on the value for L. Frequency data concerning the number of pairs of records in which the values in 17 ratios, percentages, and indices have the same interpretive directionality or range in both tests were tallied for all 72 pairs of protocols. The results are shown in Table 57 with the eight target pairs in which the value for L was .85 or less shown as a separate group.

As indicated in Table 57, the interpretive directionality or range remained the same for seven variables (*EB, D, Adj D, FC:CF + C, a:p, M^a:M^p,* and $X + \%$) in all 8 pairs of the target records in which L was less than .85 in both protocols and in 7 of the 8 pairs for three other variables (*eb, Zd,* and *L*). These findings seem important because a difference of

Table 56.   Correlation Coefficients for Two Groups of 36 Subjects Each Tested between 4 and 30 Days

Variable	Description	Group LO $R < 14$ in One Protocol r	Group AV $R > 14$ in Both Protocols r
R	No. of Responses	.36	.87
P	Popular Responses	.62	.89
Zf	Z Frequency	.53	.82
F	Pure Form	.48	.79
M	Human Movement	.44	.87
FM	Animal Movement	.28	.74
m	Inanimate Movement	.36	.28
a	Active Movement	.41	.88
p	Passive Movement	.22	.83
FC	Form Color Response	.34	.89
CF	Color Form Responses	.49	.71
C	Pure C Responses	.33	.59
CF + C	Color Dominant Responses	.38	.84
Sum C	Sum Weighted Color	.27	.86
T	Texture Responses	.54	.91
C'	Achromatic Color Responses	.28	.78
Y	Diffuse Shading Responses	.09	.40
V	Vista Responses	.62	.89
Ratios & Percentages			
L	*Lambda*	.46	.83
X + %	Extended Good Form	.81	.92
Afr	Affective Ratio	.49	.89
3r + (2)/R	Egocentricity Index	.51	.87
EA	Experience Actual	.44	.86
es	Experienced Stimulation	.23	.71
D	Stress Tolerance Index	.76	.92
Adj D	Adjusted D Score	.61	.93

as many as eight answers occurred between the Test 1 and Test 2 records in this group. However, it is equally important to note that the interpretive directionality or range shifted in between three and six of the eight protocols for eight other variables. In other words, even when *Lambda* is less than .85, the data for many of the variables that are important to interpretation are probably not valid.

The findings are much more negative when the value for *Lambda* exceeds .99. The same interpretive directionality or range existed for only two variables (*D* and *X + %*) in three-fourths or more of the remaining 28 target records. In fact, the proportion of pairs among those 28 protocols in which the same interpretive direction or range is found in both records is significantly lower than in both of the other groups for nine variables, and significantly lower than the control group for three additional variables.

These findings, although derived from relatively small samples, highlight the potential hazards that can exist in working with brief protocols, whether in a clinical or research setting. It seems clear that the majority of brief records will not have the level of reliability prerequisite to the assumption of interpretive validity. These results suggest that the interpretation of the structural data of a brief test should be avoided.

Table 57. Frequencies and Percentages for Three Groups Showing the Number of Pairs of Protocols in Which the Values for 17 Variables Fall in the Same Interpretive Range in Both Tests

| Variable | Target Groups $R < 14$ in One Protocol | | | | Control Group $R > 14$ in Both Protocols ($N = 36$) | |
| | $L < .86$ in Both Protocols ($N = 8$) | | $L > .99$ in Brief Protocol ($N = 28$) | | | |
	Freq	%	Freq	%	Freq	%
EB	8	100	11*	39	33	92
eb	7	88	13*	46	35	97
D	8	100	21	75	35	97
Adj D	8	100	16*	57	36	100
a:p	8	100	15*	53	34	94
$M^a:M^p$	8	100	13*	46	33	92
FC:CF + C	8	100	9*	32	36	100
Afr	5	63	7	25	35*	97
3r + (2)/R	6	75	11*	39	35	97
L	7	88	6*	21	34	94
X + %	8	100	24	86	36	100
X − %	5	63	18	64	32	89
Zd	7	88	13*	46	32	89
W:d	3	38	7	25	30*	83
W:M	2	25	6	21	31*	86
ALL H CONT	4	50	11	39	33*	92
ISOLATE:R	6	75	20	71	35	97

*Proportional Chi-square yields $p < .05$.

The data do seem to support the hypothesis that *Lambda* can be used as a source from which to estimate the probable reliability for a few, *but not all,* variables in brief records.

The composite of a low number of responses plus a high *Lambda* can represent the performance of a highly resistive subject who is simply attempting to avoid the many demands of the test situation. In effect, these performances depict *subtle refusals* to take the test. On the other hand, a high value for *Lambda* can represent a very marked response style that is basic to the personality structure. Unfortunately, there is no easy way to distinguish between the low *R*, high *L* record that illustrates resistance from the low *R*, high *L* record that reflects a valid indicator of a coping style. Thus, when records such as these occur, the interpreter will, at best, be very hard pressed to differentiate characteristics that are trait-like versus those that might be situationally provoked.

It seems clear that all short records pose potential problems for the interpreter. Even if *Lambda* has a value of .85 or less, the data for many structural variables are likely to be misleading. Thus, as noted in Chapter 3, protocols in which the number of responses is less than 14 should probably be discarded on the premise that they are unreliable and as such are not interpretively valid. There will be some obvious exceptions, but these will be the protocols of severely disturbed patients in which the X + % is extremely low, the X − % is quite high, and two or three bizarre responses occur, *and for which other data exist confirming the magnitude of the disability*.

As noted earlier, encounters with brief records occur much more often than might be expected. Some reflect a form of subtle resistance to the test, but in other instances, the brief record simply may be the result of a subject following instructions very concretely and failing to generalize from encouragement given during Card I. Some subjects, especially young children, want to go through the test as quickly as possible and their haste produces a short record. Whatever the cause, a record of less than 14 answers should not be accepted. In fact, it should not even be inquired, as per the instructions in Chapter 3.

BEGINNING WITH THE SUICIDE CONSTELLATION

If a subject is age 15 or older, the interpretation should always begin by inspecting the value for the Suicide Constellation. The reason for this approach is the *S-CON* does not fall into any of the clusters of variables, probably because it is an array of variables from several clusters which, as a collective, has an actuarial usefulness in detecting those who have features similar to individuals who have effected their own death. Some groupings of items in the *S-CON* have a conceptual similarity, but the entire listing does not.

Unfortunately, it has no demonstrated usefulness for subjects who are age 14 or under, and earlier attempts to develop a similar constellation for younger subjects have not been successful. In fact, neither the original data set from which the *S-CON* was developed (Exner & Wilie, 1977) nor the cross-validation data set that was used to modify the constellation (Exner, 1986) contain subjects under the age of 18. However, a study of the few available records of 15- and 16-year-old subjects who effected their own death within 60 days after having been administered the Rorschach indicates that about two-thirds were correctly identified by the *S-CON*.

The early identification of the potential for self-destructive behavior is a persistent challenge for the clinician. The classic works of Shneidman and Farberow (1957) and Farberow and Shneidman (1961) have demonstrated clear relationships between demographic and/or behavioral variables and effected suicide, and it is unlikely that any test data, taken alone, will provide a greater discrimination of suicidal risk. Nonetheless, those data often are not available; thus, when test data can provide clues concerning this risk, they should be taken seriously as a warning to conduct a more extensive evaluation of the issue.

Any review of the research literature concerning suicide reveals a host of methodological and interpretive problems. Criterion variables often differ considerably, and data from suicidal subjects are often collected too long before, or too long after, the critical event. Possibly even more important is the matter of *intent,* which is extremely difficult, if not impossible, to judge at a very precise level. Some suicides are effected by means that ordinarily are not expected to produce death, such as taking 12 or 15 aspirin, but such deaths do occur. On the other hand, there are people who survive self-inflicted gunshot wounds to the head. It seems unlikely that the intent to die was greater for the aspirin-taker than for the gunshot victim, yet on a purely demographic basis, the former is recorded as an effected suicide, whereas the latter is recorded as merely an attempt. Although some of these problems are potentially solvable, research concerning suicide is confounded by the scientific issue of prediction. Studies concerning suicide are really postdictive or retrospective, usually based on data collected from subjects who have been identified by other sources as suicidal (most commonly by reason of a prior attempt) or, in fewer instances, are based on data collected before the attempted or effected suicide. Thus even if a potential predictor is discovered, moral commitment to prevention clearly takes precedence over the scientific fantasy to test the predictor by letting events run their full course.

The complexity of features that promotes self-destruction is such that no single variable (or small group of variables) can be expected to be accurate in identifying suicide potential. This point is made quite well in a thorough review of the pre-1970 literature concerning Rorschach data and the suicidal subject (Goldfried, Stricker, & Weiner, 1971). They note that research has focused on single signs, such as the color-shading response (Applebaum & Holzman, 1962); multi-sign approaches (Piotrowski, 1950; Martin, 1951; Sakheim, 1955; Fleischer, 1957); content indicators (Lindner, 1946; White & Schreiber, 1952; Thomas et al., 1973); symbolic content (Sapolsky, 1963); and the use of signs and content combined (Hertz, 1948, 1949). Although many of these studies have demonstrated statistically significant differences between suicidal and nonsuicidal subjects, the actual number of *true positive cases* identified is often less than two-thirds, whereas the number of *false positive cases* often exceeds one-third. Thus although the findings from such studies are important, their clinical utility is often quite limited.

During the first 5 years after the Rorschach Research Foundation was created, 41 protocols became available that had been administered within 60 days prior to an effected suicide. That sample was increased to 59 in 1975 by the response to a solicitation letter that was sent to 108 clinical installations throughout North America, requesting the records of subjects meeting this criterion. The structural data were computer searched for all possible combinations of variables, and variable frequencies, to detect those appearing in at least 30 of the 59 records. The records were also subdivided using the method by which death was invoked as a crude index of intent or lethality, in an attempt to determine if that issue might be confounding to any findings. Class I suicides were defined as those in which the act employed a tactic that is almost certain to produce death, and for which essentially *no* rescue time is available after the act is initiated (explosives, jumping from great heights, cutting vital organs, etc.). Class II suicides involve an act that also has a very high probability of producing death, but some rescue time is available after the act is initiated (hanging, ingestion of most poisons, drowning, etc.). Class III suicides were defined as those in which the act has a very low probability of invoking death, and considerable rescue time is available after it is initiated (inhaling gases, cutting nonvital organs, ingesting analgesics or soporifics, etc.).

Whenever a cluster of six or more items appeared in 30 or more records of the target group, the computer would randomly draw three control groups of 50 subjects each, one consisting of schizophrenics, one of inpatient depressives, and one of nonpatients. The control groups were searched for the same constellation of items found in the target group, and chi-squares were calculated to determine whether the frequencies for the target group were significantly different from the controls. In the course of these analyses, several constellations of variables were discovered in more than 30 of the target protocols; however, only three differentiated that group from *all* three control groups at a statistically significant level, and one of those had considerably greater discriminatory power. Consequently, that group of 11 variables was incorporated into the format of the Comprehensive System and identified as the Suicide Constellation (Exner & Wylie, 1977). An expectancy table revealed that, *using a cutoff of eight or more positive variables,* it correctly identified 44 of the 59 suicide cases (75%), while identifying 10 of the 50 depressives (20%), six of the schizophrenics (12%), and none of the nonpatients as *false positives.* When reviewed by Class of act, it correctly identified 14 of 19 Class I subjects (74%), 20 of 24 Class II subjects (83%), and 10 of 16 Class III cases (63%). If the cutoff is lowered to 7, it correctly identifies more than 80% of the target sample; *however,* the number of false positives from the control groups also increases substantially, and includes 58% of the depressive sample, 38% of the schizophrenics, and even 8% of the nonpatients as false positives. Thus the cutoff of eight has been employed as the critical point at which the data appear sufficient to warrant concern.

During the period from 1977 to 1984, additional protocols, meeting the criterion of having been administered within 60 days prior to an effected suicide, accumulated in the data pool of the Rorschach Research Foundation. Most were contributed by alumni of Rorschach Workshops, the continuing education section of the Foundation. By 1984, the number of new records had reached 101 and provided a reasonable sample against which to test the validity of the original finding. The new protocols include 41 males and 60 females, ranging in age from 19 to 55 years, with an average of approximately 30 years. They were also subdivided into Class of act, using the same criteria as in the original study, to provide some index of intent. Three groups of 101 subjects each, one consisting of inpatient depressives, one of schizophrenics, and one of nonpatients, were randomly drawn from the protocol pool to use as controls. Frequency distributions for each of the 11 variables in the *S-CON* were generated for each of the four groups, plus the three subgroups in the target sample. Variables were ranked within each group and subgroup from 1 (most frequent) to 11 (least frequent). A stepwise discriminant function analysis was also used to evaluate the respective power of each variable to discriminate within each group, and to establish classification weights. Five other variables were also tested for discriminant power because they occurred with substantial frequencies among the target subjects. They included $MOR > 3$, $AG > 2$, $An + Bl > 2$, $Afr < .40$, and $T = 0$.

The first series of analyses indicate that the original 11 variable constellation did identify 75 of the 101 suicides cases correctly (74%), while misidentifying as false positives only 12 of the 101 depressives (12%), six of the 101 schizophrenics (6%), and none of the nonpatients, *if the cutoff of eight positive variables is applied.* As in the original study, a cutoff of seven increased the "correct" rate by about 10%, but also inflated the number of false positives from the two psychiatric groups to unacceptable levels (depressives = 31%; schizophrenics = 19%). The additional analyses yielded some other important findings. First, when four of the five other variables were added into the constellation, both separately and collectively, the number of correct identifications in the target sample did not improve. They are $AG > 2$, $An + Bl < 2$, $Afr < .40$, and $T = 0$. However, the addition of the fifth variable, $MOR > 3$, improved the discriminating power of the *S-CON* significantly. When added to the original constellation, and continuing to use the cutoff of eight positive variables, the correct identification of the suicide group was increased to nearly 80%, whereas the number of false positives among the three control groups did not increase.

A second yield from the added analyses, and especially from the discriminant functions analysis with $MOR > 3$ added, concerned the Egocentricity Index. In the original constellation, it was defined as positive when having a value of less than .30. In the 1977 sample, it was the third most powerful contributing variable and did correlate significantly, independent of other variables, with effected suicide ($r = .32$). In the 1984 sample, when defined as positive by a value of less than .30, the weighted rank dropped to eight in relation to all 12 variables and, taken alone, it failed to correlate significantly with effected suicide ($r = .20$). A further examination of the data revealed that a somewhat bimodal feature existed in the distribution of scores for the Index in the target sample. In the 1977 sample, 40 of the 59 subjects had Egocentricity Index scores of less than .30, whereas 9 others had scores higher than .40. When the upper group was added in an experimental trial to define the variable as positive, no improvement in the discrimination occurred, and thus the possibility of using upper and lower cutoffs to define the variable as positive was discarded. In the 1984 sample, however, only 61 of the 101 subjects had scores of less than .31, *and 27 others had scores greater than .44*. On the other hand, most subjects in the schizophrenia and nonpatient control groups had Egocentricity Indices falling between .20 and .36. Thus by altering the criterion for the Index as a positive variable in the *S-CON* to the bimodal cutoffs of less than .31 or greater than .44, a refinement of the discriminatory power of the constellation is realized, without significantly increasing the false positive rate among controls. The discriminatory power of the revised 12 variables *S-CON* is shown in Table 58.

It will be noted that if the cutoff of eight positive variables is applied, 83% of the target group are identified correctly, including more than 90% of the Class I subjects, 76% of the Class II subjects, and nearly 80% of the Class III subjects, while misidentifying only 12% of the depressive controls, 6% of the schizophrenic controls, and none of the nonpatients. As with the 1977 sample, a cutoff of seven improves the target identifications by more than 10%, but also more than doubles the proportion of false positives among the two psychiatric control groups, and includes the false positive identification of one nonpatient subject.

It is important to stress that, although the *S-CON* seems quite useful for the identification of some subjects who seem at high risk for self-destruction, or a preoccupation with self-destruction, a *false negative rate* of more than 15% exists within the target sample when the cutoff of eight is applied, and a *false positive rate* of more than 10% exists among depressive controls. These data confirm the earlier caution that the *S-CON* is by no means infallible. If eight or more variables are positive, it should be taken as a warning, and further exploration of the possibility of self-destructive features should be pursued expeditiously. Conversely, if the *S-CON* contains fewer than eight positive variables, it should *not be misinterpreted* as signifying that no suicidal risk element is present.

STRATEGIES IN ADDRESSING CLUSTERS OF DATA

Once a protocol has been judged to be interpretively valid and the *S-CON* has been reviewed, a decision is required concerning the interpretive routine to be followed. The order by which each data cluster is evaluated will vary from record to record, but the order should never be random. The decision concerning the search strategy is not quite as simple as once seemed to be the case. During an earlier phase of development of the *Comprehensive System* (Exner, 1978), it was logically concluded that all interpretive routines should begin with a review of the data for four variables (*EB, EA, eb,* and *es*) that had been designated as the *Four Square*. The rule of beginning with the Four Square was based on the logic that the four variables constitute the basic source of information regarding the core features of personality that relate to coping styles and capacity for control. The practice of beginning the interpretation with the Four Square worked well for many records, but there was a second group of protocols in which hypotheses formed early into the interpretation required modification or, in some instances, abandonment as findings from other test data unfolded. This unexpected need to backtrack and reorganize hypotheses posed problems for the interpreter as it required a change in set and a

Table 58. Frequency of Cases Identified by Number of Positive Variables in a 12-Item Constellation, from an Effected Suicide Group, Subdivided by Classification of Method Employed, Plus Three Control Groups

Group	12		11		10		9		8		7		6		5 or less	
	N	%	N	%	N	%	N	%	N	%	N	%	N	%	N	%
Effected Suicides																
Combined N = 101	1	1%	14	14%	19	19%	49	49%	84	83%	95	95%	99	98%	101	100%
Class I N = 36	0	—	8	22%	11	31%	18	50%	33	92%	35	97%	36	100%	36	100%
Class II N = 46	1	2%	6	13%	7	15%	21	46%	35	76%	42	91%	45	98%	46	100%
Class III N = 19	0	—	2	11%	2	11%	9	47%	15	79%	16	84%	16	84%	19	100%
Control Groups																
Inpatient Depressed																
N = 101	0	—	0	—	0	—	2	2%	12	12%	26	26%	44	44%	101	100%
Schizophrenic																
N = 101	0	—	0	—	1	1%	3	3%	6	6%	16	16%	33	33%	101	100%
Nonpatients																
N = 101	0	—	0	—	0	—	0	—	0	—	1	1%	2	3%	101	100%

reintegration of findings, and sometimes created confusion about how best to weigh findings in the total picture. Any of these challenges, if not properly addressed, risks the richness of the interpretive yield.

In studying many protocols in which hypotheses generated from the data of the Four Square required modification, it became apparent that the recommended tactic for beginning interpretation had failed to appreciate two facts that have become much more apparent as research findings have continued to unfold. First, while the *EB* does provide information regarding coping preferences, there are other stylistic features of the personality that can supersede that preference, or have a more dominating impact on decisions and/or behaviors. Second, in some cases the data of the Four Square may present a less accurate picture because other psychological features (usually pathological) have altered the organization and/or functioning of the person substantially.

After considerable research (Exner, 1991), 11 *Key* variables have been uncovered that, when set in an order of dominance or priority, appear to define the best order of cluster review. The 11 Key variables, in their order of dominance, are:

1. *SCZI* is greater than 3.
2. Depression Index is greater than 5.
3. *D* Score is less than Adjusted *D* Score.
4. *CDI* is positive.
5. Adjusted *D* Score is in the minus range.
6. *Lambda* is greater than .99.
7. At least one reflection answer is present.
8. *EB* is introversive.
9. *EB* is extratensive.
10. Passive movement is greater than active movement by more than one point.
11. The *HVI* is positive.

In effect, the presence of a given Key variable predicts which combination of two or three clusters of data will yield the data sources that will contribute the most substantial information about the core psychological features of the subject. Generally, these are features that will be given considerable emphasis in forming any description of the subject. They are dominant elements of personality structure and have a major impact on the psychological organization. They exert a significant influence on the way in which other features are organized and usually afford considerable direction to the psychological functioning of the subject.

SELECTING THE INTERPRETIVE STRATEGY

The findings about Key variables reaffirmed the notion that the interpretive search for all protocols should not follow the same routine. They suggested that more logical search strategies could be developed in which the interpretive routine would flow systematically and avoid backtracking and reorganization of hypotheses. In such a format, the first bits of data that are evaluated should provide some information concerning the core elements of the personality structure and/or response styles of the subject. Thus, the decision about which cluster of data to use as the starting point is important because the yield should form a centerpiece in the network of descriptive statements that will ultimately be generated. In turn, the first cluster selected usually should provide direction for the order by which the remaining clusters will be reviewed.

An examination of the 11 Key variables suggests that they reflect two sorts of data. Although five of the variables ($SCZI > 3$, $DEPI > 5$, D Score $< Adj\ D$ Score, $CDI > 3$, $Adj\ D$ Score < 0) deal with personality structure, they also focus more on the presence of psychopathology or the potential for functional disorganization. The remaining six variables involve more basic personality styles, any of which can form the cornerstone of organization and functioning. The 11 Key variables, and the recommended interpretive search strategies that should be employed are shown in Table 59.

The Key variables shown in Table 59 are listed in an order of priority. In other words, the first Key variable that is positive defines the interpretive routine for the record. Most of the routines are straightforward, but in some cases the entire routine cannot be defined by simply using the first positive Key variable and subsequent Key variables, or Tertiary variables must also be used before the complete routine is established. Each of the strategies or routines follows in a logical sequence so that each new finding merges neatly with those already developed.

Each of the strategies or routines shown in Table 59 is both empirically and logically developed. These routines are empirical in the sense that the first two or three clusters reviewed are likely to yield the greatest amount of information concerning the core features of the subject and logical in the sense that the sequence is designed so that each new finding merges neatly with those already developed. It is important to note that the 11

Table 59.   Interpretive Search Strategies Based on Key Variables

Positive Variable	Typical Cluster Search Routine
$SCZI > 3$	Ideation > Mediation > Processing > Controls > Affect > Self-Perception > Interpersonal Perception
$DEPI > 5$	Affect > Controls > Self-Perception > Interpersonal Perception > Processing > Mediation > Ideation
$D \rightarrow Adj\ D$	Controls > Situation Stress > (The remaining search routine should be that identified for the next positive key variable or list of tertiary variables)
$CDI > 3$	Controls > Affect > Self-Perception > Interpersonal Perception > Processing > Mediation > Ideation
$Adj\ D$ is minus	Controls > (The remaining search routine should be that identified for the next positive key variable or list of tertiary variables)
$Lambda > 0.99$	Processing > Mediation > Ideation > Controls > Affect > Self-Perception > Interpersonal Perception
Reflection > 0	Self-Perception > Interpersonal Perception > Controls (The remaining search routine should be selected from that identified for the next positive key variable or list of tertiary variables)
EB = Introversive	Ideation > Processing > Mediation > Controls > Affect > Self-Perception > Interpersonal Perception
EB = Extratensive	Affect > Self-Perception > Interpersonal Perception > Controls > Processing > Mediation > Ideation
$p > a + 1$	Ideation > Processing > Mediation > Controls > Self-Perception > Interpersonal Perception > Affect
HVI Positive	Ideation > Processing > Mediation > Controls > Self-Perception > Interpersonal Perception > Affect

search strategies are not markedly discrete. Three of the clusters—ideation, mediation, and processing—are always in tandem because they are interrelated. Likewise, the clusters pertaining to self-perception and interpersonal perception also are always in tandem because of their interrelationship.

TERTIARY VARIABLES AS STARTING POINTS

Some protocols may not contain any positive Key variables. When this occurs, the starting point can be selected from positive findings among numerous tertiary variables. Unlike the Key variables, tertiary variables do not have much predictive power. They do tend to highlight which cluster will yield the most significant information about a subject but do not predict which subsequent clusters will contain the most supplementing information. Thus, the search routines developed from them are general guidelines for beginning, but they should not be regarded as inviolate. Table 60 provides a list of the Tertiary variables that are used most frequently to determine the initial interpretive search pattern when *none* of the key variables are positive. The recommended search pattern can be altered in some cases, but probably should occur only under unusual circumstances.

Table 60.   Interpretive Search Strategies Based on Positive Tertiary Variables

Positive Variable	Typical Cluster Search Routine
OBS Positive	Processing → Mediation → Ideation → Controls → Affect → Self-Perception → Interpersonal Perception
DEPI = 5	Affect → Controls → Self-Perception Interpersonal Perception → Processing → Mediation Ideation
EA > 12	Controls → Ideation → Processing → Mediation → Affect → Self-Perception → Interpersonal Perception
$M \to O$, or $M^p > M^a$, or *SUM*6 *SPEC SC* > 5	Ideation → Mediation → Processing → Controls → Affect → Self-Perception → Interpersonal Perception
SUM SHAD > *FM* + *M*, or *CF* + *C* > *FC* + 1, or *Afr* < 0.46	Affect → Controls → Self-Perception → Interpersonal Perception → Processing → Mediation → Ideation
X − % > 20%, or *Zd* > +3.0 or < −3.0	Processing → Mediation → Ideation → Controls → Affect → Self-Perception → Interpersonal Perception
3*R* + (2)/*R* < .33	Personal Perception → Interpersonal Perception → Affect → Controls → Processing → Mediation → Ideation
MOR > 2, or *AG* > 2	Personal Perception → Interpersonal Perception Controls → Ideation → Processing → Mediation → Affect
T = 0 or > 1	Personal Perception → Interpersonal Perception Affect → Controls → Processing → Processing → Ideation

CASE ILLUSTRATION

The procedure of selecting the interpretive search routine may be illustrated by using the L.S. protocol, presented earlier in Chapter 10. The Structural Summary for L.S. is shown in Table 61.

Table 61. Structural Summary for Protocol L.S.

```
==================================================================================
LOCATION              DETERMINANTS                       CONTENTS      S-CONSTELLATION
FEATURES         BLENDS           SINGLE                               NO..FV+VF+V+FD>2
                                              H   = 4, 0               NO..Col-Shd Bl>0
Zf    = 13       m.CF             M   = 3      (H) = 0, 0               NO..Ego<.31,>.44
ZSum  = 39.5     FM.FD.FT         FM  = 3      Hd  = 2, 0               NO..MOR > 3
ZEst  = 41.5     m.FY             m   = 0      (Hd)= 0, 0               NO..Zd > +- 3.5
                 FM.FD            FC  = 1      Hx  = 0, 0               YES..es > EA
W     = 8        M.m             CF  = 2      A   = 8, 0               YES..CF+C > FC
 (Wv  = 0)                        C   = 0      (A) = 0, 1               NO..X+% < .70
D   = 16                          Cn  = 0      Ad  = 2, 0               NO..S > 3
Dd  = 1                           FC'= 0       (Ad)= 0, 0               NO..P < 3 or > 8
S   = 1                           C'F= 0       An  = 0, 0               NO..Pure H < 2
                                  C'  = 0      Art = 1, 0               NO..R < 17
   DQ                             FT  = 1      Ay  = 1, 0               2.....TOTAL
.........(FQ-)                    TF  = 0      Bl  = 0, 0
  +  = 9    ( 0)                  T   = 0      Bt  = 2, 1               SPECIAL SCORINGS
  o  = 16   ( 0)                  FV  = 0      Cg  = 1, 0                  Lv1    Lv2
v/+  = 0    ( 0)                  VF  = 0      Cl  = 0, 0      DV  =  0x1    0x2
  v  = 0    ( 0)                  V   = 0      Ex  = 0, 0      INC =  0x2    0x4
                                  FY  = 1      Fd  = 0, 0      DR  =  1x3    0x6
                                  YF  = 0      Fi  = 0, 1      FAB =  0x4    0x7
                                  Y   = 0      Ge  = 0, 0      ALOG=  0x5
      FORM QUALITY                Fr  = 0      Hh  = 1, 0      CON =  0x7
                                  rF  = 0      Ls  = 0, 1         SUM6  = 1
      FQx  FQf  MQual  SQx        FD  = 0      Na  = 0, 0         WSUM6 =  3
  +  = 2    0    2    0           F   = 9      Sc  = 3, 1
  o  = 22   9    2    1                        Sx  = 0, 0      AB  = 1    CP  = 0
  u  = 1    0    0    0                        Xy  = 0, 0      AG  = 0    MOR = 0
  -  = 0    0    0    0                        Id  = 0, 1      CFB = 0    PER = 1
none=  0    --   0    0           (2) = 8                      COP = 3    PSV = 0
==================================================================================
                 RATIOS, PERCENTAGES, AND DERIVATIONS

Core                              Affect                Interpersonal
R = 25           L =  0.56        FC:CF+C = 1: 3        COP = 3      AG = 0
--------------------------------- Pure C  =   0        Food    = 0
EB = 4: 3.5  EA =  7.5  EBPer= N/A Afr    =0.56        Isolate/R =0.16
eb = 8: 4    es =  12   D   = -1  S       = 1          H:(H)Hd(Hd)= 4: 2
         Adj es =   9  Adj D =  0 Blends:R= 5:25       (HHd):(AAd)= 0: 1
--------------------------------- CP      = 0          H+A:Hd+Ad =13: 4
FM = 5 :  C'= 0   T = 2
m  = 3 :  V = 0   Y = 2
                                 Mediation       Processing        Self Perception
Ideation                         P   = 8         Zf  =13           3r+(2)/R=0.32
a:p  =  8: 5   Sum6  =  1        X+% =0.96       Zd  = -2.0        Fr+rF   = 0
Ma:Mp =  4: 1  Lv2   =  0        F+% =1.00       W:D:Dd = 8:16: 1  FD      = 2
2AB+Art+Ay= 4  WSum6 =  3        X-% =0.00       W:M = 8: 4        An+Xy   = 0
M-   =  0      Mnone =  0        S-% =0.00       DQ+ = 9           MOR     = 0
                                 Xu% =0.04       DQv = 0
----------------------------------------------------------------------------------
  SCZI = 0    DEPI = 2    CDI = 1    S-CON = 2    HVI = No    OBS =YES
==================================================================================
```
Copyright (c) 1976, 1985, 1990 by John E. Exner, Jr.

Following the list of Key variables in Table 59, it will be noted that neither of the first two (*SCZI, DEPI*) are positive. The value for the *SCZI* is zero and the value for the *DEPI* is 2. The third Key variable ($D < Adj\ D$) is positive. The D Score is -1 while the Adjusted D Score is zero. Therefore, as specified in Table 59, the interpretive routine will begin with the cluster of variables that focus on the issue of controls. Once the review of the variables in the controls cluster has been exhausted, the search will turn to the array of variables concerning situational stress.

As noted in Table 59, the remaining interpretive search strategy is not defined. This is because the Key variable $D <$ Adjusted D simply indicates the presence of some situationally related stress. It is for this reason that the first cluster to be reviewed concerns controls. Questions regarding the overall capacity for control and general tolerance for stress become quite important as does information concerning the impact of the current situational stress, some of which will be provided by studying the array of variables related to situational stress. But neither of those data sets are likely to provide more salient information about some of the core features of the psychological organization or personality of the subject. It is for this reason that it is necessary to continue searching through the list of Key variables for another that is positive. The next positive Key variable, or in some instances the first positive tertiary variable, will be used to define the remainder of the interpretive strategy.

The data for the L.S. record reveal that none of the remaining Key variables are positive. The *CDI* value is only 1, the Adjusted *D* Score does not have a minus value, the value for *Lambda* is only 0.56, and there are no reflections in the record. The *EB* is neither introversive or extratensive. For either of those styles to be indicated, the value for one side of the *EB* must be at least two points greater than the value for the other side if *EA* is 10 or less, or more than two points if the value for *EA* exceeds 10. The sum of passive movement is not greater than the sum of active movement, and the Hypervigilance Index (*HVI*) is not positive. Thus, it becomes necessary to move to the list of Tertiary variables to determine the appropriate search routine.

The first tertiary variable (*OBS*) is positive, indicating the presence of an obsessive style. Thus, the interpretive strategy for the L.S. record will be:

Controls → Situation Stress → Processing → Mediation → Ideation
→ Affect → Self-Perception → Interpersonal Perception

The L.S. record will be used to illustrate how the data points in each cluster are addressed in the context of the overall interpretation in subsequent chapters. However, before moving to those data, it is important to review the interpretive importance of the Key variables as each one, whether or not it dictates the interpretive searching routine, will often highlight the presence of significant features that can have a major impact on the psychological organization and functioning of the subject.

REFERENCES

Applebaum, S. A., and Holzman, P. S. (1962) The color-shading response and suicide. *Journal of Projective Techniques,* **26,** 155–161.

Exner, J. E. (1978) *The Rorschach: A Comprehensive System. Volume 2: Current research and advanced interpretation.* New York: Wiley.

Exner, J. E. (1983) Rorschach assessment. In I. B. Weiner (Ed.), *Clinical Methods in Psychology,* (2nd Ed.). New York: Wiley.

Exner, J. E. (1986) *The Rorschach: A Comprehensive System. Volume 1: Basic foundations,* (2nd Ed.). New York: Wiley.

Exner, J. E. (1988) Problems with brief Rorschach protocols. *Journal of Personality Assessment,* **52,** 640–647.

Exner, J. E. (1991) *The Rorschach: A Comprehensive System. Volume 2: Interpretation,* (2nd Ed.). New York: Wiley.

Exner, J. E., Martin, L. S., and Mason, B. (1984) *A review of the Suicide Constellation.* 11th International Rorschach Congress, Barcelona.

Exner, J. E., and Weiner, I. B. (1982) *The Rorschach: A Comprehensive System. Volume 3: Assessment of Children and Adolescents.* New York: Wiley.

Exner, J. E., and Wilie, J. R. (1977) Some Rorschach data concerning suicide. *Journal of Personality Assessment,* **41,** 339–348.

Farberow, N. L., and Shneidman, E. S. (Eds.) (1961) *The Cry for Help.* New York: McGraw-Hill.

Fleischer, M. S. (1957) Differential Rorschach configurations of suicidal patients: A psychological study of threatened, attempted, and successful suicides. Unpublished doctoral dissertation, Yeshiva University.

Goldfried, M., Stricker, G., and Weiner, I. B. (1971) *Rorschach Handbook of Clinical and Research Applications.* Englewood Cliffs, N.J.: Prentice-Hall.

Hertz, M. R. (1948) Suicidal configurations in Rorschach records. *Rorschach Research Exchange and Journal of Projective Techniques,* **12,** 3–58.

Hertz, M. R. (1949) Further study of "suicidal" configurations in Rorschach records. *Rorschach Research Exchange and Journal of Projective Techniques,* **13,** 44–73.

Lindner, R. M. (1946) Content analysis in Rorschach work. *Rorschach Research Exchange,* **10,** 121–129.

Martin, H. (1951) A Rorschach study of suicide. Unpublished doctoral dissertation, University of Kentucky.

Piotrowski, Z. (1950) A Rorschach Compendium: Revised and Enlarged. *Psychiatric Quarterly,* **24,** 543–596.

Sakheim, G. A. (1955) Suicidal responses on the Rorschach test. *Journal of Nervous and Mental Disease,* **122,** 332–344.

Sapolsky, A. (1963) An indicator of suicidal ideation on the Rorschach test. *Journal of Projective Techniques and Personality Assessment,* **27,** 332–335.

Shneidman, E. S., and Faberow, N. L. (1957) *Clues to Suicide.* New York: McGraw-Hill.

Thomas, C. B., Ross, C. D., Brown, B. S., and Duszynski, K. R. (1973) A prospective study of the Rorschachs of suicides: The predictive potential of pathological content. *The Johns Hopkins Medical Journal,* **132,** 334–360.

White, M. A., and Schreiber, H. (1952) Diagnosing "suicidal risks" on the Rorschach. *Psychiatric Quarterly Supplement,* **26,** 161–189.

CHAPTER 15

Key Variables I—
SCZI, DEPI, CDI

Anytime one of the Key variables is positive, an initial hypothesis should be formulated that is in accord with the positive finding even before beginning the study of data in the specific clusters. As noted in the preceding chapter, the first five Key variables tend to focus on features that signal the likelihood of pathology, or at least the potential for psychological disorganization. Obviously, each also conveys some information about personality structure, but the presence or potential for disorganization is usually the more critical element when attempting to flesh out a valid portrait of the psychology of the subject. Two of the five, the Schizophrenia Index (*SCZI*) and the Depression Index (*DEPI*), connote the likelihood of a serious pathological state when they are positive. Two others, *CDI* > 3 and *AdjD* is minus, indicate the presence of a psychological organization in which a marked potential for disorganization exists. The last, *D* < *AdjD,* suggests the presence of some situationally related stress that may impede typical levels of functioning, sometimes quite severely. The material in this chapter focuses on the first three (*SCZI, DEPI, CDI*) because when they are positive, they often highlight some features regarding the psychological organization that contribute significantly to both diagnosis and treatment planning.

THE SCHIZOPHRENIA INDEX (*SCZI*)

The approach to interpretating the *SCZI* should be similar to that used with the Suicide Constellation. If the value is not positive, it *does not* necessarily rule out schizophrenia, but simply indicates that there is no firm actuarial data on which to develop a postulate that schizophrenia is present. Conversely, if the value for the *SCZI* is positive, any of three hypotheses may be appropriate depending on the actual value for the Index.

If the *SCZI* value is 4, the initial hypothesis is the most conservative and equivocal, namely that it can be concluded that the subject manifests many features that are consistent with those found commonly among schizophrenics and infrequently among other subjects. This suggests that there is a reasonable likelihood that schizophrenia is present and that the interpretive search will include some focus that will attempt to confirm or reject the postulate. However, the conclusion that schizophrenia is present should not be made unless the data are clearly supportive of it.

If the *SCZI* is 5, the initial hypothesis should be more definitive than if the value is 4, that is, evidence indicates that there is a strong probability of schizophrenia. The interpretive search begins with that assumption, and the routine includes focus on the manifestations of the disorder with awareness that there is some possibility that the hypothesis might be rejected as the specifics of data sets are reviewed. In these cases, the hypothesis concerning the likelihood of schizophrenia should not be abandoned in the descriptive summary unless specific findings are very compelling.

If the *SCZI* value is 6, the initial hypothesis is even more stringent. A value of 6 indicates a very strong likelihood that schizophrenia is present and the interpretive search begins with that as a given. Whereas the approach to cases in which the *SCZI* value is 4 proceeds on the assumption of a possibility, to be accepted or rejected, the approach in cases where the value is 6 proceeds on the assumption that schizophrenia is present and only extremely compelling data would cause that conclusion to be altered.

RESEARCH RELATED TO HYPOTHESES BASED ON THE *SCZI*

The issue of identifying schizophrenia has been both complex and controversial for many decades. Although most formats for the diagnosis of schizophrenia begin with the general agreement that schizophrenia involves some form of thought disorder, there is much less agreement about the way in which the disturbance is manifest, and about which added features, taken from the many that seem to characterize schizophrenia, are truly differentiating. In part, the difficulties posed in the identification of schizophrenia stem from the basic conceptualizations about schizophrenia. Khouri (1977) has pointed out the sharp differences that exist among those who purport a continuum concept of schizophrenia, and those who identify schizophrenia as a discretely different entity from all other mental dysfunctions. Moreover, conceptualizations of schizophrenia frequently differ considerably regarding the major etiological factors. Some stress the importance of a potential genetic element, whereas others afford major emphasis to environmental factors. Possibly, the diversity of opinions concerning schizophrenia is best portrayed in a series of articles, in the *Schizophrenia Bulletin,* that attempt to address the question, "What is schizophrenia?" (Meltzer & Liberman, 1982; Snyder, Kety, & Goldstein, 1982; Strauss & Carpenter, 1983; Zubin & Ludwig, 1983; Bowers & Wing, 1983; Bleuler, 1984).

Diagnostic manifestations of schizophrenia have also been at issue, except for the common agreement that thinking problems will be evident. For example, Satorius, Shapiro, and Jablensky (1974) have used frequency distributions for the presence of 12 behavioral variables, observed in a large cross-cultural group, to illustrate the schizophrenic condition. They note that 97% of the schizophrenics manifest a lack of insight, about 70% have some form of hallucination, two-thirds show signs of delusions, and about half have some form of thinking alienation. In a similar context, Carpenter, Strauss, and Bartko (1973) used a computer analysis of 360 items and 55 combinations of items to differentiate schizophrenics from nonschizophrenics. They reported that the 12 most discriminating signs include restricted affect, poor insight, thinking aloud, failure to awaken early, poor interpersonal relations, widespread delusions, incoherent speech, bizarre delusions, nihilistic delusions, lack of elation, lack of depressed facies, and unreliable information. They find that if a combination of six or more is present, two-thirds of the schizophrenics are correctly identified, whereas only 4% of the nonschizophrenics are misidentified.

Some of the difficulties in differentiating schizophrenia from nonschizophrenia arise because of attempts to refine the diagnosis—that is, differentiating categories, such as paranoid, catatonic, and such—or to delineate degrees of involvement, as in borderline or incipient schizophrenia. For example, Kety et al. (1968) and Kety et al. (1975) have suggested the notion of a spectrum of schizophrenias. Their conceptualization is based mainly on a series of investigations that have involved elaborate record keeping about adopted children, a design that permits some separation of the genetic element from environmental influences. The spectrum concept is not markedly different from the older notion of a family of schizophrenias (Bleuler, 1911) and is directed at a group of disorders that varies in severity, but all of which appear to be genetically related. In the "hard" or "firm" area of the spectrum lie disorders labeled chronic schizophrenia, borderline states, and some acute schizophrenia disturbances. In the less firm or "soft" area of the spectrum appear some of the acute schizophrenia reactions, the schizotypal personality, and the schizoid style. Although the notion of the spectrum is primarily a research classification, its relation to previously developed conceptualizations of schizophrenia requires attention in any Rorschach-related research involving the differentiation of the condition.

Andreasen (1989) has provided an excellent summary regarding the changing definition of schizophrenia. She notes that it has become very narrow and, as such, limits the diagnosis to severe forms. She also points out that, at the same time, there has been a greater acceptability of the notion of a schizophrenia spectrum. One segment of this spectrum includes psychotic boundary disorders. These include the schizophreniform disorder, delusional disorders, brief reactive psychoses, and the schizoaffective disorder in which there is a persistence of psychotic-like symptoms without affective symptoms. Another segment of the spectrum includes the schizotypal, schizoid, and paranoid personality disorders.

Whatever the approach to classification, it is clear that the diagnostician, regardless of the technique employed, confronts a substantial task in attempting to differentiate schizophrenia. Haier (1980) has reviewed a variety of approaches to diagnostic decisions concerning schizophrenia and points out that not everyone uses the same criteria for the diagnosis, and many criteria are unreliable. Haier has also noted that when methods designed essentially for research purposes are compared, such as the *Research Diagnostic Criteria* (Spitzer, Endicott, & Robbins, 1978), *New Haven Schizophrenia Index* (Astrachan et al., 1972), *Carpenter and Strauss Flexible Criterion* (Carpenter, Strauss, & Bartko, 1973), the *St. Louis Criterion* (Feighner et al., 1972), and the *Taylor and Abrams Criteria* (Taylor & Abrams, 1975), the agreement among the sets about who is schizophrenic differs considerably and, on the average, agreement is moderate to low. Because the DSM criteria for schizophrenia is derived mainly from the Research Diagnostic Criteria (RDC), it will probably form the basis for most diagnostic decisions concerning schizophrenia in the immediate future. As Haier has noted, it tends to narrow the concept of schizophrenia away from the spectrum concept so that the notion of a unitary disease is also diminished. At the same time, the increasing emphasis on biological factors may ultimately lead to a more precise definition of subtypes.

Accurate diagnosis of schizophrenia is important, mainly because of the intervention consequences. The bulk of recent research on the treatment of schizophrenia indicates that the response to intervention is generally much more positive if the treatment includes a somatic core, predominantly some form of antipsychotic medication (May, 1968; Hogarty et al., 1974; May, Tuma, & Dixon, 1976; Exner & Murillo, 1977). There are findings that suggest some kinds of schizophrenic subjects may not respond favorably to drug treatment (Klein, Rosen, & Oaks, 1973; Rappaport et al., 1976), and although the data may be somewhat equivocal, they highlight the importance of a thorough description of the patient before intervention planning is finalized. As Keith et al. (1976) have emphasized, a description focusing on data from the assessment of cognitive functioning and social interests, plus interpersonal skills, can be especially important in determining an intervention model. The results of the Boston Psychotherapy Study with schizophrenics (Stanton et al., 1984; Gunderson et al., 1984), also appear to suggest that accurate diagnosis of schizophrenia *plus* a meaningful description of assets and liabilities may be critical to the ultimate determination of the intervention plan.

RORSCHACH MANIFESTATIONS OF SCHIZOPHRENIA

There have been many attempts to identify Rorschach variables that will afford a valid differentiation of schizophrenia (Rapaport et al., 1946; Piotrowski & Lewis, 1950; Theisen, 1952; Watkins & Stauffacher, 1952; Beck, 1965; Weiner 1966). All have achieved some success, but with less than consistent uniformity. Diversity in results has often been the result of heterogeneity of samples and of varying emphasis on different subcategories in the overall scheme of classification. Weiner, (1966, 1977) has offered a compelling argument that the most accurate use of the Rorschach for identifying schizophrenia will be one in which the test variables will be conceptually linked to the entity. In other words, as features of the condition are identified and clarified, Rorschach data can be approached in terms of which variables best reflect those features. It is essentially this approach that has been used in the study of Rorschach manifestations of schizophrenia.

Although listings of features of schizophrenia sometimes differ sharply in length and/or content, almost all include reference to four basic characteristics—*inaccurate perception, disordered thinking, inadequate controls,* and *interpersonal ineptness.* There are several Rorschach variables that relate to these features, either directly or indirectly. However, none of these variables is exclusive to schizophrenia. For instance, many psychiatric groups have inadequate controls, such as some histrionics, borderline personalities, impulsive styles, inadequate personalities, and so on. Similarly, several psychiatric groups, such as schizoids, immature personalities, and some character disorders, tend to be inept in social relationships. *But no group, other than schizophrenia, has been defined or conceptualized as having both the problems of disordered thinking and inaccurate perception.* It is because of this that data concerning these two features have been the focus in studying Rorschach manifestations of schizophrenia, and those findings have formed the basis from which the Schizophrenia Index has evolved.

Inaccurate Perception   Schizophrenics typically have some difficulty perceiving their world and themselves accurately. Their perceptual distortions are often reflected in poor or inappropriate judgment. They have difficulty in assessing their own experience realistically and, as a consequence, tend to act in odd or strange ways, say things that are out of place, and harbor farfetched ideas. In the most extreme form, perceptual distortions create the basis for hallucinatory experience; that is, the more a person distorts the reality of what is seen, heard, smelled, and so on, the greater the probability that they will experience sensory impressions for which there is no realistic external stimuli.

Four of the variables included in the mediation cluster, P, $X+\%$, $F+\%$, and $X-\%$, relate to the issues of conventionality and perceptual accuracy. Two of these, the $X+\%$ and the $X-\%$, are especially important in detecting problems in perceptual accuracy. The first identifies the proportion of instances in which the translation of the stimulus field is atypical, whereas the second indicates the proportion of those atypical translations that involve perceptual-mediational distortion. The mean $X+\%$ for nonpatients, both adults and children, is about 80%, with a standard deviation of 10% or less. It is the *only* variable that has consistently high long-term retest reliability during the developmental years (Exner, Thomas, & Mason, 1985). Thus if the $X+\%$ falls below 70%, it signals a tendency to translate the world in an unconventional manner. If it falls below 60%, that tendency is very marked and is probably impairing effective adjustment. The mean $X-\%$ for nonpatient adults and children falls between 4% and 8%, with standard deviations between 4% and 6%. When it exceeds 15%, considerable distortion is indicated, and if it exceeds 20%, the distortion is probably of a potentially disabling magnitude. The inpatient depressive reference sample has a mean $X+\%$ of 53% and a mean $X-\%$ of 20%. The character disorder group has a mean $X+\%$ of 58% and a mean $X-\%$ of 20%. The schizophrenic reference sample has a mean $X+\%$ of 40%, and a mean $X-\%$ of 37%, both of which are significantly different from either of the other two psychiatric groups.

Disordered Thinking   This is probably the most clinically obvious feature among schizophrenics. Incoherent or disordered thought can take many forms. Sometimes, it may manifest as a disruption in the sequence of thoughts. In other instances, it will be noted by a predominance of unreasonable conclusions concerning cause-and-effect relationships, or in bewildering abstract preoccupations, or in very idiosyncratic symbolism or by persistent and very marked overgeneralizations. The $M-$ responses and the six Critical Special Scores appear to capture many of these forms of disarray when they occur in the Rorschach.

$M-$ responses occur with a relatively low frequency among most groups, except schizophrenics. They appear in only 22 of the 700 adult nonpatient records (3%), 57 of the 180 character disorder records (32%), and 127 of the 315 inpatient depressive protocols (40%), as contrasted with 256 of the 320 schizophrenic records (80%). If $M-$ does appear in the record of a nonschizophrenic, the probability is that the frequency will be 1. Only 1 adult nonpatient, 12 character disorder subjects, and 49 inpatient depressives gave more than one $M-$, so that the means for $M-$ for those groups of .03, .47, and .58 respectively, are relatively low. Conversely, 149 of the 320 schizophrenic records contain more than one $M-$, and the mean for the group is 2.4.

Similarly, the frequency of the Sum of the six Critical Special Scores tends to be significantly lower among most all groups as compared with schizophrenics. For example, although about 81% of the nonpatient adults do have at least one of these Special Scores in their record, the mean for the group is 1.6, and the mode is 1. All 180 of the character disorders protocols contain at least one of these Special Scores, and the mean for the group is 2.62, with a mode of 2. Similarly, all 315 of the depressive records have at least one Critical Special Score, and the mean for the group is 3.4, with a mode of 3. All of the protocols for the schizophrenia reference group contain Critical Special Scores, the mode being 4, and the mean for the group, 5.07, is significantly greater than that of any other group. Schizophrenics not only give more of the Critical Special Scores, but they also tend to give more of those with higher weighted values. The mean $WSum6$ (44.69) is more than two times greater than for the depression reference group (18.2) and nearly four times greater than for the character disorders reference group (11.43).

As with the issue of perceptual inaccuracy, evidence of disordered thinking, taken alone, does not indicate schizophrenia. It merely indicates that a thinking problem is present that may or may not be similar to that found in schizophrenia. Several other groups, such as some drug-related conditions, schizotypal personality disorders, and some forms of affective disturbance, commonly manifest some problems in thinking and often have significant elevations in either or both the Sum of the six Critical Special Scores, or the *WSum*6. It is for this reason that the *SCZI* includes data concerning *both* perceptual inaccuracy and disordered thinking.

When the Comprehensive System was published in 1974, it did not include any of the Special Scores, or the $X-\%$. Thus early attempts to identify structural data that might differentiate schizophrenia were doomed at the start. Nonetheless, a series of studies were conducted during the next four years focusing on the issue of correctly detecting the presence of schizophrenia. Five of the six Critical Special Scores were added to the System in 1976 (Exner, Weiner, & Schuyler, 1976) and a host of discriminant analyses, using various combinations of variables related to perceptual inaccuracy and problems in thinking were completed. Ultimately, an experimental schizophrenia index fell into place (Exner, 1978).

At about the same time that the experimental Index was defined, The Research Diagnostic Criteria (*RDC*) became available for use to identify schizophrenia (Spitzer, Endicott, & Robins, 1977, 1978). Prior to that time, the schizophrenia sample at the Rorschach Research Foundation had been selected using the Inpatient Multidimensional Psychiatric Scale (*IMPS*), plus the reports of significant others as recorded in the Katz Adjustment Scale (*KAS*). A composite score had been employed, using the "Schizophrenia Disorganization" Score of the IMPS, and a symptom score derived from the *KAS*. The RDC appeared to be well standardized, with high interrater reliability, and obviously would be the forerunner of the classification decisions for the pending DSM-III. Thus it was selected to be the validating criterion against which the experimental index would be tested.

During the next five years, the experimental index evolved gradually into a formula that included five variables. It was tested against various samples of first-admission patients ultimately diagnosed as schizophrenic by the *RDC* criteria (Exner, 1981, 1983), a relatively small sample of children (Exner & Weiner, 1982), and a sample of inpatient schizophrenics collected in Spain (Vives, 1983). As a result of these various tests of the experimental index, a sixth special score (*DR*) was added, which seemed to strengthen the efficacy of the formula, and in 1984 the original *SCZI* was published. It involved five issues to be tested with possible scores for the index ranging from 0 to 5.

The original *SCZI* proved quite useful, with accuracy rates varying between 72% and 89%, depending on the sample studied, and with false positive rates that appeared to be relatively modest, ranging from zero to 12% depending on the group studied. However, after the 1980 publication of DSM-III, a new emphasis was placed on accurate diagnosis of the affective disorders and personality disorders and false positive rates appeared to increase among those groups. During the same time, it was noted that the false positive rates were higher than expected among adolescents with histories of drug abuse or acting-out behaviors. Thus, while a score of 5 continued to confirm the likelihood of schizophrenia, scores of 4 were more questionable, and often included many false positives.

Investigations designed to strengthen the *SCZI* began in 1986 and several combinations of variables were developed that improved both true positive and false positive rates. However, it was only after the research concerning Level 1 and Level 2 Special Scores was completed and the $S-\%$ formulated that the improvements became more substantial. Following from a large number of correlational and discriminant function analyses, it became apparent that at least 10 variables loaded positively in attempting to correctly identify the presence of schizophrenia.

Subsequently, more than 50 discriminant function analyses were conducted, each involving a variety of subject samples that included nonpatients, schizophrenics, nonschizophrenic patients. The objective of each analysis was to determine the best weightings and/or cutoff scores for the 10 variables that would produce the largest percentage of true positive cases and the smallest percentage of false positives among the various control samples. The control samples included both inpatients and outpatients, as well as adults and children. The best combination of the variables, weightings, and cutoffs resulted in the new *SCZI*, which involves 10 variables that are used in the six tests that comprise the current *SCZI*.

As noted earlier, the critical value in the *SCZI* is 4. A value of 4 indicates that there is a significant probability that schizophrenia is present but the possibility of a false positive also exists. Values of 5 or 6 are more definitive. Either of those values indicate a strong likelihood of schizophrenia being present and a very low probability of a false positive finding. This is probably best illustrated by the results of a "Monte Carlo" procedure. The procedure involved five random drawings. In each draw, 100 subjects were randomly selected from each of five groups consisting of: (1) DSM-III diagnosed first-admission schizophrenics ($N = 1238$), (2) DSM-III-SADS diagnosed first-admission major affective disorders ($N = 1421$), (3) outpatients beginning treatment for the first time ($N = 926$). The outpatients represent a variety of diagnoses, but more than half had depression as one of the presenting symptoms. (4) Adolescent behavior disorders ($N = 764$), and (5) adult nonpatients ($N = 1364$). The program for the procedure was written so that after a record was included in one draw, it would be excluded from the pool and not available for subsequent draws. The results are shown in Table 62.

The false positive rates vary from 0% to 11% depending on the group studied. However, 76 of the 105 false positive records (72%), have *SCZI* values of 4. It is for this reason that *SCZI* values of 4 must be approached with caution. False negative rates are also relatively modest, ranging from 12% to 22% across all five draws. Most of the false negative protocols, 67 of 83 (81%) have fewer than 17 responses. Another group that may have a higher frequency of false positives is the schizoaffective disorder. Prior to DSM-III, this condition was considered as a type of schizophrenia because of the marked peculiarity in thinking and was included as part of the "hard" spectrum concept. The protocol pool of the Rorschach Research Foundation includes only 63 cases that, by DSM-IIIR standards, are unequivocal for the diagnosis of schizoaffective disturbance. Thirteen of the 63 have an *SCZI* of 5, and 22 others have four positive variables.

THE DEPRESSION INDEX (*DEPI*)

The admixture of features that are used as a basis for identifying and classifying affective problems poses a considerable challenge for any assessment instrument or technique, and the Rorschach is no exception. The *DEPI* consists of 15 variables that form the basis for the seven tests that are involved in this index. Unlike the *S-CON* and the *SCZI*, the *DEPI* value is reviewed twice, first in the scrutiny of the special indices in the context of Key variables, and second, when the cluster involving variables related to affect is assessed. The interpretation of the *DEPI* should be formulated cautiously and, like the *SCZI*, in the context of the specific value for the index. *DEPI* values of 0 to 4 are actuarially meaningless. A *DEPI* value of 5 is positive but does not yield any definitive initial hypotheses. A value of 5 indicates the subject has many of the features that are common

Table 62.　Frequency of *SCZI* Values of 4 or More for Five Random Selections of 100 Subjects from Each of Five Groups

	Schizophrenic Disorder N	Affective Disorder N	Outpatient Mixed Group N	Adolescent Behavior Problem N	Adult Nonpatient N
Draw 1					
SCZI = 6	32	0	0	0	0
SCZI = 5	29	1	1	3	0
SCZI = 4	23	6	4	3	0
Total	84	7	5	6	0
Draw 2					
SCZI = 6	31	0	0	0	0
SCZI = 5	33	0	0	4	0
SCZI = 4	22	10	4	5	1
Total	86	10	4	9	1
Draw 3					
SCZI = 6	26	1	0	1	0
SCZI = 5	34	3	2	1	0
SCZI = 4	21	5	3	6	0
Total	81	9	5	8	0
Draw 4					
SCZI = 6	34	1	0	0	0
SCZI = 5	33	1	0	2	0
SCZI = 4	21	6	2	4	0
Total	88	8	2	6	0
Draw 5					
SCZI = 6	32	1	0	1	0
SCZI = 5	24	3	1	1	0
SCZI = 4	22	7	5	7	1
Total	78	11	6	9	1

among those diagnosed as being depressed or having an affective disorder but may also simply indicate that the psychological organization of the subject can easily give rise to depression or fluctuations in mood. Other problems or symptoms may supersede this feature, and a diagnosis other than depression may be assigned depending on presenting symptoms and history. Therefore, if a *DEPI* value of 5 is noted in the sweep of the special indices, it should be disregarded in the context of initial hypotheses as its importance will be integrated later in the interpretive review of features related to affect.

　　DEPI values of 6 and 7 are much more definitive. Subjects having these values for the *DEPI* will almost always be diagnosed as having some significant affective problem (the exceptions to this occur most often among schizophrenics who are depressed but will have schizophrenia as the primary diagnosis). Thus, if *DEPI* values of 6 or 7 are present, an initial hypothesis to the effect that the subject is apparently experiencing a serious affective disturbance is warranted.

RESEARCH RELATED TO HYPOTHESES BASED ON THE *DEPI*

The challenge of developing a useful depression index has been much more complex than was involved in formulating the *SCZI*. Although the search for indices of depressive features has met with considerable success, the search for a cluster of variables that might be useful in accurately identifying those cases in which depression is included in the diagnostic label has been much more difficult. The problem seems to be twofold.

First, depression as a complaint or symptom is very common among psychiatric subjects. Depression is a more socially acceptable symptom than strange thinking, poor reality contact, or sexual dysfunctioning, and thus it is common for patients readily to concede to the experience. As an unfortunate consequence, many patients are admitted to hospitals, or to outpatient care, with the naively decided diagnosis of depression, and the initial focus of treatment centers on this feature. Second, unlike the marked features of schizophrenia, depression may in fact, be a major element in a variety of syndromes, ranging from reactive distress to the schizoaffective disturbance. As a consequence, the search for a data cluster that would discriminate the markedly depressed person from those who are simply dissatisfied, unhappy, or distressed has required the screening of different groups. These include dysthymics (neurotic depression), unipolar depressives, bipolar disorders, the schizoaffective disturbance, plus a rather significant population of subjects who are somewhat helpless in contending with the complexities of their environment.

The first experimental *DEPI* consisted of five variables that did discriminate quite effectively between depressive groups and the three control groups (Exner, 1986), but the total yield was far from spectacular. It did correctly identify about 70% of the subjects from dysthymic and unipolar groups. Unfortunately, the incidence of false positives among the control groups was considerable, ranging from 30% of nondepressed inpatients, to nearly 10% of the nonpatient sample. Anyone who worked with the experimental *DEPI* for very long can attest to the problems encountered when using it. The false negative rate was unacceptably high, often exceeding 60% for some groups of clearly depressed adult subjects and even greater when depressed children were studied (Lipovsky, Finch, & Belter, 1989).

Part of the problem stemmed from the fact that the index was overly conservative, but the problem was exacerbated by the changing definitions of depression and affective disorders that occurred between 1978 and 1990. During that period, the literature concerning affective disturbances often was marked by contradictory positions and many of the research findings, based on non-Rorschach sources, have been equivocal. Obviously, depression, as a complaint, continues to rank among the most commonly presented symptoms, but even the most stringent advocate of the DSM position will openly admit that findings of homogeneity among depressed patients are, at best, scarce.

Wiener (1989) presents an excellent review of the ambiguity, inconsistency, and overgeneralization that is evident among the current applications of the term depression, and offers harsh criticism for the DSM approach to defining features of depression. As Wiener notes, "Depression is used indiscriminantly as a label for a state, trait, sign, syndrome, disease, as a category name and, at the same time, as an explanatory concept." Much of the problem seems to occur because many view depression as having a homogeneous psychological and/or biological predisposition, and several diversified concepts of depression have been put forth, based on this assumption (Beck, 1967; Blatt, Quinlan, Chevron, McDonald, & Zuroff, 1982; Brown & Harris, 1978; Chadoff, 1974; Kendell,

1976; Millon & Kotik, 1985; Seligman, 1975; Abramson, Metalsky, & Alloy, 1989). Some identify the developmental years as the breeding ground from which a predisposition evolves, while others focus on faulty attribution, negative self-concept, adverse social interaction, or poor psychobiology. Whichever cause, or group of causes is identified, the notion of homogeneity persists. Yet, the criteria for the *DSM* diagnostic categories tend to stray far from the notion of homogeneity. Instead they reflect an amalgam of signs and symptoms from which any of a seemingly endless number of combinations will yield the same diagnosis. For instance, Wiener (1989) points out that, provided a dysphoric mood is present, there are 286 possible combinations of signs and symptoms that can lead to the diagnosis of Dsythymic Disorder.

A review of the positions and findings regarding depression easily lends itself to the conclusion that there are at least three different kinds of people who tend to be diagnosed as being depressed, or having an affective disorder, (1) those who are emotionally distraught, (2) those who are cognitively pessimistic, lethargic, and self-defeating in their behaviors, and (3) those who are helpless in the face of contending with a complex society. Obviously, these are not discrete states and considerable overlap can be expected, but some of the positions and findings do tend to support the hypothesis that they reflect *primary* features in the psychological organization of the person.

In 1986, that postulate formed the basis for a series of studies regarding the *DEPI*, with the tentative objective of creating three *DEPI*s to replace the original experimental index. The first step involved an effort to subdivide the more than 1400 cases in the protocol pool, collected from subjects diagnosed as affectively disturbed, into three broad groups using nontest data as the basis for the sort. The groups were arbitrarily defined as (1) emotionally depressed, (2) cognitively depressed, and (3) helpless. The sort was impossible for more than 650 cases because of insufficient data, but three groups ultimately were formed, each containing more than 200 subjects. Factor analyses yielded interesting but unclear findings. A five-factor solution generated two common factors for all three groups, two factors common to two groups but not the third, and one factor that made no sense at all. At best, the results suggested that the groups were probably different in some ways. The next steps involved a series of *MANOVA*s, intergroup correlational analyses, and discriminant function analyses. This time the yield was more distinct.

The data for the first two groups (emotional and cognitive) overlapped considerably, but the data for the third group were much more discrete. No matter what tactic was employed, it was impossible to empirically disentangle the first two groups, and consequently, they were collapsed into a single group ($N = 471$) that was used as a target sample from which to search out a new *DEPI*. This was done using a series of discriminant analyses and contingency tables. The third group (helpless $N = 213$) was held out to be used as a sample against which results might be tested. The findings revealed that at least 15 variables must be considered if the presence of depression or an affective disturbance was to be identified. Those 15 variables form the basis for seven tests that constitute the new *DEPI*.

The first test of the current *DEPI* focused on the sample of subjects that had been categorized as helpless, and the results were very disappointing. Only 36 of the 213 subjects (17%) showed values of 5, 6, or 7 on the new *DEPI*. This seemed very striking because the final contingency table for the *DEPI* indicated that values of 5, 6, or 7 correctly identified 402 of the 471 subjects (85%) in the target sample that had been used to formulate the index. Ultimately, the helpless sample was used for the development of the

CDI, which has proved to be a very useful index, either taken alone or reviewed as a secondary data source when considering the issue of depression.

A second test of the *DEPI* was accomplished by using the 663 subjects who could not be subdivided into the exploratory groups (emotional, cognitive, helpless) because of a lack of data. About 81% (539) had values of 5, 6, or 7, and 469 (71%) had values of 6 or 7.

Similar testing of the *DEPI* was completed using groups of schizophrenics, outpatients, character disorders, and nonpatients. Children and adolescents were included in each test. The "false positive" results have been very favorable. About 3% of nonpatient adults are positive on the *DEPI* as are less than 2% of nonpatient children. On the other hand, about 19% of schizophrenics are positive (most obtaining values of 5), as are about 13% of the character disorders (almost all obtaining values of 5). The outpatient sample has about 18% who are positive on the *DEPI* with about 78% of those having values of 5.

A review of the validation data concerning each of the variables included in the *DEPI* indicates that they reflect a substantial mixture, with each related either to a cognitive or affective feature. For instance, *MOR* responses, the egocentricity index, *FD* answers, and the intellectualization index involve a greater emphasis on cognitive activities, whereas color-shading blends, *C'* answers, or the *Afr* are much more directly related to affect. The fact that a composite was required to achieve the desired efficacy level seems to indicate that most people who are diagnosed as dysthymic or as an affective disorder will have difficulties in both areas, even though they might be differentiated as being either cognitively or affectively distressed or disturbed if some other criteria are applied.

THE COPING DEFICIT INDEX (*CDI*)

A direct by-product of the research leading to the *DEPI* is the development of the Coping Deficit Index. People who have scores of 4 or 5 on this index are likely to have impoverished or unrewarding social relationships. Generally, they are people who have difficulty contending with the natural demands of a social world, hence, the notion of coping deficit seems appropriate. These potential coping difficulties can give rise to numerous problems. Usually, those who are positive on the *CDI,* that is, having values of 4 or 5, will have histories that are marked by limited interpersonal effectiveness or success, frequent social ineptness, or even instances of social chaos. Quite often, their helplessness and/or ineptness in social situations breeds the kinds of features and experiences that might easily be translated in ways commensurate with the diagnostic criteria for some types of depression, but the depressive features usually are a by-product of the overall social coping problem. The coping limitations signified by a positive *CDI* also raise a more general question concerning capacities for control. The capacity for control is usually defined in terms of the ability to form and direct responses; however, even in cases in which that capacity appears to exist but a marked kind of social immaturity also exists, a potential vulnerability for problems in everyday living is created. This vulnerability can often contribute to control problems if they arise.

RESEARCH RELATED TO HYPOTHESES BASED ON THE *CDI*

As noted earlier, the *DEPI* was not effective in identifying very many of the subjects from the depression-affective disorders pool who had been categorized as "helpless."

Consequently, the records from the helpless group that were not positive on the *DEPI*, that is, those having a *DEPI* value of less than 5 ($N = 177$), were combined with the 69 false negatives from the original target group to create a new sample to study ($N = 246$). It was anticipated that a second depression index might be formulated by using a series of intercorrelational and discriminant function analyses.

The group did prove to be reasonably homogeneous for a grouping of 11 variables. Several mixtures of those 11 variables were tested, and ultimately it was determined that they yielded the greatest efficacy when used in a composite to test five issues and assigning one point for each issue proving to be positive. Thus, by using critical values of 4 or 5, 194 of the 246 subjects in the new target group (79%) are correctly identified, including 143 of the 177 subjects in the helpless group (81%). When this new index was calculated for the group of 663 subjects from the depression-affective disorders pool who had not been able to be subcategorized for the original analyses leading to the *DEPI*, 219 (33%) were positive, including 93 of the 124 subjects who were negative on the *DEPI*.

The fact that 79% of subjects with affective disorders diagnoses who are not positive on the *DEPI* also obtained values of 4 or 5 on this index posed some compelling data. At first glance, the variables in the index appeared to be a strange mix, but on closer study it was apparent that most have some relationship to social/interpersonal activity. A review of scores on this new index for several other groups were then calculated as a logical next step in evaluating its usefulness. The results indicate that about 3% of nonpatient adults have values of 4 or 5, although the percentages are higher among nonpatient children (6% to 24%). Between 20% and 25% of schizophrenics have values of 4 or 5, as do nearly 50% of nonadjudicated character disorders. The highest percentage of positive indices were found among three groups, inadequate personalities (88%), alcohol and substance abusers (74%), and adjudicated character disorders (69%). The collective findings led to the decision to select the label Coping Deficit to best describe the index.

The substantial percentages of positive *CDI*s among the various psychiatric groups make it reasonably clear that this new index is not a second depression index. Conceptually, the *CDI* appears to afford a measure that tends to identify those who have coping limitations or deficiencies. Additional support for that postulate is found in the data for 440 outpatients beginning treatment for the first time. Initial interviews for those patients were coded for a variety of variables, including "major presenting complaints." The presenting complaints were coded as: (1) depression, (2) anxiety, (3) ideational control, (4) emotional control, (5) somatic, and (6) interpersonal difficulties, and as many as three were entered for each subject. A sorting program was used to create two groups. The target group included all subjects for whom item 6 (interpersonal difficulties) had been coded positive, and a control group consisted of the remaining subjects for whom item 6 had not been coded as being positive among the presenting complaints. The *CDI* was calculated for the 440 records, and 125 had values of 4 or 5. The distribution of the 125 positive *CDI* records is shown for each group in Table 63.

These data do not mean that the subjects in the target group actually did have more interpersonal problems than the subjects in the other group, for that is unlikely. However, the data do suggest that the subjects who complained about interpersonal difficulties were apparently more acutely aware of those problems.

Although the *CDI* is not a depression index, the presence of a positive *CDI* among subjects diagnosed as being depressed seems to have considerable relevance for treatment planning. The reference group of first-admission inpatient depressives, shown in Chapter 12, is a random sample of 315 subjects representing approximately 25% of

Table 63.   The Frequency of *CDI* Values of 4 or 5 among Two Groups of Outpatients Sorted on the Basis of Interpersonal Complaints

	Interpersonal Complaint N = 204		No Interpersonal Complaint N = 236	
	N	%	N	%
CDI = 4	36	18%	18	8%
CDI = 5	61	30%*	10	4%
Total Positive CDI	97	48%*	28	12%

*Significantly different from other group ($p < .001$).

protocols available for that group. The selection was stratified to include approximately half who were admitted to private psychiatric hospitals and half who were admitted to public hospitals. The *DEPI* results for this sample indicate that 237 (75%) have values of 5 or more, and 80 of the 237 (34%) also have *CDI* values of 4 or 5.

In the total sample of 315 subjects, 138 (44%) have *CDI* values of 4 or more. This means that 58 of the 78 subjects (74%) who had *DEPI* values of less than 5 (false negatives) had *CDI* values of 4 or more. Stated differently, 25% of the group are positive on both the *DEPI* and *CDI*; 50% are positive on the *DEPI* but not on the *CDI*; and 18% are positive on the *CDI* but not on the *DEPI*. Taken together, the two indices identify slightly more than 93% of the total group.

None of the 315 subjects remained hospitalized for longer than 42 days. Six-month posthospitalization data were available for 271 of the 315 subjects in the sample. Those data reveal that 72 of the 271 were rehospitalized during that period. A review of the baseline records for those 72 subjects shows that 33 were positive on both the *DEPI* and *CDI*; 24 were positive on the *CDI* but not the *DEPI*; 13 were positive only on the *DEPI*; and the remaining two subjects had not been positive on either the *DEPI* or *CDI*. In other words, 79% of the relapsers had been positive on the *CDI* at the time of their first admission. This is a significantly greater proportion than the 43% of the subjects in the original sample who were positive on the *CDI*.

Obviously, many variables, both internal and external, contribute to relapse and it would be an error to assume that the 11 variables which make up the *CDI* form a nucleus of "best" predictors. Nevertheless, the disportionately high percentage of relapsers who were positive on the *CDI* suggests that issues of interpersonal skills and adjustment may not have been adequately addressed during hospitalization or in post hospitalization outpatient care. Another data set seems to support this contention.

A review of the 125 subjects who had values of 4 or 5 on the *CDI* in the outpatient sample (N = 440) reveals that 74 had been assigned a diagnosis related to an affective problem (major affective disturbance or dysthymia). An additional 157 subjects in the sample, who were not positive on the *CDI,* were also assigned affective problem diagnoses. In other words, 231 of the 440 outpatient subjects presented features of depression that were of sufficient frequency and/or magnitude to warrant an affective problems label. Some form of antidepressant medication was prescribed as a part of the therapeutic routine for 123 of the patients who were not positive on the *CDI* and 56 of the patients who were positive on the *CDI*. Follow-up data, collected during a period of 10 to 12 months after treatment began, reveals that 41 of the 56 (73%) positive *CDI* subjects treated with antidepressant medication persisted in complaints regarding depression and were still in treatment. Conversely, only 39 of the 123 patients (31%) diagnosed as having an affective problem who were not positive on the *CDI* persisted in complaints regarding depression and were continuing in treatment. Although these are very crude data, they offer a hint that patients positive on the *CDI* who manifest features of depression may not profit significantly from the routine treatments for depression, especially those pharmacologically focused, unless the treatment also includes some emphasis on social skill development.

Interestingly, deficits reflected by a positive *CDI* seem to be altered rather easily by well-planned treatment. The results of two treatment effects studies (Weiner & Exner, 1991; Exner & Sanglade, 1992) show that 46 of 70 patients (66%) who had *CDI* values of 4 or 5 at the onset of several different types of treatment were no longer positive on this index in a second Rorschach administered after 8 to 14 months of intervention. Conversely, very brief treatments, that is, ranging over two to three months, appear to have little effect on this coping deficit. Thus, while a positive *CDI* finding harks poorly for the present and immediate future of the subject, the prognosis for change is quite positive for most such subjects, given the appropriate treatment direction and opportunity.

REFERENCES

Abramson, L. Y., Metalsky, G. I., and Alloy, L. B. (1989) Hopelessness Depression: A theory based sub-type of depression. *Psychological Review, 96,* 358–372.

Andreasen, N. C. (1989) The American concept of schizophrenia. *Schizophrenia Bulletin,* **15,** 519–531.

Applebaum, S. A., and Holtzman, P. S. (1962) The color-shading response and suicide. *Journal of Projective Techniques,* **26,** 155–161.

Astrachan, B. M., Harrow, M., Adler, D., Bauer, L., Schwartz, A., Schwartz, C., and Tucker, G. A. (1972) A checklist for the diagnosis of schizophrenia. *British Journal of Psychiatry,* **121,** 529–539.

Beck, A. T. (1967) *Depression: Clinical, Experimental and Theoretical Aspects.* New York: Harper & Row.

Beck, S. J. (1965) *Psychological Process in the Schizophrenic Adaptation.* New York: Grune & Stratton.

Blatt, S. J., Quinlan, D. M., Chevron, E. S., McDonald, C., and Zuroff, D. (1982) Dependency and self criticism: Psychological dimensions of depression. *Journal of Consulting and Clinical Psychology,* **50,** 113–124.

Bleuler, E. (1950) *Dementia Praecox or the Group of Schizophrenias* (1911). New York: International Universities Press.

Bleuler, M. (1984) What is schizophrenia? *Schizophrenia Bulletin,* **10,** 8–10.

Bowers, M. B., and Wing, J. K. (1983) What is schizophrenia? *Schizophrenia Bulletin,* **9,** 495–499.

Brown, G. W., and Harris, T. (1978) *Social Origins of Depression.* New York: Free Press.

Carpenter, W. T., Strauss, J. S., and Bartko, J. J. (1973) Flexible system for the diagnosis of schizophrenia: Report from the WHO International pilot study of schizophrenia. *Science,* **182,** 1275–1278.

Chadoff, P. (1974) The depressive personality: A critical review. In R. J. Friedman and M. M. Katz (Eds.), *The Psychology of Depression.* Washington, D.C.: Winston.

Exner, J. E. (1974) *The Rorschach: A Comprehensive System. Volume 1.* New York: Wiley.

Exner, J. E. (1978) *The Rorschach: A Comprehensive System. Volume 2: Current research and advanced interpretation.* New York: Wiley.

Exner, J. E. (1981) The response process and diagnostic efficacy. 10th International Rorschach Congress, Washington, D.C.

Exner, J. E. (1983) Rorschach assessment. In I. B. Weiner (Ed.), *Clinical Methods in Psychology,* (2nd Ed.). New York: Wiley.

Exner, J. E. (1986) *The Rorschach: A Comprehensive System. Volume 1: Basic foundations,* (2nd Ed.). New York: Wiley.

Exner, J. E., and Murillo, L. G. (1977) A long term follow-up of schizophrenic treated with regressive ECT. *Diseases of the Nervous System,* **38,** 162–168.

Exner, J. E., and Sanglade, A. A. (1992) Rorschach changes following brief and short term therapy. *Journal of Personality Assessment,* **59,** 59–71.

Exner, J. E., Thomas, E. A., and Mason, B. (1985) Children's Rorschachs: Description and prediction. *Journal of Personality Assessment,* **49,** 13–20.

Exner, J. E., and Weiner, I. B. (1982) *The Rorschach: A Comprehensive System. Volume 3: Assessment of children and adolescents.* New York: Wiley.

Exner, J. E., Weiner, I. B., and Schuyler, W. (1976) *A Rorschach Workbook for the Comprehensive System.* Bayville, N.Y.: Rorschach Workshops.

Exner, J. E., and Wylie, J. R. (1977) Some Rorschach data concerning suicide. *Journal of Personality Assessment,* **41,** 339–348.

Farberow, N. L., and Shneidman, E. S. (Eds.) (1961) *The Cry for Help.* New York: McGraw-Hill.

Feighner, J. P., Robins, E., Guze, S. B., Woodruff, R. A., Winokur, G., and Munoz, R. (1972) Diagnostic criteria for use in psychiatric research. *Archives of General Psychiatry,* **26,** 57–63.

Fleischer, M. S. (1957) Differential Rorschach configurations of suicidal patients: A psychological study of threatened, attempted, and successful suicides. Unpublished doctoral dissertation, Yeshiva University.

Goldfried, M., Stricker, G., and Weiner, I. B. (1971) *Rorschach Handbook of Clinical and Research Applications.* Englewood Cliffs, N.J.: Prentice-Hall.

Gunderson, J. G., Frank, A. F., Katz, H. M., Vannicelli, M. L., Frosch, J. P., and Knapp, P. H. (1984) Effects of psychotherapy in schizophrenia: II. Comparative outcome of two forms of treatment. *Schizophrenia Bulletin,* **10,** 564–598.

Haier, R. J. (1980) The diagnosis of schizophrenia: A review of recent developments. *Schizophrenia Bulletin,* **6,** 417–428.

Hertz, M. R. (1948) Suicidal configurations in Rorschach records. *Rorschach Research Exchange and Journal of Projective Techniques,* **12,** 3–58.

Hertz, M. R. (1949) Further study of "suicidal" configurations in Rorschach records. *Rorschach Research Exchange and Journal of Projective Techniques,* **13,** 44–73.

Hogarty, G. E., Goldberg, S. C., Schooler, N. R., and Ulrich, R. F. (1974) The collaborative study group: Drug and sociotherapy in the aftercare of schizophrenic patients II. Two year relapse rates. *Archives of General Psychiatry,* **31,** 603–608.

Keith, S. J., Gunderson, J.G., Reifman, A., Buchsbaum, S., and Mosher, L. R. (1976) Special report: Schizophrenia, 1976. *Schizophrenia Bulletin,* **2,** 510–565.

Kendell, R. E. (1976) The classification of depression: A review of contemporary confusion. *British Journal of Psychiatry,* **129,** 15–28.

Kety, S. S., Rosenthal, D., Wender, P. H., and Schulsinger, F. (1968) The types and prevalence of mental illness in the biological and adoptive families of adoptive schizophrenics. In D. Rosenthal and S. S. Kety (Eds.), *The Transmission of Schizophrenia.* Oxford: Pergamon Press.

Kety, S. S., Rosenthal, D., Wender, P. H., Schulsinger, F., and Jacobsen, B. (1975) Mental illness in the biological and adoptive families of adopted individuals who have become schizophrenic: A preliminary report based on psychiatric interviews. In R. R. Fieve, D. Rosenthal, and H. Brill (Eds.), *Genetic Research in Psychiatry*. Baltimore: Johns Hopkins University Press.

Khouri, P. (1977) Continuum versus dichotomy in theories of schizophrenia. *Schizophrenia Bulletin,* **3,** 262–267.

Klein, D. F., Rosen, B., and Oaks, G. (1973) Premorbid asocial adjustment and response to phenothiazine treatment among schizophrenic patients. *Archives of General Psychiatry,* **29,** 480–484.

Lindner, R. M. (1946) Content analysis in Rorschach work. *Rorschach Research Exchange,* **10,** 121–129.

Lipovsky, J. A., Finch, A. J., and Belter, R. W. (1989) Assessment of depression in adolescents: Objective and projective measures. *Journal of Personality Assessment,* **53,** 449–458.

Martin, H. (1951) A Rorschach study of suicide. Unpublished doctoral dissertation, University of Kentucky.

May, P. R. A. (1968) *Treatment of Schizophrenia.* New York: Science House.

May, P. R. A., Tuma, A. H., and Dixon, W. J. (1976) Schizophrenia—A follow-up study of results of treatment: I. Design and other problems. *Archives of General Psychiatry,* **33,** 474–478.

Meltzer, H. Y., and Liberman, R. P. (1982) What is schizophrenia? *Schizophrenia Bulletin,* **8,** 433–437.

Millon, T., and Kotik, D. (1985) The relationship of depression to disorders of the personality. In E. E. Beckham and W. R. Leber (Eds.), *Handbook of depression: Treatment, assessment and research*. Homewood, Ill: Dorsey Press.

Piotrowski, Z. (1950) *A Rorschach Compendium: Revised and enlarged, Psychiatric Quarterly,* **24,** 543–596.

Piotrowski, Z., and Lewis, N. D. C. (1950) An experimental Rorschach diagnostic aid for some forms of schizophrenia. *American Journal of Psychiatry,* **107,** 360–366.

Rapaport, D., Gill, M., and Schafer, R. (1946) *Psychological Diagnostic Testing. Volume II.* Chicago: Yearbook Publishers.

Rappaport, M., Hopkins, H. K., Hall, K., Belleza, T., and Silverman, J. (1976) Acute schizophrenia and phenothiazine utilization. I. Clinical outcome. Final Report, National Institute of Mental Health, NIMH Grant 16445.

Sakheim, G. A. (1955) Suicidal responses on the Rorschach test. *Journal of Nervous and Mental Disease,* **122,** 332–344.

Sapolsky, A. (1963) An indicator of suicidal ideation of the Rorschach test. *Journal of Projective Techniques and Personality Assessment,* **27,** 332–335.

Satorious, N., Shapiro, R., and Jablensky, A. (1974) The international pilot study of schizophrenia. *Schizophrenia Bulletin,* **1,** 21–34.

Seligman, M. E. P. (1975) *Helplessness: On depression, development and death.* San Francisco: Freeman.

Shneidman, E. S., and Farberow, N. L. (1957) *Clues to Suicide.* New York: McGraw-Hill.

Snyder, S. H., Kety, S. S., and Goldstein, M. J. (1982) What is schizophrenia? *Schizophrenia Bulletin,* **8,** 595–602.

Spitzer, R. L., Endicott, J., and Robins, E. (1977) *Research Diagnostic Criteria* (RDC) for a selected group of functional disorders. New York State Psychiatric Institute.

Spitzer, R. L., Endicott, J. E., and Robins, E. (1978) *Research Diagnostic Criteria for a Selected Group of Functional Disorders,* (3rd Ed.). New York: New York State Psychiatric Institute.

Stanton, A. H., Gunderson, J. G., Knapp, P. H., Frank, A. F., Vannicelli, M. L., Schnitzer, R., and Rosenthal, R. (1984) Effects of psychotherapy in schizophrenia: I. Design and implementation of a controlled study. *Schizophrenia Bulletin,* **10,** 520–563.

Strauss, J. S., and Carpenter, W. T. (1983) What is schizophrenia? *Schizophrenia Bulletin,* **9,** 7–10.

Taylor, M. A., and Abrams, R. (1975) A critique of the St. Louis psychiatric research criteria for schizophrenia. *American Journal of Psychiatry,* **132,** 1276–1280.

Thiesen, J. W. (1952) A pattern analysis of structural characteristics of the Rorschach test in schizophrenia. *Journal of Consulting Psychology,* **16,** 365–370.

Thomas, C. B., Ross, D. C., Brown, B. S., and Duszynski, K. R. (1973) A prospective study of the Rorschachs of suicides: The predictive potential of pathological content. *The Johns Hopkins Medical Journal,* **132,** 334–360.

Vives, M. (1983) Analysis of Rorschach data from acute and chronic Spanish schizophrenics. Workshops Study No. 291 (unpublished), Rorschach Workshops.

Watkins, J. G., and Stauffacher, J. C. (1952) An index of pathological thinking in the Rorschach. *Journal of Projective Techniques,* **16,** 276–286.

Weiner, I. B. (1966) *Psychodiagnosis in Schizophrenia.* New York: Wiley.

Weiner, I. B. (1977) Rorschach indices of disordered thinking in patient and nonpatient adolescents. IX International Rorschach Congress, Fribourg, Switzerland.

Weiner, I. B., and Exner, J. E. (1991) Rorschach changes in long-term and short-term psychotherapy. *Journal of Personality Assessment,* **56,** 453–465.

Wiener, M. (1989) Psychopathology reconsidered: Depressions interpreted as psychosocial transactions. *Clinical Psychology Review,* **9,** 295–321.

White, M. A., and Schreiber, H. (1952) Diagnosing "suicidal risks" on the Rorschach. *Psychiatric Quarterly Supplement,* **26,** 161–189.

Zubin, J., and Ludwig, A. M. (1983) What is schizophrenia? *Schizophrenia Bulletin,* **9,** 331–335.

CHAPTER 16

Key Variables II—
The D Scores:
Control and Stress Tolerance

The *D* Scores are included as two of the first five Key variables, *D* < *AdjD* and *AdjD* is minus. Both are related to issues of control and stress tolerance and constitute the basic data in the cluster related to controls and the array of data concerning situational stress. It is somewhat unrealistic to attempt to explain these two Key variables separately. Instead, it seems more reasonable to discuss the two scores collectively with the expectation that the relevance of each, as a Key variable, will unfold. One, the *D* Score, provides input regarding the current capacity for control. The second, the Adjusted *D* Score, offers information regarding the more typical or usual capacity to formulate and control behaviors. No firm conclusions can be drawn by simply examining these two data points; however, there are some general postulates that should be considered. Ultimately, other data in the cluster will be used as a basis from which to accept, modify, or reject these first tentative postulates.

As implied in the discussion concerning the *CDI,* capacity for control refers to one's ability to draw on available resources to formulate and implement decisions in a deliberate and meaningful way. If one's capacity for control is deemed *adequate,* the assumption is that, under most circumstances, sufficient resources are available to be able to initiate and direct behavior. This connotes that ongoing stimulus demands, experienced by the subject, generally do not exceed the capacities of the subject to process and respond meaningfully to those demands. In other words, most or all of the behaviors manifested by the subject are controlled and directed.

Stress tolerance is actually a by-product of the capacity for control. As capacity for control increases, so too does the ability to tolerate stress. It is very important to emphasize that adequate capacity for control, or good stress tolerance, does not necessarily equate with good adjustment. It does *not mean* that behaviors selected and implemented will necessarily be effective, adaptive, or even logical. It simply means that the person has sufficient resources accessible to be able to form and direct behavior. On the other hand, if one's capacity for control is deemed to be *limited* or *inadequate,* that is often a precursor to maladjustment as the tolerance for stress is also lowered.

The implication of limited or inadequate capacities for control is that either of two circumstances exist. One is that fewer resources are routinely accessible than expected. Consequently, the subject is vulnerable to becoming overwhelmed by the complex stimulus demands that are encountered in everyday living. If that occurs, a state of *stimulus overload* is created. Stimulus overload is a condition in which the frequency and/or intensity of stimulus demands exceeds the range of responses that can be formulated or implemented effectively. The second circumstance is one in which, even though resource availability is usually adequate, the level of stimulus demand is sharply increased, also creating an overload situation in which the demands exceed the range of responses that can be formed or delivered effectively.

In either of these circumstances, the parameters of stress tolerance are exceeded. The resulting overload state tends to disorganize some of the psychological organization and/or operations of the subject. Consequently, some behaviors are not well formulated, and others may not have sufficient follow-through in their implementation to deal effectively with the demand situation(s). Some people are in an almost continuous state of overload. They are beset with more experienced demands for responses than they can handle easily. The result is that many of their behaviors are insufficient or even inappropriate, and when new demands occur, their lives can become marked by disarray or even chaos. This is common among children, but far less so for the adult. If the subject experiencing overload is prone to manifest thinking and feelings in overt behavior, he or she will often appear distraught and/or disorganized, even to the casual observer. Conversely, those who are more prone to internalize thoughts and feelings will often experience bouts of anxiety, apprehension, uneasiness, helplessness, tension, or depression.

THE ADJUSTED *D* SCORE

Although the relation between the *D* and Adjusted *D* Scores is important, the main focus is the Adjusted *D* Score. It is the best direct single Rorschach index of the ability to maintain control under demand or stress situations, and obviously its value is quite important. Nonetheless, the interpretation of the value for the Adjusted *D* Score is also applicable to the *D* Score. In other words, whereas the Adjusted *D* provides input regarding the usual capacity for control, the *D* Score offers information about that capacity as it is now. The majority of adult subjects, both patients and nonpatients, will have an Adjusted *D* Score of 0. Subjects with an Adjusted *D* Score of 0 usually have an adequate tolerance for the stresses of everyday living, and it is only under conditions of intense, prolonged, and/or unexpected stress that their controls falter significantly.

If the Adjusted *D* Score exceeds 0, such as +1, +2, and so on, it signifies greater capacity for control and greater tolerance for stress because the resources available for use are well in excess of the demands for responses. Apparently, people with Adjusted *D* Scores greater than 0 have been able to identify more of their resources in ways that make them readily accessible than do most people. This creates an increase in the capacity for control, and as a by-product the tolerance for stress (even prolonged, intense, and/or unexpected stresses) is improved considerably. As the magnitude of the positive Adjusted *D* increases, so too do the capacities for control and the ability to tolerate stress.

At first glance, *D* Scores in the plus range may appear to be a very desirable characteristic, and for some people that can be the case. However, it is important to reemphasize that neither of the two *D* Scores have much to do with adjustment or adaptive behavior. For instance, 31% of the subjects in the schizophrenia reference sample have *D* Scores greater than 0, and 41% of that group have Adjusted *D* Scores greater than 0. Patients who have *D* and Adjusted *D* Scores greater than 0 do tend to have sturdy controls and are not easily disorganized by stress situations, in spite of their pathology. They are frequently more difficult to treat because they tend to use their resources to avoid direct confrontations with the experiences of frailty, helplessness, or discomfort that often serve to promote motivation for growth or change. If the elements that lead to sturdy control capacity, as represented by the elevated D and Adjusted D Scores, have been organized prematurely in the developmental cycle, the result can be a form of rigidity that produces an excessive distancing from many experiences that have value in extending or broadening sensitivity to, an awareness of the environment. Thus, if a pathological element becomes pervasive in the personality structure, as in schizophrenia or even in less serious conditions, the possibilities for change are reduced substantially.

On the other hand, subjects with D or Adjusted D Scores in the minus range, -1, -2, and so on, have fewer available resources than are required in light of the frequency and/ or intensity of demands made on them. They are overloaded, that is, they are experiencing more demands for response formulation than they are able to prepare and implement at the moment. The overload predisposes inefficient or ineffective functioning. At times, they may not process information adequately, may not form decisions carefully or thoroughly, or may not implement decisions fully or effectively. In effect, they are vulnerable to impulsiveness in both thinking and behavior. If only the D Score is in the minus range, the overload can be expected to be transient, but if the Adjusted D Score is in the minus range, the condition is more chronic.

People with D or Adjusted D Scores of -1 often have trouble with new situations. They tend to function best in routine and predictable environments. New or more complex situations often cause them to become distracted or inefficient and their behaviors may not be as adaptive as might ordinarily be the case. Those who fall into the -2, -3 or lower categories, are in an almost continuous state of overload. They are beset with many more experienced demands for responses than they can handle easily. The result is that many of their behaviors are insufficient or even inappropriate, and when new demands occur, their lives usually become disorganized in some ways. People with *Adj D* Scores of less than -1 usually have histories that include numerous events marked by faulty judgment, emotional disruption, and/or behavioral ineffectiveness. They are chronically vulnerable to ideational and/or affective impulsiveness and typically function adequately for extended periods only in environments that are highly structured and routine and over which they have some sense of control.

As noted earlier, an overload state is not uncommon among children, but it can be an extremely detrimental situation for the older person. The sometimes disorganized and chaotic child is usually regarded in a more acceptable light than is the disorganized or chaotic adult. The disorganized child is typically judged as being the product of limited development and the resulting lack of maturity. The same features are much less acceptable in the adult, even though the causes may be the same. Whereas a D Score in the minus range may be the result of some situational stress, an overload condition reflected in the minus Adjusted D Score *can be* the result of a perpetuated developmental failure. These are the more immature people whose lives seem to be marked by one chaotic event after another, or whose general pattern of activity will be marked by an excessive frequency of ineffective and/or maladaptive behaviors. However, *it is unrealistic to presume that minus Adjusted* D *Scores only reflect a form of immaturity.* Some people who are besieged with pathology during adulthood are gradually pushed into an overload state. As stimulus demands increase in breadth and frequency because of the pathology, resources may become overtaxed and spread too thin. This increases the potential for disorganization and, if the pathology persists, this can become a chronic state. For instance, in some cases, the history will contain information about significant achievements in complex endeavors such as educational or occupational success. High levels of achievement are extremely rare among subjects who have Adjusted D Scores in the minus range. Therefore, if a minus Adjusted D Score occurs in the record of a subject with a significant achievement history, it is reasonable to assume that the current minus Adjusted *D* Score is the result of some ongoing disorganization.

Challenging the Adjusted *D* Score   As suggested earlier, it is impractical to formulate an interpretive hypothesis concerning controls and stress tolerance solely from the data for the *D* and Adjusted *D* Scores. Whereas a *D* Score that is lower in value than that for the Adjusted *D* Score does probably signal situationally related stress, both *D* Scores are somewhat crude, and if studied in isolation may provide only limited information about the capacity for control. In fact, in some records, the *D* Scores might even render misleading information about controls or stress tolerance. Thus, the credibility of the *Adj D* Score must be challenged.

The first step in this process is to review the datum for *EA,* which is the linchpin in the controls cluster. It provides information from which to judge the validity of the Adjusted *D* Score. In other words, it serves as a reference point against which the integrity of the Adjusted *D* Score can be evaluated, and in doing so, is also an indirect referent concerning the *D* Score. *EA* provides an index of resources that are accessible to the individual and drawn on when necessary to formulate decisions and implement those decisions in deliberate behavioral activity. Conversely, *es* represents an index of demands being experienced by the subject. Thus, if the *Adj D* Score is zero, it is expected that *EA* will fall at least in the average range and that *es* will not be greater than average. Usually, plus *D* scores are produced by higher than average values for *EA*. When this is true, it reflects an abundance of available resource. It does not mean better adjustment, but merely indicates that the subject has identified and/or organized resources more extensively than is the case with most people. But how the resources are used can be an altogether different matter.

If the value for *EA* is in the average range, an *Adj D* Score of zero is expected and probably reflects a reliable and valid index of capacity for control and stress tolerance. If the value for *EA* is in the average range and the *Adj D* Score is in the *plus* range, this is an unusual finding and signals a lower than expected value for *es*. Thus, the *Adj D* Score may be misleading and requires further evaluation. If the value for *EA* is in the average range or above and the *Adj D* Score is in the *minus* range, this is an unusual finding that signals a higher than average value for *es* after it has been adjusted for stress factors. The unexpected elevation in *es* should be evaluated carefully, and conclusions regarding the reliability of *Adj D* deferred until that time.

If the value for *EA* exceeds the average range, an *Adj D* Score in the *plus* range is expected and probably represents a reliable and valid index of capacity for control and tolerance for stress. If the value for *EA* exceeds the average range and the *Adj D* Score is zero, an unexpectedly elevated *es* is present, which may indicate that capacity for control has been greater than currently indicated. This possibility should be carefully evaluated. If *EA* is significantly lower than average, it suggests more limited available resources. An *Adj D* Score in the *minus* range is not unexpected. If the *Adj D* Score is zero or greater, it is possibly misleading because people with a low *EA,* other than young children, are more chronically vulnerable to becoming disorganized by many of the natural everyday stresses of living in a complex society. They function most effectively in environments that are well structured and reasonably free of ambiguity.

A second challenge regarding the efficacy of the Adjusted *D* Score is less direct. It involves a challenge concerning the reliability of the *EA* and is derived from the data of the *EB*. It is important to keep in mind that the *EA* is simply the addition of values from both sides of the *EB*. If the *EB* is misleading, so too will be the *EA*. A zero on either side of an *EB* in which the other side contains a substantial value casts doubt on the reliability of the

EA and typically signals the presence of an unusual affective problem that may have served as a predisposition to a current stress state, *or* could be the product of a current stress state.

If the values on both sides of the *EB* are greater than zero, the resulting *EA* is probably reliable. If, however, the value for *M* is zero and the value for *Sum C* is greater than 3.0, it is reasonable to conclude that the subject is being overwhelmed or flooded by affect. This creates a major impact on thinking, especially the ability to invoke the forms of delay in ideational activity that are often necessary to maintain adequate attention and concentration while pursuing decision operations. The possibilities of either ideational or behavioral impulsiveness are increased significantly under this condition. In this circumstance, *EA* is unreliable and consequently the Adjusted *D* Score is unreliable.

Similarly, if the value for *Sum C* is zero and the value for *M* is greater than 2, the subject is investing considerable energy in a massive containment or shutdown of affect. Usually this requires much more resource than the average person has available, and thus the vulnerability to stimulus overload and consequent disorganization is considerable. Here too, the values for *EA* and the Adjusted *D* Score will be unreliable.

The *CDI* and Controls   Another very important input to any postulates concerning controls is the datum of the Coping Deficit Index (*CDI*). Even if the values for the *Adj D* and *EA* are within average limits, a positive *CDI* raises serious questions about the capacity for control and/or tolerance for stress. Subjects who are positive on this index appear to have more trouble in many coping situations. They tend to feel helpless or out of place when confronted with everyday social demands and this sense of helplessness can often give rise to behaviors that are quite similar to those manifest in overload situations. Thus, even though the Adjusted *D* Score may be zero or greater, positive *CDI* subjects frequently become disorganized and/or ineffective when confronted with social demands. In effect, this feature adds a new dimension to the issue of control and stress tolerance that must be factored in when these issues are considered.

Therefore, if the value for the Adjusted *D* has withstood the challenge based on the values for *EA* and *es* and the value for the *CDI* is less than 4, it can be assumed that a proposition based on the Adjusted *D* is sound. However, regardless of the value *Adj D,* if the value for the *CDI* is 4 or 5, it suggests that the personality organization of the subject is somewhat less mature than might be expected, which can create a vulnerability for problems in coping with the requirements of everyday living. Such difficulties usually are manifest in the interpersonal sphere and can easily contribute to problems in control when they occur.

Even if the *Adj D* value is in the *plus* range, signifying that the subject has a greater tolerance for stress than do most, and is far less likely to experience problems in control, a positive *CDI* signals a potential for control or stress tolerance problems in the interpersonal sphere.

RESEARCH RELATED TO HYPOTHESES BASED ON THE ADJUSTED *D* SCORE

The notion that some variable might be created to provide indications about capacities for control and/or tolerance for stress evolved very gradually in the development of the Comprehensive System. In the early 1970s, when the basic procedures and components of the Comprehensive System were being selected, tested, and reviewed, *EA* did not seem to fit well as an easily interpreted variable and was almost discarded. Nonetheless, sufficient data had accumulated to identify the average *EA* for adults and, prompted by Beck's (1960) findings and those of Piotrowski and Schreiber (1952) in which significant increases were reported for the values in both sides of *EB* after prolonged treatment, three retest studies were mounted, spanning an 18- to 20-month period (Exner, 1974). They involved patients and nonpatients. The retest values for *EA* among nonpatients changed very little, as did those for unimproved patients. Conversely, the retest values for *EA* increased significantly among patients who were judged as improved.

These findings seemed important enough to include *EA* into the Comprehensive System, but the usefulness of *EA* remained elusive, partly because of a conceptual error that concerned the interpretation of two variables, *Experience Balance* (*eb*) and *Experienced Stimulation* (*es*) which, at that time was erroneously called *Experience Potential* (*ep*). The *eb* was derived from a Klopfer ratio that he believed to represent response tendencies that had not yet been fully accepted or available to the subject (Klopfer, Ainsworth, Klopfer, & Holt, 1954). Klopfer's interpretation of the ratio was based mainly on findings from an investigation leading to the development of a Prognostic Scale (Klopfer, Kirkner, Wisham, & Baker, 1951) in which *FM, m,* and some shading variables were shown to load positively into an index predicting a favorable response to treatment. Both Klopfer and Piotrowski (1957) had long argued that *FM* and *m* responses reflected introversive tendencies and reflected types of primitive or less available forms of ideation, whereas some shading answers represented extratensive tendencies not fully developed. Those postulates led to the logical but erroneous assumption that if *FM, m,* and some of the shading variables did represent forms of less sophisticated, undeveloped, or unavailable response tendencies, their frequencies would diminish as *EA* increased as a function of treatment or development. In other words, they were conceptualized as representing potential. Nevertheless, sufficient data had accumulated to caution that the *ep* represented activities not controlled by higher cognitive functioning and, as such, worked on the individual to provoke responses (Exner, 1974, p. 315).

The erroneous conception regarding the "potential" element reflected in the *eb* persisted for several years even though more data accumulated to support the notion that *ep* represents an index of psychological activity not accessible to organization or control (Exner, 1978, pp. 82–86). Two laboratory studies also were completed during this period, one involving mirror tracing and one involving the pursuit rotor. The results of both seemed to argue against the potential factor and prompted the Wiener-Levy dissertation, involving a sophisticated replication of the pilot study with the pursuit rotor. The results forced a reevaluation of the notion of potential (Wiener-Levy & Exner, 1981). In addition, considerable normative data concerning children had accumulated as had most of the adult nonpatient sample; and the third retest of a longitudinal study concerning children, a host of data regarding first-time outpatients, first admission inpatients, plus follow-up testing of patients in treatment, had been collected. The composite of these data permitted closer scrutiny of the issue of potential.

The collective findings made it obvious that the use of the term *potential* had been wrong and the *ep* was relabeled *Experienced Stimulation* (*es*). Most of what had been written about *ep,* that it represents some form of impingement or demand was indeed true, but the Klopfer-Piotrowski-Exner assumption that these stimuli reflected some psychological potential was not true.

Given the new framework, it seemed important to create some formula that might express the relationship between accessible resource, as measured by *EA,* and the demands experienced by the subject, as expressed by *es.* This led to the development of the *D* Scores. The concepts or terminology used to explain the *D* Scores, such as stimulus demand and stimulus overload are not new. They have their origins in a lengthy outpouring of work in the areas of frustration, stress, emotion, and experimental psychopathology. The citations concerning this work are almost endless and probably begin with Pavlov. Some of the most direct explications of these concepts can be found in older but still valuable literature such as French (1947), Gantt (1947), Liddell (1944), Mair (1949), Maslow (1947), Miller (1944), and Selye (1956). They remain implicit in the newer literature concerning stress and/or emotion (Seligman, Abramson, Semmel, & von Baeyer, 1979; Lazarus, 1983; Lazarus & Folkman, 1984, Lazarus, 1991). Findings concerning the *EA, eb, es,* and the *Adj es,* should help to clarify the issues posed by the *D* Scores. A review of the variables related to the Adjusted *D* Score is probably the best starting point.

A number of variables contribute to the formulation of the Adjusted *D* Score. They include the *EA,* which is a summation of the values on each side of the *EB,* plus the summation of the values on both sides of the *eb* which, in turn, are adjusted to reduce any unexpected elevations for the *m* and *Y* variables. That adjustment is critical because both the *m* and *Y* variables are highly unstable and seem most directly related to situationally related stress experiences. Therefore, it is best to put those two variables aside for the moment when describing the Adjusted *D* Score as it relates to the capacity for control.

THE EXPERIENCE ACTUAL (*EA*)

Beck (1960) conceptualized the *EA,* working in part from a suggestion of Rorschach but mainly from data for subjects who had completed psychotherapy. He postulated that by summing the two sides of the *EB,* that is, the human movement answers (*M*) and the weighted values for the chromatic color responses (*FC, CF, C*), the result would provide an index of the extent to which resources are organized in a manner that makes them accessible. He noted that subjects completing treatment successfully usually have retest *EB*s that show the same directionality as in their pretreatment protocols, but the numbers in the ratio tend to be considerably larger *even though the posttreatment records were not significantly longer.* Beck argued that the increases in human movement and chromatic color answers represented the development of more inner life and affective experiences, thereby constituting a broadening of available resources. An obvious assumption underpinning Beck's hypothesis is that both human movement and chromatic color answers are related to use of resources.

Findings by Bash (1955) and Piotrowski and Schreiber (1952) lend support to Beck's concept although neither conceptualized the process. Bash administered Card IX to 28 subjects 200 times in succession, using a 5-second exposure and a 15-second interval. He found that the *M:C* ratio for 18 of these subjects gradually became nearly equal; that is, a numerical decline of one component and an increase in the other component occurred. Although a change in this experimental *EB* was noted, the numerical values comprising the *EB* remained essentially stable. Piotrowski and Schreiber studied 13 patients before and after prolonged psychoanalytic treatment. They report that both sides of the *EB* ratio increased significantly after treatment although the directions of the ratio generally remained constant, a finding comparable with that reported by Beck. One other study

(Erginel, 1972) appears to lend some support to the *EA* concept. Erginel used data from an earlier study (Kemalof, 1952) in which six series of inkblots, similar to the Rorschach, had been administered to 12 subjects on six consecutive days. Erginel illustrates that the *M* + *SumC* does fluctuate on a daily basis and interprets this as a function of mood shifts. Interestingly, the *EB*s generally appear to maintain a relatively constant direction, and the *EA*s fluctuate 4.0 or less in 50 (70%) of the 72 observations. Beck (1972) has suggested that the *EA* permits an evaluation of the *EB* that goes beyond response style.

Exner (1974) reported findings that lend some support to the Beck postulate concerning *EA*. In one study, 30 patients and 30 nonpatients were retested after an 18-month interval. The mean *EA* for the nonpatients was 6.25 at the first test and 6.75 at the second test. The patient group was subdivided into two groups on the basis of independent ratings of improvement provided by both professionals and relatives. The mean *EA*s for the unimproved patient group were 3.50 at pretreatment and 4.25 at the second test, whereas the patient group rated as significantly improved showed a mean *EA* at pretreatment of 3.75 versus a mean of 7.25 in the second test ($p < .02$). In a second study, two groups of 12 patients each were tested prior to, and at the termination of treatment. One group had been in long-term psychotherapy, averaging 131 sessions during an average interval of 20.2 months. The second group was treated using supportive and directive methods, averaging 47.4 sessions, extending over an average period of 10.3 months. Both groups received medication as deemed appropriate, but the medication was not considered as a primary treatment method. The pretreatment mean *EA*s were very similar for both groups, 4.51 for the long-term group and 4.76 for the supportive group. The posttreatment mean *EA*s are quite different, 5.51 for the supportive group versus 8.26 for the long-term group ($p < .05$).

Similar findings have been reported for larger patient samples tested first prior to treatment and retested two or more times during the following one to five years. The first focused on Rorschach changes in short-term and long-term treatment (Weiner & Exner, 1991). It involved two groups of 88 patients each. One, treated in "short-term therapy" averaged 62.1 treatment sessions, and all had terminated within 27 months after beginning treatment. Twenty-one of those subjects had values for *EA* of less than 7.0 when beginning treatment as contrasted with only 11 subjects continuing to show *EA*s of less than 7.0 when retested 27 to 30 months later. The second group was treated in long-term, dynamically oriented, therapy, averaging 224 treatment sessions by the end of 2½ years. Thirty of the 88 had *EA* values of less than 7.0 at the onset of treatment whereas only 7 had such low values for *EA* when retested after 27 to 30 months. The findings for each group also indicated that *es* tends to become lower as treatment progresses.

The second study concerned two groups of 35 subjects, each in short-term and brief treatment and focused on Rorschach changes in those forms of intervention (Exner & Sanglade, 1992). The short-term treatment group averaged 47 treatment sessions on a once-per-week basis, whereas the brief treatment group averaged only 14.2 treatment sessions. Fifteen of the short-term treatment subjects had *EA* values of less than 7.0 at the onset of intervention. At termination, the number with *EA* values of less than 7.0 was reduced to 8. Conversely, 11 of the brief treatment subjects had *EA* values less than 7.0 when beginning treatment, and 9 of the 11 continued to show these low *EA* values at termination. The values for *es* tended to become lower for almost all subjects in both groups and consequently an increase in both the *D* and Adjusted *D* Scores occurred.

The *EA* retest reliability is very substantial among nonpatient adults, regardless of whether the retest is administered after a brief interval or a much longer period. Data show *EA* retest correlations of .83 after 1 year and .85 after 3 years. Conversely, the *EA* retest correlation for a group of 30 patients retested after only 6 months of intensive psychotherapy is .70, and for the same group retested after 18 months is .58 (Exner, 1978). Similarly, the *EA* retest correlations for nonpatient children, although ranging from .80 upward when retested after brief intervals, are very modest and often not significant when the retest is administered after a period of 9 months or longer, ranging from .19 to .45 (Exner & Weiner, 1982; Exner, Thomas, & Mason, 1985). The mean values for *EA* among nonpatient children increase each year from ages 5 through 13, but rarely more than by 0.5 in any one year. These data suggest a relationship between *EA* and some of the elements of development; however, if there is an interpretive usefulness to the absolute value of *EA,* it has remained elusive. Exner, Viglione, and Gillespie (1984) have reported a consistently positive significant correlation between *EA* and *Zf. Zf* has a modest positive significant correlation with intelligence and also with the need for achievement, thus either of these elements may be integral to *EA.* However, *EA* is not significantly correlated with intelligence when the range of IQs used falls on a normal distribution from 80 to 120 ($r = .12$). On the other hand, if the IQ range is restricted from 110 to 140, the correlation is positive and significant ($r = .38$). Possibly the most conservative explanation for this finding is that more intelligent people are able to identify and organize resources in ways that make them more easily accessible.

Although *EA* does increase gradually during developmental years, *es* changes only slightly. The value for *EA* is within 2.5 points of the value for *es* in the records of 65% of the 700 adults constituting the nonpatient normative sample, yielding *D* Scores of zero. An additional 22% have *EA* values that are more than 2.5 points higher than *es,* yielding *D* Scores in the plus range. When the *EAs* relationship is adjusted to account for the situational stress variables (*m* and *Y*), 90% of the sample has an Adjusted *D* Score of 0 or greater. On the other hand, the average value for *EA* tends to be lower among patients than nonpatients, and values for *es* are often more than 2.5 points greater than *EA,* thereby creating *D* Scores of less than 0. Even when adjusted for situational stress, a significantly greater proportion of patients than nonpatients have Adjusted D Scores of less than 0.

Beck noted that *EA* tends to be highest among schizophrenics in which manifest symptoms are clinically most obvious, yet they are often most difficult to treat. Most of those patients manifest paranoid features. He suggested, "The greater the supply of inner energy, the more it is converted into pathologic symptoms, given a personality that is taking recourse to a symptomatic solution" (1960, p. 20). Other data concerning nonschizophrenics in outpatient care also coincide with this postulate. Patients who respond most rapidly to treatment typically are those who are in distress. Patients with *D* Scores greater than 0 react more casually to stress and are slower to develop the patient–therapist alliance that seems so necessary for progress. This has been one of the findings that led to the conclusion that the *D* Scores have a relation to stress tolerance.

The most crucial assumption relevant to an understanding of EA and its relation to the two *D* scores is that the two variables involved in its calculation—*M* and the weighted *Sum C*—are manifestations of the use of resource, or stated differently, are related to *deliberately* initiated psychological behaviors. The data supporting this assumption are mainly of an inferential variety, but substantial in quantity. Some have evolved from studies focusing specifically on *M* or the Chromatic Color responses, but much has generated from studies concerning the *EB,* and this information is elaborated in the next chapter.

THE ADJUSTED EXPERIENCED STIMULATION (*Adj es*)

In light of the accumulated data regarding *EA,* it seemed important to develop a crude index that would offer information concerning the impinging or demanding stimulus experiences. The data of the *eb* provided the source, and *es* was the result. When studied in relation to *EA,* and adjusted for the probability of metric variance, it proved to afford important information concerning control and stress tolerance.

As noted earlier, the *eb* is a derivation of a ratio suggested by Klopfer et al. (1951). He offered the faulty postulate that it was useful in identifying response tendencies "that are not fully accepted by, or available to the subject" at a given time. His postulate that *FM* and *m* answers relate to introversive features and that achromatic and shading answers relate to extratensive tendencies was a premise held by many Rorschachers involved in the early development of the test. The flaw in that postulate was created by the logical assumption that the process related to *M* is also related to the variables *FM* and *m* and that the process related to chromatic color responses is also related to the achromatic color and shading variables. The variety of validity studies concerning these variables, plus intercorrelational studies, offer no support for that assumption. For instance, intercorrelations between *M* and *FM* range from .11 to .19, and between .10 and .20 for *M* and *FM +m.* Similarly, the intercorrelations between Sum of Achromatic and Shading (*SH*) and *WSumC* range from .22 to .24, between *SH* and *FC* range from −.14 to −.19, and between *SH* and *CF +C* from .23 to .37 (Exner, 1983; Exner, Viglione, & Gillespie, 1984). Only the latter, .37, is statistically significant. It was found in only one sample of nonpatient adults and has not replicated in other samples.

The *eb* is entered as the sum of *FM +m* on the left side, and the sum of all achromatic color and shading variables (*SH*) on the right. The distinction of the two groupings of variables is important because, although there are no demonstrable process relationships between the variables in the *eb* and those in the *EB,* they do share some common features. As with *M,* the *FM* and *m* answers involve some form of projection, because the movement features do not exist in the stimulus field, but more important, all three also appear to relate to forms of ideation. Whereas the *M* answers concern deliberately formulated and directed ideation that is generally in the direct focus of attention, the *FM* and *m* answers apparently relate to mental activity that is provoked by demand stimuli. This mental activity usually is not in the direct focus of attention. Instead, it is a more peripheral process that tends to serve a stimulating function, like an ideational signal system that often prompts a person into action. Most of the time, it serves a useful alerting function; but if the activity becomes inordinately diverse or excessive, it can become a disruptive force. This is probably what happens in cases of insomnia, or in people who complain about "racing thoughts," or "having too many things on my mind." In these instances, the peripheral ideation tends to interfere with concentration and the subject has difficulty keeping the focus of attention on a specific target or objective. Similarly, chromatic color and the *SH* responses all relate to affect. Whereas the chromatic color answers relate to the deliberate discharge of affect, the *SH* variables relate to the experience of affect that is created by demand stimuli. These are irritating or prompting feelings created by any of a variety of psychological experiences. Some are obviously generated by need states. Others are provoked when feelings are not expressed openly or fully, and still more result from a sort of rumination about the self. Thus the *eb* is organized to provide information about the experiences of stimulus demand.

A review of previous research concerning the six variables that contribute to the *eb*, plus findings from new studies, indicated that all six variables might be useful to detect stimulus demand, but that only four of those variables reflect a more incessant or state-like condition. The remaining two, *m* and *Y*, appear to be far less stable and related to situational factors. In that context, the Adjusted *D* Score was designed so as to ignore situationally related factors by adjusting the *es* psychometrically to exclude unusual elevations in the values for *m* and *Y*, thereby giving emphasis to the four variables that relate to more chronic or persistent stimulus demand features. A review of research related to each of the four should clarify the necessity of making this adjustment.

THE *FM* VARIABLE

As mentioned earlier, both *FM* and *m* seem related to the presence of mental activity that is provoked by demand states. In that context, they are similar, yet they are also very different. The research concerning *m* indicates that it is an unstable, state-related variable, which appears to be induced by situational stress. The mental activity to which it relates seems to involve a sense of helplessness and/or loss of control. Nonetheless, it is reasonable to hypothesize that when this activity is present, regardless of the process by which it is provoked, the subject will experience some difficulties in attention and concentration, and that efforts at reasoning can be interrupted or diverted easily.

The *FM* variable, even though related to different origins than *m*, and even though similar in process, probably evokes more altering but fewer disruptive features. Such a conclusion seems logical because *FM* is reasonably stable over time. The retest data for *FM* are quite intriguing in that they show correlations ranging from the lower to upper .70s, *regardless* of whether the retest is done after a brief 3-week period or a lengthy 3-year interval. Most other Rorschach variables that have retest correlations in the .70s for long intervals will have retest correlations in the .80s, or even into the .90s over brief periods of time. The consistency of these retest correlations for *FM* suggests that, although it is reasonably stable, situational variables may also influence the process to which it relates.

Rorschach (1921) did not include a coding for animal movement in his research, and later, both Beck and Rapaport decided to follow his decision. Klopfer devised the *FM* coding and Hertz and Piotrowski adopted it into their approaches. All three, operating under the false premise that a relationship existed between *M* and *FM*, assumed that it represented a more primitive form of thinking, which is not necessarily true. However, all three also suggested that it has a relation to some awareness of impulses that are striving for gratification, which does seem to be true.

FM has been researched less than many other Rorschach variables, possibly because it did not appear in all of the earlier approaches to the test. Nonetheless, the data that have accumulated offer several consistent findings from which some seemingly valid judgments concerning the process can be made. First, *FM* has been shown to increase under diminished states of consciousness, such as those produced by alcohol (Piotrowski & Abrahamsen, 1952) and sodium amytal (Warshaw, Leiser, Izner, & Sterne, 1954). Exner, Zalis, and Schumacher (1976) studied the records of 15 chronic amphetamine users, all of whom were between the ages of 17 and 22. They note a substantially high frequency of *FM* as contrasted with a control group of 15 chronic marijuana users in the same age range. There were, of course, other differences between the two groups. The amphetamine subjects showed many of the features of the acute schizophrenic, whereas the marijuana users did not illustrate psychotic features. Nonetheless, the *FM* frequency was much higher for the first group. This finding prompted an examination of the protocols of 190 female subjects, half of whom were prostitutes. The prostitute subjects had been classified by intraoccupational socioeconomic level criteria, ranging from the very "high-priced" call girl to the addicted part-time streetwalker (Exner, Wylie, Leura, & Parrill, 1977). The streetwalkers, identified in the study as the Class V Group, consisted of only 10 subjects, all of whom were heroin addicted. They were matched, on the basis of marital status, intelligence, birth order, and educational level, with 10 controls who were not prostitutes. There were many features in the protocols of the two groups that differentiated one from another, but one major difference occurred in the frequency of *FM* answers. The 10 addicted prostitutes gave almost twice as many *FM* answers as did the controls.

Much of the data concerning *FM* suggest that the ideational process correlated with this variable is provoked by unmet need states. In theory, these would be the unprovoked thoughts that occur most often when a person is not deliberately focusing attention on a coping issue. For instance, the kinds of mental activity that keep the intended sleeper awake may be *FM*-related actions. Findings of several studies seem to offer support for this postulate.

Exner, Cooper, and Walker (1975) studied the Rorschach changes of nine *very* overweight males during a 10-day medically supervised dietary program. Each of the subjects began the program with at least 50 pounds of excess weight, and the procedure for the diet involved hospitalization, during which only the intake of fluid was permitted. The "fluid only" phase of the program was the first segment of a more extended weight-control regimen. Rorschachs were administered the day before hospitalization, and again on the 10th day of hospitalization. The average weight loss during this period was 18.4 pounds, and at least psychologically, all nine subjects were "very hungry" on the 10th hospital day. The average number of *FM* answers given in the prediet protocols was 3.77, which is not significantly different from the nonpatient norm; however, the variation *within* the sample was striking. Two subjects produced considerably fewer *FM* answers at the second testing, one moving from three to zero, and a second from four to one. One additional subject remained essentially at the same point, giving three *FM*s in the first record and four in the second. The other six subjects increased substantially for *FM* at the second test, the smallest increase being from two *FM*s at the first test to four at the second. Thus, although the data are not statistically defensible, the majority of subjects did move upward for *FM*, most showing a considerable change.

The second study in this series involved the testing of 15 juvenile offenders (Exner, Bryant, & Miller, 1975). All were tested at entry to a juvenile detention center and again at the 60th day of detention. All 15 had been sentenced to an "indeterminant period" of detention for offenses ranging from auto theft to assault, an act typically marking a series of antisocial acts in the history of the subject. Most such subjects are released from detention after 75 to 90 days, but others are detained for a considerably longer period. Thus at the 60-day interval, none of the subjects knew the probable date of release. The average number of *FM* responses at the first testing was 4.27 ($SD = 1.3$), whereas at the second testing, the mean *FM* had increased to 6.89 ($SD = 1.9$, $t = 4.68$, $p < .05$).

Ridgeway and Exner (1980) tested first-year medical school students twice. The subjects were also administered the McClelland (1953) Need Achievement Scale, and Rank Order Correlations calculated for several Rorschach variables and *NAch*. None were significant for the first test, but a rho $= .41$ ($p < .01$) was discovered between *FM* and *NAch* in the second test, which was administered 2 or 3 days before their first major anatomy examination, a situation that logically should give rise to the achievement need.

Exner (1979) paid 15 male volunteers to participate in a physical restraint study. Each was tested 1 week prior to the laboratory restraint to establish baseline data. Subjects were paid in relation to the amount of time they elected to remain in restraint. The subjects were restrained in a large wooden chair using 32 leather straps so that, when all were secured, the subject could do little more than move fingertips, toes, and eyes. Subjects were able to terminate the restraint by signaling the experimenter, using a button attached to one arm of the chair that caused a bell to ring. Prior to being released, however, the subject was administered a second Rorschach, with the examiner holding the cards. The mean *FM* for the group in the baseline data was 3.26 (*SD* = 1.64), whereas the mean *FM* in the retest was 5.42 (*SD* = 2.02), *p* < .02.

The means for *FM* are relatively consistent across age groups in the normative data, tending to hover between 4.0 and 5.0 through age 16, and are about 3.7 for adults. These findings cast considerable doubt on the postulate that *FM* is related to a more primitive form of ideation. It seems more likely that it relates to a process that is not deliberately initiated, and less well controlled or directed.

Haan (1964) reported that when *FM* exceeds *M*, there is a high correlation with several measure of defensiveness, including intellectualization, rationalization, regression, and substitution. She suggests that *FM* may reflect either an overt expression of impulse, or an internalization of behavior, oriented toward containment of the impulse. However, this defensiveness is apparently not very effective if relapse is used as a criterion. Exner, Murillo, and Cannovo (1973) followed 105 nonschizophrenic patients for 1 year following discharge from hospitalization. Twenty-four were rehospitalized during the first 12 months, and 17 had more *FM* than *M* in their discharge records, as contrasted with only nine of 81 nonrelapsers. Exner (1978) has also noted that withdrawn children tend to have more *M* than *FM*.

There are a number of studies that suggest that elevations in *FM* are related to behavioral dysfunction. Piotrowski and Abrahamsen (1952) report that subjects who give more *FM*s than *M*s tend to be much more aggressive under states of diminished consciousness, such as under the influence of alcohol or drugs. Earlier, Thompson (1948) found that *FM* is significantly correlated with MMPI measures of irresponsibility, aggressiveness, and distractability. Sommer and Sommer (1958) found a significant correlation between *FM* and assaultive behavior, and Altus (1958) reported that students scoring high on the MMPI Schizophrenia Scale give significantly more *FM* than do students scoring low on that scale. Berryman (1961) found that *FM* is related to the level of productivity in creative artists. Piotrowski and Schreiber (1952) found that the quality of *FM*s tend to change during treatment, generally becoming more assertive and less passive. They note that these changes correspond to behavioral changes in which successfully treated subjects demonstrate more "vitality and liveliness" in their actions. Exner (1978) found that a group of 480 adolescents, classified as behavior or conduct disorders, have a slightly, but not significantly, higher mean for *FM* as contrasted with nonpatient adolescents, averaging nearly six per record.

Thus, the entry on the left side of the *eb* offers some indication about mental activity that is being prompted by demand experiences, and most are expected to be *FM* related. The demands may be stress related or need related or, as is most often the case, by the composite of both. As noted earlier, this activity appears to serve a stimulating or alerting function, that tends to prompt a person into action. In that context, it can be regarded as a positive complement to coping resources. On the other hand, if the activity is excessive, it can become a disruptive force. This is probably what happens in cases in which difficulties in concentration occur or even in those instances in which the objectives of relaxation cannot be developed.

The value on the left side of the *eb* is *always* expected to be higher than the value on the right side. This is true for about 90% of nonpatient children between the ages of 5 and 14, 85% of nonpatient children, ages 11 and 16, and about 85% of the nonpatient adults. This is also true of most patient groups, although the proportions of subjects with a higher left side value tend to be less than for nonpatient groups. For instance, the reference sample of character disorders has 70% with higher left side *eb,* and the schizophrenic sample has only 59% higher on the left side. The reference sample of seriously depressed subjects includes 61% who have a higher value in the *right side of the eb.* This is not a surprising finding, because each of the four variables included in the right side value of the *eb* is related to irritating affective experiences that are created by demand situations.

THE ACHROMATIC COLOR AND THREE SHADING VARIABLES

The symbol *SH* has often been used to represent a composite value of the four variables, *C',* *T, V,* and *Y;* however, it can be somewhat misleading to those not thoroughly familiar with the Rorschach. It can be misinterpreted to imply that each of the four variables share many common features, a presumption that is *not* really true. It is true, as noted earlier, that all four are related to impinging or irritating affects, but beyond that common element they are quite different from each other. One of the four, *Y,* is highly unstable, and that is why it is essentially excluded when calculating the Adjusted *es.* Two others, *T* and *V,* are very stable for their presence or absence, and the fourth, *C',* usually has retest correlations ranging from the middle .60s to the middle .70s, but rarely higher, or lower. Like *FM* it seems to have some trait-like stability but is also influenced by state conditions.

The composite does have use as the right side value of the *eb* by providing a crude index of subjectively felt distress. Usually, the value will range between 2 and 4 among nonpatients, but it can often be higher for subjects in that group, and in patient groups. The absolute value, taken alone, has little interpretive significance unless it is inordinately higher, such as greater than 5, *or if it exceeds the value in the left side of the eb.* Either of those circumstances signals the presence of distress. However, when considering the Adjusted *es* only three of the four variables on the right side of the *eb* are critical.

THE TEXTURE VARIABLE

Texture answers appear most consistently among the records of nonpatients, both adults and children. Eighty-nine percent of all subjects in the nonpatient normative sample give at least one texture response, and most give *only* one (M = 1.03). Patients give texture answers far less frequently than do nonpatients and thus the absence of *T,* as well as elevations in *T,* are interpretively important. Klopfer (1938) was the first to recognize the importance of a separate coding for texture answers, and later Klopfer et al. (1954) suggested that it is related to needs for affection and dependency. McFate and Orr (1949) have noted that *TF* and *T* answers occur more frequently among young adolescents than in older adolescents or adults. Kallstedt (1952) has suggested that this is because young adolescents are more socially and sexually insecure. Montalto (1952) found that 6- and 7-year-old children whose mothers were more restrictive give significantly more texture answers than do those of the same ages who have democratic mothers. Breecher (1956) found more texture responses among patients who had been maternally overprotected as contrasted with those who had been maternally rejected. She suggested that maternal rejection causes a reduction in the "need to be liked."

Hertz (1948) reported that texture responses reflect a cautious sensitivity, related to a willingness to be more open with the environment. Brown et al. (1950) found that psychosomatic patients give significantly fewer texture answers than do patients being treated for other complaints. Steiner (1947) reported that unsuccessful workers give significantly more texture answers than do successful workers. Allerhand (1954) noted that texture responses correlate with an index of anxiety in an experimental induced conflict situation, although Waller (1960) was unable to find a relation between texture and scores on the Welsh or Taylor anxiety scales but did find texture related to an overall "impression" of anxiety. Potanin (1959) found that individuals who "acknowledge" dependency features prefer geometric designs with textural details significantly more than do people who describe themselves as independent. Coan (1956) studied Rorschach variables factorially, and concluded that the blends containing *M* and a texture variable relate to inner sensitivity or empathy. Exner (1978) demonstrated that when patients do articulate texture, they tend to do so with a substantially greater frequency than do nonpatients. This is probably because people who become patients are often troubled by long-standing feelings of emotional deprivation or have experienced recent emotional losses. Either will give rise to elevations in the frequency by which texture is included in answers.

For instance, Exner and Bryant (1974) found that 30 recently separated or divorced subjects averaged 3.57 texture responses (*SD* = 1.21) and that none had *T*-less protocols, whereas demographically matched controls averaged 1.31 texture answers (*SD* = 0.96). Twenty-one of the 30 separated or divorced subjects were retested after 6 months, at which time 14 reported having reconstituted or replaced the lost relationship. Those 21 subjects had averaged 3.49 texture answers in the first test, as compared with 2.64 in the second test. Similarly, Exner and Leura (1975) found an average of 2.87 texture answers (*SD* = 1.12) in a group of 23 children, ages 8 to 12, who had been placed in foster homes for the first time within the preceding 60 days because of the loss of one or both parents.

Exner, Leventrosser, and Mason (1980) found that 36 of 50 first-admission depressed patients who had at least one texture response also reported having a transitional object as a young child, such as a teddy bear, favorite blanket, and so on. Conversely, only 10 of 50 first admission depressed patients who had *T*-less records reported having a transitional object. Those data are similar to findings of Exner and Chu (1981) concerning nonpatient adults.

Subjects who have *T*-less protocols appear to have several psychological characteristics that are quite different from those who deliver texture answers. The first hint of this was noted by Leura and Exner (1976), who tested 32 foster-home children, aged 7 to 11, who had no placement lasting longer than 14 months, and a control group of 32 children of about the same intellectual level who had lived with their true parents since birth. The mean *T* for the foster-home group was 0.457 (*SD* = 0.26), *and 20 subjects produced "T-less" records.* The mean *T* for the 32 control subjects was 1.47 (*SD* = 0.52), and only three of those gave "*T*-less" protocols. A retest after four months of 16 of the 20 "*T*-less" foster home subjects showed that 15 of the 16 remained T-less. This marked difference cannot be attributed to the "failure of articulation" element. In the first testing, the 20 subjects averaged 1.4 gray/black or shading answers, with 16 of the 20 delivering such responses. Most involved C' or Y. In the retest, the 15 T-less subjects averaged 1.7 gray-black, shading answers with at least one in every record. These data appear to support the premise that, for some subjects, the affective experience of emotional or dependency needs may become "neutralized," and if this experience occurs, it takes on a durable characteristic. Pierce (1978) reported a similar finding in the protocols of 52 children who had experienced an absent parent prior to age 8. In that sample, T appeared in only seven protocols.

Exner (1978) also found that therapists tend to rate T-less patients lower in motivation for treatment during the first three months of contact than they do patients who have T in their pretreatment records. Exner, Martin, and Thomas (1983) found that T-less subjects tend to select seats in a waiting room that are more distant from a collaborator who was seated diagonally from the entry door than did subjects who gave T in their records. In fact, subjects who had elevations in T in their protocols tended to sit as close to the collaborator as possible, and frequently spoke to the collaborator, whereas T-less subjects rarely spoke during the 10-minute waiting period.

The data concerning T are quite compelling. Most nonpatients give one T response, usually an FT answer to Card VI. People who elevate for T have greater needs for closeness, and the elevation gives some indication of those needs. They apparently experience loneliness or stronger than usual needs to be dependent on others. On the other hand, people who do not give T in their records appear to be more guarded and/or distant in interpersonal contacts. They also appear to be more concerned with issues of personal space than are most people. Interestingly, T-less subjects usually will give at least one texture answer in records that are taken after 9 to 15 months of treatment, regardless of the type of intervention (Exner, 1978; Weiner & Exner, 1991; Exner & Sanglade, 1992).

THE ACHROMATIC COLOR VARIABLE

Achromatic Color responses show a higher mean among nonpatients (1.53) than the texture responses; however, they are given by a smaller proportion of subjects. Whereas T responses are given by about 89% of the normative sample, the C' variables appear in only 79% of those records. They appear in 78% of the records of depressed patients, in 70% of the Schizophrenic reference sample, and in 49% of the records of the reference sample of Character Problems. Klopfer (1938) was the first to provide a specific coding for responses in which the white, gray, or black features of the blots are used as color. He postulated that these answers correlate with a tendency to tone down affect, but cautioned that the specific process involved would be defined by the presence or absence of other test features. For instance, he hypothesized that C' answers, involving the use of white space as color, might relate to a euphoric characteristic *if* the record is also marked by a substantial number of chromatic color responses. Later, Klopfer hypothesized that the C' answers might be related to depressive features (Klopfer & Spiegelman, 1956). Rapaport et al. (1946) suggested that the process related to the C' types of response might be more conscious and defensive against direct affective expression. Piotrowski (1957) also postulated that the C' responses are related to depressive feelings but emphasized that the euphoric element is likely to be present if the responses involve white or light-gray areas of the blots, citing the findings of Weber (1937) that alcoholics give significantly more *C'* answers involving the white and light-gray areas.

Exner (1974) found that *C'* responses are given about twice as frequently by psychosomatics, obsessives, and schizoids as by nonpatients, and about three times as frequently as given by patients diagnosed as passive-aggressive or psychopathic. Exner (1974) also reviewed the pretreatment protocols of 64 first-admission affective disorders who had been placed on a "suicide watch" at the time of admission. Sixteen of the 64 made suicide gestures within 55 days of admission, and only five of those 16 records (31%) contained *C'* responses as contrasted with 34 of the 48 (71%) patients who did not make a gesture. These findings tend to support the postulate that a relationship does exist between affective constraint and *C'*. Exner and Leura (1977) found that the records of 20 adolescents being evaluated for disposition recommendations related to "acting-out" offenses contained *significantly more C'* answers ($M = 2.77$; $SD = 1.03$) than did the records of 20 nonpatient adolescents ($M = 1.12$; $SD = 0.79$) used as controls for the study, $p < .01$. Both groups were retested after 8 weeks, at which time all disposition decisions concerning the acting-out subjects had been made and implemented. The control subjects gave about as many *C'* answers in the retest as they had in the first test ($M = 1.07$; $SD = 0.87$), whereas the acting-out group gave significantly fewer *C'* responses than they had in the first test ($M = 1.11$; $SD = 0.94$). These data offer some support for Rapaport's suggestion that the process related to *C'* may be defensive. The findings also coincide with retest correlational data mentioned earlier, indicating that although *C'* is relatively stable, it is apparently subject to fluctuation under some state influences.

Some of the most compelling data concerning *C'* responses come from the normative and reference samples. As noted previously, 78% of the depressives give at least one *C'* answer, and the mean for the group is 2.16, as compared with means of 1.53 for nonpatients, 1.05 for schizophrenics, and 0.83 for the character disorder group. Exner (1978) has noted that inpatient depressives, retested at discharge when the clinical manifestations of depression have abated, usually give fewer than half the number of *C'* responses that were present in the pretreatment records, even though the retest records tend to be significantly longer. An elevation in *C'* responses has been found to be one of five variables useful in the identification of some serious depressive disturbances (Exner, 1983, 1991).

Assuming that the *C'* answer does relate to a form of affective constraint, it is important for the interpreter to evaluate the use of form in those responses. When form is dominant, as in the *FC'* response, the operations involved in the constraint are probably more cognitively controlled than when the reverse is true. The process of constraint should not be confused with anxiety, although anxiety may sometimes accompany the experience. Rather, it is like a psychological "biting of one's tongue," whereby the emotion is internalized and consequently creates some irritation. It is the irritation that is represented by the *C'* variable, which, experientially, can probably take any of several forms, ranging from a vague uneasiness or discomfort to a much more marked experience of tension.

THE VISTA VARIABLE

Vista responses were first defined by Rorschach (1923) in a passing reference to answers containing dimensional features. Klopfer and Kelley (1942) and Beck (1944) both created separate codings to account for the dimensional answers based on the shading features of the blots. Both suggested that they are related to a form of introspection. Klopfer posited that they represent efforts at taking distance to handle anxiety, whereas Beck perceived them as related to a more morose feeling tone created by depression and/or feelings of inferiority. Vista responses are the least frequently given type of shading response, occurring in only 20% of the adult nonpatient normative sample records ($M = 0.26$), 18% of the Character Disorder protocols ($M = 0.24$), and 35% of the Schizophrenic records ($M = 0.60$). It is extremely rare among young nonpatient children, appearing in only 2 of 905 records of youngsters between the ages of 5 and 11 in the normative sample. The frequency of V responses is greater among adolescents. It increases significantly at the 12-year level and approaches the mean and proportional frequency for nonpatient adults in each of the adolescent years. Vista responses appear more frequently in the records of seriously depressed subjects. The reference sample of depressed inpatients shows that 56% contain at least one V answer ($M = 1.09$). Klopfer (1946) and Light and Amick (1956) found very low frequencies of vista responses among the elderly.

Meltzer (1944) has shown that vista answers occur with a significantly greater frequency among stutterers than nonstutterers. Bradway et al. (1946) reported that vista responses are related to "treatability" in delinquent adolescent females. Buhler and LeFever (1947) found that alcoholics give significantly more vista answers than do psychopathic personalities. They interpret this to indicate that alcoholics are more self-critical. Rabinovitch (1954) has shown that vista answers are significantly correlated with the greater GSR deflections and perceptual thresholds and interprets this as reflecting an attempt to avoid unpleasant stimuli. Fiske and Baughman (1953) have noted that the incidence of vista answers tends to increase among outpatients with the length of the record.

Exner (1974) found that vista answers occur more frequently among subjects who make suicidal gestures within 60 days after being tested. Exner and Wylie (1977) found an elevation in vista responses is significantly correlated with effected suicides that occur within 60 days after being tested and included that finding as one variable in the Suicide Constellation. Exner, Martin, and Mason (1984) have cross-validated the efficacy of the Suicide Constellation using a sample of 101 subjects who effected their own death within 60 days of being tested. They found that the vista variable remains as a highly important variable in the Constellation. Exner (1974, 1978, 1991) has reported that vista answers tend to increase in records of patients who have been in uncovering forms of psychotherapy for at least 6 months as contrasted with pretreatment records. Exner (1974) has also found that patients in group psychotherapy who have vista answers in their pretreatment records tend to give more self-focusing statements during the group sessions.

The data concerning vista answers appear to support the Klopfer-Beck positions that it is related to a "taking distance," introspective process; however, it is doubtful that the relation is direct. Instead, it seems to be related to a negative emotional experience that is generated by the self-focusing behavior. Obviously, the very low frequency with which the vista answer appears makes its presence in any record interpretively important. Unlike the texture answer that is expected to appear in a record, the vista response *is not*. Its absence is generally a more favorable sign than its presence. When V is present, it signals the presence of discomfort, and possibly even pain, that is being produced by a kind of ruminative self-inspection which is focusing on *perceived* negative features of the self. Although the presence of a single FV response in an average-length record might be considered positively in the context of prognosis for early treatment motivation, the self-defacing aspects of the process that give rise to the negative feelings can be a marked obstacle to early treatment gains. Probably the only time that the presence of vista answers can be viewed positively is when the subject has been in some form of uncovering or developmental intervention for several months. In that circumstance, the intervention process is designed to promote self-inspection, much of which will focus on negative features and thus can be expected to generate the experiences of pain and/or irritation. However, vista answers are not expected to appear in the records of patients who are nearing termination. Although the process of self-inspection will undoubtedly continue after treatment, irritation and/or pain should not be a routine product of the process. This is usually indicated by the presence of another Rorschach variable (*FD*) that is also related to taking distance and self-inspecting, but which is apparently *not* related to affective experience.

THE *D* SCORE

Hopefully, the preceding discussion concerning the *EA* and the Adjusted *es* makes it clear how the Adjusted *D* Score is derived and how the components of it relate to issues of control and stress tolerance. But, as implied throughout the preceding section, there are instances in which the customary capacities for control are altered temporarily by an unusual increase in peripheral mental activity and/or subjectively felt distress. These increases in mental and/or affective activity are created by situationally related stress circumstances.

Daily living almost always involves some situational stress events with which people contend by drawing more extensively on their available resources than might usually be the case. By doing so, they deal with unexpected events such as transportation hassles, unusual occupational demands, or unexpected social requirements without becoming psychologically disorganized. Nonetheless, they do experience the irritation of the experience and if a Rorschach were administered before the stress experience ended, it is likely that some elevation in either *m* or *Y* would be noted. Even taking the Rorschach usually is moderately stressful for most subjects. That is probably the reason that occasional *m* and/or *Y* answers appear in most records. When stress experiences become substantial and remain unresolved or are perceived as very difficult or even impossible to resolve, the resulting sense of helplessness is typically reflected in Rorschach data by increases in *m* and/or *Y* responses that go well beyond the expected levels.

The basic indicator of an increase in stimulus demands being generated by unresolved situationally related stress is noted when the *D* Score is lower than the Adjusted *D* Score. As noted earlier, the two scores are always expected to have the same value; and when that is the case, the issues of control and tolerance for stress are addressed by focusing only on the Adjusted *D* Score. But when the *D* Score is less than the Adjusted *D* Score, two descriptions are required. The first focuses on the *D* Score and provides information regarding the *current* capacity for control and tolerance for stress. The second is the description of the more usual or customary capacity for control, derived from the datum of the Adjusted *D* Score.

Situational stress conditions often draw heavily on one's resources and, at times, the increase in demands will create an overload condition that can produce far less effective thinking and/or behavior than is usually the case. Even if an overload state is not created by the situational stress, its impact may often produce a less impressive or productive set of behaviors. Thus, if the *D* score has a minus value, the potential for impulsiveness in thinking, affect, and/or behavior is considerable. People with *D* scores of -1 are vulnerable to disorganization in complex or highly ambiguous situations, and this vulnerability increases as *EA* falls below the average range. If the *D* score is less than -1, the potential for disorganization is increased substantially, regardless of the value of *EA*. If this finding is positive, the presence of Pure *C* responses, *M* $-$ answers, or Formless *M* responses is also very important. The presence of one or more Pure *C* answers in this configuration suggests that some of the impulsiveness will manifest in affective displays while the presence of *M* $-$ or Formless *M* responses raises a question about whether ideational controls may be impaired because of the overload state.

Conversely, if the *D* Score value is zero or greater, there is no evidence supporting the notion that impulsiveness is likely. Nonetheless, the fact that *D* is less than the Adjusted *D* does indicate that the stress tolerance of the subject is lower than usual, and some interference may occur in the customary patterns of thinking and/or affect. The following data sets illustrate how, when a difference occurs between the *D* and Adjusted *D* Scores, the data for each are interpreted with regard to other variables in the controls cluster.

Case 1		*Case 2*	*Case 3*
$EB = 4{:}2.0$ $EA = 6.0$		$EB = 4{:}5.0$ $EA = 9.0$	$EB = 7{:}4.5$ $EA = 11.5$
$eb = 6{:}6$ $es = 12$ $D = -2$		$eb = 7{:}6$ $es = 13$ $D = -1$	$eb = 4{:}8$ $es = 12$ $D = 0$
$m = 2$ $Y = 3$ $Adj\ es = 9$		$m = 2$ $Y = 2$ $Adj\ es = 11$	$m = 1$ $Y = 5$ $Adj\ es = 8$
$AdjD = -1$		$AdjD = 0$	$AdjD = +1$

In Case 1, the *D* Score is -2, suggesting considerable overload and a marked proclivity for impulsiveness. As with Adjusted *D* Scores in this range, the subject is probably quite disorganized and very easily distracted. Moreover, the fact that the Adjusted *D* Score remains in the minus range indicates that much of the potential for impulsiveness and/or disorganization is somewhat chronic, mainly because of the lower than average *EA*. This is a subject who has limited resources and some form of situational stress has exacerbated the potential for disorganization.

In Case 2, a much different situation exists. The *D* Score is -1, indicating that, at the moment, the subject is in overload and prone to some form of impulsiveness. However, the Adjusted *D* Score is 0, and the *EA* is in the average range. Thus, while situational stresses have made the subject more vulnerable to some form of disorganization, it appears likely that under most circumstances, the subject's capacity for control and tolerance for stress essentially are no different from that of most people.

Case 3 is different from either of the other two. The *EA* indicates that this is a subject with abundant resources, but at the moment, the presence of some situationally related stress circumstance has reduced the subject's capacity for control and stress tolerance. Although the subject continues to maintain levels of control capability and tolerance for stress similar to that of most people, they are substantially less than is usually the case.

RESEARCH RELATED TO HYPOTHESES DEVELOPED FROM THE *D* SCORE

The critical variables related to a *D* Score that may be lower than the Adjusted *D* Score are *m* and *Y* (*FY, YF, Y*). They appear to provide the best evidence concerning the psychological experience of situational stress that is available in the Rorschach. From a temporal perspective, they are very unstable. In every retest study, whether short term or long term for both adults and children, the resulting retest correlations for either variable rarely exceed .50, and in most instances fall between 0 and .30 (Exner, 1978, 1983; Exner, Armbruster, & Viglione, 1978; Exner, Thomas, & Mason, 1985; Exner & Weiner, 1982). In spite of the lack of temporal stability, there are considerable data indicating that both are interpretively significant when the frequencies for either are elevated. The means for both range from considerably less than 1.0 for *Y,* to slightly more than 1.0 for *m* for various adult groups, both patient and nonpatient, and they are consistently less than 0.5 for nonpatient children. It is because the means for nonpatient adults hover at 1.0 or less for both variables that the Adjusted *es* includes one *m* and/or one *Y* if either has occurred in the protocol.

THE *m* VARIABLE

Research concerning *m* was rather sparse prior to the 1970s. It was included as a coding variable in the Klopfer, Hertz, and Piotrowski Systems, and generally posited to represent the thoughts or drives that are not well integrated into the cognitive framework. Klopfer, Hertz, and Piotrowski have suggested that *m* is probably associated with the experience of frustration, especially regarding interpersonal relations. McArthur and King (1954) found that a combination of *m* plus a preponderance of chromatic color responses differentiated unsuccessful college students, whereas Majumber and Roy (1962) reported a significant elevation in *m* among juvenile delinquents. Neel (1960), using models of motoric and ideational inhibition, found that either condition causes an elevation in *m* as compared with control subjects. She interpreted her findings as evidence for tension and/or conflict created by the inability to integrate needs with behavior. Piotrowski and Schreiber (1952) found that *m* responses tend to disappear in the posttreatment records of patients who are judged as responding successfully to treatment.

Shalit (1965) was the first to report definitive findings concerning the relation of *m* to situational stress. He was able to collect retest Rorschachs from 20 Israeli seamen under the natural stress conditions of being on a relatively small ship during a severe storm condition. All had been tested previously, about 1 year earlier, when they entered the Israeli Navy. Shalit found that the retest frequencies for *M* and *FM* remained essentially the same, but the frequencies for *m* increased significantly. He interpreted this finding as related to the stressful condition created by the storm, postulating that the elevations in *m* reflect a sense of disruption and fear of disintegration of controls. The Shalit finding posed an obvious challenge for research concerning *m;* that is, if *m* does correlate with the sense of disruption of controls under stress, the issue of helplessness or lack of control should be an important independent variable in any study designed to test the validity of his findings.

Exner and Walker (1973) retested 20 inpatient depressives 1 day before their first ECT. Fourteen of the 20 had at least one *m* in their first protocol, which had been collected within the period of 5 to 7 days after admission ($M = 1.26$, $SD = 0.83$). The retest protocols included 16 that contained *m,* with a significant increase in the mean ($M = 2.57$, $SD = 1.09$, $p < .05$). A second retest of those subjects was administered when they were discharged, and only 6 of the 20 contained *m* responses ($M = 0.39$, $SD = 0.88$), even though the records were generally longer than either of the first two tests.

Armbruster, Miller, and Exner (1974) tested 20 Army paratroop trainees on one of their first 3 days of training and retested them the evening before their first parachute jump. Three of the 20 subjects had *m* responses in their first test ($M = 0.16$, $SD = 0.48$), whereas 12 produced at least one *m* in the retest ($M = 1.68$, $SD = 0.73$). In another natural stress study, 25 elective surgery patients were tested several weeks before surgery and then retested the day before or morning of the surgery (Exner, Armbruster, Walker, & Cooper, 1975). The baseline records, collected 25 to 63 days prior to surgery, included 10 with a total of 16 *m* answers. Nineteen of the retest records contained *m* responses, for a total of 41 ($p < .02$). In addition, 13 of the baseline records contained at least one *Y* variable, for a total of 56 ($p < .01$). A second test was administered during an interval of 60 to 70 days after discharge. Fourteen *m* responses appeared in 8 of the 25 records, and only 16 *Y* determinants occurred among 10 of the protocols.

Exner (1978) found that patients in long-term psychotherapy average nearly two *m* and about one *Y* at the beginning of treatment. After approximately 9 months, those averages are nearly double, with the increases appearing mainly in the protocols of patients judged by their therapists to be encountering significant struggles and experiencing considerable distress. Campo (1977) studied 72 patients, each of whom had at least three *m* answers in their Rorschachs and concluded that elevations in *m* do not coincide with the severity of disturbance, but do correlate with severe distress experiences.

THE *Y* VARIABLE

The pre-1970s literature concerning the *Y* variable is more extensive than for *m*, but also is more contradictory. Some of the contradiction was created by the fact that each of the systematizers used different criteria and symbols for the coding of diffuse shading. Binder (1932) was the first to offer a detailed approach to the coding of achromatic and shading answers. Following his lead, each of the systematizers included a variety of scores to denote different types of achromatic and shading responses but failed to agree on the criteria for most of them, including diffuse shading, although each considered it to be an important determinant in the test. Although most of the systematizers postulated that diffuse shading answers have some relation to anxiety, they have differed concerning its form and impact. Beck (1945) suggested that diffuse shading responses reveal a painful "absence of action." Later, Beck and Molish (1967) extended this explanation, postulating that diffuse shading signals a sense of paralysis. They speculated that when the answer is form dominated, as in *FY*, the experience might be regarded more favorably, because it serves as a stimulus to action. Conversely, they argued that the *YF* and *Y* type of responses are indicative of an inability to respond. Rapaport et al. (1946) hypothesized that diffuse shading responses represent a form of anxiety of a magnitude that often supersedes other need states in forcing and/or directing behavior. Klopfer et al. (1954) postulated that diffuse shading answers represent a form of free-floating anxiety. Both positions—that is, Beck's diffuse shading-passivity hypothesis and the Rapaport diffuse shading-anxiety hypothesis—have been studied in many investigations and some support is available for each.

Buhler and LeFever (1947) were among the earliest to test the shading-anxiety postulate in their study of alcoholics. They report a significantly greater use of diffuse shading among alcoholics. Eichler (1951) and Cox and Sarason (1954) both note significant increases in the use of diffuse shading under an experimentally induced stress situation.

Similarly, Levitt and Grosz (1960) obtained significantly more *Y* responses after anxiety had been induced hypnotically. Lebo et al. (1960) treated 12 of 24 high-anxiety subjects with CO_2 and found a significant decrease in *Y* answers as compared with the untreated group. Although these studies tend to support the shading-anxiety hypothesis, numerous works contradict the hypothesis. Several studies have found no relationship between scores on the Taylor Manifest Anxiety Scale and diffuse shading answers (Goodstein, 1954; Holtzman et al., 1954; Goodstein & Goldberger, 1955; Levitt, 1957; and Waller, 1960). Schwartz and Kates (1957) used an experimentally induced stress model and found that stressed subjects gave significantly fewer *Y* variant answers than did controls. Berger (1953), Fisher (1958), and Schon and Bard (1958) each used designs in which the Rorschach was administered under "real life" stress situations and found no evidence that the *Y* variants were associated with the stressful situation. Neuringer has suggested that anxiety manifestations are probably better judged by a constellation of variables rather than by one variable such as the *Y*-type answers. A similar position is implied by Goldfried, Stricker, and Weiner (1971) in their review or Elizur's Rorschach scoring for anxiety which focuses mainly on verbalizations in the test. The data concerning shading and anxiety are obviously equivocal, and at best, may be interpreted to indicate that *Y* answers represent *some types of anxiety at times,* but cannot be routinely taken as a direct index of anxiety.

Studies concerning the diffuse shading-passivity hypothesis are less numerous than those dealing with the anxiety issue, but the findings are clearly more consistent in favoring the Beck postulate. Klebanoff (1946) found that flyers experiencing "operational fatigue" give significantly greater numbers of *Y* variants. He also noted a tendency of these subjects toward withdrawal and passivity. Elstein (1965) found the *Y* variants significantly related to passivity toward the environment. He noted that "high *Y*" subjects are more inhibited and resigned to their situation and suggests that they attempt to seal themselves off from the world. Salmon et al. (1972) report the use of a factorial model to study various determinants. They grouped all responses to gray-black features as "shading," which was probably an error. Nonetheless, they did find a striking correlation between "shading" and emotion and intellectual control, the composite of which could equal withdrawal behaviors.

Unfortunately, most of these studies failed to differentiate types of anxiety, levels of stress tolerance, or degrees of helplessness. In other words, the issue of control, or the potential for loss of control, may confound the correct interpretation of some findings. For instance, Viglione and Exner (1983) used an unsolvable anagram design to produce frustration among a randomly selected half of a group of volunteer college students. They were able to demonstrate a significant elevation in state anxiety among the subjects in his experimental group, but the Rorschachs of those subjects did not differ significantly from those of his nonfrustrated control subjects, and neither group showed elevations for *m* or *Y*, or the sum of the achromatic and shading variables. McCowen, Fink, Galina, and Johnson (1992), using a design similar to that of Viglione and Exner, have reported increases in *m* under stress conditions, whether the stress is perceived as controllable or not, and increases in *Y* when the stress is perceived as uncontrollable. Unfortunately, their findings are difficult to evaluate because no frequency data are offered in their paper and their approach to analyzing their findings consisted of parametric statistics when, in fact, both dependent variables are nonparametric.

In studies such as these, although well designed and with effective independent variables, subjects remain largely in control even though they may experience some frustration. Under more natural stress conditions, that option is not available. For instance,

Ridgeway and Exner (1980) administered the Rorschach and the McClelland Need Achievement Scale to first-year medical students shortly after they began their training. Both tests were readministered either 2 or 3 days before the subjects took their first major examination in anatomy. Significant elevations were found for both *m* and *Y* in the retest records. In another study, Exner, Thomas, Cohen, Ridgeway, and Cooper (1981) tested 54 medical inpatients 1 or 2 days prior to discharge. One group was comprised of 27 males who had been hospitalized 13 to 17 days earlier because of a myocardial infarction. Although recovered from the incident, these men would remain at some risk for at least a 90-day postdischarge interval. The Control group consisted of 27 males recovering from orthopedic surgery. Their average length of hospitalization was 19 days. Although most remained in casts, no significant risk factor existed concerning their recovery or future health. Both groups were retested during an interval of 93 to 118 days after discharge. Frequency data concerning the *m* and *Y* variables in both tests are presented for each group in Table 64. The cardiac group, continuing at risk at the time of the first test, gave more than twice as many *m* ($M = 2.15$, $SD = 1.01$) and *Y* ($M = 2.56$, $SD = 0.84$) responses than did the orthopedic group, yet 8 to 10 weeks later when the risk factor had declined substantially, the two groups did not differ significantly and both had frequencies for *m* and *Y* that were similar to the nonpatient normative data.

The means and frequencies for both *m* and *Y* are generally much higher among situational crisis patients than for any other psychiatric groups. For example, the mean *m* for 62 first-admission patients diagnosed as Acute Post-traumatic Stress Disorder is 2.74 ($SD = 1.21$) and the mean *Y* for this group is 2.87 ($SD = 1.29$). Retest data, collected 14 to 19 days after the first test, for 41 of those subjects, all judged to have improved sufficiently to be discharged, show a very significant reduction in the mean values for both variables ($m = 1.14$, $SD = 1.02$; $Y = 1.29$, $SD = 0.93$).

The issue of detecting manifestations of situationally related stress in Rorschach data is, by no means, completely resolved. It does seem obvious that elevations in either *m* or *Y* do convey some sense of stress-related helplessness and, for the moment, are probably the best indices of this problem. However, elevations in *T* sometimes reflect the emotional impact of recent loss and probably should be factored into interpretive hypotheses concerning current versus chronic capacities for control when the recent loss is confirmed by the history of the subject. In other words, in cases in which the *D* Score is less than the Adjusted *D* Score, the contribution to the difference that may be created by elevations in *T* should be considered very carefully. The data for the L.S. protocol illustrate this quite well. As noted in Chapter 14, the interpretation of the L.S. record should

Table 64. Frequency Data for *m* and *Y* for Two Tests of Two Groups of Male Medical Patients

Variable	Cardiac Group N = 27		Orthopedic Group N = 27		*p*
	Test 1	Test 2	Test 1	Test 2	
m (Total)	58[a]	22	26	21	.01
No. of Protocols	24	19	20	17	ns
Y (Total)	69[a]	25	29	21	.01
No. of Protocols	25	20	19	18	ns

[a]Significantly more than all other groups.

begin with the cluster concerning controls and the array of data concerning situationally related stress.

The data in each cluster should be approached systematically, moving in a logical progression from point to point, with the objective of formulating postulates when the accumulation of findings warrants, or ruling out the presence of some characteristics when that is appropriate. The Structural Summary page of the *Structural Summary Blank* has been organized to facilitate the procedure by placing together data for variables that are related to a single feature, such as affect, ideation, processing, self-perception, and so on. However, the composite shown in each data group does not necessarily represent all of the structural data relevant to the feature about which the cluster focuses. As noted earlier, several structural variables are related to more than one characteristic of psychological organization or functioning. For instance, the *eb* and all of the variables that contribute to its tabulation are shown in the *Core* section as it does relate to issues of control and stress tolerance. But, the *eb,* and some of the variables related to it, are also reviewed again during the study of data concerning affect and ideation. Moreover, although the structural data in a section are *always* the first to be reviewed, the interpreter often will be diverted from the structure to the sequence of scores or to the actual responses in the protocol.

Although the data of the Rorschach can be addressed blindly, with no information other than the age and sex of the subject, that tactic should usually be reserved for teaching purposes and with the knowledge that some data of the record may not be interpreted fully or correctly unless some additional history data are available. This added material should include information concerning the reason for the testing, presenting complaints, marital status, educational and occupational achievement, and possibly some information concerning family background. Any or all can be quite relevant when attempting to cast a finding in the proper perspective. This is especially true when evaluating the data from the cluster concerning controls or the array of findings regarding situationally provoked stress. Consequently, it is important to know something about the L.S. history before addressing the data.

THE L.S. HISTORY

L.S., a 26-year-old male, is married, has one child (male, one year old), and is a high school teacher. He is a self-referral to a community counseling center, complaining that he feels very tense and anxious, and suffers from insomnia. He notes that during the past six months he has been having some difficulties preparing his daily lesson plans and is worried by the fact that he will be among a group of teachers to be evaluated during the next two months concerning contract renewal. He attributes the onset of his problem to a variety of factors. He had intended to begin part-time graduate study about a year ago, but deferred the decision to do so because his wife had endured a difficult pregnancy and he felt obligated to assist with their newborn son. The child had some respiratory problems during his first year and was rehospitalized once at age four months for a three-week period. Apparently, those problems have been corrected, but the subject continues to express concern for the child's health. He also reports that his relationship with his wife has become more distant since the birth of the child, suggesting that because each has been preoccupied with the infant, they have had little time for each other. He admits that they have quarreled about the possibility of having more children—she would prefer to, he would not. Originally they had agreed on two children, and on the assumption that she would work as a substitute teacher during their early developmental years. He now feels that was an unrealistic assumption.

He is the oldest of three male siblings, all of whom are college graduates. His brother, age 24, is a chemist; and his brother, age 21, has recently entered law school. Both parents are living. The father, age 59, is a skilled blue-collar worker, and the mother, age 57, a housewife. Both are high school graduates and take considerable pride in the fact that all three sons are college graduates. His wife, age 25, is also a college graduate, having majored in elementary education and taught third grade for three years before becoming pregnant. During the second trimester of her pregnancy, she began having fluid problems and resigned her position on her doctor's advice.

He reports that he enjoys playing tennis but has not found much time to do so since the birth of his son, and because he continually is behind in his class preparation. He says that he enjoys teaching some of his classes but admits that he sometimes has discipline problems with his students. He feels that he would probably do better in a junior college position but recognizes that is impossible to obtain unless he completes an advanced degree.

THE CONTROLS CLUSTER

The controls cluster comprises seven basic variables plus frequencies for the six scores that contribute to the *eb* and *es*. Four of the seven basic variables were originally labeled as The Four Square (Exner, 1978), and at that time constituted the starting point for all interpretation. They are the *EB* (Erlebnistypus), *EA* (Experience Actual), *eb* (Experience Base), and *es* (Experienced Stimulation). Although each provides useful interpretive information, and collectively they present a relatively broad picture about several important psychological features, the composite fell short of providing a true representation concerning capacity for control. The discovery of the other three variables, the two *D* Scores and the *CDI,* has added considerably more information about controls and stress tolerance. They add critical data points from which issues of control and stress tolerance can be addressed more extensively.

When the controls cluster is reviewed at the beginning of interpretation, because the first positive Key variable is *D < AdjD, CDI >* 3, or *AdjD* is minus, there is a clear suggestion that some control problems appear to exist and the search through the variables in the cluster will address issues such as the source of the problem, the chronicity of the problem, and the extent to which the problem may be resulting from some form of disorganization. When the review of the cluster does not occur first in the interpretion, the routine proceeds with no preconceptions, but the steps are the same. The data are reviewed to determine if there are any unusual features regarding control and/or stress tolerance.

In the L.S. case, the search decision is based on the initial finding that *D < AdjD,* leading to the proposition that some situationally related stress condition exists. Among the issues to be addressed is whether the current stress has created an overload condition, and whether the subject is more chronically vulnerable to overload. The data for the controls cluster are shown in Table 65.

The *D* Score is −1 and the Adjusted *D* Score is zero. Working first from the Adjusted *D* Score, a tentative postulate is that, ordinarily, L.S. usually is able to form and direct behaviors as much as other adults. In other words, his capacity for control and tolerance for stress is usually not very different than for most adults. However, the *D* Score is −1,

Table 65.   L.S. Data for Controls and Tolerance for Stress

$EB = 4{:}3.5$		$EA = 7.5$		$D\ \ = -1$
$eb = 8{:}4$		$es = 12$	$Adj\ es = 9$	$Adj\ D = \ \ 0$
$FM = 5$	$C' = 0$	$T = 2$		$CDI\ =\ \ 1$
$m = 3$	$V = 0$	$Y = 2$		

suggesting that some situational factors have reduced his capacity for control and, in fact, he is now in overload. This increases the likelihood that, in new or more complex situations, he will not function as adaptively or effectively as might be the case if the stress situation did not exist.

When challenging the apparent validity of the Adjusted *D* Score, there are no data that question the reliability of the *EA* as the values for both sides of the *EB* are substantial. Similarly, the value for the *CDI* is only one, thereby offering no significant input to the issue of control. Thus, the earlier tentative postulates derived from the *D* and Adjusted *D* Scores seem viable. Therefore, the next issues to be addressed concern the impact of the situational stress. The array of data concerning situationally related stress for the L.S. protocol are shown in Table 66.

The difference between the *D* Score and the Adjusted *D* Score provides an estimate of the magnitude of the stress. Usually, the resulting value will be *one*. If the value exceeds one, it can be assumed that the experience of the stress is quite severe and that the impact is creating a considerable interference in some of the customary patterns of thinking and/ or behavior. In the L.S. record, the difference is one; thus, interference created by the stress can be expected to be more modest than severe. If the *D* score has a minus value, the potential for impulsiveness in thinking, affect, and/or behavior is considerable. This is the case for the L.S. protocol. Should the *D* score have been less than -1 the potential for disorganization would be increased substantially, regardless of the value of *EA*.

As noted earlier, the values for *T, m,* and *Y* are often useful in determining if the impact of the overload has specificity. For instance, if the value for *T* is 2 or more, as is the case in the L.S. record, it is possible that some of the stress is related to an experience of emotional loss. This should be confirmed easily by the recent history. If the history does not reveal an obvious recent emotional loss, the possibility of a more chronic state of loneliness or neediness should be considered and investigated more thoroughly. Obviously, such a chronic state would have little to do with situational stress effects. There is no information concerning an obvious recent emotional loss in the L.S. history; however, it is implied that some tension does exist in the marriage regarding the possibility of having a second child. While this may account for the elevation in *T*, it does not seem directly relevant to the situational stress condition.

Table 66.   Situational Stress-Related Variables for Protocol L.S.

$D\ \ = -1$	$EA\ \ \ \ = 7.5$		Total Blends	$= 5$
$Adj\ D\ = +0$	$PureC\ = 0$		Blends created by m, Y, T	$= 3$
$Sum\ T = 2$			Blends created by m or Y	$= 3$
$Sum\ m = 3$	$MQ-\ \ = 0$			
$Sum\ Y = 2$	$MQnone = 0$		Col-Shad Blds created by $Y = 0$	

If the values for m and Y are not substantially different and the value for T is 0 or 1 (or if higher values for T can be attributed to a more chronic situation), it can be assumed that the impact of the stress is diffuse. On the other hand, if the value for m is more than three times that of Y, it is likely that the overload is having greater impact on thinking; whereas if the value of Y is more than three times that of m, it is likely that the greater impact occurs on emotion. In the L.S. protocol, there are 3 m's and 2 Y's; thus, it is most likely that the effect of the stress is diffuse.

The number of Blends that contain the variables m, and Y often provides information concerning possible increases in complexity as a result of the increased stimulus demands. If there are blends created *exclusively* by the presence of the m and/or Y variables, such as *FC.FY, m.CF, m.YF,* and so on, a subtraction of the number of those blends from the total number of blends provides an estimate of the nonstress level of complexity. Usually, such blends occur no more than two or three times in most records. If the number of blends that include these variables is greater than two, the excess provides a crude, but sometimes useful index of added psychological complexity being created by the stress condition. The L.S. protocol contains a total of five blends, three of which are created by the presence of m or Y. Therefore, it is reasonable to assume that considerably more psychological complexity has been created by the stress condition.

If the subtraction of blends created by the presence of m or Y reduces the total from an above-average range to an average range or below, it is probable that the current stress is creating substantially more complexity than is common and, as such, contributes to a vulnerability for disorganization. This is the case in the L.S. record and is especially important because the D Score is in the minus range. It suggests that a significant increase in complexity has occurred which, in turn, has increased the potential for impulsive like behaviors.

The list of blends also should be reviewed for Color-Shading Blends (any that include both chromatic color and shading or achromatic color), noting any created exclusively by the combination of chromatic color plus Y, such as *FC.FY*. These blends offer some indication of the presence of situationally related affective confusion. Even if one Color-Shading blend exists based exclusively on the combination of chromatic color plus Y, it can be assumed that the stress condition has created and/or increased emotional confusion. There are no such blends in the L.S. protocol.

A SUMMARY REGARDING CONTROLS AND STRESS TOLERANCE FOR L.S.

The datum for the Adjusted D Score indicates that, ordinarily, the subject usually is able to form and direct behaviors as much as other adults. In other words, his capacity for control and tolerance for stress is usually not very different than for most adults. However, the D Score is -1, suggesting that some situational factors have reduced his capacity for control and, in fact, he is now in overload. This increases the likelihood that, in new or more complex situations, he will not function as adaptively or effectively as might be the case if the stress situation did not exist. There is also some increased likelihood that impulsiveness, in thinking, affect, and/or behavior will occur. The cause of the overload is not completely clear although the history suggests that it is occupationally related. Some tension existing in the marriage may also be contributing to the current stress situation. In either event, the effect of the stress appears to be more diffuse than specific and it does seem clear that considerably more psychological complexity than is customary has been created by the stress condition.

The psychological picture of L.S. will broaden as the other clusters of data are addressed but, before proceeding to the other data clusters for this record, it is important to review the remaining Key variables as sources of information concerning their importance in revealing the presence of basic personality response or coping styles.

REFERENCES

Allerhand, M. E. (1954) Chiaroscuro determinants of the Rorschach Test as an indicator of manifest anxiety. *Journal of Projective Techniques,* **18,** 407–413.

Altus, W. D. (1958) Group Rorschach and Q-L discrepancies on the ACE. *Psychological Reports,* **4,** 469.

Armbruster, G. L., Miller, A. S., and Exner, J. E. (1974) Rorschach responses of parachute trainees at the beginning of training and shortly before their first jump. Workshops Study No. 201 (unpublished). Rorschach Workshops.

Bash, K. W. (1955) Einstellungstypus and Erlebnistypus: C. G. Jung and Herman Rorschach. *Journal of Projective Techniques,* **19,** 236–242.

Beck, S. J. (1944) *Rorschach's Test. I: Basic Processes.* New York: Grune & Stratton.

Beck, S. J. (1945) *Rorschach's Test. II: A Variety of Personality Pictures.* New York: Grune & Stratton.

Beck, S.J. (1960) *The Rorschach Experiment: Ventures in Blind Diagnosis.* New York: Grune & Stratton.

Beck, S. J. (1972) Personal Communication.

Beck, S. J., and Molish, H. B. (1967) *Rorschach's Test. II: A Variety of Personality Pictures,* (2nd Ed.). New York: Grune & Stratton.

Berger, D. (1953) The Rorschach as a measure of real life stress. *Journal of Consulting Psychology,* **17,** 355–358.

Berryman, E. (1961) Poet's responses to the Rorschach. *Journal of General Psychology,* **64,** 349–358.

Binder, H. (1932) *Die Helldunkeldeutungen im psychodiagnostischem experiment von Rorschach.* Zurich: Urell Fussli.

Bradway, K., Lion, E., and Corrigan, H. (1946) The use of the Rorschach in a psychiatric study of promiscuous girls. *Rorschach Research Exchange,* **9,** 105–110.

Breecher, S. (1956) The Rorschach reaction patterns of maternally overprotected and rejected schizophrenics. *Journal of Nervous and Mental Disorders,* **123,** 41–52.

Brown, M., Bresnoban, T. J., Chakie, F. R., Peters, B., Poser, E. G., and Tougas, R. V. (1950) Personality factors in duodenal ulcer: A Rorschach study. *Psychosomatic Medicine,* **12,** 1–5.

Buhler, C., and LeFever, D. (1977) A Rorschach study on the psychological characteristics of alcoholics. *Quarterly Journal of Studies on Alcoholism,* **8,** 197–260.

Campo, V. (1977) On the meaning of the inaminate movement response. Ninth International Rorschach Congress, Fribourg, Switzerland.

Coan, R. (1956) A factor analysis of Rorschach determinants. *Journal of Projective Techniques,* **20,** 280–287.

Cox, F. N., and Sarason, S. B. (1954) Test anxiety and Rorschach performance. *Journal of Abnormal and Social Psychology,* **49,** 371–377.

Eichler, R. M. (1951) Experimental stress and alleged Rorschach indices of anxiety. *Journal of Abnormal and Social Psychology,* **46,** 344–356.

Elstein, A. S. (1956) Behavioral correlates of the Rorschach shading determinant. *Journal of Consulting Psychology,* **29,** 231–236.

Erginel, A. (1972) On the test-retest reliability of the Rorschach. *Journal of Personality Assessment,* **36,** 203–212.

Exner, J. E. (1969) Rorschach responses as an index of narcissism. *Journal of Projective Techniques and Personality Assessment,* **33,** 324–330.

Exner, J. E. (1973) The Self Focus Sentence Completion: A study of egocentricity. *Journal of Personality Assessment,* **37,** 437–455.

Exner, J. E. (1974) *The Rorschach: A Comprehensive System. Volume 1.* New York: Wiley.

Exner, J. E. (1978) *The Rorschach: A Comprehensive System. Volume 2. Current research and advanced interpretation.* New York: Wiley.

Exner, J. E. (1979) The effects of voluntary restraint on Rorschach retests. Workshops Study No. 258 (unpublished), Rorschach Workshops.

Exner, J. E. (1983) Rorschach assessment. In I. B. Weiner (Ed.) *Clinical Methods in Psychology,* (2nd Ed.). New York: Wiley.

Exner, J. E. (1986) *The Rorschach: A Comprehensive System. Volume 1: Basic foundations,* (2nd Ed.). New York: Wiley.

Exner, J. E. (1987) The search for projection. *Alumni Newsletter.* Asheville, N.C.: Rorschach Workshops.

Exner, J. E. (1988) COP. *Alumni Newsletter.* Asheville, N.C.: Rorschach Workshops.

Exner, J. E. (1988) Problems with brief Rorschach protocols. *Journal of Personality Assessment,* **52,** 640–647.

Exner, J. E. (1990) *EB* Pervasive (EBPer). *Alumni Newsletter.* Asheville, N.C.: Rorschach Workshops.

Exner, J. E. (1991) *The Rorschach: A Comprehensive System. Volume 2: Interpretation,* (2nd Ed.). New York: Wiley.

Exner, J. E., Armbruster, G. L., and Viglione, D. (1978) The temporal stability of some Rorschach features. *Journal of Personality Assessment,* **42,** 474–482.

Exner, J. E., Armbruster, G. L., Walker, E. J., and Cooper, W. H. (1975) Anticipation of elective surgery as manifest in Rorschach records. Workshops Study No. 213 (unpublished), Rorschach Workshops.

Exner, J. E., and Bryant, E. L. (1974) Rorschach responses of subjects recently divorced or separated. Workshops Study No. 206 (unpublished), Rorschach Workshops.

Exner, J. E., Bryant, E. L., and Miller, A. S. (1975) Rorschach responses of some juvenile offenders. Workshops Study No. 214 (unpublished). Rorschach Workshops.

Exner, J. E., and Chu, A. Y. (1981) Reports of transitional objects among nonpatient adults as related to the presence or absence of T in the Rorschach. Workshops Study No. 277 (unpublished), Rorschach Workshops.

Exner, J. E., Cooper, W. H., and Walker, E. J. (1975) Retest of overweight males on a strict dietary regimen. Workshops Study No. 210 (unpublished), Rorschach Workshops.

Exner, J. E., and Kazaoka, K. (1978) Dependency gestures of 16 assertiveness trainees as related to Rorschach movement responses. Workshops Study No. 261 (unpublished), Rorschach Workshops.

Exner, J. E., and Leura, A. V. (1975) Rorschach responses of recently foster placed children. Workshops Study No. 196 (unpublished), Rorschach Workshops.

Exner, J. E., and Leura, A. V. (1977) Rorschach performances of volunteer and nonvolunteer adolescents. Workshops Study No. 238 (unpublished), Rorschach Workshops.

Exner, J. E., Levantrosser, C., and Mason, B. (1980) Reports of transitional objects among first admission depressives as related to the presence or absence of T in the Rorschach. Workshops Study No. 266 (unpublished), Rorschach Workshops.

Exner, J. E., Martin, L. S., and Mason, B. (1984) A review of the Suicide Constellation. 11th International Rorschach Congress, Barcelona.

Exner, J. E., Martin, L. S., and Thomas, E. A. (1983) Preference for waiting room seating among subjects with elevations or absence of *T* in the Rorschach. Workshops Study No. 282 (unpublished), Rorschach Workshops.

Exner, J. E., Murillo, L. G., and Cannavo, F. (1973) Disagreement between ex-patient and relative behavioral reports as related to relapse in non-schizophrenic patients. Eastern Psychological Association, Washington, D.C.

Exner, J. E., and Sanglade, A. A. (1992). Rorschach changes following brief and short term therapy. *Journal of Personality Assessment, 59,* 59–71.

Exner, J. E., Thomas, E. A., Cohen, J. B., Ridgeway, E. M., and Cooper, W. H. (1981) Stress indices in the Rorschachs of patients recovering from myocardial infarctions. Workshops Study No. 286 (unpublished), Rorschach Workshops.

Exner, J. E., Thomas, E. A., and Mason, B. (1985) Children's Rorschach's: Description and prediction. *Journal of Personality Assessment, 49,* 13–20.

Exner, J. E., Viglione, D. J., and Gillespie, R. (1984) Relationships between Rorschach variables as relevant to the interpretation of structural data. *Journal of Personality Assessment, 48,* 65–70.

Exner, J. E., and Walker, E. J. (1973) Rorschach responses of depressed patients prior to ECT. Workshops Study No. 197 (unpublished), Rorschach Workshops.

Exner, J. E., and Weiner, I. B. (1982) *The Rorschach: A Comprehensive System. Volume 3. Assessment of children and adolescents.* New York: Wiley.

Exner, J. E., Weiss, L. J., Coleman, M., and Rose, R. B. (1979) Rorschach variables for a group of occupationally successful dancers. Workshops Study No. 250 (unpublished), Rorschach Workshops.

Exner, J. E., and Wylie, J. (1977) Some Rorschach data concerning suicide. *Journal of Personality Assessment, 41,* 339–348.

Exner, J. E., Wylie, J. R., Leura, A. V., and Parrill, T. (1977) Some psychological characteristics of prostitutes. *Journal of Personality Assessment, 41,* 474–485.

Exner, J. E., Zalis, T., and Schumacher, J. (1976) Rorschach protocols of chronic amphetamine users. Workshops Study No. 233 (unpublished), Rorschach Workshops.

Fisher, R. L. (1958) The effects of a disturbing situation upon the stability of various projective tests. *Psychological Monographs, 72,* 1–23.

Fiske, D. W., and Baughman, E. E. (1953) The relationship between Rorschach scoring categories and the total number of responses. *Journal of Abnormal and Social Psychology, 48,* 25–30.

French, T. M. (1947) Some psychoanalytic applications of the psychological field concept. In S. S. Tomkins (Ed.), *Contemporary Psychopathology* (pp. 223–234). Cambridge, Mass.: Harvard University Press.

Gantt, W. H. (1947) The origin and development of nervous disturbances experimentally produced. In S. S. Tomkins (Ed.), *Contemporary Psychopathology* (pp. 414–424). Cambridge, Mass.: Harvard University Press.

Goldfried, M. R., Stricker, G., and Weiner, I. B. (1971) *Rorschach Handbook of Clinical and Research Applications.* Englewood Cliffs, N.J.: Prentice-Hall.

Goodstein, L. D. (1954) Interrelationships among several measures of anxiety and hostility. *Journal of Consulting Psychology, 18,* 35–39.

Goodstein, L. D., and Goldberger, L. (1955) Manifest anxiety and Rorschach performance in a chronic patient population. *Journal of Consulting Psychology, 19,* 339–344.

Haan, N. (1964) An investigation of the relationships of Rorschach scores, patterns and behaviors to coping and defense mechanisms. *Journal of Projective Techniques and Personality Assessment, 28,* 429–441.

Hammer, E. F., and Jacks, I. (1955) A study of Rorschach flexor and extensor human movement responses. *Journal of Clinical Psychology,* **11,** 63–67.

Hertz, M. R. (1948) Suicidal configurations in Rorschach records. *Rorschach Research Exchange,* **12,** 3–58.

Holtzman, W. H., Iscoe, I., and Calvin, A. D. (1954) Rorschach color responses and manifest anxiety in college women. *Journal of Consulting Psychology,* **18,** 317–324.

Kallstedt, F. E. (1952) A Rorschach study of 66 adolescents. *Journal of Clinical Psychology,* **8,** 129–132.

Kemalof, S. (1952) The effect of practice in the Rorschach Test. In W. Peters (Ed.), *Studies in Psychology and Pedagogy.* Instanbul: University of Istanbul Press.

Klebanoff, S. A. (1946) Rorschach study of operational fatigue in Army Air Force Combat Personnel. *Rorschach Research Exchange,* **9,** 115–120.

Klopfer, B. (1938) The shading resonses. *Rorschach Research Exchange,* **2,** 76–79.

Klopfer, B., Ainsworth, M., Klopfer, W., and Holt, R. (1954) *Developments in the Rorschach Technique.* Vol. 1. Yonkers-on-Hudson, N.Y.: World Book.

Klopfer, B., and Kelley, D. (1942) *The Rorschach Technique.* Yonkers-on-Hudson, N.Y.: World Book Company.

Klopfer, B., Kirkner, F., Wisham, W., and Baker, G. (1951) Rorschach prognostic rating scale. *Journal of Projective Techniques,* **15,** 425–428.

Klopfer, B., and Spiegelman, M. (1956) Differential diagnosis. In B. Klopfer et al. (Eds.), *Developments in the Rorschach Technique. II: Fields of Application.* Yonkers-on-Hudson, N.Y.: World Book.

Klopfer, W. (1946) Rorschach patterns of old age. *Rorschach Research Exchange,* **10,** 145–166.

Lazarus, R. S. (1983) The costs and benefits of denial. In S. Breznitz (Ed.), *The denial of stress* (pp. 1–30). New York: International Universities Press.

Lazarus, R. S. (1991) *Emotion and adaptation.* New York: Oxford University Press.

Lazarus, R. S., and Folkman, S. (1984) *Stress, appraisal and coping.* New York: Springer.

Langmuir, C. R. (1958) *Varieties of decision making behavior: A report of experiences with the Logical Analysis Device.* Washington, D.C.: American Psychological Association.

Lebo, D., Toal, R., and Brick, H. (1960) Rorschach performances in the amelioration and continuation of observable anxiety. *Journal of General Psychology,* **63,** 75–80.

Leura, A. V., and Exner, J. E. (1976) Rorschach performances of children with a multiple foster home history. Workshops Study No. 220 (unpublished), Rorschach Workshops.

Levitt, E. E. (1957) Alleged Rorschach anxiety indices in children. *Journal of Projective Techniques,* **21,** 261–264.

Levitt, E. E., and Grosz, H. J. (1960) A comparison of quantifiable Rorschach anxiety indicators in hypnotically induced anxiety and normal states. *Journal of Consulting Psychology,* **24,** 31–34.

Liddell, H. S. (1944) Conditioned reflex method and experimental neurosis. In J. McV. Hunt (Ed.), *Personality and the Behavior Disorders. Volume 1.* (pp. 389–412). New York: Ronald Press.

Light, B. H., and Amick, J. (1956) Rorschach responses of normal aged. *Journal of Projective Techniques,* **20,** 185–195.

Mair, N. R. F. (1949) *Frustration.* New York: McGraw-Hill.

Majumber, A. K, and Roy, A. B. (1962) Latent personality content of juvenile delinquents. *Journal of Psychological Research,* **1,** 4–8.

Maslow, A. H. (1947) Conflict, frustration and the theory of threat (pp. 588–594). In S. S. Tomkins (Ed.), *Contemporary Psychopathology.* Cambridge, Mass: Harvard University Press.

McArthur, C. C., and King, S. (1954) Rorschach configurations associated with college achievement. *Journal of Educational Psychology,* **45,** 492–498.

McClelland, D. C., Atkinson, J. W., Clark, R. W., and Lowell, E. L. (1953) *The Achievement Motive*. New York: Appleton-Century-Crofts.

McFate, M. Q., and Orr, F. G. (1949) Through adolescence with the Rorschach. *Rorschach Research Exchange,* **13,** 302–319.

McGowan, W., Fink, A. D., Galina, H., and Johnson, J. (1992) Effects of laboratory-induced controllable and uncontrollable stress on Rorchach variables *m* and *Y. Journal of Personality Assessment,* **59,** 564–573.

Meltzer, H. (1944) Personality differences between stuttering and nonstuttering children as indicated by the Rorschach Test. *Journal of Psychology,* **17,** 39–59.

Miller, N. E. (1944) Experimental studies of conflict. In J. McV. Hunt (Ed.), *Personality and the Behavior Disorders. Volume 1.* (pp. 431–465). New York: Ronald Press.

Montalto, F. D. (1952) Maternal behavior and child personality: A Rorschach study. *Journal of Projective Techniques,* **16,** 151–178.

Neel, F. A. (1960) Inhibition and perception of movement on the Rorschach. *Journal of Consulting Psychology,* **24,** 224–229.

Pierce, G. E. (1978) The absent parent and the Rorschach "T" response. In E. J. Hunter and D. S. Nice (Eds.), *Children of military families.* Washington, D.C.: U.S. Government Printing Office.

Piotrowski, Z. (1957) *Perceptanalysis.* New York: Macmillan.

Piotrowski, Z. (1960) The movement score. In M. Rickers-Ovsiankina (Ed.), *Rorschach Psychology.* New York: Wiley.

Piotrowski, Z., and Abrahamsen, D. (1952) Sexual crime, alcohol, and the Rorschach Test. *Psychiatric Quarterly Supplement,* **26,** 248–260.

Piotrowski, Z., and Schreiber, M. (1952) Rorschach perceptanalytic measurement of personality changes during and after intensive psychoanalytically oriented psychotherapy. In G. Bychowski and J. L. Despert (Eds.), *Specialized Techniques in Psychotherapy.* New York: Basic Books.

Potanin, N. (1959) Perceptual preferences as a function of personality variables under normal and stressful conditions. *Journal of Abnormal and Social Psychology,* **55,** 108–113.

Rabinovitch, S. (1954) Physiological response, perceptual threshold, and Rorschach Test anxiety indices. *Journal of Projective Techniques,* **18,** 379–386.

Rapaport, D., Gill, M., and Schafer, R. (1946) *Psychological Diagnostic Testing.* Vol. 2. Chicago: Yearbook Publishers.

Raychaudhuri, M., and Mukerji, K. (1971) Homosexual-narcissistic "reflections" in the Rorschach: An examination of Exner's diagnostic Rorschach signs. *Rorschachiana Japonica,* **12,** 119–126.

Ridgeway, E. M., and Exner, J. E. (1980) Rorschach correlates of achievement needs in medical students under an arousal state. Workshops Study No. 274 (unpublished), Rorschach Workshops.

Rorschach, H. (1921) *Psychodiagnostics.* Bern: Bircher (Transl. Hans Huber Verlag, 1942).

Rorschach, H. (1923) The application of the form interpretation test. In *Zeitschrift fur die gesamte Neurologie und Psychiatrie.*

Salmon, P., Arnold, J. M., and Collyer, Y. M. (1972) What do the determinants determine: The internal validity of the Rorschach. *Journal of Personality Assessment,* **36,** 33–38.

Schafer, R. (1954) *Psychoanalytic Interpretation in Rorschach Testing.* New York: Grune & Stratton.

Schon, M., and Bard, M. (1958) The effects of hypophysectomy on personality in women with metastastic breast cancer as revealed by the Rorschach Test. *Journal of Projective Techniques,* **22,** 440–445.

Schwartz, F., and Kates, S. L. (1957) Rorschach performance, anxiety level and stress. *Journal of Projective Techniques,* **21,** 154–160.

Seligman, M. E. P., Abramson, L. Y., Semmel, A., and von Baeyer, C. (1979) Depressive attributional style. *Journal of Abnormal Psychology,* **88,** 242–247.

Selye, H. (1956) *The stress of life.* New York: McGraw-Hill.

Shalit, B. (1965) Effects of environmental stimulation on the *M, FM,* and *m* responses in the Rorschach. *Journal of Projective Techniques and Personality Assessment,* **29,** 228–231.

Singer, J. L, and Brown, S. L. (1977) The experience type: Some behavioral correlates and theoretical implications. In M. A. Rickers-Ovsiankina (Ed.), *Rorschach Psychology,* (pp. 325–372). Huntington, N.Y.: Robert E. Krieger.

Singer, J. L., and Herman, J. (1954) Motor and fantasy correlates of Rorschach human movement responses. *Journal of Consulting Psychology,* **18,** 325–331.

Sommer, R., and Sommer, D. T. (1958) Assaultiveness and two types of Rorschach color responses. *Journal of Consulting Psychology,* **22,** 57–62.

Steiner, M. E. (1947) The use of the Rorschach method in industry. *Rorschach Research Exchange,* **11,** 46–52.

Thomas, E. A., Exner, J. E., and Baker, W. (1982) Ratings of real versus ideal self among 225 college students. Workshops Study No. 287 (unpublished), Rorschach Workshops.

Thompson, G. M. (1948) MMPI correlates of movement responses on the Rorschach. *American Psychologist,* **3,** 348–349.

Viglione, D. J. (1980) A study of the effect of stress and state anxiety on Rorschach performance. Doctoral dissertation, Long Island University.

Waller, P. F. (1960) The relationship between the Rorschach shading response and other indices of anxiety. *Journal of Projective Techniques,* **24,** 211–216.

Warshaw, L., Leiser, R., Izner, S. M., and Sterne, S. B. (1954) The clinical significance and theory of sodium amytal Rorschach Testing. *Journal of Projective Techniques,* **18,** 248–251.

Watson, A. (1965) Objects and objectivity: A study in the relationship between narcissism and intellectual subjectivity. Unpublished doctoral dissertation, University of Chicago.

Weber, A. (1937) Delirium tremens und alkoholhalluzinose in Rorschachschen Formdeutversuch. *Zeitschrift fur die gesamte Neurologie und Psychiatrie,* **159.**

Weiner, I. B., and Exner, J. E. (1991) Rorschach changes in long-term and short-term psychotherapy. *Journal of Personality Assessment,* **56,** 453–465.

Wiener-Levy, D., and Exner, J. E. (1981) The Rorschach *EA-ep* variable as related to persistence in a task frustration situation under feedback conditions. *Journal of Personality Assessment,* **45,** 118–124.

Winter, L. B., and Exner, J. E. (1973) Some psychological characteristics of some successful theatrical artists. Workshops Study No. 183 (unpublished), Rorschach Workshops.

CHAPTER 17

Key Variables III—
Dominant Personality Styles

Whereas the first five Key variables usually signify the presence of pathology, disorganization, or developmental problems, the remaining six Key variables (*Lambda* > .99; *Fr* + *rF* > 0; *EB* is introversive or extratensive; $p > a + 1$; *HVI* is positive) do not. Instead, they simply call attention to the presence of one or more basic features of personality that usually are very influential in determining how decisions are formed, or how they are implemented in behaviors. In contemporary psychology, these personality features are often called response styles, although historically they have also been identified as traits or habits, or sometimes more loosely as abiding dispositions. Regardless of the nomenclature employed, these are the features that give rise to psychological and behavioral response tendencies, sometimes only in specific situations, but more often as a general preference for a particular approach to problem solving or decision making.

Some of these basic personality styles may predispose pathological thinking or behavior, but that is not inevitable. In fact, the presence of a style that may breed pathology for one person might serve to promote satisfactory adjustment or even considerable success for another. Stated differently, the ultimate effect of any style depends on two factors. One is the total psychological configuration of the personality. The second is the relationship between that unique configuration and the environment in which the individual functions.

It is naive to assume that people have only one response style that dominates *all* decision making and behavior. Personality structure is much more complex than that and, typically, personality or psychological organization is marked by many stylistic or trait-like features. One of the major strengths of the Rorschach is that it often provides data that indicate the presence of various response styles. Each of the six Key variables that constitute the main focus of this chapter reflect such styles, but they are not the only variables in the test that relate to stylistic features. Every data cluster includes some variables that may signal the presence of trait-like features that can often be quite influential to decision operations and/or the formation and implementation of behaviors, but generally, their overall impact is not as potent or widespread as is the case when one or more of the styles represented by the six Key variables are present. Thus, discussion of the other variables that indicate stylistic features will be reserved for subsequent chapters focusing on the analysis of the data clusters so as to give proper emphasis to the presence of the style in the context of the feature to which it relates.

The order in which these variables, and the styles related to them, are presented here does not coincide with the prioritized order in which they are presented in Table 59 in Chapter 14. The order in which the Key variables are listed in Table 59 relates to the best empirically derived prediction about the order of interpreting various clusters. The order in which they are presented here seems more appropriate so as to afford proper emphasis to the probable relationships and influences that will tend to exist between various styles as they exist in the psychological organization and functioning of a subject.

THE HIGH *LAMBDA* STYLE

Data concerning *Lambda* suggest that it is a crude index of the extent to which a subject is psychologically willing to become involved in a new stimulus field (Exner, 1978, 1986). Thus, when *Lambda* is low it indicates that the subject may become more involved than is customary, sometimes because of a processing style (overincorporation) but more often because of an unusual frequency of psychological demands experienced by the subject. Conversely, when *Lambda* is substantially above average, that is, greater than 0.99, it indicates the presence of a preferred response style that is oriented toward reducing stimulus situations to their most easily managed level. This often requires a narrowing or simplification of the stimulus field. In doing so, the subject tends to minimize the importance of, and/or ignore some elements of the stimulus field. People with High *Lambda* coping orientations routinely formulate behaviors that are in accord with their tendency to oversimplify complex stimulus demand situations. As a result, their behaviors, at times, may be less effective in terms of the requirements of the situation and, at times, can even run contrary to social expectations.

The behaviors of subjects who have a High *Lambda* Style often convey the impression that the simplification occurs at the input level; that is, by using a sort of psychological tunnel vision, the subject does not process all of the significant elements of a field. But this explanation does not seem viable in light of the fact that, as a group, High *Lambda* subjects, do not show any significant problems in processing, nor do they show any greater frequency of negligent processing (underincorporation). A more logical explanation suggests that the simplification is a defensive process through which some significant elements of a field are viewed as having little importance when judged against the needs of the subject plus the perceived demands of the situation. As such, those elements are afforded little or no attention in the formulation of responses.

The antecedents of the style appear to vary. In some cases, it is simply the product of a developmental lag that has caused the immaturity and social ineptness of the child to persist into adulthood. A High *Lambda* orientation is not uncommon among nonpatient children. For instance, approximately 11% to 15% of nonpatient children between the ages of 5 and 11 show this feature, but after age 11 the proportions diminish rapidly so that it appears in only 7% of 14- and 15-year-old nonpatients, in 6% of 16-year-olds, and in only 5% of nonpatient adults. For the young child, the tactic of simplification is probably quite important at times because it permits them to deal with a more easily managed world. But this tactic becomes important as the capacity for conceptualization increases and complexity becomes less threatening. In other cases, the persistences of the style into adolescence and adulthood seems to be generated by a sense of social deprivation and an excessive preoccupation with need gratification. In still other cases, the style becomes part of the product of negative sets toward the environment and becomes a tactic through which the subject manifests this negativism.

Regardless of the origins of the style, the kind of psychological functioning that it often evokes can set the stage for the formation of some behaviors that will fail to meet the demands of a situation and/or deviate from socially expected patterns. Obviously, the High *Lambda* Style can interfere with the most well-intended efforts toward social adaptation. But this is not always the case. Sometimes a response style designed to simplify external stimuli serves as adaptive, albeit defensive purpose. For example, the subject with limited intelligence, limited flexibility, or limited stress tolerance may find it important to avoid the myriad complexities posed by the world in everyday life. Narrowing stimulus fields in ways that make them more easily managed can be highly beneficial to people such as this *provided* that in doing so they do not violate social rules and expectations in ways that will breed conflict between themselves and their world.

When a High *Lambda* is the first positive Key variable in record, the interpretation of the protocol begins with the three clusters that focus on cognitive operations, processing, mediation, and ideation. The early objectives in the interpretive routine are to determine the extent to which processing is effective, mediation is conventional or atypical, and thinking is clear or clouded. This information is often crucial in determining whether the behaviors of the subject can be expected to align with or disregard social expectations.

THE RELATION OF THE HIGH *LAMBDA* STYLE TO OTHER STYLISTIC FEATURES

It is impossible to overestimate the importance of correctly identifying the presence of a High *Lambda* Style. The cutoff for such an identification of >0.99 is empirically derived, but good judgment should be exercised by the interpreter. Unfortunately, the history of the Rorschach has been marked by the flawed assumption that any number of answers, large or small, should be accepted and the record be judged as interpretable. As illustrated by the test-retest data presented in Chapter 14 concerning brief records (Exner, 1988), the composite of a low number of responses plus a High *Lambda* can also represent the performance of a highly resistive subject who is simply attempting to avoid the many demands of the test situation. In effect, these performances depict subtle refusals to take the test. Unfortunately, there is no easy way to distinguish between the low *R*, High *Lambda* record that illustrates resistance from the low *R*, High *Lambda* record that reflects a valid indicator of a coping style. This finding contributed significantly to the decision to discard records of less than 14 answers. But this may not resolve the issue of style versus resistance completely.

Obviously, the larger the number of responses, the sturdier the cutoff of >0.99 becomes in identifying the High *Lambda* Style; however, if the record is brief but within acceptable limits, such as 14, 15, or 16 answers, the interpreter might consider the possibility of extending the critical cutoff value upward, to as much as 1.1 in the instance of adults or even to 1.2 for the record of a younger subject. This is not a "hard-and-fast" rule, and the ultimate judgment should be made in light of whether or not the remainder of the protocol, (i.e., those answers that are not simply Pure *F* answers), is marked by considerable richness and/or complexity. If it is, the extended limits are probably applicable. Conversely, if it is not, the 0.99 cutoff probably is best retained to define the style.

This is a very important interpretive decision because, if the High *Lambda* Style does exist within the personality organization of a subject—especially an adolescent or adult—it tends to supersede or overlay other stylistic features. This does not mean that it will *always* dominate in decision making or in the formulation of behaviors. More likely, it will be dominant in more complex or threatening situations that are perceived by the subject as challenges to the integrity of the self-concept or obstacles to the gratification of experienced needs.

RESEARCH RELATED TO HYPOTHESES DEVELOPED
FROM *LAMBDA*

Lambda represents the proportion of pure *F* responses in the protocol, and pure *F* answers do correlate with a kind of psychological economy operation. Whenever *Lambda* is disproportionately high, that is, greater than 0.99 for adults or children, it signals that most of the responses that have been selected to deliver are generally simplistic, pure form answers. They are responses that ignore or neglect the complexities of the stimulus field. They are developed by using only the contours of the blot, thereby excluding other stimuli in the field. This should not be interpreted to suggest that pure *F* answers are undesirable; that is not the case. Almost all subjects deliver some pure *F* answers, and the failure to do so can signify a serious problem.

Rorschach (1921) was the first to note the importance of the pure *F* answer. He suggested that it was related to the attention-concentration features of the subject's thinking. Both Beck (1945) and Klopfer et al. (1954) have implied that pure *F* relates to a form of "affect delay," agreeing to some extent with Rapaport et al.'s (1946) notion that decisions related to the pure *F* response involve formal reasoning. All three suggest that the stimulus properties of the blots may create some affective and/or conflict state, and that the decision to select a pure *F* answer indicates some form of defensiveness. Rapaport suggested a parallel between Hartmann's notion of a conflict-free sphere of ego functioning, and the decision to select a pure *F* answer indicates some form of defensiveness. Neither Beck nor Klopfer accepted this position. Instead, they argued that affect and/or conflict may be present during the decision process, but that it is somehow controlled by the more deliberate and probably conscious operations.

There are a variety of empirical data that support the Beck-Klopfer position concerning pure *F*. In the developmental studies of Ames et al. (1952, 1971), the normative data of Exner and Weiner (1982), and the longitudinal study of Exner, Thomas, and Mason (1985), a relatively high proportion of pure *F* answers are found in the records of children and adolescents, with that proportion decreasing as age increases. Klopfer interpreted this as a form of rigidity, reflecting the inability of the child to exhibit emotion and/or conflict without fear or reprisal. Beck (1944), Paulsen (1941), and Swift (1945) have all reported that the proportion of pure *F* has a significant relation to intelligence; that is, the more retarded children give significantly lower frequencies of pure *F*. Significantly lower proportions of pure *F* have also been noted among epileptics (Arluck, 1940). Rabin et al. (1954) reports that the proportion of pure *F* increases under intoxication but the quality of the responses decreases. Buhler and LeFever (1947) report that alcoholics generally give a proportionally higher frequency of pure *F* answers than do psychopaths. Henry and Rotter (1956) found that more pure *F* answers are produced by subjects who have a knowledge of the purpose of the test. Hafner (1958) reports that when subjects are instructed to respond as quickly as possible, a significantly lower proportion of pure *F* answers occur. The composite of these data appear to indicate that when the subject is in the more defensive position, he or she is prone to increase the number of pure Form answers. The data also suggest that when the subject is unable to promote the necessary delays required for the formulation of the pure *F* answer (as in the organic or characterological style prone toward impulse display), the proportion of pure *F* answers will be proportionally lowered. Conversely, 26 of 35 (74%) protocols collected from closed head injury subjects tested within 60 days of the insult, have values for *Lambda* that exceed the critical cutoff of 0.99. When retested, three to five months after the first test, 18 of the 26 have values for *Lambda* that are less than 0.99 even though the average length of the record increases only slightly.

These findings also gain some support from the studies of the more severe psychopathologies. Sherman (1955), for example, notes that the incidence of pure *F* is relatively lower among the acute schizophrenics, a phenomenon which he interprets as experiencing much stress as well as struggling for some solution to the crisis state. Kelley, Margulies, and Barrera (1941) have reported a significant increase of the pure *F* frequency after one ECT treatment. Rapaport et al. (1946) have noted a significantly greater proportion of pure *F* answers among paranoid schizophrenics than among other types of schizophrenia. Goldman (1960) has found that recovering schizophrenics tend to give significantly higher proportions of pure *F* than occurred prior to remission. A significantly higher pure *F* is found among the 53 schizophrenics studied by Exner and Murillo (1973) at discharge than at admission. In another study (Exner, 1986), 109 patients, approximately half of whom had been diagnosed as schizophrenic, were evaluated at admission and again 8 to 10 weeks after discharge of hospitalization. A significant increase in the proportion of pure *F* is found after discharge. Exner and Murillo (1977) have also found that schizophrenics who remain out-of-hospital for a period of 1 to 3 years have a significantly higher *Lambda* than do schizophrenics who are readmitted during the first year after discharge.

Whereas adult nonpatients tend to give about 25% to 35% of pure *F* responses in their records, the proportions of pure *F* are considerably higher among those subjects who have histories of asocial or antisocial behaviors. For example, the average *Lambda* for the reference sample of subjects with character problems is 2.12 (*SD* = 2.39). About 68% of those 180 subjects have *Lambda*s greater than 0.99 and more than one-half of the total sample has been involved at least once in legal action. In effect, the High *Lambda* in a record of average length or greater indicates that the avoidance and/or simplification operations represented in the high frequency of pure *F* responses is probably *stylistic*. It denotes the type of person who approaches the environment in an overly economical manner; as a result, these persons often find themselves in confrontational situations. This is not necessarily because they deliberately violate rules or ignore the expectations of others. Instead, they have a psychological set, or response style that orients them to avoid, ignore, or reject stimulus complexity as much as possible. Thus they often find themselves at odds with the expectations or demands of the world. Subjects with this form of coping style will often have a lower than average *X* + % and tend to give fewer *Popular* responses, mainly because they view the environment less conventionally than do most people. Usually the histories of these subjects will include information concerning their avoidant or overly economical style. If the history is contradictory to this postulate, the high *L* in a record of average length or longer should be interpreted in the situational context; that is, the subject has apparently responded to the stress of the ambiguous task demand by being ultraconservative.

LOW *LAMBDA* VALUES

When the frequency of pure *F* answers is significantly lower than average, leading to a low *Lambda*, a much different picture is indicated, which is not necessarily stylistic but could be a by-product of other stylistic features. As noted earlier, most subjects will give some pure *F* responses. These answers, when not given excessively, can be viewed as a healthy backing away from complexity, as if psychologically resting and using a simpler approach to the task. The failure to do this raises three interpretive possibilities. First, some people have difficulty identifying the most economical ways of handling task demand. Frequently, they are victims of their unfulfilled needs, conflicts, and emotions. As a result, they do not always use their resources effectively. Their preoccupations and/or apprehensions often interfere with concentration or logical reasoning, and thus they often fail to perceive easier or economical solutions, which leads to an overinvolvement with stimuli around them. It is not a deliberate involvement, but rather an inability to back away. When this is the cause of the low *L,* there will be many other features of the record that signal turmoil.

Two other conditions can also produce a low *Lambda.* Both can be viewed somewhat more positively than the circumstance of psychological turmoil, one more so than the other. Some achievement-oriented people have the advantage of being flexible and able to adapt easily to situations. If these persons view the test as a challenge to their coping skills, they will often sacrifice economy to gain a sense of accomplishment. Therefore, they frequently reject the simpler responses and strive to deal effectively with the complexity of the stimuli. When the low *Lambda* is created by this striving, many features of the record will convey a picture of control, flexibility, adaptability, and psychological sturdiness. The $X+\%$ and the number of *Popular* responses are usually well within the average range, the *Zf* and number of *W* and *DQ* + answers are usually elevated, and typically, the *Zd* score is in the normal range.

The third condition that often produces a low *Lambda* is also related to an orientation to accomplishment, but it is created less from the sense to challenge and more from the need to avoid error or failure. It is identified by an elevated *Zd* score. If the *Zd* score is greater than $+3.0$, it indicates that the subject tends to invest more effort in organizing the stimulus field than is typical or necessary. It is a kind of cognitive inefficiency that can be either an asset or liability, depending on the circumstance in which it occurs. This characteristic is called *overincorporation,* and is described in more detail in the section concerning processing. There is a significant, positive correlation between overincorporation and a low *Lambda,* with the overincorporative style usually being the causal element. When both are noted in a protocol, other data concerning stability, reality testing, clarity of thinking, stress tolerance, and control will be the decisive elements in determining whether the low *Lambda* is cause for concern, or merely a by-product of a more firmly entrenched cognitive style.

INTROVERSIVE AND EXTRATENSIVE STYLES

Rorschach (1921) considered the Erlebnistypus (*EB*) as one of the most important characteristics of the test. He proposed that it reflects the underlying preferential response style of the individual. The *EB* represents the ratio of the Sum of the *M* answers to the Sum of the *weighted* chromatic color responses, using weights of 0.5 for *FC,* 1.0 for *CF,* and *1.5* for Pure *C.* The reason for this particular scheme of weights is not completely clear; however, it appears as though Rorschach noted that chromatic color answers occur with greater frequency than *M* responses and believed the weights should represent some equalization of those average frequencies and, at the same time, include appropriate emphasis for the color answers that minimize or exclude the use of form.

Rorschach hypothesized that when the ratio is distinctly weighed in the *M* direction, the person is more prone to use his or her inner life for basic gratifications. He termed this introversiveness but was careful to note that it is not the same as the Jungian concept of introversion. Whereas the Jungian introvert is generally conceptualized as being distanced from people and frequently perceived as isolated or withdrawn into him- or herself, Rorschach's notion of introversiveness focuses on the manner in which the resources of the person are used *but* does not necessarily imply direct overt behavioral correlates. Thus introversive persons may be regarded by others as outgoing in their social relationships, but internally, they are prone to use their inner life for the satisfaction of their important needs. At the opposite pole is the extratensive person, whose *EB* is markedly weighed on the color side of the ratio. Extratensives are prone to use the interactions between themselves and their world for gratification of their more basic needs. It is the *depth* of affective exchange that often marks the extratensive person; that is, they manifest affect to *their world* more routinely than do introversives. Rorschach also defined the ambient, that is, one whose *EB* contains equal, or nearly equal values on each side of the ratio. He postulated (erroneously, as it turns out) that the ambient may be the most flexible of the three types or styles with regard to the use of resources for obtaining gratification.

Rorschach perceived the *EB* as illustrating a constitutionally predisposed response tendency, emphasizing that the introversive and extratensive features are not opposites, but simply psychological styles or preferences. He believed that the style is a relatively stable psychological feature of the individual but also noted that various conditions could alter the response preference, either temporarily or permanently. For instance, unusual or prolonged stress conditions might elicit a transient alteration in the style, whereas some treatment effects might create a more permanent change. He also postulated that when the *EB* displays very low frequencies, such as 0:1 or 1:0, a coarctation has occurred in the development or functioning of the style or, in instances of psychopathology, may reflect a rigid defensive effort in which an almost complete paralysis of affect forms the basis of the effort.

Rorschach was not precise about how the relationship between *M* and the *WSumC* should be used to identify introversive and extratensive subjects. Instead, he used words such as "few" versus "many" but also discussed "degrees" or "intensities" of either style. He did, however, argue that when the values for each variable were within one point, or equal, the subject should be regarded as an ambient. That argument appears to have been valid when cast against empirical findings, but the magnitude of *EA* is also a critical variable in defining either of the two styles. Thus, if the value for *EA* is 10 or less, a difference of two points or more between *M* and *WSumC* does seem sufficient to differentiate introversive and extratensive subjects. If the value of *EA* is greater than 10, the difference between the two variables should exceed two points before defining a subject as being either introversive or extratensive.

As research has accumulated, much of it supports Rorschach's basic postulates concerning the introversive and extratensive styles. He was possibly too expansive in assuming that either style was *directly* linked to gratification. For instance, an introversive subject does not necessarily derive gratification from his or her inner life, nor does an extratensive subject necessarily derive gratification from affective experience or discharge. But the psychological tactics involved in each style are those typically used to gain need reduction or gratification, and the consistency of their use probably does have some secondary gratifying elements because the subject is doing that with which he or she is psychologically accustomed and comfortable.

The Introversive Style   If the *EB* indicates the presence of an introversive style, it can be assumed that, ordinarily, the subject prefers delay in formulating decisions or initiating behaviors until all apparent alternative possibilities have been considered. People such as this usually prefer to keep feelings at a more peripheral level during problem solving and/or decision making and tend to rely heavily on internal evaluation in forming judgments. They generally prefer systems of logic that are precise and uncomplicated. They usually avoid engaging in trial-and-error explorations and are less tolerant when problem-solving errors occur.

The Extratensive Style   If the *EB* indicates the presence of an extratensive coping style, it can be assumed that the subject usually merges feelings with thinking during problem-solving activity. This does not mean that thinking is less consistent or more illogical than in an introversive subject, however, the affective impact on ideation often may give rise to more complex patterns of ideation. Extratensive subjects tend to be more accepting of logic systems that are not precise or marked by greater ambiguity. Their judgments are often influenced by the external feedback of trial-and-error activity. In fact, they usually engage in trial-and-error activity and are far more tolerant than the introversive subject when errors occur.

RESEARCH RELATED TO HYPOTHESES BASED ON THE *EB*

The literature concerning the *EB* is varied and sometimes confusing because of a tendency by some to equate the notions of the introversive or extratensive styles with the behavioral expectations implied in the Jungian model of introversion-extraversion, even though Rorschach specifically disclaimed any such relationship (Bash, 1955; Klopfer, 1954; Mindness, 1955). Most investigations have focused on the two basic styles, introversive and extratensive.

Goldfarb (1945, 1949) found that children raised from very early life under impersonal institution conditions show marked extratensive features. Rabinovitch, Kennard, and Fister (1955) report significant EEG differences between extreme *EB* styles and suggest that introversive subjects show greater indices of "cortical harmony." Singer and Spohn (1954) and Singer and Herman (1954) report evidence for a relation between styles and the frequency of motor activity during a waiting period. Singer (1960), in a literature review concerning *EB,* suggests that support clearly exists for the postulate that two dimensions of constitutional temperament are represented in the ratio, one representing a capacity for internal experience and the second reflecting activity or motility. Molish (1967) suggests, in his literature review, that the elements illustrated in the *EB* have critical directing effects on most all nuances of personality and their related correlates of behavior. Both Singer and Molish cite studies demonstrating that introversives respond differently than extratensives in a variety of behavioral situations, such as problem solving, stress situations, and environmental responsiveness.

The directionality of the *EB* appears to be remarkably stable for the adult. Exner, Armbruster, and Viglione (1978) found that 77 of the 100 nonpatient adult subjects participating in their three-year retest study were either introversive or extratensive in both tests. They used a two-point or greater difference between *M* and *WSumC* as the criterion for differentiation. In the retest, only two of those 77 subjects had changed directionality. Similarly, 39 of the 50 nonpatient adults participating in the one-year retest had *EB*s in the first test in which one side of the ratio was 2 or more points greater than the other side. After one year, 38 of the 39 continued to show a difference of at least 2 points in the ratio and none changed directionality.

The directionality of the *EB* is far less stable in children over long intervals. As will be noted from examination of the data in Table 44 in Chapter 12, the majority of children ages 5 through 7 show an extratensive style, whereas 10% or less show an introversive style. Also, the percentage of children who fall into the ambient range is significantly larger through age 14 than for the nonpatient adult group. Exner and Weiner (1982) found that only 12 of 26 eight-year-olds showing an extratensive style continued to be extratensive at age 14, whereas 7 of 9 eight-year-olds who showed an introversive style continued to manifest that style at age 14. Exner, Thomas, and Mason (1985) found a considerable variability in the *EB* style for 57 subjects who were tested five times at intervals of 2 years, beginning at age eight. The composite of normative, reliability, and longitudinal data suggest that *if* the preferential features of introversiveness or extratensiveness become enduring characteristics of the personality, the stabilization will probably occur prior to early adulthood, and for most people during early to mid-adolescence.

The normative data indicate that approximately 80% of nonpatient adults are either introversive or extratensive and that the proportions of each are about the same. This distribution is quite different than found among patient groups. For instance, the schizophrenic reference group includes 60% who are introversive, only 11% who are extratensive, and about 30% who are ambient. The reference group of depressives reveals that about 25% are introversive, 18% extratensive, and 56% are ambient; and among the reference group of character problems, about 35% are introversive, 24% extratensive and 41% are ambients. These data are consistent with those previously reported for nonpatient and psychiatric groups (Exner, 1974; Exner, 1978) and support the postulate that, contrary to Rorschach's notion, the ambient is *not* the more flexible or adaptive of the three styles. On the contrary, the ambient appears to be much more vulnerable to intra- or interpersonal problems. Findings from several other studies also support this position. For instance, when the retest reliabilities of the 100 nonpatients retested after three years (Exner, Armbruster, & Viglione, 1978) were reviewed by *EB* style, the 20 ambients in the group show consistently lower retest correlations for most variables than do either of the other groups (Exner, 1978). This finding suggests less consistency in coping behaviors.

In a problem-solving study of 15 introversives, 15 extratensives, and 15 ambients (Exner, 1978), the introversives were found to perform the fewest operations before reaching the solutions. The extratensives performed more operations but were able to achieve solutions to the problems in about the same amount of time as the introversives. The ambients performed more operations than the extratensives, required significantly more time to achieve solutions than either the extratensives or introversives, and repeated more operations and made significantly more errors in the operations. These data indicate that it is impossible to distinguish whether the introversive or extratensive styles might be the more preferable or efficient, but it is clear that the ambients are the least efficient and least consistent in their behavioral patterns. These findings are consistent with those reported by Rosenthal (1954). He also concluded that although the introversive and extratensive styles of problem solving are clearly different, both are equally proficient in terms of achieving solutions.

Exner and Murillo (1975) studied 148 inpatients for a period of 1 year after their discharge from hospitalization. The Rorschach was administered at discharge and the patients subdivided into cells on the basis of the *EB* and for whether *EA* was greater than *es*. Forty-one of the patients were rehospitalized within the first 12 months, of whom 49% were ambients, and nearly 70% had values for *es* that were higher than *EA*. Exner

(1978) also followed 279 outpatients from the beginning of their treatment through a period of 28 months to evaluate changes as a function of different types of intervention. Seven modes of intervention were involved, ranging from dynamic psychotherapy to biofeedback. Evaluations concerning progress were collected at 90-day intervals from the patients, therapists, and significant others, and each patient was retested each 9 to 12 months, regardless of whether he or she had terminated treatment. The lowest mean ratings, concerning progress or improvement occurred for the ambient subjects at *each* 90-day interval during the first 12 months, *irrespective of type of treatment.* Subsequent data indicate that significantly more patients continued in, or reentered treatment if they had *EB*s showing an ambient status at termination, or at the 18-month retest.

In the long-term treatment effects study of Weiner and Exner (1991), 32 of 88 patients treated with a dynamic model of therapy were ambitents at the onset of treatment. In the second retest, taken 27 to 31 months after treatment began, only 9 continued to display an ambient status, and only 7 of those 9 were ambitents in the third retest, administered 46 to 50 months after treatment began. Conversely, 38 of the 88 patients treated using short-term methods, usually lasting 18 months or less, were ambitents prior to the onset of treatment. In the second retest, administered between 27 and 31 months after treatment began, and at a time when all had terminated treatment, 28 continued to display an ambient status in their Rorschachs, and 26 of the 28 had ambient *EB*s in their third retest administered after 46 to 50 months. Somewhat similar findings are noted in the two groups of 35 patients each studied by Exner and Sanglade (1992) with regard to brief and short-term treatment. In the brief treatment group, 18 of the 35 subjects began as ambitents. In the second retest, administered 8 to 12 months after the onset of therapy, 17 of the 18 continued to display the ambient feature. On the other hand, of the 19 subjects among the 35 subjects treated with short-term therapy who were ambitents in their pretreatment records, only 8 continued to display the ambient features in their first retest, administered 8 to 12 months after the onset of therapy, and only 5 persisted in reflecting ambient features in the second retest, administered after 24 to 27 months after beginning treatment. These findings appear to support the notion that the ambient, given the appropriate developmental framework, does become either introversive or extratensive.

Some of the major psychological differences between the two styles, introversive and extratensive, as contrasted with the absence of either style, as exists in the ambient person, are illustrated in Table 67, which compares subjects from the nonpatient normative sample. It is important to note that these data have excluded subjects *who have significant* Lambda *values.*

Similar differences can be noted in Table 68, which provides data for the same 27 variables for the outpatient sample, again, including only those subjects for whom the value of *Lambda* is not significant.

Although some differences do exist between nonpatients and outpatients within each style and in the ambient groups, the overall configuration of data for each group is highly consistent. In other words, introversive patients and nonpatients are highly similar to each other and very different from the groups of extratensive patients and nonpatients, and both groups of introversive and extratensive subjects are quite different from the two ambient groups.

These data strongly suggest that the ambient is much more vulnerable to difficulty in coping situations than either the introversive or extratensive. Their failure to develop a consistent preference or style in their coping behaviors seems to lead to less efficiency and more vacillation. Because they usually require more time to complete tasks, it is

Table 67. Statistical Comparisons for 22 Variables between 295 Extratensive, 240 Introversive, and 127 Ambitent Nonpatient Adults with Protocols in Which *Lambda* < 1.0

Variable	Extratensives				Introversives				Ambitents			
	Mean	SD	Freq.	Mode	Mean	SD	Freq.	Mode	Mean	SD	Freq.	Mode
M	2.92	0.77	295	3.00	6.47*	1.21	240	7.00	3.84^{a}a	1.22	127	3.00
FC	5.29*	1.60	295	5.00	3.25	1.39	235	3.00	3.59	1.77	123	5.00
CF	3.35*	1.03	295	3.00	1.57	0.70	227	2.00	1.66	1.02	113	1.00
C	0.10	[0.29]	28^x	0.00	0.01	[0.11]	3	0.00	0.17	[0.43]	18	0.00
WSumC	6.13*	1.04	295	6.00	3.21	1.02	240	3.50	3.71^b	1.41	127	3.50
FM + m	4.65	1.29	295	5.00	5.04	1.40	240	5.00	5.25^a	1.69	127	6.00
EA	9.05	1.60	295	8.50	9.69^a	2.07	240	9.50	7.55*	2.37	127	7.50
es	8.12	2.31	295	7.00	7.87	2.51	240	7.00	9.66*	4.25	127	9.00
Sum Y	0.65	[0.72]	153^x	0.00	0.32	[0.79]	51	0.00	0.87	[1.63]	57	0.00
Sum Shad	3.46	1.49	295	3.00	2.83	1.75	233	2.00	4.41*	3.41	127	3.00
Blends	5.77	1.59	295	6.00	4.47*	1.89	240	3.00	5.61	2.00	127	5.00
Col-Shd Bl	0.70	[0.81]	151#	0.00	0.26	[0.49]	56	0.00	0.35	[0.60]	37	0.00
Afr	0.73*	0.16	295	0.91	0.67	0.14	240	0.67	0.64	0.15	127	0.63
H	2.44	0.81	295	3.00	5.17*	1.68	240	5.00	2.50	1.23	123	3.00
All H Cont	4.72	1.32	295	4.00	6.59*	1.35	240	7.00	5.06	1.72	127	5.00
Bl	0.25	[0.47]	70^x	0.00	0.01	[0.11]	3	0.00	0.21	[0.51]	21	0.00
Ex	0.02	[0.14]	6	0.00	0.27	[0.45]	65#	0.00	0.14	[0.35]	18	0.00
Fi	0.63	[0.78]	131#	0.00	0.26	[0.49]	56	0.00	0.30	[0.58]	30	0.00
Food	0.36	[0.59]	88#	0.00	0.12	[0.33]	29	0.00	0.18	[0.50]	17	0.00
AB	0.23	[0.46]	63^x	0.00	0.07	[0.33]	12	0.00	0.17	[0.37]	21	0.00
COP	1.88	1.32	237	2.00	2.68*	1.71	201	3.00	1.65	1.28	93	2.00
CP	0.04	[0.21]	13	0.00	0.00	[0.00]	0	0.00	0.00	[0.00]	0	0.00

*F ratio indicates a value significantly different from both other groups (p < .001).
^{a} Scheffe procedure indicates significant difference from extratensive group (p < .001).
^{b} Scheffe procedure indicates significant difference from introversive group (p < .001).
#Chi-square indicates a proportional frequency different from both groups (p < .001).
^{x} Chi-square indicates a proportional frequency different from introversive group (p < .001).

logical to assume that they invest more energy in the process. In contrast, the preferential consistency that marks the introversive and extratensive styles leads to greater efficiency because the psychological routines involved are more stabilized. Consequently, people with either of those styles are apparently less vulnerable to difficulty during coping behaviors.

As noted several times above, the two styles, introversive and extratensive, are quite different from each other. In fact, they appear to be different in several neurophysiological functions. Blatt and Feirstein (1977) found that introversive subjects show greater cardiac variability during problem solving. Exner, Thomas, and Martin (1980) used a six-channel physiograph to record cardiac and respiratory rates and GSR, taken at the scalp, for two groups of 15 subjects each during a problem-solving task similar to that used in the Blatt and Feirstein study. Fifteen of the subjects were clearly introversive (M > WSumC by 4 or more points) and 15 were clearly extratensive (WSumC > M by 4 or more points). All had D Scores of 0 or +1. A baseline recording was taken during a 5-minute resting period following the attachment of electrodes. The subject was given instruction concerning the problems and permitted to work for up to 10 minutes on a

Table 68. **Statistical Comparisons for 22 Variables between 85 Extratensive, 128 Introversive and 70 Ambitent Outpatient Adults with Protocols in Which *Lambda* < 1.0**

Variable	Extratensives				Introversives				Ambitents			
	Mean	SD	Freq.	Mode	Mean	SD	Freq.	Mode	Mean	SD	Freq.	Mode
M	2.37	2.17	67	2.00	6.19*	2.17	128	6.00	4.06^a	0.48	70	4.00
FC	0.68	0.60	55	1.00	1.38^a	0.72	122#	1.00	2.31*	1.81	56	2.00
CF	2.74	1.88	69	3.00	1.23*	0.77	114	1.00	1.97	1.09	64	3.00
C	1.43	[1.39]	54#	0.00	0.09	[0.29]	12	0.00	0.34	[0.59]	20	0.00
WSumC	5.23*	2.17	85	3.00	2.06	1.02	122	1.50	3.64^b	1.13	70	3.50
FM + m	3.72*	1.54	85	5.00	4.94	2.01	128	4.00	5.00	1.48	70	5.00
EA	7.60	2.29	85	7.00	8.24	3.05	128	7.50	7.70	1.35	70	7.50
es	7.21	2.60	85	8.00	7.94	2.33	128	6.00	7.84	3.31	70	8.00
Sum Y	1.11	[1.06]	54	0.00	1.09	[0.68]	113#	1.00	0.77	[0.90]	36	0.00
Sum Shad	3.49	2.16	85	2.00	2.99	2.39	122	2.00	2.84	2.42	60	2.00
Blends	3.61	1.88	85	4.00	4.52	2.13	122	4.00	3.86	2.07	70	6.00
Col-Shd Bl	0.73	[0.93]	34	0.00	1.17	[0.89]	105#	1.00	0.71	[0.66]	42	1.00
Afr	0.52	0.07	85	0.45	0.49	0.11	128	0.50	0.57^b	0.18	70	0.36
H	1.13*	0.74	67	1.00	2.84	1.25	128	2.00	2.37	1.18	70	1.00
All H Cont	3.25*	2.27	67	3.00	6.70	2.37	128	7.00	5.11^b	1.97	70	5.00
Bl	0.61	[1.05]	28	0.00	0.00	[0.00]	0#	0.00	0.31	[0.47]	22	0.00
Ex	0.35	[0.48]	30	0.00	0.23	[0.42]	29	0.00	0.34	[0.76]	12#	0.00
Fi	0.08	[0.28]	7^x	0.00	0.48	[0.59]	55	0.00	0.46	[0.50]	32	0.00
Food	0.28	[0.70]	12^x	0.00	0.06	[0.23]	7	0.00	0.26	[0.44]	18#	0.00
AB	0.57	[0.50]	48#	1.00	0.09	[0.29]	12	0.00	0.31	[0.47]	22	0.00
COP	0.57	0.73	36	0.00	1.28^a	1.53	67	0.00	2.09*	1.47	56	2.00
CP	0.09	[0.29]	8	0.00	0.00	[0.00]	0	0.00	0.00	[0.00]	0	0.00

Underlined values indicate a significant difference from nonpatients ($p < .001$).
*F ratio indicates a value significantly different from both other groups ($p < .001$).
^{a} Scheffe procedure indicates significant difference from extratensive group ($p < .001$).
^{b} Scheffe procedure indicates significant difference from introversive group ($p < .001$).
#Chi-square indicates a proportional frequency different from both other groups ($p < .001$).
^{x} Chi-square indicates a proportional frequency different from introversive group ($p < .001$).

trial problem for purposes of adaptation. The target recordings were then taken for the next 30 minutes, during which the subject worked on two problems of increasing difficulty. The findings for the cardiac activity are similar to those of Blatt and Feirstein; that is, subjects in the introversive group showed more variability, *with a general tendency for the rate to reduce.* During a three-minute rest period between problems there was significantly less variability, and the rate tended to increase.

A similar pattern toward decrease was found for the respiratory rate of the introversives, which reversed during the 3-minute rest interval, and the GSR values also tended to become lower throughout the entire 30-minute session. The extratensive groups showed significantly less cardiac and respiratory variability during the activity phase, with *both tending to increase* shortly after beginning the task and remaining at a significantly higher level than baseline. During the 3-minute rest interval, the cardiac rate showed more variability than for the introversive group and tended to become lower, as did the respiratory rate. The GSR values for the extratensives tended to increase gradually during the first 10 minutes of the task, and remained significantly higher than the baseline throughout the 30-minute interval.

There is also some evidence to suggest that extratensives are more susceptible to distraction than introversives may be. Chu and Exner (1981) studied 20 introversive and 20 extratensive subjects, all with *D Scores of 0,* for speed and accuracy in adding columns of four-digit numbers under two conditions. All of the subjects were juniors or seniors in college, majoring in business administration, and the groups were comparable for cumulative grade point average. In one condition, subjects worked in a quiet room, whereas in the second they worked in a room with interference conditions created by random noises and flashing strobe lights. The groups did not differ for the number of columns completed or for number of calculation errors under the quiet condition; however, the introversive group completed significantly more columns and made significantly fewer calculation errors than the extratensive group under the interference condition. Some added understanding of the introversive style can be gleaned by a review of some of the research published concerning *M.*

THE HUMAN MOVEMENT RESPONSE (*M*)

It is important to caution that, although *M* has probably been the subject of more investigations than any other Rorschach determinant, many investigations have neglected some or all of the problems inherent in efforts to study a very complex variable in isolation. Although there does appear to be a common psychological element for all *M* responses, there are also many variations on that element that create some risk in generalizing from studies in which all *M*'s are ordered into a single category. For instance, almost all investigators who have focused their attention on *M* have neglected the issue of whether the subject is truly introversive or whether the group studied contains a combination of introversives, extratensives, and ambients. The common element lies in the fact that *all movement responses, human and nonhuman, involve some form of projection.* The blots do not move. Thus, the formation of a movement answer must include features that are mentally created by the subject and attributed to the stimulus field. This is why the specific content of the *M* answer takes on a special importance in the qualitative interpretation of a protocol. This factor creates a problem for the study in which all *M*'s are combined into a single category, disregarding whether they involve real or unreal figures, single or multiple figures, are aggressive or cooperative, active or passive, or are given to a tiny *Dd* area rather than to a *W* or *D.*

For instance, Piotrowski (1957) and Exner (1974) have demonstrated that differences in the characteristics of *M* do relate to differences in behavioral and interpersonal effectiveness. Subjects who give more cooperative *M*'s are generally oriented toward more socially effective behaviors. Subjects who give significantly large numbers of passive *M* are more prone to avoid decision responsibility and prefer to be more dependent on others for direction. Exner (1983) found that subjects with high frequencies of aggressive *M* answers show higher frequencies of verbal and nonverbal aggressive behaviors and are also prone to view interpersonal relationships as being commonly marked by aggressiveness. Witkin et al. (1962) found a high positive correlation between assertive *M*'s and Field Independence. Wagner and Hoover (1971, 1972) report that drama students, drum majorettes, and cheerleaders tend to give more "exhibitionistic" *M* responses. Findings such as these indicate the need for caution in generalizing results of studies in which all *M* responses are treated in the same way. Nonetheless, the quantity of research concerning *M* does tend to blend together to help gain some understanding of the process related to the formation of these types of answers.

Several studies suggest a positive relationship between *M* and intellectual operations. Most have involved the use of IQ or some other direct measure of intelligence and the frequency and/or quality of *M* responses (Paulsen, 1941; Abrams, 1955; Altus, 1958; Sommer & Sommer, 1958; Tanaka, 1958; Ogden & Allee, 1959). Schulman (1953) reports that *M* is positively correlated with abstract thinking and has demonstrated that the activity in both functions requires some delaying operations. Levine, Glass, and Meltzoff (1957) have also demonstrated that *M* and the higher levels of intellectual operation require delaying activity. Conversely, Mason and Exner (1984) failed to find significant correlations between *M* and any of the WAIS subtests for a group of 179 nonpatient adults. However, Exner, Viglione, and Gillespie (1984) did find a significant positive correlation between *M* and *Zf*. Kallstedt (1952) noted significantly fewer *M* in the protocols of adolescents than in those of adults. Ames et al. (1971) and Exner and Weiner (1982) found the means for *M* to be significantly lower in young children as contrasted with older children or adults. A gradual increase occurs in the mean for *M* at each year from age 5 through age 13. Ames (1960) has reported that the frequency of *M* responses tends to decline in the elderly, although that conclusion may be the result of overgeneralization. Data collected at the Rorschach Research Foundation from elderly subjects suggests that they should not be regarded as a single group, but should be subdivided with regard to their socioeconomic/health status. For instance, subjects over the age of 65 who live independently and report no major health problems give records that are quite similar to younger nonpatients. In fact, average *EA* values tend to be higher than the overall nonpatient sample. On the other hand, subjects over the age of 65 who live in facilities designed to provide frequent health care do have records that are somewhat more impoverished than younger nonpatients, and the average value for *EA* is somewhat lower than the nonpatient sample. A third group of elderly subjects who live in continuous health care facilities, such as nursing homes, show an average *EA* that is considerably less than either of the other two elderly groups and, as expected, the mean *M* is significantly less than for the total nonpatient sample.

The *M* has frequently been identified as an index of creativity; however, the empirical findings on this issue are somewhat equivocal. The different criteria that have been used for creativity appear to have clouded the problem considerably (Dana, 1968). Hersh (1962) has found a significant relationship between *M* and artistic talent. Richter and Winter (1966) report a positive relation between "intuition and perception" scores and *M*. Dudek (1968) has found that subjects giving a large number of *M*'s show greater ease in expressing themselves "creatively" in TAT stories and Lowenfield Mosaic Designs. By most other criteria, however, *M* and creativity appear unrelated.

The results of work concerning *M* and fantasy have been much more definitive. Page (1957) reports a direct relationship between *M* and daydreaming. Loveland and Singer (1959), Palmer (1963), and Lerner (1966) have noted that increased *M* is related to sleep and/or dream deprivation. Orlinsky (1966) has also shown a significant relation between *M* and dream recall and total dream time. Dana (1968) has also demonstrated a positive relation between *M* and fantasy. He suggests that *M* answers can represent any/or all of six different psychologic actions, including fantasy, time sense, intellect, creativeness, delay, and some aspects of interpersonal relations. Cocking, Dana, and Dana (1969) report findings that appear to confirm the relationship between *M* and fantasy, time estimation, and intellect.

The relationship between *M* and motor inhibition has been the subject of numerous investigations, essentially because Rorschach postulated the occurrence of kinesthetic activity when *M* answers are formed. Singer, Meltzoff, and Goldman (1952) found that *M* increased after subjects were instructed to "freeze" in awkward positions. Similarly, an increased *M* has been noted after an enforced period of delay (Singer & Herman, 1954; Singer & Spohn, 1954). Bendick and Klopfer (1964) report a significant increase in both *M* and *FM* answers under conditions of motor inhibition, and significant increases in *M, FM,* and *m* under conditions of experimentally induced sensory deprivation. In an earlier work, Klein and Schlesinger (1951) presented data to suggest that a relationship may exist between motor inhibition and a variety of Rorschach responses, including movement answers. In a similar context, Steele and Kahn (1969) failed to find significant increases in muscle potential with the production of movement answers. They did note, however, a tendency of subjects who produced many *M*'s to show increases in muscle potential. Possibly of greater interest is the fact that increases in muscle potential were noted accompanying almost all aggressive content answers, regardless of whether movement was involved. Motor expression has also been noted as precipitating an increase in the frequency of movement answers by Cooper and Caston (1970). They used two sets of Holtzman Ink Blots given before and after a 5-minute period of physical exercise. In general, the issue of kinesthetic activity in movement answers is, at best, only an indirect approach to the study of the psychological activity associated with their formulation, and the contribution of these works to the interpretation of *M* answers is still an open issue. Possibly, studies concerning the relationship between *M* and the delay of behavior have a more direct relevance to the interpretation of this kind of response.

Frankle (1953) and Mirin (1955) have both demonstrated that subjects who produce greater numbers of *M* tend to longer motor delays in their social adjustments. Beri and Blacker (1956) have found that mean reaction times to the blots are significantly longer for subjects giving more *M* than Color responses. Levine and Spivack (1962) report a significant correlation between the productivity of *M* and independent index of repression. Earlier, Hertzman, Orlansky, and Seitz (1944) noted that high *M* producers showed a greater tolerance for anoxia due to simulated high altitude conditions (18,500 feet) than did subjects giving low frequencies of *M*.

Some of the important data concerning the interpretation of *M* are derived from studies of various psychopathological groups. Guirdham (1936) noted that depressives tend to give lower frequencies of *M*. Schmidt and Fonda (1954) report a high occurrence of *M* among manic patients. Gibby et al. (1955) found that hallucinatory patients give significantly more *M* than do delusional nonhallucinatory patients. Thomas (1955) offers similar findings. King (1960) has shown that paranoid schizophrenics who have interpersonal delusions produce significantly more *M* than do paranoid schizophrenics with somatic delusions.

Rorschach suggested that when the form quality of *M* is poor, the likelihood of psychopathology appears to be greater. That postulate has been supported by many findings (Beck, 1945, 1965; Rapaport, Gill, & Schafer, 1946; Phillips & Smith, 1953; Molish, 1960; Weiner, 1966; Exner, 1974, 1978). Weiner (1966) has suggested that the *M*− response is probably related to deficient social skills and poor interpersonal relationships. Exner (1978) and Exner and Weiner (1982) have included the *M*− answer as one of the critical criteria for the differentiation of schizophrenia. Brain-injured subjects tend to give fewer *M*'s in their records (Piotrowski 1937, 1940; Evans & Marmorston, 1964). The presence of good quality *M*'s has been regarded as a positive prognostic indicator, especially for the seriously disturbed subject. This factor is weighed heavily in both the Rorschach Prognostic Rating Scale (Klopfer, Kirkner, Wisham, & Baker, 1951) and the Piotrowski Prognostic Index (Piotrowski & Briklin, 1958, 1961). Rees and Jones (1951) and Lipton, Tamerin, and Lotesta (1951) report that good quality *M*'s significantly differentiate schizophrenics who respond favorably to somatic treatments. Piotrowski (1939), Halpern (1940), and Stosky (1952) have all reported significant increases in the frequency of *M* among patients who show improvement versus those who do not. Exner (1974) compared the admission and discharge records of 71 schizophrenics followed in a relapse study and did not find a significant increase in *M* in the second test; however, 19 of the 71 patients who relapsed during the first year after discharge did have significantly fewer *M*'s in both of their tests as compared with the records of the 52 nonrelapsers.

Any attempt to summarize the full psychological meaning of *M* responses will probably fall short of describing the extremely complex activities to which they relate. Clearly, *M* involves the elements of reasoning, imagination, and a higher form of conceptualization. It is also contingent on a form of delay from yielding to more spontaneous translations of, or responses to a stimulus field, during which time an active and deliberate form of ideation occurs. This deliberate directing of one's inner life breeds images and/or fantasies that become the basis of decision making concerning the selection of responses to a given constellation of stimuli. Response tendencies may be thwarted and/or displaced into continuing ideational activity, or they may be externalized, either directly or indirectly, into behaviors. *M*-related activity does not appear to be a conscious process, although some of the reasoning involved probably does include a conscious focusing of attention. In effect, the presence of *M* indicates the use of a delaying tactic through which the stimulus field, and potential responses to it, are sorted more extensively than might otherwise be the case.

Obviously, the presence of *M* and/or the frequency of *M* cannot be interpreted accurately without giving consideration to several other test variables. Almost all subjects have some *M* in their records. The adult nonpatient normative data reveal that all 700 subjects in the sample have at least one *M*. Similarly, the normative for 9-year-olds indicate that all 140 subjects in that sample gave at least one *M* answer. However, the introversive subject with a record containing five *M* responses will be prone to use the delaying tactic much more frequently in decision operations than will the extratensive subject who also has five *M*'s in his or her record. This is why the data of the *EB* have such an interpretive importance.

As noted earlier, those with extratensive styles approach problem solving quite differently than do introversives. They make many more operations even though their times to decisions or solutions are not significantly different from introversives. They appear to be trial-and-error oriented, willing to make errors as a trade-off for the information they receive. Logically, it appears that they rely more on external feedback than do introversives in decision operations; however, the data supporting that assumption are sparse and indirect, and some data suggest that the postulate is incomplete, oversimplified, or erroneous. For instance, even though the extratensives use more operations in problem-solving activities, a variety of studies have failed to establish a relationship between *EB* style and various measures of Field Dependence and Field Independence. Similarly, frequency data concerning internal versus external Locus of Control are about the same for nonpatient introversives and extratensives. An extension of the hypothesis concerning the use of external stimuli by extratensives (which does have some support) is that they are more prone to invest affect into their decision operations and, as a consequence, are more likely to use interaction with the world as a source of information and/or gratification. In other words, they are more oriented to seek and/or respond to external stimuli when formulating coping responses.

To illustrate, Exner and Thomas (1982) videotaped structured 7-minute interviews of 15 extratensive and 15 introversive nonpatient college students who were volunteers participating in another study. The interviews were all conducted by the same person and followed a questionnaire format concerning attitudes about academic requirements. The tapes, replayed without sound, were rated for postural-gestural behaviors, such as leaning forward, chair turning, arm movements, hand gestures, and such, by three raters who had no familiarity with the nature of the study. The mean rating for the extratensive subjects was 15.64 (SD = 4.61) versus a mean of 8.22 (SD = 4.07) for the introversive group (p <.02).

It is very important to remember that introversive or extratensive styles that are indicated in the records of children under 13 are unlikely to persist over lengthy time periods; however, substantial proportions of the nonpatient subjects in each age group between 5 and 10 show an extratensive style, whereas very few manifest an introversive style. In fact, the proportion of introversive subjects at each age level, from 5 through 16, is consistently less than the proportion of extratensives. Interestingly, the adult nonpatient sample includes slightly more extratensive than introversive subjects. Most psychiatric groups include a substantial proportion of ambients, but the remaining subjects do not tend to divide evenly between the introversive and extratensive styles. For example, the reference sample for schizophrenics includes a relatively small proportion of extratensives, and the reference sample of depressives includes slightly more introversives than extratensives. Conversely, a review of data for 100 outpatients who have hysteroid features reveals that 54 have an extratensive style, whereas only 11 have an introversive style. Some added understanding of the extratensive style can be derived by reviewing some of the research concerning chromatic color answers.

CHROMATIC COLOR RESPONSES (*FC, CF, C*)

Rorschach (1921) proposed that responses involving the chromatic colors of the blots relate to affect. He argued that they provide some index of emotional excitability, and the extent to which the use of color is merged with form can be viewed as representing "degrees of stabilization" of affective urges. In this context, *FC* answers supposedly illustrate more modulation or control of affective displays, whereas *CF* and *C* responses are related to instances of discharge in which the emotion is considerably more pronounced and dominating. Rorschach speculated that the *CF* responses are related to actions in which far less cognitive adaptation occurs, as in circumstances when emotions such as irritation, suggestiveness, sensitivity, or empathy dominate the formation and direction of behaviors. He postulated that the pure *C* responses relate to actions marked by little or no adaptation, as in instances of impulsiveness or lability. He pointed out that the ratio of *FC* to *CF* + *C* responses might be an index of the extent to which control is present in the affective state of the individual.

Although data do support some of Rorschach's postulates, he may have been overly simplistic in suggesting the fine discriminations between the three variables, and especially concerning the differentiation between *CF* and *C*, because both have considerably less temporal stability than does the combination of the two. For example, the long-term retest studies reveal retest correlations for the combination of *CF* + *C* of about .80, whereas the correlations for either variable, taken separately, range from .51 to .66. Similarly, the short-term retest studies show correlations for the composite of *CF* + *C* ranging from .83 to .92, whereas the correlations for the variables taken separately range from .59 to .76. This does not mean that a *C* response should be regarded as equivalent to *CF. C* does seem related to a more intense, less well-controlled form of affective discharge; however, *it is erroneous to assume that the more limited control is a trait-like feature, such as an impulsive style.* The elements of control and/or proneness to impulsiveness are much more directly related to the *D* Scores. The types of chromatic color responses do reflect the aspects of modulation, or lack thereof, of emotional displays, but they *do not necessarily* relate directly to elements of control. In this framework, the *FC:CF+C* ratio does have interpretive value, as does the *Weighted SumC* entered in the *EB,* and both can provide important information concerning affective adaptability.

Chromatic color responses appear to vary considerably in terms of how much or how little cognitive effort and complexity is involved. Schachtel (1943) was among the first to argue that the perception of color involves minimal activity and defined color responses as reflecting a passive process. Rickers-Ovsiankina (1943) reviewed a significant number of research works concerning perception, and also concluded that color perception is a more immediate process than form perception, requiring less cognitive activity in the mediation of the stimulus input. Rapaport (1946) suggested that the *CF* and *C* answers represent a short-circuiting of delay functions. Shapiro (1956, 1960) reviewed a broad variety of clinical and experimental literature to define a "mode of perception" associated with the color experience. He argued that some color responses do involve more perceptual passivity, in which the cognitive functions necessary for affective delay are relaxed, and that the impact of the discharge on behavior will be proportional to the degree of relaxation that has occurred. Piotrowski (1957) has hypothesized that *FC* responses involve much more cognitive complexity, because they require delay in merging contour and color in precise ways. He has agreed that the *CF* and *C* responses represent situations in which the cognitive elements are overly relaxed, or even possibly overwhelmed by affective states.

The theory linking chromatic color responses to affective activity has often been a point of controversy. Unfortunately, much of that controversy has not focused on correlates of color responses, but rather on the concept of "color-shock," which was introduced by Rorschach and defined as a startle reaction to the chromatically colored figures. Extensive listings of indices of color-shock were developed between 1932 and 1950, including such elements as long reaction times, disruption of sequence, failure to give Popular answers, lower *R,* and so on. Much Rorschach literature of the 1940s and 1950s was marked by attempts to validate the various listings, but none were successful by contemporary research standards. Keehn (1954) reviewed many of those studies and concluded that few, if any, of the signs were actually precipitated by the color features of the blots. Crumpton (1956) noted that color-shock signs will occur as often to achromatic versions of the chromatic blots.

It is unfortunate that much research effort was devoted to studies on color-shock, and then the negative findings were translated as being directly applicable to the color-affect theory. The studies that have approached the issue more directly have generally been supportive of the concept. Klatskin (1952) found that subjects giving responses in which both color and texture are present are more susceptible to stress. Wallen (1948) found that the "affective quality" of the chromatic colors has a facilitating effect on responses.

Grayson (1956) has reported that the composite of color and form rather than color alone influences productivity. Crumpton (1956) has found that color cards tend to elicit more undesirable affect and more aggressive and passive contents than do achromatic cards. Forsyth (1959) reports that the color cards facilitate an anxiety score. Exner

(1959) has found that both *R* and content scores are altered significantly when Card I is presented in a variety of chromatic colors as contrasted with the standard gray-black version. One of the most frequently cited studies, generally used to support arguments against the color-affect hypothesis, is that of Baughman (1959). He used eight groups of subjects, administering one the standard Rorschach series; a second, an achromatic series; a third, the standard Rorschach series with a modified inquiry; and the remaining five groups, each one set of modified Rorschach cards. Although the Baughman analysis of data was quite thorough, he neglected a specific comparison of the standard and achromatic Rorschach groups for *R* to the chromatically colored cards (II, III, VIII, IX, and X). A review of his data suggest that the group responding to the standard series gave nearly 200 more answers than did those responding to the achromatic series, the majority of which were to Cards II, III, VIII, IX and X.

Another controversial approach to the color-affect hypothesis is shown in studies concerning the proportional number of answers to Cards VIII, IX and X of the test. Both Klopfer and Kelley (1942) and Beck et al. (1961) have postulated that the number of responses to the last three cards, as contrasted with the *R* to the remaining cards, gives some index of the "affective" responsiveness to one's world. Even though they have disagreed on the method for calculating this proportion (Klopfer using 8-9-10%, and Beck using the Affective Ratio), they have agreed on this basic principle. When the proportion of *R* to Cards VIII, IX, and X is high, the subject is regarded as affectively responsive, and conversely, when the proportion is low, the subject is viewed as affectively guarded and/or withdrawn from affective stimulation. Several studies have investigated this postulate but have generally reported negative findings (Sapenfield & Buker, 1949; Dubrovner et al., 1950; Allen et al., 1951; Perlman, 1951; and Meyer, 1951). Unfortunately, most of these works are marked by flaws in experimental design, such as either using a group administration technique, or a test-retest method. Exner (1962) used a matched groups design, administering one group the standard Rorschach series and the second group an achromatic version. The results clearly demonstrate that the colored cards of the standard series stimulate a greater productivity to each of the three cards. Reaction times were also generally longer to the standard chromatic series than to the achromatic versions. Although these data lend no direct support to either the color-affect, or 8-9-10% hypotheses, they do indicate that color, as a stimulus, has a substantial impact on the formulation of answers.

The developmental Rorschach literature also lends some support to the color-affect hypothesis. Many investigators have reported that the *C* response is predominant in the very young child (Halpern, 1940; Klopfer & Margolies, 1941; Ford, 1946; Rabin & Beck, 1950; Ames et al., 1952, 1971). Ames also found that *CF* responses become more dominant after year two, and remain so through year 16, although a gradual increase in *FC* answers is noted at each year level. Her findings are generally consistent with the normative data for children although other data indicate that *FC* answers have slightly higher means than the means for *CF* beginning at age 15.

Brennen and Richard (1943) reported that subjects with high *Weighted SumC* (*WSumC*) are more easily hypnotized than those with low *WSumC*. Similarly, Steisel (1952) and Linton (1954) have noted that subjects with high *WSumC* are more likely to alter their judgments in accord with the suggestions of a confederate examiner. Mann (1956) found a significant relationship between the number of words related to the environment and the *WSumC*. Exner and Armbruster (1979) found a significant correlation (rho = .48) between the *WSumC* and the total score on the Zuckerman (1971) Sensation

Seeking Scale among 30 assembly-line workers at a manufacturing plant. Weigel and Exner (1981) had 54 nonpatient office workers give preferential ratings for a series of 60 slides using a 5-point scale, with the highest value assigned for the most preferred. The group included 21 extratensives, 14 ambitents, and 19 introversives. Thirty of the slides were nature scenes or photos of buildings, and 30 involved interactions among people, or between a person and an animal, such as a boy playing with a dog. When the subjects were divided into two groups of 27 each, based on a median split of the distribution of *WSumC* scores, *no* significant difference occurred between the groups; when the 14 ambitents were discarded from the distribution, however, the remaining 20 subjects in the upper half showed significantly higher mean preference values for *both sets of slides* than did the 20 subjects in the lower half of the distribution. As might be expected, 14 of the 20 subjects in the upper half of the *WSumC* distribution are extratensive.

The interpretive value of data concerning the frequencies and types of chromatic color responses is derived mainly from the *FC:CF+C* ratio; *however,* those data only can be integrated accurately into the interpretation when studied in relation to the *D* scores, and all of the other variables related to affect. Thus further elaboration concerning the *FC:CF+C* ratio must be deferred until the cluster concerning affect is discussed.

Overall, the findings presented should contribute to a better understanding of the introversive and extratensive styles. There is, however, another issue concerning those styles that contributes significantly to any postulates or conclusions drawn concerning them. This is the issue of the pervasive style.

EB PERVASIVE (*EBPer*)

This recently developed ratio (Exner, 1990, 1991) concerns the dominance or pervasiveness of the introversive or extratensive styles in decision making and/or coping activity. As noted in Chapter 10, *EBPer* is calculated only when a marked style is indicated in the *EB*. It has interpretive relevance when the value for it is 2.5 or greater. When the *EBPer* is positive, it indicates that the style is very pervasive, and tends to manifest in almost all problem solving or coping activity, *even though the particular stylistic approach may be less efficient or even inappropriate for the specific situation.* It reflects a reduced level of flexibility that can often limit the extent to which the individual can adapt easily to new demand situations. Thus, while a dominant or pervasive style may be an asset in some situations, it is more likely to be a potential handicap for the adult who exists in a world in which a broad variety of coping situations occur routinely.

RESEARCH RELATED TO HYPOTHESES BASED ON *EBPer*

Although a great deal of information has evolved concerning the significant differences that exist between introversive and extratensive subjects, the issue of homogeneity within each style has received very little empirical scrutiny. As a result, most interpretations of the *EB* have tended to assume that the overall approach to problem solving is similar and relatively consistent within each style and that variations within a style will be produced by other psychological features. For instance, it has been demonstrated that marked differences may exist within either style for tasks requiring greater persistence (Piotrowski, 1957; Exner, 1974; Wiener-Levy & Exner, 1981). Generally, those differences appear to be related to D scores and to the magnitude of EA. In other words, as one's capacity for control and resource accessibility increases, problems in being persistent in a meaningful but frustrating task are reduced.

The type and quality of M responses and chromatic color answers, also correlates with variations within a style concerning the effectiveness and characteristics of the style. Subjects who give an above-average number of "cooperative M's" are generally more oriented toward socially effective behaviors (Piotrowski, 1957; Exner, 1987, 1988), and a positive relationship exists between assertive M's and the tendency to be field independent (Witkin, Dyk, Faterson, Goodenough, & Karp, 1962). While all introversives tend to be ideational in their coping activities, the manifestations of the style will be notably different for the introversive with a higher es and M's that are predominantly aggressive than the introversive with a higher EA and M's that are predominantly cooperative.

The behavioral variability within any group of extratensives is probably greater than that for introversives. This is because the introversive is defined by a single form of answer, the M, whereas the extratensive is defined by any combination of three types of chromatic color answers, FC, CF, and C. Thus, the extratensive whose record consists mainly of CF and C responses will probably differ considerably in coping activity from the extratensive whose record is marked by a predominance of FC responses. Again, the presence of a higher EA or higher es will contribute significantly to the manifestations of the coping activity, as will many other personality features.

The accumulated findings regarding differences within styles tend to reinforce the theoretical formulation of Singer and Brown (1977). They speculated on the possibility that the two basic dimensions of the EB, introversive and extratensive, may be constitutionally predetermined, but they also pointed to many findings in the developmental psychology literature to emphasize how these styles may be reinforced or inhibited in their "natural" development. They suggested that a revised EB, derived from more precisely defined criteria than the crude and simple ratio devised by Rorschach, could yield much information concerning the patterns of fantasy, affectivity, motility, and of the spontaneity potential in the individual's ideation and affect.

Logically, any attempt to create a revised EB should be prefaced by more information than has been published regarding the consistency or homogeneity of the introversive and extratensive styles. In other words, if other seemingly important variables are held constant, such as $FC:CF+C$, D Scores, $X+\%$, type of M, etc., are the problem solving activities within each style consistent even though the absolute values in the EB differ considerably? For example, would an introversive, with an EB of 6:1.0 manifest problem solving behaviors highly similar to those of the introversives who have EBs of 7:4.0, or 6:3.0, or 6:3.5?

The first hint that this might not be true evolved from a reexamination of the data from the problem-solving study described earlier that was first reported in the first edition of Volume 2 (Exner, 1978). It involved three groups of 15 subjects each, drawn from a college population and selected on the basis of the EB, the Adjusted D Score, and SAT Verbal Scores, which were between 575 and 600. One group was clearly extratensive, defined by $Sum\ C$ exceeding M by 3.0 or more; a second group was clearly introversive, defined by M exceeding $Sum\ C$ by at least 3.0; and the third group consisted of ambitents, defined as $Sum\ C$ being within 0.5 point of M. All subjects had Adjusted D Scores of 0 or +1, and the frequencies for each did not differ among the groups.

The problem-solving apparatus used was the *Logical Analysis Device* (LAD; Langmuir, 1958), for which the subject is provided with a display panel containing nine indicating lights arranged in a circle. Each of the nine lights is controlled manually through the use of an adjacent push button. A 10th light is located in the center of the circle and is known as the "target" light. It has no switch. Information about the relationships of the various lights is provided by an arrow diagram placed within the circle of nine indicator lights. Each arrow indicates one relationship, either between the indicator lights on the circle, or between any of these lights and the target light. The only information that the subject does not have is the nature of the relationship between two lights.

Any of three kinds of relationships may exist between two lights: (1) an effector relation (one light being activated will cause another light to activate), (2) a preventor relation (if one light is on, a second is prohibited from lighting), and (3) a combinor relation (the combination of two lights activated simultaneously will act either as an effector or preventor for a third light). The object of the task is to light the center light, using only operations created by the switches for the three lower peripheral lights.

Before the first problem, the subject is taught the rules of solution by demonstration, explanation, and practice. The subject may ask questions, take notes, and repeat practice operations. The task of finding the correct combination of operations, using only the three lower switches, is one of logical analysis, developed by trial and error, with each trial representing an experimental question posed by the subject concerning various relationships. Ultimately, the subject must synthesize the information developed from each operation to cause the target light to be turned on. The problems vary in complexity. Some may contain as few as 15 or 20 information-yielding operations, while others may have as many as 50 operations that can yield relevant information. Each is such that many other possible operations can be eliminated by logical deduction. This procedure is demonstrated and explained during the instruction period but each subject must ultimately decide how many operations will be explored, and in what sequence, before a final solution is attempted. Each operation is electronically recorded, so that the total recording provides data regarding (1) total number of operations to solution, (2) total number of extraneous or irrelevant operations, and (3) total number of repeated operations. The latter can be subdivided into repeated relevant and repeated extraneous operations. The time between operations and total time spent solving the problem are also recorded.

Subjects vary enormously in their approach to these problems. Some work in an overly systematic manner, exploring the functions for each of the nine peripheral lights even though some are often obviously irrelevant to the task. Others tend to repeat, or "verify" information over and over. Still others move almost immediately to the switches controlling the three lower lights that must ultimately be used in the final solution. This latter group, which Langmuir labeled as "organ grinders," typically has the most difficulty because they seldom pause to contemplate the results of their actions, nor do they usually alter their approach in favor of the more elementary analytic procedure provided in the initial instructions. Data accumulated for a reasonably large number of subjects suggests that problem-solving approaches can be defined along a broad continuum of efficiency that ranges from the hyperactively haphazard, crude, and redundant to the deliberately systematic, flexible, and sophisticated.

The 45 subjects were asked to solve four problems of gradually increasing difficulty, with time limits of 10, 15, 20, and 30 minutes, respectively. Two examiners were assigned randomly across subjects. Neither was aware of the basis on which the subjects had been selected. Subjects were not aware of time limits and were encouraged to continue working on the problem for as long as they desired, but the data analyses were restricted to operations performed within the time limits for the respective problems. All 45 subjects completed Problems 1 and 2 within the time limits. Problem 3 was completed within the time limit by 13 extratensives, 12 introversives, and 12 ambitents. Problem 4 was completed within the time limit by 12 extratensives, 12 introversives and 11 ambitents.

In the original analyses, the data for each problem were addressed separately, using a 3 × 3 *ANOVA,* with total operations, total errors, and average time between operations as the dependent measures. Separate analyses were performed for repeated operations, repeated errors, and total average time to completion for those finishing within the time limits. The results indicate introversives used substantially fewer operations to achieve their goal, whereas the extratensive group explored many more possibilities, often needlessly, and often with much greater replication of operations and errors, even though taking slightly less time to achieve the "target." The introversives were slower but more systematic in their decisions, and the accuracy of their decisions compensated for the slowness of operation. The extratensives were more "doer" oriented in problem solving, more willing to make mistakes but they apparently profited from those mistakes so that their solution times were generally a bit shorter than the more reflective introversives.

These results parallel the findings of Rosenthal (1954) who used the Katona Matchstick problems with groups of high *M* and high *Sum C* subjects. Rosenthal found that the high *M* group was more thoughtful and took longer finishing the task. Although the approach to the problem solving was different for the two groups, they were equally proficient in terms of achieving solutions.

On the other hand, the ambitents are clearly less efficient when compared with either of the other groups. They use more time to solution, but more important, they repeat more operations and repeat more errors than either of the other groups. In the last two problems, ambitents repeated almost twice as many errors as the extratensives, and nearly three times as many as performed by the introversives. It would appear that the ambitent needs to verify each maneuver or operation, and apparently does not profit as much from mistakes as do either of the other kinds of subjects. The ambitent is probably more prone to vacillate during problem solving, that is, tending to fluctuate between alternatives rather than manifest a consistent coping approach. The lack of consistency can breed more vulnerability to disruption under stress conditions. This does not mean that ambitents are less well adjusted or effective, but a lack of consistency can become a significant liability under various circumstances.

As noted above, a reexamination of these findings provided a hint that less homogeneity exists within the introversive and extratensive styles than might appear to be the case at first glance. It was implied above that the data suggest the introversive and extratensive groups are difficult to discriminate in terms of efficiency if time to solution is used as the criterion. But that implication is subject to challenge if the results for Problems 3 and 4 are studied separately. In the original analysis, time to solution was calculated for those two problems *only* for subjects completing the task within the allowed time limits of 20 and 30 minutes respectively. In fact, when the two groups are subdivided, using completion within the time limit as the basis for the subdivision, some of the results appear to be rather striking.

Twelve introversives and 13 extratensives completed Problem 3 within the time limit. Twelve subjects from each of those groups completed Problem 4 within the time limit. The five subjects who failed to complete Problem 3 within the time limit also failed to complete Problem 4 within the time limit. All subjects continued working until a correct solution was reached on each problem. Although the size of the noncompleting samples is far too small to attempt any statistical comparisons, the data do appear to highlight some characteristics that tend to differentiate the pervasive and nonpervasive styles.

In general, the data for the noncompleters are substantially different than for the completers in each group. For instance, the noncompleter introversives had substantially fewer total operations and much longer times between operations than the completer introversives for each problem. Likewise, the noncompleter extratensives had substantially more total operations and less time between operations than the completer extratensives. In effect, the noncompleters in each group are *outlyers* whose scores for Problems 3 and 4 tended to make the differences between the two groups appear more notable than may have been the case. In other words, while the differences between the two completer groups still seem obvious, they are less substantial and in several instances, such as seconds between operations or repeated operations, the differences are not statistically significant.

These findings stimulated a review of other characteristics of the six Problem 4 noncompleters. All had SAT verbal scores within a 15-point range; all had D Scores and Adjusted D Scores of 0; all had $X+\%$'s between 72% and 86%; all had $FC:CF+C$ ratios that contained more FC and none had *Pure C* responses; and none had Zd scores of less than 0.5. The one common Rorschach feature was that all had EBs in which the higher number was at least three times the lower number, and in three cases the higher number was four or more times greater than the lower number. A review of the protocols for 24 Problem 4 completers revealed that only two subjects had EBs in which the higher value was at least three times greater than the lower value (Exner, 1991).

The finding regarding the extensive difference between the values for M and *Sum C* among the noncompleters led to the postulate that as the magnitude of the difference between the values in the EB increases, the basic characteristics of the style become more dominating or consistent. Stated differently, the hypothesis suggests that as the difference between values in the EB becomes substantial, the dominance of the style tends to inhibit flexibility in its applications.

A post-hoc test of the hypothesis was organized by culling through more than 325 Rorschach protocols of subjects who had completed the same sequence of the four LAD problems, or a parallel series that has the same difficulty level and the same number of information-yielding operations, within the respective time limits. Those subjects completed LAD problems while participating in various projects at the Rorschach Research Foundation during the period from 1974 to 1982. The objective was to create four groups, two introversive and two extratensive, differentiated by the EB, and among which differences in demography and other major Rorschach variables would be minimal.

The sorting process yielded four groups of 13 subjects each. The classification criterion for assignment to the target groups (pervasive introversive or pervasive extratensive) was that the higher value in the EB be at least 2.5 times that of the lower value. The criterion for the control group assignment (typical introversive or typical extratensive) was that the higher EB value be less than 2.5 times that of the lower value but at least two points higher if the EA was 10 or less or at least 2.5 points higher if the EA was greater than 10. The label "typical" was selected after reviewing adult nonpatient normative data and determining that only about 25% to 28% of introversives and extratensives have a larger EB value that is at least 2.5 times that of the lower value.

The subjects ranged in age from 19 to 34 with an average for each group of between 22 and 24 years. Four from each group had been outpatients when they were tested. The other 36 were nonpatients who participated in the standardization sample or served as controls in psychiatric studies. All had completed at least 13 years of education, and the average for each group ranged between 13.6 years and 14.7 years. All had Rorschachs in which the D Score and Adjusted D Score were 0 or $+1$; had $X+\%$'s between 73% and 86%; had at least six Popular answers; had $FC:CF+C$ ratios containing as much or more

FC and had no *Pure C*'s; contained at least 10 *Zf;* and had *Zd* values no lower than −1.5 (four subjects in each of three groups and three subjects in the fourth group had *Zd* scores greater than +3.0). Table 69 shows the performance data for each group through the four problems.

The results appear to afford support for the hypothesis that basic features of the introversive and extratensive coping styles are more dominant and less flexible when the greater *EB* value is at least 2.5 times larger than the lesser value. In Problems 1 and 2, which are relatively easy problems that almost all subjects will solve within the time limits, the data for the introversive groups are very similar as are the data for the extratensive groups. As might be expected, both extratensive groups used significantly

Table 69. Means for Six Variables in Four Logical Analysis Device Problems for Introversives and Extratensives Subdivided on the Basis of *M:Sum C* Difference

	Introversives		Extratensives	
	Pervasive N = 13	Nonpervasive N = 13	Pervasive N = 13	Nonpervasive N = 13
	M	*M*	*M*	*M*
Problem 1 (10 min)				
Total operations	10.1	11.3	17.7*	16.8*
Total errors	2.8	3.6	6.4*	5.6**
Seconds between operations	20.9	20.2	13.2*	13.3*
Repeated operations	2.6	2.8	5.7*	5.4**
Repeated errors	1.5	1.9	2.1	3.0
Seconds to solution	231.6	222.4	213.9	217.5
Problem 2 (15 min)				
Total operations	19.4	20.7	31.8*	29.9*
Total errors	4.6	5.4	12.7*	12.2*
Seconds between operations	23.3	21.7	12.2*	14.1*
Repeated operations	3.9	4.4	9.1*	7.0
Repeated errors	1.9	1.8	5.8*	4.1
Seconds to solution	441.6	419.9	414.5	421.2
Problem 3 (20 min)				
Total operations	36.8	45.1	64.6*	5.9*
Total errors	10.3	13.8	27.9*	19.7***
Seconds between operations	29.7	23.6	12.3*	18.4***
Repeated operations	5.8	7.1	11.4*	7.7
Repeated errors	3.6	4.7	8.1*	6.1
Seconds to solution	1126.6	1001.9**	981.2**	963.3**
Problem 4 (30 min)				
Total operations	42.1	54.3**	77.7*	61.0***
Total errors	9.3	16.2**	31.2*	21.1***
Seconds between operations	24.8	17.6	12.3**	15.6
Repeated operations	10.8	14.3	19.5**	15.1
Repeated errors	4.6	4.3	7.1	5.4
Seconds to solution	1254.6	952.7***	1049.8**	927.4***

*Significantly different from both introversive groups, $p < .02$.
**Significantly different from extreme introversive group, $p < .01$.
***Significantly different from both extreme groups, $p < .02$.

more operations, made more errors, tended to repeat more operations, and had significantly shorter intervals between operations than the introversives. The pattern of differences shifts considerably for the last two problems.

Problem 3 is much more difficult than Problem 2 because it involves more complex combinor relationships. In Problem 3, both extratensive groups used significantly more operations than the pervasive introversive group but not the typical introversive group. In fact, there are *no* significant differences between the nonpervasive introversive and extratensive groups. Conversely, the pervasive extratensive group differed from the pervasive introversive group for all six variables and had more errors and shorter intervals between operations than the typical extratensive group. The pervasive introversive group averaged significantly more time to solve the problem than any of the other three groups. Problem 4 is even more complex than Problem 3. As with Problem 3 there are no significant differences between the nonpervasive introversive and nonpervasive extratensive groups but both differ substantially from the two pervasive groups. Actually, the performance of the nonpervasive extratensive group is more like that of the nonpervasive introversive group than the pervasive extratensive group.

An examination of the trends within groups across all four problems seems to indicate that the two nonpervasive groups profited more from the problem-solving experience, or at least tended to modify their problem-solving approaches more. The nonpervasive introversives began using more operations, made more errors, had shorter intervals between operations, and achieved solution in nearly the same amount of time as the nonpervasive extratensives. Likewise, the nonpervasive extratensives began using fewer operations, made fewer errors, lengthened the time intervals between operations, and had the lowest average time to solution for the last two problems. In other words, those in the nonpervasive groups appeared to show greater flexibility by adopting some of the problem-solving features of the opposite style and in doing so, enhanced their performance. Those in the pervasive groups did not appear to do this. Their approach to each problem was consistent with their approach to the preceding problem. In this instance, that lack of flexibility probably reduced efficiency.

These findings raised intriguing questions concerning the pervasive style and prompted a review of other data for subjects in the protocol pool. Although only about 25% of introversive and extratensive nonpatient adults do have a pervasive style, the percentages are considerably higher for some psychiatric groups. For instance, about 60% of schizophrenics are introversive and nearly two-thirds of those do have pervasive styles. Nearly half of inpatient depressives are either introversive or extratensive and about half of those subjects have pervasive styles. About 60% of character disorders are either introversive or extratensive and about two-thirds of those have pervasive styles.

Among the more striking data is the fact that when subjects from the outpatient sample are reviewed, 85% of the introversive outpatients have a pervasive style as do approximately 65% of the extratensive outpatients. Obviously, there are other important differences between the outpatients and nonpatients. Tables 70 and 71 show frequency data for nine variables, comparing nonpatient and patient introversive and extratensive subject respectively. Subjects with a High *Lambda* Style have been excluded from these comparisons because that style tends to supersede the *EB* style in many instances in which coping, decision making, or problem solving are at issue.

Obviously, both patient groups have distributions for the Adjusted *D* Score that are different than the nonpatients groups. Similarly, both patient groups give significantly fewer cooperative movement answers, offer significantly fewer pure *H* responses, tend to exhibit

Table 70.   Frequency Comparisons for Nine Structural Variables between 240 Introversive Nonpatient Adults and 128 Introversive Outpatient Adults with Protocols in Which *Lambda* < 1.0

Variable	Introversive Nonpatients		Introversive Outpatients	
	N	%	N	%
EBPer > 2.4	61	25	109	85*
Adj D Score > 0	110	46	26	20*
Adj D Score = 0	124	52	89	70*
Adj D Score < 0	6	3	13	10
COP > 2	131	55	20	16*
Pure *H* < 2	2	1	14	11*
(*FM* + *m*) < Sum Shad	15	6	27	21*
$M^p > M^a$	9	4	48	38*
p > *a* + 1	2	1	73	57*

*Chi-square shows proportional frequency difference ($p < .001$).

more evidence of irritating internal affective stimulation, and tend to show more evidence of passivity than the nonpatients. The latter is also stylistic. While it is impossible to conclude without question that the pervasive style has led to the other differences, the issue is quite compelling and provoked a review of some treatment data available for some of the subjects whose records are included in the protocol pool at the Rorschach Research Foundation using the pervasiveness issue as a classification variable.

Overall, this group consists of nearly 1000 subjects who were tested more than once in the course of treatment effects research. For many, the data include some information concerning length of hospitalization and/or number of outpatient treatment visits, premature termination from treatment, rehospitalization, treatment progress, or posttreatment progress. Two target groups were selected from this pool, using as the criterion for

Table 71.   Frequency Comparisons for Nine Structural Variables between 295 Extratensive Nonpatient Adults and 85 Extratensive Outpatient Adults with Protocols in Which *Lambda* < 1.0

Variable	Extratensive Nonpatients		Extratensive Outpatients	
	N	%	N	%
EBPer > 2.4	84	28	55	65*
Adj D Score > 0	70	24	32	38*
Adj D Score = 0	205	69	29	34*
Adj D Score < 0	21	7	24	28*
COP > 2	98	33	1	1*
Pure *H* < 2	33	11	56	66*
(*FM* + *m*) < Sum Shad	46	16	20	24
$M^p > M^a$	53	18	22	26
p > *a* + 1	2	1	6	7

*Chi-square shows proportional frequency difference ($p < .001$).

selection the fact that the baseline Rorschach included an *EB* that was either introversive or extratensive.

The first target group consists of 261 first-admission nonschizophrenics. About 70% had been hospitalized for some form of affective disturbance. None of the subjects terminated their hospitalization against medical advice (AMA) and none were transferred to other hospitals. The group was subdivided into (1) nonpervasive style or (2) pervasive style, disregarding whether the style was introversive or extratensive, and data were analyzed concerning (1) length of hospitalization, (2) confirmation of entry into posthospitalization outpatient treatment, and (3) rehospitalization within one year. The results are shown in Table 72.

The second target group consists of 239 outpatients, beginning treatment for the first time, who remained in treatment for at least four months. Presenting complaints vary considerably for this group but the majority manifest some depressive features. As with the inpatient target group, they were subdivided on the basis of nonpervasive versus pervasive style. Four dependent measures were selected for analysis. They are (1) terminations against advice, (2) terminations with a favorable outcome within one year, (3) therapist progress evaluations for the first two months, (4) therapist progress evaluations for the second two months. The results are shown in Table 73.

The credibility of the results shown in Tables 72 and 73 are clearly subject to question because so many variables, such as type of treatment, presenting symptoms, subject demography, and other personality variables have not been considered. Nonetheless, they are compelling because of their consistency. Among the inpatient group, more pervasive style subjects were hospitalized for a longer period even though there is no difference for the proportions entering outpatient care or being rehospitalized. Among the outpatients, significantly fewer pervasive style subjects terminated care within one year and proportionally more were evaluated negatively for progress by their therapists after both two and four months.

The collective data concerning those with pervasive styles seems to have sufficient substance to warrant the inclusion of *EBPer* into the *Comprehensive System*, however, it remains a crude index subject to further refinement. Ultimately, it might be possible to identify a composite of variables, which when added to the pervasive style, could predict the presence of a marked potential for pathology or difficulties in adjustment, but this would require a large sample prospective study. For the moment, it seems clear that a

Table 72. Some Treatment Data Concerning First-Admission Inpatients Subdivided on the Basis of *EBPer*

Variable	Nonpervasive *EB* N = 139		Pervasive *EB* N = 122	
	N	%	N	%
Length of hospitalization				
Less than 16 days	33	24	24	20
Between 16 and 30 days	67	48	35	29*
More than 30 days	39	28	63	52*
Entered outpatient care	131	94	117	96
Rehospitalized	36	26	27	22

*Significantly different from nonpervasive group ($p < .01$).

Table 73.   Some Treatment Data Concerning First Time Outpatients Subdivided on the Basis of *EBPer*

Variable	Nonpervasive *EB* N = 137		Pervasive *EB* N = 102	
	N	%	N	%
Terminated against advice	26	19	17	17
Favorable termination within one year	80	58	39	38*
Evaluations—1st two months				
Negative	22	16	30	29*
Neutral	51	37	28	27
Favorable	64	47	44	43
Evaluations—2nd two months				
Negative	29	21	36	35*
Neutral	26	19	15	15
Favorable	82	60	51	50

*Significantly difference from nonpervasive group ($p < .01$).

pervasive style does pose a potential liability because of the lack of problem-solving flexibility, and in the instance of the pervasive style patient, the pervasiveness of the style may well be among the targets for which treatment is considered.

THE REFLECTION-RELATED STYLE ($Fr + RF > 0$)

When the value for $Fr + rF$ is greater than zero it signals the presence of a dominating element in the self-concept of the subject. It is a narcissistic-like feature that includes a marked tendency to overvalue personal worth. This stylistic feature is natural among children but usually disappears during adolescence as formal operations begin and social relationships take on a new importance. When this characteristic persists into late adolescence and/or adulthood it continues to foment an inflated sense of personal worth that tends to dominate perceptions of the world and transactions with it. It does not automatically predispose pathology but it can impair the development of a mature balance between a healthy concern for one's own integrity and the integrity of others.

This narcissistic-like characteristic forms a basic response orientation or style that is highly influential in decisions and behaviors because of the need for frequent reaffirmation or reinforcement of the exaggerated sense of personal pride. It often contributes significantly to the development of motives for status. If success and/or recognition is achieved, it reduces the likelihood that this exquisite form of self-centeredness will promote pathology or maladjustment. On the other hand, failures to obtain reaffirmation of the high self-value usually lead to frustration and negativism, and elaborate systems of personal defense are developed through which the integrity of the naive belief concerning the extraordinary personal worth can be protected. Rationalization, externalization and denial typically form the core of these defenses. As these defenses are used excessively, they can create a predisposition to pathology and/or maladjustment. Adolescents and adults with this narcissistic-like feature often find it difficult to establish and maintain deep and meaningful interpersonal relations. In some instances, this provokes self-examining and if that occurs, internal conflict can arise reflecting a struggle to maintain the inflated self-value versus some awareness that it may not be valid. If the environment has been especially ungiving of reinforcement, asocial and/or antisocial sets can evolve rather easily.

RESEARCH RELATED TO HYPOTHESES BASED ON REFLECTION ANSWERS

Whereas reflection responses appear in about 7% of the adult nonpatient sample, the proportions tend to be higher among patient groups. For instance, about 10% of the outpatient and depressive reference sample protocols contain reflections as do 13% of the records in the schizophrenia sample. The greatest proportion occurs in the protocols of the character disorder reference group, about 20%. That proportion is not unlike those found among the records of nonpatient children in which the percentages range from 32% at age 5 to 28% at age 8, 21% at age 11, 14% at age 14, and 20% at age 16.

Reflection answers have considerable temporal stability in the records of adults. For instance, 42 subjects included in the outpatient reference group gave at least one reflection answer when first tested prior to beginning treatment. When retested between 9 and 12 months later, 41 of the 42 gave at least one reflection response. Similarly, a composite of 150 protocols, consisting of 100 nonpatients retested after three years and 50 nonpatients retested after one year, contained 17 in which at least one reflection answer was given in the first test. All 17 subjects gave at least one reflection response in their retest records.

Interestingly, the proportion of reflection responses among nonpatient adult protocols differs substantially when the group is subdivided by occupation. The largest proportion, nearly 30%, is found among the clergy. The second largest proportion appears in the records of surgeons, 24%, and nonpatients employed in the theatrical industry also give a considerable proportion of reflection answers, about 20%. The proportion is even higher for some subgroups in the theatrical industry. For instance, Winter and Exner (1973) tested 18 subjects who were very successful performing artists with no psychiatric history. The Egocentricity Index for this group averaged .48, with a range of .40 to .62, and seven of the records contained reflection answers. Similarly, Exner et al. (1979) obtained the protocols of 39 successful theatrical dancers, none of whom have any admitted psychiatric history. The mean Egocentricity Index for the group is .47, with a range from .28 to .77, and 14 of the records contain at least one reflection answer. These data seem to offer indirect evidence that the presence of the narcissistic-like feature associated with reflection does not necessarily doom a subject to pathology or maladjustment, especially if the subject is able to coexist in an environment (and/or occupation) in which a reaffirmation of high personal worth occurs routinely.

Much of the basic research related to reflection responses is intertwined with the coding for *pair* (2) responses and the Egocentricity Index ($3r + 2/R$). The separate codings for reflections (*Fr, rF*) and pairs (2) evolved somewhat fortuitously from a study comparing four groups of 20 subjects each; inpatient depressives who had made a recent suicide gesture, inpatient male homosexuals, imprisoned character disorders who had been diagnosed as antisocial personalities, and adult nonpatients drawn mainly from a college population (Exner, 1969). Frequency data revealed that reflections appeared in more than 75% of the records of the homosexual and antisocial groups, but not at all among the depressives and in only three nonpatient records. Because the reflection answers were all based on the symmetry of the blots, it was decided to tally the frequency with which the symmetry of the blots was used to report identical pairs of objects. The tally revealed that the homosexual group gave significantly more pairs than did the other groups, and that the depressives gave significantly fewer pairs than the other groups.

Raychaudhuri and Mukerji (1971) used four groups of 15 subjects each, from a prison population, to study reflections and pairs. The groups were comprised of active homosexuals, passive homosexuals, sociopaths, and controls. They found that both homosexual groups gave significantly more reflections than either of the other two groups, and that sociopaths gave significantly more reflections than the controls. They found the number of pair answers to be significantly high in both homosexual groups, *and* among controls when contrasted with the sociopathic group.

These findings provoked a hypothesis that reflection and pair answers might, in some way, be related to overinvolvement with the self. To test that postulate, a sentence completion blank was constructed following a format similar to one used by Watson in her study of narcissism (1965). An original blank of 50 stems was reduced to 30, most of which contain the personal pronouns *I, me,* or *my,* and administered to 750 nonpatient adults. Responses were scored for whether the answer focused on the self (*S*), such as, *I worry:* about my future; or focused on others (0), such as *I worry:* about the homeless people of the world. Eighty subjects, 40 with the highest number of *S* responses, and 40 with the highest number of 0 responses were administered the Rorschach by 14 examiners. Reflection answers appeared in the records of 37 of the 40 high *S* subjects as contrasted with only two records of the high 0 subjects. The high *S* group also gave nearly $2\frac{1}{2}$ times the number of pair responses as the high 0 group. The blank, entitled the *Self Focus Sentence Completion* (SFSC), was then standardized on a population of more than 2500 subjects (Exner, 1973). The 30 subjects from each extreme of the resulting distribution were administered the Rorschach by 16 examiners. Reflection and pair responses appeared more than twice as often among the 30 high *S* subjects as among the records of the high 0 group.

These findings stimulated a decision to combine the reflection and pair responses into a single variable that would also account for the number of responses in a record. This procedure involved the SFSC scores and Rorschach data for 325 nonpatient adults. The decision to weigh reflections with a value of 3 in the Egocentricity Index resulted from a discriminant function analysis designed to differentiate the strength of each of the two Rorschach variables, and the frequency for each, to identify the quintile on the SFSC distribution into which a subject would fall. The results indicated that reflections have a geometric property to identify those subjects falling in the upper two quintiles, and the weighting of 3 represents a conservative averaging of that property.

The first validation study concerning the usefulness of the Egocentricity Index focused on a behavioral index of self-centeredness. Twenty-one male candidates for an engineering position were administered several psychological tests, including the Rorschach, by examiners naive about the nature of the study. Subsequently, they were interviewed by a member of the personnel staff of the corporation to which they were applying for employment. The interviews were conducted in a 12-by-17-foot office, which had an 8-by-8-foot one-way vision mirror on one wall. Each candidate was escorted to the office by a receptionist and invited to be seated next to a desk to await the interviewer. The mirrored wall was to the left of the subject. Interviewers arrived no earlier than 10 minutes after the candidate, and during that waiting period a video camera was used to film the candidate.

The tapes were subsequently replayed, and the amount of time each candidate spent viewing himself in the mirror was tallied. The range of mirror viewing time for the group was from 6 to 104 seconds, with a median of 49 seconds.

The group was divided on the basis of these data, using a median split and eliminating the candidate at the midpoint. The average mirror-viewing time for the upper half was 68.5 seconds, and 27.1 seconds for the lower half ($p < .01$). The 10 protocols of subjects in the upper half contained 6 with reflections and 103 pair responses, whereas the 10 subjects in the lower half contained no reflections and 68 pair responses. The groups are significantly different for both variables, and for the Egocentricity Index (upper 10 = .476, SD = .13; lower 10 = .298, SD = .14, $p < .01$). The first 10 minutes of the interviews were audio recorded and then scored for the number of times the candidate used the personal pronouns, *I, me,* or *my* during that segment. The scores ranged from 57 to 148. A rank order correlation comparing that distribution with the distribution of values for the Egocentricity Index yielded a *rho* correlation of .67, $p < .01$. The subjects having given the six reflection answers had the highest frequency of personal pronoun use, ranging from 119 to 148.

Thomas, Exner, and Baker (1982) used the Gough Adjective Checklist with 225 college students. Each student responded to the ACL twice during the same session, in a counterbalanced design, once with the instruction to "describe yourself," and once with the instruction to "describe yourself as you would like to be." A difference score was calculated for each subject, and the 20 subjects falling at each extreme were recruited to take the Rorschach. The average difference score for students in the upper extreme was 9.4 and in the lower extreme was 38.9, the latter showing the greatest discrepancy between the "real" and "ideal." The mean Egocentricity Index for the upper extreme group is 48.9 (SD = .09), and 11 of the records contained 16 reflection answers. The mean Index for the group in the lower extreme is .31 (SD = .12), and none of the records contained reflection responses ($p < .01$).

Therapist reports concerning 429 outpatients, collected two months after treatment began (with therapist evaluations concerning the motivation of the subject for change), rated 38 of the 43 subjects whose pretreatment Rorschach contained one or more reflection answers negatively. During the first 12 months of that treatment effects study, more than 150 subjects terminated treatment prematurely including all 38 subjects who had reflections in the pretreatment record and who were rated negatively for change motivation by their therapists.

It seems clear that this narcissistic feature does not change quickly or easily as the result of treatment. The data from the Exner and Sanglade (1992) treatment effects study concerning brief and short-term treatment reveals that 4 of the 35 patients treated with brief therapy had reflection answers in their pretreatment records and continued to give such answers in the 8–12 month retest. Similarly, 5 of the 35 subjects in the short-term group gave at least one reflection answer in their pretreatment records and continued to give at least one such response when retested a third time 24 to 27 months after beginning treatment, even though all had terminated nearly a year earlier. The findings for those in short-term treatment are similar to those reported by Weiner and Exner (1991). In their group of 88 subjects in short-term treatment, 10 had reflection responses in their pretreatment records. The same 10 subjects persisted in giving reflection answers in the third retest, taken about four years after the first test, and two years after treatment had been terminated. Conversely, whereas 12 subjects treated using a dynamic, long-term model of treatment, had reflection answers in their pretreatment test, only 6 of the 12 continued to give such answers in their third retest, administered after four years, but it is important to note that all 12 gave reflection answers in their first retest, after 12–14 months of therapy, and 9 of the 12 persisted in giving such answers in their second retest, administered 27–31 months after beginning treatment.

It is probably important to reemphasize that the presence of this narcissistic feature does not predestine the subject to a pathological state. Instead, any evaluation of this dominating self-concept element must be cast in the context of the total person, and the environment in which he or she exists. If the person is truly superior in some ways, and if the environment affords ready acknowledgment to that fact, the narcissism probably will serve to motivate the subject to higher aspirations and potential accomplishments. Conversely, if the person does not possess those features that are admired by others, or if external reinforcements to the inflated sense of personal worth are not easily forthcoming, the needs to defend and protect the inflated sense of personal worth will often breed behaviors that go well beyond the boundaries of reality and, as such, will be likely to produce behaviors that are maladaptive and/or pathological.

THE INTERPERSONALLY PASSIVE STYLE ($p > a + 1$)

The $a{:}p$ ratio provides another variable from which a stylistic response tendency is often identified. If the value for passive movement exceeds the value for active movement by more than one point, it indicates that the subject generally will assume a more passive, *though not necessarily submissive,* role in interpersonal relations. Subjects such as this usually prefer to avoid responsibility for decision making and are less prone to search out new solutions to problems or initiate new patterns of behavior. Findings for other variables in the interpersonal cluster are often important in attempting to discern how the passive style is most commonly manifest in behavior.

RESEARCH RELATED TO HYPOTHESES BASED ON THE $a{:}p$ RATIO

Rorschach suspected that differences in the type of movement answers could be used to discriminate features of personality. He described them as being marked by *flexion or extension,* the former being defined as those in which the action is toward the center of the blot, the latter for those in which the action pulled away from the center axis of the blot. He argued that extensor movement answers reflect assertiveness, whereas flexor answers indicate submissiveness of compliance. Hammer and Jacks (1955) found that aggressive sex offenders give significantly more extensor M's, whereas the more passive offenders, such as exhibitionists, tend to give more flexor M's. Mirin (1955) found that schizophrenics giving predominately extensor M's were resistive to contradictions in a memory task, whereas those giving more flexor M's were more willing to give in to the contradictions. Wetherhorn (1956) used a special series of blots designed to provoke more movement answers and found no relationships between the extensor-flexor M's and measures of ascendancy-submissiveness, or masculinity-femininity.

Both Beck et al. (1961) and Piotrowski (1960) warned about the limitations of approaching movement answers using Rorschach's flexor-extensor concept. Beck correctly pointed out that many movement answers do not meet either of those criteria, because they are "static," such as a person standing, or sleeping, or looking. Piotrowski classified M's as favorable versus unfavorable using features such as cooperativeness, lack of restraint, confident postures, and such, and was able to differentiate effective and nonadaptive parole conduct of released army prisoners. He also evaluated successful and unsuccessful business executives and found that the successful group gave more self-assertive and confident *M* answers. Exner (1974) found that first-admission acute schizophrenics and forensic subjects gave significantly more hostile *M* and *FM* answers than other psychiatric groups, or nonpatients. He also found that when all movement answers were coded as *active* or *passive,* following a suggestion by Piotrowski, active movement responses occurred significantly more in the records of the acute schizophrenics, subjects with a history of assaultiveness (regardless of diagnosis), and a group of character disorders, whereas passive movement answers occurred more frequently in the records of long-term inpatient schizophrenics, depressives, and outpatient neurotics. He also noted that a proportional difference score, comparing the frequencies of active and passive movement answers, differentiated patients from nonpatients.

The reliability correlations for active and passive movement are generally quite high for both brief and lengthy intervals. They range from the mid .80s to low .90s for active movement, and from the upper .70s to mid .80s for passive movement. The cognitive operations with which they correlate also seem pervasive in other ideational activities. For instance, Exner (1974) paid 34 female subjects to induce a 10-minute period of daydreaming on each of 25 consecutive days, and to record those daydreams in a diary. The activity of the central figure in the daydream was scored as being active or passive, and for whether a shift from one characteristic to the other occurred. Those scores were then compared with the data from the *a:p* ratios in the Rorschachs of the subjects that had been collected prior to the onset of the daydream routine. Twenty of the 34 subjects had *a:p* ratios in which one value was more than three times that of the other, whereas 14 had *a:p* ratios in which neither value was more than twice the other. The results showed that subjects who give a large majority of Rorschach movement responses in a single direction also have the majority of daydream scores in the same direction, and have relatively few shifts in the activity of the central figure of the daydream. In other words, if the subject gave substantially more active movement answers in his or her Rorschach, the central figure in the daydream tended to be active, and the outcome was usually the result of the action of the central subject. Conversely, if the subject gave substantially more passive movement answers in the Rorschach, the central figure in the daydream usually was described in a passive role, and the outcome of the daydream was typically attributed to the actions of others. The opposite is true for the subjects who have less discrepant values for active and passive movement answers in their Rorschachs. They reported daydreams in which an almost equal mixture of active and passive characteristics are assigned to the central figure, and showed shifts from one characteristic to the other in a significant number of their daydreams.

Although assaultive subjects, acute schizophrenics, and some subjects with character problems do tend to give significantly more active movement than other psychiatric groups, research seeking specific behavioral correlates with active movement has yielded negative findings. In other words, a high frequency of active movement responses *does not* equate with an unusual frequency of active behaviors, or with any special class of behaviors. This is apparently because most people give more active than passive movement responses. Adult nonpatients give nearly twice as many active movement answers as passive responses, and that ratio is relatively consistent for most groups, including nonpatient children. Only 3% of nonpatient adults give more passive than active movement responses, and the proportions of nonpatient children giving more passive than active movement answers range from 2% to 12%, depending on the age group.

Some patient groups have higher proportions of subjects who give more passive than active movement. For example, this occurs for 21% of the subjects in the schizophrenic reference sample, 24% in the sample of depressives, and 30% in the character disorder reference group. Exner (1978) devised an index of behavioral passivity using 20 items in the Katz Adjustment Scale. The entire KAS was completed for 279 outpatients by a significant other of the patient, 9 months after treatment had been initiated. All subjects were volunteers in a long-term treatment effects study, the design of which required psychological testing and behavioral evaluations at 9-month intervals for at least 3 years, regardless of whether treatment had terminated. Examination of the Rorschachs collected at the 9-month interval revealed that 83 of the 279 subjects had a:p ratios in which p exceeded a by more than 1. Their mean score for the passivity index was 11.6 ($SD = 4.2$). A comparison group of 83 other patients was randomly drawn from the remaining 196 subjects. The mean passivity score for that group was 5.3 ($SD = 3.3$), yielding a highly significant difference between the groups ($p < .001$).

In a related study (Exner & Kazaoka, 1978), videotapes were recorded for the first two sessions of two groups of eight subjects each participating in assertiveness training. Rorschachs were administered prior to the training and revealed that 7 of the 16 trainees had a:p ratios in which p exceeded a by more than 1. The videotapes were scored for the frequencies of verbal and nonverbal dependency gestures by subject, by two groups of three raters each. One group of raters scored only the audio segment of the tapes, whereas the second group scored using both the audio and visual data. The seven subjects who began the training with the *passive* a:p ratios were scored for nearly twice as many verbal dependency statements and approximately the same number of nonverbal dependency gestures during the two sessions as were the other 9 subjects.

The findings of these studies seem to indicate that when people give significantly more passive movement responses—that is, when p exceeds a by more than 1—a tendency toward more passive and possibly dependent behaviors exists. The tendency toward dependency appears to be even more marked if the record includes at least one food response. Schafer (1954) had postulated that Fd responses are related to oral dependency characteristics. In the Exner and Kazaoka study, the four assertiveness training subjects who scored highest for dependency gestures had at least one Fd response in their records. Those findings provoked another videotape study, involving a class of 24 sixth-grade students. The class was recorded twice during one week, in both instances during art instruction. The students were learning to paint with acrylics and often had reason to request aid from the teacher. The tapes were scored for (1) requests for assistance from the teacher and (2) follow-up questions to the teacher. Contrary to expectations, the 6 students who had Rorschach a:p ratios in which p exceeds a by more than 1 did not make more requests for assistance than did the other 18 students, but 7 students, including three who had passive a:p ratios, with at least one Fd response, made nearly twice as many requests for help and asked nearly four times as many follow-up questions after the help was provided than did the other students.

A review of 54 protocols of outpatients, diagnosed according to the DSM-IIIR Axis II criteria as being "Passive-Dependent," includes 41 (79%) in which p exceeds a by more than one point; and 33 of the 41 records contain at least one Fd answer. Among 79 outpatients who, in a two-month rating after treatment began, were described by therapists as being "excessively passive" in their approach to treatment, 56 (71%) had a:p ratios in their pretreatment records in which *p* exceeded *a* by more than one point. A review of a large sample of pretreatment outpatient records ($N = 860$) reveals about 30% have *a:p* protocols in which *p* exceeds *a* by more than one point; however, that finding is somewhat misleading. When the group is subdivided by other response styles, a different picture evolves. For instance, the cells created by taking only subjects who have a High *Lambda* Style, that is, with a *Lambda* value of 1.0 or higher ($N = 304$), and then subdividing that group by the *EB* style (introversive, extratensive, ambient), reveal that 49% of the 86 introversive subjects show the passive style as do 30% of the 166 ambient subjects. But, none of the 52 extratensive subjects in this group display the passive feature. Similarly, when the remaining 556 patients in the total group, who do not have a positive *Lambda* value, are subdivided by *EB* style, 136 of 247 (57%) introversive subjects manifest this passive feature as contrasted with 20 of the 148 (14%) ambient subjects and 12 of the 168 (7%) extratensive subjects. This suggests that the tendency toward a passive style is much more common among those having an ideational style, or those who do not have a well-fixed style, than among those who are much more involved with their environment, as are typically those with extratensive styles. Thus, the presence of a passive behavioral style, as represented by $p > a + 1$, should be regarded as being much more deviant when found in the protocol of an extratensive subject, and as such, is probably much more disruptive to the psychology of the person.

THE HYPERVIGILANT (*HVI*) STYLE

If the hypervigilant is positive, a hypervigilant style can be assumed to exist as a core element of the psychological structure of the subject. The hypervigilant person uses considerable energy to maintain a relatively continuous state of preparedness. This anticipatory or hyperalert state seems to have its origins in a negative or mistrusting attitude toward the environment. People such as this probably feel quite vulnerable, and as a consequence formulate and implement behaviors very cautiously. They are quite preoccupied with issues of personal space and very guarded in their interpersonal relations. Typically they do not have sustained close relationships unless they feel in control of the interactions. They do not expect closeness and often become very suspicious about gestures of closeness by others. While this feature is not necessarily pathological, exacerbations of it often produce paranoid-like manifestations.

RESEARCH RELATED TO HYPOTHESES BASED ON THE *HVI*

The HVI evolved from attempts to validate a cluster of five variables which, at first glance, appeared to be related to paranoid characteristics (Exner, 1986, p. 470). In studying the cluster in more detail, it became obvious that the term paranoid was not really appropriate. The cluster had first been discovered during a study of 150 paranoid schizophrenics. In that sample, more than 70% were positive for all five variables and more than 85% were positive for at least four of the five. In contrast, only 13% of a comparison group of 150 schizophrenics who manifest no paranoid features had all five variables positive and only 17% were positive for four of the five. The findings seemed conceptually logical because of validational data related to each of the five variables: the absence of *T* tends to indicate more guarded and distant relations with others; an emphasis on *Hd* and *Ad* responses usually involves head, profiles, and so on; elevations in S correlate with negativism and anger; and elevations in Zf and Zd indicate extensive but cautious processing. The next step involved a review of the protocols of 20 outpatients, diagnosed as paranoid personality disorder. All five variables were positive in 12 of the 20 cases, and at least four of the five variables were positive in 16 of the cases. This seemed to confirm the initial hypothesis that the cluster did, indeed, relate to paranoid features.

Unfortunately, additional findings concerning false positive cases required that the conceptual model for the cluster to be reconsidered. First, the five variables were sometimes positive for patients who do not manifest any obvious paranoid characteristics, and four of the five variables were positive for a substantial percentage of several groups. For instance, all five appeared positive in about 10% of a randomly drawn group of 200 depressives, and four of the five were positive for nearly 20% of that group. Similarly, all five variables were positive among 10% of a randomly drawn group of 100 character disorders, and four of the five were positive in more than 30% of that group. In fact, at least four of the five variables were positive among 48 (8%) of the original normative sample of 600 adult nonpatient's records.

These findings prompted another series of discriminant function analyses for the original samples of 150 paranoid schizophrenics and 20 paranoid personality disorders plus a group of 200 randomly drawn adult nonpatients and a second group of 200 outpatients for whom considerable information regarding behaviors, relationships, and progress in treatment had been provided from three sources, (1) the patient, (2) the therapist, and (3) a significant other. This latter group provided an excellent source of cross-validational data.

The results of the discriminant function analyses for the combined group of paranoid schizophrenic and paranoid personality disorders broadened the cluster to include seven variables but also revealed that one of the variables accounted for nearly half of the variance. It is $T = 0$. Consequently, a new index was created in which the absence of T is prerequisite. If that condition is positive, the remaining tests in the index proceed, but if T is present in the record, the entire index is considered to have a negative result. Ultimately, an eighth variable was added, and in light of various studies the decision evolved to identify it as a method of detecting the presence of a hypervigilant state.

The HVI is positive for 132 of the 150 (88%) paranoid schizophrenic sample and 18 of the 20 paranoid personality disorders. But it is also positive among small segments of other groups. For example, it is positive for about 10% of the first-admission inpatient depressives reference group ($N = 315$), 7% of the character disorders reference group ($N = 180$), and about 9% of the outpatient reference sample ($N = 440$). It is also positive for about 3% of the adult nonpatient reference sample, and although it is not positive for any nonpatient children in the normative samples for ages 5 through 10, it does appear in 1% to 3% of the protocols of nonpatient children for ages 11 to 16. It seems likely that these are *not* false positive cases.

Probably the best understanding of the HVI is derived from the nontest data available for the sample of 200 outpatients mentioned earlier, which was used as one of the groups to develop the index. Only 23 of those subjects were positive on the HVI, but they form a rather discrete sample. Interestingly, only three of the 23 subjects were described by their therapist as having paranoid-like features, or by their significant other as being irrationally suspicious of others. Instead, they were uniformly identified as people who tended to be hyperalert during most of their daily routines. This hyperalertness was described by most of the therapists as like a subtle state of apprehensiveness or pessimistic anticipation in which the subject assumes a psychological preparedness even though there may be no clues or stimuli in the environment to warrant it. They tend to view the world more cynically than most and tend to avoid creating close relations with others. In fact, most are described as being more mistrusting of others, and overly concerned with issues of personal space. They are very slow to respond to treatment, and 8 of the 23 subjects terminated prematurely.

Although the general description of those positive on the HVI is derived from a relatively small sample of subjects, the striking homogeneity among the reports of therapists and significant others argues for their validity. Apparently, these are people who consider themselves to be potential victims of the environment and believe that they must be alert to avoid such victimization. Obviously, if this set or style becomes magnified or intensified as a result of pathology, more direct paranoid-like features are likely to manifest as in the instance of the group diagnosed as paranoid personality disorder and the group diagnosed as paranoid schizophrenic.

SUMMARY

The presence of any of the response styles described above will have a substantial impact on the psychological structure and functioning of a subject. If styles or traits are considered in the context of a hierarchy, any of these six features usually will dominate or afford direction to the manifestations of other traits or styles that may be present in the psychological makeup of a person. Such domination is not inevitable in every situation, as circumstances may occur in which the presence of some less important disposition will take on special importance in light of the given situation. In those instances, a style that ordinarily is less dominant may become more dominant temporarily, and as such, will be the determining factor that directs decisions and behaviors. But those episodes are transient and, in general, the more basic styles will be responsible for forming the majority of decisions and behaviors.

It is important to emphasize that some of these more dominating features are often observed among the records of children and young adolescents. While they may be quite influential with regard to the behaviors of the moment, there is no reason to assume that their presence will persist into later years because continuing growth and experience regularly lead to change in the youngster. Many children go through periods in which a High *Lambda* type approach to the world is the most economical and least demanding. Similarly, most children rely mainly on an extratensive approach to problem solving at one time or another during their developmental years. The exquisite self-centeredness of the reflection-related style is not at all uncommon in younger subjects, and a marked tendency to be passive in social situations is often a convenient method for the younger person to deal with the complexities of the environment. On the other hand, when introversiveness or hypervigilance are noted in a younger subject, there is a strong likelihood that those features will be carried on through their developmental years into adulthood.

Some subjects, both children and adults, will give protocols in which none of these six basic styles are present. If that occurs in the protocol of a child, it should not be cause for concern because some additional stylistic features can be expected to evolve with development. However, when that occurs in the record of an adult, it raises some cause for concern. Obviously, the lack of a High *Lambda* Style, a reflection-related style, a passive style, or a hypervigilant style are all positive findings; but the absence of either an introversive or extratensive style means that the subject is an ambitent, which is not a positive finding for an adult. This is the case for the L.S. protocol, and the important issue now is what are the stylistic features in the psychological organization of this 26-year-old male, and how are they manifest in his functioning? One answer to this question is found in determining the search strategy for his protocol. The first positive Key variable was $D < Adj$ $D,$ causing the beginning interpretation of his record to focus on the cluster of variables related to controls, followed by a search through the variables in the array concerning situational stress. The remaining search routine is dictated by the presence of the first positive tertiary variable, the OBS is positive. OBS is another variable that, when positive, reflects a marked response style, not necessarily as potent as those represented by the Key variables, but nonetheless, highly important to any understanding of how L.S. tends to function in most situations. A positive OBS indicates that the remaining search routine will begin with a review of the three clusters that constitute the cognitive triad, processing, mediation, and ideation. These clusters are the subject matter for the next chapter, and the L.S. protocol will be addressed in detail as each are discussed.

REFERENCES

Abrams, E. W. (1955) Predictions of intelligence from certain Rorschach factors. *Journal of Clinical Psychology,* **11,** 81–84.

Allen, R. M., Manne, S. H., and Stiff, M. (1951) The role of color in Rorschach's Test: A preliminary normative report on a college student population. *Journal of Projective Techniques,* **15,** 235–242.

Altus, W. D. (1958) Group Rorschach and Q-L discrepancies on the ACE. *Psychological Reports,* **4,** 469.

Ames, L. B. (1960) Constancy of content in Rorschach responses. *Journal of Genetic Psychology,* **96,** 145–164.

Ames, L. B., Learned, J., Metraux, R., and Walker, R. N. (1952) *Child Rorschach Responses.* New York: Harper & Row.

Ames, L. B., Metraux, R. W., and Walker, R. N. (1971) *Adolescent Rorschach Responses.* New York: Brunner/Mazel.

Arluck, E. W. (1940) A study of some personality differences between epileptics and normals. *Rorschach Research Exchange,* **4,** 154–156.

Bash, K. W. (1955) Einstellungstypus and Erlebnistypus: C. G. Jung and Herman Rorschach. *Journal of Projective Techniques,* **19,** 236–242.

Baughman, E. E. (1959) An experimental analysis of the relationship between stimulus structure and behavior in the Rorschach. *Journal of Projective Techniques,* **23,** 134–183.

Beck, S. J. (1944) *Rorschach's Test. I: Basic Processes.* New York: Grune & Stratton.

Beck, S. J. (1945) *Rorschach's Test. II: A Variety of Personality Pictures.* New York: Grune & Stratton.

Beck, S. J. (1960) *The Rorschach Experiment: Ventures in Blind Diagnosis.* New York: Grune & Stratton.

Beck, S. J., Beck, A., Levitt, E. E., and Molish, H. B. (1961) *Rorschach's Test. I: Basic Processes,* (3rd Ed.). New York: Grune & Stratton.

Bendick, M. R., and Klopfer, W. G. (1964). The effects of sensory deprivation and motor inhibition on Rorschach movement responses. *Journal of Projective Techniques,* **28,** 261–264.

Beri, J., and Blacker, E. (1956) External and internal stimulus factors in Rorschach performance. *Journal of Consulting Psychology,* **20,** 1–7.

Blatt, S. J., and Feirstein, A. (1977) Cardiac response and personality organization. *Journal of Consulting and Clinical Psychology,* **45,** 111–123.

Brennen, M., and Richard, S. (1943) Use of the Rorschach Test in predicting hypnotizability, *Bulletin of the Menninger Clinic, 7,* 183–187.

Buhler, C., and LeFever, D. (1977) A Rorschach study on the psychological characteristics of alcoholics. *Quarterly Journal of Studies on Alcoholism, 8,* 197–260.

Chu, A. Y., and Exner, J. E. (1981) EB style as related to distractibility in a calculation task. Workshops Study No. 280 (unpublished), Rorschach Workshops.

Cocking, R. R., Dana, J. M., and Dana, R. H. (1969) Six constructs to define Rorschach M: A response. *Journal of Projective Techniques and Personality Assessment, 33,* 322–323.

Cooper, L., and Caston, J. (1970) Physical activity and increases in M response. *Journal of Projective Techniques and Personality Assessment, 34,* 295–301.

Crumpton, E. (1956) The influence of color on the Rorschach Test. *Journal of Projective Techniques, 20,* 150–158.

Dana, R. H. (1968) Six constructs to define Rorschach M. *Journal of Projective Techniques and Personality Assessment, 32,* 138–145.

Dubrovner, R. J., Von Lackum, W. J., and Jost, H. A. (1950) A study of the effect of color on productivity and reaction time in the Rorschach Test. *Journal of Clinical Psychology, 6,* 331–336.

Dudek, S. Z. (1968) M an active energy system correlating Rorschach M with ease of creative expression. *Journal of Projective Techniques and Personality Assessment, 32,* 453–461.

Evans, R. B., and Mormorston, J. (1964) Rorschach signs of brain damage in cerebral thrombosis. *Perceptual Motor Skills, 18,* 977–988.

Exner, J. E. (1959) The influence of chromatic and achromatic color in the Rorschach. *Journal of Projective Techniques, 23,* 418–425.

Exner, J. E. (1962) The effect of color on productivity in Cards VIII, IX, X of the Rorschach. *Journal of Projective Techniques, 26,* 30–33.

Exner, J. E. (1969) Rorschach responses as an index of narcissism. *Journal of Projective Techniques and Personality Assessment, 33,* 324–330.

Exner, J. E. (1973) The Self Focus Sentence Completion: A study of egocentricity. *Journal of Personality Assessment, 37,* 437–455.

Exner, J. E. (1974) *The Rorschach: A Comprehensive System. Volume 1.* New York: Wiley.

Exner, J. E. (1978) *The Rorschach: A Comprehensive System. Volume 2. Current research and advanced interpretation.* New York: Wiley.

Exner, J. E. (1983) Rorschach assessment. In I. B. Weiner (Ed.) *Clinical Methods in Psychology,* (2nd Ed.). New York: Wiley.

Exner, J. E. (1986) *The Rorschach: A Comprehensive System. Volume 1: Basic foundations,* (2nd Ed.). New York: Wiley.

Exner, J. E. (1987) The search for projection. *Alumni Newsletter.* Asheville, N.C.: Rorschach Workshops.

Exner, J. E. (1988) COP. *Alumni Newsletter.* Asheville, N.C.: Rorschach Workshops.

Exner, J. E. (1990) *EB* Pervasive (EBPer) *Alumni Newsletter.* Asheville, N.C.: Rorschach Workshops.

Exner, J. E. (1991) *The Rorschach: A Comprehensive System. Volume 2: Interpretation,* (2nd Ed.). New York: Wiley.

Exner, J. E., and Armbruster, G. L. (1979) Correlations between some Rorschach variables and Zuckerman sensation seeking scores. Workshops Study No. 252 (unpublished), Rorschach Workshops.

Exner, J. E., Armbruster, G. L., and Viglione, D. (1978) The temporal stability of some Rorschach features. *Journal of Personality Assessment, 42,* 474–482.

Exner, J. E., and Kazaoka, K. (1978) Dependency gestures of 16 assertiveness trainees as related to

Rorschach movement responses. Workshops Study No. 261 (unpublished), Rorschach Workshops.

Exner, J. E., and Murillo, L. G. (1975) Early prediction of posthospitalization relapse. *Journal of Psychiatric Research,* **12,** 231–237.

Exner, J. E., and Murillo, L. G. (1977) A long-term follow up of schizophrenics treated with regressive ECT. *Diseases of the Nervous System,* **38,** 162–168.

Exner, J. E., and Sanglade, A. A. (1992) Rorschach changes following brief and short term therapy. *Journal of Personality Assessment,* **59,** 59–71.

Exner, J. E., and Thomas, E. E. (1982) Postural–gestural behaviors among introversives and extratensives during a structured interview. Workshops Study No. 292 (unpublished) Rorschach Workshops.

Exner, J. E., Thomas, E. A., and Martin, L. S. (1980) Alterations in GSR and cardiac and respiratory rates in Introversives and Extratensives during problem solving. Workshops Study No. 272 (unpublished), Rorschach Workshops.

Exner, J. E., Thomas, E. A., and Mason, B. (1985) Children's Rorschach's: Description and prediction. *Journal of Personality Assessment,* **49,** 13–20.

Exner, J. E., Viglione, D. J., and Gillespie, R. (1984) Relationships between Rorschach variables as relevant to the interpretation of structural data. *Journal of Personality Assessment,* **48,** 65–70.

Exner, J. E., and Weiner, I. B. (1982) *The Rorschach: A Comprehensive System. Volume 3. Assessment of children and adolescents.* New York: Wiley.

Exner, J. E., Weiss, L. J., Coleman, M., and Rose, R. B. (1979) Rorschach variables for a group of occupationally successful dancers. Workshops Study No. 250 (unpublished), Rorschach Workshops.

Exner, J. E., Wylie, J. R., and Kline, J. R. (1977) Variations in Rorschach performance during a 28 month interval as related to seven intervention modalities. Workshops Study No. 240 (unpublished), Rorschach Workshops.

Ford, M. (1946) The application of the Rorschach Test to young children. *University of Minnesota Child Welfare Monographs, No. 23.*

Forsyth, R. P. (1959) The influence of color, shading and Welsh anxiety level on Elizur Rorschach content analysis of anxiety and hostility. *Journal of Projective Techniques,* **23,** 207–213.

Frankle, A. H. (1953) Rorschach human movement and human content responses as indices of the adequacy of interpersonal relationships of social work students. Unpublished doctoral dissertation, University of Chicago.

Gibby, R. G., Stotsky, B. A., Harrington, R. L., and Thomas, R. W. (1955) Rorschach determinant shift among hallucinatory and delusional patients. *Journal of Consulting Psychology,* **19,** 44–46.

Goldfarb, W. (1945) Psychological privation in infancy and subsequent adjustment. *American Journal of Orthopsychiatry,* **15,** 249–254.

Goldfarb, W. (1949) Rorschach test differences between family reared, institution reared, and schizophrenic children. *American Journal of Orthopsychiatry,* **19,** 624–633.

Goldman, R. (1960) Changes in Rorschach performance and clinical improvement in schizophrenia. *Journal of Consulting Psychology,* **24,** 403–407.

Grayson, H. M. (1956) Rorschach productivity and card preferences as influenced by experimental variation of color and shading. *Journal of Projective Techniques,* **20,** 288–296.

Guirdham, A. (1936) The diagnosis of depression by the Rorschach Test. *British Journal of Medical Psychology,* **16,** 130–145.

Hafner, A. J. (1958) Response time and Rorschach behavior. *Journal of Clinical Psychology,* **14,** 154–155.

Halpern, F. (1940) Rorschach interpretation of the personality structure of schizophrenics who benefit from insulin therapy. *Psychiatric Quarterly,* **14,** 826–833.

Hammer, E. F., and Jacks, I. (1955) A study of Rorschach flexor and extensor human movement responses. *Journal of Clinical Psychology,* **11,** 63–67.

Henry, E. M., and Rotter, J. B. (1956) Situational influences on Rorschach responses. *Journal of Consulting Psychology,* **20,** 457–462.

Hersh, C. (1962) The cognitive functioning of the creative person: A developmental analysis. *Journal of Projective Techniques,* **26,** 193–200.

Hertzman, M., Orlansky, D., and Seitz, C. P. (1944) Personality organization and anoxia tolerance. *Psychosomatic Medicine,* **6,** 317–331.

Kallstedt, F. E. (1952) A Rorschach study of 66 adolescents. *Journal of Clinical Psychology,* **8,** 129–132.

Keehn, J. D. (1954) The response to color and ego functions: A critique in light of recent experimental evidence. *Psychological Bulletin,* **51,** 65–67.

Kelley, D., Margulies, H., and Barrera, S. (1941) The stability of the Rorschach method as demonstrated in electric convulsive therapy cases. *Rorschach Research Exchange,* **5,** 44–48.

King, G. F. (1960) Rorschach human movement and delusional content. *Journal of Projective Techniques,* **24,** 161–163.

Klatskin, E. H. (1952) An analysis of the effect of the test situation upon the Rorschach record: Formal scoring characteristics. *Journal of Projective Techniques,* **16,** 193–199.

Klein, G. S., and Schlesinger, H. G. (1951) Perceptual attitudes toward instability: Prediction of apparent movement experiences from Rorschach responses. *Journal of Personality,* **19,** 289–302.

Klopfer, B., Ainsworth, M., Klopfer, W., and Holt, R. (1954) *Developments in the Rorschach Technique.* Vol. 1. Yonkers-on-Hudson, N.Y.: World Book.

Klopfer, B., and Kelley, D. (1942) *The Rorschach Technique.* Yonkers-on-Hudson, N.Y.: World Book.

Klopfer, B., Kirkner, F., Wisham, W., and Baker, G. (1951) Rorschach prognostic rating scale. *Journal of Projective Techniques,* **15,** 425–428.

Klopfer, B., and Margulies, H. (1941) Rorschach reactions in early childhood. *Rorschach Research Exchange,* **5,** 1–23.

Langmuir, C. R. (1958) *Varieties of decision making behavior: A report of experiences with the Logical Analysis Device.* Washington, D.C.: American Psychological Association.

Lerner, B. (1966) Rorschach movement and dreams: A validation study using drug-induced deprivation. *Journal of Abnormal Psychology,* **71,** 75–87.

Levine, M., Glass, H., and Meltzoff, J. (1957) The inhibition process. Rorschach human movement response and intelligence. *Journal of Consulting Psychology,* **21,** 45–49.

Levine, M., and Spivack, G. (1962) Human movement responses and verbal expression in the Rorschach Test. *Journal of Projective Techniques,* **26,** 299–304.

Linton, H. B. (1954) Rorschach correlates of response to suggestion. *Journal of Abnormal and Social Psychology,* **49,** 75–83.

Lipton, M. B., Tamarin, S., and Latesta, P. (1951) Test evidence of personality change and prognosis by means of the Rorschach and Wechsler-Bellevue tests on 17 insulin treated paranoid schizophrenics. *Psychiatric Quarterly,* **25,** 434–444.

Loveland, N. T., and Singer, M. T. (1959) Projective test assessment of the effects of sleep deprivation. *Journal of Projective Techniques,* **23,** 323–334.

Mann, L. (1956) The relation of Rorschach indices of extratension and introversion to a measure of responsiveness to the immediate environment. *Journal of Consulting Psychology,* **20,** 114–118.

Mason, B., and Exner, J. E. (1984) Correlations between WAIS subtests and nonpatient adult

Rorschach data. Workshops Study No. 289 (unpublished), Rorschach Workshops.

Meyer, B. T. (1951) An investigation of color shock in the Rorschach Test. *Journal of Clinical Psychology, 7,* 367–370.

Mindness, H. (1955) Analytic psychology and the Rorschach test. *Journal of Projective Techniques, 19,* 243–252.

Mirin, B. (1955) The Rorschach human movement response and role taking behavior. *Journal of Nervous and Mental Disorders, 122,* 270–275.

Molish, H. B. (1965) Psychological structure in four groups of children. In J. S. Beck (Ed.), *Psychological Processes in the Schizophrenic Adaptation.* New York: Grune & Stratton.

Molish, H. B. (1967) Critique and problems of the Rorschach. A survey. In S. J. Beck and H. B. Molish, *Rorschach's Test. II: A Variety of Personality Pictures,* (2nd Ed.). New York: Grune & Stratton.

Ogdon, D. P., and Allee, R. (1959) Rorschach relationships with intelligence among familial mental defectives. *American Journal of Mental Deficiency, 63,* 889–896.

Orlinski, D. E. (1966) Rorschach test correlates of dreaming and dream recall. *Journal of Projective Techniques and Personality Assessment, 30,* 250–253.

Page, H. A (1957) Studies in fantasy-daydreaming frequency and Rorschach scoring categories. *Journal of Consulting Psychology, 21,* 111–114.

Palmer, J. O. (1963) Alterations in Rorschach's experience balance under conditions of food and sleep deprivation: A construct validation study. *Journal of Projective Techniques, 27,* 208–213.

Paulsen, A. (1941) Rorschachs of school beginners. *Rorschach Research Exchange, 5,* 24–29.

Perlman, J. A. (1951) Color and the validity of the Rorschach 8-9-10 per cent. *Journal of Consulting Psychology, 15,* 122–126.

Phillips, L., and Smith, J. G. (1953) *Rorschach Interpretation: Advanced Technique.* New York: Grune & Stratton.

Piotrowski, Z. (1937) The Rorschach ink-blot method in organic disturbances of the central nervous system. *Journal of Nervous and Mental Disorders, 86,* 525–537.

Piotrowski, Z. (1939) Rorschach manifestations of improvement in insulin treated schizophrenics. *Psychosomatic Medicine, 1,* 508–526.

Piotrowski, Z. (1940) Positive and negative Rorschach organic reactions. *Rorschach Research Exchange, 4,* 147–151.

Piotrowski, Z. (1957) *Perceptanalysis.* New York: Macmillan.

Piotrowski, Z. (1960) The movement score. In M. Rickers-Ovsiankina (Ed.), *Rorschach Psychology.* New York: Wiley.

Piotrowski, Z., and Bricklin, B. (1958) A long-term prognostic criterion for schizophrenics based on Rorschach data. *Psychiatric Quarterly Supplement, 32,* 315–329.

Piotrowski, Z., and Bricklin, B. (1961) A second validation of a long-term Rorschach prognostic index for schizophrenic patients. *Journal of Consulting Psychology, 25,* 123–128.

Rabin, A. I., and Beck, S. J. (1950) Genetic aspects of some Rorschach factors. *American Journal of Orthopsychiatry, 20,* 595–599.

Rabin, A., Papania, N., and McMichael, A. (1954) Some effects of alcohol on Rorschach performance. *Journal of Clinical Psychology, 10,* 252–255.

Rabinovitch, M. S., Kennard, M. A., and Fister, W. P. (1955) Personality correlates of electroencephalographic findings. *Canadian Journal of Psychology, 9,* 29–41.

Rapaport, D., Gill, M., and Schafer, R. (1946) *Psychological Diagnostic Testing.* Vol. 2. Chicago: Yearbook Publishers.

Raychaudhuri, M., and Mukerji, K. (1971) Homosexual-narcissistic "reflections" in the Rorschach:

An examination of Exner's diagnostic Rorschach signs. *Rorschachiana Japonica,* **12,** 119–126.

Rees, W. L., and Jones, A. M. (1951) An evaluation of the Rorschach Test as a prognostic aid in the treatment of schizophrenics by insulin coma therapy, electronarcosis, electroconvulsive therapy, and leucotomy. *Journal of Mental Science,* **97,** 681–689.

Richter, R. H., and Winter, W. D. (1966) Holtzman ink-blot correlates of creative potential. *Journal of Projective Techniques and Personality Assessment,* **30,** 62–67.

Rickers-Ovsiankina, M. (1943) Some theoretical considerations regarding the Rorschach method. *Rorschach Research Exchange,* **7,** 14–53.

Rorschach, H. (1921) *Psychodiagnostics.* Bern: Bircher (Transl. Hans Huber Verlag, 1942).

Rosenthal, M. (1954) Some behavioral correlates of the Rorschach experience balance. Unpublished doctoral dissertation, Boston University.

Sapenfield, B., and Buker, S. L. (1949) Validity of the Rorschach 8-9-10 percent as an indicator of responsiveness to color. *Journal of Consulting Psychology,* **13,** 268–271.

Schachtel, E. G. (1943) On color and affect. *Psychiatry,* **6,** 393–409.

Schafer, R. (1954) *Psychoanalytic Interpretation in Rorschach Testing.* New York: Grune & Stratton.

Schmidt, H., and Fonda, C. (1954) Rorschach scores in the manic states. *Journal of Psychology,* **38,** 427–437.

Schulman, I. (1953) The relation between perception of movement on the Rorschach Test and levels of conceptualization. Unpublished doctoral dissertation, New York University.

Shapiro, D. (1956) Color-response and perceptual passivity. *Journal of Projective Techniques,* **20,** 52–69.

Shapiro, D. (1960) A perceptual understanding of color response. In M. Rickers-Ovsiankina (Ed.), *Rorschach Psychology.* New York: Wiley.

Sherman, M. H. (1955) A psychoanalytic definition of Rorschach determinants. *Psychoanalysis,* **3,** 68–76.

Singer, J. L. (1960) The experience type: Some behavioral correlates and theoretical implications. In M. Rickers-Ovsiankina (Ed.), *Rorschach Psychology.* New York: Wiley.

Singer, J. L., and Brown, S. L. (1977) The experience type: Some behavioral correlates and theoretical implications. In M. A. Rickers-Ovsiankina (Ed.), *Rorschach Psychology,* (pp. 325–372). Huntington, N.Y.: Robert E. Krieger.

Singer, J. L., and Herman, J. (1954) Motor and fantasy correlates of Rorschach human movement responses. *Journal of Consulting Psychology,* **18,** 325–331.

Singer, J. L., Meltzoff, J., and Goldman, G. D. (1952) Rorschach movement responses following motor inhibition and hyperactivity. *Journal of Consulting Psychology,* **16,** 359–364.

Singer, J. L., and Spohn, H. (1954) Some behavioral correlates of Rorschach's experience-type. *Journal of Consulting Psychology,* **18,** 1–9.

Sommer, R., and Sommer, D. T. (1958) Assaultiveness and two types of Rorschach color responses. *Journal of Consulting Psychology,* **22,** 57–62.

Steele, N. M., and Kahn, M. W. (1969) Kinesthesis and the Rorschach M response. *Journal of Projective Techniques and Personality Assessment,* **33,** 5–10.

Steisel, I. M. (1952) The Rorschach Test and suggestibility. *Journal of Abnormal and Social Psychology,* **47,** 607–614.

Stotsky, B. A. (1952) A comparison of remitting and nonremitting schizophrenics on psychological tests. *Journal of Abnormal and Social Psychology,* **47,** 489–496.

Swift, J. W. (1945) Rorschach responses of eighty-two pre-school children. *Rorschach Research Exchange,* **7,** 74–84.

Tanaka, F. (1958) Rorschach movement responses in relation to intelligence. *Japanese Journal of*

Educational Psychology, **6,** 85–91.

Thomas, E. A., Exner, J. E., and Baker, W. (1982) Ratings of real versus ideal self among 225 college students. Workshops Study No. 287 (unpublished), Rorschach Workshops.

Thomas, H. F. (1955) The relationship of movement responses on the Rorschach Test to the defense mechanism of projection. *Journal of Abnormal and Social Psychology,* **50,** 41–44.

Wagner, E. E., and Hoover, T. O. (1971) Exhibitionistic *M* in drum majors: A validation. *Perceptual Motor Skills,* **32,** 125–126.

Wagner, E. E., and Hoover, T. O. (1972) Behavioral implications of Rorschach's human movement response. Further validation based on exhibitionistic *M*'s. *Perceptual Motor Skills,* **35,** 27–30.

Wallen, R. (1948) The nature of color shock. *Journal of Abnormal and Social Psychology,* **43,** 346–356.

Watson, A. (1965) Objects and objectivity: A study in the relationship between narcissism and intellectual subjectivity. Unpublished doctoral dissertation, University of Chicago.

Weigel, R. B., and Exner, J. E. (1981) *EB* style and preference for interpersonal and impersonal slides among nonpatient adults. Workshop Study No. 291 (unpublished), Rorschach Workshops.

Wetherhorn, M. (1956) Flexor-extensor movement on the Rorschach. *Journal of Consulting Psychology,* **20,** 204.

Wiener-Levy, D., and Exner, J. E. (1981) The Rorschach *EA-ep* variable as related to persistence in a task frustration situation under feedback conditions. *Journal of Personality Assessment,* **45,** 118–124.

Winter, L. B., and Exner, J. E. (1973) Some psychological characteristics of some successful theatrical artists. Workshops Study No. 183 (unpublished), Rorschach Workshops.

Witkin, H. A., Dyk, R. B., Faterson, H. F., Goodenough, D. R., and Karp, S. A. (1962) *Psychological Differentiation: Studies of Development.* New York: Wiley.

Zuckerman, M. (1971) Dimensions in sensation seeking. *Journal of Consulting and Clinical Psychology,* **36,** 45–52.

CHAPTER 18

Cluster Interpretation I— The Cognitive Triad

The cognitive triad consists of three clusters that are relatively independent of each other, and yet are often closely related. They include *information processing* (the procedures involving the input of information), *cognitive mediation* (the procedures of translating or identifying information that has been input), and *ideation* (the procedures of conceptualizing the information that has been translated). Each is related to a relatively discrete feature of cognition, but the results of the operations in one feature can have a very direct influence on the operations in either of the other two features. Collectively, they represent a continuous process that forms the basis for essentially all deliberate and/or meaningful behaviors. The relationships in the process might be illustrated simply, such as:

$$INPUT \rightarrow \quad TRANSLATION \rightarrow \quad CONCEPTUALIZATION$$
$$(PROCESSING) \quad (MEDIATION) \quad (IDEATION)$$

In reality, however, the relationships can be much more complex. For instance, the conceptualization of the translation of one input may create a set that will influence the translation of a second input or even affect how the second input is processed. Similarly, a faulty or narrowed translation of one input can lead to a faulty conceptualization and/or can impact on the processing of the next input.

The interrelationships between the processes require that the three clusters be studied collectively. Typically, the triad will be approached by beginning with the data regarding processing, then reviewing the data concerning mediation, and completing the review with the data concerning ideation. But this order may not always be practical, and in some cases it is reversed to begin with the cluster regarding ideation. This is because findings concerning ideation sometimes are critically important in forming the cornerstone for understanding the psychological complexities of the subject. For instance, if schizophrenia is suspected, the critical issues are whether thinking (ideation) is seriously disturbed and whether the translation of stimuli (mediation) is markedly inaccurate. Regardless of whether the review of the triad begins with processing or ideation, it is important to remember that the findings from each cluster often will provide important clarification for the findings from the other two clusters.

Obviously, when dealing with the data in a cluster, each datum point should be approached systematically, moving in a logical progression from point to point, with the objective of formulating postulates when the accumulation of findings warrants, or ruling out the presence of some characteristics when that is appropriate. The Structural Summary page of the *Structural Summary Blank* has been organized to facilitate the procedure by placing together data for variables that are related to a single feature, such as affect, ideation, processing, self-perception, and so on. However, the composite shown in each data group does not necessarily represent all of the structural data relevant to the feature on which the cluster focuses. As noted earlier, several structural variables are related to more than one characteristic of psychological organization or functioning. For instance, the *eb* and all of the variables that contribute to its tabulation it are shown in the *Core* section as it does relate to issues of control and stress tolerance. But, the *eb* and some of the variables related to it are also reviewed again during the study of data concerning affect and ideation. Moreover, although the structural data in a section are *always* the first to be reviewed, the interpreter often will be diverted from the structure to the sequence of scores or to the actual responses in the protocol.

INFORMATION PROCESSING

Although all of the variables in the processing cluster are interrelated, they also consist of two subclusters. One affords some information regarding processing effort or motivation (*L, OBS, HVI, Zf, W:D:Dd, W:M*), whereas the second provides more information about the quality and efficiency of the processing (*DQ, Zd, PSV,* Sequencing). Four of these variables, when they are positive, seem to be more basic or dominant in processing activity and clearly relate to stylistic or trait-like features. The four that reflect a marked kind of psychological consistency are the High *Lambda* style, a positive *OBS* or *HVI,* and the *Zd* score that exceeds +3.0, which represents a tendency to invest more effort than is customary in scanning activity. This feature has been described as *overincorporation* (Exner, 1978), as it involves an orientation to approach each new stimulus field with caution and thoroughness, even though much more effort is required. Some of the other variables in the cluster also may reflect stylistic or trait-like features in processing, but none appear to have the dominating influence that is manifested by the basic four even though they might reflect very sturdy or consistent features in the usual processing activity of the subject.

PROCESSING AND THE HIGH *LAMBDA* STYLE

As discussed in Chapter 17, if the value for *Lambda* is 1.0 or greater, it signals that a basic response style exists involving a marked tendency to narrow or simplify stimulus fields perceived as complex or ambiguous. Although this coping style reflects a form of psychological economizing that is usually more influential in mediating activity, it may affect the operations involved in processing information and as such, can create a potential for a higher frequency of behaviors that do not coincide with social demands and/or expectations. High *Lambda* introversive nonpatients appear to process no differently than Low *Lambda* introversive subjects. They organize at about the same rate and show no indications of neglect when processing a new stimulus field. On the other hand, High *Lambda* ambient and extratensive nonpatients do appear to take a more lackadaisical approach in their processing actions. They organize less than is expected and tend toward offering more simplistic answers.

Among outpatients, the pattern is somewhat different. The High *Lambda* introversive and ambient outpatients seem to display processing activities that differ very little from nonpatients in general, but the High *Lambda* extratensive outpatients appear to be much less involved, and much more casual in their processing activities.

Collectively, the data suggest that when a High *Lambda* style is present, it will not necessarily impact on the processing activities of the subject, unless the subject is *extratensive*. When the latter exists it seems probable that less effort will be expended, although there is no reason to assume that the lower effort will necessarily result in faulty input. Conversely, an effort that is lower than expected does create a potential for some negligence in processing.

PROCESSING AND THE OBSESSIVE STYLE INDEX

If the *OBS* is positive, it is very likely that the subject is prone to be perfectionistic, overly preoccupied with details, often indecisive, and likely to have some difficulty in expressing emotion, especially negative emotion. People who are positive on the *OBS* usually process information carefully and methodically. They often have an above-average number of answers that are organized (*Zf*) and frequently will be *overincorporators* in their scanning activity (*Zd* > *+3.0*). They are strongly influenced by their needs to be correct or conventional, and because of this, they tend to give more overelaborated descriptions in their use of form and often give a higher number of Popular answers. The cautious, perfectionistic tendency manifested by people with this style is not necessarily pathological; however, these features can become very counterproductive in many situations in which time pressures exist, or in which the complexity of the situation at hand seems overwhelming. When either of these circumstances occur, processing activity tends to become loose and chaotic and frequently leads to faulty mediation or translation of the situation.

RESEARCH RELATED TO THE OBS VARIABLE

The *OBS* evolved during the course of testing and cross-validating the *SCZI* and the *DEPI*, as it was important to test those indices against other psychiatric groups that included subjects who were neither schizophrenic nor seriously depressed. Among those were two groups, one consisting of 32 outpatients who had been diagnosed as obsessive-compulsive disorders, and a second group of 114 outpatients who had been defined as compulsive personality disorders. Most cases included anxiety as the presenting symptom, but 33 also were marked by impairing phobic features.

A discriminant function analysis for these 146 protocols did produce considerable homogeneity among seven conditions for six variables. In fact, when those conditions were applied in various combinations, 101 of the 146 subjects (69%) were correctly identified. Two of the conditions weigh much more heavily than do the other five (*FQ*+ and *X*+ > .89), thus the calculation of the *OBS* includes any of four combinations of variables that yield a positive finding.

An eighth condition, *EB* style = introversive, seems to be quite relevant to correctly identifying the presence of the style but is not currently included as a relevant variable. In the normative samples, the *OBS* is positive for two of the 1390 nonpatient children protocols and in 13 of the 700 (2%) nonpatient adult records. The latter include six introversive subjects, five extratensive subjects and two ambitents. However, when the data for the relatively large sample of outpatients ($N = 860$) are examined, 130 of 240 (54%) introversive subjects having a value for *Lambda* of less than 1.0 are positive on the *OBS*. Similarly, 10 of 86 (12%) of introversive subjects having values for *Lambda* greater than 0.99 are positive on the *OBS*. *None of the remaining subjects, either extratensive or ambitent* in the group ($N = 610$) are positive on the *OBS* regardless of the *Lambda* value. Likewise, the frequency of positive *OBS* findings in other groups is essentially zero. It is not positive among any cases in the schizophrenic, depressive, or character disorder reference groups.

These findings are somewhat difficult to understand. If the *OBS* style were positive only among introversive subjects, regardless of whether they are patients or nonpatients, the conclusion would be reasonably straightforward; that is, an ideational style is prerequisite for the *OBS* style. But the almost random-like distribution of positive *OBS* findings among nonpatients suggests that the style can occur in tandem with many other basic features of the personality, but it apparently creates a higher risk for problems in adjustment when it exists in the introversive subject.

PROCESSING AND THE HYPERVIGILANT STYLE

If the *HVI* is positive, it signals a state of hyperalertness. People such as this are guarded and mistrusting of the environment. They usually are very concerned about processing information and often invest excessive energy to ensure that all features of a stimulus field are surveyed carefully. In many instances, this breeds a superior processing effort; but if pathology is present, the hyperalertness often takes on paranoid-like characteristics in which overly suspicious preoccupations cause an unusual concern for details that sometimes supersedes concern for the whole stimulus field. When this occurs, the processing activity often becomes chaotic and inefficient and tends to promote faulty mediation.

PROCESSING AND THE OVERINCORPORATIVE STYLE— THE *ZD* SCORE

The *Zd* score clearly relates to processing efficiency, that is, does the input occur with relative ease and is it still accurate? Some people are able to process new material quite easily and appear to be comfortable with the process. Others seem less secure about their processing operations and exert extra effort to make sure that no salient features of a field have been neglected. Another group, comprised largely of children seem less concerned about the input and tend to scan a field somewhat haphazardly. These three groups are usually identified correctly by using the *Zd* score.

If the value for *Zd* is less than -3.0 it usually signifies an *underincorporative* form of scanning activity. In other words, the subject scans hastily and haphazardly and often may neglect critical bits or cues that exist in a stimulus field. Underincorporation creates a potential for faulty mediation and can lead to less effective patterns of behavior.

If the value for *Zd* is greater than $+3.0$ it usually indicates the presence of an *overincorporative* style. Overincorporation is an enduring trait-like characteristic that prompts the subject to invest more effort and energy into scanning activities. Although somewhat less efficient because of the added effort involved, overincorporation is often an asset because the cautious, thorough approach to scanning usually ensures that all stimulus cues are included in the input.

RESEARCH RELATED TO THE *ZD* SCORE

Approximately 77% of nonpatient adolescents and adults have *Zd* scores that fall within the range of +3.0 to −3.0. The mean *Zd* for most groups, older than age 10, hovers around zero. Younger children tend to have a greater incidence of *Zd* scores that are less than zero, and substantial numbers of 5-, 6-, and 7-year-olds will have *Zd* scores less than −3.0. When the Comprehensive System was first formulated, information concerning the interpretive use of the score was very limited. It was included in the System because deviations from the +3.0 to −3.0 range occurred much more frequently among psychiatric subjects than nonpatients, and this suggested the possibility of some problems in cognitive processing. Subsequent research has shed considerable light on that original speculation.

Exner and Leura (1974) found that children with *Zd* scores of less than −3.0 made more errors in a "Simon Says" game than did children with *Zd* scores in the +3.0 to −3.0 range. They also found that children with *Zd* scores greater than +3.0 made significantly fewer errors in the game than did children with scores in the average range. Leura and Exner (1977) found *Zd* scores of less than −3.0 in the protocols of 14 of 15 children who had been diagnosed as "hyperactive" and who had abnormal EEGs. Exner (1978) reported that *Zd* scores exceeding +3.0 appear more frequently in the protocols of subjects who have obsessive or perfectionistic personality features, whereas *Zd* scores of less than −3.0 appear more frequently in the records of subjects who manifest more impulsive-like decision operations in problem-solving behaviors. Based on the composite of findings, Exner (1978) concluded that subjects with *Zd* scores less than −3.0 have a tendency to be negligent in processing information, and this creates the probability that some of their responses will be formulated before a stimulus field is fully mediated.

The distinction between underincorporation and overincorporation, as contrasted with those with *Zd* scores in the average range, has been confirmed by several other findings. Exner and Caraway (1974) found that overincorporators are much more reluctant than underincorporators to make guesses about movie and book titles, and proverbs, when only parts of words are displayed. Bryant and Exner (1974) tested over- and underincorporators, using the Minnesota Paper Form Board. Half of each group took the test under a 10-minute time limit and the other half took the test with no time limit. They found that the underincorporators completed almost twice as many problems as the overincorporators when working under the time limit, *but* they also made about twice as many errors. Thus the scores of the two groups were not significantly different. Under the no-time-limit condition, overincorporators attempted significantly more items and achieved significantly more correct solutions. Exner and Bryant (1975) found that underincorporators performed better in a serial learning task after 10 training trials; however, when the number of training trials was doubled, the accurate recall of the overincorporators was far superior to that of the underincorporators. Bryant, Kline, and Exner (1978) found that overincorporators averaged significantly longer times to complete the Trails B test in the Halstead–Reitan than subjects with *Zd* scores in the average range.

Exner, Bryant, and Armbruster (1979) studied the eye-scanning patterns of 12 adolescents in a matching familiar figures task. Four of the subjects were overincorporators, four were underincorporators, and four had *Zd* scores in the average range. The task involved the exposure of six target faces, each for 750 milliseconds, and each exposure followed by the exposure of a field of nine faces for an interval of 750 milliseconds. Subjects were instructed to indicate which of the field faces was the same as the target face by using a light pointer. Eye activity was recorded for the 750-millisecond intervals during which the target faces were exposed. The overincorporators averaged more than twice as many scan paths (crossing a previously viewed space again) as did the underincorporators, and significantly more than those with *Zd* scores in the average range. Overincorporators and subjects with average *Zd* scores had significantly more horizontal sweeps of the target than underincorporators, and the overincorporators also showed a greater tendency to complete vertical sweeping scans than did either of the other groups. The average number of correct identifications was slightly but not significantly greater for the average group—4.9 (overincorporators = 4.3; underincorporators = 4.3).

Sixty-three of 279 outpatients (23%) followed for 27 months by Exner (1978) had *Zd* scores of −3.5 or less at the beginning of treatment. In the first retest, after 9 months, only 17 of the 63 continued to have *Zd* scores in the underincorporator range, and only four other subjects, all of whom had *Zd* scores between 0 and −3.0 in the first test, had *Zd* scores of −3.5 or less at the first retest. The 18-month retest data show that 26 of the 279 had *Zd* scores of −3.5 or less, including 20 who had similar scores in the pretreatment test. These data suggest that underincorporation is corrected somewhat easily by most forms of intervention. The data concerning overincorporation for this group is quite different. Forty-seven of the 279 patients (17%) had *Zd* scores of +3.5 or greater in the pretreatment test. At the first retest, 71 subjects, including 42 of the original 47, had scores in the overincorporative range. The 18-month retest data show that the frequency had increased to 89 and included 69 who had been overincorporative in the first retest, and 44 of the 47 who had scores in that range in the pretreatment test. The 27-month retest data are most striking, because 102 of the 279 (37%) had *Zd* scores greater than +3.0, including 42 of the original 47 and 86 of the 89 from the second retest. A closer inspection of the data revealed that all but 3 of the 24 subjects who moved into the overincorporator range in the first retest were continuing in treatment, as were all subjects who moved into the range at the 27-month retest. Thus unlike underincorporation, which appears to be altered easily, overincorporation does not appear to change as a function of intervention. This is probably because intervention, as a process, promotes a greater attentiveness to, and searching through, of stimuli.

Underincorporation appears to be a clear liability, except for the young child, because of stimulus neglect. Conversely, overincorporation can be advantageous in a variety of situations, especially those in which careful processing of information is important. Apparently, overincorporation becomes a liability when the subject has the experience that time available for processing is insufficient. Exner and Stanley (1979) used four subjects from each of the three categories in a time estimation pilot study. Subjects were seated in a totally darkened room and asked to estimate time intervals of 2, 6, and 15 minutes. The four overincorporators each underestimated the actual amount of elapsed time for 15 minutes, but not for either of the other intervals. The underincorporators had a mixed performance, with two underestimating the two-minute intervals, but overestimating the five- and 15-minute intervals, and the remaining two overestimating all three intervals.

Although overincorporation does appear frequently among people who are more obsessive or perfectionistic, it should not be misconstrued as a good "diagnostic" indicator for that feature or for psychopathology in general. About 18% of the adult nonpatient normative sample have *Zd* scores in the overincorporative range. A review of the records of 100 hysteroid outpatients, drawn randomly from the protocol pool at the Rorschach Research Foundation, reveals that 23 have *Zd* scores greater than +3.0. Similarly, 38% of the protocols in the schizophrenic reference sample, 26% of the records in the sample of depressives, and 28% of the character disorder group have this same characteristic. In addition, nearly 25% of the nonpatient children between the ages of 10 and 16 have *Zd* scores greater than +3.0. Underincorporation is most common among younger children. Nearly 30% of nonpatient children between the ages of five and nine have *Zd* scores of less than −3.0, as contrasted with only 7% of the adult nonpatient group. The schizophrenic sample shows that 26% are underincorporators, as are 25% of the depressives and 17% of the character problems. Whereas overincorporation is probably not a viable treatment objective, underincorporation should be considered as a high priority target for change when discovered in the record of an adolescent or adult because its presence, as a cognitive tactic, can be very disruptive to other operations, especially those involving complex decision making. The data suggest that it can be altered most easily by the creation of delaying tactics, using procedures such as those described by Meichenbaum (1974).

OTHER VARIABLES RELATED TO PROCESSING EFFORT

The three other variables that afford direct information concerning the processing effort are the *Zf*, the *W:D:Dd* ratio, and the *W:M* ratio, but none of the three should be interpreted separately. The *Zf* relates to organizing activity. The frequency of organizing activity provides an indication about the extent to which the subject has approached the task, using cognitive tactics that typically are more demanding than some other mediational approaches. Answers that include a *Z* score, with the possible exception of *Wo* responses to Cards I and V, require considerably more mediational effort than is required in forming a more simplistic *D* answer that avoids any blot integration. Although some basic intellectual talent is required for *Z*, the actual frequency and type of *Z* are influenced by many other features, such as *Lambda*, *OBS*, *HVI*, and/or the presence of pathology.

Adults and younger subjects usually average between 9 and 13 *Z* responses. When the frequency exceeds 13, it suggests that the processing effort has been more extensive than expected. If the frequency is less than 9, it suggests that less effort has occurred than expected, but either of those assumptions are somewhat concrete and must be reviewed in light of other processing data.

The *W:D:Dd* ratio also relates to processing motivation. As implied above, more effort is required to formulate *W* answers to 8 of the 10 blots. Conversely, *D* answers are easier to form in all of the blots except I and V. Whereas *W* responses given to most of the blots require some organizing of the figure, several relatively discrete detail segments already exist in each blot. This lends itself to the easier formulation of multiple potential answers. Thus, when selecting answers to be delivered, it seems quite probable that many more *D* answers are available. In that context, the selection of the *D* response is compatible with the natural orientation of most subjects to accomplish the task efficiently and economically. Most subjects will give fewer *W* than *D* answers, usually in ratios ranging from 1:1.2 to as much as 1:1.8.

Dd areas tend to be less discrete and/or obvious, and the majority of *Dd* answers will require that more processing effort be expended than is involved in forming a *D* response. For that reason, the frequency of *Dd* answers is usually quite low, typically ranging from 0 to 3. The reward for that extra effort is an escape from dealing with the ambiguities of some blot areas. In other words, they tend to represent a form of avoidance through which the subject tries to create a more narrow stimulus field that is easier to handle. Most subjects give at least one *Dd* response, but if the value for *Dd* is 4 or more, and the value for *Zf* is less than 13, it usually indicates that the subject prefers to deal with less complex, more easily managed stimulus fields. This finding may represent a tendency to feel uncomfortable about decision-making capabilities, but if all, or most all of the *Dd* answers include *S* it probably reflects a negativistic set of the subject toward the test or toward the environment. Any conclusions regarding *Dd* responses must be formulated only after the Sequencing of locations scores has been reviewed.

The *W:M* ratio also concerns processing motivation or effort because elevated frequencies for *W* signal the investment of more effort than might be necessary for the task. However, this should not automatically be considered as a negative finding. If the resources of the subject are considerable, the extra effort being generated in the overselection of *W*'s may, in fact, have a very modest psychological cost to the subject. In that *M* responses relate to reasoning and higher forms of conceptualization, as well as the process of giving deliberate direction to ideational focusing, the frequency of *M* responses can be regarded as a crude index of some of the functional capabilities that are necessary for achievement-oriented activities.

Overall, adults, both patient and nonpatient, average about twice as many *W* responses as *M* responses, and approximately 70% will have a *W:M* ratio that falls in the range of 1.5:1 to 2.5:1, but those figures are misleading and *should not* be used to determine a useful range for interpreting the *W:M*. Instead, any interpretation of *W:M* must be cast in relation to the data of *EB* because introversives usually give substantially more *M* than most extratensives, and ambients usually give more *M* than extratensives but significantly less *M* than introversives. At the same time, all three groups give about the same number of *W* answers. In this context, if the frequency of *W* answers is substantially greater than the number of *M* responses—that is, for introversives if the ratio exceeds 1.5:1, for ambients if the ratio exceeds 2.2:1, and for extratensives if the ratio exceeds 3:1—it probably indicates that the subject is striving to accomplish more than is reasonable in light of current functional capacities. This postulate is strengthened in cases where the DQ distribution shows a low frequency of *DQ*+ responses, which correlate with more sophisticated quality of processing. Such findings suggest that if this tendency occurs in everyday behaviors, the probability of failure to achieve objectives is increased, and the consequent impact of those failures can often include the experience of frustration.

Although this is an unusual and possibly important finding in the record of an adult, it is relatively commonplace among children. For instance, 5- and 6-year-olds will frequently have a *W:M* ratio of 8:1 or even greater, and 9- and 10-year olds often have *W:M* ratios of 4:1 or greater. Youngsters are notorious for overestimating their capacities and setting inordinately high goals. Fortunately, they are also notorious for placing little value on most of those goals and thus are usually able to deal with the consequences of failure in a more casual way so that any impact of frustration is relatively brief.

When the frequency of *W* responses is disproportionately low in relation to the *M* frequency (i.e., 1:1 or lower for extratensives and ambients, and 0.5:1 for introversives), it suggests that the subject is very cautious, and possibly overly conservative in defining objectives for achievement. However, this postulate may not be valid if the *Zf* and frequency of *DQ*+ responses are at least average. If both *Zf* and *DQ*+ are average or above average in a record in which the *W:M* ratio is disproportionately low, the issue of underestimating capabilities and/or conservative goal setting should be reviewed in the context of a possible orientation toward being overly economical. This might be revealed by the presence of a High *Lambda* style or an usually high frequency of *Dd* answers.

In general, two rules may be applied when considering the effort or motivation invested in processing. First, if any two of the following are positive—(1) *Zf* is higher than average, (2) the value for *W* exceeds the value for *D + Dd*, (3) the ratio *W:M* is equal to or greater than expected in light of the *EB* data—it can be concluded that the subject is highly motivated and makes a considerable effort in processing, especially when the information involved relates to problem solving or decision making. This feature can be an asset provided adequate resources are available. However, it can be a liability if resources are limited or if the quality, efficiency, or consistency of the processing is substandard. Second, if at least two of the following are positive—(1) *Zf* is less than average, (2) the value for *W* is less than one-half the sum for *D + Dd*, (3) the ratio *W:M* is less than expected in light of the *EB* data, it is probable that some processing will be affected by very conservative motivation and, as such, may not be very effective. This may reflect a kind of defensive withdrawal from social competitiveness that can serve a useful purpose if there are intellectual limitations or other cognitive handicaps. However, if the intellectual level is at least average, this type of set toward processing typically is the result of a negative self-image. This finding should be reevaluated during the review of the cluster concerning self-perception.

THE QUALITY AND EFFICIENCY OF PROCESSING ACTIVITY

The *DQ* Distribution   The coding for developmental quality (*DQ*) appears to be related to the willingness and/or capacity to analyze and synthesize the stimulus field in a meaningful way. Generally, a higher frequency of *DQ*+ answers is found among brighter and psychologically more complex subjects, whereas the lower level *DQv* responses, which reflect an unsophisticated, less mature form of processing, occur most frequently among children and intellectually limited and/or neurologically impaired subjects. Children under the age of 10 can be expected to give between 3 and 5 *DQv* answers, but from the age of 10 upward the frequencies decline substantially so that by age 16 a frequency of more than 2 is somewhat unusual. Adult groups, both patient and nonpatient, usually have a mode of 1 for *DQv*, although most patient groups have slightly higher means for the variable than does the nonpatient normative sample. An earlier version of the *DQ* coding included a minus code that was linked directly to minus Form Quality (Exner, 1974). Like the *DQv*, the *DQ*− was also considered as indicative of a lower level of cognitive functioning and frequently appeared in the records of seriously disturbed subjects. The combined frequency of *DQv* and *DQ*− did differentiate the more severe disturbances (Freidman, 1952; Becker, 1956; Wilensky, 1959); however, it would appear that most of the variance contributing to the differentiation can be accounted for by the *DQ*−. In other words, the discrimination was generated mainly by data concerning perceptual inaccuracy rather than the level of cognitive maturity and complexity. A hint of this was noted by Siegel (1953) who noted that paranoid schizophrenics manifest a high frequency of lower level *DQ* responses even though they tend to function at a much higher cognitive level than do other schizophrenics.

The *DQv/+* is the least frequent of the four types of answers. It appears more frequently in the records of children and adolescents than adults. It is most notable in the records of youngsters between the ages of 9 and 15. In the younger subject, it is probably a more positive sign, indicating an orientation toward a higher level of cognitive activity; however, frequencies of 2 or more in the records of adults suggest that the orientation toward a more sophisticated cognitive level is somehow aborted by problems that are apparently related to form commitment.

The *DQo* is the most frequently given answer and represents a kind of cognitive economy that does not sacrifice the quality of operations as does the *DQv*. Whereas *DQv* answers reflect a concrete, overly simplistic, and diffuse form of cognitive functioning, the *DQo* represents a more conservative, but committed, processing effort. In some ways, the *DQo* can be considered similar to pure *F* responses in that both relate to a cognitive action that avoids complexity and instead involves a straightforward definition of the stimulus field or part of it. It is for this reason that *Z* scores assigned to *Wo* responses are generally lower for the more solid blots than for *D+* responses to the same blots.

The correlation between *Zf* and the composite of *DQ+* and *DQv/+* answers, derived from the nonpatient adult sample, is significant, $r = .461$ ($p < .01$). Therefore, if *Zf* is elevated in the record of an adult or a subject in mid-adolescence, the frequencies of *DQ+* and *DQv/+* are expected to be at least average or above. If this is not the case, it signals that the effort is present, but the cognitive activity is less sophisticated and/or complex than might be expected. Obviously, if *Zf* is elevated and the frequency of *DQ+* responses is substantial, it indicates that the subject is not only working hard at the task, but doing so with a complex and sophisticated cognitive effort.

It is very important to avoid the erroneous assumption that complex and sophisticated cognitive processing is somehow synonymous with efficiency or effective adjustment. *That is not true.* The process may be very complex but not necessarily grounded in reality or oriented toward effective adjustment. Many symptom patterns evolve from very elaborate cognitive operations. Among the best illustration of this are the systematized delusional systems that are usually built through an intricate but unrealistic network of very complex cognitive activity.

Cognitive Inflexibility (*PSV*)   It has been noted earlier that the Rorschach has, at best, only limited value as an index of intelligence or providing information about discrete cognitive operations such as attention-concentration, memory operations, and such. Nonetheless, there are instances in which unusual responses or response patterns provide a strong hint that some cognitive operations are limited or impaired. These involve the responses for which the Special Scores *PSV* (Perseveration) or *CONFAB* (Confabulation) have been assigned. The criteria for coding these unusual responses should leave no doubt that they signify some sort of cognitive problem.

Perseverations are the more frequent of these two types of answers, but even so, they are uncommon, especially among adults. Approximately 5% of the subjects in the adult nonpatient sample gave *PSV* responses, but never more than one each. They appear significantly more often among adult psychiatric reference samples with approximately 12% of the schizophrenics and 21% of the depressives giving one or two, and the character problem group containing 14% who gave at least one and as many as two. *PSV*'s occur much more frequently among younger children. For instance, the sample of 5-year-old nonpatients includes 63% who gave one *PSV* answer. The frequencies of subjects giving *PSV* answers decline gradually to about age 10 and more rapidly thereafter. For instance, they appear in 21% of the protocols of nonpatient 9-year-olds, dropping to only 3% of the records from nonpatient 12-year-olds, and continuing at the 3% level for the 16-year-old subjects.

Patients with *severe* neurological impairments tend to give a higher frequency of *PSV* answers; however, they are typically of the "mechanistic" variety, that is, repeating the same answer on each of several consecutive cards. Neurologically involved patients who are only mildly or moderately impaired show no greater frequency of *PSV* answers than do psychiatric patients. The overwhelming majority of *PSV* answers (86%) are "within card perseverations." In effect, the subject delivers almost the same response as the next answer to the blot as was given previously. When this occurs, it appears to signal a failure of cognitive shifting, and the implication is that the subject has some problem with cognitive inflexibility or *rigidity* as related to information processing or decision making. Obviously, many elements such as neurological impairment, intellectual deficit, or a kind of psychological paralysis can create such a condition. The high frequency with which it occurs among younger children suggests that, in some instances, the cognitive operations have not developed to a more adult-like level. If this is true, intelligence test data may provide important clues in sorting through this finding.

If the *PSV* occurs only once in a record, it probably indicates that the subject was momentarily rigid in decision or selection operations, an event that can occur in many people. If the *PSV* frequency is 2, a careful review of non-Rorschach data related to cognitive operations is clearly in order, even if the subject shows clear and unequivocal features of a major disturbance. Whenever the *PSV* value exceeds 2, there is no question that the cognitive functioning of the subject, other than a young child, should be thoroughly evaluated as might be done by some form of neuropsychological screening.

If the *PSV* responses, regardless of frequency, are "across card perseverations," such as the subject reporting the *same* two people fighting, or the *same* butterfly, on two or three different cards, a different kind of shift failure is implied and is probably not related to cognitive limitations. Instead, these kinds of answers signal a marked preoccupation, usually provoked by a psychopathological state, and occurring most commonly among seriously disturbed psychiatric subjects. When "across card" perseverations occur, the interpreter should make a decision about whether and/or how best to pursue the implications of the responses. For example, if the content has an interpersonal feature such as people fighting, TAT stories might provide some very enlightening information. On the other hand, a carefully developed history is often the best source from which information concerning preoccupations is derived.

OTHER FINDINGS RELATED TO PROCESSING VARIABLES

1. Z Scores. Although some basic intellectual talent is required for Z, the actual frequency and type of Z are influenced by many other features. Most subjects, both adults and children, patients and nonpatients, have some type of Z in about 40% to 50% of their answers. Obviously, High *Lambda* style subjects tend to have lower Z frequencies because so many of their responses are simply pure *F*. When the Zf is low, it may indicate an intellectual limitation, but more likely it denotes a reluctance to tackle the complexity of the stimulus field. A high Zf may be the product of intellectual striving or a need to deal with the stimulus field in a more careful and precise manner. The reliability data for Zf are substantial for both brief and lengthy retest intervals. The retest correlations for

Zf range from .89 to .92 for brief intervals, and .83 to .85 for much longer periods of time. Although the *Zf* provides information about the initiative of the subject to approach the task with more effort than might be required, taken alone it can be misleading, because the levels of effort vary, and the quality of the organized product can be distributed along a continuum ranging from mediocre to very sophisticated.

For instance, younger clients tend to have about the same proportion of *Z* in their records as do adults. At the same time, younger clients usually have a smaller proportion of *DQ*+ responses than adults. In other words, there are fewer responses in the records of younger clients that involve an organization of adjacent or distant details, and more that are based on *Wo* or integrated *S* responses. This probably reflects the "devil may care" approach that frequently characterizes the way in which the child takes on a task, but it also reflects the more simplistic level of cognition that is commonplace among children. As a consequence, the *ZSums* of children are usually lower than for adults.

2. The W Response. Rorschach (1921) postulated that *W* has a relation to intellectual operations, suggesting that it denotes the ability to organize the components of one's environment into a meaningful concept. Beck (1932) did find a positive correlation between *W* and intellectual operations; however, the literature on this issue has been somewhat contradictory. Abrams (1955) reported a correlation of nearly .40 between *W* and IQ, but a substantially lower correlation was reported by Armitage et al. (1955) for the same variables. Previously, McCandless (1949) reported no significant findings in studying the *W* answer as related to academic achievement, and Wittenborn (1950) found no relationship between *W* and several measures of mental ability. Lotsoff (1953) reported that *W* is related to verbal fluency but not necessarily to intelligence per se. Holzberg and Belmont (1952) and Wishner (1948) failed to find any significant relationship between *W* and the Similarities subtest of the Wechsler-Bellevue Scale. Mason and Exner (1984) found low but statistically significant correlations between *W* and the Comprehension (.20), Similarities (.24), Digit Symbol (.20), and Object Assembly (.19) subtests of the WAIS, using a sample of 171 nonpatient adults; however, no significant relationships were discovered between *W* and intelligence. Ames et al. (1971) found that the greatest proportion of *W* answers occurs in the records of 3- and 4-year-olds, with a gradual decline in the proportion through adolescence until it approximates the general adult proportion, which is between 30% and 40% of the record.

When the location frequencies, including the *W* responses, are studied for *D*Q, the findings are much more consistent, and definitive relationships are found with different kinds of intellectual operations. Friedman (1952) found that nonpatient adults give significantly more *W*+ answers than do schizophrenics or children. Frank (1952) has shown the same to be true when nonpatients and neurotics are compared. Blatt and Allison (1963) reported a significant positive relationship between higher *DQ W*'s and problem-solving ability. Ames et al. (1971) also found that the quality of *W* responses increases through adolescence, and a similar finding is reported by Exner and Weiner (1982). In general then, although *W* can be taken as some index of motivation to deal with the entire stimulus field, its relation to more sophisticated and/or complex cognitive operations must be derived from a review of the *DQ* codes that have been included in the response.

3. The Dd Response. An elevated *Dd* frequency can be caused by an excessive number of space responses. This is not uncommon among children and adolescents. Elevations in *Dd* can also be a form of avoidance through which the subject tries to create a more narrow environment that is easier to manage. Klebanoff (1949) found that male paretics give significantly more *Dd* than do nonpatients. Schachter and Cotte (1948) reported a substantial elevation of *Dd* in the protocols of prostitutes taken shortly after their arrest. Kadinsky (1952) concluded that the relationship between *Dd* and external adjustment is negative, but between *Dd* and internal adjustment is positive. Rabin et al. (1954), using a retest method, found the *Dd* increases significantly after the ingestion of substantial quantities of alcohol. If normative data are used as a guideline, when the proportion of *Dd* is within the average range of one to three, it is probably a positive sign, showing both the initiative and capacity to back away temporarily. If the frequency is disproportionate, it can indicate a form of perfectionism or a tendency to flee from routine coping demands. *Dd* answers that include a movement determinant can be especially important because they involve projection to an unusual area. Thus they should be studied carefully for any indications of impairment to the ideational process.

Location Sequence   The final step in evaluating processing activity involves a review of how the location codes appear in the Sequence of Scores. This is to determine if the approach to processing is consistent. The positioning of *W* answers is especially important, that is, subjects who are consistent will be disposed to give most of their *W* answers either as first answers or as last answers but usually will not show a mixture of the two. A similar consistency is expected for *Dd* responses when the number of *Dd*s is elevated in a record. If the sequencing of location selections appears reasonably consistent through most of the blots, it can be assumed that processing habits are regular and predictable. On the other hand, if the sequencing patterns vary considerably across cards, it can be concluded that processing during problem solving and/or decision making tends to be irregular. While this is not uncommon among children, its presence in the record of an older adolescent or adult suggests a failure to have developed economical or efficient processing habits. While this may not be a major liability, an inconsistency in processing habits can increase the potential for faulty inputs or a reduced quality of processing activity.

THE L.S. PROTOCOL AND INFORMATION PROCESSING

As was noted in Chapter 14, the interpretive routine for the L.S. record began with data regarding controls and stress tolerance because the value for the *D* Score was less than the Adjusted *D* Score. The findings indicated that his capacity for control and tolerance for stress is usually not very different than for most adults, but some situational factors have reduced his capacity for control and he is now in overload. This increases the likelihood that in new or more complex situations he will not function as adaptively or effectively as might be the case if the stress situation did not exist. There is also some increased likelihood that impulsiveness, in thinking, affect, and/or behavior will occur. As also noted in Chapter 14, the first positive Key variable for the L.S. record, $D < Adj D$, only defined the first two groups of variables to be studied and did not define the complete search routine. Although the remainder of the routine usually will be identified by the presence of another Key variable, no other Key variables are positive in the L.S. record, requiring that the listing of Tertiary variables be reviewed to decide the order in which the remaining clusters of data should be addressed. The first positive Tertiary variable, *OBS*, indicates that the remaining clusters of data should be addressed by first examining the Cognitive Triad, beginning with the cluster regarding

Table 74.   L.S. Protocol Processing Data

L = 0.56	$W:D:Dd$ = 8:16:1	Zd = −2.0	$DQ +$ = 9
Zf = 13	$W:M$ = 8:4	PSV = 0	$DQv/ +$ = 0
HVI = No	OBS = Yes		DQv = 0

Location Sequencing

I: *W.W.Dd*	IV: *W.D*	VII: *D.D.*
II: *D.DS*	V: *W*	VIII: *W.D.D.*
III: *D.D*	VI: *W.D.D.*	IX: *D.D.D*
		X: *D.D.W*

processing. The variables from the L.S. protocol that are related to processing are shown in Table 74.

Although the positive *OBS* typically suggests a cautious, somewhat meticulous approach to processing, the data here do not confirm that to be the case for L.S. It is true that the *Zf* is slightly higher than average (13), indicating a good motivation to organize. The *W:D:Dd* ratio (8:16:1) reveals a conservative or economical approach to processing stimulus figures, but none of the remaining data indicate unusual features in the processing activity. The *W:M* is neither conservative nor excessive (he is an ambitent). There is no unexpected elevation in *Dd* answers, and the *Zd* score is in the expected range. There are 9 *DQ* synthesis answers, no *DQv* responses (suggesting the quality of the processing effort is good), and the sequence is relatively consistent with 6 of the 8 *W* answers occurring as first responses and the pattern of *D* answers falling in a consistent pattern. Overall, the data for the cluster reflect a picture of a reasonably efficient, although sometimes conservative, processing effort.

MEDIATION

One of the most important issues in describing personality functioning concerns the extent to which the subject is oriented toward making conventional or acceptable responses. Information concerning how inputs are translated provides reasonably direct evidence concerning this issue. One person can be ultraconventional while another can be overly idiosyncratic. Either of these orientations toward reality can be a liability and impede effective adaptation. At the extreme, a person may be prone to frequent distortions of perceptual inputs. Obviously, this can be a very serious impediment to efforts at maintaining effective adjustment in the environment. The value for Popular answers (*P*) and the *X + %* offer the most direct information regarding one's orientation toward making conventional translations. They are two of the nine variables in this cluster, which includes *Lambda*, OBS, *P, X + %, F + %, Xu %, X − %, S − %, CONFAB*, plus the frequency data in the Form Quality Distribution (+, o, u, −). If minus responses have occurred, they are also reviewed for homogeneous clustering (i.e., all being first or last responses within a blot, or all having the same content, or all occurring to blots with color, etc.) and levels of distortion (the degree to which the response violates the properties of the stimulus field). The data for *Lambda* and the *OBS* should be reviewed before interpreting any other data in the cluster. This is because either the High *Lambda* style or the *Obsessive* style can impact substantially on mediational activities and if either are present, they often add substance to any understanding of findings from other data in the cluster.

THE HIGH *LAMBDA* STYLE AND MEDIATION

The tendency to oversimplify that characterizes the High *Lambda* style often promotes forms of translation that ignore or distort salient features of the stimulus field. Thus, if data concerning mediation indicate translating problems for a High *Lambda* style subject, the possibility that the difficulties are related to the style must be considered carefully. For example, a low $X+\%$, an elevated $Xu\%$, and a substantial $X-\%$ are commonplace among schizophrenics. The high $X-\%$ apparently occurs because schizophrenics have difficulty in retaining the stimulus input in short-term storage, have difficulty with the retrieval of information from long-term storage, or select translations of a field that coincide with preoccupations that are pathologically based. Similar causes of problems in mediation are commonplace among other subjects with serious psychological-psychiatric disturbances, or among some subjects who are neurologically impaired. However, there are other groups who are not severely impaired who may manifest mediational problems, but the cause of the problems may be based mainly in the stylistic orientation to oversimplify. For example, when the Character Disorder Reference Group ($N = 180$) is subdivided on the basis of the High *Lambda* style, the 122 subjects with that style have a mean $X+\%$ of 57%, an $Xu\%$ of 20%, and a mean $X-\%$ of 23%. The remaining 58 subjects in the sample have a mean $X+\%$ of 67%, a mean $Xu\%$ of 17%, and a mean $X-\%$ of 16%. In other words, the presence of the High *Lambda* style appears to contribute to the selection of significantly more unconventional answers, including significantly more answers involving mediational distortion.

It is erroneous to assume automatically that the High *Lambda* style inevitably leads to mediational problems. The mean $X+\%$ for 114 adult nonpatients who have a High *Lambda* style, drawn from the entire nonpatient pool, is 74%. That is only slightly lower than the mean of 79% for the normative group of 700 nonpatients, which includes only 38 High *Lambda* subjects. Both groups have essentially the same mean $X-\%$, 8% and 7% respectively. The main difference is in the $Xu\%$, which is 14% for the nomative sample and 18% for the 114 High *Lambda* style subjects.

Thus, if the value for *Lambda* is positive (1.0 or greater), the marked tendency toward psychological economizing that frequently leads to a narrowing or simplification of stimulus fields that are perceived as complex or ambiguous, may promote negligence in the translation of information. When this occurs, it creates a potential for a higher frequency of behaviors that do not coincide with social demands and/or expectations.

Sometimes, the findings for the $F+\%$ are useful in sorting out the impact of the High *Lambda* style on mediational activity. The $F+\%$ has little interpretive use except when the value for *Lambda* is positive, and when that is the case, a comparison between the values for the $X+\%$ and the $F+\%$ becomes important. If $X+\%$ is less than 70% but $F+\%$ is 70% or greater, it suggests that when the tactic of simplification is not invoked, or fails, the subject becomes prone to translate stimuli in less conventional ways. This may occur because the subject is irritated or overwhelmed by stimulus complexity and as a consequence, attempts to deal with the problem by withdrawing from and/or distorting the nature of the stimulus situation. Conversely, if $X+\%$ is 70% or more and $F+\%$

is *less than* 70%, it is possible that the subject assumes an unconventional or distortional approach during mediation to support the oversimplification process. This is more likely to be true when the $F+\%$ is less than 60%.

THE OBSESSIVE STYLE AND MEDIATION

As noted earlier, a positive OBS signifies the presence of a marked tendency toward perfectionism and an excessive preoccupation with details. People such as this are very cautious in translating stimuli as they are strongly influenced by needs to be correct or conventional. Thus, when the OBS is positive, the data in the cluster concerning mediation are expected to be well within average limits, if not above average. The number of Popular answers and the $X+\%$ are often higher than average, and the frequency of overelaborated ($FO+$) answers is also elevated. If the OBS is positive, but some of the expectations concerning the data are not met, it indicates that the style has become counterproductive because excessive efforts to refine and/or reorganize the details of an input tend to create an interference in mediational activities. Thus, the number of $FO+$ answers may be high even though the $X-\%$ is also elevated; or the number of Popular answers may be above average although the $X+\%$ is well below average. When these unusual mixtures of data appear, they signal a chaotic mediational process that should be considered as a major treatment objective if intervention is to be planned.

BASIC DATA CONCERNING MEDIATION

The basic data concerning mediation consist of P, the $X+\%$, the $Xu\%$, the $X-\%$, the $S-\%$ and the frequency distribution of form quality scores. Collectively, they provide critical information about the issues of conventionality and perceptual accuracy.

If the number of Popular answers is at least average, it signifies that, in obvious situations, expected or acceptable responses are likely to occur. The probability of less conventional responses occurring in situations that are simple and/or precisely defined is minimal *even* if some problems in processing have been noted. If the number of Popular responses is greater than average, it may indicate that a preoccupation with conventionality exists. In other words, the subject may be overly concerned with detecting cues related to socially expected or unacceptable behaviors. This is not necessarily a liability, but can reflect a more perfectionistic or obsessive-like feature. If the number of Popular answers is lower than average, it is probable that less conventional, more individualistic responses will occur, even in situations that are simple and/or precisely defined. This is not necessarily a liability, but can be a problem if difficulties in processing are noted. The data concerning the $X+\%$ are important in determining whether this tendency contributes to, or is a feature of, a marked potential for asocial and/or antisocial behavior.

If the $X+\%$ falls between 70% and 89%, it indicates that the frequency rate for making conventional responses is similar to that of most people. If the $X+\%$ is greater than 89%, it probably indicates an unusual commitment to conventionality. While this is not necessarily a liability, it often signals an excessive preoccupation with social acceptability that can lead to a sacrifice of individuality. Elevations in the $X+\%$ may also reflect a marked tendency toward obsessiveness and/or perfectionism, even though the OBS may not be positive. If the $X+\%$ (and $F+\%$ in High L records) is less than 70%, it can be assumed that the subject is oriented toward making more unconventional translations of stimuli than do most people. This usually equates with patterns of less conventional behaviors. This tendency will be even greater if the number of Popular answers is also less than average. This does not necessarily mean that the less conventional behaviors will be unacceptable or antisocial. On the contrary, it may simply represent a strong emphasis on individualism, and might be the product of social alienation. On the other hand, it could result from more serious mediational or affective modulation problems. When this finding is positive in High *Lambda* Style records, it is often the result of a strong orientation to maintain distance from, and thus cope with an environment that is perceived as threatening, demanding, and ungiving. In other cases, the tendency to produce more unconventional behaviors can result from cognitive difficulties that may include processing and/or perceptual accuracy problems.

Sometimes the $X+\%$ is lowered because of the presence of answers that have no form. Usually, these are pure C responses. Less commonly, they are pure C', pure T, or pure Y answers, and in rare instances they are formless M responses. If the $X+\%$ has been lowered substantially by any of the first four ($C, C', T,$ or Y) answers, it indicates that affective problems are interfering with the mediation process. If the lowered $X+\%$ is created because of formless M answers, it suggests that problems in ideational impulse control are interfering with mediation.

The $Xu\%$ often differentiates the subject who is overly individualistic from those who have more serious mediation problems. Among nonpatient adults, the average $Xu\%$ is 14%, and scores between 7% and 20% are not uncommon. Unusual responses are desirable in every record, and only when the $Xu\%$ exceeds 20% should there be cause for concern. Elevated $Xu\%$s suggest that the subject is overly individualistic, which at times may be acceptable in a given environmental framework, but much of the time the environment is less tolerant and tends to view such a subject as being out of step with the world.

Minus answers reflect some sort of distortion in translating the input. Almost all subjects give some minus responses, and when the frequency is low, it probably represents no more than a glimpse into some personal preoccupation or some mediational casualness on the part of the subject. Generally, value for the $X-\%$ is expected to be less than 15% and the value for the $S-\%$ is always expected to be less than 40% unless the total number of minus answers is less than 4. If the value for the $X-\%$ is less than 15%, it can be concluded that the frequency of perceptual inaccuracy and/or mediational distortion is no greater than for most people. If the value for the $S-\%$ is 40% or more, it is likely that negativism or anger contribute significantly to these inaccuracies or distortions when they occur. If the value for the $X-\%$ falls in the range of 15% to 20%, some concern is warranted about the elevated incidence of perceptual inaccuracy and/or mediational distortion. The actual frequency of minus answers is relevant. Two or three minus responses usually is not cause for major concern. Conversely, the presence of four or more minus answers signals that a careful review of the features and distribution of those answers may be critically important to a better understanding of mediational activity. If the value for the $S-\%$ is equal to or greater than 40%, this concern should focus on the affective characteristics of the subject.

If the value of the $X-\%$ exceeds 20%, it is likely that significant problems exist that promote perceptual inaccuracy and/or mediational distortion. If the value for the $S-\%$ is equal to or greater than 40%, it is probable that negativism and/or anger contributes substantially to the problem. The data concerning affect may shed some light on this issue. If the value for the $S-\%$ is less than 40%, it can be assumed that the inaccuracy or distortion problems are more pervasive.

If the value of the $X-\%$ exceeds 70% and R is greater than 13, regardless of the value for the $S-\%$, it is very possible that the subject is attempting to exaggerate or malinger symptoms. Subjects who have an $X-\%$ greater than 70% are usually very difficult or even impossible to test and typically, will have recent behavioral histories that are consistent with the postulate than an active psychotic-like state exists. If the history does not provide clear and consistent evidence of a psychotic-like state, the probability of malingering is substantial.

Whenever minus answers occur in a record, they should be studied in terms of their sequencing. For example, if all minus form quality occurred in answers that cluster within the first three cards, it is probable that the distortions are a product of negative resistance toward the test situation. Similarly, if three or more minus answers were given and 40% or more of the minus answers involve S, and those answers are scattered throughout the sequence, it is probable that some of the distortions are the product of a chronic, trait-like negativistic orientation toward the environment which is likely to increase the probability of behaviors that may disregard social conventions or expectations. If all or most all minus answers were given to blots containing chromatic color the possibility of affective disruption must be considered. If this problem exists, it will usually be confirmed by data concerning affect, which will often include some difficulties in modulating affective displays (higher right side value for $FC:FC+C$), and in many instances a tendency to avoid emotionally toned stimulus situations (low Afr). If more than one minus answer exists and all or most all minus answers are given as first responses to the blots, it may signify a lackadaisical or hasty approach in mediation. This is especially true if subsequent answers within the blot are more conventional. Finally, if all or most all minus answers are last responses to the blots, two possibilities should be considered. The first is the more common of the two, namely, that those answers are of special significance to the subject and may be quite revealing when their characteristics or content is reviewed. A second possibility is that the subject may be prone, for any of several reasons, to exaggerate features of disturbance. This is particularly likely if the record contains more than three minus answers.

MEDIATIONAL DYSFUNCTION

Confabulations (*CONFAB*) are very rare. They do not occur among nonpatient adults or children, or in any of the adult psychiatric reference samples, except in 8 of the schizophrenia cases. Rorschach hypothesized that they represent a form of impaired perception such as might be found among intellectually limited, organic, or schizophrenic subjects. Obviously, it is a highly unique form of response in which some of the more important cognitive controls fail, or are lacking. As might be expected, research concerning the *CONFAB* is sparse. Most Rorschach examiners will never take a record that contains a *CONFAB* response unless they deal frequently with very young children or people who have notable intellectual deficits. The protocol pool at the Rorschach Research Foundation includes 17 records collected from severely retarded young adults who have Full Scale WAIS IQs of less than 65, a population for which the Rorschach is usually not applicable. Although the records are very brief and barren, 7 of the 17 do contain legitimate *CONFAB* answers. *CONFAB* responses should not be confused with autistic or bizarre responses such as are commonplace among schizophrenic or psychotic subjects. Those are coded with other Special Scores. The *CONFAB* involves a blatant overgeneralization that often disregards the natural contours of the blot. It seems to reflect a serious form of intellectual dysfunction or alogical cognitive operation, neither of which is characteristic of common psychopathological states. Obviously, if one does occur, other forms of cognitive evaluation are required.

FINDINGS RELATED TO BASIC VARIABLES IN THE MEDIATION CLUSTER

Popular Responses (*P*)   The common or Popular response was originally regarded by Rorschach as reflecting the ability to perceive and respond to the commonplace features of the blots. The high frequency with which these answers occur, at least once in every three records, seems to support that contention. Baughman (1954) found the *P* was one of the most stable features in the test, and least subject to any undue sets created by examiners. His findings are supported in a variety of retest studies reported here and elsewhere (Exner, 1978, 1983; Exner, Armbruster, & Viglione, 1978; Exner & Weiner, 1982) in which the short-term reliabilities range from .84 to .88, and over longer intervals from .79 to .86. Bourguinon and Nett (1955) and Hallowell (1956) have demonstrated that the listing of Populars holds well for other cultural groups, a finding also supported in work presented here. Leighton and Kluckhorn (1947), Honigman (1948), Joseph and Murray (1951), and Fried (1977) have all demonstrated that some responses are uniquely Popular for specific cultures; however, they are usually added Populars rather than replacements for the basic listing. Beck (1932), Kerr (1934), and Hertz (1940) all reported a low incidence of *P* among intellectually retarded subjects. Ames et al. (1971) have reported that a gradual increase in the frequency of Popular answers occurs among children as they become older, a finding similar to that found in the nonpatient sample presented here.

Theoretically, *P* has a finite limit of 13, although in rare instances subjects may give more than one *P* to the same blot, such as defining the popular *D*1 area on Card III as two men, and then defining the same area as two women in a second answer. Nonetheless, as opposed to other Rorschach variables, it is relatively easy to identify deviant frequencies. Nonpatient adults average nearly 7, with a mode and median of 7, schizophrenics average nearly 5 with a mode of 4 and a median of 5 (which is significantly lower than for nonpatients, $p < .02$). Depressives have an average of slightly more than 5, but with a mode of 4, and a median of 5, and the character disorders group averages about 5, with a mode of 6 and a median of 5. The skewness and kurtosis values of the curves for each group suggest that the distribution follows a relatively normal curve. Thus it would be expected that most adult subjects should render between 5 and 8 Popular responses. When this is not the case, the data become interpretively important.

A low frequency of Popular responses in the record of an adult, 4 or less, reflects either an inability *or* unwillingness of the subject to deliver that which may be the most obvious possible answer. *It does not necessarily signify poor reality testing,* but simply that, for some reason, the subject offered less typical responses than expected. Interestingly, the correlation between the frequency of *P* answers and the $X+\%$ is negligible, $-.02$ for 100 nonpatient adults (Exner, Viglione, & Gillespie, 1984). Thus, it does not necessarily hold true that the person oriented to giving commonplace answers will also yield a considerable frequency of Popular responses. According to these findings, the $X+\%$ can be quite substantial and yet a relatively low number of Popular answers might be included in the record. Low P, as noted above, simply indicates that a subject has not responded in the most economical or conventional manner possible in light of the requirements of the task. It may signal serious pathology, but it also may signal a more unique personality who does not violate reality, but instead tends to deal with it in a common, but not highly conventional manner. The basic key to sorting through this issue will rest with the data of the $X+\%$.

It is also useful to review the Sequence of Scores to identify those cards to which Popular responses were not given. Table 24 in Chapter 8 includes the percentages of nonpatients and nonschizophrenic patients used in developing the Form Quality Table, who gave Popular responses to the blots. As noted there, the range is considerable. More than 90% of the subjects gave the Popular response to Card VIII, whereas only about 35% gave the Popular response to Card II. Thus if P is low, it is expected that the few Populars given will involve the blots to which high percentages of Populars occur—namely, I, III, V, and VIII. If P is consistently absent to these Cards, the interpreter is likely to find other evidence indicating the presence of pathology, or a marked kind of nonconformity.

On the other end of the continuum, some subjects give an overabundance of Popular answers. If *Lambda* is positive, greater than 1.0, this may simply reflect the effort to economize described in Chapter 17. Conversely, if *Lambda* is not high, the elevation in Popular answers probably indicates an orientation toward the more simplistic and correct, and can hint of a commitment to conventionality that is well beyond that which might be expected.

Form Quality ($X+\%$, $F+\%$, $Xu\%$, $X-\%$, $S-\%$)   Form is a basic ingredient to almost all Rorschach answers. Baughman (1959), in his classic work on the stimulus features of the blots, clearly demonstrated the dominant role that form plays in the formulation of most answers. His work, and that of Exner (1959), can be viewed as offering clear evidence for the important role of this determinant. In both works, the color and shading properties of the blots were altered, sometimes causing major variations in the frequencies for the use of different determinants and/or response contents. *In both studies,* however, the proportion of responses that include form remained relatively stable. Mason, Cohen, and Exner (1985) have reported on a series of factor analyses of Rorschach data for groups of nonpatients, schizophrenics, and depressives. Although the overall factor structures were different for each group, form was consistently a dominant element in the first factor for each group.

Rorschach noted that a substantial portion of responses are Pure F and that almost all of the remaining responses will be marked by some inclusion of contour features. He postulated that the manner and quality in which form is applied in creating the response represents the subject's ability to perceive things conventionally, or realistically. In that context, he devised a scheme of differentiating the form quality of answers into + (good) or − (poor), and created the $F+\%$ to reflect the percentage of good *Pure* form responses in the record, arguing that when that percentage is low, it equates with limited perceptual accuracy and possibly poor reality testing.

Generally, the inclusion of form in a response has been considered as an "ego" or thinking operation. Rapaport et al. (1946), for example, drawing from the concepts of ego psychology, argue that the use of form denotes a process of formal reasoning in which the mediation of the stimulus calls attention to the contours. Implicit in the operation is the direction of attention, forms of control, and the making of discriminating judgments with regard to the standards of the environment. Korchin (1960) has discussed the process in the conceptual framework of perceptual organizing activity. Beck (1945) postulated that when the quality of the form use is good, the subject demonstrates a respect for reality, whereas the frequent use of poor form indicates a disregard for this element. The bulk of research concerning form quality that was published during the first 50 years after Rorschach's death focused on the $F+\%$ and gained considerable support for his contentions about it.

Form Quality-Form ($F+\%$)   As Molish (1967) has noted, the $F+\%$ tends to vary with both intellect and the affective state of the subject. Much early Rorschach research concerned its relation to intellect. Beck (1930, 1932) reported relatively high correlations between the low $F+\%$ and limited intellectual endowment. Similar findings were reported later by Klopfer and Kelley (1942) and Sloan (1947). However, studies concerning the relationship between the $F+\%$ and nonretarded subjects have yielded some contradictory findings. Several (Paulsen, 1941; Holzberg & Belmont, 1952; Abrams, 1955; Armitage et al., 1955) reported significant correlations between $F+\%$ and IQ or MA, but others (Wishner, 1948; Gibby, 1951; Taulbee, 1955) have reported that no single Rorschach variable, or grouping of variables, shows consistently significant correlations with intelligence. Those findings are consistent with the report of Mason and Exner (1984). Ames et al. (1971) found that the $F+\%$ is generally low for very young children, but that it typically exceeds 80% by the sixth year.

A review of studies concerning brain-injured subjects (Molish, 1959) indicates that substantial variations exist for form quality, a finding that Molish interpreted to represent differences in the type of damage experienced and the consequent impairment to adaptive functioning. The data concerning $F+\%$ among geriatric subjects are also somewhat mixed. Klopfer (1946), Davidson and Kruglov (1952), Ames et al. (1954), and Caldwell (1954) all noted a decline in the mean $F+\%$ in older subjects; however, Prados and Fried (1943) and Chesrow et al. (1949) reported that older subjects maintain a relatively high $F+\%$.

The most striking data concerning the $F+\%$ have generated from the studies of more severely disturbed psychiatric patients, and especially schizophrenics. Weiner (1966) pointed out: "Virtually all studies of $F+\%$ in schizophrenia and control groups have replicated the findings presented by Beck and Rickers-Ovsiankina in their historically significant 1938 contributions." In each of those studies, schizophrenics showed a mean $F+\%$ in the 60s, whereas controls yielded significantly higher means, 87.3 for the Rickers group and 83.9 for the Beck group. Similar findings have been reported by Friedman (1952), Berkowitz and Levine (1953), Knopf (1956), and Molish and Beck (1958). Sherman (1952) divided a group of 71 nonpatients and 66 schizophrenics into high and low responder groups. He found that the $F+\%$ differentiated the nonpatients from the schizophrenics regardless of record length. These accumulated findings led Beck to suggest that whenever the $F+\%$ equals 60% or lower, it is indicative of serious psychopathology, or representative of marked intellectual limitations or brain dysfunction. That suggestion coincides well with the data for the adult nonpatient normative sample, which shows a mean of 71% with a standard deviation of 17.

Goldberger (1961) used an isolation design and found that subjects with higher $F+\%$s were more capable of handling the "primary process intrusions of sensory deprivation."

Baker and Harris (1949) came to similar conclusions from a design using "speed quality" under stress. Several authors report a significant increase in the $F+\%$ as the result of therapeutic change (Piotrowski, 1939; Kisker, 1942; Beck, 1948); however, Zamansky and Goldman (1960) reported on a well-designed study of 96 hospitalized patients and found no significant increase in $F+\%$ following intervention, although a "global" analysis of the pre- and post-treatment records was significantly differentiating. Exner and Murillo (1973) found that the $F+\%$s of 53 schizophrenic subjects increased approximately 10 percentage points (which is not statistically significant) at discharge from hospitalization as contrasted with their admission records.

Although the $F+\%$ sometimes provides a valuable input to the interpretation of a record, it does have marked limitations. As Weiner (1966) has pointed out, it often represents only a small proportion of the total responses and, as such, may offer only a glimpse of how appropriately form has been used. Its value is probably limited to records in which at least ten Pure F responses occur, or when *Lambda* is greater than 1.0. When neither of those criteria are met, it signals that the $F+\%$ will be based on a very small number of responses, and thus the percentage can shift dramatically as a function of the FQ coding of one or two answers. It was for this reason that Weiner (1966) recommended the use of the Extended $F+\%$, a calculation first described by Rapaport et al. (1946) and elaborated on by Schafer (1954). It included all responses in which F was the primary feature in the determinant, such as Pure *F, FC, FC', FT,* and so on. Weiner correctly pointed out that this variable might be a more reliable measure of perceptual accuracy because it represents a larger number of answers in most protocols.

Feldman et al. (1954) reported a correlation of approximately .80 between the $F+\%$ and the Extended $F+\%$, although Cass and McReynolds (1951) had previously reported that the Extended $F+\%$ is generally higher than the $F+\%$ for nonpatient adults. Exner (1974) reported correlations of .78 between $F+\%$ and the Extended $F+\%$ among nonpatients, .73 among schizophrenics, and .62 among inpatient nonschizophrenics. That series of studies also revealed that nearly 35% of all $FQ-$ codings occur to responses in which the form feature is *not* the dominant characteristic, such as *CF, YF,* and so on. Those findings led to the decision to test a calculation that would include the form quality for all responses in the record.

Extended Form Quality ($X+\%$)   Early studies on the $X+\%$ illustrate that is does discriminate quite well among nonpatient and the more seriously disturbed psychiatric groups (Exner, 1974, 1978). The mean $X+\%$ for nonpatients, both children and adults, tends to hover around 78%. Standard deviations are typically around 10%. Standard deviations for patient groups tend to be slightly, but not significantly higher, indicating a somewhat greater dispersion of the scores. Similarly, means for patient groups tend to be somewhat lower than for nonpatients, but usually not significantly lower unless the patient group consists of seriously disturbed subjects. For instance, the mean $X+\%$ for schizophrenics is 40%, and 97% of the schizophrenics in the reference sample have $X+\%$s lower than 70%, as contrasted with only 10% of the nonpatient normative sample. Retest reliabilities for the $X+\%$ are consistently high, over both brief and lengthy intervals, usually ranging from the mid .80s to low .90s, and it is the *only* variable that shows a consistently high retest reliability when studied longitudinally from age 8 through age 16 (Exner, Thomas, & Mason, 1985). It has proven to be an important variable in the Suicide Constellation (Exner & Wylie, 1977), and a critical variable in the identification of schizophrenia (Exner, 1978, 1983, 1991; Exner & Weiner, 1982).

Interpretively, the $X+\%$ provides data that relate to the use of the form features of the blots in a commonplace, reality-oriented manner. Although some aspects of perceptual accuracy are related to it, the $X+\%$ is probably more of a measure of perceptual and/or mediational conventionality, because the calculation is based on the proportion of answers that are defined as commonplace by frequency criteria.

When the $X+\%$ is low—that is, less than 70%—it signifies that the subject tends to translate stimulus fields in ways that are more atypical. A low $X+\%$ may be caused by any of, or a combination of, three features, perceptual-mediational distortion, overcommitment to individuality, or as noted earlier, failures in modulating affective experiences or maintaining adequate control over ideational impulses.

THE PROPORTION OF UNUSUAL ANSWERS (*Xu %*)

In many cases, the low $X+\%$ is not created by an abundance of minus answers. Instead, it is the product of a high frequency of unusual (u) responses. As noted earlier, these are low-frequency answers that can be seen easily, because they do not violate the appropriate use of the blot contours. They reflect a less common way of translating the stimulus field that still abides by the demands of reality. In effect, they typify those instances in which the subject exerts some of the features of his or her individuality. When they occur in low frequencies, they are probably a healthy sign, but when they occur in excessive numbers, to the point of reducing the $X+\%$ beyond the lower limit of the average range, they can signal an excessive commitment to the self, and an unwillingness to adhere to the standards of conventionality. The difference between low $X+\%$s based on minus responses versus those created by unusual responses has been shown to discriminate "process and reactive" schizophrenics (Zukowsky, 1961), improvement among schizophrenics (Saretsky, 1963), and legally sane from legally insane murders (Kahn, 1967).

High frequencies of unusual responses occur in the records of those who, for any of a variety of reasons, feel less committed to conventionality. If the environment makes few demands on this sort of person for conformity to behavioral expectations, the consequence of the low $X+\%$ may be negligible; however, in instances when the environment is less accepting of this unconventional orientation, the likelihood of frequent confrontations is considerable. As might be expected, many subjects who run afoul of social rules and regulations have records in which the $X+\%$ is low because of an elevation in the $Xu\%$, and many also have low P and/or a higher than average *Lambda*.

Perceptual-Mediational Distortion ($X-\%$)   The $X-\%$ represents the proportion of uncommon responses in the record that disregard the appropriate use of the contours of the blots. These are the answers in which the objects specified are, at best, very difficult to see, and in many instances impossible to find. In effect, they are violations of reality. Minus responses are not uncommon, but usually occur in low frequencies. For example, nearly 87% of the adults in the nonpatient normative sample gave at least one minus answer, and the mean $X-\%$ for the group is 7%. Nonschizophrenic patient groups tend to give slightly but not significantly more minus answers. The depressive reference sample shows that 99% of those subjects gave at least one minus response. The mode for the group is 2, although the median is 4, and the mean $X-\%$ is 20%. Higher frequencies of minus responses are common among schizophrenic subjects. The reference sample of schizophrenics shows a mean for $FQ-$ of nearly 9 with the mode and median being 7, and a mean $X-\%$ of 37.

As noted earlier, it is important to try to distinguish whether the impairment is specific or diffuse. In many cases, impairments that are created by preoccupations may be revealed by a clustering of the minus responses in a specific class of contents or determinants. This is most common in protocols that have elevations in the $X-\%$, but with $X+\%$ in the average range. For instance, a review of 60 records of elective surgery patients shows the $X-\%$ to be elevated in 37 cases, but only 11 have $X+\%$s lower than 70%. Approximately 65% of their minus responses include contents of anatomy or x-ray. Similarly, Exner (1989) found that 35% of all minus answers, given by 68 males with serious physical problems, were either anatomy or x-ray answers. Many subjects who have problems in emotional control give most of their minus form quality in answers that include chromatic color determinants. If no clustering of the minus answers is detected, it should be assumed that the impairment has a more diffuse impact.

Obviously, if the $X+\%$ is low *and* the $X-\%$ is elevated, it is reasonable to conclude that the magnitude of the impairment is considerable and interfering significantly with the capacity of the subject to make appropriate responses. As the $X-\%$ increases, the greater the probability of inappropriate behavior, and whenever it exceeds 25%, the likelihood of major impairment is substantial.

Minus Responses Involving White Space $(S-\%)$ This variable evolved during the research on the *SCZI* (Exner, 1991). It is one of the 10 variables that loads significantly in discriminant function analyses that differentiate false positives from true positives. Data revealed that many false positive cases, on both the original *SCZI* and many of the subsequent experimental *SCZI*s, were created because of three variables: a low $X+\%$, a high $X-\%$, and at least one $M-$ answer. Although the proportion of false positive cases was within reasonably acceptable limits for most groups (less than 6%), it was unacceptably high among three groups, inpatient affective disorders, inpatient adolescents, and children having academic difficulties.

A sort of minus responses, card-by-card by location, for those three groups plus a target group of schizophrenics, yielded a highly significant difference. Namely, the nonschizophrenics, especially younger clients, tended to give many more $S-$ answers than did the schizophrenics. Further investigation revealed that while the absolute raw score for $S-$ answers did provide some useful discrimination, a proportional score or percentage improved the discrimination substantially. The $S-\%$ also provides information about the extent to which mediational distortions may relate to some affective interference or influence. Minus responses are quite intriguing because they defy or distort the contours of the stimulus field. During the response process, the subject has the opportunity to rescan the stimulus field often, and alter or discard potential answers that had been created during the first scan of the field. This opportunity to make internal corrections before giving an answer is an important part of the test, yet most people give some minus answers. For instance, 605 of the 700 adult nonpatients who constitute the normative sample gave at least one minus response. Earlier research suggests that many minus answers will have projected features, promoted by sets and/or preoccupations. Thus, when the $S-\%$ exceeds 40% in records that have more than three minus answers, it is reasonable to postulate that strong sets, created by negativism or anger, are contributing to mediational distortions.

THE L.S. PROTOCOL AND MEDIATION

The mediation variables for the L.S. protocol are shown in Table 75.

Table 75.   L.S. Protocol Data Concerning Cognitive Mediation

Lambda	=	0.56	*OBS*	= Pos	*Minus Features*
P	=	8	*X + %*	= .96	No Minus Responses
FOx +	=	2	*F + %*	= 1.00	
FOxo	= 22		*Xu%*	= .04	
FOxu	=	1	*X − %*	= .00	
FOx −	=	0	*S − %*	= .00	
FOxnone =		0	*CONFAB* = 0		

The manifestations of the Obsessive style seem rather obvious. The $X+\%$ is very high (96%), and the record includes two $FQ+$ responses as well as eight Popular answers. There are no minus answers and only one unusual response. Collectively, the data suggest that he is overly committed to making conventional or acceptable responses, and the cost for this is a sacrifice of his own uniqueness. People such as this often convey an impression to others of being well adjusted, but sometimes too "stiff" or conforming. They often are unwilling to accept differences among people and frequently are quite critical of those who do not conform to their expectations. Inside, they are often less content with themselves and sometimes have considerable difficulty expressing their feelings openly or directly. The fact that L.S. is able to maintain the integrity of his Obsessive style in light of the currently experienced situational stress illustrates the strength of the style and this is probably an asset for him. Often, people with an Obsessive style are prone to disorganization when in overload situations unless they have an abundance of resource available. Earlier, it was noted that L.S. has an *EA* of 7.5, which, although falling in the average range, is not especially substantial. Nevertheless, even though he is experiencing tension, anxiety, insomnia, and has some difficulty in concentration, his mediational activity shows no impairment. Data concerning ideation and affect are especially important in a case such as this because they will often shed some light on the source and/or impact of the stress and its potential for disorganizing the Obsessive style.

IDEATION

The variables in the cluster related to ideation address the issue of how the translations of inputs become conceptualized and used. Thinking involves the meaningful organization of a series of symbols or concepts. It constitutes the core of psychological activity from which all decisions and deliberate behaviors evolve. Rorschach data fall far short of uncovering the more subtle nuances of ideational activity. Nonetheless, the data in this cluster often can provide a useful picture regarding the ideational operations of the subject. Several variables are involved, beginning with the *EB* (and *EBPer* if appropriate), the data for the left side of the *eb,* and extending to the two active:passive ratios, the Intellectualization Index, the frequency of Morbid content answers, the Critical Special Scores and their quality, $M-$ responses, and finally ending with a subjective evaluation of the quality of all human movement answers. Much of the research related to thinking has been elaborated in Chapters 15 and 17. Thus, rather than create a separate section concerning research findings, studies related to specific variables will be described as the variables are discussed.

The *EB* and *EBPer*   The *EB* is a cornerstone from which to understand the characteristics of thinking as they related to decision making. This has been described in Chapter 17. Thus, if the *EB* reveals an introversive style, it suggests a person who prefers to delay until all apparent alternatives have been considered and who prefers logic systems that are precise and uncomplicated. If an extratensive style is revealed, it indicates that the person merges feelings with thinking much of the time and more complex patterns of thinking may occur that often give rise to trial and error behaviors. If the *EB* does not indicate a style (ambitent), it signifies a potential for inconsistency in decision making, a tendency to reverse decisions, and a vulnerability to errors in judgment. If either the introversive or extratensive style is pervasive, it signals a marked lack of flexibility in coping approaches that sometimes can be quite detrimental to successful problem solving or decision making. Such a finding has a direct input to understanding the ideational activities of the subject.

The Left Side *eb*   Findings concerning the data for the left side of the *eb* have also been described in Chapter 17. They contribute substantially to an understanding of ideational activity. If either *FM* or *m* is elevated, or the combination of the two yield a value that is higher than average, it is likely that deliberate and focused ideational activity will be interrupted more often than should be the case. When this occurs, attention and concentration are routinely shortened.

The *a:p* Ratio   The data from the two active-passive ratios are especially important. As illustrated in Chapter 17, the *a:p* ratio has definite implications for passivity in the interpersonal activities of a subject, but it also relates to ideational activity. Piotrowski's work (1957, 1960) suggested that a more consistent form of thinking or inner experience is common among people experiencing difficulties in adjustment; that is, less shifting occurs from the forms of ideation characterized by the active or passive designations. In other words, ideational sets that are formed are more difficult to interrupt or alter.

The results of three investigations seem to support this postulate and suggest that the data of the *a:p* ratio relate to the features of cognitive flexibility versus narrowness or constriction. Exner (1974) found that significantly larger proportional difference scores between *a* and *p* existed among unimproved patients as contrasted with improved patients, although both groups had considerable discrepancies between the values for *a* and *p* at the onset of treatment. Similarly, Exner and Wylie (1974) found that therapist ratings concerning responsiveness of patients in two treatment sessions were significantly higher for those who entered treatment with the values in the *a:p* ratio less than proportions of 3:1 than for those entering treatment with *a:p* proportions of more than 3:1. Exner and Bryant (1974) asked two groups, each consisting of 15 high school students, to write as many uses as they could formulate for each of eight items, such as a key, a toothpick, a golf tee, and so on, considered separately or in combinations. Subjects in one group all had values of five or more in one side of the *a:p* ratio, and zero in the other side. Subjects in the second group all had *a:p* ratios in which the value in one side exceeded the other by two or less. The groups did not differ for the number of uses for the items considered separately; however, the group with $a:p$ values close together recorded more than twice as many uses for the items taken in various combinations.

Thus, if the sum of the values in the ratio is four and one value is zero, it can be hypothesized that the thinking and values of the subject tend to be less flexible and more well fixed than is ordinarily the case. If the sum of the values in the ratio exceeds four, and the value on one side of the ratio is no more than twice that of other, the finding is not significant. If the sum of the values in the ratio exceeds four, and the value on one side is two to three times greater than the value on the other side, it can be presumed that the ideational sets and values of the subject are reasonably well fixed and would be somewhat difficult to alter. If the sum of the values in the ratio exceeds four, and the value on one side is more than three times greater than the value on the other side, it can be concluded that the ideational sets and values of the subject are well fixed and relatively inflexible. People such as this find it very difficult to alter attitudes or opinions, or to view issues from a perspective different than that which they hold.

The $M^a:M^p$ Ratio   The findings concerning the $a:p$ ratio suggested that a closer examination of the $M^a:M^p$ ratio might also reveal useful data concerning some of the ideational characteristics of subjects. A review of the daydream ratings of active and passive (Exner, 1974) for 34 female subjects showed that 7 of the 34 had 15 or more daydreams that were rated as passive, whereas none of the remaining subjects had more than 9 passive daydreams. Of additional interest was the finding that only 11 of the 123 passive daydreams given by those 7 subjects contained shifts in the role of the central character, that is, moving from a passive to active role or vice versa. Four of the 7 subjects had passive $a:p$ ratios, but *all* 7 had $M^a:M^p$ ratios in which the value for passive M was greater than active M than active M.

Exner, Armbruster, and Wylie (1976) recruited 25 nonpatient adults who had been administered Rorschachs for the normative sample. Each had given at least six M responses, and 13 had given more M active than M passive, whereas the remaining 12 had given more M^p than M^a. They were asked to write endings for each of six TAT stories that had been created to present dilemma situations. For example, the figure in Card 3BM was featured as having lost a job, the boy in 13B was described as having wandered away from a picnic and was lost, and so on. The story endings were scored for (1) positive or negative outcome, (2) outcomes involving new people injected into the story, and (3) outcomes initiated by the central figure of the story versus those contingent on the actions of someone else. The overwhelming majority of the outcomes were positive (88%) and did not differentiate the two groups. The 12 subjects with higher M^p added new people to 38 of the 72 endings (53%), whereas the higher M^a subjects added new people to only 17 of their endings (24%, $p < .05$). The most striking difference concerned the initiation of outcomes. Forty-nine of the 72 outcomes given by the higher M^p group (68%) were initiated by someone other than the central figure of the story. The higher M^a group did this in only 21 (29%) of their endings ($p < .01$).

Additional data contributing to an understanding of the $M^a:M^p$ ratio has been gleaned from therapist ratings. Fourteen therapists completed ratings for 56 patients after the third, sixth, and ninth treatment sessions (Exner, 1978). All had entered dynamically oriented psychotherapy. The ratings concerned a variety of treatment issues and observations, such as promptness, estimates about motivation for treatment, ease of sharing concerns, and such. Among the items included were ones concerning requests for direction, lengthy intervals of silence during the session, and impressions of a general sense of helplessness. Fifteen of the 56 patients gave pretreatment Rorschachs in which M^p was greater than M^a. The therapist ratings for that group were significantly higher for requests for direction and impressions of a general sense of helplessness when compared with those for the other 41 patients.

Exner (1978) has suggested that when M^p is greater than M^a, it indicates that the ideation of the subject, especially fantasies, will be marked much more than is common by a "Snow White" feature—that is, being more likely to take flight into passive forms of fantasy as a defensive maneuver, and also being less likely to initiate decisions or behaviors if the alternative that others will do so is available. Approximately 10% of the nonpatient adults in the normative sample have this characteristic as contrasted with 35% of the schizophrenic reference sample and 34% of the depressives and 36% of the character disorders. The percentages are much lower for nonpatient children, ranging from 8% to 15%, depending on the age group.

The Snow White feature is probably much more of a liability for introversives than for extratensives, because introversives are more prone to rely on the workings of their inner life. It is probably an even greater liability for the schizophrenic. The composite of disturbed thinking and fantasy abuse can only portend poorly for appropriate decision making. This is relevant not only to schizophrenia: Any person who engages in unusual patterns of thinking is more likely to emit poorly organized or implemented decisions.

Thus, if the value for M is greater than one and the value for M^p is one point more than the value for M^a, it indicates that the subject has a stylistic tendency to use fantasy excessively. People such as this are prone to defensively substitute fantasy for reality in stress situations much more often than most people. This form of avoidance/denial provides some temporary relief from stress by replacing an unpleasant situation with one that is easily managed. However, it also tends to breed a dependency on others because of the implicit assumption that external forces will bring resolution to the situation if it can be avoided long enough. The abuse of this tactic creates risks for any subject, but probably more so for the introversive subject because the basic coping style is being used in ways that are likely to be ineffective. If the value for M^p is two or more points greater than the value for M^a, it indicates the presence of a marked style in which a flight into fantasy has become a routine tactic for dealing with unpleasant situations. People such as this can be assumed to have a *Snow White syndrome,* which is characterized mainly by the avoidance of responsibility and decision making. They use fantasy with an abusive excess to deny reality and often, the results are counterproductive to many of their own needs. This mode of coping involves the creation of a self-imposed helplessness because it requires a dependency on others. Unfortunately, it also makes them vulnerable to the manipulations of others. The pervasiveness of this coping style is particularly detrimental for the introversive subject because the basic ideational coping orientation becomes subservient to the avoidant-dependent orientation in situations that seem overly complex or potentially stressful.

The Intellectualization Index   An original intellectualization index was calculated as $Ab + Art$ (Exner, 1987) but subsequent research concerning what was then a content score for abstract responses (ab) suggested that abstractions are more appropriately accounted for if a special score designation is used. That research also indicates that abstraction responses account for much more variance in identifying the defensive process of intellectualization and that the content category for anthropology also contributes.

Thus, a revised index, designed to account for all three variables with the special score *AB* (Abstract) weighted double was formulated in 1990 (Exner, 1990).

Reexamination of the validation criteria from which the original index was developed, mainly therapist reports collected during the first 10 weeks of treatment concerning the defensive structure of clients, indicates that values of 4 and 5 have some limited interpretive significance. Subjects with values of 4 and 5 do tend to intellectualize more often than most others but it is erroneous to assume that this defensive strategy is a major, or frequently used feature in the psychological operations of the individual. On the other hand, when the value is 6 or greater, there is a much greater likelihood that the subject does employ intellectualization as a major tactic to neutralize some of the impact of emotion. The distribution of positive Intellectualization Indices among patients is quite intriguing. It does not occur among introversive outpatients who have High *Lambda* styles and only among a small proportion (7%) of introversive outpatients with values for *Lambda* less than 1.0. On the other hand, the Intellectualization Index is positive (>5) for 12% of outpatient High *Lambda* style ambitents and 31% of High *Lambda* style outpatient extratensives. When *Lambda* is not positive, the Index is positive for 19% of outpatient ambitents and 57% of outpatient extratensives. Thus, it appears that this defensive tactic is much more common among those who become more involved with their feelings but apparently have some sense of discomfort with them.

Although this process serves to reduce or neutralize the impact of the emotions, it also represents a naive form of denial that tends to distort the true impact of a situation. In effect, it is a pseudointellectual process that conceals and/or denies the presence of affect and, as a result, tends to reduce the likelihood that feelings will be dealt with directly and/or realistically. People such as this tend to become more vulnerable to disorganization during intense emotional experiences because the tactic becomes less effective as the magnitude of affective stimuli increases.

Morbid Content Responses and Ideation   Most of the data regarding the relationship between Morbid content responses and thinking is derived from research concerning depression, and the reports of therapists working with depressed patients. The Special Score *MOR* evolved from efforts to study depression in children. Some previous efforts to use morbid content as a suicide indicator had been reported to have achieved some modest success (White & Schreiber, 1952; Sakheim, 1955; Fleischer, 1957; Thomas, Ross, Brown, & Duszynski, 1973). Extrapolating from those works, plus some of the criteria listed for the Fisher and Cleveland (1958) Penetration scoring, a listing of possible criteria for *MOR* was submitted to five judges who worked independently. Subsequently, those definitions that were selected by all five judges as reflecting some aspect of morbidity were integrated, and the resulting criteria tested for interscorer reliability, which yielded a 95% agreement among 10 scorers and 15 records that contained a total of 57 *MOR* answers (Exner & McCoy, 1981).

The retest reliability of *MOR* among nonpatient adults ranges from .66 to .71 for long-term retests, to .78 to .88 when the retest is administered during a period of 30 days or less. The reliability of *MOR* among nonpatient children, over brief intervals, is slightly higher than for adults, ranging from .84 to .94. This is probably because children tend to have a greater proportion of records in which *one MOR* appears. Only 51% of nonpatient adults have at least one *MOR* in their records as compared with between 59% and 100% of the records of younger nonpatients, depending on the age group. The mean for nonpatient adults is 0.7, with a mode of zero, whereas the means for all age groups of children and adolescents approach or exceed 1.0. This is apparently because younger clients give a greater frequency of the "flattened" animal response to Card VI, a response which is, by far, the most frequently given *MOR* by both children and adults.

Schizophrenics, character problems, and nondepressed outpatients average about one *MOR* answer, and they appear in slightly more than half of the protocols of those groups. *MOR* responses appear in 219 (70%) of the 315 protocols that constitute the adult depressive reference sample, with all 219 giving at least two *MOR* and 181 of the 219 giving three or more. Exner and Weiner (1982) found that inpatient children with a primary symptom of depression average nearly three *MOR* responses as compared with about one for other inpatient children. They were also able to retest 22 depressed inpatient children after approximately 8 months of treatment and found that the mean for that group had declined from 2.94 in the first test to 1.01 in the second test.

There is a significant negative correlation ($r = -.41, p < .01$) between *MOR* and the Egocentricity Index; that is, as *MOR* is elevated, the Index tends to be lower. A considerable elevation in *MOR,* greater than three, was found in 72 of 101 (71%) protocols collected within 60 days prior to an effected suicide. This is the group of records used to cross-validate the original Suicide Constellation discovered by Exner and Wylie (1977). A discriminant function analysis reveals that *MOR* > 3 does contribute to the differentiation of the suicide group from various control groups and, as such, it has been added as a twelfth variable to the revised Suicide Constellation (Exner, Martin, & Mason, 1984).

The pretreatment records of the 430 outpatients who volunteered to participate in the long-term treatment effects study (Exner, 1978) were coded for *MOR,* and any containing three or more *MOR* responses were used to create a separate group, disregarding presenting symptom patterns ($N = 76$). The therapist ratings for these patients, completed early into treatment, were reviewed and compared with the ratings of 76 other patients, drawn randomly from the remaining 354 subjects in the study. There was no *single* markedly consistent difference between the groups; however, a composite of nine items concerning attitudes toward the self, the presenting problem, and expectations for the future were rated significantly lower, that is, more negatively for the high *MOR* group. In other words, those patients who had more than two *MOR* responses were rated as being clearly pessimistic about their future, including the likelihood of some favorable treatment outcome.

If the value for *MOR* is 3 or higher, it is very likely that the thinking of the subject is marked frequently by a pessimistic set in which relationships are viewed with a sense of doubt and/or discouragement, and gloomy outcomes are anticipated regardless of the quality of the effort invested.

Critical Special Scores & *WSUM*6   The Critical Special Scores—that is, the Levels 1 and 2 *DV, INCOM, DR,* and *FABCOM,* plus the *ALOG* and *CONTAM*—are used to identify events in which some difficulty occurred in various aspects of thinking. None of these events, with the possible exceptions of the *DR*2, *FABCOM*2 responses and the *CONTAM,* are necessarily major causes for concern, *provided* that they occur with very low frequencies. Nearly 81% of the subjects in the adult nonpatient sample gave at least one response for which one of these Special Scores was assigned, and the mean for the group is closer to 2 than to 1. Nonpatient children tend to give more. For example, 7-year-olds average nearly 6, and 10-year-olds average slightly more than 5. Collectively, the Critical Special Scores fall on a crude continuum regarding cognitive mismanagement or dysfunction, with the *DV*1 at one end and the *CONTAM* at the other end. In general, the continuum might be conceptualized in terms of three segments, one reflecting events involving relatively mild cognitive slippage, a second portraying more serious instances of faulty thinking, and the third segment representing events involving severe cognitive dysfunction.

*DV*1 *INCOM*1 *DR*1	*DV*2 *FABCOM*1 *INCOM*2 *ALOG*	*DR*2 *FABCOM*2 *CONTAM*
MILD	SERIOUS	SEVERE

The *FABCOM*1 answers probably fall slightly to the left of the midpoint of the continuum. Generally, nonpatient adults give more of the Special Scores that are in the first segment of the continuum, that is, the *DV*1, *INCOM*1, and *DR*1 responses. Fifty-three percent of the 700 adult nonpatient records include at least one *DV*1 response, 46% contain at least one *INCOM*1 response, and 15% at least one *DR*1 response. The *FABCOM*1 appears in 16% of the adult nonpatient records, but only 7 of the 700 cases (1%) contain *DV*2 responses, 3 (.5%) contain *INCOM*2 answers, and 29 (4%) have *ALOG* responses. Thirteen (2%) have *DR*2 or *FABCOM*2 answers and none of the 700 records contains a *CONTAM*.

At the other extreme, the 320-subject schizophrenic reference sample averages more than nine Special Scores, and 227 of the 320 give at least one level 2 response including 202 (63%) that give at least one *FABCOM*2 and 35 (5%) who gave at least one *CONTAM*.

The *DV*1 appears to involve brief instances of cognitive mismanagement. Distorted language use or idiosyncratic modes of expression impede the subject's ability to communicate clearly. They appear most commonly among the records of children who have yet to develop the language skills necessary to convey an impression easily. Although not uncommon among adults, they are not expected in the record of a bright person, and when they occur, the content of the *DV*1 may carry considerable importance. Taken alone, two or three *DV*1 responses have little importance, but if they occur with a much higher frequency in the adult record, some sort of cognitive problem exists and the issue of language skills should be explored more fully. *DV*2 responses represent a more serious form of cognitive mismanagement and often will convey some sort of preoccupation that is intruding into the conceptual operations of the subject.

*INCOM*1s are the most common of the six Special Scores in the records of nonpatient adults and also appear frequently in the records of children. They signify unusual condensations of blot details in a single object and, as such, apparently indicate a form of discrimination failure, and reflect a kind of concrete reasoning. As with the *DV*1 responses, one or two *INCOM*1s, as the only Critical Special Scores in the record, usually will not be cause for concern. On the other hand *INCOM*2 answers usually go well beyond simple levels of discrimination failure. They reflect very strained logic systems that are most common among those whose thinking is seriously impacted by preoccupations and/or a marked disregard for reality.

*DR*1 responses usually represent a more moderate form of dysfunction than in either the *DV*1 or *INCOM*1. They illustrate a peculiarity in the verbiage of the subject that may be the product of poor judgment, but more likely illustrates poor control over ideational impulses. Most *DR*1 responses are detachments from the task and often consist of circumstantial-like ramblings. *DR*2 answers represent a very serious problem in ideational impulse control. They are common among various inpatient groups but appear most frequently in the records of hypomanic subjects whose affective disorganization impairs their ability to stay "on target." Larger numbers of *DR*1 answers, or even one *DR*2 answer, suggest that patterns of disjointed thinking may exist which can interfere significantly with effective decision making.

*FABCOM*1 answers typically are more serious than any of the other Level 1 responses because they involve an irrational synthesizing action. They are not uncommon among younger children but, as Weiner and Exner (1978) have noted, the frequency of *FABCOM*1's becomes markedly lower during adolescence. They appear most frequently in the records of schizophrenics, and reflect the very loose associations that often occur in thinking which is inconsistent, disorganized, and primitive. *FABCOM*1 responses often appear in the records of people with less mature forms of thinking. For instance, at least one appears in 40% of the protocols in the Character Disorders reference group. When more than two *FABCOM*1 answers appear in a record, it should be regarded as a very negative sign, unless the record is taken from a youngster under the age of 12. *FABCOM*2 answers are indicative of much more serious problems in thinking. They reflect a serious disregard for reality and suggest that the judgments of the subject often are severely flawed, or that ideational impulse control is very limited. The presence of even one *FABCOM*2 indicates that serious disruptions in conceptualizing occur frequently, and that the ideational operations of the subject will be marked by distortion. This may be the result of serious affective disruption that clouds judgment but more often is the product of chronically disturbed patterns of thought.

ALOG answers also occur with a considerable frequency among younger children, but that frequency falls markedly during adolescence. They appear in about 4% of adult nonpatient records and about 12% of the records for outpatient adults, but usually with very low frequencies of one to two. They are much more common in the protocols of severely disturbed subjects, especially schizophrenics. They represent forms of strained reasoning in which faulty cause-and-effect relationships are simplistically created and maintained. They are a mark of poor logic and flawed judgment, either of which can have substantial effects on decision operations and the formation of behaviors.

CONTAM responses illustrate the most severe form of cognitive disorganization that is detected in the Rorschach. They involve a completely unrealistic merging of experience. It may be that some form of perceptual merging also occurs, but this has never been established. It is clear that there is a fluidity of thinking which also involves strained reasoning. The process creates a product that is the antithesis of adaptive behavior. No *CONTAM* answers appear in the protocols in the depressive, outpatient, or character disorders reference groups.

Ideally, a record will contain none of the Critical Special Scores but, as has been noted earlier, the majority of subjects from almost most every group manifest one or more of these forms of slippage as they take the test. One, two, or three, especially of the less serious, is not an uncommon finding among nonpatient adults, and even more occur among nonpatient children. However, when the sum exceeds five in the record of an adult, or more than one standard deviation above the age mean for a younger client, the data are too compelling to avoid concluding that some disturbance in thinking exists. In many cases, the sum of the weightings for each of the scores can offer ready information concerning the extent to which impairment may exist (*WSUM*6).

Nonpatient adults have a mean *WSUM*6 of nearly 4 and a standard deviation indicating that 6, or even 7 may not be uncommon. If a more liberal application of two standard deviations above the mean is applied, a *WSUM*6 greater than 9 reflects less than 8% of the nonpatient sample. However, the interpretation of data concerning the Critical Special

Scores should not be approached concretely. Obviously, the presence of a combination of three *DV*s and three *INCOM*s can be regarded more favorably than if the combination consists of two *DR,* two *FABCOM,* and two *ALOG* responses. The first combination yields a *WSUM*6 of 9, whereas the second yields a *WSUM* of 24. The second combination offers reasonably clear evidence of disturbed thinking, whereas the first falls along a border of maybe or maybe not. The mean *WSUM*6 for adult nonpatients is 3.2, but for nonpatient children it is considerably higher. For instance, the mean for 5-year-olds is nearly 15, falling gradually to about 13 for 9-year-olds, about 9 for 12-year-olds, and slightly less than 5 for 16-year-olds. On the other hand, the mean *WSUM*6 is nearly 45 for the schizophrenic reference group, slightly more than 18 for the depressive reference group, about 11 for the character disorders group, and nearly 10 for outpatients.

It is also important to review whether the Special Scores cluster in any particular way, such as all, or almost all, involving the same determinants or contents. If clustering does occur, it may provide some clarification about the features of the thinking problem. For example, a review of 70 protocols of inpatients diagnosed as paranoid schizophrenic by DSM-III criteria reveals that nearly two-thirds of their Critical Special Scores appear in responses involving human content, even though human content responses constitute only about 25% of the total *R* in their records. This is not too surprising, because paranoid ideation often focuses on elements related to interpersonal relations. In a similar pattern, subjects in the depressive reference sample gave more than 60% of their Critical Special Scores in responses that also have achromatic or chromatic color determinants, even though those answers represent less than one-third of the responses that they delivered. It seems logical to postulate that this probably reflects some of the impact of their affective difficulties on their thinking.

QUALITY OF RESPONSES WITH SPECIAL SCORES

After the quantitative data for the Critical Special Scores has been studied, it is very important that each response containing a Special Score be read to evaluate degree and substance of the ideational slippage. Although the Level 1–Level 2 differentiation is designed to differentiate the bizarre from the more commonplace forms of slippage, there is no substitute for reading (hearing) the answer. The majority of Level 1 answers will sound naive or immature, as will some Level 2 answers. Quite often, a reading of the target response will afford new information concerning the sophistication, or lack thereof, that distinguishes that ideational activity of the subject. Level 2 responses and *ALOG* answers often reveal some major preoccupation but, in other instances, they will convey a remarkable distortion in judgment and/or conceptualization. The astute Rorschacher will learn rather quickly to differentiate the more pathological kinds of answers from those that are simply the product of unsophisticated thinking.

The *M* Quality   The *M* Quality distribution consists of a listing of the form quality frequencies for the human movement responses in the record. Because the frequency of *M* is usually low, ranging from 3 to 9 for the subjects in the adult nonpatient sample, most, or all of these are expected to include an appropriate use of form. As noted in Chapter 17, *M* responses appear to reflect the deliberate directing of thinking and, as such, the more they deviate from the realities of the stimulus field, the more likely the thinking activity will be marked by deviation. *M*s also include projections that, in some ways, represent some of the inner qualities of the subject. None of the subjects of the 700 in the adult nonpatient sample failed to give an *M* response, and only 22 (3%) gave *M* − responses. This is in contrast to 32% of the reference sample of character problems who gave at least one *M* −, almost 30% of outpatients who gave at least one *M* −, 40% of the depressives who had *M* −s in their record, and 80% of the schizophrenics who gave *M* − responses.

The presence of one *M* − response is sufficient to raise concern about peculiarity in ideation. If the frequency is greater than 1, the likelihood of a marked thinking problem is increased considerably. Two *M* − responses is an unusual finding, and if more than two occur, the presence of disoriented, very strange thinking is practically certain. If most, or all of the *M* − answers are passive, it increases the probability that characteristics are present from which delusional operations evolve. It is also very important to study the contents of *M* − answers carefully to determine if they have homogeneous features. This is frequently the case in reactive psychoses or in severe disturbances that include a well-fixed delusional system.

A second kind of *M* response that often signifies disturbed thinking is the one in which there is no form use. These are abstract or symbolic responses, such as, "This represents madness," or "It is the depth of depression," or "It smells delicious." They represent a form of detachment from, or marked disregard for the stimulus field, and may have features that are quite similar to a hallucinatory-like operation. *M* no-form responses are quite rare and when they occur, they should be interpreted in the same context as if a significant elevation in *M* − responses exists.

Whereas the *M* − and *M* no-form responses indicate the probability of serious problems in thinking, *Mu* responses represent an idiographic, but not necessarily peculiar form of ideation. One or two *Mu* answers can be taken as a positive sign, *if* the record also contains other *M*s in which the form features are used in a more conventional manner. If the record contains several *M*s, most or all of which are *Mu,* it may indicate that the thinking of the subject is overly unique and/or eccentric, but not necessarily maladaptive. The extent to which this may or may not be a liability must be judged in light of other personality characteristics that are indicated in the record, and especially whether there is other evidence of considerable cognitive slippage. If so, this will usually be revealed by an elevation in the number and variety of the Critical Special Scores.

Reading the Human Movement Answers The final step in evaluating ideational activity involves a reading of all of the *M* responses focusing on the quality of the responses, that is, whether they are sophisticated, commonplace, or reflect a more juvenile or primitive form of conceptualization. As with the reading of answers that contain Critical Special Scores, the objective of this procedure is to "listen" to how the subject has conceptualized. The purpose of reading the answers has nothing to do with their content, that is, the projected material. That is studied later when the data for the cluster on self-perception are reviewed. Instead, the focus is on the quality of the response. In adult records, the conceptual quality of the movement answers is expected to be at least commonplace or even sophisticated. If one or more of the *M* answers has a more juvenile or primitive conceptualization, it can be postulated that some of the thinking of the subject tends to be less mature or more unsophisticated. Conversely, human movement responses given by children or younger adolescents usually include some answers that have more juvenile or primitive characteristics. if the *M* responses of a younger subject contains none of these features, it can be postulated that the thinking of the subject tends to be more sophisticated and/or mature than is common for his or her peers.

THE L.S. PROTOCOL AND IDEATION

The variables related to ideation for the L.S. protocol are shown in Table 76. The data for the *EB* are quite important as they indicate that the subject is an ambitent. This suggests that he is not very consistent in his coping behavior, sometimes using the delay tactics of thinking through issues like the introversive but at other times merging feelings with his thinking and prone toward a more trial-and-error approach. It is likely that neither of these tactics has proven useful, and he is prone to be more indecisive, use more effort, repeat more errors, and generally be less effective in his problem-solving activities. This kind of ideational inefficiency creates a special burden for one with an obsessive style. Whereas they prefer to be methodical and systematic, the lack of consistency in coping runs counterproductive to that objective. As a result, the obsessiveness tends to create a sense of discomfort and frequent experiences in which indecisiveness promotes anxiousness and/or tension. This probably contributes to some of his reported symptoms.

The left side *eb* value of 8 is somewhat higher than expected, indicating the presence of considerable peripheral ideation that tends to interfere with attention and concentration, which is one of the symptoms that he reports. This level of interference only serves to exacerbate his already present tendencies to vacillate in decision operations. An examination of the components of the *eb* reveals that the value for *FM* (5) is within expected limits and that the increase is a product of the elevation in *m*, apparently created by the situationally related stress that he is experiencing.

The two active:passive ratios (*a:p*, $M^a:M^p$) offer no significant data. The values for *a:p* (8:5) are not disparate. Thus, there is no reason to suspect that his thinking or his values lack flexibility in spite of his obsessive style. Similarly, the $M^a:M^p$ ratio contains more active movement (4:1), which is interpretively meaningless as there are no known relationships between active movement in general and any ideational and/or behavioral activity. The value for the Intellectualization Index (4) is slightly elevated, suggesting that he does tend to use intellectualization more frequently than most people as a method of neutralizing affect, however, this is not a major defensive tactic in his personality organization. There are no *MOR* responses in the record and only one Critical Special Score, a *DR*1 coded to Response 10 on Card V. It occurred in the Response Phase, "It could be a bat or a butterfly, I think more a butterfly now that I look at it *because I said bat before.*" It is not a pathological response, but rather seems to convey

Table 76.   L.S. Protocol Data Concerning Ideation

			Critical Special Scores			
EB = 4:3.5	*EBPer* = N/A	*M* Quality				
eb = 8:4	(*FM* = 5	+ = 2	*DV*	= 0	*DV*2	= 0
a:p = 8.5	*m* = 3)	*o* = 2	*INC*	= 0	*INC*2	= 0
2*AB*+*Art*+*Ay* = 4	$M^a:M^p$ = 4:1	*u* = 0	*DR*	= 1	*DR*2	= 0
MOR = 0		− = 0	*FAB*	= 0	*FAB*2	= 0
			ALOG	= 0	*SUM*6	= 1
Responses to Be Read for Quality			*CON*	= 0	*WSUM*6	= 3
2, 6, 16, 22						

a need to convince the examiner and/or himself that he is really more flexible than might appear to be the case. There are no $M-$ responses and, in light of the data regarding the Critical Special Scores, there is no reason to suspect any serious problem in thinking.

He gave four M answers. The first is on Card I, Response 2, "It could also be a modern dance of some sort with a woman standing in the center with her hands in the air and two creatures dancing around her." This is a relatively high-quality answer. The second M occurs in Response 6, to Card III, "A couple of men bending over to lift something up." This is not an uncommon response even though it becomes overelaborated ($+$) in the Inquiry. The quality is adequate for an adult, but not nearly as sophisticated as the Card I answer. The third M appears in Response 16, to Card VII, "This way it looks like a couple of women doing the can-can." Again, the response becomes overelaborated in the Inquiry, but regardless of that feature, the quality of the basic answer is rather sophisticated at the onset. The final M answer occurs in Response 22, on Card IX, "You know, this way it looks like a person on a motorcycle or bike." It is also a fairly sophisticated answer. Collectively, three of his four M answers are of very good quality and the fourth is by no means unsophisticated.

Overall, it appears as if the ideational activity of L.S. generally is clear, unimpaired, and usually of good quality. There is no reason to believe that he is inflexible, in spite of his obsessive-like style. Probably his greatest handicap lies in the fact that he is not predictable in his ideational approaches, that is, he lacks a consistency in his approaches to coping and/or decision making. In addition, he is currently experiencing an excess of peripheral ideation that appears to be interfering with his attention and concentration. This higher level of peripheral ideation seems to be directly related to situationally related stress and can be expected to be reduced if that stress is identified and contended with effectively.

REFERENCES

Abrams, E. W. (1955) Predictions of intelligence from certain Rorschach factors. *Journal of Clinical Psychology,* **11,** 81–84.

Ames, L. B., Learned, J., Metraux, R. W., and Walker, R. N. (1954) *Rorschach Responses in Old Age.* New York: Harper & Row.

Ames, L. B., Metraux, R. W., and Walker, R. N. (1971) *Adolescent Rorschach Responses.* New York: Brunner/Mazel.

Armitage, S. G., Greenberg, T. D., Pearl, D., Berger, D. G., and Daston, P. G. (1955) Predicting intelligence from the Rorschach. *Journal of Consulting Psychology,* **19,** 321–329.

Baker, L. M., and Harris, J. G. (1949) The validation of Rorschach test result against laboratory behavior. *Journal of Clinical Psychology,* **5,** 161–164.

Baughman, E. E. (1954) A comparative analysis of Rorschach forms with altered stimulus characteristics. *Journal of Projective Techniques,* **18,** 151–164.

Baughman, E. E. (1959) An experimental analysis of the relationship between stimulus structure and behavior in the Rorschach. *Journal of Projective Techniques,* **23,** 134–183.

Beck, S. J. (1930) The Rorschach Test and personality diagnosis: The feeble minded. *American Journal of Psychiatry,* **10,** 19–52.

Beck, S. J. (1932) The Rorschach Test as applied to a feeble-minded group. *Archives of Psychology,* **84,** 136.

Beck, S. J. (1945) *Rorschach's Test. II. A Variety of Personality Pictures.* New York: Grune & Stratton.

Beck, S. J. (1948) Rorschach F Plus and the Ego in treatment. *American Journal of Orthopsychiatry,* **18,** 395–401.

Becker, W. C. (1956) A genetic approach to the interpretation and evaluation of the process-reactive distinction in schizophrenia. *Journal of Abnormal and Social Psychology,* **53,** 229–236.

Berkowitz, M., and Levine J. (1953) Rorschach scoring categories as diagnostic "signs." *Journal of Consulting Psychology,* **17,** 110–112.

Blatt, S. J., and Allison, J. (1963) Methodological considerations in Rorschach research: The *W* response as an expression of abstractive and integrated strivings. *Journal of Projective Techniques,* **27,** 269–278.

Bourguinon, E. E., and Nett, E. W. (1955) Rorschach Populars in a sample of Haitian protocols. *Journal of Projective Techniques,* **19,** 117–124.

Bryant, E. L., and Exner, J. E. (1974) Performance on the Revised Minnesota Paper Form Board Test by under and overincorporators under timed and nontimed conditions. Workshops Study No. 188 (unpublished), Rorschach Workshops.

Bryant, E. L., Kline, J. R., and Exner, J. E. (1978) Trails A and B performance as related to the *Zd* score. Workshops Study No. 259 (Unpublished), Rorschach Workshops.

Caldwell, B. M. (1954) The use of the Rorschach in personality research with the aged. *Journal of Gerontology,* **9,** 316–323.

Cass, W. A., and McReynolds, P. (1951) A contribution to the Rorschach norms. *Journal of Consulting Psychology,* **15,** 178–184.

Chesrow, E. J., Woiska, P. H., and Reinitz, A. H. (1949) A psychometric evaluation of aged white males. *Geriatrics,* **4,** 169–177.

Davidson, H. H., and Kruglov, L. (1952) Personality characteristics of the institutionalized aged. *Journal of Consulting Psychology,* **16,** 5–12.

Exner, J. E. (1959) The influence of chromatic and achromatic color in the Rorschach. *Journal of Projective Techniques,* **23,** 418–425.

Exner, J. E. (1974) *The Rorschach: A Comprehensive System. Volume 1.* New York: Wiley.

Exner, J. E. (1978) *The Rorschach: A Comprehensive System. Volume 2: Current research and advanced interpretation.* New York: Wiley.

Exner, J. E. (1983) Rorschach Assessment. In I. B. Weiner (Ed.), *Clinical Methods in Psychology,* (2nd Ed.). New York: Wiley.

Exner, J. E. (1987) An intellectualization index. *Alumni Newsletter.* Asheville, N.C.: Rorschach Workshops.

Exner, J. E. (1990) The intellectualization index $[2AB + (Art + Ay)]$. *Alumni Newsletter.* Asheville, N.C.: Rorschach Workshops.

Exner, J. E. (1991) *The Rorschach: A Comprehensive System. Volume 2: Interpretation,* (2nd Ed.). New York: Wiley.

Exner, J. E., Armbruster, G. L., and Viglione, D. (1978) The temporal stability of some Rorschach features. *Journal of Personality Assessment,* **42,** 474–482.

Exner, J. E., Armbruster, G. L., and Wylie, J. R. (1976) TAT stories and the $M^a{:}M^p$ ratio. Workshops Study No. 225 (unpublished), Rorschach Workshops.

Exner, J. E., and Bryant, E. L. (1974) Flexibility in creative efforts as related to three Rorschach variables. Workshops Study No. 187 (unpublished), Rorschach Workshops.

Exner, J. E., and Bryant, E. L. (1975) Serial learning by over and underincorporators with limited and unlimited numbers of training trials. Workshops Study No. 194 (unpublished), Rorschach Workshops.

Exner, J. E., Bryant, E. L., and Armbruster, G. L. (1979) Eye activity in a matching familiar figures task of 12 adolescents selected on the basis of *Zd* scores. Workshops Study No. 263 (unpublished), Rorschach Workshops.

Exner, J. E., and Caraway, E. W. (1974) Identification of incomplete stimuli by high positive *Zd* and high negative *Zd* subjects. Workshops Study No. 186 (unpublished), Rorschach Workshops.

Exner, J. E., and Leura, A. V. (1977) Rorschach performances of volunteer and nonvolunteer adolescents. Workshops Study No. 238 (unpublished), Rorschach Workshops.

Exner, J. E., Martin, L. S., and Mason, B. (1984) A review of the Rorschach Suicide Constellation. 11th International Congress of Rorschach and Projective Techniques. Barcelona, Spain.

Exner, J. E., and McCoy, R. (1981) An experimental score for morbid content (MOR). Workshops Study No. 260 (unpublished), Rorschach Workshops.

Exner, J. E., and Murillo, L. G. (1973) Effectiveness of regressive ECT with process schizophrenia. *Diseases of the Nervous System,* **34,** 44–48.

Exner, J. E., and Stanley, F. B. (1979) Time estimates for three intervals by 12 subjects selected on the basis of *Zd* scores. Workshops Study No. 268 (unpublished), Rorschach Workshops.

Exner, J. E., Thomas, E. A., and Mason, B. (1985) Children's Rorschachs: Description and prediction. *Journal of Personality Assessment,* **49,** 13–20.

Exner, J. E., Viglione, D. J., and Gillespie, R. (1984) Relationships between Rorschach variables as relevant to the interpretation of structural data. *Journal of Personality Assessment,* **48,** 65–70.

Exner, J. E., and Weiner, I. B. (1982) *The Rorschach: A Comprehensive System. Volume 3: Assessment of children and adolescents.* New York: Wiley.

Exner, J. E., and Wylie, J. R. (1974) Therapist ratings of patient "insight" in an uncovering form of psychotherapy. Workshops Study No. 192 (unpublished), Rorschach Workshops.

Exner, J. E., and Wylie, J. R. (1977) Some Rorschach data concerning suicide. *Journal of Personality Assessment,* **41,** 339–348.

Feldman, M. J., Gurrslin, C., Kaplan, M. L., and Sharlock, N. (1954) A preliminary study to develop a more discriminating F+ ratio. *Journal of Clinical Psychology,* **10,** 47–51.

Fisher, S., and Cleveland, S. E. (1958) *Body Image and Personality,* New York: Van Nostrand Reinhold.

Fleischer, M. S. (1957) Differential Rorschach configurations of suicidal patients: A psychological study of threatened, attempted, and successful suicides. Unpublished doctoral dissertation, Yeshiva University.

Frank, I. H. (1952) A genetic evaluation of perceptual structuralization in certain psychoneurotic disorders by means of the Rorschach Technique. Unpublished doctoral dissertation, Boston University.

Fried, R. (1977) Christmas elves on the Rorschach: A popular Finnish response and its cultural significance. IXth International Congress of Rorschach and other projective techniques. Fribourg, Switzerland.

Friedman, H. (1952) Perceptual regression in schizophrenia: A hypothesis suggested by use of the Rorschach Test. *Journal of Genetic Psychology,* **81,** 63–98.

Gibby, R. G. (1951) The stability of certain Rorschach variables under conditions of experimentally induced sets: The intellectual variables. *Journal of Projective Techniques,* **3,** 3–25.

Goldberger, L. (1961) Reactions to perceptual isolation and Rorschach manifestations of the primary process. *Journal of Projective Techniques,* **25,** 287–302.

Hallowell, A. I. (1956) The Rorschach Technique in personality and culture studies. In B. Klopfer et al. (Eds.), *Developments in the Rorshach Technique.* Vol. 2. Yonkers-on-Hudson, N.Y.: World Book.

Hertz, M. R. (1940) The shading response in the Rorschach inkblot test: A review of its scoring and interpretation. *Journal of General Psychology,* **23,** 123–167.

Holtzberg, J. D., and Belmont, L. (1952) The relationship between factors on the Wechsler Bellevue and Rorschach having common psychological rationale. *Journal of Consulting Psychology,* **16,** 23–30.

Honigmann, J. J. (1949) *Culture and Ethos of Kaska Society.* Yale University Publications in Anthropology, No. 40.

Joseph, A., and Murray, V. F. (1951) *Chamorros and Carolinians of Saipan: Personality Studies.* Howard University Press.

Kadinsky, D. (1952) Significance of depth psychology of apperceptive tendencies in the Rorschach Test. *Rorschachiana,* **4,** 36–37.

Kahn, M. W. (1967) Correlates of Rorschach reality adherence in the assessment of murderers who plead insanity. *Journal of Projective Techniques,* **31,** 44–47.

Kerr, M. (1934) The Rorschach Test applied to children. *British Journal of Psychology,* **25,** 170–185.

Kisker, G. W. (1942) A projective approach to personality patterns during insulin shock and metrazol convulsive therapy. *Journal of Abnormal and Social Psychology,* **37,** 120–124.

Klebanoff, S. G. (1949) The Rorschach Test in an analysis of personality in general paresis. *Journal of Personality,* **17,** 261–272.

Klopfer, W. (1946) Rorschach patterns of old age. *Rorschach Research Exchange,* **10,** 145–166.

Klopfer, B., and Kelley, D. (1942) *The Rorschach Technique.* Yonkers-on-Hudson, N.Y.: World Book.

Knopf, I. J. (1956) Rorschach summary scores and differential diagnosis. *Journal of Consulting Psychology,* **20,** 99–104.

Korchin, S. J. (1960) Form perception and ego functioning. In M. Rickers-Ovsiankina (Ed.), *Rorschach Psychology.* New York: Wiley.

Leighton, D., and Kluckholm, C. (1947) *Children of the People: The Navaho Individual and His Development.* Harvard University Press.

Lotsoff, E. (1953) Intelligence, verbal fluency and the Rorschach Test. *Journal of Consulting Psychology,* **17,** 21–24.

McCandless, B. B. (1949) The Rorschach as a predictor of academic success. *Journal of Applied Psychology,* **33,** 43–50.

Mason, B. J., Cohen, J. B., and Exner, J. E. (1985) Schizophrenic, depressive, and nonpatient personality organizations described by Rorschach factor structures. *Journal of Personality Assessment,* **49,** 295–305.

Mason, B. J., and Exner, J. E. (1984) Correlations between WAIS subtests and nonpatient adult Rorschach data. Workshops Study 289 (unpublished), Rorschach Workshops.

Meichanbaum, D. H. (1974) *Cognitive Behavior Modification.* Morristown, N.J.: General Learning Press.

Molish, H. B. (1967) Critique and Problems of Research. In S. J. Beck and H. B. Molish, *Rorschach's Test. II: A Variety of Personality Pictures,* (2nd Ed.). New York: Grune & Stratton.

Molish, H. B., and Beck, S. J. (1958) Further exploration of the six schizophrenias: Type S-3. *American Journal of Orthopsychiatry,* **28,** 483–505, 807–827.

Paulsen, A. (1941) Rorschachs of school beginners. *Rorschach Research Exchange,* **5,** 24–29.

Piotrowski, Z. (1939) Rorschach manifestations of improvement in insulin treated schizophrenics. *Psychosomatic Medicine,* **1,** 508–526.

Piotrowksi, Z. (1957) *Perceptanalysis.* New York: Macmillan.

Piotrowski, Z. (1960) The movement score. In M. Rickers-Ovsiankina (Ed.), *Rorschach Psychology.* New York: Wiley.

Prados, M., and Fried, E. (1943) Personality structure of the older aged groups. *Journal of Clinical Psychology,* **3,** 113–120.

Rabin, A., Papania, N., and McMichael, A. (1954) Some effects of alcohol on Rorschach performance. *Journal of Clinical Psychology,* **10,** 252–255.

Rapaport, D., Gill, M., and Schafer, R. (1946) *Psychological Diagnostic Testing.* Vol. 2. Chicago: Yearbook Publishers.

Rorschach, H. (1921) *Psychodiagnostics.* Bern: Bircher (Transl. Hans Huber Verlag, 1942).

Sakheim, G. A. (1953) Suicidal responses on the Rorschach Test: A validation study. *Journal of Nervous and Mental Disease,* **122,** 332–344.

Saretsky, T. (1963) The effect of chlorapromazine on primary process thought maifestations. Unpublished doctoral dissertation, New York University.

Schachter, W., and Cotte, S. (1948) Prostitution and the Rorschach Test. *Archives of Neurology,* **67,** 123–138.

Sherman, M. H. (1952) A comparison of formal and content factors in the diagnostic testing of schizophrenia. *Genetic Psychology Monographs,* **46,** 183–234.

Siegel, E. L. (1953) Genetic parallels of perceptual structuralization in paranoid schizophrenia: An analysis by means of the Rorschach Technique. *Journal of Projective Techniques,* **17,** 151–161.

Sloan, W. (1947) Mental deficiency as a symptom of personality disturbance. *American Journal of Mental Deficiency,* **52,** 31–36.

Taulbee, E. S. (1955) The use of the Rorschach Test in evaluating the intellectual levels of functioning in schizophrenia. *Journal of Projective Techniques,* **19,** 163–169.

Thomas, C. B., Ross, D. C., Brown, B. S., and Duszynski, K. R. (1973) A prospective study of the Rorschachs of suicides: The predictive potential of pathological content. *The Johns Hopkins Medical Journal,* **132,** 334–360.

Weiner, I. B. (1966) *Psychodiagnosis in Schizophrenia.* New York: Wiley.

White, M. A., and Schreiber, H. (1952) Diagnosing "suicidal risks" on the Rorschach. *Psychiatric Quarterly Supplement,* **26,** 161–189.

Wilensky, H. (1959) Rorschach developmental level and social participation of chronic schizophrenics. *Journal of Projective Techniques,* **23,** 87–92.

Wishner, J. (1948) Rorschach intellectual indicators in neurotics. *American Journal of Orthopsychiatry,* **18,** 265–279.

Zamansky, H. J., and Goldman, A. E. (1960) A comparison of two methods of analyzing Rorschach data in assessing therapeutic change. *Journal of Projective Techniques,* **24,** 75–82.

Zukowsky, E. (1961) Measuring primary and secondary process thinking in schizophrenics and normals by means of the Rorschach. Unpublished doctoral dissertation, Michigan State University.

CHAPTER 19

Cluster Interpretation II— Affect, Self-Perception, Interpersonal Perception

The emotions of people are often difficult to understand because of their complexity and the variety of sources from which they originate. Emotions permeate all psychological activity and contribute to a continuing chain of psychological events from birth to death. They intermingle with thinking and have an impact on judgment, decision making, and all manner of behaviors. Sometimes they are mild and sometimes they are intense. Much of the time they are easy to manage and direct, but in some instances, it is difficult to control the influence that they exert in forming or implementing behaviors.

The Rorschach variables that relate to emotion are less numerous and more indirect than is desirable in a test designed to study the psychological organization of a person. The inferential hypotheses drawn from them must be integrated with care. The objective is, to the extent possible, to determine the role of emotion in the psychology and functioning of the subject. That role differs considerably from person to person, and many issues must be addressed when attempting to gather information concerning this complex psychological feature.

The structural variables related to affect include the *DEPI*, the *EB* (and *EBPer* when appropriate), the data for the right side of the *eb*, the *FC:CF+C* ratio, any incidence of pure *C* answers, the *Affective Ratio*, frequencies for Space and/or Color Projection responses, and the myriad of data concerning blend answers. In addition to the data for the *EB*, at least four of the other variables in the cluster reflect trait-like features of the person. They include the *FC:CF+C* ratio, the *Affective Ratio*, above-average frequencies for Space responses, and the Color Projection answer.

DEPI AND AFFECT

The Depression Index actually is not a part of the Affect Cluster. It consists of a variety of affective, cognitive, and interpersonal variables, yet it must always be considered when issues of affect are at hand. Thus, even before addressing the variables that have been empirically established as being related to affect, the value of the *DEPI* should be reviewed. If the *DEPI* is positive, either of two propositions should be stated and either forms a cornerstone against which the data of the cluster are reviewed. The first is when the value for *DEPI* is 6 or 7, which implies that a significant affective problem exists that should be given careful consideration when evaluating the other data of the cluster. This has already been described in Chapter 15. It is more common to find a value of 5 among psychiatric patients, signifying that the personality organization of the subject tends to give rise to frequent and intense experiences of depression and/or affective disruption. If a *DEPI* value of 5 is noted, it requires that all other hypotheses or conclusions concerning affect must be cast in light of this feature.

THE *EB* AND AFFECT

As with the data concerning ideation, the *EB* provides important information concerning how affect impacts on some of the basic psychological operations of the subject. This is described in Chapter 17 but is worth reviewing again here in the context of feelings. If an extratensive style is present, it can be assumed that the subject usually tends to intermingle feelings with thinking much of the time and especially during problem-solving or decision-making activities. People such as this are more prone to use and be influenced by emotion than others, are more inclined to display feelings, and often are less concerned about carefully modulating or controlling those displays. If the *EB* indicates an introversive style, the subject usually prefers to keep feelings at a more peripheral level, particularly during problem solving and decision making. While they are willing to display feelings openly, they also are inclined to be more concerned about modulating or controlling those displays. Obviously, if either the extratensive or introversive style is pervasive, it has considerable importance to any understanding of the affective features of the subject.

If the *EB* fails to indicate a coping style (*ambitent*), it is likely that the emotions of the subject are inconsistent in terms of their impact on thinking, problem-solving and decision-making behaviors. In one instance, the subject's thinking may be strongly influenced by feelings, whereas in a second instance, even though similar to the first, emotions may play only a peripheral role. Because the role of emotions in psychological functioning is not very consistent, the subject is often more vulnerable to their effects.

THE *eb* AND AFFECT

The data for the right-side *eb* value are important in understanding the impact of irritating affects on the psychological activity of a subject. Usually, the left-side value for the *eb* is expected to be larger than the right-side value, but sometimes an excess of irritating affects can be present even if the left-side value is the higher of the two. For instance, if the value of *es* is 11 or less and the left-side value of the *eb* is greater than the right side, but the value for *T* exceeds 1, or the value for *C'* exceeds 2, or the value for *V* exceeds 0, or the value for *Y* exceeds 2, a hypothesis concerning experienced discomfort is in order that focuses on the variable(s) related to the discomfort. The relation between each of these variables and affect has already been described in Chapter 16. More commonly, however, distress, or an excess of affective irritation is signaled in records that have a total value for the *eb* that is greater than 3, and the right-side value is greater than the left-side value. When this occurs, each of the variables contributing to the right-side value should be evaluated to discern the source(s) of the distress and interpretive hypotheses should be formulated from those findings.

THE *FC:CF +C* RATIO

This ratio provides an index of the extent to which emotional discharges are modulated. The data of the ratio are most meaningful when studied in relation to the *D* Scores. If either or both the D Scores fall into the minus range, the capacity for control will be much more limited, and the capacities for modulation of affect will be more vulnerable to interference by even modest, but unexpected stress experiences.

Less cognitive effort is required to identify colors than forms. Thus, color responses can involve a more passive process, but when specific form demands are injected into the translation of color stimuli, it suggests that more cognitive control has been inserted into the process. For this reason, *FC* responses equate more with affective experiences that have been controlled and/or directed by cognitive elements. On the other hand, *CF* and *C* responses illustrate instances in which the subject has been more prone to give way to the affective stimulus, and inject less cognitive modulation into the translation of the stimulus field.

Thus, the *FC* response correlates with more well controlled or modulated emotional experience, whereas the *CF* answers relate to less restrained or modulated forms of affective discharge. Pure *C* answers tend to correlate with the more unrestrained ventilation of feelings; however, it is important to note that the values for *CF* and *C* are considerably less reliable when studied separately than when studied as the unit *CF +C*. Most nonpatient adults will give more, or at least as much, *FC* as *CF +C*. On the other hand, younger subjects typically will give more *CF* and *C* answers than *FC* responses. If the value for *FC* is at least one point more or as much as twice that of the *CF +C* value, *and* the value for Pure *C* is zero, it can be assumed that the subject controls or modulates emotional discharge about as much as most adults. This is an unexpected finding in the record of a subject younger than age 15 and suggests that more stringent controls are being exerted in contending with emotional display than is common among younger clients. If the value for *FC* is more than twice but less than three times that of the *CF +C* value, *and* the value for Pure *C* is zero, a tendency exists to exert more stringent control of emotional discharges than is typical of most people. This is an extremely unusual finding in the record of a subject younger than age 15. If the value for *FC* is three or more times that of the value for *CF +C, and* the value for Pure *C* is zero, it can be assumed that the subject is much more overcontrolling of emotional displays than most people. This finding usually indicates a fearfulness or mistrust of being involved in more intense affective displays.

Sometimes, the value for *FC* is at least one point more or as much as twice that of the *CF +C* value, *and* the value for Pure *C* is one. When this occurs, it indicates that the subject modulates emotional discharge about as much as other adults most of the time, but modulation lapses occur, during which discharges are less well controlled than is the case for most adults. If this finding is positive in the record of a subject younger than age 15, it suggests that attempts at more stringent control tend to falter often and may signal the presence of a conflict state concerning the use and control of emotion. Similarly, if the value for *FC* is more than twice the value for *CF +C,* and the value for Pure *C* is one or more, it signals that emotional displays are tightly modulated most of the time, but that the stringent controls are vulnerable to failure. People such as this usually have serious conflicts about emotion and at times these conflicts will contribute to a breakdown of the routine efforts at stringent modulation.

If the record of an adult has an *FC* value that is at least one point more or as much as twice that of the *CF + C* value, *and* the value for Pure *C* is greater than one, it indicates that although the subject strives to modulate emotional discharge effectively, potentially serious lapses in modulation occur frequently. This is a very unusual finding in the protocol of an adult that should be reviewed in the context of control issues. This finding is very common in the records of children or young adolescents and probably signals the presence of a conflict concerning the appropriate modulation of emotional display.

When the value for *CF + C* is equal to or as much as two points greater than the value for *FC,* and the value for Pure *C* is zero or one, it suggests that the subject is less stringent about modulating emotional discharges than are most adults. This is not a negative finding for an adult, *if* there are no problems with controls. It simply reflects a person who tends to be more obvious or intense in expressing feelings than the average adult. Although this is a common finding for most adolescents and many younger children, it is far less common for the introversive subject regardless of age. On the other hand, if the record of an adult has a value for *CF + C* that is equal to, or as much as two points greater than the value for *FC,* and the value for Pure *C* is greater than one, it indicates some potentially serious modulation problems. People such as this are often overly intense in their emotional displays and frequently convey impressions of impulsiveness. This problem could be the product of control difficulties; however, it is equally possible that it reflects a less mature psychological organization in which the modulation of affect is not regarded as being very important. Findings such as this are very common among children and represent the affective exuberance and limited modulation that frequently manifests in the behaviors of the younger subject. However, this finding is extremely unusual among introversive subjects regardless of age and, if it is noted in the record of an introversive subject, it is reasonable to hypothesize that the efficacy or integrity of the ideational style is impaired and often short-circuited by other psychological operations.

When the value for *CF + C* is three or more points greater than the value for *FC,* and the value for Pure *C* is zero, it indicates that the subject modulates emotional discharges much less than others. Adults such as this usually call attention to themselves because of the intensity by which their feelings are expressed. This is not necessarily a liability as the effectiveness or ineffectiveness of the higher frequency of less restrained emotional displays will be determined largely by the acceptability of the displays in the social environment. This is a very common finding among younger adolescents and most children. When the value for *CF + C* is three or more points greater than the value for *FC,* and the value for Pure *C* is one or more, it reflects a very notable laxness in modulating emotion. This finding is most common among children, ages 5 to 10. It is less common among older children and adolescents and is a very unusual finding among adults. When it occurs in the adolescent or adult, they often are regarded by others as overly emotional and/or less mature. If this occurs for an introversive subject, it indicates a serious problem regarding the functioning and/or effectiveness of the style.

FINDINGS RELATED TO HYPOTHESES BASED ON THE *FC:CF + C* RATIO

The stability of the directionality shown in the ratio is quite remarkable. Exner, Armbruster, and Viglione (1978) found, in their data concerning 100 nonpatient adults retested after 3 years, that if the value in one side of the ratio exceeded the other by at least 1 point in the first test, the same directionality existed in the second test. The same stability has been found in retest studies for nonpatient adults and children when the retest is administered after a briefer interval (Exner, 1986). A similar stability in the directionality for the ratio is found among inpatient schizophrenics and depressives retested as much as one year after the first test (Exner, 1983) even though all had been involved in elaborated treatment programs and most had been discharged from hospitalization. The stability of the directionality of the ratio also exists among outpatients up to at least one year of treatment (Weiner & Exner, 1991; Exner & Sanglade, 1992).

Adult nonpatients usually give at least as many *FC* responses as *CF + C,* and usually a few more *FC.* For instance, 220 of the 700 nonpatient adults in the normative sample give at least two more *FC* answers than the composite of *CF + C.* Children do the opposite, giving significantly more *CF + C* than *FC* at every age through age 12; and even into the midadolescent years, the values for *FC* are usually not much greater than for *CF + C.* Patient groups tend to have *FC:CF + C* ratios that are much more like those of younger clients—that is, with the greater number on the right side of the ratio. This is probably because most patients experience problems in emotional control more so than is common among nonpatients. There are important exceptions. For instance, analysis of the protocols of 48 outpatients, all being treated for psychosomatic problems, indicates that 27 have *FC:CF + C* ratios of 4:1 or greater, and only four have *FC:CF + C* ratios in which the value of *FC* is less than 1½ times that of *CF + C.*

A higher right-side value in the ratio should not automatically be translated as signaling *lack* of control, because that issue is probably more contingent on the elements reflected in the *D* Score, form quality, and stability of ideation. However, it does suggest that the emotional behaviors will be marked more often by characteristics of intensity or even impulsiveness. For instance, Gill (1966) found that subjects who delay responses in a problem-solving task gave significantly more *FC* than *CF + C* answers, whereas those who did not manifest delay in forming their responses gave significantly more *CF + C.* There have also been several studies in which a higher frequency of *CF + C* responses has been found to correlate with impulsive or aggressive behaviors (Gardner, 1951; Storment & Finney, 1953; Finney, 1955; Sommer & Sommer, 1958; Townsend, 1967).

Stotsky (1952) reported that treatment success is achieved more frequently among schizophrenics whose pretreatment protocols show more *FC* than *CF + C.* Exner, Murillo, and Cannavo (1973) found significant shifts from more *CF + C* to more *FC* when comparing the pre- and post-treatment records of 105 nonschizophrenic inpatients. Exner and Murillo (1975) found a significantly greater proportion of higher right side *FC:CF + C* ratios in the discharge Rorschachs of patients who relapsed within 12 months following discharge as contrasted with nonrelapsers. Exner (1978) found that 116 of 199 outpatients, who were subsequently rated as improved by significant others, had more *CF + C* than *FC* in their pretreatment protocols, but only 61 continued to have more *CF + C* in protocols that were collected 28 months after the onset of treatment.

CF and *C* responses have considerably lower retest reliabilities than does the combination of *CF + C.* Nonetheless, the presence of a Pure *C* answer in the *FC:CF + C* ratio should not be regarded lightly, except in the records of children for whom such findings are common. Any formless response signifies a failure to modulate an impulse. It may indicate lability—that is, the person is unable to intercede cognitively because the affective experience is so intense—but it can also signal an instance in which some decision has been made to give way to the impulse rather than exert the effort necessary to intercede. In either instance, the Pure C response is commensurate with emotional behaviors that essentially are void of control. If the $FC:CF+C$ ratio is marked by multiple Pure C answers, the likelihood that at least one will occur in a retest record is substantial. A review of retest data for 300 patient and nonpatient adults reveals that when only one Pure C occurred in a first test, the probability of it reoccurring in a second test is not greater than .65, but if two or more Pure Cs occurred in the first test, the probability of at least one occurring in the second test exceeds .90. Therefore, if multiple Pure C responses appear, it is very likely that some behaviors of the subject will be featured by very intense emotional characteristics. Although this may not be disabling, the tendency creates a potential for interference with effective adjustment patterns in the adult.

THE AFFECTIVE RATIO (*Afr*)

Another datum providing information about the responsiveness of a person to emotional stimulation is the index derived from the proportion of answers to the last three blots, the *Afr*. It is one of the more intriguing variables in the test because it is difficult to establish a sound conceptual linkage that easily explains why the empirical data concerning it fall as they do. The retest correlations for the *Afr* are remarkably high. They range from the mid .80s to low .90s for both nonpatient children and adults retested after brief intervals, *and the same range* is found for adults when the retest is administered after a lengthy interval. For instance, Exner, Armbruster, and Viglione (1978) found a retest correlation of .90 for the *Afr* for their 100 nonpatient adults retested after 3 years. Findings such as these make it difficult to discount the notion that some form of style is involved.

Much of the conceptual intrigue concerning the *Afr* generates from the fact that Cards VIII, IX, and X are the only totally chromatic blots in the series. The Baughman (1959) data revealed that subjects gave substantially more responses to the standard Rorschach than to a totally achromatic version, and the bulk of the difference was created by more answers to the five blots containing chromatic color. Exner (1962) also found that subjects gave significantly more responses to the last three blots when they were presented in their natural chromatic form than when they were presented in achromatic versions. The obvious conclusion is that chromatically colored stimuli tend to provoke more answers, but that offers no support of substance for the premise that a link exists between responses to chromatically colored stimuli and emotion. There are, however, some data that support that premise.

Exner (1978) subdivided the 100 nonpatient adults retested in the Exner, Armbruster, and Viglione study, using the data of the *EB* to determine if the high long-term reliability of the *Afr* is consistent by style. The division yielded 37 introversives, 43 extratensives, and 20 ambients, and the retest correlations were consistently high for all three groups, but the *mean Afr*s for the groups were quite different from each other. The mean *Afr* for the ambients actually falls between the means for the other two groups, *which are significantly different from each other* (Introversive = .62, SD = .13; Ambient = .67, SD = .11; Extratensive = .79, SD = .14, $p < .05$). Thus, each group is relatively consistent within itself, but the two extreme groups differ considerably in terms of the proportional average number of responses to the last three cards. This is an intriguing finding, because it coincides with the fact that extratensives tend to become more involved with affect in coping situations.

These findings are not substantially different than appear in the adult nonpatient standardization sample of 700 subjects. For instance, introversive subjects who also have a High *Lambda* style have a mean *Afr* of .66 (*SD* = .15) and a mode of .57. Introversive subjects who do not have a High *Lambda* style have a mean of .67 (*SD* = .14) and a mode of .50. Ambitents who have a High *Lambda* style have a mean *Afr* of .70 (*SD* = .17) and a mode of .69, while ambitents who do not have a High *Lambda* style have a mean *Afr* of .64 (*SD* = .15) and a mode of .63. Extratensive nonpatients with a High *Lambda* style show a mean *Afr* of .75 (*SD* = .05) and a mode of .77, while extratensives who do not show a High *Lambda* style have a mean *Afr* of .73 (*SD* = .16) and a mode of .91.

These data offer a strong case from which to argue that average, or expected ranges for the *Afr* must be set with regard to the data of the *EB*. In other words, extratensive subjects generally are expected to have higher *Afr* values than either of the other *EB* groups, regardless of the value for *Lambda*. The average range for the extratensives probably is best defined at falling between .60 and .95, whereas the average range for the introversives and ambitents is more likely to be from .50 to .80.

If the value for the *Afr* is in the average range, it suggests that the subject appears to be as willing to process emotional stimuli as most people. Generally, this is not a significant finding; however, if the subject tends to have chronic difficulties with the modulation or control of emotion, it may indicate a naive lack of awareness concerning either of those problems. Usually when emotional stimuli are processed, some response or exchange is required. People who have difficulties with control often find it more beneficial to avoid emotional stimuli, thereby reducing demands made on them.

If the value of the *Afr* is above average, it indicates that the subject is very attracted by emotional stimulation. This finding is more common among extratensives but not exclusive to them. It should not be considered as a liability, but rather simply reflects a stronger interest in emotion. People such as this apparently are more intrigued with, or reinforced by emotional stimuli. This can become a liability if there are problems with control and/or modulation because the tendency to seek out emotional stimuli will probably increase the frequency with which emotional exchanges are expected or required.

If the value for the *Afr* is less than average, but no more than one standard deviation below the average range, it suggests that the subject is less interested in, or less willing to process emotional stimuli. It should not be considered as a liability, but simply reflects a preference to be less involved with emotional stimuli. If other data indicate problems with modulation or control, this finding may signal some awareness of those problems and an inclination to avoid situations in which those difficulties might be exacerbated.

If the value for the *Afr* is less than average and more than one standard deviation below the average range, it indicates a marked tendency to avoid emotional stimuli. People such as this usually are quite uncomfortable around emotion and, as a result, often become much more socially constrained or even isolated. This finding is particularly important in the protocol of a child or adolescent because it suggests that many of the everyday exchanges that contribute to development are being avoided or approached with excessive caution.

FINDINGS RELATED TO HYPOTHESES BASED ON THE *Afr*

Research concerning the relationship between the *Afr* and behavior is more impoverished than should be the case for this apparently stylistic variable. Most findings are
retrospective. For instance, findings derived from the studies of nonpatients prompted a
review of the records of outpatients participating in several long-term treatment effects
studies. A total of 279 subjects, divided on the basis of the *EB* of their pretreatment
Rorschachs, include 51 ambients, 99 extratensives, and 128 introversives, with Afr
means of .73, .69, and .67, respectively; however, the *Afr* distributions for the introversive and extratensive subjects *are almost bimodal.* The introversive sample includes 36
subjects with *Afr*s of less than .40, and another 31 subjects with *Afr*s above .80. Similarly, the extratensive group includes 27 subjects with *Afr*s below .50, and 33 with *Afr*s
greater than 90. These findings suggest that although patients, as a group, or as subgroups, do not differ substantially for the mean *Afr,* they do show markedly different
distributions of *Afr* values from those found among nonpatients. In other words, patients
tend to fall at the upper and lower extremes more often. This group of patients was
retested at approximately 9-month intervals, regardless of whether they had terminated
or were continuing in treatment. At the end of the 27th month, 199 of the 279 subjects
were rated as significantly improved by significant others. A review of their third retest
Rorschachs, collected during the 27th or 28th month of the study, showed that 172 remained relatively consistent for *EB* directionality, with 10 still in the ambient range, 92
being introversive, and 69 extratensive. A review of the distribution of *Afr* values for the
introversive and extratensive subjects reveals means of .63 and .71, respectively, with
the values being *normally distributed for each group.* The bimodality that was evident in
the first testing was not apparent at the third retest. Conversely, the distribution of *Afr*
values for the 80 subjects who were *not* rated as being improved continued to show considerable bimodality, with 27 subjects with *Afr*s lower than .50, and 24 with *Afr*s higher
than .80. One of the more fascinating findings is that 38 of those 51 subjects also had
FC:CF+C ratios in which *CF+C* is greater than *FC,* but there is *no difference* among
subjects falling in the extremes for *EB* style. About as many at each end of the distribution are introversive as are extratensive. Interestingly, 19 of the 27 subjects with low
*Afr*s have Adjusted *D* Scores of zero or in the plus range, whereas 17 of the 21 subjects
with high *Afr*s have Adjusted *D* Scores in the minus range.

Following from these findings (Exner, 1978), a random draw from the protocol pool
was completed. It consisted of 300 subjects, disregarding patient or nonpatient status,
who gave Rorschachs containing at least three achromatic color responses, and 300 subjects who gave no *C'* responses. The mean *Afr* for the group with elevations in *C'* answers
was .79 (*SD* = .14), whereas the mean *Afr* for the group giving no achromatic color responses was .55 (*SD* = .16), yielding a significant difference (*p* < .01). These findings
appear quite important because they indicate that subjects who have difficulty expressing affect tend to respond more frequently to stimuli that seem to have affective properties than do subjects who do not tend to inhibit or internalize feelings. This finding is
even more important when the groups are studied for *EB* style and the frequencies and
weighted sum of chromatic color answers. The *C'* positive group included 121 extratensives, 107 introversives, and 72 ambients, with a mean *WSUMC* of 4.94 (*SD* = 1.87).
The *C'* negative group included 103 extratensives, 118 introversives, and 79 ambients,
with a *WSUMC* mean of 4.56 (*SD* = 1.93). In effect, the two samples did not differ significantly for *EB* styles or the *WSUMC.*

Some of the developmental data also appear to support the notion of a linkage between the *Afr* and receptivity to emotionally toned stimuli. The mean *Afr* for children between the ages of 5 and 8 drops from .88 to .69. It hovers in the upper .70s to mid .60s through age 16. The standard deviations at each age tend to be less than .10, and the other descriptive statistics concerning the shape of the distributions indicate that most are very close to normality. These data seem to coincide well with what is known about the easy excitability of younger children, and how that feature gradually becomes more subdued or modulated with age.

Two laboratory studies appear to support the notion that the *Afr* does relate to interest or willingness to process affective stimuli. The first (Exner & Thomas, 1984) involved 20 nonpatients. Ten had *Afr*s exceeding .80, and the remaining 10 had *Afr*s of less than .50. They were asked to rate a series of 12 artist sketches on a scale of 1 to 12, with the value of 1 assigned to "like least" and the value of 12 assigned to "like most." Six of the sketches were done in India ink (achromatic grey-black) and all six involved people in different situations. The other six were replicas of the first six but were chromatically colored. Nine of the 10 subjects with the lower *Afr*s ranked all of the achromatic versions of the pictures higher than any of the same pictures that were chromatically colored while 7 of the 10 subjects with high *Afr*s rated all of the chromatically colored versions higher than the achromatic versions. The second involved ratings of six advertising cartoons, three of which were presented in both achromatic and chromatic form (Exner, Thomas, & Chu, 1985). The raters consisted of 10 inpatients diagnosed as having a major affective disturbance, five of whom had *Afr*s less than .50 and five with *Afr*s greater than .70. The five subjects with low *Afr*s rated at least two of the three achromatic versions more favorably, while the five subjects with higher *Afr*s uniformly rated the three chromatic versions more favorably.

Thus, the style or operation represented by the Affective Ratio seems to involve a psychological receptiveness to emotionally provoking stimuli. It apparently reflects the proneness to invest effort in the cognitive processing of those stimuli, *and the level of processing itself becomes a form of response, which in turn serves as a stimulus to other responses.* It does not relate directly to the issue of affective control but can have an indirect relationship. For example, elevations signify a tendency toward overresponsiveness, whereas low *Afr*s signify avoidance tendencies. Overresponsiveness can increase the likelihood for more affective exchanges, which can tax resources. It seems reasonable to hypothesize that if resources are limited, or if ongoing stimulus demands are already substantial, added requirements for affective exchange can produce overload and consequently, may lead to control problems. Conversely, an awareness of overresponsiveness might cause some to attempt to be more constrained in exchanges to avoid overload, and overcontrol can be a consequence. Similarly, an avoidance of emotionally provocative stimuli could be the product of concerns about control. Obviously, any combination of over- or undercontrol, and under- or overresponsiveness can create a potential for affective disarray.

COLOR PROJECTION (*CP*)

The Special Score *CP* can also provide some data concerning how the subject responds to affective experience. It was first suggested by Piotrowski (1957) to account for instances in which a subject identified achromatic blot areas as being chromatic. He postulated that it represents an ingenuine emotion, that is, an attempt to deal with a feeling of help-lessness by substituting a rather transparent and unrealistic positive emotional tone. That premise has been difficult to test because the incidence of *CP* responses is infre-quent in most groups of subjects. *CP*s appear in only 13 of the 700 protocols in the adult nonpatient normative sample (1%), all of whom are extratensive, and only 7 of the 1390 records of nonpatient children (0.5%). It appears in about 4% of the records in the schizophrenic reference sample, 4% of the inpatient depressives, and 1% of the outpa-tient reference sample, but *none* of the protocols for the sample of character problems. In a larger sample of outpatients having *Lambda* values less than 1.0 (*N* = 556), *CP* ap-pears in 16 protocols, all of which are records of extratensive subjects, whereas *CP* does not appear in any of the records of High *Lambda* style outpatients.

Generally, if the value for *CP* is greater than zero it signifies that the subject often denies the presence of irritating or unpleasant emotion or emotional stimulation by sub-stituting a false positive emotion or emotional value to the situation. This is a hysteroid-like process that disregards or violates reality. Typically, people who use this process feel very uncomfortable about their ability to deal adequately with negative feelings, and frequently, they do have problems in modulating their own affective displays. They often bend reality to avoid dealing with perceived or anticipated harshness in the environment, and as a result their interpersonal relationships are prone to suffer.

FINDINGS RELATED TO HYPOTHESES BASED ON *CP*

A review of 430 records of outpatients who originally volunteered to participate in the long-term treatment effects study revealed considerably higher proportions of *CP* re-sponses than expected in several diagnostic groups. This group was targeted because therapist evaluations of the patients had been collected after each of several sessions early into treatment, and additional evaluations were obtained after more lengthy inter-vals. Forty-four of the records contained at least one *CP* answer, and some contained as many as three CPs. They appeared in protocols of patients whose primary symptom patterns were described as psychosomatic (*N* = 14), hysteroid-like problems in dealing with affect (*N* = 20), depression (*N* = 7), and obsessive-like features (*N* = 3). The therapist evaluations included a section pertaining to tactics of defense, and if this was discernible, as many as three were to be listed, such as fantasy, displacement, denial, intellectualization, and so on. Forty-two of the 44 subjects who gave at least one *CP* response were described in the evaluations as having marked tendencies to use denial as a defensive tactic. Three comparison groups of 51 patients each were randomly drawn from the remaining 385 patients in the study. In the first, 17 of the 51 were described as using denial as a defensive tactic; in the second, 14 of the 51; and in the third, 18 of the 51 were described as having this feature. Each of the three chi-squares is statisti-cally significant ($p < .02$).

Although these findings result from only one study, they seemed sufficiently com-pelling to support Piotrowski's basic hypothesis. Interpretively, it does appear to relate to an abuse of denial as a tactic to deal with unwanted emotions. Interestingly, the 44 subjects who gave *CP* responses had, as a group, a significantly higher mean for *C'* answers (4.92), than did any of the three randomly selected comparison groups (2.47 to 2.93, $p < .05$). The very low frequency with which this kind of answer occurs makes its presence even more significant, and emphasizes the necessity of carefully weaving this finding into other data concerning emotional features.

WHITE SPACE RESPONSES

Data concerning answers that include the use of white space can often add information concerning some of the affective characteristics of the subject. Rorschach postulated that the use of white space in responses represents a form of opposition or negativism, arguing that it requires an alteration in the figure–ground relationship. Beck (1945) and Rapaport et al. (1946) have endorsed this hypothesis but have also cautioned that it may simply indicate a form of contrariness that may serve to accent the idiographic features of the person. Klopfer et al. (1954) had added to this by suggesting that it can be interpreted as a form of constructive self-assertiveness, whereas Piotrowski (1957) has argued that it can represent a striving for independence. All have emphasized that when it occurs with considerable frequency, it can illustrate some impingement to reality contact.

Any interpretation of *S* must proceed cautiously in determining if the emotional complex of the subject includes an unusual negativistic, oppositional, or angry set toward the environment. One or two *S* responses should not be regarded as significant other than indicating a natural form of self-assertiveness. If the value for *S* is three or more, the finding is important but must be reviewed to differentiate trait-like hostility from situationally related negativism. For instance, if all *S* responses were given to the first two blots, it indicates that the subject was probably not well prepared to take the test and responded negativistically to the demands of the situation. Conversely, if the value for *S* is three, and at least one of the three *S* answers occurred after Card II, it suggests that the subject is disposed to be more negativistic or oppositional toward the environment than are most people. This is not necessarily a liability but can become detrimental to the formation of harmonious social relationships. If the value for *S* is four or more, and at least one of the *S* answers was given after Card III, it indicates the presence of a very negative, angry attitude toward the environment. This is a trait-like feature.

It is important to emphasize that findings concerning the presence of excessive negativism and/or anger toward the environment *do not* necessarily mean that the anger will be manifest overtly in the behaviors of the subject. An above-average number of *S* answers does not correlate with overt behavior, but this trait-like feature does have some influence on the decision-making and coping activities of the subject. People such as this often are less tolerant of the routine compromises usually required in social intercourse. If problems in control and/or modulation exist, it is likely that the more intense affective displays of the subject will include some manifestations of the highly negativistic set of the subject.

FINDINGS RELATED TO HYPOTHESES BASED ON *S* RESPONSES

Counts and Mensh (1950) used a retest model and found a significant increase in *S* after hypnotically inducing conflict. Fonda (1951) and Bandura (1954) both found a significant positive relation between *S* and oppositional tendencies. Rosen (1952) reported a significant correlation between the frequency of *S* and high *Pd* scores on the MMPI, but did not find a relationship between S and the diagnosis of psychopathy. Rapaport et al. (1946) found the highest incidence of S among paranoid schizophrenics and Molish (1955) has posited that when S appears in schizophrenic records, it represents a process through which a passive resistance to the environment is maintained. Fonda (1960) reviewed the literature concerning S and concluded that the proportion of S in the record gives some indication of the effort being devoted to the defense of autonomy.

The data for S fall on a clear J-curve for most groups. About 86% of adult nonpatients give at least one S answer, and the median and mode are both 1. At least one S appears in about 90% of the records of nonpatient children, and the medians and modes for almost every age group are similar to those for nonpatient adults. The schizophrenic reference group averages nearly 3 S responses, and the median and mode for the group are both 2. In the depressive sample, the median is 2 and the mode is 1; whereas among outpatients the median is 1.5 and the mode is zero. In the character disorders group, the median is 2 but the mode is zero.

There are some interesting differences in the frequency of records in which S is elevated when the data are studied in relation to the High *Lambda* and *EB* styles. For instance, more than one in four High *Lambda* introversive nonpatients give more than two S answers as do almost half of High *Lambda* introversive outpatients. Very few introversive nonpatients (3%) who do not have a High *Lambda* style give more than two S answers, but approximately 38% of the outpatients who do not have a High *Lambda* style give more than two S answers.

About 13% of the records of nonpatient ambitents who also have a High *Lambda* style and about 17% of nonpatient ambitents who are not positive for *Lambda* contain more than two S's. Between 25% and 30% of the records of outpatient ambitents, regardless of the value for *Lambda,* have S greater than two.

Nonpatient extratensives, regardless of the *Lambda* value, have between 13% and 18% of their protocols with S greater than two. Approximately 43% of outpatient extratensives who *do not* have a High *Lambda* style have records in which S is greater than two, but the records of outpatient extratensives who do have a High *Lambda* style include only 4% in which S is greater than two. These data are intriguing and require much more research before the differences can be understood more fully.

The most common S responses occur to Cards I (variations of a face), and II (rocket), and least frequently to Cards IV, V, VI, and VIII. Rorschach probably was only partially correct in his assumption that all S answers involve some alteration in the figure and ground relation. This does not seem to be the case for Card I, to which nearly 20% of nonpatient adults and nearly 30% of nonpatient children give some sort of face response, usually the face of a cat, a mask, or a Halloween pumpkin. That kind of answer continues to be given with about the same frequency if the white areas are colored either light or dark gray, that is, still maintaining the contrast effect for contours. However, if the contours are eliminated by coloring the white areas as a gray-black—that is, homogeneous with the immediate surroundings—the frequency of face responses is reduced to zero. Some other internal space areas are also routinely perceived as part of figure rather than ground. These include the DS3 area on Card VIII, and all of the space areas on Card IX.

The reliability data for S suggest that all space responses do not necessarily correlate with the same psychological operations, because they are quite variable. Retest correlations range from .59 to .73 for brief intervals, and from .72 to .79 for lengthy intervals. The fact that lower retest correlations are found for brief intervals provoked a decision to subdivide 165 pairs of brief interval retest protocols, from both patients and nonpatients and including adults and children, in which at least one S response appeared in the first record, into three groups: (1) those containing only WS and/or DS answers, (2) those containing only DdS answers, and (3) those containing a combination of WS and/or DS plus DdS responses.

Subsequently, a fourth group was created containing records in which all S answers appeared in Card I, or a combination of Cards I and II in the first test. The retest correlation for the group ($N = 38$) in which only WS and/or DS responses appear is .63. The correlation for the group containing only DdS answers ($N = 33$) is .71, but the retest correlation for the group containing a mixture of WS and/or DS plus DdS ($N = 94$) is .86. As might be suspected, the latter group has a mean for S (3.97, $SD = 1.1$) that is significantly greater than either of the other two groups, 1.23 and 1.41, respectively ($p < .05$). In other words, as S elevates well beyond the mean, it reflects a more stable characteristic. The retest correlation for the group of records in which all S answers occurred to Card I, or the combination of Cards I and II ($N = 28$) is only .32, which suggests that these responses are more situationally related and probably are a product of resistance to taking the test.

BLENDS AND AFFECT

When more than one determinant is present in a response, it indicates that the activity occurring in the formation and delivery of the answer was more complex than might have been expected or required. In almost every instance, this complexity will involve some sort of affective experience. In some respects, the blend response can be regarded as representing the extreme opposite of the Pure F response. Whereas Pure F denotes a simple, straightforward classification, the blend is the product of activity in which considerable analysis and synthesis of stimulus elements occurs. As noted in Chapter 16, sometimes the presence of situational stress will increase the number of blends that are given. These are answers in which the blend would not exist if either an m or Y variable had not been included. But most blends are not situationally related. In fact, among nonpatients, more than 90% of all blends given do not contain either the m or Y variables.

Slightly more than one-fifth of the responses given by nonpatient adults are blends, and all 700 subjects in the normative sample gave at least one, but those data are a bit misleading. The expected number of blends differs in relation to EB. Introversive subjects tend to give fewer blends than extratensives or ambitents. Typically, about 20% of their responses are blended, and it is somewhat unusual for the proportion of blends to exceed 25% of R. The average range for introversive subjects falls between 13% and 26%. Extratensives generally give records in which about 25% of the answers are blended, and it is not unusual for the proportion to be as high as 33% of R. The average range for extratensives is from 19% to 33%. Blends given by ambient subjects also average about 25% of R, but it is not unusual for the proportion to exceed 35%. The average range for this group is between 16% and 36%.

Nonpatient children and younger adolescents tend to give proportionally fewer blend answers, although most give at least one. In the normative data for younger clients, 13 of the 90 five-year-olds did not give blend answers, nor did 2 of the 120 twelve-year-olds and 2 of the 110 thirteen-year-olds. In other words, 1373 of the 1390 subjects gave at least one blend answer. Prior to age 10, the proportion of blends tends to be less than 20% of R, but from ages 11 to 16, the proportion increases to between 25% and 30% although, as with adults, youngsters with an introversive style usually give significantly fewer blends than ambitents or extratensives.

Of most patient groups, 85% to 90% give at least one blend, although they appear in only about 75% of the protocols of the character disorder reference sample. As might be expected, High *Lambda* style patients tend to give proportionally fewer blends than patients for whom the *Lambda* value is not positive. Exner (1974) reported that more records with no blends are found among subjects with IQ's of less than 90, but Mason and Exner (1984) found only very low, nonsignificant correlations between Verbal IQ ($r = -.03$) and Performance IQ ($r = .02$) and the frequency of blends. As might be suspected, they also found a significant negative correlation between *Lambda* and blends ($r = -.28$).

The interpretation of blends should be based on both the quantity and substance. The absence of blends in the record of an adolescent or adult is a negative sign, indicating a form of psychological narrowness or constriction. It probably also indicates less sensitivity to oneself and the environment. If the proportion of blends in the record falls below the average range in relation to *EB*, it suggests that the psychological functioning of the subject is less complex than is usually expected. This is not uncommon for subjects who have values for *Lambda* that exceed 0.99, as their basic style is oriented to avoid complexity. Nonetheless, this finding suggests the possibility of some psychological impoverishment that has a potential to create difficulties in dealing with complex emotional stimuli. If these difficulties occur, they are most likely to manifest in the modulation of emotional displays. At the other extreme, a significant elevation in the number of blends— that is, a proportion of *R* that is considerably greater than average in relation to *EB*—signals much more psychological complexity than is customary. If the subject has an abundance of resources readily accessible, the complexity might be viewed as an asset to functioning, because it suggests a greater sensitivity to stimuli. However, if available resources are more limited, or if problems in control and/or modulation exist, the complexity of functioning increases the possibility that affect can have detrimental influence on the behavioral consistency and/or stability of the subject.

All determinants, with the exception of Pure *F,* are related to operations that have some affective properties. Although the movement and *FD* determinants are more directly related to ideational activities, those activities often involve, or give rise to affect. Approximately 70% of all blends have at least one movement determinant, but less than 2% consist exclusively of movement determinants, such as *M.FM, M.m,* or *FM.m.* About 7% of all blends consist exclusively of one of the movement determinants plus *FD.* More than 90% of all blends include at least one determinant that is related directly to affective experience—that is, chromatic or achromatic color, or one of the shading determinants. In many instances, the substance of the blend provides some clue about how the affective elements are working in the psychological operations of the subject. For instance, a blend of *Ma.FC* will generally be regarded much more positively than *CF.FMp.* In the former, the delay factor is dominant and the affect apparently well modulated. In the latter, less well-modulated affect is dominant and merged with a need-related component that has a passive quality. Similarly, a blend of *Mp.FC'* suggests a form of passive affective constraint, which may not be regarded very favorably, yet it is much more positive than a blend such as *mp.YF,* which reeks of a sense of paralysis. As the number of determinants in a blend increases, so too does the complexity of operations that has been involved. About 20% of all blends involve more than two determinants, and about 5%

involve more than three determinants. These typically are elaborate responses and often have very revealing contents. If more than one-fourth of the blends in a record contain three determinants, or if the record contains one or more blends that include four or more determinants, it should be assumed that, at times, the psychological functioning of the subject is inordinately complex. While this is not necessarily a liability it can easily contribute to dysfunction if resources are limited or if problems in control and/or modulation exist.

Shading and Color-Shading Blends   There are two types of blends that are of special importance to the review of affective features. They are the *shading blend* and the *color-shading blend*. The shading blend is the response in which at least two of the achromatic and/or shading determinants are present, such as *FT.FY, FV.FC', C'F.YF,* and so on. These are very unusual responses and never expected. They appear in only 3 of the 700 records of nonpatient adults, not at all among the character disorder group, and in only 7 of the schizophrenic protocols. They are much more frequent in the records of the depressive reference sample, appearing in 29 of the 315 protocols (9%). They also appear in 21 of the 216 records of outpatients whose primary symptom pattern is depression (10%), and in 8 of 68 records of first-admission inpatient drug abusers who were tested after approximately 1 week of detoxification (12%). Because all four of the achromatic and shading variables relate to irritating or painful affective experience, the presence of two or more in a single answer probably indicates a more tormented experience that creates a very disruptive impact on most all affective functioning. In other words, it tends to dominate the affective experiences of the subject and can become very pervasive in influencing thinking. The substance of the shading blend is also important. If it contains only two of the critical variables, and one of the two is a *Y* variable, it is likely that the experience is more situationally related. On the other hand, if the critical variables do not include *Y,* the intense distress is probably much more chronic.

The color-shading blend occurs much more frequently than the shading blend. These are responses in which a chromatic color determinant and at least one of the four achromatic or shading determinants is present. At least one color-shading blend appears in 252 of the 700 adult nonpatient protocols (36%). They occur less often in the records of nonpatient children and adolescents. They appear in less than 20% of the records for most age groups in the normative samples. Color-shading blends appear most frequently in the records of depressives. More than 55% of the records in the depressive reference sample, and nearly 70% of the records of outpatient depressives in the long-term treatment effects study (Weiner & Exner, 1991), contain at least one, and nearly one-fourth of the records in both groups have three or more. In contrast, they appear in about 35% of schizophrenic records, slightly more than 40% of nondepressed outpatients, and about 28% of the character problem group.

Beck (1949) was the first to elaborate on the color-shading blend, suggesting that it represents a form of simultaneous pleasure and pain. Applebaum and Holzman (1962) found that color-shading blends appear more frequently in the records of subjects prone to suicide. Exner and Wylie (1977) also found that it does correlate significantly with effected suicide ($r = .34, p < .01$), but because of the high frequency with which it appears in other groups, it is not an effective discriminator when taken alone. Nonetheless, it does load positively into the Suicide Constellation. Applebaum and Colson (1968) have suggested that it reflects an aborted form of emotional experience. Exner

(1978) has postulated that it represents more of a mixed or confused emotional experience that, at times, can indicate the presence of ambivalence.

The retest reliabilities for *all* color-shading blends are relatively modest, ranging from .48 to .57 for lengthy retest intervals, and .55 to .67 for retests administered during a period of 30 days or less. However, as Castles (1984) has suggested, those correlations are somewhat misleading because of the Y variable. Approximately 60% of the color-shading blends given by nonpatient adults, almost 70% of those given by nonpatient children, and nearly 40% of those given by patients contain a Y variable, suggesting that a situational factor has contributed to the formation of the blend answer. When the retest reliabilities were calculated for 150 adult nonpatients retested after lengthy intervals, and divided into two groups based on whether the color-shading blends contained a Y variable, the correlations for those including Y ranged from .28 to .41; for those not including the Y variable, they ranged from .68 to .79. When the retest records of 130 nonpatient adults and children who took the second test within 30 days were divided in the same way, the retest correlations for those containing a Y variable ranged from .16 to .34, whereas the correlations for the group in which the blends did not contain a Y variable ranged from .73 to .82. These findings suggest that, as with the shading blends, the characteristic may be situationally related, even being provoked by the test-taking situation, or it may be of a more chronic nature, indicated by those color-shading blends created by the presence of a C', T, or V variable. If chronic, the element of ambivalence is much more likely to exist as a trait-like feature by which the subject often is confused by emotion and may frequently experience both positive and negative feelings about the same stimulus situation. People such as this often experience feelings more intensely than others and sometimes have more difficulty in bringing closure to emotional situations. Regardless of whether the color-shading blend appears to be situation related or chronic, its presence signals some difficulty with affect that should be noted in the context of other findings concerning affective characteristics. A confusion in feelings can mark many events, and if the mixed feelings are related to a specific situation, it does not necessarily predispose faulty or ineffective adjustment to other emotional situations. Conversely, ambivalence, as a trait-like feature, creates many more potential hazards to the maintenance of consistency in affective reactions to various classes of emotional stimulation and, as such, can greatly affect a variety of relationships in the environment.

THE L.S. PROTOCOL AND AFFECT

Data for the cluster of variables concerning affect for the L.S. protocol are shown in Table 77.

The *DEPI* value is not significant and, as noted earlier, the *EB* indicates that the subject is an ambient. This suggests that he is not consistent in how he uses affect in thinking and especially in decision making. At times, he will push feelings aside and attempt to address issues methodically and logically. In other instances, his feelings will become quite influential in his problem-solving/decision-making operations. Unfortunately, neither tactic is well developed, and thus unlike the introversive or extratensive, he is quite inconsistent in the experience and use of his emotions.

The right-side value of the *eb* (4) is not substantially elevated, but the composite of the value (2 *T* and 2 *Y*) is unusual and suggests that he is experiencing an irritating kind

Table 77.   Data Concerning Affect for the L.S. Protocol

DEPI = 2				Blends
EB = 4:3.5		EBPer	= N/A	m.CF
eb = 8:4		FC:CF + C	= 1:3	FM.FD.FT
		Pure C	= 0	m.FY
C' = 0	T = 2	Afr	= 0.56	FM.FD
V = 0	Y = 2	S	= 1	M.m
		Blends/R	= 5:25	
		CP	= 0	

of loneliness that is compounded by feelings of helplessness. This seems consistent with his report of marital discord and occupational dissatisfaction.

The *FC:CF+C* ratio (1:3) indicates that he does not modulate his emotional discharges very well and, at times, they are probably overly intense and rather obvious to those around him. On a positive note, there are no Pure *C* responses. Nonetheless, the higher right-side value in the *FC:CF+C* ratio is quite unexpected because of his obsessive style. Obsessives usually are very well controlled, sometimes overly so, and a looseness in modulation such as noted here may indicate a kind of naiveté about feelings that probably should be addressed if some form of intervention is planned.

The Affective Ratio is at the lower end of the "average" range for ambients and well below the mode for his group (.82). This may signal some awareness of his problems in dealing effectively with feelings. Whether or not that is the case, it does seem clear that he is less prone to become involved with emotionally provocative stimuli than are most ambients. There are no *CP* answers and only one space response, thus, neither of these variables contribute to the interpretive yield.

There are five blends in the record (20%), which is not unusual, and none include shading or color-shading blends. Yet, the structure of the blends is intriguing. Three appear to be situationally related (*m.CF, m.FY, M.m*). If even two of the three did not exist, the proportion would be much lower than expected for an adult, especially for an intelligent adult. This suggests that, ordinarily, his psychological operations are much less complex and/or sophisticated than might be expected. This is not unusual for a person with an obsessive style as people with that style do tend to keep things simple and uncomplicated. Unfortunately, that tendency often breeds a neglect or failure to prioritize and/or discriminate important from unimportant events, particularly emotional events. This can create a potential for difficulties in both the self and interpersonal perception spheres.

In summary, the emotional structure of L.S. does not seem to be very compatible with effective adjustment. He is inconsistent in the use of his feelings in problem solving and decision making. When he discharges emotion, it is often overly intense and probably less mature than should be the case. He is burdened with a sense of loneliness and feels somewhat helpless in light of current situational stresses. He is not particularly interested in processing emotionally toned stimuli and usually functions in an uncomplicated manner although, at present, situational factors have increased his level of psychological complexity substantially. None of these issues, taken separately, are major causes for concern; however, when considered collectively they seem to portray a person who is, at best, naive about his feelings, inconsistent in their use, and possibly even fearful of their impact. He is currently irritated by feelings of loneliness and helplessness and these probably contribute significantly to his reports of tension and anxiety. If some brief form of intervention is planned, focus should be on the issues of loneliness and helplessness; but it could be more beneficial to provide a longer form of treatment through which he might learn more about modulating his emotional displays, become more willing to process emotional stimuli, and use his own feelings more effectively in decision-making operations.

SELF-PERCEPTION

The data in this cluster provide information from which to develop a picture of self-image and self-esteem. Self-image is the view that one harbors about himself or herself. It is the product of an internal lexicon that describes the characteristics of the self, such as bright, dull, beautiful, ugly, talented, vulnerable, kind, selfish, sensitive, and so on. Some of these perceived characteristics may be reality based while others may be more imaginary. Regardless of their basis, they form a collective representation of the assets and liabilities of the person *as perceived by the person*. Self esteem has to do with the value of that collective representation when judged against external sources. It is an estimate of personal worth in relation to others, usually significant others who may be real or imagined. It is involved in both specific and general evaluations and probably has something to do with establishing achievement goals. Although these two features are interrelated, that relationship is not nearly as direct as might seem to be the case.

The reflection response is a critical element in this cluster if it is positive. The stylistic ramifications for those who have reflections answers has already been described in Chapter 17, as has some data concerning the Egocentricity Index. But a more extensive review of the Egocentricity Index is warranted here.

THE EGOCENTRICITY INDEX $(3r + (2)/R)$

The Egocentricity Index provides an estimate of self-concern and possibly self-esteem. The Index is a crude measure of self-focusing or self-attending behavior. If it falls above the average range—greater than .45 for an adult (or greater than 1 SD above the mean for the age group of a younger person)—it suggests that the subject tends to be much more involved with himself or herself than are most others. If a reflection is present in the record, it indicates that the narcissistic-like feature is strongly embedded in the psychological organization of the subject and is sustaining favorable judgments concerning the self in relation to others. If there are no reflection answers in the record, it signals an unusually strong concern with the self that easily leads to a neglect of the external world. In many cases a higher-than-average Index indicates a highly positive estimate of personal worth, but in some instances this unusual preoccupation with the self may signal a marked sense of dissatisfaction with oneself.

If the value for the Egocentricity Index is below average—.32 or less for an adult (or less than 1 SD below the age mean for a younger person)—it can be assumed that the subject's estimate of personal worth tends to be quite negative. Such individuals regard themselves less favorably when compared with others. This characteristic is often a precursor to depression. This finding is very uncommon in records containing reflection answers. If it is positive in a protocol containing one or more reflection answers, it indicates that the subject is in serious conflict regarding self-image and self-value. The likelihood of mood fluctuations is substantial and behavioral dysfunction is likely.

FINDINGS RELATED TO THE EGOCENTRICITY INDEX

Some of the basic research leading to the development of the Egocentricity Index has been described in Chapter 17. Other findings have contributed to sorting out its interpretive usefulness. For instance, Exner (1974) used ratings on the Inpatient Multidimensional Psychiatric Scale (IMPS) completed during the first week of hospitalization, and again by different raters six to eight weeks after discharge, to differentiate 180 patients into groups of "improved" and "unimproved." Rorschachs were administered at about the same times the ratings were done. The admission Rorschachs for the patients who did not have depression as a major symptom ($N = 106$) showed a mean Egocentricity Index of .474 ($SD = .11$), which is significantly higher than the mean for a nonpatient control group, .38 ($SD = .07$). The patients who did have depression as a major symptom ($N = 74$) had a mean Egocentricity Index that was significantly lower than the other patient group, .278 ($SD = .12$). The data from the postdischarge Rorschachs for the subjects rated as unimproved were very similar to the admission data (Nondepressed $M = .493$, $SD = .13$; Depressed $M = .272$, $SD = .10$). The data for the patients rated as improved showed a shift toward the mean for nonpatient controls (Nondepressed $M = .385$, $SD = .09$; Depressed $M = .324$, $SD = .10$). The improved groups are not significantly different from each other or from the control group.

The temporal consistency for the Egocentricity Index is quite substantial, with correlations ranging from the mid .80s to low .90s for both brief and long-term retests. Long-term retest correlations are considerably lower for children through age 14, after which the Index appears to have the same stability as for adults (Exner, Thomas, & Mason, 1985). The curves for the distribution of Index values usually have some skewness to the left, but with somewhat higher peaks than a normal curve. For instance, the nonpatient adult normative sample shows a mean of .39 and SD of .07; however, the mode is .36, and although the skewness is almost perfect (.01), the kurtosis is 2.91, reflecting the large number of values falling slightly to the left of the mean. Distributions for patient groups tend to be more skewed to the left but with lower kurtosis values. For example, the mean for the schizophrenic reference sample is .37, but the mode is .50; and 35% of that sample have values *less than .33,* while 36% have values greater than .44. Similarly, the data for the character disorder group show a mean of .42, a mode of .39, and 34% of the sample with values of less than .33 while 33% of the sample have values greater than .44. In other words, elements of bimodality tend to mark both samples. This is much more the case among depressives. The reference sample of depressives has a mean of .34, but a mode of .21, with 163 of the 315 subjects (52%) having values of less than .33 and 75 (24%) having values above .44.

The data for younger clients also provide some indirect support for the notion that the Index relates to self-involvement. Children are generally quite self-centered, especially during the earlier developmental years. This trait seems to be well illustrated in the gradual decline that occurs in the means for the Index from ages 5 through 16. At 5, the nonpatient children show a mean of .69, with a mode of .60. By age 9, the mean drops to .57 with a mode of .55. At age 11, the mean is .53 and the mode is .50, and by age 16 the mean is .43, with a mode of .50. Similar declines have been shown by age for children with behavior problems and withdrawn children, although the means for the former typically are higher than for nonpatients, and for the latter typically are lower than nonpatients (Exner, 1978). A similar pattern of decline for the frequencies of reflection responses appears among all groups of children, with younger children tending to give more, and mid-adolescents having about the same frequencies as adults.

Exner, Wylie, and Bryant (1974) collected peer nominations from 37 group psychotherapy patients, distributed across four groups, after the fourth month of treatment. A 30-item form was used, with the responses given anonymously, with two entries (most and least) for each item. The items ranged over a variety of interpersonal preferences and behaviors, such as most and least trusted, attending a party with, seeking advice from, loaning a car to, sensitive to others, and so on. Ten of the 37 subjects had produced reflections in their Rorschach administered prior to treatment. Seven of the 10 were consistently ranked *least* for 11 of the 30 items, and all 10 were ranked *least* for the "seeking advice from" and "telling problems to" items. Interestingly, the mean Egocentricity Index for these 10 subjects, .57, did not differ significantly from the mean Index for the 10 other subjects who received the most positive nominations (.47). Another interesting finding is that the subjects who were mentioned least frequently tended to have substantially lower indices than others in the groups. Exner et al. (1975) were unable to establish any significant relationships between the Egocentricity Index and either the Field Dependence-Independence Phenomenon as measured by the rod and frame, or Locus of Control as measured by the I-E Scale.

Data from the long-term treatment effects study (Weiner & Exner, 1991) indicate that a change from a too high or too low Egocentricity Index to the average range occurred significantly more often among patients who were rated as improved at the 27th month as contrasted with those who were rated as unimproved. Exner and Murillo (1977) were able to follow the posthospitalization adjustment of 44 schizophrenics for 36 months. They were from a group of 70 multiple admission schizophrenics who had participated in a treatment effects study and had sustained enough improvement to remain out of the hospital. The 3-year behavioral evaluations indicated that almost all were able to function with reasonable effectiveness in their environments. About half had been treated with ECT plus psychotherapy and the other half with phenothiazines and psychotherapy. The mean pretreatment Egocentricity indices for both groups were significantly higher than average—.53 and .51 respectively. At intervals of both one and three years postdischarge, the mean Index for the ECT plus psychotherapy group was in the mid .30s—.37 and .35—whereas the mean for the group treated with drugs plus psychotherapy remained consistently high—.51 and .53. In this instance, the much higher Egocentricity Index of the drug-treated group does not appear to have created a significant handicap. It seems likely that the overly self-centered person is less prone to malfunction provided that he or she exists in an environment where self-centeredness is accepted or even encouraged.

Although a high Egocentricity Index probably becomes a liability for subjects in some situations, a lower-than-average Index appears to portend far more adjustment hazards. Exner and Murillo (1975) found that 16 of 22 relapsing nonschizophrenics had Egocentricity indices of less than .30 at discharge, whereas only four of the 55 nonrelapsers from this group had an Index of less than .30. Low Egocentricity indices tend to appear with a much greater frequency among the protocols of subjects with obsessive styles, such as obsessive-compulsives, phobics, and psychosomatics. A lower-than-average Index is very common in the records of effected adult suicides, and loaded positively into the original Suicide Constellation (Exner & Wylie, 1977). This was reaffirmed in a cross-validation of the Suicide Constellation; however, it was also found that higher-than-average indices also have a discriminant function (Exner, Martin, & Mason, 1984).

VISTA AND FORM DIMENSION RESPONSES

Information about self-inspecting behavior is often important when attempting to develop a picture of self-image. Vista and Form Dimension responses both appear to relate to this process. *FD* answers generally are a positive sign, unless they occur with a substantial frequency. Conversely, as discussed in Chapter 16, vista responses signal the presence of some irritating affective experience that is being produced by self-inspection. Ideally, the record of an adolescent or adult will have no Vista answers and the value for *FD* will be 1 or 2. Such a configuration suggests that the subject engages in self-inspecting behaviors somewhat routinely, and in general, the process can be beneficial as it tends to promote reevaluation of the self-image.

Neither of these answers is expected in the protocols of young children. For instance, Vista responses do not occur in any of the nonpatient records of youngsters between the ages of 5 and 9. Two of the 120 records of 10-year-olds do contain one Vista answer; none appear in the sample of 11-year-olds; and one appears in 4 of the 120 records in the 12-year-old group. However, beginning at age 13, the frequencies increase considerably. Vista appears in nearly 10% of the records of 13s and 14s, about 11% of the records for 15s, and almost 15% of the protocols of the 16-year-old group. This is not necessarily surprising as considerable self-inspecting tends to occur during adolescence and, at times, the focus is often on elements of the self with which the subject is dissatisfied. *FD* answers occur more frequently among children and adolescents, but the proportions of records containing *FD* are modest until age 10. For example, only about 12% of 7-year-old nonpatients give an *FD* response as contrasted with 40% of 9-year-olds. Between the ages of 10 and 16, *FD*s appear in at least two-thirds of the records, and for some of the groups appear in more than 75% of the protocols. Thus, if there are no *FD* or Vista answers in the record of an adolescent or adult, it is possible that the subject may be less involved with self-awareness than is usually the case. People such as this tend to be more naive about themselves.

On the other hand, if the value for *FD* exceeds 2 *or* if the value for *V* exceeds zero, it suggests that some unusual self-inspecting behavior is occurring. This is not necessarily an atypical feature during some stages in the life cycle, such as puberty and aging, or in proximity to critical life events such as affective loss, failures, physical or psychological difficulties, and so on. Whatever the cause, this finding confirms that considerable self-inspecting is occurring. If this finding occurs in a protocol containing a reflection response, it probably signals the presence of a conflict state concerning self-image. If the Egocentricity Index is lower than average, it suggests that the unusual frequency of self-inspecting probably relates to the negative self-value held by the subject.

SOME FINDINGS CONCERNING *FD* AND VISTA

The *FD* was first identified by a separate coding in the early development of the Comprehensive System (Exner, 1974). Klopfer and Kelley (1942) had included them, but only those for which the unarticulated use of shading seemed probable. The impetus for considering a separate coding was provoked by the previously mentioned study of 64 inpatients who had been placed on a suicide watch. Those records averaged more than three *FD* responses as contrasted with about one *FD* in the records of nonpatients. Thus at first glance it appeared that *FD* might be related to depressive features common in the subject preoccupied with self-destruction. However, the records of psychiatric outpatients also contained significantly more *FD* responses than the nonpatient sample, averaging more than two. Those findings led to the postulate that *FD* might relate to introspection, the logic being that outpatients, in the therapeutic routine, are encouraged to be self-examining. Subsequently, three studies were completed, the results of which appear to support this postulate.

In the first, it was found that introversive subjects, both patients and nonpatients, average significantly more *FD* responses ($M = 2.42$; $SD = 0.94$) than do extratensives ($M = 0.93$; $SD = 0.91$), $p < .01$. This finding suggested that *FD* is related to delay and/ or internalization. In the second study, 40 subjects were selected from a waiting list at a mental health facility and randomly assigned, 10 each to four "holding" groups. They were informed that, while waiting for the assignment of individual therapists, they could participate 2 hours each week in group sessions designed to focus on treatment plans and objectives. The group sessions were videotaped and the audio material on the tapes for the first three sessions was scored by three raters who had no knowledge of the nature of the study. They used a two-dimensional grid to record whether the verbal material was self- or other-directed, and whether the content referred to the past, present, or future. The 40 subjects were divided into two groups of 20 each for the purposes of data analysis, using a median split of the distribution of *FD* frequencies. The mean *FD* for the upper half was 2.83, and for the lower half was 1.34. The ratings of the audio material revealed that the subjects in the upper half of the distribution gave significantly more self-directed statements than did the subjects in the lower half. In addition, the subjects in the upper half had significantly more statements focusing on the past and present than did those in the lower half. The two groups did not differ on two measures of egocentricity, and thus it seems reasonable to conclude that the more self-focusing statements were not simply a manifestation of self-centeredness.

In the third study, 15 outpatients, entering dynamically oriented psychotherapy, were tested a few days prior to their first therapy session and retested after the 10th session. It was hypothesized that *FD* should increase at the retest, assuming that the patients would become more involved in the introspective process. Subjective ratings of "self-awareness" were also collected from each patient's therapist after the 1st, 5th, and 10th sessions. The results show a mean *FD* of 2.06 ($SD = 1.03$) with a range of 0 to 4 in the pretreatment records. In the second test, the mean increased to 3.11 ($SD = 0.89$), $p < .05$, and the range increased to 1 to 6. The therapist ratings of self-awareness were on a 5-point scale. The correlation between *FD* and the ratings after the first session were not significant ($r = .13$); however, the correlation between *FD* and the ratings done after the 10th session were significant ($r = .37$, $p < .02$). These data seemed to offer added support to the proposition that *FD* is related to a psychological activity involving self-inspection, or at least self-awareness, and consequently the *FD* category was added into the Comprehensive System.

Data that have accumulated since 1974 have also provided support for the basic hypothesis concerning *FD*. Exner, Wylie, and Kline (1977) tested 279 outpatients prior to their first session, and retested them three times, at intervals of 9, 18, and 27 months after the onset of treatment. The patients were unequally distributed across seven treatment modalities, ranging from biofeedback ($N = 28$) to psychoanalytic psychotherapy ($N = 56$). Many of the patients involved in the briefer forms of treatment, such as biofeedback, assertiveness training, and systematic desensitization had terminated prior to the first retest, and only 54 of the 279 remained in treatment at the 27th month. The mean *pretreatment FD* for the entire group is 1.52 ($SD = 1.03$), as contrasted with a mean *FD* of 2.71 ($SD = 1.18$) at the first retest, $p < .01$. Interestingly, the mean for *vista* also increased significantly, nearly doubling from 0.89 in the pretreatment records to 1.68 in the protocols of the first retest. The 18-month retest showed a slight but not significant reduction in the mean *FD* as compared with the nine-month retest, to 2.39 ($SD = 1.18$); however, when the group was subdivided into terminated ($N = 157$), and continuing in treatment ($N = 122$) differences were discovered. The mean *FD* for the terminated group was 1.67 ($SD = 1.02$), which is similar to the pretreatment data. The mean *FD* for the group continuing in treatment was 3.49 ($SD = 1.29$), which *is* significantly higher than the mean for the second test. More important, when the 9-month retest data were reanalyzed using the 18-month subgroups, the means for *FD did not show a significant difference* (terminated = 2.51 versus continuing = 2.92).

A second important finding in the 18-month retest data is that the mean for vista decreased significantly for the total group, from 1.68 at 9 months to 0.78, and when the subgroups were reviewed, both show relatively low mean values for vista (terminated = 0.63 versus continuing = 0.94). Thus it would appear that the introspective process is facilitated by a variety of intervention methods and that, during the early phases of intervention, some of that process evokes the sorts of affective irritation associated with vista answers. Apparently, the irritation is lessened considerably as the intervention is extended or terminated; however, if intervention continues, the process of self-inspection, as reflected in the *FD* answers, remains at a higher-than-average level.

FD answers occur most frequently in the records of nonpatients. The adult normative sample shows that almost 80% gave at least one *FD* response. People voluntarily seeking outpatient treatment average nearly two *FD* answers. Conversely, the schizophrenic reference group shows that only 34% gave at least one *FD* response ($M = 0.60$), and the character disorder group has *FD* in only 23% of the records ($M = 0.33$). The inpatient depressive reference group shows a mean *FD* of 0.82, which is only slightly lower than nonpatient adults, however, *FD* appears in only 50% of the protocols in that sample. An elevation in *FD* may signal that the process is being abused to the disadvantage of the subject. For instance, the Suicide Constellation includes the item $FV + VF + V + FD < 2$. In other words, it is not only the irritating affect generated by introspection, as represented by vista answers, which is a valid predictor, but any indication of an exaggerated involvement with self-examination, as can be indicated by an elevation in *FD*.

HUMAN CONTENTS AND SELF-IMAGE

The evaluation of human content has several uses. First, the absolute frequency of all human content provides some information about interest in people. Second, a breakdown of human contents into those that are Pure *H* versus those that are *Hd* or parenthesized human figures seems to afford some indication about whether the conceptions of people, including the self, are based on actual experience or are derived more from imaginary conceptions. Third, the actual substance of human content answers often provides useful projected information about how people, and the self, are conceptualized. Probably the most critical human content datum related to self-image is the relation between Pure H and other human contents, expressed in the ratio $H:(H)+Hd+(Hd)$. All nonpatient subjects in the standardization samples, except for children under the age of 9, give more Pure H than the combination of $(H)+Hd+(Hd)$. In fact, beginning at age 12, and including the entire adult nonpatient sample, the ratio of $H:(H)+Hd+(Hd)$ usually reduces to about 3:2. In other words, adolescents and adults tend to give more "real" human responses than either imaginary or part-human answers.

Actually, the data for adults differ in relation to *EB*. The ratio for introversives typically reduces to about 3:1, while the ratio for extratensives and ambitents reduces to about 1.3:1. This is probably because introversives give more human movement answers and consequently, give more answers that contain human content. Patient groups differ significantly from nonpatients with regard to the relation of Pure H to other kinds of human content. The schizophrenic reference sample shows an average ratio of about 1.5:2; the depressive and outpatient samples have ratios of approximately 1:1.5, and the character disorders group has a ratio of about 1:2.

Weiner and Exner (1991) found that 147 of the 176 outpatients entering long-term or short-term treatment averaged about five human contents in their pretreatment records, of which about 3.5 were *not* Pure H. In the second retest taken 27 to 31 months after treatment began, and at which time all patients in the short term group had terminated, all subjects averaged slightly more than 6 human contents and only 24 continued to fewer Pure H answers than the combination of $(H)+Hd+(Hd)$. The findings in the Exner and Sanglade (1992) study of Rorschach changes following brief and short-term treatment, involving two groups of 35 subjects each, reveals that 19 of those entering brief treatment and 18 of those entering short-term treatment had fewer Pure H answers than "other" human content responses. At the second retest, taken 8 to 12 months after the baseline for the brief treatment group and 24 to 27 months after the baseline for the short-term treatment group, indicate that 16 of the 19 brief treatment subjects continued to have more human contents that were not Pure H, but that only three subjects from the short-term treatment group continued to show that configuration.

Another hint that more Pure H than other forms of human content relate to a more realistic estimate of self-image is found in the Thomas, Exner, and Baker study (1982). They used Gough Adjective Checklist with 225 college students with each student responding to the *ACL* twice during the same session, in a counterbalanced design, once with the instruction to "describe yourself," and once with the instruction to "describe yourself as you would like to be." A difference score was calculated for each subject, and the 20 subjects falling at each extreme were recruited to take the Rorschach. The average difference score for students in the upper extreme was 9.4 and in the lower extreme was 38.9, the latter showing the greatest discrepancy between the "real" and "ideal." The $H:(H)+Hd+(Hd)$ ratio for those in the upper extreme approximates 2.8:1, whereas the ratio for those in the lower extreme is about 1:1.2. Interestingly, the proportions of introversive, extratensive, and ambitent subjects are about the same for both groups.

Thus, when interpreting the $H:(H)+Hd+(Hd)$ ratio with regard to self-image, a value on the left side that is at least equal to, or greater than, the right side is desirable. If the majority of the human contents include whole figures scored H, it suggests that self-image and self-value are probably based more on experience than on imagination. This finding is generally positive, but it *should not* be translated to mean that self-image and/or self-value are necessarily accurate or realistic. Rather, it indicates that interactions have contributed significantly to formulations regarding the self. If the majority of human contents are scored *Hd* or have parenthesized human contents, it suggests that self-image and/or self-value tend to be based largely on imaginary rather than on real experience. Subjects such as this are often less mature and frequently have very distorted notions of themselves. This more limited self-awareness will sometimes serve negatively in decision-making and problem-solving activity and creates a potential for difficulties in relating to others. If one or more answers include an *Hx* content, it signals that the subject attempts to deal with issues of self-image and/or self-value in an overly intellectualized manner that tends to ignore reality. People like this often have ideational impulse control problems, and as a result many features of self-image are grossly distorted.

ANATOMY (*An*) AND X-RAY (*Xy*) CONTENTS

Another data set that can often provide information about problems in self-image or self-concern is the *An*+*Xy* content frequencies. Anatomy responses occur with a significantly greater frequency than do x-ray answers, but both appear related to issues of body concern. The *An* response, because of its more substantial frequency, has been studied in more detail than *Xy* answers, but in the overall picture they are correlated with similar features. Beck (1945) speculated that they are related to issues of body concern. Shatin (1952) found a significantly greater frequency of *An* answers among psychosomatics than is the case for "neurotics." Zolliker (1943) earlier had found a substantially high incidence of *An* answers in the records of women suffering psychiatric complications due to pregnancy. Rapaport et al. (1946) found a high incidence of these responses among "neurasthenics." Weiss and Winnik (1963) have postulated that matters of physical health may not be relevant to the interpretation of *An* answers, arguing that these answers can indicate a vicarious preoccupation with body concern without directly experiencing physiological discomfort. However, that argument seems tenuous at best. Exner et al. (1975) found elevations in *An* responses in both elective surgery patients and overweight patients beginning a stringently controlled dietary routine. In fact, the records of 331 medical outpatients and inpatients reveals a mean for *An* of slightly more than two. Draguns, Haley, and Phillips (1967) concluded from a literature review that *An* responses signal a form of self-absorption which can be the product of either autism or physiological changes such as those created by pregnancy, pubescence, or physical illness.

Nonpatient adults average about 0.42 *An* responses, and nonpatient children, through age 11, average slightly less. Young nonpatient adolescents, ages 12 to 14, average nearly 1.0 *An* answers, but 15- and 16-year-old nonpatients tend to give no more *An* responses than nonpatient adults. Patients, both adults and children, have larger proportions of records in which *An* answers occur, and have higher means for the variable, ranging from 0.98 for schizophrenics to 1.05 for inpatient depressives. About one-third of the *An* responses given by patients are *FQ*−, whereas less than 10% of the *An* responses given by nonpatients are minus answers. X-ray responses occur much less frequently among nonpatients than among patients. Only 17 of the 700 adult nonpatients in the normative sample gave an *Xy* answer, as did only 30 of the 1390 nonpatient children, all of which occurred in the protocols of youngsters over the age of 10. Among psychiatric patients, *Xy* answers occur most frequently among schizophrenics and depressed patients with problems in body functioning. Exner, Murillo, and Sternklar (1979) found an average of 2.2 *Xy* answers among 21 inpatient schizophrenics who manifest body delusions, and an average of 1.7 *Xy* answers among 17 depressed inpatients who had problems in body functioning.

Thus, if the value for the composite of $An + Xy$ is 1 or 2, some body concern may be present but should not necessarily be considered as a major issue in the psychological organization of the subject unless the answers have a minus form quality. If the value is 3 or more, it can be assumed that some unusual body concern or preoccupation is present. This finding is not uncommon among subjects who have physical problems, but if no obvious medical cause for the concern is evident in the history of the subject, it is likely to have a psychogenic origin and probably relates in some way to the overall conception of the self. If the composite includes Xy answers, the concern is probably marked by more distressful feelings, because they usually involve the achromatic or shading determinants, whereas the An responses that are not Pure F answers are more likely to involve chromatic color.

MORBID (*MOR*) RESPONSES AND SELF-IMAGE

Responses containing morbid content (*MOR*) invariably include some projected material. They are embellishments of the stimulus field that attribute features to the object that are not obvious in the field. The composite of findings described in Chapter 18 concerning *MOR* suggests these answers signal an orientation toward the self, and probably toward the environment, that is marked by pessimism; and the self-image is conceptualized by the subject to include more negative, and possibly damaged, features than is commonplace. In other words, *MOR* responses provide indirect, or sometimes direct, self-representations. Obviously, if a negative self-image exists, it can foment a tendency toward anger, dissatisfaction, and/or depression, and predispose problems in adaptation.

MOR responses are interpreted both in terms of the quantity and substance of the responses. If the value for *MOR* equals 1, the finding is actuarially meaningless. While a single *MOR* response suggests that it is unlikely that the self-image includes markedly negative features, that postulate should be evaluated by examining the substance of the answer. If the value for *MOR* is 2, it is more likely that some negative features are included in the self-concept. This finding also should be evaluated more carefully by a review of the verbal material in the *MOR* answers. This finding is somewhat unusual in a protocol containing a reflection answer and suggests the presence of conflict concerning self-image and self-value. If the value for *MOR* is 3 or more, it is reasonably certain that the self-image is marked by negative characteristics. The verbal material in the *MOR* answers should provide some additional clarification concerning the negative characteristics.

A note of caution must be injected here concerning the issue of attempts to malinger depression. Data from three studies (Meisner, 1984; Exner, 1987; Ros Plana, 1990) indicate that the value for *MOR* is routinely elevated by nonpatient subjects recruited to simulate depression in the Rorschach. Thus, any interpretation of *MOR* answers must be cast in the context of the assessment situation.

ANALYSIS OF THE VERBAL MATERIAL

Rorschach (1921) was very cautious in his estimate of the interpretive yield from the verbal material. He pointed to the fact that the test does not provoke a "free flow" of ideation but states that if unconscious or subconscious ideation did occur in the test, it would be manifest in the content. It does seem highly plausible, in light of Rorschach's training and orientation, that he would have accepted Frank's *Projective Hypothesis* (1939) as relevant to the interpretation of the test.

Lindner (1943, 1944, 1946, 1947) was among the first to make a formal argument encouraging a greater emphasis on "content analysis" than had been the case previously. He cited instances in which the scoring configurations did not provide an accurate "diagnostic" picture of psychopaths but analysis of the verbalizations did produce an accurate diagnostic picture. He also presented a series of classes of answers to different areas of the blots that could be interpreted as symbolically representative of different types of psychopathological ideation. Following from Lindner's lead, many works have focused on the analysis of content as related to diagnostic types, personality traits, and the "meaning" of specific classes of verbalizations. Some of these, especially those dealing with traits, have evolved special scorings for particular classes of contents (Elizur–anxiety, 1949; Elizur–hostility, 1949; Walker–aggression, 1951; Stone–aggression, 1953; Wheeler–homosexuality, 1949; Smith & Coleman–tension, 1956; Fisher & Cleveland–body image boundary, 1958; Holt–defense effectiveness, 1960, 1966). Unfortunately, with the possible exception of the Holt index of defense effectiveness, these scoring approaches have yielded equivocal findings. This does not negate the usefulness of verbalization analysis, but instead emphasizes the problems involved in attempting to "formalize" these data into specific categories. For example, a review of the research concerning the Wheeler 20 signs of homosexuality suggests that 6 of the 20 signs are "unquestionably poor," 6 others hold up "fairly well under empirical test," and the remaining 12 are ambiguous (Goldfried, Stricker, & Weiner, 1971). Studies attempting to equate specific classes of content with a *specific* "symbolic" meaning have been equally limited in success. Goldfarb (1945) and Goldfried (1963) both emphasize that animal contents are not universal in their symbolic meaning. Several studies (Bochner & Halpern, 1945; Meer & Singer, 1950; Rosen, 1951; Phillips & Smith, 1953; Hirschstein & Rabin, 1955; Levy, 1958; Zelin & Sechrest, 1963) have explored the postulate that Cards IV and VII represent "father and mother," respectively. Findings that have been positive are equivocal and have not been supported by more sophisticated research designs (Wallach, 1983).

The same negative findings have evolved concerning the significance of other blot stimuli, such as Cards III or X representing interpersonal connotations, or that Card VI represents sexuality. It is *very dangerous* for an interpreter to operate under these faulty assumptions. On the other hand, some contents tend to lend themselves to interpretation quite readily. For instance, sexual contents usually signify some form of preoccupation, and Pascal et al. (1950) have presented evidence to indicate that genital contents do have some universal meaning. Molish (1967) has pointed out that sexual contents are useful to interpretation because they are much more direct than symbolic. Prandoni et al. (1973) did find a greater frequency of sexual contents in the records of sex offenders but, like Molish, cautions that these types of answers have little meaning when interpreted in isolation.

One of the most common approaches to the analysis of the verbal material is based on the logical grouping of responses that appears to have a common theme, or very common characteristics. Schafer (1954) has presented one of the most comprehensive approaches to the verbal material using this method. He cites 14 broad-ranging categories, using psychoanalytic constructs, which include dependency, aggressiveness, conflicts, fears, and such, and provides illustrations of how different contents may relate to the same theme. Although some of these examples are useful only if applied in the psychoanalytic framework, such as the response of "mud" reflecting an "anal" orientation, most serve to represent a consistency of themes that can be useful regardless of theoretical orientation. For instance, Schafer suggests that answers which include references to God, police, a straw man, weak branches, and such can relate to feelings of inadequacy and/or impotency. Schafer's work is a classic of this kind and can be of use by an interpreter, regardless of orientation, because it tends to give emphasis to the "obvious" classes of responses that might "fit together" to convey idiographic needs, preoccupations, and such. Schafer also points to the importance of studying the emotional tone that is often conveyed by the wording of a subject.

Obviously, some of this is conveyed in Special Scores, such as *MOR*, or *AG*, but in many cases the repetitious use of a word or tone in describing objects can add new information. For example, a subject may consistently begin an answer by saying "Boy, this is another loser," or "I'm just no good at this," either of which might suggest a sense of insecurity or inadequacy.

Historically, most interpreters have attempted to derive some information from each response, proceeding in a methodical but often concrete response-by-response approach to the record. Although this is an admirable objective, the approach can be naive and very misleading. It is appropriate if the interpreter wants to ensure that no important information is neglected, *but it is erroneous to assume that all responses will yield some new or enhancing information.*

Most of the useful information that can be gleaned from the analysis of the verbalizations comes mainly from the *projected material.* These are the movement responses, the answers which contain material that distort or go well beyond the stimulus field, or the answers in which the objects reported are embellished. In some records, every answer will have one or more of these features; in most protocols, however, this is not the case, and the interpreter should avoid becoming burdened by trying to determine why a specific object was reported, or if there is symbolic significance in the selection of a response. As with the structural data, people tend to be redundant in their verbal behaviors *if* those behaviors are manifestations of needs or attitudes or conflicts. For example, if a thrice married and now separated woman gives responses such as "A vulgar man displaying his thing," "The ugly neckbone of a person like men have," "A vandal with a fire in his gut," and "An evil man peering into a window," it takes little more than common sense to develop the postulate that she does not care for males and probably feels threatened and/or victimized by them. These are all rich responses that involve movement or embellishments.

At the other extreme, a subject might give a sequence of answers to Cards I through IV such as "A bat," "The face of a cat," "Two dogs," "A hole in the ground," "A butterfly," "Some blood," "Two people," "A furry gorilla," and "A willow tree." This sequence of nine responses to the first four blots contains *no* movement, and there are *no* embellishments, but they are not all Pure *F* answers. The hole could involve vista or *FD*, the blood and possibly the butterfly could include chromatic color, and the gorilla response almost certainly would include texture. *Yet, none include any clear projected features.* They are essentially classification answers and, as such, contribute little or nothing to the analysis of the verbal material.

There are two other pitfalls that can occur in analyzing verbal material about which caution should be exercised. First, some interpreters are prone to read the material in the response *and* the Inquiry together, as if a single stream of ideation is represented. *This is not the case,* because the verbal material in the original response is delivered much earlier, *and under a different set of conditions than the material in the Inquiry.* When giving the original answers, the subject is operating under a fairly ambiguous set of instructions, and usually he or she will be naive to the blots. Thus projected material that occurs is issued somewhat freely, and because of that it has considerable interpretive value. The task of the Inquiry is much more structured. The subject is encouraged to more verbiage and, under this circumstance, embellishments are much more commonplace. They must be addressed with great caution and used only if there is good reason to believe that they are not provoked by the instructions of the Inquiry. Thus the analysis of the verbalizations should *always* begin by reading *vertically,* through the original responses, and ignoring the verbal material of the Inquiry while doing so. This process should generate most of the postulates that will be derived from the verbal material. Naturally, the Inquiry should not be ignored. If used conservatively, and *after* completing the review of the original responses, some of the elaborations in the Inquiry can often be quite useful in clarifying or supporting other material. But just as new information that is developed in the Inquiry is usually not included in the coding of an answer, new information developed in the Inquiry ordinarily should not be used to develop a new series of hypothesis. A second problem that the interpreter must avoid when dealing with the verbal material is the development of premature sets. It is sometimes very easy to become caught up in a single answer or two. The result can be a misleading and/or erroneous postulate that is afforded considerable weight, and in turn, other data that might support alternative or contradictory positions are ignored.

MORBID RESPONSE CONTENTS

As noted earlier, the quantity of *MOR* is quite important but it is often the substance or content of the answers that conveys a more meaningful or revealing picture concerning some of the characteristics of the self-image. For instance, in some records, a key word will occur repeatedly in the *MOR* answers, such as dead, broken, battered, or ruined. The cumulative use of such a word usually provides an important clue regarding the conceptualization of the self. Although a single response containing such a key word might be important, the more definitive conclusions are usually drawn when the same word, or very similar words, are used redundantly across several answers. Some *MOR* answers are commonplace, such as animals in a fight that have been hurt, given to Card II, or an animal that has been run over, given to Card VI, which is especially common among the protocols of children. They should not be disregarded as being meaningless, but any hypotheses generated from them should be considered as *very* tentative and not accepted into the final summary unless cross-validated by other data.

Some *MOR* responses are unique and/or dramatic and will often provide a rich input to the understanding of self-image. For instance, "The dead fetus of a woman who has just been forced to have an abortion," reeks with projected information as does, "Two little girls sitting and crying because they just got spanked for being bad." Projected material such as these examples will probably merge easily with other findings concerning self-image. In many instances, these more unique or dramatic answers also have a minus form quality, the presence of which tends to increase the likelihood that the answer is a direct projected representation of the self.

THE CONTENT OF MINUS RESPONSES AND SELF-IMAGE

Some minus responses are the product of projection. As such, they often can provide very useful insights into self-image or self-value. For example, "The face of an evil man" given to a *Dd* area on Card I cannot help but attract attention because it is minus and also because it is embellished by using the word "evil." However, some minus responses may not be products of projection. They could result from faulty processing or mediation. Thus, it is important to emphasize that the content of the minus answers should be approached very conservatively. Projected material, especially in minus answers, should be rather obvious. If it is not, the answer should be disregarded because attempts to glean meanings from contents that are unclear become counterproductive to the interpretative process.

The minus answers should be read in order and the accumulated postulates summarized after the last minus has been reviewed. In some cases, a substantial proportion of the minus answers will cluster for the content coding, such as *An* or *Sc*. When that occurs, it can be assumed that a preoccupation is being manifest through the projective process.

MOVEMENT ANSWER CONTENTS AND SELF-IMAGE

The movement responses also provide an important source of information concerning self-image. They should be read systematically, developing postulates concerning self-image when they can be appropriately formulated on the basis of obvious projected self-representation. Usually, these answers should be reviewed by studying the human movement responses (*M*) first. The reason for this is that direct self representation is more likely to be obvious if human content is involved. Once the *M* answers have been evaluated, the *FM* answers should be reviewed and then the *m* responses should be studied.

It is important to stress the need for conservatism in generating hypotheses from movement responses. The stimulus features of some blots tend to provoke movement classifications. This is especially true in Cards II (*DS*3, rocket taking off), III (*D*1, people lifting or pulling), V (*W,* a winged animal in flight), and IX (*D*3, clowns or monsters leaning or fighting). If postulates are formed because of movement answers to these areas, generally they should be based mainly on the presence of more unusual or idiographic embellishments that are included in the answers. For example, "A rocket taking off so that they can spy on people," to Card II is very different from "A rocket taking off," given to the same Card II area. Similarly, "Two people dancing," to the *D*1 area of Card II is very different from "Two people dancing in a vulgar way because they want to have sex" given to the same area.

In many instances, the projected material will manifest most directly in the homogeneity of the features of numerous movement answers, such as most being passive, aggressive, or markedly emotional. The probable validity of hypotheses generated from movement content usually can be estimated by using repetition as a basis. In other words, the more often a theme or characteristic occurs among the answers, the more likely it reflects a dimension of self-image or self-esteem. Ordinarily, the more valid postulates will be confirmed by significant structural findings. In some cases, the material in one answer may appear inconsistent or even contradictory with the material in other answers. If this occurs, none of the postulates should be discarded prematurely. Each should be afforded consideration during the summary of findings from the entire cluster, and possibly reconsidered during the summary of the complete interpretation.

EMBELLISHED CONTENT IN OTHER RESPONSES AS RELATED TO SELF-IMAGE

Another type of answer that includes projected material are the ones that contain unusual or dramatic wording, or have special embellishments that go well beyond the simple classification of an object, even though they contain no movement, have adequate form quality, and do not contain special scores such as MOR. These forms of embellishment typically involve some projected self-representation, and the material from them should be used to broaden the picture of self-image. Findings generated from embellished answers should be used cautiously and usually they will merge with other hypotheses or conclusions. However, in some records, especially those that are impoverished for movement answers or special scores, the accumulation of embellishments or unusual wording can sometimes generate hypotheses regarding self-concept that might not be formulated otherwise.

For instance, the following responses occurred in the record of a High *Lambda* style ambitent in which only two movement answers, ("Two women pulling on something" to Card III), one minus response ("Some leg bones" to Card VII), and no *MOR* answers were given. The first, to the *D*4 area of Card I was, "An elaborate statue of a beautiful woman," later inquired to reveal that "she has wide hips and a big breast, very beautiful." The second, to Card V, was, "A picture of an actress with a beautiful gown." The inquiry yielded, "Her gown is made of feathers to give an ethereal appearance." The third, to Card IX was, "The sort of crown that only a queen should wear, colorful and elaborate." The inquiry provoked only an emphasis on color and form. Any one of these answers might raise a question regarding self-image, but collectively they argue strongly for the presence of some narcissistic-like feature that may have an exhibitionistic quality. The record was taken from a man charged with the murder of a secretary who worked in an office in which the subject was also employed, and who had scorned his advances.

Most embellished answers are not as obvious as those illustrated above, but most do coincide with other findings in the protocol.

THE L.S. PROTOCOL AND SELF-IMAGE

The structural data relating to self-image for the L.S. record are shown in Table 78.

There are no reflection answers in the record and the Egocentricity Index (.32) is below the average range. This suggests that the subject does not judge himself as favorably as he does significant others in his world. This finding may relate to his sense of apprehension concerning his occupational status. His perceived occupational failure is probably even more irritating because of his obsessive style. There are two *FD* responses in the record, indicating considerable self-examining behavior, but it is not clear whether

Table 78.   Self-Perception Data for Protocol L.S.

$3r + (2)/R = 0.32$	$FD = 2$	$MOR = 0$	$Hx = 0$	$An + Xy = 0$
$Fr + rF = 0$	Sum $V = 0$	$H:(H) + Hd + (Hd) = 4:2$		$Sx = 0$

Responses to Be Read				
MOR Responses	*FQ*− Responses	*M* Responses	*FM* Responses	*m* Responses
		2, 6, 16, 22	1, 4, 8, 19, 24	5, 12, 22

these introspective activities are couched in a reality based estimate of his own potential and worth or whether they may be gauged more in light of his more negative sense of personal worth. The latter is more likely to be true. The data of the $H:(H)+Hd+(Hd)$ *ratio* suggest that he is about as interested in people as are most adults, and the presence of four Pure H responses argues that his self-image is based more on experience than imagination.

There are no $An+Xy$ or MOR answers. Thus, there is no reason to suspect an unusual body concern or any evidence suggesting that his self-concept is marked by unusually negative features. There are 12 movement responses in the record, which include four M answers, five FM answers, and three m responses. Collectively, they should provide some more definitive information concerning his perception of himself.

The first M answer appears to Card I, response 2, "It could also be a modern dance of some sort, with a woman in the center with her hands in the air and two creatures dancing around her." It is striking for its content, and the answer also affords an illustration of how some interpreters can become trapped into misleading speculation. The central figure is a woman, and some may attempt to deal with that very literally, suggesting that it may represent his wife, or some aspect of his own "feminine" identity, and so on. *However, in this instance the sex of the figure must be ignored.* It is very rare that the $D4$ area is ever identified as a man or a child. The figure probably does represent the subject, but it is the movement that conveys the projection, *not* the sex of the figure. She is standing with her hands "in the air," which seems like a passive, possibly helpless, or signaling gesture. In the inquiry, he indicates that, ". . . the hands are raised in sort of supplication," which is a pleading gesture. The creatures are dancing around. They might be playful, or celebrating, but because they are *creatures,* they are possibly threatening. If the latter is true, the response seems to be a good representation of his helplessness and the threats that he is experiencing. In the inquiry, he notes that they ". . . represent something symbolic of whatever she's doing . . . those winged animals in Greek mythology . . ." One wonders if he is referring to Pegasus, the winged horse that sprang from the body of Medusa at her death, but that sort of conjecture should remain just that and not filter into the interpretive conclusions unless other evidence clearly supports that notion.

The second M is to Card III, response 6, "A couple of men bending over to lift something . . ." It is a cooperative response, and although detailed thoroughly for form features, it is also somewhat tentative (inquiry), ". . . but I can't tell what it is, probably some big rocks." This is a fairly common answer and not much projected material is obvious. The third M is to Card VII, response 16, "This way it looks like a couple of women doing the can-can." It is a form of exhibitionistic movement, involving a historically "naughty" routine that carries sexual connotations. It may signal a desire to be more open and active, possibly including his sexuality. If so, it is easy to understand how the desire would be difficult to manifest in light of other data in the record.

The last M is to Card IX, response 22, "You know, this way it looks like a person on a motorcycle or a bike." A motorcycle is an object often associated with a more reckless lifestyle, *or* a bike, the self-propelled, more conventional object. This may signify some conflict about how best to express needs and affects.

There are five FM responses; the first on Card I, response 1, "Looks like a bat gliding along." The first, or *signature,* response can often convey quite a bit about the way in which the subject generally approaches new coping situations. It has been selected from many available and, as such, probably represents something about the decision of the subject regarding how to approach the task. His first answer has two interesting features.

The passive movement reflected in the word *gliding* is of considerable interest, especially because it coincides in an almost predictable way with previously developed hypotheses about his cautious, obsessive style. It is also notable because bats usually do not glide. They are much more active, so that this is an almost incongruous use of the word.

The second *FM* is on Card II, response 4, "It could be a couple of dogs touching noses." It is a tentative and exploratory response, involving domestic animals in a cautious, nonaggressive activity. The third *FM* is to Card IV, response 8, "It could be a gorilla sitting on a stump," later in the inquiry described as furry, and leaning backward. The classification of Card IV as a gorilla is very commonplace, thus the type of animal should not be given any special emphasis. Again, it is the movement that is important. It is passive and nonthreatening. Interestingly, to this point in the record, all of the movement, with the exception of a rocket response on Card II, has been passive or cautious. The fourth *FM* is more active, but clearly evasive. It was given to Card VIII, response 19, "You know, this top part looks like a sand crab, like it was leaping forward, going away from you." The final *FM,* to Card X, response 24, "This brown could be a deer jumping," also tends to be more avoidant, which is not inconsistent with his previous *FM* answers.

The three *m* answers tend to offer more of the same. The first, to Card II, response 5, "The center could be a rocket ship taking off and this red could be the exhaust fire," is a very common answer but a bit unusual because of the wording "exhaust fire." The second, to Card VI, response 12, although scored for active movement, is clearly a cautious, defensive, and almost a concealing type answer, "This could be a submarine cruising along in the darkness," (inquiry) ". . . like a shadowy effect . . ." The last *m* answer occurs in the inquiry for response 22 on Card IX (the motorcycle response), ". . . the way his head is formed there you can get the impression of his hair flying back in the breeze." Two of the three have a passive quality. The submarine answer is probably the most revealing of the three with its concealed defensiveness.

Collectively, the movement answers seem to convey a somewhat timid, uncertain person who is cautious, passive, and conservative on the one hand, yet sometimes interested in being more open and even reckless. He is probably not very comfortable with his conception of himself, seems to feel a need to be more guarded than should be the case. When considered in light of findings regarding his affect, it seems probable that he experiences some conflict or confusion about how best to express his needs and feelings.

Some of the embellishments to answers appear to coincide with this postulate. For instance, on Card IV, response 9, he reports, "A delicate flower." In his first answer, the bat is described as having "small feet," and even the can-can dancers are dancing on only one leg, appropriate for the scene, but nonetheless precarious. At least two answers, an emblem on Card VIII, which is described in the inquiry as like a family crest, and Teddy Roosevelt's head on Card IX are of a variety usually given by status-oriented people. Another interesting embellishment is in response 7 on Card III, ". . . those big red bowties that clowns sometimes wear." This raises a question about whether some of his affective displays are false and misleading.

Overall, the projected material, when considered in light of the structural data for the cluster plus previously developed findings, conveys the sense of a person who is rather rigid, guarded, and conforming, and probably status oriented. He is not really satisfied with his role but, is very uncertain about how to break loose from it. It seems likely that his previously noted strong needs for closeness are the result of his own overly cautious, obsessive-like behaviors, that probably include an avoidant orientation. It is likely that his marriage is less satisfying than he desires, but he feels a sense of confusion about how best to change the situation and thus, he tends to maintain a more timid lifestyle than he would prefer, and because he does not judge himself very favorably, he seems to regard each new situation as potentially threatening and is in a dilemma about how to deal with those threats. Data from the interpersonal cluster may help to clarify these issues.

INTERPERSONAL PERCEPTION AND BEHAVIOR

It is difficult to derive information from the Rorschach about how a subject perceives others and/or relates to them. Unfortunately, none of the test data reveal information about the real environment of the subject or about those with whom the subject interacts. The variables in this cluster represent some of the needs, attitudes, sets, and coping styles that often exist in people. As such, they can be quite influential in forming perceptions of the environment and interactions with it. Thus, some postulates generated from this cluster are derived from less direct and more inferential data and, as such, tend to be more general than are those derived from the other clusters.

NEGATIVE IMPLICATION VARIABLES

Several of the variables that appear in this cluster have been discussed earlier. In general, they are variables which, if positive, have negative implications concerning interpersonal perceptions and/or behavior. For instance, if the *CDI,* described in Chapter 15, has a value of 4 or 5, it indicates that the subject is probably less socially mature than might be expected. These are people prone to experience frequent difficulties when interacting with the environment that will often extend into the interpersonal sphere. Interpersonal relationships tend to be more superficial and less easily sustained, and they are often regarded by others as being more distant, guarded, inept, or helpless in their dealing with others, and tend to be less sensitive to the needs and interests of others. Positive CDI people often have histories that are marked by social chaos and interpersonal dissatisfaction and sometimes they back away from social relationships and accept a routine of limited, superficial contacts with others. If that does not occur, their ineptness makes them vulnerable to rejections by others.

Similarly, if the *HVI* is positive, it is reasonably certain that the person uses considerable energy to maintain a relatively continuous state of preparedness that is formulated in a negative or mistrusting attitude toward the environment. People such as this probably feel vulnerable, and as a consequence formulate and implement behaviors very cautiously. They are preoccupied with issues of personal space and are very guarded in their interpersonal relations; as a result, they do not have sustained close relationships unless they feel in control of the interactions. They do not expect closeness and often become very suspicious about gestures of closeness by others.

If the value for passive movement exceeds the value for active movement by more than one point, it indicates that the subject generally will assume a more passive, *though not necessarily submissive,* role in interpersonal relations. People like this usually try to avoid responsibility for decision making and are less prone to search out new solutions to problems or initiate new patterns of behavior. If Food responses (*Fd*) appear in the record, it indicates that the subject can be expected to manifest many more dependency behaviors than usually is expected. People such as this tend to rely on others for direction and support and tend to be somewhat more naive in their expectations concerning interpersonal relationships. They expect others to be more tolerant of their needs and demands and more willing to act in accord with those needs and demands. If a person such as this also has a passive style, it is reasonable to conclude that a passive-dependent feature is an important core component in the personality structure of the subject.

Another variable in the cluster that may reflect a negative feature is the texture response. If no texture answers appear in a record of a person older than 10, it suggests that the experiences concerning needs for closeness are dissimilar to those of most people. *It does not mean that the subject fails to have such needs.* Instead, it indicates that the subject is more cautious in interpersonal situations and is probably overly concerned with personal space. People such as this tend to be more guarded about creating or maintaining close emotional ties with others. On the other side of the texture variable, an unexpected elevation in T (more than one), indicates the presence of very strong needs for closeness. While most elevations in T will be the result of a recent emotional loss, it may also represent a more chronic state that might have been initiated by a loss or disappointment and perpetuated because the loss was never compensated or replaced. People who have these stronger needs for closeness tend to seek out relations with others and often become more vulnerable to the manipulations of others, especially those who are either passive or dependent.

The remaining variables in the cluster can denote either positive or negative features regarding the interpersonal world of the subject.

THE HUMAN CONTENT VARIABLES AND INTERPERSONAL PERCEPTION

If the number of human contents is in the average range in relation to the *EB* data, it can be assumed that the subject shows as much interest in others as do most people. On the other hand, if the number of human contents is less than expected in the context of *EB,* the subject probably is not as interested in others as most people. This finding is often positive for those who are emotionally withdrawn or socially isolated from their environment. When the number of human contents is greater than average in relation to *EB,* it signals a strong interest in others. Although this finding usually is positive and signifies a healthy interest in people, it can reflect a marked sense of guardedness in some. The latter is especially true for hypervigilant subjects who harbor a strong sense of mistrust for others.

Ames et al. (1971) found that human contents tend to increase gradually through each of the early developmental years to about age 10, after which the proportion remains relatively stable through adolescence. Those findings are consistent with the normative data for younger clients. When *all* human contents are considered, the data for ages 12 through 16 are not unlike those for nonpatient adults. Each of those age groups has a mean that falls between 5 and 6, and a mode of 5. The mean for the adult nonpatients is slightly more than 5, but with a mode of 6.

The absence of human content is an unusual finding, even in the records of younger children. Human content appears in all of the 1390 protocols of nonpatient youngsters. The absence of human content appears to signal a marked lack of interest in and/or detachment from people, which probably has some psychopathological features and will almost always indicate problems in identity and/or self-image (Exner, 1978).

Lower-than-average frequencies of human content are more common among subjects who do not appear to identify closely with typical social values. A significantly lower-than-average frequency of human contents has been noted by Walters (1953) in the records of criminals, and by Ray (1963) and Richardson (1963) among adjudicated delinquents. Exner, Bryant, and Miller (1975) found that the protocols of 15 adolescents, awaiting sentencing for serious assault crimes, included six with no human content and five others in which the frequency of human contents was 1 or 2. The reference sample of character disorders has a mean of less than 5 and a median of 4. Several studies (Halpern, 1940; Morris, 1943; Stotsky, 1952; Goldman, 1960; Piotrowski & Bricklin, 1961) have found positive relationships between the frequency of human contents and treatment effectiveness. Draguns, Haley, and Phillips (1967) have suggested that the frequency of human content varies with cognitive development and the potential for social relations. Their review of literature suggests that low frequencies of human contents may be an effective index from which to differentiate those who have withdrawn from social contacts. The data for the 430 outpatients in several long-term treatment effects studies seem to support this postulate. Fifty subjects who were rated by therapists as being the most isolated interpersonally had, on the average, very low frequencies of human contents ($M = 1.84, SD = 1.21$) and also had very low Affective Ratios ($M = .374, SD = .11$).

Although the frequency of human contents is important because it provides some indications about interest in people and possibly the extent to which a person identifies with the social environment, the frequency of Pure H responses adds very important information concerning views of, and attitudes toward, the social environment as they involve real figures. As noted earlier, the proportion of human contents that is Pure H usually ranges from one-third to one-half among nonpatient children, ages 8 through 11, and into adulthood, the proportion of Pure H increases significantly, to between one-half and two-thirds of all human contents. When the frequency of human contents is near or above average, but the frequency of *Pure H* is 1 or zero, that is, most or all of the human responses consist of *Hd,* or the parenthesized human contents, (H) and (Hd), it is likely that the record has been given by a child or a psychiatric subject. Only 68 of the 700 adult nonpatient records (9%) have this characteristic, as do between 7% and 11% of the records of younger nonpatients, ages 10 to 16. Conversely, 154 of the 320 schizophrenic reference sample protocols have this feature (48%), as do 149 of the 315 depressive records (47%), and 98 of the 180 records of the character disorder group (54%).

Beck (1945) suggested that an emphasis on *Hd* answers occurs in people who feel constricted in their world. Klopfer et al. (1954) felt that *Hd* answers signal a form of compulsiveness and/or an intellectual approach. Sherman (1952) and Vinson (1960) found significantly more *Hd* in the records of schizophrenics than among nonpatients. Molish (1967) has suggested that as the balance of human contents shifts in favor of *Hd,* it is indicative of a constrictive form of defense.

The frequency of the parenthesized human and animal contents typically is quite low among nonpatient adults ($M = 1.56, SD = 1.19$), but is almost twice as large for nonpatient children between the ages of 5 and 9 ($M = 3.07, SD = 1.63$). Patients with marked paranoid features average more than four ($M = 4.21$) parenthesized human and animal contents. Elevations are also common among schizophrenics and character disorders, although less so among depressed patients. Molish (1967) has pointed out that these answers may indicate forms of denial as related to the social environment. They clearly seem to indicate a detachment from the real world, and probably signal an investment in fantasy. The ratio $(H)+(A):(Hd)+(Ad)$ is designed to call attention to the frequencies of parenthesized responses. If any such responses occur, the value is expected to appear in the left side of the ratio, and with low frequencies such as 1:0 or 2:0 in the records of adults, or 2:1 or 3:0 among younger subjects. If the combined values exceed 3 for an adult, 4 for an adolescent, or 5 in the record of a youngster below the age of 13, or if the higher value is greater than 2 and falls on the right side of the ratio, it is very likely that the social environment is often misinterpreted.

The ratio of $H+A:Hd+Ad$ is included to focus on the frequency of Hd and Ad answers that occur in the record. *Hd* answers are much more common among people who are more guarded and suspicious in their views of the social environment. Sometimes, however, subjects with this feature give a very low frequency of human contents, and if only those data are considered, the presence of this characteristic might be neglected. Rorschach noted that animal contents reflect the largest single class of response. A variety of studies have confirmed that impression (Beck et al., 1950; Cass & McReynolds, 1951; Brockway et al., 1954; Neff & Glaser, 1954; Wedemeyer, 1954). Ames et al. (1971) note that about half of the responses of children and slightly less than half of those given by adolescents are of animals, and Beck et al. (1961) found an average of about 45% of responses in adult records include animal contents. The normative samples for nonpatient adults and younger subjects are consistent with those findings. Apparently, animal responses occur most frequently because this class of contents involves a very broad array of shapes, thereby increasing the probability that at least one will have some congruence with the contours of a blot or blot areas. But just as *Hd* responses occur infrequently, so too do *Ad* answers. Thus the $H+A:Hd+Ad$ ratio should always have a much larger value on the left side, at least 4:1. If the value on the right side is greater than one-fourth that of the left, it suggests that views of the social environment may be somewhat unusual. Exner and Hillman (1984) reviewed 119 protocols of patients with marked paranoid features and found that 93 (78%) have $H+A:Hd+Ad$ ratios in which the right-side value equals 50% or more of the left-side value.

THE PERSONAL RESPONSE (*PER*)

Data concerning the frequency of *PER* responses often provides some added input concerning the interpersonal perceptions and behaviors of the subject. Personal responses represent a form of defensiveness. A low frequency, zero to two, are common in many records and are not interpretively meaningful. However, higher frequencies warrant some concern.

The initial interest in this Special Score evolved during the collection of normative samples for children. Many examiners questioned whether these verbalizations should be coded as *DR,* because they often seem to be irrelevant to the response. The normative data reveal that both nonpatient children and adults tend to give at least one, but usually not more than two. For example, *PER* answers appear in about 90% of the records give by 12-year-olds, but only 7 of the 120 subjects in that sample gave more than one. Similarly, 81% of the 15-year-olds gave *PER* answers but only 9 of the 110 subjects gave more than one. About 69% of the nonpatient adults gave *PER* responses but only 49 of the 700 subjects gave more than one and only 18 gave more than two.

Like the *MOR* response, the distributions for nonpatients fall on a neat *J*-curve that has a very limited range, usually 0 to 5, but as narrow as 0 to 3 for some age groups, and a mode of 1. About 57% of subjects in the depressive reference sample gave PER answers, but more than half of those gave more than two and a few gave as many as nine. In the schizophrenia reference group about 51% gave *PER* and more than half of those gave three or more. Only about 43% of the records in the character disorders reference sample contain *PER,* but among those that do, nearly 70% have three or more *PER* answers.

A computer search of outpatient samples yielded two groups in which the mean for *PER* exceeded three. The first consists of 65 obsessive adults ($M = 3.76, SD = 1.4$), and the second is a sample of 45 male adolescents in treatment because of problems in handling displays of anger ($M = 3.69, SD = 1.2$). Only 6 of the obsessive patients and 7 of the adolescents had records in which no *PER* occurred. The modes for both groups are 3, and the ranges in each extend to 10. The data from the Thomas, Exner, and Baker (1982) study, in which 225 college students were administered the Gough Adjective Check List, revealed that the 20 subjects who had the greatest discrepancy between their "real and ideal" scores averaged 2.69 *PER* answers, whereas the 20 subjects from the opposite extreme of the *ACL* distribution average 0.7. Exner and Weiner (1982) used six assistants to record various behaviors that occurred among three fourth- and fifth-grade classes during interactive tasks assigned by teachers. Each class was observed by two raters for two 1-hour periods on each of five consecutive days. Among behaviors recorded were denial responses such as, "It's not my fault, he told me to do it," or "We would have finished if she hadn't fouled up," and so on. Subsequently, the five students with the highest frequency of denial behaviors, plus five others randomly selected from the remaining students, were administered the Rorschach by one of six examiners who were not familiar with the study. The five target students averaged 3.9 *PER* answers as contrasted with 2.16 for the control sample.

A computer search of the pretreatment protocols of the 430 outpatients who volunteered for the long-term treatment effects study (Exner, 1978) identified 82 (19%) in which *PER* appeared at least four times ($M = 5.73, SD = 1.6$). A review of the therapist ratings of those patients, for the early sessions of treatment, reveals that more than two-thirds (57) were rated as resistive, or having questionable motivation for treatment, as compared with less than 25% of a second group of 82 patients randomly selected from the remaining 348 subjects in the study ($M = 1.12, SD = 2.09, p < .01$).

The findings concerning the *PER* responses suggest that subjects giving significantly higher frequencies have some need to be overly precise in defending their self-image. On the surface, it may appear that some *PER* answers are more an indication of an openness or willingness to share information about oneself. That element may exist in some kinds of *PER* responses, such as the child who reports a butterfly, and then adds, "I caught one like this, it was really pretty." But at a different level, the *PER* provides more sturdiness to the percept, and consequently to the self. The personal commentary serves to provide reassurance, as if psychologically saying, "I know that I am right because I am drawing from direct experience," and in doing so, the subject feels able to fend off any potential challenge from the examiner. In other words, it reflects a sort of defensive authoritarianism.

Thus, if the value for *PER* is three it suggests that the subject tends to be more defensively authoritarian in interpersonal situations than most people. This does not necessarily impair interpersonal relations but does signal that the subject is probably less secure in situations involving challenges than might be preferred. If the value for *PER* exceeds three, it can be postulated that the subject is quite insecure about his or her personal integrity and tends to be overly authoritarian or argumentative when interpersonal situations appear to pose challenges to the self. People such as this are usually regarded as rigid or narrow by others and as a consequence, they often have difficulties in maintaining close relations, especially with those who are not submissive to them.

COOPERATIVE (*COP*) AND AGGRESSIVE (*AG*) RESPONSES

The values for *COP* and *AG* often provide valuable information about the sets that a subject may have concerning interactions between people. Although the two scores do not correlate with each other, it is important that the interpretation of either be formulated with regard for the data of the other. Both of these special scores were derived from some of the work and suggestions of Piotrowski (1957) who argued that *M* responses often translate directly into impressions about people and responses to them. Although undoubtably Piotrowski was correct, his hypotheses did not validate when only *M* answers were studied but were supported when all movement answers were included. The special score for aggressive movement evolved first.

Aggressive Movement (*AG*)   Kazaoka, Sloane, and Exner (1978) rated videotapes of the occupational and recreational therapy activities of seven inpatient groups for verbal and nonverbal aggressiveness. Each group, containing 10 patients, was taped for two 20-minute segments, once during occupational therapy in which the patients were encouraged to do clay construction, and once during recreational therapy in which each group was divided into two teams of five each to play basketball. The tapes were scored independently by each of three raters using the Fels Institute Aggression Scale. Rorschachs were administered to the 70 patients by seven examiners (each giving 10), who had no knowledge of the nature of the study.

The 70 subjects were divided into two equal groups twice, once by a median split of the distribution of the scores for verbal aggressiveness. The groups did not differ significantly for *AG* scores when divided on the basis of verbal aggressiveness (Upper Half = 3.07, $SD = 1.98$; Lower Half = 1.71, $SD = 1.57$, $p > .20$, *ns*). When the 15 subjects at each extreme of the verbal aggressiveness distribution were compared, however, they did differ significantly for *AG* (Upper 15 = 4.21, $SD = 2.03$; Lower 15 = 0.94, $SD = 1.09$, $p < .01$). When the division was based on the distribution of physical aggressiveness scores, the difference was more substantial (Upper Half = 3.57, $SD = 1.81$; Lower Half = 1.06, $SD = 1.13$, $p < .05$), and when the 15 subjects at each extreme of the distribution were compared, the magnitude of the difference was much greater (Upper 15 = 4.16, $SD = 1.94$; Lower 15 = 0.78, $SD = 1.08$, $p < .01$). Interestingly, when the scores for verbal and physical aggressiveness were combined and the distribution split at the median again, the two groups did not differ significantly (Upper = 4.06, $SD = 1.83$; Lower = 2.79, $SD = 1.74$, $p > .20$, *ns*), but the 15 subjects in each extreme did differ significantly (Upper 15 = 5.39; $SD = 2.01$; Lower 15 = 1.88, $SD = 1.2$, $p < .02$).

In another study, 33 sixth-grade children, who had been administered the Rorschach 2 to 3 weeks earlier, were videotaped during two 30-minute free periods in their classroom (Exner, Kazaoka, & Morris, 1979). The tapes were scored independently by two raters, using the Fels Aggression Scale, for verbal and nonverbal aggressiveness. The group was divided twice, using a median split of the distributions for verbal and nonverbal aggression, and discarding the middle subject. The mean *AG* scores for the upper half were significantly greater than for the lower half in both instances (Upper Verbal = 3.86, SD = 1.1; Lower Verbal = 1.2, SD = 0.87, $p < .05$; Upper Physical = 3.99, SD = 1.3; Lower Physical = 0.96, SD = 0.89, $p < .02$), although an analysis of the group split on the basis of the combined scores was not significant ($p > .10$).

The records of the 430 outpatients who participated in the long-term treatment effects studies include 82 (19%) that contain at least three AG answers. Therapist ratings for the early treatment sessions did not include any items specifically relating to a history of aggressive activity, but ratings were requested for manifestations of hostility during the sessions, and a second group of items concerned attitudes toward people. A comparison group of 82 subjects was randomly drawn from the remaining 348 subjects. Forty-one of the 82 target subjects were rated as manifesting significant hostility during at least two of the three sessions, as contrasted with 15 subjects from the comparison group ($p < .01$), and 51 of the 82 were rated as being markedly hostile in their attitudes toward people, as contrasted with 22 subjects from the comparison group ($p < .05$).

This composite of studies appears to support the notion that elevations in AG signify an increased likelihood for aggressive behaviors, either verbal or nonverbal, and that they also indicate attitudes toward others that are more negative and/or hostile than is customary. Quite likely, people with elevations in AG see the social environment as marked by aggressiveness, and they have incorporated that attitude or set, so that it has become a feature of their own personality, and consequently a feature that marks some of their behavior. The manifestations of aggressiveness will vary considerably, being influenced by other characteristics, such as reality testing, affective controls, concerns with conventionality or social acceptance, and stress tolerance.

It is true that a higher frequency of AG is not uncommon among prisoners convicted of antisocial crimes of violence, but higher frequencies of AG also are common in the protocols of surgeons, police officers, professional football players, and even among clergymen. This is one of the reasons that many other Rorschach variables must be considered before formulating any conjecture about above-average values for AG. The value for COP is often quite important in that context.

Cooperative Movement COP answers appear at least once in almost 80% of the 700 adult nonpatient records with introversives giving slightly, but not significantly, more than extratensives and ambitents. COP appears at least once in only about 65% of outpatient protocols, about half of the records from inpatient schizophrenics and depressives, and less than 40% of the protocols from character disorders. COP is not easily reported on some Cards. It occurs in less than 20% of the M and less than 15% of the FM answers on Cards I, VIII, IX, and X. It is almost nonexistent among answers to Cards IV and VI and has a very low frequency to Card V. It occurs most often to Card III, and next most frequently to Cards II and VII.

In two sociometric studies (Exner, 1987), one consisting of peer nominations from 25 third-year high school students, and the second consisting of the same type of peer nominations from 35 female college freshmen living in the same dormitory, subjects who had more than two COP answers were identified by their peers at a rate five times greater than other subjects as being the one who, "Is the most fun to be with," "Is the easiest to be around," "Is a class leader," and "Is the most trustworthy." Four subjects from the group of high school students and five of the college students whose records contained no COP responses were never nominated by any of their peers for any of those four items. Conversely, those nine subjects did receive the most nominations for relatively negative items such as, "Is the person I know least about," "Is a person who does not seem to have many friends," and "Is a person I would probably not vote for a class office."

COP also correlates with the group therapy process. A review of the audio recordings of 17 subjects in two groups, taken during three group therapy sessions, reveals that 4 subjects with more than 2 *COP* talked more frequently and for longer intervals, and directed remarks to more group members than did others in the groups. Six subjects with 0 *COP* responses talked least frequently and directed remarks to the therapist more often than did others in the groups.

Treatment effects data suggest that *COP* is probably an important variable regarding successful termination and/or discharge from hospitalization. For instance, a stratified random sample of 70 outpatients was drawn from the pool of subjects who had participated in a multiple retest, treatment effects studies. The criteria for selection was fourfold: (1) that each had entered treatment because of interpersonal problems, (2) that each had participated in the study for at least two years, (3) that each had terminated treatment before the 18th month, and (4) that the pretreatment protocol contained either 0 *COP* or 1 *COP*. The selection yielded 31 cases in which there was 0 *COP* in the pretreatment record and 39 cases in which the pretreatment record contained 1 *COP*.

Information concerning the subjects indicated that each had entered one of four treatment models (cognitive therapy, $N = 23$; rational emotive therapy, $N = 14$; behavioral modeling therapy, $N = 13$; dynamic psychotherapy, $N = 20$). All 70 subjects terminated treatment between the 8th and 15th month. All were retested during the 9th or 10th month after the onset of treatment, and again between the 18th and 20th month. In the 9–10 month retest, 37 gave at least 2 *COP* responses, 15 had 1 *COP* and the remaining 18 had no *COP* (none of these 18 had *COP* in the first test). In the 18–20 month follow-up, the *COP* distribution showed very little change. All 37 subjects who had 2 or more *COP* in the first retest had at least 2 *COP* in the second retest and 34 of the 37 (92%) reported a favorable interpersonal adjustment. Two of the 15 subjects who had 1 *COP* in the 10-month retest had 2 *COP* in the second retest, and the remaining 13 continued to give 1 *COP*. Twelve of these subjects (80%) also reported a favorable interpersonal adjustment but three reported recurring problems and one had entered treatment again. None of the 18 subjects who were *COP-less* in the first retest gave *COP* in the second retest. Ten of the 18 (56%) reported a favorable interpersonal adjustment, but 8 (44%) reported recurring interpersonal problems and 5 of the 8 had entered treatment again.

A second study focused on a review of follow-up data for 100 first-admission inpatient affective disorders. Among the admission protocols, 31 contained two or more *COP* answers, 36 contained one *COP* response, and 33 had 0 *COP*. All were retested at discharge, which occurred between 21 and 45 days after admission. At that time, 37 records contained two or more *COP*, 29 had one *COP*, and 34 had 0 *COP* answers. All entered or reentered outpatient care and 78 were continuing as outpatients at the time of a 9–10-month postdischarge follow-up. Favorable progress was reported by 30 of the 37 (81%) who had 2 or more *COP* at discharge. Three had been rehospitalized within 8 months of being discharged. Favorable progress was reported by 19 of the 29 subjects (66%) who had given one *COP* in the discharge; however, 6 of the remaining 10 had been rehospitalized during the first 8 months following discharge. Favorable progress was reported by only 18 of the 34 subjects (53%) whose discharge protocols contained 0 *COP*, and 9 of the remaining 16 subjects had been rehospitalized during the 8 months following discharge.

Obviously, as with *AG,* it is dangerous to interpret the presence or absence of *COP* in isolation. Findings generated from many other sources are necessary to put the *COP* data in proper perspective. For instance, preliminary findings suggest that interpersonal relationships are likely to be less stable for those whose protocols contain more than two aggressive movement (*AG*) answers even though multiple COP answers also appear in the record. Nonetheless, *COP* does seem to be a linchpin variable in the cluster of variables related to interpersonal perception.

Interpreting *COP* and *AG*   If the value for *COP* is zero and the value for *AG* is zero or one, it is probable that the subject does not perceive or anticipate positive interactions among people as a routine event. People such as this tend to feel less comfortable in interpersonal situations and they are often regarded by others as being more distant or aloof. This does not preclude mature and/or deep relationships with others, but in general, people with these *COP* and *AG* values are not perceived by others as being noticeably gregarious and they often remain more in the periphery during group interactions.

If the value for *COP* is zero or one and the value for *AG* is two, it is probable that the subject tends to perceive aggressiveness as a natural manifestation in interpersonal relationships. Subjects such as this are likely to emit more aggressive behaviors than do those with lower *AG* values. The specific characteristics of the aggressive behavior, that is, whether it will be verbal or nonverbal, socially acceptable or asocial, and so on, will vary considerably from subject to subject depending on many other personality variables. If the value for *COP* is less than three and the value for *AG* exceeds two, it is likely that much of the interpersonal activity of the subject will be marked by forceful and/or aggressive types of behavior that are usually obvious to the frequent observer. These behaviors often represent a defensive tactic designed to contend with a sense of discomfort in interpersonal situations. The characteristics of the aggressiveness will vary considerably depending on other personality variables as well as the nature of the environmental situation.

If the value for *COP* is one or two and the value for *AG* is zero or one, it can be assumed that the subject generally perceives positive interactions among people routinely and has a willingness to participate in them. Specific characteristics of the patterns of interaction usually will be defined by other features of the subject, such as coping styles and self-image. If the value for *COP* is two or three and the value for *AG* is two, it suggests that the subject is open and interested in positive interaction but that many of the interactions will be marked by more aggressive forms of exchange. About 17% of the nonpatients give two *AG* answers but more than two-thirds of those subjects also give at least one *COP* answer, and more than half give two *COP* responses. Thus, many subjects who perceive forms of aggressiveness as a natural mode of exchange between people also anticipate that exchanges generally will be positive.

If the value for *COP* is three or more and the value for *AG* is zero or one, or if the value for *COP* is more than three and the value for *AG* is two or less, it is probable that the subject tends to be regarded by others as likable and outgoing. Subjects such as this often view interpersonal activity as a very important part of their daily routine and are usually identified by those around them as among the more gregarious in group interactions. Usually, they anticipate and seek out harmonious interactions with others.

A value for *COP* of three or more and a value for *AG* that exceeds two is a very unusual finding and probably signals the presence of some conflict or confusion concerning the appropriate mode of interpersonal behavior. People such as this are likely to be less consistent and/or predictable in their interpersonal routines.

THE ISOLATION INDEX (*ISOLATE/R*)

Another datum that will sometimes provide information concerning one's views and re-actions to the social environment is the Isolation Index. Throughout Rorschach history, it has seemed logical to assume that an elevation in the frequency for any content cate-gory has some interpretive significance. This is because the frequencies for most cate-gories are very low, with the exception of the Animal and Human contents. None average more than two for most groups, except Botany which has a mean of 2.48 ($SD = 1.3$) for nonpatient adults. Many authors (Beck, 1945; Klopfer & Kelley, 1942; Rapaport, Gill, & Schafer, 1946; Piotrowski, 1957; Draguns, Haley, & Phillips, 1967; Exner, 1974) have postulated that elevations in a single category indicate some form of conflict or preoccu-pation. However, with the exception of the $An + Xy$ composite, no empirical data support this proposition. In that context, the computer searches were designed to study individ-ual content categories plus various combinations of categories as they might relate to other data available concerning subjects.

The first hint that the combination of Botany, Clouds, Geography, Landscape, and Nature categories might relate to social isolation or withdrawal occurred by studying the contents in the first protocols of the 430 outpatients who volunteered to participate in the long-term treatment effects studies. Therapist ratings for the early sessions con-tained items about social behaviors, such as frequency of social contacts outside the im-mediate family, feelings of social alienation or isolation, and so on. The correlation between a composite of these ratings and the combination of the five content categories is $r = .26$ for the entire group ($p < .01$); however, when the 100 subjects from each ex-treme of the distribution of therapist ratings were analyzed separately, the results were quite striking. For the 100 evaluated as having the most active and positive social rela-tions, the correlation with the combined frequencies of the five contents, calculated in relation to R and with the two categories Na and Cl afforded double weights is $-.51$ ($p < .01$), and for the 100 evaluated as being the least active and/or having the most negative social relations, the correlation with the index is .71 ($p < .001$).

The next clue to the significance of the *Isolate/R* Index was revealed by a review of data for other psychiatric samples. Two groups surfaced in this process, both of which have substantial percentages of protocols in which the Isolation Index exceeds one-fourth of R, and many for whom the Index exceeds one-third of R. The first is a com-bined group of 505 children and adolescents who have teacher ratings, or psychologist evaluations, indicating that they are markedly withdrawn from social contact (Exner, 1978). Of those 505 records, 423 (84%) have an Index that exceeds one-fourth of R, and 271 (54%) have an Index that exceeds one-third of R. The second group consists of 146 outpatient adults diagnosed as "schizoid," or "schizotypal personality disorder." Of the 146 records, 127 (86%) contain an Index that exceeds one-fourth of R, and 89 of those (61%) have an Index that exceeds one-third of R. These data signify that some sort of social isolation is indicated if the Index is .25 or greater. Two studies have been com-pleted to test this postulate.

Farber, Exner, and Thomas (1982) used a peer nomination design with 139 high school sophomores and juniors in an effort to identify subjects having the most limited social contact with others in their classes. The nominations included 15 items, all of which re-lated to interpersonal preferences or behaviors, such as most popular, best dancer, most friendly, most humorous, most helpful, best listener, most sensitive to others, most fun to be with, most responsible, most trustworthy, and so on. All of the items focused on positive rather than negative features. Eighteen students received no nominations, and they, plus 18 other students selected randomly as controls from the remaining 120, were recruited to take the Rorschach. Each subject received a $10 payment for volunteering. The target sample shows a mean Isolation Index of .31 ($SD = .08$), whereas the control group has a mean Index of .17 ($SD = .12$).

In the second study, a 30-item peer nomination inventory was used with 64 female college students, all of whom lived in the same dormitory at a small residential college (Exner & Farber, 1983). They had volunteered to participate in a psychological study concerning stresses of campus living in exchange for a donation toward new furnishings for one of the study rooms in the dormitory. All were administered several psychological tests and completed several questionnaires including the one concerning peer nominations. The 30 items included the 15 used in the previous study, plus 15 negative items, such as least friendly, most disruptive, most insensitive to others, most outspoken, most irritating, least responsible, most argumentative, and *least interested in being with people.* All subjects received at least two nominations, and 14 were nominated at least once as being least interested in being with people; however, nine of the 14 received at least 20 such nominations as compared with fewer than six for the remaining five subjects. Those nine subjects averaged .32, and all had Isolation Indices exceeding .25. For comparison, five randomly selected groups of nine subjects each were drawn from the remaining 55 students. In one group, three subjects had Isolation Indices greater than .25, but in the other four groups only one or zero had indices greater than .25.

About 12% of nonpatient adults have an Isolation Index that falls between 25% and 30% of R as contrasted with about 18% of schizophrenics, 15% of depressives, and 9% of the character disorders sample. A value of between 25% and 32% usually identifies the person who is less involved in social interaction. It does *not* necessarily reflect social maladjustment or conflict. In most instances, it represents less interest in or possibly more timidity about social intercourse. When the latter is true, the value for *COP* usually will be three or more, signifying that interest exists but participation is limited. When the Isolation Index is .33 or greater, it is very likely that the subject is socially isolated. Almost all subjects for whom this finding is positive have less than two *COP* responses, and most will also have a low *Afr.* People such as this usually find it difficult to create and/or sustain smooth or meaningful interpersonal relationships.

HUMAN MOVEMENT WITH PAIRS (2) AND HUMAN CONTENTS

The final steps in searching through data related to interpersonal perception involve a qualitative evaluation of all of the *M* responses that contain a pair (2) plus a review of all answers that contain human content. The former is to determine if there is any notable consistency in the patterns of interaction and to search for unusual words or word use that might contribute to postulates formed about social interaction. The latter is to focus on the nouns and adjectives that have been used to describe the human or human-like figures. Naturally, these forms of content analyses should proceed cautiously, and any hypotheses generated from them should be conservative unless clearly supported by other data in the cluster.

THE L.S. PROTOCOL AND INTERPERSONAL PERCEPTION

The data relating to interpersonal perception from the L.S. protocol are shown in Table 79.

The three variables relating to basic styles (*CDI, HVI, a:p*) are all negative and there are no Food answers. The elevation in texture answers has been noted before as indicating what may be a chronic experience of loneliness. Undoubtably, this neediness impacts on his perceptions of others and may have some influence on his interpersonal behaviors. The six human contents indicate that he is clearly interested in others and the fact that four are Pure *H* suggests that his conceptions of people are likely to be based more on experience than imagination. The number of *PER* answers is not significant, but the data for *COP* and *AG* are very important. There are three *COP* and no *AG* responses; thus it is highly probable that he perceives positive interactions between people as a routine, and he is apt to be viewed by others as likable and outgoing. This is intriguing in light of his apparent low self-esteem, discovered in the data concerning self-perception, and some of the difficulties he may be experiencing with the modulation of emotional displays, revealed by some of the data concerning affect. It raises the possibility that many of his interpersonal behaviors may be more contrived than real, possibly in accord with his basic obsessive style and particularly his clear needs to be conventional. The Isolation Index is negative. The three *M* responses that contain a pair are the *COP* answers, a modern dance with a woman in the center with her hands in the air and two creatures dancing around her; a couple of men bending over to lift something up; and a couple of women doing the can-can. Two of the three are dances, that is, contrived activity. Interestingly, one of the remaining three human contents—response 14 to Card VII, "A couple of kids"—is the kind of Popular answer that often includes *M* and *COP,* but that is not the case in this record. The other two human contents, Teddy Roosevelt, and a person on a motorcycle or bike, involve isolated figures. Neither include particularly unusual wording although the second is described as being "heavyset."

Overall, the data for this cluster, taken alone tend to raise more issues than are resolved. Clearly, he is lonely but also seems to be sincerely interested in others and quite gregarious. When these findings are cast in the light of findings from other clusters, they suggest that he may not be as outgoing as may appear at first glance, and possibly his interpersonal relationships are more superficial than he might desire. All of the findings for the L.S. protocol will be integrated in the next chapter and recommendations formulated with regard to his presenting complaints.

Table 79.   Interpersonal Perception Data for L.S.

CDI = 1	*a:p* = 8:5	*T* = 2	Human Cont = 6	Pure *H* = 4
HVI = Neg	Food = 0	*PER* = 1	*COP* = 3 *AG* = 0	*Isolate/R* = 0.16

Responses to Be Read

Human Movement with Pair	*Human Contents*
2, 6, 16	2, 6, 14, 16, 20, 22

REFERENCES

Ames, L. B., Metraux, R. W., and Walker, R. N. (1971) *Adolescent Rorschach Responses.* New York: Brunner/Mazel.

Applebaum, S. A., and Colson, D. B. (1968) A reexamination of the color-shading Rorschach Test response. *Journal of Projective Techniques and Personality Assessment,* **32,** 160–164.

Applebaum, S. A., and Holzman, P. S. (1962) The color-shading response and suicide. *Journal of Projective Techniques,* **26,** 155–161.

Bandura, A. (1954) The Rorschach white space response and oppositional behavior. *Journal of Consulting Psychology,* **18,** 17–21.

Baughman, E. E. (1959) An experimental analysis of the relationship between stimulus structure and behavior in the Rorschach. *Journal of Projective Techniques,* **23,** 134–183.

Beck, S. J. (1945) *Rorschach's Test. II: A Variety of Personality Pictures.* New York: Grune & Stratton.

Beck, S. J. (1949) *Rorschach's Test. I: Basic Processes,* (2nd Ed.). New York: Grune & Stratton.

Beck, S. J., Beck, A., Levitt, E., and Molish, H. B. (1961) *Rorschach's Test. I: Basic Processes,* (3rd Ed.). New York: Grune & Stratton.

Beck, S. J., Rabin, A. I., Theisen, W. G., Molish, H. B., and Thetford, W. N. (1950) The normal personality as projected in the Rorschach Test. *Journal of Psychology,* **30,** 241–298.

Bochner, R., and Halpern, F. (1945) *The Clinical Application of the Rorschach Test.* New York: Grune & Stratton.

Brockway, A. L., Gleser, G. C., and Utlett, G. A. (1954) Rorschach concepts of normality. *Journal of Consulting Psychology,* **15,** 178–183.

Cass, W. A., and McReynolds, P. A. (1951) A contribution to Rorschach norms. *Journal of Consulting Psychology,* **15,** 178–183.

Castles, J. (1984) Personal Communication. Alumni Workshop, Nassau.

Counts, R. M., and Mensh, I. N. (1950) Personality characteristics in hypnotically induced hostility. *Journal of Clinical Psychology,* **6,** 325–330.

Draguns, J. G., Haley, E. M., and Phillips, L. (1967) Studies of Rorschach content: A review of the research literature. Part 1: Traditional content categories. *Journal of Projective Techniques and Personality Assessment,* **31,** 3–32.

Elizur, A. (1949) Content analysis of the Rorschach with regard to anxiety and hostility. *Journal of Projective Techniques,* **13,** 247–284.

Exner, J. E. (1962) The effect of color on productivity in Cards VIII, IX, X of the Rorschach. *Journal of Projective Techniques,* **26,** 30–33.

Exner, J. E. (1974) *The Rorschach: A Comprehensive System. Volume 1.* New York: Wiley.

Exner, J. E. (1978) *The Rorschach: A Comprehensive System. Volume 2: Current research and advanced interpretation,* (2nd Ed.). New York: Wiley.

Exner, J. E. (1983) Rorschach assessment. In I. B. Weiner (Ed.), *Clinical Methods in Psychology,* (2nd Ed.). New York: Wiley.

Exner, J. E. (1986) *The Rorschach: A Comprehensive System. Volume 1: Basic Foundations,* (2nd Ed.). New York: Wiley.

Exner, J. E. (1987) A pilot study on efforts by nonpatients to malinger characteristics of depression. *Alumni Newsletter.* Asheville, N.C.: Rorschach Workshops.

Exner, J. E. (1987) Peer nominations and *COP. Alumni Newsletter.* Asheville, N.C.: Rorschach Workshops.

Exner, J. E., Armbruster, G. L., and Viglione, D. (1978) The temporal stability of some Rorschach features. *Journal of Personality Assessment,* **42,** 474–482.

Exner, J. E., Armbruster, G. L., Walker, E. J., and Cooper, W. H. (1975) Anticipation of elective surgery as manifest in Rorschach records. Workshops Study No. 213 (unpublished), Rorschach Workshops.

Exner, J. E., Bryant, E. L., and Miller, A. S. (1975) Rorschach responses of some juvenile offenders. Workshops Study No. 214 (unpublished), Rorschach Workshops.

Exner, J. E., and Farber, J. G. (1983) Peer nominations among female college students living in a dormitory setting. Workshops Study No. 290 (unpublished), Rorschach Workshops.

Exner, J. E., and Hillman, L. (1984) A comparison of content distributions for the records of 76 paranoid schizophrenics and 76 nonparanoid schizophrenics. Workshops Study No. 293 (unpublished), Rorschach Workshops.

Exner, J. E., Kazaoka, K., and Morris, H. M. (1979) Verbal and nonverbal aggression among sixth grade students during free periods as related to a Rorschach Special Score for aggression. Workshops Study No. 255 (unpublished), Rorschach Workshops.

Exner, J. E., Martin, L. S., and Mason, B. (1984) A review of the Suicide Constellation. 11th International Rorschach Congress, Barcelona.

Exner, J. E., and Murillo, L. G. (1975) Early prediction of posthospitalization relapse. *Journal of Psychiatric Research,* **12,** 231–237.

Exner, J. E., and Murillo, L. G. (1977) A long-term follow up of schizophrenics treated with regressive ECT. *Diseases of the Nervous System,* **38,** 162–168.

Exner, J. E., Murillo, L. G., and Cannavo, F. (1973) Disagreement between patient and relative behavioral reports as related to relapse in nonschizophrenic patients. Eastern Psychological Association, Washington, D.C.

Exner, J. E., Murillo, L. G., and Sternklar, S. (1979) Anatomy and X-ray responses among patients with body delusions or body problems. Workshops Study No. 257 (unpublished), Rorschach Workshops.

Exner, J. E., and Sanglade, A. A. (1992) Rorschach changes following brief and short-term therapy. *Journal of Personality Assessment*, **59,** 59–71.

Exner, J. E., and Thomas, E. A. (1984) The relation of *Afr* and preference for artist sketches. Workshops Study No. 294 (unpublished), Rorschach Workshops.

Exner, J. E., Thomas, E. A., and Chu, Y. A. (1985) *Afr* and cartoon ratings. Workshops Study No. 302 (unpublished), Rorschach Workshops.

Exner, J. E., Thomas, E. A., and Mason, B. (1985) Children's Rorschach's: Description and prediction. *Journal of Personality Assessment,* **49,** 13–20.

Exner, J. E., and Weiner, I. B. (1982) *The Rorschach: A Comprehensive System. Volume 3: Assessment of Children and Adolescents.* New York: Wiley.

Exner, J. E., and Wylie, J. (1977) Some Rorschach data concerning suicide. *Journal of Personality Assessment,* **41,** 339–348.

Exner, J. E., Wylie, J. R., and Bryant, E. L. (1974) Peer preference nominations among outpatients in four psychotherapy groups. Workshops Study No. 199 (unpublished), Rorschach Workshops.

Exner, J. E., Wylie, J. R., and Kline, J. R. (1977) Variations in Rorschach performance during a 28 month interval as related to seven intervention modalities. Workshops Study No. 240 (unpublished), Rorschach Workshops.

Farber, J. L., Exner, J. E., and Thomas, E. A. (1982) Peer nominations among 139 high school students related to the Isolation Index. Workshops Study No. 288 (unpublished), Rorschach Workshops.

Finney, B. C. (1955) Rorschach Test correlates of assaultive behavior. *Journal of Projective Techniques,* **19,** 6–16.

Fisher, S., and Cleveland, S. (1958) *Body Image and Personality.* New York: Van Nostrand Reinhold.

Fonda, C. P. (1951) The nature and meaning of the Rorschach white space response. *Journal of Abnormal and Social Psychology,* **46,** 367–377.

Fonda, C. P. (1960) The white space response. In M. Rickers-Ovsiankina (Ed.), *Rorschach Psychology.* New York: Wiley.

Frank, L. K. (1939) Projective methods for the study of personality. *Journal of Personality,* **8,** 389–413.

Gardner, R. W. (1951) Impulsivity as indicated by Rorschach Test factors. *Journal of Consulting Psychology,* **15,** 464–468.

Gill, H. S. (1966) Delay of response and reaction to color on the Rorschach. *Journal of Projective Techniques and Personality Assessment,* **30,** 545–552.

Goldfarb, W. (1945) The animal symbol in the Rorschach Test and animal association test. *Rorschach Research Exchange,* **9,** 8–22.

Goldfried, M. (1963) The connotative meanings of some animals for college students. *Journal of Projective Techniques,* **27,** 60–67.

Goldfried, M., Stricker, G., and Weiner, I. (1971) *Rorschach Handbook of Clinical and Research Applications.* Englewood Cliffs, N.J.: Prentice-Hall.

Goldman, R. (1960) Changes in Rorschach performance and clinical improvement in schizophrenia. *Journal of Consulting Psychology,* **24,** 403–407.

Halpern, F. (1940) Rorschach interpretation of the personality structure of schizophrenics who benefit from insulin therapy. *Psychiatric Quarterly,* **14,** 826–833.

Hirschstein, R., and Rabin, A. I. (1955) Reactions to Rorschach cards IV and VII as a function of parental availability in childhood. *Journal of Consulting Psychology,* **19,** 473–474.

Holt, R. R. (1960) Cognitive controls and primary processes. *Journal of Psychoanalytic Research,* **4,** 105–112.

Holt, R. R. (1966) Measuring libidinal and aggressive motives and their controls by means of the Rorschach Test. In D. Levine (Ed.), *Nebraska Symposium on Motivation.* Lincoln: University of Nebraska Press.

Kazaoka, K., Sloane, K., and Exner, J. E. (1978) Verbal and nonverbal aggressive behaviors among 70 inpatients during occupational and recreational therapy. Workshops Study No. 254 (unpublished), Rorschach Workshops.

Klopfer, B., Ainsworth, M. D., Klopfer, W. G., and Holt, R. R. (1954) *Developments in the Rorschach Technique. I: Theory and technique.* Yonkers-on-Hudson, N.Y.: World Book.

Klopfer, B., and Kelley, D. (1942) *The Rorschach Technique.* Yonkers-on-Hudson, N.Y.: World Book.

Levy, E. (1958) Stimulus values of Rorschach cards for children. *Journal of Projective Techniques,* **22,** 293–295.

Lindner, R. M. (1943) The Rorschach Test and the diagnosis of psychopathic personality. *Journal of Criminal Psychopathology,* **1,** 69.

Lindner, R. M. (1944) Some significant Rorschach responses. *Journal of Criminal Psychopathology,* **4,** 775.

Lindner, R. M. (1946) Content analysis in Rorschach work. *Rorschach Research Exchange,* **10,** 121–129.

Lindner, R. M. (1947) Analysis of Rorschach's Test by content. *Journal of Clinical Psychopathology,* **8,** 707–719.

Mason, B. J., and Exner, J. E. (1984) Correlations between WAIS subtests and nonpatient adult Rorschach data. Workshops Study No. 289 (unpublished), Rorschach Workshops.

Meer, B., and Singer, J. (1950) A note of the "father" and "mother" cards in the Rorschach inkblots, *Journal of Consulting Psychology,* **14,** 482–484.

Meisner, J. S. (1984) Susceptibility of Rorschach depression correlates to malingering. *Dissertation Abstracts International,* **45,** 3951B.

Molish, H. B. (1955) Schizophrenic reaction types in a Naval Hospital population as evaluated by the Rorschach Test. Bureau of Medicine and Surgery, Navy Department, Washington, D.C.

Molish, H. B. (1967) Critique and problems of the Rorschach. A survey. In S. J. Beck and H. B. Molish, *Rorschach's Test. II: A Variety of Personality Pictures,* (2nd Ed.). New York: Grune & Stratton.

Morris, W. W. (1943) Prognostic possibilities of the Rorschach method in metrazol therapy. *American Journal of Psychiatry,* **100,** 222–230.

Neff, W. S., and Glaser, N. M. (1954) Normative data on the Rorschach. *Journal of Psychology,* **37,** 95–104.

Pascal, G., Ruesch, H., Devine, D., and Suttell, B. (1950) A study of genital symbols on the Rorschach Test: Presentation of method and results. *Journal of Abnormal and Social Psychology,* **45,** 285–289.

Phillips, L., and Smith, J. G. (1953) *Rorschach Interpretation: Advanced Technique.* New York: Grune & Stratton.

Piotrowski, Z. (1957) *Perceptanalysis.* New York: Macmillan.

Piotrowski, Z. A., and Bricklin, B. (1961) A second validation of a long term prognostic index for schizophrenic patients. *Journal of Consulting Psychology,* **25,** 123–128.

Prandoni, J., Matranga, J., Jensen, D., and Watson, M. (1973) Selected Rorschach characteristics of sex offenders. *Journal of Personality Assessment,* **37,** 334–336.

Rapaport, D., Gill, M., and Schafer, R. (1946) *Psychological Diagnostic Testing.* Vol. 2. Chicago: Yearbook Publishers.

Ray, A. B. (1963) Juvenile delinquency by Rorschach inkblots. *Psychologia,* **6,** 190–192.

Richardson, H. (1963) Rorschachs of adolescent approved school girls, compared with Ames normal adolescents. *Rorschach Newsletter,* **8,** 3–8.

Rorschach, H. (1921) *Psychodiagnostics.* Bern: Bircher (Transl. Hans Huber Verlag, 1942).

Ros Plana, M. (1990) *An investigation concerning the malingering of features of depression on the Rorschach and MMPI.* Unpublished doctoral dissertation, University of Barcelona.

Rosen, E. (1951) Symbolic meanings in the Rorschach cards: A statistical study. *Journal of Clinical Psychology,* **7,** 239–244.

Rosen, E. (1952) MMPI and Rorschach correlates of the Rorschach white space response. *Journal of Clinical Psychology,* **8,** 238–288.

Schafer, R. (1954) *Psychoanalytic Interpretation in Rorschach Testing.* New York: Grune & Stratton.

Shatin, L. (1952) Psychoneurosis and psychosomatic reaction. A Rorschach study. *Journal of Consulting Psychology,* **16,** 220–223.

Sherman, M. H. (1952) A comparison of formal and content factors in the diagnostic testing of schizophrenia. *Genetic Psychology Monographs,* **46,** 183–234.

Smith, J., and Coleman, J. (1956) The relationship between manifestation of hostility in projective techniques and overt behavior. *Journal of Projective Techniques,* **20,** 326–334.

Sommer, R., and Sommer, D. (1958) Assaultiveness and two types of Rorschach color responses. *Journal of Consulting Psychology,* **22,** 57–62.

Stone, H. (1953) Relationship of hostile aggressive behavior to aggressive content of the Rorschach and Thematic Apperception Test. Unpublished doctoral dissertation, University of California at Los Angeles.

Storment, C. T., and Finney, B. C. (1953) Projection and behavior: A Rorschach study of assaultive mental hospital patients. *Journal of Projective Techniques, 17,* 349–360.

Stotsky, B. A. (1952) A comparison of remitting and non-remitting schizophrenics on psychological tests. *Journal of Abnormal and Social Psychology, 47,* 489–496.

Thomas, E. A., Exner, J. E., and Baker, W. (1982) Ratings of real versus ideal self among 225 college students. Workshops Study No. 287 (unpublished), Rorschach Workshops.

Townsend, J. K. (1967) The relation between Rorschach signs of aggression and behavioral aggression in emotionally disturbed boys. *Journal of Projective Techniques and Personality Assessment, 31,* 13–21.

Vinson, D. B. (1960) Responses to the Rorschach Test that identify thinking, feelings, and behavior. *Journal of Clinical and Experimental Psychopathology, 21,* 34–40.

Walker, R. G. (1951) A comparison of clinical manifestations of hostility with Rorschach and *MAPS* performance. *Journal of Projective Techniques, 15,* 444–460.

Wallach, J. D. (1983) Affective-symbolic connotations of the Rorschach inkblots: Fact or fantasy. *Perceptual and Motor Skills, 56,* 287–295.

Walters, R. H. (1953) A preliminary analysis of the Rorschach records of fifty prison inmates. *Journal of Projective Techniques, 17,* 436–446.

Wedemeyer, B. (1954) Rorschach statistics on a group of 136 normal men. *Journal of Psychology, 37,* 51–58.

Weiner, I. B., and Exner, J. E. (1991) Rorschach changes in long-term and short-term psychotherapy. *Journal of Personality Assessment, 56,* 453–465.

Weiss, A. A., and Winnik, H. Z. (1963) A contribution to the meaning of anatomy responses on the Rorschach Test. *Israel Annual of Psychiatry, 1,* 265–276.

Wheeler, W. M. (1949) An analysis of Rorschach indices of male homosexuality. *Journal of Projective Techniques, 13,* 97–126.

Zelin, M., and Sechrest, L. (1963) The validity of the "mother" and "father" cards of the Rorschach. *Journal of Projective Techniques and Personality Assessment, 27,* 114–121.

Zolliker, A. (1943) Schwangerschaftsdepression and Rorschach'scher formdeurversuch. *Schweiz Archeives Neurologie und Psychiatrie, 53,* 62–78.

PART V

Applications

CHAPTER 20

Integrating Findings to Address Issues

The material in the preceding section has focused on the many structural variables in the test, the sequencing of responses, the verbal material, and the interpretation of data within each of the clusters of variables. Findings from each cluster, taken separately, provide important information, but they do not represent the total Rorschach yield. The finished interpretation requires a careful blending of findings from each of these sources. It is not a lengthy task, requiring days of rumination, but it is one that requires thoroughness, logic, and most of all, a knowledge of people.

Possibly the most important caution to be exercised when integrating Rorschach findings concerns the interpreter rather than the test data. Most subjects who are administered the Rorschach have some presenting problem, and the focus is often oriented toward gaining some better understanding of the problem, in terms of cause, characteristic, and correction. Because of this, many reports tend to emphasize the dysfunction and, unfortunately, can be very misleading because they neglect adequate concern for the more positive or salient characteristics of the subject. The finished interpretation should capture the uniqueness of the person, including *both* assets and liabilities. It should be a *descriptive* summary from which the intelligent professional can draw some logical conclusions and, when required, make some logical predictions.

As noted in Chapter 13, the Rorschach is often not at its best when used predictively, for the data reflect the present more than either the past or the future. Thus statements about the past or the future must be of a more speculative nature. For instance, one of the greatest values of the Rorschach is its use in planning intervention. This is not because any particular Rorschach variable equates directly with a particular form of treatment, but rather because the Rorschach will reflect the liabilities of the subject. These can be conceptualized in terms of targets for intervention. The issue hinges on what features of the Rorschach will hopefully be altered as a result of treatment. At this point, the interpreter must review his or her knowledge of the variety of intervention modalities as they relate to each of the relevant targets, addressing the issue of which may be most likely to effect the desired changes.

The integration, or finished interpretation, of the data from any Rorschach should probably follow in accord with the interpretive strategy defined by positive Key or Teritary variables. In other words, it should describe the feature identified by the positive Key variable and then integrate the findings cluster by cluster in the order that they were reviewed. Usually, this will ensure that the most important elements of the personality will form the core of the description, and that subsequent features will be described in the context of those core elements. This is not, however, a hard-and-fast rule. In some cases, findings from a cluster reviewed late in the interpretation may provide critically important data that highlight or clarify postulates developed very early in the interpretive routine.

For instance, the early findings from the L.S. protocol revealed his obsessive style, the situationally caused overload state, his cautiousness in processing and his orientation toward being conventional. But, it was not until the data concerning affect and self-perception were reviewed that some of the important elements related to his symptoms were uncovered. Thus, when integrating the findings concerning his record, those elements should be emphasized earlier than might usually be the case.

THE L.S. SUMMARY

This is a person whose personality structure includes a basic obsessive feature at the core. He is well motivated to organize new information and is reasonably efficient in doing so, even though he has a more cautious, conservative, and somewhat meticulous approach. In ordinary circumstances, his capacity for control and tolerance for stress are usually not very different from that of most adults. In other words, he acts deliberately and meaningfully in forming and directing his behaviors and is no more vulnerable to loss of control than most adults.

Unfortunately, some situational factors have reduced his capacity for control and he is now in an overload state, that is, he is experiencing more demands or pressures than is customary and is not always able to form and/or direct all of the responses that he feels are necessary. As a result, there is an increased likelihood that, in new or more complex situations, he will not function as adaptively or effectively as might be the case if the stress situation did not exist. This overload state has reduced his tolerance for stress and this increases the possibility that impulsiveness in thinking, emotion, and/or behavior will occur.

The cause of the overload appears to be at least twofold. The history that he gives implies that it is occupationally related; however, it seems very likely that some ongoing tension in his marriage is also contributing to the situation. In either event, the stress has created considerably more psychological complexity for him than he is accustomed to or able to deal with easily.

Although his obsessiveness has contributed in some ways to his present problems, they appear to have been predisposed more directly by three other basic features in his personality structure. First, he is not very consistent in his decision making. At times, he tries to stop and think things through, keeping his feelings aside, and relying on a logical evaluation of issues involved. In other instances, he merges his feelings with his thinking, tending to let them have a priority in his decisions and typically this provokes forms of trial-and-error approaches. Most well-adjusted adults ultimately learn to rely mainly on either of these approaches, but not both. When someone becomes inconsistent in using these tactics, neither of them proves especially useful and the result is a tendency to be more indecisive, use more effort, repeat more errors, and generally be less effective in decision-making activities. This kind of decision-making inefficiency creates a special burden for one with an obsessive style. Whereas they prefer to be methodical and systematic, the lack of consistency in coping runs counterproductive to that objective. As a result, a sense of chronic discomfort is created and frequent experiences occur in which indecisiveness promotes anxiousness and/or tension. This probably accounts for some of his reported symptoms. There is no doubt that he has difficulty in attention and concentration because the situationally related stress that he is experiencing serves to exacerbate his already present tendencies to vacillate in decision operations.

Second, some of his problems appear to have an emotional basis. In general, his emotional structure does not seem to be very compatible with effective adjustment. Not only is he inconsistent in the use of his feelings in decision making, but when he discharges emotion, it is often overly intense and probably less mature than should be the case. Obsessive people usually prefer to be very well controlled, sometimes overly so, and a looseness in modulation such as noted here may indicate a kind of naiveté about feelings. In other words, the findings seem to portray a person who is unsure about his feelings and probably fearful of their impact. He is not particularly interested in processing emotional stimuli and usually tries to function in an uncomplicated manner. He seems to be unaware about how best to express needs and feelings and at present, situational factors have increased his level of emotional complexity well beyond that which he would prefer. He has marked feelings of loneliness, and the current stress has introduced feelings of helplessness that only serve to exacerbate his confusion about emotion and contribute significantly to his reports of tension and anxiety.

He does tend to intellectualize more frequently than most people as a method of neutralizing some of his feelings; however, this is not a major defensive tactic in his personality organization. This raises a question about whether some of his affective displays are false and misleading. In general, his thinking seems to be clear, unimpaired, and usually of good quality; however, the fact that he is not predictable in his approaches to decision making probably reduces the overall advantages that might otherwise be derived from his clear and good-quality thinking.

The third element that has predisposed his present condition concerns self-image. He does not judge himself as favorably as he does significant others in his world. This finding may relate to his sense of apprehension concerning his occupational status. His perceived occupational failure is probably even more irritating because of his obsessive style. He does engage in considerable self-examining behavior, but it is not clear whether these introspective activities are couched in a reality-based estimate of his own potential and worth or whether they may be gauged more in light of his more negative sense of personal worth. It is clear that he is strongly committed to making conventional or acceptable responses, but a cost for this is a sacrifice of some of his own uniqueness. Obsessive people often try to convey an impression to others of being well adjusted, but sometimes they present themselves as being too conforming. Frequently, they are unwilling to accept differences among people but inside, they are often less content with themselves and sometimes have considerable difficulty expressing their feelings openly or directly. In effect, he appears to be a somewhat timid, uncertain person who is cautious, passive, and conservative on the one hand, yet interested in being more open and even reckless at times. He is probably not very comfortable with his conception of himself and seems to feel a need to be more guarded than should be the case. When considered in light of findings regarding his emotions, it seems probable that he experiences conflict and confusion about how best to express his needs and feelings. This has probably contributed to his marital plight and the development of his strong sense of loneliness.

Undoubtably, this neediness impacts on his perceptions of others and may have some influence on his interpersonal behaviors. He is clearly interested in others and his conceptions of people seem to have a reality basis. He perceives positive interactions between people as a routine, and he is apt to be viewed by others as likable and outgoing. His interest in others appears to be quite sincere, but he may not be as outgoing as may appear at first glance; and possibly, his interpersonal relationships are much more superficial than he might desire. In fact, they are probably more contrived than real, possibly in accord with his basic obsessive style, and particularly in light of his clear need to be conventional.

The fact he is able to maintain the integrity of his obsessive style while currently under considerable situationally related stress illustrates the strength of the style, and this is probably an asset for him. Often, people like this are prone to disorganization when in overload situations. Thus, although he is experiencing tension, anxiety, insomnia, and has some difficulty in concentration, his ability to translate new inputs in conventional ways shows no impairment and his thinking remains clear.

Overall, this is a somewhat rigid, guarded, conforming, and probably status-oriented person. He is not really satisfied with his self-image or the role in which he has cast himself but is very uncertain how to change. It seems likely that his cautiousness and indecisiveness about how to deal with others has created an avoidant orientation and one of the by-products is a marriage that is less satisfying than he desires. But he feels confused about how best to change the situation, and thus he tends to maintain a more timid lifestyle than he would prefer; because he does not judge himself very favorably, he seems to regard each new situation as potentially threatening and is in a dilemma about how to deal with those threats.

It is obvious that some form of supportive intervention is required to alleviate the immediate situationally related stress. In that process, focus on his occupationally related apprehension and dissatisfaction are probably the least threatening targets; however, the issue of marital tension must be broached ultimately and the possibility of marriage counseling might be considered. It would be misleading, however, to suggest that either a brief supportive therapeutic and/or a marriage-focused intervention will resolve all relevant issues. Either may increase his sense of insecurity and/or reduce his sense of loneliness, but the core predispositions of the present problem will remain essentially unchanged. Optimally, a longer form of treatment would be more beneficial through which he might learn to be more consistent in his decision-making operations, more comfortable about expressing his feelings, and gradually become more secure in his self image. In that context, it is important to emphasize that he is an obsessive person and any form of longer term treatment is unlikely to break through that hard-fixed style. In other words, the therapist must be willing to work within that mode without expecting major changes in the basic style. Most obsessive people are more comfortable with an ideational approach to decision making and less comfortable with direct emotional confrontations. Given that as a consideration, cognitive-developmental intervention will probably have a greater promise of success than will uncovering or affective expression forms of intervention.

CASE ILLUSTRATIONS

Five other clinical cases are included in this chapter. They are neither simple nor complex, but rather, represent some of the most common assessment issues that are often posed to those responsible for the assessment of the majority of patients for whom the Rorschach might be an appropriate assessment tactic. They have been selected to provide an illustration of what the Rorschach, used properly, can and cannot reveal concerning issues of diagnosis, describing personality, and formulating recommendations concerning intervention and/or disposition. They have also been selected because they portray the manner in which the interpretative strategy differs from the approach to the test data as was illustrated in the L.S. protocol.

PROTOCOL 1: A QUESTION CONCERNING TENSION AND DEPRESSION

Referral   C.F. was referred by a psychologist who had seen her previously for about 5 months supportively, shortly after the breakup of her first marriage. He had not had any contact with her for approximately 2 years, during which time she had remarried and gave birth to a daughter. He had treated her, during their earlier contact with supportive methods, believing that her symptoms at that time, "nervousness and depression," were related to the divorce action.

He now wonders if he may have been "remiss" in terminating her and states in the referral, "She currently complains again of tension and depression, plus occasional spells during which she loses her sense of time and place and feels overwhelmed by her emotions. She has not actually had lapses of memory but is very vague for events that occur during these periods. I would appreciate an independent evaluation of her personality and any guidance you may offer about the most appropriate treatment plans."

History   C.F. was born and raised in a large metropolitan area. She graduated from high school with honors and completed 1 year of college in a local liberal arts school, on scholarship, before she married for the first time. She is a reasonably attractive, 25-year-old blonde, slight in build, but conscientious in dress so as to maximize her physical assets. She is the oldest of four children, having three younger brothers, the oldest of whom is a recent college graduate, and the younger two who are still in high school. Both parents are living. The father, age 51, is an industrial salesman, and the mother, age 50, a housewife. The parents expressed disappointment at C.F.'s early marriage; she was 19 at the time, and had just completed her first year at college. Her marriage lasted approximately 3 years and according to her statement, her husband, who was her own age, "just didn't want much from life. We were incompatible and I doubt that we would have married if I hadn't gotten all caught up in him being a football hero." She indicates that he demanded "too much of my time and didn't give me any freedom to do the things that I wanted." Shortly after her marriage, C.F. began working as a receptionist in a law firm while her husband continued in college. She states, "There were always guys after me, you know, on the prowl, and I always felt funny about it 'cause some were really nice." Ultimately, she did have two extramarital affairs, the second of which precipitated the divorce. She remarried about 5 months after her divorce, during which time she had liaisons with several men, including her present husband who is a law clerk. She became pregnant approximately 4 months after her remarriage—"It was a wonderful experience." Delivery was normal and "my husband has been a brick through the whole thing." She notes that her husband is extremely helpful with her daughter, who is now 20 months old. "I don't know what I'd do without him, they get along so well together." She says of her marriage, "We are really close, a real family, and it will be even better when I get over whatever is wrong. But right now I know there are some things that aren't right and it just keeps me on edge all of the time." She reports feelings of being confined, "Sometimes I just have to get out of the house 'cause it feels like it's closing in on me. I'm just on edge all of the time, and sometimes I just cry for no reason at all." She has been taking a variety of mild, antianxiety tranquilizers prescribed by her physician, but reports that they have not helped very much, "Some days I feel really great, but then the next day I'm all uptight again." She says that her sexual relationship with her husband is, "just like always, you know, it's o.k.," but also admits that she does not experience orgasm at each event, ". . . but I think that will get better." Her contact with her parents is infrequent "because they never wanted me to marry in the first place and were really upset when I did it again," but she writes frequently to her two oldest brothers. She suggests that her feelings of discomfort are created by "some unknown thing in my body, like some physical thing," but admits that several physicians have not detected any physiological problems. She is especially "tired" in the mornings, "I always wake up with a backache or something like that, like I couldn't sleep right," and yet she also has trouble going to sleep, "I lie awake some nights until two or three o'clock." Her menstrual cycle is normal although she does complain of "severe cramps, like a knife cutting into me" during the first day or two of menstruation. She does not want any more children "immediately," but speculates that she might have four or five more "if I can get myself straight."

Protocol 1. 25-Year-Old, Married, One Child, Housewife

Card	Response	Inquiry	Scoring
I	1. Oh gee; it ll a bf	E: (Rpts S's resp) S: The W thg ll tht bec of the way the outside is the wgs & the body is in the middl	Wo Fo A P 1.0
	S: Do u want more? E: Take your time, you'll probably find something else too.		
	2. Well it cb, a cats face too, hissing	E: (Rpts S's resp) S: These r the ears & the eyes & mouth r the white parts, it has puffy cheeks too lik it was hissing lik cats do	WSo FMªo Ad 3.5 AG
	3. This cntr prt c.b. the body of a wm w.o. a head	E: (Rpts S's resp) S: I can c the body part here (points), c these r the legs & the breasts but there's no head	Do Fo Hd MOR
II	4. Wow, look at the color, it ll blood on these dogs, or mayb its paint, yes that's it they have been playing in the paint & got it all over them	E: (Rpts S's resp) S: I don't kno why I said bld at first cause it doesn't ll that but it does ll paint that these dogs, c thyr playg, touchg their noses & thyv got paint on their legs	D+ CF.FMªo (2) A, Art P 3.0 COP
	5. Ths top red paint might be a part of the body, lik inside, maybe a kidney, there's one on each side	E: (Rpts S's resp) S: Well it ll a kidney, the way its shaped E: I'm not sure I c it as u do S: Kidneys just ll that, the roundness like that	Do F− (2) An
III	6. It ll 2 cannibals & theyr carrying a pot up to this fire, its red, like fire, like a bonfire	E: (Rpts S's resp) S: The fire is back here & they r carrying ths pot E: I'm not sure I c the cannibals S: Rite here, c, 2 black men, lik cannibals, thyr tall & lanky like cannibals, lik I've seen on TV lots of times	D+ Mª.FD.C.FCo (2) H, Fi, Hh P 4.0 COP, PER

Protocol 1 (Continued)

Card		Response	Inquiry		Scoring
V	7.	If u turn it ths way the dark part ll an ugly bug	E:	(Rpts S's resp)	Do F − A
			S:	Well it might be a spider with the big eyes, sort of the bulging kind & the legs here	
IV	8	I'd have to say a monster man of s.s., all covered w fur, see all those lines, like fur	E:	(Rpts S's resp)	Wo FTo (H) P 2.0
			S:	It's a great big monster lik in science fiction, all furry w big legs & a head that almost isn't even there, just a littl thing & a big tail too	
V	9.	Oh, a child dressed in a rabbit suit, standing to get her picture taken, it looks furry (Rubs Card)	E:	(Rpts S's resp)	D+ MP.FTo (H), Cg 2.5
			S:	Its lik a littl girl going to a party lik for halloween, she has a bunny hat & this fur suit like a bunny, ths other stuff doesn't count	
	10.	It cld b another bf too	E:	(Rpts S's resp)	Wo Fo A P 1.0
			S:	It has the wgs here & the bunny hat wld b the feelers	
	11.	There r 2 legs too, one on each side	E:	(Rpts S's resp)	Do Fo (2) Hd
			S:	They just ll legs, lik u c in a stocking ad or s.t.	
VI	12.	I'm not sure what ths top c.b. but the rest ll a piece of fur, (rubs card) you can almost feel it	E:	(Rpts S's resp)	Do TFo Cg
			S:	It's lik an unfinished coat or fur jacket or s.t., it really hasn't taken shape yet altho these c.b. arm parts here, its just a piece of fur	
V	13.	If u turn it ths way ths part ll 2 birds in a nest, waiting to be fed, u just c the heads stickg up	E:	(Rpts S's resp)	Dd+ FMPo (2) Ad, Bt 2.5
			S:	Its their heads (points) & this is the nest & they r just lik waiting for the mother bird	

548

VII	14. Ths is a littl girl who just had her hair fixed & she's lookg at herslf in the mirror	E: (Rpts S's resp) S: She has a pony tail that's probably held up w a comb or pins, she's really cute. I don't kno what the lower part is, it doesn't count	D+	Mᵖ.Fro Hd P	3.0
	15. It c.b. rain clds too	E: (Rpts S's resp) S: Oh, I d.k. why I said that, they just look all black lik rain clouds, there r 4 of them or mayb 6 I guess	Wv	C'Fo Cl	
VIII	16. Oh, ths is pretty, its like a candy house	S: Well all different kinds of candy put togthr to ll a house lik in fairy tales, the diffrnt colors r diffrnt candies & the white parts r frosting E: I'm not sure I c it as u do S: Here is the roof & the windows & the door, its not supposed to ll a real hous, but lik a fairy tale house	WS+	CF.C'Fu Fd	4.5
	< 17. If u turn it ths way it ll a beaver stepping over some stones & thgs seeing himself reflected in the water	E: (Rpts S's resp) S: Its an A lik a beaver or s.t. but its funny all pink lik that, mayb it's a reflect fr the sun that gives that color Its lik in the forest, very colorful, & he's just walkg along, lik a crossing of the stream or pool of water	W+	FMᵃ.Fr.FCo A, Na P	4.5
	18. There c.b. a skeleton in there too, lik a rib cage	E: (Rpts S's resp) S: Rite here (points) u can see the spaces in it, it just ll s. bodies ribs	DSo	Fo An	4.0
IX	19. My God, more colors, I can c a waterfall in a canyon	E: (Rpts S's resp) S: Its in the cntr, u can c the water falling, its set back in the jungle, all this green stuff, the pink part doesn't count tho, there is a cliff in front of it all colored by the sun & the waterfall in back in the distance	D+	mᵖ.CF.FDo Na	2.5
	20. There are 2 unborn children here in the pink	E: (Rpts S's resp) S: I said unborn bec they r pink thy hav the big heads & the littl bodies, lik twins	DO	FCo (2) (H)	

Protocol 1 (Continued)

Card	Response		Inquiry	Scoring
21.	This thg in the cntr ll s.t. I hav on my desk to put papers on, its a sharp spike	E: S:	(Rpts S's resp) I brought it home when I quit working, it is s.t. u just poke the hole thru the paper & the pink wld b the base tht holds it	Do Fo Id PER
22.	Wow, it ll s.b. thru paint all over the place, a mess	E: S:	(Rpts S's resp) It just ll paint spattered all over when I first lookd at it, mayb its an artist's palate	Wv C Art
23.	Ths c.b. spiders here	E: S:	(Rpts S's resp) They hav all those legs that ll a spider to me, don't thy ll that to u?	Do Fo (2) A P
24.	These cb fried eggs, 2 of 'em, thyr yellow cuz they were cookd in butter	E: S:	(Rpts S's resp) Lik they were fried in butter cause thy'r yellow, ths is the yoke part & ths is the white only its yellow bec of the butter	Do CFo (2) Fd
25.	Ths other yellow parts c.b. rose buds	E: S:	(Rpts S's resp) Thyr pretty lik littl roses waiting to open, just the buds & the littl stem, like yellow rosebuds	Do FCo (2) Bt

550

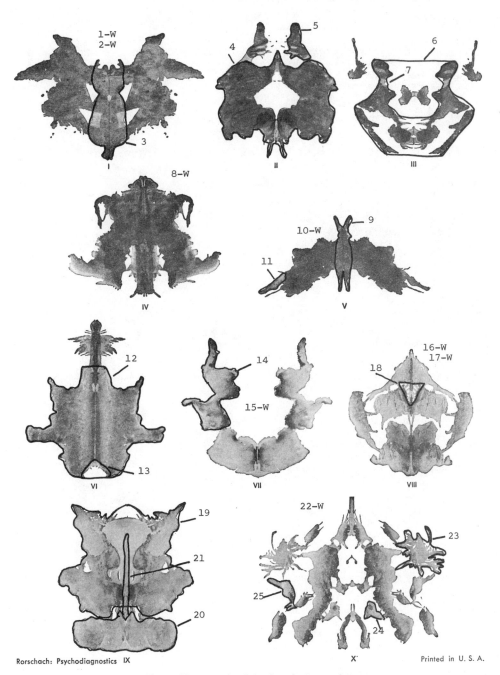

Figure 17.   Location Selections for Protocol 1.

Table 80.   Protocol 1—Sequence of Scores

CARD	NO	LOC	#	DETERMINANT(S)	(2)	CONTENT(S)	POP	Z	SPECIAL SCORES
I	1	Wo	1	Fo		A	P	1.0	
	2	WSo	1	FMao		Ad		3.5	AG
	3	Do	4	Fo		Hd			MOR
II	4	D+	6	CF.FMao	2	A,Art	P	3.0	COP
	5	Do	2	F-	2	An			
III	6	D+	1	Ma.FD.C.FC'o	2	H,Fi,Hh	P	4.0	COP,PER
	7	Do	1	F-		A			
IV	8	Wo	1	FTo		(H)	P	2.0	
V	9	D+	7	Mp.FTo		(H),Cg		2.5	
	10	Wo	1	Fo		A	P	1.0	
	11	Do	10	Fo	2	Hd			
VI	12	Do	1	TFo		Cg			
	13	Dd+	33	FMpo	2	Ad,Bt		2.5	
VII	14	D+	2	Mp.Fro		Hd	P	3.0	
	15	Wv	1	C'Fo		Cl			
VIII	16	WS+	1	CF.C'Fu		Fd		4.5	
	17	W+	1	FMa.Fr.FCo		A,Na	P	4.5	
	18	DSo	3	Fo		An		4.0	
IX	19	D+	2	mp.CF.FDo		Na		2.5	
	20	Do	6	FCo	2	(H)			
	21	Do	9	Fo		Id			PER
X	22	Wv	1	C		Art			
	23	Do	1	Fo	2	A	P		
	24	Do	2	CFo	2	Fd			
	25	Do	15	FCo	2	Bt			

Copyright (c) 1976, 1985, 1990 by John E. Exner, Jr.

Table 81. Protocol 1—Structural Summary

```
========================================================================
LOCATION           DETERMINANTS              CONTENTS     S-CONSTELLATION
FEATURES        BLENDS                                    NO..FV+VF+V+FD>2
                              SINGLE                      YES..Col-Shd Bl>0
                                         H   = 1, 0       YES..Ego<.31,>.44
Zf   = 13       CF.FM         M   = 0     (H) = 3, 0       NO..MOR > 3
ZSum = 38.0     M.FD.C.FC'    FM  = 2     Hd  = 3, 0       NO..Zd > +- 3.5
ZEst = 41.5     M.FT          m   = 0     (Hd)= 0, 0       NO..es > EA
                M.Fr          FC  = 2     Hx  = 0, 0      YES..CF+C > FC
W    = 8        CF.C'F        CF  = 1     A   = 6, 0       NO..X+% < .70
  (Wv = 2)      FM.Fr.FC      C   = 1     (A) = 0, 0       NO..S > 3
D    = 16       m.CF.FD       Cn  = 0     Ad  = 2, 0       NO..P < 3 or > 8
Dd   = 1                      FC' = 0     (Ad)= 0, 0       NO..Pure H < 2
S    = 3                      C'F = 1     An  = 2, 0       NO..R < 17
                              C'  = 0     Art = 1, 1      YES..Pure H < 2
   DQ                         FT  = 1     Ay  = 0, 0       NO..R < 17
.........(FQ-)                TF  = 1     Bl  = 0, 0        4.....TOTAL
  +  =  8  ( 0)               T   = 0     Bt  = 1, 1
  o  = 15  ( 2)               FV  = 0     Cg  = 1, 1      SPECIAL SCORINGS
v/+  =  0  ( 0)               VF  = 0     Cl  = 1, 0        Lv1     Lv2
  v  =  2  ( 0)               V   = 0     Ex  = 0, 0     DV  =  0x1    0x2
                              FY  = 0     Fd  = 2, 0     INC =  0x2    0x4
                              YF  = 0     Fi  = 0, 1     DR  =  0x3    0x6
                              Y   = 0     Ge  = 0, 0     FAB =  0x4    0x7
                              Fr  = 0     Hh  = 0, 1     ALOG =  0x5
   FORM QUALITY               rF  = 0     Ls  = 0, 0     CON =  0x7
                              FD  = 0     Na  = 1, 1        SUM6  = 0
     FQx  FQf  MQual  SQx     F   = 9     Sc  = 0, 0        WSUM6 = 0
 +  =  0    0    0     0                  Sx  = 0, 0     AB  = 0    CP  = 0
 o  = 21    7    3     2                  Xy  = 0, 0     AG  = 1    MOR = 1
 u  =  1    0    0     1                  Id  = 1, 0     CFB = 0    PER = 2
 -  =  2    2    0     0                                 COP = 2    PSV = 0
none=  1   --    0     0      (2) =  9
========================================================================
               RATIOS, PERCENTAGES, AND DERIVATIONS

R = 25          L  = 0.56
------------------------------  FC:CF+C = 3: 6    COP = 2    AG = 1
                                Pure C  =    2    Food      = 2
EB = 3: 8.5  EA = 11.5  EBPer= 2.8  Afr  =0.67    Isolate/R =0.32
eb = 5: 6    es = 11      D   = 0    S    =   3    H:(H)Hd(Hd)= 1: 6
         Adj es = 11  Adj D  = 0    Blends:R= 7:25  (HHd):(AAd)= 3: 0
------------------------------  CP      =    0    H+A:Hd+Ad  =10: 5
FM = 4 :  C'= 3   T = 3
m  = 1 :  V = 0   Y = 0
                          P   = 8      Zf  =13      3r+(2)/R=0.60
a:p    = 4: 4   Sum6  = 0   X+% =0.84   Zd  = -3.5   Fr+rF  = 2
Ma:Mp  = 1: 2   Lv2   = 0   F+% =0.78   W:D:Dd = 8:16: 1  FD  = 2
2AB+Art+Ay= 2   WSum6 = 0   X-% =0.08   W:M = 8: 3   An+Xy  = 2
M-     = 0      Mnone = 0   S-% =0.00   DQ+ = 8      MOR    = 1
                            Xu% =0.04   DQv = 2
------------------------------------------------------------------------
 SCZI = 1    DEPI = 3    CDI = 2    S-CON = 4    HVI = No   OBS = No
========================================================================
```

Copyright (c) 1976, 1985, 1990 by John E. Exner, Jr.

INTERPRETIVE ROUTINE FOR PROTOCOL 1

The first positive Key variable is that at least one reflection response is present, but as noted in Chapter 14, when this is the first positive key variable it does not determine the entire search strategy. It only defines the first three clusters to be addressed, self-perception, interpersonal perception, and controls. The remainder of the routine must be determined in light of the next positive key variable, or if no other key variables are positive, the first positive tertiary variable. In this protocol, the next positive key variable is the *EB*, which indicates an extratensive style. Therefore, using Table 59 in Chapter 14 as the guide, the cluster concerning affect will be fourth in the search order, followed by the three clusters in the cognitive triad. Thus, the complete interpretive routine will be:

$$\text{Self-Perception} \rightarrow \text{Interpersonal Perception} \rightarrow \text{Controls}$$
$$\rightarrow \text{Affect} \rightarrow \text{Processing} \rightarrow \text{Mediation} \rightarrow \text{Ideation}$$

SELF-PERCEPTION—PROTOCOL 1

The data relevant to self perception for Protocol 1 are shown in Table 82.

The presence of the two reflection answers indicates that a marked narcissistic-like tendency to overvalue her personal worth is a nuclear element of her personality. It is a dominating psychological influence that, although not necessarily pathological, has a significant influence on her perceptions of the world and the people in it. It impacts on her decisions and behaviors and creates a need for status that sometimes will exceed realistic expectations. It also tends to generate elaborate systems of defense, especially rationalization and denial, that are used to ward off threats to the integrity of her inflated self-value. Her continuing need to reaffirm her lofty self-value makes it difficult to create and/or maintain deep interpersonal relations as others often reject the deferential role that they are expected to take.

The very substantial value for the Egocentricity Index (0.60) affirms the subject's strong self-centeredness and suggests that she attends to the external world much less than do most adults. She is clearly very self-focused. There are two *FD* responses, suggesting that she engages in self-examining behavior at least as much as most adults. Usually, this finding is positive but, in this instance, must be considered in light of her seeming exquisite self-centeredness. Thus, while it typically signals a tendency to reevaluate self-image, in this case it may merely indicate a process through which the inflated self-image is being reaffirmed. Some support for that postulate seems evident in the data for the $H:(H)+Hd+(Hd)$ ratio, which includes only one pure H response. It

Table 82.   Self-Perception Data for Protocol 1

$3r + (2)/R = 0.60$	$FD = 2$	$MOR = 1$	$Hx = 0$	$An + Xy = 2$
$Fr + rF = 2$	Sum $V = 0$	$H:(H)+Hd+(Hd) = 1:6$		$Sx = 0$

Responses to Be Read				
MOR Responses	*FQ*− Responses	*M* Responses	*FM* Responses	*m* Responses
3	5, 7	6, 9, 14	2, 4, 13, 17	19

suggests that her conceptions of people, including herself, tend to be based much more on imagination than real experience.

The presence of two *An* answers signifies more body concern than is common and probably relates to her current complaints. There is one *MOR* response, which is actuarially meaningless, but in this instance is intriguing because it is somewhat incongruous with the reflection answers and the very high Egocentricity Index. It occurs to Card I, response 3, "This center part could be the body of the woman without a head." In the Inquiry, she affirms "the body part . . . legs and breasts but there's no head." At best, this is a *soft MOR*. There is no death, destruction, or injury and yet, there is an implication of damage or incompleteness. People without a head do not function well and there may be such an implication here; however, this is very speculative and means little unless some other data support this postulate.

There are two minus answers, the first to Card II, response 5, ". . . a part of the body . . . maybe a kidney," and the second to Card III, response 7, ". . . an ugly bug . . . [inquiry] . . . might be a spider with big eyes." Neither are especially revealing although both have more of a negative content than might be expected.

She gave three *M* answers. The first is to Card III, response 6, "It looks like two cannibals and they're carrying a pot up to this fire; it's red like a fire." In the Inquiry, she notes that she has seen cannibals on TV "lots of times." Cannibals feed off other people as do people who need some reassurance of their worth. The second is to Card V, response 9, ". . . a child dressed in a rabbit suit, standing to get her picture taken, it looks furry [inquiry] . . . a little girl going to a party . . ." This answer has several tentative meanings. First, it is a child who is to be gloried on film. Second, the child is concealed beneath a false exterior that conveys warmth, and third, "she" is going to a party, a potentially happy event. The third *M* answer is to Card VII, response 14, ". . . a little girl who has just had her hair fixed and she's looking at herself in the mirror," clearly conveying her excessive self-concern. It is interesting to note that two of the three *M* answers identify children rather than adults and the third, even though a cooperative form of movement, does not involve any adult, but rather cannibals.

Collectively, the three *M* answers seem to convey less maturity and, to some extent, forms of denial. They are not answers commonly given by adults. Instead, they are more juvenile and raise a question about whether she really does identify herself in an adult role.

There are four *FM* answers, the first to Card I, response 2, ". . . a cat's face too, hissing . . . [inquiry] hissing like cats do." It is the only aggressive movement answer in the record and occurred after being prompted by the examiner for added responses. The second, is to Card II, response 4, "Wow, look at the color, it looks like blood on these dogs, or maybe it's paint, yes that's it thy have been playing in the paint and got it all over them, [inquiry] I don't know why I said blood at first 'cause it doesn't look like that but . . ." This is the type of answer that reeks of denial through which something unpleasant is converted into something much more acceptable. The third *FM* answer is to response 13, Card IV, ". . . birds in a nest, waiting to be fed . . . [inquiry] . . . waiting for the mother bird." It is a very regressive and dependent answer. The fourth is to Card VIII, response 17, and is the second reflection response, ". . . a beaver stepping over some stones and things and seeing himself reflected in the water . . . [inquiry] it's a reflection from the sun that gives that color . . ." Again, the self-glorification is emphasized.

The single *m* answer is to Card IX, response 19, "My God, more colors, I can see a waterfall in a canyon . . . [inquiry] . . . all colored by the sun and the waterfall back in the distance." This conveys a sense of passivity and concealment, and yet still made colorful by something or someone else.

The embellishments included in many of her answers are also very telling. For instance, several of her answers include verbiage that tends to be somewhat inappropriate for an adult, "Oh gee . . . Wow, look at the color . . . This top red paint might be . . . Oh, a child . . . you can almost feel it . . . Oh, this is pretty . . . My God, more colors . . . Wow, it looks like . . ." All of these comments have a hysteroid quality, much more like the child than the adult. Some of the substance of some answers has a similar quality—dogs playing in paint, she has a bunny hat and a fur suit, a candy house . . . like in a fairy tale, somebody threw paint all over the place. Two other answers seem important because of their contents. The first is to Card IX, response 20, ". . . two unborn children . . . [inquiry] I said unborn because they're pink," and her last answer to Card X, ". . . rose buds . . . [inquiry] They're pretty like little roses waiting to open . . ." Both convey a sense of indefiniteness, that is, waiting for things to come, or possibly wishing for things in the past.

INTERPERSONAL PERCEPTION AND BEHAVIOR—PROTOCOL 1

The data relevant to this cluster are shown in Table 83.

The *CDI* and *HVI* are both negative and the data for the *a:p* ratio are not actuarially relevant, although on a more subject level it seems worthy to note that the number of passive answers equal the number of active answers. The presence of the two *Food* answers is quite important as they signal strong needs for dependency. In addition, there are three texture answers that convey a marked sense of loneliness and intense needs for closeness. This is very important because there is no direct evidence of significant emotional loss in the history. There has been a divorce but there has been a remarriage. On the other hand, she reports feeling confined, notes that she is somewhat distant from her parents, and implies that her husband may be the primary caretaker for their child, "I don't know what I'd do without him, they get along so well together." It seems possible that she may feel somewhat neglected and uncared for, and has no easily available resource to gratify her own strong emotional needs.

The substantial number of human contents (7) indicates that she is very interested in others, but the presence of only one pure *H* also indicates that she probably doesn't understand people very well. There are two *PER* responses, which is not significantly high, but does suggest that, at times she may be more defensively authoritarian than are most adults. The presence of the two *COP* answers is a positive finding and the presence of one *AG* response seems of little significance, except for the fact that it followed a

Table 83.   **Interpersonal Perception Data for Protocol 1**

CDI = 2	a:p = 4:4	T = 3	Human Cont = 7	Pure H = 1
HVI = Neg	Food = 2	PER = 2	COP = 2 AG = 1	Isolate/R = 0.32

Responses to Be Read	
Human Movement with Pair	Human Contents
6	3, 6, 8, 9, 11, 14, 20

challenge by the examiner. This raises a question about whether she commonly responds to challenge in that manner.

The Isolation Index is positive (0.32), which is unusual for someone strongly interested in others, but not unusual for someone who is very self-centered and who does not understand people very well. It suggests an impoverished interpersonal world, a finding that does not bode well for a married person. The single human movement answer containing a pair is cooperative but also involving unusual people (cannibals). Similarly, the human contents generally reflect a more limited or even distorted conception of others (a woman without a head, cannibals, a monster man, a child dressed in a rabbit suit, two legs . . . in a stocking ad, a little girl, and two unborn children).

CONTROLS—PROTOCOL 1

Data pertaining to issues of control and stress tolerance are shown in Table 84.

Table 84.   Controls and Stress Tolerance Data for Protocol 1

EB = 3:8.5		EA = 11.5		D = 0
eb = 5:6		es = 11	$Adj\ es$ = 11	$Adj\ D$ = 0
FM = 4	C' = 3	T = 3		CDI = 2
m = 1	V = 0	Y = 0		

The D Scores are both zero, suggesting that, usually, she has enough resource available to participate meaningfully in forming and directing her behaviors. Her tolerance for stress is like that of most adults and typically her controls will not falter unless stress is unexpected and intense, or quite prolonged. Examination of the EA and EB offer no evidence to challenge the validity of the D Scores, even though the value for the Adjusted es is rather substantial. In fact, if the values for texture and C' were not so elevated, there is some possibility that the Adjusted D Score might actually be higher, but that is a conjecture based on an assumption that, under different circumstances, the value for T might be only one and the value for C', no more than two. In any event, the data, as they exist, indicate that there are no reasons to be concerned about her capacity for control or her tolerance for stress at this time.

AFFECT—PROTOCOL 1

The data related to affect for this record are shown in Table 85.

The Depression Index is not positive but most of the remaining variables in the cluster yield very important findings. The EB (3:8.5) reveals an extratensive style, indicating that she is very prone to merge her feelings with her thinking during problem solving or decision making. The value for $EBPer$ (2.8) signifies that this is a pervasive style and she is not very flexible about its use. Thus, she is a very intuitive person, oriented toward forms of trial-and-error activity when seeking solutions, and probably very willing to display her feelings openly. While the presence of a consistent style is usually an asset, the lack of flexibility concerning its use can become a liability at times, particularly those situations in which a more thoughtful approach, reasonably free of feelings, has a

Table 85.   Data Concerning Affect for Protocol 1

			Blends
DEPI = 3			
EB = 3:8.5	EBPer = 2.8		M.FD.C.FC'
eb = 5:6	FC:CF+C = 3:6		M.FT
	Pure C = 2		M.Fr
C' = 3 T = 3	Afr = 0.67		CF.FM
V = 0 Y = 0	S = 3		CF.C'F
	Blends/R = 7:25		FM.Fr.FC
	CP = 0		m.CF.FD

significantly greater likelihood of producing desired results. The pervasiveness of the style becomes more of a liability because of two other features.

First, the right-side value of the *eb* is considerable, being greater than the left-side value. This signals the presence of distress, and those irritating feelings will undoubtably play some role in her judgments and decisions from time to time. This finding is not unexpected in light of her complaints about being on edge all of the time, crying for no apparent reason, tired in the mornings, and suspecting that she has undetected physical problems. The second feature is some potentially serious problems in modulating her emotional discharges, as reflected in the data for the *FC:CF+C* ratio (3:6), which includes two Pure *C* answers. People such as this often are overly intense in their emotional displays and frequently convey impressions of being impulsive. When there are no problems in control, as is the case here, it signifies a less mature psychological organization in which the issue of modulating affective displays is not regarded as being very important. The quality of the two Pure *C* responses tend to convey this kind of looseness: fire and splattered paint. It seems likely that people around her will be inclined to regard her as too emotional and probably immature.

The *Afr* is in the average range for an extratensive indicating that she is as willing to process emotional stimuli about as much as most adults; however, there are three *S* answers, suggesting that she is somewhat more negativistic or oppositional toward the environment than are most people. This could be a product of her feelings of loneliness and isolation, but whatever the cause, it creates a detriment to the preservation of harmonious relations with others.

The number of blends is not inordinately high for an extratensive person, but there are two color-shading blends in the record. This indicates that she often finds emotions to be confusing and probably experiences both positive and negative feelings about the same situation. People such as this tend to experience feelings more intensely and frequently have difficulty bringing closure to emotional situations.

INFORMATION PROCESSING—PROTOCOL 1

Data related to processing for this record are shown in Table 86.

The data for *Lambda,* the *HVI,* and the *OBS* are not relevant. The substantial *Zf* (13) indicates that she does strive to organize at least as much as most adults, and the *W:M* confirms a sound achievement orientation. However, the *W:D:Dd* ratio indicates that she is a bit more cautious or conservative than might be expected. The presence of eight *DQ +* answers is favorable, but the two *DQv* answers suggest that some of her processing activity is less mature than is common for adults.

Table 86.   Processing Data for Protocol 1

L = 0.56	$W:D:Dd$ = 8:16:1	Zd = −3.5	$DQ+$ = 8
Zf = 13	$W:M$ = 8:3	PSV = 0	$DQv/+$ = 0
HVI = No	OBS = No		DQv = 2

Location Sequencing

I: W.WS.D	IV: W	VII: *D.W*
II: *D.D*	V: *D.W.D*	VIII: WS.W.DS
III: *D.D*	VI: *D.Dd*	IX: *D.D.D*
	X: W.D.D.D	

The Zd score (−3.5) signals underincorporation; that is, she tends to scan stimulus fields hastily or in a haphazard manner and, at times, will neglect critical stimulus cues. This creates a potential for faulty mediation and can contribute to less effective patterns of behavior. The sequencing is reasonably consistent. She begins 4 of the 10 cards with W answers and the remaining 6 with D responses. There is a bit of inconsistency on Cards V and VII to which W answers are given after D responses. This is particularly unusual for Card V and probably reaffirms the importance of her first answer to that blot (a child dressed in a rabbit suit).

COGNITIVE MEDIATION—PROTOCOL 1

The data relevant to mediation are shown in Table 87.

Table 87.   Data Concerning Cognitive Mediation for Protocol 1

Lambda = 0.56	*OBS* = Neg	*Minus Features*
P = 8	$X+\%$ = .84	5, 7
$FQx+$ = 0	$F+\%$ = .78	
$FQxo$ = 21	$Xu\%$ = .04	
$FQxu$ = 1	$X-\%$ = .08	
$FQx-$ = 2	$S-\%$ = .00	
FQxnone = 1	$CONFAB$ = 0	

The data for this cluster are very similar to that expected in the protocol of a nonpatient. The sizable number of Popular answers indicate that, when given obvious cues, she makes very conventional responses. The $X+\%$ is well up into the average range and the $Xu\%$ is somewhat lower than usual for an adult. The presence of two minus answers is not uncommon, and when they are reviewed (kidneys in response 5; an ugly bug in response 7), neither are serious distortions of the blot areas involved.

IDEATION—PROTOCOL 1

Data regarding ideation from this record are shown in Table 88.

The findings from the cluster regarding affect have already established that she is not very oriented to the procedures of delay and thinking things through before coming to a decision or taking action. In fact, it seems rare that she will do so, because her

Table 88.   Data Concerning Ideation for Protocol 1

EB = 3:8.5	EBPer = 2.8	M Quality		Critical Special Scores		
eb = 5:6	(FM = 4 m = 1)	+ = 0	DV = 0		DV2 = 0	
a:p = 8:5	M^a:M^p = 1:2	o = 3	INC = 0		INC2 = 0	
2AB+Art+Ay = 2		u = 0	DR = 0		DR2 = 0	
MOR = 1		– = 0	FAB = 0		FAB2 = 0	
			ALOG = 0		SUM6 = 0	
Responses to Be Read for Quality			CON = 0		WSUM6 = 0	
6, 9, 14						

extratensive style is so pervasive. Thus, her thinking usually will be the product of ideational and affective activities that have merged. A major issue concerning this product is how extensive is the influence of her previously noted emotional looseness. As it turns out, the data in this cluster generally are more positive than negative.

The values for FM (4) and m (1) are not unusual indicating that there is no evidence of higher-than-expected levels of peripheral ideation. Similarly, the a:p ratio (4:4) offers no evidence of inflexibility in her attitudes or values. Probably the most negative finding is derived from the M^a: M^p ratio (1:2), which suggests that she does tend to use fantasy as an escape from reality more often than most people. This is a form of ideational denial that provides temporary relief by replacing unpleasant and/or uncontrollable situations with ones that are easily managed and free of stress. However, it breeds a dependency on others because there is an implicit assumption that, somehow, external forces will resolve the unpleasant issues if they can be avoided long enough. Nonetheless, she does not appear to be overly involved with intellectualization, and the single MOR answer is irrelevant to issues concerning her thinking. There are no critical Special Scores in the record, an unusual finding for most nonpatient adults.

Thus, it must be concluded that her thinking is reasonably clear and coherent. Even the quality of her thinking must be judged to be at least adequate in light of her three M answers, even though the content of all three provide a more negative input concerning her perceptions of herself and others. The first (cannibals) is fairly complex and the other two (child in a rabbit suit; little girl who just had her hair fixed) are immature in terms of content, but rather elaborate in terms of quality. A similar impression is gleaned if the entire record is read. There is a reasonably good quality to the manner by which she forms and articulates answers even though many are marked by naive and sometimes even childlike characteristics.

SUMMARY—PROTOCOL 1

The psychological picture that has unfolded reveals an extremely self-centered person whose narcissistic orientation appears to have a dominating influence in most of her psychological functioning. She seems to be quite immature, having a naive conception of herself and others. She has strong needs to be dependent on others; however, her attitudes toward, and awareness of others, are not well founded in real experience and, as a consequence, her interpersonal world lacks both depth and maturity. In effect, she often finds herself isolated in a world in which she would like to participate more but, unfortunately, tends to define that participation only in terms of her own needs and wants.

Actually, she has considerable resource available to her that permits her to act mean-ingfully and deliberately when forming or implementing decisions, and usually she is not easily disorganized by stress experiences. Many of her decisions, however, are too focused on herself and this probably causes others to back away from her. When things go wrong, she usually will externalize blame, or in some instances even deny the pres-ence of the negative event. In some instances, she often takes flight into fantasy for the specific purpose of avoiding responsibility and/or confrontations.

She is heavily committed to the experience and use of emotion as a way of living. Sadly, she apparently has never learned to value the importance of modulating her feel-ings. As a result, she often does not exert much control over her emotional discharges, and this permits her emotions to become overly intense and/or influential on her much more often than should be the case. Many of her feelings are confusing to her, and some are marked by considerable negativism or hostility. Thus, although her thinking is clear and her perceptual accuracy is well within acceptable limits, many of her behaviors are quite likely to be inefficient or even maladaptive even though she is quite aware of con-ventionality and motivated, at least in part, to make acceptable responses. Her failure to inject effective modulation into her emotional displays stems from her inordinate, child-like self-centeredness, and the immaturity that it has perpetuated. This lack of develop-ment has produced a marked tendency to be excessively dependent, and probably demanding on others for decisions and direction.

Currently, she is experiencing considerable distress. Some of the distress appears to be occurring because she is attempting to conceal and internalize some of her intense feelings, but much of it stems from a strong sense of loneliness and may even include an anticipated sense of abandonment or rejection. It seems likely that her first marriage probably failed, at least in part, because she made excessive demands on her husband, and her current marriage may be marked by more difficulties than initially meet the eye. Her strong needs for closeness plus her overall immaturity, cannot help to make the car-ing for a newborn a task that is difficult if not threatening. It seems impossible to avoid the speculation that some of her apparent sense of loneliness may result from the fact that her husband is devoting time to the care of their child and, consequently, has less time to give to her.

In effect, she portrays a very narcissistic, immature, histrionic personality, caught up in a centrifuge of often confusing and/or conflicting intense feelings, attempting to cope with them, as well as with everyday responsibilities, in her persistently immature, deny-ing, and sometimes emotionally inappropriate manner. She often wants to do what is correct and appropriate, but she is frequently hindered from this objective by her own immaturity, her naivieté about people, and her strong needs to reaffirm her unrealisti-cally inflated sense of personal worth.

It seems quite likely that her therapist was remiss in attributing many of her earlier presenting characteristics to the stresses of the breakup of her first marriage. Possibly, if he had continued to see her, some of her current long-standing problems would have been more apparent. In any event, she is now in another difficult time. He could elect some form of supportive treatment, but the magnitude of her developmental liabilities, plus the inten-sity of her pleas of helplessness seem to make this a poor choice for intervention. Even if the support were to bring some relief, the likelihood of a recurrence of symptoms is con-siderable. Thus it seems reasonable to make two recommendations. First, it is appropriate and necessary to evaluate the status of her marriage more thoroughly than is possible from the history she provides. It is possible that the undercurrents of her problems have not yet interfered with her relationship with her husband, but that seems unlikely. If this postulate is true, a form of marital therapy, as a support, could be in order. Second, and regardless of the first, she should be in a form of developmental therapy.

There are several approaches that could be useful, ranging from some of the long-term cognitive approaches to the more psychodynamically insight-oriented approach. It is important, however, to note that patients who have a strong narcissistic orientation usually do not come to treatment seeking change within themselves. Instead, they seek support during current crisis situations and ultimately want therapists to help them change the way that the world responds to them. Thus, considerable tolerance on the part of the therapist is required and any tactics that might be directed to change from within should be avoided until a strong therapeutic bond is created.

It also seems appropriate to recommend consideration of a female therapist, especially if the evaluation of the marriage confirms signs of weakness or open conflict. She now sees herself as a child, or at least assumes a role that is much more typical of the dependent child than the adult woman. She has also been rejected by at least one male in her life, and that could cause her to be overly cautious and/or denying with a male therapist. Conversely, working with a female therapist might offer her a new opportunity to explore her identity from a different perspective, and in a situation that avoids many of the hazards that could be created by her earlier experiences with males, including her previous therapeutic experience.

PROTOCOL 2: A QUESTION OF ADOLESCENT WITHDRAWAL

Referral   This 17-year-old male was admitted voluntarily to a private psychiatric hospital on the encouragement of his parents and after one interview with a consulting psychiatrist. The parents have been increasingly concerned about him for approximately $1\frac{1}{2}$ years, during which he has become more withdrawn from them, his siblings, and from friendships that he had developed during his earlier school years. They have been informed by some of his teachers that he seems detached and uninterested, and as a result, his grades have dropped from A's and B's during his first year in high school, to C's and D's during his recently completed third year. He has attributed this to a lack of interest and has responded to their efforts to encourage him by more withdrawal. For the past several months, he has isolated himself from his family by remaining in his room except for meals, listening to music, or by taking long rides on his prized 10-speed bicycle. Shortly before his admission, he had been repairing a tire on his bicycle and suddenly took a sledgehammer to it, ruining it completely. It was this event that precipitated the psychiatric consultant, and the recommendation by the psychiatrist that he be hospitalized for evaluation. After 8 days of hospitalization, the staff consensus favored a tentative diagnosis of "Borderline Personality Disorder," with a recommendation for long-term outpatient care. At that time, psychological evaluation was requested to assist in identifying treatment objectives.

History   The subject is the third child, and oldest son in a family of five children. His older sisters are ages 22 and 20, the older being married and living out of the home, and the second a college junior still living at home. His younger siblings are ages 8 and 6. The considerable disparity between his age and that of his next younger sibling is created by the fact that his mother, now age 44, suffered from vascular problems following his birth and was encouraged to avoid further pregnancies. Once the condition cleared, after several years of medical care, she and her husband agreed to have "one more" child. The youngest child was, according to the mother, "very unexpected but very welcome." The father, age 48, owns a small construction firm. There is no psychiatric history in the immediate family, but the mother does report that two of her close relatives, an uncle and a cousin, have both been hospitalized for long periods because of "nervous breakdowns." The subject has been hospitalized since shortly after beginning his senior year in high school. He expresses some confusion about the destruction of the bicycle, suggesting that he lost his temper because one of the bolts that was disconnected could not be refitted in place. He argues that it was "a dumb thing to do," but when pressed on the issue he notes that the bike "was getting old anyhow and sometimes it wouldn't do the things I wanted it to." He discounts his poor school performance during the past two years as unimportant and the result of "lousy teachers who are only in it for the money." He says that he has promised himself to do better in the current year "and when I get back I'll really show them what I can do." He admits to some experiences of depression, but suggests that is common for "people struggling to grow up." He says that the concern of his parents about his lost friendships is "unimportant" because most of the young people with whom he associated in the past are "too out of it." He accuses them of being "just into dope a lot," and implies that he has tried several drugs but finds them offensive. He claims that he has "dated" frequently, but his parents feel this is not true. He indicates that he has not had any "real" sexual experience, "but I've fooled around a little." He feels that his current problems with his parents are "just a misunderstanding, they're great and we'll work it all out, really we will." He admits that he does not get along well with his siblings but then adds, "They're really o.k. too, and we can get along better." He feels very apprehensive about being in the hospital but suggests, "It'll maybe get some people off my back while I sort things out. It could be a good thing, maybe." He denies any strangeness in his thinking or hallucinatory experiences. His parents report a relatively normal developmental history and no serious medical illnesses, and indicate that, until the episode with the bike, they had not observed any loss of temper since his preschool years.

Protocol 2. V.M., 17 Years Old

Card	Response	Inquiry	Scoring
I	1. A face w 4 eyes, lik u carv a pumpkin	E: (Rpts S's resp) S: Ther's the top 2 eyes & thes r the bttm 2 eyes & ths is the nose. The way the bttm eyes get lighter ll a smile too. Ths r the ears & cheeks (points), its lik a face tht wld b carvd in a pumpkin	WSo FYo (Hd) 3.5 INC
	E: Most peopl c mor thn 1 thg 2. They do? Well, it ll s.k. of flying object	E: (Rpts S's resp) S: I can't defin wht kind, but here r its wings & it ll its in flt. Its not wrkg too hard at it since its wgs r'nt fully spread. It mite b a bat E: I'm not sure I c it lik u do S: How can u tell if someone is sick or not from these, c its the W thg	Wo FMªo A P 1.0
II	3. It ll a face & a wide open mouth, spittg bld	E: (Rpts S's resp) S: Hr r the eyes & ths r the eyebrows. The mouth is here & leads into the nose here. E: U mentioned a face spittg bld S: Like s.o. is screaming & spitting up bld rite here the red spots (D3)	WS+ Mª.CF− Hd, Bl 4.5 MOR
	4. It also ll a grave w a cross at the tombstne, a blk cross on top of the white tombstn	E: (Rpts S's resp) S: Ths prt here (white) is the dirt like u r lookg at it from a distance. Ths is the grave hr & up here is the cross. Ths line here (points) cuts the grave from the tombstn	DS+ FC'.FD−ld 4.5

564

Card	No.	Response	Inquiry	Loc.	Determinant(s)	(2)	Content	P	Z	Special Scores
III	5.	Ths ll to me lik 2 girls pulling on s.o.'s face	E: (Rpts S's resp) S: Ths is the girl, her head, breast & legs. Ths ll the face thyr pulling on, the eyes, nose & mouth. Its in the proc of being torn apart by ths 2 girls. The eyes r bulging out of the guy's face. The girls r pulling him w their arms	D+	Ma.FD−	(2)	H.Hd	P	3.0	FAB2, AG, MOR
	6.	Ths 2 thg here r broken guitars	E: (Rpts S's resp) S: On either side here, it ll s.o. has smashed them fr a side angle so the neck is hanging off, & the bttm is bent lik a boot, lik its guts r hanging out, lik the wire & other stuff, thts rite here (points)	Do	Fu	(2)	Id			MOR
IV	7.	Tht ll, uh, ll one of thos guys in a "Keep on trucking" poster. Coming out of his body is a dragon	E: (Rpts S's resp) S: Its taken fr a vantage, horizon type drawing. Thes r his feet & hr r his arms & thy r a little deformed. His head has little shape but its ther. That's the dragon comg fr betwn his legs, or sk of monster E: I'm not clear abt the vantage, horizon type drawing S: Lik if u keep lookg at it, it gets thinner & thinner so tht u don't c it anymore.	W+	FDu		(H),(A)	P	4.0	FAB, MOR, DV
V	8.	Tht ll a bf	E: (Rpts S's resp) S: Hr r its antlers & wgs & there r the legs or whatevr u want to call them	Wo	Fo		A	P	1.0	INC

Protocol 2 (Continued)

Card		Response		Inquiry	Scoring

9. It also ll it cb a man w wgs & antlers. He's got a line running rite dwn the middle of him

E: (Rpts S's resp)
S: Yeah, her's his head & antlers & legs. Ths drk line running dwn him is from where they made the inkblot

Do Fo H INC2

VI 10. It ll s.k. of machine & its speared half the sun

E: (Rpts S's resp)
S: Yeah, ths is the machine, ths prt here. Ths line running dwn the middle is what u'd get in the machin to run it. Its s.k. of drill & its got half the sun. Thr r flames coming fr the sun so its got half the sun

W+ m^a u Sc, Na 2.5 FAB2

11. Its also a plain inkblot

E: (Rpts S's resp)
S: It ll s.b. put ink on a pc of paper & folded it togthr. Thy prob fooled around a littl by pushg the ink around to get the shades, then they opned it up & said "wow, I've made s.t." but there's no real shape to it.

Wv Y Art

VII 12. It ll 2 Egyptian girls doing an Egyptial dance

E: (Rpts S's resp)
S: Yeah, here's their heads w their hair up. It comes over their forehead. Here's the chin, u can't c the mouth well. Thes r their arms out lik that, u can c them fr the head to the waist, ths dwn here is nothing

D+ M^a o (2) Hd P 3.0 DV2

13. Or it c.b. 2 gals rockg on rockg chairs

E: (Rpts S's resp)
S: Thes r rockg chairs balanced on the corner, mayb rockers lik blks of wood w a rounded bttm. The girls r the same as before & they just kinda rock on it.

W+ M^p o (2) H, Hh P 2.5

VIII 14. Ths ll 2 bears clmbg either side of a mt, 2 pink bears, or red, whtevr tht is

E: (Rpts S's resp)
S: Here r the bears & thyr in motion, going up the side of the mt. Thy r on opposite sides of the mt.

W+ FM^a.FCo (2) A.Ls P 4.5 INC

566

15. In the mt is a face of an Eskimo, or Indian type ruler or god. It ll the bears hav their paws on his hair

E: (Rpts S's resp)
S: Yeah, here r his eyes & his nose here. Ths green area is his mouth & he's got all the lines of his face, he's even got a littl paint on his face, lik littl green bits of paint on it here. Ths is his hair, its long hair, the bears hav opposite paws on his hair

$D+$ $FM^p.FC-$ (2) Hd, ALs P 3.0 FAB2

IX 16. It ll 2 profiles of Alfred Hitchcock

E: (Rpts S's resp)
S: 2 bad profiles, rt here is the forehead & ths white part is his eye, ths is his nose & mouth is ths littl indentatn, he's got a pimple on his chin

DSo Fu (2) Hd 5.0

17. Or, the head of a pig thy killed in Lord of the Flies

E: (Rpts S's resp)
S: The same prt again, but use the pink & orange, lik a profile of tht pig thy stuck on the stake (D1) & its drippg bld down here (D4), the pink color, but evaporating up here (D3), there's one on each side w the stake (D5) in the middl . . .
E: Evaporating?
S: Lik all the juice inside is evap up into the air
E: (Rpts S's resp)

$W+$ $m^p.CF-$ (2) $(AD), Bl$ 5.5 MOR, INC2

X 18. Ths is just all kinds of bugs, yeah thts wht it is

E: (Rpts S's resp)
S: Yeah, all kinds of bugs. Ths 2 blue ones r bugs & up hre ths 2 ll crawly brwn bugs. E.t. in the pic. gives more life to the bugs, u can detect their presence easier

$W+$ FCo (2) A 5.5 DR

19. It's also got a face in it

E: (Rpts S's resp)
S: Hr r the eyes & the nose w a moustache like parts of the face & if u turn it upsid dwn get exactly the same, c?. here r the nose, eyes & moustache again

$DdSo$ $F-$ Hd

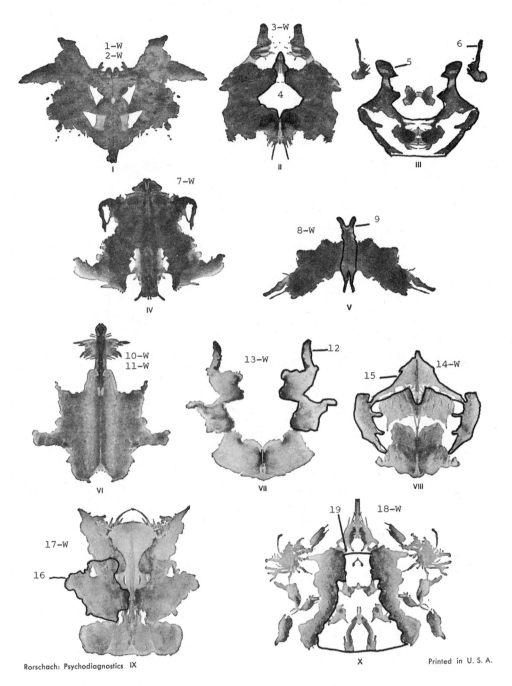

Figure 18.   Location Selections for Protocol 2.

Table 89.   Protocol 2—Sequence of Scores

CARD	NO	LOC	#	DETERMINANT(S)	(2)	CONTENT(S)	POP	Z	SPECIAL SCORES
I	1	WSo	1	FYo		(Hd)		3.5	INC
	2	Wo	1	FMao		A	P	1.0	
II	3	WS+	1	Ma.CF-		Hd,Bl		4.5	MOR
	4	DS+	5	FC'.FD-		Id		4.5	
III	5	D+	1	Ma.FD-	2	H,Hd	P	3.0	FAB2,AG,MOR
	6	Do	2	Fu	2	Sc			MOR
IV	7	W+	1	FMp.FDu		(H),(A)	P	4.0	FAB2,MOR,DV
V	8	Wo	1	Fo		A	P	1.0	INC
	9	Do	7	Fo		H			INC2
VI	10	W+	1	mau		Sc,Na		2.5	FAB2
	11	Wv	1	Y		Art			
VII	12	D+	2	Mao	2	Hd	P	3.0	DV2
	13	W+	1	Mpo	2	H,Hh	P	2.5	
VIII	14	W+	1	FMa.FCo	2	A,Ls	P	4.5	INC
	15	D+	4	FMp.FC-	2	Hd,Ls,A	P	3.0	FAB2
IX	16	DSo	1	Fu	2	Hd		5.0	
	17	W+	1	mp.CFu	2	(Ad),Bl		5.5	MOR,INC2
X	18	W+	1	FCo	2	A		5.5	DR
	19	DdSo	30	F-		Hd			

Copyright (c) 1976, 1985, 1990 by John E. Exner, Jr.

Table 90.   Protocol 2—Structural Summary

```
=================================================================================
LOCATION            DETERMINANTS              CONTENTS        S-CONSTELLATION
FEATURES         BLENDS        SINGLE                         YES..FV+VF+V+FD>2
                                          H   = 3, 0            NO..Col-Shd
Bl>0
Zf    = 15      M.CF          M  = 2     (H)  = 1, 0          YES..Ego<.31,>.44
ZSum  = 53.0    FC'.FD        FM = 1      Hd  = 5, 1          YES..MOR > 3
ZEst  = 49.0    M.FD          m  = 1     (Hd) = 1, 0          YES..Zd > +- 3.5
                FM.FD         FC = 1      Hx  = 0, 0           NO..es > EA
W     = 11      FM.FC         CF = 0      A   = 4, 1           NO..CF+C > FC
  (Wv = 1)      FM.FC         C  = 0     (A)  = 0, 1          YES..X+% < .70
D     = 7       m.CF          Cn = 0      Ad  = 0, 0          YES..S > 3
Dd    = 1                     FC'= 0     (Ad) = 1, 0           NO..P < 3 or > 8
S     = 5                     C'F= 0      An  = 0, 0           NO..Pure H < 2
                              C' = 0      Art = 1, 0           NO..R < 17
   DQ                         FT = 0      Ay  = 0, 0           6.....TOTAL
........(FQ-)                 TF = 0      Bl  = 0, 2
  +  = 11  ( 4)               T  = 0      Bt  = 0, 0          SPECIAL SCORINGS
  o  =  7  ( 1)               FV = 0      Cg  = 0, 0              Lv1    Lv2
  v/+ = 0  ( 0)               VF = 0      Cl  = 0, 0          DV   = 1x1    1x2
  v  =  1  ( 0)               V  = 0      Ex  = 0, 0          INC  = 3x2    2x4
                              FY = 1      Fd  = 0, 0          DR   = 1x3    0x6
                              YF = 0      Fi  = 0, 0          FAB  = 0x4    4x7
                              Y  = 1      Ge  = 0, 0          ALOG = 0x5
   FORM QUALITY               Fr = 0      Hh  = 0, 1          CON  = 0x7
                              rF = 0      Ls  = 0, 2          SUM6  =12
       FQx  FQf  MQual  SQx   FD = 0      Na  = 0, 1          WSUM6 = 48
  +  =  0    0     0     0    F  = 5      Sc  = 2, 0
  o  =  8    2     2     1                Sx  = 0, 0          AB   = 0    CP  = 0
  u  =  5    2     0     1                Xy  = 0, 0          AG   = 1    MOR = 5
  -  =  5    1     2     3                Id  = 1, 0          CFB  = 0    PER = 0
  none= 1   --     0     0    (2) =  9                        COP  = 0    PSV = 0
=================================================================================
                    RATIOS, PERCENTAGES, AND DERIVATIONS

R = 19          L = 0.36          FC:CF+C = 3: 2     COP = 0      AG = 1
---------------------------------  Pure C  =    0    Food    = 0
EB = 4: 3.5   EA =  7.5  EBPer= N/A  Afr   =0.46      Isolate/R =0.21
eb = 6: 3    es =  9     D  = 0    S       = 5        H:(H)Hd(Hd)= 3: 8
         Adj es =  7   Adj D  = 0  Blends:R = 7:19    (HHd):(AAd)= 2: 2
---------------------------------  CP      = 0        H+A:Hd+Ad =10: 8
FM = 4  :  C'= 1   T = 0
m  = 2  :  V = 0   Y = 2
                         P  = 8      Zf   =15          3r+(2)/R=0.47
a:p   =  6: 4  Sum6  = 12  X+% =0.42  Zd  = +4.0       Fr+rF = 0
Ma:Mp =  3: 1  Lv2   =  7  F+% =0.40  W:D:Dd =11: 7: 1 FD    = 3
2AB+Art+Ay= 1  WSum6 = 48  X-% =0.26  W:M =11: 5       An+Xy = 1
M-    =  2     Mnone =  0  S-% =0.60  DQ+ =11          MOR   = 5
                           Xu% =0.26  DQv = 1
---------------------------------------------------------------------------------
   SCZI = 5*    DEPI = 5*    CDI = 1    S-CON = 6    HVI =YES   OBS = No
=================================================================================
```

Copyright (c) 1976, 1985, 1990 by John E. Exner, Jr.

INTERPRETIVE ROUTINE FOR PROTOCOL 2

The first positive Key variable is the *SCZI,* which has a value of 5, warning of the possibility of schizophrenia. As noted in Chapter 15, when the *SCZI* is 5, regardless of whether the subject is an adult or child, the likelihood of schizophrenia is considerable, and the probability of a false positive is somewhat remote. There are other conditions that could produce a schizophrenia-like record, such as an active or very recent toxic psychosis, especially if amphetamines have been involved, a major affective disturbance that has created a psychotic-like state, or some neurologically related conditions, especially those in which a recent insult has created much disorganization. In this instance, the subject denies any extensive drug history. The *DEPI* is positive but only with a value of 5, which is very unlikely to coincide with an affectively induced psychotic state, and there is no evidence of a significant neurological impairment. Obviously, a recommendation in the report should call for a careful drug screen, in spite of the subject's denial of drug use. For the moment, however, the positive *SCZI* value must be weighed carefully, and because it is the first positive Key variable, it defines the interpretive routine as:

Ideation → Mediation → Processing → Controls → Affect
→ Self-Perception → Interpersonal Perception

IDEATION—PROTOCOL 2

The data related to ideation for Protocol 2 are shown in Table 91.

The *EB* (4:3.5) reveals that he is an ambitent. Thus, his ideational activity is less consistent than is expected for an older adolescent. At times, he delays decisions, pushes feelings aside, and tries to think things through, but in other instances his feelings merge into his thinking and become very influential, often promoting forms of trial-and-error behaviors. In that neither of these approaches are well developed, both are less effective, and he often finds himself indecisive or reversing previously reached judgments. He is vulnerable to errors in judgment and prone to repeat those errors more often than people who are more consistent in their decision-making activities.

The left-side value of the *eb* is not unusual, consisting of four *FM* answers and two *m*, suggesting that there is no reason to believe that he is impinged upon by an excess of peripheral ideation. Similarly, the data for the *a:p* and M^a:M^p ratios and the Intellectualization Index are unremarkable. On the other hand, there are five *MOR* responses indicating that his thinking and attitudes are marked by a strong sense of pessimism. This undoubtably influences his patterns of thinking and his decision operations.

The data concerning the critical Special Scores are probably the most striking in the cluster. They appear 12 times in his 19 answers and include seven Level 2 answers. Collectively, they yield an extremely high Weighted Sum of 48, which leaves no doubt concerning the presence of seriously disordered thinking. Disturbance of this magnitude usually involves very flawed judgment, distorted conceptualizations, disorganized patterns of decision making, and a flow of thinking that is often bizarre. However, such a conclusion should be tested by reading the responses containing critical Special Scores, mainly to determine the degree to which elements of bizarreness are obvious, as usually is the case in the answers scored as Level 2, or whether they reflect less mature, or even playful forms of organization. It is naive to assume that all of the responses falling into

Table 91.   Data Concerning Ideation for Protocol 2

		M Quality	*Critical Special Scores*			
EB = 4:3.5	*EBPer* = N/A					
eb = 6:3	(*FM* = 4 *m* = 2)	+ = 0	*DV*	= 1	*DV2*	= 1
a:p = 5:5	M^a:M^p = 3:1	*o* = 2	*INC*	= 3	*INC2*	= 2
2AB +Art +Ay = 1		*u* = 1	*DR*	= 1	*DR2*	= 0
MOR = 5		− = 2	*FAB*	= 0	*FAB2*	= 4
			ALOG	= 0	*SUM6*	= 12
Responses to Be Read for Quality			*CON*	= 0	*WSUM6*	= 48
3, 5, 10, 12, 13						

one category represent equal degrees of slippage or dysfunction. Some obviously reflect more disruption than others, even though they may be in the same category. In most cases, when schizophrenia is present, the element of strange or bizarre thinking is very striking in some of the responses. They are not simply unusual, but tend to stand out like 'a beacon in the way that they reflect the disordered thought.

The first is an *INCOM* in response 1, "A face with four eyes, like you carve a pumpkin." Few, if any, people carve four eyes in a pumpkin and thus, the *INCOM* is appropriate, but it seems less mature than bizarre. The second occurs to Card III, response 5—two girls pulling on someone's face—which is also one of his *M* answers. It is a *FABCOM2* response and quite bizarre. The next is to Card IV, response 7, which is a poster of a guy with a dragon coming out of his body, also scored as a *FABCOM2;* it also stretches the imagination well beyond reality and is also scored as a *DV* because of his description, ". . . taken from a vantage, horizon-type drawing." The fifth is a rather immature *INCOM* in response 8, antlers on a butterfly. The sixth, also to Card V, response 9, reflects much more slippage, a man with wings and antlers, scored as an *INCOM2*. The next, to Card VI, response 10, is a machine that has speared half the sun, a *FABCOM2* that seems void of any good judgment. On Card VII, response 12, he reports girls doing an Egyptial dance, a fairly obvious neologism. There is a simplistic, immature *INCOM* on Card VIII, response 14, pink bears, and a much more serious manifestation of slippage in the next answer to the same card, a face and bears having their paws on his hair, scored as a *FABCOM2*. The eleventh is given to Card IX, response 17, all the juice is evaporating into the air, scored as an *INCOM2,* and the last is a rambling *DR* in response 18, to Card X, everything in the picture gives more life to the bugs, you can detect their presence easier. Several of these might be given by the very young child who has poor judgment and little concern for reality, but even such a child would not give all of them. Collectively, they reflect the kind of strange logic, faulty associations, and possibly even delusional operations, that mark the ideation of a severely disturbed person.

The record also contains two *M* − answers, one of which has already been mentioned (two girls pulling on someone's face). The first *M* − was given to Card II, response 3, a face and a wide-open mouth, spitting blood. Although that answer might not be judged as a seriously disordered and bizarre as many others, it simply adds more data to confirm the presence of disordered thought. Thus, the findings concerning ideational slippage clearly coincide with that found commonly among schizophrenics. The same forms of slippage are extremely uncommon among affective psychotics but could exist in the record of a toxically induced psychosis, or even a reactive psychosis following an extreme trauma, but none is suggested by the history. Obviously, the need for a drug screen is critical.

Actually, the quality of his thinking, disregarding the bizarre features, is not unsophisticated. All of his *M* answers are synthesized and reasonably complex, which probably reflects a substantial intellect that seems to be confirmed by the fact that he had received A's and B's during his first year of high school.

COGNITIVE MEDIATION—PROTOCOL 2

The data relevant to issues of mediation are shown in Table 92.

The findings for *Lambda* and the *OBS* are not relevant. He gives a substantial number of Popular responses (8), which suggests that when he is in obvious situations, expected

Table 92.   Data Concerning Cognitive Mediation for Protocol 2

Lambda	= 0.36	*OBS*	= Neg	*Minus Features*	
P	= 8	*X + %*	= .42	3, 4, 5, 15, 19	
FQx+	= 0	*F + %*	= .40		
FQxo	= 8	*Xu%*	= .26		
FQxu	= 5	*X − %*	= .26		
FQx−	= 5	*S − %*	= .60		
*FQx*none	= 1	*CONFAB*	= 0		

or acceptable responses are likely to occur. It should be noted, however, that two of the eight Popular answers also include a minus form quality. In other words, he will sometimes ruin even the expected or acceptable behavior. In fact, the low $X+\%$ (.42) suggests that he probably displays a higher-than-usual frequency of behaviors that disregard social demands or expectations. This disregard for conventionality is due in part to his tendency to overpersonalize in translating stimuli as reflected by the well-above-average $Xu\%$ (.26), but another major source appears to be significant problems in perceptual accuracy and/or distortion that occur when he translates stimuli, as illustrated by the $X-\%$ (.26).

The considerable $S-\%$ (.60) may be an important finding. Three of the five minus answers involve S. Totally, there are five S responses spread throughout the record, suggesting that some of the distortions are the product of a chronic, trait-like, negativistic orientation toward the environment. Such an orientation is likely to increase the probability of behaviors that may disregard social conventions or expectations. It is also important to note that all five minus responses occur to blots containing chromatic color (II, III, VIII, and X). Neither of these findings rules out the possibility of schizophrenia, but they are less common among schizophrenics. Whether or not schizophrenia is present, it does seem clear that affective elements contribute significantly to mediational problems.

None of the minus answers involve a complete distortion of the blot. They include face responses on Cards II and X, a grave and tombstone on Card II, and spoiled Popular responses on Cards III and VIII. Four of the five include human contents, and the fifth (the grave and tombstone) carries a human association. This sort of homogeneity among minus response contents is not unusual among schizophrenics, especially if there is a fixed delusional system, or if marked paranoid features exist.

INFORMATION PROCESSING—PROTOCOL 2

The data for the cluster related to processing are shown in Table 93.

A hypervigilant style is present, indicating that much energy is invested to maintain a relatively continuous state of preparedness. When pathology is in evidence, such as is the case here, this core style typically creates the basis from which marked paranoid features evolve. Thus, it is likely that a form of paranoid schizophrenia is present.

The manifestations of the hypervigilant style are obvious in the other data regarding processing. The $W:D:Dd$ ratio (11:7:1), the $W:M$ ratio (11:4), and Zf (15) all signify a high level of motivation to process new information or information related to problem solving or decision making. Similarly, the Zd score (+4.0) reveals an overincorporative

Table 93.   Processing Data for Protocol 2

L = 0.36	$W:D:Dd$ = 11:7:1	Zd = +4.0	$DQ+$ = 11
Zf = 15	$W:M$ = 11:4	$PSV = 0$	$DQv/+$ = 0
HVI = Pos	OBS = Neg		DQv = 1

Location Sequencing

I: WS.W	IV: W	VII: *D.W*
II: WS.DS	V: W.D	VIII: W.D
II: *D.D*	VI: W.W	IX: *DS.W*
		X: W.DdS

style, which involves a considerable investment of effort and energy into scanning activities. It reflects a cautious and thorough approach to ensure that all stimuli are included in the input. Actually, the quality of the processing activity is quite good as depicted by the presence of 11 *DQ+* answers, but unfortunately, sophisticated processing does not necessarily equate with more effective mediation, ideation, or adjustment.

CONTROLS AND STRESS TOLERANCE—PROTOCOL 2

Data relevant to the issues of capacity for control and tolerance for stress are shown in Table 94.

Both *D* Scores are 0, denoting that he has adequate capacities for control, and ordinarily will have sufficient resources accessible from which to formulate and implement responses. The data for the *EA, EB,* and Adjusted *es* provide no reason to challenge the validity of the *D* Scores. At first glance, this finding may seem incompatible with the presence of schizophrenia, but it is not. The capacity for control has little to do with the direction or quality of thinking, or the accuracy of perception. It simply indicates that, under most circumstances, he is not overwhelmed by the features of his disturbance.

The history tends to be commensurate with this finding. The bicycle incident is the only strikingly bizarre event reported, and during 8 days of hospitalization few, if any, indicators of serious disturbance have appeared. Thus, if he can avoid intense and/or prolonged stress experiences, the issue of behavioral control is not a significant problem for him. This can be viewed as both an asset and a liability. It is an asset because it does permit him to avoid being thrown into frequent psychotic episodes, but it is a liability because it also provides the capacity to conceal, from himself and others, the magnitude of his disorder. One consequence of this is that it may create some obstacles to effective treatment. For example, during the past several months he had attempted to isolate himself from others, and has done so with some degree of success. This may indicate that he has some awareness of his plight, and especially of the need to avoid stress. It illustrates

Table 94.   Controls and Stress Tolerance Data for Protocol 2

EB = 4:3.5		EA = 7.5		D = 0
eb = 6:3		es = 9	Adj es = 7	$Adj\ D$ = 0
FM = 4	C' = 1	T = 0		CDI = 1
m = 2	V = 0	Y = 2		

how his capacity for control permits him to avoid being overwhelmed, albeit that his tactic of doing so has only limited effectiveness, and over longer periods of time is maladaptive.

On the other hand, his capacity for control may be somewhat more fragile now than is usually the case. Although the *D* Score is 0, there are two *m* and two *Y* responses, indicating that he is experiencing situationally related stress, probably as a result of being hospitalized. He *is* feeling some loss of control and a sense of being unable to make responses. The *EA,* although in the average range, is not particularly substantial. If he is impinged upon by more stress experiences, such as might result from prolonged hospitalization, or conversely, by discharge into a threatening environment, his controls could be overwhelmed. Thus, although his controls are currently sufficient, they may be more marginal when viewed in the context of future stress levels he can be expected to experience as a result of being carefully scrutinized.

AFFECT—PROTOCOL 2

Data related to affect for this case are shown in Table 95.

The *DEPI* of 5 indicates the current personality organization is very similar to that of persons who have frequent and reasonably intense experiences of affective disruption which usually occur in the form of considerable distress and/or depression. When the *DEPI* has a value of 5, the actual manifestations of depression may not be obvious, or even among presenting complaints. He does admit to some experiences of depression but tends to make light of them. This suggests that he prefers to avoid confrontations with his feelings and, obviously, is not very willing to share them with others.

The already established fact that he is an ambitent indicates that he is inconsistent in the way that his emotions impact on his thinking, problem solving, and decision making. Interestingly, the data for the *FC:CF+C* ratio (3:2) indicate that he modulates his emotional discharges about as much as do most adults; however, it is also important to note that both of the *CF* answers involve blood, which are somewhat more primitive kinds of responses that tend to have less modulation than is reflected in the *FC:CF+C* ratio. This leads to the speculation that there is a potential for more emotional volatility than meets the eye. The seemingly impulsive-like destruction of his bicycle may add some support to this postulate.

The very low *Afr* (.46) denotes his tendency to avoid processing emotionally toned stimuli. This seems to be quite important as it may signify a subtle awareness of the problems that he encounters when dealing directly with feelings. For instance, a review

Table 95.   Data Concerning Affect for Protocol 2

DEPI = 5				*Blends*
EB = 4:3.5		*EBPer* = N/A		*M.CF*
eb = 6:3		*FC:CF+C* = 3:2		*M.FD*
		Pure *C* = 0		*FM.FC*
C' = 1	*T* = 0	*Afr* = 0.46		*FM.FC*
V = 0	*Y* = 2	*S* = 5		*FM.FD*
		Blends/*R* = 7:19		*FC'.FD*
		CP = 0		*m.CF*

of the responses that he gives to the five blots that contain chromatic coloring yields a dismal picture. Collectively, 10 of his 19 answers were given to those blots. They include all 5 of his minus answers, 6 of his 7 blends, 4 of his 5 S responses, and only 2 of the 10 answers have ordinary form quality. These findings seem to leave no doubt that, under emotional provocation, his functioning is far less than adequate. The five S responses convey a strong, negative attitude toward the environment, and suggest that, inside, he is boiling with anger. Blends comprise about 37% of his answers, indicating considerable psychological complexity. This is not unusual for an ambitent, but only one appears to have been created by situationally related factors ($m.CF$), and five of the seven involve ideationally related variables. It is also of interest to note that all three of his FD answers are blended.

SELF-PERCEPTION—PROTOCOL 2

The data related to issue of self-perception are shown in Table 96.

Table 96.   Self-Perception Data for Protocol 2

$3r + (2)/R = 0.47$	$FD = 3$	$MOR = 5$	$Hx = 0$	$An + Xy = 1$
$Fr + rF = 0$	Sum $V = 0$	$H:(H)+Hd+(Hd) = 3:8$		$Sx = 0$

		Responses to Be Read		
MOR Responses	$FQ-$ Responses	*M* Responses	*FM* Responses	*m* Responses
3, 5, 6, 7, 17	3, 4, 5, 15, 19	3, 5, 12, 13	2, 7, 14, 15	10, 17

The Egocentricity Index (.47), is beyond the expected level, suggesting that he is very self-focusing. This seems to be reaffirmed by the presence of three FD responses, signaling that he is quite involved in self-inspecting behaviors. The 11 human contents denote a very strong interest in people, but only three of the 11 are Pure H, indicating that his conceptions of people, including himself, are based much more on imagination than on real experience. There are five MOR responses, indicating that his self-image is marked by many negative features and that he may perceive himself as damaged in some way. The contents of the MOR answers seem to confirm the latter (response 3, a face spitting blood; response 5, this ll face they're pulling on . . . it's in the process of being torn apart; response 6, the neck is hanging off and the bottom is bent; response 7, here are his arms and they are a little deformed; response 17, the head of a pig that they killed).

Faces and heads are involved in four of his five minus responses. On Card II, it is "a face and a wide-open mouth spitting blood"; to Card II, "a grave with a cross at the tombstone . . ."; to Card III, ". . . two girls pulling on someone's face . . . [inquiry] . . . the eyes are bulging out of the guy's face . . ."; to Card IX, "the head of a pig they killed in the *Lord of the Flies* . . . [inquiry] . . . it is dripping blood . . . but evaporating up here . . . like all the juice inside is evaporating . . ."; to Card X, ". . . a face in it . . . [inquiry] . . . if u turn it upside down u get exactly the same . . ."

Two of the four human movement answers include minus form (face spitting blood, girls pulling on someone's face) while the remaining two are ordinary form: response 12 ". . . two Egyptian girls doing an Egyptial dance," and response 13, ". . . two gals rocking on rocking chairs" that are [inquiry] "balanced on the corner." All are strange and probably reflect the strangeness that he experiences about himself. The four *FM* answers also signify strangeness: response 2, "some kind of flying object . . . [inquiry] not working too hard . . ."; response 7, ". . . Coming out of his body is a dragon . . . [inquiry] . . . coming from between his legs . . ."; response 14, ". . . two bears climbing either side of a mountain, two pink bears . . ."; response 15, ". . . it looks like the bears have their paws on his hair." Similarly, the two *m* answers convey the same elusive, confused picture of self-concept; response 10, ". . . some kind of machine and it's speared half the sun," and response 17, ". . . all the juice is evaporating up into the air." None of the movement answers convey any solid sense of self. Essentially all are distorted in one way or another, and collectively, they present a picture of an individual who is very confused about who he is and what he is. In fact, at least one (the dragon coming out of his body) and probably two others (the machine that speared the sun and the juice evaporating into the air) seem to suggest a marked confusion about sex role and sexuality in general.

INTERPERSONAL PERCEPTION AND BEHAVIOR—PROTOCOL 2

Data relating to issues of interpersonal perception are shown in Table 97.

Table 97.   Interpersonal Perception Data for Protocol 2

$CDI = 1$	$a{:}p$ = 5:5	T = 0	Human Cont = 11	Pure $H = 3$
$HVI =$ Pos	Food = 0	$PER = 0$	$COP = 1$ $AG = 1$	*Isolate/R* = 0.21

Responses to Be Read	
Human Movement with Pair	*Human Contents*
5, 12, 13	1, 3, 5, 7, 9, 12, 13, 15, 16, 19

The positive *HVI* indicates a general mistrusting attitude toward others. People such as this feel quite vulnerable and are very cautious in their interactions. Typically, they are preoccupied with issues of personal space and are very guarded interpersonally. They do not anticipate close relations and usually become very suspicious about gestures of closeness by others. A core variable in the *HVI* is the absence of *T,* which relates to a lack of experienced needs for closeness that are common to people. This does not mean that the needs do not exist, rather that they are far less comfortable in close relationships, especially tactile relationships. Thus, even though he has a very strong interest in others, as illustrated by the 11 human contents, it is likely that the interest is more of a defensive preoccupation than desire for closeness. The only *COP* answer is also aggressive (2 girls pulling on someone's face). Answers in which both cooperative and aggressive movement occur have not been studied carefully, but since both are forms of projection, it does seem logical to assume that they reflect conflict, or at least confusion about interpersonal relationships.

Most of the 11 human contents also signify confusion about people. They include a pumpkin face with four eyes, someone screaming, spitting up blood, two girls pulling on someone's face, a "Keep on trucking" poster with a dragon coming from between his legs, a man with wings and antlers, Egyptian girls doing an Egyptial dance, two gals rocking on rocking chairs that are balanced on the corners, the face of an Eskimo or Indian type ruler, profiles of Alfred Hitchcock, and a face that looks exactly the same if you turn it upside down. None are typical responses and emphasize the lack of understanding that he has about people.

SUMMARY—PROTOCOL 2

It seems very apparent that this young man is quite disturbed. His thinking is confused and disordered, and he is very prone to distort reality rather severely. It seems very likely that he is a paranoid schizophrenic. He is inordinately affected by emotionally toned stimuli. Emotions seem to torment him and exacerbate his confused identity. He has become extraordinarily guarded in perceiving and dealing with people, and resorts to a form of psychological isolation as a way of defending himself from the threats posed by a world that he cannot contend with easily. He is obviously bright and has learned to draw on his resources in ways that permit him to maintain a facade of a withdrawn eccentric, but not severely disturbed, person. Beneath that facade, which tends to work well when he is not under unusually intense stress, is a very fragile and frightened person who is overly guarded about people and very confused about his own role in his environment. It seems quite probable that the prospect of assuming an adult role in life is becoming overwhelming to him. He has struggled to retain controls, but that battle has a considerable cost and he is gradually losing in his fight for stability.

The overall psychological picture is one of gradual deterioration, with an increasing probability that he will manifest overt characteristics of schizophrenia soon unless he is relieved of pressures to engage in a "normal" pattern of social interaction. The staff diagnosis of borderline personality disorder and the recommendation for long-term outpatient care is completely unrealistic. It seems clear that he is much more disturbed and fragile than is conveyed by simple preliminary observations and interviews, and the predictable consequences are a major disruption to his current form of cautious adaptation to his world. His hypervigilant-paranoid state cannot help but ultimately reduce his tolerance for new stress, because it requires a major commitment of many of his resources.

Intervention in a case such as this requires careful planning, plus a very tactful entry to the process. He is probably extremely unwilling to admit to any major problems and apparently was admitted only for evaluation. The "news" that he has a major disturbance may be met with considerable resistance, and any efforts to involve him into an active treatment program can be expected to be received with similar results. His statement at admission that his hospitalization will, ". . . maybe get some people off my back while I sort things out," forewarns of some of the difficulties that may be encountered by those who seek to help. Nonetheless, as with most all schizophrenics, there is a need to provide antipsychotic medication and stabilize him on the routine by which it is taken. But, before that can happen, there must be some concessions; first by the professional staff, who must be willing to share with him their understanding of the severity of his problem, and second by him and his family, who also must acknowledge the severity of the problem. If the professional staff are able to work around his marked paranoid guardedness, the prospect of outpatient care, designed to help him restructure his life and provide a continuing support system, may be viable. At the moment, he is probably a very frightened, confused, angry young man, and a form of supportive intervention that openly identifies the magnitude of his problem and offers a positive prospect for the future can be extremely helpful to him.

PROTOCOL 3: A QUESTION OF PSYCHOSOMATIC INVOLVEMENT

Referral   This 23-year-old female was referred for evaluation by her physician after reviewing the results of a neurological examination that he had requested. The neurological referral was made after her fifth visit to him during a 4-month period. Her initial complaint had been feelings of fatigue, but during each of the last two visits she also reported an increasing frequency of headaches. The neurological examination included an EEG and a CT-Scan, plus a neuropsychological examination. All results were negative, and the consulting neurologist recommended a psychiatric evaluation, suggesting that the headaches are probably psychosomatic. The data from the neuropsychological evaluation yielded a WAIS Verbal IQ of 136, with Scaled Scores ranging from 14 on Digit Span to 18 on Information, and a Performance IQ of 131, with Scaled Scores ranging from 11 on Picture Arrangement to 17 on Object Assembly. Her Wechsler Memory Quotient is 123. She made no errors on the Aphasia Screening Test, and her performances on the various tests of the Halstead-Reitan are all within normal limits.

History   The subject is the oldest of three children, having a sister, age 19, who is in her second year of college, and a brother, age 17, who is in his third year in high school. Both parents are living. Her father, age 47, is a journalist. Her mother, age 44, is a housewife. According to the subject, there is no psychiatric history in the immediate family. The developmental history she provides is unremarkable. She ranked second in her high school graduating class and went on to obtain a B.A. degree in sociology from a prestigious university, graduating magna cum laude at age 21. Shortly thereafter, she obtained employment with an advertising firm for which she continues to work. Currently, she is the leader of a six-member team responsible for designing and constructing layouts for TV and magazine advertising. She was promoted to her current position approximately 10 months prior to the evaluations. She states that she enjoys her work and feels that she has made several close friendships with her co-workers.

   She maintains her own apartment and reports a history of varied social-emotional relationships. She notes that, as a high school student, she dated frequently but had no sustained emotional ties. During college, she also dated frequently and did have one "prolonged" relationship during her sophomore year. Her first sexual experience was at age 18, during her first year at college, and since that time has engaged in intercourse with a variable frequency, ". . . depending on how much I get involved with the guy." She notes that she has manifested some poor judgment about sex, having become pregnant during the summer following her junior year in college. She learned of her pregnancy shortly before her senior year began and struggled with the idea of having an abortion. She decided against this and withdrew after completing the first semester of her senior year, at the onset of her third trimester of pregnancy, to live in a home for unwed expectant mothers. She was supported in this decision by her parents who she describes as being ". . . terrifically understanding about the whole mess." Early into her pregnancy, she had considered retaining custody of the child but ultimately decided to place the child, a female born during the spring, for adoption. She describes her decision as, "I know in my heart that I did the right thing. I don't believe that I could have given her everything that she needed and then both of our lives would have gotten worse. I know that she's in a good home because they are very careful about placement." She went on to add that she would like to have information about her daughter from time to time, but realizes that is impossible. She returned to the university during the summer following the birth and graduated in August.

She discounts the possibility that her headaches are related to the decision to relinquish custody of her daughter, "If they are really psychological, they are because I'm not happy with myself now." She freely admits to having several disappointments in her more recent emotional life, noting that most of the men with whom she becomes involved do not meet her standards, "I don't think I expect too much, but they all seem so immature, and I want more than that in a relationship." None of the relationships that she has established with men since her graduation have lasted longer than 6 months, and she has consistently refused propositions to "live in." She does want to marry and looks forward to having children. She notes that she had headaches during high school and college, ". . . usually when I felt the pressure of exams," but argues that they were "different" from the ones she now experiences. She describes them as being "more dull," in contrast to the current ones, which she characterizes as having a rapid onset and being one-sided, ". . . usually on the left, but not always." She says that now they occur with a much greater frequency, often four to six times per week. She says that the pain is "very sharp" and admits that her physician has chided her because she tends to abuse antipain medication that he has prescribed.

Protocol 3. A 23-Year-Old-Female

Card		Response	Inquiry	Scoring
I	1.	Ugh, ths re me of a witch burning of s.s., lik in Salem E: Take your time, u'll probably find somethg else too	E: (Rpts S's resp) S: The witch is in the cntr w her arms up in the air, its a vague outline bec of all the smoke rising all around her. The fire isn't obvious but the smok is billowing all around her, all dark	$W+$ $M^p.m^a.YFu$ $(H), Fi$ 4.0 MOR
	2.	I suppose it c.b a bf too but is all ruined w holes in it	E: (Rpts S's resp) S: These c.b. wgs (points) but thy r pretty ragged, its dead I suppose bec of the holes in the wgs	WSo Fo A P 3.5 MOR
II	3.	This is grotesque, I thk it c.b. 2 people fiting & both are badly injured	E: (Rpts S's resp) S: Thy ll twins bec thy'r the same on each side, thy r surely hurtg e.o. bec of the bld on their heads & all over their lowr prts, c all the red, it c.b. prehistoric men in a death struggle, bent in agony, neither wants to lose in spite of those wounds	$W+$ $M^a.CFo$ 2 (H) BL 4.5 $MOR,$ AG
	4.	The cntr c.b. water in a pit or puddle	E: (Rpts S's resp) S: I thk of the white prt as the water & its down in this pit, the sides around it seem to go in E: Go in? S: The different colors give it a sense of depth	$DdSv/+$ VFo Na 4.5
III	5.	My God, ths ll 2 ghouls, thy r tugging at a baskt of bones	E: (Rpts S's resp) S: It struck me rite away lik that, 2 indescribable creatures, lik in sc fict having torn some poor A apart & now thy'r fiting over the bones	$D+$ M^ao 2 $(H),$ An P 3.0 $MOR,$ AG

581

Protocol 3 (Continued)

Card	Response		Inquiry	Scoring
IV	6. Some creature lying down, lik from sc fict all cvrd w moss or s.t., mayb fur, yes mayb fur or moss, a vague hulk w the feet towd u	E: S:	(Rpts S's resp) The feet r so big he must be lying dwn w the ft toward u & it ll moss all over him, its not real, just a sc fict creature lying there, lik a martian	W + $M^P.FT.FDo$ (H) Bt P 4.0
V	7. Well, the most I can mak of it is a bat swooping down lik to get s.t., like to grab it	E: S:	(Rpts S's resp) The wgs wide sprd & its all dark black, lik it was at nite, it has claws out here (points)	Wo $FM^a.FC'o$ A P 1.0 AG
VI	8. Ths thg c.b. roots	E: S:	(Rpts S's resp) It was almost an afterthot, thy just ll roots of a bush or tree	Do Fo Bt
	9. My first impression was of a totem pole, lik the Indians worship	E: S: E: S:	(Rpts S's resp) I supp thy don't really worship the pole but what it stands for I'm not sure how u c it It has wgs & ths (points is the pole)	Do Fo Ay
VII	10. It ll fried food to me, not really chicken or shrimp, mayb shrimp, u can c the roundedness of the pieces, mayb scallops, yes two on each side	E:	Yes, probably scallops, thy'r breaded, several pieces, 4 of them, 2 on each side, like a pattern, just up here (points), the way thy r painted on here makes them ll thy'r dimensional	Do FVu Fd
VIII	11. Ths ll s.t. from an Anat book, an illustration of different parts of the human insides	E: S:	(Rpts S's resp) The rib cage is there, c the spaces in betwn the ribs (points) & the pink c.b. lungs or kidneys & the lowr part the stomach, its all colorful the way an Anat illustr is in the bio. texts	WS+ FCo An, Art 4.5
	12. The lowr part c.b. ice cream too, orange & strawberry mixed in a bunch	E: S:	(Rpts S's resp) Just a scoop of mixed ice cream as if it were made that way, I'v never seen it lik this tho	Dv CF.YFo Fd

IX	v 13.	Ths way its an explosion, lik an atomic explosion with the flames & smoke shooting out all over	E: (Rpts S's resp) S: Well it has the mushroom cloud & there is fire (orange) & smoke (green) all over, the different colors of the green give the impr of the layers of smoke	$W +$ $m^a.CF.VFo$ Ex,Fi 5.5
X	14.	A maple seed has landed in a puddle of water	E: (Rpts S's resp) S: It's rite here (points) & the white is the puddle of water, its just laying there with no place to root	$DdS +$ $m^p o$ Na 6.0 MOR
	15.	A crab has caught a bug	E: (Rpts S's resp) S: Ths blue prt is the crab & the little grn prt is the bug, the crab has caught it & will eat it I suppose, it has no chance to get away bec of all the legs of the crab	$D +$ $FM^a o$ A P 4.0 AG
	16.	A cocker spaniel, 2 of thm, waiting for s.t. to happen, just sitting there	E: (Rpts S's resp) S: It ll one on each side, as if thy were just sitting & waiting, c this is the frmt leg	Do $FM^p o$ 2 A

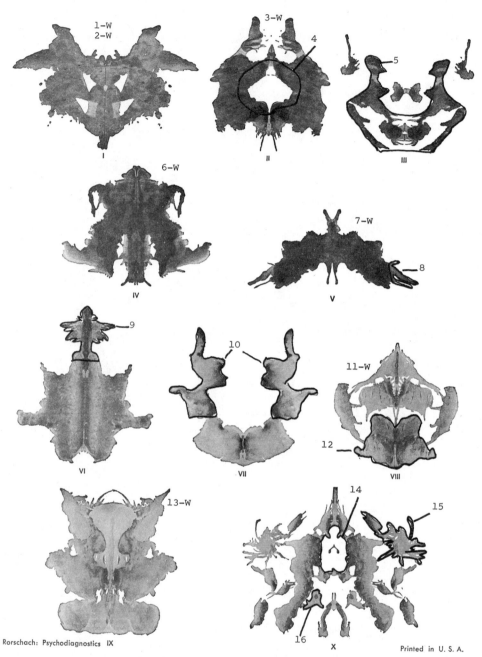

Figure 19.   Location Selections for Protocol 3.

Table 98.   Protocol 3: Sequence of Scores

CARD	NO	LOC	#	DETERMINANT(S)	(2)	CONTENT(S)	POP	Z	SPECIAL SCORES
I	1	W+	1	Mp.ma.YFu		(H),Fi		4.0	AG,MOR
	2	WSo	1	Fo		A	P	3.5	MOR
II	3	W+	1	Ma.CFo	2	H,Bl		4.5	MOR,AG
	4	DdS/	99	VFo		Na		4.5	
III	5	D+	1	Mao	2	(H),An	P	3.0	MOR,AG
IV	6	W+	1	Mp.FT.FDo		(H),Bt	P	4.0	
V	7	Wo	1	FMa.FC'o		A	P	1.0	AG
	8	Do	10	Fo		Bt			
VI	9	Do	3	Fo		Ay			
VII	10	D+	2	FVo	2	Fd		3.0	
VIII	11	WS+	1	FC-		An,Art		4.5	
	12	Dv	2	CF.YFo		Fd			
IX	13	W+	1	ma.CF.VFo		Ex,Fi		5.5	
X	14	DdS+	29	mpo		Na		6.0	MOR
	15	D+	1	FMao		A	P	4.0	AG
	16	Do	2	FMpo	2	A			

Copyright (c) 1976, 1985, 1990 by John E. Exner, Jr.

Table 99.   Protocol 3—Structural Summary

```
================================================================================
LOCATION              DETERMINANTS            CONTENTS      S-CONSTELLATION
FEATURES                BLENDS        SINGLE                 YES..FV+VF+V+FD>2
                                                H   = 1, 0   YES..Col-Shd Bl>0
Zf    = 12        M.m.YF            M   = 1    (H) = 3, 0   YES..Ego<.31,>.44
ZSum  = 47.5      M.CF              FM  = 2    Hd  = 0, 0   YES..MOR > 3
ZEst  = 38.0      M.FT.FD           m   = 1    (Hd)= 0, 0   YES..Zd > +- 3.5
                  FM.FC'            FC  = 1    Hx  = 0, 0   YES..es > EA
W   = 7           CF.YF             CF  = 0    A   = 4, 0   YES..CF+C > FC
(Wv = 0)          m.CF.VF           C   = 0    (A) = 0, 0   NO..X+% < .70
D   = 7                             Cn  = 0    Ad  = 0, 0   YES..S > 3
Dd  = 2                             FC' = 0    (Ad)= 0, 0   NO..P < 3 or > 8
S   = 4                             C'F = 0    An  = 1, 1   YES..Pure H < 2
                                    C'  = 0    Art = 0, 1   YES..R < 17
    DQ                              FT  = 0    Ay  = 1, 0     10.....TOTAL
........(FQ-)                       TF  = 0    Bl  = 0, 1
+   = 9  ( 1)                       T   = 0    Bt  = 1, 1    SPECIAL SCORINGS
o   = 5  ( 0)                       FV  = 1    Cg  = 0, 0         Lv1     Lv2
v/+ = 1  ( 0)                       VF  = 1    Cl  = 0, 0   DV   = 0x1     0x2
v   = 1  ( 0)                       V   = 0    Ex  = 1, 0   INC  = 0x2     0x4
                                    FY  = 0    Fd  = 2, 0   DR   = 0x3     0x6
                                    YF  = 0    Fi  = 0, 2   FAB  = 0x4     0x7
                                    Y   = 0    Ge  = 0, 0   ALOG = 0x5
   FORM QUALITY                     Fr  = 0    Hh  = 0, 0   CON  = 0x7
                                    rF  = 0    Ls  = 0, 0        SUM6  = 0
     FQx  FQf  MQual  SQx           FD  = 0    Na  = 2, 0        WSUM6 = 0
+  =  0    0     0     0            F   = 3    Sc  = 0, 0
o  = 14    3     3     3                       Sx  = 0, 0
u  =  1    0     1     0                       Xy  = 0, 0   AB   = 0     CP  = 0
-  =  1    0     0     1                       Id  = 0, 0   AG   = 5     MOR = 5
none=  0   --     0     0           (2) =  4               CFB  = 0     PER = 0
                                                            COP  = 0     PSV = 0
================================================================================
                   RATIOS, PERCENTAGES, AND DERIVATIONS

R = 16         L =  0.23            FC:CF+C = 1: 3    COP = 0    AG = 5
--------------------------------    Pure C  =    0    Food      = 2
EB = 4: 3.5  EA =  7.5   EBPer= N/A  Afr     =0.60     Isolate/R =0.38
eb = 6: 7    es = 13     D  = -2     S       =    4    H:(H)Hd(Hd)= 1: 3
             Adj es = 10  Adj D =  0  Blends:R= 6:16   (HHd):(AAd)= 3: 0
--------------------------------    CP      =    0    H+A:Hd+Ad = 8: 0
FM = 3  :  C'= 1   T = 1
m  = 3  :  V = 3   Y = 2
                      P   = 5       Zf  =12          3r+(2)/R=0.25
a:p    = 6: 4   Sum6  = 0   X+% =0.88   Zd  = +9.5   Fr+rF   = 0
Ma:Mp  = 2: 2   Lv2   = 0   F+% =1.00   W:D:Dd = 7: 7: 2   FD = 1
2AB+Art+Ay= 2   WSum6 = 0   X-% =0.06   W:M = 7: 4   An+Xy = 2
M-    = 0       Mnone = 0   S-% =1.00   DQ+ = 9      MOR   = 5
                           Xu% =0.06   DQv = 1
--------------------------------------------------------------------------------
  SCZI = 1     DEPI = 6*    CDI = 2     S-CON =10*   HVI = No   OBS = No
================================================================================
Copyright (c) 1976, 1985, 1990 by John E. Exner, Jr.
```

S-CON—PROTOCOL 3

Before reviewing the list of Key variables to determine the appropriate search strategy, it is very important to note the positive Suicide Constellation (10), which suggests a marked preoccupation with self-destructive thoughts. In that she is an outpatient, immediate action should be taken to explore this probability, especially because her presenting complaints include no indication of serious depression or suicidal thinking. It should be made clear that she has many of the characteristics common to those who have effected their own deaths. There is always the possibility that the Constellation has identified a false positive, particularly if substantial depression is present; however, it would be foolhardy to ignore the finding. Usually, a brief interview, conducted by a skilled professional and focusing on the issue, will uncover inclinations toward self-destruction, even if information developed in earlier interviews has failed to do so.

INTERPRETIVE ROUTINE FOR PROTOCOL 3

The first positive Key variable is the *DEPI,* which has a value of six. This signifies that her personality structure include features that predispose frequent and intense episodes of emotional disruption. Typically, patients with a *DEPI* value of this magnitude have a major affective disorder, or at the very least, will be diagnosed as having dysthymia, assuming that schizophrenia is not present. Thus, the interpretive strategy for this record will be:

Affect → Controls → Situational Stress (because the *D* Score is less than the Adjusted *D* Score) → Self-Perception → Interpersonal Perception → Processing → Mediation → Ideation

AFFECT—PROTOCOL 3

The data concerning affect for this record are shown in Table 100.

When the *DEPI* is positive, and especially if the value is six or seven, it is always useful to review the 14 tests that comprise the Index to determine if there is any notable homogeneity among the positive variables. Six of the tests include variables (vista, color-shading blends, *S, Afr* < .46, sum shading > *FM* +*m*) related directly to affective features. Six others (*FD,* Egocentricity Index, Blends < 4, *MOR,* Intellectualization Index) are related more to cognitive features, while the remaining two (*COP,* Isolation Index) concern interpersonal attributes. Usually, when a major affective disturbance is involved, a review of the 14 tests will reveal a heterogeneous mixture of positive variables, but in some cases a clear majority of the positive tests relate either to affective or cognitive features. When this occurs, the finding is often useful in understanding the nature of the affective disruption identified by the positive *DEPI* and can be particularly important when considering treatment alternatives. In this case, the subject is positive for 8 of the 14 tests, of which 4 are affective (vista, color-shading blends, *S,* sum shading > *FM* +*m*), 2 are cognitive (Egocentricity Index, *MOR*), and 2 are interpersonal, a mix

Table 100.   Data Concerning Affect for Protocol 3

DEPI = 6			*Blends*
EB = 4:3.5	*EBPer* = N/A		*M.m.YF*
eb = 6:7	*FC:CF* +*C* = 1:3		*M.FT.FD*
	Pure *C* = 0		*M.CF*
C' = 1 *T* = 1	*Afr* = 0.60		*FM.FC'*
V = 3 *Y* = 2	*S* = 4		*m.CF.VF*
	Blends/*R* = 5:25		*CF.YF*
	CP = 0		

that does not show much consistency. Thus, it is likely that the affective problem is related to, and intrudes on all three general areas.

The *EB* identifies her as an ambitent. Therefore, the use of her emotions in her thinking is inconsistent, sometimes impacting markedly on her judgments and decisions and at other times playing only a peripheral role. The right-side value for the *eb* is greater than the left side, signaling considerable distress, especially because the value (7) is considerably greater than expected. The substantial number of vista answers appears to be the main source of the elevated value and signifies that she is engaging in considerable self-examining behavior, and apparently is focusing mainly on features that she regards as liabilities. The result is negative, irritating affect and, in this instance, is probably quite tormenting.

The *FC:CF+C* ratio (1:3) indicates that she does not modulate her emotional discharges very well. When they occur, they tend to become overly intense and, at times, become very intrusive in her thinking, decisions, and behaviors. When she releases affect, it is likely that those around her are very aware of her feelings. Although none of the color answers are Pure *C*, the contents of the three *CF* answers tend to be more primitive or juvenile than is expected of bright adults (blood, food, fire). There is no reason to believe that she avoids emotionally provoking stimuli as the *Afr* is within the average range. A very important finding concerns the Space responses (4). They suggest a very negative, oppositional, and probably hostile attitude toward the world, and undoubtably, that hostility intrudes into much of her thinking and behavior. There are 6 blends in this relatively brief record of 16 answers (38%), which is not necessarily unusual for an ambitent, but high nonetheless. It signifies considerable complexity in her current psychological operations. Two of the blends simply may be manifestations of her current stress, but even if they are discounted, at least one color-shading blend remains (*m.CF.VF*), indicating a confusion about feeling and the frequent experience of ambivalence.

CONTROLS, STRESS TOLERANCE AND SITUATIONAL STRESS—PROTOCOL 3

The data related to issues of capacity for control and tolerance for stress are shown in Table 101.

Her situation is made more complex by the presence of some reasonably intense situational stress. The *D* Score is −2, but when adjusted, becomes 0. Under ordinary conditions, she usually has enough available resource to form meaningfully and direct responses. The *EA*, (7.5) though not substantial, is average, and the values in the *EB* give no cause to challenge the validity of the Adjusted *D* Score. Thus, typically, she is able to handle stresses about as well as most adults. However, the current situation is quite different. The *D* Score of −2, which is created because of three *m* and two *Y* responses,

Table 101. Controls and Stress Tolerance Data for Protocol 3

EB = 4:3.5		*EA* = 7.5		*D* = −2	
eb = 6:7		*es* = 13	*Adj es* = 10	*AdjD* = 0	
FM = 3	*C'* = 1	*T* = 1		*CDI* = 2	
m = 3	*V* = 3	*Y* = 2			

indicates that she is experiencing serious problems in control and the corresponding feelings of helplessness often produced by such problems.

The magnitude of the stimulus overload state is so extensive that it is very likely she often experiences demands to which she is unable to make well-organized responses. In many instances, her decisions may not be formulated fully, or her efforts to implement responses may be marked by some disorganization. Her tolerance for stress in this state is very limited and easily exceeded. She is especially vulnerable to impulsiveness in new or unexpected situations that go beyond the easily recognized structure of daily routines. It might be speculated that the increase in the frequency and intensity of her headaches is the product of the situationally related condition. On the other hand, the situational condition could, itself, be the result of an increasing awareness of frequent intense depressive episodes and her inability to contend effectively with them. In either event, the impact of the current stress is severe and creating considerable interference in some of her customary patterns of thinking and/or behavior. Two of her blend answers seem stress related, suggesting that her level of complexity has been increased by the situational elements, and of the two, one is a color-shading blend, implying that her ambivalence or confusion about feelings has also intensified because of situationally related factors.

It is important to note that the history she provides includes no mention of any situationally related stress-producing features. She was promoted approximately 10 months earlier and maintains that she gets along well with her colleagues. She admits to an erratic love life, but there is no evidence of recent loss or disappointment. If the history is accurate, the current stress may well be more internally created than produced by her interactions with the world. If so, the potential consequences of the positive Suicide Constellation become much more ominous.

SELF-PERCEPTION—PROTOCOL 3

Data concerning self perception for this record are shown in Table 102.

The low Egocentricity Index (.25) indicates that she regards herself less favorably when she makes comparisons of her own worth to that which she perceives for others, especially those significant to her. The issue of the three vista responses has been addressed earlier but probably should be assessed again in conjunction with the one *FD* answer. In other words, one-fourth of her 16 answers contain evidence of self-inspection. This is extraordinarily disproportionate and probably signals an almost obsessive kind of rumination about the self, which clearly leads to distress. Added to these findings are the morbid content answers (5) which denote that the self-image includes some very negative, unwanted features that promote a pessimistic view of the self and the world, and

Table 102. Self-Perception Data for Protocol 3

$3r + (2)/R = 0.25$	$FD = 1$	$MOR = 5$	$Hx = 0$	$An + Xy = 2$
$Fr + rF = 0$	Sum $V = 3$	$H:(H)+Hd+(Hd) = 1:3$		$Sx = 0$

Responses to Be Read				
MOR Responses	*FQ*− Responses	*M* Responses	*FM* Responses	*m* Responses
1, 2, 3, 5, 14	11	1, 3, 5, 6	7, 15, 16	1, 13, 14

become very influential in many decisions. Collectively, these are the ingredients from which dysphoric experiences evolve quite easily, and because all three are relatively stable variables, it seems likely that she has been experiencing considerable depression for quite some time.

There are only four human contents in the record and only one is Pure *H,* suggesting that her conception of herself is grounded much more in imagination than reality. There are also two anatomy responses, indicating that she probably has much more body concern than is common for an adult, however, this is not unexpected in light of her presenting complaints.

The record is very rich in projected material, especially the *MOR* responses. Actually, *MOR* is scored in four of the first five answers. She begins the test with a morbid, negative response, ". . . a witch burning of some sort . . . [inquiry] . . . a vague outline because of all the smoke rising all around her . . ." It probably reflects both her feelings of negativism about herself and her sense of helplessness about it. The sense of damage is conveyed again in the second answer, ". . . a butterfly too but it is all ruined . . . [inquiry] . . . it's dead I suppose . . . ," and again in the third answer, ". . . two people fighting and both are *badly* injured [inquiry] . . . they are surely hurting each other . . . in a death struggle, bent in agony . . ." The morbidity persists in the fifth answer, ". . . two ghouls, they're tugging at a basket of bones [inquiry] . . . two indescribable creatures . . . having torn some poor animal apart and now they're fighting over the bones." The other *MOR* answer occurs in response 14, "A maple seed has landed in a puddle of water [inquiry] . . . it's just laying there with no place to root."

Three of her four *M*'s are included in the *MOR* responses (witch burning, people fighting, ghouls tugging) while the fourth is her only answer to Card IV, "Some creature lying down . . . covered with moss or something, maybe fur or moss [inquiry] it looks like moss all over him." Technically, it is not a *MOR* answer but certainly hints at morbidity and also an obvious conflict that she seems to have about herself (whether she is covered with fur or moss; whereas fur has a protective and desirable feature, moss has no protective property and is prone to grow in dank places).

Two of her three *FM* answers have aggressive contents. The first, to Card V, ". . . a bat swooping down like to get something, like to grab it." The second, in response 15, is also aggressive, but at the same time, conveys a marked sense of helplessness, "A crab has caught a bug [inquiry] . . . and will eat it I suppose, it has no chance to get away . . ." Her third animal movement response is her final answer (16) and has a helpless and somewhat ominous quality, "A cocker spaniel, two of them, waiting for something to happen, just sitting there."

Two of the three *m* answers are also included among the *MOR* responses (smoke billowing, seed laying). The third, to Card IX, is ". . . an atomic explosion with the flames and smoke shooting out all over." All three reflect a clear lack of control. Some of her other elaborations probably add information about her negative and pessimistic sense of self. For instance, she begins three of the first five answers with negative comments: (1) ugh, (3) this is grotesque, (5) my God. Her response to Card VI is quite intriguing: ". . . a totem pole like the Indians worship [inquiry] I suppose they don't really worship the pole but what it stands for . . ." It seems quite symbolic although the meaning is not fully clear. On a simplistic level it may raise questions about sexual preoccupations, but on a different level it could relate to some confusion about status.

INTERPERSONAL PERCEPTION AND BEHAVIOR—PROTOCOL 3

Data related to interpersonal perception are shown in Table 103.

Table 103.   Interpersonal Perception Data for Protocol 3

$CDI = 2$	$a{:}p = 6{:}4$	$T = 1$	Human Cont $= 4$	Pure $H = 1$
$HVI = $ Neg	Food $= 2$	$PER = 0$	$COP = 0$ $AG = 5$	$Isolate/R = 0.38$

Responses to Be Read

Human Movement with Pair	*Human Contents*
3, 5	1, 3, 5, 6

The data for the *CDI, HVI,* and *a:p* ratio are not relevant. The two Food responses are very important because they signal a strong dependency orientation and the presence of a *T* response, albeit unusual (Card IV), confirms that she does experience needs for closeness. The number of human contents (4) is about average for an ambient and illustrates an interest in others, but the presence of only one Pure *H* signifies that her understanding of people is very limited and probably not well founded in real experience. One of the most important findings in this cluster is the absence of *COP* responses and the very large number of *AG* answers (5). They indicate that she perceives aggression as a routine part of interpersonal life, and her own interpersonal activity usually will include forceful and/or aggressive behaviors that, typically, will be obvious to even the casual observer. This does not mean that they will be asocial or antisocial, but her current overload state, plus the fact that she does not modulate her emotional displays very well, does suggest that they will be less well controlled and probably somewhat intense.

It is not surprising to note a positive Isolation Index (.38). Such a finding might be predicted from her history, but even if the history were not available, most of the accumulated data regarding her emotions, her self-image, and her aggressiveness do not support predictions of deep, close relations with others. The only human movement answers containing a pair are both aggressive and morbid (people fighting in a death struggle and ghouls fighting over bones), and none of her human contents are positive (a witch, prehistoric men, ghouls, and a science-fiction creature covered with moss).

INFORMATION PROCESSING—PROTOCOL 3

The data related to processing activity are shown in Table 104.

Table 104.   Processing Data for Protocol 3

$HVI = $ Neg	$W{:}D{:}Dd = 7{:}7{:}2$	$PSV = +9.5$	$DQv/+ = 9$
$L = 0.23$	$W{:}D{:}Dd = 7{:}7{:}2$	$Zd = +9.5$	$DQ+ = 9$
$Zf = 12$	$W{:}M = 7{:}4$	$PSV = 0$	$DQv/+ = 1$
$HVI = $ Neg	$OBS = $ Neg		$DQv = 1$

Location Sequencing

I: W.WS	IV: W	VII: *D*
II: W.DdS	V: W.D	VIII: WS.D
III: *D*	VI: *D*	IX: W
		X: *DdS.D.D*

The value for *Lambda* is quite low. Pure *F* responses, when not used excessively, can be viewed as a healthy backing away from complexity, as if psychologically resting and using a simpler approach to the task. The failure to do this raises three interpretive possibilities. First, some people have difficulty identifying the most economical ways of handling task demand. Generally, they are victims of their unfulfilled needs, conflicts, and/or emotional turmoil. Their preoccupations and/or apprehensions interfere with concentration or logical reasoning, and they fail to perceive easier or economical solutions, which leads to an overinvolvement with stimuli around them. It is not a deliberate involvement, but rather an inability to back away. Usually, when this is the cause of the low *L,* there will be many features in the record that signal turmoil, as is the case here.

Two other conditions can also produce a low *Lambda.* Both can be viewed more positively than the circumstance of psychological turmoil. Achievement-oriented people have the advantage of being flexible and able to adapt easily to situations. If they view the test as a challenge, they often sacrifice economy for accomplishment and they frequently reject simpler responses and strive to deal effectively with the complexity of the stimuli. When the low *Lambda* is created by this striving, many features of the record will convey a picture of control, flexibility, adaptability, and psychological sturdiness, which is not the case here. The third condition that often produces a low *Lambda* is also related to accomplishment, but it is created less from the sense to challenge and more from the need to avoid error or failure. It is the overincorporative style that prompts the subject to invest more effort in organizing the stimulus field than is necessary. It is a cognitive inefficiency that can be either an asset or liability, depending on the circumstance. When overincorporation exists, other data concerning stability, reality testing, clarity of thinking, stress tolerance, and control are decisive elements in determining whether the low *Lambda* is cause for concern, or merely a by-product of the firmly entrenched cognitive style. She is an overincorporator as reflected by the *Zd* score (+9.5) and thus, it is possible that there has been a chronic tendency to become overly involved with stimuli; but it has probably been exacerbated by her emotional turmoil, so that now, her failure to economize more often may increase her overall vulnerability.

Actually, the other data in the cluster, including the overincorporative style, can be regarded positively. The *Zf, W:D:Dd,* and *W:M* ratios all indicate that she is well motivated in processing efforts and the overincorporative style signifies that she works hard to make sure that all cues are included in the input process. Nine of her 16 answers are synthesized, demonstrating good quality processing. There is one *DQv* answer (ice cream), which may reflect the occasional impact of her strong dependency needs on her processing activities. The sequencing of location selections is quite consistent. All but one of her *W* answers are first responses, and all remaining answers are *D* except for one *Dd* answer that she gives at the beginning of Card X.

COGNITIVE MEDIATION—PROTOCOL 3

Data related to mediation for this record are shown in Table 105.

The five Popular responses indicate that she is able to make commonplace translations of new stimuli, but possibly more important is the fact that the *X*+% is 88% and the record contains only one minus, and one unusual answer. A question was raised earlier about

Table 105.   Data Concerning Cognitive Mediation for Protocol 3

Lambda = 0.23	OBS = Neg	Minus Features
P = 5	X + % = .88	11
FQx + = 0	F + % = 1.00	
FQxo = 14	Xu% = .06	
FQxu = 1	X − % = .06	
FQx − = 1	S − % = 1.00	
FQxnone = 0	CONFAB = 0	

whether her marked tendencies toward aggressiveness might manifest in asocial or antiso-cial activity, especially in light of her problems in modulating emotional displays. The data concerning mediation argue strongly against that possibility. She is very attuned to convention, and seeks to make sure that most of her behaviors will fall into that frame-work. In fact, she may be a bit too committed to making conventional and/or acceptable responses and could be sacrificing some of her own individuality to do so.

IDEATION—PROTOCOL 3

The data related to ideational activity are shown in Table 106.

Table 106.   Data Concerning Ideation for Protocol 3

EB = 4:3.5	EBPer = N/A	M Quality	Critical Special Scores			
eb = 6:7	(FM = 3 m = 3)	+ = 0	DV = 0		DV2 = 0	
a:p = 6:4	M^a:M^p = 2:2	o = 3	INC = 0		INC2 = 0	
2AB +Art +Ay = 2		u = 1	DR = 0		DR2 = 0	
MOR = 5		− = 0	FAB = 0		FAB2 = 0	
			ALOG = 0		SUM6 = 0	
Responses to Be Read for Quality			CON = 0		WSUM6 = 0	
1, 3, 5, 6						

The findings concerning her thinking include several positive features, but there are three detrimental characteristics that warrant careful consideration. The first is her in-consistency in problem solving/decision-making operations reflected by the data of the *EB*. As an ambient, she often requires more time to come to closure on issues, is prone to make more problem-solving errors, and is also prone to repeat errors more often than should be the case. Ordinarily, this might not be a major hazard for an extremely bright person, but when impinged upon by considerable turmoil, it may serve to contribute to the turmoil. For instance, all 4 of her *M* answers appear as first responses to each of the first 4 cards and are included in the sequence of her first 6 answers. They reflect the tactic of delay and thinking things through common to the introversive style. The same 6-answer sequence also includes 4 of her 5 *MOR* contents, 3 of her 5 *AG* contents, 3 of her 5 Popular answers, and 6 of the 12 responses containing *Z*. Following Card IV, the an-swers tend to be less sophisticated, less well organized, and more dominated by affective characteristics and/or the *FM* and *m* variables that are related to peripheral ideational activity. The latter are present in each of her last 4 answers. In fact, the last 10 answers contain only 2 Popular responses, the only minus response, the only *DQv* response, and proportionally far fewer organized answers. It is almost as if the ideational style gave rise to more disruptive experiences, causing her to discard that approach in favor of one involving less quality, but through which she could avoid direct focus on her negative self-image and interpersonal turmoil. This finding gives rise to the speculation that, under different conditions, her preferred style may be more introversive, but that the marked affective disarray has interfered with that tendency.

The second negative feature marking her thinking is peripheral ideation. The left-side value in the *eb* is only six, which is within expected limits, but half of that value is comprised of *m* answers suggesting that a considerable increase in this kind of mental activity has occurred because of situationally related factors. Substantial increases in peripheral ideation, such as this, often impair attention and concentration considerably.

The third detriment to her thinking may be the most important for the moment. It is the large number of *MOR* answers (5), which indicates that her thinking is almost chronically infiltrated by a strong pessimistic feature. Invariably, this impacts on her conceptualizations and becomes very influential in her decisions. Her thinking is filled with gloom and doom and can only serve to intensify the experiences of emotional disruption when they occur.

On a more positive note, the *a:p* ratio offers no reason to suspect unusual inflexibility in her thinking or attitudes, the $M^a:M^p$ ratio is not positive, and the Intellectualization Index only has a value of two. More important, there are no critical Special Scores and no *M* − answers. Thus, her thinking, except for the marked pessimism, remains reasonably clear and unimpaired, and even though the content of her *M* answers is more negative than positive, the quality of those four responses is quite sophisticated and commensurate with what might be expected from a highly intelligent person.

SUMMARY—PROTOCOL 3

This is a very seriously depressed woman who seems to be hanging onto her world by her psychological fingertips. A suicide potential is very real and immediate attention to this issue is required. It is important to note that she has visited her physician five times during a four-month interval, complaining first about fatigue and subsequently about headaches that have increased in frequency and intensity. These symptoms are probably indirect pleas for help and not simple manifestations of a psychosomatic involvement. She is in considerable pain, but apparently some threads of a need to present herself in ways that do not threaten her integrity further inhibit her from sharing the torment that is present. Instead, she has resorted to a previous symptom pattern, headaches, to seek attention and support.

It seems clear that the depression she experiences has been present in a serious form for quite some time, and is increasing in both frequency and intensity. She is not very consistent in her problem-solving or decision-making activities and this becomes an added burden in light of her turmoil. She does not modulate her emotional displays very well and is often more intense and less well controlled in her use of feelings than is expected of a bright adult. She harbors a great negativism or anger toward the world, and this will often influence her judgment and decisions. Currently, the impact of her chronic depression has become even more disruptive because of some situationally experienced stress. The cause of the latter is not clear. It could relate to some new interpersonal disappointment, or it could be the product of an increasing awareness about many of her own deficiencies. It could also be the product of the accumulated experiences of frustration that she has encountered. In any event, it has placed her on the brink of major disorganization. Her stress tolerance is badly impaired and she is very prone to impulsiveness. Her current state of substantial stimulus overload creates continual hazards to her efforts at effecting functioning, and although she often makes a strong effort to contend with her pain, it ultimately becomes overwhelming and causes her to drift into less mature forms of passive resignation concerning her plight.

She is, and has been, continually battered by a very negative self-image and the consequences of a prolonged struggle with herself. She ruminates about her negative features and has a conceptualization of herself filled with features that she does not like and which, in her thinking, cause others to reject her. She sees the world and interpersonal relationships as being marked by aggression and apparently will often manifest aggressiveness in her contacts with others, albeit in forms that are usually within socially acceptable limits. This tactic, when added to the fact that she has never developed a reality-based conception of people, serves to ensure that her interpersonal relations are superficial and short-lived. She has strong needs to be dependent on others and her failure to experience the close relationships that she would prefer only exacerbates these needs. The cyclical experiences of failure in interpersonal relations have served to reinforce her negative self-image and further reduce the value she places on her personal worth.

She is very intelligent and still able to use some of her more sophisticated cognitive operations very effectively. She processes new information very thoroughly and in a sophisticated manner. She is extremely "conventionality oriented" when translating new information, almost too much so, and this may be causing her to abrogate some of her own individuality. She wants to conform, but, in her own eyes, has never achieved that objective. In spite of her horrendous emotional turmoil, her thinking remains clear, although it does seem impaired at times by a terrible pessimistic attitude toward herself and the world. She does not expect positive outcomes regardless of her own effort.

The antecedents to the depression are not fully clear, although it seems obvious that the distinction between her perceived self-image and her hopes and expectations constitute the seeds from which the turmoil has grown. Similarly, her interpersonal failures, especially those involving closeness and dependency, have added to the growth. Although she denies that her decision to relinquish custody of her daughter plays any role in her current state, that issue should not be overlooked as an important predisposing factor.

In light of the suicide potential and the current state of psychological overload, it would be foolish to disregard her very precarious state. Both are factors that argue strongly against initiating efforts at intervention without providing considerable structure and continual support for her. Hospitalization, at least for a brief period, seems warranted. She needs to be eased into a recognized pattern of intervention supports, including well-defined preliminary objectives, that she can clearly understand and will help her to acknowledge the pain now bottled up inside. This should not require any lengthy period and can also become a platform from which planning for outpatient care can occur. Outpatient treatment will be lengthy and should focus first on tactics that will break into the pessimistic cognitive links that continually reinforce her negative sense of self. Ultimately, treatment must focus on the development of new interpersonal strategies and a more effective use of her feelings as they impact on her, on her decision making, and on her interactions with others.

PROTOCOL 4: A QUESTION OF IMPULSIVENESS

Referral   This is a court referral, the subject having been indicted on one count of aggravated assault and one count of attempted homicide. He is alleged to have attempted to strangle his "live-in" girlfriend during an argument concerning the dinner that she had prepared. She states that he had been drinking during the afternoon preceding the event and became obstreperous after watching a football team on which he had bet lose a game. She says that he began swearing and threw a beer can across the room. When she suggested that they have dinner, he calmed for awhile, but then began to complain about the food, then about her housekeeping habits, and then about her clothing. Subsequently, he struck her on the side of her head and then kicked her after she had fallen to the floor. He then grabbed her by the throat and began strangling her but, at the same time, apparently attempted to have intercourse with her. She had screamed several times when he was hitting her and a neighbor, living in an apartment across the hall came into the apartment (the door was unlocked) and "tackled" the subject as he was on top of the woman. Shortly thereafter, the building superintendent arrived and assisted the neighbor in subduing the subject. By that time, the woman was unconscious and an ambulance and police were called.

The consulting psychologist was asked to act as an *amicus curiae* to the court in a pretrial hearing, during which the defense intends to offer a plea of "not guilty," based on the premise that the subject acted during a state of diminished capacity that was created either by a neurological or psychiatric condition. The subject claims to have only limited memory for the event and also claims a history of similar behaviors, some of which resulted in a psychiatric discharge from military service. A specific question posed by the court is whether evidence exists that would favor a decision by the court for commitment for further evaluation, ordering a separate sanity trial, or to proceed with routine trial action.

History   L.H. is an impressive-looking 32-year-old male of medium height and weight. He stands out as well groomed and neat. He has a husky voice and a ready smile that seems to have "cooperativeness" written all over it. He picks his words carefully, and after a short while in the interview, it becomes obvious that he wants to make a good impression. Prior to psychological evaluation, he had a complete neurological examination that yielded negative findings. He is the third child, and oldest son, in a family of four. His father was an accountant and the mother a housewife. His older sisters, now ages 38 and 40, both married shortly after completing high school. Both parents are deceased, the father at age 58 of a coronary, the mother at age 59 from cancer. He does not know the whereabouts of his younger brother, age 29. L.H. is a high school graduate and has taken "a few" college courses "here and there." He has marked memory lapses for his various jobs but estimates that he has held "at least a dozen," all of which fall into the "blue collar" category except one as a salesman in an appliance store. He currently works as a forklift operator in a storage warehouse but also claims to make "a lot of extra money" from gambling and "things like that."

He describes his sex history with some rather grandiose claims of conquest, "I'd never get married with all the available women around . . . Women just seem to want to fall into bed with me . . . No kidding doc, I haven't paid my own rent in two years . . . I guess I'm lucky to have the natural talent that women go for." He claims his first sexual experience occurred at age 11 when he was seduced by "an older girl." He says that he may have fathered "a kid or two," but has not definite knowledge of any of his past loves giving birth. Most of his jobs have lasted less than one year, and he admits to being fired twice for fighting with supervisors. He freely admits to the attempted strangulation of the girlfriend with whom he had been living for about 8 months, "I don't know what happened, one minute we were o.k. and the next minute I was like a wild man, I went crazy." He claims that similar events have happened at least twice, both times leading to some assault on females. He openly admits to problems with his temper and says that, "It got really bad when I was in the Army. I lasted only four months after they drafted me." Military records indicate that he was discharged with a diagnosis of "Schizoid Personality with epileptoid features." He says that he does drink frequently, "Mostly beer," and that he has tried drugs but did not like the effects. He claims that each time he has a "severe" temper control problem, he has no memory for the event. He expresses remorse concerning the attempted strangulation of his girlfriend. He states, "It's about time that I got some help because this temper is really bad and I don't want to hurt anyone, not really."

Protocol 4   32 Year Old Male

Card	Response	Inquiry	Scoring
I	1. Holy Christ: I d.k. what ths is, mayb its a naked wm in the cntr w her hands up, like a model	*E*: (Rpts *S*'s resp) *S*: Yeah, the more I look at it the more it ll that. Here's her hips & it ll the hands in the air, as if she's modeling s.t., but if she naked what's she modeling? That's a thought isn't it. *E*: Can u show me a bit more so that I c it the way u do? *S*: Well, c here is the outline, u can't c her head, mayb its back lik she was laughing, she looks pretty sexy to me doc.	*Do* *M*°o *H,Sx* *DR*
	E: (Most people c more than 1 thg) *S*: Gee, I don't c nothg else.		
II	2. Oh u'r really kidding me aren't u? Am I supposed to tell u wht ths really ll to me? (*E*: Yes) Well doc ths is a good one, ths bttm prt ll some a-a- well I was gonna say pussy, but I'll say vagina to make it a littl bettr, how's that?	*E*: (Rpts *S*'s resp) *S*: I heard somewhere if u c tht stuff u'r preoccup'd w it, is that right? *E*: Can u show me how u c it? *S*: Well it has the fuzzy look to it lik there was hair, I'm tryg to b honest about it cause I hav a big responsibility to try & get bettr	*Do* *FTo* *Hd,Sx* *DR*
	3. Ths top prt ll a bldy thumb	*E*: (Rpts *S*'s resp) *S*: Well it's all red lik bld, & its shaped lik a thumb, mite hav had an accident, there's really 2 of them, 1 on each side	*Do* *CF*− (2) *Hd. Bl* *MOR*
III	4. Thy ll 2 wm doing s. t. in ths pot, no wait a minute, its lik	*E*: (Rpts *S*'s resp) *S*: Yeah, lik she's makin bad apples in her	*W*+ *M*ᵃ*.Fro* (*H*), *Hh, Art* *P* 5.5 *AB*

598

	Response	Inquiry	Scoring
	a witch, lik in snow white & she's doing s.t., brewing s.t. in the pot & lookin in the mirror	den & thes red thgs r lik decorations, sort of symbols of her cult, lik trophies or s.t. E: Decorations? S: Just thgs on the wall, I d.k. what.	
IV V5.	Ths is some old tattered & torn hide, mayb it was a jacket once but now its all ruined from being weathered	E: (Rpts S's resp) S: The W thg ll tht, altho the arms r gone I guess, it ll its all greasy & beat up E: Greasy & beat up? S: Yeah, c the drk splotches on it c.b. grease & its all ragged around the edges	Wv YFu Cg MOR
V 6.	Ths ll a bat bearing down on a target w his feelrs stretch'd out ready to strike	E: (Rpts S's resp) S: It apparently sightd its prey & now its about to gobble it up E: Can u show me how u c it? S: Sure, c the wgs (points) & the body, it looks stiff, lik it's ready to strike	Wo FM^a_o A P 1.0 AG
VI 7.	Well, I said I'd b honest, u'll prob lock me up & throw away the key, but ths top prt ll a man's—well—his sex organ, penis that is	E: (Rpts S's resp) S: Its ths top thg, I hav to admit these side thgs don't fit, at least I never saw one w feathers altho it wld b popular as hell I'll bet E: Can u tell me what maks it ll tht? S: Hell, if u don't c it u'd bettr lock me up & thro away the key, it just ll that 2 me damn it (Throws card down).	Do Fo Sx
VII 8.	ll a cpl of pieces of fried chicken to me	E: (Rpts S's resp) S: Well, thy'r sort of drumsticks altho the shape isn't really right, thy hav lik breading on them lik u get in chkn in a basket, the colorg is diff lik breadg. E: Where is it that u c them?	Do Fo Hd,Sx DR

Protocol 4 (Continued)

Card	Response	Inquiry	Scoring
		S: Ths bttm prt isn't included, altho I guess u can c it as anothr piece	
		E: U mentioned breading	
		S: Thy look ruff & drk lik breadg, lik u kno, breadg is that way	
V9.	If u turn it ths way it ll a cpl of can-can dancers going at it	E: (Rpts S's resp) S: Thy hav thyr heads touchg lik thy were in a chorus line or s.s. of specialty dance, c the legs r kicking outward so u can't c it, u can c only one on each	W+ $M^a o$ (2) H 2.5 COP
VIII V10.	Ths prt ll sherbet, its got a glassy look to it, differnt from real ice cream	E: (Rpts S' resp) S: Yeah, its all colord like sherbet, orange & raspberry I guess & its kind of grainy lik sherbet, it's not all the same coloring, grainy like	Dv C.Y Fd
<11.	ll a wolf, ready to spring at s.t., he's being reflected in a river or pond	E: (Rpts S's resp) S: C the legs here & the body & the wolf head, there's no tail tho, he's ready to spring, standg on some rocks or s.t. being reflectd dwn here I d.k. what ths (points to front prt) mite b, mayb a stump or s.t.	W+ $FM^a.Fr o$ A,Ls P 4.5 AG
IX V12.	ll the whole damn world is blowing up, u get the feelg of a lot of force	E: (Rpts S's resp) S: Lots of force, lik an atomic blast but it has so much color that it has 2 b the world or at least part of it, c all the fire here—I guess we'd b bettr off if it happened	Wv $m^a.CF o$ Ex,Fi AG, MOR, ALOG

600

13. If u turn it ths way the pink ll cotton candy, no stick but a couple of 'em, c one on each side, sticky like candy
E: (Rpts S's resp)
S: Well they'r pink & fluffy lookg, fuzzy lik cotton candy, u can't c the stick tho, just the round ball of cotton candy lik is on the stick like at a fair
E: u said they were sticky like?
S: Thy ll if u pick them up, Thy'll stick to ur fingers

Dv   CF.TFo   (2)   Fd

X 14. Well a cpl lady bugs at the top eatin on a weed
E: (Rpts S's resp)
S: They hav legs & antennae, c (points) they look pretty good lik lady bugs

D+   FMᵃo   (2)   A, Bt   4.0

15. The pink ll bld stains
E: (Rpts S's resp)
S: Yeah, they ll bld stains to me, prob dried up cause the red isn't as dark as fresh bld, just a blob of dried bld

Dv   C   Bl   MOR

16. Ths up here ll a spider tht has caught a bug in its claws & is going to devour it
E: (Rpts S's resp)
S: It has a lot of legs, I don't kno wht the grn thg is, s.k. of bug I guess, the ole spider has really got it tho

D+   FMᵃo   A   P   4.0   AG

17. Mayb a cpl dogs down here lik they were baying at the moon or s.t.
E: (Rpts S's resp)
S: C here thy r, 1 on each side, the heads are tilted up lik thy were baying like dogs do

Do   FMᵃo   (2)   A

18. Ths blue thgs ll some sex thgs lik a cpl of ovaries or s.t., if there were a—penis there they cld b testicles but there isn't any so thy must b ovaries
E: (Rpts S's resp)
S: They just rem me of that, I d.k. exactly why, I guess bec of the way they r formed there, I d.k. what that is between them tho, mayb a clitoris but that isn't where it's supposed to be

Do   F−   (2)   Sx   ALOG

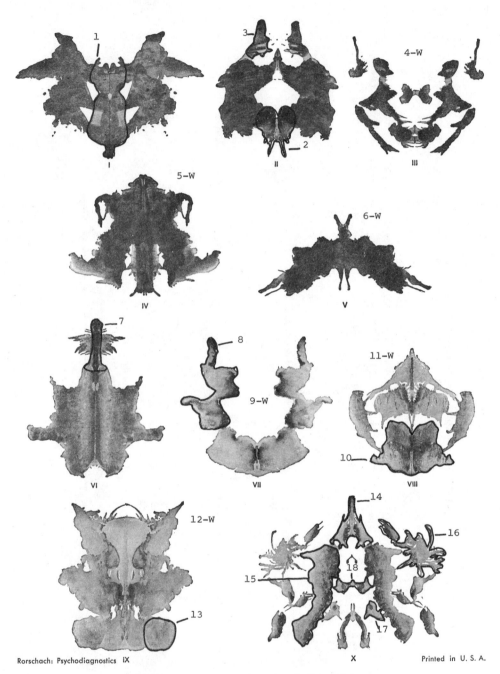

Figure 20. Location Selections for Protocol 4.

Table 107.   Protocol 4—Sequence of Scores

CARD	NO	LOC	#	DETERMINANT(S)	(2)	CONTENT(S)	POP	Z	SPECIAL SCORES
I	1	Do	4	Mpo		H,Sx			DR
II	2	Do	3	FTo		Hd,Sx			DR
	3	Do	2	CF-	2	Hd,Bl			MOR
III	4	W+	1	Ma.Fro		(H),Hh,Art	P	5.5	AB
IV	5	Wv	1	YFu		Cg			MOR
V	6	Wo	1	FMao		A	P	1.0	AG
VI	7	Do	3	Fo		Hd,Sx			INC2
VII	8	Do	2	FYu	2	Fd			
	9	W+	1	Mao	2	H		2.5	COP
VIII	10	Dv	2	C.Y		Fd			
	11	W+	1	FMa.Fro		A,Ls	P	4.5	AG
IX	12	Wv	1	ma.CFo		Ex,Fi			AG,MOR,ALOG
	13	Do	4	CF.TFo	2	Fd			
X	14	D+	11	FMao	2	A,Bt		4.0	
	15	Dv	9	C	2	Bl			
	16	D+	1	FMao		A	P	4.0	AG
	17	Do	2	FMao	2	A			
	18	Do	6	F-	2	Hd,Sx			ALOG

Table 108.   Protocol 4—Structural Summary

```
================================================================================
LOCATION              DETERMINANTS              CONTENTS        S-CONSTELLATION
FEATURES          BLENDS          SINGLE                        NO..FV+VF+V+FD>2
                                            H    = 2, 0         YES..Col-Shd Bl>0
Zf    =  6        M.Fr          M   = 2     (H)  = 1, 0         YES..Ego<.31,>.44
ZSum  = 21.5      C.Y           FM  = 4     Hd   = 4, 0         NO..MOR > 3
ZEst  = 17.0      FM.Fr         m   = 0     (Hd) = 0, 0         YES..Zd > +- 3.5
                  m.CF          FC  = 0     Hx   = 0, 0         YES..es > EA
W     =  6        CF.TF         CF  = 1     A    = 5, 0         YES..CF+C > FC
  (Wv =  2)                     C   = 1     (A)  = 0, 0         YES..X+% < .70
D     = 12                      Cn  = 0     Ad   = 0, 0         NO..S > 3
Dd    =  0                      FC' = 0     (Ad) = 0, 0         NO..P < 3 or > 8
S     =  0                      C'F = 0     An   = 0, 0         NO..Pure H < 2
                                C'  = 0     Art  = 0, 1         NO..R < 17
    DQ                          FT  = 1     Ay   = 0, 0          6....TOTAL
........(FQ-)                    TF  = 0     Bl   = 1, 1
 +   =  5  ( 0)                  T   = 0     Bt   = 0, 1        SPECIAL SCORINGS
 o   =  9  ( 2)                  FV  = 0     Cg   = 1, 0            Lv1     Lv2
v/+  =  0  ( 0)                  VF  = 0     Cl   = 0, 0     DV   = 0x1     0x2
 v   =  4  ( 0)                  V   = 0     Ex   = 1, 0     INC  = 0x2     1x4
                                FY  = 1     Fd   = 3, 0     DR   = 2x3     0x6
                                YF  = 1     Fi   = 0, 1     FAB  = 0x4     0x7
                                Y   = 0     Ge   = 0, 0     ALOG = 2x5
    FORM QUALITY                 Fr  = 0     Hh   = 0, 1     CON  = 0x7
                                rF  = 0     Ls   = 0, 1         SUM6  = 5
      FQx  FQf  MQual  SQx       FD  = 0     Na   = 0, 0         WSUM6 = 20
 +   =  0    0    0     0        F   = 2     Sc   = 0, 0
 o   = 12    1    3     0                    Sx   = 0, 4     AB   = 1    CP  = 0
 u   =  2    0    0     0                    Xy   = 0, 0     AG   = 4    MOR = 3
 -   =  2    1    0     0                    Id   = 0, 0     CFB  = 0    PER = 0
none=  2   --    0     0         (2)  = 8                    COP  = 1    PSV = 0
================================================================================
                  RATIOS, PERCENTAGES, AND DERIVATIONS

R = 18         L =   0.13          FC:CF+C = 0: 5    COP = 1     AG = 4
-----------------------------------Pure C  =    2    Food        = 3
EB = 3: 6.0  EA =  9.0  EBPer= 2.0 Afr     =1.00     Isolate/R  =0.11
eb = 6: 5    es = 11       D =   0 S       = 0       H:(H)Hd(Hd)= 2: 5
         Adj es =  9   Adj D =   0 Blends:R= 5:18    (HHd):(AAd) = 1: 0
-----------------------------------CP      = 0       H+A:Hd+Ad  = 8: 4
FM = 5 :  C'= 0   T = 2
m  = 1 :  V = 0   Y = 3
                          P    = 4      Zf    = 6       3r+(2)/R=0.78
a:p   =  8: 1  Sum6  = 5   X+%  =0.67     Zd    = +4.5     Fr+rF   = 2
Ma:Mp =  2: 1  Lv2   = 1   F+%  =0.50  W:D:Dd = 6:12: 0   FD      = 0
2AB+Art+Ay= 3  WSum6 = 20  X-%  =0.11     W:M   = 6: 3     An+Xy   = 0
M-    =  0     Mnone = 0   S-%  =0.00     DQ+   = 5       MOR     = 3
                          Xu%  =0.11     DQv   = 4
--------------------------------------------------------------------------------
   SCZI = 2    DEPI = 3    CDI = 1    S-CON = 7    HVI = No    OBS = No
================================================================================
```

Copyright (c) 1976, 1985, 1990 by John E. Exner, Jr.

INTERPRETIVE ROUTINE FOR PROTOCOL 4

The first positive Key variable is the presence of reflection answers, which designates that the interpretive routine begin with the clusters on self-perception, interpersonal perception, and controls. The remainder of the search strategy is defined by the fact that the *EB* is extratensive. Thus, the complete routine will be:

Self-Perception → Interpersonal Perception → Controls → Affect
→ Processing → Mediation → Ideation

SELF-PERCEPTION—PROTOCOL 4

Data pertaining to self-perception are shown in Table 109.

The presence of the reflection answers reveals that a marked narcissistic feature is a core element in his psychological organization. He has an exaggerated sense of self-value, which he defends through an elaborate system based mainly on rationalization, externalization, and denial. The enormously high Egocentricity Index (.78) confirms an exquisite level of self-centeredness and suggests that, at best, his interpersonal relations usually will be superficial and will endure only if they are gratifying to his needs. The absence of *FD* or vista answers suggests that he is less prone to self-examination than most adults and the $H:(H)+Hd+(Hd)$ ratio (2:5) implies that his perceptions of people and his self-image are based much more on imaginary concepts than real experience.

The significant number of sex answers (4) confirms a pronounced sexual preoccupation that already seemed evident in the history he gave. The answers are intriguing in light of the three *MOR* responses, an unusual finding in the record of a markedly narcissistic person, and indicate that his self-image may include more negative features than expected. The contents of at least two of the three *MOR* answers are also very intriguing and may provide some clarification regarding the sexual preoccupation. The first, to Card II is, ". . . a bloody thumb [inquiry] . . . might have had an accident." The second, to Card IV is ". . . tattered and torn hide, maybe it was a jacket once but now it's all ruined from being weathered [inquiry] . . . all greasy and beat up." Both of these seem to raise questions about role security while the third, to Card IX, is the only *m* answer and seems more directly related to his current plight, ". . . the whole damn world is blowing up [inquiry] . . . I guess we'd be better off if it happened." One of the *MOR* answers (bloody thumb) is also a minus answer. The second minus response is a unique sex response, the fourth in the record and his last answer in the test, ". . . some sex things like a couple of ovaries or something, if there were a—penis there they could be testicles but there isn't so they must be ovaries" [inquiry] . . . I don't know what's between them though, maybe a clitoris but that isn't where it's supposed to be." It is impossible to avoid speculating that this signals a marked preoccupation with his own sexuality.

The three human movement answers tend to be exhibitionistic and/or grandiose. The first, to Card I, is his first sex response and has an exhibitionistic quality, ". . . a naked woman in the center with her hands up, like a model," but in the inquiry a sense of vulnerability is raised, ". . . but if she's naked, what's she modeling?" The second, to Card III, is more grandiose, ". . . a witch, like in snow white . . . brewing something in the pot and looking at herself in the mirror [inquiry] . . . these red things are decorations, sort of symbols of her cult, like trophies or something." The third, to Card VII, is also exhibitionistic, ". . . can-can dancers going at it," but also hints at

Table 109. Self-Perception Data for Protocol 4

$3r+(2)/R = 0.78$	$FD = 0$	$MOR = 3$	$Hx = 0$	$An+Xy = 0$
$Fr+rF = 2$	Sum $V = 0$	$H:(H)+Hd+(Hd) = 2:5$		$Sx = 4$

		Responses to Be Read		
MOR Responses	*FQ*− Responses	*M* Responses	*FM* Responses	*m* Responses
3, 5, 12	3, 18	1, 4, 9	6, 11, 14, 16, 17	12

vulnerability in the inquiry, ". . . c the legs are kicking outward so you can't see it, you can see only one on each."

The *FM* answers tend to be more aggressive, ". . . a bat bearing down on its target [inquiry] . . . about to gobble it up," to Card V; "a wolf ready to spring at something, he's being reflected in a river or pond," to Card VIII; and three to Card X, ". . . lady bugs . . . eating on a weed," ". . . a spider that has caught a bug . . . and is going to devour it," ". . . dogs down here like they were baying at the moon or something."

Many of his answers are embellished in unusual ways, including the other two sex answers. In response 2, Card II, he states, "Oh, you're really kidding me aren't you . . . Well doc, this is a good one . . . I was gonna say pussy, but I'll say vagina to make it a little better, how's that?" The fact that he says what he said he would not say reflects how he fails to delay. It suggests that he is often aware of inappropriateness, but does little to alter his approach. This naiveté in judgment is also reflected quite well in his preface to answer 7, "Well I said I'd be honest, you'll probably lock me up and throw away the key, but this top part looks like a man's-well-his sex organ, penis that is [inquiry] . . . at least I never saw one with feathers although it would be popular as hell I bet."

While some of his answers reflect concreteness and poor judgment, others appear to be attempts to defend himself by manipulation, which seems overly obvious at times, "Oh, you're really kidding me aren't you . . . She looks pretty sexy to me doc . . . I'm trying to be honest about it cause I have a big responsibility to try and get better . . . Hell, if you don't see it you'd better lock me up and throw away the key."

INTERPERSONAL PERCEPTION AND BEHAVIOR—PROTOCOL 4

The data related to interpersonal perception are shown in Table 110.

The *CDI, HVI,* and *a:p* ratio offer no relevant information, but the three Food answers and the two Texture responses are quite important. The former signify dependency needs, while the latter indicate needs for closeness and an apparent marked sense of loneliness. Interestingly, one of the Texture determinants occurs in a sex response (Card II, vagina), while the second appears in a Food answer (Card IX, cotton candy). Both are somewhat juvenile or even primitive, and both are atypical. In a similar vein, none of the three Food answers are form dominant (fried chicken, sherbet, cotton candy) and all three involve the use of shading.

Collectively, these findings suggest an intense need system that is probably very influential in his thinking and ultimately in his perceptions of, and interactions with, people. In the interview, he conveyed a Don Juan-like attitude concerning women, "I'd never get married with all the available women around . . . women just want to fall into bed

Table 110. Interpersonal Perception Data for Protocol 4

$CDI = 1$	$a:p = 8:1$	$T = 2$	Human Cont = 7	Pure $H = 2$
HVI = Neg $= 0.11$	Food = 3	$PER = 0$	$COP = 1$ $AG = 4$	*Isolate/R*

Responses to Be Read

Human Movement with Pair	Human Contents
9	1, 2, 3, 4, 7, 9, 18

with me . . . I guess I'm lucky to have the natural talent that women go for," braggings that are not necessarily unexpected from a highly narcissistic person. Elevations in T responses are unusual and, ordinarily, occur only when the subject has recently experienced a significant emotional loss. It is possible that the flight of his girlfriend, following his attack, could provoke this sense of loss; however, it seems important to note that his interview statements make no mention of a desire for reconciliation, and he implies that his attractiveness to women makes any broken relation easy to replace. Thus, the texture answers, combined with the strong dependency needs, could signify a much more long-standing experience of affective deprivation which, when considered in light of his needs to reaffirm his exquisite self-value, could account for the Don Juan-like behaviors. If this postulate is valid, it suggests that he is the type of person whose unmet needs for closeness are so strong that few normal adult relationships could be sufficiently fulfilling.

The seven human contents imply a strong interest in others, but it is important to note that four of those include sex responses, and only two involve Pure H. Thus, his perceptions of people are not well founded and typically will have some imaginary basis. The four AG answers seem critically important in understanding his recent behavior and probably do not portend well for his future interpersonal contacts. He perceives aggressiveness to be a natural component in interpersonal relations and, although data concerning controls, affect, and mediation are very important to any hypothesis about whether the aggressiveness might be asocial or antisocial, the history already suggests that he is not overly concerned with conventionality.

The only human movement answer containing a pair is to Card VII (can-can dancers going at it . . . in a chorus line or some sort of specialty dance). It is also his only COP response. Although not an uncommon response, it seems interesting to note that his only answer denoting a positive interaction among people is one in which the action is contrived. The other human contents are all somewhat immature and most are sexual (a naked woman modeling, a vagina, bloody thumbs, a witch making bad apples, a penis with feathers, and a couple of ovaries). There seems to be no question that his conceptions of others are strange and probably very superficial.

CONTROLS—PROTOCOL 4

Data related to controls for this record are shown in Table 111.

Both D Scores are 0, indicating that, ordinarily, he has enough resource available from which to form and direct behaviors as he experiences demands for them. The data for the EA and EB provide no cause to question the validity of the Adjusted D Score. This finding does not rule out the possibility of being overwhelmed by severe stress, but at the moment he is under considerable stress. The record contains one m and three Y

Table 111.   Controls and Stress Tolerance Data for Protocol 4

$EB = 3:6.0$		$EA = 9.0$		$D = 0$
$eb = 6:5$		$es = 11$	$Adj\ es = 9$	$Adj\ D = 0$
$FM = 5$	$C' = 0$	$T = 2$		$CDI = 1$
$m = 1$	$V = 0$	$Y = 3$		

responses, causing an elevation of at least two points in the *es*. This is not surprising as he has been arrested and charged with aggravated assault and attempted homocide, yet the *D* Scores both remain 0. This places doubt on the likelihood that impulsive outbursts of rage, or other forms of intense emotional display result from frequent losses of control. At the same time, it is important to note that the *D* Scores do not address the issue of diminished states of consciousness and it is difficult, at best, to predict from Rorschach data how his capacity for control might change in altered mental states, such as produced by intoxication, or other elements.

AFFECT—PROTOCOL 4

The data concerning affect for this record are shown in Table 112.

Table 112.   Data Concerning Affect for Protocol 4

				Blends
DEPI = 3				
EB = 3:6.0		*EBPer* = 2.0		*M.Fr*
eb = 6:5		*FC:CF+C* = 0:5		*FM.Fr*
		Pure *C* = 2		*m.CF*
C' = 0	*T* = 2	*Afr* = 1.00		*C.Y*
V = 0	*Y* = 3	*S* = 0		*CF.TF*
		Blends/*R* = 5:18		
		CP = 0		

The *EB* (3:6.0) reveals the presence of an extratensive style. Thus, in most situations, he will approach stimulus demands by releasing affect and it will usually mark his thinking, his attitudes, his decisions, and his behaviors. This preferential style is also characterized by trial-and-error approaches to problem solving, and a tendency to seek gratification of his own needs through emotional exchange. The *EBPer* suggests that this is not an inflexible style, so that, at times, other options may be employed, but most of the time it is the preferred approach to decision making, and the presence of a reasonably well-established coping style is a favorable finding. However, other variables that are related to affect raise some serious concerns. The *FC:CF+C* ratio (0:5) indicates that, much of the time, he fails to use his capacities for control to modulate his affective displays in ways that are common to adults. Instead, he seems to permit his emotions to become much more intense than is common for the adult. Two of his responses are Pure *C,* and both are somewhat primitive (ice cream and blood). Their presence strongly suggests that he is the type of person who *passively gives way* to his feelings. In those situations, his emotions will often reach such levels of intensity that they direct or command the nature of his thinking and behaviors. These findings make it very likely that some of his behaviors will be impulsive-like, but it is important to distinguish those behaviors from ones that are the true product of lability, that is, when controls *are* insufficient and the person easily becomes overwhelmed by the intensity of feeling. His behaviors, even though appearing impulsive, are *not* the product of loss of control, but rather result from a failure to direct available resources in ways that will invoke modulation.

This finding seems even more important in light of the well-above-average *Afr* of 1.0 that signals a very strong interest in, and receptiveness to processing emotionally toned stimuli. Strong interests in being in or around emotional situations is not in itself a liability, but it does suggest that he may be the type of person who searches out emotional situations, possibly in concert with his orientation to gratify needs through emotional exchange. If this hypothesis is valid, it reveals that he tends to immerse himself psychologically in situations in which affective exchange or expectations are commonplace. Under such circumstances, his proneness to release affect in less controlled ways cannot help but become a significant liability, because the displays often will be too intense.

It is interesting to note the absence of Space responses in the record. In other words, there is no reason to believe that he is especially negativistic or angry, which seems a bit contrary to his reported actions; however, it is important to recognize that his view of the world is somewhat distorted and aggressiveness is a normal manifestation. No doubt, his chronic need to reassure himself about his value plus his strong needs for closeness and dependency give rise to aggressiveness rather easily. There are two color-shading blends, indicating considerable confusion about feelings or frequent experiences of ambivalence. One may be related to the current situational stress $(C.Y)$, but the second reflects a more chronic picture so that it is likely that the current stress has only exacerbated a preexisting problem.

INFORMATION PROCESSING—PROTOCOL 4

Data concerning processing activity for this record are shown in Table 113.

The data concerning processing are more negative than positive. The Zf (6), $W:D:Dd$ ratio (6:12:0), and the $W:M$ ratio (6:3), all signal a rather conservative approach to processing. He seems to be economical and this could be an asset for him. On the other hand, the *Lambda* (.13) indicates that he is not very economical. Rather, he becomes quite involved in stimuli. Similarly, the Zd (+4.5) indicates overincorporation; that is, when he becomes involved in scanning, he devotes considerably more effort than might be necessary. There is a contradiction here. On the one hand, he seems economical, but on the other, he becomes very involved with new stimulus fields and he invests more effort than required. The product of this incongruity possibly is best reflected in the DQ distribution. He does have five synthesis responses, but he also has four DQv answers, suggesting that much of the quality of his processing effort is less mature, overly concrete, and more simplistic than is expected for an adult. The sequencing data offer some confirmation of this. He is not very consistent. Three of his W answers are first responses, and two are second answers. His main approach is the economical D, which seems to be used appropriately in Cards I, II, VI, VII, and VIII, but he becomes carried

---

Table 113.   Processing Data for Protocol 4

L = 0.13	$W:D:Dd$ = 6:12:0	Zd = +4.5	$DQ+$ = 5
Zf = 6	$W:M$ = 6:3	PSV = 0	$DQv/+$ = 0
HVI = Neg	OBS = Neg		DQv = 4

Location Sequencing

I: D	IV W	VII: $D.W$
II: $D.D$	V: W	VIII: $D.W$
III: W	VI: D	IX: W.D
		X: $D.D.D.D.D$

away in Card X and generates five D answers. Thus, although he might prefer to be economical, he is not very good at it.

COGNITIVE MEDIATION—PROTOCOL 4

Data concerning mediation for this record are shown in Table 114.

Table 114.   Data Concerning Cognitive Mediation for Protocol 4

Lambda	= 0.13	*OBS*	= Neg	*Minus Features*	
P	= 4	*X* + %	= .67	3, 18	
FQx+	= 0	*F* + %	= .50		
FQxo	= 12	*Xu*%	= .11		
FQxu	= 2	*X* − %	= .11		
FQx−	= 2	*S* − %	= .00		
*FQx*none	= 2	*CONFAB*	= 0		

There are only four Popular responses, which is lower than average for the adult. This suggests that he does not translate many aspects of his world conventionally even though obvious cues are present. In a similar context, the $X + \%$ of 67% is lower than desirable, although the $X - \%$ (.11) and the $Xu\%$ (.11) are not significantly elevated. The FQx distribution contains two minus, two u, and two *no form* responses. It signifies that, in some instances, he will distort inputs, whereas in other instances, he will simply translate them idiographically or ignore them in favor of his own feelings. Although none of these features is unusual for many people, collectively, they create a significant potential for unconventional responses that can only serve to increase the overall proclivity for maladaptive behaviors. Earlier, the issue was raised about whether his aggressive propensities might be manifest in asocial and/or antisocial activities. The composite of these data leaves little doubt that issues of conventionality will probably play only a negligible role in determining how the aggressiveness is displayed.

The two minus answers are not directly homogenous for specific content (bloody thumbs, ovaries), but both are primitive and have clear sexual overtones. The first (bloody thumbs) is not a major distortion of the blot features, however, the second (ovaries) stretches the imagination considerably. It is more of a Level 2 minus answer and serves to reaffirm the sexual preoccupation and confusion that seem to mark much of his thinking and behavior.

IDEATION—PROTOCOL 4

The data related to ideation for this protocol are shown in Table 115.

Table 115.   Data Concerning Ideation for Protocol 4

		M Quality	*Critical Special Scores*			
EB = 3:6.0	*EBPer* = 2.0					
eb = 6:5	(*FM* = 5 *m* = 1)	+ = 0	*DV*	= 0	*DV2*	= 0
a:p = 8:1	$M^a{:}M^p$ = 2:1	*o* = 3	*INC*	= 0	*INC2*	= 1
2*AB*+*Art*+*Ay* = 3		*u* = 0	*DR*	= 2	*DR2*	= 0
MOR = 3		− = 0	*FAB*	= 0	*FAB2*	= 0
			ALOG	= 2	*SUM6*	= 5
Responses to Be Read for Quality			*CON*	= 0	*WSUM6*	= 20
1, 4, 9						

The *EB* (3:6.0) has already been noted from the data concerning affect. He is not the type of person who usually stops before making a decision to think things through and then test the most feasible alternative. Instead, his feelings are pervasive in his thinking and most of his decisions are intuitive and will involve trial-and-error activity. The left-side value for the *eb* suggests that there is no unusual level of peripheral ideation that may deter his attention or concentration. The *a:p* ratio of 8:1 indicates that much of his thinking and attitudes will be marked by considerable inflexibility. It will not be easy for him to view things differently or alter many of the values that he has adopted. This is quite important in light of his needs for closeness, his dependency orientation, and his sexual preoccupation. The rigidity of his thinking will probably make it very difficult to approach or alter any of these features.

The *Mᵃ:Mᵖ* ratio and the Intellectualization Index are not relevant, but is important to note the presence of the three *MOR* answers. They indicate that much of his thinking will be marked by a pessimistic attitude, and this may give rise to some of his aggressiveness. The number of critical Special Scores in the record (5) is not a major cause for concern, but the specifics are. One is an *INCOM2* (penis with wings), two others are ramblings with fairly clear sexual overtones (if she's naked what's she modeling, that's a thought isn't it; you're really kidding me aren't you . . . well I was gonna say pussy, but I'll say vagina . . . cause I have a big responsibility to try and get better), and two are concrete *ALOG* answers (it has so much color it must be the world or at least part of it; if there were a penis there they could be testicles but there isn't any so they must be ovaries). These are not pathological answers but they do illustrate shoddy, immature forms of cognitive slippage that are created by a very strong preoccupation. The contents of his *M* answers also hint at this immaturity, but the quality of the *M*'s have some sophisticated features (a naked woman in the center with her hands up like a model; a witch like in snow white . . . like she's making bad apples in her den; a couple of can-can dancers going at it . . . like they were in a chorus line or some sort of specialty dance). These are not the kind of responses given by an intellectually impoverished person. This suggests that he does have a capacity for quality thinking, but other problems tend to keep the output at a less desirable or effective level.

SUMMARY—PROTOCOL 4

There is no significant psychiatric disability from which to build a case that could be used to mitigate the circumstances concerning the assault on his girlfriend. He is a very primitive person, but not one who could be described a being easily victimized by irresistible impulses or frequent diminished states of consciousness, unless the latter is self-induced, as could be the case by the abuse of drugs or alcohol. He is not without the capacity for control, but rather, has not learned the social values of control, or is unwilling to invest the effort necessary to initiate controls when he engages in emotional discharge. He is far too self-centered to restrain himself from the prospects of immediate relief from stress, or immediate gratification of his own needs, and far too insecure in his own identity to have developed much sensitivity to others. In fact, it is likely that most of his interpersonal relations are perceived by him as sources from which to fulfill his strong unmet needs for closeness and dependency. He takes as much as possible from the relationship while giving as little as possible to it. A false sense of grandiosity, coupled with an orientation toward aggressiveness, has become an important feature in the façade that he has created to deceive himself and others and with which he conceals his own sense of inadequacy and sustains his overinflated sense of self.

The narcissistic features are probably very long-standing, perpetuated by a failure to discover many of the positive realities of the interpersonal world. Unfortunately, his experiences with people apparently have been far less satisfying than he may have anticipated or desired. Thus, he is forced to defend his unrealistic sense of self by denial, rationalization, and externalization. This permits him to continue to perceive himself as important to the world, and at the same time, account for the many disappointments that he has experienced and afford some acknowledgment of being a battered or damaged person.

He gives way to his feelings very easily. They merge with his thinking and become very influential in his decisions and behaviors, but he makes little effort to modulate their intensity. He is not very attuned to conventionality and is prone to disregard or distort it whenever doing so meets his own needs. His thinking often is overly simplistic and marked by faulty judgment. In turn, this has perpetuated his immaturity and self-centeredness, and limits the probability that he will profit from his own mistakes. In effect, his psychological organization predisposes inappropriate, maladaptive social behaviors; and inevitably, some will be characterized by his aggressive orientation. Sexual activity appears to have become a highly valued behavior, probably because it serves to counteract many of the underlying concerns that he has about masculinity.

It would not be unrealistic to describe him as a psychopathic personality, easily prone to give way to his feelings as his wants dictate, and with little or no regard for the future consequences of his behaviors. Even if this were not a forensic case, and the subject were seeking some form of treatment, it is unlikely that he would persist in any intervention routine, other than one that would be supportive and reinforcing, because the threats to him that would arise during other forms of treatment would quickly be weighed as being far greater than any gains that he might perceive possible. In that context, it seems difficult to make any recommendation to the court that might be beneficial to him in his current situation. Hospitalization for further evaluation will reveal little more than is evident here. A separate sanity trial might be demanded by the defense but should not be expected to afford any relief for the subject or his victim. Proceeding with a routine trial action will afford the subject's attorney an opportunity to present psychological findings in the context of mitigation, but if the case for the prosecution is presented well, there is little reason to assume that psychological factors will become a major element in the decision of a jury.

PROTOCOL 5: A QUESTION OF CHRONIC ANXIETY

Referral   This 28-year-old female was referred because of frequent bouts of intense anxiety. She has reported episodes of intense anxiety from time to time for approximately 4 years. Historically, both her physician and psychiatrist attributed them to the problems she experienced with a duodenal ulcer that first appeared at about age 24. She was described at that time as a tense, somewhat anxious, and very achievement-oriented person. She was treated with a variety of medications and dietary regimens for approximately 3 years, and also participated in an intervention program of systematic desensitization for about 1 year. During that time, the ulcer seemed well under control and dissipating. The ulcer flared again about 1 year prior to this evaluation and required surgery, after which she reentered systematic desensitization for a 4-month period. During a period of 5 months following her termination from that program she has been symptom free, but during the past 60 days, she has had recurring episodes of intense anxiety and apprehension that she describes as "panic attacks." There has been no reappearance of physical symptoms, but she complains of serious interference to concentration, and some sleep difficulties. The psychiatrist is requesting the evaluation before deciding on another course of intervention.

History   She is an attractive, short, dark-haired registered nurse who currently has supervisory responsibility for 6 other nurses and a supporting staff of 13 health-care providers on a 44-bed general medical ward. She holds a B.S. degree in nursing from a well-known university, and has worked at the same hospital for 7 years. Her work history is excellent. She manifests good patient relationships, accomplishes her own duties thoroughly and efficiently, and since being promoted to a "Head Nurse" position slightly more than 2 years ago, has set "commendable" standards for herself and those who work with her. She lives alone in a hospital apartment, dating irregularly. She was engaged during college to a resident physician, but "our interests didn't coincide, and so we called it off." She implies virginity but politely refuses to speak of sexual matters, "That is a personal matter that I'm not prepared to talk about now." She is the oldest of two daughters of parents who emigrated from a middle European country shortly after they married. Her family was poor during her developmental years, living in a "cold-water" flat in a large eastern city until she entered high school. By that time, her father had been able to establish himself as a skilled tradesman and purchased a small duplex house where the family still lives. She entered college on a nursing scholarship and maintained a "Dean's List" average throughout her 4 years there. She dated frequently in high school and in college but "never for very long with one person." She is very thrifty in her spending habits, preferring to "save my money for a rainy day, or in the event that my parents ever need it." She attends a Protestant church each Sunday, "more to set an example than because I have a belief. In fact, I'm probably an agnostic, although I don't go around telling everybody." Her younger sister, age 25, after having completed 2 years of college, is now married to a businessman and is currently pregnant. She describes both of her parents as the "salt of the earth." She indicates that both are very hard working, conservative, and "vigorously sincere." She says that she feels closer to her father than her mother, but is uncomfortable in making any distinction between them. She verbalizes a feeling of contempt for many of her colleagues, "who work their eight to five and get out as quickly as they can. They just don't have much concern for those who they are supposed to be serving." She has great faith in "most doctors" but admits that she has seen some who she feels would fare better in other professions. She says that she sleeps well, has no appetite problems, exercises daily, likes horseback riding, tennis, and an occasional movie.

Protocol 5 28-Year-Old Female

Card	Response	Inquiry	Scoring
I	1. Two wm, prob witches dancing @ a fig. in the cntr, it seems to b a person, quite helpless, its a wm too bec u can c her breasts and hips & she has her hands up	E: (Rpts S's resp) S: Well, the witches r on each side, the hav big dark cloaks on & they'r doing a dance, I can't really tell if its a ritual or if theyr burng her at the stake. She is just there in the cntr w her hands up	W+ M^{a-}.FC'o (2) H,(H),Cq 4.0 AG,COP (H) 4.0 AG, MOR *(The scoring of a-p is used as both features of M appear. Both are counted in the a:p ratio)*
	2. It cld b an x-ray of a pelvis too	E: (Rpts S's resp) S: Yes, the W thg ll one, its black lik an x-ray & it has the general structure of a pelvic area, u c, u get the slant of the pelvic arch here	Wo FC'o Xy 1.0
II	3. At the top it ll 2 hens preparing to fite w e.o., these red areas	E: (Rpts S's resp) S: It ll 2 hens primping for a fite u can c the heads & feet & legs	D+ FM^{au} (2) A 5.5 AG
	4. The cntr ll a temple of worship w a tower of silver or platinum	E: (Rpts S's resp) S: Ths cntr white area is the temple & ths ll the tower, it clearly has the form of a towr & its colord like silver or platinum or some other valuable metal wld b colord, its the metal part that really attracts people to the temple bec its so valuable	DdSO FC'0 Ay 4.5 DR
III	5. 2 wm fiting over s.t. valuable, it ll a basket that theyr fitg over, they must b angry the way theyr tugging so hard	E: (Rpts S's resp) S: Oh yes, these r the wm, u c the breast outline & the hi-heels, & theyr thin like wm & this is the basket, it must b full of goodies bec each wants it for her own, but neither seems able to get it	D+ M^{a}o (2) H,Hx,Cg,Hh P 3.0 AG

IV

V6. Well, ths c.b. an x-ray too, I'm not sure of what, possbly a pelvic arch again & the sacral area of the cord

E: (Rpts S's resp)
S: It's ths *W* thg, its kind of dark & it has a shape that conceivably cld b the pelvic area if u stretch u'r immag a littl. Ths prt wld b the part of the cord, & the rest the pelvis, it definitely has that kind of darknss to it like an x-ray

$Wo \quad YFo \quad Xy \quad 2.0$

V

7. 2 peopl leang against s.t., lying down w thr backs against ths thg in the cntr. I thnk thy'r wm, almost but not quite rstg back to back w thr legs stretchd out like thy wer relxg like they wrkd hard at s.t. & now theyr takg a break

S: Oh I rem ths one, I've sat lik that many times during the war when we'v had a surgery break. I use to hav a good friend who was killed in Seoul & most of the time when we couldn't rest for a long time we'd prop up like ths, u c her r the legs extendg outward

$W+ \quad M^p o \quad (2) \quad H \quad 2.5 \quad COP,PER$

VI

8. A weapon, here at the top, lik an arrow that u would thrust at someone in battle, it has a spear type tip, s.t. u wld use to hurt or maim or kill

E: (Rpts S's resp)
S: Yes, just ths top, it has a kind of dull tip lik it cld really do damage if it were misused, it just has the general characteristics of a weapon

$Do \quad Fu \quad Sc \quad DR$

9. U kno, ths cntr prt cld be a rivr or a road, far away, as if u were stdg on a mt or s.t. lookg down at it

S: Well, u hav to stretch u'r immag to c the next one, r u ready?
E: Go rite ahead
S: Well, it's just a straight line, as a road or river but its so small u'd hav to be far away to c it lik ths, c rite here (points)

$Do \quad FDo \quad Ls$

VII

10. 2 wm arguing @ s.t. w.e.o., u just c their heads, it ll thy r disagreeg @ s.t.

E: (Rpts S's resp)
S: Yes, just the head parts, mayb thy r the one's I saw earlier who were fitg ovr the basket of precious stuff, u

$D+ \quad M^a o \quad (2) \quad Hd \quad P \quad 3.0 \quad AG,PSV$

Protocol 5 (Continued)

Card	Response	Inquiry	Scoring
		can c the facial features rather dis-tinctly, especially the lips here, & ths wld b a hair piece of s.s.	
<11.	If u turn it ths way it cld b a scottie dog w his flat snout & stubby legs here	E: (Rpts S's resp) S: Its a good liknss to one, ths is the tail & the snout & the funny littl legs here	Do Fo A
VIII 12.	There's a rib cage here, at the cntr	E: (Rpts S's resp) S: Its here (points), it has a pretty good formation lik a rib cage has u can c the spaces in between	DSo Fo An 4.0
13.	The W thg seems to be s.s. of anatomy chart but I can't identify the specific prts, oh!, bettr still, it cld b internal viscera & ths bttm prt cld b s.s. of inter-nal wound, it has a bloody mass effect there	E: (Rpts S's resp) S: Well not really a chart of An, it looks much more like the visceral organs & ths orag-pink prt here ll a wound, the organs r not clerly delineatd but it could b, the colorg is so strkg par-ticulry the effect of the wound but the other parts r also colord much like the visceral organs might b E: U said the effect of the wound? S: It looks deep somehow, I supp bec its darkr there	Wv/+ CF.VFo An,Bl 4.5 MOR
IX 14.	The orange ll 2 witches hovrg ovr a cauldron lik they r argug @ wht to mix in it, thy hav peakd hats on	E: (Rpts S's resp) S: Rite here (points) thy r pointg to the cauldron here in the middle, I can't say wht's goig on but thy r appar-ently arguing about what mixture shld go in it	Dd + Mᵃo (2) (H),Hh,Cg 2.5 AG

616

15. U kno, ths cntr prt cld b a glass candl holder w a candle in it, lik u can c thru it

E: (Rpts *S*'s resp)
S: Well its rite here where the cauldron is except that it goes down further than the cauldron & u can c the candle inside it, u see thgs lik that in resturants some times, it has a milky colrg about it as if the candle was givg off lite

E: Milky coloring?
S: It's whiiish looking

DS+ FV.m^P.FC'o (2) *Sc* 5.0

X 16. 2 A's tryg to do s.t. to ths pole lik thg, mayb thyr tryg to capture it or mayb thyr tryg to climb up it or mayb thyr not sure what to do w it

E: (Rpts *S*'s resp)
S: Thy just look confused @ ths thg, thy r unknwn creatures w little legs & antennae, almst no legs at all, I can't decide what ths is, mayb its s.s. of food & thy r arguing about when to eat it, its difficult to decide

D+ FM^{a}u (2) (A),Id 4.0 *COP,DV*

17. Ths cld b a seed fr a tree, a maple tree I believe, I'm not sure but there is s.s. of tree that has seeds shaped like ths & they turn brown after thy fall

S: The seed is easier to decrib, u c it is rite here (points) & its brwn as if it were ready for plantg or whatever when they fall so as to start a new tree

Do FCo *Bt*

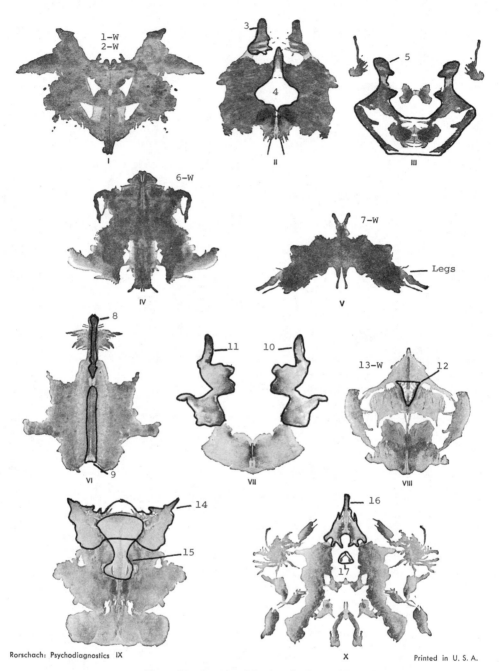

Figure 21.   Location Selections for Protocol 5.

Table 116.   Protocol 5—Sequence of Scores

CARD	NO	LOC	#	DETERMINANT(S)	(2)	CONTENT(S)	POP	Z	SPECIAL SCORES
I	1	W+	1	Ma-p.FC'o	2	H,(H),Cg		4.0	COP,AG
	2	Wo	1	FC'o		Xy		1.0	
II	3	D+	2	FMau	2	A		5.5	AG
	4	DdSo	99	FC'o		Ay		4.5	DR
III	5	D+	1	Mao	2	H,Hx,Hh,Cg	P	3.0	AG
IV	6	Wo	1	YFo		Xy		2.0	
V	7	W+	1	Mpo	2	H		2.5	COP,PER
VI	8	Do	2	Fu		Sc			DR
	9	Do	12	FDo		Ls			
VII	10	D+	2	Mao	2	Hd	P	3.0	AG,PSV
	11	Do	2	Fo		A			
VIII	12	DSo	3	Fo		An		4.0	
	13	W/	1	CF.VFo		An,Bl		4.5	MOR
IX	14	Dd+	99	Mao	2	(H),Hh,Cg	P	2.5	AG
	15	DS+	8	FV.mp.FC'o		Sc		5.0	
X	16	D+	11	FMau	2	(A),Id		4.0	COP,DV
	17	Do	3	FCo		Bt			

Table 117.   Protocol 5—Structural Summary

```
===============================================================================
LOCATION              DETERMINANTS              CONTENTS       S-CONSTELLATION
FEATURES          BLENDS        SINGLE                         YES..FV+VF+V+FD>2
                                          H   = 3, 0           YES..Col-Shd Bl>0
Zf    = 13      M.FC'         M   = 4      (H) = 1, 1           NO...Ego<.31,>.44
ZSum  = 45.5    CF.VF         FM  = 2      Hd  = 1, 0           NO...MOR > 3
ZEst  = 41.5    FV.m.FC'      m   = 0      (Hd)= 0, 0           YES..Zd > +- 3.5
                              FC  = 1      Hx  = 0, 1           YES..es > EA
W   = 5                       CF  = 0      A   = 2, 0           NO...CF+C > FC
  (Wv = 0)                    C   = 0      (A) = 1, 0           NO...X+% < .70
D   = 10                      Cn  = 0      Ad  = 0, 0           NO...S > 3
Dd  = 2                       FC'= 2       (Ad)= 0, 0           YES..P < 3 or > 8
S   = 3                       C'F= 0       An  = 2, 0           NO...Pure H < 2
                              C'  = 0      Art = 0, 0           NO...R < 17
    DQ                        FT  = 0      Ay  = 1, 0            4.....TOTAL
.........(FQ-)                TF  = 0      Bl  = 0, 1
 +  = 8  ( 0)                 T   = 0      Bt  = 1, 0           SPECIAL SCORINGS
 o  = 8  ( 0)                 FV  = 0      Cg  = 0, 3             Lv1      Lv2
v/+ = 1  ( 0)                 VF  = 0      Cl  = 0, 0      DV   =  1x1      0x2
 v  = 0  ( 0)                 V   = 0      Ex  = 0, 0      INC  =  0x2      0x4
                              FY  = 0      Fd  = 0, 0      DR   =  2x3      0x6
                              YF  = 1      Fi  = 0, 0      FAB  =  0x4      0x7
    FORM QUALITY              Y   = 0      Ge  = 0, 0      ALOG =  0x5
                              Fr  = 0      Hh  = 0, 2      CON  =  0x7
       FQx  FQf  MQual  SQx   rF  = 0      Ls  = 1, 0         SUM6  = 3
 +  =  0    0     0      0    FD  = 1      Na  = 0, 0         WSUM6 =  7
 o  = 14    2     5      3    F   = 3      Sc  = 2, 0
 u  =  3    1     0      0                 Sx  = 0, 0      AB  = 0     CP  = 0
 -  =  0    0     0      0                 Xy  = 2, 0      AG  = 5     MOR = 1
none=  0   --     0      0    (2) =  7     Id  = 0, 1      CFB = 0     PER = 1
                                                          COP = 3     PSV = 1
===============================================================================
                 RATIOS, PERCENTAGES, AND DERIVATIONS

R = 17         L =  0.21              FC:CF+C = 1: 1      COP = 3     AG = 5
-----------------------------------   Pure C   =  0       Food      = 0
EB = 5: 1.5  EA =  6.5   EBPer= 3.3   Afr     =0.55       Isolate/R =0.12
eb = 3: 7    es = 10       D  = -1    S       = 3         H:(H)Hd(Hd)= 3: 3
           Adj es = 10   Adj D = -1   Blends:R= 3:17      (HHd):(AAd)= 2: 1
-----------------------------------   CP      = 0         H+A:Hd+Ad  = 8: 1
FM = 2  : C'= 4   T = 0
m  = 1  : V = 2   Y = 1
                              P   = 3       Zf  =13          3r+(2)/R=0.41
a:p    = 6: 3   Sum6  = 3    X+% =0.82      Zd   = +4.0     Fr+rF    = 0
Ma:Mp  = 4: 2   Lv2   = 0    F+% =0.67      W:D:Dd = 5:10: 2  FD     = 1
2AB+Art+Ay= 1   WSum6 = 7    X-% =0.00      W:M  = 5: 5      An+Xy   = 4
M-     = 0      Mnone = 0    S-% =0.00      DQ+  = 8         MOR     = 1
                             Xu% =0.18      DQv  = 0

-----------------------------------------------------------------------
  SCZI = 0      DEPI = 4     CDI = 2     S-CON = 5    HVI = No   OBS = No
===============================================================================
Copyright (c) 1976, 1985, 1990 by John E. Exner, Jr.
```

INTERPRETIVE ROUTINE FOR PROTOCOL 5

The first positive Key variable is the minus Adjusted *D* Score, which indicates that the interpretation should begin with a review of the cluster concerning controls. It does not, however, define the remainder of the search strategy. That is specified by the next positive Key or Tertiary variable, which in this record is an introversive *EB*. Therefore, the complete interpretive routine will be:

Controls → Ideation → Processing → Mediation → Affect
→ Self-Perception → Interpersonal Perception

CONTROLS AND STRESS TOLERANCE—PROTOCOL 5

Data related to issues of capacity for control and tolerance for stress are shown in Table 118.

Table 118.   Controls and Stress Tolerance Data for Protocol 5

EB = 5:1.5		EA = 6.5		D = −1	
eb = 3:7		es = 10	$Adj\ es$ = 10	$Adj\ D$ = −1	
FM = 2	C' = 4	T = 0		CDI = 2	
m = 1	V = 2	Y = 1			

The Adjusted D Score of −1 indicates that she is in a chronic state of stimulus overload. As a consequence, capacity for control and ability to deal with stress effectively is less than might be expected. Some of her decisions and behaviors may not be well thought through and/or implemented, and a proclivity for impulsiveness exists. Although she is more vulnerable to control problems and more susceptible to disorganization under stress, those events are unlikely to occur in structured, well-defined situations. People such as this usually function adequately in environments with which they are familiar and in which demands and expectations are routine and predictable. The risk of losing control becomes more substantial as demands increase beyond levels for which the subject is prepared.

The EA is lower than average, especially for an introversive person. It indicates more limited available resources than might be expected, particularly in light of the fact that she is a college graduate, has a productive work history for the past seven years, and has been promoted to a head nursing position. The Adjusted D Score in the minus range is not unexpected in light of the EA as more limited resources do create a continuing potential for overload to occur. The data for the EB offer no basis from which to challenge the validity of the EA or the Adjusted D Score. Nonetheless, the findings are somewhat puzzling in light of the history.

The es is somewhat higher than expected but, actually, is not above average for an introversive adult. The left-side value of the eb is lower than expected, thus the bulk of the es value comes from the right side of the $eb,$ which reflects affective irritants. In this instance, elevations exists for both achromatic color and vista answers. Thus, findings concerning affect and self-perception will be important to an understanding of the overload condition and probably the symptom formation. However, the low EA remains a focal point of the problem, and hopefully, other data will shed light on whether it reflects some form of gradual deterioration or whether it simply represents a more chronic developmental lag.

IDEATION—PROTOCOL 5

The data relevant to ideation for this record are shown in Table 119.

A clear introversive style in indicated by the EB (5:1.5). She prefers to delay before making decisions or responses to afford time to think through the pros and cons of alternative responses that might be available in a situation. Typically, she prefers to keep her feelings aside when in coping situations so that their influence on her decisions is, at

Table 119.   Data Concerning Ideation for Protocol 5

$EB = 5{:}1.5$	$EBPer = 3.3$	M Quality		Critical Special Scores		
$eb = 3{:}7$	$(FM = 2 \quad m = 1)$	$+ = 0$	$DV = 1$		$DV2 = 0$	
$a{:}p = 6{:}3$	$M^a{:}M^p = 4{:}2$	$o = 5$	$INC = 0$		$INC2 = 0$	
$2AB + Art + Ay = 1$		$u = 0$	$DR = 2$		$DR2 = 0$	
$MOR = 1$		$- = 0$	$FAB = 0$		$FAB2 = 0$	
Responses to Be Read for Quality			$ALOG = 0$		$SUM6 = 3$	
1, 5, 7, 10, 14			$CON = 0$		$WSUM6 = 7$	

best, modest. The value of the *EBPer* reveals that this is a very marked and not very flexible coping style. In other words, she will persist in its applications even in situations in which a more intuitive and/or trial-and-error approach might be much more efficient and productive. This inflexibility can be a significant handicap unless she is in very routine and predictable situations.

As noted earlier, the left-side value of the *eb* is somewhat less than expected, consisting of only two *FM*'s and one *m*. Almost all adults give more than two *FM* answers and when the value is low, such as is the case here, questions must be raised about experienced needs and the apparent lack of peripheral ideation that they typically provoke. In some instances, low values for *FM* indicate a hasty reaction to demands created by such stimuli, but there is no evidence in the history to suggest that this may be the case. In other instances, low values for *FM* signify very modest need levels, which is unusual and often difficult to understand. The latter may be true in this case when considered in the context of her low *EA,* and if this is true, it may indicate an element of self-sacrifice that is almost counterphobic. The *a:p, M^a:M^p* ratios and the Intellectualization Index are all within expected limits, and there is only one *MOR* response in the record, albeit it is unusual and has considerable importance concerning the issue of self-perception. Considered positively, there are no reasons to believe that her ideational approaches or attitudes are inflexible, or that she uses fantasy excessively, or that her thinking is marked by considerable pessimism.

There are three critical Special Scores in the record and a *WSUM6* of 7, neither of which are cause for concern, but the characteristics of these responses are interesting and do shed some light on her thinking. Two are *DR* responses, the first occurring in the inquiry to response 4, Card II, ". . . it's the metal part that really attracts people to the temple because it's so valuable." The second is in response 8, to Card VI, ". . . it has a spear type tip, something you would use to hurt or maim or kill [inquiry] it has a kind of a dull tip like it could really do damage if it were misused . . ." The third is a *DV* in the Inquiry for response 16, to Card X, ". . . they are unknown creatures . . ." Neither of the *DR* responses are bizarre, yet they reflect a loss of distance from the task, as if she becomes caught up in her thinking in a way that detracts from its effectiveness. The *DV* is not a simple illustration of cognitive slippage. Instead, it has an almost magical quality. Collectively, they suggest that, at times, her preoccupations may interfere with the effectiveness of her ideational style.

It is important to note that her thinking seems reasonably clear, and even when she drifts from the target, there is no loss of coherency. Her *M* responses all involve a conventional use of form and their quality is very sophisticated (two women, probably witches dancing around a figure in the center; two women fighting over something valuable . . .

[inquiry] it must be full of goodies because each wants it for her own; two people leaning against this thing in the center . . . almost but not quite resting back to back; two women arguing about something . . . [inquiry] maybe they're the ones I saw earlier who were fighting over the basket of precious stuff; two witches hovering over a cauldron like they are arguing about what to mix in it). In fact, almost all of her answers have an intellectually sophisticated quality. Thus, in spite of the low *EA,* it seems clear that her ideational activity usually is complex and has considerable intellectual substance.

INFORMATION PROCESSING—PROTOCOL 5

The data related to processing activity are shown in Table 120.

Table 120.   Processing Data for Protocol 5

L = 0.21	$W:D:Dd$ = 5:10:2	Zd = +4.0	$DQ+$ = 8
Zf = 13	$W:M$ = 5:5	PSV = 0	$DQv/+$ = 1
HVI = Neg	OBS = Neg		DQv = 0

Location Sequencing

I: W.W	IV: W	VII: *D.D*
II: *D.DdS*	V: W	VIII: *DS.W*
III: *D*	VI: *D.D*	IX: *Dd.DS*
		X: *D.D*

The findings for *OBS* and *HVI* are not relevant here, although the low *Lambda* value seems important. It suggests that she does become more involved with stimuli than is customary, and the substantial *Zf* suggests a good motivation for processing. However, the *W:D:Dd* and *W:M* ratios both reflect a very conservative and economical approach to processing new information which, at first glance, may seem contradictory to the findings regarding *Lambda* and *Zf.* More than likely, she becomes very alert to stimuli, but then addresses them in a selective, economical manner. The *Zd* score reveals that she is an overincorporator, scanning very thoroughly to ensure that no critical bits of information are neglected. There is a *PSV* response, but it is not a within-card type that might signal cognitive rigidity. Instead, it is across card, conveying some sort of preoccupation. The sequencing is not very consistent. Three of her *W* responses are first answers, while two others are second responses. One of her two *Dd* answers occurs first to a blot, while the other is a second response. This may be the product of a low *EA* and the Adjusted *D* Score of −1, that is, she has difficulty maintaining a consistent approach in her processing activities. Collectively, the data concerning processing are not terrible and, in fact, offer no evidence of a major liability in this area. Nonetheless, they seem less desirable for one in a senior supervisory position.

COGNITIVE MEDIATION—PROTOCOL 5

The data concerning mediation for this record are shown in Table 121.

The importance of the low *Lambda* has already been noted in regard to processing. She does become overly involved in stimuli and, although this might be a function of her overincorporative style, it may also signal some of the affective problems noted when

Table 121.   Data Concerning Cognitive Mediation for Protocol 5

Lambda	= 0.21	*OBS*	= Neg	*Minus Features*	
P	= 2	*X* + %	= .82	No Minus Responses	
FQx +	= 0	*F* + %	= .67		
FQxo	= 14	*Xu%*	= .18		
FQxu	= 3	*X* − %	= .00		
FQx −	= 0	*S* − %	= .00		
*FQx*none	= 0	*CONFAB*	= 0		

reviewing the cluster regarding controls when issues of affective interference were raised. There are only three Popular responses in the record, an inordinately low number for an intelligent person. They appear in answers to Cards III, VII, and IX and involve an across-card perseveration. The failure to give Popular answers more often, especially to Cards I, V, and VIII, is very notable and suggests that, even when obvious cues are present, she will not always make the most conventional response. At the same time, the $X+\%$ is .82, well into the average range, suggesting that she is oriented toward conventional behaviors. There are no minus answers, and the $Xu\%$ of .18 is well within acceptable limits and indicates that she expresses her own individuality about as much as most people. In light of these findings, the low number of Popular answers could simply reflect a tendency to be more individualistic, or it could signal some form of preoccupation that does not disregard the obvious, but which supersedes the obvious in favor of responses that are more in keeping with the preoccupation.

AFFECT—PROTOCOL 5

The data related to affect for this record are shown in Table 122.

The value for the *DEPI* (4) is not actuarially positive, but it does signal that some concern should be afforded to issues related to the index. The *EB* has already been discussed; she does not like to involve feelings in her thinking and especially in her coping/decision operations. The right-side value for the *eb* (7) is quite important. It is considerably greater than the left-side value, but even if it were not, the magnitude of the value is important. She is in distress, and the elements contributing mainly to the distress consist of *C'* and vista answers. Obviously, she is internalizing much more emotion than do most people. This process usually leads to considerable subjective discomfort that may manifest as anxiety, sadness, tension, or apprehension. In this case, anxiety and

Table 122.   Data Concerning Affect for Protocol 5

DEPI = 4				*Blends*	
EB	= 5:1.5	*EBPer*	= 3.3	*M.FC'*	
eb	= 3:7	*FC:CF+C*	= 1:1	*CF.VF*	
		Pure *C*	= 0	*FV.m.FC'*	
C' = 4	*T* = 0	*Afr*	= 0.55		
V = 2	*Y* = 1	*S*	= 0		
		Blends/*R*	= 3:17		
		CP	= 0		

panic attacks constitute the main symptomotology, which is not surprising. The internalization of feelings that she would psychologically prefer to externalize creates considerable irritation that must be manifested in some way. Otherwise, it creates indirect symptoms.

The situation is exacerbated by the rumination that seems to be ongoing. She is focusing often on features of herself that she perceives to be very negative, and this only adds to the experiences of distress that she creates by holding too much emotion inside. The ulcerous condition is not surprising as internalization of emotion is very common among those who develop somatic complaints. It is important to note here that she is not a person who displays emotion very much. There are only two chromatic color responses in the record, but interestingly, the $FC:CF+C$ ratio does not show overcontrol. It is a 1:1 ratio, not much different than found in most adults, but the low values on each side convey a sense of constriction about displaying her feelings. Interestingly, the Afr is still within expected limits for an introversive person. Thus, she still seems interested in, and willing to process emotional stimuli about as much as other adults who have her marked ideational style. At the same time, it is important to note that there are three S responses in the protocol. They signal a sense of negativism and possibly even anger that does not seem to be expressed very directly. There are only three blends in the record, which is somewhat fewer than expected. She is not very complex, in spite of the chronic overload that she is experiencing. Nonetheless, one is a color-shading blend, suggesting confusion about her feelings. More important, a second is a shading blend which signals the presence of considerable pain. Overall, there is no doubt that she hurts very much, and it is, in some ways, to her credit that she has not fallen apart psychologically. But, she seems to be on the brink of emotional chaos, which will surely occur if she continues in relying on the process of internalization to handle her feelings.

SELF-PERCEPTION—PROTOCOL 5

The data concerning self-perception for this record are shown in Table 123.

The Egocentricity Index (.41) is within the average range and gives no hint that she focuses to excess either on herself or the external world. It implies that she regards herself no more or less favorably than significant others in her immediate world. Nonetheless, the two vista answers plus the one FD response indicate that she is involved with considerable self-examination, and that she probably ruminates about negative features that she perceives to exist within her. This is causing some of the considerable pain noted previously. Apparently, she has characteristics that she does not like, and her awareness of them torments her. There is a distinct elevation in $An+Xy$

Table 123.   Self-Perception Data for Protocol 5

$3r+(2)/R=0.41$	$FD=1$	$MOR=1$	$Hx=1$	$An+Xy=4$
$Fr+rF=0$	Sum $V=2$	$H:(H)+Hd+(Hd)=3:3$		$Sx=0$

Responses to Be Read				
MOR Responses	*FQ*− Responses	*M* Responses	*FM* Responses	*m* Responses
13		1, 5, 7, 10, 14	3, 16	15

answers, two of each. Usually, when significant values of this magnitude occur for this variable it signifies some sort of preoccupation that may have obsessional features.

It is important to raise the question of whether the undue emphasis on *An* and *Xy* responses could be occupation related. Usually, this is *not* the case. Nonpatient physicians, nurses, and other medical workers tend to give slightly more *An* answers—one or two—than other nonpatients, but usually they do not give *Xy* answers or, if so, no more than one. An x-ray is an exposure that permits the viewer to see through and implies a sense of vulnerability. Both of her *Xy* answers are pelvic areas, making it impossible to avoid speculation about sexual concerns, or sex role identity. Her first anatomy response, to Card VIII, is of a rib cage and does not appear to have an obvious relation to the x-ray answers except that it is described as an object that can be seen through, ". . . u can see the spaces in between." The second *An* answer to the same blot seems much more revealing, especially if a symbolic translation is applied. It is her only *MOR* answer. She begins by describing an anatomy chart, but then alters the answer, ". . . oh! Better still, it could be internal viscera and this bottom part could be some sort of internal wound, it has a bloody mass effect there," later in the Inquiry describing the wound as deep and dark. The uniqueness of the answer and the way it developed seem also to offer a strong hint about sexual issues.

The human movement answers have a rather different quality. Four of the five are aggressive and include some kind of conflict. The first, response 1, "Two women, probably witches dancing around a figure in the center, it seems to be a person, quite helpless [inquiry] . . . I can't really tell if it's a ritual or if they're burning her at the stake . . ." It is a magical answer that conveys much confusion. The second is to Card III, response 5, "Two women fighting over something valuable, it looks like a basket that they're fighting over, they must be angry . . . [inquiry] . . . it must be full of goodies because each wants it for her own, but neither seems able to get it." The third is a more positive response but also very tentative. It is to Card V, response 7, "Two people leaning against something, lying down with their backs against this thing in the center. I think they're women, almost but not quite resting back to back . . ." Certainly, the answer offers a direct implication about closeness, "almost but not quite," and may have some homosexual overtones, but that is more speculative. The fourth, response 10 to Card VII, resurrects the conflict noted in her Card III response, "Two women arguing about something with each other [inquiry] maybe they're the ones I saw earlier who were fighting over the basket of precious stuff . . ." A similar theme is present in the last *M* answer, response 14, Card IX, ". . . two witches hovering over a cauldron like they are arguing about what to mix in it . . . [inquiry] . . . I can't say what's going on but they are apparently arguing about what mixture should go in it." The presence of conflict is clear. The substance of the conflict is not, although it is difficult to resist arguing that it has to do with sex role. If she is a virgin, as implied in the history, the conflict could involve the dilemma about how to express her sex needs.

The two *FM* answers are less consistent. The first, to Card II, is ". . . two hens preparing to fight with each other . . . [inquiry] . . . primping." It is consistent with the aggressive human movement answers. The second, given to Card X, is less definite and marked more by indecision, "Two animals trying to do something to this pole-like thing, maybe they are trying to capture it or maybe they're trying to climb up it or maybe they're not sure what to do with it [inquiry] They just look confused about this thing . . . maybe it's some sort of food and they're arguing about when to eat it . . ." The single *m* is given to Card IX, ". . . a glass candle holder with a candle in it . . . [inquiry] . . . you can see the candle inside . . . it has a milky coloring about it as if the candle was giving off light." It is a rare answer and, again, seems to have a sexual quality.

Some of the other contents and embellishments also seem to have definite sexual overtones. For instance, her responses to Card II (a temple of worship with a tower of silver or platinum . . . it's the metal part that really attracts people to the temple because it's so valuable), Card VI (A weapon . . . that you would thrust at someone in battle . . . something you would use to hurt or maim or kill) and Card VIII (. . . some sort of internal wound, it has a bloody mass effect . . . the coloring is so striking, particularly the effect of the wound . . .) seem to convey an approach–avoidance attitude about sexuality. The Inquiry to her last answer is intriguing in a similar context, ". . . and it's brown as if it were ready for planting or whatever when they fall so as to start a new tree."

The rich projected material that she provides makes it impossible to avoid speculation that she has become more and more aware of her rather isolated, although occupationally successful, existence and is challenging her cautious, conventional orientation.

INTERPERSONAL PERCEPTION AND BEHAVIOR—PROTOCOL 5

The data related to interpersonal perception for this protocol are shown in Table 124.

The values for the *CDI*, *HVI*, *a:p* ratio, and the Food variable are not relevant. The absence of Texture is important and may even be critical in efforts to flesh out a better understanding of her problem. The *T*-less feature indicates that she does not experience needs for emotional closeness in ways similar to most adults. This does not mean that the needs are absent, but rather that she is less comfortable in close relationships, especially those involving tactile exchange. *T*-less people usually maintain distance from others or are particularly cautious in their relationships. They are often overly concerned with their own space and become annoyed and even angry when it is intruded upon by others.

The six human contents indicate a clear interest in others, and the fact that half are Pure *H* suggests that her conceptions of people are probably grounded in real experience. There are indications of some obvious confusion concerning the most appropriate model of interpersonal behavior. Three of her answers include *COP* features, suggesting that she tends to perceive relationships as positive. It is an attitude that usually causes one to be regarded by others as outgoing and likable. Five of her answers, however, including one of her *COP* responses contain aggressive movement (*AG*). This is a very unusual mix because the high frequency of *AG* indicates that she perceives aggressiveness as a natural manifestation in interactions. People such as this usually are quite forceful and/or aggressive in their interactions. No doubt, her orientation to making conventional

Table 124. Interpersonal Perception Data for Protocol 5

CDI = 2	*a:p* = 6:3	*T* = 0	Human Cont = 6	Pure *H* = 3
HVI = Neg	Food = 0	*PER* = 1	*COP* = 3 *AG* = 5	Isolate/*R* = 0.12

Responses to Be Read

Human Movement with Pair	*Human Contents*
1, 5, 7, 10, 14	1, 5, 7, 10, 14

responses, as noted from the data concerning mediation, ensures that her aggressiveness is not asocial or antisocial. In fact, the history becomes helpful in understanding how she might be outgoing and positive, and yet aggressive. It is noted that her work history is excellent . . . she manifests good patient relationships . . . has set "commendable" standards for herself and those who work for her. Those comments might be paraphrased to indicate that she manifests good professional relations with patients, but probably not too close, and that she sets firm and forceful standards for herself and those who work for her. She admits to feelings of contempt for many of her colleagues "who work their eight to five [who] don't have much concern for those they are suppose to be serving," and implies that she has worked with some physicians whom she judges to be less than competent. Thus, her interpersonal relationships are probably very superficial and not very rewarding to her, and the data concerning self-perception suggests that she may be quite aware of this.

SUMMARY—PROTOCOL 5

It is unfortunate that the history is not more detailed, especially concerning her interpersonal relationships, and particularly her sex history. That information is crucial to any specific treatment recommendations. Nonetheless, a fairly clear picture of her psychological organization has unfolded.

Her capacity for control is very limited and her tolerance for stress is, at best, marginal. She is in a state of chronic overload that increases the possibility of impulsiveness in her thinking and behavior. Fortunately, she is in a fairly well-structured situation with which she has become familiar during the past 7 years and in which she can function with reasonable effectiveness. But no hospital is that routine and predictable and many of her reports of anxiety and panic probably represent manifestations of her inability to respond in ways that are consistent with her own expectations.

In part, her overload state is created because she is more limited in accessible resources than is common for the adult. This seems to reflect a developmental lag that may have occurred because she sacrificed her own individuality in favor of her family's wants during earlier years, or it may simply be that she developed a strong commitment to a somewhat unrealistic Florence Nightingale type role model prematurely. Whatever the cause, there are probably many unrecognized resources available to her which, if identified, could help to resolve the overload problem. A second factor contributing to the overload is considerable distress. Much of that distress seems to evolve from a sense of dissatisfaction with herself and an inability to express her feelings in ways that are not threatening to her.

She has a well-developed ideationally oriented coping style with which she will usually push feelings aside and delay responses until she can give consideration to alternatives. Unfortunately, this stylistic approach to decision making is not very flexible and she will persist in its use, even in situations in which other tactics of problem solving might be much more efficient. At the same time, her thinking is reasonably clear and somewhat flexible, although she does have a marked preoccupation with sexuality. Her perceptual accuracy is very conventional; however, it would be erroneous to describe her as being committed to conformity. Often, she also seems to express uniqueness by avoiding obvious conforming situations. Her cognitive operations are quite sophisticated, although she may be too economical at times and probably is overly conservative in setting goals. It is clear that she is not comfortable with feelings although she does handle her emotional displays appropriately, and is as willing to process emotionally toned stimuli as most adults. Inside, however, she harbors much more negativism, or even anger, than may meet the eye.

The key to her problem appears to lie in her dissatisfaction with herself and her relations with people. Her self-image is much more negative and confused than should be the case, and it seems clear that she often approaches interpersonal exchange with more aggressiveness than is common for most adults, even though she may present a facade of cooperative outgoingness. She perceives the world as an aggressive and confusing place, and obviously is raising many questions about her role in it. Those questions appear to have evolved because she is preoccupied with her own identity. She seems to have some unresolved intrigue with sexuality that continues to pose conflicts for her.

She may be sensing the fact that her emotional isolation is atypical and, as such, is disconcerting. She may have experienced a series of disappointments in her social-emotional relationships. She may be a virgin who is struggling about that issue, or she may find herself dissatisfied with the conventional feminine role that she has attempted to play. Regardless of the cause of her dissatisfaction and preoccupation, it is very likely that her ulcer was related to one or more of these issues, and that resolution of that problem may have, in some way, removed a defense on which she often relied. The panic attacks that she describes are quite real, and can be expected to continue and probably increase in frequency until the issues of intrapersonal roles can be addressed through some form of intervention that will focus on three major issues.

The first target for treatment should probably concern her interpersonal world. She is cautious and guarded about people and needs to learn that she really can approach them more openly and less aggressively. Second, she needs avenues through which she can express her feelings more directly. She has many feelings bottled up inside and the sooner they can be confronted in a controlled manner, the fewer experiences of anxiety will occur. Third, she needs to explore her own self-image and her dissatisfactions about it. Some of this will evolve as her interpersonal and affective constraint problems are addressed, but there are probably deeper issues concerning self-image that should be addressed. Obviously, one of these concerns sexuality and her preoccupations with it. In the past, she has been involved in systematic desensitization, which really does not work well unless adequate resources are available at the onset. She has not had that advantage and that form of intervention has had only transient success. In that she is an ideational person, some form of cognitive intervention, combined with an interpersonally oriented method, such as modeling seems appropriate. Ultimately, however, some form of uncovering treatment will be necessary to promote the desired development and deal directly with the issues of sexuality.

Author Index

Subject Index